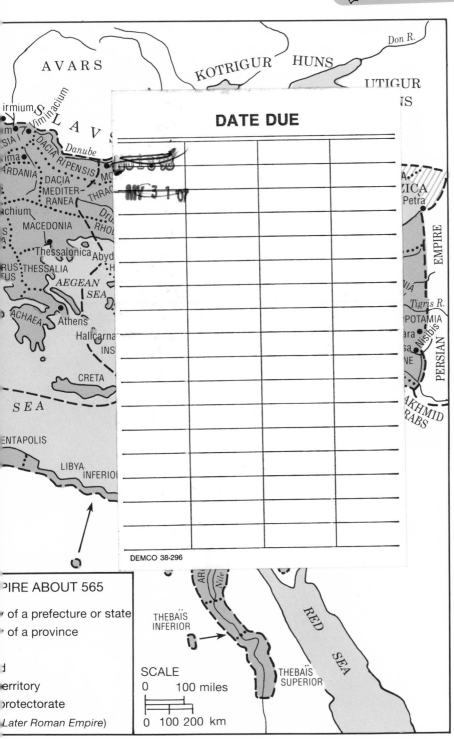

AVARS

KOTRIGUR HUNS

UTIGUR

Don R.

irmium

Viminacium

SLAVS

Danube

DACIA RIPENSIS

DARDANIA DACIA MEDITER-RANEA

THRACE

MACEDONIA

RHOD

Thessalonica Abyd

THESSALIA

AEGEAN SEA

ACHAEA Athens

Halicarna

INS

CRETA

SEA

ENTAPOLIS

LIBYA INFERIOR

Petra

EMPIRE

Tigris R.

POTAMIA

Nisibis

PERSIAN

AKHMID ARABS

DATE DUE

MAY 3 1 07		

DEMCO 38-296

PIRE ABOUT 565

of a prefecture or state

of a province

erritory

rotectorate

(Later Roman Empire)

THEBAÏS INFERIOR

Nile

RED SEA

THEBAÏS SUPERIOR

SCALE

0   100 miles

0   100 200 km

A History of the Byzantine
State and Society

WARREN TREADGOLD

A History of the Byzantine State and Society

STANFORD UNIVERSITY PRESS
Stanford, California

Printed in the United States of America

CIP data appear at the end of the book

Maps: Helen L. Sherman

Cover illustration: Four groups of saints from a
twelfth-century mosaic of the Last Judgment in
the Church of Santa Maria Assunta, Torcello. The
groups are, from the rear of the procession, at left:
(1) female saints, led by the hermit Saint Mary the
Egyptian; (2) monastic saints, led by the abbot
Saint Euthymius the Great; (3) military saints in
court costume, led by Saint Theodore the Recruit; (4) episcopal saints, led by Saint John
Chrysostom followed by Saints Gregory of
Nazianzus, Nicholas of Myra, and Basil of Caesarea. (Photo: Irina Andreescu-Treadgold)

Frontispiece: Left leaf of a twelfth-century menologium icon from the Monastery of Saint Catherine,
Mount Sinai, showing Christ and six of the twelve
great feasts of the Church at the top, with the
saints commemorated each day during the months
from September to February. The right leaf of
the same icon appears below as Fig. 207. (Photo:
Courtesy of Michigan-Princeton-Alexandria
Expedition to Mount Sinai)

IN MEMORY OF MY FATHER,
DONALD TREADGOLD
(1922−1994),
WHO PASSED ON TO ME HIS RESPECT
FOR SCHOLARSHIP, THE CLASSICS, AND
THE CHRISTIAN EAST

Contents

Tables and Maps

MAPS

Preface

Today, in the age of the monograph, the time for a general survey seems always to be the indefinite future. Yet the reader of monographs on Byzantium often senses that they presuppose a common body of knowledge, which one would expect to find in a general book. Though that book used to be George Ostrogorsky's *History of the Byzantine State*, even someone who has read it thoroughly will find that historians are now assuming information and points of view that are not in it. We have newer short histories of Byzantium, topical surveys of Byzantine civilization, and now a comprehensive reference dictionary on Byzantine subjects, but thus far no updated, detailed, and complete history.[1] This is what I have tried to supply here, within the limits of a single volume. My intended audience includes both the scholar and the general educated reader, and the student who aspires to become one, the other, or both.[2]

This book is a history of Byzantium rather than a history of modern scholarship on Byzantium, and so it is not quite the book that the mono-

---

1. See especially Robert Browning's *The Byzantine Empire* (rev. ed.: Washington, 1992) among the short histories, Cyril Mango's *Byzantium: The Empire of New Rome* (London, 1980) among the surveys of civilization, and Alexander Kazhdan's three-volume *Oxford Dictionary of Byzantium* (New York, 1991). Of two multivolume works, Aikaterine Christophilopoulou's *Byzantine History* (2 vols.: Amsterdam, 1986–93; in progress), which has reached 1081 to date, is designed as a teaching manual rather than a history, and John Julius Norwich's *Byzantium* (3 vols.: London, 1988–95) is an uncritical compilation of largely obsolete work (which, however, "makes no claim to academic scholarship," I, 28).

2. I assigned preliminary drafts of the book in two courses at Florida International University without provoking complaints, once students were assured that in Byzantine histories, as in Russian novels, no one bothers to learn all the names.

graphs seem to be assuming. Modern Byzantine scholarship, besides leaving many gaps and agreeing on some dubious propositions, has often come to conclusions that are inconsistent with each other, usually because those working on different parts of the field have reached results that turn out to be incompatible. A general book could be compiled by summarizing the modern studies and overlooking their incongruities; but the result would be a distorted picture of both the modern scholarship and Byzantium itself. A book could also be written that discussed all the contradictions and omissions in modern scholarship; but if limited to one volume it would leave little space for Byzantium, and would be of scant interest to anyone but students of modern historiography. What I have done instead is to consult the modern literature as far as it helped, to read as many of the Byzantine sources as I could, and then to write the history as I see it, following all, most, some, or none of the modern and Byzantine authorities as the case may be.

The purpose of my bibliographical survey and notes is not to satisfy bibliographers but to guide the reader to the principal works that I have used and think useful. I have described the basic sources and secondary literature in the final bibliographical survey, *not in the notes*, which are limited to references that cannot easily be found by consulting the survey. Thus many fundamental works never appear in the notes, which tend to be most abundant when the secondary literature is least satisfactory. Much that has been written on Byzantine history—as on other topics— is mistaken, repetitious, or insignificant, and the process of listing and responding to it has become a distraction from the sources and the subject. Of course, since this book itself is secondary literature, readers should use it with due caution, realizing, for example, that about a quarter of the statements that I qualify by "probably" are probably wrong.

The book differs from standard approaches in several ways, about most of which I have written other books or articles.[3] It puts less emphasis on the catastrophe of the seventh century.[4] It takes a more optimistic view of the eighth and ninth centuries.[5] It pays more attention to the army, emphasizing its survival through the seventh century and its failure to survive the eleventh century.[6] I give less prominence to Icono-

3. These I have cited fairly often in my references in order to avoid either repeating my previously published arguments or implying that my views need no justification.

4. See W. Treadgold, "The Break in Byzantium and the Gap in Byzantine Studies," *Byzantinische Forschungen* 14 (1990), 289–316.

5. See W. Treadgold, *The Byzantine Revival, 780–842* (Stanford, 1988).

6. See W. Treadgold, *Byzantium and Its Army, 284–1081* (Stanford, 1995).

clasm, the last and least of the empire's major theological controversies.[7] I make more use of statistics and numerical estimates, since despite their varying reliability and precision they are less misleading than the standard generalizations about economic decline and disappearing cities.[8] The reader will also find none of the usual judgments that grave internal defects doomed the empire long before it actually fell. Though today we can say that the fall was inevitable in the sense that nothing can be done about it any more, only from about 1360 was Byzantium so weak as to be at imminent risk of extinction.

In some other ways I differ with many Byzantinists, but probably not with most. I attach no great importance to holy men, court oratory, or official ceremonies, since none of these seems to have mattered much to most contemporaries.[9] I find modern ideologies like Marxism, Poststructuralism, or nationalism of various sorts to be unhelpful for studying Byzantium, where social classes and political and religious groups were loose, shifting, and not ideological in the modern sense. I also think that events and emperors did matter, even for the lowliest Byzantine. What the emperor did, or did not do, could rapidly confront ordinary Byzantines with economic ruin, new religious doctrines, or conquest by a foreign power. Byzantine society, originally defined by the state, was constantly changed by it.

None of these comments means that modern scholarship on Byzantium is worse than that on most other subjects. Perhaps simply because it remains underworked territory, Byzantium has inspired more than its share of studies that are both original and valid. It has had its great names, like Edward Gibbon, Charles Diehl, J. B. Bury, Ernest Stein, and A. H. M. Jones; one of them, Sir Steven Runciman, is still active. It has its outstanding contemporary historians, like Cyril Mango, Alexander Kazhdan, Alan Cameron, Michael Hendy, and Ralph-Johannes Lilie. It has teams of scholars working on important research projects in Britain,

7. To the best of my knowledge, no one has suggested that Iconoclasm had more important consequences, or even attracted more contemporary interest, than Arianism had earlier. Yet secular historians, who never call the fourth century the Age of Arianism, often term the eighth and ninth centuries the Age of Iconoclasm, at the expense of more significant aspects of eighth- and ninth-century history.

8. Interestingly, the scholars who make the most speculative generalizations, sometimes without any evidence, are often the most skeptical about statistics recorded in the sources; cf. *Byzantium and Its Army* (above, n. 6), 1–7.

9. See W. Treadgold, "Imaginary Early Christianity," *International History Review* 15 (1993), 535–45, and "Taking Sources on Their Own Terms and on Ours," *Antiquité Tardive* 2 (1994), 153–59.

France, Austria, and Australia. If the field is now endangered in America, the main reason is the decline of its leading institution, Harvard's Dumbarton Oaks Center for Byzantine Studies, which despite a huge endowment has let the number of its research professors drop to zero, its fieldwork end, and its leadership lapse.

For fellowships that supported my work on this book, I am happy to thank the National Endowment for the Humanities, the Earhart Foundation, the Wilbur Foundation, the Florida International University Foundation, and All Souls College, Oxford. My thanks for reading all or part of my text and making important suggestions and corrections go to Robert Browning, Noël Duval, John Fine, Michael Hendy, Leslie MacCoull, George Majeska, Victor Spinei, my father, Donald Treadgold, and my wife, Irina Andreescu-Treadgold. My special thanks go to Alexander Kazhdan for making hundreds of valuable comments, even though he and I hold very different views on some aspects of Byzantine history. Naturally neither he nor any of my other readers could or should subscribe to everything I say here. I also renew my thanks to my original teacher, Ihor Ševčenko, whose respect for the sources and impatience with scholarly mediocrity are needed now more than ever.

For help during my travels in the Mediterranean and in assembling the illustrations I am grateful to Chrysanthi Baltoyanni, Charalambos Bouras, Fr. Leonard Boyle, David Buckton, Helmut Buschhausen, Slobodan Ćurčić, Gianfranco Fiaccadori, Jacques Lefort, Jerko Marasović, Thomas Mathews, Denys Pringle, Eugenia Salza Prina Ricotti, Serena Romano, Bruno Tarantola, Natalia Teteriatnikov, Mehmet Tunay, Paul Williamson, and especially my wife. My thanks also go to my patient cartographer, Helen Sherman, and to my extraordinarily faithful and careful editor, Paul Psoinos, who has greatly improved the book and often acted as the research assistant I never had. Finally, my parents and again my wife have given me unstinting support during the most difficult project I have ever attempted.

This book assumes readers who want to learn about the Byzantine Empire in some detail. But why, I am sometimes asked, should anyone who is not Greek care about Byzantium? First, Byzantium shaped and passed on Christian, Roman, and Greek traditions, including Christian theology, Roman law, and the Greek classics, that still influence modern life everywhere. Byzantine traditions have had their most powerful effect on Russia and the rest of Eastern Europe, a part of the world that all of us have much more to hear from, for better or worse. Another reason for studying the Byzantines is that despite a similar background they produced a civilization often strikingly unlike that of modern Western Europe and America. As a conservative, religious, and not very materialistic society, Byzantium had weaknesses corresponding to Western strengths, and strengths corresponding to Western weaknesses. Though in its politics Byzantium often resembled a Middle Eastern dictatorship, neither the West nor anyone else has matched it in maintaining a single state and society for so long, over a wide area inhabited by heterogeneous peoples. So Byzantine history helps explain why we are as we are, and how we might be different. Some of us also find it fascinating.

Coral Gables, Florida
November 1993

Note on Transliteration

Although Latin was the official language of the Byzantine Empire until the sixth century, and many Byzantines spoke Latin until the eighth century, most of the time most Byzantines spoke Greek, and used the Greek alphabet when they wrote. Greek names can be transliterated into the Latin alphabet for an English text in four main ways. One way, the most logical but the least familiar, is to give the closest equivalent to the Byzantine pronunciation, which was roughly the same as in Modern Greek. The first emperor of the Byzantine period thus becomes Dhioklitianos, the last Konstandinos XI. A second method, which many historians now favor, is to give the closest equivalent to the ancient Greek pronunciation, which no one used in Byzantine times. This makes the emperors Dioklētianos and Kōnstantinos XI. A third method, the one most often used by the Byzantines themselves when they wrote in Latin, is to turn the Greek name into a Latin one, changing the Greek letters into their Latin equivalents and the Greek endings into equivalent Latin endings. Thus we have Diocletianus and Constantinus XI. A fourth method, long standard in English, is a modification of the third, using English equivalents when they exist and Latinizing the rest. This gives us Diocletian and Constantine XI.

Each of these methods has its advantages and drawbacks, and each can carry ideological baggage. The first tends to emphasize the link between Byzantium and modern Greece, the second that between Byzantium and classical Greece, and the third that between Byzantium and Rome. All three links are undeniable, though a tendency to minimize that between Byzantium and Rome has recently boosted the popularity of the second

Table of Greek-English Transliterations

Greek	English equivalent			
	Method I	Method II	Method III	Method IV
α	a	a	a	a
$\alpha\iota$	e	ai	ae	ae (s)[a]
$\alpha\upsilon$	af (av)[b]	au	au	au
β	v	b	b (v)[c]	b (v)[c]
γ	gh (y)[d]	g	g	g
$\gamma\gamma$	ng	ng	ng	ng
$\gamma\kappa$	g (ng)[e]	gk	gc	gc
δ	dh	d	d	d
ϵ	e	e	e	e
$\epsilon\iota$	i	ei	i	i
$\epsilon\upsilon$	ef (ev)[b]	eu	eu	eu
ζ	z	z	z	z
η	i	ē	e	e
$\eta\upsilon$	if (iv)[b]	ēu	eu	eu
θ	th	th	th	th
ι	i	i	i	i
κ	k	k	c	c
λ	l	l	l	l
μ	m	m	m	m
$\mu\pi$	b (mb)[e]	mp	mp	mp
ν	n	n	n	n
$\nu\tau$	d (nd)[e]	nt	nt	nt
ξ	x	x	x	x
o	o	o	o	o
$o\iota$	i	oi	oe (i)[f]	oe (i)[g]
$o\upsilon$	on	on	on (um)[f]	on (um)[f]
$o\varsigma$	oṡ	os	os (us)[f]	os (us)[h]
$o\upsilon$	ou	ou	u	u
π	p	p	p	p
ρ	r	r	r	r
$\dot{\rho}$[i]	r	rh	rh	rh
σ, ς	s (z)[j]	s	s	s
τ	t	t	t	t
$\tau\zeta$	dz	tz	tz	tz
υ	i	u	u	u
υ[k]	i	y	y	y
ϕ	f	ph	ph	ph
χ	kh (h)[d]	ch	ch	ch
ψ	ps	ps	ps	ps
ω	o	ō	o	o
$\omega\upsilon$	on	ōn	on (o)[f]	on (o)[l]
$\cdot$	—	h	h	h

[a] At the end of a word when customary ("Athens").

[b] Before all vowels and voiced consonants.

[c] For terms introduced only during the Byzantine period ("Monemvasia"), especially those taken from foreign languages ("Artavasdus").

Table of Greek-English Transliterations (continued)

---

d Before *e* and *i*.

e In the middle of a word.

f At the end of a word.

g At the end of a word, though when customary the *i* can be replaced by an *s* or *es* ("Federates").

h At the end of a name, though when customary the *us* can be replaced by an *e* ("Constantine") or omitted altogether ("Diocletian"), while for islands the *os* is used ("Lesbos").

i When doubled or at the beginning of a word.

j Before voiced consonants.

k When between vowels or at the beginning of a word.

l At the end of a word when customary ("Plato").

m Marking a vowel at the beginning of a word.

method. My practice here is to follow the fourth method for names, since it not only produces the most familiar forms but is appropriate for people, places, and institutions that were both Latin and Greek, like John Italus, Syracuse, or the Scholae. I use the second method for other Greek words, mainly because it is the easiest to convert back into the Greek alphabet.

The accompanying table of transliterations shows how each method works, though it cannot include all the traditional peculiarities of Method IV ("Constantinople" for "Constantinoupolis," "John" for "Ioannes," etc.).

In transliterating from the Arabic and Cyrillic alphabets, I have chosen the forms that seem best to reflect the pronunciation, except for names that have become standard in English (e.g., "Mohammed" for the prophet "Muḥammad," "Belgrade" for "Beograd"). I have rendered hačeks in medieval (but not modern) Slavic names by adding an *h* (e.g., "Dushan" for "Dušan"), and *j* and *ij* by *y* (e.g., "Kaloyan" for "Kalojan").

A History of the Byzantine State and Society

Introduction

If, as many people think, states grow old and die after a limited lifespan, Rome should have fallen long before it reached its Byzantine phase. As it was, parts of the Roman state that threw off Etruscan rule about 510 B.C. remained independent until the fall of Trebizond in 1461 A.D. In the course of those two millennia, the state naturally underwent profound changes: vast expansion, transformation into a monarchy, administrative division into eastern and western parts, the fall of the western part, and the dwindling and fragmentation of the eastern part. Yet, long after the city of Rome had been lost, something calling itself the Roman Empire remained in the East, under the rule of emperors who could trace their succession in an unbroken line back to Augustus. Modern historians have called this empire "Byzantine" because it was ruled not from Rome but usually from Constantinople, the former Byzantium.

Even though the name "Byzantine Empire" was never used at the time, the distinction it represents is a useful one. When the eastern part of the Roman Empire came to be ruled separately, it was changed by Greek cultural and political traditions, and soon by the Christian religion as well. Since this reshaped eastern empire lasted almost twelve hundred years after the division, while the western empire disappeared in less than two hundred, the changes in the eastern empire seem not to have been a serious disadvantage for its survival. But when those changes began, in the late third century, the Roman Empire, Greek customs, and Christianity were already well established in the East.

Greek tradition was the oldest of them. Nearly all the lands bordering the eastern Mediterranean Sea had passed under Greek rule by 331 B.C., when Alexander the Great finished adding Anatolia, Syria, and Egypt to his inheritance of Macedon, Thrace, and Greece. That year Alexander founded Alexandria in Egypt, a Greek city he intended to be a metropolis for his domains up to that time. Within this eastern Mediterranean realm, Alexander's Greeks were to maintain strong political, economic, and cultural influence for over a thousand years. Although Alexander conquered lands farther to the east, those were never more than superficially Hellenized, and soon slipped from Greek rule. The real successes of Hellenization took place within Alexander's Mediterranean possessions, which were almost precisely the lands that eventually became the early Byzantine Empire.

After Alexander's early death in 323 B.C., most of his empire split into three large kingdoms under three of his marshals, who were succeeded by their descendants. The largest of these kingdoms was founded in Mesopotamia and extended to Syria and Anatolia by Seleucus I the Victor, who bequeathed it to his heirs as the Seleucid Kingdom. The richest of the three kingdoms was founded in Egypt by Ptolemy I the Savior; since all his male heirs shared his name, it became known as the Kingdom of the Ptolemies. The third and weakest state, established by the descendants of Antigonus I the One-Eyed, was the Antigonid Kingdom, consisting of Macedon and a precarious and partial hegemony over Greece. Other Greek cities and leagues existed as well, among which Pergamum and Rhodes became the most powerful. Non-Greeks who were well Hellenized came to rule kingdoms in Bithynia, Pontus, Cappadocia, and even Judaea. Thus almost the whole eastern Mediterranean basin remained subject to Greek-speaking rulers, until the arrival of the Romans.

When the Romans arrived, they took over the region without much disturbing the machinery of Greek rule. First invited east by Pergamum and Rhodes, Rome conquered Antigonid Macedon, absorbed Greece, and inherited Pergamum. The Romans continued to expand inexorably until, by largely peaceful means, they had made provinces of Bithynia, Seleucid Cilicia and Syria, and Ptolemaic Cyrenaïca and Cyprus. After annexing Egypt in 30 B.C., Rome effectively became a monarchy itself, so that the agents of the Ptolemies were replaced by those of Augustus. Artificially but not absurdly, some Byzantine chroniclers later reckoned 30 B.C. as the date when the Romans had taken over "the empire" from the Greeks.

Although by then Rome held nearly all the eastern Mediterranean coastlands, Greeks and Greek speakers continued to dominate the area's administration, economy, and culture. In the eastern portion of the Roman Empire, except in the Roman military colonies established along the lower Danube, Latin was the language only of the army and of a handful of high Roman officials who were fluent in Greek as well. Greek-speaking city councils performed most administrative functions, including the collection of taxes. Just as prominent Romans acknowledged the superiority of Greek culture, so prominent Greeks acknowledged the superiority of Roman government, and few if any thought of expelling the Romans. During the first centuries of Roman rule, the Greek East was generally peaceful and prosperous.

By the time Christ began his ministry in Judaea under Augustus's successor Tiberius, both Greek culture and the Roman Empire were dominant in the East. From Saint Paul onwards, Christian missionaries preached to the Greek-speaking population of the Roman Empire, profiting from the absence of political or linguistic barriers; for three hundred years, they made most of their converts among people who spoke Greek. Although the Roman government executed Christ, Saint Peter and Saint Paul, and some other Christians, it made no systematic attempt to suppress Christianity until the third century, when its two persecutions were brief and erratic. By that time nearly every city in the eastern Roman Empire had an organized Christian community, and Christian theological literature, written chiefly in Greek, could impress even pagan philosophers. Some Byzantines later believed that God had fostered the Greek language and the Roman state for the very purpose of helping Christianity to spread.

By the late third century, however, neither Christianity, Hellenism, nor even the Roman Empire was precisely triumphant in the East. Christians were still greatly outnumbered within every region and social group, and were particularly sparse in the countryside. Even Greeks were a minority in the eastern Roman Empire; a majority spoke Greek only in the Greek peninsula, western Anatolia, the islands, the coastlands, and the largest cities (Map 1). Otherwise the principal language varied: in Egypt it was Coptic; in Syria and Mesopotamia, Aramaic; in Thrace, Thracian; and within Anatolia, Phrygian, Galatian, Isaurian, or Cappadocian. While Greek was making some progress in rural Thrace and Anatolia, where the native languages were at least of the same Indo-

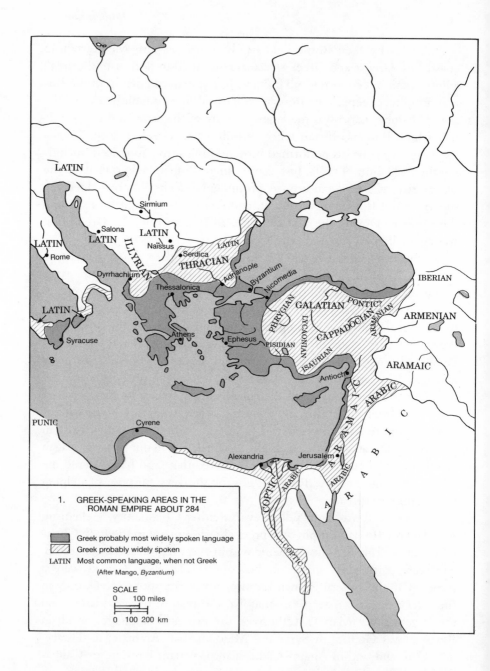

1. GREEK-SPEAKING AREAS IN THE ROMAN EMPIRE ABOUT 284

Greek probably most widely spoken language
Greek probably widely spoken
LATIN Most common language, when not Greek

(After Mango, *Byzantium*)

SCALE
0   100 miles
0   100 200 km

European family, it had a good deal less success in the countryside of Egypt and Syria, where the native languages were Hamitic or Semitic and fundamentally unlike Greek.[1]

The Roman Empire ran into serious difficulties during the third century, especially in holding its eastern provinces. The trouble began in the late second century, when an epidemic broke out, the Parthians invaded from the east, the Germans invaded from the north, and the emperors began raising the army's pay. Mostly because disease caused a decline in the taxpaying population, tax increases proved inadequate to meet the army payroll. When the government debased and overminted the currency instead, inflation set in, dislocating the economy and annoying the army as its pay sank in value. Military revolts started, followed by still more barbarian invasions.[2]

In the East, the German tribal alliance of the Goths invaded Thrace, Greece, and Anatolia, and forced the Romans to evacuate Dacia (in modern Romania north of the Danube). The Persians of the Sassanid Empire, which replaced the Parthian Empire in 226, similarly harassed Syria and took over the Roman protectorate in Armenia. The Arabs of Palmyra, repudiating Roman suzerainty, temporarily ruled Syria, Egypt, and part of Anatolia. Worse still, the commanders of the armies that fought these invaders and rebels repeatedly tried to seize power for themselves. Between 211 and 284, the Goths killed one emperor, the Persians captured another, and a third died in another epidemic; but the remaining twenty-three emperors were either certainly or probably killed by Romans, in most cases after reigning less than two years. If the empire was not yet falling, it was unmistakably in decline.

The years after 284 brought major reforms, including the administrative division between East and West, that mark the beginning of the Byzantine period. Although the West soon resumed its decline and disappeared, the history of the East was less simple, with many declines and recoveries. These are apparent from the East's gains and losses of territory. Disregarding a few administrative changes in the boundary between East and West (by defining it as it was finally set in 395) and excluding deserts, the territorial extent of each part of the Roman Empire can be plotted over time on a graph (Fig. 1).

For the East, the graph shows a moderate loss between 300 and 450, the result of defeats by the Persians and Huns. Then a major gain occurred, as much of the former western empire was reconquered by the emperor Justinian. Justinian's gains disappeared by 620, because of new

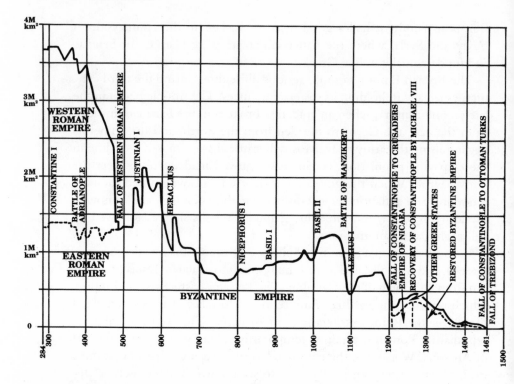

1. Graph of the territorial extent of the Byzantine empire, 284–1461.

invasions by the Germans, Persians, and Avars. By 750 another major loss occurred, as the Arabs conquered a large part of Byzantine territory. But this second decline was made good by 1050, when after many reconquests the empire was scarcely smaller than it had been in 300 or 620, and slightly larger than it had been in 450. Then came another severe decline, caused by losses to the Seljuk Turks. Interrupted by a partial recovery, this decline lasted until 1204, when Constantinople fell to the Fourth Crusade, and the provinces that remained under Greek rule were divided among several successor states. Finally the main empire and the smaller Greek states recovered for a time, before shrinking to nothing by 1461, conquered by the Ottoman Turks.

No doubt differences in population and resources can make land area a misleading guide to a state's power; but for Byzantium the graph gives for the most part an accurate picture. Each major territorial gain reflected underlying strength, and each major loss showed underlying weakness. Such strengths and weaknesses often escaped the notice of Byzantine observers, who considered the losses temporary and took the reconquests more or less for granted. But in comparison with these gains and losses of territory, most of the battles, intrigues, and ceremonies that preoccupy Byzantine sources and many modern histories were insignificant. Territorial losses and gains signaled the main turning points of Byzantine history, when the Byzantine state and the society it ruled shrank or expanded, and were forced to adapt to new circumstances.

The Byzantine state and Byzantine society did not always match each other, since the state could have weak influence over some of its subjects, but strong influence over others who lived outside Byzantine rule. Yet up to the third century, the Roman state had hardly corresponded to any single society in the East. Rome's rulers, consisting of the emperor and a select group of his officials, had little contact with most of the people they ruled. No doubt the government wished its subjects to be contented and prosperous, if only because it hoped that they would then rebel less often and pay more in taxes. But the rulers, to the extent that they thought about their subjects at all, gave most of their attention to the soldiers and to the citizens of the main cities, because those, small minorities though they were, could cause the government the most trouble.

Nor did the third-century Roman government have any great effect on the lives of most of its subjects. Outside the Latin-speaking West, the people of the Roman Empire had never had much in common with each other. Most Egyptians, Syrians, and Greeks shared no language, and shared a religion only in the sense that most of them did not repudiate the others' gods. The bulk of them were subsistence farmers living in small villages, illiterate and seldom aware of political events. They feared foreign invasions only because invaders usually ravaged and stole more than the Roman army did. Most provincials thought of the central government as an alien force, and found it rapacious and unreliable. Not even the army was happy enough with the emperors it proclaimed to keep them for more than a few years before overthrowing them.

Such were the unpromising elements from which the Byzantine Empire was to be formed. Yet even in the later third century the eastern Roman Empire retained much of its former prosperity. The invasions and state requisitions had caused only local and temporary impoverishment. The recurrences of disease seem to have brought only moderate depopulation, and may even have relieved overpopulation in some places. By ancient standards, the commerce, manufacturing, and culture of eastern Roman cities were still impressive. The worst effects of the third-century crisis had been felt in the western part of the empire, which possessed less defensible frontiers and less productive cities, and had suffered more from enemy raids and military revolts. The future of the Roman Empire lay in the East, where in 284 the army proclaimed yet another new emperor.

PART ONE

The Enlarged State and the Burdened Society

2. Aerial view of Diocletian's palace near Salona, where he retired after his abdication in 305. Its walls now enclose the center of the city of Split, Croatia, with Diocletian's octagonal mausoleum serving as the cathedral (center right, with bell tower). (Photo: Nenad Gattin, courtesy of Vinko Nikolić)

The Refoundation of the Empire, 284–337

In 283, during a war against the Persians in Mesopotamia, the emperor Carus was killed, allegedly by a thunderbolt but more probably by assassination. The Roman army proclaimed Carus's son Numerian emperor. Soon it abandoned the Persian war and slowly withdrew into Anatolia. When the army reached Nicomedia in 284, Diocles, the commander of the imperial bodyguard, announced that Numerian himself had been murdered. After executing the supposed assassin, Diocles had himself proclaimed emperor. His claims were rejected by Carus's surviving son, Carinus, who had been ruling at Rome and now led an army against Diocles. A civil war began, and early the next year the forces of the two emperors clashed at the Margus River in the middle of the Balkans. The battle went well for Carinus until he too was assassinated, leaving Diocles the temporarily undisputed ruler of the Roman Empire.

DIOCLETIAN'S NEW SYSTEM

Like most of his predecessors over the past fifty years, Diocles was a capable career officer from an obscure family in Illyricum. In comparison with similar emperors, he was a middling general but an excellent manager, with an education slightly better than average. He appears to have been around forty years old at his accession. According to plausible reports, he had been born at Salona on the Illyrian coast, to a father who was a freedman and a scribe. Appropriately for a scribe's son, he showed a liking for records and numbers, and wrote without literary pretensions. Salona was in Latin-speaking territory, but his Greek name of Diocles

3. Marble bust, probably of Diocletian (r. 284–305), now in the Istanbul Archeological Museum. (Photo: Irina Andreescu-Treadgold)

suggests Greek origins, and he was equally at ease speaking Latin or Greek. Although in 285 he Latinized his Greek name to Diocletianus, he was the nearest thing that the empire had yet had to an emperor of Greek stock.

Diocletian had no son, but decided he needed another emperor to share his powers and the dangers he faced. A preference for the Greek East may lie behind his decision to retain control over it and to entrust the Latin West to someone else. At Milan, in July 285, Diocletian adopted as his son one of his Illyrian comrades in arms, Maximian, giving him the rank of Caesar, or junior emperor. Henceforth the defense of the provinces west of Illyricum became the primary responsibility of Maximian, while the defense of Illyricum and the East remained that of Diocletian. The next year, when Maximian faced a usurping emperor in Britain, Diocletian strengthened his colleague's hand by promoting him to Augustus, the highest imperial rank.

Diocletian still kept a formal precedence over Maximian. As an expression of their relationship, Diocletian styled himself Jovius, claiming the patronage of Jupiter, king of the gods, and titled Maximian Herculius, assigning him the patronage of Jupiter's son Hercules. In practice Maximian continued to defer to his senior colleague's judgment. But each emperor maintained his own court and ran his own army and administration, with a separate praetorian prefect (in Latin, *praefectus praetorio*) as his chief lieutenant. Although the empire remained juridically one, and on occasion was ruled by a single emperor again, after 285 its eastern and western parts always had different prefects and separate administrations. From this time forward, we can follow the history of the East with only occasional attention to the West.

Before Diocletian, jurisdiction over the eastern and western parts of the empire had sometimes been separated for a time, either by a rebellion in the East, like Diocletian's own, or as an emergency measure, like Carus's entrusting the West to his son Carinus before departing for Persia. But Diocletian's arrangement was more systematic than those temporary divisions. Although for an emperor without a son to adopt an heir and title him Caesar had long been standard practice, Diocletian meant Maximian, who was only a few years his junior, to be a colleague rather than an heir. Diocletian plainly realized that, at a time when internal rebellions and external invasions had become endemic, the empire was too big for one emperor to rule and defend.

What remains striking is that Diocletian took as his own portion not the Latin West but the Greek East, to which he attached Latin-speaking Illyricum, his own homeland. Although his motives cannot be reliably reconstructed, he evidently believed that the East, with Illyricum, was at least as important a part of the empire as the West, and an appropriate domain for the senior ruler. Given the threat that the empire faced from foreign invasions and military rebellions, part of his reason was surely that the larger part of the army was stationed in the East—twenty-three of thirty-four legions as of the early third century—where it faced the empire's single strongest adversary, Persia. The East as Diocletian defined it also included the empire's best recruiting ground, in Illyricum, and its richest farmland, in Egypt.

Leaving Maximian to defend the West, Diocletian concentrated first on strengthening the frontiers in the East. He began recruiting more troops. In two campaigns he drove some Sarmatian raiders back across the Danube frontier, and built new fortifications to keep them out. In 287 he negotiated a peace with Persia, establishing a Roman protectorate over Armenia and securing the Mesopotamian border, which he defended with more fortifications. He established his principal residence at Nicomedia, where he had first taken power. On the coast of Asia Minor but facing Europe, Nicomedia was in the middle of Diocletian's eastern domains and midway on the road between the Balkan and Mesopotamian frontiers.

Diocletian hardly supposed that naming a permanent colleague would be enough to solve the problem of the empire's security. He felt that the empire, including its western part, needed a bigger army and more fortifications, and more revenue to pay for them. Probably in 287, he introduced a new system for taxation and the requisition of supplies, which also applied to the western provinces ruled by Maximian. For centuries the Romans had levied taxes of different kinds all over the empire, at widely different rates. The inflation of the previous century had slowly rendered monetary taxes almost worthless, so that the government increasingly met its expenses by requisitions of labor or goods, such as uniforms for the soldiers and grain for city dwellers. Originally such requisitions had been paid for in money at fixed rates, but as inflation made the value of the payments nugatory they had gradually ceased to be made. Under this makeshift system assessment was inefficient and burdensome, and raising taxes was difficult.

Diocletian realized that the best way of maximizing receipts while minimizing economic dislocation was to standardize the taxes and requisitions according to his subjects' ability to pay. Collecting taxes or requisitions that fell equally on each man, household, or measure of land had the obvious disadvantage that some men and households could afford to pay much more than others, and some land was far more productive than other land. Uniform rates that the rich could pay easily would ruin the poor, and rates that the poor could pay would be absurdly low for the rich and yield little revenue. Yet any assessment of land and other property according to their monetary value would rapidly become obsolete as the coinage continued to inflate.

To make a reliable assessment possible, Diocletian defined two standard units to measure tax liability. One was the *caput*—literally meaning "head," but better translated as "heading" because it was a theoretical unit for varying numbers of taxpayers. It was supposed to stand for a set amount of wealth, which happened to be well above that of the average taxpayer; it could represent the resources of many poor households, the property of several middling ones, or a fraction of the fortune of a rich man. Seemingly the wealth taken into account was limited to real estate. The second unit was the *jugum* ("yoke"), representing a set acreage of first-class plowland; apparently it could also be a larger portion of worse land or a smaller portion of better land, so that each *jugum* would be of approximately the same value. The *juga* seem to have been designed to assess requisitions of grain, and the *capita* to assess other taxes, in coin or in kind. Evidently regions that produced a large surplus of grain, notably Egypt, were assigned more *juga* and fewer *capita* than others. The quantity of grain levied per *jugum*, and tax per *caput*, could vary from year to year according to the government's needs. Yet the intent appears to have been that in a given year an equal quantity of grain should be levied per *jugum* and an equal amount of tax per *caput*, at least within the jurisdiction of each emperor.[1]

This system must have taken some time to put into effect. Each city was assigned a quota of *capita* and *juga* for its territory, and the city councils, which had always been responsible for collecting taxes and requisitions, now had to collect the taxes and requisitions that corresponded to their cities' quotas. When the system began, the quotas must have been assigned somewhat arbitrarily, on the basis of current records. But the system at least allowed an accurate census to be made, and Diocletian seems to have planned for a regular revision of assessments in five-year cycles beginning in 287, with the beginning of a thoroughgoing reassessment perhaps scheduled for 292. His plans for a reform of the coinage and of provincial administration may also have begun this early.

Although Diocletian was now primarily ruler of the East, he continued to be aware of the problems of the West. He twice conferred with Maximian at the boundary between Illyricum and Italy, where their jurisdictions met. Once the two rulers campaigned together against the Germans there. Maximian, who had taken Milan as his headquarters, maintained or restored order in most of the West, though he was unable to suppress the rebellion in Britain, which had spread to northwestern Gaul. The record of the two Augusti was by no means a bad one, particularly by the standards of the past century of disasters, but it failed to satisfy Diocletian. He therefore made another major change.

In 293 he arranged with Maximian to proclaim two junior emperors, so that each Augustus received a Caesar, sharing his epithet of Jovius or Herculius, to help rule his part of the empire. Maximian's Caesar was Constantius, his son-in-law and former praetorian prefect, while Diocletian's Caesar was his own son-in-law Galerius, who may also have been his former praetorian prefect. Like both Augusti, the new Caesars were experienced officers from Illyricum. Constantius was given the task of putting down the rebellion in Britain and Gaul, where he took Trier as his headquarters. At this time, Galerius's main headquarters seems to have been Antioch, and his main assignment to guard Syria and Egypt against the Persians, while Diocletian finished strengthening the Danube frontier.

These Caesars, despite having praetorian prefects of their own, were subject to their Augusti even within their assigned regions, which in any case were not permanently fixed. Furthermore, though Constantius and Galerius were not much younger than Diocletian and Maximian, the Caesars were designated heirs to the Augusti, perpetuating the artificial dynasties of the Jovii in the East and the Herculii in the West. This system of four emperors has since been called the tetrarchy. In fact, it sim-

4. Gold medallion of Galerius (r. 305–11), four-fifths actual size, depicting him as Caesar, the rank he held between 293 and 305, with his patron Jupiter on the reverse. (Photo: Dumbarton Oaks, Washington, D.C., copyright 1996)

ply applied the familiar practice of appointing junior emperors to the existing dyarchy. It therefore tended to confirm rather than to confuse the twofold division of the empire.

Around the time of the appointment of the new Caesars, Diocletian and his colleagues transformed the provincial administration, which had stayed much the same since the time of Augustus.[2] The former provinces, which had been fewer than fifty and of very different sizes, were replaced by about a hundred new provinces of more nearly uniform extent, population, and resources. Some fifty-five of these provinces were in the eastern empire, which was smaller in area but richer and more densely populated. The former provincial governors, who had commanded whatever troops garrisoned their provinces, were replaced by purely civil governors, while the army became subject to separate military officials.

The new provinces were further grouped into twelve large jurisdictions called dioceses, six of which were in the East. Each diocese was administered by a vicar (*vicarius*), an official who was the superior of the diocese's civil governors. Each vicar's superior was the praetorian prefect of one of the four emperors. Thus the emperors roughly tripled the number of their major officials, adding new prefectures, dioceses, and provinces and appointing military and civil officials to replace the old provincial governors. The number of lower-ranking bureaucrats also increased.

The introduction of four emperors required approximately quadrupling the imperial court, which consisted of councilors, household servants, and several administrative bureaus. Besides the praetorian prefect, whose department was in charge of the army and the requisitions levied for it, each emperor probably received a public treasurer, whose department handled his monetary revenues and mints, and a private treasurer, whose department managed his imperial estates. Each emperor also had bodyguards, messengers, and several departments to keep government records, all soon put under a master of offices (*magister officiorum*), an official probably created by Diocletian. By a rough estimate, the civil service doubled from about fifteen thousand men to about thirty thousand, of whom something more than half held posts in the East.[3]

Diocletian and his colleagues also greatly enlarged the army. Although the difficulty of recruiting and supplying soldiers probably forced them to increase it more gradually than the much smaller bureaucracy, most of the army's growth appears to have been rapid. The surviving figures that reflect it are open to some doubt, but the overall picture is clear. Starting with an army totaling some 390,000 soldiers in 285, the four emperors seem to have increased it by about half as much again, to some 581,000. Within the East, the increase seems to have been a good deal less, from about 253,000 men to 311,000, with most of the additions being made on the Persian frontier. The navy also increased, from about 46,000 seamen to about 64,000, with perhaps half of each number belonging to the East.[4]

Although earlier each provincial governor had commanded the soldiers in his province, Diocletian created military commands under dukes (*duces*). The dukes' commands, sometimes covering two or three of the small provinces created by Diocletian, formed a continuous series along the empire's land frontiers. All these ducates had forces ranging from two thousand to over twenty thousand men, usually both cavalry and infantry, and those on the lower Danube had fleets. Many of these frontier troops were quartered in new and elaborate fortifications. While the emperors could summon the dukes' troops whenever necessary, only relatively small mobile reserves accompanied the emperors at other times.

In the process of making his reforms, Diocletian reduced Italy and the city of Rome virtually to provincial status and subjected both the West and the East to the same administrative system. The Roman senate's remaining authority nearly disappeared, and senators became ineligible for all but a few governorships and other offices. Although the senators retained their wealth and personal privileges, most of the real power in the vast new machinery of government belonged to newcomers, many of them soldiers installed by the soldier-emperors. Now the empire's real capitals were simply wherever the emperors happened to be at the time, and many of their officials followed them on their travels.

Diocletian took some pains to assure that his subjects treated him and his colleagues with reverence. Ceremonial for approaching the emperors was made more elaborate, and they were guarded more closely. They were depicted in statuary as of superhuman size and strength (Fig. 5; cf. Fig. 7), and official rhetoric in their honor was especially effusive, stressing the particular favor that the gods had shown them. They described themselves as chosen by the gods, abandoning the threadbare pretense that they were leaders of a republic but diverting attention from the brutal truth that their power came from the army. Except insofar as the inapproachability of the emperor made him harder to assassinate, all this made little practical difference. The emperor had long been an absolute monarch, who after he was proclaimed by the army could rule practically as he wished until he was removed. Nonetheless, by laying public claim to the power that emperors had long had, but pretended not to have in deference to the wishes of senators and other conservatives, Diocletian strengthened the basis of his authority.

A new census of the empire's people and wealth was begun soon after 293 and apparently completed by 296. The census inspectors reassessed the persons and property of each landowner, evaluated these in *capita* and *juga*, and added the landowners' totals together to produce revised totals of *capita* and *juga* for the area administered by each city. Tax collectors then instructed each city council to provide animals, money, and even recruits for the army in proportion to its jurisdiction's *capita*, and grain according to its *juga*. Most taxes fell due annually on 1 September, the beginning of the year of the indiction (*indictio*, meaning "assessment"); but the census was also used for extraordinary requisitions. The actual collection from individual landowners was the responsibility of the decurions (*decuriones*), the city councilors. Because decurions had to supply from their own property whatever they failed to exact from others, service as a decurion often became a burden, and in some cases could mean financial ruin.

Despite the instability of the coinage, many of the taxes were either levied in money or convertible into money, with the rates adjusted to keep pace with inflation. Diocletian nonetheless intended to bring inflation to an end. Soon after his accession he had begun minting gold coins

5. Detail of the triumphal arch of Galerius in Thessalonica, from an old photograph. Galerius appears in the middle of the top register, larger than the figures around him, and in the middle of the third register, sacrificing to the gods on an altar. (Photo: Deutsches Archäologisches Institut, Athens)

at a reliable standard of purity; but these were scarce, and the inflation of the heavily debased silver coinage continued. Soon after 293 the emperors began issuing coins of undebased silver, of billon (copper with a small but fixed proportion of silver), and of pure copper. The billon and copper coins were minted in large numbers, in the hope that their values would eventually stabilize. The government seems to have had no idea that monetary stability depended on the supply of money rather than on its metallic purity.[5]

Although the new system of taxation distributed the costs of government more equitably than before, most taxpayers seem to have resented it, probably because they realized that its purpose was to increase the total burden imposed upon them. Farmers tried to evade taxes by moving to regions where they were not registered, and the wealthy avoided serving on city councils so as not to be obliged to make up the frequent shortfalls in receipts. The emperors consequently promulgated laws to bind farmers to the land they worked and to force anyone with enough property to serve as a decurion. Apart from city dwellers who owned no farmland, the main groups to escape the new exactions were army officers, civil officials, and senators, all of whom were exempt from serving on city councils. Diocletian may have extracted money from some of the exempt groups by means of lawsuits, since he is said to have prosecuted many of the rich in order to seize their wealth.[6] Despite various defects in the rules and their enforcement, however, the new system succeeded in raising more revenue and soldiers. It was to remain the basic mechanism of Byzantine taxation for centuries.

STABILITY RESTORED

Diocletian's purpose in multiplying emperors, officials, and troops, and in building more forts, was plainly to make the Roman government so strong that no rebel or invader could defeat it. But his changes in administration, taxation, and defense took years to put into full effect, and in the meantime he and his colleagues faced many challenges. Except for occasional visits to Nicomedia, Diocletian stayed in the Balkans until 296, securing the Danube frontier by campaigning, fortifying, and recruiting. Galerius spent his time in Egypt, where he put down a revolt and defeated raiders on the southern border, and in Syria, where a new Persian king, Narseh, was preparing for war. Late in 296 Narseh invaded the Roman client state of Armenia. The emperors were determined to stop him. Early the next year, while Diocletian advanced to join Galerius, the latter led his forces to help the Armenians. But Narseh defeated the Romans and forced Galerius to retreat. That summer another rebellion broke out in Egypt, perhaps provoked by the new census and taxes. Diocletian's regime suddenly looked vulnerable.[7]

Taking advantage of having a Caesar, Diocletian marched against the Egyptian rebels while giving Galerius a chance to retrieve his loss to the Persians. Advancing rapidly, Diocletian soon arrived in Egypt, where the rebels had proclaimed a usurper emperor, and began to restore order. Galerius left Narseh in Armenia for the moment and went to the Danube frontier to gather more troops. In the autumn of 297, while Diocletian pacified the Egyptian countryside and besieged Alexandria, Galerius marched into Armenia with some twenty-five thousand men. There he crushed Narseh's army, capturing the king's family and nearly capturing the king. Galerius drove home his advantage by invading lower Mesopotamia and triumphantly sacking the Persian capital of Ctesiphon the next year. Meanwhile Diocletian had starved out Alexandria and ended the Egyptian rebellion.

In 299 the Persians agreed to a treaty that recognized Armenia and its northern neighbor Iberia as Roman clients, and ceded some Persian borderlands to Armenia and Rome. Diocletian took over several small Armenian satrapies south of Armenia proper; he ruled these through their traditional satraps rather than making them a regular province. The gains from the Persians, though minor, were the empire's first new conquests in a century. More important was Persia's recognition of Roman superiority, which left the East secure against Persian attack for years to come. Meanwhile, in the West Constantius had suppressed the rebellion in Britain and Gaul and Maximian had put down another rebellion in Africa, so that the entire empire was at peace.

With his government assuming a reassuring permanence, Diocletian transferred Galerius to the Balkans, taking Anatolia, Syria, and Egypt as his own jurisdiction. Each of the four emperors now had responsibility for three of the twelve dioceses. Galerius and his praetorian prefect governed the dioceses of the Pannonias (northern Illyricum), the Moesias (southern Illyricum and Greece), and Thrace. Diocletian and his prefect governed the dioceses of Asiana (western and southern Anatolia), Pontica (northern and eastern Anatolia), and the East (Syria and Egypt). Galerius usually resided at Thessalonica in northern Greece, and Diocletian's favorite residence remained Nicomedia. Both of these nascent capitals were Greek cities on the main routes between Europe and Asia and between the Mediterranean and the Black Sea. Important though the manpower of Illyricum and the grain of Egypt were for the eastern part of the empire, Diocletian evidently regarded the Greek heartland as its political center, where both of its rulers should have their seats.

Diocletian had the highest respect for Greek traditions in religion. He encouraged the cults of the traditional Greco-Roman gods and showed little interest in the many more recent pagan cults and philosophies. His devotion to Jupiter seems to have been religious as well as political; his original name of Diocles, or "Zeus's Glory," implies that his parents had commended him at his birth to the king of the gods. His faith eventually brought him into conflict with Christianity. In 299 he and Galerius presided over a sacrifice at which the entrails of the victims failed to show the usual marks. The officiating priests charged that some Christians who were members of the court had frustrated the sacrifice by making the sign of the Cross. Accepting this explanation, Diocletian indignantly ordered all members of his court and army to sacrifice to the gods or resign their posts. This purge was not very thorough, but many Christians did leave the army and civil service in the East. Other Christians were not affected.

During the first few years of the fourth century, it became clear that Diocletian had succeeded in restoring the empire's stability. Although Galerius still needed to campaign against raiders on the Danube frontier, and similar police actions were needed in the West, there were no more major invasions. As rebellions also ceased, Diocletian became the longest-reigning emperor for over a hundred years. With ample resources from his system of taxation, he was able to construct a number of grand public buildings, particularly at Nicomedia. The greatly expanded machinery of government that Diocletian had established could evidently be sustained, and it operated more or less as he intended.

Diocletian's main failure was in his attempt to restore the currency. While his gold and silver coinage held its value, it remained rare. The far more common billon and copper coins were still subject to inflation, not because they were debased but because too many were being minted for the economy to absorb at stable rates. In 301 Diocletian ordered their nominal value to be doubled and put controls on wages and prices throughout the empire, forbidding merchants to refuse to sell at no more than the legal maximums. When the merchants refused to sell nonetheless, the edict had to be abandoned. Yet the state continued to function reasonably well, because most government revenues and payments were either adjustable or assessed in kind.

Diocletian was increasingly troubled by the spread of Christianity. In this he appears to have been influenced partly by the anti-Christian views of Galerius and partly by a growing realization of how strong Christians had become. At first Diocletian, whose overriding concern was to restore order and harmony to the empire, had tolerated Christians even in public service. As the Christians became bolder and more numerous, however, their rejection of the gods who were the emperors' patrons became hard to ignore, and Galerius's arguments in favor of a new persecution became more persuasive.

In 303, after consulting with Galerius, other high officials, and an oracle of Apollo, Diocletian had the Christian cathedral of Nicomedia demolished, and issued an edict against Christians. The edict prohibited Christian services, ordered the destruction of Christian churches and liturgical books, and deprived professed Christians of recourse to courts of law. While officially this edict applied to both East and West, in the West Maximian enforced it only sporadically and Constantius scarcely enforced it at all, so that it took full effect in the East alone. The Christians were naturally resentful. When the palace at Nicomedia burned down, the emperors of course believed charges that Christians had set the fire. Those accused were executed, and orders went out to arrest the Christian clergy. In 304, abandoning moderation, Diocletian and Galerius commanded everyone in the East, except for Jews, to sacrifice to the gods. Many Christians were imprisoned and tortured, and a number were killed, usually for particular acts of defiance. Most escaped punishment by making themselves inconspicuous.

This persecution failed to force many Christians to apostasize, and it seems to have been unpopular even among pagans. As Christians had become more numerous and familiar, most pagans had ceased to credit the old stories of Christian cannibalism, incest, and general immorality, and had found Christians to be respectable citizens with particularly sterling sexual morals. Their sufferings met with sympathy, and their determination and courage with admiration. The few hundred martyrs, who served to inspire their fellows, were not a significant proportion of church members. On the whole the persecution probably strengthened the Church.

During the worst of the persecution, Galerius was the virtual ruler of the East, because in 304, while returning from a visit to Rome to celebrate the twentieth anniversary of his accession, Diocletian became seriously ill. He only began to recover his health early in 305, and by then he was contemplating abdication. After a generally successful reign of twenty-one years, he was ready for retirement, and had a capable heir waiting to succeed him. Apparently on the argument that a reign that was long enough for him should be long enough for his colleague, he prevailed upon the western Augustus, Maximian, to retire along with him. Their joint abdication allowed Galerius to become Augustus in the East and Constantius Augustus in the West, with new Caesars as subordinates and presumptive heirs for each.

Galerius seems to have exercised considerable influence on Diocletian's arrangements. The new Caesar for the West was Severus, a friend of Galerius's and possibly his praetorian prefect, while the new Caesar for the East was Maximin, Galerius's nephew. As befitted his new seniority, Galerius was given jurisdiction over Anatolia as well as the Balkans, five dioceses in all, including the East's main administrative center at Nicomedia. Maximin received jurisdiction only over Egypt and Syria, which formed the oversized Diocese of the East. Furthermore, Severus, whose connections with Galerius were close, was assigned the dioceses of Africa and Italy, which adjoined Galerius's holdings in Illyricum.

Although the new Augustus of the West, Constantius, enjoyed a nominal precedence over his western Caesar, in practical terms Galerius seemed to be inheriting more power, not only in the East but over the whole empire. While Galerius's friends had been chosen Caesars, the claims of Constantius's son Constantine and Maximian's son Maxentius, who were both of age to rule, received no recognition. Reportedly Galerius feared he would be unable to control them, although his daughter was already married to Maxentius. Despite this rejection of hereditary succession, Diocletian and Galerius had the new Augusti adopt their new Caesars, realizing that soldiers almost always preferred the succession of sons. Diocletian's prestige was so great, and his system so well established, that when he abdicated in 305 Maximian followed his example without objection, and the old emperor's nominees for Caesar and assignments of territory were accepted without question. He resumed his Greek name of Diocles, retired to a vast palace that he had built near his presumed home town of Salona, and busied himself with raising cabbages.

His reign, if not an unqualified success, had been far more successful than any of his predecessors' for over a century. Diocletian had assumed power when the empire was in apparently hopeless disorder, and he gave up power, voluntarily, when peace and stability had returned. He had changed the empire's government and army profoundly and lastingly, and few would have disputed that the empire was the better for it. His most important changes were his great expansion of the army and bureaucracy and his reorganization of state finance to pay for them. To judge from Diocletian's success in securing the frontiers, his enlarged army was sufficient, while his new officials appear to have been enough to enforce the collection of taxes and to maintain order in the provinces. Paying for a larger army and a doubled bureaucracy was easier than might have been supposed, because most soldiers and officials continued to be remunerated at low rates. By extending and equalizing the burden of taxation, Diocletian was able to raise much more revenue without exacting more than most taxpayers could easily pay.

Admittedly, extensive new recruitment for the army and administration depleted the productive work force. Worse still, the creation of a large and powerful but poorly paid army and bureaucracy invited extortion and embezzlement in the long run. The multiplicity of emperors also carried with it a serious weakness, which Diocletian's dominating personality concealed. Having two Augusti and two Caesars instead of one Augustus was a source of strength to the empire as long as the rulers cooperated, because an emperor was always near at hand to meet foreign invasions and deter revolts, and if he ran into trouble he had colleagues to come to his aid. But that the four emperors should be content with their portions, without aspiring to more territory, troops, or revenue, or to putting their sons in place to succeed them, could hardly be taken for granted for the indefinite future.

Diocletian's original colleagues were highly talented men who held him in awe and never disobeyed him. The new Caesars appointed in 305 were men of lesser ability, and neither they nor Galerius enjoyed good relations with Constantius. Finally, for all Galerius's power, neither he nor Constantius was formally assuming Diocletian's position as guide of the whole empire, and Diocletian had no plans to continue exercising authority in retirement. Nor had the empire's economic, religious, and military problems been lastingly resolved. In spite of the imposing institutions that Diocletian had put in place, the future balance of power was not at all stable.

RENEWED CONFLICT

Intelligent and decisive, probably in his late forties, Galerius was a better general than Diocletian and almost as good an administrator. But he was too harsh and inflexible to be Diocletian's equal as a leader. From the first, Galerius tried to direct policy over the whole empire, trusting in his influence over Maximin and Severus. He began with the sensitive matters of taxation and persecuting Christians. Whereas Diocletian had registered and taxed only those who owned or worked farmland, Galerius ordered the registry of townsmen without rural property, who were to be taxed on their persons and on the people in their households. Many such townsmen were poor and deeply resented the tax. It also required the government to draw up the first full lists of city dwellers, who included many Christians. Since this census helped the government detect Christians who avoided making pagan sacrifices, Galerius was able to intensify the persecution. Maximin and Severus followed Galerius's lead; Constantius did not.

Tensions appeared almost at once. Constantine, Constantius's son by his divorced wife Helena, had been in the East for years, first serving under Galerius in Persia and the Balkans and then residing at Diocletian's court in Nicomedia. Passed over for promotion to Caesar in 305 contrary to the expectations of many, Constantine obtained leave from Galerius to join his father in Britain. When Constantius died a year later, his troops proclaimed Constantine Augustus of the West out of loyalty to his family. Constantine moved into his father's palace at Trier and applied for recognition to the eastern Augustus Galerius, excusing his assumption of power by claiming that his army had forced it upon him.

According to Diocletian's arrangements, on Constantius's death the western Caesar Severus should have become Augustus, and he and Galerius should have chosen a new Caesar. Galerius wanted to defend Diocletian's rules, and in any case he felt little affection or trust for Constantine. Yet the new emperor was showing himself conciliatory, and could only be dislodged by difficult and dangerous warfare. So Galerius offered as a compromise to recognize Constantine as Caesar of the West, while Severus became Augustus. Constantine agreed, outwardly preserving the peace, but the spirit of cooperation among the emperors had obviously weakened. Later in 306, Constantine's example inspired young Maxentius to seize power in Italy, where his father Maximian had been ruling just the year before.

The people of Rome and the other Italian cities, already resentful at losing their privileged position in the empire, were particularly annoyed by Severus's attempt to register and tax them along with other townsmen. The Romans were therefore happy to proclaim Maxentius, who summoned his father from retirement to become Augustus once more. Severus marched on Rome with a much larger force to put down the rebellion. But his troops, who had served under Maximian for years, began to desert to the rebels. Severus had to withdraw, and in 307 was forced first to surrender and then to commit suicide. Maxentius took the title of Augustus, while Maximian bestowed both the title of Augustus and the hand of his daughter Fausta on Constantine. Thus three western Augusti formed an alliance against Galerius.

East and West were now openly hostile to each other. When the enraged Galerius marched on Rome, even his soldiers began to desert to Maximian and Maxentius. Galerius reluctantly returned to Illyricum, pillaging Italy as he went. During this campaign thousands of men went over from the eastern armies to the western. Galerius still would not accept defeat, and soon had the satisfaction of seeing Maximian try to overthrow his son, fail, and seek Galerius's protection. By 308, Galerius was able to bring Maximian to a peace conference at Carnuntum, on the upper Danube, attended by the retired Diocletian.

With Diocletian's approval, Galerius decided that Maximian should abdicate, Maxentius should be deposed, Constantine should be demoted from Augustus to Caesar again, and Licinius, another friend of Galerius, should become the new Augustus of the West. Until Licinius could take Italy and Africa from Maxentius, he was to share Galerius's authority over the Balkans. The only practical effect of this decision was to create still another Augustus, Licinius. Although Galerius tried to satisfy Constantine and Maximin with the title Son of the Augusti, in the end he had to recognize them as Augusti as well. Maximian resumed his title of Augustus, making six Augusti, and took refuge with Constantine. The empire was in greater confusion than ever.

Nonetheless, the old emperors had made a wise choice in Licinius, a shrewd and flexible man in his early forties who was to outlast almost all his colleagues. When Constantine compelled Maximian to commit suicide in 310, Licinius invaded northern Italy and took part of it. He retreated only because he had to campaign against raiders on the Danube. Since by this time Galerius was gravely ill, apparently with cancer of the colon, Licinius was reluctant to leave Illyricum again. As Galerius lay in agony in 311, he considered the possibility that he might be suffering from the wrath of the Christian God. The eastern emperors had continued what Diocletian had begun, except that instead of executing recal-

6. Licinius (r. 311–24). Gold solidus, shown twice actual size, with a personification of Victory on the reverse. (Photo: Dumbarton Oaks, Washington, D.C., copyright 1996)

citrant Christians Maximin favored blinding them in one eye, laming them in one leg, and consigning them to hard labor in the state mines. But on his deathbed Galerius rescinded the edicts of persecution, which he admitted had failed, released Christian prisoners, though without restoring their property, and asked them to pray for him.

Galerius seems to have died without making definite arrangements for the succession in the East. At the news of his death, Maximin seized Asia Minor on his own initiative, leaving Licinius in possession of the three Balkan dioceses that he had ruled jointly with Galerius. Taking Diocletian as his model, Maximin made Nicomedia his headquarters, canceled the taxes Galerius had introduced on city dwellers who owned no farmland, and resumed the briefly interrupted persecution of Christians. By contrast, Licinius continued Galerius's taxation of townsmen and deathbed decision to tolerate Christians.

Since even Maximin realized that the earlier persecution had failed, he adopted somewhat more subtle measures. While he had released most Christian prisoners and did not compel Christians to perform pagan sacrifices, he forbade them to assemble or to build churches. Noticing that the church hierarchy was a source of Christian strength, Maximin imitated it by naming pagan high priests for each province and chief priests for each city. These supervised pagan rites and pressured Christians to take part in them. Maximin ordered anti-Christian propaganda to be taught in the schools and posted in public places. Finally, he encouraged and granted petitions from provincial and civic authorities to expel Christians from their regions and to imprison or execute the contumacious.

Christians were thus forced to move out of a number of eastern provinces and cities, and some martyrdoms occurred.

Although relations between Licinius and Maximin were clearly strained, for the present the two found it prudent to keep an uneasy peace with each other. While Licinius's position seemed to be the weaker, Maximin wanted to be free to campaign against Armenia, where the rapid spread of Christianity had rendered a persecuting emperor an unwelcome protector. In the West Maxentius was proposing to avenge his father's death by attacking Constantine, so that none of the four Augusti was friendly with his neighbor. So matters stood when a dispirited Diocletian died in retirement at his palace near Salona in 311. Some said he had taken his own life.

Since the unsettled situation invited alliances, Constantine offered to marry his half-sister to Licinius, and the proposal was accepted. To counter this combination, Maximin made overtures to Maxentius. In effect, Constantine and Licinius recognized each other as the only legitimate rulers of the West and the East, while Maxentius and Maximin exchanged similar recognitions. Yet any real military cooperation was difficult. The geography allowed Constantine to attack only Maxentius, and Maximin to attack only Licinius. Thus threatened, Maxentius and Licinius did not dare attack each other. Besides, each emperor was reluctant to risk invasion or rebellion in his own territory by leading many of his troops into another's domain. Nonetheless, in 312 the boldest of the emperors, Constantine, assembled an expeditionary force with which he planned to invade Italy. Constantine at least shared no border with another emperor. But his forces were definitely smaller than those of Maxentius, which still included the deserters from the East of five years before.

After the breakdown of Diocletian's two artificial dynasties protected by Jupiter and Hercules, Constantine had adopted as his patron deity the Unconquered Sun (*Sol Invictus*), whom his father Constantius had also favored. Perhaps because the cult of the sun showed some superficial resemblances to Christianity, including worship on Sundays and celebrating a divine birthday around Christmas, Constantius had been highly tolerant of Christians.[8] Constantine, whose mother Helena was a Christian, seems to have felt vaguely sympathetic to Christianity, even before his attitude changed dramatically during his march against Maxentius. Early in this campaign, Constantine saw what he thought was a vision of a cross superimposed upon the sun. He subsequently had a dream in which Christ promised him victory if his army carried standards marked

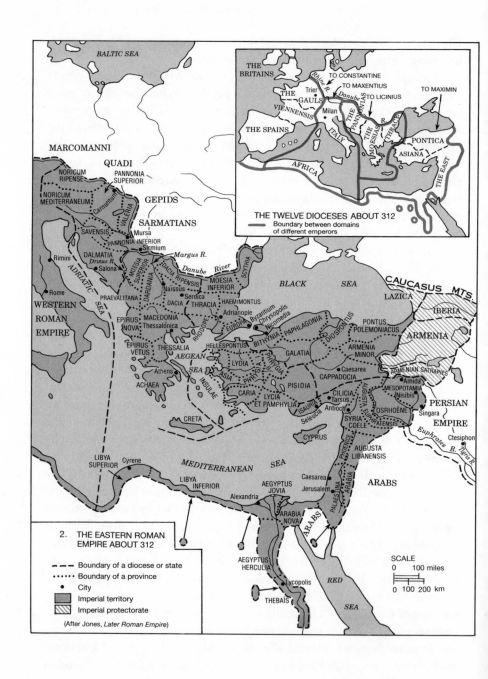

BALTIC SEA

THE
BRITAINS

TO CONSTANTINE
TO MAXENTIUS
TO LICINIUS
TO MAXIMIN

THE
GAULS

Rhine R.
Trier
Danube R.
Milan

VIENNENSIS

THE SPAINS

ITALY

THE PANNONIAS

THRACIA
THE MOESIAS

R.

PONTICA
ASIANA

THE EAST

AFRICA

THE TWELVE DIOCESES ABOUT 312
Boundary between domains
of different emperors

MARCOMANNI

QUADI

NORICUM
RIPENSE
NORICUM
MEDITERRANEUM

Carnuntum

PANNONIA
SUPERIOR

VALERIA

GEPIDS

SARMATIANS

SAVENSIS

Mursa

PANNONIA INFERIOR
Sirmium

DALMATIA

Drinus R.
Salona

Rimini

Margus R.

Danube   River

MOESIA
SUPERIOR

DACIA RIPENSIS

SCYTHIA

BLACK   SEA

CAUCASUS MTS.

LAZICA

ADRIATIC   SEA

Rome

WESTERN
ROMAN
EMPIRE

PRAEVALITANA

Naissus

DARDANIA

DACIA

Serdica

MOESIA
INFERIOR

THRACIA

HAEMIMONTUS

IBERIA

ARMENIA

EPIRUS
NOVA

MACEDONIA
Thessalonica

Adrianople

RHODOPE

EUROPA
Byzantium
Chrysopolis
Nicomedia

PONTUS
POLEMONIACUS

DIOSPONTUS

ARMENIAN SATRAPIES

EPIRUS
VETUS

THESSALIA

AEGEAN

SEA

Athens

HELLESPONTUS

BITHYNIA

PAPHLAGONIA

ARMENIA
MINOR

PHRYGIA

GALATIA

ACHAEA

INSULAE

ASIA

LYDIA

PHRYGIA

Caesarea

CAPPADOCIA

Amida

MESOPOTAMIA
Nisibis

PERSIAN
EMPIRE

CARIA

PISIDIA

CRETA

LYCIA
ET PAMPHYLIA

ISAURIA

CILICIA
Tarsus

Antioch

Seleucia

OSRHOËNE

Singara

Euphrates R.

Ctesiphon

Tigris R.

CYPRUS

SYRIA
COELE

AUGUSTA
LIBANENSIS

LIBYA
SUPERIOR
Cyrene

LIBYA
INFERIOR

MEDITERRANEAN   SEA

AEGYPTUS
JOVIA

Alexandria

Caesarea

Jerusalem

PALAESTINA

PHOENICE

ARABIA

ARABS

ARABIA
NOVA

ARABS

2. THE EASTERN ROMAN
    EMPIRE ABOUT 312

--- Boundary of a diocese or state
····· Boundary of a province
•   City

Imperial territory

Imperial protectorate

(After Jones, *Later Roman Empire*)

AEGYPTUS
HERCULIA

Lycopolis

THEBAIS

RED

SEA

SCALE
0   100 miles

0 100 200 km

with the monogram of the first two Greek letters of Christ's name.[9] Having ordered such standards for his soldiers, Constantine met Maxentius's main force just north of Rome, at the Milvian Bridge over the Tiber. There Maxentius, fighting with his back to the river, was driven back and drowned when his army panicked. Constantine took over all Italy and Africa from his dead rival.

Impressed by his brilliant victory against the weight of numbers, Constantine was henceforth a convinced Christian, though at first a poorly instructed one. He did not flatly repudiate the cult of the sun, which he apparently believed had helped him discover the true faith through his vision, and he took some care to avoid offending the pagan majority of his subjects. But he promptly restored the confiscated property of Christians, exempted the Christian clergy from taxation, and began building churches. In 313 Constantine married his half-sister Constantia to his ally Licinius at Milan. While conferring with Constantine Licinius agreed to restore church property in his domains, and when and if he conquered Maximin's territories to end the persecutions and restore church property there as well.

At just this time, Maximin unexpectedly invaded Thrace, forcing Licinius to march east with all possible speed. Since his army was outnumbered, Licinius opened negotiations, but no settlement could be reached. He therefore attacked, and after a hard-fought battle won a complete victory. Pursued by Licinius, Maximin fled south and, when he saw that he could not rally his troops, killed himself at Tarsus. Just as Constantine had become Augustus of the whole West, Licinius now became Augustus of the whole East. He not only fulfilled his agreement by ending the persecution and restoring Christian property, but punished some of the most notorious persecutors. The empire was again at peace, ruled in concert by eastern and western Augusti as in the early days of Diocletian and Maximian. The two made some efforts to coordinate their government, for example by converting the five-year tax indictions into new indictions of fifteen years, which remained standard thereafter.[10]

Yet Constantine was not content for long to be ruler of the West alone, especially because the East had more troops, larger revenues, and most of the empire's Christians. Between 313 and 315, Licinius campaigned first to secure his hold on Armenia and the satrapies on its southern border, then to drive the Goths from the Danube frontier, where he took Sirmium as his headquarters. In the meantime Constantine, whose headquarters remained at Trier, campaigned along the Rhine against the local German tribes. But by 315 he was massing troops that threatened Licinius. Constantine evidently tried to provoke a quarrel, perhaps by asserting his right to name new Caesars for both West and East. In 316 he invaded Licinius's Diocese of the Pannonias.

Although Licinius was not fully prepared for the attack, he was nearby at Sirmium with somewhat superior forces, and he advanced to meet Constantine in the middle of the Pannonian Diocese. In the ensuing battle Constantine won a major victory. Licinius retreated south, sending orders for another army to assemble at Adrianople in Thrace and vainly trying to negotiate with Constantine. Near Adrianople the two Augusti fought again in 317, and after fierce fighting Constantine again forced Licinius to retreat. But this time Licinius carefully kept his army together and threatened Constantine's supply lines. Constantine therefore agreed on a peace that gave him the dioceses of the Pannonias and Moesias and left Licinius in possession of the dioceses of Thrace, Asiana, Pontica, and the East. As the clear victor in the war, Constantine held much the larger part of the empire's territory. The concentration of troops and wealth in the East, however, gave Licinius almost as large a share of power.

For seven years Licinius ruled his remaining territories from Nicomedia. Constantine spent most of his time at Sirmium and Serdica in his new Balkan possessions, sending his eldest son Crispus as a Caesar to Trier, where he ruled Britain, Gaul, and Spain with his own praetorian prefect. Each of the Augusti watched his nearby colleague with evident suspicion. The policies of Constantine and Licinius increasingly diverged. Constantine, with somewhat larger revenues and a stronger position, appointed new officials to hear complaints of overtaxation, and probably avoided raising tax rates. Licinius, who needed all the revenue he could collect, began counting those over sixty-five as *capita* and assessed *juga* ruthlessly. Constantine showed more and more favor to Christians, in 321 declaring Sunday a holiday in commemoration of the Resurrection. Licinius, however, suspecting that the many Christians in the East favored Constantine, found an excuse for curbing their activities when their disputes began to disturb public order.

Since Licinius had extended toleration to the Egyptian church at Maximin's death, two disputes had come into the open. One had begun during the first persecution under Maximin, when Bishop Peter of Alexandria had gone into hiding. Claiming that Peter had forfeited his post by deserting his flock, Melitius, bishop of Lycopolis in Upper Egypt, moved to Alexandria and began acting as bishop, ordaining priests in the city and bishops elsewhere in Egypt. In 311 Peter returned and excommunicated Melitius for usurpation, declaring his acts and ordinations invalid. In consequence the Egyptian church split into rival churches headed by Peter and Melitius, the latter claiming to be the church of those who stood fast before persecution. This Melitian Schism persisted after Peter was martyred in 311, and it continued to plague his successor Alexander, who became bishop of Alexandria two years later.

Worse yet, early in Alexander's episcopate a local priest named Arius began preaching that Christ had not always existed, as God the Father had always existed. Arius acknowledged that Christ had existed before the world was created and time began; but he maintained that before time began the Son had been created by the Father out of nothing. Arius's formulations met with violent objections from Bishop Alexander and his brilliant young secretary Athanasius. They argued that Christ had always existed because he had come from his Father's own substance, so that before being begotten the Son had existed in the Father. They accused Arius of turning the Father and the Son into two gods, making God the Son into a different and inferior god. Arius retorted that they were the ones who were turning the Son into a second god by making him fully God.

Since neither Scripture nor any previous theological consensus addressed this matter unequivocally, Christian opinion divided. While Alexander summoned a council of Egyptian bishops that condemned Arius, Bishop Eusebius of Nicomedia called a council in his city that reversed the condemnation. When Alexander held a larger council that confirmed the condemnation, Bishop Eusebius of Caesarea in Palestine held still another council that defended Arius. Rioting broke out in Alexandria over the issue of Arianism, as Arius's doctrine was called. Though easily misunderstood, Arianism raised basic questions about the divinity and humanity of Christ that Christians clearly needed to settle among themselves.

At this point Licinius declared his impatience with Christian controversies and forbade the eastern bishops to hold further synods. To protect himself against Christian disaffection, he purged his government and army of Christians. To increase his revenues, he canceled the exemption of the clergy from service on city councils. Finally Licinius executed several bishops in Pontica, apparently on charges of plotting with the king of Armenia, which had been officially Christian since 314. Constantine protested Licinius's treatment of Christians. After Constantine briefly crossed into Licinius's Diocese of Thrace in 323 to expel some Gothic or Sarmatian raiders, Licinius protested in his turn and prepared for war.

In 324, with the excuse that he was defending Christian interests, Constantine invaded Thrace outright with about twenty thousand soldiers. In a battle near Adrianople he met Licinius, who had an army of some thirty-five thousand; but the pagan emperor fled and left most of his men to surrender. Pursuing his opponent to Byzantium, Constantine besieged him there. After losing his fleet in a naval battle with Constantine's son Crispus, Licinius evacuated Thrace, then made another stand across the Bosporus at Chrysopolis. When Constantine bested him once again, Licinius surrendered in return for Constantine's promise to spare his life. In fact, Licinius was executed a few months later on a charge of sedition. The victorious Constantine took possession of the palace at Nicomedia and the whole remainder of the empire.

CONSTANTINE'S CHANGES

By this time Constantine, aged about fifty-one, had already ruled for eighteen years, displaying remarkable luck, much personal charm, relentless ambition, and impatience bordering on instability. His skill at political maneuvering made him seem wiser than he was. Born at Naïssus in Latin-speaking Illyricum, he had acquired a serviceable if not elegant knowledge of Greek during his stay at Nicomedia in his twenties. For twelve years he had been a professed Christian, although like many Christians he had been postponing his baptism so that it could expiate not only his sins already past but any sins he might commit in the future. Unusually in a time of small families, he had four sons. The eldest, Crispus, born of a first wife who had died early, was now grown. The other three, Constantine II, Constantius II, and Constans, were the sons of Constantine's second wife Fausta, the daughter of Maximian, and still children. Despite his youth, Constantine II had been made a Caesar already, like Crispus.

Although officially Constantine ruled the entire empire, after 324 he lightened his administrative labors by ruling it through five or six praetorian prefects. One, assigned to the Caesar Crispus since 318, administered the Atlantic dioceses of Britain, Gaul, and Spain, and continued to do so while Crispus fought in the East and when he returned to the

7. Constantine I (r. 307–37; 324–37 over the East). The colossal head and hand from a statue in his basilica in the Roman Forum. (Photo: Musei Capitolini, Rome)

West afterward. Retaining a praetorian prefect attached to himself personally, Constantine appointed separate prefects to administer three regional groups of dioceses apart from Crispus's holdings. There was one prefect for the Pannonias, Italy, and Africa (with Africa sometimes receiving a separate prefect). Another prefect was assigned to Macedonia and Dacia (two dioceses that Constantine created from the former Diocese of the Moesias) and Thrace. The last prefect administered Asiana, Pontica, and the East.[11]

These three regional prefectures, besides the one assigned to Crispus, were presumably intended to be the portions of Constantine's three younger sons, who were still too young to rule them. Recognizing that Diocletian's old homeland in the Latin-speaking Pannonias belonged with the West, Constantine attached it to Italy and Africa. Interestingly, however, he left his new Diocese of Dacia, which was largely Latin-speaking, in the same prefecture with mostly Greek-speaking Macedonia and Thrace. Since he planned to live in the East and personally supervise the two easternmost prefectures with their six dioceses, Constantine seems to have wanted to include in them his own native country in Dacia. Moreover, the boundary between Dacia and the Pannonias, at the Drinus (modern Drina) River, conveniently divided the Danube frontier into a section that defended Greece and a section that defended Italy. This boundary's strategic logic later led to its becoming the frontier between the eastern and western parts of the empire.

In the process of conquering the three-quarters of the empire that he had not originally held, Constantine had assembled a large field army that was distinct from the frontier forces. This evidently consisted of the mobile reserves of Constantine and his rivals, to which they had added during the civil wars. Since his field army had served him well, and centralized reserves were easier to keep drilled and disciplined than dispersed garrisons, after his victory Constantine retained in the East a mobile force of perhaps twenty thousand men, which was separate from the border troops. Along with this field army, Constantine created a still more exclusive body of perhaps thirty-five hundred cavalry known as the Scholae, who served him as guards and agents in various capacities.[12]

Constantine's retention of the field army and the creation of the Scholae showed that despite redividing the empire into prefectures he planned to exercise authority over the whole of it. He kept by his side a bureaucracy with powers over all the prefectures. Although before 324 each emperor had maintained his own chancery, Constantine during the rest of his reign had only one master of offices, the head of the bureaus that kept imperial records. The real capital of the empire was to be wherever Constantine resided, and he took a momentous measure to emphasize that fact.

Not two months after Licinius's surrender, still in 324, Constantine formally refounded the city of Byzantium, giving it the name of New Rome. Both its name and the large area that he ordered to be surrounded by its walls show that he meant it to be a grander and more permanent capital than Nicomedia or Thessalonica had been. Less than sixty miles from Nicomedia, Constantinople had as strategic a location as its predecessor, being situated on the sea route from the Black Sea to the Mediterranean and the land route between the Persian and Danube frontiers. Its harbor of the Golden Horn was large and deep, but no better than the Gulf of Nicomedia. The new city's clear advantage over Nicomedia was its far more defensible site, on a peninsula that an easily defended wall could cut off by land.

Vital though this defensibility was to be in later centuries, however, it seems not to have mattered much to Constantine, who scarcely expected to need to defend his city. More significant to him seems to have been that it was near the site of his final victory over Licinius. Probably what he liked best was that it would be a capital of his own, lacking Nicomedia's associations with Diocletian but sharing its strategic location. Constantine emphasized the new city's connection with his dynasty by proclaiming his son Constantius II a Caesar on the day of its foundation. Constantine was doubtless pleased, and not surprised, that from the first most people called his city Constantinople.

Although Constantine transformed Byzantium so thoroughly that its old name was soon used mainly by antiquarians, Constantinople did not become an important place all at once. The emperor often left it, and took most of his officials with him. Even though it incorporated a sizable existing city with harbors, baths, a stadium, and probably an aqueduct, it remained under construction for years. Constantine laid out colonnaded streets and a forum and enlarged the stadium, known as the Hippodrome because it was intended mainly for races of horse-drawn chariots. He also built a palace—known as the Great Palace—two senate houses, buildings for state business, and perhaps three churches, including the Cathedral of Saint Irene.[13]

Unlike Diocletian, Constantine liked the idea of having a senatorial order, and wanted his New Rome to have a senate of sorts. He enrolled such Roman senators as lived in the East or were willing to come from the West, along with some administrative officials whom he raised to senatorial rank. He offered imperial land in Anatolia to any senators who would build private houses in the city, and to those who would construct tenements he promised free grain for their tenants. The free or subsidized grain that he promised to various landlords and officials in the city seems to have left them with a large surplus to sell. Constantine also encouraged Christians to settle in Constantinople, though he made no attempt to close its pagan temples.[14]

The greatest harm the foundation of the new capital did to paganism was probably financial. Constantine had been short of cash from the beginning of his reign, when he had reduced the weight of Diocletian's gold coin, known as the *solidus* in Latin or the *nomisma* in Greek, from sixty to the pound to seventy-two to the pound. Although in 324 he acquired the substantial treasury of Licinius, Constantine seems not to have been satisfied with it. To supplement it as he worked on his city, he ordered the confiscation of the treasures of the pagan temples of the East, thereby acquiring an immense quantity and variety of valuables.[15] As he gained these new resources, Constantine reorganized the empire's financial administration under two separate ministers. They were the count of the sacred largesses (*comes sacrarum largitionum*) to manage public expenditures and the count of the private estate (*comes rei privatae*) to administer imperial properties.[16]

Many temple sculptures and decorations went to adorn buildings and squares in Constantinople, like a statue of the sun god in the forum, whose face Constantine altered to resemble his own. Most of the temples' gold was minted, creating a gold currency so abundant that it could be used for most large public and private transactions. Although Constantine aggravated the inflation of the base-metal coins by reducing the weight of the copper and the amount of silver in the billon so as to mint more coins, his gold coinage established a secure medium for large-scale trade, savings, and government payments. By instituting new taxes in gold on trade and senatorial property, Constantine assured that the government's gold supply would be constantly replenished. Through most of Byzantine history the gold solidus or nomisma was to retain the purity and value that Constantine had assigned it.

Constantine naturally extended to the whole empire the privileges for Christians that he had already introduced in his previous realm, and he reinstated Christians whom Licinius had dismissed from the eastern army or government because of their religion. Soon after his final victory

8. Column of Constantine, erected at the center of his forum in Constantinople and originally topped by his statue. (Photo: Dumbarton Oaks, Washington, D.C., copyright 1996)

Constantine went even further, prohibiting all pagan sacrifices and divination throughout the empire, though in practice he did not and could
not enforce his prohibition strictly. He allowed most pagan rites that did
not include sacrifices, but he pointedly prohibited those that violated
Christian standards of chastity, such as sacred prostitution and religious
orgies. By granting official favor to Christians and only limited toleration to pagans, he reversed the legal position of the religions as it had
been under Licinius.

Although pagans were still too numerous to let Constantine enforce
Christian morality by law, he occasionally legislated in support of it. Thus
he forbade gladiatorial shows, and instead encouraged the less violent
Roman sport of chariot racing. In place of the previous rule allowing
divorce by the wish of either spouse, Constantine permitted it only in
cases of serious crime, or of the wife's committing adultery or keeping a
brothel. He allowed bishops to try legal cases on the petition of either
party. To discourage infanticide, he provided poor parents with public
grants. Constantine also showed a distinct preference for Christians in

appointing civil and military officials. But he withdrew his previous exemption of the Christian clergy from serving on city councils in the case of extremely wealthy men, many of whom seem to have sought ordination only to escape their public responsibilities. Those with an authentic vocation were eventually allowed to make themselves eligible for ordination by renouncing their property.

By this time Constantine had clearly declared himself an opponent of paganism and a partisan of Christianity. Not surprisingly, the Church welcomed his patronage and for most purposes accepted his leadership, trusting in both his guidance by God, which his vision of the Cross seemed to demonstrate, and his political instincts, which his successes seemed to prove. In the West, from a wish to promote harmony among Christians, he had already settled some disputes over ecclesiastical discipline, though he had been careful to decide for the church hierarchy and against those who challenged it. In the East he was now faced with the problems of Melitianism and especially Arianism.

Soon after the founding ceremonies at Constantinople, Constantine visited Antioch and discovered the extent of the Arian controversy. An unsubtle and impatient man, Constantine could not see why Christians needed to argue about something that had happened before time began, had passed unmentioned in Scripture, and had been overlooked by the Church for almost three centuries. Although similar views were later taken in similar circumstances by emperors with much more experience of Christianity than Constantine, such moderation almost always infuriated both sides and hindered a final resolution.

The emperor sent his main theological adviser, Bishop Hosius of Cordova, to Alexandria with an imperial letter asking Alexander and Arius to settle their differences. In Egypt Hosius found feelings far too inflamed to allow any such solution of Arianism, and discovered the Melitian controversy as well. Hosius needed to hold two councils, one at Alexandria and another at Antioch on his way back, and to promise to hold still another, larger council in 325. This Constantine decreed should be held at Nicaea, not far from Constantinople, so that he could attend himself. He apparently planned for this to be the first worldwide, or "ecumenical," council, and encouraged participation by offering to pay the expenses of all the bishops who came.

Some three hundred bishops attended, including all those who had taken a leading part in the Arian controversy to date. Far more came from the East than from the West, but the pope sent two priests to represent him, and Hosius of Cordova presided. While the majority of bishops seem not to have held strong views on the subject, the most articulate ones certainly did. The main defenders of Arius, who was present as an observer, were Eusebius of Nicomedia and Eusebius of Caesarea, the latter not quite as strongly committed as the former. Alexander of Alexandria, accompanied by Athanasius, continued to oppose Arius, and enjoyed the support of several important bishops, including Eustathius of Antioch and Hosius.

Early in the proceedings Eusebius of Caesarea introduced a carefully worded creed, based on Scripture, that neither affirmed nor denied Arius's views. No one could object to anything in it, and Constantine praised it. But Constantine had also been listening to Hosius, and proposed to add to this creed the affirmation that the Son was "of the same substance" (in Greek, *homoousios*) as the Father. This one word totally excluded Arius's doctrines, and by itself even left room for Sabellianism, the previously condemned heresy that the Father and the Son were identical. Because the emperor had suggested the word, however, the opponents of Arius seized on it eagerly, and scarcely anyone felt able to speak against it. Further clarifications were added, and the resulting Nicene Creed was signed by all the bishops except for two from Libya. They and Arius, who also would not sign, were condemned by the council and exiled by Constantine.

The council then considered the case of the Melitians. It attempted to compromise with them by recognizing Melitius as bishop of his original see of Lycopolis and arranging for the Melitian clergy to be absorbed into the regular Egyptian hierarchy, subject to Alexander's approval. This agreement almost immediately failed, as the Melitians maintained that they were the real church, guarding the faith that others had betrayed in the face of persecution. The Council of Nicaea also set rules for calculating the date of Easter, recognized the special authority of the bishop of Alexandria throughout Egypt and of the bishop of Antioch throughout Syria, and decided various other questions before concluding its sessions. The emperor regarded the council as a success. The council appeared to have discredited Arianism for good. It had reached clear though not inflammatory decisions and set a precedent for ecumenical councils to resolve future disputes in the Church.

A PARTLY FINISHED STATE

Soon after the Council of Nicaea, Hosius of Cordova returned to his see. Deprived of Hosius's advice for the first time since his conversion,

Constantine had to rely on his own unreliable religious instincts. To his confusion, he found that many bishops who had signed the Nicene Creed were expressing misgivings about the idea that the Son was of the same substance as the Father. This wording troubled not only the real Arians, but non-Arians who wanted a more conciliatory formula, or who felt that the Son was divine but inferior to the Father, or who feared the Sabellian heresy that the Son was the same as the Father. To meet all these objections, Eusebius of Caesarea concocted the argument that "of the same substance" could mean no more than that the Son came from the Father, which even Arius admitted. While this position was unacceptable to the strongest opponents of Arius, Constantine tolerated it out of a desire for unity. Only when Eusebius of Nicomedia refused to condemn Arius did Constantine exile him for plainly rejecting a decision of the council.

In 326 the emperor showed himself at his most erratic. While he was traveling to Rome to celebrate the twentieth year of his reign, his wife Fausta convinced him that Crispus, his son and her stepson, was guilty of some sexual crime, perhaps rape. Constantine had Crispus executed. But shortly thereafter he had Fausta herself killed, apparently on a charge of adultery. Rumor had it that Fausta had falsely accused Crispus of trying to seduce her, and that Constantine had discovered she had actually been trying to seduce Crispus. The emperor then issued rather unbalanced legislation prescribing savage penalties for adultery and rape, ostensibly to raise pagan morality to Christian standards. At the same time, probably as a sort of family penance, his mother Helena left on a pilgrimage to the Holy Land to distribute alms and to build churches on the sites of Christ's birth and ascension.

By the time the emperor returned to the East, sentiment in the Church was definitely turning against the party that had been victorious at Nicaea. In 327 a council at Antioch presided over by Eusebius of Caesarea deposed several bishops who opposed Arius, including Eustathius, the bishop of Antioch itself. Eustathius was accused of Sabellianism and of keeping a concubine. Impressed more by the second charge than the first, Constantine confirmed the deposition. Later that year Constantine convened another council at Nicomedia, which while recognizing the Council of Nicaea reinstated Arius and Eusebius of Nicomedia, both of whom professed their orthodoxy. Pleased that the Church's unity seemed to have been restored, Constantine wrote to Alexander of Alexandria exhorting him to receive Arius. Alexander managed to avoid doing so

9. Saint Athanasius, archbishop
of Alexandria (328–73). Twelfth-
century mosaic from the Capella
Palatina, Palermo. (Photo: Istituto Centrale per il Catalogo e la
Documentazione, Rome)

until he died in 328. He was succeeded by his secretary Athanasius, a
particularly dedicated and eloquent enemy of Arianism.

During that year and the next Constantine traveled to the West,
where he defeated the Germans on the Rhine frontier and installed his
twelve-year-old son Constantine II to replace Crispus at Trier. On returning to the East in 330, Constantine dedicated Constantinople as his
capital. It was still a makeshift sort of city, with many buildings hastily
and badly constructed, but it gained population very quickly. By 332
regular fleets from Egypt were providing it with eighty thousand free rations of grain. This was apparently enough to make free bread for some
240,000 people, but since the city still had fewer than half that many,
much of the grain must have been reexported.[17]

Whenever Constantine was in Constantinople, a large part of his field
army was stationed nearby and his bodyguard and bureaucracy resided
there with him. His court inevitably attracted petitioners, office seekers,
and others. Because the emperor continued to travel, and most of the
field army and government continued to follow him, Constantinople
was not yet a capital in the full sense of the word, as Rome had been before Diocletian. So much money and prestige had been invested in it,
however, that it seemed likely to become more important in the future.

TABLE I

The Dynasties of Diocletian and Constantine I

Emperors are in capital letters. Senior emperors of the East are in italics, with the years of their reigns marked "r." Other years are of births and deaths.

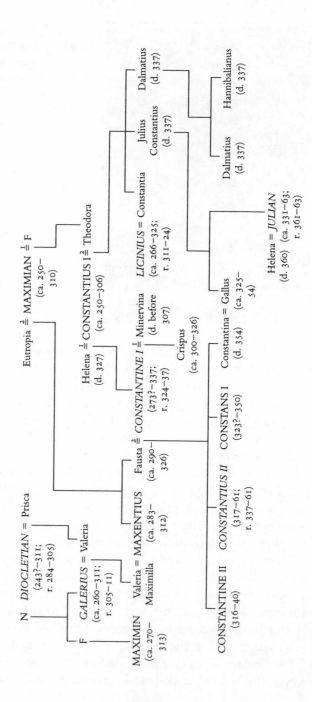

With his return to the East, Constantine became embroiled again in the Arian controversy. In pursuing ecclesiastical harmony without facing the theological issue, he constantly vacillated between a resurgent pro-Arian party and its determined adversaries. Athanasius of Alexandria steadfastly refused to receive Arius. Arius's defenders, led by Eusebius of Nicomedia, joined with the Melitians, who had elected another bishop of Alexandria of their own, in trying to persuade the emperor to depose Athanasius on several ill-founded charges. Constantine summoned Athanasius for trial, but was sufficiently impressed by his defense to acquit him in 332 with a rebuke to his enemies. When Arius unwisely threatened to start a schismatic church of his own if he were not received at Alexandria, Constantine condemned him and ordered ten *capita* added to the tax assessment of any unrepentant Arian.

The Melitians soon returned to the attack, this time accusing Athanasius, among other things, of murdering one of their bishops. By 334 this charge had been repeated often enough for Constantine to let Athanasius's enemies try him at a council at Caesarea in Palestine. The emperor dissolved the council only when Athanasius produced alive the Melitian whom he was accused of murdering. Yet as Eusebius of Nicomedia continued to press the Arians' and Melitians' charges against Athanasius, Constantine agreed to hold a council at Tyre and Jerusalem in 335, which readmitted Arius and deposed Athanasius for various alleged acts of violence.

When Athanasius arrived at Constantinople to plead his case, Constantine annulled the decision of the council. But when Eusebius of Nicomedia came a few days later and accused Athanasius of threatening to stop the fleet that brought grain to Constantinople from Alexandria, Constantine exiled Athanasius to Trier. The people of Alexandria rioted; Anthony, the most respected Egyptian monk, protested; no successor to Athanasius was named; and nothing was settled. While Eusebius of Nicomedia persuaded Constantine to order the reluctant bishop of Constantinople to give Arius communion, Arius died suddenly in 336. In the end, without repudiating the Council of Nicaea, the emperor had allowed opponents of the council to take over most of the eastern church.

By 335 Constantine, in his early sixties, was ready to put Caesars in charge of all the parts of the empire. Since the execution of Crispus he had only three sons to rule the four parts, but he made his nephew Dalmatius a Caesar to fill the vacancy. Constantine II continued to rule in the dioceses of the Gauls, Viennensis, the Britains, and the Spains. Constans took the dioceses of Italy, Africa, and the Pannonias. Constantius II received the dioceses of the East, Pontica, and Asiana. The newly chosen Dalmatius was left with the dioceses of Macedonia, Dacia, and Thrace, including Constantinople. Thus the eldest and senior Caesar, Constantine II, kept four dioceses, and the others got three each, with the one who was not even a son incongruously assigned the emerging capital. The younger Caesars, aged between eighteen and perhaps twelve, went to their respective domains to be trained in administration and warfare by their praetorian prefects and generals titled masters of soldiers. For the present Constantine remained the only Augustus, with overriding powers, but on his death the Caesars were all to become Augusti and rule in their own right.

At the time of this settlement Constantine was still vigorous. He had recently campaigned on the Danube frontier twice, defeating the Goths in 332 and the Sarmatians in 334, and in 336 he carried operations across the river, probably to build more fortifications on the north bank. He prepared an expedition against the Persians, whose ambitious young king, Shāpūr II, had begun a border war. After some raids on the Roman frontier, the Persians invaded Armenia, blinded its Roman client king, and replaced him with a Persian client. Rejecting Persian offers to negotiate, Constantine declared his intention to make his nephew Hannibalianus king of Armenia, and possibly of Persia as well. But before the emperor could march, he fell gravely ill. He died in 337 near Nicomedia, soon after receiving baptism from Eusebius, the city's pro-Arian bishop.

As an institution, the Roman Empire had changed more in the barely fifty years between Diocletian's accession and Constantine's death than in the three centuries since Augustus. Except for Constantine's adoption of Christianity, most of the change was Diocletian's doing. By greatly enlarging the government and army and providing a method of taxation to pay for it, he ended the political and military crisis of the third century, and on the whole restored stability. The empire's government had never been so large before, and, if allowances are made for its having more dangerous enemies and ruling a diminished population, it had never been so powerful.

Although the civil wars between 306 and 324 were obviously contrary to Diocletian's plans, in several ways they vindicated his judgment. During this lengthy period of hostility and open warfare between emperors, no one who was not a member of Diocletian's two dynasties rebelled successfully, no emperor from the two dynasties was assassinated, and no foreign invaders made significant inroads. The civil wars were fought between Diocletian's nominees and their chosen successors for control over his state, which itself remained proof against outside attack. The conflicts that began a year after his abdication demonstrated how brilliant Diocletian's leadership had been during the preceding twenty years. Yet these troubles also put his reforms to a test that revealed their essential durability.

In most respects, Constantine saw the strengths of Diocletian's system and continued it. Even after Constantine reunited the empire, he followed Diocletian by redividing it among praetorian prefects and masters of soldiers, with his sons and nephew as Caesars. He kept Diocletian's method of taxation, and is unlikely to have allowed the amount of revenue it raised to decrease. Although he restored the tax exemptions canceled by Licinius, Constantine also created new taxes on trade and on senators' property. He seems to have made no significant increase in the size of Diocletian's enlarged bureaucracy and army throughout the whole empire, though he transferred some troops from the West to the East for his field army.

Aside from his new counts of the sacred largesses and of the private estate, who replaced similar financial officials of the previous period, Constantine seems to have created only one important post, that of the quaestor, who drafted imperial laws. While Constantine probably added a few lesser officials, he must also have dispensed with some of those who had been attached to the courts of Maxentius and Licinius. Constantine's main changes were the transfer of the military powers of the praetorian prefects to the masters of soldiers, and the transfer of a number of units from the frontier forces to the centralized field armies. The former measure may have helped avoid rebellions, and the latter probably helped repel foreign invaders.

While Constantine retained Diocletian's system, he was often lax in maintaining it. In the long run, keeping a large field army both depleted the frontier forces and tended to reduce them to second-rate status. Constantine appears to have converted many of the frontier troops on the Danube from infantry to cavalry, presumably improving their mobility but apparently not their efficiency. Without more careful attention than Constantine gave them, the frontier forces were liable to decay, weakening the empire's first line of defense. The demoralization of the frontier garrisons may already have begun to show in the need for Constantine to campaign repeatedly on the Danube with field forces during the last years of his reign.

Unlike Diocletian, Constantine generally trusted senators, whom he appointed to many official posts. Rather surprisingly, since the senate at Rome had as a body long ceased to have more than an honorary role in government, Constantine created a second senate at Constantinople. Indeed Constantine was on good terms with most of his officials, and apparently subjected them to less thorough supervision than Diocletian had, though he made fitful and ineffectual attempts to limit corruption. In comparison with Diocletian, Constantine spent lavishly, on buildings, favorites, the Church, and charity. While his confiscation of the treasures of pagan temples paid for his extravagance, he left the government with a habit of overspending that was likely to outlast that unrepeatable accession of revenue. Moreover, his toleration of official corruption was especially dangerous now that officials were so numerous.

Constantine's conversion to Christianity was his most important change. When he first supported Christianity, in his western domains where Christians were a small minority, it must have seemed a rash move. But by the end of his reign the new official religion was spreading rapidly, and paganism was collapsing apace. Any doubts among pagans that Christians could be enthusiastic servants of the empire proved baseless. The Christians also proved magnanimous in victory, given their previous sufferings under pagan emperors. By ending the persecution of Christians without beginning a persecution of pagans, Constantine reduced violent religious conflict in the empire. By mismanaging the Arian controversy, however, he probably increased religious dissension, and certainly increased confusion. By failing to understand that Arianism was a problem that called for a clear and consistent solution, Constantine showed that his religious inspiration was of a very limited kind.

His other accomplishment of lasting significance was the foundation of Constantinople. But its importance was far from clear in 337, when the city was half built and its fate depended on what subsequent rulers chose to make of it. Yet, at least after Constantine's successors let the city establish itself, for the first time it gave the eastern part of the empire a regional capital comparable to Rome. Even though the bureaucracy that Constantine installed in the city was largely pagan, and mostly spoke and wrote Latin, both the city and the bureaucracy were inevitably influenced by the surrounding population, which was overwhelmingly Greek and increasingly Christian. Thus the rise of Constantinople helped the eastern part of the empire become more Greek and more Christian, and politically and culturally independent.

The refoundation of the Roman Empire was for the most part the work of Diocletian, a ruler with a better understanding of statecraft than Constantine. Without Diocletian's reforms, Constantine's career would hardly have been possible. Yet Constantine, whether through inspiration, good fortune, or misfortune, made some changes that were more lasting than his predecessor's. His centralization of Diocletian's army and administration, combined with his careless and extravagant management, set the pattern for years to come. Constantine's adoption of Christianity began a sweeping and permanent transformation of all of society. And his refoundation and promotion of the town of Byzantium soon brought changes that can justify our calling the eastern empire Byzantine.

CHAPTER TWO

The State Under Strain, 337–395

Constantine's long-standing plans for the succession fared little better than Diocletian's. In the absence of all three of his sons, his grieving soldiers accepted Eusebius of Nicomedia's story that the emperor had been poisoned by his half-brothers Julius and Dalmatius.[1] The army accordingly lynched Julius, Dalmatius, and Dalmatius's two sons—the Caesar Dalmatius, who had been administering the Balkans, and Hannibalianus, whom Constantine had recently named king of Armenia. The massacre included some of their other relatives, supporters, and presumed supporters. By the time the killing was over, all that remained of the dynasty were Constantine's sons and two very young nephews, Gallus and Julian. Although the army had received no formal orders, it plainly assumed that its actions would be welcome to the sons. They were finally proclaimed Augusti three months after their father's death. Constantius II and Constans, the Augusti nearest to Dalmatius's realm, divided it among themselves. Constans took Macedonia and the Dacias, and Constantius II took Thrace, including Constantinople.[2]

CONTINUITY UNDER CONSTANTIUS II

Therefore, at the age of twenty, Constantius II became the ruler of almost the whole Greek East. After his proclamation he promptly arrived at Constantinople to supervise the funeral and burial of his father. On the outskirts of the city Constantine had built a funerary chapel dedicated to the Holy Apostles, in which Constantius buried his father as he had wished, as the thirteenth apostle. The son set about following and completing his father's policies, trusting that the vast structure he had inherited would endure as long as it was properly maintained. Although not an extraordinary personality, Constantius was unusually serious and conscientious, and his habitual wariness at least showed that he was aware of the dangers he faced. Constantine had died at a delicate time, when the empire was only very partially converted to Christianity, state expenses were growing burdensome, the frontiers were becoming less secure, and corruption was spreading alarmingly through the army and bureaucracy.

Soon after their proclamation, the three brothers conferred in Pannonia to regulate their positions. Constantine II, who despite being the eldest and senior Augustus had gained nothing from the partition of Dalmatius's domain, received an ill-defined tutelage over Constans that did not extend to Constantius. Asserting their essential independence, Constantius and Constans put single praetorian prefects in charge of their dominions, reducing the number of prefectures from five to three. Constantius and Constans also kept separate field armies under masters of soldiers (*magistri militum*), of which each emperor usually had one for infantry and one for cavalry. The division of the empire was accentuated because Constantine II and Constans agreed with almost all western Christians in favoring a strict interpretation of the Nicene Creed, while Constantius followed many eastern Christians (and his father's final judgment) in rejecting it. At the beginning of his reign, however, Constantius bowed to his brothers' wishes and restored the pro-Nicene bishops whom Constantine had exiled, including Athanasius of Alexandria.

After a brief campaign against the Sarmatians on his Danube frontier, Constantius hurried east to contain the Persians, who had already invaded Roman Mesopotamia. He spent most of the next twelve years in fighting them. As when he had been Caesar, Constantius habitually resided at Antioch, which, besides being closer to the Persian front than Constantinople, was more centrally located within his territory. Having speedily restored the frontier and the Roman protectorate over Armenia, he began a series of annual campaigns against the Persians, which were mostly successful. The predominance of the Romans over the Persians established by Diocletian appeared to be holding.

By 339 Constantius felt secure enough to have Athanasius deposed as bishop of Alexandria and to replace Bishop Paul of Constantinople, a supporter of Athanasius, with Athanasius's archenemy Eusebius of Nicomedia. Athanasius and most of the eastern bishops who supported him

10. Bronze bust, probably of
Constantius II (r. 337–61).
(Photo: Musei Capitolini, Rome)

fled to Rome and appealed to Pope Julius I. In 340 the pope called a council at Rome that ordered them reinstated. But the same year Constantine II was killed while invading Italy in an attempt to impose his authority on Constans. Taking over Constantine's former possessions in Gaul and Britain kept the anti-Arian Constans occupied for some time. He was the less inclined to interfere in the East because Constantius's official position was not Arian, but merely tolerant of Arianism.

Admittedly, Constantius had selected Eusebius of Nicomedia, one of the staunchest defenders of Arius. As bishop of Constantinople, Eusebius consecrated the Arian Ulfilas bishop and sent him on a mission to the powerful tribe of the Goths, which eventually converted them to Arian Christianity. On the other hand, in 341 a council at Antioch attended by Eusebius and Constantius produced a creed that avoided endorsing Arianism and was compatible with the doctrine of Nicaea, though it omitted the Nicene formula that the Father and Son were of the same substance. When Eusebius subsequently died and supporters of the Nicene Creed rioted in Constantinople, Constantius put down the riots and cut the city's grain dole in half, but he allowed an opponent of Arianism, Macedonius, to become the city's bishop. Thus the theological position of the eastern church remained as confused as it had become in the last days of Constantine I.

At Pope Julius's request, in 343 Constans persuaded Constantius to help him resolve the confusion by conveninq an ecumenical council at Serdica. The town was just on Constans' side of the border that separated the brothers' domains, and with the western bishops united and the eastern ones divided the westerners expected to prevail. Before the deliberations could begin, however, most of the eastern bishops refused to allow the western bishops to admit Athanasius and his followers. When an effort at compromise failed, the eastern bishops withdrew to Adrianople, on Constantius's side of the border, where they held a council of their own. While the bishops at Serdica readmitted Athanasius and the other exiled bishops and reaffirmed the Nicene Creed, the bishops at Adrianople confirmed the depositions of the exiles and reaffirmed the creed of the recent Council of Antioch. Each side excommunicated the other, making the schism in the Church official.

Constans protested, and soon flatly demanded the restoration of the exiled bishops. Although Constantius had continued to prosper in his Persian campaigns, raiding across the Tigris in 343 and temporarily capturing the Persians' camp in 344, his resources were still somewhat inferior to those of his brother, with whom he certainly did not want a civil war. Constantius therefore agreed to restore most of the exiles, including Athanasius, though not to depose their replacements or to accept the Nicene Creed. In consequence the eastern church became more deeply split than ever, as many places had rival Christian communities and some had rival bishops.

Although this was by no means the sort of toleration that Constantius wanted, he accepted it for the present because he had to deal with the Goths, who invaded and raided Thrace about 345, and with Shāpūr II, who was persistently attacking the frontier strongholds of Nisibis and Singara. Showing considerable skill, Constantius negotiated a peace with the Goths whereby some of them joined the army that he used to fight off the Persians. By this time he had divided his field army into two parts with their own masters of soldiers, one kept with him and one deployed in the East to guard the Persian frontier. Shāpūr remained a stubborn adversary despite his defeats, persecuting the Persian Christians and fighting a brutal but indecisive battle with the Romans near Singara in 348.

So matters stood until 350, when Constans was overthrown and killed by one of his officers, Magnentius. The usurper gained control over all of the West but Illyricum, where Constans' master of soldiers Vetranio declared himself emperor. By marching to Serdica, Constantius was able to obtain Vetranio's abdication without difficulty, and to acquire the Army of Illyricum. Dislodging Magnentius was a more daunting task. Fortunately for Constantius, at this time Shāpūr learned of an invasion of his own eastern frontier by Kushan tribes, who would keep him busy for years. Still, Constantius did not want to leave the East without an emperor while he put down the western rebellion. Lacking a son, early in 351 he gave the rank of Caesar and the hand of his sister Constantina to his cousin Gallus, aged twenty-five, and sent Gallus to rule at Antioch. Constantius then marched west.

The civil war was hard fought. Magnentius ambushed Constantius's army just before it could enter Italy, and forced it to retreat almost to the Danube. Constantius won a battle at Mursa in Pannonia that was extremely bloody, though a report that casualties on both sides totaled fifty-four thousand is probably exaggerated. In 352 Magnentius had to abandon Italy, but only the next year did Constantius defeat him in Gaul and drive him to suicide. The empire's army was gravely weakened, and Gaul was full of German raiders. But Constantius had gained control of Constans' former prefectures of Illyricum, Italy, and Gaul, and become the empire's only Augustus.

Meanwhile Gallus had governed the East remarkably badly. After punishing a Jewish revolt with indiscriminate slaughter, he remained inactive while the indigenous tribe of the Isaurians plundered southeastern Anatolia. He executed citizens from all over the eastern prefecture on suspicion of plotting against him. When Antioch suffered from famine, Gallus first ordered the execution of all its decurions, a measure countermanded by the vicar of the Diocese of the East, then allowed the governor of Coele Syria to be lynched by a mob. Informed of Gallus's excesses by his anxious officials, Constantius gradually restricted his cousin's powers and withdrew his troops. Gallus was nonetheless able to have his remaining soldiers murder his praetorian prefect in 354. At this Constantius urgently summoned his Caesar to the West, purportedly to assume power there so that Constantius could return to the East. After some hesitation, Gallus did go to Italy, where he was tried and executed for his various derelictions.

Constantius did in fact need a Caesar for the West. Although pacifying the Rhine frontier was obviously going to take years, the Augustus wanted to concentrate on the Danube and Syrian frontiers of the East, which were also threatened. Accordingly he kept direct jurisdiction over Italy, Africa, Illyricum, and the East, but in 355 proclaimed his remaining cousin Julian as Caesar, marrying the young man to his sister Hel-

11. Constantius II (cf. Fig. 10) scattering largesse. Drawing in a calendar copied from an original of 354. (Photo: Biblioteca Apostolica Vaticana)

ena. Constantius was unaware that Julian, in the course of his education in Greek philosophy, had become a fervent pagan of a strongly idealistic and ascetical kind. For the present, however, Julian outwardly professed Christianity and seemed both respectful and competent. He was sent to Gaul to fight the Germans in the company of subordinates loyal to Constantius, who did not entirely trust his cousin's loyalty and abilities. Julian was surprisingly successful at clearing the Germans from Gaul.

Constantius remained in Italy for two more years, attempting to impose his muddled religious views on the whole empire, now that he had a free hand to do so. In 356 he issued an edict closing all pagan temples and outlawing all pagan practices, and he seems to have made much progress in enforcing it. By deposing a few western bishops and intimidating others, the emperor was able to hold councils that confirmed Athanasius's deposition as bishop of Alexandria. This imperial troops soon effected, and Athanasius went into exile once more. While driving Germans and Sarmatians out of the Danube frontier districts in 359, Constantius sponsored separate eastern and western church councils at Seleucia and Rimini. At his insistence, both adopted a creed that declared the Father and the Son to be "similar in substance" (*homoiousios*), thus allowing both the Nicene position that they were of the same substance and the Arian position that the Son's substance was somewhat different.

Later that year Constantius moved to Constantinople, which now that he was sole Augustus he intended to make into something resembling a capital. To enhance the city's legal status, he raised the rank of its chief magistrate from proconsul to prefect, as at Rome. The Constantinopolitan senate, hitherto an unprepossessing body of barely three hundred members, he increased to some two thousand by enrolling favored courtiers, Roman senators from the Balkans, and former vicars and provincial governors. The custom slowly took hold that each year one of the two consuls, now purely honorary magistrates left over from the Republic, should be an easterner named at Constantinople, while a westerner became consul at Rome.

The emperor had already rebuilt his father's chapel of the Holy Apostles, which had originally been of slovenly construction. Now he expanded his father's Cathedral of Saint Irene by joining it to a spacious new Church of Saint Sophia.[3] Saint Sophia became the city's principal church after its inauguration in 360, though Saint Irene remained the official cathedral. Constantius also held a council at Constantinople to confirm and enforce the decisions taken by his councils of Rimini and Seleucia. In an effort to insure toleration of Arians, this Council of Constantinople ruthlessly deposed and exiled many eastern bishops who rejected Arian beliefs, even if they rejected the Nicene Creed as well. The exiles included Bishop Macedonius of Constantinople, who was replaced by the strident Arian Eudoxius. The depositions ordered by this council insured that the eastern hierarchy would be outwardly obedient to Constantius. But by forcing non-Arians to approve Arianism on pain of deposition, the emperor increased hostility to the doctrine he wanted to tolerate. The large party that had expressed doubts about the Nicene Creed now began to look upon it more favorably, as a means of fighting the resurgent Arians.

Constantius's indulgence of his supporters and harshness toward others had increasingly unfortunate consequences for the government as well. By this time his expenditures were growing apace, swollen by warfare, bureaucracy, construction, and largesse. The emperor often levied supplementary taxes when ordinary revenues fell short. He also confiscated the property of many real or imagined rebels, whom he hunted down by means of informers and an enlarged corps of government agents. Constantius moreover appropriated for the central government the lands belonging to the cities, so reducing the resources available to the city councils. More anxious than ever to avoid serving, many decurions sought refuge in the enlarged senate; but Constantius made a law closing it to them, and expelling any decurions who had become senators. Because he allowed considerable embezzlement among his officials and was generous in granting confiscated lands to informers and others, the financial burden on the empire's citizens must have increased even more rapidly than did the revenue collected.

Unpopular though he may have been in many quarters, however, Constantius seemed to be at the height of his power, shielded by a large, loyal, and satisfied segment of the army and civil service. Yet he still had to reckon with Shāpūr of Persia, who had won his wars with the Kushans and remained bent on conquering Roman Mesopotamia. After briefly allying with the Armenians and sacking the important Mesopotamian city of Amida in 359, Shāpūr overran the frontier strongpoint of Singara in 360. Constantius assembled troops to lead against the Persians, and ordered Julian to send him part of the army that was stationed in Gaul. Although Julian professed willingness to send the men, he distrusted Constantius, and knew that Constantius distrusted him. The Caesar also knew that the Army of Gaul was loyal to him personally, and reluctant to serve against the Persians. With his implied approval, his officers encouraged the soldiers to proclaim him Augustus.

This was not quite a rebellion, since Julian did not claim the whole empire. But it signaled that he would take no more orders from the East. When Julian asked his cousin to recognize his title, claiming that his men had forced it upon him, Constantius refused to recognize him as anything more than Caesar. After negotiations came to nothing, Julian began to march east in 361. Constantius interrupted a campaign in Mesopotamia to march against him. Since Constantius commanded much larger forces and had shown himself a capable and determined commander, he appeared to have the advantage. But when he reached Cilicia, he fell mortally ill. As he was baptized on his deathbed, he magnanimously named Julian his successor.

DEFEAT UNDER JULIAN

So Julian, fresh from his victories in Gaul, became ruler of the whole empire at age twenty-nine, without a fight. Yet he kept some of the attitudes of a rebel, as if he had defeated and deposed Constantius II instead of succeeding as his cousin's legitimate heir. Displeased with what had been done by Constantine I and his sons, Julian wanted to curb the empire's swelling bureaucracy and the Romans' accelerating conversion to Christianity. He began immediate efforts to reverse both trends. Showing most favor to his dynasty's original cult of the Unconquered Sun, Julian lifted Constantius's ban on pagan practices, resumed public sacrifices, reopened the temples, and restored the temples' lands. Like Maximin fifty years before, Julian appointed high priests for each province and chief priests for each city. To sow further confusion in the Church, he recalled the bishops exiled by Constantius II, although he soon exiled the charismatic Athanasius again. Julian ordered no violence against Christians himself, but he took no measures against others who attacked Christians. Some pagans at Alexandria went so far as to lynch the city's unpopular Arian bishop, George.

Julian diminished the size of the central government by dismissing many imperial advisers, notaries, and spies. On the other hand, he attempted to revive the city councils by returning the civic lands that Constantius had confiscated. Julian also enrolled as decurions many wealthy men who had avoided their duties by legal or illegal means. Showing an ascetic's repugnance for Constantius's elaborate court, he purged it of many of its bodyguards and palace servants. Alone among emperors since Diocletian, Julian saw no need for a colleague of any sort to rule part of the empire.

After a stay of several months at Constantinople, where he furiously enacted these reforms, Julian traveled to Antioch, where he prepared for an invasion of the Persian Empire. Constantius had already planned an attack, and Julian wanted to win a victory so brilliant that it would vindicate paganism. In the meantime, however, his stay at Antioch was unhappy. The majority of the Antiochenes were Christians who for years had been accustomed to Constantius's splendid court, and they found an austere pagan emperor little to their taste. Although Julian induced some Christians to apostasize to gain his patronage, he made many enemies by executing Christians who damaged temples, pardoning pagans who murdered Christians, and prohibiting Christians from teaching the Greek classics. When Julian attempted to refute a prophecy of Christ by rebuilding the Jewish temple at Jerusalem, his work was destroyed by an earthquake, and perhaps by arson as well. Then the temple of Apollo near Antioch burned; Julian blamed the Christians, and closed the city's cathedral. Even among pagans, Julian's popularity began to wane.

12. Julian (r. 361–63). Marble statue now in the Louvre, Paris. (Photo: Copyright Réunion des Musées Nationaux)

In 363, after composing a tract decrying the Antiochenes' ingratitude and unwisdom, Julian left on his Persian campaign in the hope of refurbishing his reputation. This expedition was large and well prepared, despite some misgivings on the part of its largely Christian troops. Shāpūr II certainly feared it, and tried to stay out of its way. Julian planned a two-pronged invasion. He himself proceeded with the main army and a fleet along the Euphrates. At the same time Procopius, a relative of his on his mother's side, was to lead a detachment along the Tigris, enlist the empire's Armenian allies, and meet the emperor near the Persian capital of Ctesiphon. There the two armies would threaten the Persian capital, and could either sack it or impose harsh terms on Shāpūr.

The emperor duly approached Ctesiphon, transferred his fleet to the Tigris by reopening an ancient canal, and defeated a Persian force. But Ctesiphon looked unexpectedly difficult to take, and for some reason Procopius failed to appear. Uncertain of what to do next, Julian crossed the Tigris to look for Procopius's army, burning his fleet because of the difficulty of sailing it upstream. His expedition already seemed to be a failure.[4] As the emperor retreated, harried by the Persians, he was struck by a spear, apparently cast by an Arab assassin in Persian service. The wound was serious, and after a few hours Julian died of it. Since he had forgone the protection of a large retinue, he was as vulnerable to assassination as the third-century emperors; like most of them, he had a reign of less than two years. Since he had named no colleague, he had no influence over the succession. As the next emperor, the army chose a Christian, the senior officer of the Scholae.

The legal and military power of an emperor was so great that Julian had been in a position to kindle a strong pagan revival. Even his brief attempts, though too cerebral and puritanical to win wholehearted support from most pagans, left pagans more confident and Christians less so. Yet paganism, lacking the natural cohesion and missionary spirit of Christianity, was poorly suited to the task of large-scale reconversion of Christians, which was essential to making the traditional religion safe again. Outlawing Christianity had failed before, and given the large numbers of Christians in the East was probably impossible by Julian's time. Paganism's best chance would have been a long period of patient and steady pressure on Christianity while the emperor avoided dangers and defeats. Julian, in both his encouragement of paganism and his attack on Persia, had tried to do too much too fast.

His successor Jovian, aged thirty-two, inherited the melancholy task of extricating the army from Persia. Dogged by the Persians, who had stripped the land of provisions, Jovian retreated along the east bank of the Tigris, but hesitated before attempting the dangerous crossing. Shāpūr offered a thirty-year peace if Jovian would cede Singara, Nisibis, and most of the Armenian satrapies and give up the Roman protectorate over the Armenian Kingdom. In view of his army's peril and his own parlous hold on power, Jovian agreed to these terms, on condition that the Roman population of the two border cities be evacuated before they were surrendered. He managed to cross the river, found Procopius's detachment, from which he obtained supplies, then evacuated the border region.[5] Pausing briefly at Antioch to recall Athanasius and lift the legal disabilities that Julian had imposed on Christians, Jovian set out for Constantinople at the start of 364. But in the middle of Galatia he died by a freak accident. Apparently the charcoal fire that heated his bedroom suffocated him.

Again the succession was determined by the army, and especially the bodyguard, which chose another Christian officer of the Scholae, Valentinian. When he reached Constantinople a month after his accession, Valentinian named his younger brother Valens as his fellow Augustus. The brothers had been born in the Latin-speaking border province of

Pannonia Inferior, but seem to have learned Greek in the army. Perhaps because he considered himself better fit to handle the intractable problems of the West, Valentinian assigned Valens the Prefecture of the East, consisting of Constantius II's earlier domains in Egypt, Syria, Anatolia, and Thrace, while keeping Illyricum for himself. After the brothers divided the field forces between them, Valens had three field armies, one in the Emperor's Presence, one of the East, and one of Thrace, each with some twenty thousand men.

DEFEAT UNDER VALENS

Valens, who became emperor at the age of thirty-five or so with only a few years' service in the Scholae to prepare him, was younger, less talented, and much less experienced than Valentinian. Valens' main virtues were loyalty to his brother, hostility to corruption, and parsimony. These may not have been sufficient qualifications for imperial office at the time, but they were necessary ones. By the time of Valens' accession, the level of taxation, after many years of increases, is said to have risen to twice its level when Constantine arrived in the East. If the empire was to continue on its current course, it was obviously in trouble, perhaps even in danger of fiscal and military ruin. The imperial brothers, to their credit, saw that something needed to be done.

Upon taking power, Valentinian and Valens jointly enacted laws to hold down the taxes. Each reconfiscated the lands of the pagan temples and of the cities, although the temples remained open. The brothers allowed decurions to enter the senate on condition of giving their sons enough property to replace them on the councils, and permitted decurions to be ordained if they gave the councils the whole of their property. Both emperors appointed independent officials to supervise tax collection and to hear complaints of unjust taxation. Although these laws were only partly effective, by enforcing them and reducing peculation Valens was able to halt tax increases at once.[6]

After Constantius II's death, the western church had returned to its uncompromising endorsement of the Nicene Creed, which Valentinian accepted; but the eastern church remained in theological chaos. Constantius's council of 360 had put the hierarchy in the hands of the Arians and their collaborators. It had also exiled the strongly anti-Arian bishops led by Athanasius and the more hesitant bishops represented by Macedonius. Recalled by Julian, the more anti-Arian bishops had promptly

13. Valens (r. 364–78). Gold 1½ nomisma, shown twice actual size, with Valens on horseback on the reverse. (Photo: Dumbarton Oaks, Washington, D.C., copyright 1996)

reaffirmed the Nicene Creed at a council in 362, and two years later the less anti-Arian bishops met to define their intermediate position.

Valens found that many eastern sees were claimed by two or three bishops who accepted the decisions of different councils. But at Constantinople itself the death of Macedonius had strengthened the hand of the Arian patriarch Eudoxius. Influenced by Eudoxius, Valens decided to confirm the decisions of Constantius's councils, which after all were the most recent to be summoned by an emperor. Consequently Valens again exiled the bishops exiled under Constantius. This decision was primarily political, but as such it was impolitic. A wiser ruler than Valens would have seen that Constantius's attempt to conciliate the Arians had caused more division than it healed, and that merely upholding a precedent was not worth alienating the western church and the majority of eastern Christians, who opposed Arianism with varying degrees of fervor.

Although Valens had become emperor legally, he had no hereditary right to the throne. In 365, after he set out for the eastern frontier to hold the Persians to their treaty, Julian's relative Procopius was proclaimed emperor at Constantinople. Procopius's dynastic claim was so obvious that he had gone into hiding for fear of being accused of rebellion. In the end he decided that if he was going to be accused anyway he might as well rebel. He won over the troops in Thrace and the first contingent that Valens sent against him, then received more men from the Goths across the Danube. Yet most of his forces deserted him when Valens attacked him in 366. After capturing and beheading Procopius, the emperor quickly subdued the remaining rebels.

Shaken at discovering the fragility of his rule, Valens became more concerned with political opponents than ecclesiastical ones. Whereas he executed, exiled, and confiscated the property of those who had supported Procopius, he allowed Athanasius to return to Alexandria. In 367 Valens tried to assure his popularity by assessing the land tax at half the previous rate.[7] He undertook a three-year war against the Goths to punish their support of Procopius. The emperor was finally successful, and forced them to accept a treaty renouncing the tribute they had formerly received from the empire.

Valens had regained his confidence by 370, when he moved to Antioch and apparently planned to remain in the Diocese of the East. At this time he allowed the city councils of his part of the empire to regain custody of their old civic lands, evidently in return for their remitting a sum equal to two-thirds of the lands' current revenue to the central government.[8] Valens also dispatched expeditions that expelled the Persians from Armenia and part of Iberia, which they had occupied after the empire abandoned its Armenian protectorate.

These achievements seemed substantial. But the next year Valens learned with alarm that some of his pagan courtiers at Antioch, having convinced themselves by divination that his successor would be an imperial notary named Theodore, were plotting to hasten the supposedly inevitable. The prophecy was actually somewhat ambiguous, since it was that the next emperor's name would begin with the four Greek letters TH-E-O-D.[9] After a ruthless investigation, Valens put to death not only Theodore and the others implicated in the plot, but other pagans alleged to have used divination for any purpose. To deepen Valens' displeasure, the new Roman client king of Armenia proved disloyal. Valens had him assassinated.

The emperor's religious policies were now palpably failing. A new generation of strongly anti-Arian bishops had taken office in Anatolia, led by Basil of Caesarea in Cappadocia. On the Arian side, the chief theologian Eunomius of Cyzicus was making Arianism more radical by arguing that the Son was not even similar in substance to the Father. When Eudoxius of Constantinople died in 370 and Athanasius of Alexandria died in 373, the bishops whom Valens approved to succeed them faced widespread protests. In an attempt to restore order, the emperor commanded all the eastern bishops to sign copies of the Creed of Rimini and

14. Saint Basil, bishop of Caesarea (370–79). Fourteenth-century fresco in the Monastery of the Chora, Constantinople. (Photo: Dumbarton Oaks, Washington, D.C., copyright 1996)

Seleucia on pain of exile, thereby starting an ineffectual but bitter persecution of a large part of the hierarchy.

Meanwhile events outside Valens' jurisdiction took a menacing turn. In 375 Valentinian suddenly died and left the rule of the West to his sons Gratian and Valentinian II, who were dangerously young for such heavy responsibilities. At about the same time, a horde of the warlike Asiatic nomads known as the Huns arrived from Central Asia and utterly defeated the Greutungi, a loose confederation of Gothic tribes settled north of the Black Sea. The next Gothic confederation of tribes to the west, the Tervingi, after a brief attempt at resistance despaired of defeating the Huns. Instead, in 376 their principal leaders sent an embassy to Valens asking for asylum in Thrace, in return for which their men would serve the emperor as regular soldiers.

Valens agreed, hoping to economize on the army and to resettle some vacant land in northern Thrace that had been devastated by years of border warfare. A mass of Tervingi, perhaps numbering some two hundred thousand, crossed the river.[10] The Tervingi, by this time largely converted to Arian Christianity, seemed ready to honor their agreement. They promptly supplied many recruits, who were sent for training to Syria and southern Thrace. But the Roman authorities in northern Thrace, who even with goodwill would have had trouble supplying this many refugees, mistreated the Tervingi, extorting slaves from them in return for inferior food.

As tension mounted between Tervingi and Romans, many Greutungian refugees also sought asylum on Roman territory. Despite Valens' refusal, they managed to cross the Danube unopposed. Soon fighting broke out between Tervingi and Roman troops. Both groups of Goths began to plunder Roman farms. The Tervingian recruits in southern Thrace deserted and joined what had now become a full-scale revolt. Valens sent reinforcements from Syria in 377, but these, after initially confining the rebellion to northern Thrace, could not keep the Goths from breaking through to the well-cultivated farmland to the south. Appealing to his western colleagues for help, Valens arranged a truce with the Persians, recalled the bishops he had exiled, and gathered all available troops from Armenia and Syria. In 378 he marched against the Tervingi, probably with an army approaching forty thousand men.[11]

For whatever reason, Valens would not wait for a Roman army that was slowly making its way from the West, and met a united force of Tervingi and Greutungi near Adrianople. A disorderly attack by the Roman cavalry began a chaotic battle between the two large armies, in which the less disciplined Goths had the advantage over the disoriented Romans. After fighting long and fiercely, almost two-thirds of the Roman army was killed, or about twenty-five thousand men. Valens himself died, and the rest of the Romans fled. This battle of Adrianople was the most crippling and humiliating defeat suffered by a Roman army in a hundred years.

The Goths, who had also lost many men, lost still more in unsuccessful attempts to storm the walls of Adrianople and Constantinople. The Romans quickly massacred the Tervingian recruits in Syria. Nonetheless, for the time being, the battle of Adrianople had prostrated the eastern empire's field armies. Never an outstanding emperor, Valens had shown little strategic insight and run an unreasonable risk. But even a gifted ruler might have had trouble grasping and handling the threat posed by the Goths, which was like nothing the empire had seen for a century. The

TABLE 2

The Dynasties of Valens and Theodosius I

Emperors are in capital letters. Senior emperors of the East are in italics, with the years of their reigns marked "r."; emperors of the West are in roman type. Other years are of births and deaths.

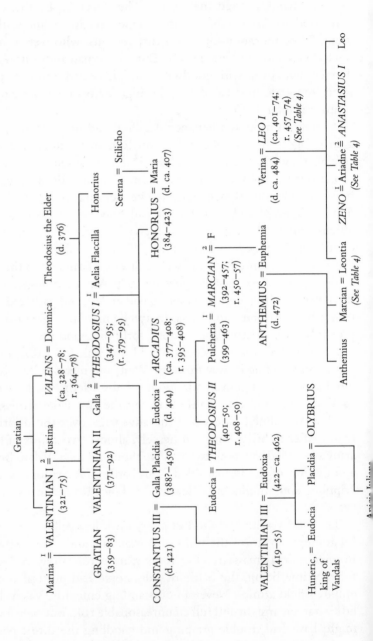

defensive machinery created by Diocletian and modified by Constantine had fallen apart, before a mass of Germans formed almost by chance.

RECONSTRUCTION UNDER THEODOSIUS

The adolescent western emperor Gratian rose to the occasion. Instead of making his younger brother Valentinian II eastern emperor, as precedent would have suggested, he turned to a capable general, Theodosius. Immediately after the battle of Adrianople Gratian put Theodosius in charge of operations in the Balkans, where the Sarmatians had crossed the Danube to join the rampaging Goths. When Theodosius brought an army from the West and crushed the Sarmatians, Gratian rewarded him with the rank of Augustus at Sirmium, early in 379. Theodosius was assigned not simply the Prefecture of the East, which Valens had ruled, but a newly defined Prefecture of Illyricum. The latter consisted of the dioceses of Dacia and Macedonia, which had formerly belonged to the West, though not Pannonia, which remained western. This addition to the East was necessary not only because the barbarians threatened Illyricum as much as they did Thrace, but because the only effective mobile troops left in the area belonged to the Army of Illyricum, which had not fought at Adrianople.

Although at his accession Theodosius was barely thirty-three, since his twenties he had served creditably in Britain under his father, also an eminent general, and he had already distinguished himself as a local commander in Illyricum by defeating the Sarmatians five years before. His parents had been rich Christian landowners in Spain and had educated him well, evidently seeing that he acquired a working knowledge of Greek. He had retired from public life in 376, when Gratian had executed his father on an obscure charge, but Theodosius never showed public rancor over this episode.[12] While he could lose his temper under extreme provocation, usually he was calm and diplomatic, and became popular with his soldiers and officials. He was probably the empire's ablest ruler since Diocletian.

He also faced the worst crisis since Diocletian's time. The Goths had established themselves in force amid the ruins of the Thracian farms, and after the battle of Adrianople they were not much afraid of the Roman army, which indeed was no longer very formidable. Because they could not return to their former lands, now occupied by the Huns, the Goths could only be removed from the empire by virtually exterminating them.

That task would require enlisting and training many more new recruits than the tax rolls could easily spare, who would need to be paid much more than the tax system could easily raise. If in fighting the Goths the Romans lost badly again, the eastern empire would be practically defenseless against the Goths, Huns, and Persians, and its very survival would be in doubt. Yet the Goths could hardly be allowed to advertise the empire's weakness by raiding the Balkans indefinitely.

For a year Theodosius recruited whatever troops he could find, including many Germans and even Gothic deserters, while patrolling the western boundary of the Prefecture of Illyricum to keep the Goths out. He replaced a military system that had usually separated infantry from cavalry with a system of unified armies for Illyricum, Thrace, and the East, and another in the Emperor's Presence, each under a single master of soldiers. Though these measures made the army look rather better, it was still too weak to fight the Goths, and its discipline and morale were especially shaky. Fortunately for the Romans, at the time of their greatest weakness their adversaries did not seize the opportunity to attack. The Goths were busy plundering Thrace. The Huns had conquered enough to keep them satisfied for the present without invading the empire. With the death of the long-lived Shāpūr II in 379, even the Persians became more pacific.

The religious divisions in the East were also growing more manageable. Like almost all westerners, Theodosius rejected Arianism, and his western colleague Gratian was becoming increasingly anti-Arian under the influence of Ambrose, the forceful new bishop of Milan. In the East, now that the bishops exiled by Valens had returned, most of the Church was ready to accept the Nicene Creed. Many of the Christians of Constantinople elected the firmly orthodox Gregory of Nazianzus, a close friend of the recently deceased Basil of Caesarea, to replace their Arianizing bishop. A council of eastern bishops at Antioch approved the Nicene formula. Though himself of the same opinion, Theodosius avoided taking concrete action against the Arians because the military danger remained acute.

In the spring of 380, the Tervingi broke into Macedonia and headed for Greece, while the Greutungi invaded Dacia and drove west. Finding his forces too feeble to repel this double attack, Theodosius requested and received reinforcements from Gratian, who hurried to the Balkans with a second detachment. The first group of reinforcements drove the Tervingi back into Thrace, and Gratian's arrival checked the Greutungi.

15. Theodosius I (r. 379–95), at center, and his court in the imperial box of the Hippodrome in Constantinople. Relief on the base of the Obelisk of Theodosius from the Hippodrome, Constantinople. (Photo: Irina Andreescu-Treadgold)

After conferring with Theodosius at Sirmium, Gratian agreed to settle the Greutungi on his own territory in Pannonia, while the Tervingi began squabbling among themselves.

During this time, Theodosius fell gravely ill at Thessalonica. Fearing that he would die, he received baptism, which like most Christians in public life he had postponed to avoid the rigors of church discipline. As it happened, he recovered; but on his recovery he became the first emperor to rule as a full member of the Church, constrained to do penance if he committed a serious sin. His deference to the ecclesiastical hierarchy correspondingly increased. He also issued an edict appealing to all his subjects to accept the full divinity of the Father, Son, and Holy Spirit, though he prescribed no penalties for those who dissented, including Arians, Jews, and pagans.

The emperor then entered Constantinople and celebrated a triumph that could be justified as an attempt to reassure public opinion, if not by any solid success. From the start he made the city more his permanent capital than his temporary residence, and outfitted the palace there with a splendor appropriate to peacetime. He also gave some attention to domestic measures, dividing the overlarge Diocese of the East by making Egypt a separate diocese under an Augustal prefect.[13] Theodosius understood that he would greatly ease the crisis if he could convince both Romans and barbarians that it was already over.

The war with the Goths was in fact dying down. Early in 381 dissension among the Tervingi became so bitter that their deposed king fled to Constantinople, and on his subsequent death his supporters joined the Roman army. While the Goths thus lost some of their strength, Theodosius continued vigorously recruiting Roman soldiers.[14] Although he had benefited from the help of the western empire and from the Goths' disunity, Theodosius deserves great credit for keeping the eastern army from disintegrating, as it had been ready to do during the worst of the emergency.

Taking advantage of his respite from war, the emperor tried to end the disorder in the Church. First he ordered Christians who did not accept the Nicene Creed to surrender their churches. Then he summoned the remaining bishops to an ecumenical council at Constantinople. This council both confirmed the Nicene Creed, with its declaration that the Son was fully divine, and added a statement that the Holy Spirit was fully divine as well. From this it followed that the Father, Son, and Holy Spirit were three persons of a single Godhead, the Trinity. The dogma of the Trinity clarified for the first time the relationship of the three persons long mentioned in the Christian formula of baptism. The bishops accordingly condemned both the Arians and those who denied the divinity of the Holy Spirit, who were termed "Macedonians" because they included former partisans of Macedonius. Agreeably with Theodosius's high regard for Constantinople, the council also awarded the city's bishop an honorary rank second only to the pope's, noting that Constantinople was the New Rome. Some now began to give him the honorific title of patriarch of Constantinople.

Although Arianism remained dominant among the Germans, this Second Ecumenical Council soon won acceptance from the great majority of Christians, perhaps not surprisingly. After all, Arianism had never been official doctrine or even a majority belief within the empire; most opponents of the Council of Nicaea had merely defended creeds that did not exclude Arianism. As Arianism grew more extreme, almost everyone had come to realize that such a controversial doctrine needed to be either adopted or condemned. Given this choice, most Christians were unwilling to deny the full divinity of Christ, and accepted the Nicene Creed. After the Council of Constantinople Theodosius forbade Arians and other heretics to build churches to replace those that they had lost, leaving them to hold services in makeshift and inconspicuous places. As a further vindication of the faith he had approved, the emperor explicitly forbade the use of pagan sacrifices for divination, a prohibition that he enforced so strictly as nearly to ban any sacrificing whatever. He thus returned pagans to approximately their position under Constantius II, after twenty years of milder treatment since Julian's day.

In 382 Theodosius concluded a treaty with the Goths, apparently including the bulk of both the Tervingi and the Greutungi. As in 376, the Goths were permitted to live in Roman territory in return for doing military service, the Tervingi in northern Thrace and the Greutungi in Pannonia. But instead of serving as regular troops in different divisions of the Roman army, the Goths were to serve under their own leaders as Roman allies ("federates," *foederati*), with virtual independence from Roman administration. From this time the Greutungian federates came to be known as the Ostrogoths, and the Tervingian federates as the Visi or, for the sake of parallelism, the Visigoths.[15]

The terms of this treaty were probably the best available to Theodosius without a fight. Though for the Goths to keep their own territory and army within the empire was dangerous, for them to loot the empire as declared enemies was still worse. If they were managed well, they might prove useful against other enemies; if they revolted later, by that time the regular Roman army might be able to fight them on more equal terms. The treaty at least reduced the risk of a Roman military collapse. After concluding it, apparently as a sign that the worst was over, Theodosius returned jurisdiction over the Prefecture of Illyricum to Gratian.[16]

The empire's security remained precarious. Less than a year after this treaty was signed, civil war broke out in the West and rebels killed the emperor Gratian, whose help had been so useful to the East. The usurper Maximus assumed power in the Prefecture of Gaul, though he conceded the prefectures of Italy and Illyricum to the young Valentinian II and his mother Justina. Theodosius was sufficiently disturbed by Maximus's rebellion to pay a visit to northern Italy in 384. When he found that matters had stabilized, however, he decided to recognize the usurper rather than pursue another civil war.

Theodosius soon returned to his residence at Constantinople, where he pursued negotiations for peace with Persia and continued to repair his army. When a large band of Ostrogoths invaded Thrace in 386, Roman troops were strong enough to kill many of them and to capture the rest. The captives were settled in vacant lands in Phrygia, well into Anatolia. Then the Persians agreed to a peace. Though under the peace treaty the Romans recognized a Persian protectorate over most of Armenia, they gained the remainder of Armenia for the empire, governing it through Armenian satraps. This shortened the eastern frontier and made it more defensible.[17]

Yet just as the East regained its equilibrium, civil war resumed in the West. In 387 the usurper Maximus invaded Italy. Valentinian II and Justina took refuge at Thessalonica, sending appeals for help that their eastern colleague could not well refuse. After allying himself with Justina by marrying her daughter Galla, in 388 Theodosius marched west, entrusting the East to his young son Arcadius under the care of his prefect of the East, Tatian. As the eastern emperor advanced, he defeated Maximus twice in Pannonia and finished him off in northern Italy. Theodosius was in control of the entire West by the end of the year. This campaign against Maximus gave impressive proof of the recovery of the eastern field army, even if many of that army's troops were now Gothic federates and other barbarians.

While he officially restored Valentinian II, Theodosius remained in the West for three years, repairing the empire as best he could. In 390 he legislated that decurions who became senators must continue to serve on their councils, and so finally stopped the principal drain on the councils' resources. Decurions could now enjoy higher rank, but without escaping their duty to collect taxes. This law applied to both East and West. During his stay in the West, Theodosius visited Rome but spent most of his time at Milan, by now the usual western capital, where he took the city's bishop, Ambrose, as his spiritual guide. In a striking demonstration of his power, the bishop made the emperor do public penance for having a crowd at Thessalonica massacred, though some of the victims had lynched a general. The next year, again under Ambrose's influence, Theodosius ordered the closure of all pagan temples and prohibited all sacrifices in both East and West. He enforced his measures against paganism more strictly than Constantius II had done, and with more effect. Soon most temples were destroyed, and paganism began to decline rapidly.

Later in 391, the emperor returned to Constantinople to rule the eastern empire, to which he again added the Prefecture of Illyricum, apart from Pannonia. During his stay in the West he had transferred a number of western mobile troops to the East, giving it an adequate mobile army for the first time since the battle of Adrianople. With these new troops he expanded the eastern Army in the Emperor's Presence into two armies of parallel organization, each about twenty-one thousand strong.[18] On the whole Theodosius had reestablished order in the East, though he still had to campaign against German marauders in Macedonia and to suppress pagan riots when the temples were closed in Egypt and Syria.

The West was less fortunate than the East. Valentinian II's disagreements with his German master of soldiers Arbogast led to the western emperor's death in 392 and Arbogast's proclamation of a puppet emperor, Eugenius. While Eugenius was nominally a Christian, Arbogast was a pagan and introduced toleration of paganism. By contrast, at the same time Theodosius was prescribing fines even for pagan worship in private, and replacing his pagan prefect Tatian with an ardent Christian, Rufinus. The eastern emperor rebuffed Eugenius's overtures for peace, and began preparations for war.

Assembling a great expeditionary force that like his earlier one was largely German, Theodosius marched west once more in 394. Again he left his son Arcadius in the East, this time under the guidance of Rufinus. Theodosius's force, unopposed as it marched through the Balkans, met the army of Arbogast and Eugenius just inside the border of the Diocese of Italy, at the Frigidus River. In a day of extremely bloody fighting, Theodosius was defeated, suffering the loss of many of his Visigothic federates. The next day, however, with characteristic determination, he joined battle once more, and in further fierce fighting he prevailed. Eugenius was killed, and Arbogast committed suicide. The entire West quickly submitted to Theodosius, who summoned his younger son Honorius to be its emperor. He intended to return to rule the East, entrusting both Honorius and the West to Stilicho, a half-German general who had married Theodosius's niece. But shortly after Honorius arrived, early in 395, Theodosius died at Milan, of dropsy.

Although at Theodosius's death the empire was undoubtedly vulnerable, the wonder is that it was no worse. Since the death of Constantine I, both state and army had suffered from civil wars, defeats by the Persians and Germans, a corrupt and inefficient bureaucracy, and perhaps even economic and demographic decline. Constantius II, Julian, Jovian, and Valens had all been competent though not brilliant rulers, with consid-

16. Silver missorium of Theodosius I, probably dating from 388, showing the emperor enthroned between his son Arcadius (right) and Valentinian II (left), with guardsmen at the sides and a personification of Earth at the bottom. (Photo: Real Academia de la Historia, Madrid)

erable understanding of the problems they faced. Their difficulties as they juggled one crisis after another mostly reflected the empire's underlying weakness and the strength of its enemies' attacks. After the battle of Adrianople, the eastern empire was temporarily in grave danger, and its imminent collapse under German and Persian pressure was conceivable. Since that battle had shown how risky it could be to fight the empire's enemies head on, Theodosius can scarcely be blamed for avoiding such attacks when he could. No doubt the original Tervingian revolt and Arbogast's proclamation of Eugenius showed the dangers of allowing Germans too much power inside the empire. But despite his strenuous efforts to recruit more Romans, Theodosius needed German troops as well, and he managed his Germans skillfully enough that they fought for him repeatedly without rebelling.

Admittedly Theodosius introduced no sweeping reforms of the many defects in the administration and army. But those defects, however easy to identify, were maddeningly difficult to correct. Theodosius's constant and successful efforts to avoid impending catastrophe left him scant leisure to plan for the long run. He nonetheless rescued the empire from the gravest peril, and restored a stability that capable and unified leadership should have been able to maintain. Although at his death his sons were too young to provide that leadership, he had supplied each of them with a capable adviser, Arcadius with Rufinus and Honorius with Stilicho. No ruler could have done much more.

The Danger of Barbarization, 395-457

What Theodosius failed to foresee was that Stilicho and Rufinus would quarrel. The late emperor had specified that his elder son Arcadius should rule the prefectures of the East and Illyricum, while Honorius, the younger son, should have the prefectures of Italy and Gaul. That much was not in dispute. But according to Stilicho, in a private conversation on the day of his death the emperor had entrusted both his sons to Stilicho's care. Stilicho therefore claimed authority over the whole empire. Rufinus refused to accept this claim, which rested on Stilicho's word alone.[1]

For the moment Rufinus controlled the administration of the East and Illyricum. But Stilicho retained almost all of the mobile armies of both eastern prefectures, which Theodosius had led against Eugenius's rebels. Just as Stilicho ruled for Honorius, who was a boy of eleven, Rufinus had effective control over Arcadius. At age eighteen, Arcadius should have been old enough to take some part in ruling; but even as an adult he was too weak of wit and will to assert himself. So at a time when strong government was urgently needed to manage the Germans, Huns, and other barbarians, both inside and outside the empire, squabbling surrogates ruled for figurehead emperors.

HOSTILITY BETWEEN EAST AND WEST

At the news of Theodosius's death, the East's lack of mobile forces became conspicuous. To exploit it, some eastern Huns crossed the Caucasus and Armenia and invaded the East, penetrating to northern Syria.

17. Arcadius (r. 395–408). Marble bust now in the Istanbul Archeological Museum. (Photo: Dumbarton Oaks, Washington, D.C., copyright 1996)

Still worse, the Visigothic federates, returning from the West to find their lands in northern Thrace under attack by the western Huns, revolted against the empire. Led by their commander Alaric, the Visigoths moved into southern Thrace. Soon they reached the suburbs of Constantinople. They were particularly dangerous because Alaric was fully aware of his opportunity. Through negotiations, Rufinus persuaded Alaric to withdraw, possibly by promising the Visigoths new land in Thessaly. In any case, that was the place they entered and began to pillage. In keeping with the role that Stilicho claimed as guardian of the whole empire, he promptly led the combined field armies of East and West into Thessaly to drive out the Visigoths. Perhaps his intervention should have been welcome to Rufinus. But the eastern prefect regarded it as a threat.

Despite Rufinus's long service as a trusted adviser of Theodosius and his authority as prefect, his power was not quite secure. The ravages of the Huns and Visigoths had hurt his reputation; many resented his

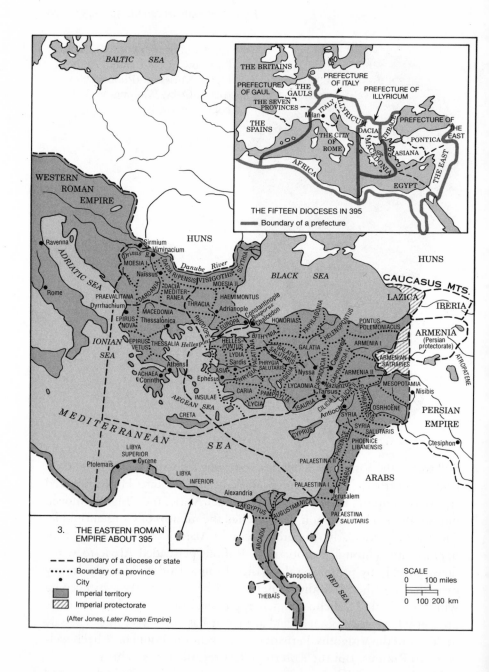

BALTIC SEA

THE BRITAINS

PREFECTURE
OF ITALY

PREFECTURE
OF GAUL

THE
GAULS

PREFECTURE OF
ILLYRICUM

ITALY

ILLYRICUM

THE SEVEN
PROVINCES

Milan

PREFECTURE OF
THE
EAST

THE
SPAINS

DACIA

THRACE

PONTICA

THE CITY
OF
ROME

MACEDONIA

ASIANA

THE EAST

AFRICA

EGYPT

THE FIFTEEN DIOCESES IN 395
—— Boundary of a prefecture

WESTERN
ROMAN
EMPIRE

Ravenna

Sirmium

HUNS

Viminacium

HUNS

Drinus R.

Danube River

MOESIA I

DACIA RIPENSIS

SCYTHIA

Naissus

VISIGOTHS

CAUCASUS MTS.

Rome

DACIA
MEDITER-
RANEA

MOESIA II

BLACK SEA

LAZICA

IBERIA

DARDANIA

PRAEVALITANA

Dyrrhachium

HAEMIMONTUS

THRACIA

Adrianople

Constantinople

Chalcedon

Bosporus

HONORIAS

PAPHLAGONIA

PONTUS
POLEMONIACUS

ARMENIA
(Persian
protectorate)

MACEDONIA

Thessalonica

EPIRUS
NOVA

RHODOPE

EUROPA

BITHYNIA

HELENOPONTUS

ARMENIA I

ADRIATIC SEA

MOESIA I

EPIRUS
VETUS

THESSALIA

Hellespont

HELLES-
PONTUS

GALATIA

GALATIA
SALUTARIS

Caesarea

ARMENIAN
SATRAPIES

IONIAN
SEA

Athens

ASIA

LYDIA

Sardis

PHRYGIA
PACATIANA

PHRYGIA
SALUTARIS

CAPPADOCIA I

ARMENIA II

MESOPOTAMIA

Nyssa

ACHAEA

Corinth

Ephesus

CARIA

LYCAONIA

Nazianzus

CAPPADOCIA II

Nisibis

INSULAE

PAMPHYLIA

ISAURIA

Tarsus

CILICIA I

CILICIA II

OSRHOËNE

PERSIAN
EMPIRE

AEGEAN SEA

LYCIA

CRETA

CYPRUS

Antioch

SYRIA

EUPHRATENSIS

MEDITERRANEAN SEA

SYRIA
SALUTARIS

PHOENICE
LIBANENSIS

Ctesiphon

LIBYA
SUPERIOR

Cyrene

PHOENICE

PALAESTINA II

Ptolemaïs

LIBYA
INFERIOR

ARABIA

ARABS

Alexandria

AEGYPTUS

AUGUSTAMNICA

PALAESTINA I

Jerusalem

PALAESTINA
SALUTARIS

ARCADIA

RED SEA

3. THE EASTERN ROMAN
EMPIRE ABOUT 395

— — Boundary of a diocese or state
· · · · · · Boundary of a province
•   City
        Imperial territory
        Imperial protectorate

(After Jones, Later Roman Empire)

Panopolis

THEBAÏS

SCALE
0   100 miles

0   100 200 km

financial exactions; and young Arcadius was too pliable to follow the same adviser consistently. Rufinus had hoped to strengthen his authority by marrying his daughter to Arcadius. But the head chamberlain, the eunuch Eutropius, enticed the emperor into marrying another candidate, the half-German and exceptionally beautiful Eudoxia. Rufinus now seems to have worried that Stilicho, after dealing with the Visigoths, might march on Constantinople and make good his claim to rule for Arcadius. In order to forestall that danger, Rufinus had Arcadius order Stilicho to leave eastern territory and send his eastern troops to the East.

Stilicho had a difficult choice to make. It was plainly in the empire's interest for him to expel the Visigoths from Thessaly. If he did so, he would have the chance to enforce his guardianship over Arcadius. On the other hand, it was also in the empire's interest to avoid an open breach between East and West. Respect for Theodosius's memory dictated that Stilicho should obey Theodosius's only son who was of an age to command. Moreover, preliminary skirmishing showed that the Visigoths were not going to be defeated easily. Therefore Stilicho chose to obey. Without formally renouncing his claim to guardianship over Arcadius, he evacuated Greece. Before doing so, he sent the eastern soldiers in his army to Constantinople under the command of a Visigoth in Roman service, Gaïnas.

Yet Stilicho had provided for his revenge. When Rufinus came out to greet the returning eastern army, Gaïnas's men assassinated him. Since Arcadius was too supine to rule, and Stilicho was far away, control over the East fell into the hands of the man closest to Arcadius, the head chamberlain Eutropius, who had already selected the emperor's wife. Although the eunuch may well have plotted with Stilicho earlier, when Eutropius took power he did not invite Stilicho to visit Constantinople or to resume fighting the Visigoths. Instead Eutropius allowed Alaric to lead his people into southern Greece without serious resistance. Invading territory that had not been raided for over a century, the Visigoths exacted tribute from Athens, destroyed Corinth, and methodically looted the Peloponnesus.

As yet unsure of his troops' abilities or loyalties, Eutropius left the Visigoths alone for the moment and concentrated on reassembling the eastern army. He reconstituted the mobile armies of Thrace, the East, and Illyricum, and the two mobile armies in the Emperor's Presence, which were called praesental armies even when the emperor was absent from them. Once these troops were safely divided into five commands, as Theodosius had intended, military rebellions were less likely, and the field armies had the flexibility they needed to fight their multiple enemies. Eutropius was still reluctant to test his troops in combat, but Greece obviously needed defending.

Probably in 397, after the Visigoths had pillaged unopposed for two years, Stilicho organized an expeditionary force and landed in the Peloponnesus to fight them. Like Rufinus before him, Eutropius feared that after defeating the Visigoths Stilicho would advance on Constantinople and take power there. The chamberlain accordingly had Arcadius declare Stilicho a public enemy, outlawing his campaign. Although Stilicho had already driven the Visigoths out of the peninsula, he was again finding them difficult opponents and withdrew once more. Then, less interested in the welfare of the empire than in avoiding the fate of Rufinus, Eutropius encouraged the master of soldiers in Africa Gildo to rebel against Stilicho and transfer his allegiance to the East. Putting down this revolt kept Stilicho busy for a year. Meanwhile Eutropius came to terms with the Visigoths. He settled them in Epirus, on the border between East and West, and gave their leader Alaric the title of master of soldiers for Illyricum. The Visigoths kept the peace but helped themselves to new arms from the diocesan armories.

Opportunistic though Eutropius could be, he was a capable official who restored stability in an uncertain situation. He appears to have worked with success to refill the depleted treasury of the eastern government, while avoiding weakening the army in the process. When the patriarchate of Constantinople fell vacant, the chamberlain obtained the appointment of John Chrysostom ("Golden Mouth"), a brilliant preacher and church reformer who became popular among the people of the capital. After other commanders had failed to check the eastern Huns who were raiding Anatolia, Eutropius finally took action. He led an army against them in person and soundly defeated them, driving them out of the empire and back across Armenia. For his victory he had himself named consul for 399, an honor never before received by a eunuch.

During his consulship, however, the Ostrogoths whom Theodosius had settled in Phrygia rose in rebellion and began raiding the surrounding parts of Anatolia. After attempting negotiations, Eutropius sent an army against them under Gaïnas, whom he evidently counted as a supporter. But Gaïnas apparently felt that he had been inadequately rewarded for murdering Rufinus. After the Ostrogoths defeated a force led by one of his subordinates, Gaïnas came to an understanding with his

18. Saint John Chrysostom, patriarch of Constantinople (398–404). Ninth-century mosaic from Saint Sophia, Constantinople. (Photo: Dumbarton Oaks, Washington, D.C., copyright 1996)

fellow Goths. With their support, he began dictating terms to the Romans. First he demanded that the emperor placate the rebels by surrendering Eutropius. Eutropius's enemies in Constantinople, who had come to include the empress Eudoxia and the prefect of the East Aurelian, persuaded Arcadius to agree. By taking refuge with Chrysostom in Saint Sophia the eunuch escaped immediate death, but he was executed not long thereafter. Aurelian took charge of Arcadius and the government.[2]

Yet by now Gaïnas wanted control of the government for himself. To secure it, he openly joined the Ostrogothic rebels and marched on Constantinople. Probably in the spring of 400, he demanded to meet the complaisant emperor at the city's Asian suburb of Chalcedon. During this audience, Arcadius accepted more demands: to make Gaïnas one of the masters of soldiers in the Emperor's Presence, to allow Gaïnas's troops to occupy Constantinople, and to name officials of Gaïnas's choice to the highest posts in the administration, removing Aurelian from the prefecture. Gaïnas therefore entered Constantinople as the master of the eastern empire, and was promised the consulship for the next year. Germans already dominated the eastern mobile forces, including the Army of Illyricum under Alaric and the Army of the East under another Visigoth, Fravitta. Although Arcadius remained emperor, he had never ruled as one and never would. Apparently Germans had taken over the whole enormous apparatus of the eastern Roman state.

During the late spring and early summer of 400 Gaïnas held Constantinople and directed the empire as he wished, but with increasing difficulty. The people of the city became more and more resentful of his power. Gaïnas found it prudent to exile rather than execute Aurelian and the other officials who had been dismissed. When the Goth asked for a single church within the walls in which he and his fellow Germans could practice their Arian faith, John Chrysostom insisted that Arcadius refuse. The emperor's refusal emboldened the Romans in the city. Rumors of Gothic reprisals against Romans provoked rumors of Roman plots against the Goths. Hoping to reduce tension, Gaïnas began to transfer his troops out of the capital. But after he and most of his army had withdrawn, the citizens rose against him, closed the gates, and massacred the Goths who were trapped inside.

Arcadius, heeding the mob, recalled his former prefect Aurelian and the other exiles. The emperor promoted Fravitta from master of soldiers of the East to master of soldiers in the Emperor's Presence, then called upon him to suppress Gaïnas as a traitor. Luckily for the Romans, Fravitta, who unlike most Goths was not an Arian but a pagan, chose to follow his own interests and obey. When Gaïnas's men tried to cross into Anatolia, Fravitta's army inflicted heavy losses upon them and forced them back. The remaining rebels turned north and crossed the Danube, only to be slaughtered by the Huns, who considerately sent Gaïnas's head to Arcadius. Power in Constantinople appears to have passed to the empress Eudoxia and a group of officials led by the count of the sacred largesses John. John was reputedly Eudoxia's lover and the real father of her son Theodosius, born at just this time. Such as they were, Romans were back in command of the empire.

Gaïnas's bid for power seems to have left the eastern authorities with an understandable distrust and dislike of German officers. Their feelings extended to Alaric and to Gaïnas's former patron Stilicho. Perhaps with John's encouragement, toward the end of 401 Alaric gave up his post as master of soldiers for Illyricum and led his Visigoths out of eastern territory. They marched straight for the western imperial capital of Milan. When Fravitta protested John's hostility toward the West, John had him cashiered and executed.[3] Now that many barbarian troops had been massacred in the East, and the chief barbarian military commanders had been removed, the eastern government had mostly freed itself from barbarian influence. Of course, Alaric's departure for Italy helped the East only by gravely imperiling the West.

Speedily concluding a campaign against some Germans who had crossed the upper Danube, Stilicho relieved Milan in early 402. After fighting an indecisive battle with Alaric, he negotiated the Visigoths' withdrawal from Italy. But Alaric remained not far to the east, probably in the territory that had become the Diocese of Illyricum in the western empire. The western government was sufficiently traumatized to move its capital from Milan to a more defensible place, the island city of Ravenna by the Adriatic coast.[4] A deadly threat hung over the West.

During this time no single personality was firmly in charge in the East, and the results were unfortunate not only for Stilicho and Fravitta but for John Chrysostom. In his efforts to reform the morals of the clergy, the patriarch of Constantinople had been exerting his ecclesiastical authority throughout Thrace and Anatolia, well beyond the traditional limits of his see's jurisdiction. The enemies he made in the process found a leader in Theophilus, the domineering archbishop of Alexandria. As head of a see that was also styled a patriarchate and had long been the most powerful in the eastern empire, Theophilus was disturbed by the rise of Constantinople to rival Alexandrian preeminence.

In 402 some Egyptian monks whom Theophilus had excommunicated appealed to Chrysostom. Although Chrysostom claimed no jurisdiction in the case, Eudoxia and the civil authorities summoned Theophilus to the capital. When Theophilus arrived in 403, he assembled Chrysostom's enemies, won over Eudoxia, and had a synod condemn the patriarch on various implausible charges. As riots broke out in Constantinople, Arcadius's vacillating advisers had Chrysostom first exiled, then recalled almost immediately, and finally exiled again in 404. Chrysostom's second exile provoked a schism, with his many defenders including Pope Innocent and the western bishops. Naturally this schism further damaged relations between East and West.

The empress Eudoxia died later the same year. Soon after the docile Arcadius had been freed from her influence, he returned to following a single competent adviser. This was Anthemius, who had been an important official for some time before he became prefect of the East in 405. If he had had full responsibility earlier, he might well have avoided provoking the enmity of Stilicho and the schism over Chrysostom. As it was, however, Anthemius had to deal with the consequences of both of those follies of his predecessors.

Thoroughly out of patience with the East, Stilicho persuaded Alaric and his Visigoths to help seize the Prefecture of Illyricum for the West. By the beginning of 407, Alaric had occupied Epirus and was waiting to be joined by Roman troops from Stilicho. But before those troops could march, several German tribes simultaneously broke through the Rhine frontier, and rebellions broke out in Britain and Gaul. Stilicho had to abandon his attempt to take over Illyricum, and Alaric withdrew to the West, forcing Stilicho to pay him compensation for his trouble. Thus the western threat to Illyricum evaporated.

Not long thereafter, Anthemius's government had the exiled Chrysostom so badly mistreated that he died. Though the schism lingered on, no one could demand any longer that John be restored to office, and the issue became the less urgent one of whether his memory should be honored. Atticus, the patriarch who had been consecrated as John's second successor in 406, quickly began conciliating John's partisans, although it took him ten years to rehabilitate Chrysostom completely. Anthemius

19. Marble frieze of lambs from the second Church of Saint Sophia, Constantinople, dating to the rebuilding begun in 406. (Photo: T. Mathews, Dumbarton Oaks, Washington, D.C., copyright 1996)

and Atticus also started a grand new Church of Saint Sophia to replace the one built by Constantius II, which rioters in favor of Chrysostom had burned two years before.

When Arcadius died in 408, he was succeeded by the seven-year-old Theodosius II, who at least for constitutional purposes was recognized as Arcadius's son. The change of sovereign from a weakling to a child merely meant that Anthemius's virtual regency became official, while he remained without effective rivals for power. Although the western emperor Honorius wanted to go east to assert his authority there, Stilicho advised him not to leave the West while Germans were spreading over part of the Gallic Prefecture and rebels had seized the rest of it. Soon afterward a military uprising resulted in Stilicho's execution, and in the massacre or desertion of most of the Germans in the Army of Italy.

Honorius's new anti-German advisers quickly repaired their relations with Anthemius. But thirteen years of estrangement from the East had inflicted terrible damage on the West. The western government was in an uproar, and Alaric and his Visigoths, joined by many German deserters from Stilicho's army, had Italy almost at their mercy. In the East, however, relative calm had returned. By failing to rule, Arcadius had allowed a good deal of maladministration. But by continuing to reign— so harmlessly that nobody had taken the trouble to depose him—he had maintained legal continuity during a troubled time. He had thereby secured the succession for Theodosius II, who during his own reign was to follow his predecessor's example of feeble rulership.

THE THREAT OF THE HUNS

For over thirty years the Huns had held the region to the north of the Danube, and for several years at least they had been united under a single king, Uldin. Yet they had not disturbed the Romans much, and had actually helped the eastern government by killing Gaïnas in 400. In 408, however, while the East was distracted by reports of an imminent Persian invasion, Uldin led his Huns across the Danube in force, near the border between the eastern and western empires. Advancing through Dacia into Thrace, Uldin refused the Thracian commander's offer of an alliance and demanded a substantial tribute from the eastern government.

Fortunately for the empire, the bait of Roman gold led some of Uldin's lieutenants to desert. The king beat a hasty retreat across the Danube, abandoning many of his men. Anthemius's government rounded them up, sold them into slavery, and carefully dispersed them in Asia. Uldin's authority was shaken badly enough to keep him north of the Danube for the time being. Then the East concluded a peace with Persia, supposedly to last for a hundred years. Under it the Romans seem to have paid the Persians a subsidy for guarding the passes in the Caucasus against the Huns, and the Persians became more tolerant of their Christian subjects.

While the East was still dealing with the Huns and Persians, the plight of the West became desperate. Gaul, Britain, and Spain remained in revolt. Alaric and his Visigoths twice besieged Rome, where they arranged the proclamation of a puppet emperor in 409. Although the western capital of Ravenna was secure from direct assault, Honorius feared betrayal by his disaffected subjects and considered taking refuge at Constantinople. Anthemius's regency managed to send four thousand soldiers to Ravenna, and they may well have saved Honorius's throne. But no one saved Rome itself, which Alaric's men captured and sacked in 410.

The fall of Rome shocked educated opinion in both West and East, and brutally revealed the weakness of the western government. Such a humiliation could scarcely have happened if the recent quarrel between East and West had not prevented Roman cooperation against the Visigoths. From this time on, the West was much inferior in wealth and power to the East, and generally known to be so. Nevertheless, over the next few years Honorius's western empire made a partial recovery. Alaric died; the Visigoths left Italy and settled in southern Gaul; and the Roman

20. The Theodosian Walls of Constantinople, begun by the prefect of the East Anthemius in 413. (Photo: Warren Treadgold)

rebels were subdued, while the capable general Constantius took over the leadership of the army and administration.

In the East the Huns remained a danger that Anthemius did not underestimate. He had the walls of the Thracian towns repaired, and built up the Roman fleet on the Danube. Not satisfied with this, in 413 he began new fortifications of great strength for Constantinople. Although the city proper can hardly have outgrown the capacious walls built by Constantine, the new walls commanded higher ground than the old ones and enclosed space for cisterns, farms, supply depots, and many refugees. The walls included both inner and outer circuits, and were plainly designed to withstand a long siege. Although Anthemius must mainly have worried about the Huns, the Anthemian Walls—more commonly but less deservedly called Theodosian—formed an almost impregnable defense against any attack from the land side, whether of foreigners or of Roman rebels. Barring some major innovation in siege warfare, these fortifications could hardly be taken without the help of a navy or betrayal from within. They not only assured that Constantinople would never fall to the Huns, but remained the empire's greatest man-made asset for centuries to come.

Not long after starting work on the walls, and probably before the new Church of Saint Sophia was consecrated in 415, Anthemius seems to have died. Much of his power passed, remarkably, to the emperor's sixteen-year-old sister, Pulcheria. Although taking a vow of virginity excused her from marrying a husband who would have impinged upon her influence, Pulcheria, like her mother Eudoxia, shared her authority with male associates. For years Pulcheria's chief collaborator was apparently the master of offices Helio. She and he increasingly relied on German and other barbarian army officers, disregarding the dangers of excessive German power that had been revealed by the revolt of Gaïnas not so long ago. In 418 Pulcheria and Helio sent the Gothic general Plinta to put down a revolt in Palestine. Afterward Plinta became one of the masters of soldiers in the Emperor's Presence for twenty years.

As a devout Christian, Pulcheria had her brother the emperor officially bar pagans from public service in 416, although she seems not to have objected so much to Arian barbarians as to pagans. Eventually Theodosius II himself began to take an interest in religious affairs, and after he married in 421 his wife Eudocia, though a former pagan, did the same.[5] That year, when the new Persian king Bahrām began to persecute Christians in his territory, Theodosius declared war on Persia, ending more than forty years of relative peace with the empire's great eastern neighbor. To guard against an attack by the Huns while some Thracian troops were off fighting the Persians, Ostrogoths were brought from Pannonia and settled in Thrace.

Operations against the Persians were largely entrusted to Ardabur, a relative by marriage of Plinta's from the Iranian tribe of the Alans. The war went somewhat better for the Romans than for their adversaries. Ardabur put Nisibis under siege, and another Roman army helped Christian rebels in Persian Armenia. But as the Romans were fighting on the eastern frontier, King Rua of the Huns took his chance to raid the dioceses of Dacia and Thrace again, passing by the recently settled Ostrogoths and forcing the government to man the new walls of Constantinople. Faced by a war on two fronts, in 422 Helio made peace with the Persians on roughly the same terms as before. This treaty, like the earlier one, was supposed to last for a century. The Huns were bought off with a small but ignominious annual tribute of 25,200 nomismata.[6]

Meanwhile relations between the eastern and western parts of the empire had worsened once again. The eastern government, in the hope of reuniting the empire under Theodosius II when Honorius died, had refused to recognize Honorius's proclamation of his general Constantius as his coemperor and heir in 421. Theodosius's government also tried to transfer ecclesiastical jurisdiction over the Prefecture of Illyricum from the pope to the patriarch of Constantinople. Although Constantius prepared the western army for war, he died before he could march.

Constantius's death brought a temporary reconciliation between West and East. Yet his widow Galla Placidia, Honorius's sister, soon quarreled with her brother and took refuge at Constantinople with her infant son Valentinian. In 423 Honorius himself died without an heir, and Theodosius II wanted to exercise his dynastic right to rule the whole empire. But the western courtiers proclaimed a new emperor, John, who was not related to the house of Theodosius. To defeat John, the eastern government decided to appeal to partisans of Galla Placidia by supporting her son's claim to the western throne.

In 424 the eastern general Ardabur and his son Aspar led an expedition to the West. At first Ardabur was shipwrecked near Ravenna and fell into John's hands. But he turned his captivity in the city to such good account that he managed to betray it to Aspar. After capturing John, Ardabur reached a settlement with John's partisans, by which one of them, Aëtius, became the leading general in the West and Placidia's son became emperor as Valentinian III. In 425 Helio traveled to Ravenna and installed Valentinian there. During Valentinian's reign the eastern and western empires maintained their alliance, which was sealed by Valentinian's betrothal and eventual marriage to Theodosius II's daughter Eudoxia.

Thus far into the reign of Theodosius, the eastern government had performed rather well, at least in comparison with what had been done under Arcadius and was being done in the West. The East had avoided internal dissension and dealt with external dangers, winning little glory but avoiding serious losses. It had even provided some protection to the Christians ruled by Persia, though the Persian king Bahrām meddled somewhat more in church affairs after he abolished the Armenian monarchy in 428. Theodosius's advisers also maintained sound finances and worked to improve the administration. In 425 state chairs were founded at Constantinople for thirty professors of grammar, rhetoric, philosophy, and law, whose main task was to train civil servants. In 429 the government appointed a commission to produce the Roman Empire's first official collection of laws, which was published nine years later as the *Theodosian Code*. But at about the time the commission started its work, Helio appears to have died, and the state began to function less smoothly.

The first sign of trouble was a new theological controversy. The patriarch of Constantinople Nestorius expressed the seemingly logical opinion that the Virgin Mary, since she had given birth to Christ only as a man, not as God, was the mother of Christ but not truly the Mother of God, as she was often called. Theodosius II supported Nestorius; Pulcheria opposed him. Many bishops, led by Cyril of Alexandria, accused Nestorius of heretically dividing Christ into separate human and divine persons. Nestorius insisted that he believed Christ to be a single person, though endowed with divine and human natures that acted separately.

A council held at Rome by Pope Celestine condemned Nestorius in 430. Nestorius protested that his doctrines had been misrepresented. He and the emperor obtained the pope's consent to hold an ecumenical council at Ephesus on the matter in 431. This council, which Cyril of Alexandria convened before a number of the bishops had arrived, deposed Nestorius for his alleged belief that Christ had two persons. Again Nestorius protested, and he won the support of a council of bishops who arrived later and voted to depose Cyril. Confusion reigned for two years. Finally the emperor and bishops accepted the decisions of Cyril's Council of Ephesus that Mary was the Mother of God, that Christ was one person, and that Nestorius was a heretic. A few bishops started a Nestorian church based in Persia that followed Nestorius's real doctrines. Many more, while thinking that Nestorius had gone too far, disapproved of Cyril's high-handedness and thought him overly eager to submerge Christ's humanity in his divinity. Theodosius II particularly resented this humiliation of the patriarch he had chosen for his capital.

In the meantime the German tribe of the Vandals had invaded the richest part of the West, its African provinces, and Galla Placidia appealed urgently for help from her nephew the eastern emperor. Responsive to her request, Theodosius sent an expedition in 431, led by his leading general Aspar. During his stay of three years in Africa Aspar was defeated once by the Vandals and did no more than slow their advance. But in the West's desperate need this was enough for him to be rewarded with the western consulship for 434. Then Aspar was recalled, probably because of the growing danger posed to both West and East by the Huns.

The Huns had gradually overrun most of the West's Danube frontier

21. Silver missorium showing the eastern general Aspar as western consul for 434 with his young son Ardabur (right) and medallions of his father Ardabur (above left) and relative Plinta (above right), now in Florence. (Photo: Soprintendenza alle Antichità, Florence)

except for its eastern anchor at Sirmium, which the eastern government took over to keep it in Roman hands. At about this time, the Hun king Rua demanded the return of some refugees who had fled from his territory to the eastern empire. But before the Roman ambassadors arrived to negotiate, Rua suddenly died and was succeeded by his ferocious nephews Bleda and Attila. These two kings frightened the Romans into agreeing to return the refugees, to double the previous tribute to 50,400 nomismata, and to promise not to make any alliance against the Huns. Given the strength of the Huns so close to eastern territory, the East sent no troops back to the West after Aspar's departure. The Vandals advanced steadily through Africa, and in 439 took Carthage, where they soon built a fleet that landed in Sicily and even threatened the coastlands of the East.

Meanwhile the balance of power at Constantinople began to shift.

The emperor's sister Pulcheria retired from government after a quarrel with the emperor's wife Eudocia. Eudocia briefly became the chief influence on Theodosius II, with the help of the prefect of the East Cyrus of Panopolis. Cyrus's main action was to strengthen the sea defenses of Constantinople to guard against a Vandal attack. But early in 440 the emperor came to suspect Eudocia of adultery, and soon afterward she retired to Jerusalem.[7] The next year her ally Cyrus was deposed as prefect of the East and forced to become a bishop. The beneficiary of these upheavals was Chrysaphius, an ambitious palace eunuch, who seems to have plotted the departures of Pulcheria, Eudocia, and Cyrus so that he could seize power. Though by his intrigues Chrysaphius had made some enemies at court, probably including the barbarian generals, his nerve and skill at maneuvering were necessary qualities for a head of government at this dangerous time.

In 441 the eastern government dispatched another expedition against the Vandals in Africa under the Gothic general Ariobindus. Aspar apparently remained in the Balkans to guard against a Hun invasion. While the expedition to Africa was away and the Huns still threatened, the Persians invaded Roman Mesopotamia, until they were bought off. Then, before the Romans had properly dealt with the Vandals or Persians, the Huns did strike, and took and destroyed the border town of Viminacium in Dacia. Although Aspar marched against them, he found it safest to buy a truce for one year. During that time the expedition against the Vandals was recalled, without ever sailing farther than Sicily.

The Huns invaded Dacia in earnest as soon as their truce expired. This time they overran the larger part of the Dacian Diocese, capturing and wrecking all its major cities, including Sirmium. They then moved into Thrace. After the master of soldiers for Thrace was assassinated because of a plot that seems not to have involved the Huns, they sharply defeated Ariobindus and Aspar. To obtain peace, the anxious eastern government had to raise the Huns' tribute to 151,200 nomismata a year, plus a lump payment of 432,000 nomismata. These had become large enough sums that the state began to curtail tax exemptions and demanded a new tax from senators to meet the expense. Attila made use of the peace to murder his brother Bleda and to unite the Huns under his formidable self.

Providentially for the empire, the Persians had barbarian enemies of their own, the so-called White Huns, who now became so menacing that Persia needed peace with Rome as much as Rome needed peace

with Persia. In 442 the two empires made a treaty ending all mutual hostilities, and prohibiting new fortifications along their common frontier.
This peace held for many years, cemented by the necessity for both powers to concentrate their forces against invaders who threatened their very
existence. Although during the five years after 442 Attila did not invade
with his main army, contingents of Huns kept raiding imperial territory,
provoking the Romans to withhold their tribute in protest. In 447, when
an earthquake damaged the walls of Constantinople, Attila demanded
that the Romans pay the tribute that they had withheld and return new
fugitives from Hun territory. As the Romans tried to negotiate instead
of submitting at once, Attila struck across the Danube with devastating
force.

The Gothic master of soldiers of Thrace Arnegisclus met Attila in
battle in the Province of Moesia II, but lost decisively and died in the
fighting. Fanning out over the Thracian Diocese as far as the coasts of
the Black Sea and the Sea of Marmara, the Huns sacked every important
town but Adrianople and Constantinople itself. In the capital the walls
were repaired in time, and a troop of Isaurians, native if uncivilized Romans, arrived as reinforcements.[8] But the Huns defeated a praesental
army under Aspar near the Hellespont, and took many captives and enormous booty. Desperate for peace, the eastern government accepted unusually harsh terms. The greater part of the Diocese of Dacia, up to five
days' march from the Danube, was to remain desolate and open to the
Huns, who could therefore cross the frontier whenever they liked. The
Romans naturally continued to pay their annual tribute, and made the
back payments Attila had demanded. With this, Attila was content to
leave the eastern empire alone for the present.

The Huns had inflicted even worse damage on Thrace and northern
Illyricum than that caused by the Goths after the battle of Adrianople.
On the other hand, the Huns appear to have killed fewer Roman troops
than the Goths had done, and they made no efforts to settle in Roman
territory. Despite their surprising talent for sacking walled towns, the
Huns could scarcely hope to storm the magnificent fortifications of Constantinople or to penetrate into Anatolia. Since Attila's power, however
great, depended on precarious authority over many subject tribes, the
Romans' best course was probably to appease him and wait for the peril
to pass. Although Chrysaphius seems to have understood this much, it
meant enduring prolonged humiliation by the Huns, which invited
carping by his opponents. Repeated defeats in battle had discredited the

barbarian generals Aspar and Ariobindus. A commander who had not suffered such setbacks, Zeno, the leader of the Isaurians and master of soldiers of the East, became a major rival of Chrysaphius.

The eunuch made still more enemies by becoming embroiled in a new theological controversy. After the Council of Ephesus, the more extreme adversaries of Nestorius had begun to contend that besides being one person Christ had only one nature. The Constantinopolitan abbot Eutyches took this view to the point of affirming that Christ's nature, since it was fully divine, was unlike that of ordinary men. Chrysaphius, long an admirer of Eutyches, won him the favor of the impressionable emperor, who had recently supported Nestorius's quite opposite opinion. The issue was a confusing one, but many Christians felt that Eutyches had gone too far in minimizing Christ's humanity.

The emperor's view notwithstanding, a council held by Patriarch Flavian of Constantinople condemned Eutyches, and Pope Leo upheld the condemnation. In the hope of reversing this result, Theodosius summoned another ecumenical council at Ephesus in 449. A supporter of Eutyches, the patriarch of Alexandria Dioscorus, presided over the council and used a band of armed Egyptian monks to intimidate his adversaries. Dioscorus thus secured a decision that Christ had only one, divine, nature. The synod vindicated Eutyches and deposed Flavian, who died on his way into exile. Though Pope Leo protested, Theodosius II set about replacing the eastern bishops who were opposed to Dioscorus and Eutyches.

Meanwhile Chrysaphius was trying to lessen the danger from the Huns by arranging Attila's assassination. Although the idea was in itself a rational one, Attila discovered the plot, and demanded Chrysaphius be surrendered to him. This would have pleased the Isaurian leader Zeno well enough, but most of those with influence in government could not stomach such a humiliating concession. Through envoys Chrysaphius managed to flatter and buy his way to a reconciliation with the Hun king, who given his own past methods was not much upset by the idea of murdering opponents. The eunuch even gained Attila's permission for the Romans to reoccupy the territory that they had evacuated in Dacia, which by this time was so devastated that the Huns had begun to lose interest in it.

Chrysaphius had actually guided the empire through the worst of the Hun crisis with some dexterity. But in preserving the empire and his authority up to this time, he had acquired an impressive array of enemies.

22. Theodosius II (r. 408–50), with personifications of Rome and Constantinople on the reverse. Gold double nomisma, shown one and one-half times actual size. (Photo: Dumbarton Oaks, Washington, D.C., copyright 1996)

One was the Isaurian commander Zeno, whom the emperor had come to suspect of sedition but could not easily strip of his command. Another enemy of Chrysaphius's was the empress Pulcheria, the first victim of his ingenuity, who had become reconciled with her brother Theodosius and had always been an ally of the still powerful general Aspar. Although the emperor seems to have supported his favorite nonetheless, in the middle of 450 Theodosius fell from his horse, injured his back, and died.

THE GROWTH OF BARBARIAN INFLUENCE

Theodosius II's death left no male survivor of the Theodosian house at Constantinople. Although in theory the western emperor Valentinian III should have inherited the eastern throne as well, he was far away and otherwise occupied. While Pulcheria had a certain claim to determine the succession as the late emperor's sister, she had little practical power as long as her rival Chrysaphius controlled the machinery of government. In order to make her claim good, she relied on Aspar and his family of barbarian generals, with whom she had worked for years. A month after her brother's death, Pulcheria made a nominal marriage with Marcian, Aspar's chief lieutenant, alleging that Theodosius had designated him the next emperor. In the absence of another strong candidate, this was enough to secure the succession for Marcian, an obscure officer of Thracian blood nearing the age of sixty. He executed Chrysaphius, and made

Aspar's son Ardabur a master of soldiers like his father. Valentinian III was displeased, and withheld recognition from Marcian for the present, but the western emperor was in no position to contest the eastern succession.

While Marcian continued the tradition set by Arcadius and Theodosius II of relying heavily on advisers, he exercised some power and showed some ability. Perhaps on his own initiative, he promptly informed the Huns that he would no longer pay them the tribute that Chrysaphius had promised. This repudiation of appeasement was not altogether foolhardy, because Attila had already declared his intention to march against the western empire. For the present, annoyed though he was, Attila stuck to his plans and invaded the West. In 451 he advanced into northern Gaul, where he was stopped, with difficulty, by a combined force of Romans and Visigoths under the western general Aëtius.

Along with Chrysaphius's policy toward the Huns, Pulcheria and Marcian repudiated the late eunuch's theological opinions. They banished Eutyches, restored the bishops who had opposed him, and summoned a new ecumenical council, though Pope Leo believed none was necessary. Marcian originally invited the bishops to Nicaea; but when he had to ward off a minor raid by the Huns, he postponed the council and moved it to the capital's suburb of Chalcedon. This council rejected the validity of the Second Council of Ephesus, which became known as the Robber Council. The Council of Chalcedon deposed Dioscorus of Alexandria and accepted the pleas of other bishops that Dioscorus had forced them to vote as they had. The bishops at Chalcedon endorsed the earlier definition of Pope Leo that Christ was a single person with two natures, one divine and one human. The council specified that Christ's natures acted in harmony, and condemned the Nestorian belief that they acted separately. The contrary belief in one nature, Monophysitism, was declared a heresy, on the argument that it denied Christ's full humanity.

The Council of Chalcedon went on to define the jurisdictions of the five greatest bishoprics, all of which were now coming to be called patriarchates. The papacy already had an authority that extended over the whole West and the Prefecture of Illyricum, and the patriarchate of Alexandria enjoyed similar preeminence in Egypt. Now the new patriarchate of Jerusalem was given jurisdiction over the three provinces of Palestine, while the patriarch of Antioch's authority was confirmed over the remainder of the Diocese of the East. Finally, the council subjected the dioceses of Thrace, Asiana, and Pontica to the patriarchate of Constantinople, which had gradually been extending its claims since being ranked second to the papacy at the Council of Constantinople of 381.

Both the dogmatic and the organizational decisions of the Council of Chalcedon aroused controversy. Pope Leo refused to recognize the jurisdictional changes on the ground that their expansion of Constantinople's authority had no basis in church tradition. The ancient churches of Alexandria and Antioch also resented the privileges awarded by Chalcedon to the newer patriarchates of Constantinople and Jerusalem. Conversely, the churches of Constantinople and Jerusalem, as the principal beneficiaries, were the most enthusiastic supporters of the changes made at Chalcedon.

While the papacy and the West gladly accepted the council's theology, which was Pope Leo's own, many in the East found it objectionable, particularly in Dioscorus's homeland of Egypt. These Monophysites found distinguishing Christ's two natures to be practically equivalent to Nestorianism, which supposedly divided Christ into two persons. But the Monophysites were also divided among themselves. A few were outright Eutychians, who followed the Robber Council of Ephesus in considering the Son's nature to be wholly divine. But most were known as "Hesitants," because they took a middle position between the Robber Council and Chalcedon, believing that the Son had a single nature but was nonetheless both divine and human. The confusion over Monophysitism after the Council of Chalcedon was therefore comparable to the confusion over Arianism after the Council of Nicaea.

By insisting on Christ's divinity, Monophysitism tended to inspire stronger devotion than Arianism or Nestorianism, which had insisted on Christ's humanity. Any devout Christian naturally considered Christ's being God more important than his being a man; affirming Christ's divinity was what made Christianity a separate religion rather than a sect of Judaism. Since the Chalcedonians and Hesitant Monophysites shared a belief that the Son was both divine and human, the possibility remained that they could somehow agree on a sense in which one nature and two natures meant the same thing. Yet feelings ran high, and the government soon learned how intractable the issue was.

During the immediate aftermath of the Council of Chalcedon, the eastern and western Roman governments were both preoccupied with the danger posed by the Huns. In 452, when Attila invaded Italy, Marcian helped the western empire, not only by sending reinforcements directly but by invading the Huns' territory north of the Danube. This aid achieved its purpose. Leaving northern Italy only half ravaged, Attila returned in a rage to prepare for an invasion of the East. Probably he would have defeated Marcian's forces, and extorted more tribute as a result. As it happened, however, he died early the next year, on one of his many wedding nights.

Attila's death began a quarrel among his sons. Although the sons still seem to have mounted some raids on Thrace, these were repulsed by Aspar's son Ardabur.[9] Within two years, the Huns' German vassals rose and defeated them, and the improvised Hun Empire started to disintegrate. The decline of the Huns was certainly to the advantage of the Germans; but what was helpful to Germans did not necessarily benefit the two Roman governments. By this time Zeno the Isaurian was also dead, removing a possible threat to Marcian but also a possible counterweight to the Germans. Under Aspar's influence, Marcian allied himself with the Germans of the Danube valley who had been outside his control, and settled many of them in the devastated region along the river. The emperor was nonetheless careful to foster divisions in the largest tribe, the Ostrogoths, recruiting some of them as federates without lands, keeping others settled in Thrace, and leaving still others in devastated Pannonia, which was nominally part of the western empire.

Acknowledging the East's assistance during Attila's invasion, the West formally recognized Marcian as eastern emperor. But in 454 Valentinian III killed his general Aëtius, and the next year Valentinian himself was murdered. The East refused to recognize his two ephemeral successors, during whose reigns the Vandals landed in Italy and sacked Rome again, carrying off Valentinian's widow Eudoxia. In 456 what was left of the western empire fell into the hands of the German general Ricimer, who kept the throne vacant while he negotiated with the East. Pulcheria had died in 453, leaving Aspar's influence over Marcian unchallenged. When Marcian himself suddenly fell ill and died at the beginning of 457, Aspar was left in a position of almost unqualified dominance. As the Theodosian dynasty ended, both parts of the empire were under the effective rule of men of barbarian stock and Arian faith, backed by predominantly German armies.

To be sure, during most of the period from the death of Theodosius I to the death of Marcian—with the notable exception of the ascendancy of Gaïnas—few Romans would have felt that they were being ruled by barbarians. A Roman was always emperor. Practically all civil servants were Romans. Barbarians hardly ever interfered in anything but military matters, and even as military officers they generally obeyed orders. Again with the exception of Gaïnas, barbarian generals had shown no tendency to betray Roman interests to barbarian enemies, nor were they

23. Triumphal column of Marcian (r. 450–57), Constantinople, which originally carried a statue of the emperor. (Photo: Dumbarton Oaks, Washington, D.C., copyright 1996)

likely to do so as long as the empire's principal enemies were the Huns, whom Germans and Alans feared as much as Romans did. Germans like Plinta and Alans like Aspar had Roman tastes, and family connections with the Roman aristocracy. Such men had no desire to hand over the Roman Empire to independent barbarian tribes.

Yet the real danger to the empire was not so much betrayal to external enemies as subversion from within. Already, in the West, Ricimer and his German comrades were temporarily doing without an emperor, and twenty years later another barbarian general was to dispense with a Roman emperor for good. Even the Romanized barbarian generals relied for support on barbarian troops, to whom they were bound by ties of race, military training, and Arian faith. Since most Romans considered an Aspar or Ricimer ineligible to become emperor, the barbarian generals' ambitions practically forced them to subvert the imperial office somehow.

After barbarians gained firm control over the empire, as at Marcian's death they seemed about to do, their kinsmen in the army would soon become a ruling class, as they were already beginning to be. Eventually the old Roman ruling class would become otiose, and ultimately the Roman order would wither. This process was already well advanced in the western part of the empire, and developments there seemed only a little ahead of those in the eastern part. In most respects, however, politics and life went on as before. Few contemporaries looked past their personal concerns to see the empire's danger clearly.

CHAPTER FOUR

The Formation of Byzantine Society, 284–457

Before Diocletian, neither the Roman Empire nor even its eastern part had formed a society of its own. Instead there was a Greek society in Greece and many of the coastlands, an Egyptian society in Egypt, a Syrian society in Syria and Mesopotamia, mixed native societies in the interior of Anatolia, and a Latinized society along the Danube frontier. The people of the eastern provinces, except for the Latin speakers along the Danube, in varying degrees regarded the Roman government as foreign, and Latin-speaking Romans took a similar view of easterners. The Roman administration, apart from extracting tribute and arranging for defense, left the eastern provincials more or less to themselves. For most purposes they were governed through their local city councils, which administered not only the cities but the rural regions around them.

Although much of this diversity persisted in the eastern provinces long after Diocletian, between his time and the middle of the fifth century both the Roman Empire and the Christian church came to exercise an unprecedented influence on the lives of the people of the East. By the mid-fifth century, easterners had more in common with each other than ever before. They had come to share a more uniform and intrusive government, a majority religion, certain cultural characteristics, and a somewhat more unified economy. The East had become a separate state, and was becoming in many respects a distinct civilization.

REGIONS AND JURISDICTIONS

Without ceasing to be united in law and theory, the Roman Empire was politically divided from the time of Diocletian. Both his twofold and his fourfold divisions persisted. With certain boundary adjustments and a few interruptions, the realms of Diocletian's two Augusti continued to be ruled by different emperors of the East and West, while the sectors of his four emperors and their praetorian prefects continued to be separate prefectures. By the fifth century, the eastern and western governments were in practice independent of each other, even if they were usually but by no means always on friendly terms.

While the African boundary between East and West remained fixed at the Libyan desert, the European boundary varied considerably before 388. The line separating the lands of Diocletian's Jovian and Herculian dynasties ran just east of Italy until 316, when Constantine forced Licinius to retreat eastward. Constantine then added all the Balkans except Thrace to his western dominions. When he conquered the rest of the East in 324, Constantine included the Balkan dioceses of Dacia and Macedonia, though not the western Balkans, in the prefecture that included Constantinople. In 337, however, Macedonia and Dacia went to the western emperor Constans, and they were generally considered to be part of the West until 379. During this time they came under the ecclesiastical jurisdiction of Rome, and remained under the pope for centuries. Then Gratian transferred Dacia and Macedonia to the eastern emperor Theodosius I to help the East recover from the battle of Adrianople. Although Theodosius returned Macedonia and Dacia to the West between 382 and 388, thereafter the East ruled the whole of the southern Balkans.

This final border between East and West corresponded about as closely to the linguistic boundary between Greek and Latin as defensive strategy allowed. The European frontier started with the almost impassable mountains of southern Dalmatia, then followed the Drinus and Danube rivers. Rivers made for easily identified frontiers, and were somewhat inconvenient for the Germans, Sarmatians, and Huns to cross. When the barbarians crossed anyway, the Balkan Mountains slowed them down, and the straits and the walls of Constantinople nearly always halted them.

In Asia the Romans had never found a truly satisfactory frontier between the mountains of Armenia and the Syrian desert. But after 363 they at least held the shortest line between those obstacles, and many strongly fortified cities behind that line. Since the Persians had scant success in taking these strongholds, Persian power remained a serious nuisance rather than a mortal threat. While the Arabs to the south liked to raid Roman territory, and divided their alliances between Rome and Persia, they were seldom numerous or hostile enough to penetrate far into Palestine.

The African frontier consisted of deserts, except for a very short line across the Nile valley at the south, where Diocletian had set the border at the first cataract. Nomadic raiders could enter Egypt from the desert, but they were so outnumbered by the settled Egyptians that they caused little trouble. To the west the settled Libyans were so few that they suffered rather more from the forays of the nomads, but even so they were in little danger of being overrun. The eastern Romans were fortunate in having no seagoing enemies of importance until the mid-fifth century, when the Vandals of North Africa began to launch some sea raids.

The eastern empire's garrison army of frontier troops (*limitanei*) was supposed to take the main part in defending these borders. It consisted of fifteen independent commands, including every significant frontier district and the inland region of Isauria, whose outlaw-infested mountains needed policing as much as a border area. With a paper strength of about 195,000 soldiers in the late fourth century, the garrison army accounted for about two-thirds of the nominal military strength of the East. The fleets, which were attached to the frontier forces, probably added another 32,000 or so oarsmen. In practice, however, the garrisons slowly deteriorated after Constantine's creation of the mobile army relegated frontier troops to an inferior status. In 372 Valens explicitly reserved the better recruits for the field army, leaving the rest for the frontier troops. The latter came to be useful mostly for police action against raiders and robbers. Some of the names on the rolls of the garrison army were of men who had died or deserted, and even many who were present were unfit for service. Few were well trained or equipped.

The real defense of the East was the army of some 104,000 field soldiers (*comitatenses*). These, unlike the frontier forces, were largely barbarians. They served in regional armies for Illyricum, Thrace, and the East, and in the two praesental armies, normally stationed in and around Constantinople along with the 3,500 guardsmen of the Scholae. The temporarily successful revolt of Gaïnas had shown that these mobile troops were not always reliable, and they had suffered some notable defeats at the hands of the Germans, Persians, and Huns. But when the field army had loyal and capable commanders, it fought adequately. Its deployment

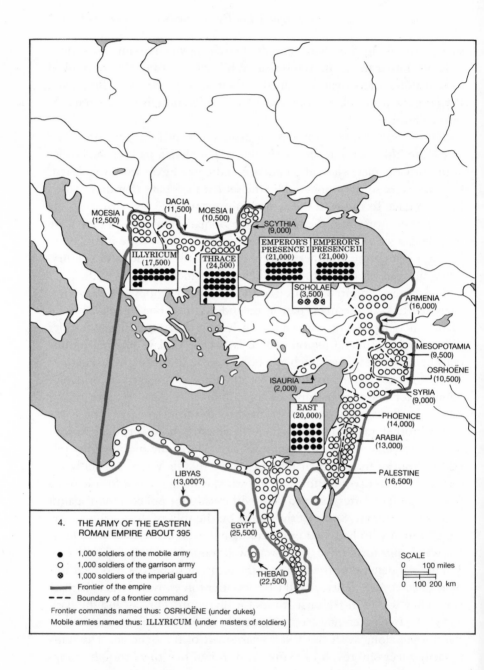

MOESIA I
(12,500)

DACIA
(11,500)

MOESIA II
(10,500)

SCYTHIA
(9,000)

EMPEROR'S
PRESENCE I
(21,000)

EMPEROR'S
PRESENCE II
(21,000)

ILLYRICUM
(17,500)

THRACE
(24,500)

SCHOLAE
(3,500)

ARMENIA
(16,000)

MESOPOTAMIA
(9,500)

OSRHOËNE
(10,500)

ISAURIA
(2,000)

SYRIA
(9,000)

EAST
(20,000)

PHOENICE
(14,000)

ARABIA
(13,000)

PALESTINE
(16,500)

LIBYAS
(13,000?)

EGYPT
(25,500)

THEBAÏD
(22,500)

4. THE ARMY OF THE EASTERN
    ROMAN EMPIRE ABOUT 395

●   1,000 soldiers of the mobile army
○   1,000 soldiers of the garrison army
⊗   1,000 soldiers of the imperial guard
── Frontier of the empire
- - - Boundary of a frontier command

Frontier commands named thus: OSRHOËNE (under dukes)
Mobile armies named thus: ILLYRICUM (under masters of soldiers)

SCALE
0   100 miles
0   100 200 km

showed the empire's most vulnerable point: four-fifths of the mobile army defended the Balkans and the capital.

Between the reigns of Diocletian and Marcian, the eastern empire at least kept the bulk of its land. By 457 it was certainly in better condition than the western empire, which had lost all of Britain, most of North Africa and western Illyricum, and much of Gaul and Spain. In the East Jovian had ceded to the Persians a smallish frontier region and the Roman protectorates over Armenia and Iberia; but Theodosius I had later annexed some of Armenia. Between the reigns of Valens and Marcian, the empire had lost control over parts of the Balkans; but by 457 it had reoccupied most of them. While the division of the empire into two seems to have hurt the West's ability to hold its territory, it had no such effect on the East. The division mostly affected the regions ruled from Constantinople in other ways.

The part of the East with the most obvious defensive problems was the Prefecture of Illyricum, consisting of the dioceses of Dacia and Macedonia. To judge from its frequent transfers between East and West before 388, and its part in conflicts between East and West afterward, the Roman governments attached great significance to it. Why they did so is not fully clear. Though in the second and third centuries it had been the empire's best recruiting ground, during the fourth century native troops became less effective, and by the early fifth century the Goths and Huns had ravaged the region so thoroughly that it cannot have had many men to spare. In any case northern Illyricum had always been poor and primitive, exporting recruits because it could hardly support them at home, while Greece, its venerable civilization notwithstanding, had long been suffering from depopulation and impoverishment. Nearly all the cities of the Illyrian prefecture, apart from its political and military headquarters at Thessalonica, were poor and growing poorer. Perhaps the Romans were slow to see that Illyricum no longer mattered as much as it once had.

Even lacking in men and riches, however, Illyricum was strategic territory. Geography made it the land bridge between East and West, and the only area that East and West could really fight over. Besides, its part of the Danube frontier was the gateway to the empire for barbarians like the Goths and Huns who traveled west from the steppes. While the straits kept the invaders from going farther east than Constantinople, they could easily go west up the Danube valley. For the eastern empire, the route through Illyricum was scarcely worth defending, as Rufinus saw; stopping invaders there mainly benefited the western empire, as

24. The so-called Golden Gate in the Theodosian Walls of Constantinople, used for triumphal entrances by victorious emperors. (Photo: Irina Andreescu-Treadgold)

Stilicho understood. Hence the long stays of the Goths and Huns in Illyricum, and the tension the territory caused between eastern and western Romans.

The case of the Diocese of Thrace, which adjoined Illyricum, was rather different. On the whole, its land was more productive. Its growing metropolis of Constantinople enhanced its political, military, ecclesiastical, and economic importance, which had previously not been great. The emperors of this time gave several Thracian villages the rank of city, partly in recognition of growth in their size and wealth. Although the Goths and Huns raided Thrace sometimes and threatened it often, they stayed only briefly and caused little if any permanent devastation or depopulation. Thrace was still a fairly backward region, but after Constantine it became less so.

The rise of Constantinople, like that of Nicomedia before it, affected Asia Minor as well. Always large and populous, Anatolia had never formed a single kingdom or province, and had never had any one metropolis. Now Constantinople became Anatolia's dominant city. It was separated from Anatolia by the Bosporus, but was linked to the Anatolian coast by frequent sailings and then to the plateau by the peninsula's principal road. By the mid-fifth century, all Anatolia was under the ecclesiastical jurisdiction, however loose, of the patriarch of Constantinople. Because the Anatolian clergy were overwhelmingly Greek-speaking, the spread of Christianity seems to have promoted the Hellenization of the interior, even as far east as Cappadocia. Thus Anatolia came closer to having a common language.

With the division of the empire into East and West, Asia Minor ceased to be a peripheral region and became a central one. The land routes that joined Constantinople with Egypt and Syria passed through Anatolia, and the main sea routes passed along the Anatolian coast. Despite some raiding by Huns from the east, Isaurians from the south, and Germans settled in the interior, Asia Minor was relatively secure in this period, much more so than Constantinople's other natural hinterland in Thrace. As the principal source of provisions and revenue within the government's easy reach, Anatolia took on added importance, especially during military crises.

For administrative purposes, Anatolia remained divided between the two dioceses of Asiana and Pontica, and united only within the larger Prefecture of the East, which included Thrace, Syria, and Egypt. Asiana and Pontica roughly corresponded to the two natural regions of Asia Minor. The fertile and populous lowlands of the west lay in Asiana, while the sparsely populated and more barren plateau of the interior lay in Pontica. The proximity of the capital tended to increase trade in the interior along the main road, but also to divert trade from the coastal cities into the port of Constantinople itself. Since the capital provided a fine market for the whole peninsula, its overall economic effect was probably positive.

The Diocese of the East, although most of its people lived in Syria, also included Isauria, Cilicia, Palestine, and Roman Mesopotamia. Apart from Isauria, which was difficult for outsiders to penetrate and control, the diocese was fairly homogeneous. It had many cities, of which Antioch was much the largest. The Cilician plain and most of the lowlands of Syria and Palestine were fertile. The hills were drier and stonier, but suitable for vines and olive trees. The ports and inland towns had the largest share of the empire's trade with the Persian Empire and India. Although Isaurian brigands harassed Cilicia, and Persian troops raided Mesopotamia, neither area seems to have been lastingly impoverished, and both may have been modestly enriched by the money spent to defend them. Palestine, one of the more peaceful parts of the empire at this time, also began to benefit from Christian pilgrimages to Jerusalem.

The patriarch of Antioch had jurisdiction over the church of the whole diocese except for Palestine, which the Council of Chalcedon placed under the patriarch of Jerusalem. Most of the peasants of the Diocese of the East and many of the townsmen spoke Aramaic, which as the main language of the country was too widespread and too different from Greek to be entirely replaced by it. The local church also used Aramaic, the language spoken by Christ and his disciples, chiefly in the dialect known as Syriac. Without becoming much more Hellenized than before, the country gradually united behind Christianity, which after all combined Greek and Semitic culture and traced its origins to Palestine and Syria themselves. Except in part of northern Palestine, the Jews had become a dwindling minority.

Egypt, which from the later fourth century formed a prefecture of its own, had been an anomalous part of the empire before Diocletian, with its own currency, much of its land nominally owned by the state, and its administration based on regions and villages rather than cities. Diocletian extended his coinage to Egypt, either sold off much of the state land or converted its rents to taxes, and introduced the empire's usual form of administration by city councils. Instead of being one great province that was the wealthiest and most populous in the empire, Egypt was split into smaller provinces comparable to those elsewhere.

Egypt continued to contribute an extraordinary levy of grain, which earlier had supplied the people of Rome but was diverted by Constantine to the people of Constantinople.[1] These large shipments, together with other taxes in cash and kind that passed through Alexandria to the new seat of government, bound the Egyptian economy more closely to that of the East, and distanced it from the West. With much the richest farmland in the Mediterranean basin, thanks to the water and silt of the Nile, Egypt had always been intensely exploited by its rulers. After Diocletian, the expanded Roman government doubtless exploited it more; but the more uniform tax system probably restrained exceptional demands on Egypt's exceptional wealth.

Although Alexandria had almost since its foundation been Egypt's capital and overwhelmingly its largest city, it was a colony of Greeks in a land of foreign culture. Outside Alexandria, and apart from a Hellenized aristocracy, Coptic was the usual language. In Egypt as in Syria, however, Christianity appealed to both Greeks and natives, and brought a measure

25. Fourth- or fifth-century Coptic textile of two Nereids, one admiring herself in a mirror. (Photo: Dumbarton Oaks, Washington, D.C., copyright 1996)

of religious unity. The patriarch of Alexandria, though a Greek prelate in a Greek city, exercised some religious leadership over the whole country. The Church was not clearly divided between Greeks and Copts; though most of the Arians seem to have been Greeks and most of the Melitians Copts, by the fifth century a large majority of Egyptians of both races had rejected both Arianism and Melitianism. Far from being a Coptic sect, Monophysitism began at Constantinople and was championed by a Greek patriarch of Alexandria. Written Coptic used a modified Greek alphabet, and the Coptic art of the Byzantine period shows a Greek influence that is absent from earlier native Egyptian art.

Except for some mob violence at Alexandria over religious questions, Egypt proper enjoyed peace and security from the reign of Diocletian to that of Marcian. Much the same was true of the far poorer Libyan provinces, a narrow corridor between the desert and coast inhabited by Greeks. But the few Libyan border troops offered an uneven defense against desert raiders. The division of the empire into eastern and western parts also meant that the Libyas became marginal territory instead of being near the center of Roman communications and trade.

In any lands of such extent and geographical diversity as those of the eastern Roman Empire, strong regional differences were bound to persist. Such things as the expanded state created by Diocletian and Constantine, the expanding and officially favored Church, the Greek language, and long-distance trade could scarcely have the same effects everywhere. Yet by the fifth century each of these elements had had its effects, and not always dissimilar ones, through every region of the eastern empire.

THE GROWTH OF GOVERNMENT

With Diocletian, centuries of easygoing Roman administration in the eastern provinces came to an abrupt end. Provincials who had scarcely known that they belonged to the empire were visited by unfamiliar tax assessors, received new imperial officials and often military garrisons, and had to meet unprecedented demands for recruits and supplies for the army. After these changes were introduced, the rebellions and invasions that had plagued the Romans during the third century abated, as Diocletian had hoped they would. Then the Roman Empire became much more like a modern state. Although the reorganized state underwent modifications and suffered setbacks, in its essentials it proved durable, and much of its structure lasted throughout Byzantine history. The radical measures taken by Diocletian were adopted by his successors, who sometimes tried to make them work better but avoided similarly radical reforms. So imposing was Diocletian's reconstruction that later rulers often left it alone when it needed changing.

By increasing the size of the army, Diocletian had inevitably increased its burden on society. At the end of the fourth century the eastern empire had some 303,000 men under arms, while the same regions had had some 198,000 before Diocletian.[2] This probably raised the proportion of the adult male population of the East that was in the army roughly from I in 25 to I in 15, a proportion that remained about the same into the fifth century. Some increase of the army's third-century strength had certainly been needed to restore order. In retrospect, however, Diocletian appears to have increased the army's size too much, especially in the West, and to have kept its pay too low throughout the empire. A somewhat smaller army with somewhat higher pay would probably have been a better solution.

With their official allowances at such minimal levels, the mass of new officers and soldiers soon found ways to increase their incomes. Commanders routinely withheld part of the pay of their soldiers and subordinates, and often kept their units under strength and pocketed the pay of the missing soldiers. Conscripts were reluctant to serve and frequently deserted. Both officers and troops extorted money from civilians, or sold them protection from enemies, creditors, or tax collectors. Soldiers also resorted to civilian occupations to supplement their earnings. Military discipline naturally suffered.

Since Constantine found that he had more than enough troops to garrison the frontiers, he felt free to keep some of them as a mobile army. The garrison troops received less pay and fewer supplies, spent much of their time farming, became almost impossible to move, and defended the frontiers poorly. The field army, having become a privileged force quartered in and near towns, got out of training, meddled in politics, and performed indifferently in the decades after its crushing defeat at Adrianople. Hiring barbarians increased the field army's effectiveness but diluted its loyalty. By 395 transfers from the West had made the eastern army larger than it had been under Diocletian by some fifty thousand men, but the eastern empire was much less secure than it had been at his retirement. The downgrading of the frontier troops had become a gradual and wasteful means of reducing the excessive cost of the army.

The need to pay a large army was what had led Diocletian to devise his system of taxation. Although the rules for assessment were applied with some regional variations, Diocletian's census did give the government its first fairly accurate idea of the wealth of the different cities and regions. Protests and fiscal difficulties in the West and Illyricum suggest that the system overassessed very poor farmers who had scarcely any surplus to pay in taxes; but most eastern farmers were prosperous enough that this problem seldom arose. The usual tax rates in the East seem to have been moderate. Probably Diocletian had planned the payroll of his army after making a reasonable calculation of what his eastern territories could afford.

To manage his system of taxation, Diocletian expanded the number of officials. But the new totals that can be estimated—around fifteen thousand for the whole of the East, of whom some twenty-five hundred were in the central bureaucracy—were not excessive given the work assigned to them.[3] As with the soldiers, however, Diocletian left the officials' pay so low as to encourage corruption. The complexities of the tax system made it difficult to detect when officials embezzled and took bribes, or when taxpayers who had or bought influence avoided full payment or any payment at all. Soon ever higher rates were needed to produce the same revenue. The emperors raised the rates and multiplied measures against corruption and tax evasion, only to be defeated by the size of the administrative machinery.

By means of laws that were frequently ineffectual but were constantly repeated and revised, the central administration sought to protect its revenues either by keeping taxpayers within their taxable category or by forcing them to provide substitute taxpayers. Although the state seldom managed to impose its will on anyone who was rich, influential, or truly desperate, the system affected even those who fled or contrived to evade their assigned payments and duties. Almost everyone had to pay something somehow. The impact of taxation was so pervasive that most people came to reckon dates by the year of the tax assessment, the indiction.[4]

Taxation fell primarily on landowners. Probably a tenth to a fifth of the land in the East belonged to the imperial estates, which produced rents for the treasury but no taxes. The East also had its large private landowners, but they were far fewer and poorer than the great landowning aristocracy of the West. By the fifth century the senates of West and East each consisted of the two thousand or so largest landholders in each region; but the annual income of an average western senator could have bought out one of the wealthiest eastern senators, and for an emperor's coronation the eastern senate was taxed about a fifteenth as much as the western. Since not even western senators owned the whole West, eastern senators can scarcely have owned a twentieth of the East.[5] Papyri indicate that in Egypt something between a tenth and a quarter of the land belonged to all the landlords living in the cities, including senators, decurions, and people of more modest means. Most of these people appear to have paid most of the taxes they owed, and some may well have been forced to pay more than their share. Since very large landholders tended to be adept at avoiding taxation, the East was fortunate to have fewer of them than the West, which found them a major fiscal problem.[6]

Most of the land in the East belonged to the peasants who worked it, who were probably affected more by Diocletian's census than by any administrative measure for centuries before. The peasants' taxes and the requisitions of their labor were regularized, often increased, and exacted more rigorously. In some cases, these may have been the first significant contributions the government had ever demanded of them. Although peasants who rented their land had their taxes paid for them by their landlords, the landlords presumably increased the rents in proportion. Landholders also made their tenants perform any labor demanded by the state, which sometimes included military service.

Nevertheless, since rural labor was scarce, landlords usually tried to protect their tenants from outright starvation, and large landholders could often evade part or all of their tenants' obligations. By doing so, they tended to force unprotected smallholders to pay more of their local assessment. Under the circumstances, during the century after Diocletian smallholders increasingly resorted to abandoning their lands, to selling them and becoming tenants, or to paying for the protection of the powerful. The government tried to curb all these practices, but without much success.

Townsmen were not subject to the head and land taxes levied in the countryside, but they paid most of the trade duties—amounting to an eighth of the value of the goods traded—because they were most dependent on imports. From the reign of Constantine onward they had to pay a further tax if they engaged in commerce. Since this tax was levied in a lump sum every four or five years, it was particularly inconvenient to pay and occasioned wide resentment. The most distressed were craftsmen, shopkeepers, laborers, and prostitutes, most of whom were poor, though a perceptible migration from the countryside to the towns is a

26. Marble bust of Eutropius, a decurion of Ephesus, now in Vienna. (Photo: From Johannes Kollwitz, *Oströmische Plastik der theodosianischen Zeit* [Berlin, 1941])

sign that poor townsmen were less miserable than poor peasants. Because the only industries of much size were operated by the government to serve its own needs, only a few merchants and shippers had wealth that was significant by the standards of rural landholders. The revenue from taxation on townsmen was small in comparison with that from rural taxation.

The state attempted to control the larger landholders by insuring that they were enrolled as decurions, the members of the city councils with the duty of collecting the taxes and forwarding the revenues to provincial officials. From Diocletian's time, those with sufficient property were compelled to serve on the councils unless they were somehow exempted. Besides being thankless, the decurions' duties were potentially ruinous because of their obligation to pay whatever taxes they could not collect. Poor taxpayers could pay only so much, and the wealthiest, many of whom were senators or officials exempt from service on the councils, could evade payment. The wealthiest and most influential decurions often aggravated the others' plight by appropriating part of the receipts for themselves. When decurions failed to deliver their cities' assessments in full, the government would collect the debts from any decurions who could be made to pay, and usually remitted arrears only when they had obviously become uncollectable. Many decurions therefore tried to gain exemption by joining the army, the clergy, the civil service, or preferably the senate, until Theodosius I ruled that not even senatorial rank could release them from their duties.

Because the civil service collected the increased assessments from the city councils, paid the enlarged army, and administered regulations of growing complexity, it grew in size, privileges, and influence. It included the staffs of the governors, vicars, prefects, ministers of the central government, and emperor. Although under Diocletian a number of military men appear to have entered the bureaucracy, later most of the civil servants came from civil-service families, the decurionate, or the lower classes in the towns. Bureaucrats were mostly paid in food, like soldiers, until their allowances were commuted to gold in the early fifth century.

Most officials were humble clerks who kept mundane records and gained slow but steady promotion by seniority. They supplemented their pay, which was hardly sufficient, with petty fees and peculation. Prospects for advancement were better for notaries, whose legal training fitted them for responsible positions, and palace servants, who could attract the notice of the emperor and his staff. These groups often collected large fees and gratuities from those who sought their help in various governmental matters, and their positions frequently gave them chances to embezzle and steal. They could then pay the fees to higher officials that were the usual price of promotion. The imperial officials and servants who did best for themselves became senators.

The senate of Constantinople was important not as an assembly, though it did sometimes meet for ceremonial purposes, but as a select and privileged social class. While it had a small hereditary core of members transferred from the senate of Rome, most senators gained admission through holding a high office, whether real or honorary. Eastern senators were therefore on average from far less distinguished families than western senators. Senators were subject to certain special levies, and were expected to pay for public games if they assumed the honorary office of praetor or consul. On the other hand, their rank assured them of deference from nearly every official, and the richest of them enjoyed overriding prestige and freedom from ordinary financial obligations.

Real influence over government policy, however, was usually limited to a few personal advisers of the emperor. Although men without important offices could have power, the highest officials were best placed to acquire it. The most consistently important minister was the praetorian prefect of the East, who administered some three-quarters of the eastern empire and was based at Constantinople with the emperor. The prefects Rufinus and Anthemius became the real rulers of the empire under Arcadius. Apart from the much less powerful praetorian prefect of Illyricum, the other chief ministers were the master of offices, who headed the clerical bureaucracy, the count of the sacred largesses, who ran the mints and paid the army and bureaucracy, and the count of the private estate, who managed the estates of the emperor. The master of offices Helio and the count of the sacred largesses John both temporarily exercised authority that, if not supreme, was at any rate superior to that of any other official.

Somewhat less important were the quaestor, who was the chief legal officer, and the city prefect of Constantinople, who administered the capital. Palace eunuchs also had extraordinary opportunities to gain dominant power, which the head chamberlain Eutropius and the lower-ranking chamberlain Chrysaphius attained. Though the masters of soldiers of the mobile armies could also be powerful, only Gaïnas under Arcadius and Aspar in the reign of Marcian gained the degree of control over the government that the greatest civil officials acquired. The high officials counted as the empire's richest and most influential men, next to the emperors. When the emperors traveled through the empire, most of these officials traveled with them; after 395, when the emperors ceased to travel much, the officials settled down with them in the Great Palace in Constantinople.

After Diocletian had reshaped society to serve state needs by his military and financial measures, his successors shored up his system with a mass of legislation. That the first official codification of Roman law occurred in this period is no accident, because with the growth of state regulation and its attendant corruption law enforcement became much more important to the government. From Diocletian to Constantine, the expansion of the army and bureaucracy brought the creation of new courts under the new officials and magistrates, providing a practical means of enforcing laws in the provinces. Although appeals to the emperor were possible in theory, his highest officials controlled access to him so tightly that they could exclude nearly anyone they chose.

During the fourth century, laws proliferated and repeated each other. When finally they threatened to overwhelm even the expanded courts, the government ordered them collected and summarized in the *Theodosian Code*. Published in 438, the code only included laws enacted since 312, when Christianity had been introduced and the new system had taken firm shape. Even after the code's publication the law remained unwieldy, subject to abuse by clever lawyers and by the governors, vicars, and prefects who ran the courts. The latter had paid high fees to obtain their posts, and expected to make a good return on their investment by collecting their own fees from litigants.

The expansion of the governmental machinery that began with Diocletian did not necessarily make the state stronger. Eventually it became so enormous that it was almost impossible to control. If the emperor was a nonentity, like Arcadius or Theodosius II, he might give up all hope of mastering the administration and allow his ministers to rule for him. The ministers, more capable than weak emperors but less secure in power, also had trouble keeping the state in hand. Although much of the elaborate system ran itself, left to itself it ran badly, as officials and soldiers embezzled and extorted more and more for themselves. If the state failed to raise the revenue to pay the army, then the army would break down, as was happening in the West by the mid-fifth century. In the East too, military revolts, urban riots, and palace conspiracies constantly threatened and occasionally broke out.

Boldly and intelligently reformed by Diocletian, the eastern Roman state worked better than the western, do doubt partly because when Diocletian conceived his reforms his experience had been primarily with conditions in the East. Yet even for the East, the superstructure was probably too large, and in any case it required constant care to keep it from growing even larger, more corrupt, less efficient, and less stable. Only a giant like Diocletian could run such a state at all well. Under merely competent rulers, like his successors before Theodosius I, matters slowly worsened. Theodosius, despite the emergencies he faced, reinforced the structure somewhat. The ministers who ruled after him guided the empire hesitantly and perilously.

THE SPREAD OF CHRISTIANITY

Despite the Romans' efforts to harmonize paganism by identifying different gods with each other and by spreading the cult of deified emperors, the dozens of cults of Greece, Rome, Anatolia, Syria, and Egypt never constituted a single faith. The fact that the cults almost always accepted each other kept religious peace but made uniformity unattainable. Of the exclusive religions, Judaism was too closely identified with a particular people to spread much beyond them, and the different sorts of dualism that professed a good and an evil god proved too antisocial to have wide appeal in the Roman world. Christianity was probably the only religion known at the time that could have won the allegiance of most of the empire's inhabitants.

During its first three centuries Christianity was always strongest in the East, where it had begun, and in the cities, which became the seats of the bishops who governed the Church. By the end of the third century, Christians formed significant groups in most of the cities of Egypt, Syria, Anatolia, and Greece, and in much of the countryside, particularly in Anatolia. They had gained a certain acceptance in society at large, and their numbers were perceptibly increasing. For the first time they became impossible for a staunchly pagan government to ignore. Even so, before Constantine Christians were a majority only in a few small cities, and they cannot have amounted to much more than a tenth of the population of the eastern part of the empire.

When Constantine bestowed his favor on Christianity, the Christian population certainly grew, but it also became more difficult to determine who was a Christian and who was not. The formal definition of church membership, those who had been baptized, certainly left out a mass of people who held Christian beliefs. Like Constantine, many Christians put off being baptized until they were dying, so as to avoid the strict penances prescribed for sins after baptism. On the other hand, also like Constantine, many did not realize at first how completely Christians were supposed to relinquish pagan beliefs and practices. Doubtless many came to the Church more through emulation of the emperor, opportunistic or otherwise, than from real understanding or conviction.

The result, leaving Judaism aside, was a religious spectrum including convinced Christians, fairly consistent Christians with some pagan beliefs, dubiously committed or poorly informed Christians, undecided persons considering Christianity, pagans sympathetic to Christianity, and pagans without Christian sympathies. All but the last group could in some sense be considered Christian. As late as 410 the zealously orthodox patriarch Theophilus of Alexandria pressed the bishopric of Ptolemaïs upon Synesius of Cyrene, a Christian Platonist who affirmed the eternity of the world and doubted the resurrection of the body.

On any reasonable calculation, Christianity made great progress under Constantine and Constantius II, while paganism receded dramatically. By the time of Julian's accession, pagans without Christian tendencies, though a majority in the East as a whole, seem to have been outnumbered in most eastern cities, including Constantinople and Antioch, if not Alexandria. By showing that paganism could still be restored as the official religion, Julian shocked Christians, revived pagan morale, and won back some waverers and opportunists to their ancestral faith. Despite the shortness of Julian's reign and its inglorious end, Jovian and Valens did not feel able to restore the antipagan laws to the full rigor that had prevailed under Constantius II; even the pious Theodosius I was slow to go that far. Nevertheless, by the later fourth century Christianity had spread widely through the countryside, and during the early fifth century its progress was unmistakable everywhere. By 457 Christians evidently formed a substantial majority in the East as a whole, and in most cities pagans were few. Paganism was a spent force, even if some of its local cults and festivals remained popular in the country.

Although occasionally groups of Christians harassed pagans or destroyed temples, the Christian government never subjected pagans to a general persecution, or even retaliated against those who had killed or maimed Christians under the pagan emperors. In the end, the loss of official status and of a clear preponderance in numbers sufficed to defeat paganism. The old religion had done without a formal organization because it had borrowed that of the state; the Roman administration had even become the model for the Christian hierarchy. After the support of the state was withdrawn, the pagan cults lost most of their property and much of their priesthood. With the growth of the Church that state patronage made possible, pagans also lost their most persuasive argument against Christianity: that most people rejected it. As soon as Christianity could no longer be assumed without argument to be absurd, the Church could shift people's attention to aspects of paganism that were problematic even for pagans.

For centuries reflective pagans had been taking an interest in problems of philosophy and morality, about which traditional paganism had very little to say. By Diocletian's time most philosophical opinion had converged in a body of beliefs known to us as Neoplatonism, which tended strongly toward monotheism. Neoplatonism explained the old gods as spirits inferior to a great divinity, who might be called Zeus, the Unconquered Sun, the One, or simply God. Thus the old gods lost most of their significance, but their presence tended to distance the supreme god from men. The old gods' reputations as thieves, liars, pederasts, and adulterers made them useless as moral judges, but the Neoplatonic supreme god seemed too exalted to take notice of petty human vices. He also seemed too far removed from human affairs to preserve individual souls after death, when according to traditional pagan belief they became ghosts in a dreary limbo. Although philosophers suggested that by leading an ascetic life one might become so spiritually pure as to merge with the great god after death, few found this a very comforting prospect. Yet attempts to present the highest deity in a form more accessible to ordinary men, like those of Julian, resulted in superstition that revived the objections to the old gods.

Christianity, by contrast, flatly repudiated the old gods, insisting that they were not only inferior spirits but evil ones as well. The Christian God who remained resembled the supreme god of the philosophers in his spiritual qualities but was more accessible and sympathetic. While some philosophers found the resurrection of the body too materialistic, it at least provided for a satisfactory afterlife; and in rejecting the eternity of the world Christianity was even less materialistic than Neoplatonism. Christian morality condemned fornication, adultery, homosexual acts, gladiatorial combat, abortion, and infanticide, all of which paganism condoned but some pagan moralists found troubling.

In short, Christianity admitted most of the innovations that paganism had been adopting and excluded most of the traditions that pagan opinion had been explaining away. Under the circumstances, traditional attachment to paganism was not an insuperable obstacle to the spread of the new faith. Although pagan traditions were strongest among the aristocracy and peasantry, eventually the former acknowledged defeat, and the latter decided that if paganism had so visibly faded something must be wrong with it. Although Judaism remained legal, laws forbade Jews to make converts or to construct new synagogues, and the line of patriarchs who had headed the Jewish community for centuries lapsed under Theodosius II.

By the middle of the fifth century, Christianity was what paganism had been in the late third century: the empire's predominant and official faith. The Church included Greeks, Egyptians, and Syrians, philosophers and illiterates, townsmen and peasants. Its organization was well defined, entrusting congregations to their priests, priests to their bishops, bishops to the metropolitans of their provinces, and metropolitans to specified patriarchs. This organization was in constant use as bishops consecrated priests, fellow bishops concentrated bishops, and groups of bishops met in regular synods and occasional ecumenical councils. Bishops had wide authority over their churches, controlled considerable property that had been donated by the faithful, and could legally arbitrate secular matters if both parties agreed. While the emperor mediated in ecclesiastical disputes and had a definite say in choosing the patriarch of Constantinople, as a rule he allowed other bishops to be elected by local clergy and laymen of influence. The Church exercised moral authority over the emperor as well, and no emperor lastingly imposed a doctrine over the opposition of most bishops.

When a religion with little doctrinal flexibility spread over so large and diverse an area, theological and jurisdictional disputes were inevitable. But in the event they caused less trouble than might have been expected. Many minor schisms and heresies quickly disappeared, and others never became more than a local nuisance. Melitians were schismatic but orthodox, and entered the fifth century as a tiny faction. Without the efforts of Constantius II and Valens to promote toleration of Arianism, it could hardly have remained an issue as long as it did, and by the mid-fifth century Arians who were not barbarians formed an insignificant group. Neither Macedonianism nor Nestorianism ever became widespread in the empire. Although Manichaeanism, an adaptation of dualism to Christianity, won a small and fanatical following,

Theodosius I legislated against it with some success. By and large Christians agreed with each other on most important issues during the first half of the fifth century, before the controversy over Monophysitism took shape.

After Constantine's conversion, Christian moral standards, which many pagans already admired, unquestionably affected some social practices of long standing in the East. The Church, long accustomed to receiving pagan converts, made few new concessions to paganism. The Church's condemnation seems to have begun to reduce the prevalence of divorce and infanticide, and ended the gladiatorial shows. Though the rules for penance were gradually relaxed, those guilty of serious sins were still barred from communion for a period of years. As before, priests were forbidden to marry after ordination, and increasingly only widowers and celibates were considered eligible for the episcopate. While the Church received enormous gifts and bequests of urban and rural

27. Saint Anthony the Hermit. Twelfth-century mosaic in the Monastery of Nea Monē, Chios. (Photo: Benaki Museum Photographic Archive, Athens)

property, the money was largely spent to minister to the poor. Most impressively, by the end of the third century Christians who wanted something more spiritual than ordinary Christian life started the ascetic movement that became monasticism.

The first monk to attract wide attention was the hermit Anthony, the son of Coptic-speaking landowners in Lower Egypt. Around the time of Diocletian's accession, Anthony divested himself of his property and withdrew into the desert to pursue a life of strict spiritual discipline. He struggled with temptations to sin, which he said he saw in the form of demons, and in the end he attained a spiritual peace that won him many admirers and imitators. He preached to those who visited him, and strongly opposed Arianism, allying himself with Athanasius of Alexandria. After Anthony's death in 356, his manner of life, made famous in a biography by Athanasius, became a model for other ascetics in Egypt, Syria, and elsewhere. Perhaps the most famous of these was Symeon the Stylite, who lived on a pillar in northern Syria for many years until his death in 459, praying and preaching to pilgrims and disciples and opposing Monophysitism.[7] Monks often took a prominent part in ecclesiastical affairs, to the point of leading riots if their ideas of orthodoxy seemed to be in danger. Intimidation by Monophysite monks proved decisive at the Robber Council of Ephesus in 449.

Groups of individual monks came to join in organized communities. The first of these was founded soon after 320 in Upper Egypt by the former hermit Pachomius. At the time of his death in 346, Pachomius guided eleven monasteries, two of them for nuns, under a set of informal rules. His example was followed throughout the East. More elaborate monastic rules were composed by Basil of Caesarea, another former hermit who had visited monasteries in Egypt, Syria, Palestine, and Mesopotamia. In the years before he became bishop of Caesarea in 370, Basil founded numerous monasteries for men and women, dedicated to living in common in obedience to an abbot or abbess. By prescribing a single way of life for monks and nuns, including both prayer and considerable labor, Basil sought to curb the laxness, pride, or excessive abstinence to which hermits could be prone. In time Basil's rules came into wide use in eastern monasteries. Although bishops and monks sometimes had their differences, on the whole the monastic movement was successfully integrated into the Church. By the fifth century monasticism was both prestigious and popular, having attracted tens of thousands of monks and nuns, and it made an important contribution to the conversion of the countryside.

28. Saint Symeon the Stylite atop his pillar. Eleventh-century miniature from the *Menologium of Basil II* (Vaticanus graecus 1613), which includes miniatures of the principal saints of the Byzantine church. (Photo: Biblioteca Apostolica Vaticana)

Many vestiges of paganism naturally remained. Despite the disapproval of theologians, astrology and divination continued to flourish among Christians eager to learn the future, and pagan festivals continued to be celebrated by Christians who respected tradition and enjoyed festivity. Although in public games chariot races displaced gladiators as the principal entertainment, theatergoers still watched almost naked actresses perform pantomimes taken from pagan mythology, which the clergy denounced in vain. Clerical disapproval had better success in shutting down gymnasiums, probably because people were less interested in stripping and competing themselves than in watching others do so. Of course some converts to Christianity paid little attention to their new religion, and many Christians did things that they themselves considered sinful. The moral authority of bishops and monks was nonetheless real, and stronger than the authority of philosophers had ever been for most ordinary people.

Since Christianity had seldom been hostile to the Roman Empire as such, few adjustments were necessary to permit Christians to serve as officials or soldiers. The main problem was that Christian tradition strongly condemned killing, and had not agreed on exceptions for war, police action, or executions. Here eastern and western churchmen tended to differ. The eastern position, as defined by Basil of Caesarea, was that those who killed, even in a just cause, should do penance and abstain from communion for three years. The western view, professed by Saint Ambrose and Saint Augustine, drew a sharper distinction between justified and unjustified killing, and generally condoned the former. The more worldly western doctrine had more success in influencing political decisions, notably when Ambrose had Theodosius I do penance for his massacre at Thessalonica. But the eastern church's scruples at least reduced the glory that had long been associated with warfare.[8] They may also have led some politicians to have their rivals assassinated rather than executed.

Given that the Church rejected beliefs and practices that had prevailed for hundreds and even thousands of years, the changes that it brought about were remarkable. Christianity gave eastern society a cohesion that it had previously lacked, gathering most people into a single religious organization and reshaping their attitudes toward morals and doctrine. Adopted consciously during Roman times rather than inherited from the prehistoric past, Christianity reshaped society in a way that would have been impossible under any form of paganism. Most Romans came to treat with deference even the Christian thinking that they did not put into practice.

HELLENISM AND ROMANISM

The designation of the East as a distinct part of the empire, the expansion of an educated bureaucracy, and the adoption of Christianity as the empire's state religion all had an influence on eastern cultural life. Many Christians were already well Hellenized, and most of them had come to respect Greek learning. Educated Romans and the Roman imperial government had always been respectful of Greeks, and aspiring bureaucrats wanted nothing better than to acquire a good education in Greek. In turn, Greek culture easily absorbed Christian and Roman elements. Yet as the bureaucracy and Church expanded, the traditional educated groups of the decurions and the pagan philosophers shrank. Overall literacy did not expand, and may even have contracted slightly. Higher Greek culture, however, continued the revival it had begun in the second century.[9]

Prolific though Greek writers had been during the second and third centuries, most of them had shown more interest in literary form than in content. They had been steeped in Homer, Euripides, Thucydides, and Demosthenes, but they had used those classic authors primarily as models for their writing style and as sources for quotations and allusions. This literary revival is most commonly called the Second Sophistic, because its favorite productions were orations in an archaizing Attic dialect, imitating the sophists of classical Athens and often discussing imaginary situations from classical Greek history. Contemporary essays, histories, biographies, satires, and epistolography were similarly rhetorical and obsessed with classical Greece. Some were nonetheless memorable, like the works of Plutarch and Lucian.

In the third century, repetitions of this sort of writing began to go decidedly stale. The main varieties of third-century literature to display originality were philosophy, which created Neoplatonism by developing a distinctive spirituality of its own, and Christian theology. Interestingly, Plotinus and Origen, respectively the third century's leading Neoplatonist philosopher and most profound Christian theologian, had studied with the same teacher at Alexandria.[10] By Diocletian's time, Bishop Methodius of Olympus was writing Platonic dialogues on Christian themes, including a *Symposium* that, in contrast with Plato's, celebrated not love but chastity.

Having assimilated much Greek philosophy, during the fourth century Christians proceeded to make other sorts of Greek literature their own. The best-educated among them retained the elaborate rhetoric of the Second Sophistic, the style that they had learned in school and that a cultivated audience would most readily accept. In using that style in the service of Christianity, however, they gave it a function that most of the rhetorical exercises of the preceding period had lacked. Pagans who defended their beliefs against Christianity also had to use their style to discuss real issues. In consequence Christianity helped restore a sense of purpose to Greek literature.

The administrative division of the empire into eastern and western parts led to decreased knowledge of Greek in the West and increased knowledge of Latin in the East. By the later fourth century this pattern was set. Saint Jerome was one of the few westerners with enough Greek to establish himself in the East, and even he wrote in Latin for a western audience after he settled at Bethlehem. On the other hand, Claudian of Alexandria moved to Ravenna and won fame as a Latin poet at the court of Honorius; Ammianus Marcellinus of Antioch moved to Rome and became the outstanding Latin historian of his time, though he gave ample attention to the East in his work. Many eastern authors who remained in the East knew Latin well because they were employed in the bureaucracy, the army, or the schools.

Since Latin remained the official language of both parts of the empire, the bureaucrats and officers of the eastern central government and army had to be able to read and write it. Yet Greek, which was much more widely spoken than Latin in Constantinople and throughout the East, inevitably came to be used in most official conversations and everyday administrative records. Greek was also the more prestigious literary language. At Constantinople the staff of the imperial library had three Latin and four Greek copyists under Theodosius I, and Theodosius II created chairs for thirteen Latin and fifteen Greek professors. Public orations, recitations, and sermons in the capital were typically delivered in Greek. It was the standard language of instruction at the East's leading schools of rhetoric and philosophy in Antioch, Alexandria, and Athens, though as the language of the law Latin was used in the main law school at Berytus (modern Beirut).

The bureaucratization and Christianization of the empire increased the need for education, if not necessarily the audience for literature. Most of the empire's population had always been illiterate, even in the towns, and many of the nominally literate knew little more than the alphabet. After Diocletian and Constantine, though basic education remained at much the same level, higher education seems to have spread. The many thousands of new civil servants and military officers in the East needed not only knowledge of Latin but fairly thorough training in literary Greek, which had already diverged significantly from the spoken language. The rapidly expanding clergy had to know the liturgy and Scriptures, which again were written in literary Greek, and soon they were expected to have some familiarity with theology. Even at the inception of monasticism the hermit Anthony showed a profound devotion to the Scriptures, and seems to have composed letters of some sophistication in Coptic.[11] The reading of sacred texts was mandatory for monks who lived under the rules of Pachomius or Basil of Caesarea, and such monks were a group that grew quickly. With the advance of Christianity even the illiterate heard the Scriptures read and sermons delivered every Sunday in church.

Not surprisingly, the most notable Greek authors of the fourth and early fifth centuries were Christians. Antipagan writings, however, ceased to be numerous or conspicuous, since most Christians considered paganism to be moribund. Their main concern was that the spread of Christianity should not lead to compromising Christian orthodoxy or morality. Most of the theology of the time therefore centered on the controversies over Arianism, Nestorianism, and Monophysitism. These heresies forced theologians to discuss Christian doctrine at length, and in particular to arrive at explanations of the Trinity and the nature of Christ.

Although from just after the time of Christ Christians had thought of God as Father, Son, and Holy Spirit, and of Christ as both God and man, only at this time did they clarify what they meant by those ideas. Hundreds of treatises were composed by dozens of theologians with varying opinions, several of whom contributed to the definition of orthodoxy adopted by the ecumenical councils. The period's most vigorous and influential theologian was Saint Athanasius of Alexandria, the leader of the opposition to Arianism. In a series of works written after the Council of Nicaea of 325, Athanasius insisted that the Father, Son, and Holy Spirit must all be equal, eternal, and fully God. He argued that if the Son and Spirit were merely created by God, as Arius claimed, they could not redeem and sanctify mankind. If created, they would be lesser beings than the Father, comparable to the lesser spirits that reflected the power of the Neoplatonists' supreme god.

Most Christians with an understanding of theology could not accept such a minimization of Christ's nature, or deny that it was almost precisely the view of Arius's follower Eunomius of Cyzicus. But some continued to resist Athanasius as well, chiefly because they feared that he did not distinguish the Father, Son, and Holy Spirit clearly enough to allow for Christ's humanity. Elucidating the Arian controversy was the accomplishment of the Cappadocian Fathers, as Basil of Caesarea, Gregory of Nazianzus, and Gregory of Nyssa came to be called, after their native province of Cappadocia in Asia Minor.

The Cappadocian Fathers' many theological works complemented each other. Basil explained Athanasius's views by specifying that the Father, Son, and Spirit, though sharing one divine substance (*ousia*), are three persons (*prosōpa* or *hypostaseis*). Gregory of Nazianzus further specified that the Son, though one person, has two natures (*physeis*), as both

29. Saint Gregory of Nazianzus, archbishop of Constantinople (379–81) and
(right) Saint Cyril, patriarch of Alexandria (412–44). Fourteenth-century
fresco in the Monastery of the Chora, Constantinople. (Photo: Dumbarton
Oaks, Washington, D.C., copyright 1996)

God and man. Basil's brother Gregory of Nyssa completed the development of these ideas by distinguishing the characteristics of the persons of the Trinity and the natures of Christ. Thus the three Cappadocians defined an anti-Arian position that permitted no doubts about the individual existence and humanity of Christ. They consequently resolved the main objections to Athanasian orthodoxy, leaving Arianism to be judged on its merits and condemned at the Council of Constantinople in 381.

Although the two Gregories' views about Christ would by themselves have excluded Nestorianism and Monophysitism, the Council of Constantinople left room for some other interpretations, and for a good deal of confusion. The principal theologian of the subsequent period was Patriarch Cyril of Alexandria, yet his works did not entirely resolve the issues. He strongly attacked any tendency to see Christ as two persons, which he called Nestorianism; but his opponent Nestorius actually believed something more subtle than the doctrines condemned by Cyril and the Council of Ephesus in 431. Furthermore, Cyril went so far in emphasizing that Christ was one person that his works encouraged others to say that Christ had one nature, even if Cyril himself had not said so. Thus after his death Cyril was claimed both for Monophysitism and for the orthodox belief in two natures of Christ that was adopted by the Council of Chalcedon in 451. Unfortunately for the unity of the Church, in the years after that council no theologian of the stature of Cyril, Athanasius, or the Cappadocian Fathers emerged to bring the Monophysite controversy to an early resolution.

Though Athanasius and Cyril were no great stylists, the three Cappadocians had received splendid classical educations and could deliver orations reminiscent of the Second Sophistic. Gregory of Nazianzus was the most eloquent, and his elaborate funeral oration for Basil of Caesarea later became the model not only for similar eulogies but for formal Christian oratory of all kinds. The patriarch of Constantinople John Chrysostom was a less formal orator but gave sermons that became classics of their genre, combining stylistic facility with spontaneity and earnestness of purpose. Similar qualities made the letters that Basil wrote as bishop of Caesarea particularly admired and used as models. Although these works were thoroughly Christian in content, Gregory of Nazianzus, Basil, and Chrysostom were all reportedly pupils of Libanius of Antioch, the most famous pagan rhetor of the fourth century and an adviser of the emperor Julian. Despite Julian's brief attempt to prohibit

Christians from teaching the Greek classics, the style of these Christian authors was as classical as that of eminent pagans.[12]

Christians with fewer stylistic pretensions than these developed their own sorts of history and biography. Bishop Eusebius of Caesarea, a reluctant defender of Arius and an associate of the emperor Constantine, wrote the first real history of the Church at a time when pagan historiography was dormant. Beginning with Christ and ending with Constantine's final defeat of Licinius, Eusebius differed from classical historians by including authentic documents, avoiding invented speeches, and generally paying more attention to accuracy than to elegance. His work later inspired several fifth-century authors to write similar ecclesiastical histories that began where it concluded.

Eusebius also inaugurated Christian biography by composing a *Life of Constantine*, though it suffered somewhat from his conflicting desires to praise Constantine and to tell the truth. The most successful work of this kind was the first real saint's life, Athanasius's biography of the Egyptian hermit Anthony. This is a concise masterpiece, which created a new type of hero. Its concern is not with conventional biographical details but with Anthony's struggle to approach the ideal of a perfect Christian life as nearly as possible. The *Life of Anthony* was widely read and imitated almost from the time of its composition. Many of its imitators sought and found a wider and less educated audience by using simpler and more colloquial language than that of their prototype.

Although this literature was produced in Greek, some of it was soon translated, not only into Latin but into the native languages of Egypt and Syria. Both Coptic and Syriac already had their own liturgies and versions of the Scriptures. From the reign of Diocletian, each of them developed its own Christian literature. Thus Anthony composed his letters and Pachomius his monastic rules in Coptic, while Ephraem of Nisibis, known as Ephraem Syrus, wrote lengthy hymns and theological poetry in Syriac. Some of the works of both men were translated into Greek. Christian Armenian literature began rather later, after the empire's annexation of western Armenia under Theodosius I. Writings in these eastern languages, which show considerable Greek influence, may even reflect an expansion of education among easterners who spoke no Greek, since little or nothing seems to have been written in Syriac, Coptic, or Armenian before.

While Christians produced the works on which most of their later theology, sermons, letters, history, and hagiography were to be modeled, pagans continued to write, though the opposition they presented to Christianity was fairly weak. The emperor Julian was probably the new religion's most determined adversary in literature as he was in politics, composing a number of hasty but intelligent orations, letters, and treatises. Eunapius of Sardis, who wrote an anti-Christian history that is mostly lost today and a collection of biographies of pagan philosophers that survives, complained bitterly about Christianity without much hope that it could be rolled back. Most Neoplatonist philosophers of the period were exploring mysticism and magic and showed little interest in anti-Christian polemic. The greatest of them, Proclus, was more aggressively pagan, but he found attacking Christianity imprudent by the time he summarized Neoplatonism in the mid-fifth century. The large band of rhetoricians were mostly pagan, but their works had little to do with religion. The finest pagan writers of the period, the rhetorician Libanius and the historian Ammianus, were generally tolerant of Christians.

The spread of Christianity and the expansion of the state affected art and architecture no less than literature. From Diocletian's reign the state had much more money to spend on public buildings, and from Constantine's reign Christians had greatly increased resources with which to build and decorate churches. At first, since little monumental art had been produced during the disruptions of the third century, artists and architects were too few to meet the burgeoning requirements of Church and state, as Constantine himself complained.[13] In comparison with the Roman Empire of the first or second century, much of the work of the early fourth century was rough and crude (Figs. 5, 6), not only because of a shortage of experienced craftsmen but because of the inexperience and lack of cultivation of the rulers and bishops who commissioned the monuments. They usually wanted something big and impressive that would redound to the glory of God, the emperor, or both. At best, as in the huge palace Diocletian built for his retirement near Salona (Fig. 2), the result was majestic. At worst, it could be positively unsafe, like Constantine's chapel of the Holy Apostles in the capital, which had to be rebuilt a few years after its completion.

Within fifty years or so, workmen had acquired the necessary skills, and patrons enough taste, to produce the desired quantity and quality of building and decoration. In the third century Christians had usually built their churches on the simple plan of a basilica, a long hall with aisles and

30. Entrance of the basilica of the Monastery of Studius, Constantinople. (Photo: R. Van Nice, Dumbarton Oaks, Washington, D.C., copyright 1996)

an apse originally devised by the state for judicial and administrative purposes. This plan long remained customary, but after many basilicas had been constructed some began to show elegance, like that built around 450 in Constantinople by Studius, a high government official (Fig. 30). By then church decoration could be technically accomplished, as in the sculpture that survives from the reconstruction of Constantinople's Saint Sophia after 404 (Fig. 19). All the cities of the empire had churches, and usually great monasteries, episcopal palaces, and charitable foundations as well. The new art became more refined, but it still tended to be bolder and heavier than the more naturalistic art of classical Greece and Rome.

The same striving for grandeur appeared in official art of a secular kind. This was only to be expected of the ceremonial structures in the capital, like the triumphal arches and columns set up by the emperors of the Theodosian dynasty (Figs. 15, 23, 24). Yet in this period many lesser cities all over the East also received grandiose gateways, squares, and colonnaded streets. Although these embellishments had some practical use as sites for commercial shops and stands, the state seems to have built them primarily to give an impression of power and prosperity. What the emperors did in the capital, the governors did in the provinces, adding

31. Marble statue of Aelia Flaccilla, wife of Theodosius I, now in the Cabinet des Médailles, Paris. (Photo: Bibliothèque Nationale, Paris)

inscriptions and statues of themselves to take the credit. Officials often built private residences of a sumptuousness that rivaled imperial palaces. Not everyone was impressed; the people of Antioch pulled down their statues of Theodosius I and his family during a riot over taxes in 387.

Despite the efforts of the emperors to look like absolute rulers, they were in practice nothing of the sort, and the ideology of a Christian empire would not allow them to be. While orators often praised the emperor with grandiloquent rhetoric that no one took seriously, Synesius of Cyrene could circulate an oration addressed to Arcadius comparing the inert emperor to a jellyfish.[14] By taking Christ as their patron instead of Zeus, the emperors accepted Christian morality and the authority of the Church, and those could be manipulated only up to a point. A Christian empire could tolerate some misrule, but not the unbridled tyranny of a Nero or a Commodus. In exchange, if the emperor was a reasonably decent man, Christian public opinion helped restrain those who might want to overthrow him. Christians also had a reason that others lacked for feeling loyalty to the empire, because they saw its value for defending and spreading their religion.

If Roman rule had ended in the East before Diocletian, it would have had remarkably few effects on eastern society. But if it had ended in the mid-fifth century, the new state religion and administrative apparatus would still have left their marks on the East. By that time most easterners had come to think of themselves as Christians, and more than ever before had some idea that they were Romans. Although they may not have liked their government any better than before, the Greeks among them could no longer consider it foreign, run by Latins from Italy. The word "Greek" itself (*Hellēn*) was already coming to mean a pagan rather than a person of Greek race or culture. Instead, the usual word for an eastern Greek had begun to be "Roman" (*Rhōmaios*), which we moderns may render as "Byzantine."

IMPOVERISHMENT AND PROSPERITY

The period from Diocletian to Marcian is difficult to characterize simply as one of expansion or degeneration, or even of stagnation. Though on the whole both the eastern Roman state and its subjects were better off than they had been during the third century, that century had been the nadir of the empire's fortunes to date. The army and bureaucracy had grown a great deal, but much of their growth was of dubious value even for the power and security of the government, and it imposed heavy costs on the empire's taxpayers. The empire could not remain powerful for long if its economy was in severe decline. But was its economy actually deteriorating very much—or at all?

Since the empire seems to have had more than enough cultivable land, the most important economic factor was the size of the population, and in particular whether it was rising or falling. Different grounds can be cited for supposing either a rise or a fall. Scattered signs seem to indicate that the empire's population had been declining somewhat even before the period 165–80, when an epidemic caused quite high mortality and was followed by another, similarly deadly epidemic in 251–66. Although the identity of these diseases is uncertain, they struck the Mediterranean with the force of new infections. They were therefore not bubonic plague, which first arrived later on, and some evidence suggests that they were smallpox and measles, which were unknown in the classical world and are not known to have arrived at any other time.[15]

These illnesses would then have become endemic, and for the Mediterranean population to build up resistance to them would have taken some time. Excess mortality from the new diseases would have decreased slowly, and could not entirely have ceased until modern times. Yet if the population had been declining before the epidemics because of a scarcity of cultivable land, afterward the land should have been more than sufficient for the reduced population, making growth possible. The earlier decline seems to have come about largely through widespread infanticide, especially of girls, which pagans found perfectly acceptable. With the spread of Christianity, infanticide seems to have become less common because the Church condemned it.

While Christianity considered celibacy the ideal way of life for the most disciplined, it also encouraged the majority who could not endure celibacy to marry and raise children. This attitude should have raised birth rates as it changed the long-standing indifference of many pagans to family life. On the other hand, by taxing heads the fiscal system inadvertently discouraged childbearing, and in some cases overtaxation must have contributed to malnutrition and famine, and so increased the death rate. Because taxation was heavier in the countryside, peasants also had an economic incentive to flee to large cities, where the death rate was always higher because of poorer nutrition and wider exposure to disease.

Some recent estimates would put the absolute size of the population of the eastern empire within the boundaries of Marcian's day at about 19 million in the second century, 18 million under Diocletian, and 16 million under Marcian.[16] Although such estimates incorporate a great deal of guesswork, the probability remains that between 284 and 457 the population remained within the range of 15 to 20 million. Yet the conclusion that the population declined during that time depends not on recorded statistics, which scarcely exist, but on the comments of contemporaries and the implications of legislation, both of them subjective and treacherous guides. Particularly suspect is the estimators' assumption that the population declined steadily from the second century to the fifth, because the main effects of the epidemics of the second and third centuries should have been felt within those centuries. If the population of the East did fall from 19 to 16 million people between 150 and 450, at the midpoint around 300 it should have been no more than 17 million.

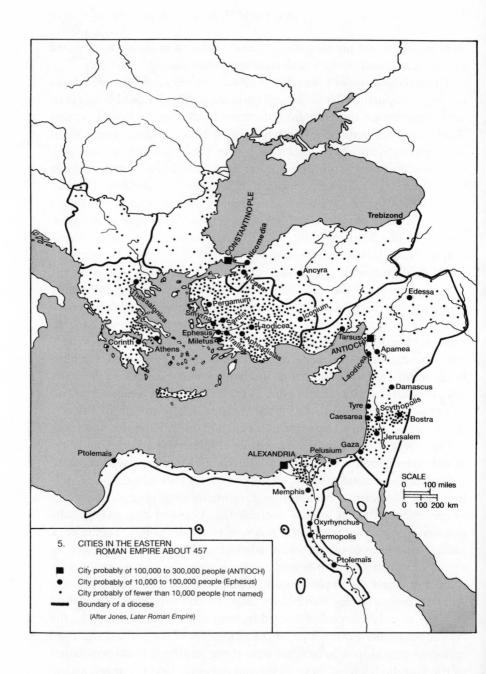

5. CITIES IN THE EASTERN
   ROMAN EMPIRE ABOUT 457

■ City probably of 100,000 to 300,000 people (ANTIOCH)
● City probably of 10,000 to 100,000 people (Ephesus)
· City probably of fewer than 10,000 people (not named)
━ Boundary of a diocese

(After Jones, *Later Roman Empire*)

SCALE
0   100 miles
0   100 200 km

Trebizond
CONSTANTINOPLE
Nicomedia
Nicaea
Ancyra
Edessa
Thessalonica
Pergamum
Smyrna
Sardis
Laodicea
Iconium
Ephesus
Miletus
Tralles
Aphrodisias
Corinth
Athens
Tarsus
ANTIOCH
Apamea
Laodicea
Damascus
Tyre
Scythopolis
Caesarea
Bostra
Jerusalem
Ptolemaïs
ALEXANDRIA
Pelusium
Gaza
Memphis
Oxyrhynchus
Hermopolis
Ptolemaïs

A recent survey of the archeological material for the countryside of the western empire suggests a moderate expansion of cultivation and rural population in the fourth century in southern Gaul and Spain, and a moderate decline in northern Gaul and Italy.[17] Though the Balkan parts of the eastern empire probably showed a decline like that of northern Gaul, which suffered similarly from barbarian raids, the more populous provinces of Anatolia, Syria, and Egypt were as peaceful as southern Gaul, Spain, and Italy. In other respects Anatolia, Syria, and Egypt are more difficult to compare with the West. Like Italy, where the population apparently declined, they had an agricultural economy so well established that it had limited potential for further development; yet they had always been more fertile and prosperous than Italy. The best guess that can be made from present evidence is that the eastern empire's population and agriculture declined a little, but not much.

If anything, the few figures preserved imply that the largest eastern cities grew somewhat between the third and fifth centuries, though such growth seems to reflect migration from the countryside rather than any general increase. Constantinople certainly expanded greatly from its start as the modest city of Byzantium. The large system of waterworks known as the Aqueduct of Valens, completed under that emperor in 373, removed the main check on Constantinople's explosive growth. By Marcian's reign the capital should have reached more than half the 375,000 that according to a prudent estimate its walls could comfortably hold; 200,000 might be a reasonable guess.[18] For Alexandria, a survey of houses taken around 500 has been used to estimate the population at 122,000, which may be somewhat low. Libanius, who should have been well informed, says that Antioch had about 150,000 people in the middle of the fourth century.[19]

By all accounts Constantinople, Alexandria, and Antioch were by far the largest cities in the East, and only they had a fully developed and correspondingly costly panoply of monuments, waterworks, baths, schools, and places of public entertainment. Their masses afforded an anonymity that attracted peasants who fled the countryside to avoid taxation. The three great cities also seem to have been the only ones in the East to benefit from government grain subsidies, and their churches ran the East's best-endowed charitable establishments. Consequently all three had sizable populations of unemployed or underemployed poor, whose numbers John Chrysostom guessed at around fifty thousand in Constantinople.[20] Although each of the three cities had some industry, and Constantinople and Alexandria were important ports, their manufacturing and trade mostly served the cities' own inhabitants. As centers for bureaucracy and luxury building, all three great cities must have consumed a much larger share of the empire's state budget and domestic product than they contributed.

The East had perhaps thirty more cities of considerable size, ranging from not much more than ten thousand to about seventy-five thousand people.[21] As the metropolis of the Balkans, Thessalonica was probably near the top of this range, but most of the rest were grouped near the bottom. While such cities were local administrative centers, they had economic roles as well. All served as markets for their surrounding regions. Some, like Nicaea and Tarsus, manufactured finished cloth, glass, metalwork, and other goods, though only the cloth can have been produced in much bulk for a wide market. The ports, like Ephesus and Palestinian Caesarea, conducted trade in local manufactures, in raw materials such as timber and stone, and in spices from India, silks from China, and other imports. Athens was largely supported by its schools; Jerusalem, by Christian pilgrimage.

But not even these moderate-sized cities were significant sources of wealth. Their traders and artisans, themselves relatively poor, lived largely

32. Ruins of Ephesus, showing the columned Arcadian Way that led to the port. (Photo: Irina Andreescu–Treadgold)

by supplying the needs of the city aristocracies, whose income came almost entirely from rural estates. The cities had hippodromes, baths, theaters, colonnades, and other amenities that were costly to build and maintain. Although these cities were not such a drain on the empire's economy as Constantinople, Alexandria, and Antioch, their principal economic function was to allow profits from agriculture to be converted into cash, which the rich and the state then spent.

The empire had about nine hundred more places with the legal status of cities, but most were so small that they are better called towns. While a handful had populations approaching ten thousand, their average size cannot have been much more than one thousand. Many had only a few hundred people, especially the former villages that the government had classed as cities for administrative reasons. As in villages, these cities' populations included many peasants who went out daily to cultivate the surrounding fields. All cities served as centers for tax collection, seats of bishops, emergency fortifications, and markets for local produce. The larger ones had theaters and baths, but very few had hippodromes. Even most of the smallest had walls, fountains, statues, and forums, occasionally with pretensions to grandeur but generally diminutive and cheaply built. The wealthy citizens, if any, were the owners of nearby estates, though the owners of any very large local estates probably lived in more interesting places. These small cities cost the government very little, and they more than paid that back by collecting the bulk of the empire's taxes.

Around the empire city councils ranged in size from about ten to over a thousand, but with so many cities so small the average can scarcely have been much over fifty. Of the roughly fifty thousand decurions, the majority would have belonged to the small cities, and these petty councilors would have had quite disproportionate fiscal obligations. The decurions in financial distress must mostly have been these, along with some from larger cities where the truly wealthy had managed to stay off the councils. Although decurions often oppressed the peasantry by charging high rents and overcollecting taxes, on the whole they were not very prosperous. Some of them were presumably the same as the middle-class city dwellers who so bitterly resented the modest taxes levied on their businesses. The real wealth was in the hands of the senators, probably still about two thousand strong in the fifth century, and of high officials with less than senatorial rank. Despite their wealth, these men paid very little in taxes, and some used their official capacities to extort and embezzle great sums.

Of Marcian's subjects, then, perhaps a million lived in cities of more than 10,000, perhaps another million in lesser cities, and roughly 14 million in villages that no one pretended were cities. Not large by modern standards, the empire's metropolises were nonetheless an economic burden, with their concentrations of unproductive poor, their small but opulent aristocracies, their expensive monuments erected by aristocrats and the government, and their corrupt officials. The about 15,000 low-ranking bureaucrats, 303,000 enrolled soldiers, and 32,000 sailors, who together headed perhaps a twelfth of the empire's households, also received sums by legal and illegal means that were in the aggregate very large. The government was also paying large additional amounts for military campaigns, fortifications, and tribute to its enemies.

The government's increased requisitions from the countryside and increased disbursements to the army, bureaucracy, and cities must have increased trade, forcing surplus crops either to be transported around the provinces or to be sold so that the proceeds could be sent around the provinces. This would have benefited the great administrative centers, other cities where large-scale building went on and mobile armies were stationed, and to some extent the outlying districts where the deteriorating frontier garrisons had their posts. The frontiers certainly needed the help, which may have been the main reason the economy of the frequently ravaged Balkan region did not collapse altogether. For other places, however, this sort of commerce was less advantageous. Since the people who carried it on did so under compulsion by the state, they tended to be impoverished rather than enriched by it, except for ingenious ones who found ways to pervert the system.

Nevertheless, by increasing the circulation of wealth, the growth of government and cities must have created many economic opportunities. The majority of easterners who lived near either the sea or navigable rivers could send goods by ship, which unlike land transportation was not so expensive as to make trade in bulk unprofitable. They could therefore exchange their own foodstuffs and other goods for some of the surplus grain that the government shipped around the empire. Careful study of the extensive ruins on the Syrian plateau along the Orontes River suggests that this region, later abandoned as unsuitable for subsistence farming, prospered during the early Byzantine period by exporting olive oil and wine and importing food.[22] Such a pattern would have let rocky land be used to grow olive trees and vines—which by themselves cannot provide a decent diet—freeing arable land elsewhere to grow grain and vegetables. In this way the benefits of a better-integrated economy should have offset some of the burdens of bigger government.

Rural depopulation, which had almost certainly occurred during the third century, should have begun to provide its own cure as labor became scarcer and therefore more valuable. Laws intended to keep smallholders from becoming tenants and to prevent tenants from fleeing can hardly have been sufficient to maintain agriculture by themselves. In the end, both landowners and the government had to limit their exploitation of the peasantry when it became counterproductive. Perhaps the best indication of this is the unmistakable though slow decline of rural slavery after the second century. Christian disapproval of slavery may have played a part, but the higher birth rate and productivity of tenants were probably more important to landholders. The number of peasants should then have ceased to fall, as more of them became free and their rents and taxes ceased to rise.[23]

Large though government expenditures were, they seem to have fallen substantially between the reigns of Diocletian and Marcian. The principal cause was a decrease in the largest single item, the military budget. While the size of the army probably remained much the same, its remuneration fell from its previous rates. First, the soldiers' regular pay, still a sizable sum under Diocletian, was disbursed in copper coins, and these depreciated so drastically in the course of the fourth century that the pay became practically worthless and was finally discontinued. Donatives, which soldiers received at the accession of the emperor and every five years thereafter, retained their value because they were paid in gold. Moreover, the state at first provided its soldiers with housing, uniforms, arms, and rations, and with horses and fodder if they were cavalrymen. By the fifth century, the soldiers received allowances in gold that allowed them to buy most of their supplies for themselves. But the frontier troops apparently received only half the allowance for rations that field soldiers had, and seem to have lived largely by cultivating vacant land near the forts where they were stationed.

The disappearance of the army's regular pay and of some of the frontier troops' allowances would have reduced state disbursements greatly, probably cutting payments to the army by more than half and the total budget by more than a quarter. No other outlays seem to have increased by an amount that would come near to equaling this decrease. Yet no large surplus piled up. Therefore revenues seem to have fallen considerably by the end of the fourth century, preventing the empire's rulers from restoring the value of regular military pay when it fell and leading them to cut the compensation of the troops on the frontier. Since at least the latter measure obviously weakened the empire's defenses where they were needed, the government must have acted under fairly strong fiscal pressure.

Estimating the budget of the empire in the fourth century is difficult, because under Diocletian most of it consisted of payments in kind, which despite their gradual conversion into cash played an important part even under Marcian. By the end of Marcian's reign the cash reserve in the treasury amounted to something over a hundred thousand pounds of gold, or 7.2 million nomismata.[24] This reserve, which was considered impressive at the time, probably represented an accumulation of small surpluses over many years. It seems to have been nearly the size of one year's revenue, which was probably around 7.8 million nomismata. Diocletian's revenue, drawn from a larger area that included western Illyricum, might have been equivalent to some 9.4 million nomismata of the standard later introduced by Constantine (Table 3).[25] Since western Illyricum was not a rich region, the probability remains that receipts in the rest of the East showed a modest decline.

In Diocletian's time the revenue of the whole empire might have been some 18 million nomismata of Constantine's standard, with the East accounting for a bit over half the total. This figure may be compared with recent estimates that the empire's revenue had a gold value equivalent to about 14.5 million nomismata around 150 A.D. and to about 22 million nomismata around 215.[26] All of these are rough estimates, and the gold values need not have corresponded closely to purchasing power; for 215 they probably exaggerated it, because silver coins were then overvalued in relation to gold.[27] Thus the revenues of 215 may have been little if any larger than those of 300. In any event, such figures indicate that the budget of the later empire was comparable in size to that of the earlier empire. If this is so, and the population had fallen as much as is usually supposed, the later empire taxed its subjects more heavily, so that the state consumed a larger proportion of the empire's wealth than before.

In comparison with the earlier empire, Diocletian's spending patterns show signs of fiscal strain. Military spending seems to have taken about 80 percent of his budget and the bureaucracy another 10 percent, though a century earlier the proportions had been around 75 percent and 5 percent. Diocletian had more soldiers and bureaucrats, but he paid them less. About 200 A.D. the empire is estimated to have had some 446,000 soldiers and sailors; but a century later the whole empire had 645,000, about 45 percent more, and the East alone had 343,000, barely 23 percent fewer. Around 200, legionaries' annual pay had been equivalent to

TABLE 3

Estimated State Budgets in the Fourth and Fifth Centuries

Date and budgetary item	Estimate (millions of nomismata)
CA. 300 (Diocletian) [a]	
pay of soldiers (311,000 × 12 nom. × ⅓) [b]	4.976M nom.
pay of oarsmen (32,000 × 12 nom. × ¾) [b]	0.48
uniforms and arms (311,000 × 5 nom.)	1.555
fodder and horses (26,000 × 5 nom.)	0.13
campaigns and other military expenses	0.5
pay of bureaucracy	1.0
other nonmilitary expenses and surplus	0.8
TOTAL	9.441M nom.
CA. 450–57 (Marcian)	
pay of Scholae (3,500 × 16 nom. × ⅓) [b]	0.075M nom.
pay of field soldiers (104,000 × 8 nom. × ⅓) [b]	1.109
pay of frontier soldiers (195,500 × 4 nom. × ⅓) [b]	1.043
pay of oarsmen (32,000 × 4 nom. × ¾) [b]	0.16
accessional donative (335,000 × 9 nom./7 years)	0.431
quinquennial donative (335,000 × 5 nom./7 years)	0.239
uniforms and arms (303,000 × 5 nom.)	1.515
fodder and horses (122,500 [c] × 5 nom.)	0.612
campaigns and other military expenses	0.2
pay of bureaucracy	0.8
grain dole	0.8
other nonmilitary expenses and surplus	0.8
TOTAL	7.784M nom.

[a] Estimated budget includes domains of both Diocletian and Galerius. For purposes of comparison, figures are converted from denarii into later nomismata struck at 72 to the pound of gold.

[b] The fractional multiplier allows for the higher pay of officers.

[c] The number includes 3,500 Scholae, 21,500 field cavalry, and 97,500 frontier cavalry (see Treadgold, *Byzantium and Its Army*, table 1, sections I–III, pp. 50–52).

over 19 nomismata; Diocletian's soldiers received about the equivalent of 12.[28] By Marcian's time, military spending had fallen to about 70 percent of the budget, but only because field soldiers drew a mere 8 nomismata in regular pay.

Therefore by 457 the empire was evidently in less comfortable circumstances than it had been in the second century. Its population had plainly decreased, and some of its farmland may well have been abandoned. While many of the wealthy and privileged evaded their taxes, much of what the poor and less privileged paid never reached the treasury, because of ever-growing extortion and theft by various officials. When the tax rates were increased through additional exactions, unprotected peasants suffered severely while influential grafters profited even more. In consequence the state imposed costs on the majority of its taxpayers that were greater than the benefits it gained for itself.[29]

Nonetheless, the eastern empire's economy was being squeezed rather than crushed. In comparison with the collapsing West, the East was prosperous and stable. Furthermore, by the reign of Marcian the eastern state's difficulties seem to have been easing. The main decrease in military pay must have been complete by the end of the fourth century, and since the government had to make no further cuts in expenditure any overall loss of revenue had presumably ceased. By that time Theodosius I seems to have halted the wholesale flight of decurions into the senate and so preserved an important part of the tax system from further erosion. Only in the later fourth century did Christianity really begin to win over the countryside, thus exposing the bulk of the population to its prohibition of infanticide and encouragement of family life. Improvements in the condition of the peasantry should also have improved birth rates. By Marcian's reign the population had probably begun growing for the first time in centuries. Finally, by this time the official rates of taxation should have stopped rising, and most taxpayers must somehow have come to terms with their obligations.

Given that the small and loosely organized government of the earlier Roman Empire had been too weak to end the third-century invasions and rebellions, the state had clearly needed strengthening. Diocletian strengthened it in the obvious way, by enlarging it. For a time his measures worked. In the longer run, however, as various Romans and barbarians discovered how to exploit the unwieldiness of the system for their own profit, the state grew weaker despite its size. On the other hand, that the eastern empire could survive such a burden was in its way a sign of economic health. The sharpening division between East and West helped to make each part of the empire more manageable, and by the fifth century the state became easier to support as the economy slowly improved. Although the western empire had become too poor and fragmented to benefit, in the East the wealth and growing cohesion of society gave the Byzantine state sound foundations for its top-heavy structure.

PART TWO

The Interrupted Advance

33. Sixth-century manuscript portrait of Anicia Juliana, flanked by personifications of Magnanimity and Intelligence, from a manuscript of Dioscorides she commissioned (Vindobonensis medicus graecus 1). (Photo: Bildarchiv der Österreichischen Nationalbibliothek)

CHAPTER FIVE

The Eastern Recovery, 457–518

In 457, when barbarian dominance of the eastern empire became almost complete, no strong dynastic ruler was at hand. For nearly a century after Valens' accession in 364, the crown had passed from father to son or, when it could not, the western emperor Gratian had named Theodosius I, and the dying Theodosius II (or at any rate his sister Pulcheria) had chosen Marcian. This sort of succession produced emperors with hereditary authority, however weak their personalities may have been, and kept the increasingly barbarian army from deciding who would be emperor. Although Marcian left no son, he was survived by his son-in-law Anthemius, the master of soldiers for Illyricum. But Aspar, firmly in control of the army in Constantinople, did not want a ruler with a hereditary claim. So great was Aspar's power that the intimidated senate apparently offered to elect him emperor, his Arianism and barbarian birth notwithstanding. Like Gaïnas before him, however, Aspar would not risk accepting the title.

Preferring to continue wielding power behind the throne, the general chose a candidate who was, as Marcian had been, a lieutenant of Aspar's in his late fifties, without a son, and seemingly undistinguished. Thus Leo, a Thracian from Dacia, was acclaimed and crowned emperor at the age of fifty-six. His title was of course Roman emperor, as Byzantine emperors were always called, but his government recognized no western Roman emperor, and at first had none to recognize. The real or fictive dynastic link that had almost always bound the East to the West was broken, and the two empires were not even allies. Though the disintegration of the western empire troubled Leo, his immediate concerns centered in

34. Colossal bronze statue, probably of Leo I (r. 457–74), now in Barletta. (Photo: From Deutsches Archäologisches Institut, *Antike Denkmäler* III [Berlin, 1913])

Constantinople. So his is as good a time as any to begin calling the eastern Romans and their empire by their modern name of Byzantine.

LEO'S STRUGGLE WITH THE GERMANS

Aspar must have known that Leo was a competent subordinate, but the Alan general seems not to have realized that his chosen emperor had the will and ability to lead. Even so, Leo began his reign with few advantages beyond his imperial title, which without dynastic prestige or a tradition of strong emperors was of uncertain value. Aspar was one of the two masters of soldiers in the Emperor's Presence, and his son Ardabur was still master of soldiers for the East. Aspar had another ally in Theoderic Strabo, his relative by marriage and the leader of the Ostrogothic federates near Constantinople. Thus barbarians seemed to control the eastern empire almost as tightly as when Gaïnas had ruled.

They had no less power in the western empire, where the German general Ricimer, probably on the theory that he had as much right to make emperors as Aspar did, put his capable lieutenant Majorian on the throne. Refused recognition by Leo and dependent on Ricimer, Majorian nonetheless began to extend imperial power outside its embattled redoubt in Italy. Preparing to contest the Vandals' control of Africa, he retook parts of Gaul and Spain from their German invaders and won over the rebellious commander of Dalmatia, Marcellinus.

By comparison Leo seemed timid, merely finding a few safe ways to differ with Aspar. The Arian general favored not only Germans but Monophysites, perhaps feeling that those the government classed as heretics should aid each other even if their beliefs conflicted. Since most of the people of Constantinople disliked both Germans and Monophysites, Leo could expect popular support if he opposed either group. But popular support might not be enough to overcome the army's opposition. So Leo was circumspect at the start of his reign, when the Monophysites of Alexandria lynched their Chalcedonian patriarch and replaced him with a resourceful Monophysite known as Timothy the Cat.[1] The emperor sent respectful letters to the metropolitan bishops of the East to solicit their views on the Council of Chalcedon and on Timothy, whom Aspar supported. As expected, almost all the bishops endorsed Chalcedon and rejected Timothy. This embarrassed Aspar, but Leo was slow to act.

Then Leo refused to pay the small subsidy due the Pannonian Ostrogoths, who were conationals of Aspar's Ostrogothic allies. Leo's gesture was somewhat spoiled when the unsubsidized Ostrogoths invaded the empire in 459; they eventually had to be bought off at the higher rate of 21,600 nomismata. Yet Leo continued to distance himself from Aspar, and chose a praetorian prefect of the East of whom the Alan disapproved. By 460 the emperor finally deposed and exiled Timothy the Cat as patriarch of Alexandria, replacing him with a Chalcedonian. Aspar's political power therefore receded, though his military power remained unimpaired.

Leo's caution proved a better way to deal with barbarian generals than his western colleague's vigorous activity. In 461, when Majorian had to abandon his expedition against Vandal Africa, Ricimer executed him and chose a weaker emperor, Severus. Never having recognized Majorian, Leo also refused to recognize Severus, but with a greater show of displeasure. The Byzantine government made a formal peace with the Vandals and accepted the allegiance of Marcellinus in Dalmatia, who threatened to attack Ricimer in Italy. But Leo, though he demanded respect from the West, had no taste for a war between the empires. Ricimer persuaded him to restrain Marcellinus, and after Severus died in 465 Ricimer and Leo began negotiations to determine the western succession.

Leo had established himself as Aspar's rival, but he could not be Aspar's master as long as the general's German friends dominated the field army. The emperor needed mobile troops he could trust, yet he also had trouble finding recruits and needed most native Byzantines as civilian taxpayers. A generation before, Theodosius II had experimented with a troop of Isaurians, unruly mountaineers who were better at fighting than at paying taxes. Although Byzantine snobs considered Isaurians barbaric, the Isaurians had lived in the empire for centuries and were unlikely to betray Byzantine interests to foreigners. Eager for allies against Aspar and his Germans, Leo summoned a company of Isaurians to Constantinople in 466.

The Isaurian leader Tarasius promptly gratified the emperor by supplying evidence that Aspar's son Ardabur, master of soldiers of the East, was plotting treasonably with the Persians.[2] The case was strong enough that Aspar could not prevent his son's dismissal. Leo did what he could to shift power from Aspar to Tarasius, who changed his name to Zeno in honor of the Isaurian general of Theodosius II. First the emperor made Zeno a commander of the imperial guard, and strengthened his hand by creating the new guard corps of the Excubitors, three hundred strong, composed largely of Isaurians.[3] The next year Leo promoted Zeno to master of soldiers for Thrace and married the Isaurian to his daughter Ariadne. Aspar found no convenient way to interfere.

Also in 467, Leo came to an agreement with the western general Ricimer. In return for a promise of help against the Vandals in Africa, Ricimer accepted Leo's choice for western emperor. This was Marcian's son-in-law Anthemius, whose plausible claim to the eastern throne Aspar had ignored. Joined by the commander of Dalmatia Marcellinus, Anthemius led a Byzantine army into Italy and took office. Leo prepared a much larger Byzantine expedition to retake Africa from the Vandals and restore the western empire's solvency. In 468 the eastern emperor sent a fleet under his wife's brother Basiliscus to attack Africa, together with a western fleet led by Marcellinus. Leo is said to have spent over 7 million nomismata, probably almost the whole reserve in the eastern treasury, to insure the success of this joint expedition of East and West. The combined force reportedly totaled some four hundred thousand soldiers and seamen.[4] While another Byzantine general advanced from Libya, Marcellinus took Sardinia. But Basiliscus negligently let the Vandals destroy most of his fleet. Marcellinus was assassinated, and the expedition fell to pieces, allowing the Vandals to seize Sicily.

This disaster crippled the West and almost bankrupted the East, but it did little harm to the reputation of either Anthemius or Leo. Some blamed the failure on Ricimer for arranging the assassination of Marcellinus; others, on Aspar for pressing Leo to give the command to Basiliscus. Shortly after the African expedition, when the Pannonian Ostrogoths attacked the neighboring tribe of the Scirians, Leo was able to overrule Aspar's preference for neutrality and send the Scirians help. The Ostrogoths won the war nonetheless, and Leo had to make peace with them. As further evidence of the empire's weakness, in 468 Persian attackers took over the Byzantine protectorate of Lazica in the Caucasus. Even these failures, however, could be blamed on Aspar as the empire's chief military commander.

Meanwhile Zeno's wife Ariadne had borne him a son. The child was named Leo, and as the emperor Leo's grandson had a strong claim to the succession. Zeno remained master of soldiers for Thrace, and the emperor named him consul for 469. As Zeno became the emperor's unquestioned favorite, Aspar lost patience. The Alan general appears to have been responsible for a mutiny that broke out in the Army of Thrace, forcing Zeno to abandon his command to save his life. Then Aspar demanded that his younger son Patricius be married to Leo's younger

TABLE 4
The Dynasty of Leo I

Emperors are in capital letters and italics, with the years of their reigns marked "r." Other years are of births and deaths.

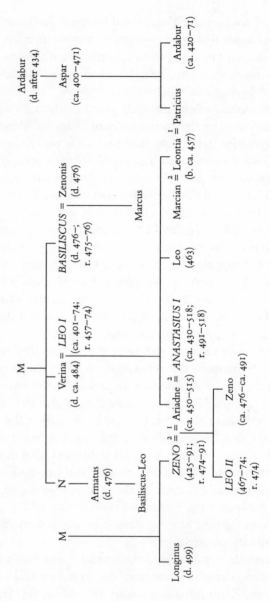

daughter Leontia and named Caesar, making him the official heir to the throne instead of Zeno's little son.

Although the emperor reluctantly complied, he was not yet defeated. Popular protests allowed him to extract a promise that Patricius would forsake Arianism. Leo rehabilitated Zeno by naming him master of soldiers for the East, and bided his time. In 470 the new master of soldiers for Thrace Anagast, who had begun a revolt, changed his mind and sent Leo letters proving that he had rebelled at the instigation of Aspar's son Ardabur. Zeno reported to Leo that Ardabur was plotting with the Isaurian guardsmen in the capital. In 471 rumors of these plots seem to have set off riots in Constantinople against Aspar, who had to withdraw to Chalcedon. Proposing a settlement, the emperor invited the general and his sons to the palace. There he had Aspar and Ardabur murdered.

The outraged Ostrogothic soldiers of the capital tried to storm the palace. When they failed, they marched off to join their fellow Ostrogoths under Aspar's relation Theoderic Strabo. This combined force of Aspar's former mercenaries and Strabo's federates elected Strabo their king. He sent to Constantinople to demand that his men be given lands in Thrace, while he himself would inherit Aspar's property and former post of master of soldiers in the Emperor's Presence. Since Leo would not agree, Strabo ravaged Thrace, besieging and capturing Arcadiopolis.

At the same time, seeing their opportunity, many Pannonian Ostrogoths left Pannonia and invaded Dacia and Macedonia. In the confusion another German tribe, the Gepids, took Sirmium. Unable to defend his European dioceses, Leo eventually made peace with both groups of Ostrogoths on unfavorable terms. He granted the Ostrogoths from Pannonia lands in the Province of Macedonia, and Strabo's Ostrogoths lands in the Province of Thrace. Although he gave Strabo the title of master of soldiers in the Emperor's Presence, Leo appears not to have let the Ostrogothic leader enter Constantinople. There Zeno became the other master of soldiers, with effective control over the largely Isaurian troops.

Thus, at the price of having the Balkans devastated yet again, Leo freed the eastern government from German control. His chosen western emperor, Anthemius, was much less fortunate. Anthemius's efforts to wrest power from his German general Ricimer began a civil war that cost the emperor his life in 472. When Ricimer died of disease soon after his victory, his power passed to his nephew Gundobad. Still hoping to free what was left of the western empire from German rule, Leo sent some troops to Nepos, the nephew of Marcellinus and his successor as commander of Dalmatia. Nepos marched on Rome without delay, drove out Gundobad, and became western emperor, ruling Italy and Dalmatia. Appointing as his chief general a Roman named Orestes, he departed to campaign in Gaul. Both imperial governments had returned to Roman control, though the western government was extremely feeble.

In 474 Leo died of dysentery, and was succeeded by his young grandson Leo II under the protection of Zeno. Leo's reign had been a very mixed success. His huge outlays in the African campaign had driven him to meet later expenses by confiscations from wealthy citizens. He had allowed the East's European provinces to be raided and in part occupied by the two bands of Ostrogoths, who remained a threat for the future. The Isaurian soldiers whom he had given so much power in the field army and the capital were a disorderly lot with questionable loyalties. Nevertheless, Leo had broken the Germans' hold on the government. That delicate and difficult task had been necessary if the eastern empire was to prosper, and perhaps even if it was to survive.

ZENO'S STRUGGLE FOR STABILITY

Since Leo II was only seven years old at his accession, his father Zeno was the real ruler and quickly had himself crowned Augustus. When the boy emperor died of disease before the end of 474, Zeno duly became sole emperor. But his position was scarcely secure. A mild-mannered

35. Zeno (r. 474–91). Gold nomisma, shown twice actual size, with a personification of Victory on the reverse. (Photo: Courtesy of the Arthur M. Sackler Museum, Harvard University Art Museums, Whittemore Collection)

and unprepossessing soldier of about forty-eight from a race of uncouth provincials, the former Isaurian chieftain was not popular in Constantinople. His only dynastic claim to the throne was through his wife Ariadne, whose mother Verina turned against him as soon as her grandson died. Yet even if the emperor inspired no fear, he proved to have a cool head and a rare talent for survival.

The empress dowager Verina took less than two months after the death of Leo II to prepare a conspiracy. Her confederates included her lover Patricius, her brother Basiliscus, the Isaurian general Illus, and the Ostrogothic general Theoderic Strabo.[5] This mighty cabal forced Zeno to flee Constantinople at the beginning of 475. He escaped into Anatolia with the imperial gold reserve and a band of loyal Isaurians. Although Verina's plan had been to make Patricius emperor and marry him, Basiliscus succeeded in taking the crown for himself and executing Patricius.

In office Basiliscus showed all the skill with which he had botched Leo's great expedition against the Vandals. He allowed the Constantinopolitans to massacre most of the remaining Isaurians in the capital. Then he gave Illus the command against Zeno, apparently without reflecting that after a massacre of Isaurians an Isaurian might not be a reliable ally against another Isaurian. As master of soldiers in the Emperor's Presence Basiliscus named his nephew Armatus, who proved a poor choice. Armatus offended his nominal colleague Strabo, hid Verina when she was suspected of plotting with Zeno, and seduced Basiliscus's wife Zenonis.

Before properly securing his throne, Basiliscus condemned the Council of Chalcedon, provoking protests by the patriarch Acacius and riots by the orthodox majority in Constantinople. Basiliscus restored the Alexandrian patriarch Timothy the Cat, pleasing many Egyptians and some Syrians but very few people close to the capital. Yet Basiliscus promptly restored orthodoxy, at the news that Zeno had rallied his forces in Isauria and won over Illus. When Basiliscus sent Armatus against the two Isaurians, even Armatus joined them, in exchange for a promise that his son would be made Caesar and Zeno's heir. Now that Zeno had the support of most of those who had driven him out in the first place, he marched back into Constantinople in 476, almost unopposed.

Despite his gentle mien, the emperor knew how to use his victory. Having promised not to execute Basiliscus and his family, Zeno let them starve in prison. Once he had kept his promise to name Armatus's son Caesar, he had Armatus assassinated and sent the son to a monastery. Except for Timothy the Cat, who died, the eastern bishops hastened to disown Basiliscus's Monophysitism. The emperor made his peace with Verina, whose daughter Ariadne seems soon to have borne him another son and heir, Zeno the Younger.[6] The emperor appointed a new praetorian prefect, Sebastian, who apparently replenished the empire's depleted treasury, if by the dubious means of selling government offices openly. Never quite deposed, Zeno reclaimed a throne that was somewhat steadier than before.

Since Theoderic Strabo had not repudiated Basiliscus, Zeno dismissed him from his titular command over the Army in the Emperor's Presence. To balance Strabo's continuing power as king of the Thracian Ostrogoths, the emperor gave Strabo's former title, again without real control over the praesental army, to the Macedonian Ostrogoths' king, Theoderic the Amal.[7] At Zeno's bidding, the Amal's Ostrogoths left their lands in Macedonia for new lands in Moesia II, adjacent to Strabo's Ostrogoths. The game of playing one set of Ostrogoths against another was rather dangerous, but less so than having the Ostrogoths united against the empire.

Meanwhile the western empire neared its end. In 475 the emperor Nepos had been driven back to his original command in Dalmatia by his general Orestes. Orestes had named his son Romulus emperor, only to be killed in 476 in a rebellion by the barbarian soldiers of the Army of Italy. The barbarians' leader Odoacer deposed Romulus, but failed to choose a new emperor. Instead Odoacer sent the western regalia to Constantinople, proposing that Zeno become emperor of both West and East, with Odoacer as his Italian commander. Nepos sent his own envoys to Zeno from Dalmatia, asking for help in recovering Italy. Given this choice, Zeno continued to recognize Nepos as the emperor legally installed by Leo I, and advised Odoacer to accept Nepos's claim. Though whatever recognition Odoacer gave Nepos was purely nominal, the eastern emperor did nothing.

There was little Zeno could have done at the time, since he could hardly spare a major force to send to Italy before he had reached a settlement with the Ostrogoths in Thrace. Although in 477 Theoderic Strabo asked to return to imperial service, Zeno distrusted him and was reluctant to pay both bands of Ostrogoths. When further negotiations failed, the next year the emperor persuaded Theoderic the Amal to join a Byzantine campaign against Strabo. The Amal arrived near Adrianople; but when the Byzantines failed to appear on time, he formed a coalition with Strabo. After preparing to fight both Theoderics, Zeno thought better of it and himself came to terms with Strabo, giving him back the Amal's title of master of soldiers in the Emperor's Presence. Declaring himself betrayed, the angry Amal plundered the Province of Rhodope. In 479 the Amal went on to loot Macedonia and Epirus, taking the city of Dyrrhachium before he was defeated by the master of soldiers for Illyricum.

In Constantinople Zeno had other supposed allies who were loyal neither to him nor to each other. His mother-in-law Verina had been plotting the assassination of the Isaurian commander Illus, who was then master of offices. When Illus found the plot out, the emperor allowed him to imprison Verina in Isauria. But this sparked a plot against Zeno by Verina's other son-in-law, Marcian, a son of the late western emperor Anthemius and grandson of the late eastern emperor Marcian.[8] After heavy fighting in the capital between Marcian's supporters and the Isaurians of Zeno and Illus, Zeno was victorious, and exiled Marcian. Theoderic Strabo seems to have been a party to the plot, because he gave sanctuary to some of Marcian's fugitive partisans. Zeno retaliated by depriving Strabo of his title once again. Though Strabo joined Theoderic the Amal in ravaging Thrace, Zeno had survived once more.

While Zeno clung to his throne, the titular western emperor Nepos was murdered in Dalmatia, the last remnant of his domain, which Odoacer's barbarians soon occupied. With Nepos the line of western emperors came to an end. Except for a piece of northern Gaul that held out a few years longer under a Roman general, independent barbarians held the whole western empire, with Odoacer ruling its core. Even if his predecessor Ricimer had ruled almost as absolutely in the name of puppet emperors or a vacant western throne, Odoacer strengthened himself by abolishing the office of western emperor. His pretense of serving under Zeno, which the emperor never accepted, was merely meant to preclude an eastern expedition to restore Roman rule in Italy. Since Zeno could not mount such an expedition at once—and would not commit himself to one by naming a titular western emperor to succeed Nepos—Roman rule lapsed in the West for the indefinite future.

That it might also lapse in the East was not unthinkable at the time. The combined forces of the Ostrogoths were a match for all available Byzantine troops. In 481 Theoderic Strabo almost succeeded in taking Constantinople by surprise. Illus manned the walls at the last moment, then foiled Strabo's attempt to cross into Anatolia. Strabo set out to raid Greece, but on the way he accidentally fell from his horse onto a spear.

36. Two fifth-century churches at Alahan in Isauria, probably built by Zeno: *left*, overall view; *right*, the interior of the rear church. (Photos: Irina Andreescu-Treadgold)

His death left his Ostrogoths in disarray, but Zeno's court also remained wracked by intrigue. His empress Ariadne plotted to murder his master of offices Illus for refusing to release her exiled mother Verina. After escaping with the loss of an ear, Illus agreed to take the post of master of soldiers for the East and left the capital, but with Verina still in his power.

As the perennial dangers of Ostrogothic invasion and political conspiracy seemed to recede somewhat, Zeno turned to a problem that was less acute but serious enough: the disaffection of the Monophysites. Heavy majorities in the West, the Balkans, and Anatolia were anti-Monophysite, and Basiliscus had found during his brief reign that most Constantinopolitans would not accept a direct attack on the Council of Chalcedon. On the other hand, in most of Syria and Egypt opposition to Chalcedon was strong. This growing division in the Church worried not only Zeno, who held no passionate views on the number of the natures of Christ, but also the patriarch of Constantinople Acacius.

In 482, when the Chalcedonian patriarch of Alexandria died, the Alexandrian clergy replaced him with a Monophysite, Peter the Hoarse. Before deciding whether to accept Peter's election, on the advice of Acacius the emperor issued an edict, styled the *Henoticon* or Act of Union, that took a deliberately ambiguous position. Condemning the extreme Monophysite Eutyches without endorsing the Council of Chalcedon that had condemned him, the edict promulgated a creed that did not specify whether Christ had two natures or one. It therefore excluded the minority of Eutychian Monophysites, who believed Christ was wholly divine, but tried to placate the Hesitant Monophysites, who believed Christ's single nature was compatible with his humanity. Zeno asked the other patriarchs to join Acacius in subscribing to the *Henoticon*, which allowed them to hold discordant views but implied mutual toleration.

Despite the objections of many of his Monophysite followers, Peter the Hoarse signed and was recognized as patriarch of Alexandria. Few Chalcedonians cared for the edict; it received the signature of an opportunistic patriarch of Jerusalem, but not of the patriarch of Antioch Calendion. Zeno was in no hurry to submit his formula to the pope in the solidly Chalcedonian West. Like previous emperors' efforts to produce ecclesiastical harmony without doctrinal unity, the *Henoticon* satisfied neither side, and had the unfortunate effect of allowing actual beliefs to diverge even further. Given, however, his uncertain grip on power, this may have been the most Zeno could have done to resolve the prevailing religious confusion. Whatever he did could be used against him. He had already been expelled from mostly Chalcedonian Constantinople by the Monophysite Basiliscus. Now, at largely Monophysite Antioch, the Chalcedonian master of soldiers Illus used discontent with the *Henoticon* to start another plot against Zeno.

The emperor learned of the plot, but he could not deal with Illus at once, because Theoderic the Amal now joined his forces with those of the recently deceased Strabo and ravaged Greece and Macedonia again. In 483 Zeno came to terms with Theoderic once more, naming him not only master of soldiers in the Emperor's Presence but consul for 484, and settling the united Ostrogoths in Dacia Ripensis and Moesia II. Pleased by the signal honor of a consulship, Theoderic came to reside in Constantinople without his men, whom he agreed to let Zeno use against Illus.

First the emperor demanded that Illus release the empress dowager Verina. After further maneuvers, Illus found a way to turn this demand to his advantage. He had the temperamental Verina proclaim Zeno's legate, the Isaurian general Leontius, a rival emperor in 484. As Chalcedonians, Leontius and Illus won over the orthodox patriarch of Antioch Calendion, though they inspired little enthusiasm among other easterners. Zeno speedily mustered a combined force of Byzantines and Ostrogoths under a barbarian general whom he trusted, John the Scythian. John made short work of the rebels. The rebel leaders escaped to a fort in Isauria, where Verina soon died and Illus and Leontius were trapped. The siege dragged on, but because of the roughness of the terrain rather than the strength of the besieged.

Among the rebels' former supporters, Zeno punished some of the satraps of Byzantine Armenia by annexing their satrapies as a province, and dethroned the patriarch of Antioch Calendion, the main eastern opponent of the *Henoticon*. As Calendion's successor the emperor recognized Peter the Fuller, who had been deposed from the see three times before for his Monophysitism. By signing the *Henoticon*, Peter formally united the eastern church behind Zeno. The emperor showed increased favor to Monophysites after the Chalcedonian rebellion of Leontius and Illus, especially because in the same year Pope Felix III condemned the *Henoticon*. By declaring the patriarch Acacius deposed and excommunicated, the pope began a schism between the eastern and western churches that corresponded with the political division between the empire and the barbarian kingdoms. The unintended effect of this Acacian Schism was to make it easier for Zeno to ignore the papacy.

Despite the Ostrogoths' help in suppressing Leontius's usurpation, Zeno's latest agreement with Theoderic broke down like the others. By 486 Theoderic was once again rampaging through Thrace at the head of his men, and the next year he pillaged the suburbs of Constantinople and cut the aqueducts. But even his united force of Ostrogoths had scant hope of capturing the city. With little to gain from further plundering of the exhausted Balkans, Theoderic made an uneasy truce with the emperor.

Zeno had never recognized Odoacer's kingship in Italy. Although he had no army available to dislodge the king, in 487 the emperor incited the Rugians, the German tribe to Odoacer's north, to invade Odoacer's domain. When the king defeated the Rugians in 488, Zeno devised a truly inspired proposal. He offered Theoderic the mission of conquering Italy and ruling it in the emperor's name. For Zeno, the arrangement offered the double advantage of punishing Odoacer and removing the Ostrogoths from the Balkans. For Theoderic it gave the emperor's sanction

37. Ivory panel of Ariadne, wife of Zeno and Anastasius I, from Florence.
(Photo: Victoria and Albert Museum)

to establish his people in Italy, which was a much more inviting country than the impoverished Balkans. Accepting the commission, the Amal led his people into Dalmatia.

Since that same year Illus and Leontius were at last captured and executed, the patient emperor had finally run out of powerful enemies. For the next three years, while Theoderic conquered Italy and besieged Odoacer in Ravenna, Zeno enjoyed the first real peace of his reign. His chief disappointment was that his son and intended heir, Zeno the Younger, died of dysentery in early adolescence, probably shortly before the emperor himself died of the same disease in 491.

Zeno's main accomplishment had been to keep his throne, against furious opposition, for seventeen years until he died a natural death. During this time he was unable to prevent the western empire from disappearing altogether. He was always in financial distress, and he allowed the Monophysites to become so strong as to make any future religious settlement difficult. Simply by surviving, however, he continued the salutary tradition of legal succession in the East, which despite many failed rebellions still stretched back to Constantine I. By the end of his reign, Zeno had also cleared the Balkans of barbarians for the first time in over a century, and had become the first emperor since Theodosius I to win more power than his ministers or generals.

ANASTASIUS'S REFORMS

Although Zeno had designated no heir after the death of his son, he was survived by his brother Longinus and his widow Ariadne. As the daughter of Leo I, Ariadne had the stronger dynastic right, and nominated the next emperor at the invitation of the senate. She chose Anastasius, an imperial chamberlain whom she knew and liked, and whom she married forty days later. Aged about sixty-one, Anastasius was not much younger than Zeno had been, and lacked administrative experience. But he was highly intelligent, cultivated, and inventive. His acquaintances already knew that Anastasius was interested in theology and sympathetic to Monophysitism, in its moderate or Hesitant form. Because of this, the orthodox patriarch Euphemius refused to crown him until he signed a promise to accept the decisions of Chalcedon. But the patriarch, having accepted Zeno's *Henoticon* himself, had to let Anastasius continue the edict's toleration of Monophysites.

At first most Constantinopolitans welcomed Anastasius, pleased that he was a true Byzantine from Greek-speaking Dyrrhachium. They had feared that the new emperor would be the Isaurian Longinus. Yet Zeno's brother had his admirers. These included, besides the Isaurian soldiers of the capital, the Blues and the Greens, factions of racing and theater fans who had been growing in numbers and enthusiasm during the fifth century. Though the young men of these factions enjoyed rioting of any sort, what really excited them was not politics, but watching and cheering the performers and athletes of their colors in the theater and Hippodrome.[9] The Blues and Greens preferred Longinus, who had paid for hiring new performers the year before, to Anastasius, who showed a puritan's dislike of the Hippodrome and theater.

The factions soon began a violent riot against Anastasius's city prefect, and set fires around the Hippodrome. Anastasius dismissed the prefect, drove the Blues and Greens from the streets, and blamed the riot, justly or not, on Longinus and the Isaurians. The emperor exiled Longinus to Egypt, also exiled the performers Longinus had hired, and expelled the Isaurian soldiers from the city. After the soldiers left, they found that the Isaurian commander in Isauria itself had already begun a revolt against Anastasius. These rebels joined their fellow Isaurians from the capital and other troops in a march on Constantinople.

To oppose them, the emperor sent the two praesental armies, commanded by a Thracian named John the Hunchback, and the Army of the East, under John the Scythian. The loyalists met the insurgents in a battle at Cotyaeum in northwestern Anatolia, and won a complete victory. The rebel Isaurians fled to Isauria, where John the Hunchback defeated them again in 492. The remaining rebels soon turned into brigands, whom John the Hunchback slowly subdued over the next few years. Although many Isaurians, Germans, and other barbarians continued to serve in the field armies, Anastasius struck a balance among them and found loyal officers to lead them. The Isaurian revolt does seem to have weakened the army temporarily; at least Anastasius chose this time to construct a defensive line some forty miles west of the capital known as the Long Walls. But suppressing the Isaurians was worth what it cost, because it finally broke the power of tribal loyalties in the mobile army.

Even after this success, Anastasius had important foreign and domestic enemies. Although Theoderic the Amal and his Ostrogoths had left the Balkans, and completed their conquest of Italy by disposing of Odoacer in 493, the European holdings of the empire soon enticed new barbarian raiders across the Danube. Also in 493 the Bulgars, a tribal coalition incorporating remnants of the Huns, invaded Thrace, defeating and killing its master of soldiers Julian. In one form or another, the Bulgars were to harry the empire during most of the rest of its history.

At home the people of Constantinople resented the emperor's Monophysite leanings and distaste for public entertainments. For one or the other of these reasons, in 493 rioters tore down the statues of the emperor and empress and dragged them through the streets. Shortly thereafter, for reasons that remain obscure, the Greens of Antioch staged a riot that for a moment unseated the administrators of the Diocese of the East.[10] While much of this trend toward rowdiness seems to have had nothing to do with Anastasius, his government had to deal with it.

The Chalcedonian majority in the capital supported the patriarch Euphemius, who began to feel his power. When the emperor asked for the return of the promise of orthodoxy that he had signed at his accession, the patriarch refused, and made independent attempts to negotiate with the papacy to end the Acacian Schism. In 496 Anastasius managed to depose Euphemius on a charge of favoring the languishing Isaurian rebels, but the deposition caused considerable popular unrest. The emperor found it prudent to select a new patriarch, Macedonius, who was a sincere though more discreet Chalcedonian. By 498 Antioch and Jerusalem had also elected patriarchs who endorsed both Chalcedon and the *Henoticon*.

Nevertheless, since he enjoyed the confidence of most of the officers and officials who might have been able to overthrow him, Anastasius had a firmer grip on power than Leo I or Zeno. Its strength increased after John the Hunchback captured the last Isaurian rebels in 498.[11] Anastasius permanently reduced the long-endemic Isaurian brigandage by settling many of the Isaurians in depopulated parts of Thrace. The emperor and his empire now enjoyed an unaccustomed freedom from rebellions.

When the Isaurian revolt finally ended, the emperor used his relative security to introduce some ambitious financial reforms. After thirty troubled years, the treasury had still not quite recovered from the costly failure of Leo's expedition against the Vandals. Anastasius set out to amass a comfortable reserve once more. With less need than his vulnerable predecessors to avoid making enemies in high places, he regulated official fees, curbed bribery, and kept close watch over military payrolls and muster rolls. Moreover, Anastasius, his count of the sacred largesses John,

38. Reformed copper follis of Anastasius I (r. 491–518), shown one and one-quarter times actual size, with the mark of value M (i.e., 40, for 40 nummi) on the reverse. (Photo: Dumbarton Oaks, Washington, D.C., copyright 1996)

and his financial adviser Marinus made several structural changes in the empire's finances.

The chief principle of these reforms was to substitute cash payments for most of the remaining payments in kind. To make the currency more flexible, in 498 John introduced the empire's first abundant and stable copper coinage in almost three hundred years. The coins were issued in clearly numbered denominations and tied to the gold coinage, which had been stable since Constantine I. By providing a means of exchange for sums much smaller than the very valuable gold nomisma, the copper coins eased both official disbursements and private payments. They were instantly popular, particularly the follis, originally valued at 210 to the nomisma. It was about the price of a pound loaf of bread, and as the largest copper coin remained in use for centuries with fairly minor fluctuations in value.

Although the government had long accepted gold for the taxes assessed in kind under Diocletian's system, Anastasius made gold payments general and regular. This wider commutation to gold benefited the state by simplifying accounting, reducing transportation costs, and avoiding spoilage of perishable goods. Taxpayers seem to have welcomed the change, because it reduced opportunities for extortion.[12] Except in Egypt, which supplied levies of grain to provision Constantinople, the government continued to collect only the payments in kind that were needed to supply soldiers stationed near the taxpayers. Even many of those supplies were purchased for cash, and most were apparently sold to the troops for cash, except for the rations distributed on campaigns.

The logical consequence of replacing taxation in kind with monetary taxation was to complete the replacement of military issues in kind with monetary allowances. Not long after 498, the state stopped free issues of the soldiers' ordinary rations, uniforms, and arms, and the cavalrymen's horses and fodder, though it continued to offer them for sale. The troops were expected to buy what they needed with their allowances. These allowances were, however, made generous enough that the soldiers much preferred them to issues in kind. This indirect increase in pay is probably the main reason the army now had no trouble attracting Byzantine volunteers, though during most of the fourth and fifth centuries it had relied heavily on conscription and barbarian mercenaries.[13]

Realizing that increases in monetary payments could lead to increased embezzlement by officials, Anastasius's counselor Marinus introduced a new administrator, the *vindex civitatis* or defender of the city. This official, who was subject to the praetorian prefect, supervised tax collection by the city council and verified the amount collected. Since *vindices* were selected according to the amounts they bid to bring in, in practice the system was a form of controlled tax farming. Even if Marinus and his men profited from the change themselves, it must have reduced local corruption and increased state revenues.[14] Also in 498, the emperor abolished the quinquennial tax on commerce, which had been a fairly small source of revenue but a hated burden for the empire's merchants and tradesmen. Anastasius used revenue from the emperor's private estates to make up for the lost income, which had supplied the quinquennial donative for the army.

The success of these fiscal reforms was swift, sweeping, and widely applauded. While modestly reducing taxation and maintaining spending, Anastasius rapidly filled the treasury. Taxpayers seem to have found payment in cash more convenient; the abolition of the quinquennial tax won universal approval in the cities, and the army's effectiveness soon improved. Though Anastasius deserves much credit for these fortunate results, they also seem to show that fiscal administration during previous reigns had been very lax. Yet the reforms could hardly have generated so much revenue so easily if the empire's subjects had not become more prosperous since the middle of the fifth century, probably because of a population increase.

Set against this economic progress, Anastasius's problems with foreign invasions and domestic disaffection became more manageable, although they continued even in 498. That year the Bulgars invaded Illyricum and defeated its master of soldiers, who lost four thousand men. Arab nomads raided Mesopotamia, Syria, and Palestine, though Byzantine border troops defeated them. The Greens rioted in the Hippodrome, and were punished by a ban on wild-animal fights. The more the factions rioted against Anastasius, the more they came to enjoy lawlessness for its own sake. Both Greens and Blues rioted the next year as well, and during the old pagan festival of the Brytae in 501 they fought each other in a particularly savage disturbance that killed more than three thousand people. The next year Anastasius banned both the Brytae and pantomime dancing. These measures, whether preventive or punitive, appear to have damped down factional violence for several years.

In 502 the Persians broke the peace that had held during the previous sixty years, when the Byzantines had needed it so much. In the interval the Persians, rather like the Byzantines, had suffered from repeated barbarian invasions, by the White Huns, and from civil discord, which had temporarily overthrown their king, Kavād. Now the restored king, in need of money to pay off the White Huns, thought the Byzantines looked vulnerable. At the time the Bulgars were raiding Thrace, and Arabs were raiding Syria and Palestine. Kavād therefore demanded tribute from Anastasius. When the emperor refused, the king invaded Byzantine Armenia, sacked Theodosiopolis and Martyropolis, and at the beginning of 503 seized the city of Amida in northern Mesopotamia.

Anastasius's reform of the army had already taken such good effect that the emperor was able to muster the almost unprecedented number of fifty-two thousand soldiers, only some ten thousand fewer than the total establishment of the two praesental armies and the Army of the East.[15] He made a treaty with the Arab raiders that gained their help against the Persians as well. Unfortunately the three field armies' three commanders mismanaged the first year's campaign by failing to cooperate with each other. But in 504, under a unifed command, the Byzantines retook Amida and raided Persian Armenia. The next year Kavād, who was fighting the White Huns again, opened negotiations for a truce. Anastasius agreed to pay the Persians the moderate tribute of 39,600 nomismata a year. He aided the victims of Kavād's invasion by rebuilding cities and reducing taxes in Mesopotamia, and in 506, when the truce became official, he took action to curb future invasions. Opposite the Persian stronghold of Nisibis he fortified the border town of Dara to

39. The Barberini Ivory, probably depicting Anastasius I, now in the Louvre, Paris. (Photo: Musée du Louvre)

make it comparably strong, though his new name for it, Anastasiopolis, never gained much currency. Dara long served its intended function of anchoring the Persian frontier.

Having made his borders relatively secure, Anastasius began to enjoy a peace troubled only by some internal tensions. In 507 the Blues and Greens began riots at both Constantinople and Antioch that needed to be put down by the army, even though the factions seem not to have been expressing any particular displeasure with Anastasius. The emperor actually appears to have been rather popular from the time of his financial reforms, until he came under the influence of Severus, a Monophysite monk born in Pisidia but trained in Syria. In 511 Severus persuaded the emperor to hold a council to depose Macedonius II, the moderately Chalcedonian patriarch of Constantinople, on a charge of Nestorianism. The next year another council deposed the Chalcedonian patriarch of Antioch, and Severus himself succeeded him. Though Severus accepted the *Henoticon*, which remained in force, his Monophysitism was unconcealed, and the emperor ceased to disguise his agreement with it.

Anastasius's favor for Monophysites caused religious riots at both Antioch and Constantinople. In 512 Chalcedonian demonstrators in the capital joined the Blues and Greens in an attempt to proclaim a new emperor. Their candidate was Areobindus, a former general married to a great-great-granddaughter of Theodosius II. But Areobindus refused to be acclaimed. The rioters were already wavering when Anastasius appeared in the Hippodrome and completed their confusion by eloquently offering to abdicate. They could not bring themselves to accept, and the emperor weathered the crisis.

Yet Anastasius's Monophysitism remained unpopular. The next year brought an organized revolt led by Vitalian, a Chalcedonian general who commanded the barbarian federates in Thrace. Vitalian forced the dismissal of one master of soldiers for Thrace, had the next one killed, and defeated a large force led against him by the emperor's nephew Hypatius, whom he captured. In 514 Vitalian marched on Constantinople. Anastasius bought him off only by appointing him master of soldiers for Thrace, paying a ransom for Hypatius, and agreeing to hold an ecumenical council the next year, presided over by the firmly Chalcedonian pope.

Thrown on the defensive, the emperor negotiated seriously with Pope Hormisdas to end the Acacian Schism, offering to accept Chalcedon. But negotiations broke down when the pope insisted on condemning the memory of the patriarch Acacius, the deviser of the *Henoticon*. When no council convened and the schism continued into 515, Vitalian marched on Constantinople again. Anastasius gave the command against the rebels to Marinus, formerly his financial adviser and praetorian prefect of the East. Despite inexperience in warfare, Marinus defeated the rebel forces, first by sea and then by land. Vitalian himself escaped to the north, but he lost most of his following, and relative peace returned to the empire. The emperor seems to have assured his popularity with the army in 516 by converting the quinquennial donative into a generous annual supplement to the soldiers' allowances.[16]

Abandoning his efforts to heal the schism with the pope, Anastasius kept the *Henoticon* in force, as he had always done. Patriarch Severus of Antioch was still powerful, and in 516 won the deposition of the last openly Chalcedonian patriarch, Elias of Jerusalem. Nonetheless, most Christians in the patriarchates of Constantinople and Jerusalem remained

orthodox, and Anastasius was by this time so aged that everyone anticipated his death. The current patriarchs of Constantinople and Jerusalem
made little secret of their Chalcedonian sympathies.

The Bulgars conducted a major raid into Macedonia and Thessaly in
517, while Vitalian remained at large in northern Thrace. On the whole,
however, the empire was at peace and well under its emperor's control.
Anastasius had achieved very substantial success when he finally died, at
the age of eighty-eight, in 518. Despite the poverty of the treasury at his
accession, at his death he left a colossal gold reserve of some 23 million
nomismata, more than three times the amount left by Marcian in 457.[17]
Anastasius was the first emperor since Diocletian to leave no serious political, financial, or military problems behind him.

This success is the more remarkable because during the reigns of
Leo I, Zeno, and Anastasius the empire had endured as many invasions
and rebellions as at any time since Diocletian's reforms. The Ostrogoths
and Bulgars had ravaged Thrace and Illyricum again and again. Lacking
strong dynastic claims to rule, the emperors had repeatedly confronted
powerful barbarians and other rebels who tried to rule for them. During
most of the period, a Persian invasion of the East, an Ostrogothic invasion of Anatolia, or simply prolonged unrest in the capital might well
have allowed Aspar, one of the Theoderics, or another barbarian to make
himself king at Constantinople. Then the eastern empire might well have
gone the way of the western.

Nevertheless, those quite conceivable disasters did not happen at a
critical juncture, and the East overcame barbarian influence, restored its
finances, and rebuilt its army. By the time the Persians did invade the
empire in 502, the Byzantines were ready and soon defeated them. However near Leo I, Zeno, and Anastasius had come to deposition—and
Zeno could hardly have come nearer—they survived to die natural deaths
while still reigning. Despite many tribulations, at the end of these years
the eastern empire held everything it had held at the beginning except
the city of Sirmium, occupied by the Gepids in 474 and eventually annexed by the Ostrogoths to their new Italian kingdom. While the empire certainly had some good luck, its weathering all these storms is also
evidence of underlying strength.

Any fair comparison of Byzantium as it was in 457 and 518 will show
a great improvement. The vastly increased resources of the state must reflect not only better management but a continuing rise in economic
prosperity, presumably encouraged by Anastasius's monetary reform.

Even the many riots of the time seem to show prosperous exuberance rather than impoverished desperation. By 518 not only was the emperor back in command of his government, but the administration and the army, which had long been in difficulties, were functioning demonstrably well. Although religious dissension remained a problem, Monophysitism seemed to be on the wane. Further proof that the recovery was real came in the next generation, when the empire scored triumphs unprecedented for four hundred years.

CHAPTER SIX

The Reconquests and the Plague, 518–565

Anastasius left an enviable legacy, but he had named no heir before dying suddenly one night in his bed. Though he might well have wanted one of his three nephews to succeed him, his family's prominence was too recent to secure their claim without his explicit declaration. Since he had kept power in his own hands and his wife was dead, no one had clear authority to choose a new emperor. The succession was therefore entirely open for the first time since the unexpected deaths of Julian and Jovian in 363 and 364. As had happened both of those times, and in the similar circumstances of 284, the imperial bodyguard had the decisive voice, and proclaimed one of its own officers.

The successful candidate, the count of the Excubitors Justin, was approved by the assembled officials and crowd after a few hours of confusion. Justin was a Thracian from a peasant family in the Latin-speaking province of Dardania, though he spoke Greek well enough. Poorly educated, passive by nature, and inexperienced in government, he was about sixty-eight, with no son to succeed him. But he had already adopted his nephew Peter, another guardsman, who had taken the name Justinian in his uncle's honor and became Justin's heir apparent. Aged about thirty-six, Justinian possessed adequate learning, extraordinary energy, and a keen sense of what the empire's new wealth and strength made possible.

THE RISE OF JUSTINIAN

Under Justin, the first native speaker of Latin to rule since Theodosius I, the imperial government took much more interest in the West.

When Justin took power, the western Roman Empire was fading from memory, the eastern church was in schism with the papacy, and the pro-papal Vitalian was still in rebellion against the imperial government. But as Chalcedonians from the Illyrian territory that was subject to the pope, Justin and Justinian were eager to end both the schism and the rebellion. Justinian also wanted the empire to exert more authority over the barbarian kings, and he may already have been hoping to recover some of the West for the empire.

The capital's Chalcedonian majority celebrated Justin's accession with demonstrations approved by the government. These compelled the patriarch John II to hold a quickly assembled synod that endorsed the Council of Chalcedon. Justin recalled the Chalcedonians exiled by Anastasius, including the former rebel Vitalian. The emperor, preferring to have Vitalian depend on imperial favor in the capital to having him conspire in Thrace, made him one of the two masters of soldiers in the Emperor's Presence. Further synods in Palestine and Syria hastened to accept Chalcedon and depose refractory bishops, among them the Monophysite patriarch of Antioch Severus. Severus took refuge in Alexandria, where the patriarch Timothy III remained at the head of a firmly Monophysite patriarchate.

While avoiding a direct confrontation with Timothy and Severus and their many followers, Justin sent an embassy to the pope to negotiate an end to the Acacian Schism. The ambassador brought conciliatory letters from the emperor, the patriarch John, and, significantly, Justinian. With Rome under Theoderic and his Ostrogoths, these negotiations were somewhat delicate. Theoderic was in his sixties; on his death the empire could reassert its claim to rule Italy, and that claim would be stronger if the schism was healed. To reassure the Ostrogothic king, Justin offered a form of adoption to Theoderic's chosen successor, his son-in-law Eutharic, and shared the consulship with Eutharic in 519. That year the Acacian Schism was healed, as specified by Pope Hormisdas, by repudiating the doctrinally ambiguous *Henoticon* and condemning the late patriarch Acacius for promoting it. After the reunion, Justin began a gradual but sustained effort to substitute Chalcedonians for the remaining Monophysite bishops outside Egypt.

Having shown himself as good a Chalcedonian as Vitalian, Justin gave the former revolutionary a reliable colleague, naming Justinian the other master of soldiers in the Emperor's Presence. At about this time the emperor appointed another of his nephews, Germanus, to Vitalian's for-

40. Justinian I (r. 527–65). Electrotype of a lost gold medallion, shown actual size, from the Cabinet des Médailles, Paris. (Photo: Bibliothèque Nationale, Paris)

mer command as master of soldiers for Thrace. Besides securing the Army of Thrace for Justin, Germanus soon won a decisive victory over Slavic raiders that established his military reputation.[1] Although Vitalian was honored with the consulship for 520, by the middle of that year his power had so diminished that Justinian contrived to have him killed with impunity.

Justinian himself became consul for 521, and bid for popularity by staging unusually splendid consular games. Himself fond of public entertainments, Justinian favored the faction of the Blues, whose partisans became his allies. His patronage emboldened them to harry their rivals the Greens more than ever, disturbing the peace in Constantinople and Antioch for several years. Presumably it was through his association with the Blues that Justinian met his mistress Theodora, a former actress in the salacious mimes they staged.

As Justinian became more influential, the empire's foreign policy became more aggressive. In 522, the Christian king of Lazica, which had been a Persian protectorate for over fifty years, offered to transfer his allegiance to the empire. Justin ignored Persian protests and accepted; in return, he suffered only some raids on Byzantine Mesopotamia and Syria by the Persians' Arab allies. In 523, when the Jewish king of Yemen massacred Christians, Justin's government persuaded the Christian king of Ethiopia to launch a retaliatory invasion. Within two years the Ethiopians had put Yemen under a Christian king subject to them, securing Byzantine access to the trade route through the Red Sea to India.

The Ostrogothic and Vandal kingdoms also began to feel the power of the Byzantine government. In 523 Theoderic, whose heir Eutharic had just died, discovered letters from some Roman senators to the emperor that apparently discussed restoring imperial rule to Italy. Among those Theoderic arrested for treason was his master of offices Boëthius, an aristocratic philosopher, whom the king executed the next year. The affair soured what had seemed to be good relations between Theoderic and the Italian nobility. To Theoderic's added discomfort, the new Vandal king in Africa, Hilderic, was corresponding with Justinian on terms so amicable as to compromise Vandal independence. Hilderic stopped Vandal efforts to convert his Roman subjects to Arianism, probably minted coins marked with Justin's portrait, and imprisoned his predecessor's queen, who happened to be Theoderic's sister.

Theoderic also protested a ban imposed by Justin on Arian worship within the empire, where most Arians were Germans and many were Goths. In 525 the king sent Pope John to Constantinople as his ambassador. Justin and Justinian received the pope with the utmost respect, had him crown the emperor again, and made a few concessions to the Arians. When John returned to Italy the next year, however, Theoderic expressed grave displeasure with the pope's friendly but not very fruitful negotiations with Justin. After imprisoning John, who died a few days later, Theoderic imposed his candidate as the next pope, Felix IV. The king himself died not long thereafter, leaving his daughter Amalasuntha to rule a discontented Italy on behalf of her eight-year-old son Athalaric.

In the meantime war broke out between the empire and Persia. Encouraged by Lazica's escape from Persian vassalage, the Christian king of Iberia tried to follow his neighbor's example. He appealed for help to Justin, who dispatched a small force; but the Persian king Kavād sent a sizable army, which expelled both the Byzantine troops and the Iberian king, and annexed Iberia to the Persian Empire. Justin responded by sending Byzantine armies to raid Persian Armenia and Mesopotamia. Although these raids were only partly successful, they demonstrated the talents of two young officers formerly in Justinian's bodyguard, Belisarius and Sittas.

Justinian gradually became virtual ruler of the empire. At first his plan to marry his mistress Theodora was frustrated by a law against marriages between senators and former actresses; but eventually he persuaded Justin to exempt repentant actresses, and the wedding took place. Despite Theodora's disreputable past, her marriage to Justinian proved stable, fortified by shared political ambition and the religiosity of the newly respectable. Public opinion knew better than to reproach the powerful pair, and as Justin's health failed visibly in 527, the senate petitioned for his nephew to be named coemperor. Justinian was duly crowned, taking sole possession of the throne when Justin died later in the year.

JUSTINIAN'S PROJECTS

Naturally Justinian became even more active after he gained full authority. Well versed in the workings of the government, army, and church, he had ideas for improvements in each of them. Although his plans were sometimes impractical, he saw many real opportunities that others missed. Occasionally vacillating, more often Justinian varied his means to pursue consistent ends. As an upstart himself, he chose his generals and officials for their merits rather than their connections. Egotistical and humorless, he was an expert employer of talented subordinates, and his best men repaid his trust with loyalty. Always he labored for what he believed, rightly or wrongly, to be the good of his subjects.

Since at his accession the empire was still at war with Persia, Justinian's first major reform concerned the troops defending the eastern frontier. After peace negotiations failed and the Persians defeated the Byzantines in 528, the emperor reorganized the Persian front, creating new commands for the border troops and a new mobile Army of Armenia. Although most of the Armenian army's fifteen thousand troops came from other mobile armies, including that of the East, new recruitment kept those forces at their original strength. Combined with the Army of the East, the Army of Armenia increased the field troops facing the Persians from twenty thousand to thirty-five thousand men.[2] By 529 Justinian entrusted the war to his two former guardsmen, making Sittas master of soldiers for Armenia and Belisarius master of soldiers for the East.

Meanwhile Justinian had appointed a commission of jurists to begin legal reforms of unprecedented scope. In 529, after scarcely more than a

41. Exterior of the Church of Saints Sergius and Bacchus, Constantinople, built by Justinian soon after he became emperor in 527. (Photo: Dumbarton Oaks, Washington, D.C., copyright 1996)

year of frenetic research, the commission published a new collection of laws, the *Justinian Code*. This was a far more ambitious work than the *Theodosian Code* of 438, which had collected only the laws from Constantine I to Theodosius II and even so included much that was obsolete. Justinian's compilation aimed to include every valid law of any date and to eliminate everything that had been superseded. It was therefore the first comprehensive legal code in the empire's history.

Justinian was delighted with the *Code*, and particularly with the prestige it would lend his name. He promptly appointed the commission's best jurist, Tribonian, both as quaestor, the empire's chief legal officer, and as chairman of a second commission that was to codify the numerous commentaries on the law.[3] The emperor was even more impressed with the chairman of the first commission, John the Cappadocian, who became his main adviser on new legislation and soon the praetorian prefect of the East. These and other new appointees started putting Justinian's stamp on the government at the expense of the traditional circle of wealthy and influential civil servants. The punitive taxes and fines levied by John and his subordinates became a significant new source of government revenue.

Justinian directed his first new laws against homosexuals, pagans, and heretics. He exempted Monophysites, whom he did not consider necessarily heretical, but he believed that attacking the rest was his duty as a Christian emperor. He dealt especially harshly with Manichaeans and with the dissident Jewish sect of the Samaritans, who mounted a serious rebellion before they were put down. Although most other religious and sexual nonconformists escaped persecution if they were discreet, some prominent pederasts were castrated, a few practicing pagans were executed, and other pagans were dismissed from official posts. Justinian prohibited pagans from public teaching in 529, dismissing many if not all pagan philosophers from their posts.

Justinian began to enjoy more military success. About 529, he adventurously sent a Byzantine expedition to the Kingdom of Bosporus in the Crimea when its king was overthrown and killed after converting to Christianity. The emperor annexed the Crimea as a province. By 530 his arrangements and appointments in the East brought the first clear Byzantine victories over the Persians for many years. Near the border fortress of Dara, Belisarius decisively defeated an invading Persian army much larger than his own. Near Armenian Theodosiopolis, Sittas defeated another much larger Persian force, and soon afterward conquered a piece of Persian Armenia. To the south, Justinian made an alliance with the recently formed Arab Kingdom of the Ghassanids in the Syrian desert. The Ghassanids were Christians and hereditary enemies of the pagan Lakhmids, who ruled a similar Arab kingdom allied with the Persians and adjoining Persian Mesopotamia. As Byzantine allies, the Ghassanids could restrain their Arab subjects from raiding Syria and Palestine, fight their Lakhmid counterparts, and raid Persian territory. Since the Ghassanids also wanted Byzantine help against the Persians and Lakhmids, the alliance was mutually beneficial.

Beginning in 530 Mundus, the master of soldiers for Illyricum, and Chilbudius, the master of soldiers for Thrace, won major victories against the Bulgars and Slavs who had been raiding the Balkans. Always the weakest point of the eastern empire, the Danube frontier became increasingly secure. Thus the Byzantine army had succeeded in defending the empire's territory, and had even modestly extended it in Armenia and the Crimea. The empire looked so strong that imperial intervention in Italy and Africa began to seem possible, not only to Justinian but to some apprehensive Ostrogoths and Vandals.

Although the Ostrogothic and Vandal rulers wanted to conciliate Justinian, by doing so they aroused fears of betrayal among their German subjects. Ostrogoths who considered their regent Amalasuntha too pro-Byzantine plotted against her and forced her to give them custody of the young king Athalaric. In 530 Vandals who feared that their king Hilderic planned to cede Africa to the empire deposed and imprisoned him, replacing him with his nephew and heir Gelimer. Justinian sent strong protests to Gelimer and considered what action to take.

The following year, after the Persians had defeated the Byzantines in Mesopotamia but lost to them again in Armenia, the Persian king Kavād died. Since his successor Khusrau wanted peace in order to consolidate his power, he opened negotiations. For his part, Justinian wanted peace with Persia so that he could invade Africa, especially because he wanted to recall Belisarius from the East to lead the invasion. During the lengthy diplomatic bargaining, Persians and Byzantines both observed a truce, and Justinian began to plan his expedition against the Vandals.

Before it left, however, at the beginning of 532, a minor incident in the capital turned into an emergency. It began when the Blue and Green factions demanded pardons for two of their members who had survived an attempt to hang them for murder. The factions' agitation soon took a more political turn. The Blues ignored the favor Justinian had shown them. Shouting the usual racing cheer of *Nika!* ("Win!"), a mob of Blues and Greens broke open the prison and burned much of the center of the city. When some leading senators gave them encouragement and arms, the rioters demanded Justinian dismiss his city prefect, his praetorian prefect John the Cappadocian, and his quaestor Tribonian. Though the emperor consented, he still failed to calm the mob. They found Hypatius, a nephew of the late emperor Anastasius, and proclaimed him emperor in the Hippodrome.

Unable to trust the regular troops in the city, Justinian considered taking refuge in Thrace, but on Theodora's advice he decided to make a stand in Constantinople.[4] By chance, he had two loyal generals in the city: Belisarius, who was preparing for the Vandal expedition, and Mundus, who was on his way from Thrace to replace Belisarius as master of soldiers for the East. These two led a few loyal troops into the Hippodrome and bloodily suppressed the rioters, whose uprising became known as the Nika Revolt. Justinian executed Hypatius, the emperor they had proclaimed, and exiled and confiscated the property of the senators who had supported the rebellion.

Although the Nika Revolt showed that Justinian was not personally

42. Relief of a chariot race from the lower part of the base of the Obelisk of Theodosius I in the Hippodrome, Constantinople, showing the four chariots of the Blues, Greens, Reds, and Whites and above these the statues and other ornaments on the central divider where the obelisk itself stood. (Photo: Irina Andreescu-Treadgold)

popular, he was doubtless right to blame it more on the senators than on the people. The son of a peasant, Justinian was impatient with the privileges of the senatorial class, and his praetorian prefect John the Cappadocian was a man of similar background and attitudes. The emperor, John, and Tribonian had already begun efforts against corruption that disturbed many high officials but few ordinary citizens. After the Nika Revolt, Justinian became even more reluctant to appoint men from senators' families to high office, and more eager to tap their fortunes for the treasury by whatever means his subordinates could devise.

The emperor continued his plans as before, adding to them the lavish reconstruction of Saint Sophia and other buildings burned down in the rioting. He kept Tribonian as chairman of his legal commission, and soon reappointed John the Cappadocian as praetorian prefect. The emperor signed a treaty with Khusrau of Persia for what was called, since it had no time limit, the Perpetual Peace. Since the Persians had raided Byzantine territory far more than the Byzantines had raided Persia, Khusrau expected to be paid, and he was. The treaty obliged Justinian to send Khusrau the ample sum of eleven thousand pounds of gold, or 792,000 nomismata; but the emperor suspended the pay of the troops on the Persian frontier, which would easily have made up the loss in a single year.[5] With peace established in the East, Justinian continued preparations for his expedition against the Vandals, despite the misgivings of his advisers, who thought the risk was too great.

The emperor also pursued a plan to reconcile some of the Monophysites, whose exiled bishops had begun to quarrel among themselves at Alexandria. Recently Julian, the exiled bishop of Halicarnassus on the

Anatolian coast, had maintained that Christ's body was by nature incapable of suffering and sin.[6] While this conclusion followed from Eutyches' original belief in a single, divine nature, most Monophysites had
long considered Eutyches a heretic and believed that Christ's nature
though one, was both divine and human. Severus, the exiled patriarch
of Antioch and the principal Monophysite leader, attacked Julian for
denying the full humanity of Christ. Soon the Monophysites were bitterly split between Severans and Julianists.

Justinian sensed a chance to do to Monophysitism what Theodosius I
had done to Arianism. Theodosius had won over those who rejected
Arius but objected to the Nicene Creed because it did not exclude
Sabellianism. When these objectors had finally realized that Sabellianism
was not a danger they accepted Nicaea, leaving the minority of real Arians to die out. Now the Severan Monophysites rejected Julian and Eutyches, but objected to the Chalcedonian formula of two natures because it did not exclude Nestorianism, which supposedly meant belief in
two persons. By reassuring the Severans that Nestorianism was not a
threat, Justinian hoped to persuade them to accept Chalcedon and leave
the Julianist minority isolated. The prize would be almost complete unity
in the Church.

To this end the emperor arranged a long conference at Constantinople between leading Chalcedonians and Severan Monophysites. Despite their long-standing disagreements over terminology and conciliar
history, the conferees' theological beliefs turned out to be surprisingly
similar, and a few Severans even accepted Chalcedon. In March of 533,
Justinian promulgated an edict condemning both Nestorius and Eutyches
and proclaiming that Christ was divine, human, and a single person. Although this edict did not immediately reconcile Severans and Chalcedonians, it set out the shared beliefs that seemed to make reconciliation
possible. Justinian hopefully continued his efforts.[7]

Three months later, in June, Belisarius sailed against the Vandals of
Africa with some eighteen thousand soldiers, most of them probably
from the Army of the East that he still commanded, and thirty thousand
sailors.[8] The Romans of Tripolitania and the Vandal commander of Sardinia had already rebelled against the Vandal king Gelimer and declared
for the emperor. In Italy the embattled Ostrogothic regent Amalasuntha was contemplating flight to the empire and needed Justinian's goodwill. She therefore allowed Belisarius to take on supplies in Sicily, even
though Byzantine success against the Vandals would obviously endanger
the Ostrogoths.

After the prefect John the Cappadocian had emphasized the dangers of the African expedition, Justinian made it small and cheap enough that it would not utterly ruin the army and treasury if it failed. On the other hand, the expedition's smallness made its failure more likely. Justinian seemed to have excessive faith in the durability of his own rule and in the abilities of Belisarius and his army. Perhaps the emperor had an exaggerated idea of the value of Africa as well. Nonetheless, Justinian believed that God favored his projects to overthrow barbarian Arians in the West and to regain former Roman provinces, and acted on his belief.

JUSTINIAN'S TRIUMPHS

Belisarius really was a commander of rare talents, including that of persuading insubordinate Byzantine armies to do things they were reluctant to do. In some ways the Vandals were also convenient adversaries. They had alienated their Roman population by long efforts to convert it to Arianism, and were so fearful of revolts and unafraid of invasions that they had destroyed the walls of all their cities except their capital of Carthage. They had been weakened both by the recent rebellions in Sardinia and Tripolitania, and by earlier Moorish raids and conquests on their borders. But the Vandals still had a larger army than Belisarius, troops scarcely worse than his, and a competent leader in Gelimer.

The Byzantine landing in Africa surprised Gelimer, who had sent most of the Vandal fleet to quell the revolt on Sardinia and could not recall it in time. As Belisarius drove on Carthage, the king executed his predecessor Hilderic and ordered three contingents of his army to ambush the Byzantines ten miles south of Carthage, at Decimum. The first contingent, led by Gelimer's brother, arrived in disorder, blundered into the Byzantines' advance guard, and was practically annihilated. The second Vandal company encountered the Byzantines' Hun mercenaries, who so terrified them that they scarcely resisted being slaughtered. Finally Gelimer came up with the largest part of his army and chased the Byzantines from Decimum. But by stopping to bury his brother, the king let Belisarius take him unprepared. As Belisarius routed him, Gelimer fled blindly in the opposite direction from Carthage, leaving its inhabitants free to welcome Belisarius.

Although Gelimer's battle plans had failed and lost him Carthage, most of his forces remained intact. He brought his fleet from Sardinia, where it had suppressed the local rebels, and he tried to win over Belisarius's Huns. Before the end of 533, however, Belisarius attacked Gelimer at

Tricamerum, not far from Carthage, and destroyed the Vandal army. After taking refuge with the Moors, Gelimer and his last few men surrendered less than a year after Belsarius had arrived. The Byzantines completed their conquest of the Vandal Kingdom by securing Sardinia, Corsica, the Balearics, and the fort of Septem on the Strait of Gibraltar.

Justinian was overjoyed. Even before Gelimer had surrendered, the emperor declared the Vandal Kingdom annexed, and made it into the Praetorian Prefecture of Africa. Belisarius returned to Constantinople in the middle of 534 with Gelimer, the other Vandal captives, and the Vandals' treasury, once plundered from the Romans and now regained. Justinian rewarded Belisarius with a triumph, an honor that only emperors had received since the time of Augustus. The gesture not only showed generosity but magnified the victory, which was certainly magnificent but not quite complete. Although the surviving Vandals had been deported and enrolled in the Army of the East, the Moors continued attacking the new African prefecture from the desert. Probably using troops from the East whom the captured Vandals were replacing, Justinian created a new Army of Africa under Belisarius's deputy Solomon. To strengthen Solomon's hand against the Moors, the emperor named him both Africa's praetorian prefect and its master of soldiers.

While making this excellent start on reconquering the West, Justinian continued his ambitious legal and administrative reforms. In 533 Tribonian's commission had published the *Digest*, an authoritative codification of earlier legal commentaries, and the *Institutes*, an official textbook for students of the law. In 534 the commission finished its work by publishing a revised and corrected version of the *Justinian Code*. The *Code*, *Digest*, and *Institutes*—supplemented by the *Novels*, Justinian's new legislation—were collectively known as the *Corpus Juris Civilis*, the Body of Civil Law. This *Corpus* became the definitive form of Roman law for the empire, and soon for the barbarian West as well.

Once this great task was completed, Justinian began to implement plans prepared by his prefect John the Cappadocian to improve efficiency and reduce corruption in the administration. John's ideas were first applied to the new Prefecture of Africa, which received a bureaucracy that was by prevailing standards both small and well paid. John's strategy was to appoint a few men of modest background who would depend upon and serve the state instead of representing and favoring the local aristocracy. His principal aim was to increase government revenue by reducing private patronage and extortion.

Following John's plans, in 535 Justinian outlawed the sale of provincial

43. The Basilica Cistern, Constantinople, built by Justinian. Engraving by W. H. Capone after T. Allom. (From Thomas Allom, *Constantinople and the Scenery of the Seven Churches of Asia Minor* [London, 1838])

governorships, a common practice that had forced governors to take bribes to recoup their investment. Along with payments to officials, the law stopped payments to the treasury, but it probably paid for itself by reducing embezzlement later. The emperor also abolished a number of offices that he considered superfluous or conflicting. These included many mere sinecures, usually held by rich senators, and the whole administrative tier of the dioceses, which had become particularly corrupt. Justinian raised the salaries of many of his remaining officials, hoping that adequate pay would help them resist corruption. The success of these reforms soon appeared in growing revenues and bitter complaints by the powerful.

Justinian's efforts to win over Severan Monophysites also made progress. His conciliatory edict of 533, which Pope John II had accepted, attracted Severus of Antioch himself to the capital for discussions. The empress Theodora, who had come to side with the Severans, appeared to be helping her husband reconcile them with the Chalcedonians. When the Monophysite patriarch of Alexandria Timothy died in 535, Theodora managed to replace him with the Severan Theodosius instead of a more popular Julianist. When the Chalcedonian patriarch of Constantinople Epiphanius died the same year, she persuaded Justinian to replace him with Anthimus, known as a Chalcedonian but friendly to the Severans. Events seemed to be moving toward a genuine union of the churches of Rome, Antioch, Alexandria, and Constantinople for the first time since the Council of Chalcedon.

Then Justinian saw his chance to make the greatest reconquest of all, that of Italy. Besides its value for Byzantine power, retaking Italy would protect the reunion with the papacy and guard the sea route to reconquered Africa. And the emperor had hopes of subduing the Ostrogothic Kingdom with little if any fighting. The Ostrogoths' regent Amalasuntha was discussing a secret proposal to hand Italy over to him. By 534 her already precarious position had become untenable with the death of her son, the adolescent king Athalaric. Needing a king at once, she chose her cousin Theodahad, who agreed to rule with her. But in 535 he had her imprisoned and murdered.[9]

When Justinian learned of the murder of his former ally, he speedily claimed the Ostrogothic Kingdom. Since Sittas was keeping the Bulgars out of the Balkans with the Army of Thrace, Justinian could spare most of the Army of Illyricum, which was again commanded by Mundus. The emperor ordered Mundus to invade Ostrogothic Dalmatia. Justinian sent Belisarius to invade Sicily with a hastily assembled army of 7,500 men.[10] While Mundus took the main Dalmatian city of Salona, Belisarius easily seized Sicily. The conquest of Sicily anchored the sea route to Africa and established a base for an invasion of Italy. In alarm, Theodahad sent Pope Agapetus to Justinian to sue for peace. But the pope had barely left when an imperial ambassador reached the king. The envoy frightened Theodahad into making a secret pact to surrender Italy to the empire.

The pope's mission had thus been superseded when he arrived in Constantinople in 536. But Agapetus stayed to demand the abdication of the patriarch Anthimus, who had joined the Severan Monophysites in refusing to accept the Council of Chalcedon. Bowing to papal authority, Justinian reluctantly obtained Anthimus's abdication and allowed the pope to consecrate a Chalcedonian patriarch, Menas. Though the pope then died, Menas held a synod that condemned Anthimus, Severus, and their followers, whom the emperor exiled from Constantinople. Still believing that only prejudice kept Severans from accepting Chalcedon, Justinian hoped that firmness might succeed better than compromise in convincing them to submit.

In the meantime an army of Ostrogoths, unaware that their king was betraying them, arrived in Dalmatia and fought an indecisive battle with the Byzantines, who withdrew after the death of their general Mundus. At this news Theodahad repudiated his agreement to surrender Italy and arrested Justinian's envoys. Then most of the soldiers in Africa mutinied against their commander Solomon, who had been unable to pay them on time from local revenues. Belisarius sailed from Sicily to Carthage, but after beginning to restore order he had to return to prevent a mutiny in Sicily itself.

Justinian reacted to these reverses with vigor. As master of soldiers for Africa he appointed his cousin Germanus, who had defeated the Slavs under Justin. Germanus arrived in Carthage with few men but all the soldiers' back pay, which soon regained the loyalty of many of the mutineers. Constantinianus, Justinian's choice to replace Mundus in Illyricum, reoccupied Salona, and the Ostrogoths abandoned Dalmatia. At this time Justinian seems to have united the navy under a new quaestor of the army, who with jurisdictions in both the lower Danube and the eastern Mediterranean could transfer ships between them as needed and control the sea.[11]

Without further delay, the emperor ordered Belisarius, despite the small number and poor discipline of his troops, to cross the straits to Italy. Fortunately for the Byzantines, the indecisive Theodahad had not reinforced the handful of Ostrogothic soldiers ordinarily stationed in southern Italy. They surrendered at once, and Belisarius rapidly advanced to Naples and besieged it. When Theodahad again sent no reinforcements, Belisarius smuggled in some troops through a broken aqueduct and took the city. At the news of the fall of Naples, the exasperated Ostrogoths deposed Theodahad and elected Vitigis, a general of some reputation, as their king.

While Belisarius marched on Rome, Vitigis had Theodahad killed. Yet instead of defending Rome, Vitigis decamped for Ravenna, where he sought legitimacy by divorcing his wife and forcing Amalasuntha's daughter Matasuntha to marry him. The four thousand Ostrogoths Vitigis left in Rome were too few to man its sprawling and dilapidated walls. When Pope Silverius persuaded the Roman people to receive the imperial army, the Ostrogothic garrison simply abandoned the city. Belisarius occupied the empire's ancient capital before the end of 536.

Belisarius's successes showed his own genius rather than the strength of his army. After detaching garrisons for Sicily and southern and central Italy, he held Rome with only five thousand soldiers. By heroic efforts, he made the walls defensible before Vitigis learned the diminutive size of the Byzantine garrison and attacked early in 537. Besieged by a much larger force, Belisarius appealed to Justinian for more men and supplies. A contingent of sixteen hundred men was on its way and soon arrived, but it was obviously not enough.

Without detailed knowledge of western conditions, the eastern government tended to underestimate the costs of reconquering the West. Expecting Africa to pay for its own defense immediately out of current revenue, Justinian had let its soldiers go unpaid until they mutinied. Seeing that Belisarius could conquer Africa in a year with eighteen thousand men, Justinian assumed he could conquer Italy with less than half as many. Although later the emperor tried to correct both mistakes, travel between East and West was dangerous in winter and slow even in summer. Germanus finished suppressing the African mutiny only in 537. By then only a few reinforcements could be sent to Belisarius before winter made sea travel unsafe.

After acquiring the huge treasure of the Vandals, Justinian was not short of money. He spent freely on buildings, reconstructing Antioch

44. Exterior of the Church of Saint Sophia, Constantinople, with the baptistery in the foreground. (Photo: Warren Treadgold)

after earthquakes in 526 and 538 and Constantinople after the Nika Revolt of 532. His most costly and celebrated monument was the new Church of Saint Sophia, dedicated in 537. In its way as boldly conceived as the conquest of Africa, this was the world's biggest church, roofed by the world's largest and highest dome. Saint Sophia made the greatest impression, but it was only one of dozens of expensive and sometimes innovative projects commissioned by Justinian. Yet the emperor might have done better to postpone some of his building until Africa and Italy were safely conquered.

During months of waiting for help in Rome, Belisarius performed marvels of improvisation to defeat the numerous besiegers and rally the unhappy besieged. His task was complicated by orders from Theodora to replace Pope Silverius with her friend Vigilius, who had been more conciliatory toward Monophysites. With good reason to believe that Justinian agreed with his empress, Belisarius deposed Silverius on a charge of plotting with Vitigis and had Vigilius elected to the papacy.

Finally, near the end of 537, ample supplies and some fifty-six hundred reinforcements arrived with John, a nephew of the former rebel Vitalian. Early in 538 John managed to seize Rimini, just south of Ravenna, frightening Vitigis into raising the siege of Rome after just over a year. By summer, seven thousand more Byzantines landed, led by the eunuch Narses, a trusted adviser of the emperor. Belisarius had already begun expanding his conquests to the north, taking Genoa and Milan with the aid of the local Romans. But Narses, invoking an ambiguity in his commission, disregarded Belisarius's orders and went off with John to conquer Aemilia.

Once the emperor had installed an apparently conciliatory pope, he tried to prepare for a comprehensive church settlement by winning over Monophysite Egypt. Severus of Antioch died in 538, and by then Justinian had deposed the patriarch of Alexandria Theodosius for refusing repeated appeals to accept Chalcedon. Theodosius's successor Paul used military force to replace the Monophysite hierarchy in Egypt with at least nominal Chalcedonians. To support Paul's efforts, the emperor made Egypt subject to five dukes with overriding military and civil powers, who had surprising outward success in suppressing Monophysitism. Officially all five patriarchates were now in communion with each other.

The conquest of Italy continued during 539, with an unfortunate interruption. The Ostrogoths, aided by some Franks, recaptured and wrecked Milan after Narses ignored Belisarius's orders to relieve the city.

As soon as Justinian received the news, he saw the necessity of a unified command and recalled Narses. The desperate Ostrogoths gained little from the destruction of Milan, and even less from another army of Franks, who in a brief raid on northern Italy harmed the Goths more than the Byzantines. After this Vitigis, never an energetic ruler, ceased to offer any effective resistance, and his men only continued a passive defense in their forts. By the end of the year, Belisarius had received reinforcements from the Army of Illyricum by way of Dalmatia, and had taken almost everything south of the Po but Ravenna, where he besieged Vitigis. Even though the city was almost impossible to take by assault, the Ostrogothic king saw no hope of relief. He opened negotiations for peace.

Thus 540 seemed to be the year when Belisarius would take the rest of Italy from the Ostrogoths, just as Solomon, reinstated the previous year by Germanus, was retaking the remainder of North Africa from the Moors. By this time, however, the emperor had begun worrying about the Persian king Khusrau, whose interest in the Perpetual Peace of 532 had diminished after he secured his throne at home. Encouraged by Justinian's preoccupation with the West, Khusrau had already allowed his Lakhmid Arab allies to raid Syria. Justinian wanted to end the Ostrogothic war in time to deter a Persian attack, or at least to have Belisarius in the East to repel one.

To bring this about, early in 540 Justinian's ambassadors offered Vitigis peace in return for half his treasury and all the land south of the Po. These terms were acceptable to Vitigis, but not to Belisarius. The general wanted to finish his conquest, and may well have feared that on his departure the Ostrogoths would invade Byzantine Italy from their remaining territory. He was able to delay ratifying the treaty until the Ostrogoths and Vitigis made another proposal. They offered to submit to Belisarius as emperor of a revived western Roman Empire. Although he was actually loyal to Justinian, he pretended to agree.

Under these false pretenses, Belisarius obtained the surrender of Ravenna, with Vitigis and his whole garrison and treasury, followed by the submission of most Ostrogoths in the north. Belisarius entered Ravenna in May, perhaps not yet aware that the Persians had invaded Syria in March. About a month later, the great general and a number of his troops were recalled to fight them. Only when he embarked for the East with Vitigis and the treasury did the Ostrogoths fully realize that Belisarius had kept faith with the emperor and betrayed them. By that time, how-

45. Exterior of the Church of San Vitale, Ravenna, completed under Justinian. (Photo: Soprintendenza per i Beni Ambientali e Architettonici, Ravenna)

ever, the reconquest of Italy was practically complete, like the reconquest of Africa. The empire had been vastly enlarged, seemingly at minimal cost.

THE PERSIAN ATTACK

The warfare in Africa and Italy had inevitably led Justinian to weaken the empire's eastern defenses. Belisarius campaigned in the West with the title of master of soldiers of the East, and apparently with a substantial part of the East's mobile army. The eastern frontier garrisons, never much better than any other border troops, decayed further after their pay lapsed at the time of the Perpetual Peace. In the Balkans, which no such treaty protected, the border troops were also in disarray, and by 539 a large part of the Army of Illyricum was away in Italy.

At the beginning of 540, the Bulgars launched a raid that met no effective opposition. From the Danube the raiders swept through Illyricum, where they took some small forts, and into Macedonia, where they sacked a small town. Bands of Bulgars reached northern Greece and southern Thrace, even making a brief raid across the Hellespont before they all withdrew. The Bulgars gathered many captives, but they caused only minor damage and took no important places. Much the greater threat was a raid on Syria, which was far richer, by the Persians, who knew how to take cities.

Aware that the Perpetual Peace might prove temporary, the emperor had strengthened the fortifications of several cities near the border and built a new stronghold at Petra to include Lazica within the frontier. Justinian had also annexed his last Armenian satrapies in 536. But this provoked an Armenian rebellion. The rebels killed the commander in Armenia Sittas in 538, before succumbing to his successor Buzes the next year. Justinian trusted that Khusrau would keep the peace for some time out of the same need to consolidate his power that had led him to make the treaty in the first place. Yet Justinian knew that he could mount a full defense against Persia only when Belisarius and his men returned.

This was also known to Khusrau, who did not see why Justinian should be the only one to collect glory, land, and loot. The Persian king hardly needed the encouragement he had received from the rebels in Byzantine Armenia and from an Ostrogothic embassy. He decided to exploit the absence of much of the Army of the East to extort and plunder money from Syria, and if possible to take a few places on the border. Before Belisarius could return, Khusrau led a strong army up the Euphrates into Byzantine territory and sacked the city of Sura. Buzes was nearby with troops from the Army of Armenia, but thought it prudent to retreat.

Justinian entrusted the defense of Syria to his cousin Germanus. The new commander, arriving at Antioch to find himself very short of men, began negotiations with Khusrau. The king agreed to withdraw in return for a payment of seventy-two thousand nomismata; but until he received it he continued advancing and extorting money from the Syrians. He sacked Beroea when its garrison deserted after years without pay. Then ambassadors from Justinian to the Persians arrived at Antioch and repudiated the terms Germanus had negotiated with Khusrau. Germanus gave up and left Antioch as the Persians approached. Though the city was defended by six thousand troops from the frontier forces, they abandoned it to Khusrau at the first Persian assault.

Thus the third city of the empire fell to the Persians, who had not captured it since the third-century crisis.[12] They pillaged Antioch,

46. Antioch (modern Antakya in Turkey), showing the ancient walls that have now mostly been destroyed. Nineteenth-century engraving by J. Jeavons after W. H. Bartlett. (From John Carne, *Syria, the Holy Land, Asia Minor, etc., Illustrated* [London, 1837])

burned most of it, and took captive the thousands of citizens who had not escaped or died. After the sack of Antioch, Khusrau informed Justinian's ambassadors that his price for peace had risen to 360,000 nomismata at once and 36,000 nomismata a year thereafter. Because this sum could not be paid immediately, the king went on to extort property from the citizens of Apamea and several other places. When he came to Edessa, he discovered that Buzes had finally prepared an adequate defense, and he accepted a moderate payment to spare the city's territory. Khusrau was ready to release his prisoners from Antioch for a larger sum, which Buzes would not allow the Edessenes to pay. At this point Justinian sent his acceptance of the king's new peace terms, but withdrew it after Khusrau attempted to take Dara as he returned.

The entire campaign was a triumph for Khusrau and a fiasco for the Byzantines. The damage done to the prosperity of Syria was considerable, but the harm to Byzantine prestige was worse. The empire's enemies could now imagine that Justinian owed his success not to Byzantine strength but merely to good fortune and one general, Belisarius. In fact, the disaster in Syria resulted from no fundamental weaknesses, but only from unpreparedness and repeated failures to agree on a coherent response to the attack. Nonetheless, the Persians, Ostrogoths, and others were right to think that Justinian's projects were straining his resources.

Among those who sensed Byzantine vulnerability was the king of Lazica, Gubazes. The Byzantine garrison and commander at the recently constructed stronghold of Petra had begun to annoy the king, who asked Khusrau to restore the Persians' protectorate over Lazica. Pleased to accept, Khusrau led his army to Lazica in 541, also persuading the Caucasian Huns to attack Byzantine Armenia. Without much fear of Byzantine retaliation, he took control of Lazica and captured Petra after a short siege. But he interrupted his campaign at the news that the Huns had been crushed by the new master of soldiers for Armenia Valerian, and that Belisarius had invaded the Persian Empire itself.

On his arrival in the East with a number of Byzantine and Ostrogothic soldiers, Belisarius had speedily put his Army of the East in order and joined forces with Buzes and the Army of Armenia. Although he had believed Khusrau was marching against the Huns rather than against Lazica, Belisarius knew a campaign of revenge would improve Byzantine morale. Passing by the strongly fortified city of Nisibis on the border, he easily seized and destroyed the next walled town of Sisaurana, capturing its garrison. He sent his Ghassanid Arab allies to raid Persian territory across the Tigris.

Since the Persians of Mesopotamia had proved as poorly prepared and disorganized as the Byzantines of Syria the year before, Buzes wanted to press on toward the Persian capital of Ctesiphon. Belisarius decided not to do so, probably because he lacked confidence in his recently reconstituted army, but also because he was alarmed by reports of his wife Antonina's plotting with Theodora in Constantinople. The two women had just forced the dismissal of John the Cappadocian as praetorian prefect by trapping him in a treasonable conversation. When Belisarius returned to the capital, they used similar means to make him tolerate Antonina's liaison with his adopted son. Belisarius's prestige was now so great that Justinian could not feel utterly sure of his general's loyalty.

In Italy Belisarius had left the Ostrogoths holding a mere scattering of fortresses north of the Po, and scarcely capable of organized resistance. Some Ostrogoths had elected a new king, Hildebad, but after defeating the Byzantines in Venetia he was assassinated by one of his Gepid allies in 541. The next nominal king was a Gepid, Eraric, who was negotiating a surrender to the Byzantines for his own benefit when he was over-thrown. In fall 541 the Ostrogoths elected Hildebad's nephew Totila, who had himself been negotiating a surrender to the Byzantines. As king, Totila agreed to fight on, but his resources were few.

Thus the empire weathered the Persian invasion. The weaknesses ex-ploited by Khusrau in Syria and Lazica, and by the Bulgars in the Bal-kans, had proved temporary and local. While the Army of the East re-covered its strength under Belisarius, Justinian's largesse rebuilt Antioch and the other cities sacked by the Persians and strengthened the Balkan forts. The formerly Monophysite Egyptians, once intimidated by Patri-arch Paul of Alexandria, accepted Paul's less abrasive but equally Chal-cedonian successor Zoïlus. Italy was almost pacified, and Justinian had just sent reinforcements, including captured Persians from Sisaurana, to increase the Byzantine advantage over the Ostrogoths. Africa was peace-ful and prosperous. Justinian's work seemed sound enough to survive any likely reverse.

THE ARRIVAL OF THE PLAGUE

Then, in October of 541, the bubonic plague made its first known appearance in the Mediterranean world. The disease spread to the Egyp-tian port of Pelusium from Ethiopia. It had probably begun either in In-dia or in East Africa; it may have reached the empire at this time because of growth in the Red Sea trade after the Ethiopians took Yemen in 525. The plague was transmitted by the bites of infected fleas from rats, or, more rarely, by the cough of an infected person. In the former case, it caused a bubonic swelling and killed some three-quarters of its victims; in the latter case, it attacked the lungs and was always fatal. The plague moved with men and rats, on ships and with armies, and had the great-est effect where men and rats were most numerous, in cities and military camps. Nothing known at the time helped much to prevent or cure it.[13]

By the spring of 542, the plague spread to most of the ports of the eastern Mediterranean, among them Alexandria, Antioch, and Constan-tinople. As the largest city, Constantinople had a particularly terrible epi-demic, aggravated by a breakdown of arrangements for the food supply. The authorities are said to have counted 230,000 dead, which would probably have been well over half the population.[14] The plague killed many government officials, probably including the quaestor Tribonian. Justinian himself fell gravely ill with it.

Just before the plague arrived, Belisarius left Constantinople at the news that Khusrau had again invaded Mesopotamia. Since the Persian king had already taken the best booty from Syria, he now intended to pillage Palestine, but he was still in the Euphrates valley when Belisarius joined Buzes and the Byzantine armies nearby. Despite having more men, Khusrau agreed to withdraw, probably because his troops too were contracting the plague. As they returned to Persia, surprising and destroying the fortified city of Callinicum as they went, the plague followed them.

It also disrupted the army of Belisarius and Buzes, and not only because it spread among their soldiers. When the commanders received word that the emperor had caught the usually fatal illness and still had named no heir, they began to discuss the succession. They feared that Theodora would choose a successor of her own instead of the army's unquestioned choice, Belisarius, who could succeed without disloyalty if the emperor died of disease. But Justinian began to recover, and reports of the officers' conversations infuriated Theodora. While her husband's condition left her in effective control of the government, she called Belisarius and Buzes to Constantinople for interrogation. There she had Buzes jailed and Belisarius stripped of his command and private guard.

Justinian's illness also freed Theodora to help Monophysites. Ever since Patriarch Theodosius of Alexandria had been deposed in 537, he had lived in Constantinople under Theodora's protection, with a group of Monophysite bishops and clergy. Avoiding needless confrontation, Justinian left Theodosius and his followers undisturbed as long as they made no new consecrations of bishops or priests. Since with the death of Severus of Antioch Theodosius had become the recognized head of the Monophysite movement, the few Monophysite bishops still in hiding were unwilling to consecrate bishops without his consent. As these bishops died off, the Monophysite hierarchy dwindled rapidly. The Monophysites' choices were thus being reduced to compromise or extinction. Theodosius himself seems to have hoped for a compromise.

Probably in the fall of 542, while Justinian was still gravely ill, the Ghassanid king of the empire's Arab allies appealed to Constantinople for a bishop. Theodora apparently felt that Justinian, though opposed to a Monophysite hierarchy in the empire, would not object to consecrations for churches outside it. She therefore had Theodosius consecrate two Monophysite bishops, nominally of Bostra in Byzantine Arabia and Edessa in Byzantine Mesopotamia. Another Monophysite missionary was sent without the rank of bishop to convert the remaining pagans in the countryside of western Anatolia.

The missionary to the pagans, John of Amida, made some seventy thousand converts in the mountains of Lydia and Caria. The titular bishop of Bostra, Theodore, limited his ministry to the Ghassanid kingdom. But the titular bishop of Edessa, Jacob Baradaeus, made it his mission to revivify Monophysitism within the empire. A charismatic monk who dressed as a beggar to elude government officials, Jacob started to consecrate a Monophysite clergy parallel to that of the official church. Although as yet he could make no episcopal consecrations, which required the presence of three bishops, Jacob began the process of converting Monophysitism from a theological tendency within the Church into a schismatic sect.[15]

Jacob's wanderings and consecrations extended far beyond his nominal see in Mesopotamia to Anatolia, Syria, Palestine, and Egypt. Though willing to use Syriac and Coptic in the Mass, he and his priests had no intention of forming local Syrian or Egyptian churches, and still hoped to take over the official hierarchy someday. Inevitably, however, their followers were not just Monophysite in theology but devoted to Jacob personally, and distrustful of the established authorities. These so-called Jacobites had little interest in any theological compromise with the emperor. The formation of the Jacobite sect was most unwelcome to Justinian, who might well have forestalled it had he not been incapacitated by the plague.

The reinforcements the emperor had already sent to Italy should have been enough to crush the Ostrogoths before the plague arrived. Early in 542, a Byzantine army of twelve thousand men drove Totila from Verona. But Justinian had again made the mistake of dividing the command. The squabbling commanders allowed themselves to be shut out of Verona, surrounded, and defeated with severe losses. Totila pressed south and defeated the Byzantines again near Florence, taking many Byzantine prisoners who joined his army. He continued south without opposition, capturing the weakly held towns and besieging Naples. The Ostrogothic king even built a navy, which succeeded in intercepting two small fleets with reinforcements from Constantinople.

By the end of 542, the plague had spread all over the East and as far as Africa and Dalmatia, if not yet to Italy. While Justinian recovered his own health, the death of large numbers of soldiers and taxpayers left men and money in short supply, especially because they were no longer managed by the ingenious John the Cappadocian. John's immediate successor as praetorian prefect of the East was plainly unequal to the task, and in early 543 Justinian replaced him with the count of the sacred largesses Peter Barsymes, who enjoyed Theodora's support.

Though less inspired and more corrupt than John, Peter managed to avoid utter insolvency during the plague. Tax revenues were presumably maintained by the usual method of assigning the lands of missing or defaulting taxpayers to their neighbors, which under the circumstances would have caused great hardship. Peter undid one of John's major reforms by resuming the sale of governorships, thus gaining immediate revenue at the price of tolerating peculation in future years. He and the emperor went to great lengths to squeeze money from the senatorial class, and were the less scrupulous because many senators had long been hostile to Justinian.

Peter also suspended the pay of the frontier troops and delayed the regular pay of the mobile troops. However shortsighted these measures may seem, the emergency required a large decrease in spending, and military pay must have accounted for about half the official budget. Justinian had already suspended the pay of the eastern frontier troops at the time of the Perpetual Peace, and had already postponed paying the field forces from time to time. Probably no other economies could have reduced expenditures enough. Whatever revenues remained were urgently needed to meet the immediate expenses of campaigns against the Ostrogoths and Persians.

At the beginning of 543, Khusrau collected a great army to invade Byzantine Armenia. To meet him, the generals who succeeded Belisarius and Buzes scraped together thirty thousand troops. But Khusrau gave up his expedition and returned to Ctesiphon when the plague again broke out in his army and one of his sons rebelled against him. On Justinian's orders the Byzantine generals used their forces to invade Persian Armenia. With no overall commander of unquestioned authority or ability, the Byzantines made a disorderly attack on a Persian fort and fell into a Persian ambush. They fled back to the empire, but the Persians were too few to pursue them.

In Italy the Byzantine command remained divided, and the soldiers were becoming ever more demoralized as they suffered more casualties and their pay fell further into arrears. After starving out Naples in early 543, Totila held most of Italy, while the Byzantines kept little more than the fortified towns of the north and center. Totila made largely successful efforts to win over the Italians, who were distressed by the length of the war and the depredations of the unpaid and poorly supplied Byzantine army. Unwilling to withdraw from Italy but unable to reinforce and supply it properly, Justinian decided to send Belisarius back as sole commander with such troops as could be spared. Meanwhile the plague reached Italy after spreading over the whole remainder of the empire.

Although in 544 the plague ended in Constantinople, it also abated enough in Persia to let Khusrau invade Byzantine Mesopotamia again. He besieged Edessa, demanding an immense sum that was refused. The Army of the East under its master of soldiers Martin thwarted repeated attempts to take the city. Even the long-unpaid frontier troops of Mesopotamia mounted an adequate defense of Dara under their talented duke John Troglita. Eventually Khusrau agreed to depart for the relatively moderate sum of thirty-six thousand nomismata. Weary of the war and weakened by the plague, both sides negotiated seriously for peace.

By 544, too late to stop the mission of Jacob Baradaeus, Justinian made another attempt to conciliate Monophysites. Among Monophysite complaints against the Council of Chalcedon were that it had seated two defenders of Nestorius, Theodoret of Cyrrhus and Ibas of Edessa, and had failed to condemn Nestorius's teacher Theodore of Mopsuestia, who had died before the council met. To answer this complaint, Justinian issued an edict with three chapters, one condemning Theodore and the other two condemning the pro-Nestorian writings of Theodoret and Ibas. Justinian expected Chalcedonians to approve this Edict of the Three Chapters, since the council had itself acknowledged that some of Theodore's works were Nestorian and had seated Theodoret and Ibas only after they had disowned Nestorius. Nevertheless, many Chalcedonians thought the edict dealt too harshly with three generally respected and long-dead theologians.

Even though the Chalcedonian patriarchs of Constantinople, Antioch, Jerusalem, and Alexandria reluctantly accepted the edict, it provoked angry protests from the churches of Italy and Africa, and Pope Vigilius refused to endorse it. This was a time when the empire especially needed the Africans' and Italians' goodwill. In Africa, the plague had struck the populous Byzantine prefecture while sparing the deserts and mountains of the Moors. The Byzantines were thus at a disadvantage when the Moors attacked in 543, enraged at a massacre of their chiefs by Sergius, nephew of the Byzantine commander Solomon. The next year Solomon died fighting the Moors and was succeeded by the unpopular and incompetent Sergius. Moors spread over the countryside, and demoralized Byzantine troops joined them.

That autumn Belisarius arrived in Ravenna with a mere four thousand reinforcements to find Italy mostly in the hands of Totila and his resurgent Ostrogoths and the Byzantine forces severely depleted. The general was also on uneasy terms with the emperor and empress, despite the recent betrothal of his daughter to Theodora's grandson.[16] At the time Belisarius took up his command, the Bulgars raided Illyricum, which was poorly defended since much of its army was still in Italy. When the Illyrian troops in Italy learned of the invasion of their homeland, they insisted on returning. Belisarius was left with utterly inadequate forces whose pay was long overdue. Some of his men deserted to Totila, who was starving out more and more walled cities.

Early in 545 the empire finally concluded a much needed five-year truce with Persia at the affordable price of 28,800 nomismata per year, all payable in advance. The truce exempted Lazica, which the Byzantines continued to claim but could scarcely hope to recover soon. This treaty and the dying down of the plague gave Justinian some hope of restoring the empire's solvency and sending reinforcements to Italy and Africa. He enacted new laws to regulate and record the taxes demanded and paid and to protect citizens against irregular requisitions by soldiers—doubtless a frequent problem with pay so far in arrears.

After the truce with Persia, the government seems simply to have canceled the pay of its frontier troops, including the arrears. In the East the border troops' modest allowances of five nomismata a year had seldom been paid since the Perpetual Peace of 532, and no border troops had received pay since the beginning of the plague in 541. Some had probably replaced field soldiers who had died of the disease. The government had ceased expecting much from the rest, and the almost 6 million nomismata that they were owed for the past four years could not be paid. Having learned to do without their pay for so long, most of them doubtless stayed where they were, continuing to defend their regions when necessary; but they had other professions and ceased to rank as regular soldiers. They had become for all practical purposes a militia.[17]

Although the pay of the field troops was also in arrears, the government seems to have continued tardy and partial payments, and in any case never repudiated its debts. Whenever a little more money was available, it went to provide reinforcements for Italy and Africa. In the spring of 545 Justinian sent some reinforcements to Africa under a new gen-

47. Mosaic of Justinian and his attendants, in the Church of San Vitale, probably of 544–45 but later reworked. The probable identifications, from left to right: six soldiers, Theodora's grandson Anastasius, Justinian's general Belisarius, Justinian, John the nephew of Vitalian (added later), Archbishop Maximian of Ravenna (later substituted for his predecessor Victor), and two deacons. Originally this mosaic and its companion (Fig. 48) probably commemorated the betrothal of Belisarius's daughter Joannina to Anastasius. (Photo: Soprintendenza per i Beni Ambientali e Architettonici, Ravenna)

eral, Areobindus. In the fall the emperor sent a larger army to Italy under John the nephew of Vitalian. But in sending these reinforcements the emperor, always fearful of revolts in the faraway West, again divided his commanders' authority. In Africa Areobindus shared the command with Sergius, and in Italy John resisted cooperating with Belisarius.

Without a unified command or back pay for the existing troops, the reinforcements for Italy and Africa did less good than they should have done. Another loss to the Moors in Africa persuaded Justinian to make Areobindus sole commander; but he was killed in a mutiny by his unpaid troops. Fortunately the mutineers, who wanted pay rather than responsibility for governing Africa, resumed their allegiance when their leader was assassinated in 546. In Italy, where Totila was besieging Rome,

48. Mosaic of Theodora and her attendants, probably of 544–45, in San Vitale. Probable identifications, from left to right: two eunuchs, Theodora, Belisarius's wife Antonina, Antonina's daughter Joannina, and five ladies-in-waiting. (Photo: Soprintendenza per i Beni Ambientali e Architettonici, Ravenna)

Belisarius planned to relieve the city by sailing into its port, while John marched overland from the south. But John busied himself with retaking southern Italy, and without his help Belisarius failed to break the siege. After the remaining citizens had starved or left, some of the garrison betrayed Rome, and the rest fled. At the end of 546 Totila occupied the almost deserted city.

That year the East was prostrated again by a disastrous harvest of the preceding autumn. As the government struggled to avoid starvation in Constantinople and Alexandria, it delayed the pay even of the armies in the Emperor's Presence. When their troops rioted, Justinian dismissed Peter Barsymes as prefect, ignoring Theodora's objections. Riots over the famine at Alexandria forced its patriarch Zoïlus to flee to the capital. In 547 Justinian had to suppress fighting between the Blues and Greens, probably for the first time since the Nika Revolt.

Despite the miserable state of the empire in general and Italy in par-

49. The Aurelian Walls of Rome, dating from the second century A.D. (Photo: Istituto Centrale per il Catalogo e la Documentazione, Rome)

ticular, the emperor disappointed Totila by refusing peace negotiations. Early in 547 the Ostrogothic king abandoned the empty city of Rome after making some gaps in its walls, and began retaking southern Italy. To the king's astonishment, Belisarius reoccupied Rome behind him, speedily restored its walls, and defended it against the Ostrogoths. Totila failed in attempts to dislodge Belisarius and to capture Belisarius's colleague John. Justinian managed to send the two struggling generals some two thousand reinforcements. The emperor could not afford even this much help for Africa, but he sent it a few troops and a fresh commander, John Troglita, who had recently shown exceptional ability as duke of Mesopotamia. John did what he could, fighting dramatic but indecisive battles with the Moors. Meanwhile the Slavs raided Illyricum as far south as Dyrrhachium. Thus the western wars dragged on, with the Byzantines neither winning nor losing.

By 548 the worst of the financial emergency was over. Early that year King Gubazes of Lazica, having found Persian protection oppressive, asked Justinian to restore the Byzantine protectorate. Since the emperor valued Lazica so much that he had excluded it from the truce of 545, he seized his chance, even amid so many pressing obligations. He sent the new master of soldiers for Armenia Dagistheus to Lazica with seven thousand men. Dagistheus and King Gubazes secured most of Lazica except for the fort of Petra, where they besieged the Persians.

In sending help to Lazica, Justinian did not neglect the West. That same spring he finally persuaded Pope Vigilius, whom he had summoned to Constantinople before the siege of Rome, to approve the Edict of the Three Chapters. In Africa John Troglita inflicted a crushing defeat on the Moors, ending their invasion. As peace returned to Africa, the emperor sent another two thousand men to Italy with the back pay demanded by the garrison of Rome. After his army's desertions and losses to the Goths and the plague, Belisarius still needed more men and money, and sent his wife Antonina to Constantinople to try to obtain them through her friendship with Theodora.

Before Antonina arrived, however, Theodora fell ill and died. At first Justinian's faithful collaborator, the empress had later prevented him from supporting capable subordinates and subverted his delicate plans to unite Monophysites and Chalcedonians. She gravely harmed church unity by allowing the mission of Jacob Baradaeus; probably she deepened the empire's financial crisis by bringing down John the Cappadocian; and she almost certainly prolonged the Ostrogothic war by plotting with Antonina against Belisarius. When Antonina appeared after Theodora's death, Justinian cut short her intrigues, which were aimed at strengthening her influence over her husband more than helping the war effort. The emperor simply recalled Belisarius, who left Italy early in 549 and retired from military service.

Apparently Justinian first assigned the Italian command to his cousin Germanus, but changed his mind when he discovered a conspiracy to make Germanus emperor. Rather than delay preparations while he investigated Germanus's guilt, the emperor transferred the command to Liberius, an elderly Italian who had served as praetorian prefect of Italy under Theoderic and more recently as prefect of Egypt.[18] Since Totila was occupied with besieging a strong garrison in Rome, Liberius seemed to have some time to prepare his expedition. Justinian's immediate concern was Lazica, where Dagistheus had defeated two Persian armies but failed to keep another from resupplying Petra. The emperor impatiently replaced Dagistheus with another elderly general, Bessas. In 550 a revolt broke out in Abasgia, a dependency of Lazica, that Bessas had to sup-

TABLE 5

The Dynasty of Justin I

Emperors are in capital letters and italics, with the years of their reigns marked "r." Other years are of births and deaths. Illegitimate descent is shown by a broken line.

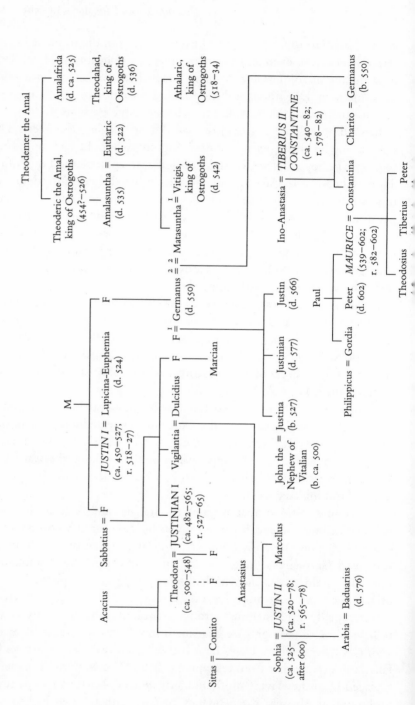

press before he could turn to Petra. With Abasgia and the rest of Lazica under control, Bessas finally subjected Petra to a strict siege.

Early in 550 soldiers in the garrison of Rome betrayed the city for the second time, again because they had not been paid. Having retaken most of Italy except for Ravenna and Ancona, Totila used his fleet to invade Sicily. Liberius hurried to the island with his half-prepared army, but he could only hold the towns against Totila, who plundered the countryside. Justinian realized that Liberius's expedition was inadequate, and now knew that Germanus bore no responsibility for the recent conspiracy. To show his confidence in his cousin, Justinian restored Germanus to the Italian command.

The emperor helped Germanus gather a large force, including new recruits and soldiers from the armies of Illyricum and Thrace. To improve his standing among the Ostrogoths, Germanus married Matasuntha, the granddaughter of Theoderic and widow of Vitigis. Germanus planned to march through Dalmatia to Italy, but had to delay his expedition when Slavic raiders invaded Dacia. They conveniently fled before him into Dalmatia, where he had already planned to march. But then Germanus died of disease, after a long career of frustrated promise. Without permission to proceed, his army wintered at Salona under the command of John the nephew of Vitalian.

From the fall of Antioch in 540 to the death of Germanus in 550 the empire had suffered repeated reverses, of which the plague was incomparably the worst. The program of reconquest, reform, and construction to which Justinian had committed the empire before the plague suddenly needed to be financed from greatly diminished resources. The resulting invasions, taxation, and reductions in spending aggravated the enormous suffering that the plague would have inflicted in any event. Some who lived through the catastrophe understandably condemned Justinian and his officers and officials.[19] In spite of everything, however, Justinian's government had staved off military and fiscal collapse until the plague ended and its ravages began to fade.

JUSTINIAN'S ACHIEVEMENTS

By 551 Justinian had collected enough men and money to invade Italy in overwhelming force. Africa was pacified. Although the truce with Persia had expired, both sides were observing it and negotiating a continuation of it, again excluding Lazica. Even Lazica was firmly in

Byzantine hands by early spring, when Bessas took Petra by assault and demolished its fortifications. The large Byzantine armies massing in Thrace and Illyricum were nearly ready to attack the empire's last two strong and active enemies, the Slavs raiding the northern Balkans and the Ostrogoths holding most of Italy.

For those commands Justinian chose somewhat curious commanders. He entrusted the campaign against the Slavs to Scholasticus, a palace eunuch without significant military experience. The choice for the Italian expedition fell on Narses, another palace eunuch, who had acquired his only important military experience while disobeying Belisarius and losing Milan in 539. Moreover, when appointed Narses seems to have been over seventy years old, like Justinian's other recent appointments Bessas and Liberius. Himself sixty-nine, Justinian wanted no more generals who were potential successors, like Belisarius, Germanus, or John the nephew of Vitalian. Once satisfied that no plotting would disrupt his campaigns, he gave his commanders full powers. Old age had not enfeebled Justinian himself, and he thought it quite compatible with military ability.

In the spring the Slavic raiders entered Thrace and defeated Scholasticus near Adrianople. But he regrouped his army and defeated them in turn, rescuing many of their captives and driving them back across the Danube. This demonstration of Byzantine power in the Balkans alarmed the neighboring Gepids. By summer they incited a horde of Kotrigur Huns from north of the Black Sea to raid Illyricum, preventing Narses from joining John at Salona. Rather than have Narses lose time and men fighting the Kotrigurs, Justinian paid for an attack on their homeland by the Utigur Huns and Crimean Goths. This forced the Kotrigurs out. When the Gepids encouraged another Slavic raid, the emperor cowed them by allying himself with their enemies to the north, the Lombards.

While John was waiting for Narses, he sent out ships to relieve the Byzantines besieged in Ancona, and not only broke the siege but destroyed the Ostrogoths' Adriatic fleet. Totila still had a fleet in the west, which was conquering Corsica and Sardinia; but he seems merely to have been hoping to persuade Justinian to make peace on acceptable terms. By fall the emperor rebuffed the last of Totila's many embassies. Narses joined John at Salona and prepared to invade Italy the next spring. He had perhaps twenty thousand men, ample supplies, and enough money to pay everything owed to the soldiers already in Italy.

When the way seemed clear for the success of the Italian expedition, the emperor received an unexpected embassy from Visigothic Spain.

Over the last three years two Visigothic kings had been murdered, while the third king, Agila, had lost Cordova to native Roman rebels. After the rebels sharply defeated Agila's attempt to retake the city, a Visigoth in nearby Seville also rebelled. This rebel, Athanagild, must have found Agila stronger than he expected, because he now asked for troops from the emperor.

Almost anyone but Justinian would have dismissed the idea out of hand. Spain was far away, and the empire had many other concerns and straitened resources. To be sure, the Italian expedition was provided for, and Justinian had just renewed his truce with the Persians until 556, again exempting Lazica. Nor could the emperor be sure of another such chance to extend his reconquests to Spain, the last Arian kingdom ruling a substantial orthodox population. Rather than let the opportunity pass, he chose Liberius, the aged general recently recalled from Sicily, to lead a small expeditionary force. It sailed for Spain in the spring of 552.

The same spring Narses marched from Dalmatia to Italy. He advanced somewhat slowly, cautious of the Franks, whom Totila had allowed to occupy much of the Po valley, and probably also of the Gepids, who were at war with the empire's Lombard allies nearby. But the Lombards inflicted a severe defeat on the Gepids, and Narses avoided the Franks by keeping close to the coast. He reached Ravenna, gathered more troops there, passed by the Goths who held Rimini, and marched toward Rome. In June he met Totila and his army at Busta Gallorum in the Apennines, where both sides readied themselves for a decisive battle.

Totila attacked first, making a cavalry charge against Narses' infantry. Harried by Byzantine archers, the Goths failed to break the Byzantine line. After heavy losses, the Goths' cavalry fled, trampling their infantry as they did so. Totila himself was fatally wounded. Of his soldiers, who included many Byzantine deserters, six thousand died in combat and many others were killed after they surrendered.[20] The few Goths who survived the battle elected one of their number, Teïas, as Totila's successor. Although some other Ostrogoths and their western fleet remained in various parts of Italy, they were far fewer than the Byzantine forces.

Continuing his progress, Narses stormed Rome, which the Gothic garrison was too small to hold. Then he turned south and besieged Cumae, where the Goths kept their treasury. As Gothic garrisons began to surrender, Teïas lashed out in despair. He killed his Roman hostages, including many senators, and massed his remaining troops for an attempt to relieve Cumae. In October Narses and the Byzantines trapped this force on a mountain in Campania, Mons Lactarius. After exhausting their provisions, Teïas and his men tried to break out of the trap. In two days of desperate fighting, the king and many of his men died. Finally Narses agreed to let the rest depart in return for a promise to leave Italy. He had reduced the Ostrogoths to an insignificant remnant and taken all their territory but Cumae, much of Tuscany, and the Po valley, which was divided between Goths and Franks. The remaining Ostrogoths, without venturing to elect another king, continued resistance only in the hope of help from the Frankish Kingdom.

Meanwhile Liberius and his troops had landed in Spain, proceeded to Seville, and joined their Visigothic ally Athanagild. When King Agila marched against them, they defeated him soundly. Liberius and Athanagild seem to have made common cause with the Roman rebels of Cordova and begun to conquer the rest of Spain. Certainly Liberius's expedition weakened Agila and strengthened the rebels. While Liberius himself returned to Constantinople, the Byzantine force stayed behind to support Athanagild. To reconquer Spain for the empire clearly required more men, but Justinian had gained a base for future operations.

Although the emperor had salvaged his reconquests, his efforts to reunite the Church seemed past saving. The Monophysite missionary Jacob Baradaeus had begun consecrating not merely priests but bishops. Disregarding Theodosius, the patriarch of Alexandria in exile at Constantinople, Jacob went to Egypt itself and found the two bishops he needed for episcopal consecrations. With them he consecrated two new bishops, for Tarsus in Cilicia and Seleucia in Isauria, with whose help he could consecrate as many more as he wished. He could now establish a Monophysite hierarchy to go with his clergy and create a complete schismatic church. Far from reconciling Monophysites and Chalcedonians, Justinian's Edict of the Three Chapters had nearly caused another schism. So many western bishops rejected it that Pope Vigilius, still detained at Constantinople, withdrew his acceptance.

The exasperated emperor invoked the ultimate remedy, summoning an ecumenical council to Constantinople in the spring of 553. Almost all the bishops who attended were from the eastern patriarchates, though a few African bishops came. Pope Vigilius stayed away rather than offend either the western hierarchy or Justinian. Endorsing the emperor's edict, the council accepted Chalcedon but condemned Theodore of Mopsuestia and the pro-Nestorian writings of Theodoret of Cyrrhus and Ibas of Edessa. At first the pope refused to approve the council's decisions, mainly on the procedural ground that the Church ought not to condemn anyone who, like Theodore, had died uncondemned. Before the end of the year, however, Vigilius gave in and accepted the council.

In Italy, as Narses finished the reconquest of Tuscany and starved out Cumae, a large force of Alamanni and Franks arrived to his north, in the region still held by Franks and Ostrogoths. These new arrivals were more interested in plunder than conquest, and in 554 they divided into two bands to raid the countryside. One of these plundered the whole east coast of Italy, then lost most of their booty to a Byzantine force and many of their men to disease. The other band raided the whole west coast, only to be practically annihilated by Narses near Capua. Narses had finished retaking everything south of the Po, except for one fort that fell the next spring. Only a few bedraggled Ostrogoths and Franks remained in the north. Justinian counted Italy as conquered, and issued an edict regulating its administration. His choice of Narses may have seemed strange when it was made, but it had been amply justified by the outcome.

Turning to Spain, the emperor apparently sent reinforcements that landed at Cartagena late in 554. By the next March their westward advance to meet their allies seems to have frightened the loyalist Visigoths into killing King Agila and proclaiming his rival Athanagild. After becoming king, Athanagild tried to thank and dismiss Justinian's soldiers. However, no doubt following the emperor's orders, they refused to leave or submit to Athanagild, and they were joined by the Romans of Cordova who had rebelled against Agila in the first place. Thus the Visigoths lost southern Spain to a combination of their former Roman subjects and the imperial troops, who held about a fifth of the peninsula.[21]

The emperor's only other major war was in Lazica, which the Persians persisted in attacking. In 555 the country's king Gubazes quarreled with the Byzantine generals and obtained the recall of Bessas. But Bessas's successor Martin also fell out with Gubazes, and had him assassinated with the emperor's permission. Justinian mollified the outraged Lazicans by replacing the late king with his younger brother Tzathes, and finally by recalling Martin in 557. That year the Persians renewed the truce again, this time without receiving tribute or excluding Lazica, where they kept only a toehold. Negotiations continued for a definitive peace treaty.

The relative calm that the empire now enjoyed was soon spoiled by a recurrence of the bubonic plague, early in 558. The disease, which had never entirely disappeared, broke out again in the eastern part of the em-

50. Interior of Saint Sophia, showing the dome and apse. (Photo: Dumbarton Oaks, Washington, D.C., copyright 1996)

pire and eventually spread to the western. The outbreak lasted six months in Constantinople. Though less acute than the earlier epidemic, it was more than enough to roll back any recovery of the population or state revenues. Peter Barsymes, reappointed praetorian prefect by 555, had to rely on his old talents for economy and extortion, including forced loans from the rich. Military pay fell behind once more. Justinian never found the money and men to complete the conquest of Spain from the Visigoths, with whom he finally made peace. A collapse of the dome of Saint Sophia in 558 took almost five years to repair, though in better times the entire church had been built in six.

Concluding that the empire was vulnerable, early the next year the Kotrigur Huns joined the Bulgars and Slavs in raiding the Balkans. Helped by the return of the Army of Illyricum from Italy, the Byzantine forces halted one band of the raiders in central Greece and drove another from southern Thrace. A third band, however, consisting of seven thousand men under the Kotrigur chief Zabergan, defeated a Byzantine army led by the same Sergius who had almost lost Africa to the Moors fifteen years before. The incapable general was himself among the captives.

Zabergan headed for Constantinople, where only the emperor's bodyguard remained to mount a defense. Justinian gave the command to Belisarius, who had been retired for ten years. Improvising an army of guardsmen, veterans, and volunteers, the great commander ambushed some of the raiders. Justinian then assumed the official command himself, though he simply paid Zabergan to release his prisoners and retreat. After the Kotrigurs withdrew, the emperor reentered Constantinople in a triumphal procession. He had won no military victory in person, but he could justly celebrate both the containment of the raiders and the empire's recovery from many other afflictions.

To avoid further Kotrigur raids, Justinian again paid the Utigurs to attack them, starting a war that proved to be the ruin of both tribes. In 561 he bought off still another coalition of Huns, the Avars, who had asked him for lands in northern Thrace. The same year Narses finished pacifying Italy by defeating some Franks and a few rebellious Ostrogoths at Verona.[22] Finally Justinian and Khusrau of Persia concluded a treaty for a peace of fifty years. Under its terms the Byzantines agreed to pay the Persians a modest annual subsidy of thirty thousand nomismata and the Persians accepted a Byzantine protectorate over all of Lazica.

The next few years were comparatively peaceful. In the spring of 562 the Bulgars made a brief raid on Thrace. The next autumn Justinian discovered and suppressed a plot against him, probably a consequence of Peter Barsymes' compulsory loans from the aristocracy. In 563 some Moors revolted in Africa, but they were quickly subdued by Justinian's nephew Marcian. Periodically the Blues and Greens rioted and fought each other. Once they made a disturbance serious enough to require police action by the emperor's nephew Justin.

The aged emperor's greatest frustration was his failure to bring Chalcedonians and Monophysites together. For a time many western bishops resisted accepting the Second Council of Constantinople as ecumenical, despite the grudging endorsement of Pope Vigilius and his successors Pelagius and John III. Eventually all but a few northern Italians gave up. By having a general council condemn a theologian and writings everyone admitted were pro-Nestorian, Justinian had attacked a minor issue with so much force that his final victory was certain. By the same token, however, the concession he had gained was too small to persuade Monophysites to abandon their schismatic church.

Seeing that his council was not enough, Justinian looked for some concession that would be compatible with the Council of Chalcedon but might still satisfy the Monophysites. In desperation he considered the formulation of the extreme Monophysite Julian of Halicarnassus that Christ's body was by nature incapable of suffering and sin, a doctrine known as Aphthartodocetism. Somehow the emperor convinced himself that this was compatible with Christ's having a fully human nature, and that the incongruous combination of both beliefs would have broad appeal. At the beginning of 565 he endorsed both Aphthartodocetism and Chalcedon in an edict so lacking in his usual acumen as to suggest a touch of senility.

Since even most Monophysites regarded Aphthartodocetism as an excessive limitation of Christ's humanity, Chalcedonians naturally opposed the edict. The patriarch of Constantinople Eutychius refused to accept it and was deposed. His replacement John III Scholasticus cleverly declared that he would not accept the edict until the other patriarchs approved it. Although none of them did so, they and John managed to avoid deposition for several months, until Justinian died, at the age of eighty-three, in November of 565.

Justinian's long and eventful reign can only be judged fairly by distinguishing the effects of his rule from those of the bubonic plague. At the time the plague appeared, Justinian had added more land to the empire

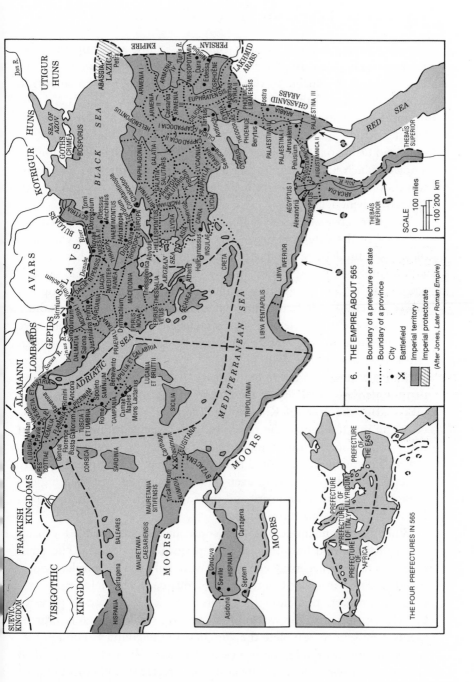

6. THE EMPIRE ABOUT 565

– · – Boundary of a prefecture or state
– – – Boundary of a province
· · · · Boundary of a province
● City
✕ Battlefield
▓ Imperial territory
▨ Imperial protectorate

(After Jones, *Later Roman Empire*)

SCALE
0   100 miles
0 100 200 km

THE FOUR PREFECTURES IN 565

PREFECTURE OF THE EAST

PREFECTURE OF ILLYRICUM

PREFECTURE OF ITALY

PREFECTURE OF AFRICA

RED SEA

MEDITERRANEAN SEA

BLACK SEA

ADRIATIC SEA

AEGEAN SEA

SEA OF AZOV

PERSIAN EMPIRE

LAKHMID ARABS

GHASSANID ARABS

UTIGUR HUNS

KOTRIGUR HUNS

HUNS

AVARS

SLAVS

GEPIDS

LOMBARDS

ALAMANNI

FRANKISH KINGDOMS

VISIGOTHIC KINGDOM

SUEVIC KINGDOM

BULGARS

GOTHS OF THE CRIMEA

BOSPORUS

MOORS

HISPANIA

Cordova
Seville
Asidona
Cartagena
Septem

Don R.

than any emperor but Trajan or Augustus. Those two imperial conquerors had begun with greater resources than Justinian's, and their conquests were less valuable to the empire than Justinian's gains in Africa, Italy, Dalmatia, and the Crimea. The treasuries of the Vandals and Ostrogoths by themselves probably covered the expense of taking and defending Africa and Italy up to 541. Under normal conditions Africa, Italy, and Dalmatia should have been easier to defend than Illyricum and Thrace, which had been in the eastern empire from the start. Justinian's stupendous reconquests therefore appeared affordable, defensible, and altogether beneficial.

No ruler, no matter how wise, could possibly have anticipated the outbreak of the plague between 541 and 544. Comparisons with medieval and modern recurrences of the same disease show that the loss of a quarter of the population in one outbreak is a reasonable guess.[23] Those deaths and the resulting economic and administrative disruption must have reduced state revenues by at least a quarter for the indefinite future, especially because the disease recurred. The plague would have been disastrous for the empire whenever it struck, with or without an effort to reconquer the West.

In dispatching his western expeditions, Justinian had assumed the risk that the Persians might attack the East in the meantime, and they did so in 540. But the costs of Khusrau's raiding in Syria and Mesopotamia were still much less than the revenues to be expected from the western conquests, which in turn could subsidize the defense of the East in the future. The reconquests should have strengthened the empire in purely military and economic terms, even without regard for the resulting extension of Byzantine authority and the suppression of barbarian Arianism that meant so much to Justinian.

When the plague broke out, with consequences incalculable for many years, Justinian and his administrators performed prudently. The main casualties of their necessary economies were Italy and the border troops, which suffered in order to prevent the collapse of the field armies defending the East. But enough soldiers were kept in Italy to preserve bases there, and once the worst difficulties were over enough reinforcements were sent to complete the conquest of the country. Though Justinian's intervention in Spain in 552 may appear overbold, by 555 it had won a rich province at very little cost. The empire would probably have reconquered the whole peninsula if the plague's recurrence in 558 had not prevented the dispatch of a few thousand more men.

Despite the plague, Justinian's reign was not utterly disastrous. In the end he lost no land and reconquered every territory his armies attempted to take. He left a more efficient administration, and his striking the border troops from the payroll brought a vital reduction in expenses without much harm to the empire's security. Justinian even left a reserve of some size in the treasury. His only clear failure was his effort to bring Monophysites back into the official church. Yet the open schism did not begin until Theodora interfered while he was incapacitated by the plague. In any case, Justinian made a more thoughtful attempt to resolve this maddening issue than any of his predecessors since the Council of Chalcedon.

Thus the reconquests did little to aggravate the effects of the plague, and even compensated for them somewhat by adding new land and people to tax. Nonetheless, the plague did terrible and lasting damage. To maintain the expanded empire with diminished resources, which each recurrence of the disease would diminish further, required ability not much inferior to that of Justinian and his brilliant ministers and generals. After almost fifty years of Justinian's effective control, through no fault of his, the empire had lost most of its capacity to expand, and some of its ability to defend itself.

The Danger of Overextension, 565–610

Outwardly glorious though the long reign of Justinian had been, few seem to have regretted its passing. The aristocracy and Justinian had never liked each other, and he had made himself increasingly obnoxious to ecclesiastics. The army resented his delaying its pay and supplies. Ordinary subjects blamed the emperor with some reason for high taxation, and with less reason for the general impoverishment caused by the plague. Justinian's great reconquests had benefited the empire and its subjects much less than might have been expected. Consequently Justinian's successors and their subjects tended to have expectations of better times, which led to initial extravagance and subsequent disappointment.

Although the suspicious old emperor had named no heir before he was on his deathbed, he had shown a good deal of favor to his nephew Justin, the husband of Theodora's niece Sophia. For more than fourteen years Justin had been curopalates, supervisor of the palace, an honorific office that he turned into an important one. Perhaps his key move was to have had his friend Tiberius promoted to count of the Excubitors. Since Belisarius had died a few months before Justinian, the only other likely heir was another Justin, son of Justinian's cousin Germanus, who at the emperor's death was away in Illyricum serving as its master of soldiers. With the Excubitors on Justin's side, the senators willingly accepted a chamberlain's story that the dying Justinian had designated his nephew Justin, and he was crowned as Justin II.

JUSTIN II'S OVERCONFIDENCE

At his accession Justin was about forty-five, with a little administrative experience and middling talent for governing. Though he seems to have realized that he was less gifted than his predecessor, Justin tried to imitate Justinian's boldness without practicing the late emperor's patience and diligence. Like most of those around him, Justin evidently underestimated how hard to rule the empire had become. His self-assured empress Sophia, whose connection with Theodora's family had helped her husband's career, aspired to have at least as much influence as Theodora had exercised over Justinian, but had even less understanding of the empire's difficulties than Justin.

At the outset of his reign, Justin won fulsome praise from his courtiers and other Constantinopolitans for departing from some of his predecessor's measures. Justin quietly abandoned Justinian's Aphthartodocetism and stopped Justinian's subsidies to the Avars, which many Byzantines found humiliating. He dispelled the government's reputation for meanness by giving large donatives to the people and promptly repaying the loans that Justinian had forced the rich to make to the state. Justin also canceled all arrears of taxation up to 560. His power seemed fairly secure, at least after he executed two senators and Germanus's son Justin on dubious charges of conspiracy in 567.

New dissension among the Monophysites encouraged Justin to make his own bid to win some of them over. Refusal to distinguish Christ's person from his nature had finally led some radical Monophysites to assert that the Trinity had not only three persons but three natures. Other Monophysites, led by the long-exiled patriarch of Alexandria Theodosius, denounced this doctrine as Tritheism, or belief in three gods, and denied that three persons of God implied three natures. This denial, however, logically undermined the main Monophysite objection to Chalcedon: that the Chalcedonian belief in two natures of Christ implied a belief in two persons.

As the Monophysites reargued their position, the emperor opened amicable negotiations with Theodosius before the patriarch died in mid-566. Next Justin and his patriarch John Scholasticus organized theological discussions at Constantinople that brought together Chalcedonians, Tritheists, and other Monophysites, including the Monophysite leader Jacob Baradaeus. These meetings continued into 567, when Justin issued an edict that, without mentioning Chalcedon, affirmed the points on

51. Silver votive cross of Justin II (r. 565–78), Vatican Treasury. Justin is in the medallion at left, and his empress Sophia in the medallion at right. (Photo: Vatican Treasury)

which all could agree. Although many Syrian Monophysite monks rejected this edict at a conference at Callinicum, Jacob Baradaeus and his Monophysite hierarchy continued to seek a compromise.

Meanwhile Justin's refusal to subsidize the Avars had no immediately adverse consequences. Rather than attack Byzantine territory, the Avars made a pact with the Lombards, the empire's traditional allies, to attack the Gepids, its traditional enemies. Even though the terrified Gepids tried to buy Byzantine help by ceding the strategic city of Sirmium, Justin let them be destroyed by the Lombards and Avars. While the Avars occupied most of the Gepids' lands, the Byzantines gained possession of both the Gepids' treasury and Sirmium, which the Avars attacked in vain.

Nevertheless, the struggle left the Avars much more dangerous neighbors than the Gepids had been, and they became the most formidable power on the Danube since the departure of the Ostrogoths. The Avars soon began an inconclusive war with the Byzantines, which Justin sent his count of the Excubitors Tiberius to fight. When the Lombards' king

Alboin understood how powerful the Avars had become, he decided to preserve his people's independence by migrating. Unluckily for the empire, he chose northern Italy as the Lombards' new home.

Now, almost simultaneously, Justinian's reconquests in Spain, Italy, and Africa came under attack, before they had properly recovered from their previous wars and outbreaks of the plague. In 567 the Visigothic king Athanagild attacked Seville and Cordova in the Byzantine Province of Spain. The next spring, Alboin led his Lombards and some other Germans into Italy, where Justin had just dismissed Justinian's old general Narses. Before winter they occupied Venetia except for the coast, and in 569 they took most of Liguria, apart from Pavia. The same year the Moorish king Garmul attacked Byzantine Africa, killing the African prefect Theodore.

During these attacks the West received no significant military or financial help from Justin, who was trying to economize whenever possible. After and perhaps because of his initial burst of munificence, Justin began a sustained effort to increase the reserve in the treasury. Though he reluctantly paid the Persians their subsidy under their treaty, he appears to have neglected the eastern armies.[1] In 569 he introduced new taxes on wine and bread, which won him a reputation for greed. He also tried to restore Justinian's ban of 535 on selling governorships, hoping that reducing corruption would save more money than the government gained from the sales.

In 571 the emperor obtained advance approval from Jacob Baradaeus and other Monophysite bishops for an edict of union. This edict equated the doctrine that Christ had one nature that was both divine and human (that is, Severan Monophysitism) with the doctrine that Christ had both divine and human natures that were united (that is, Chalcedonian orthodoxy). Thus, in a momentary triumph of common sense, Justin's Chalcedonians and Jacob's Monophysites admitted that they held the same beliefs and merely expressed them differently. On the edict's promulgation Jacob and his bishops accepted communion from the patriarch John Scholasticus.

However, because the edict implicitly endorsed the Council of Chalcedon, the Monophysite bishops failed to persuade their outraged followers to accept it. The bishops hastily withdrew their own approval to maintain their authority. Feeling betrayed, the emperor jailed as many of the bishops as he could seize, outlawed Monophysitism again, and abandoned his effort at reconciliation. He seems to have learned little from the example of his uncle Justinian, who had patiently continued negotiations with the Monophysites after worse setbacks than this.

Again unlike Justinian, Justin failed to lend his western armies even belated and partial support. From 571 to 572 the Lombards overran a large part of the Italian countryside, taking not just Pavia but Spoleto and Benevento, which formed a detached portion of the Lombard Kingdom to the south. During the same two years, Garmul's Moors defeated and killed two successive masters of soldiers for Africa. Then the new Visigothic king Leovigild attacked the northwestern part of the empire's Spanish province, taking Asidona by treachery and Cordova by surprise. These wars, along with a recurrence of the plague, indefinitely postponed the time when Byzantine Italy, Africa, and Spain could be real assets to the empire.

Rather than send eastern troops to the West, the emperor chose to attack Persia, with which Justinian and nearly all his predecessors had tried to keep the peace. Justin listened to appeals from the Armenians under Persian rule, who were plotting rebellion, and from the Turks of Central Asia, who were already raiding northern Persia. To prepare for the war, he ended his increasingly troublesome skirmishes with the Avars, probably by giving them the gifts he had refused them at the beginning of his reign. The Persian war began when the Armenians killed their Persian governor and revolted early in 572. Justin took them under Byzantine protection, stopped paying subsidies to the Persians, and curtly dismissed a negotiator sent by the aged king Khusrau.

The emperor named his cousin Marcian chief commander against the Persians and master of soldiers for the East. Marcian helped the Armenian rebels expel the Persians and sent troops to raid Arzanene, the Persian province just south of Armenia. In spring 573, Marcian invaded Persian Mesopotamia and defeated its local forces, but this was not enough to satisfy the impatient emperor. While Marcian was besieging Nisibis he received word that Justin had dismissed him, followed quickly by a report that Khusrau was arriving with a large army. The Byzantines fled in disorder. A Persian detachment raided Syria and sacked Apamea, and the Persian king laid siege to the border city of Dara. Since the Byzantine army never came to the city's defense, Khusrau took Dara by assault in November, capturing the main Byzantine stronghold on the Persian frontier.

Justin was so thunderstruck at this loss, and so conscious of his responsibility for it, that his mind gave way. As the emperor's attendants

52. The ruins of Dara in Mesopotamia. (Photo: C. Mango, Dumbarton Oaks, Washington, D.C., copyright 1996)

restrained him from jumping out of windows and calmed him by pulling him around in a little wagon, the empress turned for advice to her husband's friend Tiberius. During the emperor's manifest insanity, she and Tiberius took control of an empire threatened by Persians and western barbarians, and by another great outbreak of plague in the East. With pardonable exaggeration, contemporaries blamed Justin's arrogance and parsimony for leading the empire to disaster.

TIBERIUS'S OVERSPENDING

Tiberius and Sophia drew on Justin's large reserve to pay the Persians forty-five thousand nomismata for a one-year truce that excluded Armenia. Late in 574 Justin became lucid enough that Sophia could persuade him to appoint Tiberius as Caesar. The plague obligingly abated the day after Tiberius's appointment. At the time Tiberius was probably in his middle thirties. Since Justin was plainly not going to make a sufficient recovery to take up the burdens of office again, Tiberius became the real ruler of the empire. Like Justinian and Justins I and II, the new Caesar came from the Latin-speaking part of the Balkans. He mainly owed his promotion ahead of the mad emperor's relatives to the empress Sophia, though Justin too was an old friend of his. Their preference for him was justified by Tiberius's military abilities, but the Caesar was less gifted as an administrator.

Tiberius thought Justin's reserve in the treasury was too big, and set about using it to defend the frontiers and win for himself the popularity that Justin had lost. The Caesar accordingly gave lavish donatives, and abolished Justin's taxes on wine and bread. He confirmed Justin's ban on the sale of governorships, which may have been ineffective but was not unpopular. Like Justin, Tiberius appeased the Avars. He agreed to pay them a liberal eighty thousand nomismata a year for an alliance that would defend the Danube frontier and allow Byzantine troops stationed there to be sent against the Persians.

In 575 the Caesar began transferring soldiers from the armies of Illyricum and Thrace to the East, and offering large bounties to recruit more Byzantines and barbarians from as far away as the Rhine. Since he expected that these forces would soon allow him to defeat the Persians, he refused a Persian offer to renew the truce for five years. He settled on three years for thirty thousand nomismata apiece, again excluding Armenia. During this respite Tiberius even sent Italy reinforcements, also probably drawn from the Illyrian and Thracian armies, under Justin's son-in-law Baduarius. The Lombards looked vulnerable, since they had split into independent bands after the murder of their king Alboin and his successor Cleph, and in 576 Baduarius brought them to battle. But he lost both the engagement and his life, and the victorious Lombards conquered still more territory.

Tiberius could spare no more troops for Italy, because Khusrau had struck at Armenia, where no truce prevailed. Quickly reclaiming his rebellious Armenian possessions, the Persian king advanced into the Armenian provinces of the empire. He sacked Sebastea and Melitene; but he was shadowed by the Byzantine commander Justinian, the younger son of Germanus. Justinian finally forced the Persians back across the Euphrates, in which many of them drowned, and over the winter the Byzantines invaded Persian territory and raided Atropatene.[2] In summer 577, however, the Persians defeated Justinian in Persian Armenia. Thus the Byzantines, though they had recovered somewhat, remained weaker than the Persians. Then Justinian died, with the truce about to expire the next year.

Tiberius promoted his capable count of the Excubitors Maurice to replace Justinian as marshal of the eastern armies, including the reinforcements gathered during the truce. These consisted of large parts of the armies of Illyricum and Thrace, along with fifteen thousand new barbarian and Byzantine recruits. The recruits were no temporary mercenaries, but formed a permanent company known as the Federates, attached to the Army of the East. The addition of the Federates alone increased the regular armies on the eastern frontier by almost half.[3]

During his preparations to fight the Persians, Tiberius avoided other conflicts. When the patriarch John died, the Caesar gratified Chalcedonians by restoring the patriarch Eutychius, deposed by Justinian for resisting Aphthartodocetism. But Tiberius also accorded Monophysites toleration, which they used to quarrel among themselves after the death of Jacob Baradaeus in 578. Unable to spare troops to stop the Lombard advance in Italy, Tiberius sent more than two hundred thousand nomismata to buy the allegiance of some Lombard dukes and prevent them from electing another king. When the Slavs raided Illyricum, Tiberius used the few Byzantine forces in the area to ferry his Avar allies across the Danube. There they raided the raiders' homeland and freed some Byzantine captives.[4]

In the spring of 578, shortly before the three-year truce was up, the Persians broke it by raiding Byzantine Mesopotamia. The Byzantine general Maurice retaliated by invading Persian Arzanene. He took and garrisoned the stronghold of Aphumon, then turned south and sacked Singara in Persian Mesopotamia. Maurice's campaign showed that Tiberius had succeeded in shifting the military balance in the Byzantines' favor. Although Justin II died in late 578 without recovering from the shock of losing Dara, Maurice's victories are said to have shaken the aged Khusrau almost as badly. The Persian king died early the next year, defeated after so many victories.

Thus Tiberius became emperor in name as well as fact, celebrating characteristically by remitting a quarter of the taxes in each of the next four years.[5] Now that the empress Sophia was free of Justin but also out of office, she persuaded the patriarch Eutychius to suggest that Tiberius marry her. But Tiberius politely declined the suggestion, which would have meant divorcing his wife, and deftly frustrated Sophia's attempt to overthrow him.[6] By this time the new emperor was quite popular because of his openhandedness and success against the Persians.

His success, however incomplete, let him give some attention to the West. In 579 he sent Italy more money and a few reinforcements, which perhaps retook Classis, the port of Ravenna briefly occupied by the Lombards. The same year he aided Byzantine Spain by concluding an alliance with the Visigothic prince Hermenegild, who had converted to orthodoxy and was rebelling against his Arian father Leovigild. Meanwhile, with or without Tiberius's help, the master of soldiers for Africa Gennadius attacked the Moors and defeated and killed their king Garmul, pacifying Africa once more.

Even as matters improved in the West, they deteriorated in the East. The Avars, noticing that Tiberius had stripped the Balkans of troops, first tried to extort Sirmium from the Byzantines, then besieged it in 579. During this siege, the Slavs started an invasion of Thrace, Macedonia, and Greece that began to resemble a permanent migration. Doubtless aware of the empire's troubles in the Balkans, the new Persian king Hurmazd IV refused Tiberius's offer to make peace if the Persians gave up Dara in return for Byzantium's holdings in Iberia, Persian Armenia, and Arzanene. Meanwhile the fifty thousand Byzantine soldiers in the East were becoming difficult to pay, and threatened mutiny when their pay was overdue.[7]

The Byzantine commander Maurice responded with an offensive. In 580 he raided far beyond the Tigris, and the next year he ordered an attack on Persian Armenia and marched down the Euphrates almost to the Persian capital at Ctesiphon. He was forced to retreat, however, when a Persian army behind him raided Byzantine Mesopotamia, apparently with the connivance of the empire's supposed allies, the Ghassanid Arabs. Maurice indignantly arrested the Ghassanid king for failing to defend Mesopotamia. But by doing so he broke the empire's alliance with the Ghassanids and crippled their kingdom, exposing the eastern frontier more than ever.

As long as the Persian war dragged on, Byzantium was unable to mount a proper defense against the Avars. In early 582 Tiberius agreed to pay them the accumulated subsidies that he had withheld during the war and to cede Sirmium, after evacuating its defenders and inhabitants. This did nothing to stop the Slavs in Greece, who seem to have reached Athens around this time.[8] But the eastern frontier had priority. That June the Persians, who were raiding Byzantine Mesopotamia again, suffered a sharp defeat near the city of Constantina, lost their commander, and retreated to Dara. Maurice did not follow up the Byzantine victory, however, because he had to hurry to Constantinople.

There Tiberius lay mortally ill. Having no son, the emperor named two heirs: Maurice and Germanus, the posthumous son of Justinian's cousin Germanus. Each of them received the title of Caesar and was betrothed to one of Tiberius's two daughters. Tiberius seems to have meant to divide the empire as in 395, making Maurice emperor of the East and Germanus emperor of the West. Though the West certainly needed attention, it also needed substantial reinforcements. Perhaps Germanus declined to assume the burden of its defense without assured help from the East; or perhaps Tiberius decided at the last moment that his plan was impractical. In any case, the day before his death, he had only Maurice crowned Augustus. Tiberius died in August, leaving the empire a little stronger but considerably poorer.

MAURICE'S RETRENCHMENT

So, at the age of forty-three, Maurice became sole emperor and the husband of Tiberius's daughter Constantina. He had been born in Cappadocia, allegedly into a family of Italian origin. But he must have been a native speaker of Greek, unlike previous emperors since Anastasius. Maurice was well educated, having begun his career as a notary, and he had been a high-ranking officer since Tiberius had appointed him count of the Excubitors in 574. His military skills were unquestionable. Utterly honest and upright, he possessed a resolve that was occasionally indistinguishable from rigidity.

Although his previous victories in the East had been spectacular, Maurice had won them with a force that probably represented most of the empire's field armies from Illyricum east, plus the new company of the Federates. As emperor he found that he had one major army and three major wars to fight. His margin of superiority over the Persians was too

53. Maurice (r. 582–602). Fifteenth-century miniature from the Modena manuscript of the chronicle of John Zonaras (Mutinensis graecus 122), one of a series of portraits of Byzantine emperors in the margins that seem to be based on much earlier models. (Photo: Biblioteca Estense, Modena)

slim to let him transfer enough soldiers to expel the Lombards from Italy or the Slavs from the Balkans. Now that Tiberius had spent practically all of Justin II's gold reserve, and increased the cost of the army by recruiting the Federates, Maurice had to be much thriftier than his predecessor.

What he needed most was to force an early peace with the Persians. As eastern commander he named the former master of soldiers for Armenia John Mystacon ("the Mustached"), who apparently had the mission of completing the conquest of Arzanene. From 582 to 583 John at least secured the Byzantines' hold on the fort of Aphumon, but his progress was slowed by the rugged terrain. Maurice could not afford to keep so many troops from the Balkans indefinitely on the eastern frontier.

In spring 583 the Avars demanded an increase in their subsidy from eighty thousand to one hundred thousand nomismata. Fearing that easy acquiescence would encourage further extortion, Maurice refused. The Avars therefore invaded the empire. After capturing Singidunum and Viminacium, across the Danube from Sirmium, they raided all the way to Anchialus on the Black Sea, where they spent the winter. By the spring of 584 the emperor agreed to the increase in the Avars' subsidy, in return for their giving back the cities they had taken. Although the Slavs remained at large in the Balkans, that summer they were defeated near the Long Walls by Comentiolus, a talented junior officer leading an improvised force.

In the West Maurice tried to use the Franks to fight the Lombards in Italy, while withdrawing Byzantine support for the faltering rebellion in the Visigothic Kingdom. When the Visigothic revolt ended in early 584 with the capture of the pretender Hermenegild, Hermenegild's wife Ingund and her son escaped to the imperial province of Spain. The Byzantines used their custody of Ingund and a subsidy of fifty thousand nomismata to induce Ingund's brother, the Frankish king Childebert II, to attack the Lombards.[9] He led an expedition into northern Italy and defeated the disorganized Lombard dukes. Seeing their danger, the dukes elected a new king, Authari, to lead their defense.

After John Mystacon failed to win a quick victory in the East, Maurice gave the eastern command to his brother-in-law Philippicus. The new commander pursued fruitless negotiations with the Persians and recruited more soldiers, probably to bring the eastern armies up to strength before he had to send some troops back to the Balkans. In fall 584 Philippicus raided Persian Mesopotamia, and the next year Arzanene; but most of one of the armies in the Emperor's Presence was back in the

Balkans by 585, when Comentiolus became its commander. He used it to defeat the Slavs northwest of Adrianople, expelling them from Thrace. The Franks invaded Lombard Italy again, but lost to the reunited Lombards. The master of soldiers for Italy, now usually called the exarch, admitted failure and made a three-year truce with King Authari.

The Persians, doubtless hoping to exploit Maurice's transfer of troops from the East, prolonged negotiations, and in spring 586 raided across the frontier. Philippicus defeated them smartly near Dara. He resumed campaigning in Arzanene, with mixed success, and sent a raiding party up and down the northern Tigris valley. Yet King Hurmazd would not admit defeat, and his patience seemed justified by events in autumn 586. The Slavs attacked Thessalonica, which was suffering from both plague and famine, and the Avars suddenly broke their treaty and swept east along the southern bank of the Danube. They took most of the remaining frontier towns, and wintered in the Dobrudja.

After years of having to neglect the Balkans, Byzantium seemed about to lose control of almost the whole peninsula. The emperor summoned reinforcements from Armenia and tried to recruit more troops. In the spring of 587 Comentiolus led ten thousand men against the Avars in the Dobrudja, but after some initial success he was forced to retreat while they advanced down the Black Sea coast. They were finally stopped near Adrianople when John Mystacon arrived with troops from Armenia. The Avars returned to Sirmium, though the Slavs continued to raid Greece. Meanwhile the Byzantine conquest of Persian Arzanene proceeded with agonizing slowness.

By this time Maurice, worried by the enormous expense of providing campaign pay, supplies, and new recruits to fight two full-scale wars at once, attempted to economize. He seems to have ordered the troops to be supplied directly with arms instead of giving them the usual generous arms allowances; the effect was to reduce by a quarter the annual payment made to the troops before Easter 588. Maurice also replaced the eastern commander Philippicus with a new general, Priscus, who arrived in time to distribute the reduced pay.

The result was a general mutiny of the eastern armies. At Monocartum in Byzantine Mesopotamia the troops stoned Priscus, who had to flee for his life, and destroyed their portraits of the emperor. Even when Priscus announced the restoration of their pay, the mutineers forced the duke of Phoenice Libanensis, a certain Germanus, to accept election as their commander. Although the emperor recalled Priscus and reappointed Philippicus, the mutineers rejected their former general and began looting the surrounding region. By summer, the jubilant Persians crossed the frontier and attacked Constantina.

Impending disaster was averted by the mutineers' reluctant commander Germanus. He restored a semblance of order and drove the Persians from Constantina. Next he led his men to the border near Martyropolis, where they overwhelmed another army of Persians, most of whom were captured with their possessions. Germanus managed to send part of the loot to the emperor, who responded by giving his sanction to Priscus's restoration of their pay. When Priscus returned to the capital, Maurice, far from blaming him for the mutiny, seems immediately to have given him the command against the Avars.[10]

That summer, soon after his appointment, the Avars invaded Thrace again. After storming the city of Anchialus, they besieged Priscus in Tzurulum, uncomfortably close to Constantinople. Maurice bought them off for 57,600 nomismata, which together with some later payments interrupted the Avar war for the present. The Slavs still remained in Illyricum. In Italy the Lombard war resumed with the expiration of the truce, and the Lombards defeated another Frankish army sent by Childebert.

To the relief of almost all Byzantines concerned, the mutiny of the eastern army ended on Easter 589, when the troops received their full pay and accepted Philippicus as their commander. The only strategic loss to result from the mutiny occurred at its end, when Martyropolis was betrayed to the Persians. Philippicus made a valiant attempt to retake the strongly fortified city, but failed. Maurice soon replaced him with Comentiolus, the commander in the Balkans of two years before.

The interminable Persian war, in which Byzantine strength was usually superior, was taking its toll on the Persians as well. Probably as a diversionary tactic before the mutiny was over, Maurice had helped the new prince of Iberia mount a raid on Persian Atropatene. The Persian general Bahrām drove the raiders back into Iberia, but then he lost a battle to the local Byzantine commander Romanus. In exasperation King Hurmazd sent his general a woman's dress. This ill-timed taunt provoked Bahrām into open rebellion against the king.

Bahrām marched from Atropatene toward Ctesiphon, and early in 590 entered Persian Mesopotamia from the northeast and defeated an army sent by Hurmazd. At the news of this defeat, the Persian nobles in Ctesiphon overthrew Hurmazd and replaced him with his son, who became Khusrau II. Yet after only a brief attempt to resist Bahrām, Khusrau fled with some relatives and attendants across the Byzantine border to Circesium. Bahrām took possession of a wobbly throne in Ctesiphon, and Khusrau appealed to Maurice for aid.

If the Byzantines would restore him to power, Khusrau offered to return Dara and Martyropolis and to surrender most of Persian Armenia, including what was left of Persian Arzanene. If the Byzantines would withhold help from Khusrau, Bahrām offered them Nisibis, presumably in addition to Dara and Martyropolis. Maurice's advisers, in particular the patriarch John IV the Faster, preferred the easier and cheaper course of not assisting Khusrau. Cautious though he usually was, the emperor overruled them. Apparently he judged that a legitimate Persian king who owed the Byzantines his throne would be more likely to keep a real peace than a usurper with no reason to trust the empire.

This decision cannot have been easy to make during the prevailing financial and military troubles. The plague had returned to Syria and Italy to wreak its usual havoc. The Balkans were still occupied by Slavs and threatened by Avars, and in autumn 590 Maurice himself had to march to Anchialus to deter an Avar attack. In Italy the new exarch Romanus, the victor over Bahrām the previous year, retook most of Aemilia but was stopped before the Lombard capital of Pavia. Italy, like the Balkans, desperately needed Byzantine reinforcements that could not yet be sent.

Aiming at a clear victory in the East, the emperor marshaled his straitened resources for an expedition to restore Khusrau as king of Persia. As word of the Byzantines' preparations spread, Khusrau gained support among the Persians and was able to take Martyropolis for the empire. In spring 591 Khusrau and the new Byzantine commander Narses led the Army of the East and some Persian loyalists up to Nisibis. The city declared for Khusrau, forcing Dara to capitulate.

While the allies sent an expeditionary force down the Euphrates to attack the Persian capital, Khusrau and Narses marched east into the Persian border province of Atropatene, where they were to meet John Mystacon and another Byzantine and Persian force. Opposed by many Persians as well as the Byzantines, Bahrām abandoned Ctesiphon to the allied expedition and gathered his men to fight in Atropatene. Despite Bahrām's best efforts, in late summer the two allied forces joined south of Lake Urmia and inflicted a crushing defeat on the usurper.

Thus Khusrau regained the Persian throne. He distributed generous donatives to the Byzantine troops, who had already won immense booty for themselves. As previously agreed, Byzantium gained the rest of Arzanene, Iberia, and Persian Armenia, except for the northeastern tip around Dvin. The empire had already recovered Dara and Martyropolis. Byzantium and Persia remained at peace for the rest of Maurice's reign, and cooperated in putting down Armenian revolts. The triumphant emperor won over Iberia from Monophysitism to Chalcedonianism, and overcame some of the resistance to Chalcedon in the Armenian church, which split into Chalcedonian and Monophysite branches.

Maurice had won a splendid victory in Persia, but he still had two more wars to fight. He chose to concentrate his forces in the Balkans before reinforcing Italy. There the Lombard duke of Spoleto took several forts on the highway from Ravenna to Rome in 592, dividing the Byzantine exarchate and uniting the Lombard Kingdom. But the dogged exarch Romanus promptly retook the forts and reopened the road, keeping an alternative route open even when he lost part of the main road the next year. Romanus resisted Pope Gregory I's efforts to make a truce with the Lombards.

The Balkan troops who had been fighting the Persians must have returned by early 593, when Priscus was again the Balkan commander. His strategy was to force out the Slavs, some of whom had been settled in Illyricum for fifteen years, by attacking their homeland north of the Danube. Although the Avars protested this intervention next to their territory, the Byzantines had become strong enough to ignore the protest. Priscus led his armies across the river and twice defeated the Slavs, but they remained a stubborn and elusive enemy.

To shorten the war and reduce its cost, in fall 593 Maurice ordered the army to continue campaigning north of the Danube all winter, supplying itself from the country. However rational this plan may have seemed to the emperor, it enraged the soldiers to the brink of mutiny. Priscus, who had learned from his experience with mutineers in the East, countermanded the order and led his men to more comfortable quarters at Odessus on the Black Sea. But after Priscus's army departed, bands of Slavs returned to raid the Danubian provinces. The emperor showed his displeasure by transferring the Balkan command to his brother Peter.

Finding that he could not economize on rations, Maurice tried again to economize on pay. For the payday before Easter 594 he had Peter announce that the allowances for both arms and uniforms would be replaced by issues in kind. Knowing that merely replacing the arms allowances had set off the eastern mutiny, Maurice tried to appease the soldiers by promising that the places of men killed in action would be reserved for their sons and that disabled veterans would continue to receive allowances for rations. These measures did gratify the soldiers, but not enough to make them accept less pay. When again they threatened mutiny, Peter apparently had to restore the pay but confirm the measures meant to compensate for its reduction. Maurice ended by paying more than before.

Although Peter cleared northern Thrace of Slavs and in the autumn crossed the Danube to fight them, Maurice resented his brother's expensive concessions. The emperor removed Peter and restored Priscus at the beginning of 595. Hoping to bring the war to a speedy end, Priscus crossed the Danube and marched west toward Avar territory. The Avar khan tried to distract the Byzantines by demolishing Singidunum, but Priscus rescued and refortified the city. Evidently the khan found Priscus too strong to attack, though he avenged himself by raiding Dalmatia. The Byzantines had thus secured their Danube frontier, and Priscus seems to have forced more Slavs out of Illyricum.

Since Maurice chose to fight one war at a time, while the Balkan war continued the western provinces had to fend for themselves. In Africa Gennadius, styled exarch like his Italian counterpart, foiled a Moorish rebellion by trickery in 595. In Italy the exarch Romanus held his own

54. A fort at Limisa, Africa, built by the emperor Maurice. (Photo: Courtesy of Denys Pringle)

fighting the Lombards, but died about 596 without receiving the reinforcements needed to make real progress. His successor Callinicus, like Pope Gregory, was less aggressive.

Priscus appeared almost to have pacified Illyricum and Thrace by the fall of 597, when the Avar khan made a sudden invasion with a large army. The Byzantine armies, probably dispersed over the Balkans to subdue the Slavs, were unprepared to stop a concentrated force of so many Avars. The khan passed along the south bank of the Danube and reached the Black Sea, where he besieged Priscus in the port of Tomi. The next spring the experienced Balkan commander Comentiolus marched to the front, but had to retreat. The Avars pursued him south and captured Druzipara, most of the way to Constantinople.

The emperor personally rallied Comentiolus's army, reinforced it with the Excubitors and members of the Blue and Green racing factions, and led it to the Long Walls. Fortunately for him, the Avars had begun to catch the plague. Rather than fight further, the khan made a treaty, agreeing to withdraw from the empire in return for an increase in his tribute from 100,000 nomismata to 120,000. Maurice managed to raise the sum, though the plague had recurred not only in the Balkans but in Constantinople, Anatolia, Mesopotamia, Italy, and Africa, aggravating the empire's financial woes.

Despite everything, Maurice wanted to attack the Avars while they were still suffering from the plague, before they collected their subsidy again, and perhaps before financial exhaustion forced him to stop campaigning. In the summer of 599 the emperor boldly sent his armies into the Avar homeland north of Sirmium. While Comentiolus protected the expedition's rear at Singidunum, Priscus won four great victories, killing tens of thousands of the Avars and their allies and taking seventeen thousand prisoners.[11] The scattered Slavs who remained in Illyricum no longer posed a serious threat. Maurice had won the war in the Balkans for the foreseeable future.

The emperor ordered the Avar prisoners returned as a pacific gesture, but because he was not about to pay the Avars tribute, no treaty was necessary. While exhausting the Avars, however, the war and the plague seem also to have exhausted the Byzantine treasury. Troops were now available for an expedition to Italy, but apparently money was not. The exarch Callinicus concluded a truce with the Lombards for two years, perhaps hoping that reinforcements would be sent during that time. None were. The armies of Thrace and Illyricum, and probably the two praesental armies, remained along the Danube, keeping out the Avars and Slavs but also consuming resources that the empire could ill afford.[12]

In the winter of 602 a famine at Constantinople set off riots against Maurice that he put down with difficulty. That summer his brother Peter, again general commander of the Balkan armies, sent a contingent across the Danube to fight the Slavs. When it met with weak opposition, the emperor tried again to save both rations and ration allowances by having the armies winter in Slavic territory and live off the land. Since now the soldiers would need to do little if any fighting, Maurice hoped they would accept the order they had rejected nine years before.

Though the troops were angry, Peter refused to repeat his earlier humiliation by revoking his brother's command. The men reluctantly prepared for the crossing. But as the weather turned cold and stormy, they became irate at the prospect of wintering in such inhospitable territory. They sent legates to Peter to demand the order be rescinded. When Peter refused again, they mutinied openly and chose one of their representatives, the junior officer Phocas, as their commander. Peter fled to Maurice in Constantinople, pursued by the mutinous troops under Phocas.

Since the only defenders Maurice had for the capital were the Excubitors and the Blues and Greens, Phocas's mutineers had the upper hand. Before reaching the city, they offered the throne to Maurice's eldest son Theodosius, who was nineteen, had already been crowned Augustus, and had recently married the daughter of the former Caesar Germanus. Theodosius declined. The soldiers' second choice was Germanus himself. Germanus took sanctuary in Saint Sophia. When Maurice sent the Excubitors to remove him, a serious riot broke out. Finding the army and the capital both against him, Maurice fled to Bithynia with his family and attendants, sending Theodosius to appeal for help from Khusrau in Persia.

By this time Germanus was willing to become emperor, but the Greens opposed him because he was known as an ardent Blue. Instead Phocas was proclaimed as he entered the city. The rebel leader captured and executed Maurice, his five younger sons, and his brother Peter, Phocas's former superior. Though emperors of the West had been deposed before, and several attempts had been made to overthrow emperors of the East, Maurice was the first eastern emperor actually to lose his crown since the foundation of Constantinople.

Nevertheless, during his reign of twenty years Maurice had achieved two great victories that had seemed almost impossible, winning a highly favorable peace with Persia and securing the Balkans against the Avars and Slavs. He had persecuted Monophysites enough to advance ortho-doxy in Armenia and Iberia, while avoiding religious conflict in most of the rest of the empire. By stringent saving, he had maintained some sort of cash reserve despite prolonged wars, the extravagance of his predeces-sor Tiberius, and two great outbreaks of the plague.

Yet, probably because of his well-known rectitude, Maurice refused to manage financial crises as Justinian had, by allowing the army to fall below strength or delaying the pay of its less important divisions. In fact, since his government was never insolvent, Maurice probably needed to do no more than reconcile himself to having a depleted treasury. That might have seemed imprudent, but what he attempted proved more so. He brought his soldiers to the point of mutiny not once but four times, by announcing economies that he thought fair but he should have learned were unacceptable to them. His failure to keep the army content cost not only his own life, but the military security for which he had worked so hard.

THE BEGINNING OF DISINTEGRATION

Maurice had left the empire with no major wars but the chronic struggle with the Lombards in Italy, and a budget that could be balanced with the aid of some wit and guile, both of which his successor pos-sessed. Phocas was a Greek-speaking Thracian, aged fifty-five at his ac-cession, from a simple military family like Justinian, Justin I, Leo I, Mar-cian and other Balkan emperors before them. He was at least as firmly orthodox as any of his predecessors since Marcian. Unlike them, how-ever, he lacked experience close to the throne. Even more important, unlike every eastern emperor since Diocletian, Phocas lacked even a shred of legitimate claim to rule.

As a consequence, in spite of the enthusiastic welcome he received from the people of Constantinople, he could not feel at ease with his of-ficials and had always to fear deposition. To defend himself against at-tempts to restore Maurice or his sons, Phocas had little choice but to kill them and display their heads in the capital. Soon afterward he killed Maurice's general Comentiolus, who seems to have been unpopular with the Balkan army, and the praetorian prefect Constantine Lardys, who was disliked by the people, doubtless because of Maurice's financial mea-sures. Phocas also claimed to have captured and killed Maurice's eldest

55. Copper-alloy steelyard weight, probably a portrait bust of Phocas (r. 602–10), now in the British Museum. (Photo: Trustees of the British Museum, courtesy of David Buckton)

son Theodosius, though because his head was not displayed the rumor spread that Theodosius had escaped.

Once Phocas had disposed of the obvious heirs of the throne and those mostly closely associated with the former regime, he tried to reassure other officers and officials. He showed surprising moderation by sparing the former Caesar Germanus and Maurice's brother-in-law Philippicus, who remained count of the Excubitors. They were by no means harmless, because early in 603 they joined Maurice's widow Constantina in a plot to make Germanus emperor. They incited the Green faction to a riot that burned much of the center of Constantinople, but Phocas regained control. He kept a promise not to harm the conspirators, and simply forced Constantina and her daughters to become nuns and Germanus and Philippicus to become priests.[13] Moreover, Phocas replaced Philippicus as count of the Excubitors with Priscus, who had long been a faithful general of Maurice.

Ignoring Phocas's efforts to make his usurpation seem less revolutionary, neither the Persian king Khusrau II nor the eastern commander Narses recognized the new emperor. Khusrau imprisoned the ambassador Phocas sent to announce his accession; Narses gathered his forces in Edessa and appealed to Khusrau to join him. The general, who had helped return Khusrau to his throne twelve years before, claimed to be harboring Maurice's son Theodosius, whom he meant to reinstate as the legitimate emperor. Phocas nonetheless won the allegiance of most of the Army of the East, including the commander of Dara Germanus, probably the same Germanus who had been chosen to lead the mutineers in 588. Phocas named him master of soldiers of the East and ordered him to attack his predecessor Narses in Edessa. Before an attack could be made, however, Khusrau sent a Persian army that defeated the Byzantines, fatally wounding Germanus. The Persians put Dara under siege.

Phocas reacted with energy, concluding a new peace treaty with the battered Avars that allowed him to transfer soldiers from the Balkans to the East. He also made peace with the Lombards, who had been advancing in the Po valley. In 604 the Balkan troops came to join the eastern armies under the command of the palace eunuch Leontius, who became master of soldiers of the East. The Balkans were left dangerously exposed. Though the Avars respected their treaty, some Slavs invaded again and started harrying Thessalonica.[14]

By this time Khusrau himself arrived with an army and took custody of the supposed Theodosius from Narses. When Leontius arrived with Phocas's forces Narses fled, but Khusrau defeated Leontius near Dara, taking many prisoners and killing them all. Phocas recalled and jailed Leontius. The next year the Persians raided the border region, unopposed by Phocas's new commander, his nephew Domentiolus. Though the Persians had yet to take anything of importance, Phocas's generals could not stop them or subdue Narses, whom many believed to have the real Theodosius.

In Constantinople Theodosius's mother Constantina and father-in-law Germanus began another plot against Phocas. The conspirators included some very high officials: the praetorian prefect Theodore, the count of the sacred largesses Athanasius, and Maurice's former general Romanus. Phocas discovered the plot in June 605 and this time he retaliated savagely. He tortured and killed the officials and executed Germanus, Constantina, her three daughters, and the daughter of Germanus who had married Theodosius. When Domentiolus obtained Narses' surrender on a promise of immunity, the emperor had Narses burned alive.

Khusrau had given scant support to Narses or the young man alleged to be Theodosius. The pretender's allies were too weak and his identity too dubious to give the Persian king much hope of establishing him in faraway Constantinople. Nor did Khusrau care much for taking land he could not claim for himself. When the Persians captured Dara after a long siege, they destroyed it instead of annexing it, and they merely raided Byzantine Mesopotamia and Syria. But soon the pretender died, and the king decided to attempt some conquests at the empire's expense. In 607 Khusrau sent armies to invade both Byzantine Mesopotamia and Armenia. The first army, led by the capable nobleman Shahrvarāz, took the corner of Mesopotamia bordering Armenia, including the city of Amida. The Byzantine general Domentiolus concentrated his forces against the second army, but it routed him near Theodosiopolis. The Persians reoccupied most of what had formerly been Persian Armenia.

Phocas's defeats kept sapping his authority even after his main Byzantine opponents were dead. He tried to make himself more respectable by marrying his daughter Domentia to the count of the Excubitors Priscus, who might expect to inherit the throne since Phocas had no son. But at the wedding Phocas spoiled the effect he wanted when he took offense at the honors the Blues and Greens paid Priscus. Further to afflict Phocas, the plague returned in 608. While the Persian general Shahrvarāz took more cities in Byzantine Mesopotamia, his counterpart Shāhīn advanced through Byzantine Armenia. The plague and invasions contributed to a bad harvest and a famine.

The famine grew worse when the exarch of Africa Heraclius rebelled and stopped grain shipments from Carthage to Constantinople. The exarch had reportedly been instigated to revolt by a secret letter from Priscus, once his commander in the East. Heraclius was well beyond Phocas's reach, could assemble a sizable fleet, and led the empire's only substantial army not threatened by a foreign enemy. His exarchate and neighboring Egypt, which was lightly defended, were the empire's most fertile provinces and accounted for almost all the grain supply of the capital. Though he considered himself too old to campaign or to become emperor, his son Heraclius the Younger and his nephew Nicetas were the right age, and had military ability.

That summer, taking the Egyptian authorities by surprise, Nicetas led an army from the African Exarchate that seized Alexandria and most of Lower Egypt. Since the garrisons of the Egyptian dukes were no match for the regular soldiers of the Army of Africa, Phocas's governor of Syria Bonosus had to gather a relief force from the Army of the East. By early 609 Bonosus arrived in Egypt with troops who were desperately needed to fight the Persians.

56. Column of Phocas (on steps, at left) in the Roman Forum, from an old photograph. (Photo: Istituto Centrale per il Catalogo e la Documentazione, Rome)

After a harsh winter that prolonged the famine, Shahrvarāz occupied the rest of Byzantine Mesopotamia. Shāhīn, having conquered most of Byzantine Armenia including Theodosiopolis, invaded Cappadocia. There he defeated and killed Sergius, a relative of Phocas who may have been master of soldiers for Armenia, and swept past the master of soldiers for the East Domentiolus. Having sacked the main Cappadocian city of Caesarea, Shāhīn's Persians raided all the way to Chalcedon, across the straits from Constantinople.

Meanwhile many of Phocas's eastern troops were in Egypt battling the rebels led by Nicetas. After defeating Nicetas's deputy, Bonosus slowly reconquered most of Lower Egypt. By autumn Bonosus had reached Alexandria, where he besieged Nicetas himself. But the rebel led out an army that overwhelmed Bonosus's loyalists. Before the end of 609, Nicetas had driven Bonosus out of the country, and was able to send much of his force to Heraclius the Younger in the Exarchate of Africa. Heraclius prepared to embark with it for Constantinople.[15]

By this time Phocas's usurpation, the rebellion in Africa and Egypt, and the Persian advances in Armenia, Mesopotamia, Syria, and Anatolia had so weakened the government that public order was breaking down. Some anticipated not just Phocas's fall but the destruction of the empire. Jews in several Syrian cities started lynching Christians. Blues and Greens fought each other in Thessalonica and various towns in Syria and Anatolia. The Slavs apparently ranged throughout northern Illyricum. In the capital Phocas punished the Greens for jeering that he had taken to drink.

In 610, while Shahrvarāz advanced almost to Antioch, the Byzantine rebels took most of the rest of Syria, and Cyprus as well. At Carthage, Heraclius the Younger set sail for Constantinople with a large fleet manned by troops from Africa and Egypt. On his way he collected more supporters, apparently in Sicily, Crete, and Thessalonica. He reached and captured Abydus at the entrance to the Hellespont in September. In October he arrived before Constantinople itself.

Lacking regular troops, Phocas had to rely on the Excubitors and the Blues and Greens. Besides his son-in-law Priscus, his commanders were his brother Domentiolus, father of the general of the same name, and Bonosus, who had escaped to the capital from Egypt. But the Greens betrayed the harbor they were guarding to Heraclius, killed Bonosus, and began fighting the Blues. Priscus declared for Heraclius, whom he had reportedly favored all along. A mob lynched Domentiolus and seized Phocas, who was brought to Heraclius's ship. The story goes that Heraclius upbraided Phocas for ruining the empire, and Phocas wished him better luck. Then Phocas was beheaded.

In fact, Phocas had shown some skill simply by remaining emperor for eight years. From the onset of the plague to the overthrow of Maurice, emperors with an undisputed right to rule had struggled constantly to keep the provinces safe, the treasury solvent, and the army willing and able to fight. Given the empire's long and porous frontiers, its diminished population and resources, and the size and high pay of its army, maintaining equilibrium was very difficult, and none of Justinian's successors quite managed to do it. Under Phocas, persistent revolts against a ruler widely considered a usurper brought the empire to the verge of financial, political, and military collapse. This catastrophe, which had threatened as early as the 540's, Phocas's death did little to avert.

CHAPTER EIGHT

A Divided Society, 457–610

From the mid-fifth century until the beginning of the seventh, Byzantine society displayed remarkable vigor and resilience. It took firmer hold within its original territory, as Christianity, administrative centralization, and the Greek language all continued to spread. The state held off its internal and external enemies, and under Justinian brought large new territories in the West under the rule of Constantinople. Despite some abortive revolts, riots, and conspiracies, the empire maintained itself well until 602, and was still largely intact in 610. During most of these years, Byzantium seemed wealthy and cultured, well governed and militarily strong.

Nonetheless, when such incongruous elements, peoples, and lands combined in a single society, a number of deep divisions naturally persisted. The ruling classes were more homogeneous than their subjects, and their members tended to think their society was more cohesive than it really was. In times of peace and prosperity, the empire's people seemed to form a more or less manageable whole, and even made progress toward becoming one. But under the strain of invasions and plagues, which became frequent in the latter part of the period, Byzantium showed signs of cracking where its parts had been joined.

EAST, WEST, AND CENTER

Justinian's reconquests added still more linguistic and racial communities to an already diverse eastern empire. By 565 the reconquered territories probably included about half the population and farmland of the former western empire, though a good deal less of its total area.

Combined with the Latin-speaking lands in the Balkans, Justinian's western conquests formed a large Latin-speaking bloc. Yet Italy, Africa, and Spain were geographically and culturally distinct from each other, and still more unlike the northern Balkans, where speakers of Latin, Greek, and Illyrian lived together and had older and closer links with other easterners.

Meanwhile the organization of a schismatic Monophysite church increasingly distinguished Syria and Egypt from the Chalcedonian remainder of the empire, although Syria and Egypt also differed from each other in their languages and other traditions. Predominantly Greek-speaking Greece, Thrace, and Anatolia were left in the middle as Byzantium's geographical, cultural, and administrative center. This central region certainly had a good deal in common with the eastern and western wings, and its administrative and cultural influence on them was strong. By the end of the sixth century, however, the empire's three parts were drifting farther away from each other.

Justinian's reconquests gave the eastern empire more territory to defend and longer frontiers. The western provinces were quite distant from Constantinople, and scarcely accessible by land. Though with good weather a message could reach any of their ports in a month, sending an army was much harder, and they mostly had to see to their own defenses. In earlier times the frontiers of the African provinces, marked by the Sahara and the Atlas Mountains, had been secure enough. The Sierra Morena shielded the Byzantine province in southern Spain, and the Alps helped defend Italy. While these natural barriers should have been more defensible than the Danube or the desert border in Mesopotamia, they proved harder to defend than Justinian might have expected.

Justinian had probably planned for his Spanish province to extend to the Pyrenees, to border on the more or less friendly Frankish Kingdom. Instead Byzantine Spain had a longer and lower mountain frontier with a Visigothic Kingdom bent on destroying it. The province survived because the Visigoths were militarily weakened, divided among themselves, and disliked by their orthodox Roman subjects. Byzantine Africa's frontier never extended inland as far as Roman Africa's before the Vandal conquest. The mountains and deserts that defined the border were the homes of Moorish tribes who repeatedly harried the Byzantines. Again, the Byzantines' chief advantage was that the Moors were comparatively weak, disunited and intent on raiding rather than systematic conquest. In the end, the Byzantines defeated them.

Italy was the least safe of the western territories, though the Alps to its north were high except for their eastern spur, the Julian Alps. Through this weak point, which the Visigoths and Ostrogoths had once exploited, the Lombards invaded Italy just seven years after Narses had finished reconquering it. Byzantine Italy never had a true frontier again, nor real peace. Instead both Byzantines and Lombards uneasily held whatever land their isolated strongholds could defend. The Dalmatian frontier, which followed the Dinaric Alps, provided a fairly good shield for the land route between Italy and the original eastern empire, but the road was a slow one.

Otherwise the empire's frontiers were essentially as they had been before. The border along the Drinus, Savus, and Danube rivers often let barbarians through but remained the border nonetheless. The Taurus and Antitaurus mountains protected Anatolia, regardless of the fluctuations of the Byzantine frontier in Armenia and interruptions of the Byzantine protectorate over Lazica. In the early sixth century Anastasius strengthened the Mesopotamian frontier by fortifying Dara; Justinian protected Syria and Palestine and threatened the Persians by winning the Ghassanid Arabs as allies. Although during that century the Persians crossed the Mesopotamian frontier more often than before, this was because of their own strength and initiative rather than Byzantine weakness.

Justinian made a decisive change in the deployment of the empire's army. While he downgraded the frontier troops to a militia, he increased the field forces, mostly in the West. His only permanent addition to the eastern field forces was the new Army of Armenia, of fifteen thousand men. As Justinian reconquered the West, however, he added some forty thousand soldiers, the strength of the new armies of Italy, Africa, and Spain. The fifteen thousand men he deployed in Africa and the about thirty-five thousand he left in Illyricum and Thrace proved strong enough to keep their territories from being lost, but not from being raided. Even when expanded by Justinian to thirty-five thousand men, the eastern armies were inadequate to keep out the Persians until Tiberius II reinforced them with the fifteen thousand Federates; thereafter they were big enough, and failed only if seriously disaffected. But the Army of Italy could not repel the Lombards, who must soon have reduced its original strength of twenty thousand or so.

The old frontier forces, though no longer paid regular wages and doubtless diminished in numbers, continued to exist and to make some contribution to the defense of the East. In 534 Justinian had even established five new frontier commands in the African prefecture, though he

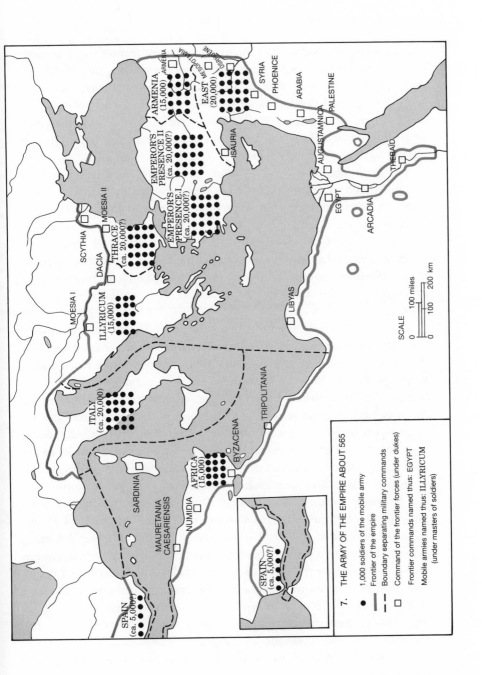

7. THE ARMY OF THE EMPIRE ABOUT 565

- • 1,000 soldiers of the mobile army
  |─ Frontier of the empire
  |¦| Boundary separating military commands
  □ Command of the frontier forces (under dukes)
  Frontier commands named thus: EGYPT
  Mobile armies named thus: ILLYRICUM
  (under masters of soldiers)

SCALE

0   100 miles

0   100   200 km

SPAIN
(ca. 5,000?)

ITALY
(ca. 20,000)

SARDINIA

MAURETANIA
CAESARIENSIS

NUMIDIA

AFRICA
(15,000)

BYZACENA

TRIPOLITANIA

LIBYAS

ILLYRICUM
(15,000)

MOESIA I

DACIA

SCYTHIA

MOESIA II

THRACE
(ca. 20,000)

EMPEROR'S
PRESENCE I
(ca. 20,000?)

EMPEROR'S
PRESENCE II
(ca. 20,000?)

ARMENIA
(15,000)

MESOPOTAMIA

OSROENE

ARMENIA

EAST
(20,000)

ISAURIA

SYRIA

PHOENICE

ARABIA

PALESTINE

AUGUSTAMNICA

EGYPT

ARCADIA

THEBAÏD

SPAIN
(ca. 5,000?)

never created any for Italy or Spain.[1] The dukes, formerly commanders only of the frontier troops, now sometimes led contingents of their region's field armies, and after the Lombard invasion Italy acquired dukes who commanded the field soldiers left in detached parts of the exarchate. In Egypt the dukes gained some civil powers as well as military ones. Interestingly, Italy and Spain, the only regions that lacked frontier troops, were also the only regions to lose their border areas.

The army held the other frontiers, with temporary lapses and frequent difficulties, until it rebelled against Maurice in 602. The overall pattern was of precarious but improving defenses in the later fifth century, much better defenses and strong offensives from about 500 to 540, then intermittent deterioration until 602, when the real crisis began. During most of this period most of the empire was at peace, though not necessarily prosperous. Conditions varied with the characteristics of local society and the different effects of warfare, heavy taxation, and the plague.

The Prefecture of Illyricum, always the poorest and most rural part of the eastern empire, was the part of the East that most resembled the West. Through the sixth century northern Illyricum continued to be mostly Latin-speaking, and to be the eastern empire's main source of military recruits. Illyricum suffered from foreign depredations as much as ever in the later fifth century, when the Ostrogoths raided or squatted in most of its territory at one time or another. After Zeno persuaded them to leave for Italy in 488, however, Illyricum enjoyed over fifty years of unaccustomed peace, disturbed only by an occasional Slavic or Bulgar raid.

During this half-century, when the Illyrian-born Justin I, Justinian, and Belisarius took command of the Byzantine government and army, the prefecture fared better than at any time since the reign of Valens. Justinian refounded the small town nearest his birthplace as Justiniana Prima.[2] The pope regained jurisdiction over the Illyrian church, after an interruption during the Acacian Schism under Anastasius I, and his jurisdiction became more important as the civil role of bishops increased. The popes exercised their authority in Illyricum through local archbishops, who in their capacity as papal deputies were called vicars. At first the only papal vicar was the archbishop of Thessalonica, but Justinian made Justiniana Prima into a separate vicariate for the northern part of the prefecture.

Beginning with 540, Bulgar and Slavic raids into Illyricum became more intense. Justinian did what he could for his homeland. He added his reconquest of Dalmatia to it, and fortified or refortified more than four hundred places in the prefecture, many far from the frontier. Although the number and location of these fortifications show that the emperor had despaired of making Illyricum fully secure, it became somewhat more peaceful in the latter part of his reign. After Justinian's death, however, the Avars joined the Slavs and Bulgars in raiding Illyricum more thoroughly. The Slavs, in particular, raided right into the Peloponnesus and settled for years in much of Greece.[3]

The combination of these raids and the plague seems to have done more harm than ever to the region's small and vulnerable towns, particularly in Greece, where Justinian's fortifications were few. With the decline of Athens, Corinth, and other ancient centers, only one important city remained, the strongly fortified metropolis of Thessalonica. Nevertheless, enough Byzantine peasants remained in the countryside, protected by the forts, to keep most of Illyricum under imperial control. Tiberius still found it the best place to recruit his new band of Federates in 575. After Maurice pacified the region in 598, it seems to have suffered little from raids up to 610.

Though sharing most of the vicissitudes of Illyricum, Thrace was a little more fortunate. Devastated by the Ostrogoths in the later fifth century, it then enjoyed a respite of peace and relative prosperity before the Slavic, Bulgar, and Avar raids began, and the plague arrived, from 540 onward. Justinian built or rebuilt over 150 forts in Thrace, providing some security. The nearness of Constantinople and of the armies in the Emperor's Presence lent some protection to the Thracian plain and its cities, but the lower Danube valley suffered as much as Illyricum from raiders in the later sixth century. Nevertheless, like Illyricum, the whole territory remained Byzantine through the reign of Phocas.

The plain of southern Thrace stretched to Constantinople, which from the mid-fifth century was the empire's largest city by a wide margin. Under the city's influence, the old Thracian language, attested for the last time in the sixth century, gave way to Greek among the people of the plain. The people of the often invaded Danube valley continued to speak mostly Latin, or at any rate a form of it. Though southern Thrace suffered less from raids than the rest of the Balkans, its denser population must have suffered more from the plague, which buffeted Constantinople repeatedly in the later sixth century.

Administratively Thrace remained part of the Prefecture of the East, along with the Asian dioceses and Egypt. After Justinian abolished the dioceses early in his reign, the prefectures had no regular subdivisions larger than the provinces, and the giant Prefecture of the East became rather unwieldy. In each of the former dioceses of Asiana, Pontica, the East, and Egypt, one of the provincial governors received the title of the old vicar of the diocese and a few of the vicar's old prerogatives. Ecclesiastical jurisdiction, which became more important as the bishops' judicial and administrative duties expanded, put Thrace and Anatolia together under the patriarch of Constantinople. As the capital's natural hinterlands, these two regions increasingly formed the empire's core.

Anatolia was much more populous and wealthy than Thrace. Except for its Armenian fringe in the east, Asia Minor remained mostly at peace from the reign of Leo I to that of Phocas. In Anatolia as in Thrace, the Greek language seems to have become dominant at this time even in the interior, where the native languages, except for Armenian in the extreme east, faded into insignificance.[4] The fifth-century rebellions in the rocky borderland of Isauria cannot have done Anatolia much harm. From Justinian's reign on, wars with the Persians were frequent in Byzantine Armenia, but the Army of Armenia and the mountainous terrain prevented the Persians from breaking through to the Anatolian plateau until 609.

The plague, however, spread throughout the Anatolian peninsula, causing widespread depopulation and apparently a good deal of lawlessness. About 548 brigandage forced Justinian to restore the police powers of the old vicar of Pontica over northern and central Anatolia, and to appoint a similar official for the inland part of what had been Asiana. Though crime then decreased, the plague returned again and again into the seventh century, no doubt carried by travelers along the post roads from one city to another. Since Asia Minor was second only to Egypt as a source of the empire's revenue, the deficit caused by the plague must have increased the region's tax burden.

Such was the empire's central portion, dominated by Constantinople and increasingly Hellenized. Here the government's control was strongest. From the rebellion of Vitalian to that of Phocas, Thrace and Anatolia harbored no serious revolts except for some unrest in the capital. Local Christians generally accepted both the Council of Chalcedon and Justinian's attempt to conciliate moderate Monophysites at the Second Council of Constantinople. After Justinian's reconquests in the West made Anatolia and the Balkans the geographical center of the empire, they found themselves more than ever in the midst of Byzantine commerce, troop movements, and culture. They therefore had special claims on the government's attention, apart from the fact that all the emperors from Leo I to Phocas came from there.

By contrast, Justinian's work of reconquest tended to relegate Egypt and Syria to the empire's military, cultural, and administrative margins. Justinian transferred troops from the East to the West, and when he added field soldiers to the eastern frontier they went to Armenia rather than Syria. He and his successors usually sent troops east only after Persian depredations had become unignorable. The reconquest of the unshakably Chalcedonian West limited the government's ability to accommodate eastern Monophysites. The Greek language spread no further in the countryside of Syria and Egypt, and much of their Syriac- and Coptic-speaking majorities joined Monophysite churches with liturgies in their own languages. The East, which seems to have been particularly hostile to the Chalcedonian usurper Phocas, was in clear danger of falling to the Persians by the end of his reign.

Yet until 540 Syria, as defined by the patriarchates of Antioch and Jerusalem, enjoyed almost complete peace and substantial and growing prosperity. From 540 on, Persian raids became frequent. Mesopotamia suffered most, Syria proper nearly as much, but Palestine far less. The Persians sacked many cities and extorted ransoms from many others. Syria's metropolis of Antioch never quite recovered from its sack in 540, which followed catastrophic earthquakes in 526 and 528 and just preceded the arrival of the plague. Justinian rebuilt Antioch and strengthened the fortifications of the main cities of Mesopotamia, and his successors spent vast sums on defending the Persian frontier. Yet Syria found peace again only after the victory Maurice won in Persia, and that peace died with him.

Although these disasters permanently impoverished the part of Syria near the coast, relative affluence continued in the highlands a bit farther inland, including much of Palestine. Damascus and Beroea, for example, seem actually to have grown in the sixth century and into the seventh. The principal reason seems to be that these dry and less populous regions had few rats and thus little trouble from the plague, which was worse than any invasion.[5] This exception to the general misery of the empire in the later sixth century suggests how fearsome the plague's results were elsewhere. Because the part of Syria hardest hit by the disease was the most Hellenized and Chalcedonian, the Monophysite minority and the dominance of the Syriac language both increased. The plague scarcely

57. Monastery of Saint Catherine at the foot of Mount Sinai, built and
fortified by Justinian. (Photo: Courtesy of Michigan-Princeton-Alexandria
Expedition to Mount Sinai)

touched the border region, whose population of sedentary and nomadic Arabs seems also to have grown.

Egypt, with its natural defenses of desert, river, and sea, remained mostly secure. Until the arrival of the plague, Egypt was the empire's richest and most peaceful region, troubled only by civil strife in Alexandria, occasional nomadic raids, and sporadic resistance to the imposition of Chalcedonian bishops on its heavily Monophysite inhabitants. Egypt remained practically free from warfare until the revolt of Heraclius reached it in the seventh century. Even that fighting cannot have caused severe disruption of Egyptian society.

The plague, however, probably hurt Egypt at least as much as any other region. The Nile valley was moist, populous, convenient to the immediate source of the plague in Ethiopia, and served by numerous boats and barges that carried rats and disease up and down the river. Egypt suffered horribly from the Black Death in the fourteenth century, and the same disease can hardly have affected it less in the sixth.[6] Worse still, the plague forced the central government to increase its demands for money and grain from the Egyptians who survived, causing famines that killed still more of them. Riots and brigandage also increased. The Libyas, however, which were poorer and drier, must have suffered less from the plague and its consequences.

If after the 540's the empire's eastern portion fared rather worse than its central region, most of the reconquered West was even less fortunate. Africa, Spain, and Italy were geographically isolated from the other provinces, though tenuous land routes did lead to Italy and Africa through Dalmatia and Tripolitania. Otherwise stretches of the open Mediterranean separated the empire's three western possessions from the main body of the empire. Except for Procopius, who had himself accompanied Belisarius to Africa and Italy, Constantinopolitan sources have scarcely anything to say about Justinian's western acquisitions, far less than about any region of the empire to the east. Nor did emperors after Justinian give the same attention to the West as to the rest of the empire.

Africa, Italy, and Spain shared Latin culture and allegiance to the papacy. But since the pope also had jurisdiction over the churches of Illyricum and the barbarian West, and some further authority over all orthodox Christendom, the patriarchate of Rome could not lend the empire's western lands much common identity. Although every educated westerner knew Latin, most African peasants still spoke Punic, while the reconquest encouraged the many southern Italians who spoke Greek to make more use of it. Africa, Spain, and Italy lacked land links with each other, and by the later sixth century invading Moors, Visigoths, and Lombards had disrupted land communications even within the three territories. Each faced military threats that preoccupied its inhabitants, administrators, and generals. The few African, Spanish, and Italian writers of the time say something about Constantinople but very little about events in the West outside their own regions.

Of the three parts of the West, Africa was the richest, as it long had been. Justinian built numerous fortifications for Africa to make up for the Vandals' demolition of most of its city walls. After a series of mutinies and Moorish invasions and raids, the Army of Africa finally secured most of the country by 579. Though the plague reached Africa and affected the coast, the drier interior should have escaped lightly, as happened in Syria. Even coastal Carthage was surely the West's largest city at the time—indeed, with the ruination of Rome, the West's only large city by eastern standards. In the later sixth century Africa sent large grain shipments to Constantinople. That rebels based in Africa could overthrow Phocas is evidence of the wealth of the exarchate and the strength of its army.

Obscure though the history of the empire's Spanish province is, its ability to survive Visigothic attacks shows that it was more robust than might have been assumed. Even though the province received little help after Justinian's death, about half of it appears still to have been in Byzantine hands in 610, including its principal port of Cartagena. Yet warfare and plague impoverished all of Spain in the period, and the Byzantine province was always unimportant to the rest of the empire.

Italy's history, position, and size made it loom larger in the central government's attention than the other western lands. It had been, if not thriving, at least self-supporting before Justinian's invasion. But the length and difficulty of the conquest, the endless Lombard war so soon after the conquest was completed, and again the plague left Italy in a worse state than any other prefecture, Illyricum included. The wars brought great destruction and the eventual loss of more than half the country to the Lombards. By the end of the sixth century, all of Italy had become depopulated. Its aristocracy of senators and decurions disappeared altogether, leaving bishops, abbots, and generals to be its ruling class.

Since Justinian was nearing the end of his reign at the time of the Ostrogoths' defeat, he was able to fortify the Italian cities much less thoroughly than those of the Balkans, Syria, or Africa. Under Justin II the Lombards invaded almost at once. After the loss of many places and grave damage to others, Byzantine Italy was left without large cities. Small but defensible Ravenna, the capital of the exarchate, was probably the peninsula's largest town. Shrunken Rome and Naples with their surrounding territories became isolated, with the pope the chief authority in the former and a local duke in the latter. The least depressed part of Italy was the far south and Sicily, where the Greek language and the sea routes to the East had never passed out of use, and became greater assets after the reconquest.

The larger size of Justinian's empire was not necessarily an economic or defensive liability. Troops and revenue could be and often were transferred from richer and safer regions to poorer and more threatened ones. From Justinian to Phocas Byzantium controlled nearly the whole Mediterranean coast, and scattered evidence suggests that trade by sea, the most economical form of premodern trade, benefited somewhat from increased security. Nonetheless, just as Diocletian had found his empire too big for one government to control, controlling the enlarged though depopulated empire of Justinian was a constant struggle.

ORDER AND DISORDER

That during the sixth century the government was able to hold these territories together at all shows that it had improved a good deal since the mid-fifth century, when it had been dangerously deficient. The scantiness of sources before Justinian makes the process of improvement hard to trace. Out of financial necessity Zeno probably reduced private corruption somewhat. By his time corruption and inefficiency may also have approached their natural limits, and even have begun to limit themselves. Petitioners will pay only so much in bribes, and utterly incompetent officials are not worth bribing. In any case, Anastasius was a vigorous reformer of the administration he inherited.

Vigilant and diligent though he doubtless was, Anastasius's main tool was monetarization. Since Diocletian the empire's revenues and expenditures had been shifting by slow degrees away from goods and toward money; but in the late fifth century they were still a tangle of payments in cash and kind, convertible at different rates under various circumstances. The system encouraged and even compelled waste and dishonesty, while frustrating efforts to stop them. Anastasius's conversion of most payments in kind to cash, with only such local exceptions as made sense, must have reduced unnecessary shipping, storage, spoilage, and confusion that had done nearly everyone more harm than good. Anastasius put some of the profits into the treasury, returned a little to the people by cutting taxes, and gave some to the army by raising their pay.

After the slow disappearance of the soldiers' salaries through the inflation of the copper coinage, and the accretion of allowances and allotments of different sorts, evaluating military pay before Anastasius is hazardous, but it was low enough to make military service unpopular among ordinary Byzantines, leading the empire to hire barbarians and Isaurians. Recruits were routinely branded to keep them from deserting. Since the allowances and allotments were minimal, particularly for the frontier soldiers, frontier troops had to make shift with other sources of income, and field troops also resorted to extortion and robbery.

The field troops became much better off when Anastasius added to the allowance or *annona* for their food three more *annonae* of equal size, one perhaps for their families, one for their uniforms, and one for their arms. Later Anastasius seems to have increased the amount of each *annona* from 4 nomismata to 5 instead of paying a quinquennial donative of 5 nomismata. The soldiers used their new allowances to buy their arms and uniforms from the state, but in a normal year the allowances much exceeded the amount they needed to remain properly equipped. Their new rate of annual pay, apparently 20 nomismata, was enough to improve both recruitment and the army's performance throughout the sixth century. The rate approximated the pay of second-century Roman legionaries, which had been the equivalent of 19.2 nomismata a year and was about what Augustus had paid auxiliaries. The frontier troops, however, received a single *annona* of 5 nomismata a year.[7]

At the same time, this increase in pay raised state expenditures and made new recruitment costly. Although the prudent Anastasius kept expenses under control, the lavish Justinian spent himself into some difficulty even before he tried to reconquer the West. His western expeditions were therefore small, and mostly formed of troops from existing eastern armies, barbarian mercenaries, and the private retainers of his generals, especially Belisarius. When the onset of the plague decreased state revenue, Justinian had to make a major reduction in military pay by striking the frontier troops from the payroll. The military effects of this measure were not grave, because the frontier forces remained in place, supporting themselves by various means to which they had already become accustomed.[8] Though each frontier soldier's wage had

been small, eliminating their whole payroll represented a significant saving for the treasury. Even so, Justinian had to struggle to meet his military payrolls, and in the process he often delayed payments and tolerated
other abuses.

While Justinian stopped paying some 225,000 frontier troops and sailors, he increased the much better-paid field army from about 104,000
to 150,000 soldiers. These men Justinian's successors also had to pay.
Though later in the sixth century the battered Italian army doubtless declined in official strength, declines there or elsewhere can scarcely have
exceeded the 15,000 men recruited by Tiberius for his Federates. When
Maurice found paying so many soldiers arduous, he thought of undoing
part of Anastasius's military pay reform. He attempted to replace the arms
allowances with issues of arms in 588, reducing cash pay from twenty to
fifteen nomismata; and in 594 he tried to replace both arms and uniform
allowances with issues in kind, which would have reduced cash pay to
just ten nomismata. The soldiers would not stand for either change.

In itself raising the soldiers' pay must have helped their morale, discipline, and effectiveness, and in the sixth century the army greatly improved on its dismal record of the fifth century. It reconquered most of
the West, and defended Byzantine territory better than before. Recruitment became far easier, conscription and the branding of recruits were
abandoned, and barbarian mercenaries dwindled to a small minority. The
sources also give the impression that soldiers resorted to extortion from
civilians less often than formerly. The sixth-century mobile armies, despite lingering defects, seem to have been the most professional force that
the empire had fielded for three hundred years.

Yet from Justinian to Phocas the army also showed a tendency to mutiny that had not been evident since the third century. The men's understandable grievance was that their pay, though in theory sufficient, was
often not paid. Justinian continually delayed payrolls; even Tiberius delayed them once; and Maurice kept trying to reduce them by one means
or another. Justinian also found ways to put off military promotions and
to discharge the older and better-paid officers. Yet he kept a close watch
on his officer corps, and probably reduced their misappropriations from
their men. If paid properly, the troops were usually content.

The bureaucracy was less so. When stronger emperors replaced the
figureheads of the first half of the fifth century, high officials lost many
of their perquisites. From the reign of Zeno, the state seems to have

taken over much of their traffic in buying and selling appointments, and Anastasius appears to have subjected their activities to closer scrutiny than ever before. Justinian, relying on a few picked magistrates loyal to himself, made systematic though occasionally interrupted efforts to curb the power and wealth of officials from the middle ranks right up to the senate.

As the emperors recovered their power after the mid-fifth century, they discouraged the senators' role as public benefactors, which could threaten the monarch's preeminence. The emperors began to subsidize the Blues and Greens, at least partly to take over the financing of the theaters and hippodromes that had been making aristocratic patrons overpopular. Zeno and Justinian named few private citizens as consuls. The last private citizen ever to assume that ancient and costly office, with its responsibility for putting on consular games, did so in 541. Afterward no senator had this chance to gain the people's favor, even if he could afford it.

Justinian was by no means the first emperor who promoted new men, reformed official abuses, or confiscated senatorial fortunes. But by doing all three at once, he caused changes more lasting than had his predecessors. With his distrust of aristocrats, pressing need for money, and extraordinarily long reign, Justinian curbed an eastern senatorial class that had attained real wealth only in recent times, and that after 541 suffered great losses in members and resources from the plague. Meanwhile the plague and the wars of reconquest ruined the originally richer senatorial aristocracy of reconquered Italy. The abolition of the dioceses also rid the empire of a large group of middle-ranking bureaucrats, though Justinian later reintroduced some elements of the diocesan organization. After Justinian, senators and bureaucrats never regained the power and wealth that they had enjoyed before him.

The sixth century also saw the final decline of the decurions, though Justinian tried at first to maintain them. After centuries of impoverishment and depletion, the city councils were obviously incapable of keeping up collections from taxpayers hard hit by the plague, which also afflicted the decurions themselves. While some men of the decurion class still helped supervise tax collection along with officials of the central government, city councils gradually ceased to meet or to have responsibility for arrears. They no longer took a part in financing civic buildings and services, which declined as the government and the Church made

58. Ruins of the Bucoleon Palace of Justinian, Constantinople. (Photo: Irina Andreescu-Treadgold)

up only part of the difference. Few of the remaining decurions were still influential in their cities, where the leaders were men of higher rank, and increasingly the bishops.

Beginning with the reign of Anastasius, bishops had a voice in choosing local officials, including provincial governors. Justinian gave bishops jurisdiction over many civil cases in their courts, and in some cases precedence over governors. The bishops and the governors alike profited from the decline of the diocesan bureaucrats above them and of the decurions below them. Justinian also gave some governors increases in pay. Other officials who gained power at the expense of the rest of the bureaucracy were Justinian's new logothetes, auditors who received a twelfth of whatever embezzled funds they could reclaim.

Finally, disturbed circumstances led Justinian and his successors to delegate more authority to the commanders of the empire's outlying mobile armies. Tiberius made his name at the head of the Army of Illyricum, and Maurice as master of soldiers for the East. The commanders of the armies of Italy and Africa, the exarchs, assumed the additional powers of civil prefects. The ability of the African exarch Heraclius the Elder to mount a successful rebellion against Phocas showed that such delegation of power could be dangerous, but it was almost a necessity in the embattled West.

Amid so much administrative change, the *Justinian Code* was obviously useful. It allowed judges, lawyers, and litigants to learn what the law was with greater ease and assurance than before. By limiting cases to one appeal, and otherwise reducing abuses, Justinian further reformed a judicial system that certainly needed improvement. Yet the *Code*, sometimes vague and confused to begin with, soon became in part obsolete. It antedated the many laws enacted later in Justinian's reign, which were never incorporated into it except as the informal appendix of the *Novels*; and it could not take into account such later developments as the growing jurisdiction of church courts. Worst of all, the *Code* (though not the *Novels*) was in Latin, and appeared just when Greek was becoming the practically exclusive language of government. By this time few law students began their studies with more than a smattering of Latin, and most of them never acquired more than a rudimentary knowledge of the language. Consequently for many lawyers and judges the law was not so much the *Justinian Code* itself as the interlinear Greek translations of it, or even Greek commentaries on it. The canon law used by the church courts had the advantage of being in Greek.

Justinian's efforts to control his empire were tireless, and surpassed in vigor and success those of nearly all his predecessors since Diocletian. If he often seemed to waver in his purpose, for example by twice dismissing John the Cappadocian, much of the reason was that he recognized the limits of his power. His immediate predecessors ran fewer risks, and his immediate successors came to more grief; none of them reigned nearly as long as he. That all of them were men of ability suggests how extraordinary he was, and also that Byzantium had in some ways become harder to rule than in the earlier years of figurehead emperors.

From late in the fifth century the army was more likely to mutiny, city dwellers more ready to riot, the upper class more discontented, and the provinces harder to control, while the Monophysites were more intractable than earlier heretics. Although Justinian's bold initiatives and the ravages of the plague were partly responsible, the empire's discontents were already evident under Anastasius. Their deeper causes were the incompatibilities between the empire's disparate elements, disruptive economic growth before 540, and even more disruptive economic decline afterward. The emperors tried to improve matters by making civil and military reforms, sponsoring circus factions, or compromising with the Monophysites. Such efforts, however, were only a little more successful than most attempts by governments to control social change.

CHURCH AUTHORITY AND ITS LIMITS

Like the state, the Church expanded, and like the state it found expansion a source of weakness as well as strength. From the mid-fifth century the Church steadily converted the empire's remaining pagans. It had marginalized them by the time of Justinian, and it overwhelmed them after the last recorded persecution of pagans in 580. The empire's Jewish population was small, and apparently growing smaller. After Justinian Arianism was a spent force even among the Germans, and few self-professed Nestorians remained in the empire, though many more lived in Persian Mesopotamia. Justinian also healed the Acacian Schism with the papacy, and by his reconquests brought eastern and western Christians within a single political and ecclesiastical structure.

Every emperor from Leo I to Phocas was devout, often to the point of religious asceticism, and all showed deference to the churchmen they considered orthodox. Throughout this period the Church exercised great authority over political, social, and cultural life. Yet on the whole, church leaders were less respected and influential than they had been when society was largely pagan. Neither they nor the emperors handled the fine points of the Monophysite controversy nearly as successfully as their predecessors had the much more fundamental issues of paganism and Arianism.

Outwardly the bishops commanded prerogatives and resources that were more extensive than ever before. With the decline of city councils, bishops were often the most powerful men in their cities, and were on a par with the provincial governors whom they helped to select. Bishops judged court cases and conducted civic business whenever those involved the Church, and sometimes when they did not. The clergy and monks, all subject to their local bishops, numbered in the tens of thousands, far surpassing the bureaucracy and approaching the army in size.

Since donations from the faithful piled up constantly and were seldom alienated, the Church was richly endowed. The churches of Constantinople, Alexandria, and Antioch possessed a great many church buildings, monasteries, and charitable institutions, besides wholly secular properties with income that contributed to church salaries and charities. Lesser sees had smaller but still substantial buildings, endowments, and incomes.

The progressive conversion of the provinces required more and larger churches, and popular devotion demanded grander ones. The late fifth and early sixth century was therefore a time of church construction unparalleled in the rest of the history of the East.

So many clerics and such sweeping activities necessarily cost large sums. Most of the money doubtless went for the Church's professed purposes, but abuses were inevitable. Although certain bishops and patriarchs lived in austere simplicity, most lived comfortably, and some lived luxuriously. To pay for an appointment as priest or bishop became a frequent practice, despite the prohibition of such simony by the Council of Chalcedon. Secular donors often retained virtual ownership of the churches that they had built.[9] As the Church gained power and wealth, it naturally lost some of its reputation for apostolic poverty and sanctity.

The reception of Christian morals by secular society continued to be an imperfect process. Pious as Justinian was, he did not attempt to bring his *Code* into agreement with church teaching in more than a few respects. He felt he had to outlaw incest and homosexual acts, and he and his wife were particularly disturbed by the sexual abuse of children, from which she had suffered personally.[10] Yet Justinian's laws limited and discouraged divorce and prostitution without prohibiting them outright. Despite the government's occasional strictures against prostitution, the licentious performances in the theater, and combats between men and animals in the Hippodrome, all of these remained popular into the following period.

Of course the Church had stricter standards than the state, and enforced them by penance or excommunication if necessary. It forbade all sexual relations outside marriage, and divorce except on the ground of adultery. Most clerics heartily disapproved of the theater, all the games at the Hippodrome (including the wildly popular chariot races), and even the public baths. But visits to such places were usually condemned as occasions of sin rather than serious sins in themselves. Church authorities generally agreed that the ideal life was that of the ascetic, removed from the world, renouncing sexuality, and devoted to God, though they acknowledged that many of the faithful were unequal to such rigors. Justinian prescribed celibacy for all bishops, and in the East the rule took hold that while married men could become priests, priests could not marry. For ordinary Christians, the Church approved a secular life, including marriage, provided that the rules against unchastity, impiety, and violence were respected.

In cases when there seemed to be no way out of breaking the rules, the eastern and western parts of the Church took somewhat divergent attitudes. In the West bishops tended to grant a dispensation, which was difficult to obtain but declared the dispensed act sinless. In the East the corresponding concept was accommodation or indulgence (*oikonomia* in Greek), which was more liberally granted but assumed that the accommodated act was still sinful. The same willingness to allow actions while condemning them appears in the eastern regulations for marriage, which usually permitted second and third marriages but forced the parties to do long penances for them. With less ambiguity, western clerics usually forbade the divorced to remarry but saw no sin in any number of remarriages by the widowed. Which of these gradually developing attitudes was the more tolerant cannot be neatly defined.

The pope and the patriarch of Constantinople had important though not irreconcilable differences with each other. The popes were suspicious of the growing power and prestige of the Constantinopolitan patriarchate, which the Council of Chalcedon had ranked next after the papacy. The papacy tacitly accepted this ranking only in 519. While the popes claimed their authority because the apostles Peter and Paul had founded the church of Rome, the patriarchs could only borrow that tradition by arguing that Constantinople was the New Rome, or evade it by arguing that ecclesiastical precedence should go to the bishop of the political capital. On its face either claim seemed to challenge papal primacy. Consequently Pope Pelagius II strongly protested when the patriarch of Constantinople John the Faster termed himself ecumenical patriarch in 588, even though John claimed no additional jurisdiction along with the title.

The Acacian Schism over the patriarch Acacius's accommodation of Monophysitism had been much more dangerous. Acacius's successors would have been glad to heal the schism if the popes had not insisted on condemning Acacius's memory, as a defense against future attempts to compromise with the Monophysites. Even after an agreement to condemn Acacius had ended the schism in 519, Justinian repeatedly tried to win Monophysites over. In the process he replaced Pope Silverius with Vigilius, held the Second Council of Constantinople, and forced Vigilius to accept its findings and to impose them upon the reluctant western church. Schism with the Monophysites was naturally a greater worry for emperors and patriarchs of Constantinople than for popes, whose jurisdiction included scarcely any Monophysites.

59. Saint John the Faster, patriarch of Constantinople (582–95). Miniature from the *Menologium of Basil II*. (Photo: Biblioteca Apostolica Vaticana)

By the early seventh century the persistence of the Monophysite controversy had become the Church's worst failure in the six hundred years of its history. After more than a century and a half of division, schismatic Monophysite churches were firmly rooted in Egypt, Syria, and Armenia. In Egypt the Monophysites formed the majority; in Syria and Armenia, an important minority. Every sort of attempt to restore church unity had failed, including persecution of Monophysites, avoiding the issue, and efforts at compromise so elaborate that today they are often given a distinct name, Neo-Chalcedonianism. Most discouraging of all, in 571 the Monophysite leaders had virtually accepted Chalcedon, only to be forced to recant by their indignant followers. Since the theological differences between most Monophysites and Chalcedonians were minute, the intractability of the controversy was remarkable.

Both Church and state doubtless made mistakes in dealing with Monophysitism, but no worse mistakes than those made in dealing with Arianism. Though without Zeno's *Henoticon*, Anastasius's forbearance, or Theodora's intervention Monophysitism might well have withered away,

Arianism had received similar opportunities from Constantine, Constantius II, and Valens. Doctrines like Monophysitism that emphasized the divinity of Christ had always had a special appeal to the pious; yet the Church had early rid itself of the most extreme heresy of that sort, Sabellianism, which held that Christ was identical with the Father. While Egyptian Christians were notoriously stubborn, many had eventually abandoned Arianism and Melitianism, and some did abandon Monophysitism. In earlier times church leaders had eventually been able to restore unity except with the most marginal groups of heretics; but in the case of Monophysitism they tried and failed.

This failure of leadership is hard to deny. No Athanasius, Cappadocian Fathers, or Cyril of Alexandria appeared at the right moment to win over the majority. Yet leading Monophysites like Severus of Antioch and Jacob Baradaeus were men of theological insight, blameless life, and even goodwill. So were Chalcedonians like the patriarch of Constantinople Menas and the patriarch of Antioch Ephraem of Amida, both of whom collaborated with Justinian. Such men had the respect of their followers, and they and others wrote extensively on the Monophysite controversy. Yet none enjoyed nearly the prestige of the great Fathers of the fourth and early fifth centuries.

In fact, from the late fifth to the late sixth century the Church had notably fewer great leaders than in the previous period, especially in the eastern patriarchates. After Saint Symeon the Stylite died in 459 his imitators made a certain impression, but the prestige of living holy men was not what it had been. A principal theme of the rather defensive biography of Saint Daniel the Stylite, who lived on a pillar near Constantinople from 460 to 493, was how God humiliated the many people the saint failed to impress. Although saints were venerated more than ever, the martyrs and ascetics of an earlier era, like Menas or Cosmas and Damian, were the ones held in highest esteem. These were the most popular subjects for hagiography.[11] While in and around Constantinople half-legendary martyrs like Christopher, Demetrius, Euphemia, George, and Theodore each had several churches dedicated to him, Daniel the Stylite had just one.

The growth of the cult of the saints actually served to reduce respect for living holy men. They could hardly hope to equal the reputed exploits of the martyrs under pagan emperors, the confessors persecuted by Arian emperors, or the first hermits of the desert. While stylitism was a strenuous attempt to achieve new ascetic triumphs, its novelty soon

60. Marble Relief of Saint Menas
from Alexandria. (Photo:
Dumbarton Oaks, Washington,
D.C., copyright 1996)

wore off. Even Monophysite leaders suffered too little persecution to gain much credit as confessors. Christians in need sought the intercession of established saints at shrines all over the empire, but relatively few can have resorted to living ascetics of unproven sanctity, especially because the most admirable tended to be the least accessible.[12] In the same way, the wealthy and comfortable contemporary church naturally commanded less respect than the humble and oppressed church of the age of the persecutions.

Much of this decline in prestige was temporary, the result of adjustment to the Church's recently acquired majority status. Late in the sixth century Gregory the Great and John the Faster became religious leaders of real stature, and were subsequently venerated as saints. They did not, however, give much attention to the Monophysite question, and they clashed with each other over John's title of ecumenical patriarch. No church leaders could wholly avoid the consequences of the drifting apart of the eastern, western, and central parts of the empire, although, like the state, the Church did better than might have been expected at holding those diverse regions together.

HIGHER AND LOWER CULTURE

In the late ancient world, any good secondary school taught the Greek classics. The basic curriculum included Homer, Euripides, Aristophanes, and Demosthenes; more advanced students also read Herodotus and Thucydides, Plato and Aristotle. In the fourth century the leading schools for higher education had been those of Athens and Alexandria, which continued to be famous into the sixth century. All these authors and institutions, of course, were thoroughly, though not self-consciously, pagan. For some time Christians who wanted to become well educated studied that curriculum and went to those schools along with pagans, even if reluctantly. In the fifth century, however, predominantly Christian schools developed, at Gaza for a time and above all at Constantinople. The influence of paganism on education elsewhere became of major concern to Christians.

By the reign of Justinian, while Christians probably formed the majority of the empire's teachers and intellectuals, the minority of pagan scholars were still numerous, prominent, and out of all proportion to the small pagan remnant of the whole population. Justinian attempted a typically decisive solution by forbidding pagans to teach in 529. His edict appears not to have ended all pagan teaching at once; but the Platonic Academy at Athens closed, and its teachers went into exile or retirement.[13] Although some pagans continued to write as pagans, they could not circulate their works safely throughout the empire.

By 600, pagan literature had become practically extinct. Oratory and formal epistolography, traditionally dominated by pagan rhetoricians, almost came to an end as Christians lost interest in them. Even the Christian sermons of the era were few, and undistinguished as rhetoric. The last notable pagan philosophers, Simplicius at Athens and Ammonius the son of Hermias of Alexandria, died in the middle of the sixth century. The leading philosopher of the next generation at Alexandria was a Christian, John Philoponus, who wrote works attacking the Aristotelian doctrines that he could not reconcile with Christianity, and defending his own brand of Tritheistic Monophysitism.[14] Thus theology began to absorb philosophy, and the professional secular scholar became rare.

Despite the decline of pure philosophy and rhetoric, learned men and accomplished writers continued to exist through the end of the sixth century. Some, like Paul the Silentiary and Agathias of Myrina, wrote classical poetry of some virtuosity on primarily secular and even erotic subjects. Contemporary histories modeled on Thucydides and Herodotus appeared regularly. Though the last of the long line of definitely pagan historians was the embittered Zosimus, who around 500 blamed Christianity for the western empire's fall, his Christian successors improved upon him in both style and analysis.

The most brilliant of the classicizing historians was without doubt Procopius of Caesarea, Belisarius's secretary. His graceful, intelligent, and detailed narrative of his superior's campaigns not only imitates but rivals Herodotus, Thucydides, and Polybius. His books on the Persian war form an animated prelude; those on the Vandal war are vivid and gripping, showing his strong sense of the role of chance in history; and those on the Ostrogothic war gradually create a powerful picture of tragedy and loss. To vent indignation against Justinian that went too far to be publishable, Procopius also wrote for the drawer his intemperate but engrossing *Secret History*, which luckily has survived. Procopius has a good claim to be Byzantium's greatest writer, and one of the great historians of the world.

The poet Agathias later wrote a classicizing history to continue that of Procopius, though it is much more pedestrian. As late as the reign of Maurice, Menander Protector and John of Epiphania produced proficient classicizing histories, now mostly lost. These and a few other secular poets and historians were nearly all government officials by profession, trained as lawyers. Although they had a good knowledge of literature and rhetoric, they were not professional scholars or teachers versed in philosophy. Procopius was not a professional either, but he evidently knew such men and strove to meet their standards. Soon afterward, as the amateur writer and scholar became the rule, the literary community lost much of its depth and diversity.

Even so, officials were obtaining fine educations in classical Greek up to the beginning of the seventh century, and a few used their erudition in their writing. After Justinian, however, even the leading authors seem somewhat less sure of their knowledge. The decline of the senatorial class affected literary circles at Constantinople by reducing patronage for and interest in literature. Knowledge of Latin was becoming rare in the East, though one last Latin poet of some talent, Corippus, migrated from reconquered Africa to the court of Justin II. When an earthquake destroyed the law school at Berytus in 551, no one rebuilt it. Once the pagan scholars and teachers disappeared, fewer Christians took their place in an academic profession that seems to have sunk in prestige.

On the other hand, from the sixth century on, literature in something close to spoken Greek became more common. The reason was hardly a spread of literacy among marginally educated groups, where it seems rather to have declined, but a decreasing ability among the educated to read and write the classical form of the language. As less educated writers predominated, they became less ashamed of their more popular language and interests, particularly as Christians became more distrustful of pagan literature and prouder of the not very elegant Greek of the New Testament.

Half-educated authors thus began to write with less fear of the scorn of better-educated critics. The chronicler John Malalas, relying on Eusebius of Caesarea and other compilers, confidently strung together myths, biblical stories, and real history. The pseudogeographer Cosmas Indicopleustes, explaining that the experts had their geography all wrong, corrected them from his own eccentric reading of the Bible. Though admittedly ancient Greek literature could draw upon a long and rich tradition of misinformation, these sixth-century attempts to substitute Christian improvisation for traditional learning were mostly new. Something like them also appears in the popular hagiography of the time, especially in accounts of posthumous miracles ascribed to saints.

Meanwhile Christian scholarship and literature took on a different shape. The middle of the fifth century turned out to be the end of the great age of the Greek Fathers, who had used their wide knowledge of secular rhetoric and philosophy to produce original and persuasive theological arguments. One peculiar exception appeared a generation or two later, significantly under the name of a much earlier figure, Saint Paul's disciple Dionysius the Areopagite. This Pseudo-Dionysius wrote quite innovative mystical theology, describing in Neoplatonic terms how the sacraments, clergy, and angels could offer Christians oneness with God. His fictive date allowed him to avoid the issue of the Council of Chalcedon, though he was more or less a Monophysite, and to gain an authority otherwise accorded only to earlier writers.

While the Council of Chalcedon coincided with the disappearance of Church Fathers, it can hardly be the only cause of the change in the writing of theology. The council did complete the official definition of the nature of Christ and thus of fundamental Christian doctrine, which might seem to have restricted the scope of theological discourse. But, like the three previous ecumenical councils, it also set off heated theological arguments that cried out for resolution by new Church Fathers. Instead the disputants argued their cases through citations from the older Fathers, who had either skirted the points in dispute or, like Cyril of Alexandria, addressed them ambiguously. As succeeding generations of theologians came to prize citations and to distrust innovation, theology became less rhetorical and more technical. Its technicality, lack of philosophical subtlety, and indifference to ancient rhetoric may well have weakened its power to convert opponents.

Accordingly clerics and monks came to know much less of the classics, but probably more of the Bible, and certainly more of the Fathers. They carefully read the new Christian classics of the fourth and early fifth centuries, including the supposedly apostolic Pseudo-Dionysius, and imbibed their doctrine if not much of their style. These later writers respected the Christian classics too much to believe that they or their contemporaries could equal the wisdom or eloquence of such giants. This was partly true, since they lacked the philosophical and rhetorical training to imitate the style or argumentation of the Cappadocian Fathers. Instead they imitated the language and discourse of the less erudite Fathers and the Bible.

Nonetheless, some learned Christian literature persisted, and apart from doctrinal matters could even innovate. The polemics of various theologians for and against Monophysitism were abundant and serious. While most popular hagiography used conventional formulas to praise obscure saints, under Justinian Cyril of Scythopolis wrote several careful and circumstantial lives of Palestinian monks, including their distinguished leader Saint Sabas, which found a certain readership. Also under Justinian, Romanus the Melode developed a metrically intricate sort of hymn, the *kontakion*, and composed wonderful examples that were admired and sung from his own time onward. Toward the end of the sixth century John Climacus wrote a practical manual for ascetics, *The Ladder of Paradise*, which became immensely popular in monasteries. In the reign of Maurice, Evagrius Scholasticus continued the fifth-century ecclesiastical histories up to his own time.

This Christian Hellenic culture exerted influence well outside the regions where most people spoke Greek. Although few westerners knew the language and most resisted attempts to conciliate Monophysites, in the end Justinian won acquiescence in his theological program from the pope and the other bishops of Italy and Africa, many of whom were chosen by the emperor and his officials and some of whom were Greeks. Coptic, Syriac, and Armenian were by now established as written languages in places with largely Monophysite churches. Yet if anything Monophysitism, which had first been formulated by speakers of Greek, strengthened Greek influence on Egyptian, Syrian, and Armenian culture.

Since Monophysites regarded their faith as the orthodoxy all Chris-

61. Saint Romanus the Melode receiving inspiration from the Virgin in a dream. Miniature from the *Menologium of Basil II*. (Photo: Biblioteca Apostolica Vaticana)

tians should adopt, their leaders, like Severus of Antioch, often wrote in Greek. Even those who wrote in Syriac, like the ecclesiastical historian and hagiographer John of Ephesus, were well versed in the Greek Fathers. Somewhat less literature seems to have been written in Coptic and Armenian in the sixth century than in the fifth, and all three literatures continued to consist largely of translations of Greek Christian texts. The patriarchate of Constantinople exerted its influence on the Hellenized clergy and monks of Syria, Egypt, Armenia, and the Latin West, though less of that influence reached the laity.

Thus Greek culture was changing in the sixth century. The number of the educated slightly contracted, the level of education declined somewhat, and middlebrow literature gained at the expense of highbrow literature. Knowledge of Latin literature declined drastically both inside and outside the empire. By 600 Greek was the only language with even a small audience for secular literature. The cultural dominance of Byzantium's Greek heartland, centered on Constantinople, was clearer than ever. Christian culture adopted its own Christian classics in place of the secular ones and grew more independent of secular culture.

As Christianity strengthened its hold on the empire from the reign of Leo I to that of Justinian, Christian art and architecture reached a peak of real splendor. Despite many problems of dating and the destruction of many monuments, the general developments seem clear. By the mid-fifth century the best Christian artists had achieved the technical expertise and majestic effects that the Church wanted. During the next hundred years the Church multiplied and refined its new art forms in a colossal building campaign. This construction exceeded any possible growth of congregations at the time. With the help of private donors and sometimes of the state, the Church enthusiastically replaced less grand buildings of the fourth century and built more monasteries and shrines everywhere, from the cities to the wilderness.

As before, the favorite type of church was the basilica, and constructing more, larger, and more elaborate basilicas became one of the empire's major industries. Quarries and brickyards, workshops and engineers must have done a thriving business. Ready-made columns, capitals, and other decorations were shipped all over the empire to adorn basilicas of standard plan. Among the largest and most lavish were two aligned basilicas in the middle of the mountains of Isauria, probably built by the Isaurian emperor Zeno (Fig. 36), and four basilicas forming a cross on a barren Syrian hill around the pillar that had once been the abode of Saint Symeon the Stylite (Fig. 62). Some builders not only multiplied the basilica but went beyond it. In the early sixth century Anicia Juliana, a wealthy private citizen of Constantinople descended from the Theodosian dynasty, joined to her palace a church of the dimensions the Bible ascribes to the Temple of Solomon. Dedicated to the ancient martyr Polyeuctus, it had sculptural decoration of riotous opulence. Envy of its magnificence seems to have spurred Justinian on to build Saint Sophia.[15]

Although sculpture has survived more often than painting or mosaic, masterpieces clearly existed in each decorative form, and by no means all of them were religious. One work that has been preserved is a sumptuous illustrated manuscript of a work on medical materials copied for the same Anicia Juliana (Fig. 33). Other art commissioned by the wealthy includes elegantly decorated textiles, silver plate, and objects in ivory. Particularly gorgeous is a huge floor mosaic from the imperial palace in Constantinople depicting fanciful scenes of country life (Fig. 63). It

62. Ruins of the pilgrimage complex of Saint Symeon the Stylite, Syria.
(Photo: R. Anderson, Dumbarton Oaks, Washington, D.C., copyright 1996)

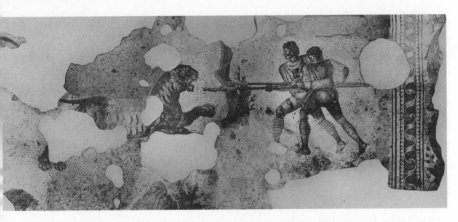

63. Detail of a tiger hunt from a mosaic floor, probably of the sixth century, in
the Great Palace of the emperors, Constantinople. (Photo: From *The Great
Palace of the Byzantine Emperors* I [Oxford, 1947])

probably belongs to the sixth century, but its combination of brilliant natural detail and elegantly artificial presentation could be found throughout the period.

Justinian continued what was already an extensive campaign of church construction on an even larger scale, and worked out a grand new style of his own. Massive domes had long been a feature of Roman architecture, and they had been erected by the builders just preceding Justinian who wanted a particularly imposing effect. Justinian liked churches roofed by large domes, often by more than one of them. In Saint Sophia he set a gigantic dome atop several half-domes, and on his second attempt managed to make it stay up. If the church was seldom copied in the decades that followed, one reason is surely that its boldness frightened off possible imitators.

By Justinian's time many artists were capable of classicizing art of the naturalistic sort, but taste seems to have changed. Even when the figures in Justinianic artwork look classical, the backgrounds are almost always stylized. Saint Sophia is full of intricate, irregular, and utterly unclassical ornamentation and structural elements (Fig. 50). Along with his architectural innovations, Justinian seems also to have patronized a more abstract style of figural mosaic. While only geometrical compositions survive from his work in Saint Sophia, a quite schematic mosaic of the Transfiguration of Christ can be seen in another of his foundations, the Monastery of Saint Catherine on Mount Sinai (Fig. 64).

Justinian's artistic style, particularly in Saint Sophia, made a strong impression on its beholders. It certainly shaped the subsequent development of the art of the Balkans and Anatolia; but it had less effect on Syria, Egypt, and the West. Even when Justinian paid for churches there, the builders were local and had their own styles, which increasingly diverged from those of the Greek heartland. The influence of Justinianic art on the empire's eastern and western wings, like that of Greek culture, was obvious but somewhat superficial.

This was all the more true because after Justinian the empire's construction boom ended. Except in some of inland Syria, few churches or other monuments date from the later sixth century. Even the construction of fortifications fell off. This trend seems also to have affected private houses, of which a number of good-sized examples survive in stone in northern Syria from the earlier period. Such art as still was produced apparently declined in refinement and cost. Both art and literature thus showed signs of deterioration toward the end of the sixth century, par-

64. Sixth-century apse mosaic of Christ's Transfiguration in the Monastery of
Saint Catherine, Mount Sinai. (Photo: Courtesy of Michigan-Princeton-
Alexandria Expedition to Mount Sinai)

ticularly in comparison with their recently thriving state. The principal
cause was presumably the impoverishment of a government and society
that had been thriving only a short time before.

EXPANSION AND DEPRESSION

The striking features of Byzantine history from the mid-fifth to the
early seventh century are a powerful advance in almost every field in the
first half of the period, followed by a gradual but unmistakable decline in
the second half. Up to about 540 the empire's army steadily emerged
from its former disarray, until Byzantium became able to make vast conquests rapidly and with moderate effort. Overcoming severe financial
embarrassment, the state gained enormous additional revenues. Private
wealth seems to have grown apace, and art and literature flourished. Justinian could fancy with some reason that his empire was capable of almost anything.

After 540 nearly everything started to go wrong. Although Justinian
completed the conquests he had begun earlier, he did so with terrible
difficulty, and at great cost in men, money, and damage to the lands he
took. At his death in 565 the only areas that the empire had gained that

it had not held in 540 were southern Spain and a few places in northern Italy. During the same interval the eastern and Balkan frontiers had become less secure. Meeting government expenses became a constant preoccupation. Private wealth substantially diminished, and literature and art began to lose their brilliance. During the rest of the century defensive and fiscal troubles persisted, until under Phocas the empire was on the brink of ruin. Although the military, economic, and cultural decline was sometimes interrupted, the long-term trend from 540 to 610 was unfavorable, and aggravated earlier tendencies toward political and social instability.

This general deterioration in the later sixth century need not have had a single cause. But it began too early to be attributable just to mistakes made by Justinian's successors, whose performance was on the whole creditable. Several possible causes can be suggested that started with the earlier part of Justinian's reign and remained significant thereafter. They include increases in spending by Justinian, the burden of defending the western reconquests, the heightened intensity of Persian and Slavic attacks, and of course the plague. Though the first three of these seem insufficient explanations by themselves, combined with each other and the plague they had a powerful impact.

In retrospect, Justinian did spend too much, and by doing so caused fiscal problems for his successors. Yet a crisis in public finance is far more likely to be an effect than a cause of a general economic depression. Justinian's spending was never absolutely reckless, and some of it was quite prudent. His building of fortifications and his subsidies to barbarians probably saved money over the long run. While his increase in the size of the field army brought a substantial and permanent increase in expenditure, it was necessary for the empire's security, and was almost offset by his stopping pay for the frontier forces. Whatever effect his considerably smaller outlay on luxury buildings and churches had, it could hardly have lingered thirty or forty years after his death. His confiscations of large private fortunes may have depressed the economy slightly, but the effect should again have been transitory. Since his one known tax increase probably raised revenues by less than 3 percent, it cannot have depressed economic activity very much.[16] As for spending on his reconquests, it cannot be counted extravagant if they produced enough revenue to cover their cost.

That they almost certainly did. The value of the captured Vandal and Ostrogothic treasuries may well have equaled the expenses of all Justinian's campaigns against the Vandals and Ostrogoths. After Justinian's reign

Africa not only paid for most of its own defense but sent large shipments of grain and a good deal of money to the East.[17] Since Italy and southern Spain essentially supported themselves, their revenues must have covered high, if not quite adequate, expenses for defense. Although efforts to make Italy and Spain fully safe might well have become a severe drain on the rest of the empire, the government could and did avoid straining its resources in this way. After 541, perfect foresight combined with disregard for Justinian's political and religious aims might have led the Byzantines to abandon Italy except for the extreme south and not to intervene in Spain. In that case, the reconquests would have shown a significant profit. As it was, at the worst they made an insignificant loss.

During the sixth century the Persians, the Slavs, and later the Avars certainly harmed the empire's economy, both by their raids and by the defensive expenditures they made necessary. Though all three powers seemed well under control by 602, the economic damage they had occasioned was nonetheless real, and contributed to the political crisis that began in that year. That in turn allowed those enemies to renew their military threats to Byzantium, even if the Avars and Slavs appear not to have recovered enough to attack before 610. That the sixth-century Avar and Persian wars led to trouble is not surprising, in view of the empire's earlier problems dealing with simultaneous fighting on both the Balkan and the eastern front. But the extent of the empire's collapse after 602 seems disproportionate, and shows Byzantium's weakness more than its enemies' strength. The military pressures were after all not so much more severe than they had been in the glorious years of Anastasius, Justin I, and the earlier reign of Justinian.

That happy age itself needs explaining, especially because it came after another troubled period when the empire had barely held its own. In fact, in the early sixth century the empire appears to have been stronger and richer than at any time since the second century A.D. The second-century prosperity had come to an end with the two epidemics between 165 and 266, which were probably measles and smallpox. As resistance to those diseases gradually spread and they became less virulent, the population seems to have stabilized by the early fifth century, and with it the economy.

Not long afterward, the population should have been able to grow appreciably for the first time in over three hundred years. Since by then there must have been ample vacant land, no overcrowding would have restrained growth. Rural slaves, whose birth rate had evidently been low, had dwindled to a small fraction of the population. Christianity encouraged the empire's great majority of married people to have children and condemned the usual means of population control, infanticide and abortion. At first, those who had many children and expected few of them to survive childhood diseases would have had larger families than they had anticipated. With land plentiful, larger families would have led to expanding the area under cultivation and to increasing rural incomes.

The population may still have grown rather slowly, but the upward trend should have been perceptible in economic activity and tax payments, and in a growing supply of labor. Increases in state revenue and army recruits under Anastasius are attested facts, yet at the same time abandonment of land and complaints of overtaxation almost disappear. This is just the sort of evidence of population growth that might be expected. Such growth would also explain the other signs of public and private prosperity at the time, including Justinian's ability to undertake so many costly activities at once.

Any economic expansion caused by population growth ended with the plague that broke out in 541. The initial impact must have been abrupt if something like a quarter of Justinian's subjects died, causing further disruption of the empire's agriculture and trade network, and subsequently a famine. Since bubonic plague has little tendency to become endemic, after the first epidemic passed the population should have begun to recover. Yet before 610 six more epidemics followed at regular intervals, cutting short each recovery and driving the population further downward after each outbreak. The process continued into the seventh century, with all its baneful fiscal and military consequences.

While the demographic evidence is inadequate to demonstrate the scale of the overall population losses caused by the plague, surviving figures can be used to trace fluctuations in the state budget. To make overall estimates of the budget during the sixth century requires the usual guesswork; but any likely mistakes should yield fairly consistent overestimates or underestimates, so that their proportional differences should be approximately valid. The same methods used to estimate a state budget of about 7.8 million nomismata under Marcian would suggest a budget of about 8.5 million nomismata in the later years of Anastasius, including a surplus of about 750,000 nomismata. A similar estimate of the state budget under Justinian around 540 would give about 11.3 million nomismata, probably with no significant surplus. Later in Justinian's reign, after payment of the frontier troops had ceased in 541, the budget can be estimated at about 8.5 million nomismata again, approximately in balance (Table 6).[18]

TABLE 6

Estimated State Budgets in the Sixth Century

Date and budgetary item	Estimate (millions of nomismata)
CA. 518 (Anastasius I)	
pay of Excubitors (300 × 40 nom. × $\frac{1}{3}$)[a]	0.016M nom.
pay of field soldiers (95,000 × 20 nom. × $\frac{1}{3}$)[a]	2.533
pay of frontier soldiers (176,000[b] × 5 nom. × $\frac{1}{3}$)[a]	1.173
pay of oarsmen (30,000 × 5 nom. × $\frac{5}{4}$)[a]	0.188
uniforms and arms (176,300 × 5 nom.)	0.882
fodder and horses (107,400[c] × 5 nom.)	0.537
campaigns and other military expenses	0.2
pay of bureaucracy	0.8
grain dole	0.8
tribute and other nonmilitary expenses	0.6
surplus	0.75
TOTAL	8.479M nom.
CA. 540 (Justinian I)	
pay of Excubitors (300 × 40 × $\frac{1}{3}$)[a]	0.016M nom.
pay of field soldiers (145,000 × 20 nom. × $\frac{1}{3}$)[a]	3.867
pay of frontier soldiers (195,500 × 5 nom. × $\frac{1}{3}$)[a]	1.303
pay of oarsmen (30,000 × 5 nom. × $\frac{5}{4}$)[a]	0.188
uniforms and arms (195,800 × 5 nom.)	0.979
fodder and horses (126,800[d] × 5 nom.)	0.634
campaigns and other military expenses	1.0
pay of bureaucracy	1.1
grain dole	0.8
other nonmilitary expenses	1.4
TOTAL	11.287M nom.
CA. 565 (Justinian I)	
pay of Excubitors (300 × 40 nom. × $\frac{1}{3}$)[a]	0.016M nom.
pay of field soldiers (150,000 × 20 nom. × $\frac{1}{3}$)[a]	4.0
uniforms and arms (195,800 × 5 nom.)	0.979
fodder and horses (127,800[e] × 5 nom.)	0.639
campaigns and other military expenses	0.5
pay of bureaucracy	1.1
grain dole	0.8
tribute and other nonmilitary expenses	0.5
TOTAL	8.534M nom.

[a]The fractional multiplier allows for the higher pay of officers.

[b]This is 90 percent of the comparable figure under Marcian, to allow for losses.

[c]The number includes 300 Excubitors and 107,100 field and frontier cavalry (90 percent of the figure under Marcian), to allow for losses.

[d]The number includes 300 Excubitors, 29,000 field cavalry (20% of 145,000 at the apparent cavalry ratio), and 97,500 frontier cavalry (including those of Africa).

[e]The number includes 300 Excubitors, 30,000 field cavalry (20% of 150,000 at the apparent cavalry ratio), and 97,500 frontier cavalry.

Thus in the latter part of Justinian's reign the empire's revenues seem to have been approximately what they had been under Anastasius, despite Justinian's greater stringency in raising revenue and his acquisition of vast territories in Africa, Dalmatia, Italy, and southern Spain. The reason cannot be that the western reconquests produced no revenue at all, and negative revenue is an impossible concept: even if the reconquests cost more money than they brought in, they would have increased the total budget. If despite all Justinian's efforts the empire's revenue was about a quarter lower in 565 than in 540, and no higher than in 518, the Byzantine economy must have been in far worse condition. Given the primitive nature of the economy, this can only mean that the total population was smaller in 565 than in 540, and about the same as in 518. In other words, a general demographic decline had offset the large population gain that would otherwise have resulted from Justinian's reconquests. Although warfare, famine, and natural disasters may have caused some of the decline, only the plague could account for losses on such a scale.

The same recent estimates that put the empire's population at about 16 million under Marcian put it at about 17 million under Phocas, or 13 million excluding the lands reconquered by Justinian. As rough approximations, these estimates seem plausible in themselves and fit well enough with earlier and later evidence. For the period between these dates, however, the estimators almost certainly err in postulating a continuous decline rather than a recovery before the plague and a sharp fall afterward.[19] By analogy with the recurrence of the bubonic plague in the fourteenth century, the disease should have caused a population decline approaching a third over the next two generations.

If so, in 540 the eastern provinces might have had some 19 million people; including Africa, Dalmatia, and most of Italy, Justinian might temporarily have ruled some 26 million souls. The 19 million people in the East in 540 would have represented an increase of roughly a fifth since 457. While in absolute terms such estimates have a wide margin for error, their value for purposes of comparison is greater, because as in the budgets errors would tend to be made in the same direction throughout. Regardless of the exact figures, both a substantial recovery before 541 and an even larger loss afterward appear practically certain.

As already noted, the impact of the plague varied markedly from place to place, so that moist, populous places often visited by outsiders were much more vulnerable than dry, lightly populated, and isolated areas. The effect of the contagion on the empire's cities was therefore disproportionately severe. The death of 230,000 people in Constantinople in 542, out of a population that cannot much have exceeded 375,000, was probably worse than average, given the size of the city and its many visitors. Yet some cities suffered not only from the plague but from destruction by the enemy, like Antioch and Rome, which were almost deserted for short intervals after their capture by the Persians and Ostrogoths in 540 and 546. Massive earthquakes killed tens of thousands at Antioch in 526 and 588, and lesser tremors also caused fatalities. Rome, which its imperial past had left with far more people than its economic role could justify, had little reason to rebound after the Ostrogothic wars depopulated it.

The cities had always attracted settlers from the countryside, and would have been especially attractive after an outbreak of plague had made urban labor scarce and housing abundant. Nonetheless, migration from the country probably did no more than reduce the net population loss of the cities to about the average for the empire, because the diminished rural population could hardly have supported undiminished cities. Accordingly the population of Constantinople in 610 could scarcely have been more than a quarter million, and was probably closer to two hundred thousand. After the disasters at Antioch the empire must have been left with just two cities, Constantinople and Alexandria, of over a hundred thousand people. Antioch, in its ravaged condition, might have been about half that size.[20]

The other real cities in the empire, those with significantly more than ten thousand people, surely decreased in number despite Justinian's reconquests, perhaps from over thirty cities to under twenty in all. The plague left regions that had previously had somewhat anemic urban life with just one metropolis of any size. Probably the only city over ten thousand remaining in Greece was Thessalonica, while Alexandria may have been the only such city in Egypt. By 610 Carthage may well have been the lone city in the whole territory retaken by Justinian with more than ten thousand people, since Ravenna is unlikely to have reached that figure. Even in Anatolia and Syria cities declined, with a few exceptions in the inland part of Syria. Though only a few towns on the Danube frontier disappeared altogether, some of the places that survived must have become mere villages. Of course, the vast mass of the population had always lived in villages, and for them life went on much as before.

The cities, as classical archeologists have noticed, were not only shrinking but losing their ancient character. To make them more defensible, the authorities or the inhabitants often contracted the circuits of the walls and abandoned outlying districts. Except in the largest cities, the theaters and hippodromes became obsolete, because no one could pay for spectacles in them. When most of the great public baths became too expensive to maintain, bathers had to resort to smaller establishments. In most cities the government and private patrons also gave up the struggle to maintain market squares, allowing merchants to set up shop along the colonnaded streets where most of their customers passed. With the decline of the decurions and of prosperity in general, only a few monuments and inscriptions went up any longer.

Yet as theaters, hippodromes, baths, squares, monuments, and temples were slowly abandoned, in their places new buildings went up to occupy vacancies in the valuable space protected by city walls. The citizens of modest means who built houses and shops there paid little attention to the old city plan and sometimes encroached upon the streets. These new arrangements need not have made life worse, or even changed it very much. Central squares had already lost much of their purpose with the disappearance of the public meetings for which they had been designed. A busy street can be as lively as a busy square; the streets accommodated trade fairs, strolling performers, religious processions on festival days, and occasional riots. People still met each other in the small baths, the street, wineshops, and church. Though tidiness and classical ideas of beauty suffered, even Justinian's buildings showed little regard for those. The new construction, haphazard but sturdy enough to leave ruins for archeologists, implies that people were far from being destitute.

Most of these changes had actually begun during the time of growing population, trade, and wealth that preceded the plague. The economic expansion seems to help explain the increased frequency of social disorder, including religious and factional rioting. Such riots had happened before, but had seldom been so severe as they became after the mid-fifth century, when many cities had large groups of young men with leisure to devote to sports, shows, carousing, crime, and following their own fashions. The gangs of Blues and Greens, who cut their hair like Huns, wore expensive and outlandish clothes in their colors, and went about armed, were only the most conspicuous of these rowdies. The idle rich looked for excitement; the idle poor looked for chances to steal some of the good things that they saw around them. Some Monophysites and Chalcedonians also seem to have liked conflict more than discussion, to the despair of those who tried to reconcile them.

These were, however, the incidental problems of an era whose prosperity is evident from the increases in construction and in the production and import of luxuries. As people who already had houses and churches built bigger and better houses and churches, new building and settlement spread in Constantinople, in provincial towns, and through the countryside. The evidence has survived best in Syria, but the pattern appears to hold for Anatolia and Egypt as well. Growth in the long-distance luxury trade from India may quite possibly have helped import the plague along the Red Sea route. Abuses that had formerly arisen because soldiers could not live on their wages, and civilians could not pay their rents and taxes, apparently decreased as everyone became more prosperous.

In the beginning the state still had to struggle, partly because it had lost most of its monetary reserve in the disastrous Vandal expedition of 468. Civil unrest and the barbarians' ravaging of the Balkans retarded the replenishment of the reserve. Even so, under Zeno fiscal embarrassment eased. That Anastasius was able to make wholesale conversions of taxes in kind to taxes in gold, without provoking protests, is a sign of earlier economic development. After cutting taxes, Anastasius amassed reserves of about 23 million nomismata, three times Marcian's reserve and a third of the record reserves of the entire empire in the first and second centuries. Anastasius's revenues of about 8.5 million nomismata seem to have been almost two-fifths of those of the whole empire at its height. Since the East had always been the empire's richer half, these comparisons suggest that it had not quite recovered all its ancient prosperity. But it was well on its way to doing so.

Drawing on Anastasius's reserves, Justinian was able to afford his impressive outlays in the early part of his reign. His reconquest of Africa, Dalmatia, and Italy up to 540 probably cost no more than the 7.4 million nomismata that Leo I reportedly spent on a far more lavish attempt to retake Africa alone. The Perpetual Peace of 532 with Persia cost 792,000 nomismata. Since Justinian spent some 300,000 nomismata on Saint Sophia in 532, the first of the six years of its construction, the whole building might have cost around 2 million.[21] Such gigantic churches as the now vanished Holy Apostles in Constantinople and the now ruined Saint John at Ephesus probably cost about a million nomismata each. Justinian obtained the Vandal treasury only in 534, and the Ostrogothic treasury in 540. Up to that time, his confiscations of private wealth seem not to have been extensive.

65. Partly reconstructed ruins of
Justinian's Church of Saint John,
Ephesus. (Photo: Irina
Andreescu-Treadgold)

The economic depression after 541 took hold by fits and starts, and even so not everything was changed. That Byzantium could sustain the ravages of the plague without an outright collapse shows how strong it had been when the plague began. At the time no one realized how lasting the effects of the disaster would be; nor could anyone have done so without knowing that the plague would recur. Even the most astute doubtless assumed that once the first outbreak had passed in 544 things would soon return to normal, as in fact they began to do. If even an informed and intelligent observer like Procopius failed to see why poverty, famine, and government exactions continued to spread after the epidemic, the population at large must also have been at a loss, and similarly resentful. In 546 the Alexandrians rioted over the famine, and the troops in Constantinople rioted because their pay was late. The Monophysites continued to be as stubborn as ever, though over the long run the plague appears to have had a somewhat sobering effect on the Blues and Greens.

The empire's great landed fortunes must have suffered not only from Justinian's confiscations, which eventually became onerous, but from a shortage of labor and the general disruption of the economy. The surviving peasants, whose labor became more valuable, may have fared better. Interestingly, however, the army continued to attract an ample supply of recruits, even when Tiberius raised its strength by fifteen thousand in 577. Service in the field forces was still so popular in 594 that the troops applauded a guarantee that their sons could inherit their places. Evidently life outside the army offered few opportunities as attractive as drawing a field soldier's pay. The frontier troops, who went on combining other professions with their service, also seem to have valued their modest privileges and supplies in kind.

Through all the fiscal troubles of the period, the government kept its revenues at a remarkably high level under the circumstances. Justin II's expenses probably fell a bit as he cut Justinian's spending on building, campaigns, and tribute, and perhaps when he lost some of his Italian troops. But Tiberius's recruitment of the Federates would have cost almost half a million nomismata annually and must have brought expenditure back to what it had been in Justinian's later years.[22] Tiberius paid his men partly by drawing on Justin II's accumulated reserve; yet even after this reserve was gone, Maurice, with whatever pains and reluctance, managed to keep paying them throughout his twenty-year reign. State bankruptcy may have threatened repeatedly between 541 and 610, but it never came. The government must have been functioning at a high level of efficiency to handle its fiscal problems so well.

Notwithstanding the economic expansion between the mid-fifth century and the mid-sixth, by 610 the empire seems to have been weaker than it had been in 457. It was larger in area, but its ability to keep what it had was in grave doubt. Its new holdings in Italy and Spain had been shrinking for decades, and it had just lost its old possessions in Mesopotamia to the Persians with alarming speed. With the atrophy of the frontier troops, the defenses of Syria and Egypt depended on the same Army of the East that had just failed to defend Mesopotamia from the Persians. Byzantium still had strengths to draw upon, especially in its Anatolian core, but the overthrow of Maurice had shaken the political equilibrium that it had maintained for so long. Heraclius had a difficult task ahead of him.

PART THREE

The Contained Catastrophe

66. Seventh-century silver plate of David and Goliath, one of a set of nine showing the life of David and perhaps made to commemorate Heraclius's victory over the Persians. (Photo: Metropolitan Museum of Art, New York)

CHAPTER NINE

Two Fights for Survival, 610–668

Heraclius is said to have accepted the crown with reluctance, and only after Phocas's son-in-law Priscus had refused it. Certainly ruling the Byzantine Empire had never been harder than it was after Phocas's execution. Even if the Byzantines still held most of the territory they had had under Maurice, nearly every frontier was in imminent peril. The Persians of Khusrau II held Byzantine Mesopotamia and threatened Byzantine Armenia, Syria, and Anatolia. The main eastern army that faced them was still in the hands of Phocas's brother Comentiolus. The Slavs already in Illyricum were looting it, and more of them had just invaded from the north.

Heraclius became emperor at the age of about thirty-six, with little experience of commanding or fighting except during the final and easiest phase of the civil war. His close associates in the capital were few; his father soon died in Africa, and his cousin Nicetas remained in the East. The new emperor had spent most of his adult life in Africa, though his family were Armenians from Cappadocia, and he had been betrothed to a young woman in Constantinople whom he married on the day of his coronation. He was prone to understandable fits of melancholy, but he had great gifts as a strategist and leader.

THE PERSIAN CONQUESTS

Heraclius had gained much credit within the empire for overthrowing the unpopular Phocas. When the late emperor's brother Comentiolus planned to march on Constantinople from his winter quarters at Ancyra, some of his own men assassinated him.[1] Heraclius named Priscus to suc-

67. Heraclius (r. 610–41) and his son the future Constantine III (r. 641), with a cross on steps on the reverse. Gold nomisma, shown twice actual size. (Photo: Dumbarton Oaks, Washington, D.C., copyright 1996)

ceed Comentiolus as commander of the troops in Anatolia, which apparently comprised the greater part of the eastern and Balkan armies. Khusrau, considering Heraclius no less a usurper than Phocas, kept pressing his invasion. The Balkans had to fend for themselves against the Slavs, since Khusrau was the more dangerous enemy.

In 611 two Persian forces advanced between Priscus's army in Anatolia and the southern army led by Heraclius's cousin Nicetas. Both Byzantine commanders, still regrouping their forces after the civil war, were far from ready to meet the Persian armies under Shāhīn and Shahrvarāz. Outmarching Priscus, Shāhīn seized Cappadocian Caesarea for the second time in two years. Well ahead of Nicetas, Shahrvarāz reached Antioch, where the Blues and Greens and Jews were running riot, and captured the great city as well. Having cut the Prefecture of the East in two, from Antioch he turned south and took Apamea and Emesa. The Persians plainly hoped to keep the broad band of northern Syria that they had taken, though in case they should fail they sent many of their Byzantine prisoners east.

That summer Priscus and Nicetas tried to expel the invaders. Nicetas brought Shahrvarāz to an indecisive battle near Emesa, which halted the Persians without driving them back. Nicetas then went to Constantinople to see Heraclius. Priscus, who seems to have had a much larger army than Nicetas, contrived to besiege Shāhīn in Caesarea over the winter. The capture of the Persians in Caesarea would have been a decisive counterblow; but Shāhīn broke out in the spring of 612. A troubled

Heraclius went to Cappadocia to inspect Priscus's army, and that fall he summoned Priscus to the capital.

Evidently Heraclius judged that his cousin had done as well as possible under the circumstances, but found Priscus delinquent. While returning Nicetas to his command, the emperor dismissed Priscus and forced him to become a monk. The new commander of the Anatolian army was Philippicus, one of Maurice's best generals, whom Phocas had forced to become a priest ten years before. Apparently not trusting even Philippicus, however, the emperor himself took command of much of the army in Asia Minor. A symbolic demonstration by the aged Justinian had been the only time a reigning emperor had marched against a foreign enemy for over two hundred years; but the emergency justified extraordinary measures.

In 613 Heraclius planned to attack the Persians in Syria from the north while Nicetas attacked them from the south. Philippicus kept a smaller force in Cappadocia to hold off Shāhīn's superior army. When Shāhīn took Melitene, Philippicus reacted by invading Persian-held Armenia, forcing Shāhīn to follow him over rugged terrain and suffer heavy losses. Meanwhile, in the main campaign, Heraclius fought a bloody but inconclusive battle with the Persians outside Antioch. They regrouped, defeated him, and forced him to abandon Cilicia. As Nicetas's campaign in the south came to nothing, Byzantium's fortunes continued to decline.

That fall Shahrvarāz captured Damascus and invaded Palestine. The Jews, who were numerous in the northern part of the country, joined him in a triumphal march to Jerusalem. Apparently the Christians of Jerusalem surrendered to him, but in the spring, after he marched south, they expelled his garrison. Shahrvarāz turned back, besieged Jerusalem, and took it by storm. In retaliation for its revolt he deported most of its Christian population to Persia, destroyed the principal churches, and carried off the supposed True Cross of Christ. Then he allowed the Jews to settle and govern the city.[2]

Although Nicetas had withdrawn to Egypt without stopping the Persians, Heraclius kept his cousin in office and continued to rely on his family. Since his first wife Eudocia had died in 612 after the birth of his son Heraclius Constantine, the emperor made a second marriage with his niece Martina. The patriarch Sergius objected that the marriage was incestuous, but Heraclius overruled him.[3] Somewhat less incestuously, the little heir to the throne Heraclius Constantine was betrothed to Nicetas's daughter Gregoria. Presumably Heraclius hoped that blood relatives would be less likely than other connections to plot against his foundering government.

In the Balkans, the local garrison army still held the main strongholds near the Danube frontier, but between and behind them the Slavs had conquered the greater part of Illyricum, including most of Epirus, Thessaly, and central Greece. They even took to the sea in canoes to attack the Cyclades. Although the Slavs belonged to different tribes, several of these united in an unsuccessful attempt to storm Thessalonica by land and sea, probably in 615. Around the same time, the Avars opened a general offensive to the empire's north, taking Salona, Naïssus, and Serdica. Not long afterward, they deported many of the local Byzantines to Avar territory near Sirmium. After the Avars had shown their strength, the Slavs resumed cooperating with them against Byzantium.[4]

By 615, the empire had lost nearly all of Mesopotamia, Syria, Palestine, and Cilicia to the Persians, and most of Illyricum and much of Thrace to the Avars and Slavs. About 615 the Visigoths also conquered most of the rest of Byzantine Spain.[5] The only major Byzantine possessions that survived more or less intact were Africa, Egypt, and Anatolia, and the latter two faced imminent Persian invasions. Since even Maurice had found paying the army onerous, the imperial treasury must have been bare indeed after fourteen years of territorial losses, economic disruption, and intensifying warfare. The fisc could have coped thus far only because the empire's richest provinces remained, a good many soldiers had disappeared from the payroll, and pay was in arrears.

Probably in the spring of 616, financial necessity drove Heraclius to pay all his salaries, including military ones, at half the previous rate.[6] Even these he paid not in gold, as was customary, but with a new silver coin minted for the occasion, the hexagram.[7] In halving the soldiers' pay, Heraclius appears to have made the change that Maurice had tried but failed to introduce in 594, substituting issues in kind for the soldiers' inflated arms and uniform allowances. Probably he similarly replaced the cavalrymen's allowances for fodder with the fodder itself. Civilian officials, less vital to the state and less able to cause trouble, seem simply to have lost half their pay. Heraclius could have succeeded in imposing such drastic measures only because the necessity was so obvious. The new hexagrams were inscribed, "God Help the Romans!"

By cutting his cash expenditures almost in half, Heraclius gave the treasury some hope of financing the long and ruinous war that stretched ahead of him. In the Exarchate of Italy, the unpaid soldiers had already

68. Silver hexagram of Heraclius and his son Constantine, shown twice actual size, with the Cross and the invocation "God Help the Romans!" on the reverse. (Photo: Courtesy of the Arthur M. Sackler Museum, Harvard University Art Museums, Whittemore Collection)

assassinated the exarch John, and at Naples the rebel John of Conza had proclaimed himself emperor. After the reform of salaries had restored the treasury's solvency, Heraclius was able to send the new exarch Eleutherius with the pay that was overdue. Eleutherius soon restored a measure of order to Italy, and executed John of Conza.

Meanwhile, in the East, Shāhīn raided Anatolia in devastating force. Again Philippicus tried to divert Shāhīn by attacking Armenia, but Shāhīn continued his march. To judge from fairly clear archeological evidence, the main body of Persians went by way of Ancyra to Chalcedon, sacking both cities, while a raiding party sacked Sardis.[8] At Chalcedon, however, Shāhīn agreed to conduct a Byzantine embassy under the praetorian prefect Olympius to King Khusrau to sue for peace. By now the Persians were in a position to dictate their terms, and had reason to fear overreaching themselves if they pursued the war. So confident, however, was Khusrau of further victories that he kept the ambassadors imprisoned and let them die in captivity.

Next Shahrvarāz invaded Egypt. The resistance was led by Nicetas, at the head of much of the Army of the East, and perhaps some of that of Africa. Nicetas had managed, with the help of the Chalcedonian patriarch of Alexandria John the Almsgiver, to negotiate a church union with the Monophysite majority, now that the Persian danger had inspired a rare spirit of cooperation among Egyptians. Nonetheless, Shahrvarāz met little opposition as he began a methodical conquest of the country.

Over the next several years, the Persians subjugated Egypt and di-

69. Saint John the Almsgiver, patriarch of Alexandria (610–19). Miniature from the *Menologium of Basil II*. (Photo: Biblioteca Apostolica Vaticana)

gested their conquests in Syria and Palestine. They made some effort to placate the population, by favoring Monophysites and expelling the Jews from Jerusalem in 617 in favor of Christian settlers. The next year the Persian advance in Egypt and a fresh outbreak of plague forced Heraclius first to charge for the grain dole that had been free since the time of Constantine, and then to suspend it altogether. In the meantime the Avars and Slavs only narrowly missed taking Thessalonica.[9]

The wonder is that no one conspired to overthrow an emperor whose failures were unprecedented in the history of the eastern Roman Empire. Perhaps the officials in a position to conspire realized that in such an extremity any internal disorder risked destroying the state and leaving nothing to rule. The exarch of Ravenna Eleutherius did proclaim himself emperor in 619, but his ambition seems to have been limited to ruling an exarchate independent of the crumbling empire. His soldiers soon assassinated him.

By 619 the Persians were besieging Alexandria. Although the city itself should have been easy to defend, its large population could not be fed once it was cut off from the rest of Egypt. While the authorities might have evacuated civilians and kept up resistance, Nicetas and the patriarch John despaired of ultimate success. Nicetas left to become exarch of Carthage, John retired to Cyprus, and Alexandria surrendered to avoid starvation. The Persians, who courted the Egyptians by recognizing a purely Monophysite hierarchy, probably finished their conquest of Egypt before the end of 620.

At this point the Persians occupied all of Mesopotamia, Cilicia, Syria, Palestine, and Egypt, and most of Armenia. This was as much Byzantine territory as they could conquer or hold at all safely. Byzantine Africa lay across a desert and too far from the center of their power in Persia and Mesopotamia; Anatolia lay across the Taurus and too near the Byzantines' heartland around Constantinople. The empire's other main enemies, the Avars and Slavs, already held most of the Balkans, apart from some coastal outposts and lowland Thrace. These northern invaders had also reached their natural limits, since they could only take and keep the coasts and southern Thrace by making a reckless attempt to overmatch Byzantine sea power and capture Constantinople.

Yet the rump of the empire in Anatolia and southern Thrace, raided by the Persians and Avars and isolated from its faraway western possessions, had sunk so low as to tempt its enemies to aim at its total destruction. Because the empire had lost almost half its land, even paying state salaries at half the old rate was straining the treasury. Again and again the Byzantine army had retreated after failing to repel the enemy. In order to show both the Byzantines and their enemies that the empire could be saved, Heraclius desperately needed to take the offensive against his strongest adversary, the Persians.

HERACLIUS'S RESPONSE

Heraclius understood and acted. He obtained the necessary money from the patriarch of Constantinople Sergius, who lent the state a great mass of the Church's gold and silver for the duration of the war. This plate the government melted down into coins. The proceeds allowed the treasury to clear its arrears, recruit new troops, hire mercenaries, and meet payrolls for several years. Even bronze statues and ornaments were coined, though they must have been used to pay for military supplies, because soldiers drew pay in precious metal. After gaining this much financial relief, Heraclius turned to reorganizing the army.

The Army of Armenia and the armies in the Emperor's Presence were in Anatolia, and appear to have kept the greater part of their manpower. The Army of the East must have suffered more, but at least half of it appears to have reached Anatolia, either by retreating overland from Syria or by embarking from Alexandria or Africa. Parts of the armies of Illyricum and Thrace may have remained in Anatolia since the reign of Phocas; the rest had been caught between the Slavs settled in the south and the Avars advancing from the north. As a result the Army of Illyricum mostly disintegrated, while the Army of Thrace retreated south with heavy losses. The Army of Africa faced the Persians in Egypt. The Army of Italy could scarcely hold its own exarchate. The Visigoths were about to swallow what little remained of both the Province and the Army of Spain.[10]

In 621 Heraclius transferred what was left of the Army of Thrace to Anatolia to combine it with the troops that were already there. Although the armies retained their old identities, for the present Heraclius reinforced and reorganized them, drilled them together, and treated them as parts of a single force. He seems not to have changed the army's fundamental structure, but he must have needed to consolidate many subordinate commands to bring battlefield formations up to strength.[11] Thus the emperor created a mobile force that probably numbered some fifty thousand men.[12]

While Heraclius was busy in western Anatolia, Shahrvarāz raided eastern Anatolia with a Persian force that apparently spent the winter around Trebizond on the Black Sea coast. In the spring of 622, Heraclius made a truce with the Avars, promising them tribute in order to free himself for a campaign against the Persians. In July the emperor led his reorganized army to Cappadocia, where he found the Persian army under Shahrvarāz. The Persian general occupied the Cilician Gates to keep the emperor out of Syria; but when the Byzantines turned toward Armenia and threatened to outflank Shahrvarāz, he followed them. After some indecisive maneuvers, the armies came to a battle, in which Heraclius defeated Shahrvarāz. Although the victory was not a crushing one, the Persians left Anatolia, and the effect on both sides' morale was considerable.[13] It was the Byzantines' first defeat of the Persians in years.

Heraclius was apparently poised to invade Persian-held Armenia, when news arrived that the Avars had broken their truce and invaded southern Thrace. The emperor returned to Constantinople, hoping to appease the Avars and unwilling to transfer to Europe the army he needed to fight the Persians. In 623, advancing to the straits, the Avar khan proposed peace negotiations at Heraclea in Thrace. When Heraclius arrived, however, the Avars barely failed in an attempt to kidnap him, and raided up to Constantinople. After sending a vast haul of booty and prisoners back across the Danube, they extorted a yearly tribute of two hundred thousand nomismata in return for a truce that left their prisoners and the greatest part of Thrace in their hands. By now they had little left to take in Europe apart from the well-fortified coastal towns, which of course included the capital.[14]

Possibly relying more on this fact than on the treaty, in 624 Heraclius prepared to depart for the East. His plan was, and may have been since 621, not to reconquer his lost provinces but to make a decisive thrust at the center of Persian power so as to force a favorable peace. His preparations show that he was ready for a long campaign. He left his twelve-year-old son Heraclius Constantine at Constantinople under the protection of the patriarch Sergius and the master of offices Bonus, and he took his wife Martina along with him.

The emperor marched purposefully to the East, where he first retook Theodosiopolis in what had been Byzantine Armenia. Then he advanced on Dvin, the capital of Persian Armenia, and surprised and sacked it. Ravaging and taking captives as he went, the emperor invaded the Persian province of Atropatene. His objective seems to have been to threaten the seat of the Persian court in central Mesopotamia, and by summer he had already come some three-quarters of the way.[15] Seeing the danger, Khusrau II had already recalled Shahrvarāz from the west and mustered a reported forty thousand men. The king led them in person to Ganzaca, the capital of Atropatene; but there he concluded that Heraclius's army was too much stronger than his, and fled south through the Zagros range. Heraclius stopped to sack Ganzaca and destroy its Zoroastrian temple, then pursued Khusrau south, taking the king's summer palace in the mountains.

By this time it was autumn, and the emperor had to decide whether to risk everything on an immediate invasion of Mesopotamia or to withdraw to winter quarters. Perhaps because he considered an invasion too perilous, perhaps because he hoped Khusrau would be ready to make peace, Heraclius chose to winter in the Persian protectorate of Albania, in the Caucasus north of Atropatene. After the emperor had sacked some Albanian towns, he was able to spend a quiet winter in the country. During his stay he released his prisoners and enlisted a number of mercenar-

70. Detail of the facade of the palace of the Persian kings at Ctesiphon in Mesopotamia, probably built in the third century, in a photograph taken before the collapse of its right wing. (Photo: From Marcel Dieulafoy, *L'art antique de la Perse* V [Paris, 1889])

ies from Albania and neighboring Iberia, Lazica, and Abasgia, all of which were mostly Christian despite their recent domination by Persia. Heraclius also seems to have acquired some fine local scouts, because in the coming years he generally knew more about the Persians than they knew about him.

By the spring of 625 Khusrau had brought his chief generals and many of his soldiers from the west. The king sent them against Heraclius in three army groups, led by Shahrvarāz, Shāhīn, and a third general, Shahraplakan.[16] The emperor marched south from Albania into Suinia, a district of Persian Armenia, while the enemy armies converged upon him. But he outmaneuvered them. He managed to defeat Shahraplakan just before Shāhīn arrived, then to rout Shāhīn's army and capture its camp. The remnants of the defeated Persian forces took refuge with Shahrvarāz.

Heraclius would probably have invaded Atropatene again if his Caucasian mercenaries had not departed, refusing to fight so far from their homelands. Without his mercenaries, Heraclius decided to retire for the winter to Byzantine Armenia and prepare an offensive for the following year. As he marched to the north of Lake Van, however, Shahrvarāz followed, encamping at Arces at the lake's northern end. From there the Persian general sent a contingent north to ambush the Byzantines. But the emperor discovered the plan in time, and launched surprise attacks that annihilated the ambushers and drove Shahrvarāz from Arces with heavy losses. Having beaten all three Persian generals, Heraclius wintered by Lake Van, not far north of Mesopotamia.

Unshakably opposed to making the concessions needed for a peace, Khusrau now imitated Heraclius's strategy of threatening his adversary's base. He raised new taxes, mobilized more soldiers, and came to an agreement with the Avars for a joint attack on Constantinople. In the spring of 626 he sent two armies to Anatolia, one under Shahrvarāz and the other under Shāhīn. Heraclius had just captured Amida in what had been Byzantime Mesopotamia when, well informed as usual, he turned to intercept the advance of Shahrvarāz into Cappadocia.

Though Heraclius caught Shahrvarāz at a bridge over the upper Sarus River, after a drawn battle the Persian escaped him and pressed on toward Constantinople. Heraclius could hardly ignore the threat to his capital; but he would not abandon the East, where the Turkish tribe of the Khazars had just invaded Persian Albania and Atropatene and seemed ideal to enlist as Byzantine allies. The emperor accordingly divided his army. Keeping a small contingent to lead to the Caucasus, he sent another part to reinforce Constantinople, and a third under his brother Theodore to stop Shāhīn. Heraclius's reinforcements arrived at Constantinople ahead of Shahrvarāz, and Theodore defeated and killed Shāhīn somewhere in eastern Anatolia.

A concerted and sustained siege by the Avars and Persians could still be a serious threat to Constantinople. By June 626 Shahrvarāz had encamped at Chalcedon, on the Asian side of the city, and the Avars and their Slavic allies had reached the land walls on the European side, cutting the Aqueduct of Valens and destroying the suburbs. The master of offices Bonus and the patriarch Sergius refused the Avar khan's demand for the capital's surrender. At the end of July the khan arrived before the city, assaulted the walls with siege machines, and prepared to ferry thousands of Persians across the Bosporus in the canoes of his Slavic followers.

This siege began to miscarry early in August. Although the Slavs succeeded in crossing to Asia, on their way back the Byzantine fleet sank their canoes and killed the Persians they carried. Next the victorious

Byzantine army of Theodore arrived. By a stroke of luck, the authorities in the capital intercepted a message from Khusrau that ordered Shahrvarāz's execution. When they showed it to the general, he understandably began to plot against his distrustful king.[17] The Avars ran out of supplies and interrupted their siege to forage. The Persians decamped, and the siege was over.

This was the turning point in the war. Shahrvarāz retired to Alexandria, kept control of his army and Egypt and Syria, and ceased to help Khusrau. Not long after the failure of the siege of Constantinople, the alliance between the Avars and Slavs broke down, and a great uprising of the Slavs crippled the Avar Khanate. By the summer of 627, the bulk of the Byzantine armies in Anatolia left to join Heraclius, who was completing the conquest of Iberia. Having made his alliance with the Khazars, with their help he defeated and killed the Persian commander Shahraplakan.

Toward the end of the summer, after his reinforcements arrived from Anatolia, the emperor had an army that was reckoned at seventy thousand men, including his Iberian and Lazican mercenaries; his Khazar allies came to tens of thousands more.[18] With barely enough time to start a campaign before winter, Heraclius took his chance while he had it. He marched rapidly through Persian Armenia and Atropatene, undeterred even when the Khazars deserted him, and burst into Assyria. Khusrau had gathered all available Persian forces under a new general, Rāhzād, who followed the Byzantines as best he could over land that they had stripped of provisions.

In December, in a major battle near the ruins of Nineveh, Heraclius defeated the Persians, killing Rāhzād and many others and capturing many more. Although the remainder of the Persian force retreated in some order, it was no match for the Byzantines. As the emperor advanced through Assyria burning royal palaces, Khusrau fled from his favorite palace at Dastagerd to his capital of Ctesiphon. At the beginning of 628 Heraclius seized Dastagerd, where he took immense plunder, much of it originally Byzantine, and freed a throng of Byzantine prisoners. Then he proposed peace.

Khusrau refused his offer. The emperor therefore burned Dastagerd and advanced on Ctesiphon, but found the Persian capital protected by a canal in high flood. Though he could have tried to force his way across at once, he chose to turn back to Atropatene to let the Persians ponder their position, aggravated as it was by the floods and an outbreak of plague. His decision proved wise. Before the Byzantines arrived at Ganzaca, Khusrau had been overthrown by his son Kavād II, who executed his father and sued for peace.

In little more than a month, both sides agreed to a treaty. It provided for the return of all prisoners and the restoration of the frontier between Byzantium and Persia as it had been in 602. These terms served the interests of both sides. Kavād had little control over Syria and Egypt, which were in the hands of Shahrvarāz, and Heraclius had good reason not to humiliate a complaisant king by demanding further concessions. In early April, the emperor freed his prisoners and left for Armenia with his empress Martina, who had accompanied her husband through all his travails.

Intending now to deal with Shahrvarāz, Heraclius wintered at Amida, which he had taken two years before. As the virtual ruler of Syria and Egypt, the Persian general was not eager to surrender his satrapy to the empire. But Kavād II died in September, apparently of the plague, and was succeeded by his young son Ardashīr III. After further maneuvering, the next summer Heraclius and Shahrvarāz met at Arabissus in southern Cappadocia and came to an agreement. Shahrvarāz would restore Egypt and Syria, along with the True Cross, which he had taken himself at Jerusalem. In return, Heraclius would give up his claim to Mesopotamia south of Amida and support the claim of Shahrvarāz to the Persian throne.[19]

Thus the Byzantines reoccupied Egypt and Syria, and Heraclius brought the True Cross gloriously back to Jerusalem in March 630. Shahrvarāz led his army to Ctesiphon the next month, killed Ardashīr III, and became king of Persia. But just two months later, conspirators assassinated the great general and replaced him with Khusrau's daughter Bōrān. Considering his agreement with Shahrvarāz moot, Heraclius took advantage of the confusion in Persia to reoccupy Byzantine Mesopotamia. He met with no opposition from Bōrān, or from the ephemeral kings who fought for power after her death in early 631. That year, the seventh after the beginning of his Persian campaign, the emperor and his faithful wife Martina returned to Constantinople for a richly deserved triumph.[20]

Heraclius's victory over the Persians was an astonishing achievement, won by a combination of patience, determination, and skill. But restoring the empire's boundaries in the East was not the same thing as restoring the empire. The Slavs still held most of the Balkans. Much of the East was devastated after years of warfare, now followed by more plague.

Shahrvarāz had put the Monophysites firmly in control of the Egyptian, Syrian, and Armenian churches, aggravating their schism with Constantinople. The war had depleted and dispersed the army, and the loan that had to be repaid to the Church apparently exceeded the booty taken in Persia.

His success had at least made the emperor sure of his reputation and talents, and he confidently threw himself into the task of repairing the empire. After the reduction of the army's size and pay during the war, expenses probably approximated the empire's diminished revenues, so that Heraclius could and did begin to pay back what he had borrowed from the Church. But he was very short of money, and economized whenever he could. Since for the present he left the Slavs undisturbed in the Balkans, he could not send the battered Army of Thrace back to its old positions, and probably left it in western Anatolia. But he did return the eastern armies to their stations, and he apparently reassembled the eastern frontier troops, some of whom may even have continued to serve under the Persians. He seems to have put Syria and Mesopotamia under military governors like the dukes of Egypt, who had both civil powers and commands over frontier troops. For several years the emperor spent most of his time at Edessa, supervising the reintegration of Egypt and Syria into the empire.

Heraclius's zeal is particularly evident from his fresh attempt to heal the all but hopeless schism with the Monophysites. The doctrine that he proposed as a compromise between Monophysites and Chalcedonians became known as Monoenergism. While accepting the Chalcedonian formula that Christ had two natures, Monoenergism ascribed to him only one energy (*energeia*), a deliberately vague term meaning something like "motivation." Though this was of course an attempt to blur the distinction between one and two natures, that distinction had always been much sharper in polemics than in theology.

The patriarch of Constantinople Sergius, a Syrian from a Monophysite family, favored Monoenergism. Athanasius, the Monophysite patriarch of Antioch since 595, accepted Monoenergism in 631 along with most of his hierarchy. That year Heraclius chose a new patriarch of Alexandria, Cyrus of Phasis, who endorsed Monoenergism; the emperor strengthened Cyrus's hand by making him not just patriarch but prefect of Egypt, with authority over its dukes. With the help of a little persecution, Cyrus managed to win the consent of most of the Egyptian church to Monoenergism at a council held at Alexandria in 633. Meanwhile a council of the Armenian church joined the union as well, and the schism seemed to have come to a miraculous end.

That Heraclius succeeded even for a moment in reuniting the Church is a sign of his immense prestige at the time. Although the empire was exhausted and fragile, it seemed likely to have a respite of some years in which to recover its strength. Persia was more exhausted still, even after it regained a fairly stable government under King Yazdgird III in 632. The weakened Avars lost another battle to the Bulgars who lived north and east of the lower Danube; the Bulgar khan Kuvrat made a treaty with Heraclius to keep their common enemy at bay. The Slavs were content to stay where they were in the Balkans, and with their divided leadership might yet be pushed back. The only significant attacks on the empire were some raids on Palestine by nomadic Arabs, who for centuries had been a mere nuisance.

THE ARAB CONQUESTS

Yet the Arabs had recently become very different from what they had been. In 622, the year of Heraclius's first offensive against the Persians, Mohammed had made his Hegira to Medina. There he founded an Arab state, based on his new religion of Islam, that spread over most of the Arabian peninsula before his death in 632. Mohammed's followers then elected a new political and religious leader, the first caliph, Abū Bakr, who finished unifying Arabia within a year. Even after expanding so much so quickly, the Muslims looked for more to conquer. The only lands adjoining the Muslim Arab state were Byzantine Syria and Persian Mesopotamia, each of which, conveniently for the Muslims, had Arabs both inside and just outside its borders.

By the autumn of 633, Abū Bakr sent four Arab armies, totaling some twenty-four thousand men, into southern Palestine. They had the help of their fellow Arabs from the border region, whom the financially embarrassed empire had recently denied their usual subsidy.[21] At first the Arab armies merely raided the countryside in force, but they were too numerous to ignore. In early 634 the local commander Sergius, probably duke of Palestine, gathered his forces and attacked the raiders near Gaza. He lost, and died in the battle.

At Edessa Heraclius recognized the danger and mustered the Army of the East and other troops under his brother Theodore. Rather than withdraw the raiders, the caliph ordered an Arab army that was then raiding

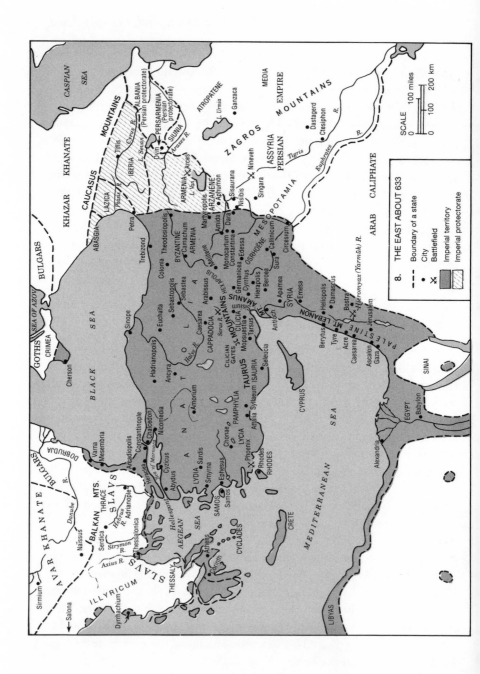

8. THE EAST ABOUT 633

- - - - Boundary of a state
• City
✕ Battlefield
[shaded] Imperial territory
[hatched] Imperial protectorate

SCALE
0   100 miles
0   100   200 km

CASPIAN SEA

MEDIA
EMPIRE

ATROPATENE
L. Urmia
Ganzaca

ZAGROS MOUNTAINS

Dastagerd
Ctesiphon

Tigris R.
Euphrates R.

ASSYRIA
PERSIAN

Nineveh

Singara

ARAB CALIPHATE

KHAZAR KHANATE

CAUCASUS MOUNTAINS

ALBANIA (Persian protectorate)
PERSARMENIA (Persian protectorate)
SIUNIA

IBERIA
Tiflis
L. Sevan
Cyrus R.
Phasis R.
Dvin
Arxes R.
Araxes R.

ABASGIA
LAZICA

ARMENIA ✕ Arces
ARZANENE
Aghinum

Petra

Trebizond

Martyropolis
Amida
Dara
Sisaurana
Nisibis
Constantina
Edessa
Callinicum
Circesium

BYZANTINE
Camachum
ARMENIA
Melitene

Theodosiopolis

Colonia
Euchaita
Sebastopolis
Sebastea
Arabissus
Caesarea
Sorus R.

OSRHOENE
MESOPOTAMIA

Germanicaea
Cyrrhus
Hierapolis
Beroea
Apamea
Sura

SYRIA
Emesa
Heliopolis
Damascus

BULGARS

SEA OF AZOV
GOTHS
CRIMEA
Cherson

BLACK SEA

Sinope

Hadrianopolis

Ancyra

CAPPADOCIA

TAURUS MOUNTAINS
CILICIAN GATES
Mopsuestia
Tarsus
CILICIA
Seleucia
ISAURIA

AMANUS MOUNTAINS

Antioch

MT. LEBANON

PALESTINE
Berytus
Tyre
Acre
Caesarea
Ascalon
Gaza
Jerusalem
Bostra
Hieronyax (Yarmūk) R.

Amorium

A N A T O L I A

Chonae
PAMPHYLIA
LYCIA
Attalia
Phoenix
Syllaeum
RHODES
Rhodes

CYPRUS

SINAI

EGYPT
Babylon
Alexandria

AVAR KHANATE

Sirmium
Naïssus
Serdica
BALKAN MTS.
THRACE
Adrianopolis
Constantinople
Chalcedon
Nicomedia
Heraclea
Cyzicus
Abydus
Sardis
LYDIA
Smyrna
Ephesus

BULGARS
DOBRUDJA
Danube R.
Varna
Mesembria
Arcadiopolis
Sea of Marmara
Hellespont

SLAVS

Strymon R.
Hebrus R.
Axius R.
THESSALY
Thessalonica

Nicomedia

SAMOS
Samos

Chonae

Athens
Corinth
CYCLADES

ILLYRICUM
Salona
Dyrrhachium

AEGEAN SEA

CRETE

MEDITERRANEAN SEA

LIBYAS

Persian Mesopotamia to reinforce them. It arrived under its energetic commander Khālid ibn al-Walīd, who became the main leader of the invasion. He joined most of the other Arabs near Bostra, which surrendered to them. That summer Theodore met them in a battle between Gaza and Jerusalem, and was soundly defeated. He returned to Edessa to face his brother's wrath.

Heraclius's theological compromise began to founder along with his fortunes in arms. Strong opposition to Monoenergism had emerged among the Egyptian and Syrian Monophysites and the Palestinian Chalcedonians, the latter led by the patriarch of Jerusalem Sophronius. Even the Constantinopolitan patriarch Sergius had become disenchanted with the theological ambiguities of Monoenergism and wrote to Pope Honorius for advice. The pope rejected Monoenergism, conceding only that Christ had one will, in the sense that he willed nothing self-contradictory. In deference to the Pope, Heraclius abandoned Monoenergism toward the end of 634. Instead he tried to regain divine favor by a halfhearted order to convert the Jews.

The next year Heraclius regrouped his forces in Syria under two new generals, Theodore the Sacellarius and Baänes. The empire's military position kept deteriorating. While the Byzantine commanders made their preparations, Damascus and Emesa surrendered to the Arabs. By early 636 the Byzantines had gathered some forty thousand soldiers and expelled the Arabs from both cities. But Khālid's Arabs then defeated Theodore, who apparently led the smaller force, near Emesa. After seeking refuge with Baänes, Theodore turned back at the news, true or false, that Baänes' army had proclaimed its general emperor. While the Byzantines were in disarray, the Arabs met Baänes' army south of Damascus, by the canyon of the river Hieromyax—in Arabic, Yarmūk. The Byzantines put up a desperate struggle, but in the end the Arabs killed many of them and drove most of the rest over a precipice to their deaths. These overwhelming defeats left the Byzantine forces in Syria incapable of further resistance.

Now fully aware of the threat posed by the Arabs, Heraclius decided to abandon Syria for the present and to concentrate on saving Egypt. Apparently he reinforced Egypt with troops from one of the armies in the Emperor's Presence under their commander John.[22] Part of the Army of the East may also have reached Egypt, while the rest of it retreated into Anatolia. Having done what he could for Egypt and his armies, the emperor left the East, ordering that the True Cross be sent to Constantinople for safekeeping.

71. The walls of Antioch from the east. Engraving by S. Lacey after W. H. Bartlett. (From John Carne, *Syria, the Holy Land, Asia Minor, etc., Illustrated* [London, 1837])

Heraclius was now over sixty, aged by anxiety, ill with dropsy, and despondent at losing to the Arabs the lands that he had just reclaimed from the Persians. Some Byzantines, perhaps including the emperor himself, thought God was punishing him for his incestuous marriage to Martina, since of their eleven children four had died and two were crippled. The emperor became so morbidly afraid of the sea that he remained at the Palace of Hieria on the Asian shore of the Bosporus, refusing to cross to the capital. He quarreled with his brother Theodore, and in late 637 punished his bastard son Athalaric and some associates for an alleged plot.

The victorious Arabs retook Damascus, advanced through Syria, and in 637 conquered its northern part, including Antioch and Beroea. At the same time they won a devastating victory over the Persians in Mesopotamia and captured Ctesiphon. Soon the new caliph 'Umar arrived to oversee the annexation of Syria to his domains. After the patriarch Sophronius sadly surrendered Jerusalem early in 638, the Arabs held all of Syria except for some beleaguered coastal cities. Egypt was isolated, and Byzantine Mesopotamia almost defenseless. The governor of Osrhoëne John, who was probably its duke, agreed to pay the Arabs one hundred thousand nomismata a year from local revenues not to cross the Euphrates. But after John had made the first payment, the emperor dismissed and exiled him, evidently for exceeding his authority. The main restraint on the Arabs was the plague, which many of them caught from the Syrians and Egyptians.

Heraclius finally returned to his capital in 638, over a bridge of boats designed to allay his hydrophobia. In a last attempt to salvage his theological compromise, he issued a statement of faith prepared by the patriarch Sergius, the *Ecthesis* ("Exposition"). The *Ecthesis* affirmed the Council of Chalcedon and the two natures of Christ, forbade further discussion of Christ's energies—which few wanted to discuss anyway—and declared, using language permitted by Pope Honorius, that Christ had one will. This doctrine of one will, or Monotheletism, differed from Monoenergism only in being slightly less muddled. Sergius died just after its promulgation, but the new patriarch Pyrrhus held a council that approved the *Ecthesis*.

In 639, after receiving no tribute from Byzantine Mesopotamia, the Arabs began their conquest of the country. They finished the task with little delay, accepting the surrender of Edessa and storming Dara. Late the same year, other Arabs invaded Egypt. The leader of this expedition, who seems already to have extorted tribute from the Egyptians, was ʿAmr ibn al-ʿĀs, one of the conquerors of Syria. ʿAmr is said to have led no more than four thousand men; once Heraclius's general John had arrived, Egypt was surely defended by more soldiers than this, even without counting the bedraggled garrison troops. But the country was still suffering from the plague, impoverished and demoralized. Since the Egyptian prefect and patriarch Cyrus had intensified his persecution of the Monophysites to force them to accept Monotheletism, a number of Egyptians were ready to cooperate with the invaders. Yet if properly defended the Nile presented the Arabs with a major obstacle.

ʿAmr easily took the coastal towns on his way, but met firm resistance near the Nile from John and the local dukes. After a furious battle in which John died, ʿAmr had to appeal to the caliph ʿUmar for reinforcements. John's successor was Theodore, perhaps the same general the Arabs had defeated near Emesa, and in any case a mediocre strategist. Before ʿAmr's reinforcements arrived, Theodore and the patriarch Cyrus gathered their forces at the fortified town of Babylon on the Nile, near modern Cairo, but remained on the defensive. By the summer of 640, ʿAmr's army had grown to about fifteen thousand men. With these ʿAmr attacked the Byzantines north of Babylon, routed them, and besieged Cyrus in the city itself.

To reinforce Egypt, Heraclius sent soldiers from the displaced Army of Thrace under its commander Marianus. But the Arabs promptly defeated Marianus and destroyed much of his army.[23] In these dire straits, the besieged patriarch Cyrus reached a tentative agreement to pay ʿAmr tribute of two hundred thousand nomismata a year in return for a truce. Cyrus traveled to Constantinople to submit these terms to the emperor, but Heraclius angrily repudiated them and exiled Cyrus.[24] The Arabs went on besieging Babylon, and defeated and killed Marianus in a second battle. As panicked Byzantine soldiers decamped from the Egyptian countryside and poured into Alexandria, the Arabs sealed their conquest of Palestine by taking Caesarea.

In Constantinople the plague had returned, and the emperor was dying of his dropsy. Along with reports of Arab advances, he received word that Pope John IV had held a council that condemned the *Ecthesis*. Heraclius's despondency, awareness of his impending death, and good sense all led him to the same decision: he abandoned the *Ecthesis*, which had already failed to appease the Monophysites and troubled many Chalcedonians. In January 641 the emperor died, an imposing but tragic figure, who had outlived his reputation and his success.[25]

Recovering from early reverses that were understandable under the calamitous circumstances, Heraclius had dealt with the Persians remarkably well. His performance against the Arabs until their victory at the Yarmūk was respectable. Afterward, increasingly broken in spirit and body, he could probably have done more to defend Syria and Mesopotamia, which were almost completely lost before his death, and Egypt, where only the coast and some isolated strongholds remained. A massive transfer of troops to Syria of the sort that Heraclius had achieved against the Persians in Armenia might possibly have overwhelmed the not very numerous Arabs. Failing that, or while that was done, paying more tribute might further have delayed or diverted the Arab conquests. Heraclius had himself paid the Avars; only in his later years did he become obsessed with refusing to make payments abroad, beginning with the modest subsidies to the Arab allies who afterward betrayed Palestine. In comparison with the cost of fighting the Arabs, not to speak of the lost revenues of Syria and Egypt, large payments could be justified.

Yet no tribute could have restrained the Arabs for very long, and Heraclius knew from experience that preparing shattered armies for a great offensive was a lengthy and difficult operation. He also knew that Anatolia was much more defensible than Syria and Egypt, and that its defense required a reserve of money and men, which were already in short supply. The field army, probably over 150,000 men in 602, by 641 seems to have fallen to some 109,000.[26] Even these soldiers were going to be hard to pay without the revenues of Egypt and Syria. A total war against the Arabs would have left the Byzantines defenseless if it had failed.

It might well have failed against the Arabs as they were by 641. They still had all the fierceness of nomads, like the Germans, Huns, and Avars who had often defeated the empire but had been too divided and disorganized to destroy its eastern part. With the foundation of the caliphate, the Arabs had gained both cohesion and organization, like the Persians who had recently come so close to destroying the empire. This combination was fearsome, especially when joined to religious fervor, and neither the Byzantines nor anyone else had yet learned how to slow its progress, let alone how to stop it.

Though Heraclius gave up some of his provinces to the Arabs, neither he nor his immediate successors lost his whole domain, as his contemporary Yazdgird III of Persia was soon to do. The failure of Yazdgird's desperate defense of Mesopotamia surely contributed to his later loss of Persia beyond the Zagros, which should have been at least as defensible as Anatolia beyond the Taurus. Even hindsight is insufficient to determine whether Heraclius's measured response to the Arab invasions was a major mistake, a minor mistake, or no mistake at all. It was in any case the decision of an informed, experienced, and intelligent strategist.

CONSTANS II'S RESISTANCE

At a time when the prevailing crisis seemed to call for vigorous and united leadership, Heraclius willed the throne jointly to his eldest son, Heraclius Constantine, and his eldest surviving son by Martina, Heraclonas.[27] Since Heraclonas was just fifteen, while Heraclius Constantine was about twenty-nine, the latter became the real ruler, as Constantine III. But Constantine suffered from an advanced case of tuberculosis. The real significance of the old emperor's will was that on Constantine's death the successor would not be Constantine's ten-year-old son Heraclius, but Heraclonas, with Martina as regent. Such an arrangement was objectionable to many people, who considered Martina's incestuous marriage invalid and her children bastards, or in any case felt that the suc-

TABLE 7

The Dynasty of Heraclius

Emperors are in capital letters and italics, with the years of their reigns marked "r." Other years are of births and deaths. Illegitimate descent is shown by a broken line.

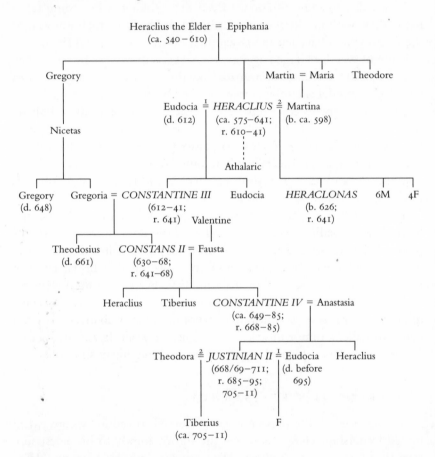

cession should pass from eldest son to eldest son in accordance with custom. Yet Martina, as the widow of the late emperor, also had her partisans, including the patriarch Pyrrhus.

Among his other afflictions, Constantine III had therefore to worry about Martina. He learned from the finance minister Philagrius that before dying Heraclius had set aside a secret fund from the treasury, administered by the patriarch Pyrrhus for Martina. This the emperor confiscated in time to meet the spring military payroll, to which the customary accessional donative added half as much again. Constantine won much goodwill by sending his soldiers a total of 2,016,000 nomismata in pay and accessional donatives, despite his straitened circumstances.

At the same time Constantine appointed Valentine, a subordinate of Philagrius, as commander of the main eastern army, which probably combined the armies of Armenia and the East. The emperor still hoped to salvage at least the coast of Egypt, perhaps by arranging a new truce. But the inept general Theodore, once again in command of whatever survived of the imperial forces, could not stop the Egyptians from squabbling, let alone the Arabs from advancing. Constantine recalled the patriarch of Alexandria Cyrus from exile, consulted him, and prepared to return him to Egypt with an army. But before this army was ready, Egyptian Babylon surrendered to the Arabs, who then put Alexandria under siege.

Constantine III died of his consumption after a reign of just over three months. His partisans spread the rumor that he had been poisoned by Martina, who took power as regent for her son Heraclonas. Yet her regime followed Constantine's plans, and sent Cyrus back to Alexandria with an army. The expedition apparently included most of the rest of the armies in the Emperor's Presence under their commander Constantine.[28] To replace the praesental armies, the government summoned the rest of the Army of Thrace to the capital from its makeshift quarters in western Anatolia.

Martina badly needed military support, because the eastern armies under Valentine were ranged against her. Apparently she was in financial straits, because she failed to match the accessional donative that the soldiers had just received from Constantine III.[29] Although she exiled Valentine's patron Philagrius to Africa, Valentine himself was beyond her reach in Anatolia. He soon led his men to Chalcedon to defend the interests of the late Constantine's young son. While the Arabs seem to have taken advantage of Valentine's absence to raid Anatolia for the first time, they were too busy elsewhere to undertake its conquest at once.

With Valentine's army encamped across the Bosporus, a mob formed in Constantinople to agitate against the government and for Constantine's son. They forced one concession after another. First the patriarch Pyrrhus had to crown young Heraclius, whom the demonstrators renamed Constans.[30] Next the mob compelled Pyrrhus to abdicate, and his steward became patriarch as Paul II. In desperation Martina offered Valentine the title of count of the Excubitors, promised another donative for his soldiers, and recalled his friend Philagrius. Nevertheless, after more than a month of disorders, Valentine entered the city and deposed Martina and Heraclonas. Valentine apparently shrank from killing a woman and child who were not so obviously guilty of usurpation as Phocas had been. Instead, borrowing penalties that had previously been inflicted for ordinary crimes, the general slit Martina's tongue and Heraclonas's nose, assuming that such disfigurements would make them ineligible to rule.

The only emperor left was Constans II, still not quite eleven years old and dominated by Valentine. Just after young Constans' accession, the patriarch of Alexandria Cyrus agreed to surrender Egypt to 'Amr by the next autumn. During the intervening year, the Arabs were to allow the Byzantine army, and any Egyptians who so wished, to evacuate Egypt undisturbed, taking their movable property with them. All the Egyptians were to pay 'Amr tribute, and the Arabs guaranteed the property of the Egyptians who chose to remain. The Alexandrians were furious with Cyrus for his capitulation, but they could hardly resist further without more help from Constantinople.

No help came from Valentine, who had other concerns. Although the mob prevented him from assuming the imperial title along with Constans, the general remained the most powerful man in the empire. In early 642 he married his daughter Fausta to the pubescent emperor and resumed his command over the eastern armies. Then he departed to chase Arab raiders out of Armenia. Left with no choice but to honor the Egyptian truce, that fall Theodore and his army evacuated Alexandria, where Cyrus had already died, and sailed for Cyprus. 'Amr rounded off his conquest of Egypt by capturing the Libyas early the next year.

After losing Egypt, Valentine's regime mounted a poor defense of the remainder of the empire. Mu'āwiyah, the Arabs' energetic governor of Syria and recently the conqueror of Palestinian Caesarea, began raiding Anatolia as far as Amorium, two-thirds of the way from the border to Constantinople. The Arabs of Atropatene—or Azerbaijan, as it began to be called—raided Armenia again; they were only driven out by the Armenian prince Theodore Ṛshtuni, whom the empire recognized as ruler of Armenia. Meanwhile, in Italy the Lombards defeated and killed the exarch Isaac, and conquered Liguria in 644. Probably that fall, Valentine again tried to make himself emperor by leading his troops into the capital, but the patriarch Paul resisted him. The unlucky general was lynched by an angry mob loyal to Constans.[31]

So it happened that Constans became effective ruler of the empire just before he turned fourteen. Surprisingly, he brought a speedy end to the weak rule that had hobbled the empire during the four unhappy years since Heraclius's death. At first the young emperor must have depended

72. Constans II (r. 641–68): *above,* gold nomisma, shown two and a half times actual size, depicting him as an adolescent, with a cross on steps on the reverse; *left,* miniature from the Modena Zonaras, depicting him as an adult. (Photos: Dumbarton Oaks, Washington, D.C., copyright 1996; and Biblioteca Estense, Modena)

heavily on advisers like his next commander of the eastern armies, another Armenian named Theodore.[32] But despite his youth Constans soon showed all the determination and ingenuity of his grandfather, together with a sense of urgency that Heraclius had sometimes lacked.

After the latest disasters, the empire's territory consisted of scarcely more than Anatolia, Armenia, Africa, and part of Italy, all in grave danger. In Constans' eyes every province was precious. He paid special attention to his family's imperiled homeland of Armenia, and he favored Armenian generals and the Armenian prince Theodore Ṛshtuni. A year after Valentine's death, the emperor even tried to recover Egypt, where

Arab rule had barely begun. As leader of the Egyptian expedition Constans chose yet another Armenian, Manuel, whom he gave the optimistic title of prefect of Egypt.

Since the Byzantines still controlled the sea, Manuel had no trouble sailing into Alexandria toward the end of 645. The Alexandrians hailed him as a liberator, having found that the caliphate levied heavier taxes than the empire and showed less respect for Monophysites. The new caliph 'Uthmān had replaced 'Amr with a less capable governor, who failed to stop Manuel from advancing into the Nile delta. But Manuel squandered his time and popularity in plundering the countryside, and the caliph reappointed 'Amr. The vigorous Arab commander gathered fifteen thousand men, with whom he forced Manuel to retreat to Alexandria and then to embark for home.

The failure of Manuel's expedition, evidently a large and expensive one, left young Constans on the defensive for several years. Already in 646 Mu'āwiyah managed to sack several fortified places in Cilicia, to make Cappadocian Caesarea capitulate, and to advance to Amorium again. He also started building a fleet for sea raids. Arabs from Egypt now raided the African Exarchate. Even worse, the African exarch Gregory, son of Heraclius's cousin Nicetas, chose this time to proclaim himself emperor. In 648 the Egyptian Arabs began a real invasion of Gregory's exarchate, while Mu'āwiyah's fleet raided Cyprus.

Then Constans' fortunes improved somewhat. The imperial fleet drove the Arab raiders from Cyprus, and the Arab invaders of Africa defeated and killed the usurper Gregory without conquering the country. They withdrew after Gregory's successor Gennadius promised them an annual tribute of some 330,000 nomismata. Gennadius also sent the usual surplus of revenues over expenditures to Constantinople, but otherwise administered Africa as he liked. Constans had not appointed Gennadius, and could not easily replace him.[33] Like Gregory, Gennadius relied on support from the African church, whose bishops were fiercely Chalcedonian. Maximus, an eloquent monk from Constantinople, had convinced them that the imperial government favored Monotheletism.

Although young Constans probably held no strong personal opinions on Monotheletism, he was trying desperately to hold together the Chalcedonian West, the central provinces, where few objected to Monotheletism, and Armenia, where Monotheletism was the chief alternative to Monophysitism. Constans tried to set a neutral course by issuing a statement known simply as the *Type* ("Edict"), which forbade discussion of how many wills or energies Christ had. But neutrality was not what Maximus and the western church wanted. Pope Martin I condemned both Monotheletism and the *Type* at a council attended by Maximus in 649. When Constans sent a new exarch of Italy, Olympius, to compel the pope to accept the *Type*, Olympius sided with the pope and proclaimed himself emperor in 650. The next year Olympius set out for Sicily, but on the way he died of the plague and his rebellion collapsed.

Arab strength continued to increase. When Constans concluded a truce with Mu'āwiyah in 651, the Arabs took advantage of it to finish off Persia and free their full energies to attack the empire. By 652 the Armenian prince Theodore Ṛshtuni, despairing of further resistance, accepted Mu'āwiyah's suzerainty. But Constans was greatly attached to Armenia. He marshaled his forces and at the age of twenty-one led them in person to the East. Neither a plot in the capital by the Armenian commander of the Army of Thrace nor a raid on Cilicia by Mu'āwiyah distracted the emperor from his campaign.[34] He subjugated both Armenia and Iberia before returning to the capital to punish the plotters. Even when Mu'āwiyah sent an army to restore Theodore Ṛshtuni the next year, the Byzantine commander Maurianus kept a hold on much of Armenia.

In the meantime Constans had reestablished his authority in Italy under the new exarch Theodore Calliopas, who arrested Pope Martin and Maximus and packed them off to Constantinople. They were charged with treason, which seems to have mattered much more to Constans than heresy or schism. An imperial court convicted Martin of abetting the usurpation of Olympius, and Maximus of supporting that of Gregory. Martin died in exile in the Crimea. The next pope, Eugenius I, neither accepted nor explicitly condemned the *Type*, and Constans was deliberately negligent in pressing the issue.

In 654 Mu'āwiyah launched a major attack on the empire with his always dangerous army and increasingly formidable fleet. The tireless Arab governor sent naval detachments to attack Cyprus and Crete, and he himself sacked Rhodes, where he looted the wreck of the wondrous Colossus. In a wide-ranging campaign, his army plundered Ancyra, took Trebizond and Theodosiopolis, and drove the Byzantine general Maurianus out of Armenia and into the Caucasus. The Arabs also sent the untrustworthy Theodore Ṛshtuni to Damascus, where he died in captivity, and replaced him with another prince, Hamazasp. Rumor had it that Mu'āwiyah planned an early assault on Constantinople by land and sea.

The next year Muʿāwiyah invaded Cappadocia, and his fleet advanced along the southern coast of Anatolia. Constans must have considered the naval attack the more dangerous, because he sailed against it with a large fleet of his own. He met the Arabs off Phoenix in Caria, lost a battle with heavy casualties on both sides, and barely escaped to Constantinople. Although the Arab fleet retreated after its victory, and on land Muʿāwiyah failed in an attempt to take Cappadocian Caesarea, the Arabs clearly retained the initiative.

But that summer a rebellion broke out against the caliph ʿUthmān, who like Muʿāwiyah was a member of the Umayyad family. The governor of Syria interrupted his campaigns against the empire to support his caliph, but within a year the rebels stormed Medina and killed ʿUthmān. When the enemies of the Umayyads elected ʿAlī the next caliph, Muʿāwiyah began a civil war to avenge ʿUthmān, and if possible to succeed him. Arab assaults on the empire ceased, leaving Constans with almost all the territory he had taken over in 644, except for the protectorate over Armenia. This alone was a substantial accomplishment in such terrible times for a man who only turned twenty-six in 656; but much more was needed to secure Byzantium's future.

CONSTANS II AND THE THEMES

At the time, Constans could hardly have known how long the Arab civil war would last, or how much damage it would do the Arabs. Since it racked the caliphate from end to end, its consequences were sure to linger for at least two or three years, and the emperor prudently counted on no more than this. To judge from later events, however, he began to formulate plans for reorganizing the army that would need several years of peace to implement safely. As it was, the Byzantine army had shown an alarming tendency to disintegrate after its sharp defeats in Syria and Egypt, and a disturbing tendency to rebel, especially in the West. Paying it must always have been difficult, and would probably become impossible if the surplus revenue from Africa was lost for long.

Constans first turned his attention to Armenia, where Prince Hamazasp, though installed by the Arabs, appealed to Byzantium as soon as he had some hope of resisting them. With this help, a Byzantine army reestablished its Armenian protectorate in 657. The next year Constans led the empire's first serious campaign against the Slavs in more than half a century. His limited objective was evidently not to make conquests, but to protect the empire's remnant of southern Thrace by weakening the Slavs on its border. This much he achieved, taking many Slavs captive.

In 659 the Arab civil war still raged, and Mu'āwiyah, afraid that Constans might exploit it further, made a generous truce with him. This time the Arabs would pay the tribute, at the daily rate of 1,000 nomismata, a horse, and a slave. While paying tribute was unprecedented for the Arabs, receiving it was quite exceptional for the empire; the Byzantines had long regarded tribute as something paid only to barbarians, but by now Constans must have needed the 365,000 nomismata a year. The treaty's best feature for the emperor was that he could depend on it for as long as chaos continued in the caliphate.

In all probability, Constans took this chance to make military arrangements for many years to come. Between 659 and 662, according to plausible guesswork, he reorganized his army into the commands that were to dominate the empire's military history for the next three centuries: the themes (*themata*). The Greek word is rather mysterious, but may mean something like "emplacements." The themes were simply the mobile armies of the previous period settled in specific districts, also called themes, which they served to defend. As the empire's territory had shrunk, most of its armies had retreated to new stations. Because all of Anatolia now needed defending, all of it received soldiers. Because Greek had become the empire's almost exclusive language, the armies acquired Hellenized names.

So the armies in the Emperor's Presence, lately known as the Obsequium ("Retinue"), became the Opsician Theme, stationed much as before in southern Thrace and northwestern Anatolia. The Army of Armenia became the Armeniac Theme, stationed in most of its original territory in eastern Anatolia, to the west of the Armenian protectorate. The Army of the East became the Anatolic Theme; but since it had lost all its original territory except Cilicia and Isauria, most of its men had taken up quarters in central Anatolia. The Army of Thrace became the Thracesian Theme, settled in western Anatolia where Heraclius had withdrawn it. Constans also created a corps of marines, the Carabisian Theme, named after a Greek word for ship (*karabis*) and based in Greece and the Aegean islands, and on the southern shore of Anatolia. This appears to have been formed from the remains of the Army of Illyricum, whose territory had included Greece.[35]

Within the boundaries of each theme, the soldiers received grants of land. From these the men were to support themselves and raise or buy their supplies, evidently including horses and fodder for the cavalry. To sell them their arms and other equipment, Constans seems to have relied on an expanded system of state warehouses that accepted goods as well as money in exchange. The land grants replaced the soldiers' issues of uniforms, arms, and horses and half of their former pay, which now fell to a mere five nomismata. Although the soldiers resided on their land grants, they were supposed to appear whenever they were summoned—at least every spring to be inspected, drilled, and paid—and to go on offensive and defensive campaigns.

Except for the count (komēs) of the Opsician Theme, the commander of each theme was titled a strategus (stratēgos, "general"). The Opsician count had his headquarters at Ancyra, the Anatolic strategus at Amorium, the Armeniac strategus apparently at Euchaïta, and the Thracesian strategus probably at Chonae, so that all four army commanders were based in central Anatolia. The naval strategus of the Carabisians had his base on the island of Samos.[36] Subordinates of each strategus, called turmarchs (tourmarchai), commanded divisions of their soldiers and territory called turmae (tourmai). Under them drungaries (droungarioi) headed subdivisions called drungi (droungoi), each with a thousand soldiers. Although for a time the civil provinces continued to exist alongside the themes, they served mainly as circumscriptions for the collection of taxes and the franchising of state warehouses. For most purposes the strategus of a theme was the governor of its region.

The one source to date the organization of the themes attributes it to the immediate successors of Heraclius, among whom Constans is the only plausible candidate.[37] The sources first mention themes by name after 662, when Constans left for a long campaign in the West with soldiers from the Opsician Theme, while the Armeniac Theme remained in the East.[38] References to themes are frequent thereafter. The earliest surviving lead seal of a state warehouse that seems to have supplied the themes probably dates to 659. Afterward such seals are common. At the same time, coins of types minted after 658 are far less common at Anatolian archeological sites than earlier coins, a sign that the state was spending much less money there.[39]

Settling the soldiers in the themes would have been possible only when they were not needed for active duty for several years, a condition that among the possible times applied only during the interval from 659 to 662. As the men took up their new places they would also have needed to fortify many of their posts; and many coins, most of them probably paid to soldiers, date a large number of Anatolian fortifications to the

73. Lead seal of Theodore, commerciarius of the warehouse of Galatia about 659, shown twice actual size. Portraits of Constans II and his son the future Constantine IV appear on the obverse with Theodore's name, and Theodore's office is given on the reverse. Theodore was probably one of the officials who first organized the state warehouses to supply soldiers settled on the new military lands. (Photo: Dumbarton Oaks, Washington, D.C., copyright 1996)

reign of Constans II, including new walls for Ephesus, Pergamum, Sardis, and Ancyra.[40] A final consideration for dating the themes' origin is that for this period evidence of the empire's internal history is worse than for almost any other time, so that the sources' silence about such a momentous change is most easily explained if the change was made then. For it to have developed through any sort of gradual evolution is practically impossible.

If this conjectural date is right, during these four years soldiers and marines were settled all over the Anatolia and southern Thrace on specific land grants. Much later sources put the value of a cavalryman's grant at a minimum of four pounds of gold and a marine's at a minimum of two; both minimums should have been enough to allow and indeed to require the men to keep tenants to do farm work for them. Infantrymen doubtless had farms that were smaller, but still big enough to support them adequately. When a soldier died, his land grant and his place on the rolls passed together to his heir, so that in principle every vacancy was filled at once.

The soldiers' grants may well have approached a fifth of the arable land of Anatolia. Some of this may have been confiscated from private owners, but most of it seems to have come from the old imperial estates, large tracts farmed by tenants that from now on practically disappear. Though handing out these estates would have deprived the treasury of their rents, eliminating half the military payroll and all the costs of military equipment should have saved considerably more. The state also saved itself the trouble of collecting the rents and distributing the equipment, because the state warehouses were apparently run by private contractors. Best of all, by spreading soldiers over the empire the system gave most regions their own defense against enemy raids. Yet the soldiers of the themes were still mobile, and from the first Constans probably planned to take many of them with him on his western expedition.

Anticipating his departure, the emperor took some preventive measures against potential troublemakers. In 661 he executed his brother Theodosius on suspicion of conspiracy, and he amputated the tongue and hand of the Chalcedonian theologian Maximus, who died in exile the next year. Though the original charge against Maximus had been political, his theology was in Constans' eyes a cause of the revolts of the western exarchs Gregory and Olympius—perhaps even of the suspected plot of Theodosius. Maximus earned the epithet "Confessor" by refusing to clear himself by accepting the *Type*. Yet Constans was not hostile to all Chalcedonians, and several years earlier he had confirmed the election of Pope Vitalian, who without accepting the *Type* remained on correct terms with the emperor.

For Byzantine purposes, the wrong side won the Arab civil war. In 661 'Alī was assassinated, and the victorious Mu'āwiyah became caliph, restoring the Umayyad dynasty. Mu'āwiyah moved the capital of the caliphate to Damascus, and resumed his plans against Byzantium with more determination than ever. When the new caliph sent an expedition to Armenia, the Armenians promptly accepted his dominion. Constans nonetheless decided that for the present he had done enough to defend the East, and prepared to leave for the West.

There the emperor meant to suppress the disturbing signs of independence in the exarchates, if possible to defeat the Lombards and Arabs who threatened them, and probably to introduce the system of military lands. Constans left his wife Fausta and his three sons behind in the capital. Although his eldest son Constantine was at most seventeen and more likely about thirteen, Constans probably saw him married before departing, and gave him real control over the government. Since Constans himself had married at eleven and begun ruling at thirteen, for him precocity was a matter of course.[41]

So in 662 Constans set sail for Thessalonica, not bothering to clear the land route from Constantinople of Slavs. From Thessalonica he marched overland to Athens and Corinth, perhaps to ready the Carabisian Theme for the expedition. The next spring Constans and much of the Opsician and Carabisian themes sailed to Tarentum in southern Italy, where they began a war against the local Lombards. The emperor exacted a nominal submission from the Lombard duke of Benevento, then marched by way of Naples to Rome. He and Pope Vitalian greeted each other cordially, but the emperor carried off a quantity of bronze ornaments from the city, presumably to buy supplies for his army. After a stay of just twelve days in the empire's ancient capital, he marched back to Naples and on to Rhegium, where his fleet carried his soldiers to Syracuse in the fall. This campaign was too rapid to accomplish much, but by showing the flag it deterred the Lombards from attacking and the Italians from rebelling for some time in the future.

Constans now took up residence at Syracuse. It was a good port within easy reach of Italy and Africa, in both of which Constans planned to strengthen his authority. Though in the East the Arabs had started raiding Anatolia again, their raids were no more than the themes could handle, and hardly required the emperor's return. In Sicily Constans began confiscating plate from the churches and levying taxes rigorously, not only from the island but from southern Italy, Sardinia, and Africa. In these regions, and perhaps also in northern Italy, he seems to have meant to establish military lands, and he managed to secure the loyalty of the Italian and African armies. When the self-appointed exarch of Carthage

74. View of Syracuse from the south, with the Great Harbor on the left, from an old photograph. (Photo: Istituto Centrale per il Catalogo e la Documentazione, Rome)

Gennadius refused to pay the additional sums Constans demanded, the exarch's own men overthrew him.

Gennadius, however, fled to Damascus and asked for aid from Mu-ʿāwiyah, to whom he had paid tribute for years. The caliph sent a sizable force with Gennadius to invade Africa in 665. Even though the deposed exarch died when he reached Alexandria, the Arabs marched on. From Sicily Constans dispatched an army to reinforce Africa, but its commander Nicephorus the Patrician lost a battle with the Arabs and re-embarked. The Arabs plundered the southern part of the exarchate before withdrawing, and even then they kept Tripolitania as a new province of the caliphate. Yet Constans seems to have regained full control over the rest of Africa, and to have distributed military lands there.[42]

While Muʿāwiyah kept Constans occupied in the West, the caliph sent more raids into Anatolia. Each year between 665 and 668 Arab raiders wintered in imperial territory. The Arabs put most pressure on the new Armeniac Theme, where their raids extended from the region called the Hexapolis in the south to Colonia in the north.[43] By 668 these Arab raids had exasperated the strategus of the Armeniacs Saborius, who noticed that Constans had been in Sicily for five years and showed no signs of returning. Saborius therefore proclaimed himself emperor near Melitene, sending one of his turmarchs to solicit Muʿāwiyah's support.

In the capital, young Constantine quickly dispatched his own envoy to the caliph to head off such a dangerous combination. Muʿāwiyah nonetheless chose to ally with Saborius in return for a heavy tribute, and prepared an army to help the rebel. While not all of Saborius's officers joined the revolt, most of the theme seems to have followed its strategus. Constantine mustered his remaining forces under Nicephorus the Patrician. Probably this Nicephorus was the same who had fought in Africa three years before, and if so Constans had sent back some of his army in the interim.

Saborius and his men marched from Melitene to Hadrianopolis at his theme's northwestern corner, most of the way on the road to Constantinople. While drilling for battle, however, Saborius fell from his horse and died, and the leaderless Armeniacs submitted to Constantine. The caliph's reinforcements arrived in the Hexapolis to find that the revolt was over. Yet it had been the first warning that Constans' creation of the themes gave their commanders a dangerous amount of power and autonomy.

Another such warning came the same summer, when a servant assassinated Constans in his bath at Syracuse, and conspirators proclaimed a

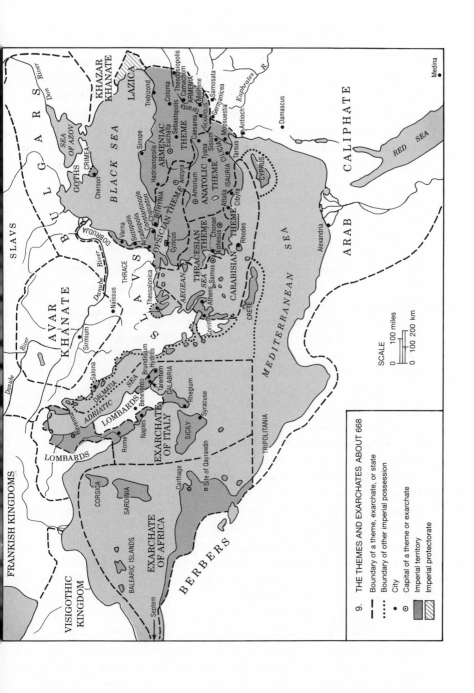

FRANKISH KINGDOMS

VISIGOTHIC KINGDOM

SLAVS

BULGARS

AVAR KHANATE

KHAZAR KHANATE

LAZICA

GOTHS

CRIMEA

SEA OF AZOV

Don River

BLACK SEA

Cherson

Sinope

Trebizond

Colonia

Theodosiopolis

Camachum

Melitene

ARMENIA

Samosata

Germanicea

Antioch

Damascus

RED SEA

CALIPHATE

ARAB

Medina

Euphrates R.

Tarsus

Mopsuestia

CILICIA

Sisium

ISAURIA

ARMENIAC THEME

Euchaita

Sebastopolis

Caesarea

Tyana

Hadrianopolis

Ancyra

Amorium

ANATOLIC THEME

Attalia

Cibyra

CYPRUS

BITHYNIA

Chalcedon

Constantinople

Cyzicus

OPSICIAN THEME

Arcadiopolis

Sozopolis

Varna

Naissus

Danube River

Sirmium

Salona

DOBRUDJA

THRACE

Thessalonica

AEGEAN SEA

Chonae

Ephesus

Samos

Athens

Corinth

THRACESIAN THEME

CARABISIAN THEME

Rhodes

CRETE

MEDITERRANEAN SEA

Alexandria

TRIPOLITANIA

ADRIATIC SEA

DALMATIA

LOMBARDS

Ravenna

Rome

Naples

Benevento

Brundisium

Hydruntum

Tarentum

CALABRIA

Rhegium

EXARCHATE OF ITALY

SICILY

Syracuse

Carthage

Site of Qayrawān

EXARCHATE OF AFRICA

CORSICA

SARDINIA

BALEARIC ISLANDS

Septem

BERBERS

LOMBARDS

SCALE

0   100 miles

0   100 200 km

9.   THE THEMES AND EXARCHATES ABOUT 668

—│— Boundary of a theme, exarchate, or state

······ Boundary of other imperial possession

• City

⊙ Capital of a theme or exarchate

▨ Imperial territory

▨ Imperial protectorate

usurper, the count of the Opsician Mizizius. Apart from the usual personal ambitions, the causes of the plot are obscure, but the emperor did
have enemies in the West. Even if he had not persecuted Chalcedonians
as such, he had punished Pope Martin and Maximus Confessor, both of
whom Chalcedonians revered as saints. He had also punished others for
associating with Martin, Maximus, and the usurpers Gregory and Olympius. Probably more to the point, Constans had demanded an extraordinary amount of revenue and obedience from the Sicilians and their
neighbors, and kept many eastern soldiers away from their new homes
for years.

In spite of all this, the rebellion of Mizizius dissipated even more
quickly than that of Saborius. After the murder of Constans, many eastern soldiers refused to recognize the usurper, and the Carabisian strategus Severus apparently gathered his fleet and fled to the East.[44] Loyal
troops from Italy and Africa converged on Syracuse and captured Mizizius, while in Constantinople Constantine IV succeeded to the throne
without challenge at the news of his father's demise. The conspirators
had overestimated the emperor's unpopularity in the army, and underestimated the solidity of his work on the themes.

By the time of his death at age thirty-seven, Constans had halted an
Arab advance that before him had surged out of control. He had also arrested the slow slide toward independence of Italy, the ancient center of
the empire and still the seat of its chief bishop, and of Africa, a great pro-
ducer of grain and wealth. By creating a new military system, he had
enabled the empire to pay a large army without the revenues of Syria,
Egypt, or even Africa. This reform came none too soon, since his confiscations and exactions toward the end of his reign indicate that the
treasury had run very short of money.

In the longer run, the themes not only secured the empire's solvency
but allowed the Byzantines to hold Anatolia for the indefinite future. If
as a general Constans fell short of Heraclius's genius, in administrative
insight he surpassed his grandfather. Between them, Constans and Heraclius had held off assaults that would easily have destroyed most states,
and might well have overcome even Byzantium's reserves of strength. To
those reserves Constans added soldiers who would fight hard to hold
their land, and who would replace themselves indefinitely. As long as
the themes lasted, the empire was safe from a repetition of its rapid collapse before the Persians and Arabs earlier in the century.

CHAPTER TEN

The War of Attrition, 668–717

To outward appearances, young Constantine IV inherited a disaster. Much of his army was far away in Sicily, where it had just murdered his father Constans II. In Anatolia another part of the army was in confusion after the usurpation of its commander Saborius, who had died only by pure accident. Arab troops sent to support the usurper were still on imperial territory. After six years, Constans' ambitious reform of the army had brought these two military revolts and no military victories of consequence. The Arabs under Muʿāwiyah continued to threaten the empire in east and west, and on land and sea.

Yet the crisis proved not to be as bad as it looked, and Constantine found himself with a rather better strategic position than the horrendous inheritances of his four predecessors since Phocas. The rebellion in the Armeniac Theme was over, and that in Sicily miscarried almost as soon as it began. Constans' work was sounder than it seemed, and Constantine IV had experience and steadiness beyond his nineteen or so years. He acted promptly to restore the order and confidence without which a large part of the army, and Africa and Italy, might have been lost.

ARAB AND BULGAR ATTACKS

At the news of his father's assassination, which must have reached him in August, Constantine decided to sail for the West. The capital always had many ships in its harbors, and most of the fleet of the Carabisian Theme seems to have reached Constantinople from the West, along with its strategus Severus. Though Constantine had just three months before the sailing season ended, he left in time and arrived safely in

75. Mosaic of Constantine IV (r. 668–85) and attendants in the Church of Sant'Apollinare in Classe, Ravenna. From left to right: Constantine's son Justinian II (r. 685–95, 705–11), Constantine's brothers Heraclius and Tiberius, the emperor himself, two archbishops of Ravenna, and three deacons. (Photo: Soprintendenza per i Beni Ambientali e Architettonici, Ravenna)

Sicily.[1] The armies of Italy and Africa had suppressed the revolt before the emperor arrived; but he could hardly have known this would happen, and even so his presence was beneficial. He gained some credit for the plotters' defeat, since the Italian and African soldiers had apparently waited for him to execute Mizizius, and he established his authority over the Opsician troops, whose loyalty had been less stout. The next spring he brought Constans' expeditionary force back to the East.

Speedily though this delicate operation was accomplished, Muʿāwiyah took advantage of it. The army he had sent to aid Saborius's rebellion seems already to have conquered the Hexapolis and wintered there; the caliph reinforced it with a large expedition under his son Yazīd. While many Opsician troops were still away from their stations, Yazīd raided as far as Chalcedon. As he returned, he captured Amorium in the Anatolic Theme, and garrisoned it with five thousand Arabs. When winter came, however, Constantine sent a force that stormed Amorium and annihilated the isolated garrison.

Not long after the eastern themes left the West, the Arabs attacked both Sicily and Africa. They sacked Syracuse, where they took, besides many prisoners, the bronze that Constans had collected during his stay. Their invasion of Africa in 670 aimed at outright conquest. Although the Arabs captured few African towns, they began building a town of their own, al-Qayrawān ("The Caravan"), to serve as a base near the heart of the exarchate. That the Byzantine forces held their ground stubbornly against such a determined enemy is some proof that Constans had strengthened them.

Muʿāwiyah also continued to harry Anatolia with land and sea raids. The maritime raiders reached the Sea of Marmara in the fall of 670 and, when unusually harsh weather overtook them, wintered at Cyzicus. They found Cyzicus an ideal camp: on a highly defensible peninsula and near to rich and poorly fortified seaside towns, including the suburbs of Constantinople. The imperial army left the Arabs undisturbed. After the raiders returned in the spring, Muʿāwiyah formed the plan of making Cyzicus a base for sustained raids over a period of years. Such raids could gather vast booty, pin down the Byzantine army and navy, and have a remote but tempting chance of taking Constantinople. To make the attempt safely, however, the Arabs would need control of the sea lanes back to Syria.

In 672 the caliph dispatched three fleets. These paralyzed the Carabisian Theme and wintered on the coasts of Cilicia, Lycia, and Lydia. The emperor understood the danger and began building warships at Constantinople. For the first time, he equipped them to use a new naval weapon, later known as Greek Fire. Invented by a recent Christian refugee from Syria, Callinicus of Heliopolis, Greek Fire was a liquid that, when shot from ships through special siphons, spread over the sea and ignited. Yet the emperor seems to have been reluctant to use this dangerous compound, which could burn friends as well as enemies.

The next year, learning that Arabs were preparing still another fleet in Egypt, Constantine sent his navy there. The Byzantines fought and won a major battle on the Egyptian coast, but the Arab fleet had already sailed. It captured Rhodes, where twelve thousand Arabs remained, preying on Byzantine shipping and preparing to grow their own food. An Arab army also took most of Cilicia, including its chief city of Tarsus. The caliph's capacity for sending expeditions seemed inexhaustible. In the spring of 674 a great Arab fleet sailed through the Hellespont, and for six months terrorized the Thracian shore of the Sea of Marmara up to the walls of Constantinople.

Although the emperor seems to have wasted no more men or ships than he could help, some resistance was necessary because the capital lacked full walls on the sea sides. In the autumn the Arabs retook Cyzicus and settled in comfortably for the winter. The next year they resumed their raids. While most of the empire's ships were defending its capital, other Arabs raided Crete, wintering there as their compatriots wintered yet again at Cyzicus. By 676, when Muʿāwiyah sent an army overland to Cyzicus under his son Yazīd, the strain began to tell on the empire.

76. The walls of Thessalonica from the east. (Photo: Deutsches Archäologisches Institut, Athens)

Already Constantine had discovered a plot by the Slav chieftain Perbundus to seize Thessalonica. When he executed Perbundus, the Slavs
attacked the city in retaliation. Since the emperor could spare only a small
fleet and few supplies, the Slavs soon reduced the Thessalonians to real
distress.[2] By this time the Lombards had also taken their chance to conquer most of Byzantine Calabria, including Brundisium and Tarentum.
Many Calabrians fled from Italy's heel to its toe, displacing the name of
Calabria from their old homeland to their adopted one.[3]

The Arabs, by spending their third successive winter at Cyzicus,
were forcing Constantine to choose between letting them sap Byzantine
strength indefinitely or risking his army and fleet in a desperate attempt
to expel them. In the summer of 677 they again raided around Constantinople, while the Slavs briefly besieged Thessalonica. Finally the
emperor decided to fight. That fall his navy put its Greek Fire into action, terrifying and routing the Arabs, many of whom were burned or
drowned. At this their fleet and army both started for home. The already
battered fleet sailed along the coast of Anatolia until it hit a severe storm

off the coast near Syllaeum, which sent almost all of it to the bottom. Before reaching Syria the Arab army was badly mauled in a battle with the forces of three Byzantine generals, probably the strategi of the Opsi-cian, Anatolic, and Armeniac themes.[4]

These Arab reverses led to still another. Since the conquest of Syria, some Christian freebooters known as Mardaïtes had been practically in-dependent on Mount Amanus between Syria and Cilicia, though they had made a nominal submission to the Arabs and robbed Byzantine Cili-cia more than Arab Syria. But the Arab conquests in Cilicia in 673 had surrounded the Mardaïtes and left them with only Arab territory to loot, and the Byzantine victories against the Arabs emboldened the Mardaïtes to rebel openly. While some of them remained on Mount Amanus, others migrated south to Mount Lebanon, an even more rug-ged retreat. There, joined by native mountaineers and slaves and escaped Byzantine prisoners from neighboring parts of Syria, they began plun-dering northern Palestine.[5]

Thus relieved from Arab attacks, Constantine prepared an expedition against the Slavs, who had diverted their attacks from Thessalonica to the northern Aegean and the Hellespont. The Byzantine army invaded the valley of the Strymon and soundly defeated the Slavs settled there. As the Slavs fled north, the Thessalonians reoccupied the Byzantine en-clave around their city, restoring the balance of power as it had been be-fore the Arabs came to Cyzicus.

Frustrated by the losses of the Arab army and navy and the rebellion of the Mardaïtes, Muʿāwiyah opened negotiations for a truce. The treaty was probably concluded in 679, specifying an Arab tribute of 216,000 no-mismata, fifty slaves, and fifty horses a year.[6] At first the treaty apparently allowed the Arabs to keep Rhodes. But the next year Muʿāwiyah died, a son of ʿAlī contested the claim of Muʿāwiyah's son and successor Yazīd, and Yazīd evacuated Rhodes to avoid further trouble with the Byzantines. Various Slavic rulers and the Avar khan also made treaties with the em-pire, which suddenly seemed far stronger than four years before.

Constantine used his respite to settle the unresolved question of Mo-notheletism. Constans II had avoided condemning the doctrine in his *Type* because he hoped to retake the eastern provinces where Monothe-letism had found some favor, and because he relied on Armenian gener-als and soldiers. Less dependent on Armenians, and with no real hope of retaking Egypt or Syria, Constantine had little reason to defend the am-biguities of the *Type*, which his western subjects resented. After friendly consultation with the pope, the emperor called a council of the eastern church for the autumn of 680.

Before the council met, Constantine announced the deposition of his brothers Heraclius and Tiberius, whom his father had crowned. Constantine wanted to establish his young son Justinian as the undisputed heir, which according to usual practice he was. But deposing unoffending junior emperors was unusual, and a body of soldiers from the Anatolic Theme arrived at Chrysopolis, opposite the capital, to demand the brothers' reinstatement. Even though Constantine had the Anatolic ringleaders hanged, he prudently restored his brothers before the council convened.[7]

When it met in the imperial palace, the council declared itself ecumenical, the Third Council of Constantinople. It could fairly do so, since it included representatives of the pope, the patriarch of Jerusalem, and the leaderless Chalcedonians of the patriarchate of Alexandria, plus the Chalcedonian patriarch of Antioch in exile, Macarius. The council prolonged its deliberations for months as the papal legates produced patristic texts to demonstrate that Christ had two wills, and Macarius produced his own texts to the contrary.

Meanwhile the Bulgars, who had long inhabited the lands between the lower Danube and the Sea of Azov, had begun to move west as the Khazars attacked them in the east.[8] By the beginning of 681 one group of Bulgars crossed the Danube into Thrace, led by their khan Asparukh, one of the sons of the late khan Kuvrat.[9] There they threatened not only to take the coastal towns still in Byzantine hands but to become enemies much stronger than the local Slavs, whom Constantine had just defeated. Determined to forestall this danger if possible, the emperor ordered troops from all five themes to cross into Thrace. Constantine led the thematic armies and fleet against the Bulgars, chased them to their fortifications in the marshes north of the Danube delta, and besieged them there.

As a standoff developed, Constantine found that camping in a marsh was bad for his gout. Entrusting the campaign to the strategi of the themes, he sailed south to take baths at the port of Mesembria. But his soldiers, thinking he had abandoned them, fled from the delta in panic. As the Bulgars pursued, and killed or wounded many of them, Asparukh advanced as far as Varna, which he captured along with the towns around it. He easily subdued the disunited Slavs and extended his khanate to the Black Sea in the east, the Balkan Mountains in the south, and the Avar

Khanate in the west. Though only a short coastal strip of this land had recently been Byzantine, the emergence of such a mighty western neighbor was precisely what Constantine had tried to prevent.

Once the Bulgars had settled south of the Danube, only a full-scale campaign outside imperial territory could dislodge them. Constantine chose to make peace, and found Asparukh willing. Before the invasion, Byzantines and Bulgars had observed a treaty that Heraclius had made with Asparukh's father Kuvrat; even now, Byzantine and Bulgar lands barely touched, and their interests were not directly in conflict. Under the new treaty the emperor accepted the Bulgars' occupation of the coast north of Mesembria and paid a presumably modest tribute, while Asparukh refrained from further conquests to the south.

The Third Council of Constantinople continued its deliberations during the Bulgar war and dispersed only in September 681. The council declared that Christ had two wills, human and divine, corresponding to his two natures, though it acknowledged that those wills could not oppose each other. Among the clerics condemned for espousing or tolerating Monotheletism were Heraclius's patriarchs Sergius and Pyrrhus, their contemporary Pope Honorius, and Macarius, whom the council deposed as patriarch-in-exile of Antioch.[10] Although these surprisingly harsh anathemas provoked lengthy discussion, the majority was eager to end the ambiguities of Heraclius's *Ecthesis* and Constans' *Type*. After more than two centuries of controversy, this council clearly affirmed the Chalcedonian doctrine that Christ was at once fully human and fully divine. Its decisions won prompt acceptance within the empire and in the western church. Since the council had completed the definition of fundamental Christian doctrine, Constantine IV gained more than the usual credit given to emperors who held ecumenical councils. He was able to depose his brothers again and, with cautious cruelty, to make them ineligible for the throne by slitting their noses.

A stroke of luck even allowed the emperor partly to offset his defeat by the Bulgars. Shortly after his council, a revolt broke out in the Avar Khanate among thousands of descendants of the Byzantines captured by the Avars during Heraclius's reign. Led by Kuver, a Bulgar whom the khan had made their chief, the fugitives left their settlements near Sirmium and migrated south to Thessalonica. Constantine welcomed them and resettled them in Thrace.[11] Around this time he also created a new Theme of Thrace from most of the European part of the Opsician Theme, though the troops defending Constantinople remained Opsician.[12] From the first the new theme's headquarters were probably at Arcadiopolis, near the border, where the strategus of Thrace was better placed to stop a Bulgar invasion than the count of the Opsician could be an Ancyra.

Then dissensions among the Arabs brought Constantine more good fortune. About 682, while the caliph Yazīd struggled to put down yet another Alid rebellion in Medina, the Christian princes of Armenia and Iberia defected from the Arabs and sought Byzantine protection for their states. The next year Arab renegades in Africa defeated and killed its Arab governor, and set up a rebel principality at Qayrawān in alliance with the Byzantines. Although Yazīd's forces suppressed the rebellion at Medina, as soon as they did so Yazīd died. The succession of his sickly son Muʿāwiyah II sparked another Alid revolt that took over most of the caliphate outside Syria. When Muʿāwiyah died in 684, his successor Marwān inherited the civil war.

Even for an emperor who liked peace, the opportunity in the caliphate was irresistible. Constantine dispatched a fleet that raided the coast of Syria, sacking Acre, Caesarea, and Ascalon while the Mardaïtes made their own raids inland from Mount Lebanon. Apparently the next fall, Constantine led an army that retook much of Cilicia and the Armenian Hexapolis, including Mopsuestia.[13] But Marwān defeated the rebels and recovered Egypt. In 685, when his successor ʿAbd al-Malik offered to pay the empire an increased tribute of 365,000 nomismata, 365 slaves, and 365 horses per year, Constantine accepted the terms.

By then the emperor was dying of dysentery. Although he presumably wanted to leave a peaceful empire to his young heir, the prudent Constantine would probably have made the truce in any case. During the twenty-three years since his father had put him in power at Constantinople, he had met dangerous Arab, Slav, Bulgar, and rebel attacks with calm determination. While he had achieved no great successes, and lost some border territory to the Arabs and Bulgars, he had freed the Church from theological disputes and preserved the empire's essential security. If Constantine might perhaps have done more, he had at least avoided trying to do too much.

JUSTINIAN II'S RISKS

Constantine's son Justinian became emperor at the age of sixteen, in an empire that had scarcely ever been smaller. He surely knew, however, that his father and grandfather had been younger than he when they took power, both of them in circumstances less favorable than his, and had acquitted themselves creditably. Justinian wanted more than that. Whatever may have moved the cautious Constantine IV to name his son Justinian, Justinian II himself felt called upon to emulate his great namesake Justinian I. From the beginning of his reign, he strove both to reconquer lost provinces and to restore imperial prestige.

Justinian had some reason to think that the time was right for a counteroffensive against the Arabs. Over the past forty years their new conquests had been few and precarious, and their civil wars frequent and serious. In 685 the caliph ʿAbd al-Malik held only Syria and Palestine, both raided by the Christian Mardaïtes, plus Egypt; the Alid rebels in Persia, Mesopotamia, and Arabia controlled more than half the caliphate. When ʿAbd al-Malik tried and failed to take Mesopotamia, the Alids invaded Palestine. By comparison with the caliphate, the empire appeared strong, solvent, and stable. Justinian showed only moderate audacity when he sought to continue his father's reconquests, circumventing the treaty Constantine had made on his deathbed.

Justinian began sensibly enough in 686 by reasserting the Byzantine protectorate over Armenia and Iberia, whose status was once more in doubt. Their two independent princes, after rebelling against the Arabs well before the treaty was signed, had been killed two years before by Khazar raiders, and the Arabs had invaded once again. Justinian sent an army under the strategus of the Anatolics Leontius that put most of Armenia and Iberia under princes subject to the empire, though the Arabs

77. Gold nomisma of Justinian II, with a cross on steps on the reverse, shown twice actual size. (Photo: Dumbarton Oaks, Washington, D.C., copyright 1996)

continued to hold parts of the two principalities. Leontius pressed on to raid and plunder Albania and Azerbaijan, which were within the territory of the caliphate but outside the control of the caliph who had made the treaty.

This campaign not only gained loot and extended Byzantine influence in the Caucasus, but persuaded the embattled 'Abd al-Malik to renew his treaty, with revisions in the empire's favor. He agreed to pay the same tribute as before, and to share the revenues of Armenia, Iberia, and Cyprus equally with the empire. In return, Justinian agreed to withdraw the Mardaïtes from the caliphate and resettle them on Byzantine territory. Some of them came from Mount Amanus that year, and others from Mount Lebanon the following spring, when Justinian went to Armenia to take up partial possession of it. Though still other Mardaïtes stayed where they were, at least twelve thousand men came to the empire, apparently with their families. These Justinian settled in the Carabisian Theme, enrolling them as permanent oarsmen for the theme's fleet.

Justinian seems then to have divided the Carabisian Theme into two parts, each with two thousand soldiers. The part in central Greece became a new Theme of Hellas with its capital at Corinth. The Carabisian Theme kept the Aegean islands, where its strategus continued to reside, along with the southern coast of Anatolia under a subordinate drungary of the Cibyrrhaeots, whose headquarters, to judge from their name, were at the port of Cibyra. The twelve thousand resettled Mardaïtes had their own commander and could man all the ships needed to carry the Carabisians' two thousand marines. Substituting Mardaïte oarsmen for temporary levies of locals must have improved the readiness and effectiveness of the reduced Carabisian Theme.[14]

Justinian also had plans for the Balkans. Probably during his march to Armenia and back, the emperor ordered the cavalry from the themes of Anatolia to assemble the following year in the Theme of Thrace for a campaign. The Bulgars had evidently been extending their influence over the Slavs of southern Thrace, in territory uncomfortably close to Constantinople and Thessalonica. Justinian meant to stop the Bulgars, and in preparation he seems to have withheld the tribute due them under their treaty.

Though ending this tribute cannot have saved much more than the Byzantines' pride, Justinian did want money, for this campaign and others. Like Justinian I, the emperor appointed energetic officials who began squeezing revenue out of the aristocracy. The emperor's chief instruments were his sacellarius (treasurer) Stephen the Persian and especially his general logothete (finance minister) the former abbot Theodotus. Theodotus collected taxes with unaccustomed rigor. He is said to have resorted frequently to confiscation, which he enforced by torture and imprisonment of the wealthy.[15]

In 688 Justinian led the assembled cavalry of the eastern themes from the capital overland to Thessalonica. On his way along the northern coast of the Aegean, he drove out the Bulgars, whose hold on the land must have been tenuous, and defeated the Slavs, who formed most of the population. Without trying to annex the region, the emperor rounded up many Slavs to resettle elsewhere. He sent at least a hundred thousand of them to the Opsician Theme. Of these Slavs, thirty thousand men were enrolled in the army and given military land grants, probably in land around Cyzicus devastated under Constantine IV by the Arabs.

Justinian apparently settled other Slavs between Thessalonica and the Strymon River, in order to expand the enclave under imperial rule. To the east of the river, southern Thrace became a no-man's-land separating Byzantine territory from the Bulgars. During this resettlement Justinian marched into Thessalonica, remained a short time in the city, and marched back, apparently by a more northerly route. As he returned, a band of Bulgars ambushed him in a mountain pass and inflicted considerable losses on his army. Yet his campaign could be counted a success if the thirty thousand captured Slavs could be incorporated into the Byzantine army, increasing it by about a third.

Leaving his Slavic recruits on their new military lands, in 689 the tireless emperor attacked the Arabs again. Although his treaty with the caliphate should still have been valid, in spite of it many Mardaïtes remained at large on Mount Lebanon, joined by Arab renegades and runaway slaves, and the caliph may have withheld his tribute in protest. Since the Arab civil war continued to rage, Justinian felt safe in sending an army that reached Mount Amanus and approached Mount Lebanon itself. ʿAbd al-Malik, who was preparing another campaign to wrest Mesopotamia from the Alids, chose to make another truce. The annual tribute he paid was reduced from a thousand nomismata per day to a thousand nomismata per week, but he apparently left the emperor a free hand in Armenia, Iberia, and Cyprus. For his part, Justinian appears to have withdrawn about sixty-five hundred more Mardaïtes with their families, though some still remained on Mount Lebanon. He enrolled those who came to him as oarsmen in his new Theme of Hellas.[16]

In his first four years as emperor, Justinian had ordered military operations every year. He had broken three treaties, made two treaties, created a theme, enrolled around 18,500 oarsmen and 30,000 soldiers, and
gained control over Cyprus, Iberia, and Armenia. This frenetic activity
had brought evident progress, but paying for the campaigns and new
troops kept the emperor's financial officials busy at their unpopular work.
And Justinian's success owed a great deal to the troubles in the caliphate.

Over the next two years 'Abd al-Malik's forces expelled the Alids from
most of Mesopotamia, captured Medina, and seemed to be winning the
civil war. Justinian kept the peace, but in 691 he removed many of the
people of Cyprus from their insecurely held island and settled them in
the still underpopulated region around Cyzicus. No doubt recalling
that Justinian I had founded a city and archbishopric named Justiniana
Prima, the emperor founded a city of Justinianopolis for the Cypriots
and gave their archbishop the combined privileges of the metropolitans
of Cyprus and Cyzicus.

The emperor soon found an excuse to escape his treaty with the Arabs.
He issued a new type of nomisma showing both his own portrait, as was
customary, and for the first time a bust of Christ. Hitherto the caliphs
had minted gold dinars that copied Byzantine nomismata down to the
emperor's portrait; but 'Abd al-Malik understandably omitted the head
of Christ from his dinars, which he began to mint in a different style and
with a somewhat lighter weight. Justinian refused the caliph's tribute on
the ground that the coins in it failed to match his own. Although the

78. Gold nomisma of Justinian II holding a cross, with a bust of Christ on the
reverse, shown two and a half times actual size. (Photo: Dumbarton Oaks,
Washington, D.C., copyright 1996)

caliph added extra coins to make up the full value, Justinian insisted on the bust of Christ. Declaring the treaty broken, he prepared for a campaign against the Arabs.

By the summer of 692, Justinian's thirty thousand Slavs had been trained, armed, and organized into a special company under their own commander Nebulus. The emperor added them to the regular thematic cavalry and led them east. But during the emperor's prolonged preparations, 'Abd al-Malik had put the Alids under siege in Mecca, mustered an Arab army, and invaded the empire before Justinian could invade the caliphate. The two armies clashed near Sebastopolis in the middle of the Armeniac Theme, with the Arabs brandishing a copy of the treaty on a spear in front of them to emphasize the justice of their cause.

The Arabs had the worst of it until Nebulus and most of his Slavic company deserted to them, allegedly because of a bribe. At this the rest of the Byzantines fled. Though the Arabs also withdrew, Justinian was irate. He disbanded the Slavic company, of whom some ten thousand men remained, and is said to have killed many of them, apparently including wives and children of the deserters. Others he sold into slavery.[17] He also imprisoned the strategus of the Anatolics Leontius, whom he seems to have held partly responsible for the defeat.

Although Justinian had to postpone his military ambitions, that very fall he sought another sort of glory. Emulating both his father and Justinian I, he announced an ecumenical council at Constantinople. No theological matters remained to be discussed; Justinian's efforts to find some in the acts of the Sixth Ecumenical Council had already failed. He nonetheless declared that a council was needed to consider questions of canon law, which the fifth and sixth councils had neglected. Because the council was meant to complete those councils' work, it has been termed the Quinisext ("Fifth-Sixth") Council.

During the two and a half centuries since the Council of Chalcedon had issued the last ecumenical canons, the practices of the eastern church had increasingly diverged from the western. The Quinisext Council came too late to harmonize such differences, but Justinian and the council's almost exclusively eastern bishops knew little of western usage. Thus the council required married men who were ordained deacon or priest to continue conjugal life, which the western church required them to renounce. The council forbade fasting on Saturdays in Lent, which the western church prescribed. Among other rulings contrary to western views, the council reduced the pope's primacy of authority to a mere precedence of honor.

Although papal legates signed the Quinisext Council's acts early in 693, Pope Sergius promptly repudiated both his legates and the council. Justinian at first tried to intimidate Sergius by having an imperial officer seize two papal officials; then the emperor sent another officer to arrest the pope himself. But the army of the exarchate supported Sergius, and would have lynched the emperor's representative if the pope had not helped him to escape. Only an army from the East could possibly have imposed Justinian's will.

After his defeat at Sebastopolis, Justinian had no soldiers to spare. His client prince of Armenia submitted without a fight to 'Abd al-Malik, who had taken Mecca and was extending his authority over Persia. Justinian himself sent columns for use in rebuilding the mosque at Mecca, since otherwise the caliph would have despoiled a church at Jerusalem.[18] But 'Abd al-Malik no longer needed the peace treaty that Justinian had broken three times. In summer 694 the caliph sent his raiders, along with the Slav deserters from the empire, to attack Cilicia, where they defeated local Byzantine troops.

Unable for the moment to win military victories, Justinian turned to building, which had been of little interest to the emperors since his model Justinian I. The emperor began with the Great Palace at Constantinople, adding a dining hall and putting walls around the palace enclosure. Since he wanted to build a courtyard for imperial ceremonies on the site of a nearby church, he demolished the church and built another elsewhere. These projects appear to have been expensive, and coming on top of military expenses they spurred Justinian's officials Stephen and Theodotus to make still more exactions from the exasperated aristocracy.

In summer 695 Justinian's reputation sank further when another Arab raid, this time on the Armenian Hexapolis, took many captives and showed that the balance of power had shifted back to the Arabs. The emperor tried to mollify the former strategus of the Anatolics Leontius, and presumably Leontius's friends, by releasing him after three years' imprisonment and naming him strategus of Hellas. Before he left Constantinople, however, the general organized a conspiracy against the emperor.

By night the conspirators seized the city's main prison, the Praetorium, and released and armed its prisoners, who included many aristocrats and military men. With their help Leontius and his followers summoned the people of the capital to Saint Sophia the next morning. They gained the support both of the patriarch Callinicus and of a large mob that shouted slogans against Justinian. Crowding into the Hippodrome, the mob pulled Justinian from the palace and proclaimed Leontius emperor.

The circumstances of Justinian's deposition suggest that the empire lacked the resources for aggressive expansion, let alone for a return to the glories of the first Justinian. At the least, making sustained conquests at this time would have required great caution. Justinian II, despite his initial successes, had made too many enemies, spent too much money, taken too many chances, and failed to see how much the seventh-century invasions had weakened the empire. In the end his projects weakened it further.

SEVEN REVOLUTIONS

The overthrow of Justinian in 695 shook the empire more severely than the three earlier revolutions of the seventh century. The murder of Maurice in 602 could not utterly shatter the East's tradition of orderly successions going back to Constantine I. The execution of Phocas in 610 seemed condign punishment for his usurpation; the rebellion in favor of Constans II in 641 served to confirm the tradition of succession from father to eldest son. But the deposition of Justinian II ended a well-established dynasty for no better reason than the emperor's unpopularity among aristocrats. Leontius's rule rested only on military support, which a number of other ambitious men could also claim since the creation of the themes.

An Isaurian, Leontius was the first man of mature age and experience to become emperor since Heraclius. Adopting the name Leo that had already belonged to two emperors, Leontius tried to act like a legitimate and moderate ruler. Though the mob wanted Justinian killed, Leontius merely slit his nose and tongue to make him ineligible to rule, exiling him to Cherson in the Crimea with some of his ministers and supporters. Leontius had even wanted to save Justinian's detested ministers Stephen and Theodotus, whom the mob burned alive.

Shunning the arrogance that had made Justinian unpopular, Leontius tolerated Arab border raids. But in 696 ʿAbd al-Malik sent an unignorable expedition against Byzantine Africa. The caliph's commander Hassān ibn al-Nuʿmān quickly took Qayrawān from the Arab renegades who held it, and by early 697 he seized Carthage, leaving what remained of the exarch's forces scattered among a few fortified towns. Though the prince of Lazica had just repudiated Byzantine suzerainty and joined the

79. Leontius (r. 695–98). Gold nomisma, shown almost two and a half times actual size. (Photo: Courtesy of the Arthur M. Sackler Museum, Harvard University Art Museums, Whittemore Collection)

Arabs, Leontius wisely gave priority to Africa, which if completely lost would be gone for the foreseeable future.

That autumn the emperor loaded the Carabisian fleet with an expeditionary force and sent it to Africa. Its commander John the Patrician boldly sailed into Carthage, taking the city by surprise while Hassān was fighting the Moors. John also cleared the Arabs from the neighboring towns. But Hassān appealed to the caliph for more troops, and when they arrived early in 698 he forced John and his men out of Carthage. The Byzantine commander sailed back to seek reinforcements; but when he reached Crete, some of his naval officers, afraid of being blamed for the campaign's failure, revolted. They proclaimed as emperor one of themselves, the drungary of the Cibyrrhaeots Apsimar, and sailed on Constantinople.

Leontius seems to have sent his remaining ships to Cyprus, to return the Cypriots from Justinianopolis under an agreement with the caliph.[19] The plague was again raging in the capital. Yet the citizens stood by Leontius when Apsimar's fleet arrived at Sycae, across the Golden Horn, and put the city under siege. That summer, however, some officers, who were said to be of foreign origin, opened a gate. The rebels stormed in, looting as they went. Apsimar, whose name was certainly foreign and probably German, became emperor under the name of Tiberius III, perhaps recalling the last emperor who had suffered no calamities. Apsimar slit Leontius's nose and relegated him to a monastery in Constantinople.

Though Apsimar had more or less adequate abilities, he had even less right to rule than Leontius, whose only real failure, the loss of Africa, was more Apsimar's fault than his own. In order to justify his usurpation, Apsimar planned a raid on the Arabs, who were then distracted by a rebellion in Persia. The emperor appointed as commander of all four Anatolian land themes the man he trusted most, his brother Heraclius, and sent him south with a large force. Traversing the passes of Cappadocia before winter set in, Heraclius invaded northern Syria. He inflicted heavy losses on an Arab army that came out from Antioch; then he raided as far as Samosata, and returned to the empire with much booty and numerous prisoners in the spring of 699.

While scoring this easy but insubstantial victory, which invited Arab retaliation, Apsimar made no effort to prevent the Arabs from taking the empire's last outposts in Africa. His only apparent contribution to the defense of the West was to form new themes of Sardinia and Sicily from existing troops. The feeble Theme of Sardinia comprised the remnants of the Exarchate of Africa, including Sardinia, Corsica, and the Balearic Islands. The Theme of Sicily comprised Sicily and Calabria, which were the parts of the Exarchate of Italy most exposed to sea raids from Arab-held Africa.[20]

The caliph soon retaliated for Heraclius's raid with a full-scale invasion of Byzantine Armenia, which he sought to add to his holdings in Armenia proper. In 700 the caliph's son 'Abdullah captured the border stronghold of Theodosiopolis and raided as far as the Hexapolis. The next year the caliph's brother Muhammad invaded the Byzantine territory east of the Euphrates in such force that its Armenian commander Baänes surrendered and its Armenian inhabitants accepted an Arab governor. Neither the emperor nor his brother Heraclius offered effective resistance.

But the Armenians themselves disliked the Arabs, and in 702 they massacred their Arab governor and his garrison, setting off a rebellion that extended far into Armenia proper and to Lazica as well. The Armenians appealed for aid to the emperor, and received some Byzantine troops. Unprepared to fight the Armenians at once, the caliph first sent 'Abdullah to Cilicia, where in 703 he fortified Mopsuestia as the Arabs' first stronghold in the region. By the next year 'Abdullah led a large army into Armenia, while another Arab army besieged Sisium near Mopsuestia. Although Heraclius attacked the Arabs at Sisium and killed or captured many of them, 'Abdullah continued subjugating Armenia.[21]

That year the deposed emperor Justinian, undeterred by the mutilation of his nose and tongue and unimpressed by Apsimar, escaped with a few of his former courtiers from exile in Cherson in the Khazar Khanate. The khan took Justinian seriously enough to marry him to a Khazar princess, who was baptized under the significant name of Theodora. When Apsimar protested, the khan was ready to hand Justinian over, but the intrepid exile and his followers escaped again, leaving his pregnant wife behind. In the autumn they sailed to the Bulgar Khanate, where Justinian was so persuasive that the Bulgar khan Tervel provided him with an army to regain his throne.

Faced with this threat, Apsimar recalled his brother Heraclius from the East to Thrace. By summer 705 Heraclius led an army near to the Bulgar frontier, but Justinian and Tervel passed right by him and marched on Constantinople. After waiting three days before the city walls without being invited in, the deposed ruler, whose courage never failed him, entered the pipe of the broken Aqueduct of Valens with some of his men. While they occupied the capital, Apsimar fled to Sozopolis in Thrace, where his army gradually deserted him. Justinian soon captured Apsimar, and executed Heraclius and his principal officers. The restored emperor sent to the Khazars for his wife Theodora and his newborn son Tiberius, and rewarded Tervel with lavish gifts and the rank of Caesar.

Justinian could claim with reason that his deposition had harmed the empire. During the usurpations of Leontius and Apsimar Byzantium had lost Africa, Lazica, part of Cilicia, and Byzantine Armenia, though it

80. Lead seal of Tervel, Bulgar khan (r. ca. 701–ca. 718), with his Byzantine title of Caesar, shown one and one-half times actual size. (Photo: Dumbarton Oaks, Washington, D.C., copyright 1996)

had regained Lazica. The Arabs had resumed their annual raids, led by Maslamah, a son of the caliph and a brilliant warrior. Three revolutions in ten years was an alarming number, especially when the Arab war was intensifying. As both the legitimate emperor and a ruler of experience and talent, Justinian had the best chance of reestablishing stability if he exercised unaccustomed restraint.

Though earlier emperors had seldom resorted to execution, Justinian's killing opponents in arms like Apsimar's officers was defensible. Early in 706, after watching games in the Hippodrome seated with one foot on Leontius and the other on Apsimar, Justinian had both of them executed as well. This too was justifiable, since Justinian's own case showed that mutilation was not enough to end an imperial career, and Phocas's execution for usurpation was a generally accepted precedent. Justinian even showed some mercy by forcing Apsimar's son to enter the Church rather than killing him. But Justinian did himself no good by executing a number of officers and officials for supporting the usurpers, and by blinding and not just deposing the patriarch Callinicus for crowning them.

Shortly after Justinian's restoration 'Abd al-Malik died, and his son al-Walīd became caliph. Walīd's uncle Muhammad finished subduing Armenia by massacring the Armenian nobles, while his half-brother Maslamah invaded Cappadocia, besieging Tyana through the winter of 707. To raise this siege, the emperor sent two strategi with a force increased by peasant irregulars; but Maslamah crushed it and sacked Tyana, deporting its inhabitants. The next year, while Justinian led a minor and unsuccessful campaign against his erstwhile Bulgar allies, Maslamah took more forts and defeated a Byzantine army near Amorium. The next year he raided Isauria. Maslamah's enthusiasm for fighting the empire appeared insatiable.

In 710 the Byzantine outpost of Cherson rebelled against Justinian with the help of the Khazars. Though the place was scarcely worth attention at a time when Anatolia was under serious attack, Justinian harbored a grudge against the notables of his place of exile, and sent a sizable fleet under Stephen the Patrician to reclaim it. Stephen easily took Cherson and executed some Chersonites, but his fleet was wrecked by an autumn storm on its way back to the capital. The people of Cherson were able to call in the Khazars once more.

This time Justinian reacted more cautiously. He was trying to put down unrest in Ravenna and Rome, and had summoned Pope Constantine to Constantinople to settle their differences over the Quinisext Council.[22] In the spring of 711 the emperor received the pope with respect and agreed that the papacy need not accept any decisions of the council that it found objectionable. Justinian was also distracted by the defection of Lazica and Abasgia to the caliph, and sent a modest expedition under Leo the Syrian, who recovered Abasgia. The emperor seems to have tried to compromise on Cherson, dispatching an embassy led by the general logothete George to negotiate a settlement with the Khazars. But the Chersonites and Khazars killed George and his party. They proclaimed as their emperor Bardanes, an exiled official of Armenian blood, giving him the Greek name Philippicus.

Since Justinian could hardly ignore usurpation, that summer he sent a third naval expedition to Cherson under Maurus the Patrician. Yet at the same time the Arabs were advancing all along the eastern frontier. Having made peace with Tervel and obtained three thousand Bulgar reinforcements, Justinian led most of the Opsician and Thracesian themes to Sinope, from which he could have attacked the Arabs in either Lazica, Armenia, or Cilicia. But there he learned that Maurus, after failing to expel the Khazars from Cherson, had joined the Chersonites in proclaiming Philippicus.

The emperor and his army started to race the usurper and his fleet back to the capital. Despite the handicap of traveling by land, Justinian nearly arrived first; but he was just short of Chalcedon when the rebels sailed into Constantinople. Philippicus had Justinian's little son Tiberius butchered, and executed Justinian's chief officials. Advancing to Justinian's camp near Chalcedon, the rebel forces persuaded Justinian's men to desert him in return for a promise of immunity. Justinian was beheaded, and Philippicus sent his head as far as Rome and Ravenna as proof of his death.

Justinian's second fall was due not so much to his excesses, which during his second reign were not great, as to the uncertainties caused by the three revolutions before it. The fourth revolution made matters even worse, destroying whatever remained of dynastic legitimacy. Philippicus evidently tried to justify himself by circulating an account of the expeditions to Cherson that exaggerated Justinian's cruelty and folly. But Philippicus had outdone Justinian in savagery by killing not only his predecessor's advisers but his son besides.

Like many other Armenians, Philippicus favored Monotheletism. When he entered the capital, he expressed his wish to repudiate the anti-Monothelete Sixth Ecumenical Council. Barely two months later, at the beginning of 712, he deposed the patriarch Cyrus for defending the council and issued an edict rejecting it. Most of the rest of the clergy accepted the edict, reluctant to brand the emperor a heretic. Along with the usual motive of cowardice, some may have felt that the empire could not afford a theological controversy at such a time.

By 712 Maslamah and the other Arab commanders had finished conquering Cilicia and the Byzantine lands east of the Euphrates. Philippicus tried to save the region of Melitene by sending Armenians to settle it, but Maslamah easily drove them from their exposed position. The Arabs pushed the empire's frontier back from the Taurus to the Antitaurus and raided far into Anatolia. In the Armeniac Theme they sacked Amasia and reached Gangra; in the Anatolic Theme they sacked Misthia and apparently stayed the winter. Meanwhile the Bulgars raided Thrace as far as Constantinople. In the spring of 713 the Arabs captured Antioch in the Anatolic Theme, the Bulgars raided again, and the Italians, enraged at Philippicus's edict against the Sixth Ecumenical Council, expelled his officers from Rome.

After all these Byzantine reverses, the count of the Opsician Theme George Buraphus, who had gone to Thrace to ward off the Bulgars, concluded that Philippicus was ripe for deposition. The day before Pentecost the count sent officers to the capital who entered the palace, seized Philippicus during his siesta, and blinded him, inflicting a mutilation harder to ignore than slitting of the nose or tongue. The conspirators doubtless meant for the crowd that gathered next day at Saint Sophia to acclaim George; but they lost control of events. The protoasecretis Artemius, head of the imperial chancery, received the crowd's acclamation and the throne under the imperial name of Anastasius II.

Anastasius seems to have chosen his new name in honor of the capable bureaucrat Anastasius I, whose prudence he emulated. He punished conspiracy and strengthened his own hand by blinding both George and the officer who had blinded Philippicus. Anastasius sent Philippicus himself to a monastery in Constantinople and exiled the plotters to Thessalonica. Without delay the emperor revoked Phillipicus's edict and recognized the Sixth Ecumenical Council. He replaced most of the strategi who had served Philippicus, choosing as strategus of the Anatolics Leo the Syrian, who had regained Abasgia for Justinian II.

The emperor gave his full attention to the Arabs who were pushing ever farther into Anatolia. In 714, when Maslamah invaded the region

81. Anastasius II Artemius (r. 713–15), with a cross on steps on the reverse. Gold nomisma, shown two and a quarter times actual size. (Photo: Dumbarton Oaks, Washington, D.C., copyright 1996)

of Ancyra in the Opsician Theme, Anastasius sent an embassy to the caliph Walīd to negotiate a truce, or at least to discover the Arabs' intentions. When the ambassadors returned to report that the caliph planned a land and sea assault on Constantinople, Anastasius began repairing the city's fortifications and putting in supplies. He appears to have given the city its first full defenses by completing the sea walls.

Although Walīd died early in 715, his brother and successor Sulaymān eagerly pursued his plans against the Byzantines. That spring the emperor learned that an Arab fleet had sailed to Phoenix in the Carabisian Theme to cut wood for more warships. Anastasius promptly ordered an expedition to assemble at Rhodes under his general logothete John the Deacon, and from there to attack the Arabs across the strait. Once on Rhodes, however, the troops from the Opsician Theme rebelled against Anastasius, perhaps out of resentment for his blinding of their count George two years before. They killed John, scattered his expedition, and sailed to Adramyttium in the Thracesian Theme. There they found and proclaimed emperor the local tax collector Theodosius, despite his attempts to escape that dangerous honor.

While the caliph Sulaymān assembled a vast army under Maslamah to conquer the empire outright, the Byzantines fought still another civil war. Anastasius left the capital in the hands of friendly officers and marched to Nicaea to confront the Opsician rebels on their home ground. But Theodosius's supporters rallied most of the Opsician troops, marched and sailed to Chrysopolis, and began naval attacks on Constantinople. Toward the end of the summer the rebels crossed to Thrace, gained admission to the capital by treachery, captured Anastasius's officers, and plundered the city. Anastasius remained at Nicaea into the fall, when he agreed to abdicate, become a monk, and go into exile at Thessalonica in return for a promise of immunity.

Theodosius III, an incapable and unwilling emperor, found himself facing a full-scale Arab invasion and continuing resistance to his rule in the Anatolic and Armeniac themes. Nominally loyal to Anastasius II, the Anatolic strategus Leo the Syrian was allied with the Armeniac strategus Artavasdus against Theodosius. So matters stood in 716, when two Arab armies invaded Anatolia while an Arab fleet advanced along the coast from Cilicia. Leo, a native of Germanicea in the borderland that had recently become Arab territory, knew both Arabic and the Arabs. During long and duplicitous negotiations, Leo outmaneuvered the Arab commander Maslamah and kept him out of Amorium.

That summer Leo had himself acclaimed emperor with Artavasdus's support. The frustrated Maslamah left Leo's territory for the Thracesian Theme, where the Arab army captured Sardis and Pergamum and spent the winter. Impatient to bring the civil war to a close, Leo marched on Constantinople himself. At Nicomedia he met and captured a group of Theodosius's officials, including the emperor's young son. Without harming them, he advanced to Chrysopolis and opened negotiations with Theodosius. The latter agreed to abdicate in favor of Leo and to enter the Church with his son, once given assurances that they would not be harmed. At the beginning of spring 717, Leo entered the capital as Leo III.

Although this seventh revolution was the most merciful and best justified of the lot, the government remained disrupted as Maslamah's forces threatened Constantinople. Political anarchy had unquestionably harmed the empire's defense against the Arabs, whose advance had seemed to stall before Justinian II's first deposition. But the Arab attacks would in any case have intensified after the end of their own civil war, and those attacks had in their turn harmed the emperors' reputations and the Byzantine army and treasury. With far more men, land, and wealth than Byzantium, the Arabs had begun to concentrate all their strength against it. Now they threatened to extinguish the empire entirely by capturing its capital.

CHAPTER ELEVEN

The Passing of the Crisis, 717–780

The Arabs' plan in 717 was not to raid in force, as in 674, but to take Constantinople outright. The caliph Sulaymān had said as much. The army and navy on their way to the city were led by the Arabs' best general, Maslamah, and are said to have reached the staggering totals of 120,000 men and 1,800 ships.[1] These forces outnumbered the entire army and navy of the empire, and were more than enough to blockade Constantinople completely. If the Arabs could take the center of Byzantine resistance at the capital, their way would be clear to complete the conquest of Anatolia that they had already begun. After a long civil war, to say nothing of seven violent revolutions over the past twenty-two years, Byzantium was ill prepared to meet them.

CHANGE UNDER LEO III

The Byzantines' main advantage was their latest emperor. Leo III, experienced but still vigorous at the age of about forty, had repeatedly extracted himself from almost hopeless situations as the Byzantine commander in Abasgia and then as strategus of the Anatolic Theme. In the latter post he had already bested Maslamah by his diplomatic and military skills and knowledge of the Arabs. As a Syrian who had probably been raised a Monophysite, Leo may have been suspect to some Byzantines; but he professed orthodoxy and was much too sensible to attempt religious innovations at such a time.[2] Leo inspired considerable loyalty in the army, and counted among his allies the Armeniac strategus Artavasdus, who married Leo's daughter Anna.

Three years earlier, Leo's former patron Anastasius II had finished the capital's sea walls and begun stockpiling supplies. Leo seems to have bought time to complete his own preparations by further negotiations with Maslamah. In the meantime the emperor secured an alliance with the Bulgars, who evidently feared that the caliphate would make a more aggressive neighbor than Byzantium. They undertook to harass the Arabs whenever possible. At the beginning of summer, when Maslamah crossed the Hellespont at Abydus and marched across Thrace sacking cities, he was dogged by the Bulgars along his way.

In July 717 Maslamah put Constantinople under a thorough siege on the land side.[3] Parallel to the Theodosian Walls the Arabs built two complete siege walls, the inner one to confine the Byzantines and the outer to keep the Bulgars out of the Arab encampment in between. At the start of September, the Arab fleet arrived to begin a blockade by sea. As most of this fleet sailed past the city and up the Bosporus, Leo sent ships to attack its rear with Greek Fire. The Arabs were horrified to see their rear guard of twenty ships with two thousand men burned or sunk. Afterward the Arab fleet stayed clear of the Byzantine fire ships, remaining in a harbor halfway up the European side of the Bosporus until winter came.

Since the Arabs had no plans for a frontal assault, as soon as they abandoned their plans for a sea blockade their numbers and the passage of time began to work against them and for the Byzantines. The Byzantines could bring in food for themselves by boat, but their land and sea raiders and their Bulgar allies prevented the Arab army in its camp and the Arab fleet in its harbor from venturing out to do much foraging. Moreover, the winter of 717–18 was freakishly harsh. As snow lay on the ground for over three months, many of the Arabs and their horses, camels, and livestock died of cold. The Arabs also rapidly consumed their supplies.

In the spring the caliph 'Umar II, who had succeeded Sulaymān, sent new fleets from both Egypt and Africa to resupply the besiegers, and another army through Anatolia to reinforce them. At this news, the strategus of Sicily Sergius assumed the capital was as good as lost and proclaimed emperor one of his officers, Basil Onomagulus, who was renamed Tiberius. With months of campaigning weather ahead, 400 Arab ships from Egypt and 260 from Africa, carrying both food and arms, entered the Sea of Marmara. To avoid the Byzantines' Greek Fire, they put in on the Asian shore, just south of Chalcedon.

The crews of these ships were native Egyptians and Africans, over-

82. Leo III the Syrian (r. 717–41).
Miniature from the Modena
Zonaras. (Photo: Biblioteca Estense,
Modena)

whelmingly Christian and ill disposed toward their Muslim rulers. Once they found themselves near Constantinople, many of them took to their landing boats and escaped to the city, where they declared their allegiance to the emperor. Leo gladly received them and sent them back with his own fleet, which captured the Arabs' supplies and sank their ships. Encouraged by this partial success, Leo was able to dispatch a small expedition to Sicily, where the army surrendered its rebel officers and order was restored. Though the Byzantines recovered some Italian forts that the Lombards had taken in the confusion, this does seem to be the time when the empire effectively lost Sardinia and the islands dependent on it.[4]

Meanwhile the army of Arab reinforcements had crossed Asia Minor and reached Nicaea. But Leo stationed Byzantine soldiers in the hills around Nicomedia, who ambushed the advancing Arabs, killed many of them, and sent the rest fleeing back to the frontier. By this time the Byzantines were bringing ample supplies into Constantinople, while Maslamah's men were starving. An epidemic broke out in the Arabs' camp, and thousands of them were killed by Bulgar attacks. The caliph 'Umar ordered a retreat, and after thirteen months the Arabs raised the siege on 15 August, the Feast of the Dormition of the Virgin, whom the Byzantines gave credit for saving the city. Though Maslamah's exhausted troops returned across Anatolia unopposed, on the return voyage many Arab ships sank during a storm in the Sea of Marmara. Still more of them burned when a volcano near the Aegean island of Thera showered them with ash. A few more fell into the hands of the Byzantines.

Thus the great Arab offensive ended in fiasco, partly through their bad luck, partly through Leo III's nerve, but largely because of the defensive strength of Constantinople and its distance from the caliphate. So complete was the Arabs' failure that it allowed Leo to go on the offensive. He sent a fleet that sacked Laodicea in Syria, and an army that forced the Arabs to evacuate much of the border region. The Byzantines reoccupied part of western Armenia, and the caliph had to refortify Mopsuestia and Melitene against them.

Despite Leo's victories, however, in 719 the former emperor Anastasius II tried to overthrow him. Anastasius seized power at Thessalonica, where he had retired as a monk, and gained a promise of help from the Bulgars, who may have felt poorly rewarded for their services to Leo. Anastasius also expected support from several officials who had served him; but they were betrayed to Leo. When Anastasius came to Heraclea in Thrace with a Bulgar army and fleet, Leo persuaded the Bulgars to abandon the expedition. The emperor captured and executed Anastasius and punished his partisans, one of whom had been the count of the Opsician. That powerful command went to Leo's son-in-law Artavasdus.

The triumphant Leo crowned his son Constantine junior emperor in 720, and celebrated by introducing a new silver coin, the miliaresion. It replaced the hexagram introduced by Heraclius, which had passed out of use. Evidently modeled on the Arab dirham and valued at twelve to the gold nomisma, the miliaresion filled a need for a coin worth more than the copper follis but less than the nomisma, which since the seventh century seems to have been tariffed at 288 folles. The miliaresion became a stable element of the coinage.

The Arabs resumed their raids as before, in spite of all their recent losses. Beginning with 720, the next caliph, Yazīd II, sent raiders every year into the Anatolic and Armeniac themes. First the Arabs defeated the Byzantines in the part of Armenia recently reclaimed for the empire, though the next year the Byzantines defeated the Arabs in Isauria. In

722, possibly with the emperor's encouragement, the Khazars began a war with the Arabs in Armenia; but not even this interrupted Arab raids on Asia Minor.[5] When Leo tried to raise taxes in Italy to pay for the Arab war, he found himself defied by Pope Gregory II and unable to control Rome.

The emperor seems to have taken the common Byzantine attitude that such setbacks were evidence of divine wrath that needed appeasing. In 722 he tried forcing the empire's Jews to accept baptism. Even that precaution, however, failed to stop the Arabs from sacking Iconium the next year and finishing their reconquest of Byzantine Armenia by taking Camachum. Not long afterward, Leo began to consider another possible reason for God's anger: that the use of icons of Christ and the saints might violate the biblical commandment against idolatry.

This idea had its partisans at the time. The news that Yazīd II had banned Christian icons in the caliphate in 721 may have shamed some Christians with the thought that an infidel was forcing them to do something they should have done by themselves.[6] Within the empire, the leading opponents of icons were two bishops in the Opsician Theme, Constantine of Nacolea and Thomas of Claudiopolis. The patriarch Germanus rebuked them for their opinion, and though it was shared by an adviser of Leo's named Beser, a Syrian refugee from the caliphate, thus far the emperor showed no clear signs of agreement. Yet the prestige that he and the empire had gained by foiling the Arab siege seemed to be dissipating. An expedition led by his exarch from Ravenna failed to regain control of Rome, and the Arabs had the better of their battles with the Khazars, raided Cyprus in 725, and sacked Caesarea in the spring of 726. Even though God had spared the Byzantines outright destruction, he still seemed to be displeased with them.

Apparently that same spring, Leo concentrated his efforts to placate God on a revised law code, the *Ecloga* or Selection—selected, naturally, from the *Justinian Code*.[7] Besides being much shorter and in Greek, the *Ecloga* modified a number of Justinian's provisions "in the interest of greater humanity," as Leo observed in its preface. Thus the *Ecloga* outlawed abortion and restricted the use of execution. But it prescribed the death penalty for homosexual acts, and greatly expanded the use of mutilation as a punishment. The inspiration for these measures, and for the *Ecloga*'s limiting the grounds for divorce, seems to have been a relentlessly literal reading of the Bible.[8] Of course, the main argument against icons was of the same sort.

83. Icon of the Virgin and Child between Saints George (left) and Theodore, from the Monastery of Saint Catherine, Mount Sinai. (Photo: Courtesy of Michigan-Princeton-Alexandria Expedition to Mount Sinai)

That summer the submerged volcano just west of Thera, which had been intermittently active since 718, erupted violently. For days the crater spewed smoke, ash, and chunks of lava over the Aegean and as far as the coasts of Macedonia and Anatolia. A great many Byzantines must have seen or heard of the effects of the eruption. Most probably believed that it was an unmistakable sign of divine anger, and it persuaded the emperor to heed the arguments that God disapproved of icons. Leo began by ordering the removal of the icon most closely associated with the emperor, a picture of Christ over the main entrance to the palace, the Bronze Gate (*Chalkē*).

Probably Leo thought that by removing icons he was suppressing an abuse that had no serious theological justification. He saw no need to consult the Church, and he appears to have been surprised by the depth of the popular opposition he encountered. The few soldiers he sent to pull down the icon from the gate were overcome the moment they did so by an outraged mob that lynched several of them. Although Leo prudently avoided executing any of the murderers, he dealt them penalties ranging from fines to mutilation, and continued to follow the course he had chosen. Apparently in an edict, he condemned the possession of icons of the saints, though not of those of Christ.[9]

At first Leo seems to have made little effort to enforce his condemnation, which was especially unpopular in the Church, in Greece, and in Italy. The patriarch Germanus kept his dissent quiet, but Pope Gregory, who was already almost independent, publicly rejected Leo's orders. After Gregory took his stand, the troops of the Italian Exarchate overthrew their officers, killed the exarch Paul, and only refrained from choosing their own emperor because the pope was opposed. Worse still for Leo, early in 727 the men of the Theme of Hellas and the islands of the Carabisian Theme did proclaim another emperor, Cosmas. They mustered their fleets and sailed on Constantinople. Even if the naval revolt was not begun to defend icons, it surely exploited iconophile sentiment.

As the rebels approached the capital, Leo attacked them with a fleet of his own armed with Greek Fire. This had its usual devastating effect, burning many ships and frightening the survivors into surrender. Leo beheaded the rebel emperor Cosmas. Apparently at this time Leo transferred the headquarters of the Carabisian Theme from the Aegean islands to the land of the less rebellious Drungus of the Cibyrrhaeots in southern Anatolia. The Carabisian Theme became known as the Cibyrrhaeot Theme, though its headquarters were later moved from Cibyra to Attalia.

Leo had barely put down this rebellion when a large body of Arab raiders struck far into Asia Minor. They sacked Gangra and pressed on to besiege Nicaea in the Opsician Theme. They had damaged the walls and seemed poised to take the city, when one of the officers of the Opsician count Artavasdus dramatically smashed an icon of the Virgin. The Arabs withdrew. Declaring that the destruction of the icon had saved Nicaea, the emperor sharpened his criticism of iconophiles, the patriarch Germanus in particular.

Although Leo's doctrine soon became known as Iconoclasm ("Icon-breaking"), the emperor still took no strong measures against icons. He dispatched a new exarch to Italy, Eutychius, who with the aid of diplomacy established himself shakily in the exarchate and made an uneasy peace with Pope Gregory. The Arabs continued to raid Anatolia, but their war with the Khazars increasingly distracted them. By 730 Leo could claim to have restored the peace and stability that Justinian II had squandered, and was ready to impose Iconoclasm on the empire.

Curiously, what Leo called at the beginning of 730 was a council of courtiers, not a church council. Those summoned included the patriarch Germanus and presumably other clerics, but Leo seems not to have trusted in his support throughout the hierarchy. He therefore relied mainly on his own authority as an emperor chosen by God, or at any rate not promptly removed by him. Germanus declined to attend, on the ground that a doctrinal question could only be decided by an ecumenical council. When the assembly adopted Iconoclasm, the elderly patriarch abdicated and was replaced by his assistant Anastasius, who agreed to accept Iconoclasm as the price of his promotion. All depictions of religious persons, including Christ, now fell under the ban, though the Cross could be depicted, if it was not part of a crucifix.

The emperor had many images that were in public view destroyed or covered, and he confiscated valuable church plate, altar cloths, and reliquaries decorated with religious figures. But he took no harsh measures against the retired patriarch Germanus or other iconophile bishops or officials. A few of them left office or left Constantinople; most kept their disagreement with the emperor to themselves and went on as before. Although the emperor wanted to end the open veneration of icons that he thought was offensive to God, neither he nor any of the numerous Byzantines who disagreed with him seems to have been eager for a confrontation, or to have seen a major theological issue at stake.

Among Christians beyond Leo's control, Iconoclasm won no known

84. Saint John of Damascus (left), writing with his stepbrother Saint Cosmas. Miniature from the *Menologium of Basil II*. (Photo: Biblioteca Apostolica Vaticana)

adherents and caused much indignation. Near Jerusalem the Chalcedonian monk John of Damascus wrote in Greek to argue that whatever was done to an icon applied to the person it depicted, thus absolving iconophiles of idolatry and accusing iconoclasts of sacrilege. John's arguments spread not only in the caliphate but into the empire. In the West Pope Gregory II refused to recognize either the new patriarch Anastasius or Iconoclasm, so that Leo's authority at Rome almost completely lapsed. In 731 Gregory's successor Gregory III called an Italian synod that condemned Iconoclasm as a heresy.

Iconoclasm notwithstanding, the Arabs kept on raiding Anatolia. By 733 they had driven the Khazars out of Armenia and invaded the Khazar Khanate, and they repeatedly raided well into the Anatolic and Armeniac themes. That year Leo made a grand gesture to ally himself with the Khazars against their common enemy, by marrying his young son and heir Constantine to a daughter of the Khazar khan. Constantine's bride was baptized under the name of Irene; but the khan himself remained pagan, and Leo never sent him help.

Also in 733, the emperor tried to regain control over Rome by sending a large fleet under the strategus of the Cibyrrhaeots Manes. This fleet was shipwrecked in the Adriatic. Unable for the present to muster another expedition, Leo punished the pope as best he could. He confiscated the sizable papal estates in Sicily and Calabria and raised taxes there, perhaps putting into effect the tax increases that Gregory II had frustrated eleven years before. At the time Leo appears to have been revising tax assessments throughout the empire, and by this act he probably made the tax rates of the Theme of Sicily, though not of what was left of the Italian Exarchate, uniform with the eastern themes.

More momentously, this was probably the time when Leo revoked papal jurisdiction over the empire's western territories and awarded it to the patriarchate of Constantinople.[10] This act deprived the popes of their traditional ecclesiastical authority not only over Sicily and Calabria, but over Byzantine Greece and the Aegean islands. With this punishment of the pope, the Byzantine hierarchy gained authority over regions that had rebelled against Leo in the past and were not at all enthusiastic about Iconoclasm. But Leo had to leave Ravenna to the pope, whose authority there was at least as strong as the tenuous hold of the exarch Eutychius. Unintentionally, the emperor had fitted the boundary of the patriarchate of Constantinople to what was for centuries to be the real western boundary of the empire.

Leo managed rather than solved the long-standing problems of holding Italy and protecting Anatolia. The Arabs, after further warfare with the Byzantines and Khazars, in 737 forced the Khazar khan temporarily to submit and convert to Islam. Soon they were raiding as far as the Thracesian Theme. About 738 the Lombards seized Ravenna, though the exarch Eutychius quickly recovered it with the help of his subordinate duke of Venetia and the support of the pope.[11] But by annexing the Lombard Duchy of Spoleto, the Lombard king Liutprand left the remnant of the exarchate surrounded by a revivified Lombard Kingdom.

Arab raiders who reached the Thracesian Theme in the spring of 740 finally provoked Leo into marching out against them. The emperor seems to have seen an opportunity for a victory, since he brought along his young son Constantine to share in the glory. Probably choosing his ground carefully, Leo fell upon an Arab force of some twenty thousand near Acroënus in the Anatolic Theme, killed most of them, and put the rest to flight. Even though the undaunted Arabs were back raiding the next year, Leo finally had a victory that he could ascribe to God's approval of Iconoclasm.

This was fortunate for him, because in the fall of 740 a devastating earthquake, which iconophiles naturally attributed to God's anger with Iconoclasm, struck Constantinople and parts of Thrace and Bithynia. Its epicenter was probably near the western end of the Sea of Marmara, since the tides were affected and the worst destruction was around Nicomedia and in some towns in Thrace. Many died and many buildings fell at Constantinople, where some sections of the land walls collapsed. Leo turned the disaster to fiscal advantage by adding a tax surcharge of a twelfth to repair the walls. The walls were soon repaired, but the surcharge became permanent.

In June 741, Leo died of dropsy, after a reign that had to be judged successful by recent standards. He had saved Constantinople from a determined Arab attack, defended the empire tolerably well, and survived several rebellions. He also died in bed after the longest reign since Constans II, who had himself been murdered. Leo had inherited an empire on the verge of disintegration and restored it to stability. He had also begun an avoidable theological controversy, but so far not a very acrimonious one. If his exploits had not convinced most people that Iconoclasm was right, he had not done badly enough to prove to them that Iconoclasm was wrong.

CONFLICT UNDER CONSTANTINE V

Since the last seven imperial successions had been violent, the peaceful accession of Leo's son Constantine would itself have been a significant achievement. It seemed to be happening when Constantine, then twenty-two years old, was crowned at Constantinople. His hereditary claim as the second member of his dynasty, while hardly overpowering, was better than anyone else's. Yet if inheritance was set aside, the obvious claimant was Artavasdus, long the commander of the great Opsician Theme and Leo III's son-in-law and chief ally.[12]

The young emperor was astute and active, and wary of Artavasdus from the start. He immediately declared a campaign against the Arabs, who were apparently raiding Anatolia as usual. Scarcely a week after his coronation, at the beginning of summer, he led his troops out of the capital, which he entrusted to the magister Theophanes Monotes ("One-Ear"). When the emperor reached Bithynia, he summoned Artavasdus for a conference on the Arab campaign. Artavasdus arrived, but fell upon Constantine's men near Dorylaeum and routed them. Constantine's

85. Constantine V Name of Dung (r. 741–75). Miniature from the Modena Zonaras. (Photo: Biblioteca Estense, Modena)

commander Beser, Leo III's iconoclast counselor, was killed. The emperor himself escaped.

Announcing that Constantine had died in the battle, Artavasdus won over Theophanes Monotes in the capital and Monotes' son, the strategus of Thrace. Monotes arrested those who remained loyal to Constantine and received the usurper into the city, where the patriarch Anastasius crowned him. Probably without condemning Iconoclasm explicitly, Artavasdus courted its opponents, who seem to have included most of the capital's clergy and officials, by allowing icons to be restored.

Meanwhile Constantine fled to Amorium and gained the support of the Anatolic and Thracesian themes. By fall he led them to the Bosporus; but without a fleet he could not cross the straits, and had to withdraw to Amorium for the winter. Thus the empire was divided in two, with the Anatolic and Thracesian themes backing Constantine and most of the rest backing Artavasdus. The usurper crowned his older son Nicephorus coemperor and named his younger son Nicetas general commander of Asia Minor, with his headquarters in the Armeniac Theme.

In 742 Artavasdus himself led his forces from the Opsician Theme into the Thracesian. Constantine advanced to meet him near Sardis, where he defeated his rival and sent him fleeing back to Constantinople. Though Artavasdus's son Nicetas led an army into the Opsician from the Armeniacs, Constantine also defeated Nicetas in a bloody battle near Modrene. In September Constantine crossed the Bosporus, and his strategus of the Thracesians Sisinnius crossed the Hellespont. They joined in besieging Artavasdus in the capital.

This siege evidently lasted over a year. Artavasdus sought help from the caliphate, but without success. He sent a fleet to gather supplies, but Constantine's Cibyrrhaeots captured it near Abydus. Artavasdus sallied out against the besiegers, but he was defeated with heavy losses, Theophanes Monotes among them. After an attack on the Cibyrrhaeots had failed, Artavasdus's son Nicetas tried to relieve the capital, only to be defeated and captured by Constantine near Nicomedia. By fall 743 the people of Constantinople were starving, and Artavasdus had to let many of them leave. In November Constantine finally made a surprise assault on the capital and seized it. He captured Artavasdus himself not long afterward.

This civil war of two years and a half was the longest the empire had seen since Heraclius fought Phocas. The caliphate might well have exploited it, with grave consequences, if the Umayyad dynasty had not been suffering from its own dissensions and the beginning of a rebellion led by the family of the Abbasids. As it was, Constantine could hardly ignore how close he had come to deposition. Through the rest of his reign he was highly suspicious of iconophiles and possible conspirators among his officials.

At first the emperor showed a politic moderation toward Artavasdus's many defeated partisans. Though he had a right to execute usurpers, he simply blinded the rebel, his two sons, and some ringleaders. Since blinding avoided breaking the biblical commandment against killing but incapacitated the victim for political purposes, it became the usual penalty for serious state crimes. Constantine merely confiscated the property of some other conspirators, and left the patriarch Anastasius in office after a public humiliation. Soon afterward, however, Constantine blinded his own ally Sisinnius on a charge of conspiracy, showing how little he trusted those around him.

Probably during the next two years, while the Arabs remained divided among themselves, Constantine broke up the enormous Opsician Theme, which Artavasdus had commanded. Since its creation from the two armies in the Emperor's Presence, it had been not only the empire's largest theme by far but perilously close to the seat of government. Besides Artavasdus's revolt, it had played a part in the assassination of Constans II and the depositions of Philippicus and Anastasius II. Constantine V now made sure that the Opsician would never wield such power again. In the process he created a branch of the army distinct from the themes, known as the tagmata ("regiments").

The tagmata founded by Constantine totaled eighteen thousand men, most of them presumably redeployed soldiers from the Opsician Theme. The names of their six divisions were those of older units of guards or garrison troops, which had been much smaller and may now have provided the tagmata with loyal officers. Most tagmatic troops seem to have continued holding military lands, as they had when they were thematic soldiers. While some tagmatic soldiers moved to the capital, where the old guards and garrisons had been stationed, most continued to live within the borders of the themes of the Opsician and of Thrace. But all had commands that were independent of the themes and a function that was different from theirs.

The two main tagmata were the Scholae and the Excubitors, previously regiments of guardsmen that had declined into insignificance. They now became crack cavalry units of four thousand men each, designed to accompany the emperor on his campaigns. Soldiers from both the Scholae and the Excubitors were stationed on both sides of the Bosporus, so that they were almost impossible to assemble secretly for conspiracies. A third tagma of four thousand cavalry, the Watch (*Vigla* in Greek), was upgraded from an earlier patrol unit (*vigilia* in Latin). The Watch could go on campaigns, but it usually remained in the capital along with two other garrison units of two thousand infantry each, the Walls and the Numera, both expanded from earlier units of a similar sort. Another division, the Optimates, consisted of two thousand muleteers intended to transport the baggage of other troops during campaigns. A unique unit somewhere between a tagma and a theme, the Optimates resided in a small district in Bithynia that was named for them, though soldiers of the Scholae and Excubitors lived there as well.[13]

The creation of the tagmata had three main results. It made plotting against the emperor more difficult, because the troops near the capital were now dispersed among various themes and tagmata with different commanders. Second, the tagmata gave the emperor an easily assembled striking force that Constantine worked to make especially effective and loyal, sufficient in itself for a small campaign and for the core of any large expedition. Finally, moving new tagmatic troops into Thrace probably allowed Constantine to advance the Thracian frontier at the expense of the local Slavs. This he seems to have begun to do before 746.

In that year, taking advantage of spreading rebellions in the caliphate, Constantine went on the offensive against the Arabs, in the process perhaps using the tagmata for the first time. With little opposition, he took Germanicea, his father's birthplace, and the nearby towns of Teluch (Doliche) and Sozopetra.[14] The emperor made no effort to hold these places; he simply expelled the Arab garrisons and took away many of the Christian inhabitants to settle in Thrace. Constantine had nevertheless made the Byzantines' first successful land invasion of the caliphate since

718. The way seemed open for more advances on the Anatolian and Thracian frontiers, when suddenly the bubonic plague returned in force.

This new outbreak of the plague had first reached Byzantine territory in the fall of 745 in Sicily and Calabria. By the next year it spread to Greece and the islands. In 747 it arrived in Constantinople, where it raged for a year and caused immense loss of life. Constantine gave up military operations and retired to Bithynia to avoid infection.[15] By the time the disease abated the next summer, a large part of the city's population had perished. Reacting with typical vigor, the emperor brought in new settlers from Greece and the islands to replace the dead.[16] Thus the Byzantine capital began to recover.

Meanwhile the Arabs were also suffering from the plague, and the Abbasid rebels were making steady progress. In 749 the rebel leader Abū'l-'Abbās was proclaimed in Mesopotamia as the caliph al-Saffāḥ. The next year Saffāḥ's forces inflicted a crushing defeat on the Umayyad caliph Marwān II. Marwān was killed later that year. Constantine seized his chance for another easy victory while the Abbasids were pacifying the caliphate. In 751 he besieged the key stronghold of Melitene, forced its surrender, and demolished it, taking booty and many prisoners from the city and the surrounding region.[17] The emperor again settled his Christian captives in Thrace, where he was busily reoccupying and re-fortifying towns, probably including the long-lost city of Adrianople.

While Constantine won victories on his eastern frontier and extended his northern one, he suffered a setback in Italy. In 751 the Lombard king Aistulf seized Ravenna and the pitiful fragment of the exarchate around it. Although Constantine sent an embassy to Aistulf demanding the return of his land, the king knew he had little to fear from the empire. Venetia and a few isolated outposts were still more or less subject to the Byzantines, and the pope had never quite repudiated Byzantine rule; but only the Theme of Sicily, including the toe and heel of Italy, could properly be counted as Byzantine territory any longer. For years Constantine sent ambassadors to the Lombards, the Franks, and the pope attempting to recover Ravenna, but he never ventured military action.[18] His real interests lay in the East.

CONSTANTINE V'S ICONOCLASM

After the alarming revolt of Artavasdus, for ten years Constantine had shored up his rule by dividing the Opsician Theme, forming the tagmata, and winning military glory from the Arabs. During this time he evidently continued the prohibition of religious images introduced by his father Leo III, but did nothing more. By 753, however, the emperor felt able to take a step that his father had never taken or perhaps even contemplated. After formally consulting his advisers, Constantine summoned a church council to condemn the veneration of icons not merely as an abuse but as a heresy.

The church hierarchy had professed Iconoclasm for twenty-three years, apart from the interlude under Artavasdus, when the patriarch Anastasius and doubtless some other bishops had temporarily restored icons. Anastasius died shortly before the council convened in early 754, and the emperor made no move to replace him before it met. It was a curious gathering, held without a patriarch of Constantinople or representatives from the pope and the orthodox eastern patriarchs, none of whom had accepted Iconoclasm. Although the emperor wanted the council to be considered ecumenical, no earlier ecumenical council had been so naked an instrument of imperial authority.

For six months the bishops deliberated at the imperial Palace of Hieria near Chalcedon, under the presidency of the archbishop of Ephesus Theodosius, son of the long-deposed emperor Tiberius III Apsimar. Besides compiling a collection of scriptural and patristic references unfavorable to icons, the Council of Hieria endorsed a splendidly sophistical theological argument promoted by the emperor. According to it, an image of Christ must show him either as both God and man confused, implying Monophysitism, or as a man distinct from God, implying Nestorianism. The council therefore condemned iconophiles as heretics, singling out the patriarch Germanus and John of Damascus for special anathemas. In its final session, the council endorsed Constantine's choice as the new patriarch of Constantinople, Constantine of Syllaeum.

In sharp contrast with most past emperors, who had tried to reduce divisions in the Church, by holding the Council of Hieria Constantine created a question of heresy where few had seen one before. Although the council encouraged iconoclasts, before long it heightened iconophile opposition and fanned a controversy that was to rage for almost another century. Since icons had already been banned, all Constantine really gained from his council was firmer control over the Byzantine church and justification for harsher measures against iconophiles. These he seems to have felt he needed, after the shock of seeing his patriarch and other iconophile officials desert him for Artavasdus. Yet for the pres-

86. The effect of Iconoclasm on ecclesiastical seals during the eighth century: *above*, lead seal of Archbishop Peter of Thessalonica, with a bust of Thessalonica's patron Saint Demetrius, 1.5 times actual size; *below*, lead seal of Archbishop Anastasius of Thessalonica, Peter's successor, with no portrait, 1.5 times actual size. (Photos: Dumbarton Oaks, Washington, D.C., copyright 1996)

ent he launched no persecution of iconophiles, probably hoping that the council would be enough to intimidate them.

In 755 Constantine again attacked across the Arab frontier, taking the border fort of Camachum and the Armenian city of Theodosiopolis. Camachun he garrisoned and kept, but he deported the Christians of Theodosiopolis to Thrace, as he had previously done with those of Melitene.[19] His main objective in the East seems to have been to gather settlers for Thrace, where his spreading colonization roused the Bulgars to make a raid the next year. In 757, after some indecisive skirmishing in Cilicia, Constantine agreed to a truce and exchange of prisoners with the Arabs, which freed him to campaign in Europe.

Apparently after defeating Bulgar raiders, in 759 the emperor attacked the Slavs west of Byzantine Thrace, and conquered some of their lands. The next year he planned to deter future Bulgar attacks by invading the Bulgar Khanate. While sending a fleet that ravaged the Danube delta, Constantine led his army to the border at Marcellae, where he joined battle with the Bulgars. He drove them from the field, but casualties were heavy on both sides. The emperor agreed to receive Bulgar hostages and grant a truce, especially because the Arabs had just raided the southern Armeniac Theme and killed its strategus.

After two years of peace, however, in 762 the Bulgars hanged the leaders who had made the truce and chose others hostile to the empire. Many Slavs fled from the new Bulgar chiefs to the emperor, who settled them among the Optimates. To exploit the divisions among the Bulgars, Constantine prepared a second land and sea expedition against them in the spring of 763. He shipped some nine thousand cavalry, probably drawn from the tagmata, to the Danube delta while he led another army to Anchialus on the Black Sea.[20] There he fought another bloody battle with the Bulgars and defeated them. The Bulgars killed their khan Teletz for his defeat, then deposed their khan Vinekh for trying to make peace with Constantine.[21] Vinekh fled to the emperor, who raided Bulgaria again in 765.

Although to many Byzantines Constantine's victories must have seemed to betoken divine favor, his Iconoclasm remained deeply unpopular among his officials. Those in civil or ecclesiastical office could hardly express dissent, but monks were bolder. Stephen, a hermit on Mount Auxentius overlooking Chalcedon, became the moral leader of the iconophiles. As the emperor noticed his courtiers' admiration for Stephen, he grew not merely exasperated but fearful of an iconophile plot. In fall 765, Constantine ordered Stephen's arrest and let a mob led by soldiers of the Scholae lynch the courageous hermit. The emperor began a persecution of Stephen's followers and of monks in general, and demanded that everyone in public life, from the patriarch Constantine on down, take an oath not to venerate icons.[22]

In June of 766, Constantine launched another land and sea expedition against the Bulgars, sending a fleet to Anchialus as he had in 763 while he marched northward along the coast. But in July a storm wrecked the fleet. After burying his drowned men, the emperor returned to Constantinople looking much less favored by God. Lashing out at his opponents, at games in the Hippodrome he ordered monks to parade holding nuns by the hand. A few days later, he was enraged to discover a full-

87. The martyrdom of Saint Stephen the Younger (top) and his companions. Miniature from the *Menologium of Basil II*. (Photo: Biblioteca Apostolica Vaticana)

blown plot against him by iconophile admirers of the martyred Stephen.

The conspirators he detected first were nineteen important officials. They were led by Constantine Podopagurus, who as postal logothete was the minister in charge of internal security, and his brother Strategius, who commanded the new and putatively loyal Tagma of the Excubitors. Other plotters included the strategi of Thrace and Sicily, and the count of the reduced but still powerful Opsician Theme. The emperor had all these men paraded in the Hippodrome, the two Podopaguri beheaded, and the others blinded. After further investigation, he also had the city prefect Procopius flogged and the patriarch Constantine jailed.

Realizing that legislating Iconoclasm without enforcing it had antagonized his officials without cowing them, the emperor began a general persecution of iconophiles. He went so far as to condemn sacred relics and prayers to the Virgin and saints, though none of these had been rejected by his Council of Hieria. He appointed new officials of unquestioned loyalty, including the eunuch Nicetas as patriarch, the ardent iconoclast Michael Lachanodracon as strategus of the Thracesians, and other military commanders. This was probably the time when Constantine divided the Opsician yet again, making it one of the smaller themes after more than half of it became the new Bucellarian Theme. In autumn 767 the emperor had the deposed patriarch Constantine humiliated and abused in the Hippodrome, and finally beheaded. Besides making a determined effort to destroy the remaining icons and some relics, the emperor launched an indiscriminate persecution of monks and nuns, maiming or killing a number of them and razing or confiscating their monasteries.

While attacking iconophile officials and monks, the emperor curried favor with the tagmata and the people of the capital, many of whom he had recruited or settled there himself. He lodged soldiers in confiscated monasteries and entertained them riotously at court. He greatly expanded the city's water supply by restoring the Aqueduct of Valens, damaged by the Avars in 626. Food became abundant and cheap in city markets, reportedly because the treasury hoarded so much gold that farmers became desperate for cash to pay their taxes. At Easter 769 Constantine relieved the shortage of money somewhat by scattering gold through the streets of Constantinople at the coronation of his third wife Eudocia as Augusta. Later that year, he sumptuously celebrated the betrothal and marriage of his son Leo, making Leo's bride Irene another Augusta.

After a decade of relative quiescence, the Arabs resumed serious raiding in 770, when they sacked Laodicea Combusta in the Anatolic Theme and deported its population. The next year they raided again and took more captives, while the Byzantines retaliated by raiding Armenia. In 772, when the Arabs advanced by land to besiege Sycae in the Cibyrrhaeot Theme, Constantine ordered forces from the Anatolics, Bucellarians, and Armeniacs to bar their retreat. But the Arabs routed the Byzantines and returned with their booty. The emperor asked for a truce from the caliph Mansūr, without result.

Though these Arab victories could have been taken as signs of divine displeasure with Iconoclasm, Constantine had silenced all iconophile opposition. His loyal strategi spread his persecution of monks through all but the border areas of the empire. In the Thracesians, the strategus Michael Lachanodracon confiscated all monastic property and forced every monk and nun to marry on pain of blinding and exile. By 772 he had eradicated monasticism within his theme. Constantine did not go so far in the rest of the empire, but he approved what Lachanodracon had done.

To gain more military glory, the emperor planned to attack not the Arabs but the more vulnerable Bulgars. In spring 774 he sailed for the Danube delta with a large fleet that apparently carried the tagamata, while the cavalry from the themes advanced on land. The Bulgars promptly sued for peace. Constantine agreed, perhaps because the sailing weather looked perilous. But he kept the cavalry from the themes in the forts of Thrace, and seems to have looked for a pretext to attack again. In the fall he found one. His spies informed him that the Bulgar khan Telerig was sending troops to deport from the border region some Slavs who were apparently friendly to the empire. The emperor quickly assembled his army, ambushed the Bulgars near the frontier, and crushed them.[23]

In spring 775 Constantine began still another land and sea expedition against the Bulgars, this time avoiding the dangers of the weather by leading his army on land. A storm nonetheless destroyed much of his fleet off Mesembria, and the emperor retreated. Though the khan Telerig made friendly overtures, these turned out to be a ruse to discover the identities of the imperial spies in the khanate, whom he killed. In late summer, Constantine started a retaliatory expedition, but when he reached Arcadiopolis he was stricken with a fever and boils on his legs. The emperor died on his way back to the capital.

Constantine's had been an extraordinary reign, but his success had been decidedly mixed. Although he had exploited the Abbasids' overthrow of the Umayyads to win some easy victories from the Arabs, he had gained nothing of importance but Camachum and some Christian settlers for Thrace. In Thrace he had expanded and strengthened Byzantine holdings somewhat and given the Bulgars better than he got, but even against them he gained no decisive advantage. In forcing outward acceptance of Iconoclasm on his officials by a reign of terror, he had begun a bitter and avoidable theological controversy. Iconophiles, who later dubbed him "Name of Dung" (*Kopronymos*), rejoiced at his death, rumoring that he himself had seen it as divine punishment. Yet Constantine also had his partisans, particularly in the army, and his memory lingered long after him.

LEO IV'S MODERATION

Constantine's twenty-five-year-old son became the emperor Leo IV, sometimes known as the Khazar because his mother was the Khazar princess Irene. Early in his reign, Leo naturally lacked the experience

TABLE 8

The Dynasty of Leo III

Emperors are in capital letters and italics, with the years of their reigns marked "r." Other years are of births and deaths unless indicated otherwise.

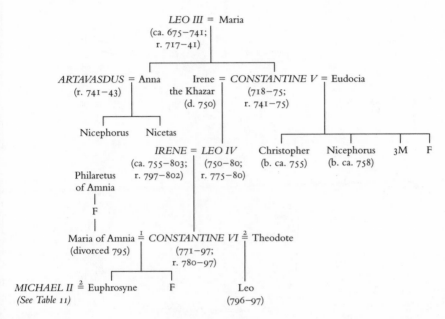

and authority with which his father had overawed opponents. Constantine had made matters worse by granting Leo's slightly younger brothers Christopher and Nicephorus the rank of Caesar, which could make them rallying points for strict iconoclasts if Leo was too conciliatory to iconophiles. Yet the iconophiles, who included many officials and Leo's own wife Irene, needed placating. A careful and resourceful man, Leo tried to moderate the divisions left behind by his father.

At his accession Leo discovered and confiscated a vast fund of gold intended for the use of his younger brothers, and used it to give generous donatives to the army and the people of the capital. At the next army payday, in the spring of 776, Leo encouraged troops from the tagmata and themes to demand the coronation of his little son Constantine as his heir. He crowned his son only after extracting an oath that they would defend the boy's right to the throne, excluding Leo's brothers. Just a month later, Leo's brother Nicephorus was discovered in a plot backed by some imperial bodyguards and grooms. With the consent of his

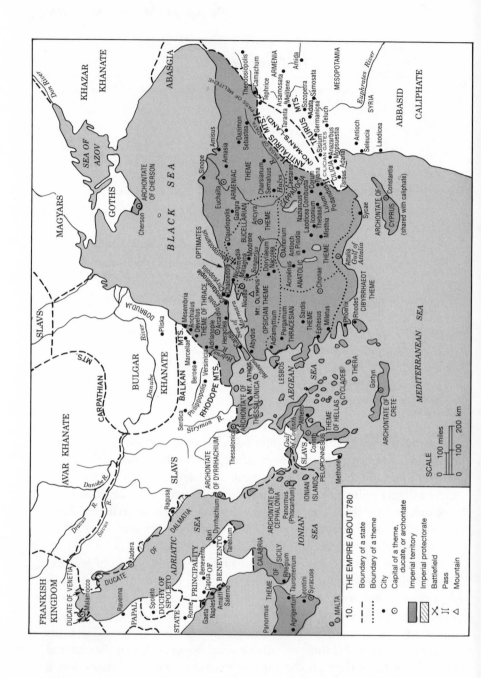

10. THE EMPIRE ABOUT 780

- – – – Boundary of a state
- · · · · · Boundary of a theme
- ⊙ City
- ⊙ Capital of a theme, ducate, or archontate
- (shaded) Imperial territory
- (hatched) Imperial protectorate
- ✕ Battlefield
- ⨝ Pass
- △ Mountain

FRANKISH KINGDOM

AVAR KHANATE

SLAVS

PAPAL STATE

DUCHY OF SPOLETO

DUCATE OF SPOLETO

PRINCIPALITY OF BENEVENTO

Rome ⊙
Spoleto
Benevento
Capua
Gaeta
Naples
Amalfi
Salerno

DUCATE OF VENETIA
Malamocco
Ravenna

ADRIATIC SEA

DALMATIA
Jadera
Ragusa

Bari
Tarentum

CALABRIA

THEME OF SICILY
Panormus (Phiscardum)
Rhegium
Tauromenium
Leontini
Syracuse
Agrigentum

MALTA

IONIAN SEA

ARCHONTATE OF DYRRHACHIUM
Dyrrhachium
Panormus (Phiscardum)

ARCHONTATE OF CEPHALONIA

IONIAN ISLANDS

Methone

THEME OF THE PELOPONNESUS

SLAVS
Corinth
Gulf of Corinth
Athens

THEME OF HELLAS

CYCLADES

THERA

AEGEAN SEA

ARCHONTATE OF CRETE
Gortyn

MEDITERRANEAN SEA

BULGAR KHANATE
Pliska
Serdica
Philippopolis
Beroea

CARPATHIAN MTS.

AVAR KHANATE

Danube R.
Drava R.
Sava R.

SLAVS

Danube River

DOBRUDJA

BALKAN MTS.
Mesembria
Anchialus
Develtus
Marcellae
Versinicia
Adrianople
Arcadiopolis
Heraclea

RHODOPE MTS.
Strymon R.

THEME OF THRACE

Thessalonica
ARCHONTATE OF THESSALONICA
MT. ATHOS

LESBOS

BLACK SEA

Cherson ⊙
ARCHONTATE OF CHERSON

GOTHS

SEA OF AZOV

Don River

KHAZAR KHANATE

MAGYARS

ABASGIA

Sinope
Amisus
Amasia
Euchaita

OPTIMATES

Constantinople
Chalcedon
Nicomedia
Nicaea
Malagina
Modrene
Sangarius
Dorylaeum
Nacoleia
Amorium

BUCELLARIAN THEME
Claudiopolis
Gangra
Ancyra

ARMENIAC THEME
Charsianum
Semaluos
Caesarea
Corum

OPSICIAN THEME
Mt. Olympus
Adramyttium
Pergamum

THRACESIAN THEME
Sardis
Ephesus
Miletus

ANATOLIC THEME
Acroënus
Antioch in Pisidia
Chonae

CAPPADOCIA
Nazianzus
Nyssa
Podandus
Tyana
Loulon

Attalia
Gulf of Attalia

CIBYRRHAEOT THEME
Phoenix
Rhodes

ARCHONTATE OF CYPRUS
(shared with caliphate)
Constantia

Sycae
Adana
Tarsus
Mopsuestia
CILICIA
Anazarbus
CILICIAN GATES
Sisium
Germanicea
Adata

TAURUS MTS.
ANTITAURUS MTS.
(NO-MAN'S-LAND)
PASS OF MELITENE

Camachum
Theodosiopolis
Tephrice
Sebastea
Dazimon

ARMENIA
Arsamosata
Melitene
Samosata

MESOPOTAMIA
Amida

Euphrates River

SYRIA
Antioch
Seleucia
Laodicea

ABBASID CALIPHATE

SCALE
0 ——— 100 miles
0 —— 100 —— 200 km

Halys
Iconium
Misthia
Thebasa
Laodicea Combusta

officials and troops, Leo stripped Nicephorus of the title of Caesar and exiled the other plotters to Cherson.

His position considerably strengthened, the emperor made efforts to propitiate the Church. Even though he kept the decrees of the iconoclast Council of Hieria in force, he abandoned Constantine's later measures against both monasticism and the invocation of the Virgin and saints. Leo began to appoint abbots to major bishoprics, and at least some of his appointees were secret iconophiles. He was apparently following the usual policy of emperors to reduce theological controversy, unlike his father, who had exacerbated it.

In the summer of 776, Leo made his bid for military renown by sending troops to raid the caliphate. They sacked Samosata on the Euphrates and took captives, but this provoked a retaliatory Arab raid that reached Ancyra. In spring 778, anticipating another Arab raid, Leo sent a force drawn from all the themes of Asia Minor under Michael Lachanodracon, who was still strategus of the Thracesians. Lachanodracon advanced to Germanicea, where he took Christian captives, plundered the land, and defeated an Arab army that came out against him. Leo celebrated his victory in Constantinople and settled the captives in Thrace. The next year, after Leo sent raiders who destroyed the Arab fort of Adata, the caliph Mahdī angrily ordered a counterraid. The Arabs marched all the way to Dorylaeum in the Opsician Theme; but Leo had his men hold the forts and burn provender, until the Arabs ran out of fodder and retreated in disappointment to rebuild Adata. The Bulgars were also in disarray, since their khan Telerig had fled to Leo in 777.

So far Leo seemed to be skillfully managing not only the empire's enemies on both frontiers but the Byzantines on both sides of the iconoclast question. Early in 780 the emperor showed still more favor to iconophiles when on the death of the patriarch Nicetas he chose a successor of known iconophile sympathies, Paul of Cyprus. Not two weeks after Paul's consecration, however, Leo discovered that his chief chamberlains had smuggled icons into the palace for the use of the empress Irene. The realization that his own servants kept secrets from him enraged and alarmed the emperor. He had the offending chamberlains flogged and paraded down the main street of Constantinople; one died from the punishment, and the others were forced to become monks. Leo rebuked Irene, rejected her claims of innocence, and stopped living with her as his wife. The estrangement of the imperial couple lasted through the summer.

Probably Leo intended to reconcile with his wife after she had been sufficiently humiliated to repent. But before he did so, his rather promising reign ended with his sudden death in September. Allegedly the young emperor had developed an insane desire for a votive crown that Heraclius had once donated to the treasury of Saint Sophia. When Leo seized the crown and put it on, boils broke out on his head, causing a fatal fever. Such was the story circulated by the empress Irene, who emerged from her disgrace to become regent for her son, the new emperor. In fact, her husband's opportune death and her account of it were more than suspicious. Probably Leo had still not wrested full control of his household from Irene, and agents loyal to her disposed of him.[24]

By this time the worst perils of the empire were past. Since the failure of the Arab siege of Constantinople in 718, the empire was no longer fighting for its life; and since the end of the revolt of Artavasdus in 743, a measure of political stability had returned. After leaving Constantinople in 748, the epidemic of plague that had been recurring for two centuries finally came to an end in the East. After the fall of the Exarchate of Italy in 751, no more provinces seemed to be threatened with outright conquest, and Constantine V had even managed to annex a little territory in Thrace from the Slavs. The Byzantine army could defeat the Bulgar army about half the time, and sometimes even defeated the Arabs.

The first three emperors of the Syrian dynasty deserve credit for putting down plots and restoring an orderly succession after the preceding anarchy. Leo III weathered an arduous siege of Constantinople; Constantine V showed that the Byzantine army could go on the offensive, and Leo IV waged war competently through his generals. The three rulers' great failure was Iconoclasm, a doctrine that Leo III imposed on a hostile church and unenthusiastic populace, and that Constantine V made pointlessly offensive to dissenters. Yet even Iconoclasm was on the wane in 780, and other trends seemed more favorable than unfavorable. After overcoming several serious threats to its existence, Byzantium was clearly going to last for some time to come.

CHAPTER TWELVE

The Shrinking of Society, 610–780

What happened to the Byzantine Empire during the seventh and eighth centuries was indisputably calamitous. From being a Mediterranean-wide power stronger than any of its neighbors, it shrank to a mainly Anatolian state far weaker than the neighboring caliphate. Byzantium's losses in men and wealth were staggering. With the Arab conquest of Egypt, Syria, and Africa the empire lost three of its four richest regions, and in Alexandria and Antioch two of its three largest cities. Most remnants of Italy, including Rome, later passed from Byzantine rule. The buffer of Illyricum almost entirely fell away, while the whole buffer of Armenia went. Once difficult to attack from the European side and almost invulnerable from the Asian, the vital capital at Constantinople came under assault from both directions. Every sector of the frontier collapsed, and no district of the empire was fully safe from conquerors or raiders.

Despite these severe reverses, the empire survived as a great power. Foreign enemies never succeeded in taking Constantinople, or in conquering any substantial part of Anatolia. The central government and army, though each went through various crises, never distintegrated or ceased to function. After initial failures against the Persians and Arabs in the first half of the seventh century, the Byzantines slowed the invaders' momentum and finally halted it. Even if the setbacks of the seventh century revealed grave weaknesses at the outset, Byzantium's ability to fight on after losing so much demonstrated enduring strengths.

LOSSES AND DEPREDATIONS

The empire's major territorial losses ended with the fall of the Exarchate of Italy in 751. Since Byzantine control over the exarchate had been tenuous since the Arab siege of Constantinople in 718—and none too firm before that—this loss was less consequential than it appears on the map. The Arab siege also seems to have been the time when Sardinia and Corsica escaped the empire's orbit. Apart from Italy, Byzantium's last significant losses had come in the early years of the eighth century in Cilicia and Armenia, which had long been endangered and in large part conquered by the Arabs. Just before losing those eastern possessions, the empire had in 698 lost the last of its holdings in Africa, though these had been imperiled and shrinking as early as 670.

In fact, the empire's truly catastrophic losses, the Arab conquests of Syria, Mesopotamia, and Egypt, went back to the decade from 633 to 643. Before that had come the ruinous, though ultimately unsuccessful, Persian onslaught of 603 to 620, which had also taken Syria, Mesopotamia, and Egypt while the Avars and Slavs were occupying most of the Balkans. Thus most of what the empire lost during the whole of the seventh and eighth centuries had first been lost by 620, and was gone for good by 643. During the next century and a half the only major loss was the gradual slippage of isolated Africa and Italy from imperial control. Otherwise the empire held almost all its land with astonishing tenacity.

The territory that remained was whatever could best be defended from Constantinople. The capital's natural hinterlands were the Thracian plain and Anatolia; within this area the Byzantines had the advantage over any enemy in supplying and moving troops, not to speak of a strong incentive to prevent enemies from making conquests. The line of the Taurus and Antitaurus mountains formed a clear natural barrier in the East. In the West the much lower Balkan and Rhodope ranges were the first natural obstacles, but they ran in unhelpful directions from west to east and provided little defense for the Hebrus valley between them. The Thracian lowlands that the Byzantines kept thus extended to the beginning of the Balkan range on the Black Sea and the beginning of the Rhodope range at the Hebrus River. The rest of the empire in 780 consisted only of the islands and coastal areas of the eastern Mediterranean that the Byzantines could hold with sea power.

The empire had also lost its old frontiers, without really establishing new ones. Until the early seventh century, though the desert borders were ill defined, Byzantine forts had been within sight of Persian strongholds in northern Mesopotamia and of Avar outposts across the Danube. However approximate or porous these frontiers may have been, they were understood by both sides to exist. In 780 the Byzantines had no similar understandings with the Arabs and Bulgars. The empire and the caliphate were separated by a shifting, depopulated no-man's-land, which included nearly the whole barren region between the Antitaurus and Taurus. The Byzantine possessions in Europe and the Bulgar Khanate were separated by a vast region, comprising most of the Balkan peninsula, that was inhabited by Slavic tribes; a few of these had loose alliances with their Byzantine or Bulgar neighbors, but most were entirely independent. Along with its frontiers, the empire had lost its frontier troops, the former *limitanei*.

Byzantium nonetheless retained approximately half of its field army, a remarkable proportion after so many defeats and withdrawals (Table 9).

TABLE 9

Field Army Units in 565 and 773

Unit in 565	Strength	Unit in 773	Strength	Loss, 565–773	Percent Loss
Praesental[a]	40,000?	old Opsician[b]	34,000	6,000?	15?
East	20,000	Anatolics	18,000	17,000[c]	49[c]
Armenia	15,000	Armeniacs	14,000	1,000	7
Thrace	20,000?	Thracesians	8,000	12,000?	60?
Illyricum	15,000	old Carabisian[d]	4,000	11,000	73
Italy	20,000?	Sicily	2,000	18,000?	90?
Africa	15,000	(lost)		15,000	100
Spain	5,000?	(lost)		5,000?	100
TOTALS	150,000		80,000	85,000[e]	52[e]

NOTE: For the explanation of figures questioned in this table, see Treadgold, *Byzantium and Its Army*, 59–63.

[a]The two armies in the Emperor's Presence, each with about 20,000 men.

[b]The elements of the original Opsician Theme, which by 773 were divided into the themes of the (new) Opsician (4,000), the Bucellarians (6,000), and Thrace (6,000), and the tagmata of the Scholae (4,000), Excubitors (4,000), Watch (4,000), Numera (2,000), Walls (2,000), and Optimates (2,000).

[c]This takes into account the 15,000 Federates added to the Army of the East ca. 577, which expanded its strength to 35,000. If the Federates are disregarded, the loss becomes 2,000 (10%).

[d]The elements of the original Carabisian Theme, which by 773 were divided into the themes of the Cibyrrhaeots (2,000) and Hellas (2,000).

[e]This takes into account the 15,000 Federates added to the Army of the East ca. 577. If the Federates are disregarded, the loss becomes 70,000 (47%).

In 773 the empire still had some 80,000 men, serving in units descended from the field forces that had numbered about 150,000 in the later years of Justinian. Most of the losses had occurred by 641, when the amount of the payroll indicates that the field army numbered some 109,000. Since that figure would have included African and Italian troops that disappeared by 773, after 641 the strength of the eastern armies must have held nearly steady. Indeed, most of the troops lost between the sixth and eighth centuries would have belonged to the destroyed or almost destroyed armies of Illyricum, Italy, Africa, and Spain, which under Justinian had totaled some 55,000 men. The eastern armies' strength seems to have fallen by barely a third, even taking into account the 15,000 Federates that Tiberius II had added to their total around 577.

All the eastern armies retreated in some degree of order, even when forced to abandon all their former posts. The old Army of Thrace probably lost something over half its men to the Avar and Slavic invasions, but it did not disintegrate. Around 621 Heraclius transferred its remaining 8,000 or so soldiers to western Anatolia, where it developed into the Thracesian Theme. Also hard hit was the Army of the East, including Tiberius's Federates, which declined during the Persian and Arab wars almost by half, from 35,000 to 18,000. That half Heraclius and his successors nevertheless managed to evacuate to central Asia Minor, where it became the Anatolic Theme. The Army of Armenia, though it abandoned most of its old stations, retreated the shortest distance and suffered least. Of its original strength of 15,000, 14,000 reached stations in northeastern Asia Minor and became the Armeniac Theme.

The two armies in the Emperor's Presence, despite their frequent use in dire emergencies, seem to have kept 34,000 of the about 40,000 men that they had had at first. These remained united in the giant Opsician Theme, which corresponded to their former peacetime stations in Thrace and northwestern Anatolia, until Constantine IV separated the Theme of Thrace from it around 681. Even then the Opsician Theme was overlarge, as its prominent role in rebellions showed, until Constantine V divided the great bulk of its soldiers among the six new tagmata and the new Bucellarian Theme. The roll of the army was completed by the little Theme of Sicily, surviving from the Army of Italy, and the themes of Hellas and the Cibyrrhaeots, apparently salvaged from the Army of Illyricum. A few hundred more soldiers served in outposts outside the regular themes, in territories commanded by archons and called archontates.

The distribution of troops was quite different from that in the earlier period. Now every part of the empire had its garrison. Instead of being concentrated on the frontiers as before, soldiers were most numerous around Constantinople and in western Anatolia, which were far from the Arabs. Although the tagmata could function as a mobile force, their concentration near the capital shows the government's anxiety to protect the Byzantine heartland. Conversely, the relative scarcity of troops near the eastern border seems to betray a feeling that Arab raids were practically unstoppable, though some troops were needed there to prevent Arab conquests.

Covering almost the whole empire, the themes became the empire's chief administrative jurisdictions, replacing both prefectures and provinces. The system of prefectures had inevitably broken down when enemies conquered almost everything but the Prefecture of the East. Although tax collectors were assigned groups of old provinces as circumscriptions as late as the reign of Leo III, in such cases the provinces were mere geographical expressions. From the time of Constans II's military reforms, the themes were the real provinces, and the themes' strategi the real provincial administrators. After the division of the overly large and diverse Opsician Theme, most themes defined natural regions and were suitable for civil as well as military administration.

One such region was the Theme of Thrace. From the Avar invasion to the mid-eighth century it had consisted of a continuous coastal strip about fifty miles deep, forming an empty wedge with Slavs settled in the middle. Bulgar and Slavic raids damaged and depopulated the cities even in the region that remained Byzantine. Security began to return, however, when Constantine V filled in the wedge by reclaiming the interior of the Thracian plain between 744 and 759. In the process he rebuilt and repopulated the cities, including Adrianople after he recovered it, and made Thrace once again into an effective buffer and a major source of food for the capital. Constantine also resettled Constantinople itself after the earthquake of 740 and the plague of 747 to 748. Soon it must have begun to grow again, and it remained despite its tribulations a great city, now the only one the empire had.

Across the straits, more extensive and more secure farmland than in Thrace, and probably a more important source of supplies for the capital, was to be found in northwestern Asia Minor. All of this region lay within the Opsician Theme until the creation of the Bucellarian Theme and the district of the Optimates. These portions of the old Opsician Theme, together with the Thracesian Theme to the south, had always

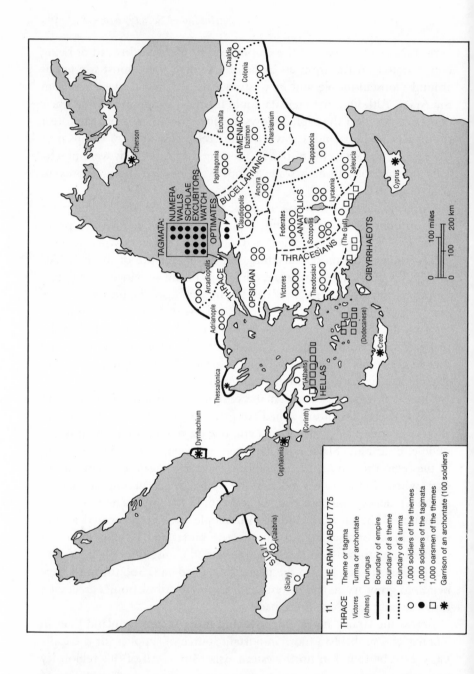

11. THE ARMY ABOUT 775

THRACE	Theme or tagma	
Victores	Turma or archontate	
(Athens)	Drungus	
	Boundary of empire	
	Boundary of a theme	
	Boundary of a turma	
○	1,000 soldiers of the themes	
●	1,000 soldiers of the tagmata	
□	1,000 oarsmen of the themes	
✳	Garrison of an archontate (100 soldiers)	

Labels on map:

Chaldia
Colonia
Cherson
Euchaita
ARMENIACS
Dazimon
Charsianum
Cappadocia
Paphlagonia
Seleucia
Cyprus
TAGMATA:
NUMERA
WALLS
SCHOLAE
EXCUBITORS
WATCH
OPTIMES
BUCELLARIANS
Ancyra
Lycaonia
Claudiopolis
ANATOLICS
Federates
Sozopolis
(The Gulf)
Arcadiopolis
THRACE
CIBYRRHAEOTS
OPSICIAN
Victores
THRACESIANS
Theodosiaci
Adrianople
(Dodecanese)
Thessalonica
Crete
(Athens)
HELLAS
(Corinth)
Dyrrhachium
Cephalonia
SICILY
(Calabria)
(Sicily)

100 miles
0   100   200 km

been the richest and most populous parts of Anatolia, containing valleys with the peninsula's most fertile land and its largest concentrations of cities, and no doubt the larger part of its population. Yet the archeological evidence is clear that most of these relatively numerous cities grew a good deal smaller during this period, and the population of their surrounding countryside presumably declined as well.

Western and northwestern Asia Minor, however, were the parts of the empire that enemy attacks damaged least. Much of the Thracesian and Opsician themes remained untouched by raiders throughout the seventh and eighth centuries. Although the Arabs ravaged some coastal areas of the Thracesians and the Opsician between 670 and 677 and some interior cities of the Optimates and Bucellarians between 716 and 718, otherwise their raids were infrequent and brief. In western Anatolia many cities never fell to the Persians or Arabs at all, most others fell only once, and the rural areas were barely affected. The southern coast of Asia Minor, which became the Cibyrrhaeot Theme, suffered from Arab sea raids more often than the western coast, but even it was usually at peace. Thus the richest part of the empire was seldom raided, and military insecurity seems not to have been the main reason for the shrinkage of most Byzantine cities.[1]

The Anatolian plateau, which included the eastern part of the Bucellarians but lay mostly within the Anatolic and Armeniac themes, had always been poorer and more rural than the lowlands to its west. Most of its less fertile land was better suited to raising animals than to growing crops. The plateau probably became poorer still in this period, because it was the object of the great majority of Persian and Arab raids. Nonetheless, the Arab raiders usually advanced only a short distance through the passes of the Taurus and Antitaurus, and returned as soon as they had rustled as much livestock as they could comfortably drive home.

Just inside the Cilician Gates through the Taurus, Arab raids could be an annual occurrence, and led the hapless inhabitants of that part of the Anatolic Theme to dig themselves underground shelters in the soft rock. The raiders afflicted the southern part of the Armeniac Theme only a little less often. The more determined raiders penetrated far into both themes, and sacked almost all the towns at one time or another, often repeatedly. Many cities shrank to mere forts, and as such became military bases and places of refuge. Yet over most of the plateau the raids were not so frequent as permanently to deplete the herds of sheep and cattle, and the pastures were practically indestructible for longer than a single season.

88. The Anatolian plateau, north of the Cilician Gates. (Photo: Irina
Andreescu-Treadgold)

Life changed more in the empire's remaining islands and coastal enclaves, which after the early seventh century were increasingly cut off
from their mainlands and hinterlands. This mattered least for the Archontate of Cherson, which had always been isolated, and the Aegean
islands, which were near Anatolia. Except for the campaigns between
670 and 677, the Arabs seldom raided the islands of the Cibyrrhaeot
Theme. Crete, an archontate independent of the Cibyrrhaeots, was similarly fortunate. The Arabs' difficulty in sustaining maritime campaigns
is evident from their settling for a condominium with the Byzantines on
Cyprus, which lay closer to Arab naval bases than to Byzantine ones.

The Theme of Hellas was just a scrap of Greece, surrounded by primitive Slavic tribes who seldom attacked the Byzantines but also had little
of value to trade with them. Hellas might almost as well have been an island, since it was linked with other Byzantine territories only by sea
routes. The once great city of Thessalonica was even more isolated, lacking a Byzantine hinterland of any size; too small to be a theme, it ranked
as an archontate. While the Slavs near Thessalonica had foodstuffs to sell
the city and were willing to trade with it, its relative prosperity also
tempted them to try to seize it, and they sometimes made raids right up
to the city walls.

Still tinier and more remote were the scattered outposts to the west that had become the archontates of Cephalonia and Dyrrhachium. The Theme of Sicily, which included the heel and toe of Italy as well as Sicily proper, was actually one of the safer and more prosperous parts of the empire, and was only rarely raided by the Arabs.[2] Although far from Constantinople, Sicily had good harbors and many speakers of Greek, who may well have become a majority by the eighth century after two hundred years of Byzantine rule. Communication by sea between Sicily and the rest of Byzantine territory remained frequent.

Less closely linked to the empire were the ducates of Dalmatia, Venetia, Naples, Amalfi, and Gaeta. Unlike Sicily, none of these seems to have had imperial troops stationed in it or more than a minority of Greek speakers among its Latin-speaking population. But these ducates continued to recognize the government in Constantinople and to enjoy good diplomatic and commercial relations with Byzantium. Until 751 the Exarchate of Italy also consisted of a sizable territory in central Italy, with a significant garrison. After 754 the former territory of the exarchate was subject to the papacy, which though hostile to Iconoclasm avoided declaring its independence from the empire.

People in most of the empire's lost provinces remained more or less aware of their religious and cultural connections with Byzantium, which the Byzantines also recognized. Constantine V did much to cut off the empire from its former subjects to the west and east by imposing Iconoclasm, a doctrine nearly all of them rejected, at a council that excluded their bishops. Yet the Byzantines still considered the Exarchate of Italy to be theirs, and vaguely hoped to recover it with the help of the pope, who held it, the Franks, who had given it to the papacy, or the Lombards, whose king fled from the Franks to Constantinople in 774. The Italians and even the Franks had a persistent respect for the empire.[3]

Under Arab rule, Armenia, Syria, Egypt, and Africa remained predominantly Christian through the eighth century.[4] Merchants, monks, and other travelers regularly made their way by sea and land from the empire to the caliphate, despite the intermittent state of war between them. Many Armenians and some Syrians settled in Byzantine lands and became prominent in the imperial army and government. Byzantine officials and chroniclers could have a detailed knowledge of events in the caliphate, and many Syrian and Armenian churchmen knew Greek and were interested in events in the empire. In 718 the Egyptians and Africans sent to besiege Constantinople felt themselves Byzantine enough to desert to Leo III. Earlier and later, various emperors invaded the caliphate to bring Syrian and Armenian settlers back to settle in Byzantine territory. Christians on both sides of the border could easily imagine an eventual Byzantine reconquest of Armenia and Syria.

During the seventh and eighth centuries the empire lost nearly all of its territories that had been either impoverished or hard to reach from Constantinople. During the long military crisis Syria, Egypt, Africa, and mainland Italy had proved too far away to hold, while most of the Balkans had seemed not to be worth the enormous effort needed to hold it. After these losses, the empire's remaining lands were more cohesive, more defensible, and economically viable. They were also overwhelmingly Greek in culture and orthodox Chalcedonian in religion. The empire thus became smaller, leaner, and tougher, unlikely to lose much more territory and even capable of regaining a little of what it had lost in Thrace and Armenia.

THE REORGANIZED STATE

Such a severe reduction in the empire's extent naturally caused the Byzantine government to become smaller. Some of this shrinkage was almost automatic, since lost provinces no longer needed to be administered or defended, but the process was still painful. One military emergency after another had to be met from dwindling assets and in conditions of social, economic, and political disruption. Byzantium was nonetheless able to adapt its government and army to meet its radically different needs. The achievement was an impressive one, evidently the result of astute decisions by individual emperors, officials, and generals. That much of what was done cannot now be traced in the few surviving sources in no way implies that it happened through some slow evolution or by accident.

Much the worst problem the government faced was maintaining its army out of its diminished resources. Even in the late sixth century, supporting the soldiers had been so difficult that attempts to reduce their cost had toppled the emperor Maurice. Heraclius seems to have bought time about 616 by enacting a reform unsuccessfully attempted by Maurice: substituting issues of arms and uniforms for half the cash pay of the troops. Even this reduced rate of payment, however, was very hard to maintain, and Constans II seems to have halved it again, discontinued the issues of uniforms and arms, and stopped supplying the cavalry with horses and fodder. Basic military pay thus sank to just a quarter of what it had been before 616, one *annona* of five nomismata instead of four *an-*

nonae totaling twenty nomismata. This much the state could at last afford.

The army could hardly have survived on this less than subsistence wage had the soldiers not received land grants in the themes, probably between 659 and 662. Most of the land needed for the grants seems to have come either from the imperial estates, which henceforth almost disappeared, or perhaps from landholders who were compensated with imperial estates elsewhere so as to disperse the soldiers more evenly over the empire. Since later evidence shows that the military lands were well distributed, and large enough to provide an adequate income, the government appears to have planned for the themes with care.

Apparently given only modest plots, the infantry had to live as farmers, raising enough to support and equip themselves. They served mostly in their own regions except on short campaigns abroad, when they received additional pay. But the cavalry were more prosperous, with estates valued at a minimum of four pounds of gold, or 288 nomismata. This sum would have bought about 144 acres of plowland, enough to support at least a half-dozen families of relatives, hired hands, tenants, slaves, or others with an obligation to provide the cavalryman's food, arms, uniform, horse, and fodder. Though most of the cavalry surely did some farm work in peacetime, in principle they were always ready for service.

The thematic troops, a mixture of cavalry and infantry, belonged not only to specific themes, but to specific regions of those themes with their own troops. The larger themes had subdivisions called turmae, which were named for the city or region in which their troops were based, or for the army division from which they had been formed. For example, the senior turma of the Anatolic Theme was called the Federates, since its men were descended from the Federates recruited by Tiberius II for the Army of the East and later settled around the Anatolics' headquarters at Amorium. The other divisions of the Anatolics were the turmae of Sozopolis, Lycaonia, Seleucia, and Cappadocia. Small themes like Hellas and the Cibyrrhaeots had only one turma. Each turma was commanded by a turmarch subject to the authority of the theme's strategus.

Then every theme and turma had at least two drungi under drungaries, each commanding a thousand men in a smaller part of the theme. For instance, the Cibyrrhaeot Theme had one drungus on the southern coast of Anatolia and another in the Aegean islands, and the Theme of Hellas had one drungus based at Corinth and another at Athens. More junior officers served under the drungaries and commanded smaller groups of troops, but in this period the drungaries were the most junior officers with responsibility for definite territories. Thus each theme and each of its turmae and drungi had a commander and soldiers responsible for defending it. The archontates too had small garrisons, apparently of a hundred soldiers apiece, commanded by their archons.

Each theme's strategus had the duty of assembling his scattered troops when his theme was either attacked by the enemy or summoned for a campaign by the emperor. Strategi also received their themes' payrolls from the capital and distributed them to their men. But since the men no longer depended much on their pay, strategi could do without the payrolls and rebel rather easily. Two strategi did so as early as 668, when the themes were just a few years old. Apart from many failed revolts, themes were behind the successful revolutions of 695, 698, 713, 715, and 718, as well as Artavasdus's almost successful rebellion of 741. The Opsician Theme alone fomented four of these eight rebellions, before Constantine V prudently split it up.

Despite their tendency to revolt, the themes defended the empire well. From the time of their creation around 660, they greatly slowed and in the end stopped the catastrophic losses of land and men of the previous half-century. Except for the exarchates of Africa and Italy, where thematic organization may not have been put into full effect, the themes suffered scarcely any losses of manpower or territory. The troops defended their land with much persistence, if little heroism. Although soldiers died, the land remained, to be inherited by others along with the military obligations attached to it. Though the themes won few battles, their main accomplishment was to survive raids rather than to prevent them.

For the offensive operations that the themes performed poorly, Constantine V created the tagmata. Generally smaller than the themes and in closer contact with the emperor, the tagmata also proved to be more loyal. The main tagmatic commanders, the domestics of the Scholae and Excubitors and the drungary of the Watch, were more like lieutenants of the emperor than independent generals. Only the emperor commanded all eighteen thousand men of the six tagmata, who were normally too widely dispersed to engage in any plot against him. Since the tagmata were almost certainly derived from the Opsician Theme and were paid together with the themes, their soldiers seem to have possessed military lands, just as thematic soldiers did.[5]

In the Carabisian Theme Constans II appears to have created a permanently organized fleet, which the empire had lacked since its earlier fleets had become part-time forces along with the frontier troops. The Carabisian Fleet served Constans rather well on his western expedition, but was no match for the much larger Arab fleet created by Muʿāwiyah. Between 686 and 689 Justinian II improved the fleet by dividing it into the Cibyrrhaeot Theme in the east and the Theme of Hellas in the west, and especially by providing it with professional oarsmen, the Mardaïtes. Yet these two thematic fleets were small and remote from the capital, which continued to be defended only by a makeshift fleet of the old sort. Like other themes, the naval themes were liable to rebel, as the Carabisians did in 698.

Military necessity, and the need to keep the loyalty of the army, induced the emperors of the seventh and eighth centuries to command troops in person. Heraclius firmly broke with the custom, prevailing since the fourth century, that even emperors who had been generals before their accession stayed away from the field of battle. Until 695 the Heraclian dynasty seemed to have the army under control, and the usurpation of Phocas seemed to be an isolated exception to the series of legal successions going back to Constantine I. The subsequent seven revolutions, most of them perpetrated by the themes, shattered that tradition forever. Though Leo III founded a dynasty, he was himself a rebel, and both his son and his grandson faced serious revolts within a year of their accessions. Henceforth emperors had to take care if they were to remain emperors.

In the middle years of the seventh century, when the army was reorganized into themes, the civil administration was reorganized into more numerous and less powerful ministries.[6] The formerly preeminent office of praetorian prefect of the East was simply abolished; the other prefectures had lapsed with the loss of most of Illyricum and the organization of Italy and Africa as exarchates. The once mighty position of master of offices became the honorific rank of magister. The count of the private estate disappeared along with the great imperial estates, while the count of the sacred largesses was replaced by the sacellarius, a mere supervisor of the officials who actually ran the administration.

The chief of those officials were three ministers called logothetes. The postal logothete (*logothetēs tou dromou*), who somewhat resembled the old master of offices, took charge of communications, embassies, and internal security. He was usually the empire's most important civil official. The general logothete (*logothetēs tou genikou*) was responsible for taxation; and the military logothete (*logothetēs tou stratiōtikou*), for paying the army. The protoasecretis kept government records. The great curator and two treasurers cared for whatever state properties remained, most of them palaces and factories. Other officials had various minor duties. The quaestor continued to be the principal legal official, and the city prefect still administered Constantinople and judged legal cases there. Some palace officials, most of them eunuchs, remained important because of their daily contact with the emperor.

The senate seldom met and was little more than a collective name for the highest dignitaries, though sometimes it went through the motions of recognizing the emperor's accession or ratifying some act of his. The emperor granted officials and courtiers several titles of rank besides that of magister, including patrician, protospatharius, and spatharius. Most of these titles, which replaced the senatorial ranks of the earlier period, had previously been names of offices or military commissions. They bestowed prestige that might be more important than the powers of an office, but that was highly dependent on the favor of the emperor.

Although the bureaucracy had more high-ranking officials than in the fourth to sixth centuries, as a whole it was considerably smaller. From about twenty-five hundred in the earlier period the central bureaucracy shrank to about six hundred by the eighth century, while the provincial officials, once around fifteen thousand, dwindled to a handful as the strategi and their military subordinates became the real administrators. Probably around the mid-seventh century when the new logothetes appeared, some drastic reduction must have been made in the administration, fitting it to the empire's reduced territory and revenues, and to its increased reliance on military government.

Heraclius's halving of the salaries seems to have continued to apply to the higher ranks, and Constans II's further halving of military pay may well have affected the chief military commanders. Whereas the prefect of Africa had drawn annual pay of one hundred pounds of gold in the mid-sixth century, later even the very highest officers, such as the strategus of the Anatolics, seem to have received only forty pounds of gold a year, though this still came to a princely 2,880 nomismata. On the other hand, at some point the pay of the lower civil officials was apparently more than restored, so that later they received at least 18 nomismata a year, the living wage that many had lacked in the sixth century.[7] This change may also have been made by Constans II, when he reduced military pay but more than compensated the soldiers with military lands. Since the wealthiest Byzantines of the eighth century were far poorer than those of the sixth, even the lowered salaries of senior

89. Seventh-century mosaic of Saint Demetrius between two local officials, from the Church of Saint Demetrius, Thessalonica. (Photo: From F. Uspensky in *Izvestija* 14 [1909])

officials would have been attractive. The bureaucracy thus became smaller and better paid, a combination likely to promote efficiency and discourage corruption.

Yet the bureaucracy had other troubles in the eighth century. Education had unquestionably deteriorated, and the efficiency of the bureaucracy must have declined along with it. The revolutions between 695 and 718 had brought a number of purges, and mutual distrust damaged relations between the iconoclast emperors and their mostly iconophile officials. Though Leo III took at least a partial census in 733, tax records appear to have been badly kept after so much disruption, so that a good deal of what was theoretically due either went uncollected or was embezzled by tax collectors or others. The average tax collected from each subject appears to have dropped considerably since the sixth century, even though depopulation should have left taxpayers with more land, and Leo III had raised the rates by a twelfth in 740.

The many losses of territory and shifts in population during the seventh and eighth centuries inevitably made the population harder to tax. Many taxpayers on the rolls must have become impossible to locate, while the rolls left out many recent immigrants to the empire. The enormous revenues of the imperial estates, most of them conveniently collected in rents from rich tenants, almost entirely disappeared. Although soldiers with military lands had to pay monetary taxes, they were free from the irregular requisitions needed to support the postal service and military campaigns. The state granted tax exemptions for lands devastated by raids, which during this period were frequent in many places.

In early Byzantine times most of the empire's richest men had resided in large cities, particularly Constantinople, within easy reach of the government. Their influence gave them some protection from taxation under weak emperors, but not from the determined exactions of a Diocletian or a Justinian. After the seventh century, most of the empire's largest landholders were to be found on the Anatolian plateau. There a number of them assembled vast estates, probably because they were the only ones with the resources to survive Arab raids and to provide protection to their tenants.[8] Such magnates lived far from the capital, exercised considerable local authority, and were not easy to tax.

With the disappearance of the class of decurions who had supervised taxation in the earlier period, the state came to deal directly with collectors who were in effect tax farmers. They were businessmen and had to be allowed to make a profit, as the decurions had not been supposed to do. The new tax collectors were of two main types: agents (*dioikētai*), who collected the land tax from the empire's many small farms, and commerciarii, who levied trade and market duties on many small business transactions and ran the state warehouses. The tax districts were no longer cities in the old sense, which had included many neighboring villages; now taxes were levied on individual settlements, the great majority of which were villages themselves. Since responsibility for paying a village's taxes now lay with all its villagers rather than with decurions in the nearest town, collecting taxes must have taken more time than before, and corruption and inefficiency were probably common. Government revenue and control would have decreased accordingly.

Under pressure from the long military crisis, the whole administration had been reduced in size and simplified. The change is evident in Leo III's *Ecloga*, which is a much briefer and rougher document than the long and elaborate *Justinian Code*. While the *Ecloga* was much needed and was well suited to its times, that is precisely the point. A smaller government, ruling an empire harried by ceaseless enemy raids and frequent full-scale wars, could hardly keep up the sophisticated administrative apparatus of the sixth century, and wisely gave up the effort to do so. Nevertheless, the eighth-century emperors seem to have neglected their administration more than was necessary or desirable, especially the iconoclasts who found that most of the bureaucracy was iconophile.

THE SHAKEN CHURCH

During the seventh and eighth centuries the emperors clashed repeatedly with the Church. Admittedly, in the very worst crises, when Constantinople itself was under siege in 626 and from 717 to 718, Church and state stood together against the enemy. But at other times when the empire was in danger, the pervasive suspicion that military defeat implied divine displeasure led to religious discord between Church and state and within each of them. The disputes centered on heresies that were not spontaneous growths, like those of the previous period, but were in large part invented by emperors: Monoenergism, Monotheletism, and Iconoclasm.

Of these, Monoenergism and Monotheletism were the less artificial. By promoting them Heraclius tried to compromise with Monophysitism, a heresy that had enjoyed strong support in the East for almost two centuries, during which many attempts to reconcile it with orthodoxy had failed. Monoenergism, despite the new formula it advanced, differed little from the studied ambiguities that had failed already. Monotheletism was something more, a coherent doctrine more or less compatible with the Council of Chalcedon but excluding the sort of clear distinction between Christ's divine and human natures that Monophysites abhorred. The patriarchs Sergius and Pyrrhus and many other churchmen welcomed one or both of the doctrines.

Heraclius's best argument for winning adherents to his theological compromises was that God had given him victory over the Persians. When the Byzantines saw that God had stopped aiding the emperor against the Arabs, many lost faith in his theology. Heraclius and Constans II backed away from Monotheletism because of its unpopularity, but they avoided condemning it, which might have seemed an admission that the empire's defeats were a punishment for heresy. After Byzantine fortunes improved a bit, Constantine IV found it easier to repudiate his great-grandfather's failed experiment. When more misfortunes nonetheless followed, Philippicus managed to bring Montheletism back, only for a moment but with surprisingly little resistance from the demoralized hierarchy.

Although Iconoclasm had few partisans before Leo III adopted it, Leo was surely not the only one at the time who felt that the empire's military reverses and internal strife were punishments from an angry God. Many Byzantines were probably ready to consider the possibility that Iconoclasm might help. After Leo's defeat of the Arab siege of Constantinople his prestige was great. Leo appears to have expected less opposition than his doctrine actually aroused, but in most of the empire the opposition was passive. Only at Leo's death, with the revolt of Artavasdus, did Constantine V learn the full extent of iconophile sentiment in the capital.

Constantine still bided his time for over a decade before declaring the veneration of icons a heresy at the Council of Hieria in 754. Although he presumably intended to intimidate iconophiles, he seems rather to have provoked them. By 765 their activities spurred him to begin a persecution, which led in turn to a broad-based iconophile plot the next year. At this the emperor sharpened his persecution and extended it to monks in general, until the religious controversy with the least theological substance had paradoxically become the bitterest and bloodiest. Leo IV sensibly tried to reduce tensions after Constantine's death.

Although each party doubtless believed that God was on its side, the dispute developed more and more into a struggle over how much control emperors should have over the Church in particular and society in general. The reason was not simply that the emperors had imposed Iconoclasm on a mostly unwilling church and society. By denying pictorial representations of Christ and his saints a place in Christian worship, iconoclast doctrine tended to assign God and the saints a restricted role in the world. Moreover, especially because the iconoclast emperors made conspicuous use of portraits of themselves, Iconoclasm gave emperors wider authority than bishops, who represented Christ, or monks, who imitated Christ and aspired to be saints.[9]

These natural if not quite inevitable implications of iconoclast theology, at first imperfectly grasped by each side, became evident in the reign of Constantine V. Under him opposition to Iconoclasm increasingly became opposition to Constantine, and loyalty to him came to require Iconoclasm. Constantine was also able to turn his persecution of iconophiles to political and economic advantage, using it to bend the episcopate and bureaucracy to his will and to confiscate large amounts of ecclesiastical and, particularly, monastic property. For the time being he did cow his enemies, since he faced no more conspiracies after his harshest persecutions began in 766.

Yet in the somewhat longer run the emperors could hardly continue persecuting so many of their subjects, including most of the traditional leadership of Church and state. The events that preceded Leo IV's death in 780 showed that even many of the officials closest to the emperor remained iconophiles at heart. The Syrian dynasty had to struggle to

90. An iconoclast whitewashing an icon of Christ compared with the centurion who pierced Christ's side. Ninth-century miniature from the Chludov Psalter (State Historical Museum, Moscow, add. 129). (Photo: Weitzmann Archive, Dumbarton Oaks, Washington, D.C., copyright 1996)

maintain Iconoclasm, which conflicted with most of Byzantine theological, ecclesiastical, and political tradition. Indeed, Leo III and Constantine V appear to have favored Iconoclasm partly because up to the early eighth century the Church had been gaining power at the emperors' expense.

While the emperors lost battles and land to foreign enemies, and then repeatedly lost their thrones, the Byzantine church produced some leaders of greater stature than had been seen since the early fifth century. The patriarch of Constantinople Sergius I was Heraclius's adviser, ally, banker, and virtual regent during the siege of Constantinople of 626. Sergius's successor Pyrrhus was also an influential figure before his opponents brought him down in 641, though his memory, like Sergius's, suffered from his connection with Monotheletism. Among patriarchs of Alexandria, John the Almsgiver won general admiration and Cyrus of Phasis widespread hatred, but both were powerful men. Patriarch Sophronius of Jerusalem was also a force in both theology and politics. Later the patriarch of Constantinople Germanus I won credit for resisting Leo III's Iconoclasm for several years. Germanus, Sophronius, and John the Almsgiver all came to be venerated as saints.

At the same time, certain monks gained more authority as leaders of opposition to emperors. During the seventh century the outstanding example was Maximus Confessor, who infuriated Constans II by his stout resistance to toleration of Monotheletism. Maximus was the man most responsible for discrediting that heresy, which was condemned soon after his death. In the eighth century, the most effective opponents of Iconoclasm were two monks: outside the empire John of Damascus perfected the iconophiles' theological argument, while within the empire Constantine V reportedly considered Stephen the Younger a mortal threat not just to Iconoclasm but to the emperor's own rule. Maximus, John of Damascus, and Stephen also gained recognition as saints.

In the seventh century the growing prestige of monks brought an abundance of biographies of contemporary saints. After a century and a half when long-dead martyrs had been hagiographers' favorite subjects, in the early seventh century John Moschus wrote his *Spiritual Meadow*, a collection of anecdotes about contemporary monks that became a devotional classic. Maurice's patriarch John IV the Faster also found his hagiographer at this time. In the middle of the seventh century the Alexandrian patriarch John the Almsgiver became the subject of a charming life by one of the most popular Byzantine hagiographers, Leontius of Neapolis on Cyprus. Authors also continued to recount the exploits of earlier saints, notably in the *Miracles of Saint Demetrius*, which describes how faith in that early Christian martyr rescued Thessalonica from its seventh-century perils.

Appropriately enough, the thriving hagiography of the seventh century was accompanied by an increased use of icons of saints.[10] Both hagiography and icons were symptoms of the growing popularity of monks and clerics, which seems to have helped provoke the eighth-century emperors' Iconoclasm. Under Iconoclasm hagiography withered, since most potential hagiographers and potential subjects of hagiography were iconophiles and monks, whom the iconoclast emperors hindered from circulating iconophile literature of any sort.

Yet Leo III was by no means irreligious, and not even Constantine V wanted to be thought so. Most of the original inspiration for Iconoclasm was biblical, a continuation of the efforts of earlier emperors to Christianize society. After outright paganism had disappeared from Byzantine territory and the empire's chief enemies became Zoroastrian Persians, Muslim Arabs, and pagan Avars, Bulgars, and Slavs, Christianity became a distinguishing feature of the Byzantines. Heraclius made much of liberating the True Cross from the Persians, and the Virgin was supposed to have helped Leo III raise the siege of Constantinople.

91. Seventh- or eighth-century encaustic icon of Saints Paul, Peter, Nicholas, and John Chrysostom, from the Monastery of Saint Catherine, Mount Sinai. (Photo: Courtesy of Michigan-Princeton-Alexandria Expedition to Mount Sinai)

As Byzantium became more Christian during the seventh and eighth centuries, the Byzantine church developed its first formal code of canon law. By the early seventh century the Church had already made collections of conciliar canons and imperial laws affecting religion. Under Heraclius an anonymous editor organized these into a comprehensive though still unofficial compilation, the *Nomocanon*. To this work Justinian II's Quinisext Council added its own disciplinary canons. The part of Leo III's *Ecloga* that deals with Christian morals is scarcely distinguishable from canon law. Church influence is discernible in the *Ecloga*'s replacing the death penalty with mutilation, which gave offenders more time to repent before they died. Feeling against execution was so strong that emperors punished even most of their political opponents only by mutilating them, though mutilated plotters could obviously remain dangerous.

The Quinisext Council and the *Ecloga* were attempts to make prevailing moral legislation more stringent. The Quinisext raised standards for the behavior of the clergy, by forbidding them to remarry, lend at interest, or wear secular garb. It also put new restrictions on the laity, prohibiting various kinds of superstition or license such as fortune-telling, lighting bonfires at the time of the new moon, or painting pornographic pictures. Despite the council's condemnations, prostitution, gambling, and the theater remained legal. But the *Ecloga* did outlaw seduction, abortion, and sodomy. It also endorsed ecclesiastical views by restricting the grounds for divorce and requiring the bride's consent to marriage as well as the groom's. Leo III considered his iconoclast edict a measure against superstition, and it received church sanction under Constantine V in his supposedly ecumenical Council of Hieria.

The continuing vigor of the Byzantine church is apparent from its lingering influence in the lost provinces of Armenia, Syria, and Egypt. Although many Syrians and most Egyptians and Armenians belonged to schismatic churches with Monophysite sympathies, Chalcedonian orthodoxy kept footholds throughout the East. By the reign of Leo III, the caliphs again permitted the appointment of orthodox patriarchs of Antioch, Jerusalem, and Alexandria; they and their clergy were styled Melchite, after the Arabic word for "emperor," because they belonged to the emperor's church. Alexandria kept a separate Coptic patriarch and Antioch a Jacobite one; only the orthodox patriarch of Jerusalem presided over a see that was mostly orthodox. Near Jerusalem the Monastery of Saint Sabas, where John of Damascus retired and wrote in Greek against Iconoclasm, attracted monks from the whole orthodox world.

Nor was the Byzantine church totally estranged from the schismatic

Coptic, Armenian, and Jacobite churches. In the mid-seventh century an anonymous Mesopotamian Jacobite wrote a Syriac apocalypse, ascribed to the fourth-century bishop Methodius of Olympus, predicting that the emperor would soon reconquer his lost lands with God's help. Translated into Greek, this Pseudo-Methodius influenced a long line of later Byzantine prophecies.[11] Most Armenians looked to the nearby Byzantines as possible protectors. In the later eighth century the Jacobite and Coptic churches, separated from the Byzantines by language, geography, and theology, became less familiar with Byzantium, but still not unsympathetic to it. Some even convinced themselves that Constantine V agreed with them, though he was no Monophysite and they were no iconoclasts.

That Iconoclasm lacked known adherents among Christians anywhere outside the empire is another sign that it was more an imperial ploy than an outgrowth of any church tradition. It made an especially bad impression on the popes, who had usually been allies of the emperors. Pope Vitalian had welcomed Constans II to Rome despite their disagreement over the *Type*, and Justinian II had welcomed Pope Constantine to Constantinople despite their clash over the Quinisext Council. Leo III broke this alliance with his iconoclast edict and subsequent removal of Sicily, Calabria, and Greece from papal jurisdiction. The schism that resulted, along with the empire's definitive loss of central Italy, was ominous for the future, but neither side wanted it to be permanent.

Only the minority of Christians who converted to Islam in Syria and Egypt seem to have concluded from the Muslim conquests that Christianity was wrong, or even in need of fundamental changes. Before Iconoclasm, the usual explanation for Muslim success had been the Christians' sins, a deduction that led to an even more rigorous and devout Christianity. Iconoclasm was partly a reaction to intensified religious feeling and practice, insofar as these had increased the power of the Church; yet the iconoclast emperors tried not so much to reduce religiosity as to subject it to their authority. Even in this they gained no more than the partial and superficial acquiescence of most of their subjects.

CULTURAL DISRUPTION

The invasions of the seventh and eighth centuries naturally had social consequences. An eastern Roman society that had long remained fairly stable, subject only to gradual change, suffered disturbances unparalleled since the coming of Roman rule. Most of the natives of Italy, Africa,

Egypt, Syria, and the Balkans eventually found themselves outside the empire altogether. Even within the empire many people of all classes became refugees, losing the bulk of their property and their places in society, while dispossessed refugees from lost territories came to join them. Raids, invasions, plagues, and other disasters destroyed old fortunes and made a few new ones. Several times the emperors purged the Church and the bureaucracy. Records of every sort came to be kept less well, and traditions of many sorts broke down.

Although Greeks had always attached less importance to family tradition than Romans had, in the early Byzantine period Latin-speaking Byzantines of senatorial rank had used family names and kept track of their genealogies. During the seventh century, when legal privileges ceased to be hereditary, senatorial rank lost whatever remained of its old meaning, as lesser ranks like that of decurion had already done. Although being the son of an official with a title was still useful for obtaining one's own office and rank, the process was no longer virtually automatic. By the late eighth century no family names of the Roman type seem to have remained in use, and no authentic connections back to the old nobility appear to have been traceable.

Unlike the bureaucracy of the capital, the decurions disappeared as a class. A provincial aristocracy still existed, but it no longer manned city councils or discharged administrative functions. As the towns became smaller and the countryside less secure, some aristocrats seem to have moved to fortified houses in the country to look after the estates that had always been the foundations of their wealth. But the invasions probably ruined many landholders, turning them into much more modest farmers. Most of the leading citizens who remained in Thessalonica, Ephesus, or Cherson appear to have been merchants of modest means.

From the seventh century onward, many provincial magnates were from families that had relocated from lost territory and were often Armenian. They seem to have merged with whatever remained of the older provincial aristocracy. Many of the provincial notables of the time served as officers of the themes, either because their wealth helped them acquire commissions or because their commissions helped them acquire wealth. Yet as the interests of the leading provincials shifted from city to country and from the administration to the army, their ideal became military distinction rather than civic prominence, and they ceased to need more than an elementary education.

This provincial aristocracy had its own family loyalties, and toward the end of the eighth century it occasionally developed its own family names, such as Podopagurus and Lachanodracon. These families also seem to have had more children than the old urban aristocracy had had, and not only because the plague affected the countryside less than the cities. In pursuing military careers and managing dispersed estates large families were an advantage, and size could add to a family's power and wealth rather than dilute and divide them. A large family from the provinces could continue to be prolific when it settled in Constantinople or reached the imperial throne. Maurice, Heraclius, and Constantine V each had more children than any earlier emperor since Constantine I.

While the civil service kept some of its traditions, it lost power when Heraclius cut its pay in half, and its numbers declined during the seventh century. Since the most important bureaucrats lived in Constantinople, their families would have suffered greatly from the outbreaks of plague that wracked the city. They had to live through frequent changes of emperor and theology, and each revolution ruined some of the less adept or more principled. The patriarch Germanus, the son of a high official, continued his career through the seven revolutions between 695 and 717, even accepting Philippicus's Monotheletism, only to abdicate in 730 when he decided that Leo III's Iconoclasm was too much for him. By the end of Constantine V's reign, after the last terrible bout of the plague, Constantinople seems to have had few citizens of wealth and influence left, certainly far fewer than the rich and powerful senators under Justinian I.

The small and largely pagan class of professors, in severe decline after Justinian's measures against paganism, probably survived no later than the fall of Alexandria to the Arabs in 642. During Heraclius's reign higher education was still available at Constantinople, where Stephen of Alexandria, some of whose works survive, taught philosophy and possibly medicine, perhaps as the occupant of a public professorial chair. Stephen, however, seems to have been an isolated figure in his own time and to have left no proper successor. The literary community at Constantinople had declined by Heraclius's reign, and was to decline further after him. In the provinces there came to be no reading public worthy of the name.

Private primary and secondary schools still existed, and individual scholars with more advanced knowledge remained, holding civil or ecclesiastical office or eking out a living as private schoolteachers. But now only by going to considerable trouble could one obtain even a basic higher education, whether it was the legal training that had been the traditional preparation for a career in government or the literary and philosophical study that had been the mark of a truly learned man. The

92. Eighth-century solar table from the Vatican Ptolemy (Vaticanus graecus 1291), showing Apollo in his chariot, the months, and the signs of the zodiac. (Photo: Biblioteca Apostolica Vaticana)

number and quality of primary and secondary schools must also have declined. The consequences were surely declines in the number of Byzantines at every level of education above illiteracy. Fewer men became even minimally literate; fewer learned correct literary Greek and practical mathematics; and even fewer gained as much as a smattering of the classical Attic language. The potential readership for all kinds of literature accordingly shrank. The writers who could compose middlebrow works became fewer, and those who could write correctly in the Attic dialect dwindled to a handful.

Besides a lack of attested professors, evidence of deteriorating education includes a near cessation of copying manuscripts and of writing classical Greek during the seventh and eighth centuries.[12] From the early seventh century, Justinian's *Code* was generally used not in the original Latin but in one of its Greek translations. After a few expert officials had with difficulty distilled some of it into the *Ecloga* of 726, the full *Code* was seldom used even in Greek. Knowledge of Latin in the bureaucracy became limited to the few scribes and interpreters needed to conduct diplomatic relations with the pope and the Lombards and Franks.

A reduced need for educated men cannot have been the only reason for this decline in education. Although the state needed fewer officials than before, it still needed enough of them to support good secondary schools and a regular public law school. Yet at least the law school failed to survive, so that officials became less able to perform such obviously practical functions as keeping track of tax receipts. The Church still needed clergy for its congregations all over the empire, and it continued to value informed theological treatises, edifying hagiography, and beautiful hymns. But after the early seventh century few clergymen were capable of writing such works.

Strictly speaking—and many Byzantines did speak strictly—neither the state, the Church, nor the aristocracy had ever needed any professors of literature and philosophy. Formerly the state and the aristocracy had supported them nonetheless, regarding higher learning as a matter of prestige. Heraclius, who continued to think this way, sponsored philosophical study and still had his panegyrists, but his successors paid less attention to such things. Lack of money cannot have had much to do with the lapse of higher education, since Heraclius was as financially embarrassed as his successors were. Professorial salaries were in any case tiny in comparison with other public expenses. Apart from the state, even the reduced aristocracy could easily have paid several more years of tuition for its sons than it did.

Yet the decline of education acquired its own momentum, diminishing with each generation the number of those who could appreciate the effects of more schooling on a man's writing, speeches, or performance in office. The decline steepened when Leo III alienated and Constantine V persecuted iconophile monks and civil servants, thus marginalizing most of what remained of the empire's educated class. Already in 692 the Quinisext Council had to condemn people who cut up, threw away, or boiled down into perfume biblical and patristic manuscripts, saying nothing of secular ones.[13] By 726 Leo III lamented in his *Ecloga* that many officials were unable to understand the existing law books.[14] But neither the Church nor the state seems quite to have grasped the causal connection between apparently useless education on the one hand and useful and meritorious knowledge on the other.

For some years early in the seventh century, a few men educated during the earlier period continued to write literature in the high Attic style. Under Heraclius, Theophylact Simocatta, a civil official with a proper legal education, wrote the last of a series of classicizing Greek histories that stretched back to the third century. His elaborate but graceless work stops with the accession of Phocas, though it includes a preface in praise of Heraclius as a patron of scholarship. No similar history continued Theophylact's during the rest of the period up to 780.

George of Pisidia, a deacon on the staff of Saint Sophia, wrote poems of some length and distinction in the classical manner, both on Heraclius's victories and on religious subjects such as the creation of the world. George's numerous works survived and earned much praise. But they were not imitated, apparently because his younger contemporaries lacked the learning to do so. The so-called *Acathist Hymn* in honor of the Virgin, perhaps completed by the patriarch Sergius to celebrate the failure of the Persian siege of 626, was much loved and admired, and has been sung in churches ever since. But its genre, the *kontakion* in the style of Romanus the Melode, became rare after the mid-seventh century, apparently because it was too difficult for later hymnographers to master. A somewhat less intricate sort of hymn, the *kanōn*, became current toward the end of the seventh century. Its leading composers were Andrew of Crete, who may have invented it, and John of Damascus.

Theology too declined during this period. Even Maximus Confessor, who served Heraclius as an imperial secretary before he became a monk, was no stylist, though he wrote voluminously and showed some originality in developing the case against Monotheletism. After him the patriarch Germanus, who was the son of an official and had been educated in the mid-seventh century, became a theologian of only middling profundity, best known for his sermons. Germanus, Stephen the Younger, and other opponents of Iconoclasm were remembered for the clarity rather than the subtlety of their arguments.

One sign of the empire's cultural decline was that the main religious writers in Greek were increasingly to be found in the caliphate. The theologian Anastasius of Sinai, a combatant of every heresy from Monophysitism to Nestorianism, spent most of his life in Arab-held Egypt and Syria. The hymnographer and homilist Andrew of Crete was born and became a monk in Arab-held Syria before migrating to the empire in the late seventh century. The most important theologian of the period, John of Damascus, never set foot on Byzantine-ruled territory. In his time his Palestinian Monastery of Saint Sabas was a more important center of religious learning than any remaining in the empire. No major iconoclast theologian emerged anywhere—except for Constantine V, who found a hearing for reasons extraneous to his theological skills.

Even in the eighth century, however, literature never lapsed altogether. A few chroniclers, whose work survives only in later compositions that made use of it, preserved the historical record, with little detail but without a gap. Theirs must be among a number of contemporary works that are lost today, especially because iconoclasts and iconophiles assiduously destroyed each other's writings. One anonymous composition, the *Brief Historical Notes* on the monuments of Constantinople, does appear to survive from the later eighth century. A middlebrow work of fabricated scholarship bordering on idiocy, it at least shows that some audience for new writing remained in the capital.[15]

The proof of cultural decline was not that some writing of this time showed ignorance—ignorant and lazy authors are always with us—but that so little showed erudition. More than half a millennium after the Second Sophistic had revived Greek literature, the regular system of higher education had vanished from the Greek world, seemingly taking along with it philosophy and science, formal history and oratory, and secular poetry and epistolography. Yet all of these had been thriving under Justinian I, just two centuries before. Even if the change primarily affected the small fraction of the population who were literate, they dominated the government and ecclesiastical hierarchy, and determined the future historical record.

Art and architecture followed a pattern similar to that of literature. After definitely falling off in the later sixth century, Byzantine luxury building almost entirely ceased during the empire's seventh-century crisis. So definitive was the cessation of building in the empire that the main Byzantine quarries were abandoned. Strangely, however, a number of fine churches continued to be built for some years in occasionally Byzantine Armenia. While the emperors husbanded their resources for defense, perhaps the weaker Armenians, despairing of defending themselves, spent their money on efforts to placate God.

In the mid-seventh century the Byzantines had to build many new fortifications, but most of these were hasty constructions of mortar and rubble, lacking the architectural pretensions of earlier fortresses faced with brick or stone. The stone needed for the strongest city walls was scavenged from earlier buildings and even from statues.[16] After the Avars cut the Aqueduct of Valens in 626, it remained out of service for over a century, though it had been Constantinople's main source of fresh water. The first large-scale construction recorded in the capital after the seventh-century hiatus is Anastasius II's strengthening of the land and sea walls in preparation for the Arab siege that came in 717. Most of the workers on such fortifications were probably soldiers rather than artisans.

Paintings and mosaics were much cheaper than buildings, and the

93. The Church of Saint Irene, Constantinople, showing a mosaic of the Cross added by Constantine V to the apse. (Photo: Dumbarton Oaks, Washington, D.C., copyright 1996)

cheapness of small wooden icons of saints may have made these especially popular before Iconoclasm. The iconoclasts destroyed many of them, but the few that remain reveal at most a slight deterioration of technique between the sixth and seventh centuries (Fig. 91). The accomplished seventh-century mosaics that happen to survive in the Church of Saint Demetrius at Thessalonica show what an isolated and embattled town could still do at the time to honor its patron saint in his principal church (Fig. 89). Some excellent silver work survives from the reign of Heraclius (Fig. 66), and the coins of Justinian II and the usurpers who followed him are as elegant as any Byzantine emperors ever struck (Figs. 77, 78, 79, 81).

   Iconoclasm was of course bad for figural religious art, but apart from that Constantine V was something of a patron of the arts and architecture. After the earthquake of 740 he not only restored the walls of Constantinople but rebuilt much of the Church of Saint Irene, serviceably if not gracefully (Fig. 93). He also went to great pains to restore the derelict Aqueduct of Valens in 767, importing workmen from all over

94. Eighth-century Byzantine mosaic of an imaginary landscape from the Umayyad mosque, Damascus. (Photo: Dumbarton Oaks, Washington, D.C., copyright 1996)

the empire. That he could not find skilled labor closer to hand showed how little building had been going on before him.

While destroying religious images, Constantine patronized symbolic or secular art. Rather than leave damaged or empty the places where icons had been in churches and monuments, he decorated them with crosses, which Iconoclasm permitted, or with flowers, birds, animals, or landscapes. When Constantine had scenes of the six ecumenical councils removed from the Milium (the milestone in Constantinople from which road distances were measured), he replaced them with scenes of the Hippodrome. The mosaic cross that he put in the apse of his restored Saint Irene is still there. His mosaic landscapes were probably much like the rather abstract ones still to be seen in the Umayyad mosque at Damascus, which had been executed by Byzantine mosaicists at a somewhat earlier date (Fig. 94). One illuminated manuscript of some beauty even survives from the late eighth century, containing some brief astronomical tables taken from Claudius Ptolemy (Fig. 92).

Despite a clear regression in education, literary creativity, and literary and technical skill, Byzantium's dark age was much less dark than that of the contemporary West. Although because of shrinking readership few new manuscripts needed to be copied, most old manuscripts were preserved in the libraries of Constantinople until the following period. The Byzantines continued to possess almost every literary work that they had known in the sixth century, the loss of Alexandria and its great library notwithstanding. Secular officials and clergymen still received at least a mediocre education, which was enough to allow them to perform their duties. A select few even became well educated, as the subsequent period was to show. Competent mosaicists and painters continued to produce artworks, though fewer and cheaper ones than before. The branches of literature and art that suffered most were historiography and architecture, which between them have given some modern historians and archeologists an exaggerated impression of cultural disruption in this period.

ECONOMIC CONTRACTION

The disasters of the seventh and eighth centuries inevitably battered the empire's already declining economy. The plague recurred until its last recorded appearance in 767, in southern Italy. Yet well before that date the disease seems to have become less virulent than it had been in the sixth century, as the population built up immunity to it and became less urbanized. The severe epidemic at Constantinople under Constantine V seems to have been exceptional. At the same time, lighter taxation and an abundance of land would have encouraged rural families to have more children. By the seventh century the death toll of most of the bouts of plague was probably no greater than the population growth since the previous outbreak.

The main reason for Byzantium's decreasing wealth and population was of course conquest by the empire's enemies. The lost lands of Italy, the Balkans, and Armenia were of no great economic value and may well have cost more to defend than they produced in revenue. But Syria, with its trading cities and exports of olive oil and wine, must easily have paid for its own defense, which had shielded the whole eastern part of the empire; Syria became the heartland of the caliphate under the Umayyads. Egypt and Africa, neither of which had been costly to defend before the Arabs came and both of which had exported large amounts of grain, were even greater losses than Syria.

All told, the empire's territory in 780 was smaller than it had been in

610 by about two-thirds. Its losses in population and productive capacity should have been significantly less than that, because the Anatolian and coastal lands that remained were richer than those lost in Armenia, Italy, and the Balkans, roughly comparable to those of Syria and Africa, and not vastly poorer than those of Egypt. Nonetheless, the empire must have lost more than half its population and a similar proportion of its production. If it had about 17 million people under Phocas, it probably had some 7 million under Leo IV, with almost the entire decrease attributable to conquest by the enemy.[17]

Enemy conquests alone, however, would not have decreased the proportion of the empire's subjects who lived in cities. By the end of the sixth century Anatolia and southeastern Thrace had been nearly as well urbanized as Syria, and more urbanized than any other part of the empire. At the beginning of the seventh century, almost half the empire's real cities, those with at least ten thousand people, had lain in regions that would still be part of the empire at the end of the eighth century. A fairly complete list of the empire's bishoprics in 787 shows that very few cities in this area had ceased to exist since the early Byzantine period.

Nevertheless, on average the cities that remained to the empire in the late eighth century were certainly much smaller than before the plague first arrived, and probably a good deal smaller than before the Persian and Avar invasions, when they had already been shrinking. Various invaders and raiders, chiefly Persians and Arabs, sacked most of the empire's cities at one time or another, sometimes more than once. These depredations, and several earthquakes, caused damage that because of the prevailing emergency the Byzantines never managed to repair. The Byzantines' main concern was naturally to fortify their settlements as quickly as possible, walling in the smallest area that could protect the population from raiders and linking the walls to a citadel that could withstand a determined attack. The authorities moved some cities to more defensible sites, and contracted the majority of others to their most defensible portions. Most of this work of fortification seems to date from the reign of Constans II, as part of the process of settling the themes on military lands.

Some formerly important cities dwindled to towns of a few thousand people, huddled beneath a citadel in a small walled area that excluded the ruins of their former civil monuments. Such towns had a bishop and a few merchants among their inhabitants, and still served as centers for defense and some tax collection; but they had much less need than before of goods from their surrounding countryside. Such was the fate of

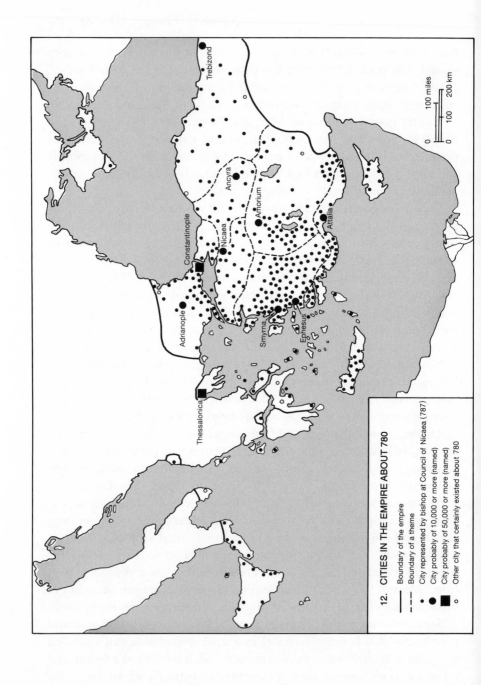

12. CITIES IN THE EMPIRE ABOUT 780

—— Boundary of the empire
- - - Boundary of a theme
● City represented by bishop at Council of Nicaea (787)
● City probably of 10,000 or more (named)
■ City probably of 50,000 or more (named)
○ Other city that certainly existed about 780

Trebizond
Ancyra
Amorium
Attalia
Constantinople
Nicaea
Adrianople
Smyrna
Ephesus
Thessalonica

0   100 miles
0 100 200 km

Athens and Corinth, which the Slavic invasions of the sixth century had already diminished and the Slavic migrations of the seventh century left as isolated outposts. The impoverished little Theme of Hellas could no longer support any true cities, even at the theme's headquarters at Corinth.

Several of the main Anatolian cities suffered similar contraction, often after Arab raids had devastated them. Pergamum never really recovered from being sacked by the Arabs in 716, nor Sardis from its sacking both then and by the Persians in 616. After the earthquake of 740 wrecked Nicomedia, it remained mostly in ruins. Aphrodisias declined drastically in the mid-seventh century, destroyed either by an earthquake or by the Arabs. Except for Nicomedia, whose functions as a port and market had been assumed by Constantinople, all these places had been inland market towns, dependent on overland trade that had evidently contracted.

On the other hand, a few cities appear to have grown a little. Slightly later evidence indicates that Amorium in the Anatolic Theme had about thirty thousand people and Adrianople in the Theme of Thrace about twenty thousand.[18] Neither place had been a particularly large city before the seventh century, when Amorium had been sacked by the Arabs and Adrianople was probably lost to the Slavs. Yet after Constantine V repopulated Thrace Adrianople soon became its chief stronghold. Amorium, headquarters of the empire's biggest theme after the Opsician was divided, counted as the greatest city of Asia Minor. Attalia, also a middling city in ancient times, similarly came to be a sizable fortified port as the headquarters of the naval Theme of the Cibyrrhaeots. Such military centers would both have protected their populations and given them an economic function in supplying local troops. Yet most major cities neither grew nor utterly shriveled, but retained some of their importance and a bit less than half their original size.

Such was surely the case with Constantinople. Its population may be guessed at around a hundred thousand in 780, though at its nadir in 748, just after the plague ended and before the new settlers arrived, it must have been substantially smaller. That Constantinopolitans needed an aqueduct by 767, but had not needed one since the Avars had cut it in 626, suggests that the city was larger in the late eighth century than in the early seventh. No doubt Constantinople's population was still much smaller than its maximum of about 375,000 before the plague of 542, but that plague would already have reduced it to less than half that figure. Recurrences of the plague and the end of the grain dole in 618 must have caused further reductions. A hundred thousand was nonethe-

less a sufficient population to maintain urban life, and the capital continued to have its Hippodrome, theaters, small baths, and large markets, besides its city prefect and even its senate of sorts. The city remained the
empire's greatest port and political and military hub, still the residence
of the emperor and now the headquarters of the tagmata.

Like Constantinople, Thessalonica fell to no enemy during this period and retained the full circuit of its old walls despite a considerably diminished population. Although the advance of the Slavs isolated Thessalonica from the rest of the empire on land, the city attracted refugees
from the remainder of the Balkans. Its isolation insured its administrative
autonomy as an archontate, and its excellent port on the sea route between the capital and the West continued to be vital for the empire's
trade and naval defenses. Since it seems likely to have remained somewhat larger than Amorium, Thessalonica probably became the empire's
second city after the fall of Alexandria.

Besides Attalia, several old Anatolian ports remained prosperous. Ephesus, which held an important commercial fair on the feast of its patron
Saint John, was probably the largest of these. Though its walled circuit
had contracted to half its size since its devastation by an earthquake
around 614, it still had space for more than twenty thousand people.
While Ephesus was probably the main port of the western Anatolian
plain, which had always been the richest part of the peninsula, the region could nonetheless support another sizable port at Smyrna. Neither
Ephesus nor Smyrna seems to have fallen to invaders. Although the Arabs
did sack Trebizond in 654, its functions as a port for northern Anatolia
and a trading station with the East sufficed to keep it a place of some size.

Alongside Amorium in the Anatolic Theme, a few old market towns
in the interior of Anatolia remained places of some consequence by becoming the headquarters of themes. Nicaea, though damaged by the
earthquake of 740, never fell to the enemy, kept the original circuit of its
walls, and became the capital of the reduced Opsician Theme by 766.
Ancyra, sacked by the Persians in 616 and the Arabs in 654, nonetheless
served as the capital first of the Opsician Theme and then of the new
Bucellarian Theme. The headquarters of the Armeniac and Thracesian
themes, apparently at Euchaïta and Chonae, were considerably smaller
towns, overshadowed as they were by those themes' major ports and en-
trepôts at Trebizond and Ephesus.

Thus within the remaining territory of the empire the number of
cities scarcely decreased at all. The number of cities of ten thousand or

more might have fallen from about fifteen to about ten, and the overall urban population probably dropped to roughly half the previous percentage. Most inland market towns fared rather badly; most ports fared somewhat better; and most military centers fared rather well. Unless raiders practically emptied a region of its Byzantine inhabitants, as occurred near the empire's Thracian and Anatolian frontiers, the fortified settlements could survive even chronic insecurity, as the people used them to take refuge.

With the partial exception of Constantinople, not even the more populous of these places were cities in the old style, administered by city councils, covering large areas, laid out with wide and straight streets, and equipped with civic monuments like hippodromes, theaters, and large public baths. Continuing trends already evident in the later sixth century, eighth-century cities were led by their bishops, covered areas that were reduced to fit defensible walls, and had mostly narrow and crooked streets, with few public buildings aside from churches, most of which were small.

Trade by land had evidently fallen off. Land transport had always been costly, especially for food, which was bulky in relation to its value. Up to the sixth century, large-scale trade in food by land had been necessary, both to feed the large inland cities and to furnish farmers with money to pay their taxes and to buy goods not available in their villages. From the seventh century onward, most cities in the interior shrank, and farmers produced almost all of what they needed for themselves. Since the empire was by no means overpopulated, most families could probably have farms that were ample for their needs. Even for a prosperous smallholder, however, selling his produce for enough cash to pay his taxes could be a serious problem.[19]

The large landholders of the Anatolian plateau must have produced some surplus for sale. But the plateau chiefly produced livestock, which could take itself to market cheaply on the hoof, as fruit and vegetables could not. This difference in the cost of transport may have been the main reason the market towns on the Anatolian plateau fared better than those in the plain. Supplying soldiers with food, horses, and fodder should also have been a significant enterprise on the plateau. Few magnates remained in the valleys, where the profits to be made from agriculture were quite modest.

Since goods could be carried least expensively by ship, trade by sea seems to have declined less than trade by land. Commerce continued

95. The main denominations of coins in the eighth century, all shown actual
size, with obverses on the left and reverses on the right. *Top row*: Gold nomisma,
worth ½72 pound of gold: *obverse*, Constantine V and his son the future Leo IV;
reverse, Constantine's then deceased father Leo III. *Second row*: Gold semissis,
worth ½ nomisma: *obverse*, Artavasdus (r. 741–43); *reverse*, cross. *Third row*:
Gold tremissis, worth ⅓ nomisma: *obverse*, Leo III; *reverse*, Leo's son the future
Constantine V. *Fourth row*: Silver miliaresion, worth ½12 nomisma: *obverse*, the
legend "Constantine [VI] and Irene, Emperors in God"; *reverse*, cross. *Fifth
row*: Copper follis, worth ½24 miliaresion: *obverse*, Leo IV (r. 775–80) and his
son the future Constantine VI; *reverse*, Leo's then deceased grandfather Leo III
and father Constantine V, with the obsolete mark of value **M** (for 40 nummi).
Bottom row: Copper half-follis, identical in type with the follis, except for being half-size and worth half as much, so that the mark of value **M** is meaning-
less. (Photos: Dumbarton Oaks, Washington, D.C., copyright 1996)

with the caliphate, which had money to buy the products of Byzantine artisans, as well as spices from India and silks from China to sell the Byzantines. Constantinople still needed large amounts of food and had citizens rich enough to buy some luxury imports. Business could also be done in the islands and along the coasts, where transport costs could be kept low. Some supplies for the army were also sent by sea.

Yet the total volume of trade must have declined greatly. The decline seems apparent from the substantial decrease in the amount of coin that survives from this period, which must reflect a real decrease in coins in circulation. The decline is less pronounced in the gold and silver coinage, the nomisma and miliaresion, which corresponded to the Arab dinar and dirham and were suitable for foreign trade. These were also the coins in which taxes were collected. But the copper coinage, which was the main medium of everyday exchange, decreased enormously. The copper follis became much rarer, and most of its fractions disappeared.

This decrease in the coinage was probably not so much an effect of the shrinkage of trade as a cause. Since barter is more convenient for wholesale transactions than for retail, a lack of small coins would have rendered trade in inexpensive items more difficult, though shop and tavern keepers probably kept accounts for their customers until they could be paid in goods or gold, and offered or accepted small items as change when neither party had coins. The government, however, minted coins not to oblige petty traders but to serve its own fiscal purposes, primarily the payment of the army. Since Heraclius had cut the army's cash pay by half, and Constans II by half again, the government minted and distributed much less money than before.

Heraclius also seems to have substituted issues of arms and uniforms for the soldiers' lost pay, while Constans substituted military land grants both for the lost pay and for the issues of arms and uniforms. Consequently after Constans the soldiers had to support themselves, and to supply their arms and uniforms, chiefly from the produce of those military lands. The otherwise mysterious state warehouses attested on many lead seals from Constans' reign onward probably sold the troops equipment not only for cash, but also for whatever produce the men had to offer and the warehouses could sell at a profit.

The commerciarii who ran these warehouses are known from their seals to have sold slaves, gold, and silk as well, and probably dealt in all sorts of wares. Since they collected trade duties of a tenth on all imports—reduced from the eighth levied earlier—they doubtless accepted the duty in kind when goods were bartered, then sold what they had collected. As businessmen, the commerciarii should also have been willing to buy goods from ordinary farmers who needed cash to pay their taxes. The warehouses therefore seem to have both accommodated and facilitated barter, serving as clearinghouses for goods that would otherwise have been difficult to buy or sell. Such a natural economy, however, would still have tended to discourage trade by land in agricultural goods, since transporting and storing food is much less convenient than carrying and keeping coins. Besides, the commerciarii, as virtual monopolists in many areas, presumably insisted on profits that were high enough to discourage voluntary trade. While the economy adapted to the new system, many towns and large landholders must have suffered.

Yet the state achieved its purpose, which was to continue supporting a large army despite a much smaller population and tax base. Such a shift from cash payment of the troops to the system of military lands and warehouses, bringing with it a shift to a much less monetarized economy, was the only practical means of defending what was left of the empire. Western feudalism, which entirely substituted grants of land for cash payments, was a more extreme form of the same solution. Byzantium at least managed to maintain some payments to its soldiers, some control over their supplies, and fairly tight control over the highest officers, who were still paid high salaries and were usually shifted from post to post before they became too well entrenched. Although military revolts grew more common and more serious, the state retained most of its authority.

It also avoided bankruptcy under exceptionally adverse circumstances. The territories lost between 610 and 620 must have accounted for over half the empire's total revenue, while more than half the empire's army survived and was desperately needed. Heraclius managed to support it by drastic reductions in state salaries, unprecedented borrowing from the Church, and extraordinary measures such as melting down bronze statues. Then he gained a respite when he recovered Egypt, Syria, and Byzantine Mesopotamia from the Persians. After these fell to the Arabs, the fact that the army was paid at a lower rate than before made weathering the crisis somewhat easier. During all this time at least Africa remained safe and continued to contribute revenue. State finances must nonetheless have been precarious until the system of military lands was introduced around 660.

This transformed the fiscal situation. Neither the seven revolutions between 695 and 717, nor the loss of Africa that accompanied them, nor the determined Arab attacks that culminated in the siege of Constantinople of 717 caused a severe financial crisis, let alone a fiscal collapse. The treasury is reported to have been full in 711, and it was positively bulging between 768 and 775.[20] Although Leo III raised taxes in southern Italy in 733 and throughout the empire after the earthquake of 740, he seems to have taken these measures without any urgent fiscal need. Nothing indicates that the state suffered from financial embarrassment at any time between the reigns of Constans II and Leo IV.

We have seen that in 641 the army probably numbered some 109,000 men, down from 150,000 in 565. This reduced number, paid at half the sixth-century rate, would have had a payroll of about 1.5 million nomismata, down from about 4 million in the later years of Justinian. But Heraclius still had to pay for many costly campaigns, and to supply his men with uniforms and arms, even if at less cost than the inflated arms and uniform allowances of the previous period. His total expenditures might thus have fallen from Justinian's about 8.5 million nomismata to perhaps 3.7 million in 641. Yet even this level of spending could be sustained only with great difficulty. Byzantium had already lost Egypt, whose revenue the Arab conquerors recorded at some 2 million nomismata.[21] The lost lands of the Balkans, Syria, Armenia, and Mesopotamia must have accounted for about as much again. Soon the Arabs threatened Africa as well; if it could pay the Arabs tribute of 330,000 nomismata in 648, its total revenue cannot have been much less than a million, more than a quarter of the empire's remaining income. This sum the empire had to be prepared to do without on short notice.

Any estimates of the empire's cash revenue during the subsequent period will considerably understate the resources of the government, because granting the use of military lands in return for military service amounted to a large payment in kind to the army. Yet rough estimates can illustrate how the government coped with its fiscal crisis and how the amount of money in circulation would have declined. The introduction of the military lands by 662 would have cut military expenditures by more than half, since besides replacing half the men's regular pay the lands covered the uniforms, arms, and remounts previously provided at government expense. The army payroll alone would have dropped to about 700,000 nomismata. Given that the government had somehow kept afloat before 662 and later weathered the loss of the revenues of Africa without further retrenchment, Constans II should have run a fair-sized surplus by the end of his reign. His budget then may be estimated at about 2 million nomismata.

TABLE 10

Estimated State Budgets in the Seventh and Eighth Centuries

Date and budgetary item	Estimate (millions of nomismata)
CA. 641 (Heraclius)	
pay of soldiers (109,000 × 10 nom. × ⅓)[a]	1.453M nom.
uniforms and arms (109,000 × 5 nom.)	0.545
fodder and horses (21,800[b] × 5 nom.)	0.109
campaigns and other military expenses	0.8
pay of bureaucracy	0.5
other nonmilitary expenses	0.3
TOTAL	3.707M nom.
CA. 668 (Constans II)	
pay of soldiers (109,000 × 5 nom. × ⅓)[a]	0.727M nom.
campaigns and other military expenses	0.5
pay of bureaucracy	0.5
other nonmilitary expenses and surplus	0.3
TOTAL	2.027M nom.
CA. 775 (Constantine V)	
pay of bodyguards (400 × 72 nom. × ⅓)[a]	0.038M nom.
pay of soldiers (80,000 × 5 nom. × ⅓)[a]	0.533
pay of oarsmen (18,500 × 5 nom. × ⅗)[a]	0.116
uniforms, arms, and rations (18,400[c] × 10 nom.)	0.184
fodder, horses, and mules (14,400[d] × 5 nom.)	0.072
campaigns and other military expenses	0.2
pay of bureaucracy	0.4
other nonmilitary expenses	0.2
surplus	0.2
TOTAL	1.943M nom.

[a] The fractional multiplier allows for the higher pay of officers.
[b] Assuming that the cavalry were about 20 percent of the total of 109,000.
[c] The number includes 400 bodyguards and 18,000 soldiers of the tagmata.
[d] The number includes 400 bodyguards and 14,000 soldiers of the cavalry tagmata.

Justinian II would have increased expenses by adding his 18,500 Mardaïte oarsmen, apparently paid the same 5 nomismata apiece as soldiers, for a total of a bit less than 100,000 nomismata. By the end of Constantine V's reign, the loss of the African and Italian exarchates would have eliminated their revenues but also the expense of paying their embattled armies. Constantine's military payroll therefore dropped back to some 700,000 nomismata, including the oarsmen and some bodyguards. Because the revenues of Africa must normally have exceeded the costs of defending it, its fall should have reduced the empire's surplus revenue. Yet Constantine ran a sizable surplus, and despite his major losses in the West his revenue still seems to have been near 2 million nomismata, roughly what it had been under Constans (Table 10).[22] Most if not all of Constantine's surplus can be explained by his confiscations from iconophile monasteries and the tax increases enacted by Leo III. This being said, the government was meeting its basic expenses without causing its taxpayers noticeable distress.

Under the circumstances, 2 million nomismata is a very respectable cash revenue for the empire to have collected in the later eighth century. In absolute terms it represented a fairly large amount of money in circulation; in relative terms, it was something like a quarter of the empire's revenue in 565, which had been drawn from almost three times the territory and more than twice the population. Moreover, if the army and bureaucracy had been paid in cash at the sixth-century rates, the budget in the late eighth century would have been not 2 million nomismata but around 4 million. Yet at the later date the army and bureaucracy performed little worse, and put a much lighter burden on both the treasury and the taxpayers.

The consequences were a less monetarized economy with less trade, and a less urbanized and much more militarized society. Although the transformation was not total, it was obvious in the empire's social, economic, political, and cultural life. The army loomed larger, and its leaders took over the government by force not only in 602 but seven times after that, leaving aside some unsuccessful but quite troublesome rebellions, like that of Artavasdus.[23] An important part of the empire's land passed from the state to its soldiers. Thus the government, and Byzantine society at large, devoted a bigger share of its smaller resources to the army, leaving much less for other purposes. The cost in several respects was great, but Byzantium could hardly have survived in any other way.

PART FOUR

The Long Revival

96. David playing the harp, inspired by the personification of Melody while personifications of Echo(?) and the Mount of Bethlehem listen. Tenth-century miniature from the Paris Psalter (Parisinus graecus 139). (Photo: Bibliothèque Nationale, Paris)

CHAPTER THIRTEEN

Internal Reforms, 780–842

In 780 Leo IV's widow Irene and her nine-year-old son Constantine VI seemed unlikely to provide strong leadership. The unpromising precedent was Martina's brief regency for Heraclonas in 641, and like Martina Irene had powerful enemies. Irene was also an iconophile, whereas the army, government, and clergy had been officially iconoclast for fifty years. As a woman, she felt unable to lead the army, which had become the most important part of the state, nor would the army have accepted her if she had tried. The two eldest sons of Constantine V were in their early twenties and prime candidates for the throne; the second of them, Nicephorus, had already conspired against Leo IV. Even if they did not seize power, someone else might try to rule for young Constantine instead of the empress, and in any case she was supposed to step down as soon as her son was ready to rule. Many knowledgeable people must have doubted Irene would last that long.

THE NEW REGIME OF IRENE

Yet Irene, an orphan in her mid-twenties from the shrunken provincial town of Athens, had keen political instincts, a strong will, and some devoted allies in the bureaucracy. The precariousness of her position seems to have given her a sense of urgency. A month and a half after her husband's death, she foiled a plot, led by the postal logothete and the domestic of the Excubitors, to put Constantine V's second son Nicephorus on the throne. The empress exiled the conspirators and had Nicephorus and his four brothers ordained priests to make them ineligible

97. Irene (r. 797–802), with her son Constantine VI (r. 780–97) on the reverse. Gold nomisma, shown twice actual size. (Photo: Dumbarton Oaks, Washington, D.C., copyright 1996)

to rule. She gave the vacated office of postal logothete to a loyal and capable eunuch, Stauracius, and secured her support within the bureaucracy. Without yet trying to abolish Iconoclasm, Irene began to select iconophile bishops, and was soon able to count on the backing of the Church.

In 781 the strategus of Sicily rebelled, and the Arabs attacked Cappadocia. Rather than depend on the generals appointed by her husband, Irene assigned the operations to palace eunuchs whom she knew and trusted. These soon put down the Sicilian revolt and saw to the defense of Cappadocia, though the veteran Thracesian strategus Michael Lachanodracon was the one who actually defeated the Arabs near Caesarea. The next year, the exasperated caliph Mahdī sent his son Hārūn al-Rashīd to invade Anatolia with an army that reached the stupendous total of 95,793 men. To oppose him, Irene seems to have appointed her most trusted eunuch, the postal logothete Stauracius.

After Hārūn had raided almost to Constantinople, Stauracius managed to trap him in the valley of the Sangarius. When Stauracius agreed to negotiate, however, a disloyal Byzantine general betrayed him to the Arabs. Irene accepted a truce that cost her tribute of 160,000 nomismata a year in order to ransom her adviser. At least this humiliating treaty let the empress replace military commanders of dubious loyalty with commanders who proved to be faithful to her.

Irene promptly turned her attention to the Balkans, where she had Stauracius redeem his reputation in 783 by leading an expedition against the Slavs. He marched from Constantinople through Thessalonica to the Peloponnesus, cowing the Slavs and collecting booty and tribute. The next year Irene herself and young Constantine toured Thrace with an army, refounding Thracian Beroea under the name of Irenopolis, and reaching Philippopolis, well west of the old frontier. Without running much risk or quite leading her troops, the empress gained in a year as much Thracian territory as Constantine V had won in his whole reign. The Byzantine campaigning continued in 784.

Irene had an opportunity to move against Iconoclasm that same year, when the patriarch Paul fell ill, and on his deathbed called for an ecumenical council to condemn Iconoclasm. He also proposed, presumably with Irene's approval, that his successor be the protoasecretis Tarasius. After Paul's death, Irene summoned a group of clergy, officials, and others who endorsed the choice of Tarasius. To the dismay of some of them, Tarasius accepted the patriarchate only on condition that an ecumenical council be held. The change from Iconoclasm was a wrenching one for a ruler so new and insecure as Irene to impose, but she proceeded in the attempt with determination.

Before the council, the empress threw off the humiliation of paying tribute to the caliph, and in retaliation the Arabs kept the eastern patriarchs from sending delegates to Constantinople, and resumed raiding from their base at Adata. But in the winter of 786 the Armeniac strategus Nicephorus learned that floods had damaged Adata's walls, and took his chance to destroy the city. In the spring Irene and Constantine accompanied another army to Thrace, where they continued pushing back the Slavs.

Leaving this army to its work, the victorious empress and her son returned to the capital in time to convene their ecumenical council in the Church of the Holy Apostles. By now the army's commanders were loyal to Irene; but many of the troops of the tagmata still honored the memory of the iconoclast Constantine V, under whom they had served for years. A mob of them gathered outside the church when the council had barely begun, and rowdily demanded its immediate end. After gauging her strength and finding it wanting, Irene dissolved the council and dismissed its delegates.

Despite her apparent failure, the empress briskly announced a campaign against the Arabs, ordering the tagmata to set out for the East. When they obeyed, the empress had Stauracius lead loyal troops from Thrace into Constantinople. Then she sent to the tagmata in Anatolia and discharged some fifteen hundred of them for their recent rioting against her council. She conducted this operation so skillfully that the soldiers obeyed without resistance. She then replaced the chief icono-

98. The Second Council of Nicaea (787), with the patriarch Tarasius (left of
cross), Constantine VI (right of cross), seated bishops, and a condemned iconoclast below. Miniature from the *Menologium of Basil II*. (Photo: Biblioteca
Apostolica Vaticana)

clast bishops and reconvoked her council at Nicaea, the site of the First
Ecumenical Council.

This Second Council of Nicaea went as Irene intended. She remained
in the capital, leaving the patriarch Tarasius to preside. The bishops present, who except for legates from abroad had almost all tolerated Iconoclasm, allowed even well-known iconoclasts to recant. Citing passages
from the Fathers that approved the veneration of icons, the council condemned Iconoclasm and the iconoclast Council of Hieria. The bishops
held their last session in Constantinople, where they hailed Constantine VI and Irene as the new Constantine and the new Helena. Irene
overruled Tarasius and others who wanted harsher punishment for former iconoclasts, and her clemency was matched by a remarkable absence
of open iconoclast resistance. After almost sixty years of official Iconoclasm, not a single prominent person is known to have defended the
doctrine once it ceased to be official.

Having restored the icons and secured the frontiers, Irene had only to marry off her son and let him take power to complete a successful regency. Constantine VI was already betrothed to the Frankish princess Rotrud, the daughter of Charlemagne. In 787, when Constantine was sixteen and Rotrud about thirteen, Irene asked for her to be sent east; but Charlemagne was too fond of Rotrud to let her go. A year later, giving up on the match, Irene held a competition among suitable Byzantine candidates, at which she and Stauracius selected a wife for her son, the granddaughter of a saintly provincial magnate. This bride show seems to have made a favorable impression, and set a precedent.[1]

Yet Irene showed no sign of conceding her son the power to which he was entitled, and he began to resent both his subordination and the wife who had been forced upon him. As sympathy for him spread at court, his mother suffered several reverses in 788. Arab raiders defeated the Anatolic army near the Cilician Gates, and the Bulgars ambushed another Byzantine army on the Strymon River, where it had advanced. When Irene sent one of her eunuchs to expel the Franks from the Principality of Benevento, the Beneventans and Franks defeated and killed him. Although she then made an alliance with Benevento and created a new Theme of Macedonia to keep the Bulgars out of western Thrace, her military reputation was tarnished.[2]

By 790 Constantine thought he saw his chance. He directed a plot against the logothete Stauracius, naively supposing that his mother was being manipulated by the eunuch. But Stauracius discovered the conspiracy and informed Irene. She confined her son to his quarters, and demanded the army swear to keep Constantine from power as long as she lived. The generals stood by Irene, and most of the soldiers reluctantly took the oath, until the Armeniacs objected. Irene sent the drungary of the Watch Alexius Musele to persuade the Armeniacs, but they deposed their strategus Nicephorus, forced Alexius to take his place, and proclaimed Constantine sole emperor. At this news the four other Anatolian land themes also deposed their strategi and rallied to Constantine. Irene bowed to necessity and released her son.

Constantine VI took power at age nineteen, with the support of most of the soldiers, but with little capacity to rule. He found his responsibilities daunting, and remained deeply attached to his mother. Although he confined her to her palace and exiled Stauracius, he never deposed her or most of her supporters. After starting and then interrupting expeditions against both the Bulgars and the Arabs within a single campaigning season, at the beginning of 792 he released Irene, recalled Stauracius, and ordered his troops to acclaim his mother along with himself. When the Armeniacs refused to acknowledge Irene, as they had before, Constantine angered them further by imprisoning their former strategus Alexius Musele. The young emperor led another expedition against the Bulgars, but met with a disastrous defeat near Marcellae.

In disgust at Constantine's incompetence, some of the tagmata proclaimed his uncle Nicephorus emperor, priest though he was. Apparently on the advice of Irene and Stauracius, the young emperor blinded Nicephorus, slit the tongues of Nicephorus's brothers, and blinded Alexius Musele. This subdued the tagmata, but the Armeniacs remained in revolt until the next year, when Constantine won his first victory by defeating them for defending his interests better than he had done himself. He discharged a thousand of them, whom he branded on the face with the words "Armeniac Conspirator." In the confusion, however, the Arabs seized the Armeniac border fort of Camachum and raided the Anatolic Theme.

Irene and Constantine shared power uneasily despite their reconciliation. In 795 the emperor repudiated his wife Maria, whom he had never liked, and married again in defiance of canon law. Though the patriarch Tarasius kept his disapproval quiet, Constantine's supposed adultery was denounced by two respected monks, Plato of Saccudium and his nephew Theodore, who were relatives of Constantine's new wife and friends of Irene. The pair of them fomented opposition to the marriage for two years, beginning the so-called Moechian ("Adulterous") controversy, until Constantine finally imprisoned Plato and exiled Theodore.

Since the emperor's remarriage remained unpopular and his government indecisive, most of his officials and generals came to prefer the still powerful Irene. In 797, as the Arabs raided Anatolia again, she and her allies plotted against Constantine. At first he escaped their attempt to seize him; Irene was about to ask her son for terms, when her fellow conspirators managed to capture the young emperor and blind him. Although they claimed that he survived the blinding and lived on in confinement, he almost certainly died of his wounds. This sordid revolution left Irene the only ruler, the first woman ever to reign over the Roman Empire by herself.

Yet from this time Irene appears to have lost much of her old spirit, perhaps from a lasting sense of guilt. The Byzantines by and large accepted her position, but it was unprecedented and vulnerable. To make clear that she alone was the sovereign, she awkwardly called herself emperor rather than empress in official documents, and struck coins with her portrait on both sides. She had to leave the succession open, since any man she adopted or married would immediately become a rival. The empress found only churchmen and eunuchs fairly safe. She recalled the monks Plato and Theodore with her apologies, and divided her trust between two eunuch patricians, the former logothete Stauracius and the newly prominent Aëtius.

Irene's assumption of power soon provoked a plot in favor of the ordained and mutilated sons of Constantine V, though they found so little support that Aëtius readily arranged their exile to Athens. But the Arabs too sensed Irene's weakness, and in 798 made their boldest raids in sixteen years, reaching Ephesus in the Thracesian Theme and sacking Malagina in the Opsician. The empress asked the caliph Hārūn al-Rashīd for peace, and appears to have renewed the immense tribute she had temporarily agreed to pay in 782. The following year plotters in Athens tried to free the unlucky sons of Constantine V, but only caused the rest of them to be blinded.

Irene tried to shore up her support by distributing donatives to the people of Constantinople, and seems to have exempted the Church from paying the taxes due on its secular tenants and their farms. She also invited Plato of Saccudium and his nephew Theodore to take over the venerable but almost deserted Monastery of Studius in Constantinople. Theodore used his position as abbot to become a forceful religious leader, and turned Studius into the head of a family of monasteries distinguished by strict discipline and Christian scholarship.

The empress fell seriously ill in 799, and her eunuch advisers Aëtius and Stauracius began to plot to determine the succession. Even when she recovered, the plotting continued. By the next year, Stauracius was planning to seize the throne for himself, apparently on the theory that a eunuch was no less fit to reign than a woman. But his conspiracy ended when he died of disease, leaving Irene without a counterweight to the formidable power of Aëtius, now strategus of the Anatolic Theme.

Meanwhile Pope Leo III crowned Charlemagne emperor at Rome on Christmas Day 800. Although the Frankish ruler had recognized Irene as sovereign of the Roman Empire in a treaty just two years before, the pope argued that a woman was ineligible to be emperor, so that Charlemagne was simply filling a vacancy. Charlemagne had no intention of deposing Irene, but reports of his coronation further weakened her authority at Constantinople, which she tried to restore by distributing more donatives and abolishing trade duties in the capital. She sent Charlemagne an embassy, and in 802 elicited a remarkable proposal. The Frankish emperor, then a widower, offered to marry Irene. The marriage would settle their conflicting claims to be emperor and would legally unite the Byzantine and Frankish empires. What this could have meant in practice was and is quite unclear, but the empress was willing to consider it.

Her courtiers were not. By this time Aëtius was strategus of both the Anatolic and Opsician themes, and his brother Leo was strategus of both Thrace and Macedonia. Since Leo was not a eunuch, Aëtius hoped to make him emperor. But other officials, among them the domestic of the Scholae Nicetas Triphyllius, opposed Aëtius and made their own bid for power. While Charlemagne's ambassadors were still in the city, Nicetas and his allies seized the Great Palace, captured Irene, and proclaimed the general logothete Nicephorus emperor. Irene accepted her deposition with dignity and was exiled to a convent she had founded.

The twenty-two years of Irene's rule, with and without her son, brought important changes. Unlike her predecessors since Leo III, who had found most of their support in the army, Irene had relied heavily on her civil officials and clergy. On the whole the results served the empire rather well. Arab raids were no worse than before, and most of Slavic-held Thrace was retaken. Religious peace returned with the condemnation of Iconoclasm, and the reserve in the treasury remained adequate despite Irene's largesses. Auspiciously for the future, the clergy and bureaucracy recovered their confidence and began restoring the empire's system of education and administration.

NICEPHORUS'S EXPANSION

The plotters who overthrew Irene had chosen a man of great ability. The new emperor Nicephorus had not only managed state finance for several years as general logothete, but seems also to have been the strategus of the Armeniacs who had sacked the Arab stronghold of Adata in 786. Allegedly descended from the Arab princely line of the Ghassanids, at the age of something over fifty he remained active and inventive. Familiar with the government and known for his piety, he was well regarded by most officials and clergy. Although he was a usurper, Nicephorus and his partisans could reasonably plead that they had acted to avert the usurpation of Aëtius's brother, and within a month of his coronation

99. Nicephorus I (r. 802–11). Miniature from the Modena Zonaras. (Photo: Biblioteca Estense, Modena)

Nicephorus relieved Aëtius of his commands in the Anatolic and Opsician themes. The emperor put all five land themes of Anatolia under the strategus of the Thracesians Bardanes Turcus, probably because Nicephorus was stopping Irene's tribute to the caliph and anticipated Arab raids.

In 803 Bardanes' men proclaimed their commander emperor, and he accepted on behalf of the exiled Irene. Yet his revolt looked more serious than it was. The Armeniacs remained loyal to Nicephorus, who had probably once been their strategus. Though Bardanes advanced to Chrysopolis, he withdrew at the news of Irene's death. As his adherents began deserting to Nicephorus, Bardanes was persuaded to surrender and become a monk. His surrender ended the rebellion, though the caliph Hārūn took advantage of it to lead a raid and had to be bought off with more tribute.

The next year Hārūn raided again, but in 805 he needed to suppress unrest in Central Asia and made a truce with Nicephorus. The emperor exploited the caliph's absence to launch campaigns in both East and West. First his strategus of Hellas retook the western Peloponnesus from the Slavs, resettling it with Byzantines who claimed descent from those who had left the region two centuries before. Then Nicephorus sent an army from the Armeniacs to besiege Melitene, and another from the Anatolics into Cilicia, where it sacked Tarsus. Meanwhile, probably with Nicephorus's encouragement, the people of Cyprus rebelled against the

Arabs who governed them jointly with the empire. The annexation of the western Peloponnesus proved lasting and profitable, though the attacks against the Arabs had to be abandoned when Hārūn abruptly returned from the East.

Early in 806 the patriarch Tarasius died, and Nicephorus replaced him with another Nicephorus, who like Tarasius was a former bureaucrat. Theodore of Studius and his uncle Plato disapproved of the choice of a layman as patriarch, and abhorred what happened next. The emperor had his new patriarch rehabilitate the priest who had been defrocked for solemnizing the second marriage of Constantine VI. Since this priest, Joseph of Cathara, had persuaded Bardanes Turcus to abandon his rebellion against Nicephorus, the emperor was in his debt; but for Theodore and Plato no such service could expiate complicity in Constantine's adulterous remarriage. Without open protest, they arranged to avoid communion with the patriarch Nicephorus. When the emperor tried to mollify them by appointing Theodore's brother Joseph archbishop of Thessalonica, he too avoided communion with the patriarch. This revived the Moechian controversy, if only clandestinely.

The emperor also had other difficulties in 806. The dukes of Venetia and Dalmatia renounced their allegiance to the empire and submitted to Charlemagne, whom Nicephorus had never recognized as emperor. With the defection of Venetia the empire lost its last foothold in northern Italy. At the same time, the caliph Hārūn invaded Cappadocia with a gigantic force of 135,000 men and sacked two forts. Unable to match such numbers, which seem to have set a record for an enemy invasion of Byzantium, Nicephorus negotiated another truce with Hārūn for the moderate tribute of 30,006 nomismata.[3]

In spite of these setbacks, Nicephorus made further ambitious plans for the West. Encouraged by his easy annexation of the western Peloponnesus, the emperor aimed to make Byzantium the dominant power in the Balkan peninsula by a combination of military campaigns and peaceful resettlement. In 807, while a Byzantine fleet reestablished Byzantine authority in Venetia and Dalmatia, Nicephorus led his first foray into the Balkans. Although he had to interrupt his march to suppress a conspiracy, his army went on to take the region of Serdica from the Slavs. In the meantime his forces in the Peloponnesus put down a Slavic rebellion, which seems to have been fomented by an Arab fleet.

Both to increase his revenue and to prepare for a wider resettlement of the Balkans, the emperor began a new census. This seems to have been the first major revision of the tax rolls since 733, and was surely needed. It counted households, land, livestock, and slaves, and investigated previous tax payments. Having already canceled Irene's remission of urban trade duties, Nicephorus now seems to have canceled all existing tax exemptions. He also ordered churches, monasteries, and charitable institutions to pay the land taxes Irene had remitted, including arrears from the first year of his reign. Those unable to pay the lump sums he demanded had part of their land confiscated.

While these reforms made taxation more equitable, they also displeased many people who had benefited from earlier underassessments and exemptions, particularly churchmen. Not surprisingly, in 808 Nicephorus discovered and punished a plot against him by a group of disgruntled clergy and civil servants. Although Theodore of Studius and his followers were not directly implicated, the emperor lost patience with them and demanded that they accept communion from the patriarch Nicephorus. When they refused, they were condemned by a church council and exiled.

As the emperor continued his expansion at the expense of the Slavs, the Bulgar khan Krum became alarmed. Early in 809 Krum's men surprised and defeated a Byzantine army on the Strymon, then sacked and wrecked Serdica. Nicephorus retaliated at once by leading an army that surprised and sacked the Bulgars' capital of Pliska. The emperor marched on to Serdica, but when his troops refused to do the heavy construction work needed to rebuild it he had to bring them back to Constantinople to restore discipline. Meanwhile the Byzantine commander in Venetia withdrew because of Frankish pressure and local disaffection.

With his gains in the West in jeopardy, Nicephorus issued a momentous edict. He chose thousands of families, mainly in Asia Minor, and ordered them to migrate during the fall and winter to the Balkans. There he created or reorganized four themes. He split the Theme of Hellas in two, extending the northern part into central Greece and making the southern part a new Theme of Peloponnesus. He expanded the archontates of Cephalonia and Thessalonica into themes, which together with the extension of Hellas covered the whole of Greece. The garrisons of the new themes of Peloponnesus and Cephalonia, known as the Mardaïtes of the West, were apparently drawn from the Mardaïte oarsmen of the Theme of Hellas.[4] Nicephorus also strengthened the central army by adding a new tagma, the Hicanati.

The arrival of these settlers, unwilling though many of them were, gave the new territories a Byzantine population and a garrison sufficient to deter Slavic uprisings. Before long the settlers turned most of Greece from a Slavonic-speaking land into a Greek-speaking one. The treasury profited doubly, from the taxes the settlers began to pay and from the sale of their former lands in other parts of the empire. The emperor avoided hoarding the revenue by ordering the principal shipowners of the capital to take out large loans from the state.

These annexations, resettlements, and reorganizations both solidified Byzantine control over Greece and increased the army by ten thousand men. Together with Nicephorus's sack of Pliska, they intimidated the Bulgars for the present. In 810 the emperor sent his new strategus of Cephalonia with a fleet to Dalmatia and Venetia, which he quickly regained for the empire. Dalmatia now seems to have been turned into an archontate under direct Byzantine rule. Venetia received a new and loyal duke, who made his ducate more defensible by moving its capital to the island settlement thereafter known as Venice.

Having achieved so much by his boldness, Nicephorus planned a great campaign against the Bulgars in 811. Its purpose was apparently to cripple the Bulgar Khanate and to annex some of its borderlands. The Arabs were distracted by a civil war between two sons of the late caliph Hārūn. Although Arab raiders did manage to surprise and destroy Euchaïta in the Armeniac Theme, Nicephorus blamed this on the theme's strategus Leo the Armenian, whom he banished, and went ahead with his plans in the Balkans.

Nicephorus's Bulgarian expedition included most of the tagmata and much of the themes, and was probably larger than any earlier Byzantine army in living memory. The khan Krum sued for peace, but was rebuffed. After waiting long enough near the border to terrify the enemy, the emperor led his troops to Pliska, slaughtered its garrison, and took the Bulgars' capital for the second time. Bulgar reinforcements arrived too late to help and were also destroyed. Again Nicephorus refused Krum's offers of peace. The Byzantines plundered Pliska and its countryside, then turned west toward Serdica.

Krum mustered what was left of his army and laid an ambush. When the Byzantines entered a river valley in the Balkan Mountains, the Bulgars hastily blocked both ends of it with log palisades.[5] Nicephorus decided not to risk an immediate assault on the barriers, and kept the army's plight secret to avoid panic. But the second night the Bulgars attacked. The emperor fell among the foremost. The rest of the army fled in terror, miring itself in a marsh, with soldiers trampling each other before some finally blundered over one of the palisades. A great many died in the rout, including the domestic of the Excubitors, the drungary of the Watch, and the strategi of the Anatolics and of Thrace, while the domestic of the new Tagma of the Hicanati was captured. The rest escaped south to Adrianople.

Nicephorus, whose skull Krum turned into a drinking bowl, was the first emperor to die in battle since Valens in 378. He had been aggressive to the point of recklessness, and at last he took one risk too many. His defeat was naturally a blow to the empire, and seemed to his enemies a judgment on his rashness and greed. Yet his boldness and economy had regained and resettled most of Greece and effectively reformed the system of taxation. In coming years these initiatives proved far more important than Nicephorus's terrible end.

RENEWED DISSENSION

Although Nicephorus's son and coemperor Stauracius was already in his late teens, he had received a serious wound near his spine during the Bulgar attack. The army's surviving officers proclaimed him emperor in the hope that he would recover; but even before he arrived in the capital his legs became paralyzed, and his recovery appeared unlikely. Though Stauracius wanted to be succeeded by his wife, his chief officials preferred his sister's husband, the curopalates Michael Rhangabe. Stauracius's attempt to have Michael blinded only hastened his brother-in-law's proclamation. Stauracius was carried off to a monastery after a reign of just over a month.

In his late thirties, handsome and cultivated, Michael Rhangabe had wide backing in the Church and civil service, no important enemies, and, given Stauracius's obvious disability, a hereditary claim to the throne. But Michael was amiable to a fault, lacking in judgment and easily led. To win popularity he began giving away Nicephorus's savings and rewarding those whom Nicephorus had punished. The emperor restored Theodore as abbot of Studius, recalled Leo the Armenian and made him strategus of the Anatolics, and counted both Theodore and Leo among his numerous close advisers.

The emperor seems to have done whatever he had been told most recently. On the advice of the patriarch Nicephorus, Michael began executing the Athingans, heretics who followed some Jewish practices, and

100. The proclamation as emperor of Michael I Rhangabe (r. 811–13) and his son Theophylact (left), by being raised on a shield. Twelfth-century miniature from the Madrid manuscript of the chronicle of John Scylitzes (Matritensis graecus 26–2). (Photo: Biblioteca Nacional, Madrid)

the Paulicians, dualists who believed the God of the old Testament was evil. But Michael called a halt to the killing when Theodore of Studius insisted the heretics be given time to repent. On the advice of many, in-cluding the pope and of course Theodore, the emperor had the unfor-tunate Joseph of Cathara defrocked once more, ending the Moechian Schism. Michael also came to an agreement with Charlemagne, recog-nizing him as an emperor, though not as emperor of the Romans.

Michael put off dealing with the triumphant khan Krum until Krum besieged the frontier town of Develtus. When Michael finally set out against the Bulgars in 812, he was too late to prevent Develtus's surren-der. His exasperated soldiers mutinied, and the people of northern and western Thrace began to flee their homes. Some tagmatic soldiers even tried to proclaim the blinded sons of Constantine V, but Michael's gov-ernment cashiered them. After occupying nearly all of Irene's and Nicephorus's annexations in Thrace, Krum offered peace. But since the khan demanded the Byzantines hand over some Bulgar deserters who had become Christians, the patriarch Nicephorus and Theodore of Studius persuaded Michael to refuse. Then Krum took and sacked Mesembria, the last remaining Byzantine border stronghold, and executed all his captives who refused to renounce Christianity. This forced the emperor to muster a larger force in the spring of 813.

Even when Michael joined his army near Versinicia in Thrace, he refused to attack the outnumbered Bulgars for over a month. Meanwhile the troops he had dismissed from the tagmata rioted in Constantinople, and the army at Versinicia became disgusted with the emperor's inaction. At last prodded by his generals, Michael ordered an attack. Yet once it had begun he hesitated to join it, and Leo the Armenian's Anatolics turned to flight, setting off a rout. Despite Leo's conduct, which was either negligent or treacherous, Michael left him with the defeated army and decamped for Constantinople. The soldiers proclaimed Leo, who accepted with a becoming show of reluctance. After waiting until Leo actually arrived at the capital, Michael abdicated. Leo exiled him to a monastery together with his sons, who were castrated to prevent their aspiring to the throne.

Leo V the Armenian seems to have been in his late thirties when he was crowned. Born into a noble family in Armenia, in his youth he had fled to the empire with his parents, enrolled in the Anatolic army, and begun a brilliant rise. When Bardanes Turcus took command of the Anatolian themes in 802, he had evidently married one of his daughters to Leo. Yet when Bardanes rebelled Leo deserted to the emperor Nicephorus, who first promoted him and then exiled him for incompetence against the Arabs. Leo had found favor with Michael Rhangabe even before Michael became emperor, and there are grounds to think that his wife Barca became Michael's mistress.[6] By the time Leo overthrew Michael his career had been highly checkered, and his failure to sign a pledge to maintain church doctrine particularly disturbed iconophiles. Shrewd and dynamic, he had few principles but many talents.

By this time the threat from the Bulgars had grown to alarming proportions. After investing Adrianople, Krum reached the walls of the capital within a week of Leo's coronation. The khan demanded tribute in return for his withdrawal. The emperor agreed to negotiations, but used them to try to assassinate Krum. The enraged Krum then devastated the suburbs of Constantinople and sacked many of the towns of southern

Thrace, including the refugee-swollen city of Adrianople, where he took forty thousand captives. He withdrew without meeting any resistance from Leo.

While biding his time, the emperor sought to reassure his subjects. Having divorced his apparently adulterous wife, he married Theodosia, an aristocratic Armenian well regarded by the clergy. At the same time Leo crowned his first wife's son Symbatius, aged about ten, and renamed him Constantine. Thus the army acclaimed Leo and his son as Leo and Constantine, a combination that inevitably recalled the iconoclasts Leo III and Constantine V and their military victories. Yet Leo V did nothing about Krum, who in early 814 sacked Arcadiopolis and other Thracian towns that his earlier raiding had missed, and organized the empire's former border region as a new province of his khanate. That spring Krum planned a full-dress siege of Constantinople. Before he could begin, however, he died of a cerebral hemorrhage. His successor soon died as well, and the Bulgar threat receded.

Leo now told his advisers his opinion that recent emperors had suffered defeat because they venerated icons, unlike the victorious iconoclasts of the eighth century. Leo therefore proposed to restore Iconoclasm. When his advisers did not venture to disagree, the emperor appointed a theological commission with the secret purpose of preparing for an iconoclast council. Its head was John the Grammarian, a learned young monk. The patriarch Nicephorus studiously ignored the emperor's obvious intentions until the next autumn, when Leo asked him to consider the commission's findings.

As the patriarch resisted, Leo had soldiers remove the icon of Christ over the Bronze Gate of the palace, which Irene had restored. In alarm some leading clerics met in the patriarchal palace on Christmas Eve to pray for the icons' preservation. Though at first Leo denied that he was an iconoclast, early in 815 he forced Nicephorus to abdicate and go into exile. The emperor chose another patriarch, who held a synod that reaffirmed the iconoclast Council of Hieria of 754. Leo exiled those who dissented openly, including many bishops and Theodore of Studius. Destruction of icons began. As usual, most people raised no objection to what the government wanted, though many disapproved.

Not long after Leo restored Iconoclasm, the new Bulgar khan Omurtag executed all his Byzantine captives who refused to renounce Christianity. When the khan raided Thrace again, and rebuffed an imperial embassy, Leo had little choice but to fight him. After thorough preparations, in spring 816 the emperor marched as far as the ruins of Mesembria. He encamped near the Bulgars, pretended to flee, then ambushed them as they pursued him. He killed or captured much of the Bulgar army, driving his victory home by raiding their khanate. A few months later Omurtag agreed to a thirty-year peace, renewable every ten years, that restored the frontier more or less as it had been in 780. The Bulgars kept most of the Thracian conquests of Irene and Nicephorus, but withdrew from some of northern Thrace.

After making this peace, Leo worked hard to rebuild the devastated themes of Thrace and Macedonia. In 817, seeing the caliphate still torn by rebellions, he sent a fleet to raid the coast of Egypt and led an army that retook the border fort of Camachum, lost under Constantine VI. About 818 the Vikings known as the Rus' seem to have made their first known raid on the empire, plundering the northern coast of Anatolia. Apparently to ward them off, around 819 Leo converted two turmae of the Armeniacs into independent commands with naval squadrons, the Theme of Paphlagonia in the west and the Ducate of Chaldia in the east.[7] On the whole Leo ruled well. He could maintain that God was rewarding his Iconoclasm, and his successes actually won over some iconophiles.

Leo still had his enemies. In exile Theodore of Studius organized a network of iconophiles who were detained, in hiding, or concealing their opinions; the latter group included most of Leo's civil service. About 820 the emperor discovered and punished a conspiracy against him in Constantinople. He was also suspicious of his domestic of the Excubitors Michael the Amorian, who was married to the sister of Leo's divorced wife and continued to grumble about Leo's divorce and remarriage.[8] Near the end of 820, agents of the postal logothete uncovered a plot by Michael against Leo. The emperor imprisoned Michael and ordered him burned alive, but the empress Theodosia obtained a stay of the execution till after Christmas. This postponement allowed the prisoner to rally some undetected plotters. They butchered Leo in church on Christmas morning and castrated his sons, releasing Michael and proclaiming him emperor.

In this fashion Michael II the Amorian, also known as the Stammerer, ascended the throne while still in chains. He was about fifty, capable but unprepossessing, from a ranching family near Amorium with no great wealth and some taint of the Athingan heresy. Though Michael shared many of Leo V's associates, the bureaucracy seems to have preferred him

101. Leo V the Armenian (r. 813–20) and (right) Leo's murderer and successor Michael II the Amorian (r. 820–29). Miniatures from the Modena Zonaras. (Photos: Biblioteca Estense, Modena)

to Leo, perhaps because he had not been the one to bring back Iconoclasm. But Leo's victories had made him popular among the army in Asia Minor, and at the news of his murder the Anatolic Theme proclaimed Thomas the Slav, who had once served with both Leo V and Michael II under Bardanes Turcus. With as good a claim to the throne as Michael, Thomas was not really a rebel. The Bucellarian, Paphlagonian, and Cibyrrhaeot themes accepted him at once as Leo's successor and avenger, and at the beginning of 821 a civil war broke out.

Michael held the European part of the empire and the Optimates, the Opsician, the Thracesians, the Armeniacs, and Chaldia. Although he hesitated to change church doctrine and was himself no iconophile, he needed iconophile support against Thomas. So he stopped the persecution, recalled the exiled bishops, and even offered to restore the patriarch Nicephorus if he would ignore the whole question of icons. When Nicephorus declined, Michael appointed an iconoclast, but the emperor's Iconoclasm was always lukewarm.

After winning over the Thracesians and seizing the eastern Armeniacs along with Chaldia, the pretender Thomas had to interrupt his campaign to repel Arab raids on the Anatolics and Cibyrrhaeots. By striking into Arab-held Armenia and taking Theodosiopolis, he not only stopped the raids but convinced the caliph Ma'mūn to recognize him as emperor. Ma'mūn allowed Thomas to recruit Christians from Armenia and Syria and to have himself crowned by the orthodox patriarch of Antioch. Though Thomas's troops were largely iconoclast and most iconophiles stood by Michael, the pretender gained some gullible adherents by insinuating that he was really Constantine VI, whose fate after 797 remained obscure to most Byzantines.

By this time Thomas had won the nominal submission of the themes of southern Greece and Sicily, and he assembled a fleet under Leo V's nephew Gregory Pterotus. Intending to attack the capital, Thomas marched from the Thracesian Theme to Abydus, crossed the Hellespont, and was acclaimed by the themes of Thessalonica, Macedonia, and Thrace. By now he had far more troops, ships, and territory than Michael, who held only the capital and most of the Opsician and Armeniac themes. In fall 821 Thomas put Constantinople under siege by land and sea. He would surely have won the war at once if someone had opened a gate for him.

Since nobody did, and his assaults on the walls failed, Thomas wintered in Thrace, maintaining his siege by land. In spring 822 further attacks on the city ended in a naval defeat for Thomas. His admiral Pterotus tried to desert, and had to be captured and killed. That summer Thomas received more ships from the western themes, only to have Michael burn many of them with Greek Fire and capture others. On the other hand, Michael was himself unable to break out of the capital.

The embattled emperor persuaded the Bulgar khan Omurtag to attack Thomas. Omurtag's invasion forced the pretender to raise his siege, and while he was defeating the Bulgars his fleet surrendered to Michael. Early the next year, when Thomas's men were starting to desert, Michael mustered his forces from the Opsician and Armeniac themes, met Thomas's army in the field, and routed it. By fall he had starved out Arcadiopolis and captured and executed Thomas. The emperor's troops put down his last opponents in Anatolia in the spring of 824, more than three years after the beginning of the civil war.

Michael did what he could to reunite the empire. He pardoned nearly all Thomas's former partisans and spread the story that Thomas, far from being an avenger of Leo V, had rebelled before Leo's death. The recently widowed Michael strengthened his claim to the throne by marrying Constantine VI's daughter Euphrosyne, whose dynasty was associated with legitimacy, military success, and Iconoclasm, though she was herself an iconophile. Michael even won two small victories against the Arabs by sending a fleet that raided the Syrian coast and an army that sacked Sozopetra. His commanders defeated or bought off the raiders the caliph sent in retaliation in 825.

Yet the civil war had weakened the army, and most of all the navy. Before the navy could fully recover, in 826 a rebellion broke out in Sicily. The next year the rebels appealed for help to the independent Arab emir of Qayrawān in North Africa. The Arabs sent by the emir soon took most of the island and besieged Syracuse. Michael dispatched the imperial fleet to Sicily in spring 828. But it had scarcely left the Aegean when a band of Arab freebooters, who had come from Spain by way of Alexandria, landed on the almost defenseless island of Crete.

This second band of Arabs smashed the makeshift fleet that was mustered against them and began occupying the island. Rather than forfeit Crete, the emperor sent to Sicily for his main navy, which had just raised the siege of Syracuse. It returned in the fall of 828, attacked the Arabs on Crete, and was routed. Giving up on Crete for the present, Michael sent his remaining naval forces to Sicily, which they mostly cleared of Arabs in 829. Meanwhile the emperor recruited new marines who at least drove the Arabs of Crete out of the Cyclades.

So matters stood when Michael II died of kidney failure in the fall of 829. Confronted with a civil war more ferocious than any since Heraclius's against Phocas, then invasions of Sicily and Crete when his fleet was at its weakest, Michael had offered creditable resistance. For that matter, Leo V had capably rescued Thrace from its worst invasion since the seventh century. On the other hand, by deserting Michael I Leo had aggravated the Bulgar threat, and by restoring Iconoclasm he had redivided a Church that had almost healed. Although Michael II had eased that division, his coup had set off the civil war. Probably his greatest contribution to the empire was to die in bed and leave a son nearly ready to succeed him.

THEOPHILUS'S AMBITIONS

Michael's son Theophilus was sixteen when he took power along with his stepmother Euphrosyne. Though reportedly born in Amorium, he had grown up in the capital, for the last nine years as heir apparent. His father had entrusted his education to John the Grammarian, probably because of John's reputation for learning rather than his Iconoclasm.

In any case, John trained his pupil to be both a committed iconoclast and an unusually cultured man. Theophilus was intelligent, a bit over-confident, and determined to have a glorious reign. Though Michael had specified that Euphrosyne should at first be coruler, Theophilus acted independently from the outset. He began a building program surpassing that of any emperor since Justinian I, renovating the sea walls of Constantinople and constructing elaborately decorated new palaces. Striving to be known for his justice, he announced that every week he would ride across the city, inspect the markets, and hear the complaints of anyone who wished to see him.

In 830 Euphrosyne selected girls to compete in a bride show for her stepson, as her grandmother Irene had once done for her father Constantine VI. Theophilus made the most of the spectacle, assembling the contestants in a splendid hall that he had just erected in the palace and offering a golden apple to his choice. The new empress Theodora was beautiful, sensible, and adaptable, and suited him well; but Theophilus seems not to have realized that his bride, like his stepmother, was an iconophile. Having provided her stepson with a wife who shared her theology, Euphrosyne retired to a nearby convent to venerate icons.

As soon as he became sole ruler, Theophilus astonished his courtiers by executing Leo V's surviving assassins, who had put his own father on the throne. While asserting that the murder of any emperor deserved death, Theophilus seems also to have had a genuine regard for Leo, who had been his godfather and fellow iconoclast, and a more successful soldier than Michael II. Theophilus tried to emulate Leo's prowess. In 831 he and his domestic of the Scholae Manuel the Armenian defeated some Arab raiders in the Armeniac Theme and celebrated a triumph.

This, however, simply provoked more Arabs to raid the Anatolic Theme and defeat the emperor there. The same year the Arabs on Sicily seized the island's second city of Panormus. After these reverses, Theophilus learned late in 831 that iconophiles were circulating a pamphlet predicting his imminent death. Treating the matter as a conspiracy, the emperor administered beatings to the monk Methodius, who had probably written the pamphlet, and to the deposed bishop Euthymius of Sardis, who died of his injuries.[9] Henceforth Theophilus regarded iconophiles with open hostility.

In 832 Ma'mūn invaded Cappadocia, disdaining Theophilus's attempt to make peace. The emperor arrived with an army and suffered another defeat. A second Byzantine request for peace was also ignored, and in

TABLE 11

The Amorian Dynasty

Emperors are in capital letters and italics, with the years of their reigns marked "r." Other years are of births and deaths unless indicated otherwise. Illegitimate descent is shown by a broken line.

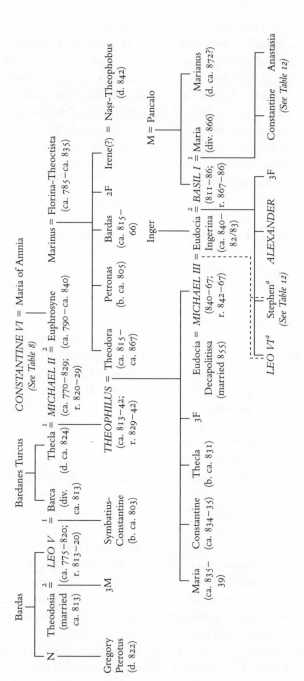

[a]Reputed to be son of Basil I, but probably illegitimate son of Michael III.

833 the Arabs began to build a permanent base at Tyana, on the Byzantine side of the Taurus. The caliph announced plans to construct a chain of such strongholds until he reached Constantinople. In the face of this mighty and implacable enemy, the emperor decided to resume persecuting iconophiles, which after all had seemed to help Leo V.

Theophilus had a church council reaffirm Leo's iconoclast synod of 815, then ordered imprisonment for all who refused communion with iconoclasts and expropriation for all who harbored such recalcitrants. He jailed many of the surviving iconophile leaders, had a few beaten to death, and drove others into hiding. The persecution was in effect by the summer of 833, when Ma'mūn arrived in Cappadocia to prosecute his war to the end. The end came a month later, when the caliph suddenly died and his successor al-Muʿtaṣim ordered the base at Tyana destroyed and the Arab army withdrawn. Theophilus apparently took this as a divine reward: as soon as he had begun to persecute iconophiles, God had struck his enemy dead and ended the invasion. The emperor became surer than ever that Iconoclasm was God's will and insured temporal success.

The next winter fortune favored Theophilus again, when the caliph's army expelled some of the religious renegades called Khurramites from the Zagros Mountains of western Persia. Many Khurramites were slaughtered or enslaved, including most of their women, but some fourteen thousand men under their leader Naṣr made their way across Armenia to the empire. They offered to convert to Christianity and serve in the Byzantine army. Theophilus gladly accepted, and married one of his wife's sisters to Naṣr, who took the Christian name of Theophobus ("Godfearing"). The emperor enrolled the Khurramites in new companies known as the Persian Turmae and distributed them among the themes, where an imperial edict required widows and spinsters from military families to marry the converted Persians. Thus the strength of the Byzantine army rose by almost a sixth.

Paying the new soldiers was easy enough, because the treasury was brimming with gold. By this time the emperor was adorning his throne room with sonorous golden organs that were played for visitors, mechanical gold lions that roared, and a gold plane tree filled with singing gold birds. Soon afterward he added several large apartments to the Great Palace, decking them with marble and mosaics. Yet the state gold reserves remained ample. Evidently they were a product both of Ni-

102. Copper follis of Theophilus (r. 829–42) of the type first minted about 835, shown actual size, with the reverse inscribed "Theophilus Augustus, You Conquer." (Photo: Dumbarton Oaks, Washington, D.C., copyright 1996)

cephorus's financial reforms and of steady economic growth over a number of years.

Theophilus seems to have helped increase such growth around 835, even if by accident. He began to mint copper folles, the main coins used for small purchases, at roughly six times the former rate. The advantage for the government was clear, because even though it increased the copper coins somewhat in size it still exchanged them for gold at a quite favorable rate. The convenience for merchants and shoppers should have been plain to anyone. While Theophilus may well have learned of a shortage of change on his regular visits to the markets, his principal reason for the increased minting was probably his love of gold. In any case, his pride in his new coins is evident from their inscription: Theophilus Augustus, You Conquer.

Yet in 835 Theophilus failed to conquer twice. When he sent a fleet against the Arabs in Sicily, they captured most of it. When he led an army against Arab raiders on the frontier, they defeated him and looted his camp. A year later, however, he sent a fleet that brought back from Bulgaria some forty thousand Byzantines who had survived or were descended from those captured by Krum more than twenty years before at Adrianople. When the Bulgars raided Thrace in retaliation, the emperor dispatched an army under his Caesar Alexius Musele, whom he had just betrothed to his daughter. Musele reclaimed a coastal strip between Thessalonica and Thrace that the empire had surrendered under the treaty of 816.[10] The khan nonetheless agreed to renew the treaty for another ten years.

In 837 Theophilus decided to raid the caliphate while most of the Arab army was attacking the remaining Khurramites in Azerbaijan. Taking Naṣr-Theophobus with his converted Khurramites and the domestic of the Scholae Manuel with the tagmata, Theophilus is said to have mustered some seventy thousand men, probably more than in any expedition since Heraclius's day. Crossing the Antitaurus, Theophilus sacked

Sozopetra and Arsamosata and extorted tribute and hostages from Melitene. He returned to celebrate a triumph in Constantinople. When the caliph's army drove the last Khurramites out of Azerbaijan, many of them fled to the empire to join their fellows, swelling the Persian Turmae to thirty thousand men.[11]

The caliph Mu'taṣim was livid at Theophilus's raid, and prepared for revenge the next year. The confident emperor still felt able to send Musele with an army to fight the Arabs in Sicily in spring 838. Apparently trusting Iconoclasm to defend him, Theophilus chose his old mentor John the Grammarian as patriarch of Constantinople and intensified his persecution of iconophiles.[12] After having them all anathematized by a council, Theophilus ordered all icons destroyed. Even lesser measures had seemingly sufficed to abort Ma'mūn's invasion in 832.

At the beginning of the summer, Mu'taṣim invaded the empire through the Cilician Gates with fifty thousand men, while thirty thousand more advanced through the Pass of Melitene. The Arabs' stated objective was Amorium, probably both the largest city of Anatolia and Theophilus's birthplace. Leaving a large garrison to defend the city, the emperor, Theophobus, Manuel, and forty thousand troops prepared to meet the Arabs. Before the Arab armies could join each other, the Byzantines attacked the smaller Arab force near Dazimon in the Armeniac Theme.

The Byzantines had the advantage in numbers, but the Arabs had ten thousand expert Turkish cavalry, whose expert archery routed their opponents. The emperor was almost surrendered to the Arabs by some of Theophobus's Persians, and was only rescued by Manuel, who suffered a mortal wound in the process. As the Persians rebelled and proclaimed Theophobus emperor at Sinope, Theophilus had to hurry to his capital to end rumors that he had been killed. Left unopposed, the Arab forces sacked Ancyra and converged on Amorium. Theophilus sued for peace in vain. After a short siege, the caliph stormed and burned Amorium. Of the seventy thousand or so defenders, inhabitants, and refugees who swelled the city, about half were killed. Only then did news of a revolt in the caliphate force Mu'taṣim to withdraw with his booty and prisoners.

Even though the Arabs failed to exploit their sack of Amorium, and other emperors had suffered worse defeats, this campaign permanently refuted the argument that strict Iconoclasm insured military success. The young emperor became gravely ill at the shock, and even when his health began to return he was too dejected to fight the Arabs or Theophobus's rebels. After his unanticipated reverses, Theophilus became ob-

103. Theophilus (at left) and the Arab caliph al-Ma'mūn (r. 813–33; at right). Miniature from the Madrid Scylitzes. The action, which is to be read from right to left, shows the caliph sending an ambassador to the emperor with a letter requesting a visit from the celebrated Byzantine scholar Leo the Mathematician. These events, if historical at all, seem to belong to the subsequent caliphate of al-Muʿtaṣim (r. 833–42). (Photo: Biblioteca Nacional, Madrid)

sessed with learning the future, in which he no longer felt confidence. Informed that John the Grammarian's cousin Leo the Mathematician could predict the future by astrology, the emperor made him head of a public school in the Magnaura Palace. In the hope of hearing reassuring prophecies, the anxious ruler consulted not just Leo but his cousin the patriarch, who was an alchemist and diviner, and even Methodius, the iconophile monk long imprisoned for predicting Theophilus's death.

Even while he was keeping Methodius in the palace, the emperor was outraged to discover that his stepmother Euphrosyne was venerating icons with his daughters in her convent. He forbade the girls to pay further visits to the iconophile empress dowager. Theophilus vented his anger by tattooing the faces of the iconophile monks Theophanes and Theodore with verses accusing them of heresy, and by branding the hands of the icon painter Lazarus with iron plates. Theophilus's wrath extended to his Caesar Alexius Musele, whom he recalled from Sicily and jailed on suspicion of disloyalty. Only a rebuke from the patriarch John persuaded the emperor to rehabilitate Alexius.

Late in 839 Theophilus finally led an army against Theophobus and his Persian rebels at Sinope, and brought them to terms. The thirty thousand Persians became ordinary thematic soldiers and were dispersed among the existing themes and some newly founded districts. Macedonia, Thrace, the Optimates, and the seven Anatolian land themes each received two thousand of the Persians. The turmae of Seleucia and Cappadocia in the Anatolics and the Turma of Charsianum in the Armeniacs became new districts known as cleisurae ("mountain passes"), each receiving two thousand more Persians. The archontates of Dyrrhachium and Cherson likewise gained the rank of themes, expanded territories, and two thousand men apiece, who were either Persians or troops from elsewhere whom the Persians replaced. Cherson, renamed the Theme of the Climata ("Districts"), appears to have been meant to meet a growing threat from the Rus'.[13]

The new Persian troops strengthened almost every vulnerable point on the frontier, except for the Armeniacs' Turma of Colonia, which was for some reason left out. While resettling the Persians, Theophilus also tightened the organization of the themes. Previously themes had had no smaller divisions than the drungi of 1,000 men. Now each drungus was divided into five banda with 200 men each, of whom 50 were cavalry and 150 infantry. Each new bandum had its corresponding territory and headquarters, and a commander known as a count, who could assemble its soldiers to face attacks more quickly than before.

Finally, Theophilus drew on his overflowing treasury and approximately doubled his troops' pay. In the process he greatly increased his minting of gold coins. Ordinary soldiers, who had been paid five nomismata a year since about 662, were now to receive one nomisma a year for each year of their service up to a maximum of twelve. This increase in pay to an average of about nine nomismata a year allowed the troops to buy better equipment and improved their morale, practically ending the military revolts that had long been common. After these military reforms, which were completed early in 840, the Byzantine army became a far more powerful, flexible, and reliable instrument than it had been before.

Already in 840, Arabs raiding the new Cleisura of Cappadocia suffered unusually heavy casualties fighting the Persians stationed there. Theophilus seems to have elevated Cappadocia to a theme as a reward for its exploits. In spring 841 Arabs making another raid on Cappadocia met local forces who drove them back through the Cilician Gates and defeated them in Arab Cilicia. That summer, other Arabs trying to raid the Cleisura of Charsianum came upon local troops who drove them out through the Pass of Melitene and sacked Adata and Germanicea. That fall Arab raiders from Crete who landed near Miletus in the Thracesian

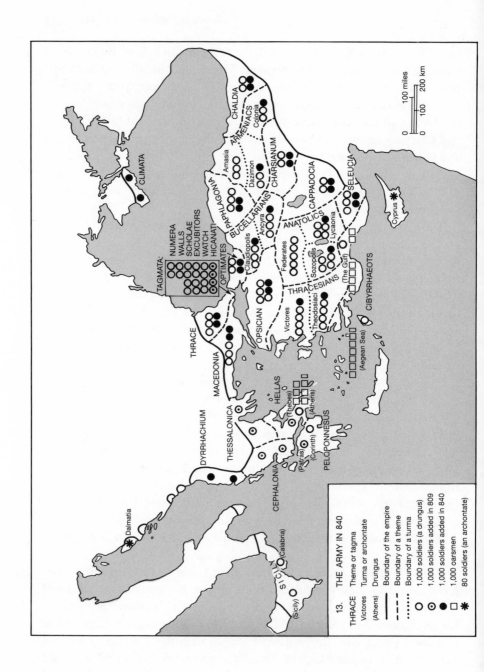

TAGMATA: NUMERA
WALLS
SCHOLAE
EXCUBITORS
WATCH
HICANATI

CLIMATA

CHALDIA
ARMENIACS
Colonia
Amasia
Dazimon
CHARSIANUM
CAPPADOCIA
PAPHLAGONIA
BUCELLARIANS
Ancyra
ANATOLICS
SELEUCIA
Cyprus
Claudiopolis
Lycaonia
OPTIMATES
Federates
Sozopolis
(The Gulf)
Victores
Theodosiaci
CIBYRRHAEOTS
THRACESIANS
THRACE
OPSICIAN
MACEDONIA
(Aegean Sea)
DYRRHACHIUM
THESSALONICA
HELLAS
(Thebes)
(Athens)
Patras)
(Corinth)
PELOPONNESUS
CEPHALONIA

Dalmatia

SICILY
(Calabria)
(Sicily)

13.   THE ARMY IN 840

THRACE   Theme or tagma
Victores   Turma or archontate
(Athens)   Drungus
─────   Boundary of the empire
─ ─ ─   Boundary of a theme
· · · ·   Boundary of a turma
○   1,000 soldiers (a drungus)
◉   1,000 soldiers added in 809
●   1,000 soldiers added in 840
□   1,000 oarsmen
✳   80 soldiers (an archontate)

100 miles
200 km
0   100
0

Theme were annihilated by the Thracesians. Never had unaided thematic armies defended their land so well.

Yet Theophilus had little chance to make use of his new military power, because his health had become too poor for him to lead an army. By the beginning of 842, he was dying of dysentery. His sole surviving son, Michael, was an infant. Among plausible usurpers, Alexius Musele had prudently retired to a monastery, but the emperor took the precaution of having Theophobus the Persian secretly executed. On his deathbed the emperor delivered an eloquent exhortation to his officials to defend the rights of his wife and son. Then he died, probably just before his twenty-ninth birthday.

Theophilus had had his failures and some merely superficial successes, but he had also done much to restore the empire's power and self-confidence. He made good use of his chances to enlist the fugitive Khurramites and to rescue Byzantine refugees from the Bulgars. Although he left a vast gold reserve of some 7 million nomismata, late in his reign he realized that gold could be used for better purposes than overfilling the treasury or redecorating the throne room, and that winning wars was more a matter of military strength than of militant Iconoclasm.[14] His increased minting of both gold and copper coins provided the monetary basis for expanding trade, and with it the economy. Most important were his reforms of the army. They reduced the danger of military revolts, and not only strengthened Byzantine defenses but prepared Byzantium to go on the offensive against the Arabs.

CHAPTER FOURTEEN

External Gains, 842–912

History repeated itself when, as in 780, an icono-clast emperor was succeeded by his iconophile widow and her underage son. Like Irene, Theodora was in her late twenties and capable both of leading and of inspiring loyalty. But she was less ruthless than Irene and had less need of drastic methods, with a son who was just two years old, no obvious rivals, and several able advisers. She relied on her brothers Bardas and Petronas, her relative Sergius Nicetiates, and especially the postal logothete Theoctistus, who as a eunuch could serve the empress without suspicion of scandal or of designs on the throne. Having served as a high official throughout the reigns of both Michael II and Theophilus, Theoctistus became even closer to Theodora than Stauracius had been to Irene.

STABILITY UNDER THEODORA

Theodora seems always to have been an iconophile and saw no reason to delay the restoration of icons, which most of her advisers favored. To save her husband's reputation and disarm opposition, she circulated a story that Theophilus had repented of Iconoclasm on his deathbed. She made her move in 843. The empress held not a council of bishops, nearly all of whom had needed to profess Iconoclasm for many years, but an as-sembly of selected officials and clerics, which met at the house of Theoc-tistus. These condemned Iconoclasm simply by accepting the Second Council of Nicaea of 787. They deposed the patriarch John the Gram-marian and elected as his successor Methodius, the long-imprisoned iconophile monk. The day of this iconophile assembly, the first Sunday of Lent, has ever since been celebrated in the eastern church as the Sunday of Orthodoxy.

Since the iconoclasts had not merely erred but had defied the decrees of an ecumenical council, Methodius deposed nearly every bishop in the empire, even though most of them except John the Grammarian abjured Iconoclasm.[1] Among those deposed was Leo the Mathematician, whom Theophilus had taken from his school at the Magnaura Palace and made bishop of Thessalonica. With money provided by Theodora's brother Bardas, Leo returned to the headship of the Magnaura, where he taught philosophy and three other professors specialized in geometry, astronomy, and grammar.[2] Though not the only school in Constantinople offering an advanced education, the Magnaura was probably the only institution with more than one teacher, and its imperial patronage helped increase the prestige of scholarship.

Just a week after the iconophile assembly, the empress sent her minister Theoctistus and her relative Sergius Nicetiates on a great expedition to retake Crete from its Arab conquerors. Meant to show that orthodoxy could win victories, the expedition began well, landing safely, besieging the Arabs, and setting up a Theme of Crete. Then Theoctistus heard a rumor that Theodora intended to name another emperor, possibly Bardas, and hastened to the capital, leaving the army in Crete under Sergius.

The rumor proved false, but before Theoctistus could return word came that the emir of Melitene ʿAmr was heading for Constantinople with a large force. The logothete therefore mustered an army and met the Arabs at the Mauropotamus in the territory of the Optimates.[3] In mid-battle some Byzantines deserted to the Arabs, Theoctistus was beaten, and the Arabs raided up to the Bosporus. Meanwhile the Arabs on Crete counterattacked and killed Sergius, wrecking the Byzantine expedition. Theoctistus, who held Bardas responsible for encouraging the desertions at the Mauropotamus, persuaded Theodora to expel him from the capital.

Theoctistus's reverses did him little harm. His influence was unchallenged after the death of Sergius and the disgrace of Bardas. He made the islands of the Cibyrrhaeots into a separate Theme of the Aegean Sea, which at least restrained the piracy of the Arabs of Crete. The caliphate was losing control over its border provinces, and though the emir ʿAmr

104. Saint Methodius, patriarch of Constantinople (843–47). Drawing made between 1847 and 1849 by Gaspare Fossati of a ninth-century mosaic in Saint Sophia, Constantinople, that was later destroyed during an earthquake. (Photo: Archivio Cantonale, Bellinzona)

of Melitene continued to penetrate the weak defenses of the Byzantines' Turma of Colonia, his resources were mainly local. Few iconoclasts remained to blame the Byzantine defeats on the icons.

While ordinary iconoclasts were disappearing, the same was not true of Paulicians, the dualist heretics of eastern Anatolia, whose rejection of the whole material world made them iconoclasts as well. Determined to extirpate their heresy, not long after restoring the icons Theodora ordered the army to execute recalcitrant Paulicians and confiscate their property. Thousands of Paulicians died; some converted, but many escaped under the renegade officer Carbeas to ʿAmr of Melitene. ʿAmr settled them along his border, where other Paulicians had already fled. In the empty lands between the empire and the caliphate they founded a splinter state under Arab protection.

Although in 845 the Arabs martyred some captives from Amorium who refused to convert to Islam, this gesture was mostly one of frustration. When the emir of Tarsus attempted another raid, the strategus of Cappadocia defeated him. Arab raids died down in the East; only in Sicily, which was too far from Constantinople to reinforce and resupply easily, did the Arabs go on defeating Byzantine forces. After the thirty-year treaty with the Bulgars expired in 846, the Byzantines repulsed a

105. Saint Ignatius, patriarch of Constantinople (847–58, 867–77). Detail of a ninth-century mosaic in Saint Sophia, Constantinople. He is beardless because he was a eunuch. (Photo: Dumbarton Oaks, Washington, D.C., copyright 1996)

Bulgar raid on Macedonia and Thrace and forced the khan to make a new treaty.

Iconoclasm had naturally left scars, but chiefly by compromising the Church, which had been unable to throw off an acknowledged heresy by the usual method of holding a council. In the process of replacing the iconoclast hierarchy, Methodius offended the monks of the Studius Monastery, who found many of his hastily appointed bishops unsuitable. When Methodius died in 847, his successor Ignatius reconciled the Studites but offended Methodius's partisans by deposing one of them, the bishop of Syracuse Gregory Asbestas. The Church remained disturbed and weakened.

Byzantium enjoyed relative peace except for Sicily, where Theodora tried and failed again to drive the Arabs back in 848. In 851 the emir of Tarsus ʿAlī the Armenian began three years of summer raids, but he seems not to have done much damage. Theodora retaliated by sending a fleet that raided the coast of Egypt in 853 and 854. The next year a Byzantine army invaded the Emirate of Tarsus and sacked Anazarbus, taking almost twenty thousand prisoners. Theoctistus killed some of them who refused to convert to Christianity, probably in delayed revenge for the deaths of the Byzantine captives from Amorium. Although the Bulgar treaty was about to expire again, after making bellicose noises the Bulgar khan Boris renewed it.[4]

On the whole Theodora's regency seemed to be a successful one, but it was soon to expire, since Michael III had turned fifteen. To his mother's and Theoctistus's despair, the adolescent emperor's main interests were drinking, chariot racing, and his mistress, Eudocia Ingerina. Hoping to steady him by marriage, the empress and her minister prepared the customary bride show. They allowed Eudocia to compete but disqualified her, perhaps because they required virginity of their candidates. Instead they married Michael to the blameless but colorless Eudocia Decapolitissa.[5] Annoyed by this forced marriage, Michael allied himself with Theodora's brother Bardas, whom he recalled to the capital after years of disgrace. With Michael's agreement, Bardas had his enemy Theoctistus assassinated. The distraught Theodora raged at her son, who for several months tried vainly to placate her. In early 856 Michael had himself proclaimed sole emperor, officially ending her regency.

On her retirement Theodora was justly proud of her accomplishments. Her government with Theoctistus had skillfully resolved the iconoclast controversy and gained the upper hand over the caliphate and Bulgaria. While keeping up Theophilus's high rate of military pay, Theodora had maintained a small budgetary surplus and modestly increased Theophilus's gold reserve to 7.8 million nomismata. Although she might have prolonged her regency by dealing with her son as Irene had dealt with Constantine VI, she wisely refrained from any damaging struggle for power.

PROGRESS UNDER MICHAEL III

Thus Michael ostensibly began to rule for himself. At age sixteen he was as old as his father Theophilus had been at his accession, but Michael had none of his father's seriousness. He continued to care chiefly for wine, sports, practical jokes, and his beloved Eudocia Ingerina, though he avoided scandal by staying married to his wife. He left most of the work of governing to his uncle Bardas, who became both a magister and the domestic of the Scholae. Bardas's brother Petronas also emerged after a period of inaction to become strategus of the Thracesian Theme and the empire's foremost general.[6]

The Paulician leader Carbeas, in the twelve years since he had fled the empire, had organized his fellow heretics into an effective army. From an enclave around the fort of Tephrice between the empire and the emirate of ʿAmr of Melitene, the Paulicians joined ʿAmr's Arabs in occasional raids on the Armeniac Theme. But theirs was a minor power. In 856, provoked by a raid, Petronas plundered the Emirate of Melitene as far as Amida in northern Mesopotamia and returned by way of Tephrice. Though he probably captured no towns and certainly did not end Arab or Paulician raiding, Petronas took many captives and penetrated farther into Arab territory than any Byzantine commander since the seventh century.

After Michael expelled his mother from the palace and confined her to a convent in 857, the sober patriarch Ignatius found himself out of place at Michael's rollicking court. In 858 Ignatius denied Bardas communion for seducing his own son's widow, an act that church law counted as incest. The patriarch also refused the emperor's request to tonsure Theodora against her will. At this the emperor forced Ignatius to abdicate. To replace him, Bardas selected the protoasecretis Photius. A layman when he was chosen, Photius had a reputation for vast learning in both secular and religious subjects. He was an enemy of Ignatius, whose ignorance he had ridiculed, and a friend of Gregory Asbestas, whom Ignatius had deposed as bishop of Syracuse. In pointed repudiation of Ignatius, Photius had Gregory Asbestas consecrate him patriarch.

Having disposed of their opponents, Bardas and Michael made another raid on the Emirate of Melitene in 859, and sent a fleet that raided the Egyptian coast. The next year ʿAlī of Tarsus invaded Cappadocia, and Michael set out against him. But the emperor had to turn back when a band of Rus' attacked Constantinople, and though a storm forced the Rus' to withdraw the Arabs took advantage of his distraction.[7] Ships from Crete raided the Cyclades and Peloponnesus, and the fleet of Tarsus surprised and sacked Attalia, headquarters of the Cibyrrhaeot Theme. By land ʿAlī of Tarsus, ʿAmr of Melitene, and ʿAmr's Paulician ally Carbeas all made raids, with ʿAmr advancing all the way to the Black Sea port of Sinope. Their raiding seems finally to have induced Michael's government to create a new Theme of Colonia in the weak spot on the border opposite Tephrice and Melitene.[8]

Realizing that Photius's appointment as patriarch had been somewhat irregular, Bardas and Michael requested and received legates from Pope Nicholas to gain his recognition. Though the legates arrived and recognized Photius at a council in 861, the pope decided they had exceeded their authority, and the question remained undecided. The influence of

Bardas, who in 862 won the rank of Caesar, was enough to keep Photius in office; but relations between pope and patriarch turned unfriendly. To exacerbate them further, in 862 the prince of Moravia, a new Slavic state that lay northwest of Bulgaria, asked for Byzantine missionaries to replace the Frankish mission he already had. When the pope declared Photius's consecration invalid the next year, Photius sent Moravia a mission headed by two brothers, Constantine, later known as Cyril, and Methodius. Moravia therefore became a missionary battleground between the eastern and western churches.

That summer an Arab army ordered by the caliph al-Mustaʿīn and accompanied by ʿAmr of Melitene plundered Cappadocia. When the main expedition turned back, ʿAmr continued the raid with his own forces. The emperor arrived with an army and fought a drawn battle with ʿAmr north of Nazianzus, but failed to stop him from reaching and sacking Amisus on the Black Sea. Near there, however, a large force under Petronas surrounded and killed ʿAmr and most of his men. Then the army of Charsianum caught and killed most of the rest of ʿAmr's army, including his son.[9] Next the Byzantines invaded Arab Armenia, where ʿAlī the Armenian had recently been transferred from Tarsus, and killed ʿAlī as well. The Paulician leader Carbeas also lost his life, probably in one of these battles. In a single summer's campaign, the Byzantines had eliminated their three most formidable enemies in the East. Michael rewarded Petronas with the title of magister, and upgraded Charsianum from a cleisura to a theme.

Meanwhile Byzantium extended its influence into Moravia, where the missionaries Constantine-Cyril and Methodius arrived in fall 863. As natives of Thessalonica, they had long known the language spoken by the Slavs just north of their city. Before his departure Constantine-Cyril, an able scholar and probably a student of Photius, apparently invented the first Slavonic alphabet (later known as Glagolitic) and began preparing Slavonic translations of liturgical texts. Introducing a Slavonic liturgy instead of the Latin Mass, Constantine-Cyril and Methodius replaced Frankish clergy as the heads of the Moravian church.

The following year Bardas and Michael began an apparently unprovoked land and sea campaign against the Bulgars. The expedition may have retaken nothing more than Mesembria, but it impressed the Bulgar khan Boris.[10] He concluded an alliance with the Byzantines and accepted his own Byzantine missionaries. By 865 Boris himself received baptism under the name of Michael, taking the emperor as his godfather. When some pagan boyars rebelled against him, Boris-Michael captured and executed them. In return the Byzantines evidently allowed him to annex some Slavic territory between Bulgaria and the empire, since friendly Christian states seemed to need no buffer between them. Within three years, the Byzantines had joined both Moravia and Bulgaria to the Byzantine church and the Byzantine influence that went with it. The pagan Bulgars and the Slavs they ruled gradually became the Christian, Slavic-speaking people we may now call the Bulgarians.

Though Bardas had governed capably for a decade, he never gained full control over his nephew Michael III. The irresponsible and extravagant emperor spent his time with athletes and drinking companions, and his favorite was the affable but cunning Basil the Macedonian. When Bardas had the emperor dismiss his grand chamberlain, Michael bestowed the post on Basil.[11] Then, early in 866, Michael apparently discovered that his mistress of long standing, Eudocia Ingerina, was pregnant. Rather than divorce his neglected wife or let his child be born out of wedlock, the emperor had Basil divorce his own wife and marry Eudocia. This was a marriage in name only, since Eudocia continued to be the emperor's mistress, and Basil was assigned a mistress of his own, the emperor's eldest sister Thecla. Michael seems also to have wanted his child by Eudocia to be his heir instead of Bardas, who as Caesar was next in line for the throne.[12]

In the spring of 866 Bardas planned a sea campaign to retake Crete, the base for Arab piracy in the Aegean. His expeditionary force, including Michael and Basil as well as Bardas, assembled at a camp near Miletus in the Thracesian Theme. Instead of embarking for Crete, however, the emperor had Basil kill Bardas, alleging that Bardas had been plotting himself. Returning to the capital, Michael then adopted Basil and made him junior emperor, though Basil was almost thirty years his senior. Eudocia's child proved to be male, and received the imperial name Leo. While Michael celebrated the birth of his natural son and adoptive grandson with chariot races, he pointedly warned Basil not to presume upon his position.

Without Bardas, and with Basil far from secure in his place, the empire's government drifted. The schism with the papacy went on. When Photius refused to appoint a separate patriarch for the Bulgarian church, the Bulgarian khan Boris-Michael turned to the pope and received Frankish missionaries from him. In Moravia Constantine-Cyril and Methodius sided with the papacy against the patriarch Photius. The Paulicians

106. Michael III the Drunkard (r. 842–67) and (right) Michael's murderer and successor Basil I the Macedonian (r. 867–86). Miniatures from the Modena Zonaras. (Photos: Biblioteca Estense, Modena)

began raiding Anatolia under their new leader Chrysocheir, nephew and son-in-law of the late Carbeas. The Cretan Arabs raided throughout the Aegean Sea, and the Sicilian Arabs terrorized not only the remnants of Byzantine Sicily and Calabria but even Dalmatia, where they put Ragusa under siege in 866. Since Michael was running huge budgetary deficits, more than half of which went to his favorites, by 867 he had to melt down the gold ornaments of the palace to meet his army payroll.[13]

In frustration over Bulgaria's defection to the papacy, Photius held a council in late summer that declared Pope Nicholas deposed on the ground that various western church practices of long standing were heretical. These included fasting on Saturdays, using unleavened bread in the Eucharist, and excluding married men from the priesthood. Photius particularly condemned the *filioque*, a phrase in the Latin form of the Nicene Creed specifying that the Holy Spirit had proceeded from the Son as well as the Father. Thus the patriarch attacked the whole western church. He also raised a difference that had no real theological consequences but was almost impossible to resolve, because no scriptural passage says anything directly relevant to the origin of the Holy Spirit.[14]

Within a month of this council, Basil the Macedonian had Michael murdered while the emperor was, as often, in his cups. Although Michael's reign had seen the empire make some major advances, most of the credit belonged to Theodora and Theoctistus until 855, and afterward to Bardas and Petronas. Aside from leading an occasional army, Michael's main acts had been to squander money and to approve the murders of Theoctistus and Bardas. By first favoring and promoting Basil and then threatening him, Michael helped provoke his own murder.

BASIL'S VICTORIES

Since Basil the Macedonian had already been crowned junior emperor, he automatically became sole ruler on Michael's death. Though of Armenian stock, Basil was called the Macedonian because he had been born in the Theme of Macedonia, in late 811.[15] He and his parents, who seem to have been prosperous peasants, were carried off by the Bulgar khan Krum in 813. Basil therefore grew up in Bulgaria, from which he only escaped in 836 with the other Byzantine refugees whom Theophilus returned to Thrace. Basil later went to Constantinople and built a career on his brawn and conviviality. A relative of the empress Theodora hired Basil as a groom and introduced him to Michael III, who made him head of the imperial stables. From this post Basil rose to be grand chamberlain, coemperor, and finally emperor at age fifty-five.

Basil's talent for scheming turned out to be useful in ruling, and as emperor he tried to overcome his lowly origins and tortuous rise to power. But that rise left him married to Michael III's former mistress Eudocia Ingerina, whose two sons, Leo and Stephen, were almost certainly Michael's. Basil chose not to pursue his valid but embarrassing case for divorcing Eudocia. His heir was in any case his eldest son Constantine, whose mother was evidently Basil's first wife. Basil crowned Constantine junior emperor, but he never liked Leo, and he had Stephen castrated and dedicated to the Church.

Basil moved promptly to settle the empire's unprofitable quarrel with the papacy, deposing and exiling the patriarch Photius and repudiating Photius's recent council condemning the pope. After reinstating Photius's predecessor Ignatius, Basil asked the new pope Hadrian II to send legates for a council to reunite the eastern and western churches. The emperor nonetheless recognized Photius's ordinations to avoid upheaval among the Byzantine clergy.

Finding that Michael III had left an utterly inadequate gold reserve of less than a hundred thousand nomismata, Basil soon restored the government's solvency. He paid his accessional donatives from his own fortune and that of his wife Eudocia, which Michael had presumably given them from the treasury in the first place. By demanding back half of Michael's recorded gifts to other favorites, Basil raised more than 4.3 million nomismata, well over a year's revenue. Thereafter he spent prudently, and had no further fiscal difficulties.

Although Chrysocheir and his Paulicians were now raiding as far as the outskirts of Nicomedia, Nicaea, and Ephesus, Basil gave priority to saving the empire's possessions in Dalmatia and Sicily from the Arabs. Early in 868 he sent two fleets with reinforcements, one to beleaguered Syracuse and the other to besieged Ragusa. The second fleet frightened off the Arabs before it arrived, and its main task during a stay of a year at Ragusa was probably to set up a Theme of Dalmatia; this theme, even if it lacked a regular garrison, was a sort of pledge to defend the region.[16] When the other fleet landed in Sicily, however, the local Arabs defeated it disastrously. Basil reacted by making an anti-Arab alliance with the Frankish emperor Louis II and Pope Hadrian, sending his fleet from Dalmatia to help them besiege Arab-held Bari. But quarreling between Byzantines and Franks hampered the siege, and the Byzantines abandoned it in 869.

Photius's schism with the Papacy had done some harm to the Byzantine church. Pope Hadrian gained jurisdiction over both Bulgaria and Moravia when he made Methodius archbishop of Moravia after Constantine-Cyril's death at Rome. The pope even demanded that the eastern church anathematize Photius and his council and repudiate all his ordinations. Basil and his bishops reluctantly agreed to these terms at a council in late 869, but they won a more important point. While the council still sat in early 870, Boris-Michael asked it whether Bulgaria should be subject to Rome or to Constantinople. With a majority of Byzantine bishops, the council returned the Bulgarian church to the Byzantine patriarchate. The Serbs also requested Byzantine missionaries and became subject to Constantinople.[17] The pope protested the council's decision, and without renewing the schism remained unfriendly to the empire.

Basil's alliance with the emperor Louis II lapsed as well, leaving Byzantium dangerously exposed in the West. The Sicilian Arabs conquered Malta in 870, and when Louis drove the Arabs from Byzantine Calabria he claimed it as his own. These reverses seem to have convinced Basil that he needed a stronger navy. He apparently recruited four thousand professional marines with their own military lands to serve in the Imperial Fleet, which earlier seems to have carried only ordinary troops from the themes and tagmata. The marines were to form a powerful naval force at Constantinople that could be used in both West and East.[18]

After Chrysocheir's Paulicians rebuffed an offer of peace in 870, the emperor marched against them the next spring, but they defeated and almost captured him. The next year Chrysocheir raided up to Ancyra. Unwilling to risk leading another Paulician campaign in person, Basil sent his son-in-law Christopher, domestic of the Scholae.[19] Christopher dispatched troops from the Armeniacs and Charsianum who caught up with Chrysocheir near Dazimon. They put the Paulician leader to flight, pursued him almost to Sebastea, and finally killed him after one of his own men had betrayed him. Chrysocheir's head was brought to Basil in Constantinopie.[20]

Although some Paulicians remained ensconced in their stronghold of Tephrice, they and their Arab allies were now on the defensive. The emperor led an army east in 873, hoping to take Melitene. The Arab city of Taranta surrendered before he arrived, and he sent a detachment south that sacked Sozopetra and Samosata before returning. Then he put Melitene under siege, but the Arabs defeated him and forced him to withdraw. Basil made the best of his retreat by marching through the territory of the Paulicians and destroying several forts.

The upstart emperor used these modest exploits to advertise himself. He celebrated a triumph at Constantinople for his sack of the Paulician forts and his subordinates' raids on the Arabs. He proclaimed the conversion of the empire's Jews, perhaps as a thank offering for his victories.[21] He was particularly gratified to discover that the former patriarch Photius had prepared a genealogy showing that the emperor's ancestors, far from being peasants as everyone had thought, were Arsacid kings of Armenia. Recalled from exile and restored to favor at court, Photius became tutor to the four sons of Basil and Eudocia.

By this time the strengthened Imperial Fleet was ready. About 873, when the Arabs of Crete raided to the end of the Aegean, the fleet sailed from the capital under its commander, the drungary Nicetas Oöryphas, and routed the raiders off Cardia. A year later, when the Cretan Arabs plundered the western Peloponnesus, Oöryphas sailed from Constantinople once more, had his men drag their ships across the Corinthian isthmus, and defeated the Arabs in the Gulf of Corinth. Next, apparently in 875 and with the help of the Imperial Fleet, the Byzantines conquered Cyprus. Ending the old agreement sharing the island with the Arabs, Basil made Cyprus a theme.[22] In 876, when the people of Bari appealed for aid against the Arabs after the death of Louis II, the Byzantines occupied the city and evidently added it to the Theme of Cephalonia.[23] The Imperial Fleet may have contributed to this fourth naval victory as well.

In 877, however, when Syracuse was blockaded by the Arabs and needed reinforcement, the emperor kept the fleet busy transporting marble for a splendid church to celebrate his reign. An imposing five-domed structure next to the palace, it was known as the New Church, and was dedicated to Christ and four saints whom Basil considered his patrons. Meanwhile the aged patriarch Ignatius died, and the emperor replaced him with the former patriarch Photius, who won over most of the Byzantine church and avoided a new schism with the disapproving pope John VIII.

The next spring Basil finally sent ships to Syracuse, but too late. Before they arrived, the Arabs stormed the city, the main Byzantine stronghold on Sicily. Though the Byzantines still held a scrap of the Sicilian coast around Tauromenium, most of the island seemed to be gone for good, because the empire's growing power was very difficult to project as far away as Sicily. The loss of Syracuse was doubly humiliating for Basil because it could probably have been saved by diverting the Imperial Fleet from its construction work.

In the East the Byzantines kept their advantage over the Arabs. The emperor helped restore his prestige by leading an army that pillaged the region of Melitene.[24] When the Arabs of Tarsus tried to raid Cappadocia, local Byzantine troops fell upon them near Podandus and wiped them out. Early in 879 the Byzantines pursued this victory by invading the Emirate of Tarsus and defeating the Arabs outside Adana. That summer Basil, accompanied by his son Constantine, led another army into Arab territory. They plundered Germanicea and Adata and apparently sent troops that raided into northern Mesopotamia. The emperor seems also to have sent a detachment under his son-in-law Christopher that at last took Tephrice, destroying what remained of the Paulician state. On returning to the capital Basil and his son celebrated a triumph warranted by their generals' achievements, if not by their own.[25]

Just after this triumph, however, Constantine suddenly died. His father was distraught, especially because the heir to the throne was now Leo,

107. View of the walls of the Paulician stronghold of Tephrice (above the modern town of Divriği). (Photo: Warren Treadgold)

evidently a son of Michael III. Next in line was Basil's real son Alexander, whom the emperor crowned; but Leo had been crowned already and could not easily be removed, and Basil's attachment to Constantine had been deep. In his grief the emperor turned to the patriarch Photius, who declared the dead prince a saint and began building a monastery dedicated to him. The bishop of Euchaïta Theodore Santabarenus, a protégé of Photius, is said to have comforted Basil by purporting to conjure up Constantine's ghost.

Late in 879 and early the next year, Photius held a council in Constantinople to settle the differences between the eastern and western churches. Pope John had offered to recognize Photius as patriarch if he apologized for his previous usurpation and surrendered jurisdiction over Bulgaria. After Photius deleted these conditions from the Greek translation of John's letter, the council recognized Photius and his ordinations. The pope was displeased, but no schism resulted. For the first time, Photius had won acceptance as patriarch without serious dissent.

The papacy and Byzantium could ill afford a quarrel while the Sicilian Arabs were on the attack. After taking Syracuse, the Arabs made further raids on southern Italy, the Peloponnesus, and the Ionian islands. In 880 Basil sent the Imperial Fleet against them under its drungary Nasar, who destroyed or captured nearly all the raiders' ships near Methone. After sailing around Sicily, Nasar landed at Rhegium, joined troops sent from as far away as Thrace and Macedonia, and drove the Arabs out of several towns in Calabria. The army went on to capture Tarentum from the Arabs.

In spring 882 the emperor led another expedition against Melitene, which he had long wanted to take. But he was driven out by Arab troops from Germanicea and Adata. An Arab attack on Cyprus forced Basil to give up his theme there, restoring the previous division of sovereignty over the island. In compensation the emperor seems to have created a new Theme of Samos from part of the Theme of the Aegean Sea.[26] Though the balance of military power had definitely been shifting in the Byzantines' favor, their advantage over the Arabs was still precarious.

Nor were the emperor's family troubles resolved. When Basil's heir and supposed son Leo turned sixteen in 882, his mother Eudocia held the usual bride show for him. She chose a saintly relative of hers, Theophano, whom the young emperor detested. With no love for Leo, Basil had no hesitation in forcing him to marry Theophano. Soon Eudocia died, and her death and Leo's unhappy marriage increased the hostility between Basil and his heir. When Theophano complained about Leo's mistress Zoë Zaützina, Basil thrashed Leo and married Zoë to someone else.[27] A year later Photius's ally Theodore Santabarenus accused Leo of plotting to kill the emperor. Basil blinded or exiled Leo's alleged confederates, confined the prince to the palace, and would have blinded him had he not been dissuaded by Photius and Stylianus Zaützes, the father of Leo's mistress. The facts are inevitably obscure, but given that Leo could expect to succeed the aging emperor before long, he had less reason to plot than Basil had to fabricate a charge against him.

Among those dismissed for plotting with Leo was the domestic of the Scholae Andrew, but he had to be reinstated after his successor was killed attacking the Arabs of Tarsus.[28] Luckily for Basil, the Arabs were too badly divided to exploit their victory. The emperor won some valuable support in the East by making an alliance with the new King of Armenia Ashot the Great, after the caliph let the Armenians restore their monarchy in 884.[29] The next year the emperor felt able to shift a large force from the Anatolian themes to Italy under the capable general Nicephorus Phocas, who reconquered several Calabrian towns.

Basil also undertook an ambitious revision of the empire's laws. The first result was the *Eisagōgē* ("Introduction"), a summary of Justinian's *Corpus* with additions probably by Photius. The *Eisagōgē* was meant not only to replace Leo III's *Ecloga* by restoring some earlier statutes, but also to introduce a much more comprehensive version of Justinian's laws that Basil was planning. The emperor promulgated the *Eisagōgē* about 886.[30] By that time his researchers had already prepared Basil's Greek version of Justinian's *Corpus*, which was almost ready to be promulgated.[31]

At age seventy-four, however, Basil was courting disaster by keeping Leo imprisoned but not disinherited. In spring 886 the emperor discovered and punished a conspiracy by the domestic of the Hicanati John Curcuas and many other officials, in which Leo was not implicated. Since the prince could scarcely be disinherited three years after his alleged offense, Basil reluctantly granted his advisers' wish that Leo be released and rehabilitated. A month later, Basil was dead. According to the official story, he was injured by a giant stag while hunting with Leo's friend Zaützes and some other dignitaries. Yet the details given were wildly improbable, and the dying emperor claimed an attempt had been made on his life. This time the evidence points to a plot on behalf of Leo, who had little enough reason to like or trust Basil.

At Basil's death the empire was militarily and financially stronger than he had found it. It was a bit bigger, after several conquests in southern Italy and on the eastern frontier, and the strengthened Imperial Fleet had made its possessions more secure. Of the major problems Basil had inherited, he virtually disposed of two, the Paulicians and the Photian Schism; he also held off the Sicilian and Cretan Arabs, except for losing Syracuse. He extended Byzantine influence over Bulgaria and Armenia, and intimidated the Arabs of the declining caliphate. Basil had mastered the government despite a humble background and a weak claim to the throne, and if he had managed his family less well, it was an almost hopeless tangle.

LEO VI'S FRUSTRATIONS

After so many vicissitudes, Leo VI succeeded Basil in 886, shortly before his twentieth birthday. His misfortunes had left him with an abiding hatred of Basil's friends and a determination to defend his own interests. Sensitive and cultivated, Leo liked leisure and women, though not the wife Basil had imposed on him. At first he entrusted most of the business of governing to advisers, above all Stylianus Zaützes, his mistress's father,

108. Leo VI the Wise (r. 886–912). Gold nomisma, shown 2.4 times actual size, with the Virgin on the reverse. (Photo: Courtesy of the Arthur M. Sackler Museum, Harvard University Art Museums, Whittemore Collection)

whom Leo made a magister and the postal logothete. Yet Leo was a competent and responsible ruler, despite some reluctance to assert himself because of his youth.

As Basil had prescribed, Leo gave his brother Alexander the formal status of a colleague, but since the brothers disliked each other Alexander had no influence. Leo seems to have been sure that his father was Michael III; one of his first acts as emperor was to have Michael reburied among the imperial tombs in the Church of the Holy Apostles. Leo appointed his brother Stephen patriarch instead of Basil's ally Photius, whom he dismissed. In 887 Zaützes had Photius exiled and Theodore Santabarenus blinded for their part in Basil's imprisonment of Leo. The emperor apparently recalled Nicephorus Phocas from Italy, perhaps because the general had been Basil's choice. After Phocas's departure the Lombards of Benevento seized Bari with Arab help, but the Byzantines soon recovered it.

Notwithstanding his hatred of Basil and Photius, Leo continued their codification of the laws. Taking over what Photius had prepared, Zaützes supervised work on a revised Greek version of Justinian's *Corpus*. Based mostly on earlier translations and commentaries, it included the *Code*, *Digest*, *Institutes*, and *Novels*. This massive compilation, omitting portions considered obsolete and rearranging the rest into sixty books, was promulgated in 888 and became known as the *Basilica*, the Imperial Code. Zaützes supplemented the *Basilica* with a number of novels, new laws occasioned by changes that had occurred since the sixth century. Leo thus provided the empire with a far more complete body of law than the summaries in the *Ecloga* and *Eisagōgē*.

In 891 the emperor sent an army to southern Italy under Symbaticius, strategus of the combined themes of Macedonia, Thrace, and Cephalonia and Longobardia. As the name Longobardia suggests, Symbaticius was to use his themes to conquer Lombard territory. After a short siege he captured the troublesome Lombard city of Benevento, annexed it, and made it his headquarters. But while much of the Byzantine fleet was in Italy, the Arabs of Tarsus raided across the border and made a sea raid on the Cibyrrhaeot Theme. The Cretan Arabs raided the coasts of the Peloponnesus and the Aegean islands, and about 892 plundered Samos and captured its strategus.

Meanwhile Boris-Michael of Bulgaria had retired to a monastery, abdicating in favor of his eldest son Vladimir. But Vladimir showed hostility to the empire, making an alliance with the Franks, tolerating the old pagan religion of the Bulgars, and persecuting his country's Byzantine clergy. Boris-Michael put an end to this flirtation with paganism in 893 by leaving his monastery and deposing and blinding his son. The old khan summoned a council of boyars that settled the succession on his third son Symeon, himself a former monk. Yet Symeon, though a Christian, was hardly pro-Byzantine. He favored a native Bulgarian clergy, replaced Greek with Slavonic as the official language of the Bulgarian church and state, and regarded the empire with suspicion.

Leo's chief minister Zaützes, whose administrative talents had won him the exalted new title of basileopator, was much more interested in domestic than in foreign affairs.[32] In 894 he unwisely persuaded Leo to make the empire's trade with Bulgaria a monopoly controlled by Zaützes' friends in Thessalonica. Symeon protested against this scheme, and after receiving no satisfaction invaded the Theme of Macedonia. The emperor sent a sizable army against him, but Symeon routed it, killing its commander and many officers. This was the first Bulgarian victory over the Byzantines in eighty years.

Since the Anatolian themes were fending off raids by the Arabs of Tarsus, the emperor sent an ambassador to the Magyars, a people of Finnish origin who bordered Bulgaria on the east, to propose a joint attack on Symeon. The Magyars agreed. Making a truce with Tarsus, in 895 Leo readied an army under Nicephorus Phocas, now domestic of the Scholae, to invade Bulgaria by land. The Imperial Fleet was to ferry a Magyar army across the lower Danube. Leo sent an embassy to offer Symeon peace, but Symeon jailed the ambassador. Phocas therefore made his invasion, and when Symeon marched against him the Imperial Fleet landed the Magyars in the Dobrudja. Symeon had to take refuge in Dristra on the Danube while the Magyars plundered as far as Preslav, where Symeon had transferred the Bulgarian capital from Pliska. On the Magyars' return they sold their Bulgarian captives to the Byzantines. Symeon sued for peace.

The emperor was eager to accept, being distracted by an Arab invasion of Armenia and the loss of Benevento to the Franks of Spoleto. He withdrew his forces and sent the noted scholar Leo Choerosphactes to make terms with Symeon. Yet as soon as Symeon found himself free from invaders, he imprisoned Choerosphactes. Next the khan persuaded the Pechenegs, a Turkish people to the northeast, to join him in driving the Magyars from their lands. Fleeing through the Bulgarian territory north of the Danube, where the Bulgarians seem to have had few troops or settlers, the Magyars migrated to the middle Danube plain. There they set about conquering Moravia and ceased to trouble the Bulgarians.

Symeon released Choerosphactes but insisted that Leo return all Bulgarian captives as a condition for negotiations. No sooner had the emperor returned them than the khan jailed Choerosphactes again. The emperor assembled his army, but on Zaützes' advice he replaced Nicephorus Phocas as domestic of the Scholae with the less experienced Leo Catacalon.[33] In the spring of 896 Symeon invaded the Theme of Macedonia once more, met Catacalon in battle at Bulgarophygon, and trounced him. Catacalon escaped with difficulty; many other Byzantines were killed or captured, and Symeon devastated the Thracian countryside and took many more prisoners.

In detention the long-suffering ambassador Leo Choerosphactes negotiated an acceptable if inglorious treaty. Symeon returned some 120,000 soldiers and civilians in exchange for an annual tribute, and retained the outposts he had overrun along the frontier. These losses led Leo to reorganize the border themes. He created a Theme of the Strymon from the eastern part of the Theme of Macedonia, and a Theme of Nicopolis from the part of the Theme of Cephalonia on the Greek mainland.

The Bulgarian war left the empire in some disarray. The Arab governor of Azerbaijan took Kars, capital of the empire's Armenian allies, who had to make an unfavorable peace. The garrison of Cherson briefly rebelled, and killed its strategus.[34] In 897 the Arabs of Tarsus sacked the

109. The empress Saint Theophano, first wife of Leo VI. Miniature from the *Menologium of Basil II*. (Photo: Biblioteca Apostolica Vaticana)

headquarters of the Theme of Cappadocia at Corum. Already unsuccessful, Zaützes was further discredited when his son and other relatives made a failed attempt to kill Leo.

Suddenly, however, the empress Theophano died, freeing the emperor to marry his mistress Zoë, Zaützes' now widowed daughter. Rumor had it that both Theophano and Zoë's husband had been poisoned, and their deaths certainly came at a convenient time for the Zaützes family.[35] Leo married Zoë in 898, as soon as he decently could. While Zaützes regained his influence, Byzantine military weakness lingered. The Arabs of Tarsus defeated a Byzantine fleet, destroying many ships and killing some three thousand men, then raided the Cibyrrhaeot Theme by land.

Despite his marriage, the emperor became impatient with his powerful minister, and punished two of Zaützes' cronies for corruption. In 899, both Zaützes and empress Zoë Zaützina died. When Zaützes' relatives plotted again to kill Leo, they were betrayed by one of their servants, the Arab eunuch Samonas, and Leo tonsured or exiled the lot of them. On the whole Zaützes and his family and friends had neglected foreign affairs and mishandled domestic administration. From the time of their fall Leo took a more active role in governing, and governed better than they had.

LEO VI'S EXPANSION

In spring 900 the emperor sent an army into the Emirate of Tarsus that advanced to Tarsus itself, overwhelmed its army, and captured its emir. Then the caliph al-Mu'tadid put down a rebellion at Tarsus and scuttled the emirate's navy. While the Arabs suffered defeats and weakened themselves, Leo persuaded an Armenian princely family to enter his service and to cede their principality to the empire. The emperor made it into the new Theme of Mesopotamia.[36] This was the first eastern acquisition of his reign, and seems to have given him an appetite for more. Leo began to look for ways to expand at the Arabs' expense.

The widowed emperor still lacked a male heir, apart from his hated brother Alexander. Though ordinarily the Church condemned third marriages, the patriarch Anthony allowed Leo to marry a third empress, the celebrated beauty Eudocia Baeana. This exasperated Alexander, who vainly plotted against his brother. But Eudocia died in 901, while giving birth to a son who also died. Since the new patriarch Nicholas Mysticus declared that a fourth marriage would be worse than fornication, Leo took a mistress. She was Zoë Carbonopsina ("Coal-Eyes"), whom he saw no reason to marry unless she produced a son.

Early in 901, a Syrian fleet under the apostate Christian Damian of Tarsus sacked the port of Demetrias in Greece, and the Sicilian Arabs sacked Rhegium, driving off a fleet sent from Constantinople.[37] Leo nonetheless sent two expeditions to the East that year. The first, led by the Armeniacs' strategus Leo Lalacon, expelled the Arabs from part of western Armenia. The second landed on the coast of the Emirate of Tarsus and ravaged almost to the Euphrates. In 902 the emperor sent the domestic of the Scholae Leo Catacalon to western Armenia, where he sacked Theodosiopolis.[38] These victories outweighed the Arab conquest of Tauromenium, which the Imperial Fleet might have prevented had it not been carrying stone again to build a church in the capital.

These eastern campaigns damaged Arab defenses all along the border and allowed Leo to annex much of the frontier zone. There he created the new Cleisura of Sebastea, and shifted the boundaries of other themes.[39] In making his changes, Leo never divided the banda of two hundred men each, but he ceased to use drungi of a thousand men, creating more turmae instead. Within each bandum he increased the number of cavalry from forty to fifty, raising the number of thematic cavalry from a fifth to a quarter. Thus some five thousand infantry became cavalry, and about six thousand new soldiers were enlisted, most of them probably Armenian refugees. With ample lands available for the new soldiers and cavalry, Leo strengthened his army at moderate expense.[40]

Although Leo's reign was prospering, the fact that he could only have a legitimate son by breaking canon law estranged him from the patriarch Nicholas and encouraged conspiracies. An attempt to assassinate Leo in church almost succeeded in 903. The would-be assassin died under torture without implicating anyone, but the emperor suspected his patriarch. The next year Samonas, Leo's loyal agent since he had revealed the second plot of the Zaützes family, was caught trying to flee to the Arabs under obscure circumstances, though Leo soon pardoned him.[41]

That spring Leo sent a large expedition against Adata, which might well have taken the city had it not turned back when an Arab fleet from Syria threatened Constantinople. This fleet, under the former Christian Leo of Tripoli, chased off the Imperial Fleet, sacked the customs station at Abydus, and reached the Sea of Marmara. The drungary of the fleet Himerius forced Leo of Tripoli to retreat, but while Himerius cautiously pursued, the enemy made for Thessalonica, the empire's second city. The Arab admiral surprised the Thessalonians as they were frantically repairing their sea walls. Himerius and his fleet found no way to intervene, and an appeal to the neighboring Slavs produced few volunteers. After a brief siege, the Arabs stormed the sea walls, looted Thessalonica for the first time, and killed or captured about half its people. The Arabs returned to Tripoli by way of Crete and Cyprus with many thousands of captives, who were sent to Tarsus to be exchanged for Muslims captured by the Byzantines.[42]

Throughout this devastating raid, no major Byzantine army or navy fought the Arabs. Probably to retaliate for the sack of Thessalonica, and to take Arab captives to exchange for the Thessalonians, Leo's general Andronicus Ducas raided the region of Germanicea and defeated the Arabs of Tarsus late in 904. The next year, after lengthy negotiations, the Arabs agreed to an exchange of prisoners. The sack of Thessalonica showed no real Byzantine weakness, merely slowness to react to a surprise attack.

Meanwhile the emperor's mistress Zoë Carbonopsina gave birth to a son, named Constantine. To become heir to the throne, Constantine had to be legitimized, by Leo's taking Zoë as his fourth wife. The prospect that Leo would do so apparently provoked a conspiracy between the patriarch Nicholas, who opposed any fourth marriage, and the success- ful general Andronicus Ducas, who wanted the throne for himself. The emperor had planned that after the exchange of prisoners in Cilicia An- dronicus should join the drungary of the fleet Himerius in attacking the Arabs. But the Byzantines broke off the prisoner exchange, apparently when Samonas discovered and thwarted Ducas's plot. Himerius defeated the Arab fleet without the help of Ducas, who fled with some followers to the Anatolic Theme. One of Ducas's men deserted to the emperor with a letter from the patriarch Nicholas that gave his approval to the conspiracy.

The patriarch's reaction confirms that the letter was genuine. Aware that Leo knew of his treason, Nicholas agreed to baptize Leo's son at the beginning of 906. When Ducas abandoned his rebellion and fled to the Arabs, the emperor ventured to marry Zoë Carbonopsina and crown her Augusta. The patriarch played for time, afraid that Leo would de- pose him as soon as he either granted or refused an indulgence. Leo cleverly appealed to Pope Sergius III, since the western church permit- ted remarriages as often as one was widowed. Leo's expert ambassador Choerosphactes also obtained legates from the eastern patriarchs to make the necessary accommodation for the emperor.

Shortly before the eastern and papal legates arrived with the indul- gences and dispensation in 907, the emperor forced Nicholas to resign, and persuaded the respected Euthymius to become patriarch. Euthymius condoned the fourth marriage, or Tetragamy, but he imposed a long penance on the emperor, defrocked the priest who had celebrated the wedding before it had been dispensed, and refused to proclaim the em- press in church. The patriarch also insisted that Leo should explicitly outlaw fourth marriages for the future, which the emperor did in a revi- sion of the *Eisagōgē* titled the *Prochiron* ("Handbook").[43]

After his marriage, Leo's fortunes began to improve. Though the Rus- sian prince Oleg made a sea raid against Constantinople in 907, Leo bought the Russians off before they did much harm.[44] The next year he crowned his son Constantine emperor and completed the exchange of prisoners with the Arabs that Ducas's rebellion had interrupted three years before. He also pardoned and received back from the caliphate

110. Detail of a tenth-century mosaic, probably of Leo VI (cf. Fig. 108) as a penitent because of his fourth marriage, above the imperial door of Saint Sophia, Constantinople. (Photo: Dumbarton Oaks, Washington, D.C., copyright 1996)

many of Ducas's followers, including Ducas's son Constantine. The emperor appointed Ducas's former confederates to commands on the eastern frontier, making Constantine Ducas strategus of Charsianum and having the Armenian lord Melias conquer land that became the Cleisura of Lycandus, south of Sebastea. Leo also created the new Cleisura of Leontocome ("Leoville"), the town he founded on the site of the Paulician stronghold of Tephrice. These changes gave the empire some excellent Armenian soldiers, more territory, and a strengthened frontier.[45]

Further to avenge the Arab sack of Thessalonica, in 910 Leo sent the drungary of the fleet Himerius to sack the Syrian port of Laodicea. The Byzantines allied themselves with the Christian powers of southern Italy against the Sicilian Arabs, and in 911 Leo appointed a separate strategus of Longobardia to prepare for an offensive. The emperor also launched a more ambitious project, the reconquest of Crete from the Arabs. He mustered the Imperial Fleet, ships and marines from the naval themes, cavalry from the Scholae, Thracesians, and Sebastea, and Armenian and Russian mercenaries, the latter hired under a treaty just made with Prince Oleg.[46]

Since nothing could do more to strengthen Byzantine sea power than the reconquest of Crete, Leo spared no expense. His expeditionary force totaled 119 ships and about forty-three thousand men, and its campaign pay alone amounted to some 239,000 nomismata. It sailed that autumn under the drungary of the fleet Himerius, apparently with the plan of wintering on Crete. But the caliph's admirals Leo of Tripoli and Damian of Tarsus gathered their own fleet and surprised Himerius off Chios, where they defeated him soundly and wrecked his armada.[47] This news must have been a severe blow to the emperor, who fell ill of a disease of the intestines and died in the spring of 912.

Although Leo suffered many reverses, on the whole his reign was a successful one. He sponsored the *Basilica*, the greatest legislative achievement since Justinian I, and other works on law, protocol, and strategy that won him the epithet of the Wise. While he never led an army, he made the empire's first major territorial gains in the East since the seventh century, and expanded and improved the army for the first time since the military reforms of Theophilus. Despite much bad luck, Leo even left a more or less legitimate son, whom on his deathbed he anxiously commended to his hostile brother Alexander.

CHAPTER FIFTEEN

The Gains Secured, 912–963

Alexander became senior emperor and effective ruler, since his nephew Constantine was only six. At age forty-one, Alexander might have expected to reign for years. But he was ill, perhaps with testicular cancer, and childless. Estranged from his wife, he cared mostly for hunting, drinking, and his mistress.[1] Above all he resented his long exclusion from power under his brother Leo VI. Probably fearing that he had only a short time to live, Alexander made some major changes on his accession. He deposed the patriarch Euthymius and restored Nicholas Mysticus, who had scores of his own to settle.[2]

The emperor allowed Nicholas to hold a council that deposed and exiled Euthymius and his many supporters in the hierarchy. In return the patriarch suggested the emperor refill the treasury, which Leo's Cretan expedition had depleted, by confiscating about a million nomismata from the Euthymian bishops. The bishops frustrated this plan by giving their money to the poor. Despite his scruples over Leo VI's fourth marriage, Nicholas reinstated the priest who had been defrocked by Euthymius for performing it, and allowed Alexander to tonsure his wife and marry his mistress. The emperor expelled Leo's widow Zoë Carbonopsina from the palace, and tonsured the admiral Himerius, who was her cousin.

In 913, when the Bulgarian khan Symeon demanded his yearly tribute under the treaty of 896, Alexander refused it, probably out of false economy. The khan prepared for war, but his preparations lasted longer than the ailing emperor. Since the patriarch wanted to keep his enemy Zoë from returning when the emperor died, he wrote to the domestic

III. Alexander (r. 912–13). Tenth-century mosaic in Saint Sophia, Constantinople. (Photo: Dumbarton Oaks, Washington, D.C., copyright 1996)

of the Scholae Constantine Ducas, who was mustering the tagmata against the Bulgarians, encouraging Ducas to seize power. To Nicholas's surprise, however, on his deathbed Alexander assigned his little nephew a board of seven regents, headed by the patriarch and excluding Zoë.

THE RIVAL REGENTS

Once Nicholas became regent, he had no use for Constantine Ducas, but Ducas's ambition had been aroused. He arrived with a few of his men just three days after Alexander's death. The imperial bodyguards, loyal to the young emperor Constantine VII, backed the patriarch rather than the general. When Ducas tried to storm the palace, he and his son were killed, and Nicholas had their partisans massacred, exiled, or tonsured. Though Zoë had returned to the palace, Nicholas sent her away again, extracting oaths from the leading officials and bishops never to recognize her as empress.

Yet with the death of Ducas the army had lost its commander in chief and its will to fight. The patriarch could do little more than exhort Symeon of Bulgaria not to invade. That summer, as the Arabs raided Anatolia and their governor of Azerbaijan captured King Smbat of Armenia, the khan led his army unopposed up to Constantinople. When he came to the city walls, he began to negotiate with Nicholas. After haughtily claiming the Byzantine throne, Symeon apparently settled for his tribute under the treaty, the betrothal of his daughter to Constantine VII, and his own coronation as emperor of the Bulgarians, not the Romans.[3] These concessions, especially the glorious title of emperor, induced Symeon to return home.

Now Nicholas faced an array of opponents, including critics of his humiliating agreement with Symeon, soldiers outraged at the fate of Constantine Ducas, and partisans of the former patriarch Euthymius and empress Zoë. The regent acted as decisively as he could, sending southern Italy help against the Arabs and forcing Zoë into a convent.[4] In early 914, however, Zoë concocted a plot with her supporters, who included the grand chamberlain Constantine. The empress's men drove Nicholas out of the palace, and she took his place as the principal regent.

Though Zoë also wanted Euthymius to replace Nicholas at the patriarchate, Euthymius declined. After three weeks she accepted Nicholas as patriarch in return for his proclaiming her Augusta and reconciling with Euthymius. Since Zoë was unwilling to confirm either her son's engage-

112. Constantine VII Porphyrogenitus (r. 913–59) and his mother Zoë Carbonopsina, with Christ on the reverse. Gold nomisma, shown twice actual size. (Photo: Dumbarton Oaks, Washington, D.C., copyright 1996)

ment to Symeon's daughter or Symeon's imperial title, the Bulgarian ruler revived his claim to the Byzantine throne. A Byzantine officer betrayed Adrianople to Symeon, but the empress promptly bribed the garrison to hand it back.

Despite the threat from the Bulgarians, Zoë answered an appeal for help by Ashot II of Armenia, who had come to Constantinople after the death of his captive father Smbat. In 915 a Byzantine army defeated Arab troops from Tarsus, Germanicea, and Samosata, took thousands of prisoners, and evidently returned Ashot to Armenia. The cleisurarch of Lycandus, Melias the Armenian, appears to have shown such valor in this campaign that Zoë made his cleisura a theme.[5] Meanwhile the reinforcements that Nicholas had sent to Italy joined their Italian allies to clear the last Arabs from Calabria.

In 916 Symeon raided the themes of Thessalonica and Dyrrhachium. The Arabs of Melitene and Tarsus also raided the eastern frontier, but the next year Zoë made a truce with them and decided to attack Symeon. The strategus of Cherson John Bogas paid the Pechenegs to attack the Bulgarians from the north, while the domestic of the Scholae Leo Phocas, son of Nicephorus Phocas, gathered a great force from the tagmata and themes, including Melias and his Armenians. As Phocas set out by land, the drungary of the fleet Romanus Lecapenus sailed to the mouth of the Danube to ferry the Pechenegs across.

When Bogas brought the Pechenegs to embark, however, he quarreled with Lecapenus. Losing patience, the Pechenegs seem to have begun conquering Bulgaria north of the Danube, and in any case gave no help to Phocas. Symeon attacked Phocas's unsupported army near Anchialus and routed it; many Byzantines died, and Phocas himself barely escaped to Mesembria. Again Symeon marched on Constantinople. Although Phocas reassembled his army and encamped near the city, Symeon made a night attack and defeated him once more.

After these two victories, Symeon would accept nothing less than his daughter's marriage with Constantine VII. The empress still refused. She proposed to Prince Peter of Serbia that he join the Magyars in attacking Bulgaria from the west. On discovering this plan, Symeon turned to invade Serbia, where he captured Peter and replaced him with his brother Paul.[6] Next Symeon seems to have raided northern Greece. Encouraged by the Byzantines' reverses, the Arabs of Tarsus raided the eastern frontier, and the African Arabs sent a fleet that sacked Rhegium.

After all these failures, by early 919 Zoë's regency looked doomed, and at age thirteen Constantine VII was too young to rule. Some sort of coup seemed imminent. The domestic of the Scholae Leo Phocas and his brother-in-law the grand chamberlain Constantine were rumored to be plotting to seize power and depose the young emperor. The emperor's tutor Theodore, in a desperate attempt to protect his charge, sent a letter asking the drungary of the fleet Romanus Lecapenus to help. Though he had not shown much military skill, Romanus was the highest-ranking commander who had not lost to the Bulgarians, if only because they had no navy. Moreover, Romanus's fleet was a handy instrument for controlling Constantinople.

Sensing a threat to the influence of the Phocas family, the grand chamberlain Constantine tried to send Lecapenus's fleet away from the capital. But when he arrived to pay the fleet before its departure, he was seized by Lecapenus, who had not yet taken sides but wanted to stay in the game.[7] With the grand chamberlain in captivity, Theodore had his imperial pupil return the regency to the patriarch Nicholas. No sooner had Nicholas become regent than he deposed Leo Phocas as domestic of the Scholae. In frustration Phocas turned to Romanus Lecapenus.

Professing to be everyone's friend, Lecapenus became the arbiter of this convoluted struggle for power. He sailed to the palace at the invitation of Theodore and took possession. Young Constantine, with his tutor's approval, appointed Lecapenus a magister and the head of the imperial bodyguard. Scarcely a month later, Lecapenus married his daughter Helena to the pubescent emperor and assumed the title of basileopator, while Lecapenus's son Christopher took over the bodyguard. Among the claimants for power, Romanus had chosen himself.

Outmaneuvered, Leo Phocas began a rebellion at nearby Chrysopolis. But Romanus had control over the emperor. Phocas's troops kept deserting to Romanus, until Phocas himself was captured and blinded in Bithynia. Romanus easily thwarted another plot by Phocas's friends. Symeon of Bulgaria, enraged that Romanus and not he had become Constantine's father-in-law, advanced through Thrace to the Hellespont, but captured nothing of importance. In 920 Romanus sent a Serbian pretender, Zacharias, to fight Symeon's ally Paul of Serbia, and though the attack failed it kept Symeon busy for a year.

As the fog of intrigue began to clear, Romanus held a council to end the lingering schism in the Church between partisans of Nicholas and Euthymius. While forbidding fourth marriages and disapproving third marriages, the council recognized Euthymius's indulgence of Leo VI and restored the Euthymian bishops to their sees. Soon after uniting the Church, Romanus had Zoë tonsured once again on a charge of trying to poison him, and a little later exiled Constantine's tutor Theodore on a charge of conspiracy. Suddenly the father-in-law of the emperor had run out of rivals.

Early in the autumn Romanus had his son-in-law appoint him Caesar, and later the same fall he had Constantine and the patriarch Nicholas crown him emperor. Romanus crowned his wife Theodora Augusta at the beginning of 921. Two months later, Romanus gave himself precedence over Constantine VII, who at fifteen would otherwise have been nearly ready to rule. Two months more and Romanus crowned his eldest son Christopher junior emperor, leaving the precedence between Christopher and Constantine ambiguous.[8] Thus the period of uncertainty ended, with Romanus Lecapenus firmly in power.

THE GAINS OF ROMANUS LECAPENUS

Romanus was about fifty in 921, experienced, shrewd, and active. His Armenian family took its name from its home town of Lacape, near Melitene, which when he was born may well have been in Arab territory.[9] His father Theophylact had been a peasant who joined the Byzantine army and gained a place in the imperial bodyguard as a reward for his services to the emperor Basil. Romanus himself made his career in the navy, rose to be strategus of Samos, and after the naval disaster of 911

113. Romanus I Lecapenus (r. 920–44), with a cross on the reverse. Pierced copper pattern for a silver miliaresion, shown twice actual size. (Photo: Trustees of the British Museum)

succeeded Himerius as drungary of the Imperial Fleet. Romanus was so adept at intrigue that he reached the throne without a single murder and without deposing Constantine VII.

Understandably confused by the intricacies of Byzantine politics since 913, some provincials and foreigners failed to see that in Romanus the empire had at last acquired a strong leader. In Italy revolts broke out in both the Theme of Longobardia and the Theme of Sicily and Calabria. The rebels in Calabria assassinated their strategus, and the rebels in Longobardia summoned the Lombard prince of Capua, who killed their strategus and conquered their theme. The Slavs in the Peloponnesus rebelled, and Symeon of Bulgaria marched on Constantinople again.[10]

Not far from the city walls, however, the Byzantine army surprised and defeated Symeon, who decided to raid the towns of Thrace instead. Apparently he then interrupted his campaign at the news that Paul of Serbia had thrown off Bulgarian suzerainty. Symeon released Paul's cousin Zacharias, who had been imprisoned in Bulgaria since his attack on Paul the previous year, and installed him in Serbia despite his recent alliance with Romanus. Meanwhile the strategus of the Peloponnesus brought his rebellious Slavs to heel, the Calabrians gave up their revolt, and the rebels in Longobardia and the prince of Capua began to negotiate their submission to the empire.

By spring 922 Symeon was done with Serbia for the moment and marched on Constantinople once more. Outside the city walls he encountered the tagmata, led by the domestic of the Scholae Pothus Argyrus, and the imperial marines, under the drungary of the fleet Alexius Musele. This time the Bulgarians surprised and defeated the Byzantines. Argyrus fled, and Musele drowned trying to escape. The khan seems to have ravaged the region for two months until the tagmata surprised and sacked his camp. Then he invaded northern Greece, and sent some of his Slav allies to stir up the still restive Peloponnesus.[11]

In place of the vanquished Argyrus, Romanus named a domestic of the Scholae of outstanding ability, his fellow Armenian John Curcuas. The emperor gave priority to ending a revolt in Chaldia, where Curcuas spent 923 rooting the rebels out of their mountain fortresses. In the meantime the Arabs raided Anatolia, and Symeon besieged Adrianople. As food ran out, some of the citizens let Symeon into the city, but he had scarcely established a garrison there when Romanus expelled it. The Byzantines' old enemy Leo of Tripoli raided the Aegean, but the Imperial Fleet defeated him soundly.[12]

Symeon saw that he was making no appreciable progress. He tried to obtain the sea power necessary to threaten Constantinople by means of a treaty with the Fatimid caliph of North Africa; but Romanus captured the Bulgarian ambassadors and came to his own agreement with the Fatimids. In 924 the Bulgarian ruler prepared the largest expedition he could muster against Constantinople, which even if it failed to seize the city might at least force a favorable peace. That summer, while the Arabs raided Anatolia, Symeon advanced on Constantinople, devastating Macedonia and Thrace as he went.

Once the khan reached the city walls he agreed to negotiate. After preliminary talks with some high Byzantine officials, including the patriarch Nicholas, he obtained a carefully arranged interview with the emperor Romanus.[13] If Symeon had ever seriously hoped to become Byzantine emperor, he must have seen his error by now; nor could he hope to marry his daughter to Constantine VII, who had already married the daughter of Romanus. Symeon therefore sulkily accepted a truce in return for an offer of tribute, and marched back to Bulgaria. By the next year his Slav allies left the Peloponnesus, and except for a few forts on the Black Sea the Byzantine frontier was restored.

Gradually peace returned to the empire. Romanus arranged a truce and exchange of prisoners with the Abbasid caliph at Baghdad. The Calabrians made their own truce with a Fatimid army that had been raiding their territory. The powerful patriarch Nicholas died, allowing Romanus to name a nonentity to the patriarchate until his eight-year-old son Theo-phylact, who was intended for it, came of age to assume it. The emperor took as his chief adviser the capable Theophanes the Protovestiarius, probably a eunuch.

Symeon then attacked Zacharias of Serbia, who had resumed his original alliance with Byzantium. Although at first Zacharias defeated Symeon's army and killed its generals, a second Bulgarian expedition forced Zacharias to take refuge in neighboring Croatia and annexed Serbia outright. The khan seems to have celebrated his victory in 926 by taking the title of emperor of the Romans and Bulgarians, and declaring the archbishopric of Bulgaria an independent patriarchate. Next he sent a large army against the Croats. But to his surprise they annihilated it, leaving Bulgaria weakened and humbled.

The emperor took advantage of Symeon's defeat to shift his attention to the Arabs in Armenia. Armenia was not only Romanus's homeland but that of his three leading generals: the domestic of the Scholae John Curcuas, Curcuas's brother Theophilus the Strategus of Chaldia, and Melias the Strategus of Lycandus. By spring 926 the emperor demanded tribute from the regions just beyond his borders. When it was refused, he sent out John Curcuas and Melias, who broke into Melitene and sacked most of it, except for the citadel. By 927 the shaken emir of Meli-tene accepted Byzantine suzerainty and agreed to send troops to fight with the imperial army.[14] The Byzantines pressed on to sack Samosata, and Curcuas advanced all the way to Arab-held Dvin, east of the pro-Byzantine kingdom of Ashot II.

The same year Symeon of Bulgaria died and was succeeded by his young son Peter, whose uncle served as his regent. In spite of all his ex-ploits, Symeon had left Bulgaria depleted of soldiers and surrounded by enemies. He had lost the Bulgarian lands north of the Danube to the Magyars and Pechenegs, and after his death his only important conquest, Serbia, speedily regained its independence. The new Bulgarian govern-ment was weak, and a plague of locusts spread famine through the coun-try.[15] The Bulgarian regency opened negotiations with Byzantium, and Romanus, who had never wanted to fight the Bulgarians, agreed to terms that were flattering for them but inexpensive for him. He appar-ently recognized the Bulgarian patriarchate, married his granddaughter Maria to the emperor Peter, and undertook to pay a modest subsidy, supposedly to support Maria in Byzantine style. In return the Bulgarians freed their many Byzantine captives.

The famine in Bulgaria was the precursor of a famine in Byzantium. While the locusts probably reached Byzantine territory as well, much worse was the terrible winter of 927–28, which brought four months of frost. Many died of the cold, and others starved because their animals and crops had frozen. Romanus built makeshift shelters for the homeless poor of Constantinople, and distributed money to those unable to buy food at the high prices that prevailed. Food shortages must have lasted at least until the next harvest. Many small farmers could feed themselves only by selling their farms to wealthy military, civil, or ecclesiastical officials. Most of the sellers became tenants on their former lands, paying rent to their new landlords.

This process alarmed Romanus, who feared the new owners would contribute less than their fair share of taxes to the village assessments. Any sales of military lands also endangered the system that supported the army. Apparently that very spring, the emperor promulgated an edict specifying that anyone who sold land must first offer it to his relatives and fellow villagers, and in any case not sell it to powerful outsiders.[16] Yet this law must have come after many sales had already been made, and often the eligible purchasers would have been too poor to buy at the prices the sellers needed.

Notwithstanding the famine, Romanus's offensive against the Arabs continued, led by just the sort of military officers who were buying out smallholders. Later in 928 John Curcuas raided the part of Armenia south of the independent kingdom. The town of Chliat surrendered, and many Arabs fled. Melias the Strategus of Lycandus then plotted to have Armenians infiltrate the nominally subject city of Melitene and betray it to him. Though the Meliteneans foiled this stratagem, they soon accepted a Byzantine garrison. Panic spread along the Arab frontier north of Mesopotamia.

After these successes the Byzantine offensive faltered. One reason was probably the famine, which impoverished the ordinary soldiers who had military lands. Italy too was a distraction, since the Sicilian Arabs were raiding and the next year the Lombards of Capua and Salerno occupied much of the Theme of Longobardia. The prospect of a Byzantine conquest of northern Mesopotamia also seems to have galvanized Arab resistance. At all events, when John Curcuas invaded Armenia again in 929, the governor of Azerbaijan defeated him and pursued him back to Byzantine territory. When Melias attacked Samosata the following year, the governor of the Mesopotamian frontier drove him off.

In 931, when the imperial army raided southern Armenia, the Arabs of Tarsus exploited the army's absence to sack Amorium, far inside Anatolia. The Byzantines returned from Armenia to seize Samosata; but just after they took the city, the Arab governor of the Mesopotamian frontier arrived with a large force. Unprepared to defend Samosata and distrustful of their nominal vassals in Melitene, the Byzantines had to abandon both cities. The Arabs' surprisingly successful raid from Tarsus probably led Romanus to make the adjacent Cleisura of Seleucia a theme. During the next year efforts against the Arabs were hampered by two revolts in the Opsician Theme led by a renegade named Basil, who was finally executed.[17]

Amidst these unaccustomed reverses, Romanus's eldest son and heir Christopher died, to his father's great grief. At least in 933, after two undistinguished patriarchs and one long vacancy, Romanus made his son Theophylact patriarch at the age of sixteen. Though Theophylact was an embarrassingly young and worldly prelate, whose main interest was in horses, the corrupt Pope John XI approved his appointment, especially because Romanus asked for papal legates to assist in the consecration. The Byzantine hierarchy, having neither a rival claimant nor strong doctrinal objections, acquiesced.

That summer, evidently after careful preparations, the Byzantines went back on the offensive in the East. They spread panic among the Arabs, methodically conquering or destroying every fort around Arab-held Melitene and Samosata. In spring 934 the domestic of the Scholae John Curcuas led an army that with Melias and his Armenians totaled around fifty thousand men. These put Melitene under a strict siege. Though while this siege occupied the domestic and most of the eastern army a horde of Magyars invaded Thrace through Bulgaria, they were bought off by Romanus's adviser Theophanes the Protovestiarius.

Meanwhile Curcuas and Melias starved the people of Melitene into submission and seized and devastated Samosata. The Byzantines seem to have meant to ruin Samosata without trying to hold it; but Melitene, which had long been a border stronghold of the Arabs, was to become one for the Byzantines. Curcuas allowed only those who were Christians or would convert to Christianity to stay in the city, giving the remaining Muslims safe-conduct into Arab-held territory. By claiming for the crown most of the region of Melitene, the emperor prevented it from becoming the sort of border barony that Leo VI had created toward the end of his reign, and that Melias still held at Lycandus.

114. The walls of Melitene (modern Eski Malatya). (Photo: Irina Andreescu-Treadgold)

By this time the emperor appears to have grown distrustful of over-powerful officers and officials. During the five years since the great famine, they had concentrated much more land in their hands, despite the edict he had issued against them. Romanus promulgated a stricter edict in 934, specifying that lands purchased illegally since 928 must be returned to the sellers without compensation. Even land legally purchased had to be restored in return for the purchase price, minus deductions for income taken from the land since the time of the sale. While this edict surely had some effect, a number of powerful men doubtless managed to defy it, as they had the law of 928.[18]

After the conquest of Melitene, Romanus sent a small expedition to demand that the Lombard prince of Capua leave the Theme of Longobardia, most of which he had held for five years. At first the prince hesitated, unsure whether the emperor could project his growing power as far as Italy. Romanus therefore sent a larger expedition the next year, and to increase the pressure on the Lombards made an alliance with the new Frankish king of Italy, Hugh of Provence. By 936 the prince of Capua decided to evacuate Longobardia.

With Melitene's fall, the family of the Hamdanids became the main power in what remained of the Arab border region. While expanding their control, the Hamdanids fought and defeated the tribe of the Banū Ḥabīb in northern Mesopotamia. Rather than submit to their enemies, by 936 the Banū Ḥabīb migrated to the empire, accepting Christianity and joining the Byzantine army. Since they had twelve thousand cavalry but no infantry, they were hard to fit into the existing thematic structure, and apparently to accommodate them Romanus created five themes of a new kind, consisting entirely of cavalry. These themes formed a continuous chain protecting the most exposed part of the border. Except for the Theme of Melitene, most of the themes' territory was probably conquered by the Banū Ḥabīb for themselves.[19]

In 936 John Curcuas marched again on Samosata. An Arab army was mustered against him by the gifted young Hamdanid general styled Sayf al-Dawlah, or the "Sword of the Dynasty" of the Abbasids. But Sayf's position was not yet secure, and an Arab rebellion forced him to turn back after merely sending supplies to Samosata. Curcuas forced the city to surrender, razed it, and sent its people away under a safe-conduct. Yet the Byzantines were to hear much more from Sayf al-Dawlah, who established himself as governor of the frontier district of Amida. Two years later, Sayf seized the Byzantine fort of Charpete near Melitene. Though John Curcuas, who was in the area with a large army, hurried to drive the Arabs out, Sayf managed to cut off and defeat the Byzantine advance guard, forcing Curcuas to withdraw.

In 939 Romanus, not yet much disturbed by Sayf al-Dawlah, sent an expedition to aid some Sicilian Arabs who had rebelled against their Fatimid masters. The Byzantines also tried to take Theodosiopolis, now an Arab-held salient between the new Theme of Derzene and the Armenian kingdom allied to the empire. As the Byzantine army built a fort opposite the city, the Arab garrison appealed to Sayf al-Dawlah, who gathered an army and set out. Taken by surprise, the Byzantines demolished their fort and withdrew while he was still in southern Armenia. Though Sayf al-Dawlah interrupted his march when he heard the siege had been raised, he went into winter quarters nearby.

The next spring Sayf demanded submission from all the Armenian princes, both the nominal vassals of the caliph and the independent rulers like King Abas, brother and successor of Ashot II. Since Sayf was content with formal gestures, most of them submitted at once, and most others soon followed to avoid a dangerous isolation. After subduing Armenia in this sort of way, the Hamdanid general invaded Byzantine territory and raided up to Colonia. Finally John Curcuas arrived, relieved Colonia, and chased the audacious Arab out of the empire. The Byzantines retaliated by raiding northern Mesopotamia.

In spring 941 Curcuas mustered his forces in Anatolia for an offensive on the eastern frontier. Before they went far, however, the fleet of the Russian prince Igor made a surprise attack near the capital, breaking the treaty made in 911. The tagmata were away with Curcuas, and the Imperial Fleet was warding off Arab pirates in the Aegean. The anxious emperor recalled Curcuas, and in the meantime dispatched his adviser Theophanes the Protovestiarius with fifteen ships and Greek Fire. The fire frightened the Russians away from the Bosporus, but they landed on the north coast of the Optimates, where they began to raid. When Curcuas arrived with his army he repeatedly defeated their parties, but only toward the end of summer did they embark. Now that the bulk of the Imperial Fleet seems to have arrived, Theophanes caught the Russians and almost annihilated them. The grateful emperor rewarded Theophanes with the office of grand chamberlain.

The next winter the Byzantines raided northern Syria almost to Aleppo, the ancient Beroea. Though the Arab rebellion had collapsed in Sicily, many of the rebels fled to the Byzantines, who no longer had to pay tribute to the Fatimids. On the mainland, having betrothed the infant son of Constantine VII to the bastard daughter of King Hugh of Italy, Romanus sent a fleet to help Hugh drive Arab pirates from Provence. The Byzantines destroyed the pirates' fleet with Greek Fire.

That autumn John Curcuas invaded Armenia. His army was large, though perhaps smaller than the eighty thousand reckoned by the terrified Arabs. The domestic made only a raid in force, but ongoing civil wars kept the Arab powers of the region from offering much resistance. Curcuas began by sacking Arzen and Martyropolis in southern Armenia. He wintered in enemy territory, and by spring was in northern Mesopotamia. There he sacked the cities of Amida, Dara, and Nisibis, capturing the inhabitants and piling up booty. In the summer he went on to besiege Edessa. The domestic offered to spare the city if it surrendered the Mandylion, a cloth bearing a supposedly miraculous image of Christ that had long been the city's talisman. While the largely Christian Edessenes considered the matter and consulted the powerless caliph, Curcuas busied himself with raiding more of Mesopotamia and sacking Resaïna. The Arabs could do nothing against him.

As a reward for Curcuas's victories, the emperor thought of making a marriage between Curcuas's daughter and his grandson and namesake, Constantine VII's son Romanus. Though young Romanus was already engaged to Hugh of Italy's bastard daughter, the aging emperor had repented of the humiliating match, and even of excluding his son-in-law Constantine from power. The old man made a will stating that Constantine was next in line for the throne, ahead of Romanus's surviving sons Stephen and Constantine. The proposed marriage alliance with Curcuas would give the retiring Constantine VII a strong protector. By the same token, this prospect aroused fear and envy of Curcuas and Constantine among Romanus's relatives and courtiers. They insisted the emperor not merely abandon the marriage but replace Curcuas as domestic of the Scholae with Pantherius, a relative of the Lecapeni.

Despite his rather spineless compliance, in 944 Romanus was outwardly victorious. The Edessenes brought themselves to give up the Mandylion, and the grand chamberlain Theophanes brought the wonderful relic to Constantinople in late summer. In the East the empire was triumphant, and elsewhere it was at peace with the Bulgarians, Magyars, and Russians. That autumn Romanus celebrated the marriage of Hugh of Italy's daughter to Constantine VII's son, even though the bridegroom was just

115. Ivory plaque of Constantine VII's son Romanus II and his bride Bertha-Eudocia crowned by Christ, now in the Cabinet des Médailles, Paris. Both Romanus and Eudocia are shown older than they actually were, but Romanus's beardlessness shows that he was a child. (Photo: Bibliothèque Nationale, Paris)

five years old. However peculiar the marriage was, it implied that Constantine was heir to the throne.

As Romanus's health worsened, preparing for a good death became his main concern. He took monks as his main counselors, persecuted Jews and Monotheletes, and remitted some 137,000 nomismata that the citizens of Constantinople owed the treasury. But once he had deprived himself of John Curcuas, the force behind most of his victories, Romanus began to look as old and weak as he was. His new domestic Pantherius, after trying to prove himself by sacking Germanicea and Pagrae near Antioch, was soundly beaten by Sayf al-Dawlah.[20]

Romanus's sons Stephen and Constantine, contemplating their impending obscurity, decided to make a desperate grab for power. Soon before Christmas 944, with the help of some sympathetic courtiers, they forced their father into a monastery on a nearby island, where he could pursue his acts of contrition without harming their interests. As the elder son, Stephen meant to become senior emperor, either keeping Constantine VII in continued subordination or tonsuring him like Romanus. At the news of Romanus's forced retirement, however, a mob gathered before the palace, demanding to see Constantine VII.

Rather than risk lynching as rebels against both their father and the legal and hereditary ruler, the Lecapenus brothers recognized Constantine's seniority. They still tried to control the government, but their sister Helena encouraged her imperial husband to make his own bid for power. Constantine VII quickly replaced the defeated domestic Pantherius with Bardas Phocas, brother of the Leo Phocas whom Romanus had bested twenty-five years before. In January 945, when the Lecapenus brothers plotted to kill Constantine at breakfast, he had them abducted at dinner, sending them to join their father in his monastery.

Romanus's fall, however inglorious, subtracted nothing from the achievements of a prudent and victorious reign. Romanus and his talented subordinates, after letting Bulgaria wear itself out, exploited the caliphate's decline to enlarge the empire. The Byzantine church was united, if not uplifted, under Romanus's son Theophylact. The empire's great families had become richer, but not so mighty as to escape most government control. Although Romanus had lacked a dynastic right to rule, he had emerged when he was needed. He had dealt more generously with Constantine VII than other usurpers had done with their predecessors, and so left less rancor behind him.

MORE GAINS UNDER CONSTANTINE VII

After all these vicissitudes of fate, Constantine became the real ruler of Byzantium at the age of thirty-nine. During the years when he had been unable to govern the empire, he had commissioned books on governing it, uncritical and disorganized compilations though they were. Not surprisingly in view of his experiences, Constantine was a retiring and unassuming man. Yet he had common sense, a loyal and intelligent wife in Romanus's daughter Helena, and a right to the illustrious epithet of Porphyrogenitus ("Born in the [Imperial] Purple"). Few knew or cared any longer that he had also been born out of wedlock to an emperor who was probably illegitimate himself. In any case, Constantine had much the best claim to the throne of anyone then living.

The new emperor was only moderately bitter against the Lecapeni. He castrated or tonsured various members of their family, and crowned his own small son Romanus as his sole coregent and heir. About 946 he discovered a plot by the patriarch Theophylact Lecapenus and the grand chamberlain Theophanes to restore old Romanus. Although the patriarch successfully resisted deposition, Constantine exiled Theophanes and the other conspirators. Curiously, he chose as his new grand chamberlain the old emperor's bastard son Basil, a eunuch who was close to the empress Helena and became a faithful and canny counselor.

Constantine claimed that under the Lecapeni the empire had been misgoverned, and sent inspectors to every theme who collected reports of local officials' oppression of the poor.[21] But Constantine's main measure to help the poor was a reaffirmation of Romanus's land laws. In spring 947 Constantine issued an edict ordering powerful landholders to restore the lands they had acquired illegally since the great famine, almost twenty years before. Strict enforcement of this edict probably helped provoke a plot in favor of Stephen Lecapenus by some palace officials, which Constantine firmly suppressed. A year later old Romanus died in his monastery, and the Lecapeni began to be forgotten.

Warfare between Byzantines and Arabs died down during the first three years of Constantine's rule. While the emperor was busy establishing himself, Sayf al-Dawlah was fighting the Ikhshidids of Egypt for control over Syria and Tarsus. The Byzantines only resumed raiding in the spring of 948, when Sayf al-Dawlah held the frontier region as emir of Aleppo and the Ikhshidids held Damascus and southern Syria. Al-

116. Ivory plaque of Constantine VII crowned by Christ, now in the State Museum of Fine Arts, Moscow. (Photo: Victoria and Albert Museum)

though Sayf defeated the first Byzantine army that raided across the Syrian border, his border fort of Adata was then taken and demolished by the strategus of Cappadocia Leo Phocas, son of the domestic Bardas.

For 949 Constantine planned a campaign to reconquer Crete. Well aware of the costly failure of the Cretan campaign of 911, Constantine planned a smaller, cheaper, and more cautious expedition. He assigned ships to keep watch all over the Aegean and Mediterranean, as far away as Umayyad Spain and Fatimid Africa. With so many ships and men on guard duty, the remainder of the navy carried just 4,100 troops from the themes and tagmata to Crete. Thus the Anatolian themes remained near their regular strength, which probably surprised Sayf al-Dawlah when he attacked the Theme of Lycandus that spring. The Byzantines drove him out, and went on to sack the border town of Germanicea and to defeat an army from Tarsus that resisted them. Leo Phocas raided almost to Antioch and repulsed a force led by Sayf's lieutenant. Theophilus Curcuas, John's brother, finally conquered the Arab outpost of Theodosiopolis, which became a theme.

The expedition against Crete sailed as planned, apparently that summer, under the drungary of the fleet Constantine Gongylius. He landed on the island without opposition from the Arabs, whom the Byzantines' elaborate preparations apparently overawed. But Gongylius failed to fortify his camp or to reconnoiter the Arabs. They took his force by surprise, killing much of it and capturing much of the rest with his camp. He and the smaller part of his fleet ignominiously fled. Though this fiasco was largely the result of Gongylius's incompetence, the whole expedition was too small and timid. Having wasted so many ships on defending himself in case he failed, the emperor prepared to fail.

No doubt encouraged by the Byzantines' losses on Crete, the next year Sayf al-Dawlah set out on an unusually ambitious raid with some thirty thousand men, including a contingent from Tarsus. He entered the empire near Lycandus and devastated much of the Theme of Charsianum. In the valley of the Lycus in the eastern Armeniacs he defeated the domestic Bardas Phocas. But as Sayf returned, Leo Phocas ambushed him in a mountain pass between Lycandus and Germanicea. The emir lost some eight thousand men and was almost taken himself. Spurning an offer of peace from the emperor, Sayf raided again in 951, invading the regions of Melitene and Lycandus before a Byzantine army and early snow forced him to retire. Meanwhile the emperor sent more men to southern Italy, only to have them defeated by the Arabs, who occupied

TABLE 12

The Macedonian Dynasty

Emperors are in capital letters and italics, with the years of their reigns marked "r." Other years are of births and deaths unless indicated otherwise. Illegitimate descent is shown by a broken line.

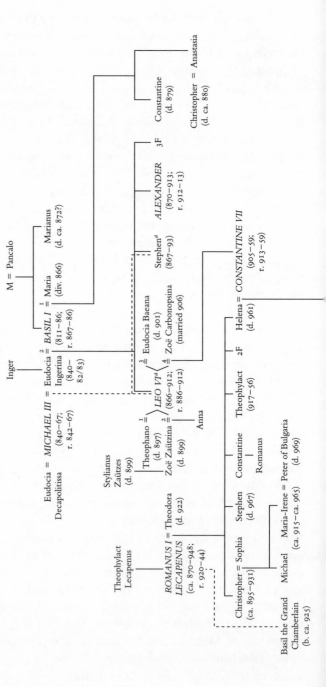

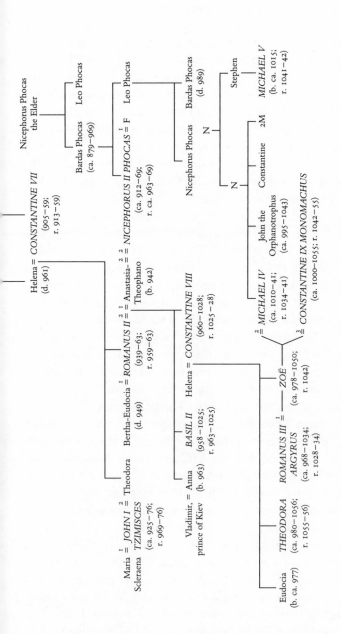

ªReputed to be son of Basil I, but probably illegitimate son of Michael III.

Rhegium. Unlike Sayf al-Dawlah, however, the Sicilian Arabs quickly accepted Constantine's peace proposals.

The following year Sayf set about repairing his ruined border fortresses of Germanicea, Adata, and Samosata. The domestic Bardas tried to stop him, but was repulsed. That fall, the domestic made a raid on northern Mesopotamia and southern Armenia, only to be routed again. The next spring Sayf raided Byzantine territory once more, defeating and capturing the domestic's son Constantine Phocas, who died in prison at Aleppo. The emir restored Adata in 954, brushing aside another attack by the domestic Bardas, and rebuilt Samosata, completing the restoration of his frontier. At this the emperor finally realized the incapacity of Bardas Phocas, who despite Byzantine strength had lost all his battles with the Arabs. Still attached to the Phocas family, Constantine chose Bardas's son Nicephorus Phocas as the new domestic of the Scholae.

As these wars dragged on, Constantine commissioned more books, restored the Great Palace, fussed over imperial ceremonies, and administered competently. When the patriarch Theophylact Lecapenus died in 956 after a fall from one of his beloved horses, the emperor chose the monk Polyeuctus as his successor, the first spiritual leader at the patriarchate in years. Then the emperor's son Romanus, who had been widowed at the age of ten, fell in love with the statuesque daughter of the owner of a tavern. To end much less shocking liaisons, the empress Theodora and emperor Basil had forced marriages on their heirs that brought ruin to themselves and plagued the empire long afterward. Out of passivity or wisdom, Constantine let his son marry the woman he loved, blandly pretending that she was well born. The bride took the name of Leo VI's first wife Saint Theophano, whom she in no way resembled.

The war with the Arabs took a turn for the better as the leadership of the army improved. In spring 956 the brilliant young Armenian John Tzimisces, then probably strategus of Mesopotamia, planned a raid on Amida. To foil it, Sayf al-Dawlah left his cousin to guard Syria and invaded Tzimisces' own territory. Tzimisces retreated, but seized the pass to Sayf's rear. In a furious battle in the midst of a rainstorm, the Arabs killed some four thousand Byzantines and put the rest to flight. Yet at the same time Leo Phocas defeated and captured Sayf's cousin, whom he sent to Constantinople.[22] Early that fall, when Sayf sent the fleet of Tarsus to raid the Cibyrrhaeots, the Cibyrrhaeots attacked it with Greek Fire, captured many of its men, and went on to raid around Tarsus.

In 957 the domestic Nicephorus Phocas besieged and destroyed Adata, which Sayf al-Dawlah had rebuilt just three years before. When Sayf planned a retaliatory expedition, Nicephorus bribed some of the emir's retainers to abduct him; though the plot was betrayed, it aborted the campaign. Sayf returned in a rage to Aleppo to punish the plotters and massacre his Byzantine captives. By this time he must have begun to see that he was losing his war with the Byzantines.

As the empire's prestige grew, the Russian princess Olga, Igor's widow and regent for her young son Svyatoslav, visited Constantinople. She was baptized under the name of Helena by the patriarch Polyeuctus, and though she failed to convert her whole country she built up a Russian church of some size.[23] The Magyars, still not grasping how strong the empire was, raided Thrace again in early 958 and were crushed by an army drawn from the themes of western Anatolia. Propitiously for the future, young Romanus's wife Theophano gave birth to a boy, who was named Basil after the founder of the Macedonian dynasty.

In late spring John Tzimisces raided southern Armenia and northern Mesopotamia, sacking Dara. When Sayf al-Dawlah sent an army of some ten thousand against him, Tzimisces killed about half of them and captured more than half the rest. By autumn the grand chamberlain Basil arrived with reinforcements, and he and Tzimisces besieged Samosata, which the fall of Adata had left exposed. They stormed and demolished it. When Sayf counterattacked, they put him to flight and slaughtered or captured much of his army, sending the captives to be paraded in Constantinople. The Byzantines had clearly broken through the emir's Syrian frontier.

In Italy they as usual did worse, since the Arabs raided Calabria again and defeated them. But while returning to Sicily the Arabs were shipwrecked, and the Fatimids agreed to a truce. In 959 the Byzantines raided through the hole they had made in the Syrian frontier and reached Cyrrhus, which they sacked. Meanwhile the emperor prepared for another expedition against Crete, hoping to redeem the only real failure of his reign. In making his preparations he increased the size of the navy, and probably created a new naval Theme of the Cyclades.[24]

In the autumn of 959, however, Constantine VII died. Despite supposedly fragile health, he had lived for fifty-four years, reigned for forty-six, and ruled for fifteen. Although not particularly vigorous, he was certainly an adequate ruler, and deserves some credit for the successes over which he presided. If he led no military expeditions, no reigning emperor had taken the field since Basil I had failed to distinguish himself there. Without bothering to get in his generals' way, Constantine maintained and made good use of an already strong army and some outstanding commanders. His territorial gains were fairly small, but his generals had faced down a mighty adversary in Sayf al-Dawlah.

THE INHERITANCE OF ROMANUS II

The empire now enjoyed that rarity in its history, an undisputed succession from father to grown son. At age twenty Romanus II already had a son of his own, whom he crowned in 960. Critics took young Romanus's love of pleasure and of his wife Theophano for signs of frivolity, and disapproved when he sent his mother and sisters to convents and replaced some of his father's officials. Yet his chief adviser and grand chamberlain was a capable adviser of Constantine's, Joseph Bringas, and Romanus continued to make use of his father's great generals.

From the first, Romanus seems to have planned to step up the war with the Arabs. He divided the Scholae into eastern and western commands, naming Nicephorus Phocas domestic of the East and Leo Phocas domestic of the West; the name of the Scholae was usually omitted from both titles. The emperor apparently also divided the Excubitors into eastern and western contingents, adding new recruits to both of these divided tagmata.[25] The domestic of the East now became the chief military commander in Asia and the domestic of the West a similar commander for Europe, thus dividing the overriding powers of the former domestic of the Scholae. On the advice of Bringas, Romanus finished

117. Romanus II Porphyrogenitus (r. 959–63), with Christ on the reverse. Gold nomisma, shown twice actual size. (Photo: Dumbarton Oaks, Washington, D.C., copyright 1996)

his father's preparations for another Cretan expedition, and the next summer dispatched Nicephorus Phocas to Crete with an overwhelming force.[26]

Besides hundreds of small craft, it included 307 warships, about two and a half times as many as in 949 or 911. The oarsmen and soldiers together are said to have numbered seventy-seven thousand, almost twice as many as in 911 and three times as many as in 949. Learning from the mistakes of his father and grandfather, the emperor used every available ship to put a large enough army on the island. Nicephorus landed safely on Crete, killed a reported forty thousand Arabs, and put their well-fortified capital of Chandax under siege.

Sayf al-Dawlah took advantage of the absence of Nicephorus and his army to raid Asia Minor with about thirty thousand men. Rather than withdraw the Cretan expedition, the emperor sent east the domestic of the West Leo Phocas, who had recently defeated a Magyar raid in Thrace. That autumn the emir sacked the fort of Charsianum, but Leo managed to take up a position behind him. In a pass through the Taurus, Leo ambushed the Arabs and killed or captured almost all of them.[27] Once more Sayf himself escaped, but his power had suffered a crushing blow. The emperor celebrated a well-earned triumph for Leo.

The winter of 961 was unusually cold, and after a dry summer and plagues of locusts it brought famine. A conspiracy formed in the capital; but Romanus's government detected the plotters and shipped in food from the provinces. On Crete both besieged and besiegers suffered horribly. Yet Nicephorus persisted. The Magyars invaded Thrace again, but the government defeated them without recalling Nicephorus. At the beginning of spring he stormed Chandax, broke through its wall, and forced its surrender, capturing the Cretan emir and the treasures amassed during more than a century of piracy. The island became a theme, and missionaries set about reconverting it to Christianity.

Nicephorus Phocas enjoyed a triumph in Constantinople that was even more glorious than his brother's. Almost at once, however, he returned to the East to fight the Arabs. Before Sayf al-Dawlah could begin to recover from his defeat, Nicephorus hoped to cripple both the Emirate of Tarsus and the Emirate of Aleppo. After extensive preparations, early in 962 he led an army into Cilicia, where he confronted the Arabs with superior numbers at a season when they expected no attack.[28] Nicephorus first arrived at Anazarbus, which he forced to surrender and demolished. Overwhelming the troops of the emir of Tarsus and captur-

118. View of the citadel of Aleppo, with the city in the foreground. (Photo: C. Mango, Dumbarton Oaks, Washington, D.C., copyright 1996)

ing a number of border forts, he returned to Cappadocia to celebrate Easter. On Nicephorus's departure, Sayf marched to Cilicia, where he reclaimed the weakened emirate for himself. But he left before autumn, when Nicephorus invaded Cilicia again, accompanied by John Tzimisces and a reported thirty thousand cavalry and forty thousand infantry.

First the domestic of the East sacked Sisium; then he crossed into Syria proper. He surprised Germanicea and Teluch, and sent a detachment that took Manbij, the ancient Hieropolis. Preparing to defend Aleppo with an improvised militia, Sayf al-Dawlah sent his best troops to meet Nicephorus north of the city. Nicephorus evaded them, drove on Aleppo, and before its walls routed Sayf and his makeshift force. As Sayf fled, pursued by Tzimisces, Nicephorus began a siege. Since the Aleppines were squabbling and their walls were dilapidated, after just three days the Byzantines broke into the city, burning and looting it except for its citadel.

At the end of 962 Nicephorus withdrew, laden with booty and re-splendent with glory. Neither he nor the emperor seems to have intended to hold any of the land he had ravaged, but only to exhaust and humiliate the Arabs. This they had certainly done. As Sayf al-Dawlah returned to his smoldering capital, Nicephorus retired at a leisurely pace to Cappadocia. When he arrived on Byzantine soil at the end of winter, he was astonished to learn that the young emperor had died, having strained himself on a hunt.

Romanus's courtiers were quick to condemn him, especially for hunting in Lent. Yet he died at the early age of twenty-three, after a reign of three and a half years of almost unparalleled military triumph. At his death Crete was firmly in Byzantine hands for the first time since 828, and a Byzantine army had entered Aleppo for the first time since 637, when it had been Beroea. Following established practice, the territory conquered was of modest extent, and the campaigning mostly defensive in purpose. The main aim of the conquest of Crete was to stop Arab piracy; Nicephorus Phocas's other campaigns, like all the empire's eastern offensives for three centuries, were meant to punish and deter raids on Anatolia. By 963 the Arabs were apparently helpless, while the Byzantine army seemed able to ward off any attack. Only the Byzantine succession was in doubt.

CHAPTER SIXTEEN

The Great Conquests, 963–1025

Romanus II's sudden death, coming when his elder son Basil II was just five years old, plunged the empire back into political uncertainty. Romanus's widow Theophano was supposed to be regent for her sons Basil and Constantine; but real power lay in the hands of the grand chamberlain Joseph Bringas, whose relations with the empress were strained. The domestic of the East Nicephorus Phocas, encamped at Tzamandus after his recent victories, had the greatest reputation with the army and almost everyone else. Needing a counterweight to Bringas, the empress wrote secretly to Nicephorus, urging him to press on to Constantinople for the triumph he deserved.

Phocas came and celebrated his triumph. He then accused Bringas of plotting against him, claimed sanctuary in Saint Sophia, and won over the patriarch Polyeuctus. With the patriarch's help, Nicephorus had his command as domestic of the East confirmed before he returned to Cappadocia. The chamberlain in his turn wrote to John Tzimisces, strategus of the Anatolics and the empire's second most famous general, asking him to take Phocas's place as domestic of the East. But rather than challenge Nicephorus, who was his uncle, Tzimisces went straight to him with the letter. The two generals summoned the Anatolian armies to Caesarea, where they proclaimed Nicephorus emperor in early summer. Then they marched on Constantinople.

While Bringas mustered the European troops to resist, as Phocas approached the capital he was joined by his brother Leo and other prominent officers. Bringas brought every available ship to the European shore to prevent Nicephorus from crossing the Bosporus, and even seized Nicephorus's aged father Bardas as a hostage. Yet the forces ranged against the chamberlain proved too strong. Bardas escaped to Saint Sophia; riots in Nicephorus's favor broke out in the city; and after three days of fighting, a mob overcame Bringas's soldiers. Basil Lecapenus, Bringas's predecessor as grand chamberlain, invited Nicephorus into the city, where the patriarch crowned him.

THE CONQUESTS OF NICEPHORUS II

Thus Nicephorus Phocas became coemperor, an office for which he was splendidly qualified. A man of fifty-one, he had held the army's main command for nine years with the greatest distinction, and was a member of the empire's leading military family. While his skills were chiefly military, he understood administration and taxation well enough, and had already shown his competence at intrigue. Pious and abstemious, an admirer of the monk Athanasius of Mount Athos, he respected the Church without letting it dominate him. Since he had no surviving sons of his own, he recognized the rights of the young emperors Basil II and Constantine. As for their mother Theophano, Nicephorus was a widower, and seems already to have arranged to marry her.

Nicephorus rewarded a number of his partisans who were men of ability. He made his brother Leo postal logothete with the rank of curopalates, and gave his own previous post of domestic of the East to John Tzimisces. The emperor restored Basil Lecapenus as grand chamberlain, replacing the exiled Bringas. Phocas honored his father Bardas with the title of Caesar, which at Bardas's advanced age could hardly affect the succession. After a month Nicephorus married Theophano, making the little emperors his stepsons.

Sayf al-Dawlah was ill, and the Arab frontier was in the grip of a famine, probably caused by bad weather but aggravated by the recent Byzantine incursions. In the fall Sayf nonetheless launched three raiding parties, one of which reached as far as Iconium. The domestic of the East Tzimisces retaliated with a winter raid on Cilicia. Defeating the Arabs near Adana, he briefly besieged Mopsuestia. Tzimisces withdrew only when his own troops began to suffer from hunger, early in 964.

Nicephorus himself spent the winter in Constantinople, planning expeditions to Cilicia and Sicily and issuing new laws. He had already quarreled with the patriarch Polyeuctus, who disapproved of his marriage to Theophano and rejected his proposal to count death fighting Muslims as a sort of martyrdom.[1] These disputes may have given Nice-

119. Nicephorus II Phocas (r. 963–69). Miniature from the Modena Zonaras. (Photo: Biblioteca Estense, Modena)

phorus more reason to legislate against the growing accumulation of church lands, which were difficult to tax, often remained uncultivated, and sometimes included illegally donated military holdings. Expressing his indignation at the greed of many monasteries to acquire property, the emperor forbade new gifts of land to the Church and the foundation of most new religious institutions. In keeping with his desire for a less worldly church, he allowed donations of movable property to existing institutions that were in need, and encouraged the foundation of simple monasteries called *laurai* in deserted places. He himself endowed the monastery on Mount Athos known as the Greatest Laura, which had just been founded by his spiritual adviser Athanasius. As a rebuke of the patriarch Polyeuctus, the emperor made the Greatest Laura independent of all ecclesiastical authority.

That spring Nicephorus left for Caesarea to muster his forces for another attack on Sayf al-Dawlah. He also dispatched his expedition to Sicily, hoping to aid the last Christians resisting Arab rule there. This force landed near Messina under Nicephorus's nephew Manuel, but the Arabs mauled it on both land and sea, killing Manuel and resuming their raids on Calabria. Probably too few ships had been sent, since those

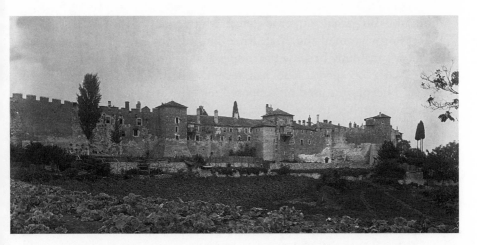

120. Overall view of the Monastery of the Greatest Laura, Mount Athos.
(Photo: Collection Gabriel Millet)

remaining in the East were enough to clear Cyprus of Arabs. They brought the island fully under Byzantine rule in preparation for an invasion of Cilicia.[2]

Later that autumn Nicephorus invaded Cilicia in force.[3] Like Tzimisces before him, he besieged Mopsuestia, aware that if it fell the Arabs would find Tarsus untenable. Arab Cilicia's only defense was its persistent famine, which forced the emperor to raise his siege after fifty days and return to Caesarea early in 965. The desperate Arabs offered tribute, but Nicephorus rebuffed them and returned to Mopsuestia in the summer. He stormed the city, captured and deported its people, and moved on to Tarsus. When the Tarsiots surrendered in return for safe-conduct to Antioch, Nicephorus occupied their city as well, completing the reconquest of Cilicia.

The emperor created new themes of Cyprus, Tarsus, and Mopsuestia. Several other themes established to the east probably date from this time, and served to protect Cilicia.[4] Nicephorus allowed the inhabitants who were or would become Christians to remain in the reconquered region, recruited soldiers for its garrisons, and encouraged other Christians from Syria and Armenia to settle there, even if they were Monophysites.[5] That fall the emperor returned to Constantinople for another well-earned triumph.

Around the beginning of 966 Nicephorus received embassies from Sayf al-Dawlah, who asked for a truce and exchange of prisoners, and from the Bulgarian emperor Peter, who requested his usual subsidy. Nicephorus granted the Arab truce but angrily refused the Bulgarian subsidy, apparently because the money had been given to support Peter's wife Maria Lecapena, who had recently died. Though Peter backed down, Nicephorus used his supposed temerity as a pretext for war. The emperor marched to the Bulgarian frontier and destroyed several forts. Yet because he was eager to return to the East, he sent an ambassador to the Russian prince Svyatoslav of Kiev, whom he paid to attack Bulgaria.[6]

By early fall the Byzantines were raiding northern Mesopotamia from Amida to Nisibis. The emperor himself ravaged northern Syria, moving from Manbij to Aleppo and on to Antioch. He besieged Antioch for a week, but turned back when he ran short of supplies. The Arabs were nonetheless in despair. The Emirate of Aleppo was disintegrating, and its celebrated emir Sayf al-Dawlah died early in 967. Probably before returning to Constantinople, Nicephorus ordered an expansion of Byzantine holdings in Armenia. The prince of Taron had just died, and his sons ceded their inheritance to the empire as a theme in return for Byzantine titles and offices.[7] Nicephorus seems to have joined Taron to the empire by creating over a dozen new Armenian themes in the intervening territory, under the general command of his nephew Bardas Phocas as duke of Chaldia.[8] Though these tiny Armenian themes were neither rich nor populous, they advanced the Byzantine frontier up to Arab Mesopotamia, and each of them provided a few more troops for the next attack on the weakened Arabs.

The famine that afflicted the Arabs now reached Byzantium, and like the previous famine led many poor peasants to sell their land. Nicephorus issued an edict providing that only the poor could buy land from the poor, and that the rich could buy land only from the rich. This may also be the date of two laws designed to protect the soldiers' military holdings. One law reserved as military lands, not to be sold to others, the property of some Armenians who had fled the new themes rather than become Byzantine subjects. A second law created a new class of cavalry with heavy armor, supported by military lands worth a minimum of twelve pounds of gold, three times the minimum for ordinary cavalry. In most cases, this measure probably meant that neighbors with military land contributed to the heavy cavalryman's expenses. These heavy cavalry, who bore some resemblance to western European knights, were to form small contingents of shock troops for Nicephorus's armies.[9]

To pay for his great campaigns and for organizing his new themes, the

121. Gold tetarteron (lightweight nomisma), shown 2.2 times actual size, with Christ on the obverse and the Virgin and Nicephorus II (cf. Fig. 119) on the reverse (as a sign of humility). (Photo: Courtesy of the Arthur M. Sackler Museum, Harvard University Art Museums, Whittemore Collection)

emperor made requisitions of various kinds. To reduce expenditure, he minted a new nomisma called the tetarteron. This was one-twelfth lighter than the standard but counted as a full nomisma for some government payments, reducing their value by a twelfth. Tetartera may well have been used to pay the many inactive soldiers of the older themes, whom Nicephorus did not need for his campaigns.[10] The tetarteron did little harm to commerce, because the coin was not debased and nomismata normally circulated by weight to allow for wear. Yet Nicephorus's increased demands and reduced payments were noticed and resented, especially in a time of economic distress. During protests in the capital in spring 967, some citizens jeered and threw bricks at the emperor.

Nicephorus's inviting the Russians to attack Bulgaria proved to be a false economy. In summer 967, Prince Svyatoslav arrived on the Danube, crushed the Bulgarian army, and blockaded part of it in the fortress of Dristra. This defeat prostrated the Bulgarian emperor Peter, who was powerless to resist further. Svyatoslav decided the country was to his liking. He occupied Little Preslav and settled in comfortably for the winter. Alarmed at the prospect of a powerful Russian principality stretching from Kiev to the Byzantine border, in early 968 Nicephorus made an alliance with the Bulgarians. When the Pechenegs attacked Kiev, probably at the emperor's suggestion, Svyatoslav had to leave Bulgaria to fight them off.

Byzantium acquired another troublesome neighbor in Otto I, the recently crowned German emperor. By 968 Otto had established his suzerainty over the Lombards of Capua and Benevento, up to the borders of Byzantine Calabria and Longobardia. Otto wanted a marriage alliance between his son and a Byzantine princess, but Nicephorus's ambassadors put him off. To speed the negotiations, Otto invaded the Theme of Longobardia, then sent his ambassador Liudprand of Cremona to Constantinople. When the Byzantines rebuffed Liudprand, Otto raided both Longobardia and Calabria. Nicephorus placed the two themes under a new naval commander, styled the catepan of Italy, and sent reinforcements.[11]

Neither Svyatoslav nor Otto, nor continuing famine in the empire, kept Nicephorus from making another Arab expedition in the autumn of 968. He raided the region of Martyropolis, crossed northern Mesopotamia, and probably took Edessa, making it a theme.[12] Advancing into northern Syria, he appeared before Antioch, then turned south and sacked Hama (Epiphania) and Homs (Emesa), from which he took the head of John the Baptist. After raiding and taking prisoners up to strongly fortified Tripoli, he occupied the main coastal fortresses to its north. Returning to Antioch, which he had now surrounded, the emperor established a strong force at the nearby fort of Pagrae to besiege the city. He gave responsibility for the whole eastern frontier to Peter, a capable eunuch, with the title of stratopedarch ("commander of the army"), and assigned the command at Pagrae to another general, Michael Burtzes. Nicephorus then dismissed much of his force, since provisions were too scarce to supply it, and went back to Constantinople. The siege of Antioch continued through the winter.

Early in 969 Peter of Bulgaria died, and his son Boris II inherited the tottering Bulgarian Empire. Having defeated the Pechenegs, Svyatoslav led his army back to Bulgaria and made short work of the Bulgarians. He seized the Bulgarian capital of Preslav, capturing Boris and his family, then finished the conquest of eastern Bulgaria by taking and devastating Philippopolis in the south. Though Svyatoslav had not yet attacked Byzantine territory, his attitude became more and more menacing. His expanded Russian state threatened the Byzantines far more than Bulgaria had done.

Elsewhere the Byzantines carried all before them. The new catepan of Italy Eugenius defeated Otto's forces and captured his ally, the Lombard prince of Capua. The duke of Chaldia Bardas Phocas invaded the remnant of Arab Armenia and destroyed its capital at Manzikert. That fall, after a blockade of almost a year, Michael Burtzes broke into Antioch, and with the aid of Peter the Stratopedarch captured the city. The emperor received the news in Constantinople with mixed feelings, since he was sorry not to have taken Antioch in person. Yet no obstacle seemed to remain to Nicephorus's conquering northern Syria, and he is said to have thought of retaking Jerusalem.

All these victories won Nicephorus surprisingly little credit at home. Besides being blamed for the famine, he was on bad terms with several important people. Michael Burtzes returned to Constantinople to find Nicephorus displeased that he had exceeded his orders by storming Antioch. The domestic of the East John Tzimisces resented the emperor's transferring eastern operations from him to Peter the Stratopedarch. Worst of all, the empress Theophano had become bored with her austere husband, whose personality was quite unlike her own. She preferred the charming Tzimisces, whom she had persuaded Nicephorus to summon to the capital. Tzimisces and the empress therefore plotted to kill Nicephorus, marry, and rule together. They won over Michael Burtzes and a number of other generals and courtiers, including the powerful grand chamberlain Basil Lecapenus. Two months after the fall of Antioch, Theophano let Tzimisces and his confederates into the palace. After a moment of alarm when they found Nicephorus's bed empty, they discovered the ascetic emperor asleep on the floor in front of his icons, and murdered him.

Nicephorus II died after a dozen years of military triumphs, begun when he was general and pressed home when he was emperor. He had wrecked the Emirate of Aleppo, swept away the bases for Arab raids on Anatolia, and replaced them with a wall of Byzantine themes. He had regained Antioch, which was the ancient capital of Syria, the seat of its patriarch, and the gate to the rest of the country. Although years of warfare had impoverished and depopulated most of these conquests, the land would eventually recover, and the Arab danger would never be the same again. Nicephorus had won his eastern wars through a determination that verged on recklessness, especially when he exchanged peaceful Bulgarians for dangerous Russians on his northern border. Yet without his neglect of other frontiers, and willingness to court unpopularity, he might have failed to crush the Arabs before they could rally.

THE CONQUESTS OF JOHN TZIMISCES

Tzimisces' murder of Nicephorus was an almost unprecedented and unjustifiable crime. John replaced officials who were Nicephorus's partisans before they could organize resistance in the army, and announced that any rioting would be punished by death. Fortunately for Tzimisces, the patriarch Polyeuctus had been one of Nicephorus's chief critics, and saw the danger of a power vacuum at Constantinople. But Polyeuctus had some principles, and refused simply to condone John's marriage to Theophano and coronation as emperor. He demanded as a condition for crowning John that he distribute his private fortune to the poor, exile Theophano, and punish the other murderers of Nicephorus. John willingly gave up his property, exiled the empress, and selected two assassins to execute. At this the patriarch declared John absolved of his sins by virtue of his anointing at the coronation.[13]

John Tzimisces thus supplanted Nicephorus II as coemperor and guardian of the young emperors Basil and Constantine. Unlike Nicephorus, who had overthrown nobody, married the reigning empress, and restored order when he was needed, John was for all practical purposes a usurper. Yet those who knew him liked him. An energetic man of forty-four, he was short, but had blond good looks that the Byzantines much admired. He had a reputation for piety and generosity. His

122. John I Tzimisces (r. 969–76). Miniature from the Modena Zonaras. (Photo: Biblioteca Estense, Modena)

family was Armenian, but well connected with the Byzantine military leadership. His grandfather had been the domestic of the Scholae Bardas Phocas; his great-uncle had been the domestic of the Scholae John Curcuas; and his mother had been the sister of Nicephorus II. Tzimisces combined Nicephorus's military talents and experience with a congeniality Nicephorus had lacked. John was also lucky in having the three years' famine end about the time he took power, since like most people the Byzantines tended to blame their government even for misfortunes utterly beyond its control.

John exiled Nicephorus's brother Leo Phocas and Leo's two sons, Nicephorus the Patrician and Bardas the Duke of Chaldia. Early in 970, two months after John's coronation, the patriarch Polyeuctus died at an advanced age, and the emperor chose a successor less inclined to challenge emperors. But the emperor kept his fellow plotter Basil Lecapenus as grand chamberlain, giving him the main responsibility for the empire's internal affairs. His own former post of domestic of the East Tzimisces gave to his first wife's brother, Bardas Sclerus. Despite his earlier resentment of the stratopedarch Peter, the emperor kept him in place, since Peter seemed about to cap his exploits at Antioch by storming Aleppo.

From their capital's citadel the harried Aleppines sued for peace. They formally ceded the Syrian coastlands that Nicephorus II had begun to occupy. What remained of the Emirate of Aleppo between Hama and the Euphrates became a Byzantine dependency, paying tribute to Constantinople under an emir approved by the emperor. Byzantine territory now reached to the confines of the Fatimid Caliphate, which had taken Egypt and had just captured Tripoli, and of the Hamdanid Emirate of Mosul in northern Mesopotamia. Tzimisces had designs on both Muslim states.

The emperor seems to have reorganized the army on the eastern frontier, which Nicephorus had left split among more than thirty tiny themes. Early in John's reign, these frontier themes were grouped under three ducates. The Ducate of Chaldia remained in the north, though it seems to have lost its authority over most of the Armenian themes to a new Ducate of Mesopotamia in the central sector. Antioch became a ducate for the southern region, including two new themes around it and the various themes of Cilicia and southern Syria. John appears to have strengthened these ducates further by giving them authority over seven more themes, carved out of the older themes nearest the border.[14]

To free himself for operations in the East, John sought negotiations with Otto I, who had invaded the Theme of Longobardia again, and Svyatoslav, who was massing troops in eastern Bulgaria. Otto was happy to make peace when Tzimisces released the prince of Capua and agreed to marry his niece Theophano to Otto's son. Svyatoslav took diplomacy as a sign of weakness and demanded a high tribute, threatening otherwise to attack Constantinople. The emperor saw that war with the Russians was necessary and began preparing for it. He recruited a new tagma of four thousand men, known as the Immortals, and mustered his other troops. He sent a force of some twelve thousand to guard the Thracian frontier, under the domestic of the East Bardas Sclerus and the stratopedarch Peter.[15] Probably that summer, a force of Russians and Bulgarians crossed the border and met Bardas's army in battle near Arcadiopolis. After fierce fighting, the Byzantines killed many Russians and drove the rest back.

At this point the former duke of Chaldia Bardas Phocas raised a rebellion to avenge his uncle Nicephorus II. Escaping from confinement at Amasia, Bardas rode to Caesarea in Cappadocia, where he found many members and friends of the Phocas family to proclaim him emperor. Bardas's father Leo and brother Nicephorus tried to help him from their own places of exile, but Tzimisces had both of them imprisoned and partly blinded. The emperor dispatched Bardas Sclerus into Anatolia to suppress the rebellion, using troops gathered for his Russian campaign. Sclerus encamped at Dorylaeum in the Opsician, while Phocas encamped at the appropriately named Bardaëtta in the Anatolics.[16] Avoiding combat, Sclerus gradually lured away most of Phocas's men, captured others, and finally persuaded Phocas himself to surrender with a promise he would remain unharmed. Phocas was tonsured and banished.

Once this revolt was over, Tzimisces connected himself with the legitimate dynasty by marrying Constantine VII's daughter Theodora, who was released from the monastic vows that Romanus II had forced on her and her sisters. The emperor sent Bardas Sclerus to winter with his army in Thrace, where the Russians had begun to raid. At the beginning of 971, however, a Fatimid army arrived before Antioch and besieged it. Tzimisces ordered a force to be gathered from the troops along the border, which defeated the Arabs and made them raise the siege.[17] During all this time the emperor had merely held his own, and his victories had been defensive, and won by others.

In his war with Svyatoslav John was determined to do better. After thoroughly drilling his troops, early that spring he marched against the

Russians, accompanied by his domestic Bardas Sclerus and his grand chamberlain Basil Lecapenus. Tzimisces led perhaps forty thousand men, including his Tagma of the Immortals, and sent a fleet of some three hundred ships to attack the Russians in the rear on the Danube.[18] Despite long preparations and many warnings, the Byzantines took the over-confident Russians by surprise. John drove straight on the former Bulgarian capital of Preslav and defeated the Russians there, killing some eighty-five hundred of them and shutting up the rest in the town. Next the Byzantines stormed Preslav, killing more Russians and freeing the Bulgarian emperor Boris II.

Renaming Preslav Joannopolis after himself, John advanced to Dristra on the Danube, where Svyatoslav was entrenched with the main Russian army. After a sharp battle that ended in a complete Byzantine victory, Tzimisces blockaded Svyatoslav in Dristra. The Byzantine fleet sailed up the Danube to make the siege complete, and determined sallies by the Russians failed to break it. Nor was the emperor deterred by an attempted coup by the partly blinded Leo Phocas, who was arrested and completely blinded. Three months of siege, heavy Russian losses attempting to break out, and utterly exhausted supplies reduced Svyatoslav to suing for peace. When Tzimisces agreed to let the prince withdraw safely to Kiev with a supply of grain, distribution of the grain revealed that of an original sixty thousand Russians only twenty-two thousand remained.

After Svyatoslav's departure, the emperor garrisoned Dristra and renamed it Theodoropolis for Saint Theodore Stratelates, who had allegedly appeared to help the Byzantines during the siege. Finally John returned to Constantinople to celebrate his triumph. He forced Boris II to abdicate and annexed most of Bulgaria outright. The emperor created six themes in western Bulgaria, all with new garrisons, and on the pattern of the eastern frontier seems to have divided the six earlier border themes of the West in two. Authority over these small themes was apportioned between new ducates of Adrianople and Thessalonica, so that the eastern and western Balkans each had a duke with wide powers.[19] In a single year's campaigning, John had gained the empire a vast and fertile territory, providing a deep buffer for Thrace and advancing the frontier to the lower Danube for the first time since the early seventh century.

Evidently planning to make all of Bulgaria Byzantine, the emperor not only ended the Bulgarian monarchy but reduced the Bulgarian patriarchate to an archbishopric and subjected it to the patriarchate of Constantinople. In western Bulgaria, however, four sons of a local Bulgarian governor, Count Nicholas, maintained a precarious independence in the region stretching from Ochrid (ancient Lychnidus) to Serdica. Though they provided a home for the dispossessed Bulgarian patriarch, none of them proclaimed himself emperor; they were simply known as the Cometopuli, or Sons of the Count. Even taken together, their holdings were a mere rump of the old Bulgarian Empire.[20]

With Byzantine power at a peak, in the spring of 972 Otto I celebrated the marriage between his son and heir Otto II and Tzimisces' niece Theophano. This alliance was beneficial to both sides. While securing the empire's possessions in Italy, which were otherwise bothersome to defend, the marriage was flattering to Byzantium and to Tzimisces in particular. Although some of Otto's courtiers grumbled that Theophano was not a relative of the legitimate Macedonian dynasty, the German emperor considered any Byzantine princess a prize.[21]

123. Ivory plaque of the German emperor Otto II (r. 973–83) and his wife Theophano in Byzantine style, now in the Musée de Cluny, Paris. (Photo: Copyright Réunion des Musées Nationaux)

At last Tzimisces seemed to be free to please himself and fight the Arabs. That fall he and his domestic of the East Melias invaded the Emirate of Mosul, which lay just across the Euphrates from Byzantine territory. The emperor sacked and burned Nisibis, then turned north and besieged Martyropolis. Since it held out, Tzimisces returned to Constantinople, leaving Melias on the frontier to continue the war.[22] Probably meaning to finish his conquest of Bulgaria before devoting full attention to the war in the East, Tzimisces sent an expedition up the Danube. His generals extended Byzantine control to the Morava (Margus) valley, where he created new themes of Ras and Morava.[23] After these conquests imperial territory almost encircled the domains of the Cometopuli, which looked doomed.

But in the summer of 973, when the domestic Melias was besieging Amida, the forces of the emir of Mosul defeated and captured him. After Melias died in captivity early the next year, the emperor massed his forces to avenge his domestic of the East. Tzimisces marched to the Theme of Taron in 974 to begin his campaign. The independent Armenian princes, afraid that he meant to annex more of their land, accepted the leadership of King Ashot III, who negotiated a hasty alliance with the emperor.[24] Joined by ten thousand allied Armenian troops, John invaded the Emirate of Mosul once more. Ravaging and plundering widely, he extracted tribute from Martyropolis and Amida, passed through the deserted city of Nisibis, and pushed on in the direction of Mosul. The emir, who was embroiled in a civil war, agreed to pay the empire an annual tribute. The emperor celebrated another triumph in Constantinople.[25]

Having subjected the Emirate of Aleppo and humbled the Emirate of Mosul, in spring 975 John attacked the strongest of the Arab powers, the Fatimid Caliphate. First he and his domestic of the East Bardas Sclerus took Apamea, which the Emirate of Aleppo had apparently lost to the Fatimids. Next Tzimisces invaded southern Syria, then under Fatimid rule except for some rebels around Damascus. The emperor advanced to Baalbek and captured it from the rebel leader Alp Tikīn. Tikīn agreed to pay Tzimisces an annual tribute of 60,000 dinars and received him into Damascus. From Damascus Tzimisces paid a brief visit to Galilee, where he climbed Mount Tabor to see the place of Christ's Transfiguration. While he was there, several cities sent him tribute, including Tiberias, Acre, and Caesarea. Discouraged from further advances by Fatimid troops stationed along the coast, the emperor turned north to

Berytus, which surrendered to him. After receiving more tribute from Sidon, he sacked Byblus and raided around the Fatimid stronghold of Tripoli.

The emperor had campaigned thus far to win glory and plunder, and to weaken the Fatimids for the future, rather than to conquer territory permanently. During the summer, however, he settled down to subjugate and annex the coast between Antaradus and Antioch. Despite Nicephorus II's conquest of the main towns, and the Aleppines' cession of the whole seaboard to the empire, several fortresses had remained in Arab hands. Tzimisces reduced them and organized and garrisoned new themes along the coast.[26]

In a letter to his ally Ashot III, the emperor declared that his real goal had been Jerusalem. Though that would scarcely have been attainable during this year's campaign, as a future objective it seemed well within reach. Just as Nicephorus's campaign of 968 had prepared for John's full conquest of the coast between Antioch and Tripoli, John's campaign of 975 was probably meant to prepare for the later conquest of Tripoli, the rest of the Syrian coast, and quite possibly Jerusalem as well.

For the present, Tzimisces returned to Constantinople. On his way back he is said to have noticed with displeasure that a large part of Cilicia had been acquired from the state as private property by the grand chamberlain Basil Lecapenus. According to a plausible rumor, Basil learned that the emperor was planning to investigate, and had him poisoned to forestall the investigation. John was already ill when he arrived in the capital, and at the beginning of 976 he died.

Tzimisces' death, at the height of his powers, interrupted the great projects of his reign. He still had more of Bulgaria and Syria to conquer, though not much more than he had already occupied. He had more to do to organize his conquests, but nothing suggests that he was unequal to the task. He left Byzantium not only much bigger than before, but more secure than it had been since the early sixth century. Tzimisces had been lucky in his career, but not in the timing of his death. In six years he had shown a genius and enthusiasm for conquest unmatched by any other Byzantine emperor, even Nicephorus II. Had he died at sixty instead of fifty-one, he might well have taken the rest of Syria and Bulgaria, and perhaps even campaigned in Egypt. Byzantium still had fine generals and vast resources, but a John Tzimisces was practically irreplaceable.

THE STRUGGLES OF BASIL II

In 976 Basil II was eighteen, an age by which several emperors had begun to rule for themselves. But the grand chamberlain Basil Lecapenus was disinclined to share power with him, and after the reigns of Nicephorus Phocas and John Tzimisces the army and administration were used to a firm and mature hand. No one saw a need to remove Basil II or his brother Constantine, both of whom seemed to be idle, pleasure-loving, and ready to take advice. Constantine married early; Basil II spent his bachelorhood in various love affairs.[27] The grand chamberlain indulged the brothers by recalling their mother Theophano from exile, though she never gained much influence at court.

Widely blamed for the deaths of both Nicephorus Phocas and Tzimisces, and unable as a eunuch to reign himself, the grand chamberlain had formidable enemies. Chief among them was the domestic of the East Bardas Sclerus, Tzimisces' former brother-in-law and close ally. The chamberlain attempted to demote Sclerus from domestic of the East to duke of Mesopotamia, and to separate him from his lieutenant Michael Burtzes by making Burtzes duke of Antioch. Sclerus's replacement as domestic of the East was to be the eunuch Peter the Stratopedarch. After first seeming to accept his demotion, Sclerus rebelled.[28]

In the summer Bardas Sclerus had himself proclaimed emperor at Melitene, presumably hoping to become coemperor with Basil II and Constantine. Most of the army along the eastern border joined Sclerus, who also gained the support of the emir of Mosul. In the rest of Anatolia the domestic Peter and Michael Burtzes mustered loyalists for the government in Constantinople. Probably that autumn, they met Sclerus in battle near Lycandus. But he put them to flight. Sclerus's forces captured Burtzes, who joined their side and won over much of central and southern Anatolia, including the fleet of the Cibyrrhaeots.

In 977 the grand chamberlain sent another army under the eunuch Leo the Protovestiarius to Cotyaeum. Leo joined Peter and tried to encourage desertions from the rebels with money and privileges, the method used to subvert the rebellion of Bardas Phocas seven years before. But buying partisans for a bastard eunuch proved harder than rallying supporters to the great Tzimisces. Leo won few adherents, and Sclerus advanced to the Lake of the Forty Martyrs in the Anatolics. Leo resorted to surprise. Marching rapidly along the road from Cotyaeum, he bypassed Sclerus's army and made for the East, the homeland of most of Sclerus's men. Fearing for their homes, some of them deserted to Leo. Sclerus sent an advance party under Burtzes that caught up with Leo, only to suffer a severe defeat. Nevertheless, when Sclerus arrived with his main army he crushed the loyalists, capturing Leo and killing Peter.

As most of Asia Minor joined Sclerus, he marched to Nicaea and besieged it. In preparation for a siege of Constantinople, the Cibyrrhaeot fleet took the Aegean islands, and was about to enter the straits when Basil Lecapenus dispatched the Imperial Fleet from the capital. It sailed through the Hellespont, fought the Cibyrrhaeots off Phocaea, and swept them from the seas. After Sclerus occupied Nicaea, allowing its starving garrison to decamp, the empire was split almost precisely between rebels in Anatolia and loyalists in Europe and the islands. Sclerus advanced to the Bosporus, but had no fleet to ferry him across.

These troubles allowed the deposed Bulgarian emperor Boris and his brother Romanus to escape from Constantinople and make for western Bulgaria. Though a Bulgarian border guard mistook Boris for a Byzantine and killed him, Romanus reached the Cometopuli, who had apparently reoccupied the themes of Ras and Morava, securing their hold on western Bulgaria. The Cometopuli apparently recognized Romanus as their titular emperor even though he was said to be a eunuch. Romanus exercised little if any power, but they found him useful for winning Bulgarians to the cause of independence from Byzantium.[29]

The civil war with Bardas Sclerus led to other calamities for the empire. The Sicilian Arabs began ravaging Byzantine Calabria and Longobardia. The Emirate of Aleppo seems to have stopped paying tribute to the Byzantines in 977. The next year tribute from the Emirate of Mosul ceased when its emir was overthrown by the Buwayhid sultan of Baghdad and fled to Sclerus and his rebels. The sultan may also have taken Byzantine Edessa at the same time. Aggravated by the civil war, another famine spread through Byzantine territory.[30]

Early in 978 the desperate Basil Lecapenus made up his mind to turn to Bardas Phocas, exiled to Chios eight years before. Although Phocas was a dangerously good general, a safely bad one would have had little chance against Sclerus; at least Phocas hated Sclerus for suppressing his revolt against Tzimisces and ruining his career. So, after swearing extravagant oaths to be loyal, Bardas Phocas was given the task of defeating Bardas Sclerus, with the title of domestic of the Scholae of the East. Since both the Scholae and the East were in the hands of the enemy, Phocas had to gather troops from Constantinople and the western themes.

When Phocas tried to cross the Hellespont, he found the Asian shore well defended by Sclerus's son. Returning to Constantinople, he managed to slip by Sclerus and cross the Bosporus. Phocas set out at once for Caesarea, in his family's homeland of Cappadocia. On his arrival he attracted many followers, among them Michael Burtzes, who changed sides once again. Marching west to face Phocas, Sclerus met him in battle near Amorium at the end of spring. After heavy losses on both sides, Phocas retreated to the east. Both generals regrouped. That fall Sclerus attacked Phocas again at Basilica Therma in the Theme of Charsianum. For the second time both armies suffered severely, and again Phocas retreated farther east. Even he seemed unable to crush the rebellion.

During the winter, however, Sclerus's duke of Antioch joined Phocas, and the Iberian prince David of Upper Tao sent Phocas twelve thousand cavalry. In the spring of 979 Phocas felt strong enough to attack Sclerus farther west in the Theme of Charsianum, at Aquae Saravenae.[31] This time Phocas won. Sclerus's weary rebels dispersed, and Scle-

124. View from the sea of the monastery known as Iberon ("of the Iberians"), Mount Athos. (Photo: Dumbarton Oaks, Washington, D.C., copyright 1996)

rus himself fled to Baghdad. By autumn only a few pockets of rebel resistance remained. David of Upper Tao was rewarded with possession of Theodosiopolis for life, and his Iberians founded a great monastery on Mount Athos with booty they had taken from the rebels.[32] But the chief credit for putting down the rebels went to Bardas Phocas, who celebrated a triumph at Constantinople.

The empire's strength was such that even the wounds of four years of civil war healed quickly. The famine seems to have abated. The Cometopuli had seemingly conquered only the exposed themes of Ras and Morava, though the most energetic member of the family, Samuel, was raiding Thessaly by 980. In the East the empire had lost nothing apart from Edessa, and in fall 981 the domestic Bardas Phocas campaigned against Aleppo, forcing its emir to resume paying tribute. Although early in 982 the German emperor Otto II invaded Byzantine Italy, in Calabria Fatimid raiders defeated him in a battle so bloody that both Germans and Arabs withdrew. By the end of the year a new catepan of Italy had restored Byzantine control.

Bardas Phocas was now the leading man in the army, if not quite in the empire. In 983 he rescued the Emirate of Aleppo from an attack by the Fatimids and exacted double tribute, sacking Homs when it failed to pay its share. Two years later, when the tribute from Aleppo was past due, Phocas raided Aleppine territory and besieged Apamea. The rumor spread among the Arabs that Phocas's real objective was to conquer the emirate outright, deporting its Muslim population. Then suddenly he received orders to retreat, not from Basil the Grand Chamberlain but from Basil the emperor.

The twenty-seven-year-old Basil II had long resented the power of Basil Lecapenus, and in the latter part of 985 he put the grand chamberlain under house arrest. The emperor probably halted Phocas's campaign at the same time to avert the danger of Phocas's diverting it to Constantinople. He transferred authority over Byzantine Syria to a new duke of Antioch, Leo Melissenus. While rumors of plots circulated in the army, Fatimid troops seized the fort of Balaneae on the Syrian coast, and Samuel of Bulgaria took Larissa, the chief city of Thessaly. Yet Leo Melissenus soon recaptured Balaneae, and by early 986 the emperor sent Basil Lecapenus into a secure exile. The next duke of Antioch was Bardas Phocas himself, who accepted his demotion from domestic and renewed the treaty with the Emirate of Aleppo. Thus Basil II accomplished the delicate business of taking full power.[33]

Eager to prove that he could fight, the young emperor took Samuel's conquest of Larissa as an opportunity. In the summer of 986, without calling on his eastern armies or Bardas Phocas, he set out with Leo Melissenus for Serdica, one of Samuel's principal strongholds. Leaving Leo to guard the passes back to Byzantine territory, Basil put Serdica under siege. Though Samuel hastened to its defense from Greece, he stayed in the hills, only daring to harass the Byzantines' foraging parties. Yet Basil lacked military experience, and his western troops seem to have been inferior to the crack eastern regiments. As the siege failed to make progress, his army ran short of supplies. A report that Melissenus was plotting against him in the rear convinced the emperor to retreat. Then, on the return march, reports that the Bulgarians had seized the passes sent the soldiers into a panic. The Bulgarians ambushed the frightened Byzantines in the pass of Trajan's Gate, and massacred many of them. Basil escaped ingloriously with the survivors.

When news of the young emperor's defeat reached Baghdad, the Buwayhid sultan let Bardas Sclerus return to the empire and bid for power again. In return Sclerus granted the sultan a treaty of alliance and some Byzantine forts in southern Armenia.[34] In the winter of 986–87 Sclerus and his followers made their way to Melitene. There he won many Byzantine and Armenian supporters and a contingent from the Marwanids, the Muslim Kurds who held southern Armenia. This second rebellion of Sclerus appeared to be growing no less fearsome than the first.

The emperor gave the task of subduing it, with the title of domestic of the East, to Bardas Phocas. Phocas massed his troops in the Theme of Charsianum, but in the summer he used them to proclaim himself emperor. He promptly entered into negotiations with Sclerus. Sclerus agreed to recognize Phocas as emperor in exchange for extraordinary powers over Byzantine Syria and Mesopotamia. The young emperor therefore faced a coalition between the original rebels and the army he had sent against them. In desperation he appealed to the Russian prince Vladimir of Kiev, the only neighboring ruler who seemed strong enough to make a difference. Basil's lure was the hand of his sister Anna. It was an extraordinary offer, because no pagan ruler, and few Christian ones, had ever married a Byzantine princess.[35]

The emperor was certainly in the gravest peril. The rebels' power looked so overwhelming that at a meeting to ratify their agreement Phocas felt able to seize and imprison Sclerus and carry on alone. Phocas took over most of Sclerus's forces and allies, and almost all of Anatolia, along with Cherson. By the middle of 988 his men occupied Chrysopolis on the Bosporus, and he besieged Abydus on the Hellespont himself. Basil II held only the European provinces, where the Bulgarians were advancing, and the weaker part of the army, which the Bulgarians had crippled. With more than half the empire's revenues going to Phocas, the central treasury was dangerously depleted.[36]

In these circumstances Basil sealed his alliance with Vladimir of Kiev. Leaping at the chance to marry Anna, Vladimir converted to Christianity and dispatched six thousand men across the Black Sea. Over the summer the marriage of Vladimir and Anna took place in Kiev along with a mass baptism of Russians, and the Russian auxiliaries arrived in Constantinople. Basil made them into a permanent mercenary company known as the Varangian Guard.[37] Basil also sent an army by sea to Trebizond under the Armenian general Gregory of Taron. Gregory marched south and gathered recruits, most of them probably Armenians who had backed Sclerus before he had been betrayed. The opening of this eastern front forced Phocas to send his son Nicephorus east, where he obtained a thousand Iberian reinforcements from David of Upper Tao.

At the beginning of 989 Basil crossed the Bosporus and made a night landing with his Varangians at Chrysopolis. There he surprised the rebels, killed many of them, and captured most of the rest with their commander, whom he impaled. The emperor thus scored his first personal military victory. Although Phocas's son Nicephorus did defeat Gregory of Taron, at the news of Basil's success Nicephorus's men dispersed. That spring the emperor and his brother Constantine marched to relieve the siege of Abydus. After the armies had faced each other for several days, Basil made a surprise attack. As Phocas tried to rally his forces, he suffered a seizure and fell dead on the field.

Phocas's death left Basil the victor. He showed little mercy, massacring some of Phocas's men and executing others. Meanwhile Russian troops from Kiev seem to have taken Cherson from the rebels, looting it thoroughly in the process.[38] Though Basil celebrated a triumph, many rebels remained at large, and they found a leader when Phocas's widow released Bardas Sclerus from his prison near Melitene.[39] Sclerus proclaimed himself emperor again, allied himself with Phocas's sons Leo and Nicephorus, and resumed the alliances with the Arabs and Armenians that Phocas had taken over from him. Yet Sclerus was old and tired, and his men were demoralized and scattered. That fall he and Nicephorus Phocas accepted a pardon offered by the emperor's brother Constantine. Leo

125. Silver miliaresion, shown one and three-quarters times actual size, commemorating the victory of Basil II (r. 963–1025) and his brother Constantine VIII at Abydus in 989: *obverse,* bust of the Virgin *Nikopoios* (Granting Victory) with the inscription "Mother of God, Help the Emperors"; *reverse,* inscription "Glorified Mother of God, the One Who Trusts in You Does Not Fail." (Photo: Courtesy of the Arthur M. Sackler Museum, Harvard University Art Museums, Whittemore Collection)

Phocas tried to hold out at Antioch, but the Antiochenes betrayed him to Basil. He was exiled, and Basil was at last the unchallenged emperor.

These three years of civil war, coming just seven years after the earlier war with Bardas Sclerus, shook the empire badly. The army was depleted and disorganized; the treasury was exhausted. Samuel's Bulgarians exploited the disorder to expand east and south, taking Preslav and Pliska, raiding down to Thessalonica, and in 989 seizing nearby Beroea. The Russians returned Cherson to Basil in ruins. The Arabs of Sicily had resumed raiding Byzantine Italy. Luckily for the empire, across the eastern frontier the Hamdanids, Marwanids, and Buwayhids had been too busy fighting each other to attack the Byzantines.

Despite ending in a victory that did Basil much credit, the second civil war soured his character for good. He turned his back on the distractions of his youth, which he apparently decided he could no longer afford. He became cruel and austere. After what he regarded as repeated betrayals by his generals and advisers, the emperor distrusted almost anyone powerful. Though past thirty, he remained unmarried, probably to avoid meddling by a wife or her relatives. He was particularly suspicious of ambitious generals, like those who had revolted against him, of Iberians and Armenians, who had allied themselves with the rebels, and of the Bulgarians, who by defeating him had set off the revolts.

BASIL II'S SUCCESSES

Although at first Basil was as much interested in revenge as in restoring the empire, the two aims turned out to be compatible, and his resentments were neither blind nor intemperate. About the spring of 990, he sent an expedition to punish the Iberians for their support of Bardas Phocas. After one Byzantine victory, David of Upper Tao sued for peace, offering to submit to the empire and to will it all his possessions, since he had no son. Basil accepted the terms and gave David the rank of curopalates. As the emperor's agent, David set about conquering lands from the Muslims to add to his legacy.

The next year Basil began a methodical war against the Bulgarians. Trying to avoid risking defeats or ambushes of the sort he had suffered at Trajan's Gate, he concentrated on retaking the territory that Byzantium had held at John Tzimisces' death. Apparently he began by attacking Samuel's conquests in northern Greece. Basil soon captured the nominal Bulgarian emperor Romanus, and slowly reduced the fortresses that Samuel had occupied over the years, Larissa presumably among them.[40]

While pursuing his Bulgarian war, Basil left sufficient forces in the East with the duke of Antioch Michael Burtzes, who helped defend the Byzantine protectorate of Aleppo against an attack inspired by the Fatimids. In 992 Basil also sent an army against the Marwanids of southern Armenia, probably in retaliation for their help to Bardas Sclerus, and forced them to pay tribute. While the Byzantines were occupied with their campaigns against the Bulgarians and Marwanids, a Fatimid general made another attack on Aleppo, defeated Burtzes near Antioch, and incited the Muslims of Laodicea to revolt; but Aleppo itself held out, and Burtzes subdued and deported the rebels after the Fatimid army withdrew.

The emperor continued campaigning against the Bulgarians in 993, making an alliance with the Serbian prince of Dioclea against them.[41] Within a year Basil recaptured Beroea, and seemed to be ready to raid Samuel's heartland around Ochrid. Then the Fatimids attacked Aleppo once more. Although Basil reinforced Burtzes, who again marched to Aleppo's defense, the Fatimid army routed him, killed five thousand of his troops, and put Aleppo under a close siege through the winter. The desperate Aleppines appealed to the emperor in Bulgaria.

As he prepared to return to the East, Basil seems to have entrusted the Bulgarian war to Gregory of Taron as duke of Thessalonica.[42] In spring 995 the emperor reportedly mustered forty thousand men and hurried to Aleppo with an advance guard of seventeen thousand.[43] Merely at the news of his approach, the Fatimid forces raised the siege, which had almost starved the city out, and retreated south. Basil could easily have annexed Aleppo, but he chose to strengthen it. Remitting the year's tribute, he reconquered the emirate's cities that had fallen to the Fatimids, including Apamea and Homs. Next he besieged Tripoli. Its Fatimid governor agreed to accept a Byzantine protectorate like that over Aleppo, but the Tripolitanians repudiated him and his concessions. For the present Basil contented himself with rebuilding the neighboring Byzantine fortress of Antaradus, which the Fatimids had destroyed. He also arrested and replaced the unsuccessful Burtzes as duke of Antioch. After this brief and businesslike campaign, the emperor returned to his capital.

There Basil attended to domestic affairs, which he seems to have neglected somewhat during the campaigns. In 996 he named a new patriarch of Constantinople after a four-year vacancy, and promulgated a new law against officials who acquired land from smallholders. Reaffirming Romanus I's law of 934 that ordered those who had bought land from the poor to return their purchases without compensation, Basil extended the law to former smallholders who had become rich, and allowed the land to be reclaimed at any time, abolishing a forty-year statute of limitations. Basil also voided all grants of imperial estates made by Basil Lecapenus, unless they had received the emperor's explicit approval.[44] Although in this legislation Basil did only a little more than his predecessors, he cannot have forgotten that landholding families like the Scleri and Phocades had caused him so much trouble. He took care to confiscate the enormous estates of Eustathius Maleïnus, a former ally of Bardas Phocas, when Eustathius died. Basil probably remained at Constantinople for a time after promulgating his law, in order to enforce it vigorously and to organize the lands he reclaimed into imperial estates.

The emperor may also have been reluctant to return to Bulgaria because the Fatimid caliph al-ʿAzīz was building a fleet to send against Byzantine Syria. But in spring 996 the ships burned in their harbor near Cairo; the Egyptians blamed merchants from the nominally Byzantine port of Amalfi. When the caliph sent another fleet and an army that besieged Antaradus, the new duke of Antioch Damian Dalassenus easily broke the siege and raided around Tripoli. Then al-ʿAzīz died, and his successor was only a boy. Rebellions against the Fatimids broke out at Damascus and Tyre in 997, with both sets of rebels appealing to Basil. He sent ships to Tyre, but avoided involvement as far inland as Damascus.

The same year Samuel of Bulgaria raided around Thessalonica. He captured the son of its duke Gregory of Taron, and when Gregory tried to rescue his son he was himself ambushed and killed. Having disabled the western Byzantine forces, Samuel retook Beroea and several places in northern Thessaly, and started raiding Greece. The emperor then put the Bulgarian war into the hands of a new domestic of the West, Nicephorus Uranus, who arrived at Thessalonica to learn that Samuel had reached the Peloponnesus. Uranus marched through Thessaly, made Larissa his base, and in the Sperchius valley met Samuel returning from the south.[45] Uranus made a night crossing of the rain-swollen river, surprised the Bulgarians, and slaughtered almost all of them.

Samuel himself and his eldest son were wounded, and made their way back to western Bulgaria with scarcely any troops.[46] The Bulgarian leader sued for peace, offering to make his territories a client state. Basil was ready to agree; but then Samuel apparently heard that his nominal sovereign Romanus had died in captivity in Constantinople. The news seems to have emboldened Samuel to proclaim himself Bulgarian emperor and renew his resistance, weakened though the Bulgarians obviously were.

As the emperor planned to resume fighting the Bulgarians himself, in 998 the Fatimids recaptured not only the part of Syria that had rebelled against them but Apamea, a possession of Aleppo. When the duke of Antioch Damian besieged Apamea, he was fatally wounded, and the Fatimid forces routed his men. The emperor tried to negotiate a settlement with the Fatimids, and went on with his campaign against the Bulgarians. By early 999 he avenged his defeat of thirteen years before by attacking and capturing Serdica and its surrounding fortresses, which he probably added to a new Theme of Philippopolis. After his return, finding that diplomacy had failed with the Fatimids, Basil felt compelled to go east in person. To avoid entrusting the powerful European army to any single commander, he divided it between two generals, Nicephorus Xiphias and Theodorocanus.

In autumn 999, the emperor arrived in Syria with his Varangian Guard and Nicephorus Uranus. Basil quickly cleared the Fatimids from the region of Apamea, garrisoning the fort of Sizara with Armenians to watch the frontier for the future.[47] He besieged Tripoli again, but as before that Fatimid stronghold withstood him. Appointing Uranus duke of Antioch, Basil retired to Cilicia for the winter. He appears to have created two new themes north of Aleppo, filling a gap left by the loss of Edessa and screening Cilicia from future raids.[48] Though he prepared to resume his campaign the following year, his expedition had already persuaded the Fatimids to negotiate seriously for peace.

The Bulgarian emperor Samuel seems to have taken advantage of the absence of Basil and Uranus to seize Dyrrhachium, probably by treachery. As its governor, Samuel appointed Gregory of Taron's son Ashot, whom he had captured in 997 and married to his daughter. Samuel also conquered the Serbian Kingdom of Dioclea and attacked the Theme of Dalmatia, which was only rescued when the Venetian doge took control in the emperor's name in the spring of 1000.[49] Then Basil's forces struck hard against Samuel's possessions in eastern Bulgaria. The two Byzantine commanders Nicephorus Xiphias and Theodorocanus captured Preslav, Pliska, and Little Preslav, all of which became themes.[50]

Basil would probably have returned at once to fight Samuel if the Iberian prince David of Upper Tao had not died that same spring. Since the emperor was David's heir, he hurried to Upper Tao and annexed it as a new Ducate of Iberia before the neighboring princes could claim it. The prince with the best claim, Bagrat III of Abasgia, was consoled with the title of curopalates and lifetime possession of some of David's border territories. After taking his Iberian inheritance, early in 1001 the emperor concluded a ten-year truce with the Fatimids which, given that they had proved unable to make conquests from him and he wanted none from them, served the interests of both sides. Once it was made, Basil entrusted the defense of the eastern frontier to Nicephorus Uranus and returned to fight the Bulgarians.

Apparently while Basil was preparing his campaign, Ashot of Taron escaped by ship from his unwanted post as Samuel's governor of Dyrrhachium, and helped arrange the city's surrender to the emperor.[51] After its recovery, Basil marched by way of Thessalonica into Samuel's possessions in northern Greece. He not only retook Samuel's recent conquests but captured Edessa, which had probably been Bulgarian for more than a century. In spring 1002 he marched to Vidin, Samuel's chief fortress on the Danube, and invested it closely.

By summer the garrison of Vidin was desperate. Too weak to relieve it, Samuel tried to draw Basil away by a raid to the south. He made a rapid attack on Adrianople, surprised it when it was undefended, and sacked it. But by this time the emperor had taken Vidin, and he avenged himself by sacking several of the Bulgarians' border forts on his way back to Constantinople. The next spring Basil retaliated more sharply by raiding far into Bulgaria. He defeated Samuel near Scopia, and sacked both Samuel's camp and Scopia itself before returning to his capital.

126. Basil II triumphing over his enemies. Contemporary illumination from the Venice Psalter (Marcianus graecus 17). (Photo: Biblioteca Marciana, Venice)

There Basil enacted a new law against large landholders, purportedly to meet the expenses of the Bulgarian war. He ordered that when small-holders defaulted on their taxes, their neighbors with larger holdings should pay not just their share but, seemingly, the whole of the unpaid sum. Since this law applied to many church lands, the patriarch Sergius II and much of the clergy protested it; but the emperor merely promised to revoke the law once the Bulgarians submitted.[52] The treasury may still have been straitened, as this law implies, because the civil wars with Bardas Sclerus and Bardas Phocas had been followed by expensive and not very profitable campaigns in Iberia, Syria, and Bulgaria. In the West the emperor had largely left the task of defense to the doge of Venice, who had to rescue Bari from an Arab siege in fall 1003.[53]

The next year Basil made a fourth campaign against Samuel, perhaps only a raid in force, before interrupting the war to give the battered Bulgarians a chance to submit.[54] He had restored the empire's territories in both East and West to roughly what they had been at the death of John Tzimisces. Though Basil had not retaken Tzimisces' themes of Morava and Ras, he had conquered Edessa in Greece and Serdica, as Tzimisces probably had not. Conquest for its own sake meant little to Basil; his largest acquisition, the Ducate of Iberia, had been the unplanned result of his revenge on its prince. With his enemies punished and his frontiers secure, after eighteen years of almost constant warfare the emperor gave himself and his empire a needed rest.

BASIL II'S CONQUESTS

This period of relative calm lasted for some years, during which the treasury filled comfortably. Basil seems to have made occasional raids on the Bulgarians, presumably still hoping that Samuel would accept a Byzantine protectorate, as he had once offered to do. Otherwise the emperor showed a reluctance to fight that bordered on apathy. In 1008 he showed no concern when Georgia was united under Bagrat III, though the heir to such a kingdom would obviously be tempted to keep the lands that since 1000 were due to the empire on Bagrat's death. When the Hamdanids began a war to recover Aleppo from a new dynasty that had displaced them, Basil refused to intervene on behalf of his clients. He also renewed his treaty with the Fatimid caliph al-Ḥākim for another ten years, and kept the peace despite Ḥākim's order in 1012 destroying all the churches in his caliphate.

By that time the emperor had resumed raiding western Bulgaria. Probably he was exasperated with Samuel's persistence; perhaps Samuel had done something further to provoke him, such as raiding northern Greece. Still Basil made no effort to conquer Samuel's remaining territory outright, contenting himself with ravaging it through the pass of Clidium ("The Key") between the Strymon and Axius valleys. When

Basil arrived at this pass in the summer of 1014, he found Samuel barricaded before it with an army, and learned that another Bulgarian force was marching on Thessalonica. The duke of Thessalonica Theophylact Botaniates put the second Bulgarian army to flight and joined the emperor at Clidium. While Basil attacked Samuel's palisade, the strategus of Philippopolis Nicephorus Xiphias led a detachment unnoticed through the hills, encircling the Bulgarians.

Samuel and his son barely managed to slip away to the fort of Prilep, and almost his whole army was trapped. Even after killing many of the Bulgarians, the Byzantines took fifteen thousand prisoners. Marching through the pass, Basil besieged the fort of Strumitsa, and sent Botaniates to clear the Axius valley south to Thessalonica. While burning the palisades that the Bulgarians had built across the valley, however, Botaniates and his men fell into a Bulgarian ambush and were slaughtered. The news enraged Basil. Evidently to avenge their deaths, he blinded all his fifteen thousand Bulgarian captives except for one in each hundred, whom he left with one eye to guide the others to Prilep. At the sight of his blinded army, Samuel suffered a heart attack, and died two days later.

Unaware of this, Basil returned to the Strymon valley, where the Bulgarian fort of Melnik surrendered to him. Since the campaigning season was coming to an end, he withdrew toward Constantinople. But at Mosynopolis he heard of Samuel's death, and realized how critical the Bulgarians' position had become. He seized his chance and marched by way of Thessalonica to invade western Bulgaria from the south. When Samuel's son and heir Gabriel Radomir offered no resistance, Basil advanced to Bitola, where he burned a palace of Samuel's. After sending a detachment that took Prilep and garrisoned it, he returned by way of Edessa to Thessalonica only at the beginning of 1015.

Though during the winter Gabriel seems to have retaken Edessa with help from its people, in the spring Basil returned, recaptured the town, and deported its inhabitants. In desperation Gabriel offered to become a Byzantine client; but Basil suspected the offer was treacherous and rejected it. He entrusted the Bulgarian war to the joint command of Nicephorus Xiphias and the duke of Thessalonica Constantine Diogenes. They set about besieging the fort of Moglena, which surrendered when Basil arrived later in the year. He resettled the defenders in Armenia.

At this point the emperor Gabriel was assassinated by his cousin John Vladislav, who took the Bulgarian throne and offered to submit to Basil. The emperor accepted the submission, which was probably what he had wanted all along, and withdrew. But soon afterward Basil received a report that John was trying to trick him, apparently by a surprise attack on Dyrrhachium. In a rage the emperor dispatched troops to raid the plain north of Bitola, and drove on the Bulgarians' capital of Ochrid, blinding all the prisoners he took.

While John attacked Dyrrhachium without success, the emperor sacked Ochrid. Basil wanted to press on toward Dyrrhachium and join some partisans of the murdered Gabriel in the hills; but he turned back when he learned that the Bulgarians had ambushed and massacred his men near Bitola. Routing the Bulgarians there, he ordered the campaign continued by Nicephorus Xiphias and the new duke of Thessalonica David Arianites, who soon took Strumitsa. The Bulgarians' empire was in ruins when Basil returned to Constantinople at the beginning of 1016.

As long as he was fighting the Bulgarians, Basil remained reluctant to intervene elsewhere. That winter the new king George of Georgia, refusing to surrender the lands that his late father had held only for life, attacked the Ducate of Iberia and defeated a Byzantine army. In response Basil did no more than contribute a fleet to a Russian raid on the moribund Khazars, which he possibly meant as a warning to the Georgians. Even when the civil war at Aleppo let the Fatimids occupy the city, Basil refrained from breaking the truce, though he showed his displeasure by banning trade between Byzantium and the Fatimid Caliphate.

The emperor spent the campaigning season of 1016 in a fruitless siege of the Bulgarian fortress of Pernik. The next spring he besieged Castoria. The Bulgarian emperor John planned an attack on Dristra in alliance with the Pechenegs, but at the mere report that Basil was preparing to come the Pechenegs gave up the alliance. As John moved south, Basil marched against him with Constantine Diogenes, who was again the duke of Thessalonica, and routed the Bulgarians near Edessa. Once more Basil returned to Constantinople only after the onset of winter, at the beginning of 1018. With the Bulgarian war going so well, the emperor sent substantial reinforcements to Longobardia, where a citizen of Bari named Meles had raised a rebellion.

That winter the Bulgarian emperor John was killed in another attempt to take Dyrrhachium. As at the death of Samuel, Basil mustered his forces at once and headed for Bulgaria. This time his success was even greater than before. When he reached Adrianople, the commander of the eastern Bulgarian fortresses, including Pernik, simply capitulated. Other Bulgarian boyars followed his example, accepting Byzantine ranks from Basil. When the emperor arrived at Strumitsa, he met the patriarch of Bulgaria David, who not only submitted but announced the surrender of John's widow Maria. Where Basil had only sought a client state, he now had been offered full possession, and accepted it.

The emperor marched peacefully through the middle of western Bulgaria, installing David Arianites at Scopia as duke of Bulgaria. At Ochrid Basil found Maria and many more boyars, all of whom pledged their loyalty to him. He claimed the Bulgarian royal treasure, which he distributed among his troops; but he let the Bulgarian patriarchate at Ochrid continue as an independent archbishopric, and allowed the Bulgarians to go on paying their taxes in kind at the rates collected by Samuel. Though at first three of John Vladislav's sons and some other Bulgarians tried to resist in the hills, they soon surrendered as well. Basil pardoned them all, except for imprisoning the governor of Epirus Nicolitzas, who had deserted from Byzantine service. In Nicolitzas's former territories Basil created two new themes, plus a third in the region of Castoria.[55]

Bulgaria, long the only power in the Balkans that rivaled Byzantium, had utterly collapsed. From Castoria the emperor made his way overland to Athens, where he gave thanks for his victory in the Parthenon, in its Byzantine form a church dedicated to the Virgin. That autumn he traveled to Constantinople to celebrate a triumph, which notwithstanding all his victories was only his second on record. The patriarch Sergius reminded him of his promise to abrogate at the end of the war his law penalizing large landholders, but Basil kept the law in force. No one dared contradict him.

The conquest of Bulgaria put the empire in a position of commanding power. In Italy the catepan Basil Bojoannes drove Meles from Longobardia, and in 1019 Bojoannes secured the theme's northern frontier by building the new fort of Troia. One last Bulgarian chieftain held out at Sirmium, but he was confronted, invited to negotiate, and assassinated by Constantine Diogenes. Sirmium became a ducate, and the neighboring princes of Croatia and Serbia became Byzantine clients. Byzantium had become undisputed master of the Balkan peninsula.

The emperor was now free to deal with affairs in the East however he wished, and the easterners knew it. As usual when he had the upper hand, he was conciliatory. He ended his boycott of Fatimid trade by 1020, when the Fatimid governor of Aleppo rebelled and sought Byzantine protection. As for George of Georgia, despite his attack on the Ducate of Iberia Basil merely asked him to surrender the lands overdue

127. View of the ruins of Ani,
through the main gate. (Photo:
Warren Treadgold)

since his father's death. Unable to believe he would be forgiven, George foolishly allied himself with the Fatimids and the Armenian king Smbat-John of Ani against the empire.

The emperor set out for his recovered client state of Aleppo early in 1021, to ward off a Fatimid attack. But the mysterious disappearance of the caliph Ḥākim, who was presumably murdered, allowed Basil to turn on George of Georgia. Too terrified to submit, George retreated into Abasgia. The emperor devastated much of Iberia and Armenia, blinding the prisoners he took as he had done in Bulgaria. In the winter he retired to Trebizond and prepared to attack Abasgia with a fleet. At this George and Smbat-John sued for peace.

George agreed to give up the lands that had long been demanded of him and to become Basil's client. The neighboring Principality of Kars also became a Byzantine protectorate, and Smbat-John even agreed to bequeath his Kingdom of Ani to the empire. This made Byzantine dominance of the Caucasus so patent that King Senacherim of Vaspurakan ceded his kingdom to Basil outright to protect it from raids, probably by Muslims from Azerbaijan. So in the spring of 1022 Basil marched back to the Caucasus, claimed his new lands, and set up a Ducate of Vaspurakan. After winning the war in the north, he had ostensibly won the war in the east.

Yet while Basil was in Armenia, a revolt broke out in Asia Minor. Its leaders were Basil's long-serving general Nicephorus Xiphias, then strategus of the Anatolics, and Nicephorus Phocas, son of the rebel Bardas, who was proclaimed emperor. Despite all his victories, many people had reasons for resenting the emperor, and by this time he was sixty-four, with his only male heir a brother nearly as old as he. Nicephorus Phocas cannot have been much younger than Basil, but he had a large family and many friends in Cappadocia. The rebels also seem to have been in league with George of Georgia and Smbat-John of Ani, who withdrew their promises to the emperor.

As Basil gathered troops to oppose the rebels, in late summer Xiphias had Phocas assassinated in the hope of becoming emperor himself. But since most of the rebels had been loyal to Phocas, they surrendered to the emperor, whose men captured Xiphias. Basil soundly defeated George and imposed the original terms on both the Georgian king and Smbat-John, taking George's son as a hostage. In consideration of Xiphias's earlier services, Basil exercised mercy and merely exiled the rebellious general, but other rebels were executed or blinded. Again victorious, the emperor returned to Constantinople before the end of 1022. He appears to have celebrated his triumphs by a temporary remission of land and hearth taxes, still without revoking his law on large landholders.

Byzantium now enjoyed another interval of relative peace. During Basil's absence in the East the German emperor Henry II had invaded Longobardia, but Henry withdrew after some indecisive sieges. A raid in the Aegean Sea by a Russian freebooter came to nothing.[56] Another civil war in Aleppo gave the Fatimids a shaky hold on the city again, and apparently provoked Basil to renew his ban on trade with the caliphate. In any case, the new dynasty of the Mirdasids drove the Fatimids from the city in early 1025, allied themselves with Byzantium, and extended their power as far south as Baalbek. No one could ignore the fact that the empire had become the main power in both Syria and Armenia.

Of all its frontier regions, only in Italy was Byzantium not absolutely supreme. Even though Basil turned sixty-seven in 1025, he wanted to accomplish one more project, an expedition against the Arabs of Sicily. Sicily was, after all, the empire's one important loss of the past two centuries that had yet to be regained. Basil sent a large army ahead of him under the eunuch Orestes the Protospatharius, which joined the forces of the catepan Bojoannes in Calabria. The emperor was preparing to follow and conduct the campaign in person, when he suddenly fell ill and died.

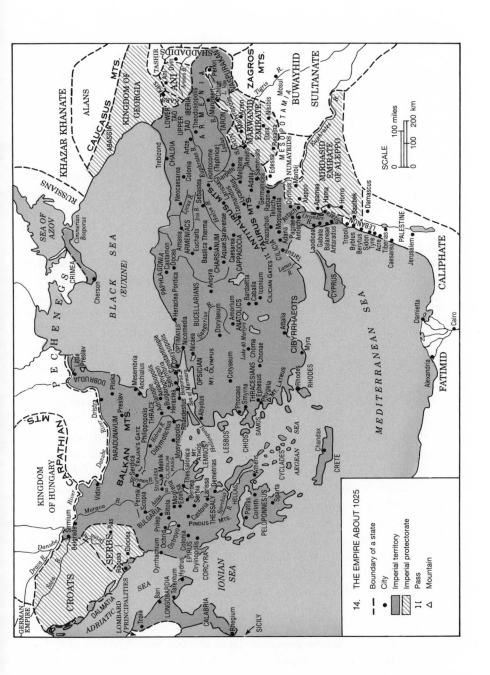

14. THE EMPIRE ABOUT 1025

Basil II had reigned for sixty-two years and ruled for forty-nine, spans unequaled by any earlier Byzantine or Roman emperor. His hand was sometimes slow, but it was steady. A careful restorer and a reluctant conqueror, he was willing to fight, but seldom eager. He purposefully recovered and consolidated the hasty gains of Nicephorus II and John Tzimisces, but had little interest in expanding beyond them. His preference was for an empire surrounded by peaceful client states. He annexed much of Iberia and Armenia through cessions and bequests that he had not demanded. He conquered western Bulgaria only because its rulers refused the protectorate he would have granted them almost to the end.

Basil's strengths as a general were persistence and caution. After 986 he never fell into another ambush, though he campaigned for years in unfamiliar and mountainous terrain. Yet he needed many years to subdue the makeshift state of western Bulgaria. He was no born tactician like Nicephorus II or John Tzimisces, who could sweep his enemies from great stretches of land in a single campaigning season. Basil was not merely cautious himself, but kept his generals on a tight rein. His precautions nevertheless succeeded in frustrating the sort of plot that had brought down his two more flamboyant predecessors. What is striking about Basil's military record is not so much its brilliance as its consistency.

At his death, after leaving two years of land and hearth taxes uncollected, Basil had turned a gold reserve that was low in 998 and none too high in 1003 into a vast hoard of some 14.4 million nomismata.[57] This staggering sum must have been amassed mostly by taxation, since Basil kept none of the Bulgarian treasury for himself and the rest of the booty and tribute he collected could hardly have been on this scale. His law of 1003 making large landholders liable for all taxes in default must have meant that the treasury collected virtually all the taxes owed to it. Though Basil may still have needed money when he made the law, he must have had more than enough by 1018, when he broke his promise to cancel it. By then his main purpose was presumably to emulate the emperors since Romanus I in restricting large estates. At a time when the great families had become stronger than ever, his vigilance kept them under firm control.

For all his undoubted success, Basil showed little breadth of vision. His driving motive for wars on the Iberians and Bulgarians was evidently revenge for their having fought against him. His memories of the revolts of Bardas Sclerus and Bardas Phocas lay behind his strictness with other magnates. At the head of the mightiest and wealthiest state in the western world, Basil remained obsessed with military and financial security. Even his provisions for the future were shortsighted. Unlike previous emperors, for whom an heir had been an urgent concern, Basil not only remained unmarried and childless himself but arranged no marriages for his brother's daughters, who were the last survivors of his house. Instead he looked forward with equanimity to the rule of his niece Zoë, a frivolous old maid.[58] Probably Basil thought he had left the empire so strong it could take care of itself. In this he was very nearly right.

CHAPTER SEVENTEEN

The Expansion of Society, 780–1025

Between the eighth and eleventh centuries the empire made a recovery unparalleled in history for so ancient a state. It almost doubled its territory, expanding from its Anatolian heartland into Armenia, Syria, and Mesopotamia, and conquering almost the whole Balkan peninsula. Its borders were surrounded by client states, and its political and ecclesiastical influence spread out as far as the vast lands of Russia. In 780 Byzantium had been weaker than either the Abbasid Caliphate or the Frankish Kingdom of Charlemagne, and the Bulgar Khanate posed a serious threat to the few Byzantine possessions in the Balkans. By 1025 none of those three rivals even survived in a recognizable form, and the empire was stronger than all its neighbors.

While the Byzantines made these gains, their society became if anything more unified. No important heresy troubled the Church after Iconoclasm faded away in the mid-ninth century. Within another century, the schisms over Photius and the Tetragamy were also put to rest. Even after all its conquests, the empire was overwhelmingly orthodox Christian, and predominantly Greek-speaking. Military mutinies and urban riots became rare; the famines of the mid-tenth century seem to have come to an end, and the emperors had curbed the depredations of the empire's large landholders. Although political crises still occurred, most of them were soon resolved. Legally the Macedonian dynasty reigned without interruption from 867, even when its members reigned alongside Romanus I, Nicephorus II, and John Tzimisces. After the disasters of the preceding period, these achievements were doubly impressive.

ANNEXATIONS AND ASSIMILATION

The empire's great conquests were the work of several emperors who followed no single plan and sometimes no plan at all. Before the reign of Nicephorus II the acquisitions were mostly defensive, intended either to establish buffer zones around the empire or to remove nests of pirates or raiders. The expansion also tended to be opportunistic, as an emperor or even a general took his chance to seize or occupy whatever he could. Before 963 nearly all the territory retaken and held had formerly been no-man's-land along the Anatolian and Balkan frontiers, most of which was hilly, poor, and almost empty of inhabitants.

Thus Irene's annexations in Thrace were deliberate but limited, serving to protect the capital and its hinterland from Bulgar raids. Nicephorus I seems to have been inspired by an unexpected victory in the Peloponnesus to reoccupy most of Greece; his conquests, though of economic value in themselves, helped defend Hellas, Thessalonica, and Cephalonia. Theophilus, who cared more for victories than for conquests, annexed only a little territory, in order to resettle his Khurramite refugees, reopen the land route from Thrace to Thessalonica, and protect Dyrrhachium and Cherson. Basil I's small conquests in Italy and the East were by-products of wars meant to stop Arab and Paulician raiders. The new eastern themes of Leo VI and Romanus I were partly intentional annexations, partly windfalls when Armenians and Arabs came over to the empire, but primarily useful for barring Arab raiders from Anatolia. Romanus II conquered Crete, as his predecessors had repeatedly tried and failed to do, chiefly to eliminate its pirates.

The reign of Nicephorus II marked the beginning of an expansion that went beyond defensive needs. Although Nicephorus's acquisitions in Cilicia, Cyprus, and his Armenian themes had definite military advantages, they seem also to have been meant as bases for his subsequent conquests around Edessa and Antioch. Since neither of those cities had been a major base for Arab raiders, Nicephorus evidently wanted them for their own sake, probably because of their venerable Christian past; he reportedly hoped to take Jerusalem as well. John Tzimisces, who expressed the same hope, seems to have enjoyed the process of conquest more than any other emperor. His annexation of eastern Bulgaria exceeded any defensive purpose, and the conquests he coveted in Palestine would have caused more defensive problems than they solved. Basil II

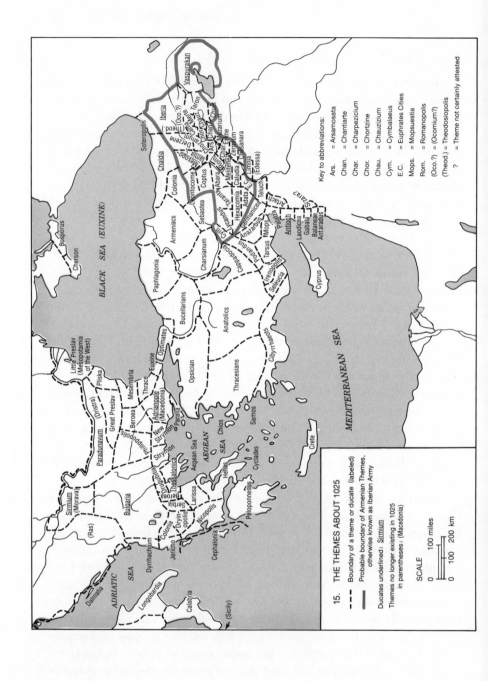

15. THE THEMES ABOUT 1025

- - - Boundary of a theme or ducate (labeled)
━━━ Probable boundary of Armenian Themes,
      otherwise known as Iberian Army

Ducates underlined: <u>Sirmium</u>

Themes no longer existing in 1025
in parentheses: (Macedonia)

Key to abbreviations:

Ars. = Arsamosata
Chan. = Chantiarte
Char. = Charpezicium
Chor. = Chortzine
Chau. = Chauzizium
Cym. = Cymbalaeus
E.C. = Euphrates Cities
Mops. = Mopsuestia
Rom. = Romanopolis
(Oco.?) = (Ocomium?)
(Theod.) = Theodosiopolis
? = Theme not certainly attested

SCALE

0   100 miles

0   100   200 km

BLACK SEA (EUXINE)

MEDITERRANEAN SEA

ADRIATIC SEA

AEGEAN SEA

Aegean Sea

Vaspurakan
Iberia
Soteropolis
Chaldia
Colonia
Sebastea
Armeniacs
Charsianum
Paphlagonia
Bucellarians
Anatolics
Optimates
Opsician
Thracesians
Cibyrrhaeots
Cappadocia
Lycandus
Seleucia
Tzamandus
Tarsus
Anazarbus
Mopsuestia
Antioch
Laodicea
Gabala
Balaneae
Antaradus
Cyprus
Teluch
Artach
Melitene
Edessa
Samosata
Bosporus
Cherson

Thrace
Euxine
Macedonia
Strymon
Paristrion
Thessalonica
Beroea
Dryinopolis
Nicopolis
Cephalonia
Larissa
Hellas
Chios
Samos
Cyclades
Peloponnesus
Crete

Little Preslav
(Mesopotamia of the West)
Great Preslav
Pliska
Mesembria
Beroe
Philippopolis
Adrianople
New Macedonia
Serbia
Bulgaria
Sirmium (Morava)
(Ras)
Dyrrhachium
Dalmatia
Longobardia
Calabria
(Sicily)
Jericho
Colonia
Paradunavum (Dnistra)

never bothered to recover Edessa in the East, but his retaliatory wars led him to complete John's annexation of Bulgaria and to take more of Iberia and Armenia.

The process of establishing thematic garrisons in the conquered regions, many of which were barren and devastated, doubtless slowed the conquests. From the time of Nicephorus I almost all the newly acquired themes were small. Leo VI created cleisurae that seem to have had as few as 800 troops, and Romanus I's eastern themes had an average of 2,400. The army is reported to have had 120,000 men in 840, and recorded figures indicate that it had about 150,000 in 963. Then the reconquests brought more rapid growth, with several large or medium-sized ducates and dozens of themes ranging from middling to tiny. The ducates and themes in Armenia totaled 50,000 men, the Immortals numbered 4,000, and the Varangian Guard was 6,000 strong. By 1025 the army must have had around 250,000 soldiers.[1] Reversing the eighth-century pattern of deploying troops toward the center, the new themes and some contingents of the tagmata were concentrated on the frontiers.

By 1025 the empire again had borders of the approximate but sketchable sort that the early Byzantine state had possessed. The Balkan frontier was quite similar to what it had been in Justinian's day: it ran along the Danube to Sirmium, then south through the mountains to include much of the Dalmatian coast, which Basil II seems to have reclaimed from Venice. In theory a part of the empire, Venice was at least an ally; and the Serbian and Croatian principalities were clients protecting the theme of Dalmatia and the ducates of Bulgaria and Sirmium. Although the Pechenegs across the Danube could be troublesome, they were no better than other barbarians at crossing a well-defended river, and they were vulnerable to attacks from the rear by the empire's Russian allies.

In the East, once the reconquests passed the natural barrier of the Antitaurus and Taurus, no easily defensible frontier could be found. Yet the Armenian massif was an obstacle, and the Armenian and Iberian themes formed a shield. Azerbaijan was hostile but fairly remote, while the Christian states of Georgia, Ani, Kars, and Sasun and the Muslim lands of the Marwanids had become clients. In northern Syria, after 970 Aleppo was usually a Byzantine protectorate and no longer a danger. Not only Tzimisces but Basil II wanted to anchor the frontier in the south by taking Tripoli from the Fatimids. Yet the Fatimids, though they were interested in Aleppo as a base for attacking Buwayhid Baghdad, never seriously tried to conquer lands that the Byzantines had annexed outright.

The most exasperating front for the Byzantines was southern Italy, where no reinforcements were ever quite enough to make the region safe. Every emperor from Michael II to Basil II would have liked to drive the Arabs from Sicily, but time and distance frustrated their plans. Southern Italy was somewhat more accessible, and the empire's naval power had been sufficient to hold the toe and heel of Italy since the time of Justinian I. After strengthening the Imperial Fleet, Basil I began to advance Byzantine holdings in Italy up the Adriatic coast. Even so, the Byzantines never succeeded in making southern Italy fully secure. Basil II hoped to do so, but died before making his expedition.

Although the empire's frontiers in 1025 represented no conscious grand design, they showed a sort of implicit logic that the different emperors had respected. Even the aggressive John Tzimisces avoided conquering Aleppo when he could have; even the cautious Basil II accepted his conquests in Bulgaria and the Caucasus rather than make them protectorates. Among lands not conquered by the end of Basil's reign, only Sicily, Edessa, and southern Syria are known to have tempted any emperor or general. Tzimisces, who had thought of conquests farther afield, never came to the point of needing to decide. Yet the Byzantines' power was such that they might well have been able to conquer inland Syria, western Mesopotamia, or even Egypt, all of which had been parts of the earlier Byzantine Empire. While all these lay some distance from the empire's center and contained few speakers of Greek, the same was true of the conquests that the empire did make in western Bulgaria, Armenia, the Syrian coast, and southern Italy.

Apparently the emperors' underlying if unspoken principle was that they would take only provinces that were mostly Christian or could promptly be made so. Bulgaria, Armenia, Iberia, and Cyprus were already predominantly Christian, and Christians seem to have remained in the majority at Antioch and Edessa.[2] The northern Syrian coast, Cilicia, Crete, Melitene, and Nicephorus I's themes in Greece seem to have had only a minority of Christians before their conquest, but their populations were small enough to be overwhelmed by Christian settlers. Since the Lebanon and Palestine still had many Christians, Tzimisces might reasonably have hoped to give them Christian majorities through a campaign of conversion, deportation, and resettlement. By the eleventh century, however, Egypt, inland Syria, and Mesopotamia were too heavily Muslim to be Christianized without many years of sustained effort. No emperor seems to have been ready to accept so many subjects of another faith for the foreseeable future, and Byzantines had never been very good at converting Muslims.

Although the Balkan territories gained by the empire were predominantly Christian by 1025, they remained more or less primitive. The land that had formed Bulgaria before the reign of Tzimisces included a few towns with some Greek speakers, but as a whole it was overwhelmingly rural and Slavic-speaking, with a significant minority of Romance-speaking Vlachs. This region had been backward and sparsely populated in late ancient times, and it surely remained so during the Bulgarian and Slavic occupation and the wars and raids after the reign of Symeon of Bulgaria. Despite their size, these lands' main contribution to the empire was to protect Greece and Thrace from raids.

Byzantine Greece and Thrace, expanded by the annexations of Nicephorus I and Theophilus and thereafter seldom raided, seem to have made a recovery during this time to at least their level of prosperity in late antiquity. After Nicephorus's resettlement their populations certainly increased, and with enhanced security their towns reestablished themselves and grew. Given the fertility of the Thracian and Thessalian plains, agricultural productivity and trade should have grown apace. The

128. The Monastery of the Dormition, near Orchomenus (Skripou) in Greece, constructed in 874. (Photo: Courtesy of Charalambos Bouras)

region began to have an aristocracy of some importance, who owned land in the countryside and houses in the towns. Its members were often civil officials, whether active or retired. The tenth-century famines in Constantinople, which were in any case short of catastrophic, were probably more a sign of the capital's growing size than of any deficiency in local agriculture or trade.[3]

The Anatolian coastlands of the Optimates, Opsician, Thracesians, and Cibyrrhaeots also prospered, exporting food to the capital and elsewhere. After the loss of Egypt they were always the richest and most populous part of the empire, and with the elimination of the pirates of Crete they became the safest. This fertile region seems to have been where officials most wanted to buy land and emperors tried hardest to prevent them, generally with success.[4] This hunger for land seems to show the growth of the western Anatolian population and its agriculture, both of which impressed Arab travelers. The Arabs also noticed the region's extensive trade, both by sea and by road between Attalia and Constantinople.[5]

Although the Anatolian plateau remained poorer and much less densely populated than the coast, it must have benefited more than any other part of the empire from the end of Arab raids, which had continually rustled its livestock. The increasing prosperity of this region is probably reflected in the power of its great landholders. Most of the empire's leading generals came from landholding families like Burtzes, Botaniates, Melissenus, and Sclerus in the Anatolics, Ducas and Curcuas in Paphlagonia, Maleïnus in the Bucellarians, Diogenes and Phocas in Cappadocia, and Argyrus in Charsianum. The greatest of these, the Sclerus and especially the Phocas family, could draw both on their wealth and on the loyalty of thousands of friends, clients, and peasants who lived on and near their estates. Whatever encroachments such families may have made on military lands seem to have done little harm to the many soldiers in the region, who turned out in force and fought well in both foreign and civil wars.

The eastern themes conquered between 900 and 1025 formed a long and deep defense for the Anatolian plateau. The Armenian themes in the northeast came to include most of the area inhabited by Armenians. On the whole, annexation by the empire improved the security of Armenia, which had suffered from more frequent civil wars and invasions when it was independent. Though some Armenians resisted or fled Byzantine rule, others welcomed it, and it came at the invitation of the princes of Taron and Vaspurakan. This relatively poor region exported men, and became the empire's main source of new soldiers and settlers. Even before the annexations, Armenians became a large element in the Byzantine army and acquired extensive lands on the Anatolian plateau. Some rose to be leading generals, high officials, and even emperors, like Leo V, Basil I, and John Tzimisces.

Cilicia, the northern Syrian coast, and the Euphrates valley up to Melitene were all fairly level and fertile, the richer and more populous part of what had been early Byzantine Syria. The Byzantine reconquest and deportations reduced their populations a good deal, but the emperors encouraged resettlement there by Christians, and attracted many Monophysite Syrians and Armenians.[6] This Christian if largely heterodox majority enjoyed a measure of official tolerance, and seems to have been at least as content under Byzantine as under Muslim rule.[7] In a region that had long been fought over by Muslims and Byzantines, the Byzantine conquest brought relatively peaceful conditions, though the intermittent Byzantine protectorate over Aleppo failed to prevent more warfare there. A large part of Byzantine Syria remained crown land.

From the mid-tenth century onward, the Byzantine islands included Crete and Cyprus and were finally more or less safe. Even during the worst of the Arab piracy and naval raids, however, some islands had already shown signs of economic recovery.[8] Throughout these centuries the part of the empire that suffered most from foreign raids and invasions was southern Italy, but even there the trend was toward more population and greater prosperity.[9] Despite the Arab conquest of most of Sicily early in the period, the security of southern Italy improved somewhat between the late ninth and early eleventh centuries.

By the time of Basil II's death the empire proper was screened by more protectorates and dependencies than ever before. Its military and economic power kept its old outposts of Venice, Naples, Amalfi, and Gaeta nominally Byzantine and generally friendly. Venice was friendliest to the empire, and its help in defending Byzantine southern Italy tended to conceal its almost total autonomy and its domination of Dalmatia, where the garrison was exiguous and Byzantine control was tenuous. The merchants of these Italian ports enjoyed all the privileges of Byzantine subjects, and in return they carried on Byzantine trade with the West and the Arabs that benefited the empire but that few Greek merchants wanted to pursue.

In a somewhat different class from these nominal possessions were the protectorates: Aleppo, the Marwanids, Sasun, Ani, Kars, Georgia, Serbia, and Croatia. When they were obedient, they recognized Byzantine suzerainty and refrained from actions that the emperor might think hostile. Yet for most purposes they acted as independent states. In the later tenth century, Aleppo and the Marwanids paid tribute to the empire, and Aleppo received Byzantine help against the Fatimids; but by the early eleventh century Basil II exacted no tribute from either Aleppo or the Marwanids, and expected Aleppo to handle its own defense. Ani, whose ruler had promised to will it to the empire, was for the time being just another client kingdom. Though all the Christian client rulers held Byzantine ranks and could use Byzantine seals on their documents, such privileges were mere honors, shared by Byzantine allies like Russia.

In 1025 the empire's power was so great that few neighboring powers would risk antagonizing it, and most of those that were Christian looked up to it. In the north the admirers included both the Russians, who had joined the Byzantine church, and the Magyars, who had recently accepted Christianity from the West and become known as Hungarians. The annexation of Bulgaria had removed the one state so large and near to the empire as to make tension almost inevitable. The remaining Armenian principalities could offer only token opposition, and the Lombards of southern Italy were similarly weak. What the German emperors wanted most from Byzantium was recognition, and if possible a marriage alliance. When frustrated, they might invade Byzantine Italy, but they never succeeded in taking much of it or holding any of it. The German emperors most interested in Italy were those most respectful of Byzantium, the Ottonians, who married one Byzantine princess and negotiated for another to marry Otto III.

The Arabs feared the Byzantine army, but as Christians became a minority in Arab Syria, upper Mesopotamia, and Egypt, Byzantine influence weakened in the Fatimid and Buwayhid lands. The Byzantine reconquest hastened the process of Islamization by attracting Christians from the Muslim side of the border to settle on the Byzantine side, expelling Muslims in the opposite direction, and increasing the Muslim powers' fear of Christians as potential allies of Byzantium. When Basil II contented himself with the eastern lands the empire had held at the death of John Tzimisces, he abdicated most of the empire's responsibility for the remaining Christians in Muslim territory. Not even the Fatimid persecution and the destruction of the Holy Sepulcher at Jerusalem changed Basil's mind. Though Nicephorus II or Tzimisces would probably have shown more concern, neither of them had begun the effort needed to draw Egypt and inland Syria back into the sphere of Byzantine influence.

This phase of territorial expansion therefore left the empire strong and secure but with few unfulfilled ambitions for conquest. The only likely prospects for annexation were the rest of Armenia, most of which was due to be inherited in any case, Sicily, and Edessa. Incorporating these three seemed easily within the empire's capabilities. Taking anything more would either annex harmless and not very valuable buffer states, or involve the empire in strenuous wars followed by difficult attempts at assimilation. In the absence of important new enemies, the military system that had first defended and then expanded the empire had finally come to exceed the empire's needs.

THE PARTNERSHIP OF EMPEROR AND ARMY

In comparison with the preceding period of jarring adjustments and military revolts, from the middle of the ninth century the emperors and army worked together comfortably. The army had never been stronger, but it overthrew no emperor after the dithering Michael I Rhangabe in 813. When underage emperors inherited the throne, the army produced as their colleagues Romanus Lecapenus, Nicephorus Phocas, and John Tzimisces; but this simply showed that the army preferred strong leaders to weak regencies, not that it was rebellious. After the hereditary emperors had come of age, the army did show a tendency to back the heirs of Romanus I, Nicephorus II, and Tzimisces—namely Stephen Lecapenus, Bardas Phocas, and Bardas Sclerus. But none of the latter actually became emperor, and none had any desire to weaken the imperial office that he wanted for himself. Even unwarlike emperors took some interest in the needs of the army, and even crowned generals showed some respect for the Macedonian dynasty. Both hereditary and military rulers also worked to restrain the growth of large estates and to strengthen the empire's defenses.

From the late eighth century, with the appearance of the first Byzantine family names, the provincial aristocracy of central Anatolia gained in wealth, influence, and military rank. By the early tenth century aristocrats dominated the chief posts in the army, with the strategi often

129. Fresco of the future emperor John I Tzimisces (right rider) and his future domestic of the East Melias (left rider) as generals leading soldiers for Nicephorus II Phocas, from the Pigeon House Church, Cappadocia (near modern Göreme). (Photo: Irina Andreescu-Treadgold)

commanding themes where they had many estates, tenants, and retainers. Thus the army developed a leadership whose power was in some measure independent of the emperor. At intervals, usually when an emperor looked as if he was somehow weak or becoming weaker, a few high officers would choose a leader who tried to seize the throne. The emperor was nevertheless the one who chose the commanders, and in most cases he could remove at will any general of dubious loyalty or excessive power.

Beginning with Romanus I, the emperors also tried to keep the magnates under control by forbidding them to buy out small landowners. This effort continued even under Nicephorus II, whose family of the Phocas was probably the greatest landholding family of them all. Though most magnates naturally favored their relatives, they did not necessarily favor other magnates. The Phocas and Sclerus families were rivals; if one of them rebelled, the other usually preferred to join the emperor rather than back the rebellion. These two families split the loyalties of the magnates of Anatolia. The larger number of magnates opposed the Phocades, because as the most powerful family they inspired just as much envy and fear among their peers as in the central government.

In fact, the main concern prompting the emperors' tenth-century land laws was probably not with the magnates' long-established ranches on the Anatolian plateau, not even with those of the Phocas family in Cappadocia. Instead the laws were directed against newly rich and influential officials who were trying to join the ranks of the magnates by acquiring farmland from smallholders, including soldiers, and evading taxation on it. Although some of these new buyers were military officers, most of them appear to have been palatine, civil, and ecclesiastical officials.[10] Responsible generals wanted to protect the military lands that supported the army, and the tax revenues that furnished its pay. Responsible emperors wanted the same. If parvenus, bureaucrats, and clerics threatened the basis of the army's strength, they could expect most of the Anatolian aristocracy to side against them and with the emperor.

After the long and dangerous revolts of Bardas Phocas and Bardas Sclerus, Basil II was particularly wary of the magnates. He excluded the Phocas family from high military ranks, usually appointed generals to commands where they held no land, and often divided commands between two generals who could provide a check on each other. But not even Basil tried to do without aristocratic generals like Damian Dalassenus and Constantine Diogenes. The military traditions, connections, and experience of the magnates were the qualities that made good generals. Nearly all of these aristocrats had as strong an interest in Byzantine military success as the emperor had, because victories won them booty and protected their otherwise vulnerable Anatolian estates from Arab raids. The emperors and the magnates needed each other.

Protected by the emperors and led by the magnates, the system of themes introduced in the seventh century adapted to changing conditions surprisingly well. The process of breaking up themes, begun in the eighth century with the creation of the tagmata and carried further in the ninth and tenth centuries, almost eliminated revolts by individual units, though not broad-based plots by leading commanders. The themes continued to frustrate enemy raids, and joined with the tagmata to make increasingly effective offensive forces. Reconquered territory was organized into small themes or added to existing themes, which not only maintained the conquests but provided more troops for further expansion.

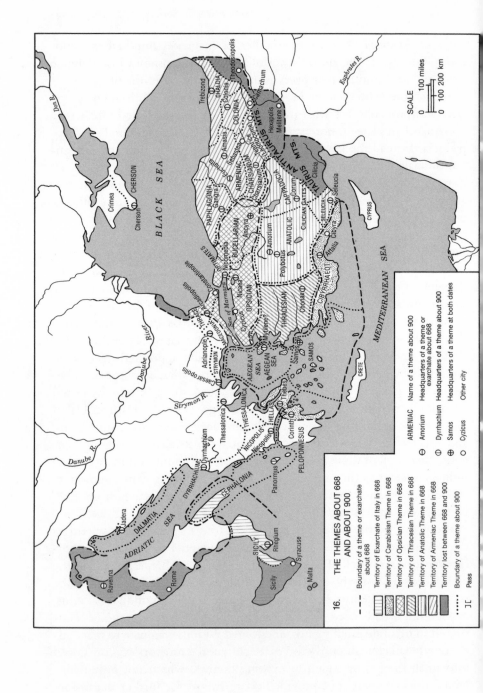

16. THE THEMES ABOUT 668
AND ABOUT 900

- ‒ ‒ ‒ Boundary of a theme or exarchate about 668
- Territory of Exarchate of Italy in 668
- Territory of Carabisian Theme in 668
- Territory of Opsician Theme in 668
- Territory of Thracesian Theme in 668
- Territory of Anatolic Theme in 668
- Territory of Armeniac Theme in 668
- Territory lost between 668 and 900
- ······· Boundary of a theme about 900
-)(Pass

ARMENIAC Name of a theme about 900
Amorium Headquarters of a theme or exarchate about 668
Dyrrhachium Headquarters of a theme about 900
Samos Headquarters of a theme at both dates
Cyzicus Other city

The only military units that seem to have been entirely lost during this period were a few of Tzimisces' small themes that scarcely had time to establish themselves before they were overrun.[11] The Theme of Sicily was only driven from the island after a dogged defense lasting for almost a century, and even then held its part of the Italian mainland.

Several military reforms helped the army adapt to its changing functions. Nicephorus I probably recruited the first new army units since the sixth century, the new Tagma of the Hicanati and three themes in Greece. Theophilus increased the soldiers' numbers further and almost doubled their pay, making the whole army a much more professional force. He also made the themes more flexible by dividing their thousand-man drungi into two-hundred-man banda, and by turning the main sectors of the eastern frontier into independent cleisurae. Basil I strengthened the Imperial Fleet by giving it its own permanent marines, causing a great and almost immediate improvement in the empire's naval forces.

Leo VI increased the proportion of the cavalry, thus making the themes more suitable for offensive warfare. The same emperor began to create smaller themes on the eastern frontier that allowed the empire to annex land by gradual increments. Nicephorus II contributed a new sort of heavily armed cavalry, and conquered a host of little themes on the frontier. John Tzimisces created the new Tagma of the Immortals and tightened control over Nicephorus's many small themes and his own by grouping them under dukes. Basil II began using foreign mercenaries on a significant scale by enlisting the Varangian Guard, and soon made the ethnarch, or commander of foreigners, an important officer. All these changes tended to enhance the army's offensive capabilities.

Although the army grew enormously, most of the increase occurred toward the end of this period, probably because by then the empire had the money and manpower to spare. The process began with the 10,000 new soldiers enrolled by Nicephorus I in 809 for his Greek themes and his new Tagma of the Hicanati, though the 4,000 of them in the Peloponnesus and Cephalonia evidently came from the Mardaïte oarsmen of Hellas. Theophilus's 30,000 new recruits were all Khurramite refugees from the caliphate. During the rest of the ninth century, the only additions to the rolls were Basil I's 4,000 marines for the Imperial Fleet. When Basil founded the Theme of Dalmatia he sent it no new troops. During the first half of the tenth century, apart from the 12,000 Arab refugees of the Banū Ḥabīb, the army gained only about 14,000 men, 6,000 of them probably Armenian natives of the new themes they garrisoned. Only from 963 to 1025 did the army expand rapidly by some 90,000 men, most of them Armenians with a scattering of other foreigners.

While the army certainly grew much stronger between 780 and 1025, the final figure of 250,000 or so on the rolls is misleading. Field armies in the great campaigns of the later tenth century seldom had more than 40,000 soldiers, about a third of them cavalry. That was usually enough; more men were hard to supply for long. The empire could field two such forces at a time, and still leave enough troops behind to defend its territory. After Tzimisces created the Immortals, the tagmata alone probably had 36,000 men, 24,000 of them cavalry. The Varangians made another 6,000. Among the themes, the troops with most fighting experience and nearest to hand for campaigns were the over 100,000 men added to the frontiers between 900 and 1025. Most of the 96,000 men of the themes dating from before 900 were hardly needed, apart from the naval themes and those in Italy and the Crimea, which were still exposed to attack.

As the interior themes became almost immune from invasions or raids, they seldom needed to fight at home. Even after Leo VI increased the proportion of cavalry in the themes to a quarter, the interior themes were top-heavy with infantry, who had done good service as garrison troops when their regions were frequently raided but were not much needed for campaigns. When Romanus I settled the Banū Ḥabīb on the border and Nicephorus II garrisoned Tarsus, the emperors apparently gave their new themes no infantry whatever. In all likelihood some other frontier themes were also composed mostly or entirely of cavalry. The interior themes could of course have been kept in training by calling them up by turns for service on campaigns. But with plenty of seasoned soldiers available in the tagmata and frontier themes, the effort scarcely seemed worthwhile. Already in the campaigns against Crete of 911 and 949 many soldiers of the nearby Thracesian Theme were passed over in favor of troops from the tagmata and eastern frontier themes. The obvious explanation is that the Thracesians had become worse troops than the others.

While most soldiers who served on expeditions received campaign pay, all soldiers seem to have received the same regular pay whether they fought or not. The annual rate was five nomismata for an ordinary soldier until 840, when Theophilus changed it to one nomisma for each year of service up to twelve. By Leo VI's day, soldiers seem to have been paid a flat rate of nine nomismata a year. This rate, though only about half what was needed to support a family adequately, produced a large payroll when multiplied by 120,000 to 250,000 men. By the late tenth century the government was receiving very little service in return for these payments to the interior themes, as the emperors must have realized.

One possible solution would have been to transfer to the borders men whose families had lived in the interior for centuries. Yet by doing this Nicephorus I had raised loud complaints, and his successors, with less need for manpower, seem not to have repeated the experiment. Another possibility was simply to strike some soldiers from the rolls. But this would have meant either taking away their military lands, leaving them destitute and rebellious, or granting them at least some of their land without military obligations. The emperors were unwilling to give up something for nothing, especially because they might need the soldiers in some future crisis or campaign. The tenth-century legislation against selling military lands must have been largely directed at these soldiers of the interior themes, because the requirements of active service should have forced most of the others to maintain their lands.

In an effort to get some value for all this regular pay, the government sometimes demanded money from soldiers who were on the rolls but did no service. The principle had long been established that holders of military land could provide and equip someone else to serve in their place, and the next step was to ask for cash instead of the soldier. As early as 921 Romanus Lecapenus asked the soldiers of the Theme of Peloponnesus to pay five nomismata apiece, or half that if they were very poor, rather than go on a campaign in Italy. In 949 Constantine VII asked for four nomismata apiece from some cavalry of the Thracesians who were not joining his expedition against Crete. When Nicephorus II declared that heavy cavalrymen were to be supported by military lands worth twelve pounds of gold rather than the usual four pounds, in most cases two cavalrymen who stayed at home probably bought heavy arms and armor for a third cavalryman who campaigned. Thus the government traded unneeded manpower for better equipment or more revenue, an eminently practical solution. Though such practices could weaken the army if carried too far, in 1025 the army was still strong.

During this period the civil service had less influence than the military establishment, and grew only modestly as its responsibilities expanded along with the empire. The bureaucracy continued to include a postal logothete for diplomacy and domestic security, a general logothete for taxation, a military logothete for the army payroll, a great curator for imperial property, and a city prefect for Constantinople. Yet these ministers' authority gradually diminished, and from the end of the ninth century the postal logothete ceased to be the most important civilian official. In the tenth century that distinction usually belonged to the grand chamberlain, who was a palatine official rather than a civil servant. His influence depended on his presence in the Great Palace, particularly when the emperor was underage or away on campaign, and reflected the fact that power had become more concentrated in the imperial office.

One official who kept his importance was the quaestor with his legal responsibilities, since after the codifying work of Basil I and Leo VI the emperors continued to exercise their legislative authority. The *Basilica* again gave the empire a comprehensive law code, which Leo's novels brought more or less up to date. These laws' promulgation ended a long period in which the empire's legislation had been so hard to consult that few new laws had been made and many existing laws had become dead letters. The main concern of the novels of Leo's successors in the tenth century was with land tenure, though they also regulated various judicial matters. To provide for stricter enforcement of the laws, the emperors named more judges in both the capital and the themes.

As state property began to grow again after almost disappearing in the seventh century, it came to be entrusted not to the great curator or general logothete but to new officials. The first major acquisition, the estates of the Mangana confiscated from Michael I after his deposition, received their own curator.[12] The treasury began to keep much of the property it confiscated, and the state kept much of the land in the themes it annexed from the tenth century onward. In 996 Basil II repossessed the imperial estates acquired or given away by Basil Lecapenus. Crown land was administered by a new domestic logothete, whom Basil II made independent of the general logothete.[13] The revenues from imperial estates must have been largely responsible for the vast surplus piled up in the treasury by 1025.

That surplus, like the ability to support such a large army, is a sign that the civil service was working efficiently through almost all of this period. After some disarray and demoralization in the chaotic seventh and eighth centuries, the bureaucracy's training and morale began to recover during the reigns of Irene and Nicephorus I. Both Nicephorus and Theophilus made particular efforts to stem corruption. The reduction of enemy raids would have reduced the number of temporary tax exemptions, while the land legislation of the tenth century would have made taxes easier to collect. After Basil II apparently decreed that richer members of tax assessment districts would have to pay when poorer members defaulted, the tax collectors must have been able to find someone to make up almost all the taxes that were due.

No doubt many civil servants used their power and influence to embezzle state funds, to finagle grants of state land, or to buy out smallholders or soldiers in violation of the land laws. The legislation of Romanus I and Basil II makes prominent mention of civilian dignitaries when listing those who tried to buy land illegally. John Tzimisces was indignant that Basil Lecapenus had granted himself huge tracts of state land in Cilicia, and Basil allegedly poisoned Tzimisces to keep him from reclaiming them. On the other hand, the emperors seem to have cared much less about limiting the holdings of civil servants in the Balkans, where land was more plentiful and large landholders might even help bring in settlers. Most estates of civil officials grew up in the Balkan part of the empire.[14]

Though after the ninth century the officer corps became difficult for outsiders to break into, the leadership of the bureaucracy and especially of the palace staff were more open to new talent. The emperors became familiar with many of the men serving them in Constantinople, even some of low rank, and took more interest in promotions there. By contrast, Theophilus's pay increase appears to have made the army more conservative, so that an immigrant like Leo V or a prosperous peasant like Michael II was less likely to reach the highest ranks. The Lecapeni rose in two generations, but they got their start when Romanus I's father entered Basil I's bodyguard, which was practically a palatine post. Within the palace, Basil I himself had advanced quickly from obscurity to be head of the imperial stables and then grand chamberlain. Because laws against castration made eunuchs rare but they were still preferred for palatine offices, they had particularly good opportunities, and they could help their relatives rise in government. Bureaucrats from newly prominent families were often more ambitious than generals from established ones and, lacking inherited wealth, were eager to secure their position by investing their savings in land.

The number of state employees had burgeoned since the eighth century. By 1025 the empire's officials, officers, soldiers, and oarsmen must with their families have exceeded a million souls. Those outside the system, who received no money from the state and had no superior officer or official to protect them, were easily exploited by bureaucrats and especially by tax collectors. Although the civil service and palace staff were relatively small, and mostly composed of humble clerks or custodians with little chance of making an illegal fortune, the richest bureaucrats and dignitaries bore watching, especially at a time when the government was acquiring so much money and land. Through most of these years, in fact, the emperors seem to have watched their bureaucracy vigilantly, sensing that it could endanger their power and that of the army. The emperors and military officers were strong enough to keep the civil service in check, as long as they had the will to do so.

THE PARTNERSHIP OF EMPEROR AND CHURCH

From the fourth to the early ninth century the empire had endured one theological controversy after another, and over a dozen emperors defended positions that were later branded heretical. After worsening during the Iconoclasm of the eighth century, the tension between Church and state began to ease, and by 1025 the Byzantine church was more united than ever before, and more obedient to the emperor. It also possessed great wealth, most of it in land, which the emperors beginning with Nicephorus II tried to limit but not to confiscate. At the same time, the conversion of the Bulgars, Serbs, and Russians made the Byzantine church much larger, spreading the empire's influence far beyond its borders.

After much tension between the earlier iconoclast emperors and the clergy and monks, in restoring the icons the empress Irene allied herself with the Church and monasticism. Under her, particularly through the efforts of Theodore of Studius, monasteries became stronger and more independent. Yet in the Moechian controversy Theodore also started a new type of dispute over imperial control of the Church. He not only rejected the remarriage of Constantine VI but refused communion with clergy who accepted it, until Michael I finally settled the dispute on his terms. Theodore showed the power that spiritual authority could have, but even many clerics doubted that the principles at stake in the Moechian controversy were worth the trouble they caused.

130. Saint Theodore of Studius. Eleventh-century mosaic from the Monastery of Nea Monē, Chios. (Photo: Benaki Museum Photographic Archive, Athens)

The restored Iconoclasm of the early ninth century was more sympathetic to the clergy than eighth-century Iconoclasm had been. Leo V and his iconoclast successors won over most bishops and monks and found a church leader of some stature in the learned John the Grammarian. By the time Theophilus began his sporadic persecution, Theodore of Studius and most iconophile bishops were dead, and even iconophile monks seemed to be a dwindling group. Yet Iconoclasm never had a strong base in the Church, and Theodora found it easy to abolish. Even though the bishops of iconoclast times were deposed wholesale in 843, scarcely any of them defended Iconoclasm after its condemnation on the Sunday of Orthodoxy. It was to be the last great heresy to disturb the Byzantine church.

At first Iconoclasm left most ordinary priests discredited for accepting it, while the new hierarchy, largely composed of monks, was inexperienced and unsure of its authority. Quarrels over ordinations arose under the patriarch Methodius, continued under his successor Ignatius, and became worse when Michael III replaced Ignatius with Photius. After the pope rejected Photius, Photius excommunicated the pope for the supposed heresy of following the customs of the western church. This Photian Schism was short, because Basil I soon returned Ignatius to the patriarchate, but the pope then insisted on deposing the clergy Photius had ordained. Although Photius restored his deposed clerics when he resumed his patriarchate on Ignatius's death, all his ordinations were disputed after Leo VI deposed him again. Even after they were finally accepted and official unity was achieved by the end of the century, resentment lingered between former partisans of Ignatius and Photius.

Such acrimony exacerbated the controversy over the Tetragamy, Leo VI's fourth marriage in 906. The dispute was as much over the validity of the ordinations of the patriarch Euthymius, Leo's replacement for Nicholas Mysticus, as over Leo's marriage and the legitimacy of Leo's heir, both of which the pope and Euthymius conditionally accepted. When Leo died, his brother Alexander reinstated Nicholas and deposed Euthymius's clergy. The controversy dragged on until 920, when Romanus I prodded Nicholas into recognizing Euthymius's ordinations and dispensation of the marriage. By that time the original political implications of the controversy had long ceased to matter.

After these disputes, the Church and emperor seem to have taken some care to prevent further controversy. The Church left the emperors relatively free to handle the succession and relations with the western church, while the emperors avoided uncanonical marriages and depositions of churchmen. After Nicholas Mysticus's death the emperors also chose less assertive patriarchs. The strongest of them, Polyeuctus, made little effort to stop essentially political measures that affected the Church, like Nicephorus II's law on church lands. Polyeuctus only insisted on spiritual principles, as when he rejected Nicephorus's idea that to die fighting Muslims amounted to martyrdom. Polyeuctus required John Tzimisces to do penance for his murder of Nicephorus, but crowned John emperor afterwards. Such a division of authority, with Church and state minding their own business, became widely accepted.

Through most of this period the church hierarchy was dominated by monks. As former laymen, the patriarchs Nicephorus and Photius were exceptions, but they enjoyed less prestige than their rivals Theodore of Studius and Ignatius, and eventually had to defer to them. Monks were not necessarily less tolerant than others. Photius was harsher with iconoclasts than Ignatius, and in the Tetragamist controversy Photians like

Nicholas Mysticus condemned Leo VI's marriage while Ignatians like Euthymius condoned it. The key to positions in these controversies was usually the partisans' loyalty to their leaders, rather than to a set of principles. Since monks tended to enjoy the greatest spiritual authority, first for their opposition to Iconoclasm and later for their personal sanctity, parties led by monks had an advantage.

The monks' influence became stronger as they formed larger communities. After Theodore's Monastery of Studius in Constantinople was temporarily taken over by the iconoclast emperors, opposition to Iconoclasm became centered in the monasteries of Mount Olympus in Bithynia, not far from the capital. After the restoration of orthodoxy, Studius recovered some of its former prestige, and Mount Olympus kept the importance it had gained. Monasteries also multiplied on Mount Latrus near Ephesus, and from the end of the tenth century on Mount Athos near Thessalonica. Monks on mountains were far enough from the world to escape many of its distractions, but close enough to influence it. The influence they sought was in the first instance spiritual rather than political.

During the early ninth century, the Church was inevitably preoccupied with Iconoclasm to some extent. Since the main theological arguments had already been made on each side, theologians like the exiled patriarch Nicephorus devoted themselves mostly to polemics. The struggles of iconophile saints, most of whom were monks, provided subjects for hagiography for many years to come; but naturally the earliest lives were more vivid and stirring than the later ones, which became formulaic and conventional. The Photian Schism and the Tetragamy produced more polemics, and deeply felt lives of the embattled monastic patriarchs Ignatius and Euthymius.

Monks took a leading role not only in determining theology but in shaping a whole view of Christian life that had lasting effects on the Byzantine church. Theodore of Studius's writings, prescribing reading and manual labor for his monks, continued to guide the activities of many monasteries besides Studius. In the tenth century, however, Athanasius of Mount Athos began to place more value on contemplation. By the year 1000 the abbot Symeon the New Theologian was advocating a search for personal salvation and closeness to God that was to become a widely shared ideal in monasteries, and touched the secular clergy and laity.[15]

The period's outstanding religious achievement was the conversion of the Slavs, for which both Church and state could claim credit. Byzantine missionary activity had more or less lapsed after the sixth century, when the empire's last pagans had been converted. Although Nicephorus I's reoccupation of much of Greece led incidentally to converting its pagan Slavs, the mission of Constantine-Cyril and Methodius to Moravia in 863 represented a new departure. Even though the Moravian church became subject to the papacy and was largely destroyed by the Magyars at the end of the century, this mission set the pattern for the conversion of Bulgaria and other Slavic countries. Constantine-Cyril evidently invented the Glagolitic alphabet, later simplified into the Cyrillic, and translated the liturgy into a dialect comprehensible to most Slavs, Old Church Slavonic, thus creating an important missionary tool.

The mission of Constantine-Cyril and Methodius, originally the idea of the prince of Moravia, awoke the Byzantines to the possibilities of missionary work. The Byzantine mission to Moravia also helped convince the Bulgar khan Boris that as a pagan he was missing something important, without which his state would be more backward than its neighbors. Although the Bulgarians worried about absorption by Byzantium, the example of more distant Moravia showed that accepting Byzantine missionaries could be compatible with political independence. Nonetheless, the mission that arrived in Bulgaria in 864 did bring a measure of ecclesiastical and cultural subordination. Attempts by the Bulgarians to assert their independence included two pagan uprisings, Boris's experiments with western missionaries, and the khan Symeon's declaring himself an emperor and his archbishop a patriarch. The end result was annexation to the empire, but only because the Bulgarian emperor Samuel and his successors had refused to accept a protectorate.

The Serbs, who asked for Byzantine missionaries and converted not long after the Bulgarians, had less to fear from the empire and more from Bulgaria. Their efforts to ally with the Byzantines against the Bulgarians had indifferent success, but they managed to avoid any lasting Bulgarian conquest, and survived the fall of Bulgaria to become clients of the Byzantines. To their northwest the Croats, despite brief submission to the patriarchate of Constantinople in the late ninth century, became a part of the western church; but they, like the Serbs, accepted Byzantine political suzerainty after the fall of Bulgaria. The only independent people in the region who were not Slavs, the Hungarians, accepted Byzantine missionaries in the mid-tenth century, and though their final conversion came from the West they remained friendly to the empire.

Russia was much too large and too distant from Byzantium to fear annexation, but it also had little need of an alliance with the emperor. By the early tenth century the Russians' raiding and trading had given them a familiarity with the empire and its religion, and by 911 some of them were serving as Byzantine mercenaries. Some progress was made toward Christianizing Russia after the visit and conversion of Princess Olga in the mid-tenth century. Nicephorus II considered the Russians friendly enough to hire them to attack Bulgaria in 966; but he misjudged them. John Tzimisces had to teach them a healthy respect for Byzantine power. Alone among the Slavs, however, they were finally converted to Christianity not at their own request but at that of the emperor, when Basil II offered a marriage alliance. A Byzantine princess was a great favor, which Basil would probably not have accorded a ruler nearer the empire for fear of conceding a claim to the Byzantine throne. With the marriage as an inducement, Vladimir became an enthusiastic Christian and loyal ally, establishing a Russian hierarchy subject to Constantinople.

The conversion of the Slavs, despite its far-reaching significance, was no more the result of conscious planning than the empire's territorial expansion was. Unlike the contemporary western church, Byzantium sent out no missionaries on its own initiative into pagan and hostile lands. Its success was consequently the more remarkable, evidence of the strong impression that the Byzantines made on their neighbors and that the missionaries made on their converts. While converting fewer people than western missionaries—who were then spreading their faith to Croatia, Hungary, the northern Slavic lands, and Scandinavia—the Byzantine church spread more than Christianity. It brought its converts to accept a degree of cultural and political leadership from the empire.[16]

The closeness of the Byzantine church to the imperial government probably explains the failure of the Byzantines in the East to convert any large number of Muslims. Because the state refused to accept more than a few non-Christian subjects, most of the Muslim populations of Syria or Egypt would have needed to convert before being conquered, an obvious impossibility. To repopulate the areas that the empire did annex, the emperors extended tolerance to Jacobite and Armenian Christians, leaving the Church in the East divided and ill prepared to win converts from Islam. Nor did either Muslims or Christians easily forget that for centuries the tide of conversion in the East had run against Christianity.

Even worse than Islam, to Byzantine thinking, was the dualism of the Paulicians, whose belief that the whole material world was the evil creation of an evil God differed radically from orthodox Christianity. After Theodora drove the Paulicians from the empire, Basil I mostly eliminated them from the eastern frontier by forced conversion and deportation when he conquered their statelet. But some Paulicians had traveled or were deported to the Balkans, where they won converts of their own. In the first half of the tenth century, the Bulgarian priest Bogomil developed a Bulgarian strain of dualism, which rejected the sacraments and the Bulgarian church along with the rest of the world. Despite being persecuted and condemning marriage and procreation, Bogomilism spread on the strength of its cynical spirituality. By the time of the Byzantine conquest, Bogomils were a sizable though clandestine group in Bulgaria.

Except for the period of Iconoclasm and the brief Photian Schism, the Byzantine church remained in communion with western Christians throughout these centuries. Constantine-Cyril sided with the pope against Photius, and Greek monks from southern Italy founded monasteries in and near Rome that were obedient to the papacy. Yet the eastern and western churches were developing and making their converts separately, and often as rivals. The Photian Schism highlighted some of the differences between the two, in particular the addition of the *filioque* to the Creed, which could be misconstrued as an important theological disagreement over the Holy Spirit. The Byzantine controversy over the Tetragamy showed not only the discrepancy between East and West in rules about marriage, but a claim by the popes to jurisdiction over Byzantine affairs that many Byzantines resented. The close identification of the Byzantine church with the state carried the danger that Christendom might split between those who acknowledged imperial authority and those who did not.

CULTURAL REVIVAL

Even before these military and missionary successes, while the iconoclast controversy still simmered, Byzantine education and scholarship had begun to recover. Notwithstanding the military crises of the seventh and eighth centuries the empire had maintained a functioning civil service, along with the schools that trained it and the books needed for teaching; yet the civil service, the schools, and the books had all been deteriorating. Without an improvement, most books would eventually have been lost as the old papyri on which they were written decayed, and the schools and bureaucracy would slowly have broken down. By the mid-eighth century the bureaucracy seems already to have been keeping its tax records badly, while interest in history had become so rare as to endanger its transmission. Since the time of Justinian I, both Church and state had come to think of learning as a luxury at best, and at worst as impious or pagan.

Iconoclasm seems to have helped change that attitude. The iconoclasts, insisting that their doctrine was fully compatible with orthodox Christian tradition, cited some isolated passages from the Church Fathers that looked unfavorable to religious images. After Irene took power in 780, the iconophiles adduced their own patristic quotations, which favored images. This set up an argument about the numbers of the citations, their precise meanings, and the contexts in which they were found. The research required was not easy, because the Fathers have little to say about images, and some of the most relevant passages were in obscure places. By the time of the Second Council of Nicaea of 787, iconophiles had discovered that learning could be useful, at least for defending icons.

Also around 780, inspired by the restoration of icons, a number of people from civil-service families entered monasteries, where Theodore of Studius, among others, had them read Christian literature. The growth in the number of readers required more copying of manuscripts. For this purpose, the monks of Studius and its allied monasteries apparently adapted the cursive script long in use in the bureaucracy, creating the minuscule hand.[17] Unlike the uncial script previously used for copying books, minuscule used lowercase letters, linked them, and left spaces between words. Minuscule was therefore quicker to write and, with the words divided, easier to read. It also made books cheaper, because it fitted more words onto less parchment in less time. Parchment had become the usual material for books since Byzantium had lost its source of papyrus with the fall of Egypt, and though this made books more expensive it also made them much more durable.

As copying and reading revived, so did literature. Besides polemics against Iconoclasm and lives of the saints who had defended icons, iconophiles produced the first historical works written for many years.

131. Page from the eleventh-century *Menologium of Basil II* with a miniature of
the empress Theodora restoring the icons. The title at the top of the page is
in uncial letters, but the text is in minuscule. (Photo: Biblioteca Apostolica
Vaticana)

The most important was that of Theophanes Confessor, a civil servant turned iconophile monk. By 815, Theophanes compiled a chronicle arranged in annual entries from 284 to 813, which in turn continued a chronicle by his friend George Syncellus that began with the Creation.[18] While Theophanes' prose is artless, and one of his main purposes was to denounce iconoclasts, he took considerable care with his chronology, and his entries beginning with the later reign of Heraclius provide much more information than any other surviving narrative.

A distant second best is the short history of the years from 602 to 769 by the patriarch Nicephorus, another former bureaucrat. Its main claim to distinction is that Nicephorus wrote it in something very like ancient Attic Greek. He may well have owed his nomination as patriarch partly to the impression this history made on Nicephorus I. The emperor, who had been general logothete before his accession, appears to have valued both learning and an efficient bureaucracy. As ambitious men learned that scholarship could advance them to the highest civil and ecclesiastical posts, its popularity spread.

After 815 the iconoclast emperors wanted their own men of learning to refute the iconophiles, and had the incentives to win scholars to their cause. Among intellectuals who won promotion under the iconoclast emperors were the patriarch John the Grammarian, the archbishop of Thessalonica Leo the Mathematician, and Ignatius the Deacon, a literary scholar who became archbishop of Nicaea. The emperor Theophilus was the main patron of all three. After discovering that Leo's fame had spread to the caliphate, the emperor made him head of a newly founded school at the Magnaura Palace, the empire's first known public school since the reign of Heraclius. Leo's knowledge of geometry, mechanics, and medicine not only seems to have contributed to the empire's international prestige, but also had practical applications. For example, Leo devised a warning system of watch fires linking the Arab frontier with the capital, which was capable of transmitting twelve different messages.

Another purpose Theophilus found for erudition—perhaps the most important in his eyes—was foretelling the future. This John the Grammarian reportedly did by alchemy in an underground laboratory, Leo the Mathematician by astrology, and the patriarch Methodius from ancient books. Theophilus's interest in prophecy was widely shared. Methodius probably prophesied the deaths of Leo V, Michael II, and Theophilus himself, the last inaccurately, and took his monastic name from Saint Methodius of Olympus, wrongly believed to be the author of a famous prophetic text. Methodius was soon revered as a saint, and though Leo the Mathematician was sometimes accused of paganism, after the disappearance of actual paganism such charges were more or less rhetorical.

Once these theological, scientific, and pseudoscientific benefits had convinced most leaders of the Church and state that learning was valuable, it could be pursued for its own sake. John the Grammarian and Ignatius the Deacon may have been careerists who shifted from orthodoxy to Iconoclasm according to the times, but their enthusiasm for erudition is beyond doubt. Leo the Mathematician taught for years in relative obscurity before Theophilus discovered him, and seems to have cared little for high office. After 843 he served both as head of the School of the Magnaura and as its professor of philosophy.

The greatest polymath of the age was Photius, whose interests lay more in literature and theology than in science. He was the son of an iconophile bureaucrat, Sergius Confessor, who probably wrote a history of the years from 741 to 828 that survives in tantalizing fragments.[19] Seemingly in 845, when Photius was in his early thirties, he compiled a gigantic account of his reading, later known as the *Bibliotheca* ("Library").[20] Despite that title, only some of the nearly four hundred works he reviews seem to have been in his private library, while for the rest he relied on notes from his reading or on his memory. Photius follows no particular order, and apparently never read over the text that he dictated or had copied from his notes; but his comments are intelligent, and his summaries can be invaluable, because about half of what he read is now lost. The books go as early as Herodotus and as late as his father's history, but the great bulk date from the Second Sophistic to Justinian's reign. Photius had a special love for history, rhetoric, novels, and odd and obscure information of all kinds.

Photius exploited his knowledge through the rest of his career, first as protoasecretis and then as patriarch. While never a teacher by profession, he made his house a scholarly salon and had a circle of disciples; probably among them was Constantine-Cyril, whom Photius later chose for the mission to Moravia. During his first patriarchate, Photius composed learned sermons and letters, including a long letter of theological advice to Boris-Michael of Bulgaria. During his first exile, Photius wrote more scholarly work, most of it collected in his *Amphilochia*, answers to

132. Photius, patriarch of Constantinople (858–67, 877–86), seated, with his friend Amphilochius. Late ninth- or early tenth-century miniature from the title page of Photius's *Amphilochia* (Lavra codex 449). (Photo: Courtesy of Kurt Weitzmann)

largely theological questions compiled for his friend Amphilochius. During his second patriarchate he was deeply involved in Basil I's recodification of the laws, and during his final exile he wrote a treatise on the procession of the Holy Spirit, opposing the *filioque*. Everyone acknowledged Photius's erudition, though his enemies claimed he had acquired it from a Jewish magician in return for denying the Cross.

Photius tutored Leo VI, and without winning his affection shaped him nonetheless. As emperor, Leo sponsored the completion of the *Basilica*, and produced orations and a long military treatise that go under his name and appear to be partly his work. Later Byzantines attributed oracles to him, sometimes confusing him with Leo the Mathematician.[21] Even if the leading scholar under Leo, the archbishop of Caesarea Arethas, was far less reflective and perceptive than Photius, the number of learned-men was clearly rising. Interest in classical literature remained lively, the copying of manuscripts proceeded apace, and new lexica to aid in reading them were prepared. The School of the Magnaura may have lapsed, but private schools multiplied.

Leo VI's son Constantine VII, a scholar among emperors but no emperor among scholars, was mainly interested in compiling reference works. He was far more a patron of writing than a writer, because most of the works attributed to him are virtually copied from earlier sources, and even that work appears to have been done by Constantine's assistants. His *On Ceremonies* is an informative if untidy source for imperial ceremonial and much else. His *On Administering the Empire* is a jumble of disjointed facts, and his *On the Themes* mostly copies texts that had long been obsolete. The history Constantine sponsored, known as Theophanes Continuatus because it begins where Theophanes ended, blends numerous sources for the ninth century, with some stylistic elegance but very little critical sense. Perhaps the project closest to Constantine's heart, of which only a fraction survives, was the so-called *Excerpta*, a giant collection of extracts from old historians on fifty-three ill-assorted subjects, each a book in itself. Although Constantine's compilations are a mine of information today, they had a very limited circulation among later Byzantines.

Some similar works in which Constantine took no part reached a wider readership. The chronicle of Symeon the Logothete appears simply to paraphrase its sources, but it at least avoids distorting and confusing them as Theophanes Continuatus does. Its author was perhaps the same as Symeon Metaphrastes, who paraphrased the lives of earlier saints in a more learned style. An anonymous scholar or scholars compiled the *Suda* ("Moat"), an alphabetized encyclopedia with useful biographical entries on ancient and Byzantine authors, which despite its length was copied a number of times. From the standpoint of world literature, the most important of these compilations was the *Palatine Anthology*, a collection of thousands of poems that range from antiquity to the tenth century, and from inept to immortal.[22]

These works and the manuscripts copied along with them preserved much the greatest part of earlier Greek literature that has survived to the present. Yet the revival of learning brought only a modest revival of literature, and for a time it seems actually to have stifled literary creativity. Reading so many older works, most of them late ancient rather than classical, led educated Byzantines to affect a style that was even more archaic and allusive than before. The exuberant discoveries of Photius were followed by the dutiful cataloguing of Constantine VII, who appears sometimes to have forgotten that writing could be useful or even beautiful. The scholars researching earlier times tended to lose interest in the present, and only a few educated Byzantines wrote original literature. One was the abbess Cassia, a defeated contestant in Theophilus's bride show of 830, who composed hymns and epigrams. Another was Leo the Deacon, who in the late tenth century revived the tradition of contemporary history by skillfully recording the glorious years from the accession of Romanus II to the death of John Tzimisces.

Probably by the early eleventh century, an unknown author created a refreshing work that is unique in Byzantine literature. Perhaps drawing on ballads by wandering bards, of whom he may himself have been one, he composed a sort of epic poem, the *Digenes Acrites* ("Double-blooded Frontiersman"). It has an unmistakable liveliness, though its style is difficult to judge because it now survives only in later versions. The poem begins with the story of an Arab emir who carries off the daughter of a Byzantine noble family. For love of her, he deserts to Byzantium and turns Christian, and they marry. Their son Basil, the poem's hero of mixed Arab and Byzantine blood, shows himself a hunter and warrior of superhuman strength. Eloping with the daughter of the strategus of Cappadocia, he finally settles on the Euphrates frontier, where he meets either Basil I or Romanus I, depending on the version of the poem. The events are legendary, but the poem surely reflects the real interests of the Anatolian aristocracy in romance, hunting, warfare, beautiful houses, and fine objects.

As the empire became wealthier, its art and architecture naturally benefited. The production of small artworks had never ceased, but by the late eighth century Byzantine skills in monumental construction had grown rusty. Lack of recent experience seems to show in the rather clumsy Church of Saint Sophia at Thessalonica, apparently built by Irene after Stauracius's successful campaign of 783 in Greece (Fig. 133). The church is heavy and boxlike, and since its original dome soon collapsed it may not even have been structurally sound.[23] Irene is also said to have constructed a palace in Constantinople, and her successors were active restorers of churches and fortifications. Theophilus was the first great imperial builder since Justinian II, and the greatest since Justinian I. Many of Theophilus's new towers for the sea walls of Constantinople survive, along with the foundations of a suburban palace that John the

133. The Church of Saint Sophia, Thessalonica, before its twentieth-century restoration, from an old photograph (with minaret deleted). (Photo: Courtauld Institute, London, and the British School at Athens)

Grammarian helped him build in the Arab style. In the absence of modern excavations, Theophilus's sumptuous additions to the Great Palace, like his roaring gold lions and other ornaments, are known only from written descriptions, but both buildings and ornaments long continued to impress visitors to the palace.

The level the arts attained under Iconoclasm can be judged from the large and accomplished mosaics that Photius put up soon after the icons' return in Saint Sophia at Constantinople. Although previous emperors seem to have left the church without figural decoration, perhaps fearing that the architecture would dwarf the figures, the iconophile patriarch placed a magnificent Virgin and Child in the apse with flanking angels (Fig. 134). Other emperors and patriarchs added to the church's mosaics, and the work, though dwarfed, is uniformly splendid. Basil I also had ambitions as a builder, which led him to make further additions to the Great Palace, repair thirty-one churches, and build eight new ones in and around Constantinople. Basil's most ambitious construction was the five-domed New Church, dedicated in 880, which set an example for later emperors.[24] Leo VI's contribution was a church dedicated to his sainted wife Theophano. Romanus I's conventual Church of the Myrelaeum survives today, unlike the churches built by Basil and Leo, even if its present condition preserves little of its former grandeur (Fig. 135).

Aristocratic patrons emulated the emperors, building themselves palaces and founding their own churches and monasteries in Constantinople. Buildings of some size and pretensions began to go up in the provinces again. At first provincial magnates and ecclesiastics limited themselves to small structures with competent but simple decoration (Fig. 128). But by the tenth century the monasteries of the Greatest Laura and Iberon on desolate Mount Athos were building more impressive churches (Figs. 120, 124). By 1028, a retired strategus could erect a

134. Ninth-century mosaic of the Virgin and Child in the apse of Saint Sophia, Constantinople. Note the flanking angel at right; another angel has been lost at left. (Photo: Dumbarton Oaks, Washington, D.C., copyright 1996)

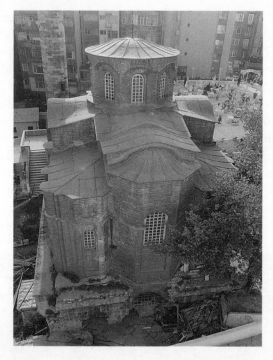

135. Monastery Church of the Myrelaeum, Constantinople, built by Romanus Lecapenus. (Photo: Irina Andreescu-Treadgold)

church in Thessalonica that emperors might have envied two centuries earlier (Fig. 136).

Most of this artistic activity took up where the sixth century had left off, and owed little if anything to models from the ancient world. But in the tenth century some ivories and manuscript illuminations show the influence of classical models, at first copied hesitantly, then with some confidence. Evidently the emperors and civil officials who were reading ancient literature had become interested in ancient art, probably by looking at old illustrated manuscripts, and ordered illustrations of a similar kind. Some of the illuminations of a Bible commissioned by the sacellarius Leo in the mid-tenth century come close to classical art. The miniatures of a roughly contemporary Psalter now preserved at Paris are even more classical and beautiful (Fig. 96). The early eleventh-century *Menologium of Basil II* has hundreds of elegant classicizing miniatures by nine painters who, exceptionally for Byzantium, signed their work (Figs. 28, 59, 61, 69, 84, 87, 98, 109, 131).[25]

136. Church of Our Lady of the Coppersmiths, Thessalonica, built in 1028.
(Photo: C. Mango, Dumbarton Oaks, Washington, D.C., copyright 1996)

By 1025 the cultural revival had reached the point where whatever survived from earlier times had been rediscovered, and secular education was valued by almost all civil officials, most generals and bishops, and many abbots. Since scholars made no use of pagan learning to challenge Christian beliefs, most churchmen thought study of the ancients was at worst a useless distraction, and at best useful for writing sermons and understanding theology. Authors and artists had become more numerous and better trained than before, while their readers and patrons had become not only more numerous and more sophisticated but richer. Although the art and literature of the period was mostly derivative, it was continuing to develop along with its reputation and its public.

ECONOMIC GROWTH

The population seems to have expanded throughout this period, and only partly because of the new conquests. The latest estimate, largely based on analogies with western Europe, indicates that the empire's inhabitants increased from roughly 7 million in 780 to roughly 12 million in 1025.[26] If this is correct, the population would nearly have kept pace with the doubling of the empire's land area. Yet most of the empire's new territory had been very sparsely populated, especially in the Balkans. Under Byzantine rule this land received more settlers, but many of those came from the empire's earlier possessions. Since even the lands that sent out settlers became more densely populated, a steady natural increase must have been occurring. With the end of the long period of plague from the mid-sixth to the mid-eighth century, the population of the empire's Anatolian heartland probably returned to its former level, and in time exceeded it.

There was ample space to accommodate more people. In 839 land appears still to have been available throughout the empire, since Theophilus had little trouble settling the thirty thousand former Khurramites with their families all over fifteen themes and cleisurae. Theophilus sent two thousand former Khurramites apiece even to the most densely populated regions: the district of the Optimates and the themes of Thrace, Macedonia, the Opsician, and the Thracesians. Although he sent none to the themes in Greece and Italy, his reason can hardly have been that those lightly populated regions had no room. About 870 Basil I could still find military lands for four thousand new marines of the Imperial Fleet not far from Constantinople.

Basil admittedly had some imperial estates in Thrace to draw upon, and he gave his marines lands worth only two pounds of gold, not the four pounds standard for marines in the naval themes. After his reign few if any additions seem to have been made to the army within the empire's original territory. When the tagmata were expanded in the later tenth century, their new troops were apparently put in outlying areas instead of being stationed near the capital. By the tenth century, the emperors' efforts to stop the rich from buying the lands of the poor must reflect a hunger for land among men with money and influence. Though that century's famines were temporary, resulting from bad weather, locusts, and troop movements, such conditions would not have caused mass starvation unless the population had been relatively dense, unable to grow much more than it needed to survive even under normal conditions.

Since the greatest burst of conquest coincided with the apparent end of the famines about 978, matters may have been improved by outmigration to the lands that were newly conquered or secured. While most new settlers in the East and some in the West seem to have been Syrians and Armenians, the majority in the West appear to have been Byzantines. Nicephorus I compelled many Byzantine civilians to settle in Thrace and Greece. When civil officials were prohibited from buying land in Asia Minor, they acquired it in the less populous parts of the Balkans, and probably attracted settlers there to work it. After Bardas Sclerus submitted to Basil II in 989, the emperor moved him and his family from the Anatolics to Didymotichus near Adrianople, where they were expected to help fight the Bulgarians.[27] Although Byzantines were ordinarily reluctant to leave their old homes, starvation was a powerful incentive, and the mediocre soil of the Anatolian plateau could only provide food for a fairly sparse population. Greece and Thrace were the nearest, safest, and most fertile regions with available land.[28]

A high rate of natural increase implies large families. The strong family feelings of the aristocracy, apparent from the spread of family names, were probably part of a development that included Byzantines of lower rank as well. The great misfortune of the hero of the *Digenes Acrites* was childlessness, which had been common and seldom lamented in earlier times. Although unlike an aristocrat Leo VI needed no sons to administer his estates or to marry to friends, and he already had an heir in his brother Alexander, he still thought having a son and heir was worth a church schism. Emperors of earlier centuries, had they considered a brother inadequate, would simply have adopted a successor or married one to a daughter. But adoption seems to have had little appeal for the Byzantines of this period, and even a daughter's grandson had the deficiency of not carrying on the family name.

Complete lists of families are rare even for emperors, since women and those who died as children tended to pass unrecorded, but some large families were plainly to be found. Philaretus, grandfather of Constantine VI's first wife Maria, had three children and seventeen grandchildren living in 788, while a peasant who was his neighbor is said to have had nine children.[29] Theophilus's wife Theodora was one of six children who lived to maturity. Although Theophilus died in his late twenties, he had seven children, all but two of whom survived childhood. Basil I allegedly had eight children, of whom all but two were probably his. Photius was one of five adult brothers. Romanus I had eight grown children, one of them illegitimate. Most laymen who failed to marry probably had a definite reason for their celibacy. Ambitious scholars, for example, may have wanted to be eligible for a bishopric, an appropriate reward for a man of learning. Despite their lay status, the learned and unmarried Tarasius, Nicephorus, and Photius attained the patriarchate itself.

Demographic growth need not always have been as rapid in the cities as in the countryside. Since the traditions of the old decurions had been broken, no one in provincial towns cared to pay for fine public buildings or lavish games. Only Constantinople had the emperor and various resident officials to finance the more luxurious amenities of urban life. The main reason for living in a town was therefore business rather than pleasure. Merchants, bishops, and provincial officials needed to reside in cities, and attracted people who depended on them or had dealings with them. But the great Anatolian magnates seem to have found less to interest them in the few cities of the Anatolian plateau than in their country houses, among the villagers who farmed their lands.

In the coastlands of Asia Minor and the Balkans, where landholdings were smaller and towns closer together than on the plateau, landowners found urban life more attractive. Some magnates there were retired civil officials, used to living in cities and unaccustomed to the country, and though they needed to supervise their lands they could still live in the nearest town. As early as the later eighth century, the Tesseracontapechys family of Athens was important enough to have a family name and to send their relative Irene to Constantinople as the bride of the emperor's son. By the tenth century even little Sparta had a class of notables, who contributed to building a church and played polo in an open space in the town.[30]

Cities surely grew, and except on the Anatolian plateau the urban population probably grew nearly as fast as the rural. The growth seems to have been greatest in ports and in the Balkans. The population of Constantinople may well have doubled, to about two hundred thousand. Thessalonica recovered quickly from its sack in 904 to resume its place as the empire's second city, benefiting from the reconquest of its natural hinterland in western Bulgaria. Since during the sack the Arabs are said to have killed fifteen thousand Thessalonians and captured thirty thousand, the normal population might have been around a hundred thousand.[31] Adrianople, with a normal population of perhaps half the forty thousand the Bulgars captured there in 813, should have recovered and grown as the Byzantines conquered more of its Thracian hinterland.[32] Among smaller places, Athens and Corinth should have had well over ten thousand people by 1025. Demetrias in Thessaly, said to have been a major port before and after it was sacked in 901, cannot have been much smaller.[33]

Cities in the Anatolian coastlands appear also to have prospered. Although the main harbor of Ephesus was silting up, the city began to make use of the nearby harbors of Phygela and Anaea. The obvious alternative port for the western Anatolian plain was Smyrna, which presumably grew as well.[34] Nicaea, not far from the sea, remained an important place on the main land routes from Attalia and the East to Constantinople. As the seas became safer and the Syrian coast was reconquered, the naval base and road terminus of Attalia grew to be a major center for trade with the Arabs. Trebizond had the same function for trade with Armenia, Georgia, and points farther east.

On average, the few cities on the Anatolian plateau seem to have grown less than Byzantine cities in general. After Ancyra and Amorium were sacked by the Arabs in 838, Amorium never fully recovered, though Ancyra regained much of its importance as a trading center after some rebuilding by Michael III.[35] Both cities were partly replaced as military headquarters by Cappadocian Caesarea, which profited from the shift of military operations to the East. When the Arab raids ended, the cities of central Anatolia lost their function as places of refuge for the surrounding populations, and since most local magnates chose to live in the countryside, even rural prosperity did not necessarily lead to much urban growth.

The empire's newly acquired lands already had cities of some size, which after suffering during the wars of conquest would have profited from the return of peace. The largest place to be reconquered was Antioch, an important trading city not only in early Byzantine times but throughout the period of Arab rule. After its resettlement by the Byzantines, Antioch became the metropolis of the whole frontier region and probably the third city of the empire, behind Thessalonica.[36] Tarsus, Melitene, and Theodosiopolis were also repopulated to become respectively the main cities of Cilicia, Byzantine Mesopotamia, and Byzantine Armenia, all regions connected by trade routes with the East. Bari, the capital of Byzantine Italy, and Chandax, the capital of Crete, were both sizable ports. Although Venice, Naples, and Amalfi were bigger and richer, they were also essentially independent states.

Nearly all the cities just mentioned should have had populations no smaller than ten thousand, though only Constantinople and perhaps Thessalonica would have exceeded one hundred thousand. Smaller cities seem to have shown a pattern that resembled the larger ones, with most growth in the Balkans, somewhat less growth in coastal Anatolia, and still less on the Anatolian plateau. In the Balkans many places like Sparta and Patras became real towns for the first time since antiquity; and almost their whole population was a gain, because they had been practically deserted before their recovery from the Slavs. In the recently conquered parts of Syria, Mesopotamia, and Armenia, most towns seem to have recovered to roughly their maximum under Arab rule.

As always, the great majority of Byzantines lived in villages. Since these, like the cities, had become independent tax districts with their own assessments, the government tried to protect the poorer villagers from being bought out or forced to pay more than their share by their richer neighbors. Basil II apparently made the greatest landowners in each village, including nonresidents, responsible for any deficit in tax collection, so that in this respect they came to resemble the decurions of early Byzantine times. Some villages even gained a wider administrative role as the headquarters of banda, the subdivisions of themes introduced by Theophilus in 840. Such villages would have had resident counts, and almost all villages must have had resident cavalrymen, who with their military lands should have been among the more prosperous villagers.

Agriculture appears to have expanded rather more quickly than trade at this time, because trade was regarded with suspicion by the state and was subjected to considerable interference and regulation. The emperors wanted no profiteering at the expense of their revenues or their subjects. Nicephorus I taxed merchants strictly, forcing them to buy land from the state and to accept interest-bearing loans from the treasury. By the time of Leo VI's *Book of the Prefect*, anyone engaged in most sorts of commerce in Constantinople, from working silk to selling groceries, had to be enrolled in a guild and to follow regulations enforced by the city prefect. Membership in a guild had some privileges, but most of those advantages were simply penalties for outsiders. Systematizing guild rules seems to have been largely the work of Leo VI, who liked to legislate and regulate, as appears from his novels and the disastrous monopoly over Byzantine trade with Bulgaria that he imposed in 894. Overregulation of Byzantine commerce was surely one reason that freer merchants from Venice, Naples, and Amalfi began to dominate the empire's overseas trade with Italy, and to take over much of its trade with the caliphate.

Yet other emperors seem to have had less interest in regulation than

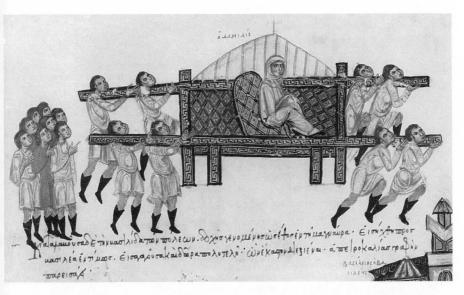

137. The widow Danelis borne in a sedan chair by her slaves. Miniature from the Madrid Scylitzes. (Photo: Biblioteca Nacional, Madrid)

Leo VI did, and internal and overland trade remained in Byzantine hands. Internal Byzantine trade evidently expanded along with the cities, the Byzantines' wealth, and security on the seas. Besides the luxury goods for the rich that had always been the mainstays of long-distance trade, a significant traffic developed in clothing, food, livestock, and other articles for the less prosperous. Around 850 Basil I was patronized by the wealthy Peloponnesian widow Danelis, who had apparently made her fortune by raising sheep and having slaves weave the wool into clothing and rugs. Provincial cities like Thessalonica, Ephesus, and Trebizond, and even small towns like Euchaïta and Chonae, held commercial fairs on the feast days of their patron saints. Constantinople, with many permanent markets and shops, needed no fairs. As its population grew, however, it required larger supplies of food and other goods that stimulated the economy of much of the empire.

During this time the growth of state revenue was surprisingly strong. The estimates that expenditures were about 1.9 million nomismata in 775, 3.1 million in 842, 3.9 million in 959, and 5.9 million in 1025 have substantial margins for error (Tables 10 and 13). But the proportions cannot be far wrong, given the great increase in both the size of the army and its rate of pay.[37] Not only could the state meet its increased

TABLE 13

Estimated State Budgets in the Ninth, Tenth, and Eleventh Centuries

Date and budgetary item	Estimate (millions of nomismata)
CA. 842 (Theophilus)	
pay of bodyguards (400 × 72 nom. × ⅓)[a]	0.038M nom.
pay of soldiers (120,000 men)[b]	1.294
pay of oarsmen (14,600 men)[b]	0.148
uniforms, arms, and rations (24,400 × 10 nom.)[c]	0.244
fodder, horses, and mules (20,400 × 5 nom.)[d]	0.102
campaigns and other military expenses	0.2
pay of bureaucracy	0.5
other nonmilitary expenses	0.5
surplus	0.06
TOTAL	3.086M nom.
CA. 959 (Constantine VII)	
pay of bodyguards (1,200 × 72 nom. × ⅓)[a]	0.115M nom.
pay of soldiers (144,000 × 9 nom. × ⅗)[a]	1.555
pay of oarsmen (34,200 × 9 nom. × ⅜)[a]	0.346
uniforms, arms, and rations (29,200[e] × 10 nom.)	0.292
fodder, horses, and mules (21,200[f] × 5 nom.)	0.106
campaigns and other military expenses	0.3
pay of bureaucracy	0.6
other nonmilitary expenses and surplus	0.6
TOTAL	3.914M nom.
CA. 1025 (Basil II)	
pay of bodyguards (1,200 × 72 nom. × ⅓)[a]	0.115M nom.
pay of soldiers (247,800 × 9 nom. × ⅗)[a]	2.676
pay of oarsmen (34,200 × 9 nom. × ⅜)[a]	0.346
uniforms, arms, and rations (43,200[g] × 10 nom.)	0.432
fodder, horses, and mules (35,200[h] × 5 nom.)	0.176
campaigns and other military expenses	0.4
pay of bureaucracy	0.8
other nonmilitary expenses	0.6
surplus	0.35
TOTAL	5.895M nom.

[a] The fractional multiplier allows for the higher pay of officers.
[b] For complete payrolls, see Treadgold, *Byzantium and Its Army*, pp. 129–34.
[c] The number includes 400 bodyguards and 24,000 soldiers of the tagmata.
[d] The number includes 400 bodyguards and 20,000 soldiers of the cavalry tagmata.
[e] The number includes 1,200 bodyguards and 28,000 soldiers of the tagmata.
[f] The number includes 1,200 bodyguards and 20,000 soldiers of the cavalry tagmata.
[g] The number includes 1,200 bodyguards and 42,000 soldiers of the tagmata.
[h] The number includes 1,200 bodyguards and 34,000 soldiers of the cavalry tagmata.

obligations, but by 1025 it had plenty of money to spare, as is evident from the enormous surplus of 14.4 million nomismata in its treasury. Even more remarkably, by then Basil II had waived two years' worth of land and hearth taxes, which should have been worth about 8 million more nomismata.

Had those taxes been collected, Basil II would probably have equaled the record surplus of Anastasius I in 518. Basil's revenue should also have been about half the record set by Justinian I around 540. Though Basil's army at the end of his reign was almost three-quarters the size of Justinian's in 540, he paid it at considerably lower rates, benefiting from the continuing system of military lands. His financial position was accordingly far more comfortable than Justinian's. Even allowing for the imprecisions in the estimates, the revenue raised from each subject under Basil II must have been comparable to that in early Byzantine times. Again allowing for imprecisions in the estimates, state revenue must have risen a good deal faster than population between 780 and 1025.

Yet after Nicephorus I's reforms tax rates seem not to have been raised, and complaints of overtaxation were relatively rare. Such complaints as did occur came from large landowners, and resulted from legislation that was meant to limit their power rather than to swell government revenues. Basil II's moratorium on hearth- and land-tax collection, which was obviously advantageous to taxpayers, might be construed as an effort to reduce overtaxation; but this seems unlikely, given the absence of widespread complaints or an increase in rates in earlier years. The most probable explanation of Basil's remissions of taxation is that with the end of the Bulgarian war, the government simply needed no more money. Thus with the same tax rates the state was raising revenues that were much higher than before.

Part of the difference can be explained by the rents from crown lands, which certainly grew under Basil II, but most of it must represent an increase in tax receipts. These depended on the number of households, the amount of land under cultivation, the quantity of livestock, the value of trade transactions, and the efficiency and honesty of tax collection. The number of households, which seems not quite to have doubled, would account for only about half the gain in revenues, which practically tripled. The rest of the gain must be the result of increases in the other four variables, and probably in all of them. More land was brought under cultivation, animals bred faster than their owners, trade expanded, and tax collection became more efficient and honest. All of these would have benefited ordinary Byzantines as well as the treasury. As oxen for plowing multiplied, they at least would have increased agricultural productivity, despite the Byzantines' relative indifference to improving agricultural techniques.

One major benefit for both agriculture and trade in the period was increased monetarization. This was largely the work of Theophilus, who increased the gold coins in circulation by nearly doubling the army's pay, and minted copper coins at about six times the previous rate. Although copper coins were a small part of the total money supply, they were important for everyday transactions, which could now be conducted with money instead of by barter. Theophilus's successors maintained his level of minting the copper coinage, and as they expanded the army their payrolls probably increased the gold in circulation more quickly than the population grew. While Nicephorus II's introduction of the lighter-weight tetarteron may have created some confusion for a few people who did not weigh their coins, his successors made their tetartera clearly distinguishable from their full nomismata, and no emperor of this period reduced the purity of the gold coinage. A more abundant and convenient currency allowed farmers to sell more produce in the cities, to the profit of both the rural and the urban economy.

Although the empire's economy had grown greatly since the ninth century, in 1025 it was still capable of further growth. The conquest of Bulgaria was very recent at the time, and most of the Balkans had an abundance of unoccupied but fertile land, with a barter economy that further monetarization could develop to advantage. The empire's new eastern conquests must also have been less than fully exploited. Even Greece and Thrace had space for more people. Many possibilities remained for expanding trade with the empire's Arab, Italian, and Slavic neighbors. Of course, any additional conquests in Syria or Italy would expand the economy along with the empire.

Yet already the government had more money than it knew how to use. A permanent reduction in taxes had little appeal for the emperors, since the money might after all be needed in the future. The tradition of monumental building on the scale of Saint Sophia had lapsed. If the cash were simply given away, the recipients might become rivals for power. During the later tenth century, the empire spent its money on campaigns to conquer new territory, and on paying more troops to defend the conquests. Consciously or unconsciously, Nicephorus II and John Tzimisces did for the state what most Byzantine aristocrats did with surplus wealth: they invested it in land. Then the income from the new lands brought still more surplus wealth. By the early eleventh century, the military reasons for more conquests were not pressing, but the economic reasons remained. Basil II, though content to forgo some tax revenues temporarily, soon started spending again on his Sicilian campaign. His successors, if they stopped making conquests, would need to decide what to do with their resources. The problem was more difficult than it looked.

PART FIVE

The Weak State and the Wealthy Society

138. Icon of the Annunciation from the Monastery of Saint Catherine, Mount
Sinai. (Photo: Courtesy of Michigan–Princeton–Alexandria Expedition to
Mount Sinai)

CHAPTER EIGHTEEN

Erratic Government, 1025–1081

The immediate succession to Basil II was automatic, because his brother Constantine VIII had long been coemperor. At age sixty-five Constantine had taken no known part in government since his twenties, but when he ruled alone his ideas proved rather different from his brother's. He levied the two years of land and hearth taxes left uncollected by Basil, and began to make lavish gifts to his favorite courtiers. He failed to reinforce the troops Basil had sent against Sicily, which withdrew after landing near Messina. He distrusted some of Basil's generals, several of whom he blinded for real or imagined conspiracies, including the duke of Vaspurakan and leading members of the Burtzes, Phocas, and Sclerus families. Yet Constantine took no more care than Basil to name a competent successor. Only when he was near death in the fall of 1028 did he hastily marry his second daughter Zoë to his city prefect, Romanus Argyrus.

ADMINISTRATIVE DRIFT

Since Constantine's eldest daughter Eudocia had become a nun, Zoë had the best dynastic claim to rule, and the long reign of Basil II had confirmed popular attachment to the Macedonian dynasty. Women had ruled for themselves before—Irene and Theodora with skill, Martina and Zoë Carbonopsina at least with energy. Constantine's daughter Zoë had neither quality. At forty-nine she was also past childbearing age, although she hoped she was not and strove with some success to keep a youthful appearance. A more promising choice for the succession would

139. Constantine VIII (r. 1025–28). Gold nomisma, shown twice actual size, with Christ on the reverse. (Photo: Dumbarton Oaks, Washington, D.C., copyright 1996)

have been her younger sister Theodora, who was more intelligent, and at age forty-five might just have been able to bear a child. But she refused to marry Romanus because he already had a wife, whom Constantine VIII packed off to a convent with the reluctant consent of the patriarch Alexius.

Romanus III Argyrus, a civil official of about sixty from a not very distinguished family of Anatolian magnates, was a recognized mediocrity.[1] Constantine's advisers reportedly dissuaded the dying emperor from choosing the more capable Constantine Dalassenus, a former duke of Antioch, thinking they would have more influence over a weak emperor.[2] Like Constantine VIII, Romanus made lavish presents and donatives. He revoked Basil II's law making magnates liable for unpaid taxes in their tax districts, forgave debts to the treasury, and tolerated embezzlement by his tax collectors. Though Romanus amnestied the generals imprisoned by Constantine and Basil, the army seems to have disliked him. He soon discovered that Constantine Diogenes and other leading officers were plotting with the princess Theodora, who may have planned to marry Diogenes. After tonsuring Diogenes and Theodora and imprisoning the other conspirators, the emperor apparently thought a major conquest would be his best insurance against future military conspiracies.

Romanus's interest fixed itself not on Sicily, whose Arabs were raiding Calabria again, but on Syria. The Mirdasid Emirate of Aleppo, despite its nominal status as a Byzantine client, had been fighting border skirmishes with the duke of Antioch Michael Spondyles. Then, in spring 1029, the Fatimids invaded Mirdasid territory and defeated and killed the emir. Some Byzantines mistook this for a chance to strengthen their hold over Syria. The patriarch Alexius summoned Jacobite bishops to Constantinople to impose orthodoxy on them, and Spondyles sent an army against the Mirdasids, who defeated it handily. Although they wanted peace and promised tribute, the emperor replaced Spondyles and planned to annex their emirate, which held the part of northern Syria that the empire did not.

Romanus offered to buy Aleppo from the Mirdasids and give them another city in exchange, but they refused. After lengthy preparations, Romanus personally led an army against Aleppo in the summer of 1030. His lack of military experience showed in his insistence on campaigning when the heat was worst and water scarcest. The troops became disorderly, fell into two ambushes, and finally fled along with the emperor. About ten thousand died, and most of the imperial baggage train was lost. Yet the Mirdasids used their victory with moderation, partly because they feared another campaign in retaliation, partly because the Byzantine frontier was well defended by the valiant strategus of Teluch, George Maniaces.

As soon as the emperor left, Byzantine fortunes improved. Imperial troops made a successful raid north of Aleppo, and the Mirdasids again offered peace. In spring 1031 they returned to being Byzantine clients, paying an annual tribute. In the autumn the Marwanid emir, who had taken Edessa but felt unable to hold it, surrendered that sizable city to George Maniaces, now promoted to strategus of the Euphrates Cities. Even when the emir changed his mind and tried to retake Edessa, Maniaces held it for the empire. The Byzantines regained some forts north of Tripoli that they had lost, and made an alliance with Tripoli's emir, who had rebelled against the Fatimids. None of these successes owed anything to Romanus.

After an expensive campaign of church building to win God's favor, in spring 1032 the emperor began another expedition to Syria, presumably hoping to exploit the troubles of the Fatimids. He turned back, however, in the middle of Anatolia on hearing that Constantine Diogenes and Theodora were plotting again in their monasteries. Before Romanus's return Diogenes committed suicide rather than implicate others under torture, but the expedition had already been aborted. Meanwhile Asia Minor and Armenia suffered the first famine recorded in more than fifty years. The Sicilian Arabs invaded Calabria, killed the catepan of Italy, and raided Corcyra. Though the strategus of Nicopolis defeated them, the next year the Arabs returned, along with the famine in Anatolia and a Pecheneg raid across the Danube.

Blamed for all these misfortunes whether he was responsible for them or not, Romanus grew unpopular. He had also offended Zoë by limiting her spending and taking a mistress. The empress in turn took a lover, Michael the Paphlagonian, a younger brother of the eunuch John the Orphanotrophus, head of the imperial orphanage. According to plausible reports, Zoë and Michael began poisoning the emperor, who became frail and ill. In spring 1034, when Romanus took too long in dying, they had him drowned in his bath. His death aroused no public distress or protest, and the next day, with the help of a large donation, Zoë persuaded the patriarch Alexius to marry her to Michael and to crown him emperor.

Michael IV the Paphlagonian was probably in his mid-twenties, since he was said to be young but had already established himself as a money changer. Inexperienced in government and suffering from epilepsy, he was under the influence of his brother John the Orphanotrophus, who had introduced him to Zoë. John himself was experienced and shrewd, but cared most for the interests of his relatives, including three younger brothers besides Michael. The family was an obscure one, with few allies but John in the army or bureaucracy.

The accession of the lowborn Michael and his relatives was particularly unwelcome to Constantine Dalassenus, who knew he had almost been chosen emperor instead of the murdered Romanus. Worried that Dalassenus would start a revolt in his retirement in the Armeniacs, John lured him to the capital with guarantees of safety and promises of honors. But that summer John blamed Dalassenus for a revolt that one of the emperor's brothers suppressed at Antioch. Alleging a plot, the orphanotrophus exiled not just Dalassenus but other leading members of the aristocracy.[3]

At first Michael's reign went rather badly, especially in comparison with the empire's recent strength and prosperity. The Arabs sacked Myra in the Cibyrrhaeots; the Pechenegs raided up to Thessalonica; and the Serbs repudiated Byzantine suzerainty. The famine persisted, as hail damaged trees and crops, and locusts ravaged the Anatolian plains. In 1035 the locusts reappeared, bringing the fourth straight year of poor harvests.[4] When Michael repeated Romanus III's error by trying to tighten his control over Aleppo, the Aleppines drove off the governor he tried to send them. Michael seemed to be as unsatisfactory an emperor as Romanus had been.

Yet the Byzantine army remained strong. The Cibyrrhaeot strategus killed or captured the Arab pirates who raided the coast of the Thracesians in 1035. By that time, after intermittent warfare, the duke of Vaspurakan secured his province by capturing the Muslim enclave of Perkri. The next year the Byzantines fought off a joint attempt to retake Edessa by the Marwanids and Numayrids, while the Fatimids made another ten-year peace with the empire. When the Pechenegs raided the Balkans again, they seem to have frightened the Serbs back into Byzantine clientship. About 1037 the Mirdasids of Aleppo renewed the Byzantine protectorate over their territory, and the Numayrids formally ceded Edessa to Byzantium.

John the Orphanotrophus appeared to be the real ruler. When a drought caused a food shortage in Constantinople, he imported grain from Greece. Since Zoë was unable to bear the emperor an heir, John had the imperial couple adopt his nephew, Michael the Caulker, who received the rank of Caesar. Zoë resented John's power and tried to have him poisoned in 1037, but he discovered and thwarted her plot. John then sought to take the place of the patriarch Alexius, alleging Alexius's election had been uncanonical because the metropolitans had not ratified it. The patriarch frustrated this plan by observing that if his election was invalid, so were all his ordinations and his coronation of Michael IV himself.

The orphanotrophus and the emperor tried to advance their reputations through a great expedition to reconquer Sicily. The campaign seemed to have a good chance of success, because the Arabs on the island had been fighting each other and the Byzantine commander was the brilliant general George Maniaces. Maniaces embarked in the spring of 1038 with a force of Varangians, who included both Scandinavian and French Normans, and other mercenaries. Gathering additional troops from Byzantine Italy, he invaded Sicily. His men captured Messina, defeated the Arabs, and began taking towns in the west and south of the island.

In the meantime the emperor's epilepsy grew worse, and he developed a severe case of dropsy. He tried to placate God by frequenting Saint Demetrius's shrine at Thessalonica, and building or rebuilding other churches. In 1039 he gave donatives to every priest and monk in the empire, and to every child whose parents made him its godfather. The orphanotrophus offset these expenses by selling offices, adding surcharges to the land tax, and demanding cash for the taxes that the Bulgarians had always paid in kind.[5]

In Sicily Maniaces continued to advance, and in early 1040 he took Syracuse by storm and refortified it. But at this point his French Normans, dissatisfied with their pay, left for the Italian mainland and raised a revolt. They helped take Bari for some other malcontents, among them Argyrus, son of the old rebel Meles. Before Maniaces could deal with them, John the Orphanotrophus had him arrested on suspicion of conspiracy. John was alarmed because the Bulgarians had just rebelled, setting off a crisis that Byzantine plotters might exploit.

John himself was mostly responsible for the Bulgarian revolt, because his demands that the Bulgarians pay taxes in cash had caused general consternation among them. The rebels seized Belgrade and proclaimed a new emperor of Bulgaria, Peter Delyan. He was probably a son of the late Bulgarian emperor Gabriel Radomir, though some Byzantines claimed he was an impostor. Peter soon drove south and took Scopia, headquarters of the Ducate of Bulgaria. The duke of Dyrrhachium Basil Synadenus marched against the rebels, but was himself accused of conspiracy and removed by the emperor Michael.

At this, Synadenus's largely Bulgarian troops rebelled against their new duke and proclaimed one of themselves, Tichomir, as another Bulgarian emperor. But when Peter proposed an alliance of the two rebel armies, an assembly of both chose Peter as their leader and stoned Tichomir, giving Peter control over both Dyrrhachium and its army. The ailing emperor retreated to Constantinople pursued by the Bulgarians, who ambushed and captured his baggage train. Peter sent troops south that captured Demetrias and defeated the strategus of Hellas near Thebes, and most of the Theme of Nicopolis joined the Bulgarians out of disgust with the local tax collectors. Thanks to John's repeated blunders, the Bulgarian Empire seemed to be reborn.

Better at internal security than foreign policy, the orphanotrophus quickly apprehended plotters in the Anatolics and at Constantinople who tried to profit from the turmoil.[6] Yet he failed to catch the strategus of Theodosiopolis Alusian, a son of the last Bulgarian emperor John Vladislav, who made his way across Asia Minor and joined Peter in Bulgaria. Peter sent Alusian with fourteen thousand men to besiege Thessalonica. When he was defeated there, however, Alusian had Peter blinded and took over his revolt. By this time, near the beginning of 1041, the emperor Michael had mustered his troops and led them to Mosynopolis against the fractious Bulgarians. The Bulgarian pretender advanced to meet him, but decided to submit in return for a pardon. The revolt collapsed, and the exhausted emperor celebrated a triumph that owed more to the squabbles of Bulgarian leaders than to his own efforts.

The Bulgarian insurrection showed that in a short time the enlarged empire had grown alarmingly flabby. During the revolt the Serbian prince of Dioclea repudiated his vassalage, seized some Byzantine border territory, and defeated the new duke of Dyrrhachium. After the recall of Maniaces, most of the Byzantine army in Sicily left to fight the Norman rebels, letting the Arabs recapture Syracuse. Although the Byzantines retook Bari when the rebel Argyrus changed sides, the Normans defeated them repeatedly and captured their catepan. When Smbat-John of Ani died in 1041, leaving his kingdom to the empire as he had promised, his nephew defeated the Byzantine army sent to claim the inheritance.

Toward the end of the year, in these unpromising circumstances, Michael IV died of his diseases, and was succeeded by his nephew and adopted son Michael the Caulker. Michael V, who seems to have been about as young as his predecessor had been at his accession, was more active but less cautious. He had promised to rule in subordination to his adopted mother Zoë, with the help of his uncle John the Orphanotrophus. But the new emperor was closest to John's brother Constantine, a former domestic of the East, who had been envious of John for some time. The emperor gave Constantine the rank of nobilissimus, just below Caesar.

Michael V wanted to be his own master, and in early 1042 he boldly exiled John and most of his family, except for Constantine the Nobilissimus. In need of allies to replace his relatives, he reinstated many of those John had exiled or imprisoned, including Constantine Dalassenus and George Maniaces. The emperor promptly sent Maniaces back to Italy, where Argyrus had rejoined the Normans to take Bari and the Arabs were retaking the last of Maniaces' conquests on Sicily. Michael also planned to exile his adopted mother Zoë. Although the men the emperor was promoting were more capable than those he was removing, he acted too hastily, underestimating his need for John's cunning and Zoë's legitimacy.

That Easter the emperor relegated Zoë to a convent on a charge of trying to poison him. This ungrateful treatment of the niece of Basil II enraged many ordinary citizens. Riots broke out in the streets, and mobs wrecked the houses of relatives of the emperor and his uncle. In a des-

140. Zoë (left) and her sister Theodora (r. 1055–56), when they reigned together in 1042. Gold nomisma, shown twice actual size, with the Virgin and Child on the reverse. (Photo: Dumbarton Oaks, Washington, D.C., copyright 1996)

perate effort to appease the crowd, Michael and Constantine recalled the empress to the palace. But the protesters, who won over the patriarch Alexius, brought Zoë's sister Theodora from her convent and proclaimed her empress. They seized the emperor and his nobilissimus and blinded them.

This extraordinary popular uprising left Zoë and Theodora as the only rulers, with Zoë the senior empress. Yet Zoë had neither the ability to rule alone, nor, after she had made some extravagant donatives, even the inclination. Still pleasure-loving, from the first she seems to have wanted to marry a third time. She considered the candidacy of Constantine Dalassenus, but found him too forceful. When another candidate suddenly died, she selected Constantine Monomachus, a well-born widower exiled for plotting against Michael IV. Zoë brought Monomachus to the capital, married him, and had him crowned emperor.

CONSTANTINE IX'S INDOLENCE

Like the three emperors before him, Constantine IX Monomachus had been chosen for his weaknesses. Yet with an engaging personality and a suitable age of about forty, he seemed a passable ruler. Sixteen and a half years after the death of Basil II, the frontiers remained roughly as they had been; the army could still fight reasonably well, and the treasury held a substantial gold reserve. Although corruption may have spread in the bureaucracy, John the Orphanotrophus had made sure sufficient revenue was collected. Constantine entrusted the everyday business of government to a competent administrator, the scholar Constantine Lichudes, whose position became known as that of mesazon ("manager"). After his years in exile, Monomachus looked forward to an easy and happy reign.

The naturally generous emperor enjoyed promoting men to high office, and appointed many more than the usual officials. Emperors had long bestowed honorary offices without salaries, or sold titular offices with salaries too low to recoup the purchase price; but Constantine seems to have been the first not merely to sell but to give away titular offices with salaries, and even to make them transferable.[7] These sinecures were apparently distributed on a scale that became a real financial drain, in some cases for the indefinite future.

Although Constantine was considerate of Zoë, he already had a mis-

141. Constantine IX Monomachus (r. 1042–55) and his wife Zoë presenting offerings to Christ. Contemporary mosaic in the gallery of Saint Sophia, Constantinople. (Photo: Dumbarton Oaks, Washington, D.C., copyright 1996)

tress, Maria Scleraena, from the noble Sclerus family. Since he had kept from marrying her when he was twice widowed only because the Church disapproved of third marriages, Maria was practically his wife, and she had followed him into exile. He soon brought her to the capital, with Zoë's permission. Next to the house he gave her he began reconstructing the magnificent Monastery of Saint George of the Mangana, visiting Scleraena during his frequent inspections of the work. To please Scleraena's brother, a personal enemy of George Maniaces, the emperor appointed a new catepan of Italy to replace the great general.

When his replacement arrived in the early autumn, the outraged Maniaces had himself proclaimed emperor. At Bari Argyrus and his Normans, who had been fighting Maniaces, cleverly announced their loyalty to Constantine. Concluding that his chances would be better in the Balkans, Maniaces sailed with his army to Dyrrhachium in the late winter of 1043. The local forces surrendered, fled, or joined the rebellion. Having tried and failed to negotiate with the rebel, the emperor mustered his troops, but he was so distrustful of his generals that he chose a palace eunuch to lead the expedition. In late spring Maniaces advanced toward the capital, and clashed with the imperial army at Ostrovo on the road to Thessalonica.

There, just as his men were putting their opponents to flight, Maniaces was wounded, and died on the battlefield. His soldiers dispersed, and the rebellion was over. Yet Constantine had barely celebrated his triumph when some four hundred ships arrived from Russia, probably sent to help Maniaces and surely hoping to profit from his revolt.[8] Now that he was dead, the Russians offered not to attack if they were paid a thousand nomismata per vessel. Constantine refused. In the ensuing battle in the Bosporus, the Byzantines burned many of the Russian ships with Greek Fire, and drove off the rest. Constantine, with more luck than skill, had surmounted two major challenges to his rule.

A year later, in 1044, the emperor sent an expedition to claim Ani from its usurping king. With the help of the neighboring Shaddadids of Dvin, the Byzantines forced Ani to surrender by the next spring, and the Kingdom of Armenia was added to the Theme of Iberia. But to avoid sharing his gains with his Shaddadid allies, Constantine then ordered an attack on Dvin, which failed. At the same time a major new Muslim power from the East, the Seljuk Turks, raided Vaspurakan and defeated and captured its duke. Yet the emperor sent tagmatic troops in 1046 to fight not the Seljuks but the Shaddadids, the allies he had betrayed. Thus the emperor ignored his enemies and fought his friends.

142. Interior of the monastery Church of Nea Monē, Chios, built by Constantine IX. (Photo: Courtesy of Charalambos Bouras)

Meanwhile, in the Balkans, some twenty thousand Pechenegs fled across the Danube from another Turkish tribe, the Uzes, and entered Byzantine service under their leader Kegen. The following winter, which was unusually cold, another hundred thousand–odd Pechenegs migrated across the frozen Danube under their chief Tyrach, this time to raid imperial territory. With the help of Kegen, the duke of Adrianople Constantine Arianites defeated Tyrach's raiders. Instead of killing or deporting them, the emperor had the Pechenegs disarmed, baptized, and settled in the underpopulated hills northwest of Serdica, hoping to use them as mercenaries. Apparently in consternation at this dangerous settlement, the western tagmata rebelled; but they accepted an amnesty after Monomachus seized and tonsured their candidate for emperor, Leo Tornices.[9] Both the western and the eastern frontier remained unsettled.

In 1047 Constantine, who liked to patronize religion and culture, inaugurated his Monastery of Saint George of the Mangana and handsomely expanded higher education. Perhaps on the advice of his erudite minister Lichudes, he founded a school of philosophy under the polymath Constantine Psellus, and a school of law under another leading scholar, John Xiphilinus. By this time the emperor was rapidly exhausting the treasury that he used to buy support. He was also suffering from gout, and demoralized after the death of his mistress Scleraena.[10] His lack of ability was becoming painfully evident.

In late summer troops from the western tagmata rescued Leo Tornices from his monastery, brought him to Adrianople, and proclaimed him emperor. Tornices marched on the capital, announcing that he meant to marry the junior empress Theodora. The emperor, with hardly any good troops in the capital, hastily recalled the eastern tagmata who were fighting the Shaddadids in Armenia, but they needed time to arrive. Fortunately for Constantine, Tornices had scarcely any money. He was forced to let his men pillage Thrace, and the Constantinopolitans feared similar treatment if they admitted him. Despite winning some skirmishes outside the walls of the capital, Tornices waited in vain for an invitation to enter, and his soldiers started to desert to the emperor. After retreating to Arcadiopolis, Tornices lost time besieging Rhaedestus. When the eastern tagmata arrived, the emperor was able to buy the loyalty of most of the rest of Tornices' men. Finally, after taking refuge in a church, Tornices was blinded on Christmas.

While most of the eastern tagmata were away confronting Tornices, a large band of Seljuk Turks raided Armenia in early 1048. They ravaged Taron and Iberia before the duke of Iberia Catacalon Cecaumenus ambushed them in Vaspurakan and nearly wiped them out. Then still more Seljuks raided through Vaspurakan into Iberia, where they destroyed the town of Artze and defeated Cecaumenus. The emperor tried to reinforce Armenia by sending a force of fifteen thousand Pecheneg mercenaries from Serdica; but these were barely across the Bosporus when they mutinied, swam the strait, and returned to Thrace. They led the main body of their fellow Pechenegs to the region of Preslav, which they found more pleasant and fertile than the land they had been given around Serdica. When the emperor arrested Kegen on a charge of conspiracy, his Pechenegs joined the others, defeated the western tagmata, and began looting the Thracian countryside.

In 1049 Constantine, having accepted the Shaddadids as clients and made a truce with the Seljuk Turks, brought the eastern tagmata west again to fight the rebel Pechenegs. The Pechenegs twice defeated forces drawn from the combined tagmata, and the second time they killed the domestic of the West Constantine Arianites. A year later the emperor released Kegen and sent him to negotiate with the Pechenegs; they simply murdered their former leader. At last the ethnarch Nicephorus Bryennius, with a force of Varangians and other mercenaries, surprised the Pecheneg raiders and massacred enough of them to interrupt their raids.

Around the time the old Augusta Zoë died in 1050, the emperor replaced Constantine Lichudes with another mesazon, the young eunuch John. The new minister cast off whatever restraint Lichudes had exercised on the emperor's prodigality. Under John's administration, if not earlier, Constantine began to reduce the gold in his nomismata by about a quarter—to eighteen karats from twenty-four—making the first important debasement since the third century. Constantine's main purpose was probably to decrease the regular pay of the inactive thematic soldiers, because the campaign pay of soldiers on active duty had always been variable. Yet this aim could have been better achieved by reducing the weight of the nomisma, as Nicephorus II had done. Since both debased and pure nomismata weighed the same, the adulteration was almost impossible to measure accurately, and the inevitable result was inflation. Though debasement cut payrolls, it also cut taxes as soon as taxpayers began using the debased coins, even when tax collectors found ways to make up some of the difference.[11]

Increasingly the government relied not on the thematic soldiers, who were out of training, but on the tagmata, mercenaries, clients, and independent allies. In Italy the former rebel Argyrus was named catepan in 1051 and enlisted the papacy as an ally against the Normans. Around 1052 the prince of Dioclea, who had been fighting the empire, made peace as an ally rather than a client. After driving an army of the tagmata and Varangians from Preslav, the Pechenegs agreed to a thirty-year peace, this time as independent allies settled within the empire's borders. In Syria the Mirdasids continued to hold Aleppo and to shield the Byzantine border as clients who were virtually independent. In Armenia the Shaddadids were clients of the same sort.

Seemingly content with such defenders, around 1053 Constantine permanently relieved some fifty thousand troops in the Armenian themes of their military duties in return for regular cash payments.[12] This meant demobilizing about a fifth of the army. Though in theory the Armenians could have been returned to active service if they were needed, no one seems to have expected this to happen, and they soon become ordinary civilians. Yet some of these troops had defeated Turks as recently as 1048, and they should have been among the most experienced thematic forces. They were also stationed on a front that needed defending against the Seljuks. Constantine's government probably chose to take payments from the Armenian themes precisely because their men were still accustomed to serving; in themes where no one in memory had fought, the men might well have refused to pay, or even rebelled. In any case, the decision to demobilize the Armenian themes was made for financial rather than military reasons, and some knowledgeable contemporaries thought it was a catastrophic mistake.[13]

Constantine's substitutes for thematic troops were not necessarily effective. The alliance between the Byzantines and the papacy failed, and the Normans defeated the catepan Argyrus and captured the pope in 1053. The Seljuks used their interval of peace with the empire to force Azerbaijan and the Shaddadids into vassalage, and to sack Kars. The Seljuk leader Tughrul raided Byzantine territory in person in the spring of 1054, attacking the Armenian themes that had just been demobilized. He plundered Vaspurakan, sacked Perkri, and sent raiding parties through Iberia, Taron, and other places before turning south to conquer the Buwayhids. Though the proof of his folly in dismantling the Armenian themes could scarcely have been clearer, Constantine did nothing.

Meanwhile some papal legates to Constantinople became embroiled in a bitter argument with the patriarch Michael Cerularius. Cerularius insisted on traditional Byzantine practices in churches throughout the empire, especially in Armenia, where unleavened bread had long been used in the Eucharist as it was in the West. Exasperated by the patriarch's intransigence, the papal legates excommunicated him. While the emperor tried to calm the dispute, demonstrations in the capital supported the patriarch, who excommunicated the legates. These personal condemnations did not end all communion between the eastern and western churches, but they ruined the emperor's alliance with the papacy and raised intractable issues that could plague any relations with the West.

By this time Constantine had become too ill to intervene further. As he lay dying at the beginning of 1055, his minister John, then postal logothete, summoned the duke of Bulgaria Nicephorus Proteuon as a likely successor. However, he ignored the fact that one last representative of the Macedonian dynasty was still alive: the elderly empress Theodora. Her partisans brought her from the convent where she had retired, and proclaimed her just before Constantine's death. Constantine's failures were so glaring that his wishes carried little weight.

At the age of about seventy-five, Theodora was obviously not going to be a vigorous ruler who could make the military and administrative reforms the situation required. But she could have chosen such a ruler through adoption or a nominal marriage. Instead, she decided to keep her power by ruling alone. She exiled the postal logothete John, his choice for emperor Nicephorus Proteuon, and the ethnarch Nicephorus Bryennius, whom the western tagmata seem to have wanted to proclaim. She also dismissed some other prominent generals. Yet she avoided debasing the coinage further, cut spending, and appointed a competent chief minister, Leo Paraspondylus.[14]

Theodora exercised all the usual imperial prerogatives, including the nomination of bishops. Though the empresses Irene and Theodora had done as much in the eighth and ninth centuries, now the patriarch Michael Cerularius objected, and pressed the empress to take a husband. Theodora was preparing to dismiss Cerularius when she fell mortally ill in the summer of 1056. Her advisers persuaded her to adopt another successor whom they could control, the sexagenarian military logothete Michael Bringas. In this way Theodora's death ended the ancient Macedonian dynasty without properly replacing it.

After brushing aside a feeble rebellion by Constantine IX's cousin Theodosius Monomachus, the new emperor Michael VI presided over Theodora's advisers. He was on bad terms with the Anatolian generals, perhaps because as military logothete he had been paying the army with Constantine's debased nomismata. Apparently the value of military pay had fallen even for generals, while wholesale promotions had more than compensated civil officials for the debasement. Early in 1057 the Norman mercenary leader Hervé rebelled when Michael denied him advancement, though he and his men were soon captured by the Seljuk Turks and handed over to the emperor.

That Easter, Michael denied requests for promotions by a group of Constantine IX's generals, led by the former stratopedarch of the East Isaac Comnenus and the former duke of Antioch Catacalon Cecaumenus. Probably the emperor refused them for fear they would plot against him later; but his refusal provoked them to plot at once, with wide support in the officer corps. Choosing Comnenus as their leader, the conspirators hastened their preparations after one of them, the domestic of the West Nicephorus Bryennius, was blinded for giving his men extra pay. Later the same spring, a gathering of soldiers proclaimed Isaac Comnenus emperor on his family estates in Paphlagonia.

Reinforced by Byzantine, Varangian, and Norman troops gathered by Cecaumenus from his own estates near Colonia, the rebel army marched to Nicaea. By their departure they left eastern Anatolia open to the Seljuks, who raided up to Colonia and sacked Melitene. Most of the Anatolian army went over to Comnenus, and the rest fled to Constantinople. In late summer Michael VI mustered his forces, including most of the tagmata, and sent them against the rebels at Nicaea. After a fierce battle, the rebels defeated and drove off the loyalists, and the emperor's attempts to negotiate failed. Finally he abdicated on the advice of the patriarch Michael, who received Isaac into the capital and crowned him.[15]

ABORTIVE REFORMS

Although the succession had often been manipulated earlier behind the facade of the Macedonian dynasty, strictly speaking Isaac Comnenus was the first usurper to take power in more than two centuries. He minted coins that showed him holding an unsheathed sword; he ruled by right of conquest. But since the Macedonian dynasty was extinct and Michael VI had abdicated, Isaac's position was scarcely more irregular than that of Romanus Lecapenus or John Tzimisces had been. Even some civil officials acknowledged that the empire needed the changes that Isaac seemed determined to make. Aged about fifty, he was energetic, alert, and self-possessed, a much more imposing figure than his sorry predecessors since Basil II. Isaac tried to end the corruption and inefficiency that had become ingrained in the administration during the past thirty-two years. While his ultimate aim was presumably to strengthen the army, for the present he devoted himself to refilling the treasury.

143. Isaac I Comnenus (r. 1057–59). Gold nomisma, shown twice actual size, with Christ on the reverse. (Photo: Courtesy of the Arthur M. Sackler Museum, Harvard University Art Museums, Whittemore Collection)

After paying the troops their usual accessional donative, Isaac disappointed any of them who expected their pay to be raised. On the other hand, he lowered the salaries of some civil servants by demoting them, and seems to have stopped paying the honorary officials altogether. He named new controllers for the tax districts, who strictly collected both the current taxes and a large accumulation of arrears. Isaac seems to have considered most of the thematic troops past saving, since he made no effort to enforce the laws that had protected their military lands. But he reclaimed imperial estates misappropriated by private persons, and even canceled a number of grants of crown lands made by Michael VI and Constantine IX.

Apparently Isaac took back all imperial estates that had been granted to churches and monasteries, which under Nicephorus II's law of 964 were forbidden to receive land from anyone.[16] The confiscation of church lands angered the patriarch Michael Cerularius, who was trying to extend his already considerable power and prestige. In 1058 the emperor prepared charges against Cerularius, exiled him, and was about to bring him to trial when the patriarch unexpectedly died. Isaac chose as his successor Constantine Lichudes, the former minister, partly because the emperor wanted to recover the imperial revenues that had been assigned to Lichudes by Constantine IX.[17]

Preoccupied with collecting or saving money, as of 1059 Isaac had done little or nothing to revive the army. Meanwhile the Norman leader Robert Guiscard, who had made his own alliance with the papacy, conquered most of Byzantine Italy. In Anatolia the Seljuks sacked and destroyed Sebastea, far inside the empire. The Hungarians invaded the Balkans, apparently to stop raids by the Pechenegs settled in Byzantine territory. Unable to ignore an outright invasion, Isaac gathered his forces and marched to Serdica. The Hungarians and most of the Pechenegs agreed to make peace—though the Hungarians seem to have kept Sirmium—and the emperor defeated a recalcitrant Pecheneg band along the Danube. As he returned, however, many of his troops drowned in a rain-swollen river.

That autumn Isaac returned to Constantinople disheartened. He found his remaining tasks daunting, his position isolated, and his opponents numerous. Soon he became ill, and feared he was dying. Since Isaac's only son was already dead, the scholar Psellus persuaded him to become a monk and abdicate in favor of Constantine Ducas, a fellow conspirator against Michael VI. By attacking abuses without benefiting the army,

Isaac had made enemies whom he lost the nerve to face down. Yet he had been right to think sweeping changes were needed. He had probably planned first to collect an adequate gold reserve and then to restore the army's pay and discipline, a plan that made sense but required time and care.

Constantine X Ducas, who took power at the age of fifty-three, was another emperor chosen for his affability and passivity. He relied on his brother and Caesar John Ducas, on Psellus, and on his wife Eudocia Macrembolitissa, the late Michael Cerularius's niece. Seeing how much the bureaucracy, the Church, and the citizenry of the capital resented Isaac's reforms, Constantine restored most of the ranks and salaries that had been lowered or abolished. Perhaps as a result, in spring 1060 he narrowly escaped assassination by plotters who apparently wanted to restore Isaac.[18] Yet Constantine shared Isaac's concern about the empire's finances. He tried to raise tax receipts, and he avoided further debasement of the nomisma.

The army continued to decay. In 1060 the Normans took Rhegium and Tarentum, reducing Byzantine Italy to little more than the coast around Bari. The emperor sent an army that recaptured Tarentum and most of southern Longobardia while Robert Guiscard was off conquering Sicily; but on Robert's return in 1062 the Normans recovered their losses. The next year the Seljuk sultan Tughrul was succeeded by his nephew Alp Arslan, and though the new sultan's main interest was in Muslim Syria, his Turks wanted to exploit the vulnerability of Byzantine Armenia and Asia Minor. In 1064 he led an expedition that not only raided but actually conquered Ani from the empire. The prince of Tashir submitted to the Turks in despair, and when the prince of Kars tried to save his land by ceding it to the emperor, his people surrendered to the Turks. That fall the Uzes crossed the Danube in tens of thousands, swept aside the Byzantine troops who opposed them, and raided as far south as Thessaly.

By winter this last demonstration of Byzantine impotence had so humiliated the emperor that he made a show of leading a tiny army into Thrace. Fortunately for him, the Uzes began to suffer from disease, hunger, and the attacks of the local Pechenegs and Bulgarians, and withdrew of their own accord. The next year Constantine allowed some Uzes to settle in western Thrace as allied troops like the Pechenegs. While the Pechenegs and Uzes remained restive in the Balkans, the Seljuk Turks kept ravaging the East, and the Normans held most of the

Catepanate of Italy. In 1066 a rebellion broke out in Thessaly against the bumbling emperor; to stop it, he had to end a surcharge he had added to the taxes, perhaps to compensate for debasement of the coinage.[19] Constantine's health began to fail, and he died the next spring, when the duke of Serdica Romanus Diogenes was already plotting against him.

Since Constantine's son Michael VII was young and backward, under his father's will his mother Eudocia served as regent, having sworn not to remarry or otherwise to promote another emperor. She frustrated the conspiracy of Romanus Diogenes and exiled him. Yet the empire obviously needed a stronger ruler than Michael was likely to become. Bolder than ever, Turkish raiders sacked and burned Caesarea, and on their return raided across Cilicia and around Antioch. Seeing the empire's danger, the patriarch, now the former law professor John Xiphilinus, released the empress from her oath and persuaded her to remarry.

Wisely forgiving the recent plot of Romanus Diogenes, Eudocia married him at the beginning of 1068.[20] In his mid-thirties, vigorous, decisive, and handsome, Romanus IV, son of Basil II's general Constantine Diogenes, came from an old Cappadocian military family.[21] Though Romanus ruled only as the husband of Eudocia and the protector of Michael VII, Eudocia appears to have loved her new husband, and Michael had no capacity to challenge anyone. For the moment, Romanus seemed strong and popular enough to ignore the resentment of the Caesar John Ducas.

Romanus was the first emperor since Basil II to give the army his full attention, which it certainly needed. Consulting with his generals, he

144. Romanus IV Diogenes (r. 1068–71). Miniature from the Modena Zonaras. (Photo: Biblioteca Estense, Modena)

speedily gathered the western tagmata, Pechenegs, Uzes, and some mercenaries, and brought them to the Opsician and Anatolic themes. There he began calling up what he could of the thematic soldiers of Asia Minor. After many years of neglect, the rolls were incomplete and the men inexperienced and badly armed; but by offering ample campaign pay, Romanus managed to muster and drill a sizable force. He seems not to have tried to muster the demobilized Armenian themes, whose territory had been partly overrun.

That summer, while Turkish bands raided Byzantine Syria, the emperor led his enlarged forces to the mountains that commanded the Syrian lowlands. During his advance the Turks evaded him and sacked Neocaesarea to the north, but Romanus led a detachment that defeated some of them near Tephrice. In the fall he marched into Syria, sending troops to Melitene to guard his rear. These failed to stop the Turks, who raided all the way to Amorium and sacked it. In Syria, however, Romanus besieged and captured the lost Byzantine border fort of Artach and the Arab border town of Manbij. His improvised army, though clumsy at catching raiders, had proved able to win a battle and take fortifications.[22]

At the beginning of 1069 the emperor returned to Constantinople, sending some Norman mercenaries to guard the Armeniacs under their leader Robert Crispin. Crispin, dissatisfied with his pay, robbed the local tax collectors, then defeated the troops that were sent against him. Though afterward he submitted and was dismissed, his men still plundered the upper Euphrates until Romanus arrived with an army in the spring. Then the emperor pursued the Turks who were raiding nearby, and killed some and drove others eastward.

Leaving the Armenian general Philaretus Brachamius to hold the line of the Euphrates with a large force, Romanus marched farther east, meaning to attack the Turkish border fort of Chliat. The Turks attacked and defeated Philaretus's army and crossed the river, forcing Romanus to turn back. The emperor failed to catch the raiders, who reached and sacked Iconium in the Anatolics before some Armenian troops ambushed them on their return. Meanwhile the Seljuk sultan Alp Arslan seized Manzikert, opposite Chliat. Undefeated in the field, Romanus returned to his capital without having stopped the Turks in either Armenia or Anatolia.

By 1070, when the emperor made no campaign, the magnitude of his problems had become evident. Some generals wanted simply to abandon the devastated Armenian themes and to concentrate on defending

Anatolia proper.[23] Romanus disagreed. He asked Alp Arslan for a truce, and an exchange of Manbij for Manzikert. During the negotiations, however, some renegade Turks defeated and captured the eastern commander Manuel Comnenus near Sebastea, then deserted with him to the emperor. When Romanus refused to surrender these deserters, other Turks raided all the way to the Thracesian Theme, where they sacked Chonae.[24]

Romanus decided he could only prevail by intimidating his Turkish and Byzantine opponents with a major victory. For the present he resigned himself to the loss of Italy, where the Normans took Bari in the spring of 1071. He replenished the treasury somewhat by reducing the gold in the nomisma from eighteen to sixteen karats, a debasement that at least had an emergency to excuse it.[25] Assembling an army of perhaps a hundred thousand thematic, tagmatic, and mercenary troops, far more than the Turks could muster, he set out for Armenia to conquer Chliat and recapture Manzikert. On his arrival in late summer, he took Manzikert by surrender, and sent a force under the Norman mercenary Russell of Baillieul against Chliat.

The sultan Alp Arslan, who had been besieging Edessa, marched back and chased Russell's army from Chliat. Then he met Romanus's more numerous forces near Manzikert. After several days of harrying by the Turks, the emperor still hoped to destroy them, and refused their offer of a truce. He advanced, attacked, and drove them back, until in the evening he ordered a withdrawal to his camp. Then Andronicus Ducas, son of the Caesar John, spread the word that Romanus had fled. This turned the withdrawal into a rout, which left the emperor and those around him to be captured by the Seljuks.[26]

The sultan, admiring Romanus's dignity in defeat, gave the captive emperor tolerable terms, especially because most of the Byzantine army had escaped. In return for his release, Romanus reportedly agreed to an alliance, an indemnity, an annual tribute, and the cession of Manzikert, Edessa, Manbij, and Antioch. Alp Arslan promptly freed him, so that he could reestablish his power and fulfill his promises. In Constantinople the news of Romanus's release pleased the empress Eudocia, but not the Caesar John Ducas. Supported by the Varangians, John proclaimed Michael VII sole emperor, put Eudocia in a nunnery, and declared Romanus deposed.

Starting with a Turkish escort supplied by the sultan, Romanus gathered the remnants of his army and advanced to Docea in Paphlagonia before he learned of his deposition. The Caesar's younger son Constantine Ducas marched against Romanus, and with the help of the Norman mercenary Crispin defeated him near Amasia. After wintering in his native Cappadocia, Romanus went to Cilicia to join his duke of Antioch; but Andronicus Ducas and Crispin arrived and defeated and captured the duke. At this Romanus surrendered on a promise of immunity. During the next summer, however, the Caesar had him blinded so brutally that he died of his infected wounds.

Although Romanus may have been rash at Manzikert, his sense of urgency had been greatly needed. He saw that a simple withdrawal from Armenia would not help, because without an effective army not even the Byzantine heartland would be safe. Inheriting long-inactive thematic troops that were quite unready for combat, he managed to give them some rudimentary training while campaigning with them. He had no time to restore them as a defensive network to hold Anatolia, where most fortifications were in such disrepair that they could not be defended; but he almost turned the themes into an offensive force that could hold Armenia and its more defensible border forts. Unlike the lesser men who brought him down, Romanus understood how vulnerable the sprawling empire had become.

MILITARY DISASTER

Michael VII Ducas, though past twenty, was still unfit to rule. His uncle John Ducas had some talent for conspiracy, but none for governing. So both relied on the postal logothete Nicephoritzes, a clever eunuch, to marshal the empire's waning resources against its multiplying enemies. Romanus IV's generals still held much of the East, and Alp Arslan took Romanus's death as grounds to repudiate his treaty and to restart the war. The Pechenegs were raiding Thrace yet again. Some Bulgarian nobles at Scopia proclaimed a new emperor of Bulgaria, Constantine Bodin, son of the Serbian prince of Dioclea. The Byzantine government gave priority to suppressing the Bulgarian rebellion, which was accomplished by early 1073.

At this point Alp Arslan died, and his son Malik-Shāh inherited the Seljuk Sultanate. The Turks seem to have seized Manzikert quickly along with eastern Armenia, but they failed to take most of the rest of the frontier. Romanus's old general Philaretus held the themes around Melitene for himself, apparently commanding most of the eastern tagmata.[27] Other

145. Michael VII Ducas (r. 1067–78; relabeled as Nicephorus III [r. 1078–81]) and his wife Maria of Alania. Miniature from a contemporary manuscript of the homilies of Saint John Chrysostom (Coislinensis 79). (Photo: Bibliothèque Nationale, Paris)

independent generals defended Taron and Edessa, while Michael's government kept a shaky grip on Antioch. Since Michael had married the Georgian princess Maria of Alania, he had an alliance with Georgia that helped him hold neighboring Theodosiopolis. Between Theodosiopolis and Philaretus's satrapy, however, the Turks took both banks of the Euphrates from Artze to Tephrice. This was a wide enough breach to let a steady stream of invaders into Asia Minor, where after Romanus's death the thematic troops seem to have disintegrated entirely. The central government could call upon little more than the western tagmata. The course of the Turkish invasion sadly vindicated Romanus's judgment that the frontier was more defensible than the interior.

Probably in the spring 1073, the young domestic of the East Isaac Comnenus, nephew of the late emperor of the same name, led a small army to drive the Turks from Cappadocia. He was accompanied by Russell of Baillieul, leader of the Norman mercenaries since Crispin's death. But in mid-campaign Russell deserted with his men. While the Turks defeated Isaac and occupied most of Cappadocia, Charsianum, and Chaldia, Russell took over the Armeniac Theme, paying himself from its taxes but at least keeping out the Turks. The next spring the logothete Nicephoritzes, now in full control of the emperor, gave the Caesar John the unenviable task of fighting Russell. John met the rebel where the Sangarius River bends east, and was captured when his own Norman mercenaries joined their comrades. His son Constantine mustered a force to rescue him, but suddenly died.

In possession of the Armeniacs, the Bucellarians, the Optimates, and the Caesar, Russell proclaimed John emperor near Nicomedia, apparently with John's consent. In self-defense, Nicephoritzes actually called in the Turks from Cappadocia. They captured both Russell and John, but released them for a ransom. Next the Turks raided the Bucellarian and Anatolic themes. While John prudently became a monk, Russell resumed his rebellion in the Armeniacs. Without dependable troops, the Byzantines seemed powerless before the Turks.

Probably in 1075, the government gave Alexius Comnenus, the even younger brother of Isaac, a special command, not against the Turks but against Russell. Alexius paid a Turkish leader to kidnap the rebel and hand him over. Yet this was far from welcome to the Armeniac population, left defenseless against Turkish raids. In Chaldia the local magnate Theodore Gabras managed to expel the Turks after a brief occupation; but this seems merely to have driven them farther west.[28] They now spread over the Armeniacs, Paphlagonia, and the Optimates, right up to the Bosporus.

With no more than a few thousand troops left in Anatolia, Michael and Nicephoritzes tried to recruit some new soldiers, including a new Tagma of the Immortals to replace the eastern tagmata.[29] To make up for the taxes lost to the Turks along with the land, the government drastically debased the nomisma from sixteen to nine karats, leaving it just three-eighths gold.[30] The authorities also confiscated property from the Church and from landowners, made the sale of grain a state monopoly, and stopped subsidizing the Pechenegs. But about 1076 the unpaid Pechenegs joined in a revolt with the duke of Paradunavum Nestor, who had suffered from Nicephoritzes' confiscations. Ignoring the rebels in Paradunavum, the authorities turned to suppressing protests by the western tagmata, whose rations were late. As the Turks tightened their grip on northern Anatolia unopposed by the government, refugees poured into Constantinople, causing a severe famine.[31]

By fall 1077, Michael's regime was in such conspicuous collapse that new revolts broke out in both Europe and Asia. Troops in the Anatolics proclaimed their strategus Nicephorus Botaniates, while the western tagmata proclaimed the former duke of Dyrrhachium Nicephorus Bryennius. From Thrace Bryennius marched on the capital; but he offended the citizens by looting the suburbs, and had to retire to Adrianople for the winter. Opinion in Constantinople then shifted toward Botaniates, who occupied Nicaea. As the emperor's partisans deserted him, Michael VII became a monk in the early spring of 1078, and his general Alexius Comnenus received Botaniates into Constantinople. When Botaniates left Chrysopolis, the Asian suburb of the capital, the advancing Turks sacked it.

Although the empire desperately needed a ruler with the energy to expel the Turks, Nicephorus III Botaniates was a well-meaning but doddering veteran, who was far past his prime at age seventy-six.[32] His utmost efforts were needed to restore even a modicum of order. While allowing the unpopular Nicephoritzes to be tortured to death, the emperor bestowed ranks and donatives liberally on his supporters and tried to win over the remaining rebels. He offered the rank of Caesar to Bryennius, who controlled Thrace, and the titles of domestic of the East and duke of Antioch to Philaretus Brachamius, who held Cilicia, Byzantine Syria, Byzantine Mesopotamia, and the mountains up to the Antitaurus. Cut off from the capital by Turkish-held territory, Philaretus

TABLE 14
The Comnenus and Ducas Dynasties

Emperors are in capital letters, and Byzantine emperors are in italics, with the years of their reigns marked "r." Other years are of births and deaths.

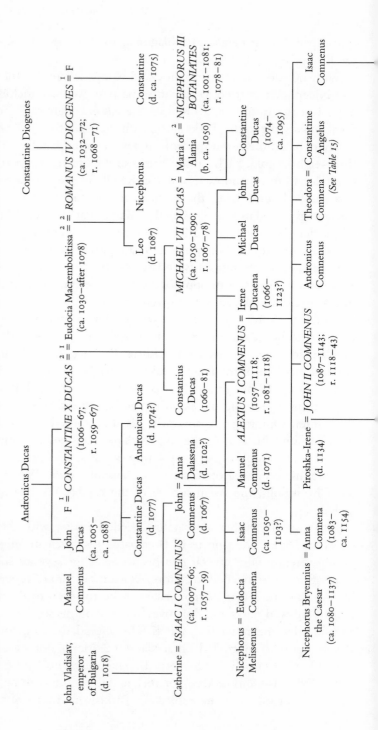

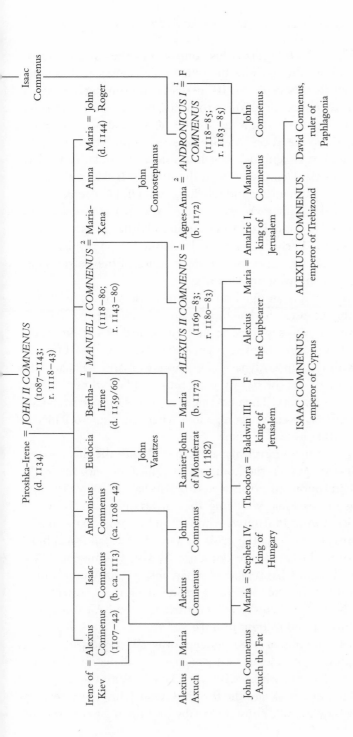

accepted his titles, which legalized his control over the eastern tagmata and Antioch without diminishing his actual independence. Bryennius, with more troops than Nicephorus III, persisted in claiming the throne.

The emperor therefore hired Turks to strengthen his army, put it under Alexius Comnenus as domestic of the West, and sent it against Bryennius. Thanks to the Turks, Alexius defeated, captured, and blinded the rebel. The end of Bryennius's rebellion forced the duke of Dyrrhachium Nicephorus Basilacius, who held the western Balkans, to choose between recognizing Botaniates and rebelling himself. He decided to revolt, and refused the emperor's offer of the rank of nobilissimus. But near Thessalonica Alexius defeated and captured Basilacius as well. After Alexius drove out the Pechenegs who had exploited these revolts to raid Thrace, a single emperor again ruled Europe south of the Balkan range and most of coastal and western Anatolia.

Yet that emperor was an aged and childless usurper. In 1079 Michael VII's brother Constantius had himself proclaimed emperor at Chrysopolis, by troops he was supposed to be leading against the Turks. Although his rebellion soon collapsed, it persuaded Nicephorus III to associate himself with the Ducas dynasty. He chose to marry Michael VII's wife, Maria of Alania, whose beauty was renowned but whose husband was still alive in a monastery. The marriage scandalized the patriarch Cosmas and many others. Even Maria repented when the emperor failed to name her son Constantine as his heir.

Botaniates' government never managed to deal with the finances, except by reducing the gold in the nomisma to a third, or with the Turks, who occupied still more of northwestern Anatolia. In 1080 they took Theodosiopolis in Armenia, widening their invasion route. They met with no opposition from Philaretus, who had all he could do to hold his own lands against them.[33] As the crisis deepened, that fall Nicephorus Melissenus, brother-in-law of the domestic Alexius Comnenus, began yet another rebellion in what remained of Byzantine Asia Minor. Enlisting the help of the Turks, he took and garrisoned a series of towns from Dorylaeum to Nicaea. When the emperor tried to send Alexius against the rebel, Alexius refused to fight his relative.

Around the beginning of 1081, Nicephorus III stupidly chose his nephew Nicephorus Synadenus as his successor, alienating both the Ducas family and Alexius, whose wife was a Ducas. With the support of the empress Maria of Alania and the former Caesar John Ducas, Alexius and his brother Isaac began a conspiracy. Absconding to Thrace, the two

Comneni gathered an army and had Alexius proclaimed emperor. While Melissenus led his own rebel army to the Bosporus, Alexius too marched on Constantinople, where he was admitted by some German mercenaries. Bowing to necessity, Nicephorus III abdicated in favor of Alexius and entered a monastery.

After centuries of capable emperors had brought Byzantium to an apex of power under Basil II, a mere fifty-six years of misgovernment had squandered half the empire's territory, nearly all of its huge army and ample treasury, and a long tradition of growing security and stability. The preponderance of incompetent emperors after Basil was striking, but no accident. Powerful bureaucrats and generals had guarded their influence by repeatedly promoting nonentities to the throne, undermining the few leaders who showed some initiative. The prevailing prosperity had doubtless produced a larger and richer crop of officials than before; but they could never have exercised their power so irresponsibly under emperors as strong as Basil II—or as George Maniaces would probably have been. By the time the officials had had their way, the state had been so thoroughly wrecked that repairing it required not just a competent ruler, but a political and military genius.

CHAPTER NINETEEN

Improvised Reconstruction, 1081–1143

Alexius Comnenus was by all accounts a remarkable man. Still just twenty-four, he had led armies for six years with surprising success. But the preeminence of so young a general also showed a shortage of talent in the army, which now consisted of little more than remnants of the western tagmata, the Varangians, and a few other mercenaries—in all, probably fewer than twenty thousand men. The scattering of rowdy troops Alexius led into Constantinople proceeded to loot the city. Along with this pathetic force, Alexius took over an empty treasury and the crumbling fragments of an empire. Before he could hope to regain what had been lost, he had to put a stop to further losses. At least his boldness was suited to the unprecedented emergency, which made long experience matter less than Alexius's steady nerves, sound instinct, and willingness to try whatever seemed necessary. He had seized power unscrupulously in chaotic times, but he practiced the saving virtue of clemency to his enemies. Though many of his associates distrusted him, few hated him, and all respected his abilities. Lacking rivals of comparable stature, he strove to keep any from emerging.

ALEXIUS COMNENUS'S SURVIVAL

Amid the ruins of the state and army, Alexius relied most on his powerful relatives and those of his wife Irene, a member of the more or less legitimate Ducas dynasty. For a moment he thought of strengthening his claim to the throne by divorcing Irene and marrying Maria of Alania, the voluptuous wife of his two predecessors. But he relented before the opposition of the Ducas family and their allies, who included the patri-arch Cosmas.[1] Since as yet Alexius had no children, he named as his heir Constantine Ducas, the young son of Maria and Michael VII. Alexius's most trusted adviser was his mother Anna Dalassena, whom he en-trusted with full administrative powers while he concentrated on mili-tary campaigns.

The emperor not only gave his mother much of the responsibility for raising money, but began to provide for members of his family in a way that was apparently new. He granted them the right to collect and keep the taxes from designated private lands without the intervention of the government. This may not at first have seemed much different from the well-established practice of granting public lands with a tax exemption; no taxes reached the treasury in either case, and the innovation merely allowed grants to be made where the state held no land. The danger was that this practice might weaken the state further by giving some of its powers to influential subjects.

Among the recipients of such concessions was Alexius's brother-in-law Nicephorus Melissenus, who had been in arms against Nicephorus III but ended his revolt in return for the tax revenues around Thessalonica and the title of Caesar. As Caesar, Melissenus could have expected to rank just after the emperor; but Alexius created the higher rank of se-bastocrator for his brother Isaac, with new ranks just below that of Cae-sar, such as panhypersebastus and protosebastus, for other members of

146. Alexius I Comnenus (r. 1081–1118). Miniature from a contem-porary manuscript of a refutation of heresies by Euthymius Zigabenus (Vaticanus graecus 666). (Photo: Biblioteca Apostolica Vaticana)

his family. Melissenus stayed loyal to Alexius despite the devaluation of his title.

While the emperor secured his grip on the Byzantine government, he lost control over his Turkish allies, who kept for themselves his former holdings in northwestern Asia Minor. These lands stretched from Nicaea, which became the capital of the Seljuk leader Sulaymān, to Smyrna, soon the headquarters of the ambitious emir Chaka. Sulaymān began to call himself sultan of Rūm—Turkish for Rome—and claimed authority over the other Turks in Anatolia in place of the legitimate Seljuk sultan Malik-Shāh.

Only pockets of the peninsula remained Byzantine, and those were partly outside Alexius's authority. A makeshift force guarded what had been the district of the Optimates. Troops from Paphlagonia garrisoned Pontic Heraclea. Troops from Cappadocia and elsewhere held the Cibyrrhaeot Theme, the southern part of the Thracesian Theme, and the western part of the Anatolic Theme. Philaretus Brachamius was still ensconced on what had been the eastern frontier, in a separate domain including Cilicia, Antioch, and Edessa. Chaldia formed another fiefdom under Theodore Gabras, surrounded by Turks on the land side. The Turks thus held most of Asia Minor, and were advancing into the rest of it.

Except for Paradunavum, occupied by the Pechenegs and their local allies, Byzantium still held its European provinces; but these were threatened by another enemy. Robert Guiscard, the Norman duke of Sicily and southern Italy, had been plotting against the empire ever since the fall of Michael VII, whose son had been betrothed to Robert's daughter. Robert kept at his court a Byzantine monk alleged to be the deposed Michael, and was already preparing an invasion when Alexius was crowned. That same spring Robert's son Bohemund landed an army at Aulon in Epirus. The new Norman state was so strong, and the old empire so weak, that Robert posed a real threat to Constantinople.[2]

Alexius reinforced Dyrrhachium, the main Byzantine base in Epirus, and mustered such an army as he could. He withdrew his troops from Heraclea Pontica and the Anatolic Theme, practically conceding Asia Minor to the Turks. He hired still more Turkish mercenaries. He even broke a previous prohibition by enlisting twenty-eight hundred Paulician heretics from Philippopolis, making them into an inauspiciously named Tagma of the Manichaeans.[3] Alexius begged for help from Venice, from disaffected Normans, and from the German emperor Henry IV, who was an enemy of the Normans' ally Pope Gregory VII.

Robert Guiscard seized Corcyra and besieged Dyrrhachium. Though a Venetian fleet arrived and destroyed the Norman navy, Robert continued the siege through the summer. Alexius gathered a force of some size but poor quality to march to the rescue himself. Arriving in the fall, he boldly attacked the Normans, but suffered a total defeat when his Turkish mercenaries deserted. The Manichaeans appear simply to have run for home.[4] Whatever was left of the old western tagmata was lost, and many of the Varangians fell. The emperor escaped almost alone.

That winter, as 1082 began, Robert captured not only Dyrrhachium but most of northwestern Greece, with Castoria. Alexius hastily assembled another army at Thessalonica, though he failed to persuade the Manichaeans to return. To pay his new men, he further adulterated the already debased coinage, collected contributions from his family, and confiscated plate from the Church. When the clergy protested, he distracted them by trying and condemning for heresy the philosopher John Italus, who had also opposed the confiscations.

Only Alexius's diplomacy was working. At his urging the German emperor invaded the Papal State, and Norman rebels subsidized by the Byzantines rose in Apulia. Robert returned to Italy to help the pope and put down the rebellion, leaving his son Bohemund to pursue the campaign against Byzantium. In the spring Alexius marched out against Bohemund, who was besieging Joannina. Bohemund defeated him. The emperor retreated to Ochrid and regrouped, only to be vanquished again. He marched doggedly to Arta, attacked Bohemund from the south, and lost once more. By autumn the Normans held most of northern Greece and western Bulgaria up to the Axius valley, and were besieging Larissa. The Byzantine army seemed helpless.

The desperate Alexius granted his Venetian allies extensive trading privileges, including a commercial colony at Constantinople and exemption from trade duties. He also hired seven thousand new Turkish mercenaries. In spring 1083, he finally chased the Normans from Larissa, scoring his first victory against them. Bohemund, finding himself checked in the field and out of money, returned to Italy to ask for help. That summer, when the Venetians seized Dyrrhachium for the Byzantines, some of the Norman army began to desert to the emperor. As the rest fell back, Alexius retook Castoria. Once the Venetians had occupied Corcyra the next spring, Greece was almost free of Normans.

Despite his hard-won victory, Alexius continued to be criticized for his confiscations from the Church. He began repaying them in installments, but one of his critics, Metropolitan Leo of Chalcedon, went on complaining that melting down plate decorated with religious figures amounted to Iconoclasm. Soon the emperor uncovered a conspiracy by his civil and military officials, which he suppressed with tact. He dismissed and imprisoned his unreliable Tagma of the Manichaeans, but this set off a rebellion by their fellow Paulicians, who escaped to the Pechenegs in northern Thrace and joined them in raiding Byzantine territory. Moreover, Robert Guiscard was as determined as Alexius, and in autumn 1084, having disposed of his own rebels, the Norman duke landed again in Corcyra with his sons. At first beaten by the Venetian and Byzantine fleets, Robert defeated them in turn and wintered on the island. The next year he landed on Cephalonia. But there he fell ill and died, at an advanced age. His sons abandoned his campaign against the empire.

Although Alexius now held all of Greece, the Pechenegs remained in Paradunavum, and the Turks had almost completed their conquest of Asia Minor. Sultan Sulaymān advanced from Nicaea through the Anatolic Theme to northern Syria. With no hope of help from Alexius, the scattered Byzantine commanders slowly succumbed to the Turks. The strongest of them, Philaretus Brachamius, lost Antioch by early 1085 and Edessa in 1086, although he kept some territory around Germanicea. The highlands of Cilicia were in the hands of another Armenian warlord, Ruben. Theodore Gabras held Trebizond and most of Chaldia. Little more than the ports of Attalia, Ephesus, and Pontic Heraclea remained subject to Alexius in Asia Minor. Most of the rest was part of Sulaymān's renegade Sultanate of Rūm.

Sulaymān was advancing into Syria in 1086 when he was killed near Aleppo by the soldiers of the legitimate Seljuk sultan Malik-Shāh. Yet his rival's death did not give Malik-Shāh control over the Turks in Asia Minor, where Sulaymān's son Kilij Arslan remained at large. Since the sultan's real interest was in conquering Fatimid Egypt, he wanted to withdraw the Turks from Anatolia, and he offered Alexius aid in reconquering it in return for a marriage alliance. Although the emperor was suspicious of the sultan's offer and unwilling to marry his infant daughter to a Muslim, he did manage to regain the port of Sinope from the Turkish ambassador. He also retook Nicomedia.

At this point Alexius had to send his meager forces to drive Pecheneg raiders out of Thrace. He had to make further confiscations from the Church as the fighting dragged expensively on. In spring 1087, when the Byzantines defeated another Pecheneg raid, the emperor decided to make the effort to retake Paradunavum, where the Pechenegs had established themselves with a collection of Paulicians, Vlachs, and other local rebels.[5] That summer, rebuffing an attempt by the Pechenegs to negotiate, he led an army to Dristra on the Danube. There he was routed almost as badly as at Dyrrhachium, and fled with a handful of men.

Luckily for Alexius, at just this time the Pechenegs were defeated by the Cumans, another Turkish people from north of the Danube. His humiliation was nonetheless severe, and he had to put down another conspiracy against him. He did not dare crown his son John, born right after the defeat, for fear that displacing Constantine Ducas as his heir would offend the Ducas family.[6] During the next three years the Pechenegs raided nearer and nearer Constantinople. Struggling to rebuild his army, Alexius recruited two thousand sons of the soldiers recently fallen in battle and made them into a new Tagma of the Archontopuli.[7] He also hired more mercenaries from the West, where the Byzantines' reverses had shocked the new pope Urban II into restoring friendly relations.

The Seljuk Turks had lost all respect for Byzantine arms, and were beginning to advance beyond Anatolia into the islands. By 1090 Chaka, the emir of Smyrna, had built himself a fleet and seized Chios and part of Lesbos. At about the same time another Turkish chieftain took Ephesus. The Byzantine dukes of Cyprus and Crete revolted.[8] A naval expedition sent against Chaka failed miserably, and the Pechenegs mauled the inexperienced Tagma of the Archontopuli. Chaka sent to the Pechenegs to suggest that they coordinate their attacks with his to finish off the empire. His perception of Byzantine weakness was only slightly exaggerated.

Still giving priority to Europe, in spring 1091 Alexius enlisted the help of some Cumans and gathered an army to oppose the Pechenegs raiding Thrace. He brought the raiders to battle at Lebunium, near the mouth of the Hebrus. There the Pechenegs were routed, trapped, and almost all slaughtered or captured. Alexius settled the survivors around Moglena, northwest of Thessalonica. As soon as the Cumans returned to their lands north of the Danube, the emperor was able to bring the Byzantine frontier back up to the river for the first time in fifteen years. Yet he had to put down still another officers' plot against him, and his problems remained daunting.

Alexius began rebuilding the empire's naval power. He gained a little control over the Pontus by naming its potentate Theodore Gabras as duke of Trebizond, and by detaining Theodore's son in Constantinople as a virtual hostage. The emperor sent a naval expedition that retook

Chios from Chaka, who had overextended himself somewhat by capturing Samos and Rhodes. In the spring of 1092 Alexius named his brother-in-law John Ducas grand duke of the fleet. This appointment proved a success, and John drove Chaka's forces from the islands by the summer. Next Alexius sent him against the rebellious dukes of Crete and Cyprus. John recovered both islands with surprising ease, since the Cretan troops killed their duke and most of the Cypriot soldiers abandoned theirs.

Even though the emperor had made no progress in recovering Asia Minor, at least the Balkans and the islands were cleared of invaders and the empire's disintegration seemed to have ceased. Again the Seljuk sultan Malik-Shāh offered Alexius a marriage alliance, with the idea of regaining control over the Anatolian Turks and withdrawing them from Asia Minor. But during the negotiations the sultan died, and his sons began fighting with each other. Sulaymān's son Kilij Arslan reigned as an independent sultan of Rūm at Nicaea, joined in eastern Anatolia by an equally autonomous emir known as Dānishmend.

When Alexius finally felt strong enough to crown his little son John his successor in place of Constantine Ducas, the emperor celebrated by creating a new coinage. Its main denomination was an almost pure gold coin, the hyperpyron. At 20½ karats, it was worth about seven-eighths of the old undebased nomisma, and more than any other coin minted within memory. The hyperpyron was supplemented by lesser coins of electrum (mixed gold and silver), billon (mixed silver and copper), and copper. Though the new coinage was somewhat more complicated than the one upset by debasement earlier in the century, it was far less con-

147. Gold hyperpyron of Alexius I, shown 1.5 times actual size, with Christ on the reverse. (Photo: Dumbarton Oaks, Washington, D.C., copyright 1996)

fusing than the ragbag of coins it replaced, and had the advantage of providing a wide variety of denominations.[9]

Alexius, who preferred pacifying land in Europe to reconquering it in Asia, campaigned in 1093 against the Serbian prince of Ras, Vukan, who was raiding Byzantine Bulgaria. Vukan agreed to a treaty when the Byzantines arrived, but began raiding again after they left. On a second campaign against Ras in 1094, the emperor frustrated another officers' plot against him led by Nicephorus Diogenes, the young son of the emperor Romanus IV. When Alexius resumed his march toward Ras, Vukan sent hostages and made a peace that he kept. Near the end of the year, a church council at last rid Alexius of the charge of Iconoclasm and pacified his principal critic Leo of Chalcedon.[10]

Thus far Alexius's main achievement had been to survive all these invasions and plots, and to keep the empire from the internal collapse that had frequently threatened it. He had repaired the finances enough to restore a sound coinage, and to pay a modest-sized army of foreign mercenaries and native recruits. This army had proved capable of recovering and defending the empire's possessions in the Balkans and the islands. But whether the Byzantines would ever regain much more than their few coastal enclaves in Anatolia remained in doubt. The plot of Diogenes may well show the exasperation of officers whose Anatolian homeland Alexius had done nothing to recover.

ALEXIUS AND THE FIRST CRUSADE

Byzantine relations with the West had improved after the failure of the Norman invasion. Death had removed the eastern and western churchmen who had excommunicated each other in 1054, and their successors were not pursuing any further theological disputes. For years the emperors had relied on western mercenaries, who now formed the bulk of the Varangian Guard. The popes cared enough about eastern Christians to deplore Byzantine losses to the Turks. Early in 1095 Alexius sent ambassadors to Pope Urban, then presiding over a council at Piacenza, to appeal for more Christian troops to keep the Muslims at bay. The pope took the request more seriously than the Byzantines expected. He conceived a plan aimed at expelling the Muslims from much of the Christian East.

Alexius's immediate concerns were more limited. When the Cumans invaded with a Byzantine claiming to be another son of Romanus IV, the emperor captured and blinded the impostor and drove the Cumans

148. Anna Dalassena's Monastery of Christ Pantepoptes ("All-seeing"), Constantinople. (Photo: Irina Andreescu-Treadgold)

back across the Danube.[11] That summer Alexius finished elaborate fortifications and a canal just south of Nicomedia, which he evidently meant to be his frontier with the Turks. Since around this time his powerful mother Anna retired to a monastery she had founded, he apparently planned to give more of his attention to civil administration and to rest from his years of hard fighting.

That fall, however, during a council at Clermont in France, Pope Urban announced a great expedition to free not only the eastern Christians but Jerusalem itself. Serving in this army would count as full penance for all a man's confessed sins. The project ignited instant enthusiasm. In the following months it attracted a growing number of eager recruits from among the lords, knights, and even peasants of western Europe. This force mounted the First Crusade, planning to march across the Balkans to Constantinople, across Anatolia to Antioch, and across Syria to Jerusalem.

The astonishing news that not a modest band of mercenaries but tens of thousands of Crusaders were about to descend on the empire alarmed the emperor, with some reason. Among the Crusaders were Normans led by Bohemund, whom Alexius had fought in Greece not a dozen years before. The Crusaders, reportedly more numerous than Alexius's army, could if they wished conquer a great deal of Byzantine territory—perhaps all of it. Even without making conquests from the empire, if they conquered part of Turkish Anatolia they would make stronger and more dangerous neighbors than the disunited Turks. And even if they handed much of Anatolia over to Alexius, he lacked the soldiers to hold it securely.

Although the emperor saw the Crusade as more a threat than an opportunity, he had to handle it with great care. Feeding the Crusaders and keeping them in some sort of order was no easy task. The first of them to arrive in the summer of 1096 were an impoverished but impassioned rabble of peasants whom the pope had not wanted to send but had been unable to restrain. On their way across Hungary and on the road from Belgrade to Constantinople they had often resorted to robbery to feed themselves. Seeing that they were no soldiers, the emperor advised their leader Peter the Hermit to wait near Nicomedia until the main crusading army came up. But not even Peter could keep them from attacking the Turks, who massacred most of them. The emperor gave asylum outside Constantinople to those who escaped.

The real army of lords and knights began to arrive in Constantinople late in the year. They marched along the roads from Belgrade and Dyrrhachium, accompanied by Byzantine military escorts of Pechenegs and other mercenaries. During early 1097, as some Crusaders waited in the suburbs of the capital for the arrival of the others, bitter disputes arose over pillaging by the Crusaders and over the emperor's delaying their supplies. The crusader army may have come to some five thousand cavalry and thirty thousand infantry; the Byzantines might have been able to muster half that many.[12]

The emperor had the lords swear to give him any land they took that had been Byzantine before the Turkish invasion, and apparently to hold anything more as his vassals. This was a good bargain for the empire, especially because Alexius was not undertaking to join the expedition to Jerusalem. Yet one of the stated purposes of the Crusade had been to help the Byzantines, and the Crusaders' main ambitions for conquest were in Palestine. Given the practical range of Alexius's power, their oath of vassalage for Palestinian conquests they might make amounted to little more than a pledge of friendship.[13] Though Bohemund cleverly asked Alexius to appoint him domestic of the East, a post that would have given him an excuse for remaining in Anatolia, Alexius politely put him off.

To reach Palestine, the Crusaders had to pass through western Anato-

lia, and that meant fighting the sultan of Nicaea, Kilij Arslan. The Crusaders and Byzantines first marched against Nicaea itself, which lay on
the main road to the East. Kilij Arslan hurried from Melitene, where
he had been fighting the troops of Dānishmend, to reinforce his well-
fortified capital. But the Crusaders had already invested it before the first
reinforcements arrived. When the sultan made a determined attack on
the besiegers, they defeated him smartly and drove him off. Just as the
Crusaders were about to storm the city, the Turkish garrison surrendered to the Byzantines on lenient terms. Alexius shared some of the
sultan's treasury with the rather disappointed Crusaders, then sent them
on their way.

They marched southeast from Nicaea in two groups. Near Dorylaeum Kilij Arslan attacked their vanguard and pressed it hard. It held
out, however, until the rear guard came up and routed the Turks again,
capturing their camp. The outfought sultan gave up active resistance,
simply ordering the Crusaders' route to be stripped of supplies before
they arrived. At Dorylaeum, on the edge of the Anatolian plateau, the
Crusaders had in any case reached the limit of the territory that Alexius
could hold behind them. As they marched through the towns of Polybotus, Philomelium, and Iconium, neither they nor the small Byzantine
contingent with them attempted to establish garrisons.

In late summer, near Cappadocian Heraclea, the Crusaders encountered the forces of Dānishmend and easily chased them away. Next the
Crusaders approached Cilicia, where the mountains were held by Armenian Christians under the sons of the recently deceased warlords Philaretus Brachamius and Ruben. By the previous agreement, the Byzantines claimed these Armenians as the emperor's subjects; the Crusaders
raised no objection. The main part of the army marched by way of Caesarea to the Cilician highlands, where the Armenians formally accepted
the emperor's authority.

Some of the Crusaders were eager to start taking land for themselves.
Led by Baldwin of Boulogne, they turned south to the Cilician plain,
where they defeated the Turks but squabbled over their conquests. They
decided to avoid further discord by moving on. After the crusader contingents met again at Germanicea, Baldwin and most of his men departed
for Edessa, answering an appeal from an Armenian prince who had driven
out the Turks. Baldwin pushed aside the prince, married an Armenian,
and set himself up as count of Edessa and Samosata. Though as former
Byzantine possessions these had been promised to Alexius, they were so

far beyond his reach that he made no protest. The rest of the army advanced to Antioch, which they invested in the middle of autumn.

While the Crusaders besieged Antioch, Alexius sent a force under his brother-in-law John Ducas to retake the coastal plain of western Anatolia. Supported by his fleet, John first marched on Smyrna, where Chaka seems still to have been emir.[14] The Turks surrendered Smyrna in return for a safe-conduct out of the city, though some who stayed behind were lynched after one of them assassinated the Byzantine governor. Probably in early 1098, Ducas marched to Ephesus. There the Turks chose to fight outside the walls, perhaps because they feared betrayal by the Greek inhabitants if they were besieged. John put the Turks to flight, captured some two thousand of them, and occupied Ephesus, Sardis, and Philadelphia. By the time he reached Laodicea, where the population welcomed him, he apparently could not spare the soldiers to garrison more towns. So he passed through Laodicea and Choma without leaving commanders behind, only stationing a few troops at the obscure fort of Lampe.[15] Next Ducas advanced to Polybotus, where the Turks from Smyrna had taken refuge, and defeated them again.

At Polybotus John evidently waited for Alexius, who had been sacking Turkish-held cities south of Nicaea, probably including Dorylaeum. Since the emperor destroyed these places rather than garrisoning them, his plan must have been to create a no-man's-land between Turkish territory and his own. When he arrived at Philomelium, a bit farther than John had gone before him, Alexius ordered the Christian population to return along with him, taking all their movable possessions. The emperor seems to have left a garrison at Acroënus, but only as a forward outpost.[16] The campaigns of John Ducas and Alexius nonetheless marked the restoration of Byzantine power in northwestern Asia Minor.

At the beginning of June, the Crusaders finally took Antioch when some of its Turks betrayed it to Bohemund. Yet a Turkish army arrived almost at once to besiege the former besiegers, who hastily appealed to Alexius. The emperor could probably have made a speedy march to Attalia, which was still Byzantine, then along the coast to Cilicia and Antioch, where he might well have restored effective Byzantine rule. But Alexius had taken as much of Anatolia as he could comfortably hold, and he concluded from what he heard that the Crusaders were doomed. He therefore returned to his capital.

Contrary to Alexius's expectations, the Crusaders broke the siege of Antioch with a daring sally. While the knights led by Count Raymond of Toulouse defended the Byzantines' right to Antioch, after months of quarreling Bohemund won possession of it, since the emperor made no effort to make good his claim to the city. Alexius protested, and some Crusaders do seem to have handed over the nearby port of Laodicea to Byzantine forces from Cyprus.[17] In any case, most of the Crusaders left Antioch early in 1099 for Palestine, which the Fatimids had recently taken from the Turks. Though Alexius now declared he was ready to join the Crusade, the Crusaders pressed on to Jerusalem without waiting for him. They stormed it in July, attaining their goal.

Just before the fall of Jerusalem, a large fleet had set out from Pisa, as much to exploit the Crusade as to aid it. The Pisans behaved like pirates, raiding Byzantine islands in the Ionian Sea and the southern Aegean. They joined Bohemund of Antioch in besieging Byzantine Laodicea, until Raymond of Toulouse forced them to stop. The emperor was busy at the time taking full possession of Trebizond, whose warlord Theodore Gabras had been captured and martyred by Dānishmend. Then Alexius sent an army across Anatolia, which in early 1100 took the coast of Cilicia from Bohemund.[18]

Bohemund retaliated by replacing the Greek patriarch of Antioch with a Frenchman. The prince would probably have tried to retake the land he had lost to the Byzantines, if he had not received an appeal from the Armenians in Melitene to save them from an attack by Dānishmend. As Bohemund hurried north to take over the city, he fell into a Turkish ambush. Just before he was captured, he managed to send for help to Baldwin of Edessa. In his turn, Baldwin arrived in time to rescue Melitene but not Bohemund. Then he left for Jerusalem to succeed his late brother as its king. Dānishmend kept Bohemund in captivity at Neocaesarea, to Alexius's relief.

In 1101 three new contingents of Crusaders arrived in Constantinople. The first, mostly Lombards, tried to rescue Bohemund, against the advice of Alexius. After taking Ancyra and leaving it to the emperor, they were cut to pieces by Dānishmend's army in the lower Halys valley. The second army, unable to catch up with the first, headed south from Ancyra and was destroyed by Kilij Arslan near Heraclea. The third army tried to join the second and met the same fate. A few men from each group escaped to blame the emperor, who had urged them to march together and take less dangerous routes. Alexius's only gain was Ancyra, which was too isolated to be kept. Kilij Arslan now established the capital of his sultanate at Iconium, blocking the main road from Constantinople to the East.

149. Ruins of the palace of the Seljuk sultans at Iconium. Engraving by Lemaitre after Ch. Texier. (From Charles Texier, *Asie mineure* [Paris, 1862])

Bohemund's nephew and regent Tancred made Alexius's supposed treachery a pretext to seize both Byzantine Cilicia and the Byzantines' ally Raymond of Toulouse. As the price of his release, Raymond had to let Tancred besiege Byzantine Laodicea, which fell in early 1103. At the height of Tancred's success, however, Bohemund returned from captivity and reclaimed Antioch, having made an alliance with Dānishmend and collected his ransom without help from his ambitious regent. Alexius had also put in a bid for Bohemund, and no one believed it was out of friendship.

The emperor now had few friends outside the empire, and a number of enemies within it. Around this time he had to suppress another plot against him, led by four brothers named Anemas.[19] Again Alexius demanded that Bohemund surrender Antioch and the coast of Cilicia, and in autumn 1103 sent another expedition to enforce his demand. The Byzantines retook the Cilician coast, but most of the Armenians in the mountains joined the Crusaders, and Bohemund captured Germanicea from Alexius's few Armenian allies early in 1104. The emperor's friend Raymond of Toulouse died while besieging Tripoli, and the duke of Trebizond rebelled against Alexius with the support of Dānishmend.

Then the emperor's luck improved. In May the Turks defeated Bohemund and his allies from Edessa near Ḥarrān (the ancient Carrhae). A Byzantine fleet took its chance to seize Laodicea. Alexius lost an enemy and Bohemund an ally when the emir Dānishmend died. After these reverses, Bohemund made Tancred regent of Antioch again and left for France and Italy to seek help, not against the Turks but against the Byzantines. Alexius learned that Bohemund planned a direct invasion of the empire from Italy, like the one made by his father, Robert Guiscard.

Both sides began prolonged preparations and a strenuous search for allies. Bohemund won over Pope Paschal II, married the daughter of Philip I of France, and enlisted a body of Italian and French adventurers. The emperor withdrew his troops from Cilicia and Laodicea, which Tancred soon captured. Alexius asked for ships from Venice and married his son and heir John to a cousin of the king of Hungary, Piroshka, who received the Greek name of Irene.[20] The emperor also hired mercenaries from Kilij Arslan, and protected his rear somewhat by recovering Trebizond in 1106.

In the autumn of 1107 Bohemund and his men landed again in Byzantine Epirus and besieged Dyrrhachium, reportedly with thirty-four thousand men. Profiting from his previous experience with the Normans, Alexius avoided a pitched battle. Instead he used Byzantine and Venetian ships to supply Dyrrhachium and deny supplies to Bohemund. The next spring Alexius barricaded the passes around Dyrrhachium and practically besieged the Normans. A year after his landing, with his army suffering from hunger and disease, Bohemund sued for peace. He agreed to surrender the Cilician coast and Laodicea to the empire, to become the emperor's vassal for all his other possessions, and to restore the Greek patriarch of Antioch.

The prince of Antioch returned to Italy in failure, but the treaty became a dead letter. Since Bohemund stayed in Italy, Tancred remained the real ruler of Antioch and ignored the treaty. Yet Alexius had disposed of a serious invasion, humbled Bohemund, and discouraged future western attacks on Byzantium. Tancred's interests were confined to northern Syria, and even there he was feuding with King Baldwin of Jerusalem, Count Baldwin of Edessa, and the son of the late Raymond of Toulouse who became count of Tripoli. Tancred was in no position to attack the empire.

After defeating Bohemund, Alexius finished restoring order to his system of taxation, a task he had begun with his reform of the coinage. Since the late eleventh century, the influence of rich taxpayers, the powerlessness of poor ones, and the prevailing monetary confusion had led tax collectors to convert the taxes into debased nomismata at rates ranging from a quarter of the intended tax to four times as much. By 1109 Alexius managed to enforce a standard rate for computing the taxes, and seems to have gained much more revenue by raising taxes for the rich than he lost by lowering them for the poor.[21]

The Sultanate of Iconium grew weaker after the death of Kilij Arslan in 1107, but this was not entirely to the Byzantines' advantage. Nomadic Turks reoccupied the no-man's-land Alexius had created along the border and began raiding Byzantine territory. Around 1110 a local Byzantine force drove them out of the border fort of Lampe, which they had taken; but this provoked a major Turkish raid, which the outnumbered Byzantines only halted by an ambush outside Philadelphia. Asia Minor needed more attention than Alexius was giving it. His commander at Acroënus, Michael of Amastris, began a revolt, though it seems to have consisted mostly of fighting the Turks without the emperor's permission. After sending an expedition that forced Michael to surrender, Alexius pardoned him at once.

The emperor was now in declining health, and more worried about Crusaders than about Turks. In 1111 he tried to stop piracy from Pisa by making a treaty with the city, reducing trade duties for its merchants and giving them a trading colony in Constantinople like the Venetians'. After Bohemund died that spring, the emperor sent to Tancred to demand the surrender of Antioch. When Tancred of course refused, the emperor sent an ambassador to Tripoli and Jerusalem to buy help against Antioch, but had no success. In 1112 Tancred died of disease and left his principality to his nephew.

That year the sultan of Iconium Shāhānshāh, son of Kilij Arslan, sent a major raid into the Byzantine corner of Anatolia.[22] Some of his raiders penetrated almost to Ephesus before being turned back by the Byzantines. The next year the Turks raided again in force, this time to the north. They thoroughly plundered the region of Nicaea and Prusa, and sacked Cyzicus and Adramyttium. The duke of Nicaea attacked them but was captured. Only when the raiders were returning did the emperor meet them near Cotyaeum, defeat them, and rescue the duke.[23] Obviously Byzantine Anatolia was not yet safe.

In the following years both the sultan and the emperor mustered their forces for a real war. In spring 1116 Turkish raiders again looted northwestern Asia Minor, until the emperor mustered an army and defeated them near Poemanenum. He stayed in the region all summer, but even so he had to fight off more raiders near Nicomedia. As even more Turks appeared around Nicaea, Alexius decided to draw them off by a campaign into Turkish territory. From Dorylaeum south, the emperor razed settlements and deported the remaining Greek population to Byzantine territory. After the Turks failed to stop his advance, the sultan himself met him in a fierce battle near Philomelium. Alexius won, and Shāhān-shāh made a treaty agreeing to halt the raids. Though the sultan was soon deposed and murdered by his brother Mas'ūd, the Turks were cowed for the moment, and Alexius returned in triumph, with ample booty and thousands of Greek refugees.

After this campaign the emperor, who had suffered from gout and asthma for some time, became gravely ill. He had always been a merciful man, but as he faced death in 1117 he became reluctant to restrain the stricter members of his clergy. He allowed them to try for heresy and depose Bishop Eustratius of Nicaea, a student of John Italus whom the emperor had long protected. Alexius also permitted the burning alive of the Bogomil leader Basil, which his clemency had long delayed.[24] As his death approached, the emperor was slow to reject his wife's irresponsible proposal to disinherit his son John in favor of the Caesar Nicephorus Bryennius, husband of his eldest daughter Anna. According to John himself, whose word was accepted, Alexius decided for his son just before dying in August.

That Alexius left the empire stronger than he found it is beyond doubt. He displayed great skill in repelling invasions, foiling conspiracies, and restoring order when general disintegration was a constant threat. Yet his early perils seem to have made him too wary of helping the Crusaders, or of strengthening his army by more recruitment. While some Crusaders and military officers certainly did want to overthrow him, cautious cooperation with them would probably have reduced that danger, and might even have let him retake most of Asia Minor before the Turks made it fully their own. By the end of his reign, he had allowed the Turks to become firmly entrenched on the Anatolian plateau.

Alexius, however, had been born too late to remember when all of Asia Minor was secure and the army was a mass force of native Byzantines. The coastal regions that he recovered were much the richest and most populous parts of Anatolia; armies moving into the interior encountered poorer land, rougher terrain, fewer Greeks, and more Turks. A completely restored empire would have had larger revenues, but not a much larger surplus; and keeping it would have meant sharing power with more generals and officials, some of whom were hostile to the Comneni. The results would have been better for many Byzantines, especially for those abandoned in Turkish territory, but not necessarily better for Alexius and his relatives. Knowing all this, Alexius put his own and his family's interests ahead of the empire's.

JOHN II AND NORMALCY

John II Comnenus was thirty when he became senior emperor. Although he had every right to the throne as Alexius's eldest son and junior emperor, he had won it in spite of his mother Irene, his elder sister Anna, and some other relatives. For several months he had to worry that they still might overthrow him. Yet they missed their chance, because their candidate for emperor, Anna's husband Nicephorus Bryennius, was less ruthless and decisive than his wife. In early 1119 John obtained proof of their plot to murder him. He temporarily confiscated their property, and permanently discredited their claims. Irene and Anna were forced to retire to a convent, while Nicephorus himself remained free. John, like his father, was alert to his enemies but merciful to them.

Otherwise John's policies differed somewhat from Alexius's. He re-

150. John II Comnenus (r. 1118–43) and his wife Piroshka-Irene, presenting offerings to the Virgin, with their son Alexius (d. 1142) barely visible at far right, around corner. Contemporary mosaic in the gallery of Saint Sophia, Constantinople. (Photo: Dumbarton Oaks, Washington, D.C., copyright 1996)

fused to renew the trading privileges of the Venetians, alleging that they had defied Byzantine officials in their colony in Constantinople. He also tried to expand Byzantine control in Anatolia beyond the periphery that had satisfied Alexius. John saw that frequent offensives were the best way to reduce Turkish raids, and he sought further conquests to shield the Byzantine coastlands and to join them with each other by land routes. While at Alexius's death northwestern Anatolia formed a solid block of territory, it was still separated from Byzantine-held Attalia by the Turks who occupied Caria. The Danishmendid emir Ghāzī also seems to have cut off Trebizond at this time, capturing its dynast and duke Constantine Gabras. John ransomed Constantine, but as long as Trebizond was isolated it could not be under secure Byzantine control.[25]

The emperor therefore began an offensive against the Turks. In 1119, provoked by a Turkish raid on the southern part of the Thracesian Theme, he set out to clear the whole Meander valley. He campaigned with his friend John Axuch, a Turk taken prisoner in childhood and brought up as a Christian, who held the title of grand domestic. The two of them took Laodicea, which had become a Turkish base after the Byzantines failed to garrison it under Alexius. Later, probably in 1120, the emperor seized the stronghold of Sozopolis which commanded roads to both Laodicea and Attalia. Before returning to Constantinople John opened the way to Attalia, separating the Turks of Caria from the Sultanate of Iconium.

Yet John could not give all his attention to Asia Minor. Apparently in 1121, a large raiding party of Cumans and Pechenegs crossed the Danube, and the emperor spent the next winter at Thracian Beroea negotiating with them. They agreed to make peace, but in the spring John rather treacherously attacked and crushed them, selling some into slavery and enrolling others in his army. Then, in autumn 1122, the Venetian doge paused on his way to the crusader states to avenge his loss of privileges by besieging Corcyra. He failed to take the island, and by spring gave up and sailed for the East. But after a year and a half he sailed back to raid Rhodes and winter on Chios, and in 1125 he looted several more Aegean islands before returning to Venice. The empire's navy, clearly inferior to its army, never ventured to attack the Venetians.

The next year, the duke of Trebizond Constantine Gabras, who had long enjoyed unusual autonomy, openly rebelled. The governor to Gabras's west, Cassianus, also rebelled at about the same time in Paphlagonia, so that most of the Black Sea coast was in revolt. When the Venetians raided Cephalonia, the emperor decided he had too many enemies and made peace with them in August. He restored the privileges Alexius had granted Venice, and officially it became a Byzantine ally once more. Not long afterward, the emperor cut his spending on the ineffective Byzantine fleet, preferring to use his resources on land in Asia Minor.

Probably in summer 1127, before John could deal with the rebels along the Black Sea, the Hungarian king Stephen II invaded the empire, angry that the Byzantines were harboring his fugitive uncle.[26] The king sacked Belgrade and Nish, and continued ravaging as far as Serdica and Philippopolis until the emperor drove him off. A year later John crossed the Danube and defeated the Hungarians on their home ground near Sirmium; but after he left, the Hungarians counterattacked, and the Serbs of Ras repudiated Byzantine suzerainty. The emperor marched back and defeated and subjected the Serbs. Although he made only a feint against Hungary before winter set in, he managed to win a peace from Stephen, whose uncle had died in the meantime.

By 1130 the emperor was ready to return to Anatolia. His preparations seem to have frightened the Paphlagonian rebel Cassianus into ceding his lands to Ghāzī, who was also allied with Constantine Gabras of Trebizond. John apparently began his operations by strongly fortifying the town of Lopadium in the northwest, where the Turks were raiding again.[27] Lopadium became the imperial headquarters for military recruitment and training. Next John marched against Ghāzī; but on his way he discovered a plot by his younger brother, the sebastocrator Isaac, who fled to the Turks. Probably doubting the loyalty of his men, John returned to Constantinople to punish the conspirators.

In exile Isaac Comnenus solicited the help of the emperor's various rivals in Anatolia. He visited in turn the Danishmendid emir Ghāzī, the rebel duke Constantine Gabras, Sultan Mas'ūd of Iconium, and the Armenian king Leo of Cilicia, the heir of Ruben. But none of these potentates made up his mind to back the pretender. Once John had secured his position at home and mustered a stronger army than before, he made a land and sea expedition to Paphlagonia in autumn 1132. There he massacred Turkish settlers, captured Castamon, where the Comneni had once had their estates, and apparently recovered the seacoast. Then he crossed the Halys, raided Turkish territory, and collected submissions from some of Ghāzī's governors. John celebrated a triumph in his capital the next year.

Ghāzī's response seems to have been to help the Turks of Iconium at-

151. The Monastery of Christ Pantocrator ("Ruler of All"), Constantinople, with its three connected churches. (Photo: Dumbarton Oaks, Washington, D.C., copyright 1996)

tack Sozopolis, the fort that guarded John's conquests in the south. Although that campaign failed, Ghāzī soon besieged and retook Castamon. The emperor began another campaign in the summer of 1134, but interrupted it when he heard of the death of his wife Piroshka-Irene. Yet Ghāzī died at almost the same time, leaving the Danishmendid realm in disarray. The emperor returned to attack Gangra, south of Castamon, before going into winter quarters. He took both Castamon and Gangra by surrender in 1135.

The next year the victorious emperor dedicated an imposing monastery and hospital to Christ Pantocrator, on a prominent hillside in the capital.[28] Intended as a thank offering for his victories over conspirators and the Turks, the Pantocrator became the family monastery of the Comneni, following the tradition of dynastic monasteries established in the two preceding centuries. Its construction showed that the treasury had recovered nicely from the crisis of the late eleventh century, which seems not to have allowed comparable outlays by John's father Alexius.

The emperor had yet to retake Trebizond and Cilicia, which Alexius had held insecurely, or Antioch, which Alexius had claimed. Antioch seemed about to fall into John's lap in late 1136, when its widowed princess offered it and her daughter's hand to John's youngest son Manuel.

The Crusaders thwarted her plans by marrying the heiress to a French-man, Raymond of Poitiers, but this at least gave the emperor a pretext to intervene. John also wanted to punish the Armenian king Leo, who had taken the Cilician plain from the Principality of Antioch and was be-sieging Byzantine Seleucia to his west. Mustering a force of Byzantines, Pechenegs, and Turks, John brought it by land and sea to Attalia.

The emperor and his sons marched against Leo's little Armenian King-dom in spring 1137. John speedily retook the Cilician plain and besieged Leo in Anazarbus, where the mountains began. The town surrendered after a Byzantine bombardment of just over a month, though the king escaped into the Taurus. John pushed on to Antioch, and set his siege machines to batter it as well. The new prince Raymond readily agreed to take John as his overlord instead of the king of Jerusalem, and even to exchange Antioch for a principality stretching from Aleppo to Homs if John would help him conquer it.

The emperor accepted this somewhat equivocal surrender, hoping to gain not only Antioch but a powerful crusader protectorate behind it. Before trying to conquer Raymond's new fief, however, the emperor marched back to Cilicia, where he captured King Leo and his sons and

152. The citadel of Anazarbus from the south, showing the ancient city walls in the foreground. (Photo: Irina Andreescu-Treadgold)

sent them back to Constantinople. John annexed the Cilician plain, and the Armenian princes in the mountains became Byzantine vassals. Early the next year the emperor returned to Antioch, where he marshaled the first joint force of Byzantines and Crusaders since the First Crusade.

In the spring he led this army against Aleppo, but arrived a little too late to surprise its Turkish garrison. He therefore turned south and besieged Sizara, in the midst of the lands he intended for Raymond. The Byzantine siege engines broke through the town walls, but the citadel held out against the listless Crusaders, who preferred keeping Antioch to making conquests instead of it. The emperor accepted a nominal submission from Sizara and retreated. Then he entered Antioch, but withdrew when Raymond's men began a riot and news came that the Turks were raiding Cilicia. John expelled the raiders and marched back to his capital, having won much glory but not so much real advantage.

The emperor's successes did impress his renegade brother Isaac, whose eight years of plotting had come to nothing, enough that he requested and received a pardon early in 1139. The Danishmendid Turks, less impressed by the emperor, raided the lower Sangarius valley. After chasing them away, John massed his forces at Lopadium again for a major campaign. Never properly defeated, the Danishmendids had evidently retaken Paphlagonia and were still backing Constantine Gabras of Trebizond. The emperor could make no better use of his victorious army than to fight them.

In late spring the emperor began his march along the Black Sea coast. He spent the rest of the year on his way, presumably because he had to drive out Turks and establish garrisons as he went. At the beginning of 1140 he reached the Danishmendid stronghold of Neocaesarea and besieged it. But the place was strong, and the winter turned harsh; the Byzantines ran short of supplies, and a son of John's brother Isaac deserted to the Turks. After six months John raised the siege, but he sent a contingent against Gabras that finally regained Trebizond for the empire.[29] By the time the emperor returned to his capital early in 1141, he had recovered the entire Pontic seaboard.

That year John rested his army at his camp at Lopadium and recruited more troops for another expedition. He pursued negotiations with the German emperor Conrad III, whom he wanted as an ally against the Normans of Sicily, and engaged his fourth son Manuel to marry Conrad's sister-in-law. Meanwhile the Danishmendid emir died, and his domains broke up into separate emirates. John took this as a chance not to destroy

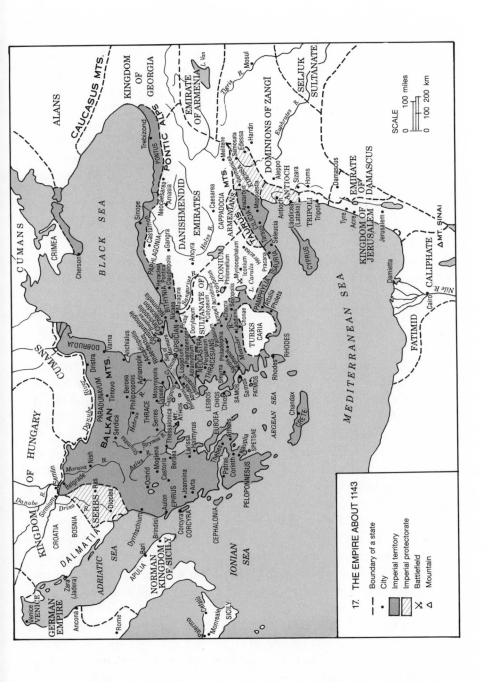

17. THE EMPIRE ABOUT 1143

the Danishmendids, whose remaining lands were fairly barren, but to turn his back on them and campaign against the rich city of Antioch.

The emperor and his sons marched south in the spring of 1142. Evidently meaning to secure a land corridor between the rest of Byzantine territory and the southern coast, they chased Turkish raiders from Sozopolis and paused to conquer the islands of Lake Caralis. The islanders, who had come to terms with the Turks of nearby Iconium, at first resisted, and seem to have submitted to the Turks again soon after John left. When the emperor came to the southern port of Attalia, his eldest son and heir Alexius suddenly died, and the grieving father had his second and third sons take the body back to Constantinople. During the voyage John's second son died as well.

The emperor determinedly pushed on toward Syria. The count of Edessa offered to become a Byzantine vassal and was accepted; but this time John demanded that Prince Raymond surrender Antioch before receiving other lands in exchange. While Raymond made excuses, John wintered in Cilicia and recaptured some mountain forts from the Turks. With only two sons left, he considered giving his younger son Manuel the title of junior emperor with responsibility for Cyprus and the coast from Attalia to Antioch. Apparently John had begun to see that his land corridor joining the southern Anatolian coast to the rest of the empire would never be truly safe, and thought of this means of protecting his southern possessions.

In early spring, before he could deal with Antioch, the emperor supposedly pricked himself with a poisoned arrow while hunting near Mopsuestia, and became deathly ill. Although most Byzantines in the camp wanted him to confirm his elder son Isaac as his heir, most of the western mercenaries supported the younger son Manuel, who was betrothed to a German and known to favor westerners. On his deathbed John was said to have chosen Manuel, who unlike his brother was present in the camp. In fact, the whole episode is suspicious. Manuel's supporters may well have manipulated the succession, or even caused John's death. Some complicity by Raymond of Antioch is also possible.[30]

Like his father, John II left the empire stronger than he found it, but not quite as strong as it looked. He improved the army and gave it a base at Lopadium from which it could guard much of Byzantine Anatolia. But the army remained a relatively small force to defend so large an empire, and the navy had become dangerously weak. John amassed a gold reserve that might better have been spent on expanding the army and navy. He took great interest in Syria, and attempted to cooperate with Crusaders, as long as they served as his vassals. Yet this cooperation achieved nothing of importance, and his intervention weakened Antioch and Edessa, both of which needed all their strength to resist Zangī, the vigorous Turkish governor of Aleppo. Involvement with the Crusaders distracted John from trying to take more of Turkish Asia Minor, which unlike Antioch would have made the empire more defensible.

To most contemporaries, however, John's choices seemed reasonable ones. By this time few Byzantines survived who longed for the lands lost to the Turks. The Sultanate of Iconium and the Danishmendid domains seemed to be in terminal decline even without Byzantine intervention; much of what they held was wasteland, and their Greek population was by now accustomed to Turkish rule. So John gave priority to subduing rebels, including the Crusaders who kept Antioch in defiance of their treaties and promises. When he died, Byzantium could defend itself, and was as big and prosperous as anyone could recall. That was good enough for John and most of his courtiers. Like his father Alexius, John was a man of limited ambitions, a brilliant manager rather than a great ruler.

CHAPTER TWENTY

Diminishing Security, 1143–1204

At the accession of Manuel Comnenus Byzantium could still be considered the leading power in the Mediterranean, but only by a narrow margin. While militarily stronger than each of its neighboring states, it was weaker than several combinations of them. More ominously, most of them belonged to either a western or a Muslim group, each of which had more in common with fellow westerners or Muslims than with Byzantines. The empire needed some firm allies to avoid the danger of an overwhelming enemy coalition. Since for religious reasons alliances with the Turks could hardly be solid and lasting, the only real possibilities were westerners.

With a Hungarian mother and a German fiancée, Manuel was well aware of opportunities both to ally with westerners and to make conquests from them. When he became emperor at age twenty-four, his intelligence and charisma were already evident. They may also have tempted him to jockey for temporary advantage instead of planning for the empire's long-term security. Manuel shared the military and political adroitness of his father and grandfather, but not their patience with the more mundane tasks of internal administration. He was at ease with westerners, rather too ready to believe in Byzantine superiority over them, and not quite wary enough of their power.

MANUEL'S NORMAN WARS

Manuel's somewhat irregular succession was managed with little trouble. He speedily sent his father's old friend, the grand domestic John

Axuch, to secure Constantinople. Axuch proclaimed Manuel and detained the two most likely aspirants to the throne, Manuel's disinherited
brother and ambitious uncle, both named Isaac. Manuel's older sister
Maria helped foil a plot by her husband the Caesar John Roger, a half-
Norman. Only some three months after his father's death did Manuel
reach the capital, where he was crowned. There he met his fiancée
Bertha, recently arrived from Germany, neither beautiful nor lively, and
not much to his Mediterranean taste. He delayed the marriage but continued the engagement, since he favored his father's plan to use the Germans against the Normans of Sicily and the French of Antioch. Roger II
of Sicily asked him for a marriage alliance, but after thinking it over
Manuel refused it.

Probably in 1144, after a brief campaign to drive the Turks from Bithynia, the emperor sent a land and sea expedition to Antioch to punish its
insubordination. The Byzantines defeated Prince Raymond and ravaged
his principality. They also kept him from lending vital help to Edessa,
which fell to Zangī's Turks. The fall of Edessa left Raymond so exposed
to Turkish attacks that he traveled to Constantinople and recognized the
emperor as his overlord, and Manuel considered this a success. Yet the
advance of the Turks in northern Syria threatened Byzantine Cilicia, and
excited western plans for a new Crusade that the Byzantines did not want.

When the German emperor Conrad protested Manuel's delay in mar-

153. Gold hyperpyron, shown one and two-thirds times actual size, of Manuel I
Comnenus (r. 1143–80) with his patron Christ Immanuel on the reverse.
(Photos: Dumbarton Oaks, Washington, D.C., copyright 1996)

rying Bertha, Manuel had to choose between taking an unattractive wife and giving up an enticing alliance with Germany. He chose to marry Bertha in early 1146, renaming her Irene. He found he could bear her somber temperament cheerfully enough if he consoled himself with various mistresses, especially his niece Theodora Comnena. But he showed his wife outward respect, and his alliance with Conrad became his main means of dealing with the West. The alliance of Byzantines and Germans was an obvious threat and provocation to Roger of Sicily, whose kingdom lay between them and whose peaceful overtures Manuel had rebuffed.

Manuel's immediate plans were to campaign against the Turks. While the Syrian Turks were in disarray after Zangī had been murdered in 1146, Sultan Mas'ūd of Iconium was probing Byzantine territory all along his frontier. Repulsed from Malagina to their north, Mas'ūd's Turks took Pracana to their south and raided the Thracesian Theme to their west. After mustering his army at Lopadium, the emperor marched far into Mas'ūd's sultanate. He defeated the Turks at Acroënus, seized their base of Philomelium, and ravaged up to the walls of Iconium itself. But when the Danishmendids reinforced the sultanate, Manuel retreated by the shore of Lake Caralis, beating off Turkish counterattacks with some difficulty. As the emperor returned to Constantinople, Mas'ūd opened negotiations that led to the return of Pracana.

By this time, to Mas'ūd's alarm and Manuel's discomfiture, preparations for the Second Crusade had begun in the West. German Crusaders crossed the Danube frontier in the summer of 1147, led by their emperor Conrad III. Although Conrad was now Manuel's relation by marriage, his men inevitably plundered on their way. The empress Bertha-Irene had to intercede to stop fighting between Byzantines and Germans outside Constantinople. Then French Crusaders under Louis VII of France crossed the Danube and caused the usual trouble supplying themselves. Worst of all, while Manuel was occupied with the Crusaders, Roger of Sicily sent a fleet that seized Corcyra and raided Greece, sacking Thebes and Corinth.

The German Crusaders were eager to advance, and Manuel was glad to see them off. Without waiting for the French, and ignoring Manuel's advice to march across the Thracesian Theme, Conrad led most of his men into the Sultanate of Iconium. Near Dorylaeum the Turks put him to a rout from which he barely escaped. He and many of his surviving men then joined Louis VII in marching through the Thracesians, but at Ephesus Conrad fell ill and returned to Constantinople. Louis and the

154. Roger II of Sicily (r. 1101–30 as count, 1130–54 as king). Detail of a twelfth-century mosaic in the Church of the Martorana, Palermo. (Photo: Istituto Centrale per il Catalogo e la Documentazione, Rome)

others went on by way of the insecure corridor of Byzantine territory from Laodicea to Attalia, suffering from Turkish attacks, hunger, and winter weather. By spring 1148 both Louis and Conrad arrived in Syria annoyed with each other and with Manuel.

Manuel's main concern was the Sicilian Normans' invasion. To stop them, he built a large fleet and asked for help from the Venetians. He confirmed their previous trading privileges and allowed them to expand their trading quarter at Constantinople. In return, a Venetian fleet was to join the Byzantines in besieging the Normans on Corcyra. As the emperor was setting out, however, the Cumans made a raid across the Danube, and he turned to chase them off. Then he delayed his expedition to spend Christmas at Thessalonica with Conrad III, who had left the failed Second Crusade. The two emperors agreed on a joint effort to expel the Normans from southern Italy.

In spring 1149 Manuel arrived at Corcyra, which the Byzantines and Venetians had still not recaptured. When the allies quarreled and began to fight each other, Manuel subdued the Venetians and forced the Normans to surrender the island. He wanted to invade the Norman Kingdom that very summer; but King Roger persuaded the Serbs of Ras to repudiate Byzantine suzerainty and attack the Serbs of Dioclea, who appealed to the empire for help. The emperor marched against the rebels, defeated them, and took Ras before returning to Constantinople for the winter.

Manuel prepared his fleet to attack the Normans the next year. But then the Hungarians came to the aid of the Serbs of Ras, Mas'ūd's Turks raided the Thracesians, and the Armenian king Theodore II advanced in Cilicia.[1] Manuel also took his chance to buy the remnant of the County of Edessa, after Nureddin, Zangī's son and successor as ruler of Aleppo, had blinded its count and killed the prince of Antioch.[2] Yet Manuel's eastern purchases, which extended from Cilicia to Samosata, began falling to Nureddin and Mas'ūd almost as soon as he bought them, and the emperor was too busy in the West to defend them. He defeated the Serbs, returning them to vassalage, then invaded Hungary and sacked Semlin and Sirmium, forcing Géza II of Hungary to make peace in 1151.

Meanwhile Manuel had ordered the grand domestic John Axuch to sail to Ancona, a city just north of the Norman Kingdom that was subject to Conrad III and friendly to Byzantium. But John never made the crossing. The weather was bad, and the Venetians opposed Manuel's designs on Sicily, fearing they would give Byzantium control over both shores of the Adriatic and so over Venetian trade. Manuel and Conrad nonetheless agreed on a joint German and Byzantine campaign against Sicily in 1152. Yet early that year Conrad died, and the expedition had to be abandoned.

Since Nureddin had now conquered all Manuel's purchases in Syria and Theodore II had taken most of Cilicia, Manuel had to turn his attention to the East. The emperor sent the now widowed Caesar John Roger to propose marriage to the widowed princess of Antioch; but he was a maladroit lover, and she refused him. Manuel sent an army to Cilicia under his cousin Andronicus Comnenus; but Andronicus, though an accomplished lover, was no warrior, and lost the rest of Cilicia to Theodore. The frustrated emperor paid Mas'ūd to attack Theodore; but Theodore defeated the sultan in 1154.

Roger II died the same year, and his son William I became king of Sicily. William made peace with the Venetians and tried to make peace with Manuel, but was rebuffed as his father had been. Manuel had bought the favor of some disloyal Norman nobles, and approached the new German emperor Frederick Barbarossa and Pope Hadrian IV, both of whom were hostile to the Normans. William too had his diplomats, and persuaded Géza of Hungary to invade the empire, in concert with a plot by Manuel's cousin Andronicus. Géza withdrew, however, when Manuel arrested Andronicus, and the king made peace after the emperor marched to the Danube in the spring of 1155.

That year a Byzantine fleet finally landed at Ancona, and Manuel launched the invasion of the Norman Kingdom that he had planned for so long. Backed by a rebellion among the Norman nobles, the Byzantines overran the coast down to Bari by the end of the year. To gain additional help, Manuel made an alliance with the Genoese, granting them reduced trade duties and a commercial quarter at Constantinople. Byzantium seemed to be punishing the Italian Normans for the rebellion they had started more than a century before.

The next spring, however, King William routed the outnumbered and overextended Byzantines as they besieged the citadel of Brindisi. Most of the expeditionary force was captured. The Norman rebels, the pope, and the Genoese came to terms with William; and Frederick Barbarossa spurned Manuel's offer of an alliance. This costly campaign gained the emperor nothing but a reputation for overreaching himself. William sent a fleet that raided Euboea in 1157; Manuel responded by sending John Axuch's son Alexius to Ancona to hire more mercenaries and allies against William. Yet by now neither Byzantines nor Normans expected to gain much by continuing the war.

Manuel's main interest had already shifted to Syria. The young king Baldwin III of Jerusalem wanted to marry a Byzantine princess, and offered an alliance that might help the emperor recover both Cilicia and Antioch. So in spring 1158 Manuel agreed to a peace with William of Sicily. By this time the emperor had spent some two million hyperpyra on his Norman projects.[3] In the unlikely event of their success, they would merely have added Apulia to the empire's collection of endangered outposts. The Italian war had made Manuel enemies in Europe and distracted him from defending his holdings in Asia. It was quite unnecessary, since both Roger II and William had been ready to make peace from the start. In the end, the war's futility became clear even to Manuel.

MANUEL'S SHIFTING ALLIANCES

In the summer of 1158, the emperor sent his brother Isaac's daughter Theodora to Palestine, where she married King Baldwin of Jerusalem. This was probably the time when Manuel, who was preparing an expedition to Syria but running short of money, changed procedures for paying the army. In place of regular pay, he granted various soldiers and officers the right to collect taxes in certain places, sometimes including rents from crown lands. Such a grant, resembling those given by the emperor Alexius to his relatives, was called a *pronoia* ("provision"), and its recipient may be termed a pronoiar. Manuel recruited many soldiers by this means, and the army he mustered does seem to have been the most formidable Byzantine force in memory.[4]

That fall Manuel himself led his army south, defeating some Turks on the way. He managed to surprise Theodore II of Cilicia, who fled before him while the Byzantines occupied the Cilician plain. Prince Reginald of Antioch, who had recently joined Theodore in raiding Cyprus, now hurried to submit to the emperor. Soon Manuel accepted both Reginald and Theodore as his vassals, though he reduced Theodore's kingdom to the Cilician highlands. Manuel made a triumphal entrance into Antioch at Easter 1159, and prepared to march with the Crusaders against Nureddin in Aleppo. But the Turkish leader too sued for peace, and Manuel, having gained his main aims in Cilicia and Antioch, granted generous terms. To the Crusaders' disappointment, Nureddin kept the former lands of Edessa he had taken from Manuel, and simply surrendered his many Christian prisoners. The emperor led his army back through the Sultanate of Iconium; but he suffered more than he had expected from harrying by the Turks of Mas'ūd's son and successor Kilij Arslan II.

This seemingly glorious expedition simply recovered ground that Manuel had lost earlier, and it showed the persistent strength of the Sultanate of Iconium, the enemy nearest the Byzantine heartland. The following winter the emperor ordered several attacks on the Turks and led forays from the Opsician and Thracesian themes, without much result. The Turks of Caria, over whom the sultan had some influence, pillaged Laodicea and took Phileta near Attalia. In 1160, to prepare for fighting Kilij Arslan, Manuel began to hire new western mercenaries. He also sent for more troops from his vassals in Serbia, Armenian Cilicia, and Antioch, and from his ally King Baldwin of Jerusalem. Since Manuel's empress Bertha-Irene had just died, his ambassador also sought a new empress in the Crusader states, and he married Princess Maria of Antioch, who unlike the late Bertha was renowned for her beauty.

By the next year, under attack from both the Danishmendids and Nureddin, Kilij Arslan began to negotiate with the emperor. Before any settlement was concluded, however, Manuel's reinforcements arrived

155. Manuel I and his second wife, Maria of Antioch. Contemporary miniature from the *Acts* of the Council of Constantinople of 1166 (Vaticanus graecus 1176). (Photo: Biblioteca Apostolica Vaticana)

from Syria, led by his nephew John Contostephanus. Invading the sultanate from the south, John sharply defeated the Turks. In spring 1162 the chastened sultan came to Constantinople in person to make peace. As usual outward submission went most of the way to satisfying Manuel, though Kilij Arslan did let some Christian bishops be consecrated in his sultanate.

In spite of his undoubted flair, the emperor's policies displayed a mixture of belligerence and weakness. When the Pisans and Venetians in Constantinople attacked the Genoese quarter, Manuel abolished the Pisan and Genoese quarters, but not the Venetian, probably because Venice was so strong. When King Theodore II invaded the Ducate of Cilicia, alleging the murder of his brother by its duke, Manuel restored peace by replacing the duke. On the death of Géza II, Manuel intervened in the Hungarian succession, rejecting Géza's son Stephen III in favor of Géza's brother Stephen IV. Stephen IV was crowned at the beginning of 1163, but lasted only six months before he had to take refuge in the empire. After sending an army to Belgrade, Manuel came to an agreement with Stephen III.

This agreement was a curious one. Manuel seems to have tried to gain some Hungarian territory by using the Byzantine succession as a lure. He betrothed his eldest daughter Maria to Stephen's younger brother Béla. The Hungarian prince seemed likely to inherit the empire under this arrangement, since Manuel still lacked a legitimate son. Béla went to Constantinople, took the name of Alexius, and received the new title of despot. He was to have as his patrimony Dalmatia and the region of Sirmium, plus Bosnia to connect the two.[5] Within a year this ambiguous arrangement led to a war over Béla's lands, which Manuel claimed as the possessions of a Byzantine functionary but Stephen refused to give up.

The emperor took seriously his claims on Hungarian territory. Even though Nureddin had just defeated a combined force of Crusaders, Armenians, and Byzantines near Antioch, Manuel merely sent some reinforcements there and marched in person to Sirmium with Béla-Alexius. King Stephen promised to cede the disputed land; but early in 1165 he took Sirmium back. Manuel led another army to Sirmium and sent another expedition to Dalmatia and Bosnia, conquering them all. Stephen accepted his losses, and Manuel formally named Béla-Alexius his heir.

Neighboring powers saw Manuel's conquest of Sirmium, Bosnia, and Dalmatia as a major Byzantine victory. The Russians of Galicia, who had backed Stephen III, now returned the emperor's cousin Andronicus when he escaped from prison in Constantinople. The Venetians asked and received money from Manuel for an alliance against Frederick Barbarossa that was forming under the pope. Pope Alexander III even considered withdrawing recognition from the German Empire and declaring Manuel the only true emperor.

Manuel grasped at this proposed honor, however insubstantial and troublesome it might seem. In early 1166 he held a council in Constantinople that rebuffed Byzantine critics of western theology, and he offered the pope financial aid and reunion with the western church in return for an imperial crown from Rome.[6] Not surprisingly, the negotiations were slow and complex. In 1167 Manuel actually offered to name Alexander to the vacant patriarchate of Constantinople. Yet this proposal raised even more problems, and in the end the pope shrank from the drastic step of trying to abolish the western empire.

Although the Byzantines had to drive the Hungarians out of Sirmium again in 1167, by that time Manuel's attention was turning back to the East. His treaty with Kilij Arslan had curtailed Turkish raids on western Asia Minor, but the emperor realized that this respite was unlikely to last. He used it to resettle and refortify the region of Adramyttium and Pergamum, which became the Theme of Neocastra ("New Forts"), between the Thracesian and Opsician themes.[7] The emperor renewed his ties with Jerusalem by marrying his grandniece to its new king, Amalric, but Manuel's rascally cousin Andronicus almost wrecked the alliance. Freed and sent to Cilicia as its duke, Andronicus first seduced the prince of Antioch's sister, who was also Manuel's sister-in-law. Then Andronicus absconded with state funds to the Kingdom of Jerusalem, where he seduced the dowager queen Theodora Comnena, Manuel's niece and his own. Finally Andronicus eloped with Theodora to Nureddin, outraging Crusaders as well as Byzantines.

Amalric and Manuel nonetheless agreed on a joint land and sea expedition to conquer Egypt. The country was wealthy and still largely Christian, and its enfeebled Fatimid caliphs had already promised Amalric tribute. In 1168, prodded by his vassals, Amalric invaded without waiting for a Byzantine fleet to help him. After advancing as far as Cairo, he withdrew when a Turkish force sent by Nureddin took over the country. The next year Amalric joined a second Byzantine fleet in besieging Damietta; the siege dragged on until the Byzantines ran out of supplies and had to abandon it. Nureddin, left in possession of Egypt, ruled it through his Kurdish governor Saladin.[8]

In 1169 Manuel's empress Maria bore him his first legitimate son, whom he named Alexius. The infant naturally supplanted the provisional crown prince Béla-Alexius, whose marriage to the emperor's daughter had been delayed in case it might not be needed. In good health at fifty, Manuel could reasonably hope to live until his son came of age. His new sense of security seems to have inspired him to confront the Venetians, whose quarter in Constantinople was becoming disturbingly large, rich, and independent. The year after his son's birth, Manuel restored the commercial quarters of the Genoese and Pisans, but the Venetians retaliated by destroying the new Genoese quarter. When they failed to agree to Manuel's demands for damages, he decided to act. Just eight days after crowning his son in 1171, he had every Venetian in the empire arrested and expropriated. Those taken are said to have numbered twenty thousand, half of whom were in the capital.[9]

This was of course an act of war. Venice incited the Serbs of Ras to rebel against the empire, and equipped and dispatched a fleet that captured some ports in Byzantine Dalmatia, plundered Euboea, and wintered on Chios. But there an epidemic broke out in the Venetians' camp, forcing them to abandon their campaign. Byzantium gained an ally in 1172, when Stephen III of Hungary died and was succeeded by Béla-Alexius, now Béla III, who married Manuel's sister-in-law. The emperor marched against the Serbs of Ras, whose prince Stephen Nemanya promptly submitted, and the Byzantines soon retrieved most of their losses in Dalmatia. With surprising ease, Manuel seemed to have rid himself of the Venetians.

On the other hand, Manuel now appeared to be neglecting the East. In Cilicia the empire's possessions fell to the new Rubenid king Mleh, an ally of Nureddin. The emperor's ally Amalric of Jerusalem tried to recover Cilicia for him, but Nureddin thwarted the attempt. Yet Nureddin and Amalric both died in 1174, and the next year Mleh was murdered. Mleh's murder allowed Duke Isaac Comnenus, the emperor's grandnephew, to advance from Byzantine Isauria to recapture the Cilician plain. Thus the Byzantines regained what they had lost.

The emperor broke his truce with Kilij Arslan in 1175, apparently because the sultan had refused his claim under their treaty to a share of some recent conquests from the Danishmendids. Occupying some largely deserted borderlands of the sultanate, Manuel rebuilt and refortified Dorylaeum in the north, Siblia in the south, and probably Cotyaeum between them.[10] He also sent an expedition to Amasia, whose

Turks had rebelled against the sultan and offered to submit to the emperor. While Kilij Arslan tried to negotiate, in 1176 Manuel dispatched another force against Amasia and mustered an unusually large army to lead against Iconium itself.

Marching up the Meander valley and on toward Iconium, in the pass of Myriocephalum Manuel fell into a Turkish ambush. He learned of the failure of his expedition against Amasia when the Turks displayed its commander's severed head. At Myriocephalum the fighting was heavy, and many men died on both sides. The Byzantines lost their baggage and supplies, and were in much the more precarious position; yet the sultan was reluctant to incur the risks of further fighting with a desperate adversary. So the emperor was able to extricate himself and his men with little more than a promise to dismantle Dorylaeum and Siblia.[11] He demolished Siblia on his way back to the capital.

The main importance of the battle of Myriocephalum was psychological. After so much apparent progress under Manuel, the empire and its army had performed no better against the Turks than at the beginning of his reign. This defeat seemed to show what many had long suspected: that the emperor's talent was for style rather than substance, and that he owed his earlier success mostly to luck. Yet the actual damage done to the empire was not great. Siblia was a small place, and once out of Turkish territory Manuel refused to destroy his more important conquest of Dorylaeum. His army could soon be restored by hiring more mercenaries.

The army did in fact recover quickly. When the sultan sent raiders down the Meander in 1177, the emperor's nephew John Vatatzes annihilated their main force, and seems to have been named grand domestic as a reward. This victory emboldened Manuel himself to expel the Turks from Panasium, south of Cotyaeum, though Byzantine forays farther to the south were driven back. That fall Manuel sent the Crusaders a fleet to mount another Egyptian campaign. Though it found the Crusaders unready, it helped convince the count of Flanders to broker a marriage between Manuel's son and the daughter of Louis VII of France. The emperor took comfort from this prestigious engagement, and from his daughter's betrothal to a son of the marquis of Montferrat in northern Italy.

Nevertheless, Manuel never forgot his defeat at Myriocephalum. As he approached sixty, he began to feel his age. He came to a grudging and tentative agreement with Venice in 1179, freeing most of his Venetian prisoners and discussing compensation for their property. When the

Turks besieged Claudiopolis that fall, Manuel found the energy for a campaign, and relieved the city; but the next year his health began to fail. The emperor hastily married his underage son to Agnes of France, renaming her Anna, and married his daughter to Rainier of Montferrat, renaming him John and appointing him Caesar. Manuel even reconciled with his renegade cousin Andronicus Comnenus, who returned from Turkish territory, swore an oath of loyalty to Manuel's son Alexius, and became duke of Paphlagonia. Having made these arrangements, in September Manuel died.

His had been a long and brilliant reign, and the gains he made were more evident than his failures. On the whole he had maintained the empire's prestige. He gained a little land in Dalmatia, Bosnia, and Asia Minor. He made alliances with the Hungarians, Crusaders, and French, though he antagonized the Normans, Germans, and Venetians. He left the treasury depleted, but not empty. He and his father and grandfather had ruled for a century without interruption; and now that the Comneni had multiplied and intermarried with other leading families, rebellions had died down and the government seemed stable. If the army's performance was uneven, it had been so for a long time. If corruption was a problem, it was little worse than before. Byzantium remained slightly stronger than any of its neighbors.

THE FALL OF THE COMNENI

At first the power behind the eleven-year-old Alexius II Comnenus was his mother, Maria of Antioch. Though at her husband's death she became a nun under the name of Xena ("Foreigner"), Maria kept her vocation from interfering with her life. She immediately took a lover and adviser, the protosebastus Alexius Comnenus, a nephew of her late husband. This was something of a scandal even by contemporary standards, and neither the empress nor her lover showed much talent for ruling; but what her subjects seemed to resent most was that Maria-Xena was a Norman and favored Pisan and Genoese merchants. Since several prominent Comneni felt excluded from power, her support in the imperial family was weak.

A conspiracy soon formed around the late emperor's daughter Maria and her new husband, the Caesar Rainier-John. In February they plotted to assassinate Alexius the Protosebastus, and presumably then to rule for Alexius II. The plotters were detected and arrested, but the Caesar and

156. John II (cf. Fig. 150), Manuel I (cf. Fig. 155), and Alexius II Comnenus (r. 1180–83). Miniatures from the Modena Zonaras, which after its text concludes with the reign of Alexius I continues its portraits of later Byzantine emperors in groups at the end. (Photo: Biblioteca Estense, Modena)

his wife escaped and barricaded themselves in Saint Sophia with the patriarch Theodosius, defended by Georgian and Italian mercenaries and a crowd of ordinary citizens. There they remained for two months, amid growing unrest, until they surrendered in return for amnesty.

The feebleness of Maria-Xena's regency became patent. Béla III of Hungary retook Byzantine Dalmatia, Bosnia, and Sirmium, while the Serbian prince Stephen Nemanya repudiated Byzantine suzerainty. In Asia Minor Kilij Arslan II conquered an extensive border region. He definitely severed the empire's tenuous land link with the southern coast, taking Cotyaeum, Sozopolis, and everything up to Attalia. The Armenian king Ruben III advanced into Byzantine Cilicia. Even more ominously, in Paphlagonia Manuel's elderly and disreputable cousin Andronicus Comnenus began collecting partisans to make his own bid for power.

Although Andronicus moved slowly, Maria-Xena was even slower than he. She only sent out an army against him in early 1182, under Andronicus Angelus, another cousin of Manuel's. The rebel Andronicus defeated the loyalist, who then joined the rebellion. The Imperial Fleet, apart from some ships manned by Italian mercenaries, also sided with the rebels. When Andronicus Comnenus advanced to Chalcedon, riots in his favor broke out in the capital. At length the imperial guard arrested and blinded the protosebastus, dealing the regency a fatal blow.

A mob took the protosebastus's arrest as a signal to attack the Pisan and Genoese quarters. It massacred the merchants, their families, and their clergy, including a papal legate, and sold the survivors into slavery. The emperor Manuel had set a partial precedent for such action by temporarily abolishing the Italian commercial quarters, and the Italians were especially blamed for supporting Maria-Xena's regency; but plainly many people in the capital had resented and envied the foreign merchants for years. Some of the Italians escaped by ship, and sacked towns and monasteries along the Aegean coast in revenge. Andronicus Comnenus made no attempt to stop the massacre, but stayed at Chalcedon to avoid responsibility for it.

After the disturbances died down, Andronicus arrived in the city and claimed the regency. He faced no immediate opposition in Constantinople. The troops in the Thracesian Theme continued to resist under the grand domestic John Vatatzes, and defeated an army that Andronicus sent against them; but a few days later John died of disease, and the Thracesian loyalists submitted to Andronicus. The regent celebrated by having Alexius II recrowned with ostentatious respect. Andronicus appeared to have many allies, and at first his regency was no more irregular than several others that had ruled for underage emperors.

Yet the many scandals of his earlier career had earned Andronicus a reputation for shiftiness. When Manuel's daughter Maria and her husband Rainier-John fell ill and died, Andronicus was widely believed to have poisoned them. Some officials were also disturbed when the regent forced the empress Maria-Xena into the convent where she supposedly belonged. By early 1183 Andronicus Angelus, changing sides again, formed a plot with the grand duke of the fleet, the postal logothete, and other prominent officials who distrusted Andronicus Comnenus. On finding them out, the regent had most of them blinded, imprisoned, or exiled, though Angelus escaped with his sons to the Kingdom of Jerusalem.

After this broad-based conspiracy, Andronicus was ready to suspect anyone around him, and seems to have punished several innocent people. When Béla of Hungary overran the Morava valley and took Serdica, the regent blamed Maria-Xena, who happened to be Béla's sister-in-law, and had her drowned. Young Alexius II raised no objection even to the

157. Andronicus I Comnenus (r. 1183–85), Isaac II Angelus (r. 1185–95, 1203–4), and Alexius III Angelus (r. 1195–1203). Miniatures from the Modena Zonaras. (Photo: Biblioteca Estense, Modena)

execution of his mother. The patriarch Theodosius abdicated in despair, leaving Andronicus to choose his replacement. In late summer Andronicus Angelus's sons Theodore and Isaac returned from their refuge in Palestine and raised a rebellion at Nicaea, attracting many Byzantine supporters and some Turkish mercenaries. To handle this emergency, Andronicus Comnenus had his partisans insist he be crowned coemperor. The regent took the crown in September, after protestations of reluctance.

Andronicus became emperor at age sixty-five, but he remained almost as vigorous, charming, unscrupulous, and irresponsible as during his many previous adventures. Although as regent he had practiced uncharacteristic prudence, his coronation emboldened him. He promptly had Alexius II strangled. Next he married his victim's widow, the eleven-year-old Agnes-Anna of France, more than half a century his junior. Declaring himself a reformer, Andronicus tried to curb corruption, which seems to have become rife. He reduced extortion by appointing honest provincial governors, raising their salaries to cover their expenses. Even his enemies admitted that he judged cases without regard for wealth or rank. His main aim was apparently to tighten the central bureaucracy's control over powerful landholders, and especially over taxation.

To reduce the number of his enemies, the emperor opened negotiations with the Venetians, allowing their merchants to return to Constantinople and promising compensation for their confiscated property. That winter a Byzantine army forced the Hungarians to retreat toward Belgrade, and in spring 1184 the emperor transferred troops to Anatolia to put down the rebellion of the Angeli. He joined the army as it besieged the rebels in Nicaea. Although Isaac Angelus surrendered that city in return for immunity, the emperor seized Prusa from Theodore Angelus, blinded him, and executed or mutilated a number of the other defenders. Such reprisals soon brought the revolt to an end.

Around the beginning of 1185, the former duke of Cilicia Isaac Comnenus, ransomed by Andronicus after the Armenians conquered his ducate in 1183, proclaimed himself emperor on Cyprus. Andronicus retaliated by having two of Isaac's relatives stoned and impaled. Then the emperor uncovered a plot in favor of Alexius Comnenus, a bastard son of Manuel who had married a bastard daughter of Andronicus. The emperor hanged or blinded the alleged conspirators, and soon blinded his son-in-law. Andronicus's punishments grew more frequent, cruel, and indiscriminate.

The mounting disorder in the empire attracted the interest of King William II of Sicily, William I's successor. In June he launched an invasion, purportedly to help a young Byzantine who claimed to be the murdered Alexius II.[12] The Normans first attacked their favorite targets of Dyrrhachium and Corcyra, which they took easily. While their army advanced overland to Thessalonica, their fleet sailed through the Aegean to complete the siege of the city. Distrusting his generals, the emperor divided relief forces among different commanders, who failed to cooperate. The duke of Thessalonica David Comnenus put up a listless defense, let the Normans undermine the walls, and finally surrendered when Andronicus sent orders for his dismissal. The Normans sacked the city thoroughly, and occupied it in preparation for a march on Constantinople.

At the news of the fall of Thessalonica the emperor kept his nerve, but he was concerned more with suppressing internal opposition than with stopping the Normans. He arrested the relatives of David Comnenus and ordered the arrest of the amnestied rebel Isaac Angelus, who was living quietly in the capital. When the emperor's men arrived, Isaac managed to kill one of them and escape to Saint Sophia. There he attracted a sympathetic crowd, which the next day forced the patriarch to crown him emperor. Andronicus tried to flee by ship, but was apprehended.

158. William II, king of Sicily (r. 1166–89) presenting the Cathedral of Mon-
reale to the Virgin. Detail of a contemporary mosaic from the cathedral, Mon-
reale. (Photo: Dumbarton Oaks, Washington, D.C., copyright 1996)

Isaac allowed Andronicus to be tortured and mutilated in the palace, then slowly dismembered alive by a mob in the Hippodrome. The mob also looted 170,000 hyperpyra from the treasury.[13] Others blinded Andronicus's two sons, one of whom died of his wounds. Breaking with the moderation and mercy of the earlier emperors of his family, Andronicus had unleashed savagery and popular violence that in the end were turned against him. Essentially an opportunist, he discredited and destroyed both himself and his dynasty. Worse still, by convincing foreigners that Byzantium was both treacherous and vulnerable, he practically invited invasions like that of the Normans.

THE FALL OF THE EMPIRE

Despite the horrendous death that he countenanced for his predecessor, Isaac II Angelus was on the whole a decent and moderate man. Mild-mannered and pleasant, just under thirty at his accession, he had middling intelligence, a bit of military experience from his rebellions, and many connections with the nobility. Unfortunately for him, this quite ordinary ruler had to deal with a chaotic administration, a depleted and plundered treasury, crumbling frontiers, and a Norman invasion that threatened to become a conquest of the whole empire.

Less suspicious than Andronicus had been, Isaac put his armies under the undivided command of a capable general, Alexius Branas. Branas found that the Normans had divided their army into three parts: a garrison for Thessalonica, a contingent farther east on the Strymon River, and a main force around Mosynopolis, farthest along the road to Constantinople. Branas first attacked the Normans around Mosynopolis, caught them off their guard, and drove them back with heavy losses. Encouraged by this success, the Byzantines attacked the Normans on the Strymon, and crushed them as well, capturing their commanders. In all ten thousand Normans are said to have been killed, and four thousand captured. The rest abandoned Thessalonica. After a foray into the Sea of Marmara, the Norman fleet also withdrew. For the present, the worst danger was over.

As the Normans retreated to Dyrrhachium, Isaac tried to restore good relations with the empire's neighbors. He made a truce with the sultan Kilij Arslan, whose Turks had just raided Neocastra. Making peace with Béla of Hungary, the recently widowed emperor married Béla's young daughter Margaret, who took the Byzantine name of Maria. The Hungarians withdrew to the Danube, while the Byzantines accepted their loss of Manuel's acquisitions in Dalmatia, Bosnia, and Sirmium. In spring 1186 the emperor led a campaign that recaptured Dyrrhachium from the Normans, and sent an expedition against the rebel Isaac Comnenus in Cyprus. Thus far, with some luck, Isaac II had begun his reign with distinction.

The Byzantines landed safely on Cyprus, but the Norman admiral Margaritone arrived and seized their ships, allowing Isaac Comnenus to capture their army. Margaritone went on to take many of the Aegean and Ionian islands.[14] Meanwhile a revolt had broken out among the Bulgarians and Vlachs in the Balkan Mountains.[15] Its leaders, the Vlach brothers Asen and Peter, exploited resentment of a special levy to celebrate the emperor's wedding with Margaret-Maria. The emperor soon drove the rebels across the Danube; but they won support among the Cumans that enabled them to recross the river. Isaac gave the command against Asen and Peter to his uncle, the sebastocrator John Angelus Ducas, who won several skirmishes before he was recalled on suspicion of conspiracy. The rebels defeated the next expedition sent against them, and proceeded to take over most of Paradunavum. It became an independent Bulgarian state under Vlach rule.

The emperor still seemed to be holding his own. In early 1187 he made an alliance with the Venetians, restoring all their privileges and promising to pay 100,800 hyperpyra in compensation for their losses. Further to improve his relations with the West, Isaac married his sister Theodora to the marquis of Montferrat's son Conrad. The emperor gave the command against the rebels in Bulgaria to the hero of the Norman campaign, Alexius Branas. But Branas had the army proclaim him emperor, marched on Constantinople, and put it under siege. After briefly panicking, Isaac borrowed money from the city's monasteries and entrusted its defense to his new brother-in-law Conrad of Montferrat. Conrad and Isaac sallied out with a makeshift force and defeated and killed Branas.

Then Conrad left for Syria, where Saladin had taken Jerusalem. As westerners rallied to their crippled crusader states, William of Sicily made peace with Byzantium, though Admiral Margaritone still held Cephalonia in his own right. In autumn 1187 the emperor made another campaign against the Bulgarians of Asen and Peter, defeated some Cumans, and advanced to Serdica and back. The next spring Isaac campaigned up to the Danube and captured Asen's wife. The rebellion in Bulgaria still seemed containable, and the Byzantine army was holding together.

During his Bulgarian campaign, however, the emperor learned that an Anatolian magnate, Theodore Mangaphas, had rebelled in the Thracesians, while a Third Crusade was forming that would pass by Constantinople. In early 1189 Isaac tried to suppress Mangaphas's rebellion before the Crusaders appeared; but they began to arrive while he was besieging Philadelphia, forcing him to hurry back. The leader of the main army of the Third Crusade was the empire's former rival the German emperor Frederick Barbarossa. As usual, the Crusaders were strong enough to pose a serious threat to Byzantium.

Although Frederick rejected attempts by the Bulgarian rebels and Stephen Nemanya of Serbia to enlist his help against Isaac, the two emperors regarded each other with deep distrust. Isaac suspected Frederick of wanting to conquer Byzantium, while Frederick suspected Isaac, who was negotiating with Saladin, of wanting to destroy the crusader army. The Byzantines barricaded their passes against the Crusaders, but the Crusaders occupied Philippopolis and repulsed three thousand Byzantine troops who tried to recover it. When Isaac detained some German ambassadors, Frederick plundered much of Thrace and seized Adrianople. Peace was made only in early 1190. That spring, after invading the sultanate and sacking its capital of Iconium, Frederick drowned in a river in Isauria.

After Frederick's departure Isaac made another expedition against the Bulgarian rebels, who had overrun more of Thrace.[16] Although he lost a number of his men in an ambush, at least he recovered Varna, Anchialus, and Serdica and established the empire's frontier along the Balkan Mountains. Apparently that fall, the emperor campaigned against Stephen Nemanya and drove him from the Morava valley. Near Belgrade he met his father-in-law Béla of Hungary, who remained friendly. In 1191 more Crusaders sailed under the English king Richard the Lionhearted, but they left the Byzantines undisturbed, except for conquering Cyprus from the rebel Isaac Comnenus.

Yet rebels continued to plague the empire. Theodore Mangaphas, though forced out of Philadelphia, took refuge with the Turks and led Turkish raids on the Thracesians. Another pretender claiming to be Alexius II gained Turkish support and raided the Thracesians until he was assassinated. A third Pseudo-Alexius appeared in Paphlagonia, and another rebel in Bithynia. Both were suppressed, but several more minor rebellions broke out as the unrest gathered its own momentum. Never had Byzantium suffered from so many regional rebellions, as local magnates and pronoiars sensed the impotence of the central government.

Under such circumstances, Isaac II had all he could do to defend his throne. Piracy became rampant in the Aegean, and overwhelmed the small Byzantine fleet. In 1192 Isaac restored the commercial privileges of the Pisans and Genoese, hoping to restrain the pirates who came from those cities. Fortunately for the empire, its neighbors had troubles of their own. The sons of Kilij Arslan of Iconium fought among themselves both before and after their father's death in 1192, and one of them surrendered Theodore Mangaphas to the emperor. By the next year Asen and Peter of Bulgaria also quarreled with each other.

To exploit the dissension among the Bulgarians, the emperor dispatched an expedition under his cousin, the grand duke Constantine Angelus. After defeating the Bulgarians raiding Thrace, however, Constantine had himself proclaimed emperor at Philippopolis. He was blinded when his own men betrayed him to Isaac, but the Bulgarian raids became worse than ever. In 1194 the Bulgarians mauled the Byzantine army near Arcadiopolis and took Serdica. Isaac appealed to his father-in-law Béla of Hungary, who agreed to help campaign against the Bulgarians the next year. The emperor duly set out in the spring; but when he reached Cypsela in Thrace he fell victim to a plot carefully laid by his older brother Alexius. Deserted by his courtiers, Isaac himself was blinded.

Alexius III Angelus's successful usurpation was a further blow to the empire. Despite some shortcomings, Isaac had put down several rebels, avoided military disaster, and restored the empire's solvency, even as he started to pay reparations to the Venetians for their losses under Manuel. Aged about forty-two at his accession, Alexius III had less energy and ability than his younger brother, and could expect still less loyalty from his subjects and family.

In returning to the capital to be crowned, Alexius abandoned the joint campaign with the Hungarians. He made lavish gifts to his fellow conspirators, but stopped paying the Venetians the compensation Isaac had promised, even though a mere 28,800 hyperpyra remained outstanding. Alexius faced a new rebellion that very summer, when yet another false Alexius II appeared in Bithynia, backed by the Turks. While Asen of Bulgaria raided Thrace and defeated the Byzantines near Serres, repeated expeditions against this Pseudo-Alexius failed. Even when his

TABLE 15
The Angelus Dynasty

Emperors are in capital letters, and Byzantine emperors are in italics, with the years of their reigns marked "r." Other years are of births and deaths. Illegitimate descent is shown by a broken line.

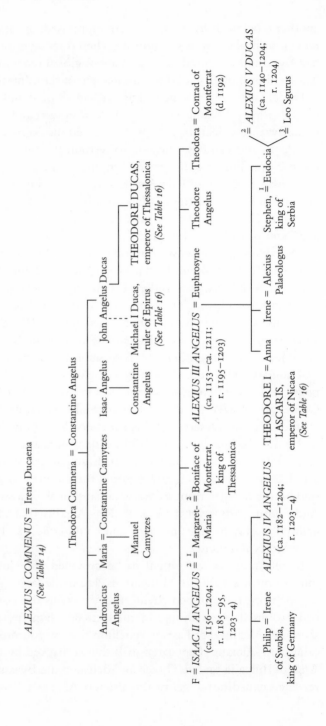

ALEXIUS I COMNENUS = Irene Ducaena
(*See Table 14*)

Theodora Comnena = Constantine Angelus

Maria = Constantine Camytzes   Isaac Angelus   John Angelus Ducas

Andronicus Angelus

Manuel Camytzes

Constantine Angelus   Michael I Ducas, ruler of Epirus (*See Table 16*)   THEODORE DUCAS, emperor of Thessalonica (*See Table 16*)

F = ¹ *ISAAC II ANGELUS* ² = Margaret- ¹ = Boniface of Montferrat, king of Thessalonica
(ca. 1156–1204; r. 1185–95, 1203–4)   Maria

ALEXIUS III ANGELUS = Euphrosyne
(ca. 1153–ca. 1211; r. 1195–1203)

Theodore Angelus   Theodora = Conrad of Montferrat (d. 1192)

ALEXIUS IV ANGELUS
(ca. 1182–1204; r. 1203–4)

THEODORE I = Anna LASCARIS, emperor of Nicaea (*See Table 16*)

Irene = Alexius Palaeologus

Philip = Irene
of Swabia, king of Germany

Stephen, ¹ = Eudocia ² = *ALEXIUS V DUCAS*
king of Serbia   ³ = Leo Sgurus
(ca. 1140–1204; r. 1204)

rising ended with his assassination, probably in 1196, the Turks raided Paphlagonia, the Meander valley, and Bithynia.

That year Asen was murdered by his nephew Ivanko, who seized the Bulgarian capital of Tirnovo and called in the Byzantines. Handed a splendid opportunity to recover Bulgaria, the Byzantine army mutinied on its way, letting Asen's brother Peter claim the throne and drive out the assassin, who fled to the empire. Next the Byzantine commander at Strumitsa, a Vlach named Chrysus, raised his own revolt. The emperor made two halfhearted campaigns against him, then granted him generous terms in 1197. Peter of Bulgaria was soon succeeded by his energetic brother Kaloyan ("Handsome John"), who continued raiding far into Thrace.

Events in the West now took a menacing turn. Henry VI of Germany, son of Frederick Barbarossa, married his brother Philip of Swabia to Isaac II's daughter Irene, widow of a Norman prince. By allying himself with Alexius's deposed and blinded brother, Henry was openly challenging the Byzantine emperor. Along with his father Frederick's hostility to Byzantium, Henry had inherited the Norman Kingdom of Sicily and its own rivalry with the empire. Henry threatened to reclaim the Normans' former conquests in northern Greece unless Alexius paid him 360,000 hyperpyra to mount a Crusade.

After bargaining the blackmail down to 115,000 hyperpyra, Alexius ordered a special levy, the German Tax, to collect it. When the people of the capital refused to contribute, he stripped ornaments from the old imperial tombs to make up the sum. The money was never sent, since just then Henry VI died, and his Crusade was abandoned. Henry's heir was the even more hostile Philip of Swabia, but a German civil war kept him from any efforts to avenge his father-in-law Isaac II. Alexius nonetheless found it prudent to renew the Byzantine alliance with the Venetians in 1198.

To deal with the Bulgarian raids, Alexius gave a command at Philippopolis to Ivanko, the killer of Asen, who had taken the Byzantine name of Alexius and been betrothed to the emperor's granddaughter. Ivanko recruited and trained an army of his fellow Vlachs, rebuilt forts, and kept the raiders at bay. But in 1199 he too rebelled. He captured the first general sent against him, the emperor's cousin Manuel Camytzes, then sold his captive to Kaloyan of Bulgaria. The Byzantine army refused to fight Ivanko. Resorting to his skills at intrigue, the emperor lured the troublesome Vlach to a meeting and had him murdered in the spring of

1200. This disposed of one rebel, but did nothing to increase respect for Alexius III.

Revolt followed revolt. That summer Michael Ducas, bastard son of the emperor's uncle John Angelus Ducas, rebelled with Turkish help and pillaged the already devastated Meander valley. The old rebel Theodore Mangaphas somehow returned from captivity and reestablished himself in the Thracesian Theme. In 1201 Kaloyan of Bulgaria freed his prisoner Manuel Camytzes, who joined Chrysus and another local commander in further revolts in Thrace and northern Greece. To their south a local magnate, Leo Sgurus, rebelled in the Peloponnesus. Riots broke out in Constantinople. One set of rioters plundered the treasury and momentarily hailed as emperor John Comnenus Axuch the Fat, a great-grandson of John II.

Worst of all, that autumn Isaac II's son Alexius fled Byzantium on a Pisan ship. Before Christmas the prince arrived at the court of his sister Irene and her husband, the German king Philip of Swabia. There young Alexius met another of his relations by marriage, Marquis Boniface of Montferrat. The prince pleaded for help to recover the Byzantine throne for his blinded father and himself. Although Philip was busy in Germany, Boniface was already planning to go east with an army, because he had just been chosen to lead the Fourth Crusade. The three men almost certainly discussed diverting the Crusade to Constantinople, but Boniface lacked the authority to do it by himself. Early in 1202 Prince Alexius traveled to Rome and asked Pope Innocent III for support. Knowing that the last three Byzantine emperors had all been usurpers, the pope rejected young Alexius's claims. He also made a point of prohibiting Boniface of Montferrat from turning the Crusade against Christians, obviously including the Byzantines.

The knights of the Fourth Crusade planned to gather that summer in Venice, where the Venetians had contracted to ferry them to Egypt for a total of eighty-five thousand silver marks. But many fewer Crusaders came than had been expected, and those who did come could raise just fifty-one thousand marks. Under their contract, they were responsible for the whole sum. The Venetian doge Enrico Dandolo offered to let them postpone payment of the balance if they would conquer the Christian port of Zara from the Hungarians for him. Despite the pope's explicit prohibition, the Crusaders agreed, and took Zara. The outraged pope excommunicated the Venetians, but forgave the Crusaders when they claimed they had acted under duress.

159. Mosaic of Old Saint Mark's of about 1261, from the facade of the Cathedral of San Marco, Venice. (Photo: Irina Andreescu-Treadgold)

While the Crusaders wintered at Zara, an embassy arrived from Philip of Swabia with a tempting offer from Prince Alexius. If the Crusaders would make him and his father emperors at Constantinople, he would accept the authority of the pope over the Byzantine church, contribute ten thousand soldiers to the Crusade, and pay the Crusaders and Venetians two hundred thousand marks, the equivalent of eight hundred thousand hyperpyra.[17] The Venetians, though their treaty with the reigning emperor was not five years old, found the offer irresistible. Isaac II's deposition seemed shocking to westerners unfamiliar with Byzantine politics, since in the West rulers were almost never overthrown. The leading Crusaders accepted the terms with the enthusiastic support of the doge and Boniface of Montferrat, and over the strong protests of the papal representative. The pope sent his own protest, to no avail.

The sum promised by Prince Alexius could easily have been raised during the reign of Manuel, who had spent two and a half times as much trying to conquer Norman Sicily. But since then much tax revenue had been signed away to soldiers, dignitaries, and monasteries. The empire had lost extensive border territories to the Turks, Armenians, Serbs, and Bulgarians. Moreover, though in 1202 Alexius III had recovered much of Thrace by capturing Chrysus, driving out Camytzes, and making peace with Kaloyan of Bulgaria, parts of Anatolia and Greece were still in revolt and paying no taxes. By this time what young Alexius had promised was far more than the reserve in the treasury, as the Venetians must at least have suspected.

In spring 1203 the Crusaders set sail, soon to be joined by Prince Alexius, their candidate for the Byzantine throne. They put in at Dyrrhachium, Corcyra, Euboea, and Abydus, all of which submitted to them and their pretender. In late June they arrived off Constantinople with about ten thousand soldiers, and perhaps as many Venetian oarsmen. Alexius III's army seems to have been larger than the Crusaders', and not so much worse as to negate the advantage of the city's magnificent walls. But the emperor conducted a feeble defense, allowing the Crusaders to sail into the Golden Horn and attack the vulnerable sea walls alongside it. When the Venetians overran a section of the sea walls in mid-July, the emperor fled to Thrace with the crown jewels and some seventy-two thousand hyperpyra.

The chief officials hurriedly freed the blind Isaac II and acclaimed him, persuading the Crusaders to stop their assault. A delegation of the Crusade's leaders came to inform Isaac of his son's promises. Despite his undisguised dismay at their extravagance, Isaac had no choice but to confirm them. The Crusaders demanded Prince Alexius be crowned co-emperor, and he was. Aged about twenty-one, without experience in government, Alexius IV needed to satisfy the exorbitant demands of a mighty western army, while placating subjects long resentful of westerners and government exactions. It was a practically impossible task.

After his coronation, Alexius announced the reunion of the churches, made frantic confiscations, and managed to pay half of what he owed: one hundred thousand marks, or four hundred thousand hyperpyra. The Venetians took half of this as their share. The Crusaders had to pay out almost all of their portion to clear their various debts. They were therefore impatient to receive the balance, and could scarcely believe that Alexius, ruling a city far richer than any they had seen before, did not have the money. Yet, even after confiscating the fortunes of his enemies and plundering church treasuries, he fell well short. The Venetians never offered to take payment in installments or in land, though by now anyone with financial expertise must have seen that the alternative would be war.

Alexius frankly told the Crusaders that the people of the capital would not tolerate any additional levies, and pointed out that his deposed uncle still controlled most of Thrace. The Crusaders agreed to stay until the next spring, but only for still more money. Some of them joined the emperor in a campaign in Thrace, where they plundered several towns but failed to dislodge Alexius III. During their absence, rioting and fires broke out in Constantinople, as hostility between Byzantines and westerners grew. Pope Innocent, with no power or desire to restore Alexius III, insisted that Alexius IV fulfill his promises and allow the Crusade to proceed. Yet after making some modest additional payments the young emperor discovered that he could pay no more, and said as much. Byzantine troops began to skirmish with the crusading army.

By the beginning of 1204 Alexius had exasperated Crusaders and Byzantines alike, and Isaac II's mind began to fail under the strain. In January both father and son were overthrown by the chief Byzantine critic of the Crusaders, Alexius Ducas Murtzuphlus. Full of energy despite his age of about sixty-five, Alexius V was clever and decisive, and gained the support of most Constantinopolitans. The treasury, however, was much barer than before, and the Crusaders far less tractable. Since Murtzuphlus killed Alexius IV, and Isaac II died, the Crusaders could no longer demand the young ruler's restoration.[18] But they did demand 360,000 hyperpyra, which by their reckoning they were owed. On the emperor's

160. Alexius V Ducas Murtzuphlus (r. 1204). Miniature from a thirteenth-century manuscript of the history of Nicetas Choniates (Vindobonensis historicus graecus 53). (Photo: Bildarchiv der Österreichischen Nationalbibliothek)

refusal, the Crusaders decided to try to seize both the city and the empire for themselves.

They started their attack in early April. Hostilities were fierce but short. Within a few days the Crusaders breached the sea walls and set a fire that spread through the city. Byzantine resistance abruptly collapsed. On 13 April the emperor fled, his Varangians surrendered, and the enemy poured into Constantinople. For three days the Crusaders looted and devastated it. They reckoned the value of their booty at over 900,000 marks, or 3.6 million hyperpyra, from which they paid off the Venetians.[19] With the flight of what remained of the Byzantine bureaucracy and garrison, the empire's central authority melted away. The patriarch of Constantinople John X fled to Thrace. Though Alexius V and Alexius III still lived, by the test of administrative continuity the empire had ceased to exist.

If the Fourth Crusade had not been diverted, under circumstances no one could have clearly foreseen, Byzantium would of course not have fallen in 1204. All the same, the emperors beginning with Manuel Comnenus had alienated the Venetians, the rulers of Germany, and many other westerners, leaving all of them ready to divert a Crusade. The empire had no reliable allies to whom it could turn in such a crisis. With its army weakened and its treasury impoverished, Byzantium could neither defeat the Crusaders nor buy peace from them. Finally, even before the Crusaders came, the empire had been suffering from an unprecedented rash of rebellions, which were both a cause and an effect of its internal decay. Byzantium's own dissensions invited the Crusaders to its capital, and left it at their mercy.

CHAPTER TWENTY-ONE

A Restless Society,
1025–1204

Taken as a whole, the eleventh and twelfth centuries were a time when the empire underwent a stunning political and military decline. From the peak of its power at the death of Basil II, in just 60 years Byzantium lost its heartland to some disorganized nomads, and was reduced to fighting for its life again. After 120 years more, the empire came to pieces and fell to a small foreign army assembled almost by chance. Yet, even while the revival of the state was interrupted and reversed, the Byzantine economy continued to expand, and literature and art flourished. Thus the empire grew richer, more cultured, and weaker at the same time.

These developments are less paradoxical than they may seem. Prosperity and education do not by themselves win wars. A thriving private economy need not lead even to filling the public treasury, let alone to political and military strength. On the contrary, more wealth can bring social tensions that undermine a state. In its combination of economic and cultural advance and political instability, eleventh- and twelfth-century Byzantium shows similarities to the city-states of classical Greece and Renaissance Italy, which succumbed just as suddenly to outside invaders.

GROWING REGIONALISM

The Byzantine losses in the later eleventh century, and again in the later twelfth, did less damage to the empire than might have been expected. For one thing, some of the losses lasted for only a fraction of the period. The Turks did not start to conquer western Anatolia in earnest until 1081, and the Byzantines had recovered it by 1098. This occupation of as little as fifteen years by a handful of Turks caused no catastrophic disruption; neither the Turkish occupation nor the Byzantine reconquest was particularly destructive. The Normans held substantial parts of the Balkans even more briefly, from 1081 to 1084 and from 1185 to 1187. The sole successful rebellion in Bulgaria began only in 1185 or 1186. Regional revolts became truly intractable later still, and even most of those soon failed, or seemed likely to fail until the Fourth Crusade supervened.

More significantly, the land Byzantium lost was on average much poorer, less developed, and less populous than the land that was continuously held or quickly recovered. The only two lost regions with real prosperity, southern Italy and northern Syria, had been border zones that were difficult and expensive to defend. The Anatolian plateau and the region north of the Balkan Mountains had always been relatively poor and sparsely settled. These losses were consequently far less serious than those of the seventh century, which included the large and wealthy provinces of Syria, Egypt, and Africa. Although then the empire had lost well over half its population, cities, and farmland, it kept most of each throughout the eleventh and twelfth centuries. While the earlier military disasters had brought on a dark age, the reverses between 1050 and 1200 did nothing of the sort.

Yet in the seventh century the foreign invasions had left the empire more cohesive, and the same was not true in the eleventh and twelfth centuries. The Turkish and Norman conquests lost the empire some Armenians in Armenia and some Italians in Italy, but each group had been Hellenized to some degree, and neither was very large or troublesome. For most of this period the empire retained its Bulgarians and Vlachs, though they became more restive and sometimes rebelled. The Pechenegs also settled in Byzantine territory and made unruly subjects. Nevertheless, the problem of disunity was not primarily ethnic. The worst disputes were among Greeks, in the capital itself and in heavily Greek provinces.

In Asia Minor one reason for the unrest was admittedly the Turkish invasion, which not only damaged the empire's security but deprived it of anything that could properly be called a frontier. Although its borders would never have satisfied a modern surveyor, earlier Byzantium had been surrounded by rivers, mountains, or deserts that more or less marked off the land that the Byzantine government administered and taxed. Much of this was open to raids, but when enemies raided they at least knew that they were on Byzantine soil. The Danube continued to be such a frontier on the empire's north until Asen and Peter set up their restored Bulgarian state; even then, the Balkan Mountains marked a rough limit to Byzantine territory. For the rest of the Balkan peninsula the boundary was the sea, except for a fairly short and mountainous stretch in the west that separated Byzantium from the Serbs.

For this period historical cartographers can and do draw lines on the map of Asia Minor that separate cities and regions known to be Byzantine from those known to be subject to the Seljuk sultan or the Danishmendid emirs.[1] However helpful such lines may be to provide orientation, they are nonetheless modern abstractions. There was not a frontier but a frontier zone. Many of the Turks, those called *Turkmen* in Turkish, were nomadic herders with no real homes or rulers, who raided not only Byzantine settlements but Turkish ones as well. The Turkmen particularly infested the border regions, where no one was in full control. Although such Turks were neither skilled in taking fortified places nor much interested in doing so, they liked booty, particularly livestock, and could penetrate almost anywhere in Byzantine Anatolia, with or without the encouragement of a sultan or emir.

After losing almost everything in Asia Minor but some parts of the coasts, in the wake of the First Crusade Alexius I reoccupied the northwestern lowlands up to the edge of the central plateau. These valleys were much the richest part of the peninsula, and may have held as many as half its inhabitants, especially after Alexius brought in refugees from neighboring regions. John II opened land corridors from the Byzantine northwest to the Pontus and Pamphylia, and from Pamphylia on to Cilicia and Antioch. Manuel filled in the region of Dorylaeum. But from time to time the Armenians or Crusaders took Cilicia, and later the Turks captured various border outposts.

The result during the twelfth century was a large block of territory in the northeast and sometimes discontinuous ribbons of borderland along the coasts. The Turks occupied part of the coast of Caria, and often raided to the sea elsewhere. In the eastern part of the peninsula the Turkish interior was separated from the Pontus in the north by the Pontic Alps and from Cilicia in the south by the Taurus Mountains; but no comparable barrier screened the west at any point. Turks always moved freely across John II's corridor between Sozopolis and Attalia. Since even after campaigning there John considered making Pamphylia, Isauria, and

161. View of the Pontic Alps, showing the Monastery of the Virgin of Sumela (center). (Photo: Irina Andreescu-Treadgold)

162. View of the Taurus Mountains near the Cilician Gates. (Photo: Irina Andreescu-Treadgold)

Cilicia a separate domain for his son Manuel, the link between the two parts of Byzantine Anatolia was obviously tenuous. Ships were the chief means of communication between them, and throughout each coastal strip. The absence of a border always tempted the Turkmen to expand a little more, and the magnates to establish their independence in between the empire and the Turks.

Without forgetting about the lost territories altogether, the government took differing degrees of interest in them, with priorities that seem somewhat strange to a modern observer. Among the regions never retaken, the emperors appeared to long most for Antioch and southern Italy, which would have been the hardest to take, to hold, and to tax. Efforts to reclaim them harmed and antagonized westerners who might otherwise have made useful allies. On the other hand, no emperor tried or even seriously contemplated reconquering the interior of Asia Minor, land that once recovered would have protected the plains and coasts and made the whole empire easier to defend. The Turks there were often weak and disunited, and never made reliable allies. The same money and effort spent fruitlessly on Antioch and Norman Italy, if devoted consistently to Asia Minor, might well have been enough to push the Turks back to the Euphrates.

Of course the emperors had their reasons, if not always good ones, for acting as they did. They knew that central Anatolia was poorer than northern Syria or southern Italy, and they may not have realized that it could produce more net revenue because of its size and defensibility. Reconquering the Anatolian plateau at the easiest time to do so, under Alexius I, would have required both enlarging the army and turning over much of the reconquered land to the dispossessed magnates, thus strengthening possible rivals of the House of Comnenus. No doubt the emperors cared about defending their rights against the Normans of Sicily, who had rebelled when they were imperial mercenaries, and against the Crusaders of Antioch, who had sworn to hand over any Byzantine territory they took. Finally, once the Balkans had become the main part of the empire after the Turkish conquests, the emperors considered westerners a greater military threat than Turks. Even though this belief seemed vindicated by the Fourth Crusade, matters might have been otherwise if the Byzantines had fought less with westerners and recaptured more of Asia Minor.

The interior of Anatolia, abandoned by the emperors except when they resettled its Christians elsewhere, grew more Turkish and Muslim. Families of Turkish settlers followed the first invaders, and settled down to lives as herders in a region well suited to pastoralism. The Turks' children by native women were raised as Turks. By raiding, or simply by herding, the Turks forced out many of the native Christian herdsmen, cultivators, and townsmen, who had never been very numerous. Most of the old magnates found refuge in the Balkans and eventually despaired of returning. In 1204 the Christians in Turkish Anatolia were probably still in the majority, but the tide was running strongly against them. The growing Muslim population became another reason for the emperors, always reluctant to rule Muslims, not to attempt reconquest of the plateau.

Among areas the emperors did reconquer, Cilicia was the hardest to keep. It was far from Constantinople, near crusader Antioch, largely mountainous, and settled by Armenians who had their own military and religious leaders. Philaretus Brachamius first held the region with many Byzantine troops, themselves heavily Armenian. The Rubenid princes and other Armenian chieftains put up stiff resistance to Byzantines, Crusaders, and Muslims alike. In 1099 the Rubenids started styling themselves kings of Armenia. The empire never regained much more than the coastal plain of Cilicia, which the Rubenids periodically descended to recapture. By 1183 they had taken it for good.

The Pontus, despite having a Greek majority, was almost as insubordinate as Cilicia. But its less exposed position made it more peaceful, and its trade with the East may have made it somewhat richer. During most of the period from 1075 to 1140 local magnates from the Gabras family were its virtual rulers, sometimes as Byzantine governors, sometimes as rebels allied with the Danishmendids. When Constantinople fell in April 1204, two grandsons of Andronicus I, Alexius and David Comnenus, were already conquering the Pontus with the help of their aunt, the Georgian queen Tamara.[2] While this Alexius Comnenus claimed the title of Byzantine emperor, his new realm is usually called, after its capital, the Empire of Trebizond. Soon it took over what remained of the Byzantine Crimea, which had probably become independent from Constantinople by 1198.[3] Alexius and David Comnenus of Trebizond also had designs on Paphlagonia, where their family had its ancestral estates and their grandfather had launched his successful revolt.

To the west of Paphlagonia Byzantine holdings in Anatolia became not just a coastal strip but a major part of the empire, comprising nearly all of the old Opsician and Thracesian themes. Here Turkish settlement had never taken root, and though Turkmen raids could reach anywhere they mostly affected the fringes, especially the Meander valley in the south. The Thracesian Theme had long been rich farmland with small and middling landholders. But it was affected by a general trend toward large landholding at this time, and when it became a border zone in the twelfth century it evidently acquired some military magnates, three of whom were in revolt by 1204.[4] The Opsician Theme continued to have many estates held by families of officials in the nearby capital. These and other inhabitants of the Opsician supported the abortive rebellion of the Angeli in 1183. In spring 1204 some of them rallied to Theodore Lascaris, son-in-law of Alexius III, who professed allegiance to the deposed emperor.[5]

During this whole period Constantinople was prosperous, and Thrace prospered along with it. The Turkish invasion of Anatolia left Thrace the most secure part of the empire, and so the natural resort for Anatolian refugees. The growth of trade benefited Constantinople as the empire's largest market, and enriched the Thracian towns that lay along the land and sea routes between Constantinople and western Europe. The interior of Thrace suffered somewhat from raids by the Pechenegs and

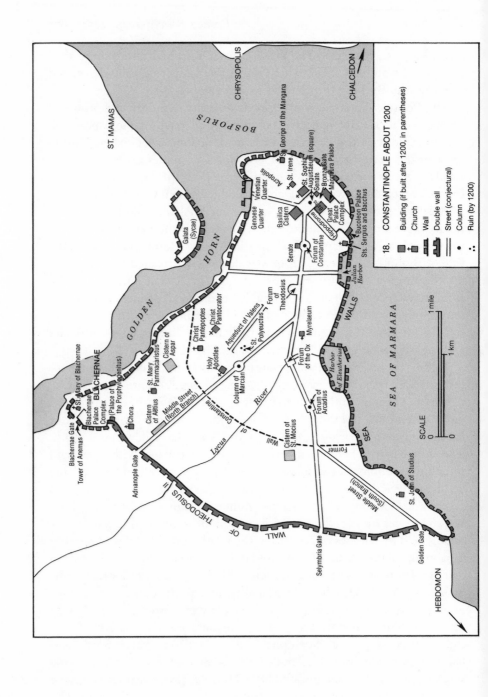

18. CONSTANTINOPLE ABOUT 1200

Building (if built after 1200, in parentheses)
Church
Wall
Double wall
Street (conjectural)
Column
Ruin (by 1200)

ST. MAMAS

CHRYSOPOLIS

CHALCEDON

BOSPORUS

GOLDEN HORN

Galata (Sycae)

Acropolis

Venetian Quarter

Genoese Quarter

St. George of the Mangana

St. Irene

St. Sophia
Augustaeum (square)
Senate
Bronze Gate
Magnaura Palace

Basilica Cistern

Hippodrome

Great Palace Complex

Bucoleon Palace
Sts. Sergius and Bacchus

Senate

Forum of Constantine

Julian Harbor

Christ Pantepoptes

Christ Pantocrator

Aqueduct of Valens

Forum of Theodosius

Myrelaeum

Cistern of Aspar

St. Polyeuctus

St. Mary of Blachernae

BLACHERNAE

Blachernae Palace Complex
(Palace of the Porphyrogenitus)

Blachernae Gate
Tower of Anemas

Chora

Cistern of Aëtius

St. Mary Pammacaristus

Holy Apostles

Column of Marcian

Forum of the Ox

Harbor of Eleutherius

WALLS

SEA OF MARMARA

Adrianople Gate

Middle Street (North Branch)

Wall of Constantine

Lycus River

Cistern of St. Mocius

Forum of Arcadius

SEA

Former

Middle Street (South Branch)

St. John of Studius

Selymbria Gate

WALL OF THEODOSIUS II

Golden Gate

HEBDOMON

SCALE

0   1 km

0   1 mile

Cumans, and later by the Bulgarians and Vlachs of Asen and Peter; but its prosperity seems to have persisted. Dominated by the capital and the estates of imperial relatives and government officials, Thrace seldom produced truly local rebels, though armies that happened to be there sometimes revolted. Most of Thrace found itself opposing the governments of Alexius IV and Alexius V, but only because it stood by Alexius III after his deposition.

Greece was comparatively tranquil during these years, and evidently saw strong growth of its population, agriculture, manufacturing, and trade. Although northern Greece was twice invaded by Normans, its countryside and even its looted metropolis of Thessalonica appear to have recovered quickly; Norman and Venetian raids on the rest of Greece and its islands were similarly transitory. Greece had a local aristocracy that was growing in numbers and wealth, but not in inclination to revolt until just before 1204. Then unsettled conditions allowed Manuel Camytzes in the north and Leo Sgurus in the south to raise rebellions.

The larger Greek islands were at least as prosperous as the mainland, but their geography made them harder to control. Both Crete and Cyprus temporarily rebelled against Alexius I. The renegade Isaac Comnenus seized Cyprus in 1185, exploiting the prevailing anarchy to hold it until its conquest by Crusaders six years later. Given the remoteness of the two islands, however, the emperors' holding them through most of this period represented something of an achievement. Corcyra was the Byzantine island most exposed to attacks from the Normans and Venetians, but the Byzantines held or recovered it each time either power attacked until the Fourth Crusade.

North of Greece, what had been Bulgaria remained remarkably loyal after its revolt from 1040 to 1041, especially considering that it was neglected by most of the emperors and raided by Pechenegs, Cumans, Serbs, and Hungarians. Most of the Morava valley stayed in Byzantine hands past 1200, despite its distance from Constantinople. Paradunavum did not even join the earlier Bulgarian revolt, and its defection between 1076 and 1091 was the work not of its natives but of its Byzantine duke and the Pechenegs. The rising that finally restored a separate Bulgarian state was led by Vlachs. Apparently the Byzantines had subdued or won over most of the Bulgarian Slavs, who must still have been the main ethnic group in the region.

Of course, Byzantium's external enemies were the ones who finally brought it down. The empire had seldom been on friendly terms with its neighbors in the past, but as its margin of superiority dwindled it needed more friends and fewer enemies. Yet Byzantine diplomacy continued to jockey for temporary advantage rather than nurture durable alliances. The emperors' marriage connections with the Hungarian kings, plagued as they were by dynastic and border disputes, served mostly to threaten the Serbs, who became even less reliable clients than before. Although relations with Russia were better, Russia came to matter less as it broke up into petty principalities. To the west the empire never made a lasting choice of allies among Venice, Pisa, and Genoa, or among the papacy, the German Empire, and the Norman Kingdom. Byzantium's most consistent policy, enmity with the Normans, caused only harm to the Byzantines, who kept hostilities alive long after the Normans were ready to make peace. The principal interests of the empire actually conflicted with none of these western powers, and none was as hostile to the Byzantines as the Byzantines were to it.

The same broadly true of the crusader states of Syria, seemingly natural allies of the empire against the Turks. From time to time Crusaders and Byzantines did collaborate, to mutual advantage. More often they frustrated each other, because of the Byzantine preoccupation with Antioch and the tensions that were inevitable when foreign armies marched across the empire. Yet Byzantine territory was so vulnerable, and so much more tempting than Syria, that the Crusaders showed some restraint by not attacking the empire more than they did. The Byzantines' often friendly relations with Turkish rulers, without much reducing raids by Turkmen, aggravated the Crusaders' distrust of the empire. The Byzantines had some allies among the Armenians, but used them mostly to fight other Armenians, the Rubenids. No emperor seems to have thought of joining the hardy Rubenids, the resurgent Georgians, and the Crusaders of Edessa and Antioch to cut off, contain, or even destroy the Anatolian Turks. Yet each Christian power would have had much to gain by such a result, and none of them more than Byzantium.

During the eleventh and twelfth centuries, in the East as in the West, the Byzantines followed no coherent strategy. If Byzantium was trying to divide and rule, it failed, since its neighbors fought the empire more than they fought each other. The problem was not really an obsession with prestige rather than power, as is sometimes said, because those two were compatible concerns, and not even Manuel let matters of prestige alone lead him into adventurism. Although he would certainly have liked the pope to recognize him as the only emperor in Christendom, by the time this became a subject of negotiation Manuel had given up on conquering the Norman Kingdom, and he can scarcely have thought of invading Frederick Barbarossa's empire. The Byzantines were, if anything, not ambitious enough. The failures of Byzantine foreign policy after 1025 largely resulted from a reluctance to conquer more territory. Most emperors worried that their already fractious empire might become too big and strong for them to dominate.

TENSIONS AT THE CENTER

During this period the wealth and power of the empire's landholding and commercial classes increased, although in an economy based on agriculture the landholders remained well ahead of the merchants. The magnates' share of land and official posts continued to grow until the empire began to have a hereditary ruling class, as before it had not. The aristocrats' acquisitiveness overwhelmed the tenth-century land laws designed to protect smallholders, which the government stopped enforcing. Meanwhile merchants and manufacturers became richer and more influential than ever, and obtained an unprecedented number of high titles, sometimes by purchase. They also seem to have fomented most of the period's riots and attacks on Italian traders. The advancement of magnates and traders left little room for officials or officers risen from the ranks, who had long been characteristic of Byzantium and the chief source of its imperial dynasties. By 1204 tenants on others' estates seem for the first time to have outnumbered independent smallholders. The ordinary subject steadily lost ground to the businessman and the grandee.

Because such men were harder to rule than ordinary subjects, the power of even the most determined and capable emperors tended to diminish, or at least became harder to use. As the Macedonian dynasty died out, the imperial office was further weakened by poor leadership and contested successions. Only briefly represented on the throne before, the landed aristocracy produced seventeen of the period's twenty-two emperors, including the Ducas, Comnenus, and Angelus dynasties. The merchant class contributed its first two emperors, Michael IV and Michael V. Conspiracies and revolts became more frequent, and a dozen of them succeeded. In no time this short had Byzantium had so many emperors, or seen so many overthrown. The number is particularly striking because during more than half of the period the first three Comneni enjoyed long reigns and overcame all the plots against them. Earlier and later rulers were much less fortunate.

Naturally the emperors tried to protect themselves. The Ducas family began, and the Comnenus family generalized, the practice of assigning the highest posts to relatives, including relatives by marriage from other powerful families and foreign ruling houses. This policy was partly successful, since the throne did pass from father to son once in the Ducas dynasty and three times in the dynasty of the Comneni. Yet even relatives could and did plot against the emperor, serving as rallying points for disaffected Byzantines and foreigners. Both the Comnenus and the Angelus dynasties suffered from internal dissension and eventually destroyed themselves.

Nevertheless, the emperors managed to keep most magnates and merchants under control most of the time. In the eleventh century the emperors usually favored the merchants and the traditional bureaucrats as counterweights to the Anatolian magnates. As a rule the government avoided appointing magnates to the civil service, preferring less prominent and less prosperous families from the Balkans. At the same time the emperors permanently and drastically decreased the size of the army, which had an aristocratic officer corps, and allowed the Turks to keep inland Asia Minor, where the military magnates had had most of their estates.[6]

During the Turkish invasion, probably to reduce aristocratic disaffection, the emperors granted refugee landholders from Asia Minor estates in the European part of the empire. During this process, however, the magnates appear to have become poorer, less attached to their land, and more dependent on the emperor.[7] Although the Comneni were Anatolian magnates themselves, they retook scarcely any of the Anatolian plateau and showed little favor to aristocrats who were not their relatives. The commercial class, after its political advances during the eleventh century, was largely excluded from power under the Comneni, and faced mounting competition from Italian traders. Admittedly, the emperors granted trading concessions to Italians, let the army decline, and lost Anatolia primarily because of incompetence or political pressures, not a wish to thwart Byzantine merchants and aristocrats. Yet governments more sympathetic to magnates and traders would probably have acted otherwise.

Even though the quarter million or so soldiers on the army's rolls in 1025 were far more than the empire needed, it did need the forty-two thousand troops of the tagmata, Varangians, and Imperial Fleet, plus many of the thematic troops along the frontiers. At first the government seemed to be maintaining the soldiers it needed and letting the rest of the themes deteriorate, a reasonable solution that let the empire defend

163. Ruins of the family castle of the Comneni at Castamon (modern Kasta-monu), Paphlagonia. (Photo: I. Ševčenko, Dumbarton Oaks, Washington, D.C., copyright 1996)

itself and even expand modestly. But Constantine IX, frightened by the military revolts of Maniaces and Tornices and running out of money, not only demobilized the themes guarding the Armenian frontier but significantly debased the currency that paid all the soldiers. Without disbanding existing units, Constantine and his successors preferred foreign mercenaries, who were fewer, more easily hired and dismissed, and presumptively more loyal to those who paid them.

The eleventh-century combination of a handful of foreign mercenaries and an enormous and inactive native force proved expensive and inefficient. What made it truly disastrous, however, was the demobilization of the Armenian themes, which opened a gap that the Turks used to enter Anatolia. The Turkish invasion and the monetary inflation of the later eleventh century caused the almost complete dissolution of the old army of the themes and tagmata. Most of its land grants, insofar as they were not lost to the enemy, seem simply to have become private possessions of the former soldiers. What remained was a small professional force of Byzantines and foreigners, chiefly Normans and Pechenegs.

Alexius I, having lost most of his troops in several battles, by 1100 assembled an army that varied in size from year to year, but might at its largest have had some twenty thousand men.[8] The only important unit to survive from the earlier period was the Varangian Guard, replenished by hiring new mercenaries. Even it had come to include more men from Scandinavia, Germany, and England than from Russia, and was probably smaller than its old strength of six thousand. Alexius also hired various other westerners and Turks. His army had many Byzantine soldiers as well, hired like mercenaries for regular pay; but Alexius's new tagmata of the Manichaeans and the Archontopuli were ineffective and short-lived, though he established them with twenty-eight hundred and two thousand men respectively and apparently meant for them to last. Later native regiments seem to have been smaller, and intentionally impermanent.

Foreign soldiers soon learned how to revolt and ceased to be much more obedient than natives. Not a few foreigners, like the Turkish Alexius Axuch or the half-Norman John Roger, became for all practical purposes Byzantines, speaking Greek, joining the Byzantine church, and taking Byzantine wives. Yet by and large, once Alexius I restored order during the first part of his reign, his professional soldiers fought loyally and well. They were good enough fighters that their numbers could be kept low, making them both controllable and affordable. Under John II and Manuel, however, these soldiers appear to have become more numerous, and correspondingly expensive. John tried to economize on the navy after making peace with the Venetians in 1126; but with a reduced fleet the Byzantines could no longer hold their own against the Normans, and Manuel built up the fleet again in 1148. Manuel's method of economizing while expanding the army was to make wider use of pronoia grants of state revenues.

Ordinary pronoia grants seem to have provided a soldier with somewhat more income than the former military lands of a cavalryman, on which they were probably modeled. Pronoiars, unlike earlier cavalrymen, received no direct pay. As before, the soldiers received revenue at its source, but now they collected taxes instead of rents. As before, troops were distributed over the empire's territory and had a personal stake in defending it. Although in using land to support soldiers, and sometimes nobles, pronoia grants resembled western fiefs, in most respects they were different. Pronoia grants covered revenues rather than the land itself, were at this stage not heritable, and formed incidental parts of a traditional state system rather than a parallel system of essentially personal obligations.

Pronoiars were easier to dismiss than holders of military lands, and less likely to turn into farmers, because the pronoia lands were not their own. Nor could magnates easily buy up pronoia grants. Yet such grants, unlike grants of taxable military estates, deprived the state of all income from the land concerned. Pronoiars also seem to have been harder to drill and to muster than mercenaries, and more inclined to join regional rebellions. Pronoia was always a convenient means of providing for new recruits, because signing away rights to taxes involved no immediate outlay. Over the longer run, however, the system provided poor value for money, and contributed to the many military, political, and financial troubles that began late in Manuel's reign.[9]

Although this army of pronoiars and mercenaries was very different from the thematic and tagmatic forces it replaced, its commanding officers resembled the older ones. Even after the Scholae disappeared along with the other tagmata, the domestics who had once commanded the Scholae remained; the army's commanders in chief in Anatolia and the Balkans were still called domestics of the East and West, unless a single grand domestic held both commands. The dukes who had commanded groups of themes eventually supplanted the strategi altogether, taking charge of the mercenaries and pronoiars stationed within their ducates. Around 1092 a new officer, the grand duke, gained jurisdiction over most of the empire's islands and coastlands along with command of the navy.

The mercenary corps were often termed tagmata, and as the number of foreign mercenaries grew the ethnarch who had commanded all of them was replaced with separate leaders for each tagma. Apart from foreign mercenaries who headed tagmata of their countrymen, aristocrats continued to hold most high military commands throughout the period. From the time of Alexius I, such commands tended to be reserved for members of the imperial family and its connections by marriage; but those connections came to include a great part of the aristocracy. As the prestige of the imperial dynasty grew, descendants of female members sometimes used their family names as well, like John Comnenus Axuch, whose mother was a Comnenus, or John Angelus Ducas, whose grandmother was a Ducas. Some sons even preferred to use the maternal family name alone, like John Angelus Ducas's bastard son Michael Ducas.

Under the weak emperors of the eleventh century, the high officials of the central bureaucracy exercised considerable, though precarious, power. One of them briefly became emperor, the former military logothete Michael VI Bringas, while the postal logothete Nicephoritzes became the chief adviser of Michael VII. But as magnates, merchants, and the imperial family gained in power, simply holding high office in the bureaucracy became a matter of less consequence. The logothetes declined in importance and were made subject to a single logothete of the secreta ("departments"), who was sometimes the same as the general controller or mesazon. Traditional officials such as the postal logothete continued to administer, but lost the role they had often had in shaping policy. After the ascendancy of Nicephoritzes, and perhaps partly in reaction to it, eunuchs began to lose the prominence they had enjoyed in government since the beginning of the Byzantine period.

The themes continued to exist as civil provinces, often merged or subdivided to make their sizes more uniform after the empire's territorial losses. At least in some places, certainly in the Pontus, turmae and banda survived as civil divisions of themes. As many themes became smaller, some of them came to consist only of a single city and its surrounding region. With the disappearance of the strategus, the civil governor of a theme was titled a judge or praetor and combined administrative, judicial, and financial responsibilities. Naturally he was less powerful than the duke of his region, who sometimes took over civil administration as well. When conditions became more unsettled in the late twelfth century, dukes increasingly became both the civil and the military governors of themes.

In the eleventh century, members of the commercial class received or purchased many offices that brought with them both senatorial rank and large salaries. Although mostly without administrative duties, these posts implied not just prestige but some influence, corresponding to the multiplying wealth of the recipients. Their promotions and salaries seem to have kept pace with the debasement of the coinage in the eleventh century, while military pay fell behind. The rise of such upstarts scandalized not only landed aristocrats but ordinary officials. Even if Isaac I terminated the salaries of these honorary offices during his short reign, Constantine X restored them. Although Alexius I and the other Comneni continued such titular appointments, they accorded less importance to all senatorial officials, whether active or honorary. The sale of offices appears also to have spread to real administrative posts, damaging the efficiency of the bureaucracy. In the twelfth century the honorary positions with real power were those reserved for members or relatives of the imperial family, such as sebastocrator, Caesar, protosebastus, and, after Manuel I, despot.

Many imperial relatives enjoyed princely revenues, either granted in direct payments or through pronoia. Perhaps the earliest grant of state revenues to a relative was that around Thessalonica assigned by Alexius I to his brother-in-law, the Caesar and former rebel Nicephorus Melissenus. Several other such recipients later plotted or revolted, including the duke of Crete Nicephorus Diogenes, who had a grant in his ducate, the Caesar John Roger, who had a grant north of Thessalonica, and the Caesar Rainier-John of Montferrat, who had a grant around Thessalonica. The duke of Paphlagonia Andronicus Comnenus, with a grant in his ducate, and the sebastocrator Alexius Angelus, with some sort of grant in Constantinople itself, managed to seize power as emperors.[10] Evidently such concessions, besides draining imperial revenue, carried with them a dangerous degree of independence. The emperors seem to have known as much, since they generally kept the grants in the family and restricted them to regions away from the frontiers.

Given that one man needed help to rule even a diminished empire, the emperors had to rely on some group or other. Noble birth had be-

164. Marble relief of an emperor, probably John II Comnenus (cf. Figs. 150, 156). (Photo: Dumbarton Oaks, Washington, D.C., copyright 1996)

come so esteemed that lowborn generals or bureaucrats might not have commanded respect or obedience. Family ties had become so important that relatives seemed safer than outsiders, whose loyalties would be to their own families. Others who had to be trusted could be rendered somewhat more trustworthy by making them relatives by marriage. Foreign marriage alliances seemed to offer further protection, because most of the new relatives would be abroad.

Yet no one was entirely reliable. The emperors themselves, aristocrats that they were, wanted to believe that their relatives would put family ties ahead of ambitions for the imperial office. But in this the emperors were often deceived. They would probably have been well advised to put more trust in generals and bureaucrats chosen from the ranks. In any case, the army and bureaucracy, which were vital to running the empire, could not be staffed entirely from the reigning dynasty. By appointing their relatives indiscriminately, the emperors merely managed to undermine their government.

THE CHURCH AND THE WEST

The church hierarchy, like the bureaucracy with which it had much in common, gained some influence in the eleventh century, then lost most of it under the Comneni. Patriarchs of Constantinople had usually been stronger under weak emperors and weaker under strong ones, and this pattern continued in an accentuated form. The five patriarchs before the accession of Alexius I in 1081 had unusual independence and power. Thereafter patriarchs counted for little, as the emperors dominated church affairs. Throughout the period, whether weak or strong, both patriarchs and emperors became less tolerant than before of foreigners who failed to follow established orthodox practices.

When Basil II chose a new patriarch just before his death, dispensing with the customary ratification by the hierarchy, he doubtless expected Alexius of Studius to be at least as compliant as the patriarchs of the previous hundred years. As might have been expected, Alexius did reluctantly agree to the empress Zoë's three scandalous marriages, the first to the divorced Romanus III, the second the day after Romanus's murder, and the third despite the Church's condemnation of third marriages. Yet Alexius managed to survive an attempt by the powerful John the Orphanotrophus to take his place, and played an active part in the popular movement that overthrew Michael V.

Constantine IX chose the next patriarch Michael Cerularius as an old friend and a fellow conspirator against Michael IV. A relation of the Ducas family, as patriarch Cerularius enjoyed broad popular backing in Constantinople, especially when he opposed westerners. His defense of his prerogatives led him to break with the papacy, even though Constantine wanted the pope as an ally. Later Cerularius quarreled with the empress Theodora over her ecclesiastical appointments, encouraged Michael VI to abdicate in favor of Isaac I, and attacked Isaac for reclaiming crown land from the Church. Isaac, more decisive than the other emperors of the time, exiled Cerularius and was preparing to depose him when the prelate died. For all his energy, Cerularius lacked the patience and prudence necessary for the formidable task of permanently advancing patriarchal power. If anything, he alerted future emperors to the danger of having insubordinate patriarchs.

Michael's next three successors, all men of some distinction, exerted their influence with more circumspection. Yet the second of them, the noted scholar John Xiphilinus, ventured to absolve the empress Eudocia from her oath not to remarry, disregarding the opposition of the Ducas dynasty and its supporters. The third patriarch, Cosmas, a monk from Jerusalem, discreetly opposed Nicephorus III's marriage to Maria of Alania after her husband Michael VII had been made a monk. Cosmas later helped prevent Alexius I from marrying Maria, who by that time had two living husbands. After doing so, however, the patriarch avoided further conflict by abdicating.

While the unusually short imperial reigns before 1081 coincided with long patriarchates, the longer imperial reigns afterward brought patriarchates that were on average of unparalleled brevity. Of the twenty patriarchs between 1081 and 1204, most shrank from the least involvement in politics. Even so, opposition from emperors or clergy led eight patriarchs to abdicate or be deposed. These were Cosmas I, his successor Eustratius, three patriarchs under Manuel Comnenus, Theodosius Boradiotes under Andronicus Comnenus, and two patriarchs under Isaac II, one of whom abdicated twice. Perhaps the bravest of the lot, Theodosius, after trying to prevent some of the horrors of Andronicus's reign, gave up in impotent despair. At a time when popes exercised more power than ever, patriarchs of Constantinople were even more vulnerable than usual.

At first the prestige of monks was also fairly low. Magnates expanding their estates gained virtual possession of many monasteries through a practice known as *charistikē* (roughly, "favor").[11] Originally meant to provide impoverished monasteries with patrons who could restore them to solvency, such grants began to give the patrons the right to draw income from well-endowed institutions. The patriarch Alexius of Studius limited the process somewhat by forbidding bishops to give their own diocesan monasteries in *charistikē*. But his order did not apply to independent monasteries, most of which fell under *charistikē* before the end of the century. When Archbishop Leo of Chalcedon was deposed in 1084, he criticized not just Alexius I's melting down church plate but all lay usurpations of church property, *charistikē* included. Shamed by Leo, Alexius's patriarch Nicholas Grammaticus also began to oppose *charistikē*. After Leo recovered his see in 1094, emperors and patriarchs continued to regulate and restrict the practice until it became rare.

Monasteries began to be founded with the stipulation that they should be administered only by their abbots, subject neither to *charistikē* nor to interference from lay founders, bishops, or even the patriarch.

165. Monastery of Saint John, Patmos. (Photo: Courtesy of Charalambos Bouras)

Perhaps the most respected monk of Alexius I's time, Saint Christodulus, founded a self-governing monastery of this sort in 1088 on the small
Aegean island of Patmos. Patmos's Monastery of Saint John kept its
independence and vigor, and became a model for others. At the same
time, pursuit of the mystical communion with God favored by Symeon
the New Theologian increasingly led individual monks to live apart
from each other. The result of more mysticism, however, was sometimes lax discipline, as monks determined their own way of life. The
monasteries regained much of their wealth, but rather less of their spiritual prestige.

The religious writers of the eleventh and twelfth centuries, though
fairly numerous, were also limited in their influence. In the case of hagiography this is hardly surprising, since apart from some leading monks
like Christodulus of Patmos the time produced few suitable subjects.
Otherwise churchmen wrote letters or orations that were chiefly concerned with secular topics. The great Christological issues were settled,
and the Church usually had less control than the emperors over the theological and disciplinary issues that remained. Besides *charistikē*, such
matters included controversies over philosophical inquiry, Bogomilism,
the Armenian and Syrian churches, and of course the western church.

Byzantine philosophers could come under suspicion of deviating
from Christian doctrine at any time. Even under an easygoing patron of
learning like Constantine IX, Constantine Psellus and John Xiphilinus
retired as professors and became monks when they were accused of het-
erodoxy. Neither was formally condemned, and eventually Psellus returned to favor at court under his monastic name of Michael, while
Xiphilinus became patriarch. But the successor to Psellus's professorship
of philosophy, John Italus, fared worse. He suffered largely because he had
offended Alexius I, by supporting the emperor's critics in the Church. In
1082, against the wishes of both the former patriarch Cosmas and the sitting patriarch Eustratius Garidas, the emperor had a synod convict Italus
of heresy. Even if Italus helped provoke the charges by his incautious use
of Neoplatonist language, he is most unlikely to have espoused the pagan views for which he was condemned. Yet the emperor found many
who were ready to believe the worst of an intellectual and a westerner,
since Italus ("the Italian") was from southern Italy, and half Norman.

Alexius himself had nothing against education. In 1107 he founded a
patriarchal school in Constantinople to train clergy, with one professor
each for the Gospel, the Epistles, and the Psalms. Alexius was not even

suspicious of philosophers as such. He appointed Italus's student Eustratius to the archbishopric of Nicaea, and both the emperor and his patriarch regretted Eustratius's deposition for heresy by a synod in 1117. At a time, however, when secular and western influences seemed to be challenging the Byzantine church, suspicion of intellectuals was widespread among both clergy and laity. And some intellectuals actually were unorthodox. A council in 1157 forced the titular patriarch of Antioch, Soterichus Panteugenus, to recant his rejection of eucharistic transubstantiation. The imperial secretary Michael Glycas, partly blinded for plotting against Manuel Comnenus, later maintained that the Eucharist, even though it was the Body and Blood of Christ, was perishable. In spite of this seeming inconsistency, Glycas escaped clear condemnation.

The Church could scarcely be at ease with the growing interest in astrology, alchemy, and divination that was typical of the period. Though there was a Christian tradition of prophecy that went back to the Old Testament, a pagan tradition also existed, and the prophecies current at this time were at best secular ones. Psellus himself was fascinated by alchemy, astrology, and demonology.[12] Many emperors and empresses habitually consulted prophecies. The most famous such work, perhaps compiled around 1100, consisted of oracles attributed to the emperor Leo VI, who was often confused with the somewhat earlier scholar Leo the Mathematician.[13] The emperor Manuel named his son Alexius because of a prediction that his dynasty would rule as long as its emperors' names began with the letters A, I, M, and A, in that order.[14]

Although the main body of the Byzantine church had ceased to be troubled by heresy, organized dissenters still existed on the empire's periphery. The Church's efforts against them were persistent but largely ineffective. The most extreme heretics, the Paulicians and Bogomils, held their own, and Bogomilism spread further in the Balkans. The patriarchs Alexius of Studius and Michael Cerularius labored strenuously and harshly to convert the Syrian and Armenian Monophysites, without perceptible success. In fact, Armenian and Syrian deviations from orthodoxy, never pronounced, had over the years approached the vanishing point; but the Byzantines refused to tolerate even minor divergences like the Armenians' use of unleavened bread in the Eucharist. The resulting antagonisms did not directly help the Turkish invasion, which Armenians outdid other Byzantines in resisting. Yet the intransigence of the Byzantine church helped sustain Armenian separatism under the Rubenids, and led many Armenian, Syrian, and Egyptian Christians to ally with the Crusaders. After a last attempt by Manuel to negotiate reunion with the Armenians failed, the Maronite Christians of Syria united with the western church in 1187, temporarily followed by the Armenians ten years later.

The schism with the papacy that began in 1054 resulted from no new differences of any importance. The schism put Byzantium at a diplomatic disadvantage, as most emperors beginning with Constantine IX realized, and brought no discernible benefits to the Byzantine church. Divergences between East and West over the *filioque*, married priests, fasting on Saturdays, unleavened bread, and so on had not prevented church unity in the past. While many Byzantines and westerners found each other vaguely unsavory, this too was nothing new. Nor, until 1204, did Byzantines and westerners do anything to each other that justified lasting acrimony. The personal excommunications exchanged under Michael Cerularius should have lasted no longer than the lifetimes of the participants. Yet the schism of 1054, which might easily have been prevented, proved surprisingly hard to end.

Although the schism would have been easiest to heal early on, it was followed by papal support for the Norman rebels against Byzantium in southern Italy. The popes wanted the Normans as allies for reasons that had nothing to do with antipathy to the Byzantines, but naturally the Byzantines regarded any assistance given to rebels as a hostile act. Relations between the empire and the Normans and papacy improved somewhat under Michael VII, only to deteriorate again when the pope excommunicated Alexius I for usurpation and the Normans invaded the Balkans. Urban II lifted the excommunication of the emperor in 1089, but the churches were not formally reunited before the First Crusade set out in 1096.

By that time the schism had lasted almost half a century, and some Byzantines and westerners had come to think that there must be good reasons for it, even if few were able to tell what precisely those reasons might be. In any case, new reasons seemed to be at hand. The assertive papacy and mighty crusader armies looked threatening to a Byzantine church and state that were already on the defensive against the Turks and Normans. Increased familiarity with Italians and Crusaders made Byzantines more conscious that westerners not only had different ways, which might have been tolerable, but actually believed that their ways were superior. The establishment of the western church in crusader Syria and Palestine, where the Greek patriarchs of Antioch and Jerusalem were replaced with westerners, was a particular Byzantine grievance.

Alexius I, however much he distrusted Crusaders, had some hope of restoring church unity, and understood that Urban II was trying to help him. But Urban's successor Paschal II favored the Norman enemies of the empire. After Alexius made peace with them, he negotiated seriously with Paschal for a reunion of the churches, suggested that the pope send him an imperial crown, and sponsored debates between Byzantine and western theologians at Constantinople in 1112 and 1114. Yet disagreements remained, especially over the papal primacy. Most Byzantine clerics would concede no more than a primacy of honor, while popes demanded at least their former jurisdiction over doctrinal and disciplinary appeals from the East. When John II held another debate in 1136, the Byzantine and western theologians admitted that their beliefs about the Holy Spirit were compatible, but the Byzantine disputant insisted that popes had no right to add the *filioque* to the Creed. Some Byzantines also raised heated objections to the western use of unleavened bread at communion. In the end neither Alexius nor John was ready to incur the unpopularity of imposing unity on the Byzantine church.

Manuel, who liked westerners better, attempted more. He saw his chance in the open conflict between Pope Alexander III and Frederick Barbarossa. In 1167 Manuel tackled the dispute over papal jurisdiction, which he saw as the crucial difficulty, by offering to appoint the pope as patriarch of Constantinople in return for being crowned emperor of both East and West. Manuel may have meant this more as a gesture of goodwill than as a serious proposal. It would have meant the abolition of the German Empire, which was barely conceivable, and the virtual suppression of the patriarchate of Constantinople, which the Byzantine church would never have accepted. In the later twelfth century the emperors and popes found it easier to leave matters as they were.

Unfortunately, many ordinary westerners and Byzantines exaggerated the significance of this half-schism, which corresponded neatly but deceptively to older differences between the churches in practice and attitude. The schism aggravated and seemed to excuse animosities that were essentially cultural and social, or even commercial and political. On the other hand, once the schism had gone on for so long, the popes and emperors had no obvious means of healing it, and may have chosen the least irritating course by allowing it to continue. Even ending the schism would not have changed the fact that Byzantine and western culture were developing in almost total independence from each other. As the two civilizations diverged further, they became prouder of their differences.

CULTURAL FERMENT

Byzantine learning and literature, always more advanced than those of the West, kept ahead of the western advances now often called the Twelfth-Century Renaissance. In comparison with westerners, Byzantine scholars began with a better command of their classical heritage, and drew on an ancient Greek culture from which the West's Latin culture had originally been derived. By the same token, the Byzantines were so pleased with their existing knowledge that they saw less need for extending, deepening, or modifying it. Yet such self-satisfaction had been a greater obstacle before 1025, when Byzantine scholarship had gone nearly as far as it could go on traditional lines. In the eleventh and twelfth centuries Byzantine writers became readier to write original works of literature. When they did, they found a readership that, if still small, was larger, better educated, and more sophisticated than any that had existed since the sixth century.

Although most Byzantine schools continued to be private, Constantine IX's public schools of law and philosophy, founded in 1047, noticeably enhanced the status of higher education. Their professors, while doing little if any formal teaching, served by their example to attract talented students.[15] The first holders of the professorial chairs, Xiphilinus and Psellus, were like the mesazon Constantine Lichudes members of an enthusiastic coterie of bright young scholars. All three of these men had important careers in public life, Xiphilinus and Lichudes as patriarchs and Psellus as an imperial adviser. Psellus's successors in the philosophical chair included John Italus and a patriarch of the late twelfth century, Michael III. Later the patriarchal school founded by Alexius I raised both the level and the reputation of theological studies. Unlike the ephemeral School of the Magnaura in the ninth century, these institutions proved durable, and may well have lasted up to 1204.

The most brilliant classical scholar of the time was Michael Psellus; yet in his voluminous writings he was more interested in showing off his learning than in making it accessible to others. The most active philosopher was Psellus's student John Italus; but much of his work was lost after his condemnation. In the twelfth century two somewhat lesser intellects made more enduring contributions to the study of the Greek classics. These were John Tzetzes' bizarre commentary in verse on the classical allusions in his own letters, and Eustathius of Thessalonica's gargantuan commentaries on Homer. Besides preserving much ancient lore that would otherwise have perished in the sack of Constantinople in 1204, Tzetzes and especially Eustathius differ from most earlier Byzantine scholars in adding their own interpretations and observations to a body of notes that had accumulated since Hellenistic times.

A new originality also appears in several of the many histories that began to be written in the mid–eleventh century, following a period of silence. Curiously, Byzantine historians almost entirely missed the opportunity to celebrate the great campaigns and conquests of Basil II, which would seem to make a stirring subject. The first surviving account of them is by a Byzantine Syrian, Yaḥyā of Antioch, who wrote in Arabic, concentrated on Syria, and despite some narrative skill failed to put events into a wider perspective. The first Greek narrative of Basil's reign appears in the quite conventional chronicle of John Scylitzes, which continues the older work of Theophanes Confessor into the late eleventh century. Byzantine historiography fully awoke only when Byzantine scholarship did, and by then the days of real military glory were over.

Michael Psellus's extraordinary historical essay, the *Chronographia*, covers the worst period of decline in the eleventh century. His interest in military matters was minimal, and he loved to praise himself and had to praise the reigning emperor Michael VII; but Psellus knew that most emperors after Basil II had misgoverned the empire, and he seldom palliates their failures in domestic affairs. His account is most remarkable for being Byzantium's first political memoir. Less meticulously composed than his various orations and discourses, it is consequently fresher. By and large it presents neither encomia nor invectives, but perceptive character sketches of rulers he knew well. A better mind, if not a better man, than those around him, Psellus reveals in passing much of what went wrong at the self-centered Byzantine court.

Besides his contemporary Michael Attaliates, who treats much the same period in a direct and conscientious manner, several notable historians followed Psellus. In the early twelfth century John Zonaras compiled an unusually analytic general history, beginning with the creation of the world and ending with the death of Alexius I. Although this sort of thing had often been done before in commonplace chronicles, Zonaras writes with acuity and elegance, clarifying ambiguities in his sources, giving his own opinions, and adding his own description of Alexius's reign. Around the same time, the Caesar Nicephorus Bryennius, probably grandson of the rebel of the same name, began a well-informed account of the troubles of the late eleventh century. Left unfinished at his death, it was continued by his wife Anna, eldest daughter of Alexius I.

The title of Anna Comnena's history, the *Alexiad*, suggests a prose epic on Alexius's life and reign. Yet it presents no stock panegyric of the father Anna loved and admired. Usually she praises Alexius for virtues he really possessed, and dramatizes events that were in fact dramatic. Since Alexius's successes were obvious and his failures far less so, she seldom needed to distort her narrative. Her careful writing and her understanding of character and politics hold the reader's interest through occasional passages of prolixity. After choosing the promising subject of Alexius's almost miraculous reversal of the empire's disintegration, she shaped it into the finest work of historical art since Procopius's *Wars*. Anna set a high standard for the Byzantine historians to come.

In the late twelfth century, the imperial secretary John Cinnamus wrote a less original though very competent history in praise of John II and Manuel. Despite its merits, his work suffers by comparison not only with Anna's but with that of his younger contemporary and fellow offi-

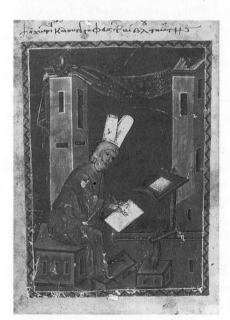

166. Nicetas Choniates. Miniature from a thirteenth-century manuscript of his history (Vindobonensis historicus graecus 53). (Photo: Bildarchiv der Österreichischen Nationalbibliothek)

cial Nicetas Choniates. Beginning with the death of Alexius I, when the empire seemed secure, Nicetas's history covers the increasingly alarming events up to and just beyond the fall of Constantinople to the Crusaders. Although toward the end Nicetas expresses understandable indignation at the Fourth Crusade and a deep sense of loss at its ravages, his judgment is complex throughout. He manages to bring court gossip and political commentary into a balanced narrative, combining the livelier features of Psellus's memoirs with Anna's more formal composition. His subject, like Psellus's, is a period of severe social and political decline; but unlike Psellus, Nicetas shows a clear recognition of what was happening.

Even if no other formal prose of the time equals the histories of Psellus, Anna, and Nicetas as literature, much of it shows similarly personal touches, usually somber ones. One example is the memoir that the eleventh-century official Cecaumenus addressed to his sons, telling them what he had learned in public life; the tumultuous politics that Psellus rather enjoyed his contemporary Cecaumenus found merely dangerous. Among the most original Byzantine works is the Lucianic dialogue *Timarion*, in which an anonymous twelfth-century satirist describes with rather black humor a visit a Byzantine of the time made to Hades and its inmates. Even the epistolographers of this period reveal much more than their predecessors about what their lives were like. Collections of letters survive from, among others, the scholar John Tzetzes, writing from Constantinople; Metropolitan Theophylact of Ochrid, writing from his see; and Nicetas's brother Michael Choniates, writing from his archbishopric at Athens. All three complain bitterly, Tzetzes about his poverty and the bishops about their rustication in the provinces.

These years also saw poets more memorable than any since the seventh-century George of Pisidia. The spirited poems of Christopher of Mytilene in the eleventh century were followed by the more famous compositions of Theodore Prodromus in the twelfth. Theodore composed elegant but fairly conventional court poetry, much of it a valuable historical source for the reigns of John II and Manuel. But Prodromus also broke with tradition by writing poems in a Greek close to the medieval spoken language, pretending in turn to be a henpecked husband, the head of an overlarge family, an ignorant monk, and a scholar, all of them poor and begging from the emperor. Theodore is known as well for a parody of Greek drama, *The Battle of the Cat and the Mice*, and one of the first verse romances written since pagan times, *Rhodanthe and Dosicles*, set in a dreamlike classical Greece.

Prodromus belonged to a whole circle of poets. Two of them wrote classical love stories in verse, which either inspired his or were inspired by it.[16] Around this time an anonymous poet appears to have put the *Digenes Acrites* into something like its present shape, with a delight in romantic love and family ties that suited twelfth-century taste. In its warlike and self-confident spirit, however, the poem belongs to the age before the Turkish conquests, and has its setting in the lost lands of the Anatolian plateau and the Euphrates valley, among the great Anatolian magnates of the old type. Most eleventh- and twelfth-century literature was more personal and sophisticated, intended for an urban readership and often for the imperial court in particular.

Like literature, art and architecture continued to develop luxuriantly throughout the period. The custom of building dynastic monasteries in Constantinople, begun by Romanus I with the modest Myrelaeum, led to more monumental and lavish foundations under Romanus III Argyrus, Michael IV the Paphlagonian, and Constantine IX Monomachus. Described by Psellus and others with fulsome superlatives, the monasteries of these three emperors in the capital have disappeared, except for the substructures of Constantine's Saint George of the Mangana. The Nea Monē ("New Monastery"), Constantine's somewhat smaller foundation on Chios, remains (Fig. 142). Not since Justinian I had emperors built consistently on such a scale. Models for these new and larger churches seem to have come partly from the earlier period and partly from Armenia and Georgia, the homeland of much of the Byzantine aristocracy.

Others followed the emperors' example in the provinces. The possessiveness that led to the practice of *charistikē* also inspired aristocrats to memorialize themselves and their families with fine religious buildings. The most imposing examples that survive are the monasteries of Daphne near Athens (Fig. 167) and Hosius Lucas near Thebes. Many more monasteries and parish churches, especially in Greece and Cappadocia, show how the prosperous Byzantines of the time made foundations in proportion to their means. By contrast, cathedrals, as the churches of bishops for which donors could not take full credit, were usually left as they had been, or simply patched up when necessary.[17]

Decorative arts kept pace with architecture. Impressive churches called for splendid decoration, which to the Byzantines meant marble and mosaic, besides the gold, silver, and silk accoutrements that have since been lost. The rich interior of Nea Monē shows even in its present state what imperial patronage could do (Figs. 27, 130). Its mosaics are

167. Monastery of Daphne, near Athens. (Photo: Courtesy of Charalambos Bouras)

executed in a stately and accomplished style, like the mosaics of its founder Constantine IX and his empress Zoë in Saint Sophia (Fig. 141). Comparable facility appears in the best manuscript illumination of the period, like a particularly skillful miniature of Michael VII and his empress Maria of Alania (Fig. 145). The latter two examples seem to have been so highly prized that in the mosaic Constantine had his own head and name substituted for those of its original subject, Zoë's first husband Romanus III, while in the miniature Michael VII was relabeled as Nicephorus III, Maria's second husband.[18] In spite of their high quality, these portraits are static, in traditional ceremonial fashion.

Some idea of Byzantine crown jewelry can be gathered from the gold and enamel part of the Holy Crown of Hungary, still a national treasure of that country (Fig. 168). It depicts Michael VII and the Hungarian king Géza I, the crown's original donor and recipient. Besides producing such state gifts for foreign rulers, in the eleventh century Byzantine masters seem to have traveled outside the empire more than before. Some went to Venice, where they helped plan and decorate its vast Church of Saint Mark, modeling it on the Church of the Holy Apostles in Constantinople (Fig. 159). Others went to Russia, where they worked on its great Cathedral of Saint Sophia in Kiev. The empire's artists and architects had become numerous enough to spare at home, and celebrated enough to be in demand abroad.

The invasions of the late eleventh century seem to have had only a temporary effect on Byzantine art, except in the regions that were actually lost. Financial difficulties interrupted imperial building of the most ambitious sort, but Alexius I's mother Anna Dalassena managed to erect the small but elegant Monastery of Christ Pantepoptes ("All-seeing") before 1100 (Fig. 148). Alexius himself built a new imperial palace at Blachernae on the Golden Horn, which became the emperors' main residence.[19] By the reign of John II, the Comneni were able to build the vast Monastery of Christ Pantocrator ("Ruler of All"), whose triple churches have loomed over Constantinople ever since (Fig. 151). Their

168. The Holy Crown of Hungary: *left*, front view, showing enamel plaques of Michael VII Ducas (r. 1067–78), his son Constantine Ducas, and Géza I, king of Hungary (r. 1074–77); *right*, detail of Michael VII. (Photos: From Patrick Kelleher, *The Holy Crown of Hungary* [Rome, 1951])

architecture is quite traditional, perhaps meant to reassure the beholder that nothing much had changed since the mid-eleventh century.

Twelfth-century figural art shows the more personal touch seen in the literature of the time. In comparison with the Saint Sophia mosaics of Constantine IX and Zoë, those of John II and Piroshka-Irene have a more individualized and natural appearance (Fig. 150). Even a monumental marble relief from Constantinople, of an emperor who is probably John II, looks more like a human being than its formalized composition might suggest (Fig. 164). Some later works verge on preciosity. The Byzantine mosaicists who worked in Norman Sicily produced mosaics for the cathedral of Cefalù that look elegant and spiritual but also slightly weak (Fig. 169). The delicacy of the angel and Virgin in a contemporary icon of the Annunciation from Mount Sinai is more appropriate to the subjects, but the folds of the robes and the tiny birds in the foreground seem overdone (Fig. 138). As Byzantine art became more

169. Apse mosaic of Christ from the cathedral, Cefalù. (Photo: Istituto Centrale per il Catalogo e la Documentazione, Rome)

innovative and self-conscious, it began to equate excellence with refinement, and refinement is easy to carry too far.

In western Europe, twelfth-century artists, writers, and scholars were also showing more appreciation for originality. But there the Church played a greater role in the revival of education, literature, and art, and nobles a smaller one. While the Byzantine church and monasteries enjoyed less independence than the papacy and western monastic orders, the Byzantine aristocracy was much better educated and more urbanized than the western feudal nobility. Yet despite the erudition of its ruling classes, Byzantium made no major improvements in agricultural, military, or architectural technology, as western Europe was doing at just this time. The Byzantines continued to think that theirs was the more accomplished civilization, and in intellectual terms they were right. Yet little of their new knowledge was of a kind that could help them to defend themselves.

WEALTH AND TRADE

Throughout these years, both Byzantium and the West were becoming richer, and trade between them increased steadily. The fairly abundant evidence almost all points the same way, even if modern scholars have taken some time to recognize the extent of the empire's prosperity.[20] Although western Europe was rapidly growing wealthier and more populous than it had been, right up to 1204 westerners who visited Byzantium marveled at the size and affluence of its cities, affirming that Constantinople was far bigger and richer than any western metropolis. The West's largest and wealthiest city was almost certainly Venice, which like some other Italian ports depended heavily on trade with the empire. The Italians needed trade with the Byzantines far more than the Byzantines needed trade with the Italians.

The steady natural increase in the Byzantine population that had begun in the late eighth century seems to have continued with scarcely any interruption through the eleventh and twelfth centuries. The obvious explanation for the dramatic spread of large landholding and the dwindling of peasant proprietors is demographic growth. As the population grew, land came to be in shorter supply and higher demand, and the rich naturally competed for it more successfully than the poor. As peasants divided their plots among more numerous children, they became poorer, and needed to sell their land more often. As agricultural labor became more abundant, its value declined, and peasants had to accept whatever terms landlords gave them. Records from Mount Athos clearly document such rural population growth in the region east of Thessalonica.[21] Both peasants and aristocrats seem to have had large families. We also hear of more illegitimate children than before, at least at the highest social levels.

The Turkish conquests, though they cost the empire a number of subjects in Asia Minor, Armenia, and Syria, also pushed many refugees into the regions that remained Byzantine. The totals can only be estimated—and no better than usual, since the more abundant evidence for the period includes only the most scattered population statistics. The set of estimates used in earlier chapters indicates that the empire had some 12 million people in 1025 and some 5 million just before the reconquest of Anatolia started in 1097. Even on this reckoning, the total would have risen to some 8 million in 1143 after the reconquests of Alexius I and John II, and would still have been over 7 million on the eve of the Fourth Crusade. But these estimates depend on an apparently exaggerated view of the disruption caused by the Turks, and more likely estimates would be 10 million in 1143 and 9 million around 1200.[22] In any case, except during the few years when the Turks occupied almost all of Anatolia, Byzantium kept control over most of its subjects. The total must have come to at least as many as the empire had had when its demographic recovery began in the eighth century.

Constantinople appears to have spread over almost as much of its walled area as at its height under Justinian I, a fact that suggests an estimate of some 300,000 inhabitants around 1200.[23] The city was reckoned at 400,000 or more by a leader of the Fourth Crusade who, even after seeing Venice, with a population of around 100,000, found the Byzantine capital of staggering size.[24] In a city this big, the reported 10,000 Venetian merchants resident in 1171 could be jailed or expelled without being able to offer serious resistance, or making much difference when they were gone. If the capital's population neared its sixth-century zenith, and other Byzantine cities had grown roughly apace, the conclusion seems to follow that the empire was even more urbanized in the twelfth century than six hundred years before, when it had had about three times as much territory and many more subjects. Urbanization should also have progressed since 1025, when the empire had about twice as much land and appreciably more people.

170. Byzantine cities of the northern Aegean, the Bosporus, and the Sea of Marmara on the twelfth-century map of al-Idrīsī (Parisinus arabicus 2221). The map is oriented in the usual fashion of medieval Arabs so as to put north at the bottom and south at the top. (Photo: Bibliothèque Nationale, Paris)

The sources, while supplying few statistics, give a good deal of evidence that cities had become larger and more prosperous. By the twelfth century, the Arab geographer al-Idrīsī and the Jewish traveler Benjamin of Tudela, listing only places on certain routes, between them call more than two dozen Byzantine cities large, populous, rich in trade, or some combination of the three. Idrīsī gives no figures. Benjamin gives informed estimates, but only for Jews, evidently meaning adult males. His highest numbers are 2,500 for Constantinople, 2,000 for Thebes, 500 for Thessalonica, 400 for Halmyrus, Rhaedestus, Chios, and Rhodes, and 300 for Corinth and Samos.[25]

If we multiply Benjamin's figures by four to arrive at the total number of Jews, then by three on the assumption that no more than a third of each city was Jewish, we have a minimum figure of 24,000 for Thebes, and 3,600 to 4,800 for the places with 300 to 400 Jews. Such minimums may be much smaller than the actual figures, since Constantinople surely had far more than 30,000 people and Thessalonica far more than 6,000.

Although in 1219 the population of the port of Lampsacus is recorded at just 163 adult males, for a total of around 650 people, this was an insignificant town that neither Benjamin nor Idrīsī mentions, even though it lay on a route that both describe.[26] Callipolis, just across the Hellespont from Lampsacus, is called large and populous by Idrīsī, and is said by Benjamin to have had 200 Jews.[27] Yet not even Callipolis was known as one of the empire's larger cities.

The impression given by the sources is that most towns grew during the eleventh and twelfth centuries, until each region of the empire had one or more cities of some size. The growth was evidently stronger in the less urbanized Balkans than in Asia Minor.[28] The central location of Thessalonica made it the real metropolis of the Balkans, and though it remained considerably smaller than Constantinople it seems to have grown at least as fast. Even Constantinopolitans thought of it as a real city and did business at its great annual fair. At this time it should have reached something like 150,000 people, with its sack in 1185 causing only a temporary decrease. After Thessalonica the size of cities seems to have dropped off a good deal. Perhaps the best guess for third place is Nicaea, which like several other regional metropolises would have had a population in the range between 30,000 and 100,000. Besides Nicaea for the Opsician Theme, these were apparently Smyrna for the Thracesian Theme, Adrianople for Thrace, and Thebes for southern Greece, with perhaps Trebizond for the northern coast of Anatolia and Attalia for the southern.[29]

Additional towns in the more populous of these regions must have had about 10,000 to 30,000 people. Such were probably Philadelphia and Ephesus for the Thracesians, Philippopolis and Rhaedestus for Thrace, Prusa and Nicomedia for the Opsician, Halmyrus for northern Greece, and Athens, Corinth, Nauplia, and Patras for southern Greece, which seems to have been particularly prosperous. The main cities of some lesser regions should also have belonged to this group: Heraclea Pontica for Paphlagonia, Chandax and Rhodes for the Aegean islands, Arta for Epirus. A few more towns of over 10,000 may have existed, but probably not in the still backward northern Balkans, where even Ochrid and Belgrade seem to have been smaller. Yet even many small towns were much bigger than they had been.

Agricultural production seems to have expanded satisfactorily in this period, with new land being brought under cultivation to meet the demand for more food. Despite the growth of the whole population and especially of cities that imported food, famines were rare. That of 1032 to 1037 apparently resulted from a combination of locusts and freakish weather. Although the exceptional disruptions of the Turkish invasion caused another famine around 1076, on the whole the empire seems to have managed to feed its many refugees. By the twelfth century Greece was exporting grain, meat, and wine to Italy. The northern Balkans and the Aegean islands appear to have raised enough sheep, cattle, swine, and poultry to replace the products of the lost Anatolian plateau.[30]

Unlike some cities before the seventh century, the cities of this time received no government subsidies worth mentioning and had to earn enough to buy their own food. Their principal products were probably textiles. Benjamin of Tudela describes weaving as the trade of many Jews, and notes that Thebes was the center of the silk industry in Greece.[31] Urban manufactures also included pottery, glass, metalwork, bricks, furniture, manuscripts, and various other objects, some of high artistic

171. Twelfth-century Byzantine ceramic plate, showing a griffin attacking a hare. (Photo: Dumbarton Oaks, Washington, D.C., copyright 1996)

quality.[32] Constantinople continued to make products of all kinds, including the empire's finest luxury goods. As always, however, trade was bigger business in Constantinople than manufacturing. In the eleventh century enough men made money from trade in the capital to buy the senatorial ranks that scandalized the landholding aristocracy.

Although plainly Italians were doing a brisk business trading with the empire, especially after Alexius I exempted Venetians from trade duties in 1082, our western sources' few references to Byzantine merchants are no proof that such merchants were few.[33] If they had been, the measures taken against Italians by John II, Manuel, and Andronicus I would have severely disrupted the Byzantine economy; yet no source suggests that anything of the sort occurred. The trade duties of a tenth of the value of merchandise that natives had to pay were not so crushing a burden as to outweigh local connections and familiarity with local conditions. Byzantine businessmen must have dominated the empire's internal trade, particularly away from the coasts, where Italians seldom ventured but most Byzantines lived. Byzantine merchants still had a large share of trade with the Muslims in the eleventh century, and are unlikely to have lost all of it in the twelfth.[34] Nonetheless, the Byzantine government's perverse policy of reverse protectionism, charging most Italian traders lower duties than natives, obviously hurt native traders. What the trade concessions to Italians did not do was decrease state revenue appreciably.

Arriving at an absolute estimate of the budget in this period is difficult, even though scattered statistics are more common than before. The military payroll, always the largest single item, can no longer be estimated by multiplying the number of soldiers by the average rate of pay, not only because neither number is known, but because the number of soldiers and their pay varied widely, especially after many men received pronoia grants. Those grants, and others given to members of the imperial family, diminished the revenues that passed through the capital but should be included in the total, because they met state expenditures and the state kept track of them. Yet the budget cannot be said to have included outright tax exemptions, which seem to have become more common at this time. The fluctuating value of the coinage is also a problem in the later eleventh century, though less so after 1092, when the hyperpyron was stabilized at about seven-eighths of the value of the old nomisma.

All this having been said, if the empire had a population of about 12 million and revenues of about 5.9 million nomismata in 1025, there is no obvious reason why the empire of 1150, with a population perhaps five-sixths that of 1025, should have had revenues much less than five-sixths of the earlier figure. If so, the later total would have been some 4.9 million old nomismata, or some 5.6 million new hyperpyra. Although a good deal of this would never have reached Constantinople, most of it must have, to judge from the sums that the government could pay out right up to the Fourth Crusade. Manuel reportedly spent 2.16 million hyperpyra on his schemes against the Normans of Sicily. He also spent 150,000 hyperpyra in 1158 on the marriage of his niece Theodora to Baldwin III of Jerusalem, including her dowry. Under Isaac II the campaign pay of the army that fought the Normans in 1185 was 288,000 hyperpyra.[35] Even with the empire at its poorest in 1203, Alexius IV managed to pay 440,000 hyperpyra to the Crusaders and Venetians, since the next year they demanded only 360,000 as the balance due on the 800,000 hyperpyra they had been promised.

The great bulk of the revenue continued to come from the land. In 1168 Benjamin of Tudela was apparently told that the trade duties of Constantinople, with the rents of state markets and shops, came to a mere 20,000 hyperpyra a year.[36] The loss to the treasury caused by the exemptions from trade duties granted to the Italians, which were in effect at the time of Benjamin's visit, has been calculated at under 50,000 hyperpyra a year.[37] In 1219 the tiny port of Lampsacus yielded 1,671¼ hyperpyra, all but 51¼ from agriculture.[38] In the twelfth century the total revenue of Corcyra is said to have been 108,000 hyperpyra, while a figure for the revenue of Cyprus of about 50,000 hyperpyra seems to represent only the surplus forwarded to the capital.[39] The revenue of Corcyra, doubtless drawn overwhelmingly from land taxes, would have been around a fiftieth of the revenue of 5.6 million hyperpyra estimated for the whole empire. For all its military and political troubles, Byzantium remained rich until 1204, when its wealth still dazzled and tempted the Crusaders.

Yet even if the empire had not fallen victim to the Fourth Crusade, by 1200 its problems of regional separatism, central maladministration, military weakness, and diplomatic ineptitude were acute. Alexius I, John II, and Manuel had managed to control their refractory magnates, merchants, and bureaucrats and to keep their foreign enemies at bay by dint of family solidarity and strong leadership. Toward the end of the twelfth century, as during most of the eleventh, the emperors were unequal to their tasks. Their incapacity was not entirely fortuitous, because some of their officials wanted inadequate emperors on the throne. Nonetheless,

without the Fourth Crusade, the realization that continuing chaos was
bad for almost everyone would probably have given a capable ruler the
chance to replace the Angeli, and to restore something like the equilibrium of the days of the Comneni. Until 1204 Byzantium always had the
makings of a great economic and military power, however badly it was
employing them.

When Constantinople fell, matters became at once vastly worse. Much
wealth was destroyed or stolen in the city, and Byzantine impotence
became patent. The Crusaders and Venetians grew more powerful, and
Bulgarians, Serbs, Turks, and separatist rebels seized their shares of the
spoils. Worst of all, Byzantium lost its central government, which had
organized a successful resistance to its enemies so many times before.
Most of the provinces were as yet unconquered, and they had supplied
much the largest part of the Byzantines' wealth; but they were already
falling into the hands of regional potentates, and even a generally recognized leader would have found them hard to marshal against the invaders. As it was, with Alexius III discredited, no one had a strong claim
to the succession, and none of the separatists had more than local authority. How much of what had been the empire would remain under
Byzantine rule, or even if any would, was very much in doubt.

PART SIX

The Failed Restoration

172. Interior of the Church of the Virgin Paregoretissa ("Comforter") at Arta, showing Christ Pantocrator in the dome. (Photo: From Cyril Mango, *Byzantine Architecture* [New York, 1976])

CHAPTER TWENTY-TWO

The Successor States,
1204–1261

The Fourth Crusade left the Byzantine world in utter confusion. Since the empire had never been a Greek national state and violent successions were nothing new, at first many provincials failed to see that what had happened was a foreign conquest, and not a somewhat irregular revolution. The Crusaders promptly chose an emperor who was to assume control over the Byzantine church, bureaucracy, and provinces as the successor of Alexius IV. Although the better-informed Byzantines and Venetians realized that the old empire was gone, not even they knew quite what was going to take its place.

In March 1204, before the Crusaders and Venetians made their final assault, they had agreed to let a college of six Crusaders and six Venetians choose a new emperor. The emperor elected was to receive a quarter of both Constantinople and the empire as his domain. The forces of the Crusaders and the Venetians would each receive half of the remainder to hold 25 fiefs in vassalage to the emperor. If a Crusader was elected emperor, as everyone assumed would happen, a Venetian was to be patriarch of Constantinople. After taking the city, but apparently before electing an emperor, the Crusaders and Venetians divided the land among themselves. In broad outline, the partition put the imperial domain in Asia Minor and some of Thrace, the crusader fiefs in Greece, and the Venetian fiefs in the islands, some ports, and Epirus.[1]

In May the electors did choose a Crusader emperor, but not Marquis Boniface of Montferrat, who had led the Crusade and expected to be elected. Boniface had already moved into the Great Palace, attracted some Byzantine supporters, and arranged to marry Isaac II's widow Margaret-Maria. He had earlier family connections with both the Angeli and the Comneni, and was a man of energy and ability. But the Venetians wanted an emperor who would be easier to control, and joined with some French and German Crusaders to outvote Boniface's Italian followers. They selected the thirty-one-year-old Count Baldwin of Flanders, who was duly crowned.

THE EMERGENCE OF SUCCESSORS

At first Baldwin, whom Byzantines called the Latin emperor, held only Constantinople and its immediate hinterland. The rest of the empire was subject partly to its bewildered Byzantine governors, and partly to a bewildering crew of rebels and deposed emperors. Alexius V reigned at Tzurulum in eastern Thrace. The previously deposed Alexius III was at Mosynopolis, from which he controlled western Thrace and the region of Thessalonica. Kaloyan of Bulgaria ruled to the north of the two Alexiuses. The rebel magnate Leo Sgurus held the parts of Greece around Nauplia, Corinth, and Thebes. Crete was apparently held by the men of Boniface of Montferrat, whom Alexius IV seems to have granted it in pronoia during his brief reign.

Rhodes was under another Byzantine magnate, Leo Gabalas. Attalia had been seized by the Italian condottiere Aldobrandini. Three more magnates held the Meander valley: Sabas Asidenus around Priene, the old rebel Theodore Mangaphas around Philadelphia, and in the east Manuel Maurozomes, who had given refuge to the fugitive sultan Kaykhusraw. Northwestern Anatolia was held by Theodore Lascaris, a son-in-law and nominal partisan of Alexius III. The Pontus had just fallen to David and Alexius Comnenus, grandsons of the emperor Andronicus who had been lynched nineteen years before. Alexius Comnenus now proclaimed himself Byzantine emperor at Trebizond.

The Byzantine resistance therefore included three men who claimed to be emperor, Alexius III, Alexius V, and Alexius of Trebizond. Of these Alexius III seemed the most plausible. He certainly hoped to retake Constantinople, and with his son-in-law Theodore Lascaris he could claim footholds in both the Balkans and Asia Minor. But he had been a disappointing ruler and had fled from the Crusaders early on. Alexius V had fled later, but after accomplishing even less. Alexius of Trebizond, descended from a widely detested usurper, was far away in a peripheral province. Although Kaloyan of Bulgaria also called himself emperor and was thinking of bigger things, few Byzantines thought of him as one of

173. Four ancient bronze horses looted from the Hippodrome, Constantinople, in their position on the facade of the Cathedral of San Marco, Venice (cf. Fig. 159). (Photo: Osvaldo Böhm)

themselves. The rebel magnates had purely local ambitions. Byzantium appeared to be smashed beyond repair.

By the same token, the Latin emperor Baldwin had a hard task to create a Latin empire that would be nearly comparable to the Byzantine one his men had wrecked. The Latins had already ruined their new capital by plundering it and giving much of the booty to Venice. The Venetian doge Enrico Dandolo was not even Baldwin's vassal, though many other Venetians were. Boniface of Montferrat, disappointed at losing the imperial election to Baldwin, remained suspicious of him, though Boniface was consoled with the promise of a vassal kingdom around Thessalonica, then held by Alexius III. After first welcoming the Latin capture of Constantinople as a means of reuniting the Church, Pope Innocent discovered how brutal the conquest had been, and condemned the sack of the city and the Crusaders' plundering of Byzantine church property.

Once elected, Baldwin found himself one of many adventurers, and only a little stronger than the others. That summer he attacked his most formidable Byzantine enemies, the deposed emperors Alexius III and Alexius V. Fleeing west, Alexius V very reasonably sought an alliance with Alexius III, whose deposer he had after all deposed. Alexius III accepted the offer and married his daughter Eudocia to Alexius V, then had his new ally blinded. This stupid act threw away the best chance for an early and effective Byzantine resistance to the Latins. As Baldwin marched to Mosynopolis, Alexius III retreated before him.

But the Crusaders could be as pigheaded as the Byzantines. The Latin emperor insisted on marching to Thessalonica, ignoring the protests of Boniface, whose kingdom it was supposed to be. Boniface retaliated by attacking Baldwin's men around Adrianople. This dangerous dispute was hastily arbitrated by the crusader barons and the Venetians. Boniface agreed to leave Baldwin's domain and to sell Venice his holdings in Crete for a thousand marks, while Baldwin let Boniface occupy Thessalonica and help the Crusaders claim their fiefs in Greece. Toward the end of the summer, the confused Thessalonians received Boniface as their king.

Among the Byzantines accompanying Boniface was Michael Ducas, the cousin of Alexius III who had rebelled against him in 1200. In early autumn, however, Michael left for Epirus to answer an appeal from a local governor related to him. Arriving to find his relative dead, Michael stayed at Arta to organize Byzantine resistance in Epirus. Mountainous Epirus, though not rich, was easy to defend against the Latins, and Michael, though a bastard, had his connection with the Angelus dynasty in his favor, and a driving ambition at a time when many others were uncertain what to do next.

Meanwhile Alexius III retreated to Greece, where he joined forces with the rebel magnate Leo Sgurus. Sgurus married Alexius's daughter Eudocia, undeterred by Alexius's treatment of her previous husband Alexius V. Alexius V was now dead, having been captured after his blinding and killed by the emperor Baldwin. Before the Byzantine alliance between the deposed emperor and the rebel magnate had taken definite shape, King Boniface of Thessalonica advanced into Greece. He captured Alexius III and drove Sgurus into the Peloponnesus, besieging him in the Acrocorinth, Corinth's almost impregnable upper town. Thus the two former Byzantine emperors, Alexius III and Alexius V, were put out of contention.

While Boniface expanded his vassal Kingdom of Thessalonica, the emperor Baldwin took over his designated holdings in Thrace and prepared to claim his Anatolian domains from Theodore Lascaris. Theodore, apparently still professing loyalty to his father-in-law Alexius III, had organized an army in the northwest. But Theodore had plenty of Byzantine rivals to his rear. The rebel magnates remained active in the south, while the self-proclaimed emperor Alexius of Trebizond had sent his brother David with an army that captured coastal Paphlagonia. Against this divided Byzantine opposition, the Latins crossed the Hellespont and defeated Lascaris near Poemanenum, south of the Sea of Marmara. They went on to besiege Lascaris's city of Prusa.

The Latins were apparently carrying everything before them. Michael Ducas of Epirus submitted to Pope Innocent to protect his fledgling state. Kaloyan of Bulgaria also made an agreement with the pope, accepting the authority of the papacy in return for a royal crown from Rome. As a nominal member of the western church, Kaloyan then offered an alliance to the Latin emperor Baldwin. But Baldwin refused, annoyed that Kaloyan had been taking border territory in Thrace.

The Crusaders seemed to need no allies. In early 1205 Baldwin's brother Henry led reinforcements into Asia Minor, captured Adramyttium, and defeated the magnate Theodore Mangaphas. In the Balkans King Boniface of Thessalonica conquered Euboea, central Greece, and most of the eastern Peloponnesus, where he continued besieging Sgurus in the Acrocorinth. The western Peloponnesus fell to some Crusaders recently arrived from Syria, who defeated an army apparently brought from Epirus by Michael Ducas.[2]

Rebuffed by the emperor Baldwin, Kaloyan of Bulgaria incited the Byzantines in Latin Thrace to revolt. They expelled the Latins from Adrianople and several other towns. Baldwin, with whatever troops his brother had not taken to Asia Minor, marched on Adrianople and besieged it. In April Kaloyan arrived with his army and attacked the Latin emperor. The Bulgarians routed the overconfident and outnumbered Latins, killing many of them and capturing Baldwin himself. The aged doge Dandolo died soon afterward. After so much rapid success, suddenly the Latin Empire seemed on the verge of collapse.

Baldwin's brother Henry hurried back to Constantinople to assume the regency of the Latin Empire and call for help from the West. He had to abandon practically all his conquests in Anatolia to Theodore Lascaris. Kaloyan, who already held most of Thrace, turned on the Kingdom of Thessalonica and sacked Serres before King Boniface could arrive from the Peloponnesus. But Kaloyan made the mistake of mistreating and fighting his Byzantine allies, and the Latins profited by recapturing some of Thrace. Since Kaloyan failed to exploit his victory, the main beneficiary of the Latin rout was Theodore Lascaris. The Latins had already broken the power of one of his rivals, Theodore Mangaphas, whom Lascaris soon took prisoner. When Alexius of Trebizond's brother

174. View of Nicaea (modern Iznik) from the east, showing the walls running along the edge of the town and Lake Ascania in the background. (Photo: Irina Andreescu-Treadgold)

David sent an army against Theodore, Lascaris defeated it and captured its commander. Probably after this victory, Theodore proclaimed himself Byzantine emperor at Nicaea.[3]

Now that the new emperor of Nicaea had defeated the forces of Alexius of Trebizond, while Alexius III was Boniface's captive, Theodore had as good a claim as anyone to the imperial title. Aged about thirty-one, with no less ability than his rivals and more vision, Theodore had already built up a functioning successor state in northwestern Anatolia from next to nothing. Later in 1205 the Nicene emperor defeated his two competitors to the south, Sabas Asidenus and Manuel Maurozomes. By early 1206 Theodore made peace with Maurozomes, who kept only the border forts of Chonae and Laodicea as a vassal of the recently restored sultan Kaykhusraw. Theodore tried to secure his claim as the leading Byzantine pretender by inviting the exiled patriarch of Constantinople John to leave the rebel-held part of Thrace for Nicaea. But the patriarch would not desert his embattled countrymen, and in any case died in spring 1206.

The same spring Kaloyan raided Thrace with a ferocity that drove the Byzantine rebels into the arms of the Latin regent Henry. The rebels surrendered Adrianople to Theodore Branas, a Byzantine general in Henry's service, and allowed Henry and his men to reoccupy most of Thrace. Having learned that his brother Baldwin had died in Bulgarian captivity, Henry had himself crowned Latin emperor. Although the Latin Empire he inherited was gravely weakened, he was a much more gifted leader than his brother and set about regaining what had been lost.

Henry tried to restrain Theodore Lascaris of Nicaea by allying with David Comnenus, the last Byzantine rival bordering on Theodore's territory. The Nicene emperor was marching on David's city of Heraclea Pontica when the Latins attacked him from the rear, and he had to turn back to chase them off. In the winter the Latins invaded Theodore's lands again, capturing Nicomedia and Cyzicus from him. He retaliated by persuading Kaloyan to attack Latin Thrace. In spring 1207 Henry had to withdraw troops from Anatolia to rescue Adrianople from the Bulgarians. To obtain a badly needed truce from Theodore, the Latin emperor agreed to return Nicomedia and Cyzicus to him.

By this time all the surviving combatants were becoming exhausted. The Latins seemed to have Kaloyan at bay, until the Bulgarians ambushed and killed Boniface of Thessalonica in late summer. Kaloyan was besieging Thessalonica when he too suddenly died in the early autumn. Since both Boniface and Kaloyan left only underage sons, a group of rebellious barons took over Thessalonica, and Kaloyan's nephew Boril usurped the Bulgarian throne. Both Bulgaria and Thessalonica were incapacitated.

By early 1208 the major players eliminated some minor ones from the game and made matters a little less chaotic. Leo Sgurus, cornered on the Acrocorinth by the Latins, committed suicide by riding his horse off a cliff. The sultan Kaykhusraw took Attalia from the freebooter Aldobrandini. Venice and its vassals finished conquering most of the islands except Crete, which had been seized by the Genoese. Theodore Lascaris chose a patriarch, nominally of Constantinople but resident at Nicaea, who crowned him emperor, nominally of the Byzantine Empire but at Nicaea for the present.

That summer the Latin emperor Henry crushed a raid by Boril of Bulgaria, secured Thrace, and took Philippopolis. Henry then marched against the rebel barons of Thessalonica. In the first part of 1209 he suppressed their rebellion by a combination of diplomacy and warfare, installed his brother Eustace at Thessalonica as regent for Boniface's infant son, and received the homage of the Latin vassals throughout Greece. To avoid trouble with the resurgent Latins, Michael Ducas of Epirus married his daughter to Eustace and made a formal submission to Henry.

175. View of Trebizond (modern Trabzon) from the east, showing the walls and the Black Sea in the background. (Photo: C. Mango, Dumbarton Oaks, Washington, D.C., copyright 1996)

After several years of anarchy, the principal powers within former Byzantine territory had established themselves. Except for Genoese Crete, independent Rhodes, and Turkish Attalia, nearly all the lands that had been Byzantine around 1200 were in the hands of four rulers.[4] The emperor of Nicaea Theodore ruled western Anatolia. The emperor of Trebizond Alexius held the Crimea and the northern Anatolian coast, including Paphlagonia under his brother David. Michael Ducas, content to do without a title, ruled Epirus. The remainder of Greece and almost all of Thrace were subject to the Latin emperor Henry and his vassals, who had subdued the Bulgarians and made the Latin Empire the leading state in the region. Though the three main Byzantine successes held about half of what had been Byzantine territory, they remained rivals.

THE RISE OF EPIRUS

The balance of power was therefore unstable. After his successes in Greece, the Latin emperor Henry returned to fighting Theodore's Empire of Nicaea. Henry tried to catch his adversary in a vise by making an alliance with the sultan Kaykhusraw, whose lands lay on the other side of Nicaea. Henry's new vassal Michael Ducas of Epirus paid the Latins a ransom for his cousin, the deposed emperor Alexius III, then sent him to Kaykhusraw, who agreed to help him take Nicaea. Michael's main aim was presumably to harm Theodore, who as the leading Byzantine pretender was Michael's competitor. Michael cannot have cared much about Alexius, against whom he had rebelled nine years before, or about the Latins, whom he attacked almost immediately.[5] Never faithful for long to any ally, Michael caused as much mischief as possible, trusting that Epirus was more defensible than his rivals' domains.

Michael therefore invaded the Kingdom of Thessalonica, beginning with Thessaly on their shared border. The pope excommunicated him, ending his nominal adherence to the western church, and the emperor Henry marched against him in 1210. Michael protected his rear by accepting the suzerainty of the Venetians, who held Dyrrhachium and claimed Epirus under the partition treaty of 1204. But the Venetians were no more interested in helping Michael than he was in helping them. While the Venetians concentrated on capturing Crete from the Genoese, Henry drove Michael out of Thessaly and forced him to become a Latin vassal again.

To balance Henry's alliance with Kaykhusraw, Theodore of Nicaea allied himself with Boril of Bulgaria. Thus Bulgaria, the Latin Empire, the Nicene Empire, and the Sultanate of Iconium were all hostile to their neighbors but allied with their neighbors' neighbors. Boril attacked Henry's vassal Kingdom of Thessalonica, but Henry defeated him. Theodore prepared a fleet to attack Constantinople, but Kaykhusraw attacked him, accompanied by the persistent Alexius III. The Nicene emperor managed to muster two thousand men, eight hundred of them Latin mercenaries, and in late spring 1211, near Antioch on the Meander, won a decisive victory, killing Kaykhusraw and capturing Alexius III. This battle let Theodore force a peace on Kaykhusraw's son and successor Kaykā'ūs. Alexius III lived out his days in a monastery at Nicaea.

That fall, however, when the triumphant Theodore was about to attack the Latins, Henry anticipated him by invading across the Hellespont. In a battle near the mouth of the Rhyndacus River, Henry defeated Theodore. The Latin emperor occupied the northwestern corner of Anatolia, and only had to stop because he ran out of men to garrison his conquests. Since Theodore was also short of men, the two emperors made peace, probably in 1212. The Latin Empire had gained the coast from

Adramyttium to Nicomedia, with a hinterland extending to Achyraüs, but these new possessions were still precarious, because the Empire of Nicaea held everything to the south of them.

While the other powers fought in the East, Michael of Epirus made good use of his time, and seems to have taken western Thessaly from the Kingdom of Thessalonica. Having repudiated Venetian suzerainty, he captured Venetian Dyrrhachium. His growing power began to unsettle his neighbors. In 1213 a papal legate negotiated an alliance between Bulgaria, which was still nominally obedient to the pope, and the Latin Empire. But the new allies Boril and Henry fought not Michael but the Serbs, without success. Michael went on to conquer Corcyra from the Venetians in 1214.

Theodore of Nicaea, after recovering from his defeat by the Latins, attacked David Comnenus, the brother of Alexius of Trebizond. Theodore took David's capital of Pontic Heraclea and forced him to flee to Sinope, where the sultan Kaykā'ūs fell upon David, killed him, and took the city. When Alexius of Trebizond arrived and recaptured Sinope, he was himself captured outside the walls. To regain his liberty, Alexius had to surrender the city and become the sultan's vassal. While Turkish possession of Sinope screened the Empire of Trebizond from further attacks by Nicaea, henceforth Alexius's claim to be Byzantine emperor rang hollow, and the Empire of Trebizond ceased to be of more than local importance.

Around the beginning of 1215 Michael of Epirus was assassinated, after a career characterized by few scruples or pretensions but some notable achievements. The successor to Michael's nameless throne was not his young son but his half-brother Theodore Ducas, who unlike Michael and his son was of legitimate birth. Probably in his early thirties, Theodore of Epirus was as unscrupulous as his brother and even more energetic. He taxed his subjects harshly and campaigned tirelessly. From the first, he seems to have had his eye on the great city of Thessalonica, which if added to his state in Epirus could make it a major power. Starting with the intervening territory, Theodore Ducas soon attacked the Bulgarians, from whom he conquered Ochrid and the upper Axius valley. The Latin emperor Henry marched against Ducas, but died at Thessalonica in spring 1216.

Although Henry had marshaled the Latin Empire's limited resources with consummate skill, he left no son or heir apparent. After an interval, the Latin barons elected the husband of his sister Yolanda, Peter of Courtenay, who was then in France. Pursuing the war with Epirus that his predecessor had begun, Peter gathered an army and landed near Dyr-rhachium in 1217, while sending his pregnant wife to Constantinople by ship. But Peter fell into an ambush set by Theodore Ducas. Theodore captured almost the whole Latin force and probably killed Peter, since the emperor was never heard of again and everyone presumed him dead. Next Theodore marched south and finished conquering Thessaly from the Latins.

In Constantinople Peter's presumptive widow Yolanda ruled as empress, but she and her empire were far from secure. She lost her last ally when Boril of Bulgaria was overthrown in 1218. Fortunately for her, in 1219 Theodore of Nicaea agreed to extend the prevailing truce and to marry her daughter. Later that year Yolanda died. Because her eldest son refused the uncomfortable Latin throne, the succession passed to her second son Robert of Courtenay. Young and indecisive, Robert arrived in Constantinople, by way of Bulgaria, only in 1221.

Late that autumn Theodore Lascaris of Nicaea died, and since he had no son was succeeded by his son-in-law John Ducas Vatatzes, aged twenty-nine.[6] Although Vatatzes had considerable talent as a ruler and commander, his right to the throne was disputed by two of Lascaris's brothers. He found it best to make his headquarters in the south at Nymphaeum, out of the Latins' way. Early the next year came the death of the last of the original successors, Alexius Comnenus of Trebizond, whose self-proclaimed empire had become an isolated vassal of the Seljuks. The most ambitious Byzantine ruler seemed to be Theodore Ducas of Epirus.

Theodore had already conquered Serres and practically all of the Kingdom of Thessalonica but Thessalonica itself. Without claiming the title of emperor for himself as yet, he refused to recognize the imperial titles of Nicaea or Trebizond, or the ecclesiastical authority of the patriarch at Nicaea. As Theodore besieged Thessalonica, its desperate Latins kept calling for aid from Constantinople. In 1224 the dithering Latin emperor Robert divided his forces, sending some to help the Lascaris brothers against John Vatatzes of Nicaea, and others to retake Serres from Theodore and relieve Thessalonica. But the Latins abandoned the siege of Serres on learning that Vatatzes had defeated their comrades and overrun most of Latin Anatolia, and near the end of the year the Latins of Thessalonica surrendered to Theodore Ducas. Now Theodore had the second city of the old Byzantine Empire in his possession, and somewhat more territory than the emperor of Nicaea.

Theodore Ducas's conquest of Thessalonica spurred John Vatatzes of

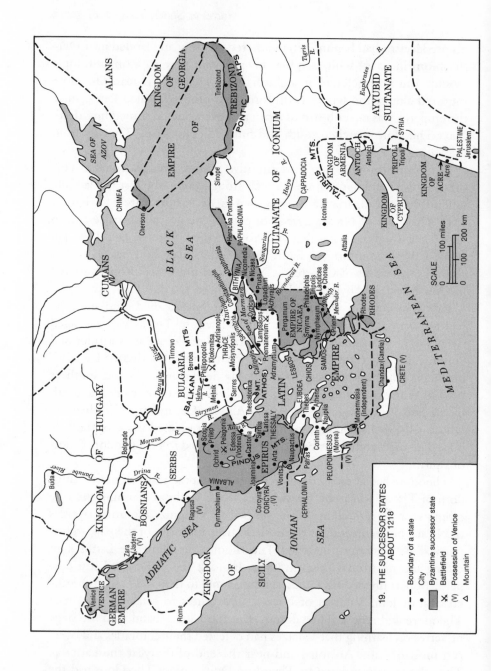

ALANS

SEA OF
AZOV

CRIMEA

Cherson

BLACK   SEA

CUMANS

KINGDOM OF GEORGIA

EMPIRE OF

TREBIZOND

Trebizond

PONTIC   ALPS

Sinope

Heraclea Pontica

PAPHLAGONIA

Daphnusia

BITHYNIA

Nicomedia

Prusa

SULTANATE   OF   ICONIUM

Halys R.

CAPPADOCIA

Iconium

Sangarius R.

TAURUS MTS.

KINGDOM OF ARMENIA

ANTIOCH

Antioch

AYYUBID SULTANATE

Tigris R.

Euphrates R.

PALESTINE

SYRIA

TRIPOLI

Tripoli

Jerusalem

KINGDOM OF ACRE

Acre

KINGDOM OF CYPRUS

Rhyndacus R.

Pergamum

EMPIRE OF NICAEA

Smyrna

Nymphaeum

SAMOS

Priene

Meander R.

Philadelphia

Laodicea

Chonae

Tripolis

Antioch

RHODES

Rhodes

MEDITERRANEAN   SEA

Attalia

SCALE

0   100 miles

0   100   200 km

Timovo

BULGARIA

Beroea

Philippopolis

BALKAN MTS.

Klokotnitsa

Adrianople

THRACE

Mosynopolis

Constantinople

Izmid

Cyzicus

Sea of Marmara

Selymbria

Lampsacus

Callipolis

Lopadium

Achyraïs

Poemanenum

Pergamum

Adramyttium

LESBOS

Nicaea

Danube River

Belgrade

Morava R.

Drina R.

SERBS

BOSNIANS

KINGDOM OF HUNGARY

Buda

Danube River

Hebrus R.

Melnik

Serres

Strymon R.

MT. ATHOS

Thessalonica

THESSALY

Larissa

ARTA MTS.

EPIRUS

Arta

Vonitsa

Naupactus

Skopje

Prilep

Pelagonia

Ochrid

Edessa (Vodena)

Castoria

Serbia

PINDUS

ALBANIA

Ioannina

Corcyra

CORCYRA

Dyrrhachium

CEPHALONIA

IONIAN   SEA

Ragusa (V)

Zara (Jadera) (V)

Venice

VENICE

GERMAN EMPIRE

Rome

KINGDOM OF SICILY

ADRIATIC   SEA

EUBOEA

CHIOS

Thebes

Athens

Corinth

Nauplia

Patras

PELOPONNESUS (Moera) (V)

Monemvasia (independent)

Chandax (Candia)

CRETE (V)

LATIN

EMPIRE

19.   THE SUCCESSOR STATES
      ABOUT 1218

- - -   Boundary of a state
  •   City
  ▨   Byzantine successor state
  ⚔   Battlefield
  (V)   Possession of Venice
  △   Mountain

Nicaea to win more victories of his own against the Latins. He finished occupying their Anatolian lands west of Nicomedia, and began building the fleet he would need for a serious attempt on Constantinople. Impressed by John's efforts, early in 1225 the Byzantines of Adrianople invited him to take over their city. John sent a force that expelled the Latins and occupied the land from the Hellespont to Adrianople, winning himself a beachhead in Europe.

A few months later, however, Theodore Ducas arrived with a much larger army that had already captured western Thrace. Theodore's victories persuaded John's forces to hand over Adrianople and their part of Thrace without a fight. After prudently concluding an alliance with John Asen II of Bulgaria, who appears to have occupied Philippopolis, Theodore took most of the rest of Thrace and drove the Latins back to the walls of Constantinople.

If the principal interest of the Byzantine successor states had been to drive out the Latins, the time was ideal for a coalition of the ruler of Thessalonica and the emperor of Nicaea. Together they could almost certainly have taken Constantinople and southern Greece, restoring the empire with approximately its borders of 1200. But since neither was willing to concede the title of emperor to the other—or even to wait to fight over it until the empire had been recovered—any attempt on Constantinople by one met with the other's opposition. As it was, Theodore's advance led his rivals to unite against him. Vatatzes sided with the Latin emperor Robert, and Asen of Bulgaria opened negotiations with the Latins. Backed by John Asen and John Vatatzes, and defended by the walls of Constantinople, Robert and his Latins began to look difficult to dislodge. Theodore accordingly hesitated. Vatatzes occupied himself with repelling Turkish attacks on the Meander valley.[7]

Apparently in the summer of 1227, Theodore had himself crowned emperor by the metropolitan of Ochrid, since the Greek metropolitan of Thessalonica refused to crown him out of loyalty to the patriarch of Nicaea.[8] Theodore was after all a cousin of the emperors Isaac II and Alexius III, and stood on the threshold of Constantinople. John Asen seems to have warned Theodore not to attack the city; the Bulgarian emperor wanted to marry his daughter to the underage heir to the Latin Empire, Peter of Courtenay's posthumous son Baldwin. The emperor Robert was no obstacle, since he died in 1228 after quarreling with his barons. Yet the barons feared that Asen would himself take over the em-

176. The citadel of Thessalonica from the north. From an old photograph.
(Photo: Deutsches Archäologisches Institut, Athens)

pire if he became the emperor's father-in-law. They therefore elected another emperor, the aged former king of Jerusalem John of Brienne, who was to be succeeded at his death by young Baldwin. While John took his time in arriving, the emperors Asen of Bulgaria and Theodore of Thessalonica both held back from marching on Constantinople. Each doubtless feared that if he besieged the city the other would attack him.

In spring 1230, Theodore broke the deadlock by invading not the Latin Empire but Bulgaria, obviously hoping to clear his way to Constantinople by defeating Asen. Asen advanced to meet him, and the two armies clashed at Klokotnitsa, near Philippopolis. Asen won a crushing victory and captured Theodore. The Bulgarians overran the inland part of Theodore's holdings in Thrace, then the Strymon and Axius valleys along with Serres and Ochrid. The shattered Empire of Thessalonica kept only Thessaly and the Aegean coast up to the mouth of the Hebrus. Epirus proper became practically independent under Michael II Ducas, bastard son and namesake of the first Michael Ducas. Asen soon ended Theodore Ducas's imperial career by blinding him for plotting in prison. Although Theodore's brother Manuel escaped the Bulgarians and took power at Thessalonica, without Theodore and his army the Empire of Thessalonica became a minor state, and practically a Bulgarian client.

THE RISE OF NICAEA

With Theodore Ducas's defeat, John Asen's Bulgaria and John Vatatzes' Nicaea were left as the main powers in what had been Byzantium. Only suspicion between them preserved the feeble Latin Empire until John of Brienne arrived to lead it in 1231. Abandoning hope of winning Constantinople peacefully, the Bulgarian emperor began negotiating with Vatatzes. In 1232 Asen renounced the union of the Bulgarian church with Rome that had lasted almost thirty years. The next year Asen let Vatatzes' patriarch at Nicaea take jurisdiction over the bishops in the Empire of Thessalonica. Yet the understanding between Bulgaria and Nicaea still fell short of being an alliance.

For his part, avoiding conflict with Asen, Vatatzes tried to strengthen his state in other ways. Having defeated the Turks in the Meander valley, he aided a revolt by the natives of Crete against the Venetians, and conquered Lesbos, Chios, and Samos from the Latins.[9] With these acquisitions, a resident Byzantine patriarch, and a new currency of traditional if somewhat debased hyperpyra, Vatatzes' Empire of Nicaea was beginning to resemble the old Byzantine Empire.[10] Vatatzes opened negotiations with Pope Gregory IX, proposing a reunion of churches in return for the surrender of the Latin Empire. But in 1233 the Latin emperor John invaded Nicene territory while Vatatzes' forces were fighting Leo Ga-

177. Gold hyperpyron, shown twice actual size, with a seated Christ on the obverse and John III Ducas Vatatzes of Nicaea (r. 1221–54) and the Virgin on the reverse. (Photos: Dumbarton Oaks, Washington, D.C., copyright 1996)

balas of Rhodes. The next year, after reducing Rhodes to vassalage, Vatatzes abandoned his negotiations with the papacy and made an anti-Latin alliance with Asen.

This pact was sealed early in 1235 when Asen married his daughter Helena to Vatatzes' son Theodore, though both bride and groom were underage. The recently restored Bulgarian patriarch at Tirnovo and the patriarch at Nicaea recognized each other. Asen and Vatatzes agreed to partition the Thracian part of the Latin Empire, assigning Vatatzes the southern sector with Constantinople. After Vatatzes had taken the territory from Callipolis to Tzurulum and Asen everything to the north, Constantinople was the only part of Thrace left in Latin hands, and the two emperors advanced to besiege it. But the Latin emperor John defeated the besiegers. The next year they returned, only to fail again.

In 1237 John of Brienne died at an advanced age, while his successor Baldwin II was in Italy begging for help. Though the time was plainly ripe for another allied assault on Constantinople, the Bulgarian emperor, perhaps hoping to take the city for himself, broke his agreement with Vatatzes. After inviting his daughter back from Nicaea for a visit, Asen kept her in Bulgaria, made a treaty with the Latins, and joined them in besieging the Nicene outpost of Tzurulum. Asen made more trouble for Vatatzes by releasing the blinded emperor of Thessalonica Theodore Ducas, and himself marrying Theodore's daughter. Theodore slipped into Thessalonica and raised a revolution against his brother Manuel, who was exiled to Turkish territory. To disarm those who objected that an emperor could not be blind, Theodore called his young son John emperor of Thessalonica, and ruled in his name from the nearby town of Edessa.

Late that year, however, an epidemic broke out in the Bulgarian capital of Tirnovo, killing the Bulgarian patriarch and Asen's wife and eldest son. Taking this as a sign of divine wrath at his treachery, Asen renewed his agreement with Vatatzes, ended his siege of Tzurulum, and returned his daughter to Nicaea. Vatatzes had a second stroke of luck when Theodore Ducas's brother Manuel escaped to Nicaea. Vatatzes agreed to help Manuel regain Thessalonica from Theodore, and in early 1239 landed him in Thessaly. But Theodore bought Manuel off by allowing him to govern Thessaly under the suzerainty of Thessalonica.

Later that year young Baldwin II of Courtenay finally marched back from the West. He had raised an army by levies from his ancestral lands in France and by the virtual sale of Christ's Crown of Thorns, taken from Constantinople.[11] Distracted by the first appearance of the Mongols on the Danube, Asen disregarded his alliance with Vatatzes and let Baldwin pass through Bulgaria unmolested. The Latin emperor enlisted the help of Cumans who had fled the Mongols, and in 1240 captured Tzurulum from Vatatzes' forces. Vatatzes responded with a naval campaign that seems to have taken Nicomedia from the Latins.

Asen died the next year, leaving the Bulgarian throne to regents for his young son Koloman. Asen's death freed Vatatzes from a strong and unpredictable neighbor; but it also gave more freedom to Theodore Ducas and his nephew Michael II Ducas of Epirus, who had taken Thessaly when its ruler Manuel died. Vatatzes invited Theodore to Nicaea, apparently to discuss an alliance of the two leading Byzantine powers against the Latins and Bulgarians. But at Nicaea Vatatzes put Theodore under arrest. He kept the peace with Bulgaria, and made a two-year truce with the Latins. He also won over the Cumans in Thrace, who joined the Nicene army in return for lands along the empire's Anatolian borders.[12]

In spring 1242 Vatatzes led his Cumans on a major expedition against Thessalonica, taking the captive Theodore along with him. Avoiding Bulgarian territory, Vatatzes advanced through the coastal strip of the Thessalonian Empire and put its capital under siege. The siege of Thessalonica had barely begun, however, when news came from Nicaea that the Mongols had invaded the Sultanate of Iconium. Though Vatatzes kept the report to himself, he was worried enough to cut his campaign short. He annexed only the Thracian coast between the mouths of the Strymon and the Hebrus, and had Theodore persuade his son John to give up the title of emperor for the title of despot, under Nicene suzerainty. Having extracted these concessions, Vatatzes released Theodore and returned to Nicaea.

As it happened, the Mongol invasion turned out well for Vatatzes. Without harming his empire, the Mongols wrecked the Sultanate of Iconium and reduced it to vassalage, also gaining the submission of the Empire of Trebizond. Yet for the present Vatatzes had lost interest in fighting Thessalonica, where the despot John was succeeded by his brother Demetrius in 1244, or the Latins, whose emperor Baldwin had returned to the West to beg for more money. In 1244 Vatatzes, having renewed his truce with the Latins until 1245, married Constance-Anna, daughter of the German emperor Frederick II. The emperor of Nicaea seemed content to be the greatest of the petty rulers of the Byzantine world.

TABLE 16

The Lascaris Dynasty and the Thessalonian and Latin Emperors

Emperors are in capital letters, and emperors of Nicaea are in italics, with the years of their reigns marked "r." Other years are of births and deaths. Illegitimate descent is shown by a broken line.

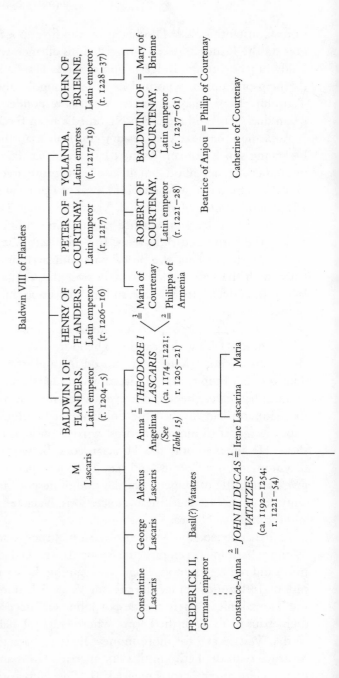

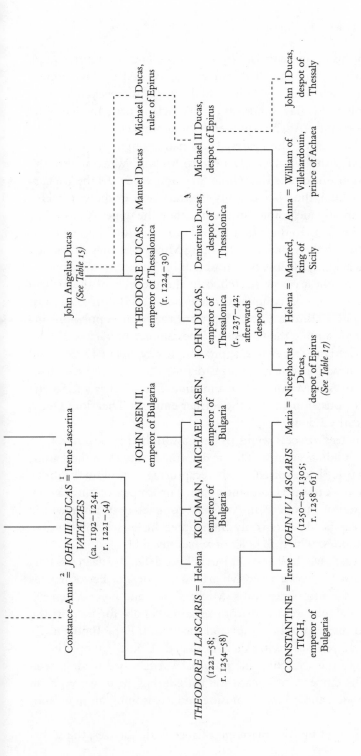

Constance-Anna $\overset{2}{=}$ *JOHN III DUCAS* $\overset{1}{=}$ Irene Lascarina
VATATZES
(ca. 1192–1254;
r. 1221–54)

John Angelus Ducas
(See Table 15)

Manuel Ducas   Michael I Ducas,
ruler of Epirus

THEODORE DUCAS,
emperor of Thessalonica
(r. 1224–30)

Michael II Ducas,
despot of Epirus

JOHN ASEN II,
emperor of Bulgaria

KOLOMAN,   MICHAEL II ASEN,
emperor of   emperor of
Bulgaria   Bulgaria

JOHN DUCAS,   Demetrius Ducas,
emperor of   despot of
Thessalonica   Thessalonica
(r. 1237–42;
afterwards
despot)

THEODORE II LASCARIS = Helena
(1221–58;
r. 1254–58)

Maria = Nicephorus I
Ducas,
despot of Epirus
(See Table 17)

Helena = Manfred,
king of
Sicily

Anna = William of
Villehardouin,
prince of Achaea

John I Ducas,
despot of
Thessaly

CONSTANTINE = Irene   *JOHN IV LASCARIS*
TICH,   (1250–ca. 1305;
emperor of   r. 1258–61)
Bulgaria

Vatatzes kept his peace with Bulgaria until the end of summer 1246, when the emperor Koloman died and was succeeded by his younger brother Michael Asen, who was only a child. This news reached Vatatzes as he was patrolling his new lands on the Thracian coast. Evidently he sensed an opportunity. After a moment's hesitation over breaking his treaty, he attacked Serres, the nearest Bulgarian stronghold. Serres surrendered so readily that Vatatzes advanced to Melnik. When it also surrendered, he went on to take the whole Strymon valley. As the Bulgarian Empire crumbled, the Nicene army overran most of the upper Hebrus valley, apparently including Adrianople, then the upper Axius valley with Scopia and Prilep. To the west Michael of Epirus took his chance to seize Ochrid. Before the year was out, young Michael of Bulgaria signed a treaty acknowledging the loss of almost half his empire to Vatatzes.

The Empire of Nicaea now stretched to the foothills of the Balkan Mountains. These startling conquests, made from the Bulgarians in just three months with enthusiastic backing from the local population, inspired a conspiracy among the Greeks of Thessalonica in Vatatzes' favor. The plotters invited the emperor to approach the city, opened a gate, and let him march in with his men. Vatatzes deposed the despot Demetrius and exiled him to Asia Minor. While annexing Thessalonica and its environs, the victorious emperor left the former emperor Theodore Ducas in control of nearby Edessa.

Although Vatatzes' success seems to have astonished even himself, he lost no time in building upon it. The next spring he attacked the Latins, with whom his truce had expired. Easily recapturing Tzurulum, he drove the Latin troops back toward Constantinople. The Empire of Nicaea now held as much land in Europe as in Asia, and completely surrounded the old Byzantine capital. Vatatzes only interrupted his attack to reinforce his vassals on Rhodes, which the Genoese had invaded.

Probably in 1248, Michael II of Epirus acknowledged Vatatzes as emperor.[13] In return Vatatzes named Michael a despot and betrothed his granddaughter Maria to Nicephorus, Michael's son and heir. When the Latin emperor Baldwin returned from pleading vainly for help in the West, he found his empire bankrupt and moribund. Pope Innocent IV began negotiating seriously with Vatatzes to cede Constantinople in return for reuniting the churches, the proposal Vatatzes had made fifteen years before. The emperor of Nicaea was patient. He spent two years on recapturing Rhodes, and on incorporating and garrisoning his new lands in the Balkans.

Despite Michael of Epirus's marriage alliance with Vatatzes, the ambitious despot and his tireless uncle Theodore were not yet convinced that the emperor of Nicaea could defend his recent conquests. In late 1251 they invaded the Axius valley, took Prilep, and advanced on Thessalonica. Vatatzes speedily mobilized and reached Thessalonica early the next year. As Michael and Theodore fled before him, he besieged and took Edessa. Although his progress became more difficult as he entered the Pindus Mountains, by the end of 1252 Vatatzes took Castoria and received the surrender of many of Michael's men.

To end the war he had started but could not finish, Michael agreed to restore Prilep to Vatatzes and to cede the regions of Edessa, Castoria, and Ochrid and the hinterland of Dyrrhachium. Accepting Nicene suzerainty once more, Michael handed over his son Nicephorus as a hostage, and his uncle Theodore as a prisoner. The aged former emperor died in custody at Nicaea. The Despotate of Epirus had again become a minor power, and the Empire of Trebizond remained one, though its emperor Manuel retook Sinope about 1254.[14] The Empire of Nicaea was bigger and stronger than ever.

That autumn, however, as John Vatatzes pursued his negotiations with the papacy to take the Latin Empire without a fight, he and Pope Inno-

178. Ruins of the palace of the emperors of Nicaea at Nymphaeum (modern Kemalpaşa), where John Vatatzes died. (Photo: Irina Andreescu-Treadgold)

cent both died. Vatatzes had profited from being the most decisive of a gaggle of squabbling competitors. Though he owed much of his success to kidnapping blind Theodore Ducas and betraying little Michael Asen, his rivals were no more fastidious, only less bold. Vatatzes was admittedly more an opportunist than a planner. If he had directed the efforts he had devoted to Bulgaria and Epirus against the Latins, he would probably have retaken Constantinople, creating a more defensible state with friendlier neighbors. He nonetheless doubled the size of the Empire of Nicaea, converting it from one of several more or less equal successors into the dominant heir of Byzantium.

THE RETURN TO CONSTANTINOPLE

Vatatzes' son and successor Theodore II, who used his mother's surname of Lascaris, was thirty-one at his father's death. The new emperor, although an epileptic and often unwell, was cultivated and intelligent. If Theodore was somewhat more aware of the dangers of his position than of its opportunities, the dangers were certainly there. The Empire of Nicaea's new possessions excited the envy of its rivals, and a coalition of those rivals might well outmatch the empire. Theodore could hardly count on having the leisure to take Constantinople by siege or assault.

Michael Asen of Bulgaria, though half Theodore's none too advanced age, hoped to reclaim from him at least some of Vatatzes' conquests. At the beginning of 1255 Asen invaded the upper Hebrus, Strymon, and Axius valleys, capturing a number of forts. Theodore reacted vigorously. He led an army to Adrianople, sacked the Bulgarian town of Beroea, and thrashed a Bulgarian force near Melnik, which he retook. Although Theodore left behind an army that the Bulgarians then defeated, on his return in spring 1256 he defeated them again. Asen made peace and gave up what little remained of his gains.

Michael of Epirus, who had been scheming to turn the Bulgarian invasion to his own advantage, now tried to protect himself by marrying his son Nicephorus to Theodore's daughter Maria. Michael sent his wife Theodora to make the arrangements with the Nicene emperor, who was staying at Thessalonica. As the price of this marriage, Theodore demanded Dyrrhachium and the Greek town of Serbia. Theodora, fearing Theodore would keep her as his prisoner if the negotiations failed, agreed. Her husband Michael had to surrender both towns. That autumn the wedding took place amid mutual distrust, and Theodore returned to Nicaea.

Never friendly to the Nicene Empire, the despot of Epirus now had a real grievance. In spring 1257 he fomented a revolt against Theodore in Albania, north of Epirus, backing the rebels with his army. With the help of the Serbs, Michael overwhelmed the Nicene troops under the future historian George Acropolites, and drove them back to Prilep. To meet this emergency, the emperor sent his best general Michael Palaeologus. But since he suspected Palaeologus's loyalty as well, Theodore gave him few reinforcements. After an initial victory, Palaeologus was unable to relieve Prilep, where Acropolites surrendered. Theodore recalled Palaeologus and imprisoned him.

Michael of Epirus was advancing on Thessalonica when he was attacked from behind by the regent of Sicily Manfred, bastard son of the late Frederick II. Manfred's troops landed in Albania and captured most of the country, plus Corcyra, by early 1258. Rather than make peace with Nicaea or fight on two fronts, Michael offered Manfred the hand of his daughter Helena, agreeing to consider Albania and Corcyra her dowry. Manfred accepted with pleasure. Michael married his second daughter Anna to the strongest Latin ruler of the Peloponnesus, the prince of Achaea William of Villehardouin. Theodore of Nicaea countered by marrying his daughter Irene to the Bulgarian emperor Constantine Tich, who had taken power after the murder of Michael Asen.

Late that summer, with the war still undecided, Theodore II died of his epilepsy. Though he had stoutly defended his father's conquests, he had failed to build much upon them, and Constantinople still seemed an elusive prize. Theodore left his seven-year-old son John Lascaris as emperor, and the grand domestic George Muzalon as regent. But the Nicene aristocracy disliked Muzalon, and after a regency of nine days he was assassinated. The new regent was the general Michael Palaeologus, recently freed from prison. While trying to negotiate with Michael of Epirus, at the beginning of 1259 Palaeologus invoked the supposed emergency to have himself proclaimed coemperor.

Once crowned, Palaeologus acted, sending his brother John to Thessalonica to face the Epirotes and their motley alliance of Albanians, Serbs, Germans, and Latins. First as grand domestic and then as sebastocrator, John Palaeologus surprised the Epirote army and put it to flight near Castoria. John followed up his victory by reoccupying the upper Axius valley, Ochrid, and southern Albania, which he took from the forces of Manfred of Sicily. The war was, however, far from over. Toward the beginning of summer, Michael Ducas of Epirus mustered his soldiers, Manfred's Germans, and Villehardouin with his Latins. The

179. *First row:* Alexius IV Angelus (r. 1203–4), Alexius V (cf. Fig. 160), and Theodore I Lascaris of Nicaea (r. 1205–21). *Second row:* John III Ducas Vatatzes of Nicaea, his son Theodore II Lascaris of Nicaea (r. 1254–58), and Theodore's son John IV Lascaris of Nicaea (r. 1258–61). Miniatures from the Modena Zonaras. (Photo: Biblioteca Estense, Modena)

three companies advanced to Pelagonia, south of Prilep; but there, with John Palaeologus approaching, the mismatched allies quarreled. Michael Ducas's bastard son John of Thessaly deserted to the Nicene side, and Ducas himself withdrew.

At Pelagonia John Palaeologus fell upon the remaining Latins and Germans and routed them, capturing William of Villehardouin and many others. The victorious sebastocrator occupied Thessaly and sacked the Latin city of Thebes. Next his deputy Alexius Strategopulus overran nearly all of Epirus. Alexius took Michael Ducas's capital at Arta, freed the captured general Acropolites, and sent Ducas fleeing to the Latin-held island of Cephalonia. Of the Epirote possessions, only the city of Joannina and the port of Vonitsa held out.

With his conquest of Epirus nearly complete, John Palaeologus returned to the East, summoned to receive promotion to despot and presumably to help attack Constantinople. In spring 1260 Michael Palaeologus did try to take the city, with the help of a Latin baron captured at Pelagonia. First the Nicene troops took the nearby Latin outpost of Selymbria. Their Latin collaborator failed to open one of the gates of Constantinople as he had promised, but they attacked the northern suburb of Galata. Meeting with no success, they granted the Latin emperor Baldwin a year's truce.

The Nicene forces needed their truce, because Michael of Epirus had reconciled with his son John. The two recovered Arta, relieved Joannina, and invaded Thessaly. Michael Palaeologus had to send his brother John back to the West, and even so Nicaea kept little more there than it had held three years before. Yet the Nicene emperor's intention had been to contain Epirus, as he had done, rather than to conquer it, as his generals had almost managed to do. Unlike his two predecessors at Nicaea, Michael put reclaiming Constantinople ahead of humbling Epirus. Early in 1261 the emperor signed a treaty with Genoa, Venice's main trading competitor in the East. He granted the Genoese sweeping commercial concessions in Nicene ports in return for help in taking Constantinople.

The emperor sent Alexius Strategopulus to reconnoiter the city's walls in July, before the truce with the Latins expired. As Strategopulus approached, however, he was astonished to learn from the local Greeks that nearly all the Latin army and Venetian fleet were away from Constantinople, making a surprise attack on the Nicene island of Daphnusia, off Bithynia. Modest though his forces were, Strategopulus decided to take his chance. He had his informants enter the city by night. They killed some sentries, broke open a gate, and gave the signal to Alexius and his men, who rode into the sleeping city. The Latin emperor Baldwin fled by boat. When the Venetians tried to resist, Alexius burned their commercial quarter, forcing them too to flee with their families and whatever property they could save. After fifty-seven years of Latin rule, the Byzantines had come back to Constantinople.

Three weeks later, the emperor Michael made his triumphal entry into the city, and saw it for the first time in his life. Though he had not personally accomplished or ordered the recovery of the capital, he had attempted the task the year before, and had been preparing to try again. By contrast, despite decades of Latin weakness, earlier claimants to the Byzantine throne had never made a determined attack on the city. While several of them had advanced almost to its gates, they had always stopped to fight each other rather than the Latins. Even Vatatzes had held back from an assault on Constantinople.

After taking the city Michael Palaeologus became known as Michael VIII to his subjects, counting his predecessors at Nicaea as Byzantine emperors in exile. Although modern scholars have followed this tidy practice, it tends to distort events through hindsight. The Nicene emperor Theodore I Lascaris was not the direct successor of Alexius V, but one of many Byzantines who tried their luck after the Fourth Crusade. Had Theodore's successors not returned to Constantinople, no one could reasonably call Theodore more than emperor of Nicaea. The title of Byzantine emperor could just as well have gone to the emperors of Trebizond or Thessalonica, if they had captured Constantinople, or to any other Greek who had taken the city. The government that Michael VIII brought to Constantinople had begun its history at Nicaea rather than developed from the Byzantine administration destroyed by the Crusaders. Nevertheless, by 1261 the Byzantines had regained more than they might have dared hope in the aftermath of 1204.

CHAPTER TWENTY-THREE

The Restored Empire, 1261–1328

In 1261 Michael VIII Palaeologus took over the better part of the land that had been Byzantine before the Fourth Crusade. He held the old empire's core in western Anatolia, Thrace, and northern Greece, with its two main cities of Constantinople and Thessalonica. He had also captured the principal lords of Latin Greece, including the prince of Achaea William of Villehardouin. Imperial armies were battling the despot Michael II Ducas for Epirus and Thessaly. The other states holding some former Byzantine territory, the Seljuk Sultanate and the little Empire of Trebizond, were enfeebled vassals of the Mongols. The Seljuk sultan Kaykā'ūs II had just fled to Michael VIII, leaving no successor worthy of the name. Thus the emperor was clearly stronger than his rivals, with hopes of making further conquests at their expense.

Although Michael's administration and army were creations of the emperors of Nicaea rather than inheritances from Byzantium, this was not entirely bad for him. The Byzantine institutions of 1204 had functioned a good deal worse than those of Nicaea had come to do. Michael had a satisfactory reserve in his treasury, and an army that for fifteen years had managed to hold almost as much territory as Michael now possessed. If parts of the restored empire had suffered severe devastation, an interval of peace could be expected to cure that. Michael's worst problem was that almost sixty years of war had left unprecedented divisions and grievances among Byzantines, and between Byzantines and Latins. Creating a unified state under such circumstances would not be easy.

THE LABORS OF MICHAEL VIII

The times called for the utmost care and tact, and those Michael Palae-ologus possessed. Aged thirty-six at his accession, he was alert, persuasive, and ruthless, the most gifted Byzantine ruler in more than a century. He began his reign in the empire's ancient capital with a flurry of activity. For a ruler of lesser talent this might have been a fatal mistake; but Michael was impatient for good reasons. He wanted to impress his opponents with his power at once, and to recover as much of the old empire as possible before a coalition could form against him. Although he debased the hyperpyron a bit more, from sixteen to fifteen karats, at least he spent the proceeds wisely.[1] He needed to restore the walls of Constantinople, and even his outlays to refurbish and repopulate the city bought prestige worth having.

The emperor struck a quick and hard bargain with William of Ville-hardouin and his barons. To win his freedom William had not only to swear an oath of vassalage to Michael but to cede him a foothold in the Peloponnesus, secured by the almost impregnable promontory of Monemvasia and the fortified town of Mistra. The emperor organized four

180. View of Monemvasia from the mainland, with the isthmus that forms its "only entrance" (*monē embasia* in Greek) at right. (Photo: Collection Gabriel Millet)

military units from among the new Byzantine subjects. Constantinople and its environs contributed the Thelematarii, soldiers provided with land or pronoia grants, the Gasmuli, marines serving for pay, and the Proselontes, oarsmen supported by land grants on the coasts and islands. The recovered part of the Peloponnesus contributed the Tzacones, marines who drew pay but also held modest land grants near Constantinople. Michael built more ships, and seems to have put all four companies of new soldiers into action within a year.[2]

At his coronation in Saint Sophia Michael took his little son Andronicus as his colleague, excluding the young heir for whom he was supposed to be regent, John IV Lascaris. Since John would be a natural rallying point for any critics of Michael, the emperor removed and blinded him at the end of the year. When this became known early in 1262, the patriarch Arsenius excommunicated Michael, and some irregular troops on the Anatolian border proclaimed a blind boy alleged to be John. Michael seems to have suppressed the revolt by enrolling the rebels as regular soldiers.[3] The excommunication was more troublesome, because it prevented the emperor from taking part in any religious service or ceremony.

The pope released William of Villehardouin from his oath to Michael, on the valid argument that it had been sworn under duress. William, the Venetians, and the deposed Latin emperor Baldwin then joined in an alliance against the emperor. In spring 1262 Michael responded with three major military expeditions, one each to fight Villehardouin, the Venetians of the Aegean islands, and Michael of Epirus. The army sent to Epirus, again under the despot John Palaeologus, merely kept the enemy on the defensive. The fleet took some of the smaller islands from the Venetians, plundered others, including Paros and Naxos, and even made a brief landing on Crete. The expedition to the Peloponnesus, carried by Genoese ships, landed at Monemvasia and began taking Latin forts.

By autumn Constantine Tich of Bulgaria invaded Thrace, making the reasonable calculation that these three campaigns must have the Byzantine army fully occupied. Tich was wrong. Michael had more troops in Constantinople, and even if they were newly recruited they still rolled the Bulgarians back to the Balkan Mountains. There the Byzantines took over Bulgaria's borderlands, capturing Philippopolis, Anchialus, and Mesembria. By the end of the year, the Byzantine army and navy had distinguished themselves, holding their own against the Epirotes and Latins and defeating the Venetians and Bulgarians. Only in Asia Minor, where the Turks were raiding, was Michael forced to neglect the empire's defenses.

In spring 1263 the energetic emperor launched fresh attacks on Epirus and on the Latins of the Peloponnesus. When Michael's brother John prepared another campaign, Michael of Epirus submitted, accepting imperial suzerainty over southern Epirus and Thessaly. The emperor also reinforced his army in the Peloponnesus, which advanced almost to the Latin capital of Andravida before being driven back. When the Venetians defeated a Genoese fleet off the Peloponnesian coast in the summer, the emperor blithely took his chance to annul his burdensome treaty with Genoa.

A year later Michael sent his brother John against the Turkish raiders in Asia Minor. John cleared the Turks from the lower Meander valley, the most vulnerable part of Byzantine territory. During John's absence, however, the despot Michael of Epirus repudiated his settlement and attacked the empire again. The emperor himself mustered an army and marched west. The despot again submitted before the Byzantines' arrival, and married his widowed heir Nicephorus to the emperor's niece Anna Cantacuzena.

While returning through Thrace, the emperor had to flee a sudden raid by the Mongols of the Golden Horde, the subordinate Mongol Khanate that ruled north of the Danube. They had been summoned by the deposed Turkish sultan Kaykā'ūs, whom the emperor had detained at Aenus, and they returned northward after Kaykā'ūs was surrendered to them. But the ex-sultan left behind his retinue, most of whom became Christians and entered Byzantine service. Michael enrolled them in a regiment of some one thousand, known as the Turcopuli, or Sons of Turks. Thus Michael escaped repeated dangers, and even turned them to his advantage.

After achieving so much, the emperor seems to have temporarily exhausted his financial reserves. The Byzantines' campaign in the Peloponnesus ground to a halt when their unpaid Turkish mercenaries deserted to the Latins. John Palaeologus returned from fighting the Turks before his work was done. In spring 1265 Michael asked the Venetians for a truce, and settled for a peace of exhaustion. Yet he had made good his claim to be the Byzantine emperor. Epirus had challenged him in vain, and Trebizond ceased to impinge upon Byzantine affairs when its emperor Manuel died and it lost Sinope again.

Since the patriarch Arsenius refused to lift his excommunication on

181. Statue of Charles I of Anjou, king of Sicily (r. 1265–85), now in the Palazzo dei Conservatori, Rome. (Photo: Musei Capitolini, Rome)

any terms but Michael's virtual abdication, the emperor finally lost patience and had a council depose the patriarch. Arsenius still had many defenders. His undistinguished successor, after excommunicating him on a charge of conspiracy, was dismissed himself after a year. The next patriarch, the respected abbot Joseph, received the emperor back into the Church as a penitent early in 1267. But many of the clergy went into schism, refusing to accept Arsenius's deposition.

Meanwhile the Byzantines had acquired an enemy stronger than those they had been holding at bay. Manfred of Sicily had lost his life and kingdom to Charles of Anjou, younger brother of Louis IX of France and an ally of the papacy. Charles captured Manfred's Greek possessions in Corcyra and northern Epirus, and sought to enlarge them. In 1267 he made a pact with the exiled Latin emperor Baldwin, promising to help Baldwin retake Constantinople in return for lordship over the Peloponnesus. Charles married his daughter to Baldwin's son and heir, and his son to the daughter and heiress of William of Villehardouin, Charles's new vassal in the Peloponnesus. For the moment, however,

Charles was too busy establishing himself in Sicily to pursue plans against the Byzantines.

Anticipating an attack by Charles, Michael VIII wanted peace with everyone else. He made no attempt to annex Epirus at this date, despite the death of Michael Ducas, whose legitimate heir Nicephorus had lost Thessaly to his half-brother John the Bastard. Even when John attacked the empire and was defeated, the emperor took only eastern Thessaly from him and gave him the title of sebastocrator. Michael made peace with the Genoese as well, granting them a colony in Constantinople's suburb of Galata and enabling them to found another major colony at Caffa in the Crimea.[4] Peace with Genoa led in spring 1268 to a five-year truce with the Venetians, who merely received the right to rent property in the empire. The emperor also won over Constantine Tich of Bulgaria, who married Michael's niece Maria Cantacuzena and was promised Anchialus and Mesembria if the marriage produced an heir. The promise must have seemed safe, because a fall had paralyzed Tich from the waist down.[5]

By 1269 Charles of Anjou had secured the Kingdom of Sicily and made alliances with Hungary and Serbia, and was planning a crusade against Michael VIII. Michael persuaded Charles's brother Louis IX to insist on a crusade against Muslims; but when Louis died on a North African crusade in summer 1270, Charles was left free to fight the empire. Desultory warfare between Byzantium and the Latins had already begun. The Latins of Euboea raided the coast of Anatolia, and the Byzantines raided Euboea in return. The emperor landed an army in the Peloponnesus, and Charles sent reinforcements. Then an earthquake wrecked Byzantine Dyrrhachium, allowing Charles's troops to occupy the damaged city in 1271. Soon Charles held almost all of Albania, a suitable base for a march on Constantinople.

Next Charles concluded an alliance with Constantine Tich of Bulgaria, who had somehow produced an heir and was demanding Anchialus and Mesembria from Michael. Charles also allied with John the Bastard of Thessaly, who repudiated Byzantine suzerainty. Michael's brother John Palaeologus led a land and sea expedition against the rebel, probably in spring 1273. Though by bringing in Latins from Athens the bastard routed the imperial army, the imperial navy destroyed a Latin fleet from Euboea that tried to exploit the defeat. After this drawn result John Palaeologus died, depriving Michael of his best general.

As the empire's enemies multiplied, Pope Gregory X asked Michael for delegates to negotiate a reunion of churches. To avoid further delay, they were to attend an ecumenical council already called for 1274 in France. The emperor could not refuse without offending the pope and inviting a crusade by Charles of Anjou, whom the pope was restraining. Because the Byzantine hierarchy stoutly opposed any union, Michael mustered some plausible delegates only after prolonged persuasion and intimidation, which provoked the patriarch Joseph to withdraw from his functions. In summer 1274 a Byzantine delegation of junior bishops and senior officials arrived at the Council of Lyons. They brought a letter from Michael VIII accepting union and all western doctrines and recognizing western church practices, but requesting that eastern church practices be allowed to continue as before. The union was ratified on Michael's terms.

The Union of Lyons made Charles of Anjou's crusade impossible, since Michael was no longer in schism with the West. Even as the Council of Lyons met, the Byzantines attacked Charles's foothold in Albania. They overran the interior, including the town of Berat, and reached the coast, capturing Buthrotum. Reinforcements from Charles held Aulon and Dyrrhachium only with difficulty. In the meantime the emperor opened an offensive against the Aegean islands under the tenacious Italian mercenary Licario. Licario's steady gains, especially in Euboea, and a simmering rebellion in Crete led the Venetians to renew their truce with Michael. Licario, who had little use for truces, went on taking islands anyway.[6]

Although the Union of Lyons was a diplomatic triumph, most Byzantines considered it an unwarranted surrender of their prerogatives to the western church. The emperor appointed a unionist patriarch, John Beccus, who persecuted enough to force the outward acquiescence of the hierarchy and bureaucracy. This, however, left the Byzantine church with two large groups of schismatics: the Josephites loyal to the antiunionist patriarch Joseph, and the Arsenites, also antiunionist but loyal to the memory of the late patriarch Arsenius. Almost all eastern Christians outside the empire rejected the union, including the separatist rulers of Trebizond, Epirus, and Thessaly.

John of Thessaly went so far as to hold an antiunionist council attended by dissidents from Byzantium.[7] Another dissenter was Michael's niece Maria, the real ruler of Bulgaria because of her husband Tich's paralysis. Probably in 1276, Maria ordered an attack on the empire, demanding the promised surrender of Anchialus and Mesembria. She withdrew her troops only when the emperor induced the Mongols to raid Bulgaria. The next year a Byzantine expedition against John of Thessaly miscarried when some of its leaders refused to fight opponents of the Union of Lyons. The union seemed to be more trouble than it was worth.

Undaunted, in 1278 Michael declared Nicephorus of Epirus replaced by his fugitive brother Demetrius-Michael, who married a daughter of the emperor but settled in Constantinople. Michael also proclaimed a new ruler of Bulgaria, John Asen II's grandson John Asen III, who married another of the emperor's daughters. The emperor sent Asen with an army to Bulgaria, where Maria had been ruling for her infant son since her husband's recent death in a rebellion. To defend herself, she married the rebel leader Ivailo, but the pair were soon besieged in Tirnovo by the Byzantines and their Mongol allies. Meanwhile Nicephorus of Epirus took Buthrotum from the empire and appealed for help to Charles of Anjou, and in early 1279 became Charles's vassal and surrendered Buthrotum to him. Thus the opportunistic despot joined a western Crusader against Byzantium in the name of resisting union with the western church.

Michael's determination began to show some benefits. In Bulgaria the Byzantines took Tirnovo, captured the empress Maria, and crowned their candidate John Asen III emperor. Although Asen was deposed within a year, his successor George Terter took over a country wracked by revolts and Mongol raids, and was in no position to oppose Byzantium. In Greece Licario, now Michael's grand duke, had taken all of Euboea but Venetian Chalcis, and most of the other islands except Venetian Naxos. He also captured the Latin duke of Athens. Michael seemed to have weathered the worst of the antiunionist storm.

In 1280 the emperor launched three campaigns to secure his borders. He sent his younger son Constantine against some Serbian raiders, who had reached Serres but fled at Constantine's approach. Michael himself went to Asia Minor, where he expelled Turkish raiders from around Nicaea and fortified the west bank of the Sangarius. Michael's older son Andronicus marched south, chased off more Turks, and rebuilt and repopulated the ruined city of Tralles, setting the frontier at the Meander. While the emperor and his son were still in Anatolia, Charles of Anjou's troops in Albania laid siege to the Byzantine fortress of Berat. But the emperor sent strong reinforcements, who in spring 1281 ambushed Charles's army, captured its commander, and sent it fleeing back to the coast. Although Dyrrhachium and Aulon held out, the rest of Albania

182. Palace of the Porphyrogenitus (now known as the Tekfur Saray), Constantinople, probably built for Michael VIII's younger son Constantine. (Photo: Irina Andreescu-Treadgold)

seems to have fallen to the Byzantines. Michael then resumed his campaigning against the Turks.

Charles was incensed at this defeat, and he had just won the election of a friendly pope, his fellow Frenchman Martin IV. Martin declared that Michael VIII had failed to achieve a genuine reunion of churches, since most Byzantines rejected it. Confident of papal support, Charles made fresh plans for a crusade against Byzantium. In the summer he enlisted Philip of Courtenay, heir to the Latin Empire, and the Venetians, who were irate at the depredations of Licario. That fall the pope excommunicated the emperor. Charles scheduled his expedition for the next year. Although the empire had been fighting well against Frenchmen and Venetians separately, this coalition of both was alarmingly reminiscent of the Fourth Crusade.

Even while making another campaign against the Turks in Anatolia, Michael turned his diplomacy against the would-be Crusaders. He incited another rising against Venice on Crete, and backed a plot against Charles by Peter III of Aragon, brother-in-law of Charles's victim

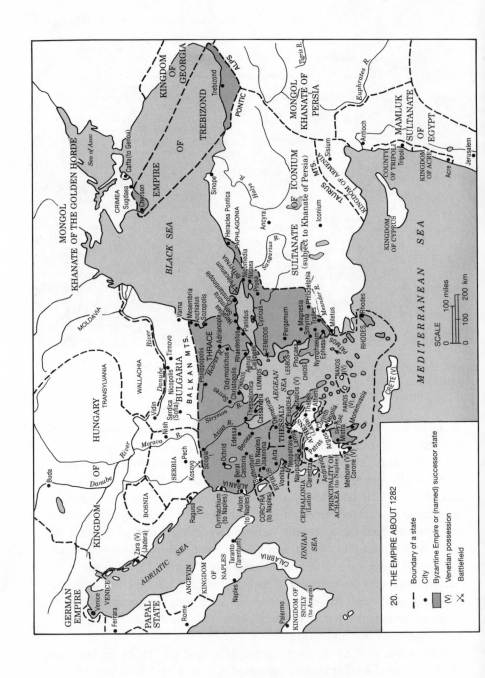

GERMAN EMPIRE

PAPAL STATE

Rome
Ferrara

Venice
VENICE

ADRIATIC SEA

ANGEVIN
Naples
KINGDOM OF NAPLES
Taranto (Tarentum)
CALABRIA

KINGDOM OF SICILY (to Aragon)
Palermo

IONIAN SEA

Buda

HUNGARY

TRANSYLVANIA

WALLACHIA

MOLDAVIA

MONGOL KHANATE OF THE GOLDEN HORDE

Nish
Ragusa (V)
Zara (V) (Jadera)
SERBIA
Pech
Kosovo
BOSNIA
Vidin
Nicopolis
Serdica (Sofia)
BULGARIA
Tirnovo
Danube River
Morava R.
Arta
Argos R.

Sea of Azov

CRIMEA
Sugdaea
Caffa (to Genoa)
Cherson

BLACK SEA

Trebizond

EMPIRE OF TREBIZOND

KINGDOM OF GEORGIA

ALPS

PONTIC MTS.

MONGOL KHANATE OF PERSIA

Tigris R.

Euphrates R.

Sinope
Heraclea Pontica
PAPHLAGONIA
Halys R.
Ancyra
Sangarius R.

SULTANATE OF ICONIUM (subject to Khanate of Persia)

Iconium

TAURUS MTS.

KINGDOM OF ARMENIA

Sisium

Antioch

COUNTY OF TRIPOLI
Tripoli

MAMLUK SULTANATE OF EGYPT

KINGDOM OF ACRE
Acre
Jerusalem

KINGDOM OF CYPRUS

MEDITERRANEAN SEA

Varna
Mesembria
Anchialus
Sozopolis
THRACE
Philippopolis
Adrianople
Hebrus R.
Rhaedestus
Didymotichus
Christopolis
Serres
Strymon R.
Thessalonica
Cassandria
Berrhoea
Edessa
Ochrid
Castoria
Scopia
Berat
Valona (to Naples)
Dyrrhachium (to Naples)
Aulon (to Naples)
Bathrotum (to Naples)
EPIRUS
Joannina
Neopatras
THESSALY
CEPHALONIA (to Naples)
CORCYRA (to Naples)
Clarentza
PRINCIPALITY OF ACHAEA (Latin) (to Naples)
Andravida
Patras
Methone (V)
Corone (V)
Mistra
Monemvasia
Sparta

BITHYNIA
Nicomedia
Nicaea
Prusa
Constantinople
Selymbria
Heraclea
Cyzicus
Pergamum
Magnesia
Smyrna
Phocaea
Nymphaeum
Ephesus
Tralles
Meander R.
Philadelphia
Miletus

Panidus
Aenus
TENEDOS
LESBOS
LEMNOS
CHIOS
PATMOS
SAMOS
NAXOS
PAROS (V)
RHODES
CRETE (V)

AEGEAN SEA

EUBOEA
CHALCIS (V)
Thebes
Athens
Neopatras
LA(?)
Corinth
Naupactus
Naupion

20. THE EMPIRE ABOUT 1282

- - - Boundary of a state
•   City
▓   Byzantine Empire or (named) successor state
(V)   Venetian possession
✕   Battlefield

SCALE
0   100 miles
0   100   200 km

Manfred. The emperor is said to have paid Peter sixty thousand hyper-pyra to foment a revolt in Sicily. If so, the money was well spent. In the early spring of 1282, when Charles was still preparing his crusade, a re-bellion known as the Sicilian Vespers broke out at Palermo. The whole island rose against Charles and called in the Aragonese. Charles had to abandon his crusade, and could barely hold a truncated Kingdom of Naples on the Italian mainland.

With Charles humbled, Bulgaria crippled, and the Turks pacified for the moment, Michael VIII turned to the separatist Byzantine states. Af-ter intense negotiations, he gave the emperor John II of Trebizond the hand of his third daughter and the title of despot, which implied sub-mission to the empire. With studied ambiguity, John agreed to dress as a despot while in Constantinople for the wedding, and back in Trebizond began to style himself emperor of the East rather than of the Romans. That autumn Michael mustered an expedition against the contumacious John of Thessaly. The emperor contracted dysentery and his wife begged him to rest, but he pressed on into Thrace. There he died, at the age of fifty-eight.

In difficult circumstances, Michael VIII had rebuilt an empire that could hold its own against its many enemies. After retaking Constan-tinople, it gained territory in northern Thrace, Albania, the Aegean is-lands, and the Peloponnesus. It lost nothing but some border outposts in Anatolia, despite fighting on as many as six fronts—against the Turks, the Bulgarians and Serbs, Charles of Anjou, Epirus and Thessaly, the Latins of Greece, and the Venetians in the Aegean islands. Michael taxed and spent furiously, but after his single debasement of the coinage he seems to have kept his budget precariously in balance. His reunion of churches, however troublesome at home, was of some use for his foreign policy. He remained true to the union till his death, unwilling to aban-don his unionist hierarchy and hoping for a more sympathetic pope. Yet the restored empire suffered, like its twelfth-century predecessor, from a lack of reliable allies. To maintain itself, it needed leaders nearly as bril-liant as Michael.

THE FAILURES OF ANDRONICUS II

Michael's son Andronicus II became senior emperor at age twenty-four, after some military experience in Asia Minor. He was cautious, conscientious, devout, and weak. Michael VIII reportedly thought that his younger son Constantine would have made a better emperor, but shrank from tampering with the succession when the empire had so many other problems. For his part, Andronicus condemned his father's unionism, refused to bury Michael in consecrated ground, and lost no time in repudiating the Union of Lyons and reinstating the patriarch Joseph. Andronicus also seems to have considered Michael's treasury reserves inadequate. At the start of his reign, he nominally increased them by debasing the hyperpyron another karat, making it fourteen karats of gold to ten of alloy.

Even a wiser ruler than Andronicus might have taken his chance to abandon the Union of Lyons. Andronicus's personal dislike for it was shared by many other Byzantines, some of whom were bitterly hostile, and the reigning pope had disowned it. Yet such a union, so easy to undo and so hard to restore, seemed to be the only hope of normalizing relations with the West and averting new crusades against Constantinople. Similarly easy and dangerous was Andronicus's debasement of the coinage. The reputation of the hyperpyron was already sinking at home and abroad. In 1284 Andronicus's further debasement led the Venetians to mint a rival coin of equal weight and pure gold, the ducat. It quickly displaced the empire's currency as the standard for Mediterranean trade.

The same year Andronicus restarted the expedition against Thessaly that his father's death had interrupted. He financed it not out of the treasury but by levying a tax of a tenth on the revenues of pronoiars, presumably in return for excusing them from the campaign. He was therefore using his pronoiars not as soldiers but as tax farmers, having them remit a tenth of the taxes but letting them keep nine-tenths for doing nothing. The expedition to Thessaly took the port of Demetrias, then withdrew to escape an epidemic. Yet something was accomplished. Nicephorus of Epirus resumed his allegiance to the empire, persuaded by his wife Anna, Andronicus's cousin. Anna also helped Andronicus kidnap Michael Ducas, the heir of John of Thessaly. The emperor hoped to marry one of his nieces to the captive prince, who indignantly refused.[8]

At first the empire's enemies seemed to be growing fewer. In 1284 the widowed emperor married Yolanda, daughter of the marquis of Montferrat, renaming her Irene. The marquis was heir to the long-defunct Latin Kingdom of Thessalonica, and as a dowry he gave up his claim. The next year Charles of Anjou died, and the emperor signed a truce with Venice. As an indemnity for their losses to Byzantine privateers, the Venetians accepted twenty-four thousand hyperpyra, about a third of what they had asked, and they regained only the modest privileges granted them by Michael VIII. The truce did give them secure access to the Crimea, where their colony of Sugdaea began to compete with Genoese Caffa.

Andronicus assumed that he was now at peace with the West for the foreseeable future, and could turn to reuniting the Byzantine church and filling the treasury. After Venice ratified the truce, a Byzantine council condemned the *filioque* and the Byzantine unionists, including the former patriarch John Beccus. Even this, however, failed to appease the Arsenite schismatics, and it made any future attempt to improve relations with the western church harder still. Next the emperor practically dismantled the Byzantine navy. He dismissed most of his father's companies of the Gasmuli and Tzacones, who as marines had supported both the navy and the army. Since by this time the invaluable Licario had either retired or died, Andronicus planned to rely mostly on the Genoese fleet, just as he preferred foreign mercenaries to Byzantine pronoiars. He seems not to have realized that foreign troops needed to fight alongside natives if they were to stay under control, and that losses of land and taxpayers could erase any savings made by ceasing to defend them.

For a time, however, Byzantium enjoyed a measure of peace and even military success. Though the Turks had retaken Tralles in Asia Minor, most of their forays seemed to be raids rather than conquests. The Byzantines slowly gained land in the Peloponnesus. By 1288 they recovered Dyrrhachium and Aulon from the Angevin Kingdom of Naples, and their old enemy John of Thessaly died, leaving two infant sons and a widow who recognized Byzantine suzerainty. The emperor also negotiated to marry his son and heir Michael to Catherine of Courtenay, heiress of the defunct Latin Empire, hoping finally to settle the western claim to Constantinople.

Then Turkish penetration of Anatolia grew worse. Probably in early 1291, the emperor inspected both the Sangarius frontier and Nymphaeum, which since the loss of the Meander valley had become a border fort. During Andronicus's absence, Charles II of Naples, son of Charles of Anjou, persuaded Nicephorus of Epirus to throw off his allegiance to the empire. The emperor had a Genoese fleet land a Byzantine army in Epirus; but Nicephorus called in Latins from the Peloponnesus who defeated it. Probably around the same time, Stephen Milutin of Serbia took Scopia and the upper Axius valley from the empire.[9]

As affairs in the Balkans deteriorated, Andronicus returned from Asia

183. Michael VIII Palaeologus (r. 1261–82), Michael's son Andronicus II
Palaeologus (r. 1282–1328), and Andronicus's son Michael (IX) Palaeologus.
Miniatures from the Modena Zonaras. (Photo: Biblioteca Estense, Modena)

Minor in 1293, giving his nephew Alexius Philanthropenus an extraordinary command to fight the Turks. Alexius did well. Within a year he
was campaigning in the Meander valley and had recaptured Miletus. He
strengthened his army by enlisting defeated Turks and refugees from
Crete. The only problem was that this army's loyalty was to Alexius, not
to Andronicus. In autumn 1295 they proclaimed Alexius emperor. The
empire was spared a civil war only because some of the rebels took a
bribe and blinded him.

The next year Andronicus married his son Michael to an Armenian
princess, since the proposed marriage with the Latin heiress Catherine
had foundered on western hostility. Charles of Naples had sealed his anti-
Byzantine alliance by marrying his son Philip of Taranto to the daughter
of Nicephorus of Epirus. Philip took over his father's holdings in Greece,
and received from his new father-in-law the Epirote coast between Vonitsa and Naupactus, with suzerainty over the rest of Epirus and Thessaly. For a second time Nicephorus had mortgaged his state to the Latins
to keep it independent of Byzantium. He died in 1296, leaving his little
son Thomas in the care of his widow, Andronicus's cousin Anna.

Byzantine weakness was beginning to show. The same year the Venetians, at war with Genoa but supposedly at peace with the empire, attacked and burned the Genoese colony in Constantinople's suburb of
Galata. Outraged at this attack on Byzantine territory, the emperor con-

fiscated Venetian property in his capital and took the Genoese side in the war. But since the empire lacked a navy, the war simply allowed Venice to pick off the many islands Licario had reconquered for the Byzantines. Probably the same year, the advancing Serbs captured Dyrrhachium, recently retaken from Naples. Although Andronicus sent an expedition against the Serbs in 1297, its general made no progress and recommended negotiations.

As the Turkish advance resumed in Asia Minor, the emperor gave the command to his cousin John Tarchaniotes, uncle of the previous commander Philanthropenus. John arrived in 1298 and began rebuilding the army, redistributing pronoia grants and enforcing the duties of pronoiars. The next year Andronicus went to Thessalonica to negotiate with Milutin of Serbia. The Serbian king gladly made peace, and apparently returned Dyrrhachium, in return for the hand of the emperor's daughter Simonis. The patriarch objected that Simonis was only six, that this would be Milutin's fourth marriage, and that Milutin's third wife was still alive; but the emperor wanted the alliance. The dubious bargain was struck by annulling Milutin's second and third marriages because he had contracted them before his first wife's death.[10]

The reforms of the Anatolian commander John Tarchaniotes made him so unpopular that he had to flee to the emperor in 1300. Andronicus apparently concluded that Byzantine troops were incapable of defending Anatolia. To replace them, in 1301 he settled some sixteen thousand Alan refugees in Thrace, where they would take no land from the Byzantines of Asia Minor; his plan was that the half of them who were fighting men should serve against the Turks. The emperor provided his Alans with military equipment by taxing the Byzantines of Thrace, including pronoiars, and the next year organized them into two contingents. One was sent to Nicomedia under his general Muzalon; the other, to Magnesia (near Smyrna) under Andronicus's son and heir Michael, then twenty-five years old.[11]

Accompanied by too few Byzantines to keep good discipline, the Alans proved unruly soldiers. Soon after arriving in Anatolia, they began to desert and return to their families in Thrace, plundering Byzantine territory as they went. Since Muzalon's Alans were nearer Thrace than Michael's, many more of them were able to get away. By summer, Muzalon was left with just two thousand men. Near Nicomedia he was attacked by the local Turkish emir Osmān, and badly defeated. Osmān began conquering the countryside for his nascent state, known after a form

of his name as the Ottoman Emirate. Byzantium had acquired a dangerous new adversary.

Young Michael kept most of his Alans together until he reached Magnesia, where he too began to suffer desertions. Though he still wanted
to attack the Turks, his advisers persuaded him that the danger was too
great. As the Turks advanced around him, his army melted away, until in
the winter he fled to Pergamum. By this time much of the Byzantine
population was panicking and abandoning the country to the Turks. By
early 1303, as the Turks advanced in Asia Minor and a revolt broke out,
Andronicus apparently tried to shore up his army by confiscating land
from magnates and the Church and giving it to the soldiers outright.[12]

To obtain a ten-year truce from the Venetians, the desperate emperor
let them keep their conquered islands and promised them seventy-nine
thousand hyperpyra as compensation for their confiscated property. In
the midst of the crisis, the emperor's wife Yolanda-Irene demanded that
he grant her sons Thessalonica, which she considered her inheritance
from her father. When Andronicus refused, she retired to the city and set
up a rival court there, in effect severing Thessalonica from Byzantium.

Seeing the empire's distress, a body of mercenaries from Aragon offered Andronicus their services. They called themselves the Catalan
Grand Company, and had fought well on Sicily for the king of Aragon.
The Catalans' captain Roger de Flor now proposed that the emperor
hire their fifteen hundred horse and five thousand foot at the exorbitant
annual rate of some three hundred hyperpyra for each cavalryman and
half as much for each infantryman. This was almost three times what the
Alans received, and probably put the Catalan payroll higher than the
empire's whole revenue.[13] Yet the emperor accepted the terms. He made
an advance payment, and granted Roger the title of grand duke and the
hand of his niece Maria Asen.

Arriving in autumn 1303, Roger and his men wintered at Cyzicus.[14]
The next spring they joined the remaining Alans and set out. Although
the Alans deserted as usual, the Catalans routed the Turks wherever they
went, from Cyzicus in the north to Ephesus in the south. Unfortunately
for the Byzantines, the Catalans also used their mastery of the field to
pillage the native population. In late summer Roger attacked Byzantine
Magnesia, while his fleet raided the Byzantine islands of Chios and Lesbos. At this the emperor recalled the Catalans, supposedly to fight the
Bulgarian emperor Theodore Svetoslav, who had invaded Thrace. The

Catalans settled in for the winter at Callipolis, away from both Turks and Bulgarians but well positioned to blackmail the emperor.

In the fall thirteen hundred more Catalans from the West landed at Callipolis and demanded to be hired. Andronicus felt unable to refuse. Roger demanded his men's pay, which was already late. The emperor went to great lengths to raise the money, imposing a new tax on crops and exacting a third of the revenues of his European pronoiars. He also debased the hyperpyron to twelve karats, making it just half gold, and equated it with new silver coins that were even more overvalued.[15] But the Catalans rejected the coins, and the tax set off a rebellion in Bithynia. Despite everything, Andronicus fell short of the sum he owed.

Early in 1305 the emperor proposed that Roger take the title of Caesar, leave for Asia Minor, and rule as a fief whatever he could take, the region of Prusa and Nicaea apparently excepted. After extorting even more money, Roger consented. Before departing in the spring, the new Caesar paid a state visit to the junior emperor Michael, who was guarding Adrianople against the Bulgarians and disapproved of his father's indulgence of the Catalans. In Michael's camp, presumably with his knowledge and quite possibly on his orders, an Alan mercenary stabbed Roger to death. The junior emperor showed his approval of the murder by having Roger's escort massacred.

Yet killing the Catalans' leaders merely served to enrage the rest of them. The Catalans elected new commanders, butchered the Byzantines of Callipolis, and spread terror through the surrounding country by land and sea. When Michael tried to stop them, they defeated him twice in little more than a month. During a third battle, the Alans and Turcopuli in Michael's army deserted, and the Catalans made short work of the remaining Byzantines. Michael himself was wounded and fled.

The Catalans stormed through Thrace, joined by Turks from Anatolia and the rebel Turcopuli. The Alan deserters pillaged on their own, and the Bulgarians invaded again, taking Mesembria and Anchialus. The Turks swarmed over Asia Minor and captured Ephesus. Supposedly to help against the Turks, the Genoese began seizing Byzantine ports and islands; their merchants took over Chios, Phocaea, Adramyttium, and Smyrna, while their privateers occupied Rhodes. Genoa showed no readiness to return any of these. Most Byzantine towns had to see to their own defense. Rioting broke out at Constantinople against Andronicus, who seemed incapable of action.

At this point, the Epirote regent Anna surprised everyone by disowning her lord Philip of Taranto in favor of her cousin the emperor. Although she had chosen a time when Andronicus could least afford to help her, she defeated the Latins and drove them from Epirus. Reacting promptly, Philip himself landed in Greece in 1306. Even after disease forced him to withdraw, he made Anna agree to return the corner of Epirus she had retaken. His forces also took Dyrrhachium from the stricken empire. Byzantium seemed to be disintegrating.

All through 1306 the Catalans and their Turkish allies devastated Thrace, destroying what they could not steal and selling their captives into slavery. Andronicus asked for help from Genoa, but when a Genoese fleet asked for the preposterous pay of three hundred thousand hyperpyra, the emperor had learned enough to decline. He tried to buy a truce from the Catalans for one hundred thousand hyperpyra, but they refused.[16] The Catalans, though they caught and massacred the last of the Alans, went on ravaging Thrace, forcing the surrender of Rhaedestus and briefly besieging Adrianople. They disrupted farming so badly as to cause a famine.

By early 1307 the need for grain from Bulgaria forced Andronicus to make peace with its emperor Theodore Svetoslav, who married Andronicus's granddaughter Theodora and kept Mesembria and Anchialus. Finally the famine began to affect even the Catalans, who had in any case nearly exhausted the loot to be had from Thrace. In late spring they and their allied Turks abandoned Callipolis and marched west to an unravaged part of the empire. By late summer they established themselves in Cassandria, just south of Thessalonica, and began plundering around their new base.

The Catalan raids and the advance of the Turks in Asia Minor convinced some westerners and even some Byzantines that the empire was doomed. Pope Clement V backed a crusade against Byzantium proposed by Charles of Valois, brother of Philip IV of France and husband of the Latin heiress Catherine of Courtenay. Charles had already won over the Venetians. He enlisted the Catalans at Cassandria as his vassals, and was actually encouraged in his plans by some despairing Byzantine officers in Anatolia. The pope granted supposedly Byzantine Rhodes to the crusading order of the Hospitalers, who conquered it from the Genoese.

In spring 1308 the Catalans attacked Thessalonica, the residence of Andronicus's estranged empress Yolanda-Irene. But they failed to take the city, and Charles of Valois kept postponing his crusade. The next

184. Facade of the Palace of the Grand Master of the Hospitalers (first building at left), Rhodes. (Photo: Istituto Centrale per il Catalogo e la Documentazione, Rome)

spring their Turkish allies left to pillage Thrace again, and the Catalans marched south and ravaged Thessaly. The Thessalian ruler John II managed to nudge them out of his domains by 1310, when they were hired by the Latin duke of Athens. The next year they killed the duke and conquered his duchy, where at last they settled down.

By then Charles of Valois's crusade had come to nothing, like Charles of Anjou's crusade before it, and the Venetians had made another truce with the emperor. The Turks formerly allied with the Catalans kept looting Thrace and defeating the junior emperor Michael until 1311; but then Andronicus retired his hapless son from the command, and appealed to his son-in-law Milutin of Serbia. Michael's retirement improved the empire's fortunes somewhat. Milutin sent two thousand Serbs, who crushed the Turks near Callipolis in 1312. A year later the frustrated Charles of Valois bestowed the hand of his daughter Catherine and his claim to the phantom Latin Empire on Philip of Taranto, who had divorced his Epirote wife. Since Philip had bargained away his part of Greece to make the match, he found himself without the resources for a crusade. So Byzantium was left with a sort of peace.

Andronicus had tried to save money by doing without a navy or much of an army, and had failed abysmally. Apart from bankrupting the treasury in a hopeless effort to pay the Catalans, the results were the devastation of the European part of the empire and the loss of nearly all the Asian part. The empire's remaining holdings in Asia Minor were a scrap of Bithynia and the isolated city of Philadelphia. Except for the Empire of Trebizond and some Genoese ports, the Turks held the rest. In proportion to Byzantium's diminished size, the disaster was comparable to the loss of nearly all of Anatolia in the decade after 1071.

At last, however, the emperor roused himself to salvage the wreckage of his empire. He was able to accumulate a modest reserve in the treasury, and to rebuild a small native army. After he had finally disposed of the forty-five-year Arsenite Schism in 1310, the Byzantine church was held together by a single set of bishops and a general dislike of Latins. The emperor recovered control of Thessalonica after the death of his empress Yolanda-Irene in 1317. Epirus and Thessaly were allied to Constantinople, because John II of Thessaly was married to a bastard daughter of the emperor, and Thomas of Epirus to a daughter of the emperor's son and heir Michael.

In 1318 Thomas of Epirus was murdered by his nephew, Nicholas Orsini of Cephalonia, and John of Thessaly also died. Since neither John nor Thomas had children, the Ducas dynasty became extinct. Hoping to replace it, Orsini took up residence at the Epirote capital of Arta, joined the eastern church, and married Thomas's widow Anna. But the empire had a strong claim to both separatist states. A Byzantine army occupied northern Thessaly, while a Thessalian magnate recognized Byzantine suzerainty to the south. Northern Epirus declared for the emperor, and the next year Orsini ceded it in return for imperial recognition as despot at Arta. Thus Byzantium gained some territory and became the sole surviving state ruled by Greeks, with the minor and distant exception of Trebizond.

FAMILY RIVALRY

The empire was at peace, and still had control over most of the best farmland in the Balkans. By careful collection of the taxes, Andronicus and his officials raised revenues to a million hyperpyra, even if those hyperpyra were only half gold. The emperor made plans to enlarge his tiny standing army to a thousand mercenaries in Bithynia and two thousand in the Balkans, and to expand his exiguous navy to twenty ships.[17] Apart from the Turks, who were divided among themselves, no major foreign enemies threatened the empire. It had prospects for expansion into the parts of Epirus, Thessaly, and the Peloponnesus feebly held by the Latins. The succession was settled for the foreseeable future, first on the emperor's son Michael, then on Michael's dashing son Andronicus, who had recently married and been crowned coemperor.

Just when the empire's luck was improving, young Andronicus's adventures caused a tragic accident. One night in 1320, when he was in bed with a noblewoman at her house, his bodyguards killed a man who wanted to see him. They had assumed the victim was a rival lover; but he turned out to be Andronicus's younger brother Manuel. The terrible news prostrated the brothers' father Michael, who died soon afterward. Old Andronicus, furious with his grandson and namesake, refused to confirm him as heir to the throne after Michael's death. The emperor openly considered choosing his second son Constantine.

Tensions mounted between the two Andronicuses. Since the elder had suffered many failures, had recently increased taxation, and was past the age of sixty, the younger Andronicus attracted a number of well-born young supporters. In spring 1321 the grandson fled the capital for Adrianople, where he had himself proclaimed senior emperor as Andronicus III. The people of Thrace eagerly joined him when he exempted them from their new taxes. He attracted an army of volunteers, and gave them pronoia grants taken from partisans of his grandfather. With this force at his back, Andronicus III appeared outside Constantinople.

The revolt had lasted little more than a month, without open fighting, when Andronicus II came to terms. The old emperor recognized Andronicus III's authority over all of Thrace between Selymbria and Christopolis, keeping only jurisdiction over foreign affairs. Although the grandson accepted the arrangement, it was an awkward one, dividing the empire's forces and humiliating the senior emperor. In the autumn he won over two of his grandson's leading partisans, one of whom plausibly claimed that the young emperor had seduced his wife. This support emboldened the loyalists to counterattack.

Neither side had the strength, or perhaps even the desire, to crush the

TABLE 17

The Palaeologus Dynasty

Emperors are in capital letters, and Byzantine emperors are in italics, with the years of their reigns marked "r." Other years are of births and deaths. Illegitimate descent is shown by a broken line.

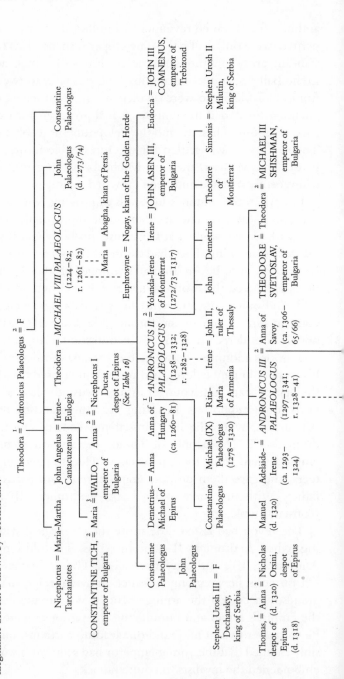

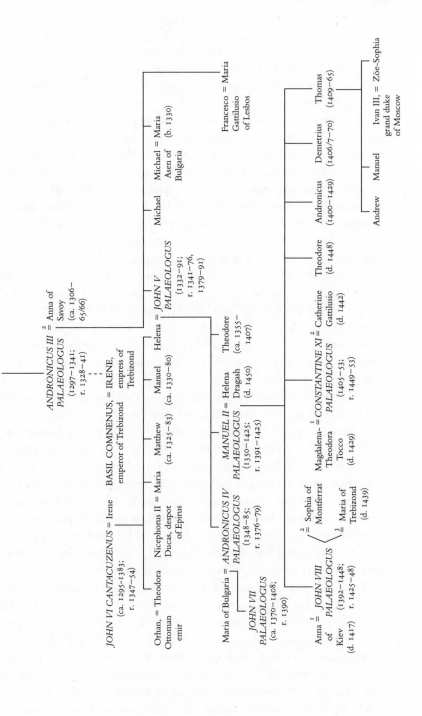

ANDRONICUS III = Anna of
PALAEOLOGUS 2 Savoy
(1297–1341;   (ca. 1306–
r. 1328–41)   65/66)

JOHN VI CANTACUZENUS = Irene   BASIL COMNENUS, = IRENE,
(ca. 1295–1383;   emperor of Trebizond   empress of
r. 1347–54)   Trebizond

Orhan, = Theodora   Nicephorus II = Maria   Matthew   Manuel   Helena = JOHN V   Michael   Michael = Maria
Ottoman   Ducas, despot   (ca. 1325–83) (ca. 1330–80)   PALAEOLOGUS   Asen of
emir   of Epirus   (1332–91;   Bulgaria
                                                        r. 1341–76,   (b. 1330)
                                                        1379–91)

Maria of Bulgaria = ANDRONICUS IV   MANUEL II = Helena   Theodore   Francesco = Maria
             PALAEOLOGUS   PALAEOLOGUS   Dragash   (ca. 1355–   Gattilusio
             (1348–85;   (1350–1425;   (d. 1450)   1407)   of Lesbos
             r. 1376–79)   r. 1391–1425)

JOHN VII
PALAEOLOGUS
(ca. 1370–1408;
r. 1390)

            Anna = JOHN VIII   Magdalena- = CONSTANTINE XI = Catherine   Theodore   Andronicus   Demetrius   Thomas
             of   PALAEOLOGUS   1 Theodora   PALAEOLOGUS   2 Gattilusio   (d. 1448)   (1400–1429)   (1406/7–70)   (1409–65)
             Kiev   (1392–1448;   Tocco   (1405–53;   (d. 1442)
          (d. 1417)   r. 1425–48)   (d. 1429)   r. 1449–53)

              2 = Sophia of   Andrew   Manuel   Ivan III, = Zöe-Sophia
                 Montferrat   grand duke
              3 = Maria of   of Moscow
                 Trebizond
                 (d. 1439)

other. While Andronicus III was the more popular claimant, his tax exemptions had left him much the poorer of the two. He was dependent on contributions from his friend John Cantacuzenus, a wealthy landowner in Thrace, until Thessalonica declared for him in spring 1322. That summer the two emperors agreed again to rule the empire jointly. Andronicus III took up residence at Didymotichus in Thrace, and his grandfather remained at Constantinople. Bitterness naturally lingered.

After this agreement was arranged, the Bulgarians seized Philippopolis and advanced to Adrianople. The territory invaded was the portion of Andronicus III, who retaliated with the help of John Cantacuzenus, his grand domestic. Andronicus and John first took back Mesembria, which had revolted from Bulgaria. In 1323 they lost it again, but retook Philippopolis. The next year the war died down as the Mongols of the Golden Horde raided both Bulgaria and Byzantium. The Bulgarian emperor Michael Shishman married young Andronicus's sister Theodora, widow of his predecessor Svetoslav, and made peace with the empire.

In 1324 old Andronicus tried to rescue Philadelphia, his last Anatolian town south of Bithynia, which had long been surrounded by Turks. He gave this seemingly impossible mission to his old general Alexius Philanthropenus, who had been blinded and disgraced twenty-nine years before. Yet blind though he was, Alexius had such a reputation among the Turks that he managed to reach and save the city. His feat, like the Catalans' success against the Turks, suggests that competent leadership could have held all of Byzantine Anatolia. By this time, however, Philadelphia was an island in a Turkish sea, over a hundred miles from the nearest Byzantine outpost at Prusa, which was itself besieged. A vigorous campaign in Bithynia by John Cantacuzenus, probably in 1325, failed to penetrate to Prusa. Though Andronicus III wanted to march in person to raise the siege of the city, his grandfather distrusted him and would not cooperate. To the grandson's indignation, in spring 1326 Prusa surrendered, and became the capital of the Ottoman Emirate.

That year the governor of Thessalonica John Palaeologus, Andronicus II's nephew, declared his independence with the support of his son-in-law, the Serbian king Stephen Dechansky. Andronicus II appeased the rebel with the title of Caesar, and when John died around the beginning of 1327 made a treaty with the Serbian king. Young Andronicus, however, afraid that the Serbian alliance might be turned against himself, came to his own agreement with Shishman of Bulgaria. These alliances made by each emperor against the other showed that Byzantium was practically split in two. The rule of two emperors satisfied neither party, and both expected more conflict.

In early autumn Andronicus III moved from Didymotichus to Selymbria, nearer the capital. His grandfather ordered the patriarch Isaiah to excommunicate him, but the patriarch refused and was suspended from his functions. The grandson tried to make a clandestine entry into Constantinople, but failed. Andronicus II called in the Serbs, who advanced as far as Thrace. Andronicus III chased them off, and took Thessalonica early in 1328. After this victory, most of the old emperor's forces in the West joined Andronicus III.

Just as the young emperor seemed to be gaining the upper hand, his supposed ally Shishman of Bulgaria sent troops to help the embattled Andronicus II. Again young Andronicus forced his enemy to withdraw, then marched on Constantinople once more. The Venetians were blockading the harbors in a dispute with the Genoese, leaving the citizens disgusted with their impotent government. On a night in late May, some of them betrayed the city to the young emperor and his general Cantacuzenus. Their troops kept fairly good order, and they let the old emperor abdicate with his dignity intact.

Andronicus II had been a thoroughly mediocre ruler when Byzantium needed an outstanding one. Beginning with a treasury that was straitened but solvent, he ordered economies the empire could not afford. His reductions in the army and navy cost him most of the Anatolian provinces and exposed the Balkan ones to devastation by the Catalans. He inherited an empire that seemed capable of recovering its twelfth-century extent, and left one that seemed unable to recover even the lands he had inherited. Even when he tried to correct his mistakes after 1311, he still seems to have hoarded gold as an end in itself, and he showed only the most limited strategic sense. No doubt Andronicus's luck was sometimes bad, but it could easily have been worse. Either Charles of Valois or Philip of Taranto might have mounted a full-blown crusade against the badly weakened empire, and conquered it outright. That with such a record Andronicus managed to reign for so long was also his good fortune—though not the empire's.

CHAPTER TWENTY-FOUR

The Breakdown, 1328–1391

When Andronicus III Palaeologus defeated his grandfather, Byzantium was a reasonably compact state in Thrace and northern Greece, with not too distant outliers in parts of the Peloponnesus and Bithynia. Its land was generally fertile, with some good ports and the two great cities of Thessalonica and Constantinople. Its only rivals in Greece were some petty Latin fiefdoms, more threatened by Byzantium than threatening it. Its northern neighbors, Serbia and Bulgaria, seemed to have reached their natural limits, having taken all the lands mostly inhabited by Slavs. Although the Turks were poised to take the rest of Bithynia, they lacked the sea power to launch a serious invasion of Europe. Costly though the civil war had been, it had enlarged the Byzantine army and given it battle experience. So the empire seemed to have a future, if not perhaps a glorious one.

RECOVERY UNDER ANDRONICUS III

Before Andronicus became sole emperor at age thirty-one he had proved himself a competent military commander. Half Armenian and a quarter Hungarian, he had acquired some western tastes from his second wife Anna, daughter of the count of Savoy. He had great personal charm; his love of action and impatience with obstacles had won him much support, and were needed at the time. While he could be irresponsible and frivolous, he had a flawed ruler's redeeming grace: a talent for delegating authority. His best friend and closest adviser was the grand domestic John Cantacuzenus, only a little older than he, but much steadier. The emperor and his general soon restored order to the government, and began to reduce corruption by appointing new judges. Amid the confusion left by the civil war, however, they had some difficulty in choosing allies among their neighbors, and in deciding where to direct their energies.

After repelling an invasion of Thrace by Shishman of Bulgaria, Andronicus and Cantacuzenus decided to give priority to fighting the Ottoman Turks. In spring 1329 they mustered an army of some four thousand men and set out to raise the Ottoman sieges of Nicomedia and Nicaea. Those two cities and Heraclea Pontica, the empire's last holdings in Bithynia, were well fortified and might yet be anchors for a small Byzantine province in Asia Minor. Not far along the road to Nicomedia, the emperor's army met an Ottoman force at Pelecanum. Most of the Turks remained in the nearby hills, and the Byzantines drove off the few who ventured down to fight. But the Byzantines were unwilling to advance while Turks remained behind them. During some indecisive skirmishes, the emperor was slightly wounded, and rumors that his wound was mortal set off a panic. The Ottomans fell on the army and mauled it badly before Cantacuzenus ferried it back to Constantinople.

Although the emperor and his adviser gave up their campaign against the Ottomans after this defeat, they were quick to respond when the people of Chios rebelled against their Genoese rulers. Andronicus arrived on the island with a fleet, expelled the Genoese, and reclaimed their nominal fief for the empire. Next he sailed to Phocaea on the Anatolian coast, where the Genoese hastily admitted his suzerainty. The emperor made treaties with the local Turkish rulers, the emir of Saruhan to the north of Phocaea and the emir of Aydin to the south. Andronicus saw that the Emirate of Aydin, which had just taken Smyrna from the Genoese and was becoming a naval power, might make a useful ally against the Genoese and Ottomans.

Seeing that the emperor was busy in the East, the Serbs besieged Ochrid. Andronicus sent an army that chased them off, and in 1330 he planned a joint expedition with Shishman of Bulgaria against Serbia. When the Serbs struck first, and defeated and killed Shishman, Andronicus coolly turned on Bulgaria and seized Mesembria and Anchialus for himself. But the Bulgarians retook both cities the next year, and the fall of Nicaea to the Ottomans diverted the emperor's attention to Asia. There the Ottomans were hostile, and the other Turks and Genoese seemed unreliable allies. The empire needed more friends.

185. Andronicus III Palaeologus (r. 1328−41) and (right) Andronicus's wife
Anna of Savoy, mother of John V. Contemporary miniatures now pasted into a
later manuscript (Stuttgart codex historicus 2-601). (Photos: Württembergische
Landesbibliothek, Stuttgart)

Looking to the West, in 1332 Andronicus joined the Hospitalers of
Rhodes and the Venetians in a Holy League against the Turks of Aydin.
The league was to have a fleet of twenty galleys, half of them Byzantine, making Byzantium the senior partner in an alliance with western
powers. The emperor also reopened negotiations for a reunion of the
churches. The problem was that Andronicus was not at all sure he wanted
to fight the Turks. He had a treaty with Aydin, and in 1333 he made a
truce with the Ottoman emir Orhan, paying him twelve thousand hyperpyra a year to spare Nicomedia.[1]

That year the Byzantine vassal who ruled Thessaly died. The Byzantine governor of Thessalonica and the despot John Orsini of Epirus (who
had overthrown his brother Nicholas) both rushed in to seize whatever
they could. In the autumn the emperor arrived in person, expelled Orsini's garrisons, and conquered Thessaly down to the Catalan Duchy of

Athens, winning a significant prize. After the emperor returned to Constantinople, however, a rebel governor captured Ochrid and Castoria with the aid of King Stephen Dushan of Serbia. When Andronicus had the rebel assassinated, Dushan made peace, ceding Castoria but keeping Ochrid. Thus Byzantium advanced a little in Greece, but lost a little to Serbia.

In 1334 the Holy League defeated the pirates of Aydin without help from the promised Byzantine ships. The following year the Genoese of Phocaea repudiated Byzantine suzerainty, attacked Byzantine Chios, and invaded Byzantine Lesbos. Andronicus razed the walls of Genoese Galata in retaliation, then blockaded the Genoese in Phocaea and Lesbos. During these sieges John Cantacuzenus reached an agreement with the emir of Aydin Umūr, who became his fast friend. Assisted by Umūr's ships and troops, the Byzantines soon forced the Genoese to surrender Phocaea and drove them from Lesbos.

While Byzantium held its own, Trebizond and Epirus declined. Andronicus married his bastard daughter Irene to the emperor Basil Comnenus of Trebizond in 1335. Two years later the Epirote despot John Orsini was poisoned by his Byzantine wife Anna, who became regent for her little son Nicephorus. At this juncture the Albanians rebelled against Byzantium, and the Ottomans took Nicomedia. Andronicus ignored the loss of Nicomedia, but the next spring he and Cantacuzenus set out for the West with two thousand mercenaries from their new ally Umūr of Aydin. After these Turks made short work of the Albanians, Andronicus was encouraged to invade Epirus. Anna simply capitulated, and the Byzantines marched in.

However, some of Anna's courtiers contrived to carry off her son Nicephorus to Italy. There he fell into the hands of Catherine of Valois, the widow of Philip of Taranto, who was the heiress to the Latin Empire and a claimant to Epirus. In 1339 Catherine fomented an Epirote revolt against Byzantium and sent young Nicephorus to head it. The Byzantines resisted the rebellion, and the following year the emperor arrived with Cantacuzenus. After a siege of Arta, the charismatic Cantacuzenus won over the rebels and secured Epirus. He and the emperor marched back to Thessalonica with Nicephorus, who was betrothed to Cantacuzenus's daughter Maria.

Both Byzantines and Latins recognized the empire's recovery of Epirus as a triumph. The same year the emperor received an appeal from his daughter Irene, who had seized power at Trebizond after the death of her husband Basil, to send her a new husband to rule Trebizond. Better yet, the Latin lords of the Peloponnesus decided to take the emperor as their suzerain instead of Catherine of Valois, provided that their rights were respected. Once these lords submitted, the Catalans of Athens were likely to follow. Andronicus seemed about to become master of the whole Balkan peninsula south of Serbia and Bulgaria, with no remaining Latin rivals on land.

The emperor also kept negotiating for church union, but the talks had set off a theological dispute. In discussing the *filioque*, the Byzantine legate Barlaam of Calabria had diplomatically observed that no human argument could settle questions about the essence of God. To this a monk from Athos, Gregory Palamas, objected that God could be known by other means.[2] Palamas meant Hesychasm, a belief among Athonite monks that by repeating a short prayer, bowing their heads, and holding their breath they could see the light surrounding God himself.[3] When Barlaam learned of Hesychasm, he denounced it as a delusion; but Palamas defended it, insisting that the light the Hesychasts saw was a means of knowing God, if not of seeing him. As feelings rose, Barlaam accused Palamas of the heretical belief that the light around God was uncreated, and thus a sort of fourth person of the Trinity. A council held in early June 1341 rejected Barlaam's charge and forbade further discussion of the matter.

A few days after the council, and before the Latin delegates arrived from the Peloponnesus, Andronicus suddenly fell ill and died in his mid-forties. His had been on the whole a successful reign. The empire had won in Epirus, Thessaly, and the islands more than it had lost in Bithynia and around Ochrid. Its army had fought at least as well as the armies of its neighbors, with the possible exception of the Ottoman Turks. Better still, more gains were within reach in Greece, and the real architect of Andronicus's success, the grand domestic John Cantacuzenus, remained in good health. Loyal to his friend's memory, Cantacuzenus seemed the ideal protector for Andronicus's son John.

THE GREAT CIVIL WAR

John V Palaeologus obviously needed a regent, since he was only nine when he succeeded his father. Eleven years earlier, during a grave illness, Andronicus III had declared that if he died John Cantacuzenus should rule for the child the empress Anna was expecting.[4] The emperor had also tried and failed to persuade his comrade to be crowned coemperor. Although in 1341 death seems to have overtaken Andronicus before he could set up a formal regency, the grand domestic took charge of the government, which he had largely run for years. But he refused to be crowned coemperor, as the grand duke Alexius Apocaucus suggested. Apparently Cantacuzenus feared the dissension his coronation might cause.

The grand domestic needed to leave on campaign almost at once. At the news of Andronicus's death, Turkish pirates from Saruhan attacked the Thracian coast, Dushan of Serbia advanced on Thessalonica, the Albanians around Berat revolted, and the emperor John Alexander of Bulgaria threatened to invade. Cantacuzenus was also eager to claim the allegiance of the Latin barons of the Peloponnesus and to send Michael Comnenus, a member of the Trapezuntine dynasty long resident at Constantinople, to rule Trebizond. Any delay risked the failure of both of these projects, and losses on every Byzantine frontier.

While he prepared his expedition, Cantacuzenus held another synod on Palamism, as Palamas's defense of Hesychasm had begun to be called. Although Palamas's critic Barlaam had left in disgust for Italy, another monk, Gregory Acindynus, kept up the opposition to Palamism. Acindynus's concern was less with Hesychasm than with Palamas's insistence on the superiority of mystical knowledge to philosophical argument. Despite having been friendly with both Barlaam and Palamas, Cantacuzenus supported the council's decision to affirm Palamism and condemn Acindynus.[5] Perhaps he was aware that compromises on theology had almost always failed in the past.

The grand domestic marched out, drove off the Turks, and persuaded the Bulgarians and Serbs to make peace. At Didymotichus he accepted the submission of the Latin delegates from the Peloponnesus. He could scarcely have been more successful. But during his absence the emperor's mother Anna, the patriarch John Calecas, and the grand duke Alexius Apocaucus all developed their own ambitions for the regency. Apocaucus even plotted to seize the young John V until, after little more than a month, Cantacuzenus returned and arrested him. Apocaucus apologized, and Cantacuzenus had him released at the request of the empress.

In early autumn, Cantacuzenus set out to take possession of the Latin Peloponnesus, realizing that if he waited longer the opportunity might be lost. Yet once the great general had gone, Apocaucus began plotting again. He enlisted the support of the empress and patriarch, along with

186. The grand duke Alexius Apocaucus. Miniature from the Paris
Hippocrates of 1345 (Parisinus graecus 2144). (Photo: Bibliothèque
Nationale, Paris)

others who resented Cantacuzenus's position. The grand duke encouraged mobs to ransack the houses of Cantacuzenus's wealthy family and
friends in the capital. Next Apocaucus, the patriarch, and the empress
organized a regency. The empress, whose right to rule seemed clearest,
dismissed Cantacuzenus as grand domestic and ordered his army to return, a month after its departure.

With this ample provocation, Cantacuzenus, then at Didymotichus,
had himself proclaimed coemperor. He had to give up on claiming the
Latin Peloponnesus. He could do nothing to help Michael Comnenus at
Trebizond, who was overthrown and imprisoned after a reign of barely
a week. Despite his professed allegiance to John V, Cantacuzenus was
branded a rebel by the regency, which held both the capital and the underage emperor. Although Cantacuzenus's fellow aristocrats knew he
had a good case, he seemed plainly in the wrong to many others. Some
also found loyalty to the emperor an attractive pretext for despoiling
magnates.

Thus the leading men of Adrianople, the nearest city to Didymotichus, declared for John Cantacuzenus, only to have an urban mob loot
their houses and expel or imprison them in the name of John V. Apocaucus applauded the uprising, and sent his son Manuel to be Adrianople's governor. Mobs in other cities in Thrace similarly drove out and
plundered aristocrats who favored Cantacuzenus. The patriarch further
undermined the pretender by excommunicating him. Though Cantacuzenus still had the larger part of the army, some of his soldiers deserted

him. He stopped the Bulgarian emperor Alexander from seizing Adrianople, but failed to take the city for himself. By this time popular feeling had forced most provincial governors to support the regents, except in recently conquered Epirus and Thessaly, where opinion was divided.

The governor of Thessalonica, though outwardly loyal to the regency, secretly offered to surrender his city if Cantacuzenus could bring an army there. Toward the beginning of spring 1342, Cantacuzenus left a garrison at Didymotichus under his wife Irene and started for Thessalonica with his sons and most of his men. He marched down the Hebrus and along the coast. No major town joined him, and he refused to spend time on sieges. Prompt though he was, before he arrived at Thessalonica a revolution overthrew his secret ally. The city's new popular government, known as the Zealots, supported John V and accepted Apocaucus's son John as their governor.[6] Apocaucus also managed to install his own candidate as emperor of Trebizond, John III Comnenus, son of the deposed Michael. The regency seemed firmly in power.

Confronted with the vengeance of a government he considered unfit and unjust, the pretender refused to submit. Yet his only base was at faraway Didymotichus. He decided to make for Serbia, first releasing any of his soldiers who wanted to leave him. He led the remaining two thousand men up the Axius into Serbia, where King Stephen Dushan received him in midsummer. Dushan was delighted to fan a civil war in Byzantium, as long as he could set his own terms. He agreed to provide Cantacuzenus with Serbian troops and to invade the empire himself, but not to surrender any conquests he made in doing so. Though Dushan was obviously a dangerous ally, the pretender, with no other hope, accepted him.

Setting out for Didymotichus, Cantacuzenus tried to take Serres, but failed when many of his men died of dysentery. He decided to return to Serbia, provoking more desertions. Meanwhile Dushan invaded Byzantine territory with relish, capturing Edessa and Castoria. As the Serbs approached Thessaly, the Thessalians warded them off by hastily receiving a Cantacuzenist governor. After this success, the pretender tried once more to relieve Didymotichus, but turned back again when his Serbian allies began to desert him. At Didymotichus Irene Cantacuzena held out only with help from the Bulgarians, who also wanted to prolong the civil war, and from Cantacuzenus's friend Umūr of Aydin, who sailed up the Hebrus but left when the winter grew too cold for him.

In spring 1343 events began to turn against the regents. Dushan overran Byzantine Albania, and the Cantacuzenist governor of Thessaly took Epirus. Returning from another failed attempt to reach Didymotichus, Cantacuzenus received an offer of submission from the people of Beroea in northern Greece, who wanted to avoid conquest by the Serbs. After the pretender occupied Beroea, nothing to the west of him remained loyal to the regency. Cantacuzenus brought troops from his new possessions in Thessaly and Epirus to besiege Thessalonica.

The pretender's gains, however, meant that his alliance no longer benefited Dushan, who could only make further advances by invading Cantacuzenist territory. The Serbian king therefore declared for the regency and sent an army against Cantacuzenus, while Apocaucus landed at Thessalonica with reinforcements. Cantacuzenus had to retreat, and appealed for help from Umūr of Aydin. Umūr did arrive, with six thousand Turkish troops, but renewing the siege of Thessalonica proved too difficult. Instead, leaving his son Manuel at Beroea, Cantacuzenus set out with the Turks on another expedition to reach Didymotichus. This time, after more than a year, they entered the city and relieved his intrepid wife Irene.

That summer, as Umūr's Turks began to ravage Thrace, the regency grew alarmed. The empress Anna pawned the crown jewels to Venice for thirty thousand gold ducats, the equivalent of about sixty thousand half-gold hyperpyra, and appealed for a crusade by the Holy League against Cantacuzenus's Turkish allies. Without attempting a general reunion of churches, she personally submitted to papal authority. Since the Palamites tended to favor Cantacuzenus and to oppose westerners, the empress and her patriarch turned against Palamism, and imprisoned Palamas.

By spring 1344, John Cantacuzenus and Umūr held most of western Thrace. But then many of the Turks insisted on returning to Aydin with Umūr. Thus weakened, the pretender faced attacks by Dushan of Serbia from the west, Alexander of Bulgaria from the north, and Apocaucus from the east. Yet Cantacuzenus had already escaped from worse predicaments than this. His remaining Turks sharply defeated the Serbs. While Alexander contented himself with occupying the region of Philippopolis, which the regency had given him, the pretender drove off Apocaucus. Meanwhile Cantacuzenus's candidate Michael Comnenus recovered the throne of Trebizond.

As Cantacuzenus slowly made his way through the Thracian countryside, many joined him. They included the governor of Adrianople

Manuel Apocaucus, the regent's own son; but the people he had governed in Adrianople, like most townsmen, remained loyal to the regency, and had to be besieged. Though that autumn the Holy League destroyed Umūr of Aydin's fleet and occupied Smyrna, Cantacuzenus was now strong enough to do without his Turkish ally. The desperate regency lashed out at supposed Cantacuzenists in Constantinople, arresting aristocrats and holding a council that excommunicated Gregory Palamas.

Early in 1345 Adrianople surrendered to Cantacuzenus. He obtained more troops from the Ottoman emir Orhan, who had noticed which party of Byzantines was friendlier to Turks. Orhan's men helped Cantacuzenus extend his control over Thrace to the Black Sea coast. By spring Umūr, having pinned down the Holy League in the harbor of Smyrna, was able to bring still more reinforcements. They helped the pretender march on Serres, where the people favored the regency but were tightly besieged by Dushan. Cantacuzenus hoped they would prefer him to the Serbs.

He turned back, however, at the news that his archenemy Alexius Apocaucus had been lynched while incautiously mingling with his aristocratic prisoners. Sensing a chance to seize the capital, Cantacuzenus made for Constantinople, only to find that the empress and the patriarch had it well under control. Yet neither of them had the energy of Apocaucus or commanded the same loyalties. Apocaucus's son John, governor of Thessalonica, tried to join the Cantacuzenists like his brother, but he was killed by his city's Zealots. Now the regents held nothing but Thessalonica, Constantinople, and some islands.

The Byzantines' civil war was going splendidly for Stephen Dushan, who captured Serres in early autumn. The king conquered the whole region down to Mount Athos and the Aegean, cutting the empire in two. Later in the year he took the title of emperor, not just of the Serbs but of the Romans. In spring 1346 Dushan had himself crowned at Scopia by the archbishop of Pech, whom he promoted to patriarch for the occasion. Alexander of Bulgaria likewise assumed the title of emperor of the Bulgarians and Greeks. The civil war had in fact left Byzantium barely stronger than Serbia or Bulgaria, and divided at that.

When Cantacuzenus heard of Dushan's coronation, he resolved to have himself crowned as well. The ceremony was held at Adrianople, the largest city Cantacuzenus held, and performed by the exiled patriarch of Jerusalem, the highest-ranking prelate available. Cantacuzenus also held a council of bishops at Adrianople that supported Palamism and pronounced the patriarch John Calecas deposed. But Cantacuzenus still insisted that he aspired to rule only as the colleague of John V.

The newly crowned pretender moved his headquarters nearer Constantinople, to Selymbria. While the Holy League was battling his ally Umūr at Smyrna, the Genoese exploited the fighting to take Chios and Phocaea from the regents, weakening them further.[7] That summer Cantacuzenus confirmed his alliance with the Ottomans by marrying his daughter Theodora to the emir Orhan.[8] The empress Anna countered by hiring six thousand mercenaries from the emir of Saruhan, but after pillaging Thrace they deserted to Cantacuzenus.

Almost bankrupt, with no reliable allies, in February 1347 Anna turned on her coregent John Calecas, and held a council that deposed him as patriarch. The same night, however, the capital's Cantacuzenists let in their leader and a thousand of his men through a tunnel dug under the city walls. No one had the heart to fight him, nor did he want to fight anyone. After several days of negotiations, Anna agreed that Cantacuzenus should rule for ten years as senior emperor for John V, who would then become his equal colleague. John V was to marry Cantacuzenus's daughter Helena. There were to be no reprisals on either side, and all confiscated or stolen land, though not movable property, was to be restored. In this way the civil war ended, after more than five years, with a limited victory for John VI Cantacuzenus.

The war had given the Genoese Chios and Phocaea, the Bulgarians Philippopolis, and the Serbs Albania and the regions of Castoria, Edessa, and Serres. The empire's chance to take the Latin Peloponnesus had been thrown away, and Thessalonica remained practically independent under the Zealots. Popular plundering of aristocrats and the depredations of Cantacuzenus's Turks had impoverished Thrace. War expenses had exhausted the public treasury and Cantacuzenus's private fortune. Personal, social, and religious resentments lingered, even though the only consistent difference between the two sides had been over the claims of Cantacuzenus.

Yet the empire had made a quick recovery nineteen years before, after the similarly bitter and destructive civil war between Andronicus II and Andronicus III. Byzantium still held Andronicus III's important conquests in Epirus and Thessaly. John VI had pledged to become the protector and father-in-law of John V. Except for the Zealots of Thessalonica, most supporters of both sides were ready to be reconciled with each other. The battle-hardened Byzantine army seemed capable of retaking the Serbs' cheaply won and lightly held conquests, and perhaps more than those. The empire had the strength to rise again.

PLAGUE AND COLLAPSE

When John VI Cantacuzenus took power in 1347 he was about fifty-one, and had played a leading part in war and politics for twenty-five years. Brilliant and cultivated, courageous and likable, he had all the virtues of a true patrician, and a few of the failings. From the start of the civil war he had overestimated his popularity, and underestimated the numbers of his opponents. His high-minded reluctance to take the crown in 1341 had certainly not deterred his enemies, and may even have encouraged them to attack him. Nevertheless, in surmounting so many obstacles he had shown himself a formidable leader and strategist.

John VI promptly held church councils that condemned the patriarch John Calecas, rehabilitated Gregory Palamas, and endorsed Palamism. That the Palamites should prevail was only to be expected; the new emperor backed them, and their opponents were widely suspected of preferring philosophy to faith and the western church to the eastern, positions few Byzantines could condone. Yet even many churchmen felt that the Palamite triumph was too complete. The new patriarch, chosen after a delay of three months, was a Palamite monk from Athos, Isidore Bucharis.

Isidore recrowned John VI in rather pathetic style—in Saint Mary of Blachernae, since part of Saint Sophia's dome had fallen the year before, and with imitation jewels, since the real ones were pawned in Venice. A week later the emperor wedded his daughter to his young colleague John V. Cantacuzenists complained that John VI should also have crowned his sons Matthew and Manuel, who had done valiant service in the war. The emperor did reward his sons as far as he could without compromising John V's rights. Matthew received an unnamed rank higher than despot but lower than emperor, and special powers over the part of Thrace between Didymotichus and Christopolis. Manuel gained the title of despot, with a similar appanage in the Peloponnesus two years later.

Without delay, John VI wrote to demand that Dushan of Serbia surrender his earlier conquest of Serres and his recent conquest of Beroea. Their return, which would still leave Dushan with most of what he had taken before breaking his pact with Cantacuzenus, was needed to link

187. John VI Cantacuzenus (r. 1347–54) presiding at a church council in
1351. Miniature from a manuscript of 1370–75 of Cantacuzenus's theological
works (Parisinus graecus 1242). (Photo: Bibliothèque Nationale, Paris)

Byzantine Thrace with Thessalonica, and Thessalonica with Thessaly and Epirus—that is, to turn three Byzantine enclaves into a continuous block of territory. If Dushan refused to hand over Serres and Beroea, Cantacuzenus threatened war. The Serbian emperor equivocated, doubtless fearing he could not hold conquests made in such exceptional circumstances.

Toward the end of spring, however, before John VI could mount an expedition against Dushan, bubonic plague broke out in Constantinople.[9] The disease, absent from the empire for six centuries, had spread from Central Asia to the Genoese colony of Caffa in the Crimea. From there ships brought it across the Black Sea to Trebizond and Byzantium. By the end of 1347 it reached western Europe, where it was called the Black Death. If the initial outbreak of the plague killed a third of the people in Byzantium, as it did in parts of the West, its impact on the empire's manpower, economy, and finances must have dwarfed the civil war's. Worse yet, as rats carried the plague from port to port, it devastated the coastlands belonging to the empire while largely sparing the inland territories of its Serbian, Bulgarian, and Turkish rivals.[10]

Coming so soon after the civil war, the Black Death left the empire short of the money and soldiers needed to drive out the Serbs. Dushan saw his chance and pressed on to conquer Epirus. The anxious emperor solicited his wealthier subjects for contributions to the war effort; he asked the papacy for help against Serbia, proposing to reunite the churches and join the Holy League; and he somewhat inconsistently appealed to his Ottoman son-in-law Orhan and to Umūr of Aydin. But Umūr died fighting the Holy League in spring 1348; and though Orhan sent some ten thousand auxiliaries, they pillaged the land around Serres and deserted. No one else helped. In a desperate attempt to raise revenue, the emperor lowered the customs duties at Constantinople to entice traders away from Genoese Galata.

Grimly mustering an army, John used it to drive Orhan's Turks from Thrace and prepared to march against Dushan. The emperor even built a navy, not just to fight the Serbs but to subdue the Zealots of Thessalonica and to restrain the increasingly insolent Genoese. But the Genoese struck first. Indignant at John's plans to lure trade away from Galata, they sailed over to Constantinople and burned the merchantmen at anchor and the Byzantine warships in the dockyard. Despite his urgent need to march against the Serbs, the emperor had to meet this brazen assault on his capital. With his subjects clamoring for war against the Genoese, he levied new taxes, began building more ships, and besieged Galata by land. He refused to make peace on any terms short of destroying the colony's recently extended walls. Meanwhile the Serbs conquered Thessaly, where the Black Death had decimated the Byzantines and killed their governor.

Early in 1349 the Black Death abated, and the new Byzantine fleet was completed. But when John ordered an attack on Galata, the inexperienced Byzantine seamen panicked at encountering a strong wind, and abandoned most of their ships to the Genoese. The dogged emperor started building a third fleet. Simply to end disruption of their business, the Genoese agreed to pay reparations of one hundred thousand hyperpyra, to return Chios after ten years, and in the meantime to lease it for twelve thousand hyperpyra a year. Though the Genoese of Chios resisted, John defeated them and took Phocaea from them.

He also established good relations with Trebizond's new emperor Alexius III, who married John's niece Theodora Cantacuzena. When the Serbs approached Thessalonica in the middle of 1350, most of the Zealots finally brought themselves to accept John VI. Expelling some diehards who wanted to let in the Serbs, they asked him for help. The emperor set out by sea with John V, sending his son Matthew by land with an army of Ottoman mercenaries. Although Matthew turned back when his Turks deserted, the senior and junior emperors sailed into Thessalonica.

Next John VI marched into the interior. Winning over most of the local leaders, he recaptured Beroea, Edessa, and the surrounding territory before the year was out. As still more places offered to receive the Byzantines, Dushan arrived from Serbia with an army and met John VI in person. According to Cantacuzenus, they agreed to a peace; if so, Dushan broke it almost at once. Apparently the emperor decided that he was too weak to take more land from the Serbs, while they were too weak to take much more from him. In fact, Dushan recaptured only Edessa and Beroea before mutual exhaustion brought the war to a close.

Although John VI had failed to restore the empire's territorial continuity, he had at least halted the Serbian advance and ended the Zealot rebellion. On departing for Constantinople he left John V and a deputy to rule Thessalonica and its hinterland. The emperor had already given similar powers to his son Matthew in western Thrace and his son Manuel in the Peloponnesus. Such a division seemed to provide for the defense of a fragmented empire while placating both the emperor's son-in-law and his sons. Naturally the rulers were supposed to cooperate under the leadership of John VI, and for the moment they did so.

188. Stephen Dushan, king of Serbia (r. 1331–55; emperor from 1346). Contemporary fresco from the Lesnovo Monastery, now in the Republic of Macedonia. (Photo: Courtesy of Slobodan Ćurčić)

When he returned to his capital in early 1351, the emperor found a war raging between Venice and Genoa. He joined the Venetians, who offered to help him take Genoese Galata and Chios; but at the approach of a large fleet from Genoa, the Venetians abruptly fled. Finding the Venetians gone, the Genoese fleet terrorized the Byzantine coast, sacking Heraclea on the Sea of Marmara and Sozopolis on the Black Sea. Seeing John VI's woes, Dushan encouraged John V to rebel at Thessalonica; but the young emperor's mother Anna sailed from Constantinople to dissuade him. Under a settlement she arranged early in 1352, she took over Thessalonica herself; her son received Matthew Cantacuzenus's appanage in western Thrace, and Matthew moved to a new domain around Adrianople. After a bloody but indecisive sea battle with the Genoese, John VI made peace with them.

That summer John's system of imperial appanages broke down completely. John V attacked Matthew Cantacuzenus in Adrianople. The Adrianopolitans joined John V, and confined Matthew to the citadel. Forced to rescue his son from his son-in-law, John VI raised the siege with Turkish mercenaries. The patriarch Callistus tried vainly to mediate. A new civil war began, with foreign powers choosing sides. John V received four thousand soldiers from Dushan of Serbia, more troops from Alexander of Bulgaria, and a loan of five thousand ducats from the

Venetians. John VI called again on his son-in-law Orhan, and received some ten thousand Ottoman auxiliaries under Orhan's son Sulaymān.

Late in the year these Byzantines, Serbs, Bulgarians, and Turks all met in a great battle on the Hebrus. John VI's Turks won it handily, and John V retreated to the little island of Tenedos. After a failed attempt to reach the capital, in early 1353 he fled to his mother Anna at Thessalonica. Although the old agreement had been that John V was to become coequal emperor in another four years, most Cantacuzenists thought he had forfeited his rights by rebelling. At their insistence, John VI had his son Matthew proclaimed coemperor in place of John V, thus deposing his junior colleague.

Nevertheless, four generations of imperial ancestors gave John V a right to the throne that even the Cantacuzenists had long admitted. The patriarch Callistus gave up his functions rather than crown Matthew Cantacuzenus. After several months, John VI had Callistus deposed and replaced by the monk Philotheus; but the Genoese of Galata helped Callistus escape to John V, who recognized him as patriarch on Tenedos. The new patriarch Philotheus waited until early 1354, then crowned Matthew.[11] There were now rival emperors and rival patriarchs, but John VI held most of what was left of the empire.

Aware that his Ottoman allies were making themselves a nuisance in Thrace, John VI tried to dismiss them. But they were paying themselves by raiding, and expected to be paid to stop. In March, while they were considering the emperor's offer of ten thousand hyperpyra, an earthquake ruined the walls of Callipolis, near their camp. Orhan's son Sulaymān briskly occupied the city and repaired its fortifications for himself. The emperor protested to both Sulaymān and his father Orhan, raising the Byzantine offer to forty thousand hyperpyra if the Turks would leave. Orhan accepted, then failed to appear to receive the money. Evidently the Turks meant to stay.

The Ottoman occupation of Callipolis confirmed many Byzantines' worst fears about John VI's reliance on the Turks. In late November John V made his move. He sailed again for Constantinople, made a clandestine landing by night, and appealed to his supporters. They turned out to be most of the populace. Again rioters attacked the houses of Cantacuzenists. Two days later, John VI agreed to reinstate John V as his junior colleague. Ten days later, to spare the empire further agony, John VI abdicated and became a monk, leaving John V to rule.

Although John VI's short reign saw Byzantium decline from a viable power to a wreck, most of the fault was not his. His arrangements for sharing power with John V had admittedly been awkward and hazardous. But without the Black Death, Cantacuzenus would probably have defeated the jerry-built empire of Stephen Dushan, regained the upper hand, and kept control of his Turks. After the plague cost him the money and men he needed, he eventually fell prey to his many enemies. Even so, Cantacuzenus had temporarily halted the empire's decline, and restored its navy. Only another natural disaster, the earthquake at Callipolis, gave the Turks a foothold in Europe. Faced with such calamities, the underage John V and his vacillating mother would surely have done even worse.

THE REMNANT OF THE EMPIRE

John V Palaeologus was twenty-three when he became senior emperor in December 1354. Although he had shown some skill and determination in reclaiming his hereditary rights, his chief ambition remained what it had been throughout his troubled youth: to be and to stay senior emperor. His other main idea, possibly borrowed from his Italian mother, was to beg the western powers for aid. He seems never to have had much hope of restoring the ruins of his realm. That the enormous task of righting the empire overwhelmed him is understandable; but perhaps the young emperor should have struggled less stoutly to take up burdens so far beyond his strength.

189. John V Palaeologus (r. 1341–76, 1379–91). Watercolor made between 1847 and 1849 by Gaspare Fossati of a mosaic in Saint Sophia, Constantinople, that has recently been rediscovered but has not yet been cleaned. (Photo: Dumbarton Oaks, Washington, D.C., copyright 1996)

At least he sometimes had the sense to consult the former John VI, who remained at a monastery in the capital under the monastic name of Joasaph. In spring 1355, John V also reached a settlement with the younger Cantacuzeni. Matthew was to keep the title of junior emperor, to leave Thrace, and to replace his brother Manuel in the Peloponnesus. Manuel was to keep the title of despot and to receive the island of Lemnos and some additional revenues. Although these terms were favorable to John V, he made no effort to fulfill them, and seems to have plotted almost at once to murder Matthew.

The emperor quickly showed his enthusiasm for westerners. He let the Genoese keep Chios not just four more years but permanently, and lowered their rent to a derisory five hundred hyperpyra. He awarded Lesbos and the hand of his sister to the Genoese adventurer Francesco Gattilusio, and soon lost control of Phocaea as well.[12] In December John wrote to Pope Innocent VI, requesting twenty ships, five hundred cavalry, and a thousand infantry to fight his enemies for six months. In return for this modest force he pledged to reunite the churches, to join the western church himself, and to send his little son Manuel to Avignon as a hostage. John apparently meant to use this papal aid against Matthew and Manuel Cantacuzenus rather than against the Turks.

At the end of the year Stephen Dushan of Serbia suddenly died.[13] Under his incompetent son, his empire crumbled into warring principalities. Even this late, Byzantium could have profited. But John V was not the man to turn Serbia's collapse to advantage, and Matthew Cantacuzenus, who still ruled western Thrace, was busy fighting John. After marching on Constantinople without result, Matthew did try to retake Serres from the local Serbs, only to be captured and sold to the emperor.[14] The one Byzantine to exploit Serbian weakness was the former despot of Epirus Nicephorus II, now almost thirty. Arriving in his old domains without an army, Nicephorus rapidly recovered both Thessaly and Epirus and ruled them as an independent state. An emperor with more spirit than John V might have retaken all northern Greece.

Still hoping for an alliance with the papacy, which was inconsequential as a military power, John neglected other opportunities. He took no part in the Holy League, which was struggling to hold the harbor of Smyrna. In 1357 he signed a treaty with the Venetians that merely confirmed his debts of almost a hundred thousand hyperpyra. John sold Pontic Heraclea, his last Anatolian port, to the Genoese. He made no alliances with the Serbs or Bulgarians, or with Nicephorus II of Epirus, whose state disintegrated in 1359 after he died fighting Albanian rebels. The next year the Holy League was dissolved, though the Hospitalers continued to hold Smyrna. Practically unopposed, the Ottomans moved farther into Thrace from their base at Callipolis, and captured Didymotichus by 1361.

The next year they began to catch the plague, which probably killed their emir Orhan.[15] Ottoman expansion slowed while Orhan's son and successor Murād fought and eliminated his brothers. During this interval, which John never tried to exploit, other Turks followed the Ottoman lead in raiding Thrace. Even the Venetians wanted an alliance to stop the Turkish advance while it was stoppable. They proposed to forgive all the emperor's debts in return for Tenedos, which they would make the headquarters of an anti-Turkish league including Genoa and Byzantium. But John refused to surrender an island that had been loyal to him during his exile.

The emperor turned to fighting not the Turks but the Bulgarians, taking Anchialus from them in 1364. Late the next year, he sailed up the Danube to see King Louis of Hungary, who had already proposed a crusade against the Turks and begun a war against the Bulgarians. What precisely John wanted from Louis is unclear. As the first sitting emperor to visit a foreign court, John was making a grand gesture, but he gained nothing whatever. Alexander of Bulgaria, suspecting John had wanted an alliance against him, refused to let the emperor return through Bulgarian territory. John remained stranded at Vidin, impotent and humiliated.[16]

Luckily for the emperor, the next summer his cousin on his mother's side, Count Amadeo VI of Savoy, mounted a small but helpful crusade. Amadeo sailed into the straits, wrested Callipolis from the Turks, barely paused at Constantinople, and seized Mesembria from the Bulgarians. After besieging Varna, he forced the Bulgarians to send him the emperor at the beginning of 1367. To meet Amadeo's expenses, John borrowed and paid him almost 42,500 hyperpyra, to be repaid when and if John came to Rome and submitted to the pope, recently returned from Avignon. The count left Byzantium bigger by two ports and the Turks in Thrace deprived of a secure harbor. Yet since nobody prevented more Turks from crossing the Hellespont, they continued to advance. By 1369 they captured Adrianople, probably the empire's third city.[17]

Instead of fighting them, that summer the emperor left for Rome to seek help from the pope, entrusting Constantinople to his eldest son Andronicus and Thessalonica to his second son Manuel. John arrived at

Rome in the fall and made his personal submission to the western church. Collecting the money due him from Amadeo of Savoy, the following spring he sailed to Venice. After prolonged haggling, the emperor apparently agreed to cede Tenedos to the Venetians in exchange for their canceling his debts, paying him twenty-five thousand ducats (fifty thousand hyperpyra), and returning his crown jewels. Back at Constantinople, however, his son Andronicus refused to surrender Tenedos, undoing the agreement. The Venetians detained the insolvent emperor until his son Manuel redeemed him in 1371.[18]

While the emperor humiliated himself in the West to no avail, the Turks advanced through the Balkans. Just before John returned to his capital, they inflicted a crushing defeat on a Serbian army in the Hebrus valley, and forced several of the Serbian princes into vassalage. At least the emperor's son Manuel made use of the Serbs' defeat to add Serres to his appanage at Thessalonica. Manuel warded off Turkish forays by canceling half the tax exemptions of monastic lands in his appanage and assigning the revenue to soldiers in pronoia. But the emperor showed none of his son's initiative. He meekly followed the Serbs in becoming a vassal of Murād, who began to style himself not emir but sultan.

John V's submission, which entailed paying tribute, seems to have been too much for his elder son Andronicus. In 1373 Adronicus joined a son of Murād in attacking both their fathers. John may have been weak, but Murād was strong enough, and the fathers soon defeated their rebellious progeny. The sultan blinded his son, who died from his injuries, and demanded John also blind Andronicus and Andronicus's son. The emperor had the blinding done gently, leaving Andronicus with one eye and his son merely squinting. John did, however, name a new heir, his second and more loyal son Manuel.

In 1376, the vassal emperor agreed to sell Tenedos to Venice on roughly the terms Andronicus had blocked six years before. The sale, however, upset the Genoese of Galata, who retaliated against Byzantium. They helped the disinherited Andronicus escape from prison, enlist soldiers from Murād, and besiege Constantinople. This time Andronicus took the city and imprisoned John V and Manuel. As Andronicus IV Palaeologus, he repaid his allies by ceding Tenedos to Genoa and Callipolis to Murād. Though the Ottomans duly occupied the strategic city, the outraged garrison of Tenedos surrendered their island to the Venetians.

Aged twenty-eight, the one-eyed Andronicus IV was scarcely more capable than John V, and had even less room to maneuver. Before he

190. Philadelphia (modern Alaşehir). Engraving by W. Floyd after T. Allom. (From Thomas Allom, *Constantinople and the Scenery of the Seven Churches of Asia Minor* [London, 1838])

could gain control of the outlying parts of the empire, he found himself locked in a major war with Venice. In 1379 his father and brother escaped to Murād, and apparently secured the sultan's help by promising him Philadelphia, which had long held out against the Turks as a practically independent outpost. In July the Venetians ferried some Turks across the Bosporus and put John back on his throne. Andronicus fled to Galata, taking as hostages his mother Helena Cantacuzena and her aged father Joasaph, the former John VI.

Andronicus remained at Galata for almost two years, but in 1381 agreed to a treaty that restored him as heir to the empire and granted him an appanage around Selymbria. His younger brother Manuel returned to Thessalonica as its governor, and their brother Theodore became governor of the Byzantine Peloponnesus following the death of Manuel Cantacuzenus.[19] The Venetians and Genoese made peace by agreeing to turn Tenedos into a wasteland, belonging to no one. During this miserable family war, the Ottomans occupied even more of the central Balkans, which had become a welter of Serbian, Bulgarian, and Albanian fiefdoms.

Only Manuel Palaeologus, coemperor at Thessalonica, tried to resist the Turks. In 1382 he won over the various rulers of Thessaly and Epirus and invested them as imperial vassals with the title of despot. He built up an army of volunteers and seemed to have a remote chance of making Byzantium a viable state again. But Manuel's efforts alerted the Ottomans. In 1383 they took Serres and besieged him in Thessalonica. He made manful efforts to hold out. But he could obtain no aid from his father, who was inert as usual, from his brother Andronicus, who rebelled again before dying in 1385, or from his brother Theodore, who was fighting the new Navarrese rulers of the Latin Peloponnesus. The Venetians also refused to help. In spring 1387, after a siege of three and a half years, Manuel abandoned Thessalonica to the sultan.

By autumn the Turks were raiding the Peloponnesus, and by early 1389 Murād had subjected all of Bulgaria. Three Serbian princes made a stand on the border of Serbia proper. In the late spring the sultan attacked them in the region of Kosovo. A great many fell on both sides. The sultan himself was among the dead, and the Serbs have celebrated their valor in the battle of Kosovo ever since. Nevertheless, the Turks finally drove them from the field with crippling losses. Although Murād's son Bāyezīd hurried back to Anatolia to secure his succession, he left the Turks masters of the Balkans.

Bāyezīd proved to be an even more active sultan than Murād. In spring 1390 he plotted with Andronicus IV's son John, who had inherited Selymbria from his father. Backed by Turkish soldiers and Genoese ships, young John gained entrance to the capital and seized the throne, while John V barricaded himself in a fortress by the Golden Gate. The usurper became John VII Palaeologus. He was about twenty years old, with some ability but little experience. He felt deep resentment against his grandfather for damaging his eyesight, but was unable to dislodge him entirely from Constantinople. John VII also failed to gain control of the remaining Byzantine islands, where his uncle Manuel gathered troops to resist him. After five months, Manuel sailed back and retook Constantinople, rescuing and restoring John V.[20]

John VII fled to Bāyezīd. The sultan was far too powerful for John V to dare to reproach for this unprovoked meddling in the empire's affairs. Without quite having the effrontery to demand that his puppet emperor be restored, Bāyezīd meant to enforce John V's vassalage. Returning young John to Selymbria, the sultan apparently summoned Manuel Palaeologus for a campaign against Philadelphia, which had refused to surrender after the emperor had ceded it. Manuel reportedly obeyed and helped take the city. Next Bāyezīd threatened to blind Manuel unless the emperor demolished his fortress by the Golden Gate. John V sadly complied. Shortly afterward he died, of complications from gout, in February 1391.

John V's reign as senior emperor justified in retrospect the Cantacuzenists who had fought to prevent it. No doubt John had taken over the wreckage of an empire, battered by Serbs to the west and Turks to the south. Yet the efforts of Nicephorus II of Epirus, Amadeo of Savoy, and John's son Manuel at Thessalonica showed that, given the will, the Serbs and Turks could be resisted with very modest resources. Instead John let his army and navy decay, and squandered his last asset, Byzantine prestige, on ill-conceived appeals to the papacy, to Hungary, and to Venice. He made no secure alliances, and gained little from the tribute he paid the Ottomans. He neither cleared his debts nor repudiated them, neither led the Byzantine church nor reunited it with the western church that he joined. Even at John's accession, something might still have been made of Byzantium. By the time of his death, its fall could be foreseen.

CHAPTER TWENTY-FIVE

The End of Byzantine
Independence, 1391–1461

In 1391 no one could reasonably have predicted that Byzantium would last two generations more. It consisted only of Constantinople itself, some nearby ports in Thrace, a few northern Aegean islands, and part of the Peloponnesus. These enclaves were depopulated, largely autonomous, and in vassalage to the far stronger Ottoman sultan Bāyezīd, who controlled almost everything around them. The next logical step was for the Ottomans to take Constantinople and make it their capital. Whether Bāyezīd would even permit the succession of a new Byzantine emperor was uncertain. John V's son Manuel was a virtual prisoner of the sultan, and the late emperor's grandson, John VII, seemed subservient to the Ottomans. By this time the empire had sunk so low that any attempt to strengthen it risked provoking Turkish annexation.

A NARROW ESCAPE

At the news of his father's death, Manuel deftly absconded from Bāyezīd's court at Prusa, arrived at Constantinople, and was crowned in March. Although as son of the late emperor's eldest son John VII had the better claim to the throne, old John had preferred Manuel. Intelligent, urbane, and experienced, Manuel II Palaeologus was forty at his accession. As governor of Thessalonica he had resourcefully resisted the Turks, and his escape from Bāyezīd also showed some enterprise. But after so many Byzantine reverses and Ottoman triumphs, Manuel had despaired of any active resistance; the best he hoped for was to hold out until something turned up. Given the condition of his realm, his fatalism was simply realistic.

Manuel hastened to make his peace with Bāyezīd. The sultan, busy conquering the emirates of southern and eastern Anatolia, accepted him as a vassal, but on harsh conditions. He apparently raised the empire's tribute, and summoned Manuel for a campaign that very spring. The emperor left his mother Helena as regent at Constantinople and reluctantly spent the rest of the year with Bāyezīd in Anatolia. On his return, early in 1392, Manuel married a princess from southern Serbia, Helena Dragash. Though Manuel already had several illegitimate children, he seems not to have married before he succeeded to the throne. Once crowned, he was at least determined not to let his line die out. His choice avoided trouble with Bāyezīd because his bride's father Constantine Dragash was a fellow vassal of the Turks, and not a likely ally against them.

For the Byzantine emperor to be anyone's vassal was deeply humiliating. In 1392 the Russian church stopped commemorating the humbled emperor in its liturgy, ignoring the protests of the patriarch of Constantinople. Yet the danger of offending the sultan was clear. When John Shishman of Bulgaria tried to throw off Turkish suzerainty in 1393 with Hungarian help, the Turks captured him, annexed his domains, and later executed him. Nor was Bāyezīd even a reliable suzerain. Late in the year he separately summoned his Byzantine and Serbian vassals to appear before him at Serres. When they arrived and found each other all together, they feared with reason that he would murder them, taking the rest of the Balkans at a blow.

In fact, the sultan merely wanted to intimidate them. He listened to their complaints about each other, especially those against the despot Theodore, who had been using Albanian mercenaries to add Argos and other places to his holdings in the Peloponnesus. After punishing some lesser Byzantine officials with mutilation, Bāyezīd demanded Theodore serve on an expedition in Thessaly and cede Argos and Monemvasia. The rest of the vassals at the meeting were allowed to leave, shaken and suspicious. Though by treating his vassals well the sultan could have kept the peace while he made conquests farther afield, his arbitrary arrogance frightened the Byzantines into desperate opposition.

The emperor refused a new summons from the sultan and prepared for war. Theodore escaped from Thessaly, recovered Monemvasia, and gave Argos to the Venetians. The Ottomans therefore blockaded Constantinople in the fall of 1394.[1] Earlier Bāyezīd might have taken the city by surprise; but to besiege it after ample warning was much more difficult. Its land walls remained almost impregnable, and the makeshift Ottoman navy was no match for the Venetians who supplied the

191. Manuel II Palaeologus (r. 1391–1425) and his wife Helena crowned by
the Virgin, with their sons (from left to right) the future John VIII, Theodore,
and Andronicus. Miniature from a manuscript of 1403–5 of the works of
Pseudo–Dionysius the Areopagite (Louvre MS. Ivoires 100). (Photo: Copyright Réunion des Musées Nationaux)

defenders. That winter the Turks raided the Byzantine Peloponnesus and the Vlach Principality of Wallachia. The raiders sent to the Peloponnesus defeated the despot Theodore but withdrew in the spring, probably when they heard that the Wallachian prince had mauled the army sent against him.

The Ottoman siege of Constantinople and invasion of Wallachia shocked westerners into mounting the largest crusade in over a century. For the effort King Sigismund of Hungary enlisted French, Germans, Burgundians, and a few Venetians. By summer 1396 Sigismund led an army of perhaps sixteen thousand men to besiege Nicopolis in Turkish-held Bulgaria. Bāyezīd arrived at the beginning of autumn, apparently with a somewhat larger force. In a battle before Nicopolis, the Ottomans killed or captured most of the Crusaders. The vanquished Sigismund escaped down the Danube on a Venetian ship.

The Crusade of Nicopolis temporarily distracted the Turks, but the Byzantines' future looked black. The Venetians and Genoese sent only enough supplies to keep Constantinople from surrendering. In 1397, when the Turks raided the Peloponnesus again and sacked Argos, the hard-pressed despot Theodore had to sell the Hospitalers Corinth, which he had recently purchased.[2] Though the sultan's assaults on Constantinople failed, its people became so restive that betrayal was a real danger, especially when the sultan talked of restoring John VII.

In summer 1399, answering an appeal from Manuel, Charles VI of France sent a small relief force under his marshal Boucicault. Boucicault landed in Constantinople with twelve hundred men, rallied Byzantine spirits, and joined the emperor in some raids on the Turks. The marshal urged Manuel to travel with him to France and request more assistance in person. Boucicault also brought John VII from Selymbria, reconciled him with his uncle Manuel, and convinced the emperor to name John regent in his absence. So in December Manuel and Boucicault embarked. The emperor was suspicious enough of his nephew to take his empress Helena and his sons John and Theodore to the Peloponnesus, where he entrusted them to his brother Theodore. Although the emperor seems to have entertained few hopes for his tour of the West, he had no better plan, and could at least avoid being captured if Constantinople fell.

After spending the winter in the Peloponnesus, in April 1400 Manuel landed in Venice, to a warm reception. As he crossed northern Italy, he found Italian Renaissance opinion sympathetic to Greeks and enthusiastic about Greek culture. A handsome and dignified man, the emperor

192. Marshal Boucicault kneeling before the Virgin. Miniature from the contemporary *Hours of Marshal Boucicault*, now in the Musée Jacquemart-André, Paris. (Photo: Musée Jacquemart-André)

did not disappoint his public. In June he met Charles VI, who came out from Paris to greet him. Manuel sent embassies to the Spanish kings and to Pope Boniface IX at Rome, and before the end of the year, Henry IV of England welcomed the emperor in London. Everyone was gracious and respectful, and many made promises; but all had problems of their own, and no one was in a hurry to help. In 1401 Manuel returned to Paris. Aware that he would be forgotten if he went home, he stayed in the French capital into the following year.

Back in Constantinople, John VII held out with a few French auxiliaries left by Boucicault. John seems to have lost Selymbria and everything else in Thrace but the capital itself. By some accounts, he was ready to capitulate in the late spring of 1402. Just then, however, Bāyezīd had to march east to face a new enemy, Timur the Lame. A Turk who had taken over Central Asia, Persia, and Mesopotamia with a mostly Mongol army, Timur was now invading Ottoman-held Asia Minor. In July he met the sultan in a great battle near Ancyra, won a crushing victory over the Ottoman forces, and captured Bāyezīd himself.

Bāyezīd's eldest son Sulaymān escaped to Thrace, but he was far too busy salvaging the Ottoman Sultanate to resume the siege of Constantinople. Timur went on to devastate Asia Minor, restoring the independent eastern and southern emirates annexed by Bāyezīd. Bāyezīd's younger sons took over what was left of Ottoman Anatolia. As long as Sulaymān needed all his remaining strength to oppose his brothers and Timur, he was vulnerable to a concerted Byzantine and western attack on Ottoman Europe. Surely aware of this, on learning of the Ottoman defeat Manuel went first to Genoa and then to Venice for negotiations. No less aware of his danger, early in 1403 Sulaymān offered astonishingly generous terms to avert an anti-Turkish coalition.

Besides freeing Byzantium from Ottoman suzerainty, the sultan ceded it most of the Thracian seaboard, from Mesembria in the north to Panidus in the west. To this he added, apparently as an appanage for John VII after Manuel's return, Thessalonica, the surrounding coast east to the Strymon and south to Thessaly, and the offshore islands. Sulaymān also granted various concessions and privileges to the Venetians, Genoese, and Hospitalers. John VII and the westerners were delighted to receive so much for nothing. Yet the treaty served Sulaymān's purpose: it kept the Christian powers from uniting against him when he was least able to fight them.

By late spring, when Manuel and his family sailed into Constantinople, the treaty was already signed. Bāyezīd had died in captivity, and Timur had left Anatolia. Although the emperor was canny enough to see that an opportunity had passed along with the danger, he ratified the treaty. He liked John no better than before, perhaps resenting that the treaty provided his nephew with a large detached appanage around Thessalonica when Callipolis would have been more useful. Nonetheless, by the end of the year Manuel let John take up his fief. After the despot Theodore bought Corinth back from the Hospitalers in spring 1404, he held the greater part of the Peloponnesus, and Byzantium was bigger than it had been for years.

The Ottoman Sultanate was not only smaller but split between Sulaymān in the Balkans and his brothers in Anatolia. Yet the empire was itself divided into Manuel's coastal strips around Constantinople, John's coastlands around Thessalonica, and Theodore's Peloponnesus, each of which was essentially independent of the others. Sulaymān held the territory between them and most of their hinterlands in Bulgaria, Thrace, and Thessaly. He also kept contact with Anatolia through Callipolis. As the sultan had doubtless expected, Manuel's empire was a facade, with barely the resources to maintain itself.

For several years, however, the sultan had to keep fighting his brothers, while Manuel's brother Theodore died in 1407 and his nephew John VII died the next year. Manuel was therefore able to assign the Peloponnesus to his second son Theodore, and Thessalonica to his third son Andronicus. Since both sons were still children, Manuel's officials became the real administrators, and the emperor the real ruler, of both territories. More unified than before, Byzantium began to look a little less decrepit, though it was still much weaker than even a divided sultanate.

The Ottoman civil war flared up in 1409, when Sulaymān's Balkan domains were invaded by his brother Mūsā. Manuel remained true to his treaty with Sulaymān, but tried to take what advantage he could. In 1410 he almost captured Callipolis from Mūsā. Yet the emperor was weaker than either Ottoman claimant, and could not stop Mūsā from defeating and executing Sulaymān the next year. In revenge the new sultan besieged Constantinople and Thessalonica. To defend himself, the emperor lent support to a third brother, Mehmed, ferrying his troops across the straits from Anatolia. After two more years of fighting, in 1413 Mehmed defeated Mūsā and had him strangled. Since this time, by luck, the emperor had taken the winning side, Mehmed confirmed Sulaymān's favorable treaty of ten years before. Once again, however, Byzantium was trapped between a single sultan's domains in Asia Minor and the Balkans.

Unable to join his holdings together, Manuel tried at least to strengthen their defenses. In 1414 he left his eldest son John to govern Constantinople and set sail for his western territories. Repulsing a Genoese attack on the island of Thasos, he spent the winter at Thessalonica. The following year he visited the Peloponnesus, now the most prosperous part of his impoverished realm, and ordered the Isthmus of Corinth to be fortified. Exacting special levies for the work, and putting down a revolt caused by them, he spanned the isthmus with a fortification he called the Hexamilium, or Six-Mile Wall. This he hoped would give the whole Peloponnesus protection comparable to the city walls of Thessalonica and Constantinople.

The emperor returned to his capital in 1416 to find the sultan's brother Mustafa raising a revolt in the Balkans. Manuel gave Mustafa some gingerly backing, and the Venetians took their chance to destroy the Ottoman navy. But that fall Mehmed's forces defeated Mustafa near Thessalonica and sent him fleeing into the city. Manuel's son John interned the unsuccessful rebel on Lemnos, and the sultan was willing to pay around twenty thousand hyperpyra a year to keep him there.[3] Young John gradually assumed more responsibilities, and was crowned coemperor early in 1421.

Then the sultan Mehmed died. John wanted to try setting up Mustafa as sultan in place of Mehmed's son Murād II. Although the risks were obvious, success might give Byzantium a chance at real independence. The old emperor opposed such adventurism, but gave in after a dispute at court that lasted several months. So John had Mustafa released from Lemnos and brought to Callipolis, which was one of many places the pretender promised to surrender to the empire. Mustafa gained a good deal of support among the Turks, took Callipolis and Adrianople, and marched on Prusa. He met Murād in battle in early 1422, but was routed by his nephew. Murād had him pursued into the Balkans and hanged.[4]

The sultan was understandably incensed with the Byzantines. Brushing aside Manuel's attempts to make peace, he besieged Thessalonica and Constantinople through the summer. Since Murād could hardly be angrier than he was, Manuel summoned the last available Ottoman pretender, another Mustafa, who was Murād's younger brother. This Mustafa's proclamation forced the sultan to raise the siege of Constantinople. Shortly afterward, however, the old and troubled emperor suffered a stroke that partly paralyzed him, and valuable time was lost. With some Byzantine help, young Mustafa seized Nicaea. But early in 1423 Murād had this last pretender captured and strangled as well. Freed from rebellions, the sultan turned again to vengeance on Byzantium.

Having found Constantinople much too hard to take, Murād attacked the other fragments of the empire. He intensified the siege of Thessalonica, and sent an army that easily demolished the Hexamilium and raided the Peloponnesus. The Turks pressed Thessalonica so hard that its governor Andronicus gave the city to Venice in the hope of saving it.[5] The junior emperor John sailed to Venice to seek further aid. During his absence, in winter 1424 the sultan granted peace to the crippled Manuel, who was assisted by his fourth son Constantine. The Byzantines surrendered their remaining fortresses around Thessalonica and on the Black Sea, except for Mesembria and Anchialus, and pledged to pay an annual tribute of about twenty thousand hyperpyra.[6] Though these terms were far from liberal, the isolated places the Byzantines gave up would hardly have been tenable against Turkish attacks, and the tribute was probably less than the cost of further warfare. In any case, the empire had little choice. The junior emperor John, who had traveled from Italy to Hungary in his search for aid, returned with empty hands.

So when the aged and bedridden Manuel died in the summer of 1425, he left Byzantium only a bit less miserable than at his accession. Yet even after the battle of Ancyra, he had scarcely anything to work with. Perhaps he should have taken greater risks; but his son John had gambled on Murād's uncle Mustafa and lost. Manuel tried as well as he could to persuade the western powers to contribute money and men to Byzantium's defense; but even his tour of Italy, France, and England, at a time when Constantinople was in imminent danger, had brought no results. The Bulgarians and most of the Serbs were already subjects or vassals of the Turks. Under such circumstances, Manuel deserves some credit for the empire's even surviving through his long reign.

A LAST APPEAL

By the time John VIII Palaeologus became senior emperor at age thirty-two, he had already played a role in government for several years. Although his father had thought him somewhat too bold, by 1425 boldness was almost impossible anyway. The empire possessed just three scraps of land. John directly ruled the vicinity of Constantinople, with

193. John VIII Palaeologus (r. 1425–48), his brother Constantine XI Palaeologus (r. 1449–53), and an imaginary Constantine I as a reminder that the first and the last emperor at Constantinople had the same name. Miniatures from the Modena Zonaras. (Photo: Biblioteca Estense, Modena)

Selymbria and the northern Aegean islands; his brother Constantine held Mesembria and Anchialus to the north; and his brother Theodore retained the Byzantine Peloponnesus. Of these, the Peloponnesian segment was much the largest, and the only one that could be enlarged without a suicidal attack on the Turks.

Since Theodore had expressed a wish to retire to a monastery, the emperor decided to replace him with Constantine, leaving Mesembria for his younger brother Demetrius. Yet by autumn 1426, when John went to the Peloponnesus with Constantine, Theodore had changed his mind about retiring. The emperor and Constantine stayed to campaign against the Latins in the northwestern corner of the peninsula. The Byzantines first attacked Clarentza, which belonged to Carlo Tocco, ruler of Cephalonia and Epirus. After they bested him in a naval battle in early 1427, Tocco gave Constantine his part of the Peloponnesus and the hand of his daughter.

This dowry became a separate appanage for Constantine, to which the emperor added the western part of Theodore's domain. John granted his youngest brother Thomas another appanage in the northern Peloponnesus, next to the remnant of the Latin Principality of Achaea. Having apportioned the Peloponnesus among his brothers, the emperor returned to Constantinople. The ambitious Constantine soon attacked Patras, then held by a papal legate, and in spring 1429 added the city to his holdings. The same year Thomas Palaeologus defeated the forces of the aged and feeble prince of Achaea, married the prince's daughter, and became his heir. Like his two brothers who also ruled in the Peloponnesus, Thomas received the title of despot.

While the Byzantines made these small but gratifying gains, the Ottoman advance rolled on. The Turks stormed, sacked, and conquered Thessalonica in 1430, ending seven years of embattled Venetian rule. The same year the Turks captured Joannina from Carlo Tocco's nephew and successor, who became their vassal for his remaining lands around Arta. By this time the Ottoman Sultanate had practically recovered its borders as they had been before the battle of Ancyra. Whenever Murād chose to make war on the Byzantines, their position would immediately become desperate.

At least the Turks' progress reawakened concern in western Europe, reviving negotiations for church union and another crusade. In 1430 John made a tentative agreement with Pope Martin V to hold an ecumenical council. The papacy offered passage to Italy and back for an eastern delegation of up to seven hundred members, including the emperor and the patriarchs of Constantinople, Alexandria, Antioch, and Jerusalem. But Pope Martin died the next year, and his successor Eugenius IV began a power struggle with the Council of Basel that stymied negotiations with the Byzantines.

The despot Thomas inherited the last of the Principality of Achaea in 1432, so that the Byzantines finally held the whole Peloponnesus except for the Venetian ports of Nauplia, Methone, and Corone. To exploit this turn of events, the despot Constantine exchanged his appanage in the western Peloponnesus for Thomas's appanage in the north. From his new base Constantine hoped to acquire the neighboring Duchy of Athens, which had been ruled for some years by an Italian dynasty. He seemed near success in 1435, when the duke of Athens died and his Greek widow was ready to cede her duchy to Constantine. But her Latin nobles resisted, and she married a new Latin duke.

Pope Eugenius, having gained the upper hand over the troublesome Council of Basel, invited the Byzantines to a council at Ferrara in 1437. The emperor hastened to depart. Leaving his brother Constantine as regent at Constantinople, John embarked with his allotted delegation of seven hundred. Among them were the patriarch of Constantinople Joseph II, the archbishop of Nicaea Bessarion, representatives of the patriarchs of Alexandria, Antioch, and Jerusalem, and bishops from Trebizond, Georgia, Bulgaria, Wallachia, and a second Vlach principality, Moldavia. Archbishop Isidore of Kiev, a Greek from Byzantium, came by land from Russia. Traveling by way of Venice, they all arrived in Ferrara the following spring.

The council's deliberations continued into 1439, when it moved from Ferrara to Florence. After exhaustive discussion, every question was resolved, usually by an agreement to tolerate existing differences. Thus the Latin Creed continued to mention the Holy Spirit's procession from both Father and Son (the *filioque*), while the Greek Creed continued to speak of the Spirit's procession simply from the Father. Formulations of varying degrees of ambiguity permitted the eastern practice of Hesychasm, the western belief in Purgatory, and the use of either leavened or unleavened bread in the Eucharist. The most important point the eastern delegates conceded was papal authority to call ecumenical councils and to hear appeals on disciplinary matters. Although the patriarch Joseph died shortly before the proclamation of union, he left a written statement endorsing it. The emperor and all but two eastern delegates subscribed to it. The pope promised to organize a crusade the next year, and made Bessarion of Nicaea and Isidore of Kiev cardinals. The emperor and his delegates returned to Constantinople early in 1440, after achieving as much as anyone could fairly have expected.[7]

Even if the Byzantines' antiwestern feelings seem to have faded somewhat since the Union of Lyons, from the beginning the Union of Florence encountered hostility in the East. The council's opponents found a leader in one of the two delegates who had rejected it, Archbishop Mark of Ephesus. Some other delegates who had subscribed at Florence disowned the union after they returned. The emperor delayed proclaiming it in the empire, and had trouble finding a unionist who would accept the patriarchate. The patriarch chosen, Archbishop Metrophanes of Cyzicus, faced open rebellion among many of his priests and bishops. Cardinal Bessarion of Nicaea returned to Italy in dismay. Cardinal Isidore of Kiev had to flee Russia for Italy the next year. The patriarchs of Alexandria, Antioch, and Jerusalem all repudiated their delegates' consent to the union. The emperor's brother Demetrius opposed it from his appanage at Mesembria, and in 1442 attacked and besieged Constantinople with troops from the sultan. But no one betrayed the city; Demetrius gave up, and John put him under arrest. A Turkish attack on Trebizond also failed.

A civil war in Hungary delayed the promised crusade until Pope Eugenius arranged a truce in 1442. The following year the pope began preparations for the expedition, which was to include an army from Hungary and a fleet to stop any Ottoman reinforcements from crossing the straits to the Balkans. The governor of the Hungarian province of Transylvania, John Hunyadi, led a preliminary campaign, which sacked Nish and Serdica before returning home at the onset of winter. The emperor prepared for the crusade by assigning most of the Peloponnesus to his energetic brother Constantine, who meant to advance into Turkish territory if the chance came. Since the Latin Duchy of Athens lay in his way, Constantine forced it to accept his suzerainty and to repudiate that of the sultan in spring 1444. Meanwhile the Albanians and Vlachs of Thessaly rebelled against the Turks, and the Albanian leader George Castriotes, better known as Scanderbeg, raised a rebellion in Albania itself. As a crusader fleet was readied at Venice, a crusader army gathered in Buda under King Ladislas of Hungary and Poland.

The sultan Murād sued for peace. Strangely, the crusader army agreed to a ten-year truce, though only the Serbs kept its terms, which restored their independence, and the others seem only to have meant to take the sultan unawares. The crusader fleet sailed into the Hellespont according to plan. King Ladislas, assisted by Hunyadi, gathered some sixteen thousand mostly Hungarian troops, and enlisted four thousand Wallachians. In late summer these marched down the Danube valley to Nicopolis. From there they advanced to the port of Varna, which surrendered to them. The Venetians kept the sultan from crossing the Hellespont, but he managed to ferry his army across the Bosporus. In November Murād arrived at Varna with a considerably larger force than the Crusaders'. In a hard-fought battle, Ladislas was killed charging the Turks, and word of his death put the Crusaders to flight. Most of them were killed, though Hunyadi escaped.

This Crusade of Varna had come close to destroying Murād's army and setting off a general revolt in Turkish Europe. Even after its failure, Hunyadi became regent of Hungary and was eager to continue resistance. Albania remained in rebellion under Scanderbeg, and the crusader fleet was intact. The despot Constantine, who had been waiting to occupy northern Greece if the Crusaders won, decided to press on nonetheless. In spring 1445 he led an army into Thessaly and took it from the Ottomans, while Hunyadi attacked the Turks along the Danube. But Hunyadi made no progress; the crusader fleet sailed home, and the Venetians made a truce with the sultan in 1446. By autumn Murād was

free to campaign against Constantine. The sultan recovered Thessaly, reclaimed his suzerainty over Athens, and broke through the Hexamilium.
A Turkish raid on the Peloponnesus was enough to force Constantine
and his brother Thomas back into vassalage.

The tireless Hunyadi gathered another crusade of sorts by 1448, enlisting the Wallachians and Scanderbeg, who was supposed to join him
later. The Hungarian regent reached Kosovo with his Wallachian allies,
but the sultan arrived there before Scanderbeg did. When the Wallachians deserted, Hunyadi found himself outnumbered. Opting for prudence rather than glory, he fled. After this last reverse, Hunyadi lacked
the means or reputation for another crusade, and no one else seemed to
have the spirit for one. Not long afterward, in these nearly hopeless circumstances, John VIII died.

Since John never had children, and his brothers Theodore and Andronicus had predeceased him, his heir was his oldest surviving brother,
Constantine. John had tried the only plan with any likelihood of success, reunion with the western church in return for a crusade. He had
concluded as convincing a reunion as was possible, which had brought
as formidable a crusade as was feasible. If it had beaten the Turks, as it almost succeeded in doing, Constantine might well have retaken the rest
of Greece, and Serbian, Albanian, and Bulgarian rebellions might have
driven the Turks from Europe. Even if such an outcome was never probable, the melancholy alternative was to do nothing, and wait for the Turkish conquest.

THE FINAL FALL

Constantine XI Palaeologus, aged forty-three, received word that he
had inherited the empire when he was ruling as despot at Mistra.[8] The
elderly empress Helena, his mother and John VIII's, thwarted a plot by
his antiunionist brother Demetrius, and served as regent at Constantinople until Constantine could arrive. The new emperor was proclaimed
at Mistra early in 1449. A man of undoubted ability, Constantine had
already distinguished himself by his intrepid conquests in Greece. By
now, however, he had scant room to maneuver. Although he wanted to
continue the Union of Florence in the forlorn hope of further help from
the West, he needed to avoid offending the Byzantine antiunionists, and
most of all the sultan.

When Constantine arrived at Constantinople he postponed his coro-

nation, probably to avoid being crowned by the unpopular unionist patriarch Gregory. The emperor made a new truce with Murād, who accepted him as a vassal. Constantine provided for his two brothers by
slightly enlarging Thomas's appanage in the western Peloponnesus and
giving Demetrius the rest of the peninsula. Yet without Constantine's
presence to restrain them, the two despots quarreled within a year, and
the emperor had to intervene to reconcile them.

In 1451, after an inconclusive campaign against Scanderbeg's Albanians, Murād II died. His successor was his nineteen-year-old son Mehmed II. At first the young sultan confirmed his father's treaty with the
emperor, perhaps only because he wanted to establish himself before
making an attempt on Constantinople. Be that as it may, late in the year
the impoverished Constantine asked the sultan to double an annual subsidy of some twenty thousand hyperpyra that the Byzantines received for
detaining an Ottoman pretender.[9] Mehmed made this a pretext for ab-
rogating the treaty.

The next spring the sultan began building a fort he called Rumeli
Hisar, on the European shore of the Bosporus.[10] Its site was on previously
Byzantine territory, and it not only threatened ships passing through the

194. Rumeli Hisar, with the Bosporus in the foreground. (Photo: Irina
Andreescu-Treadgold)

strait but provided a good base for attacking Constantinople. Mehmed also constructed a substantial fleet. That summer he engaged a Hungarian engineer, who had left Constantine's service for lack of pay, to forge cannons capable of sinking ships and breaching city walls. The sultan obviously planned not just a demonstration, but a full-scale assault.

The emperor appealed to Venice, Genoa, Hunyadi, the king of Aragon, Pope Nicholas V, and other western powers, and to his brothers Thomas and Demetrius in the Peloponnesus. By autumn, however, the brothers were fully occupied, first by a major Turkish raid, then by an Albanian-led revolt. The pope sent Cardinal Isidore of Kiev, who brought two hundred soldiers from Naples. But the pope insisted that Constantine proclaim the Union of Florence and reinstate the unionist patriarch Gregory, who had withdrawn to Rome the previous year. Although reluctant to defy the antiunionists, the emperor felt unable to defy the papacy when western help was so desperately needed. He therefore had the Union of Florence proclaimed.

Early in 1453, seven hundred Genoese and three hundred Venetians arrived, bringing the total number of soldiers in Constantinople to some three thousand foreigners and five thousand Byzantines. Mehmed had perhaps eighty thousand men. Although the Byzantines had their walls, the Turks had the Hungarian's new cannons, including a behemoth that shot balls said to weigh twelve hundred pounds. The Turkish forces easily captured the Byzantine outposts of Thracian Heraclea, Mesembria, and Anchialus. At the beginning of April, after offering the Byzantines their lives if they surrendered, the sultan settled down to besiege Constantinople.

The siege lasted two months. Since the Turkish cannons could only fire at intervals, and the giant one could fire just seven times a day, the Byzantines were able to patch up much of the damage to the walls as it was done. Though the Byzantines too had cannons, they were slow-loading guns that killed few men, and their recoil further weakened the walls. Despite the Turkish fleet, some Genoese ships brought in supplies during the siege. The Turks tried but failed to clear a boom that had been used to block the Golden Horn, and their first assault on the damaged fortifications was also beaten back.

To evade the boom, the Turks contrived to wheel some ships overland around the wall of Galata. These they launched at the far end of the Golden Horn, forcing the defenders to man the sea walls on that side. Still the Turks could not break the boom or penetrate the walls. While losing many men, they inflicted remarkably few Christian casualties. Late in May, the sultan again offered to spare the defenders in return for capitulation, or even to raise the siege for an exorbitant tribute, apparently a hundred thousand hyperpyra a year.[11] Since the emperor could not raise such a sum even once, the Christians fought on.

The sultan ordered a massive assault before daybreak on 29 May. By this time the largest Turkish cannon had gravely weakened the defenses just south of Blachernae. The moat was filled with rubble, and both the inner and the outer wall had partly collapsed. Mehmed sent three waves of troops against the weakest point, but they suffered terrible losses without penetrating the city. Then they wounded the Genoese commander, Giovanni Giustiniani. When he was brought down from the walls, his troops began to flee, and the Turks broke in through a nearby gate. As the enemy swarmed into the city, most of the Italians escaped in their ships, but almost all the Byzantine soldiers fought to the death, the emperor Constantine among them.[12]

The sultan let his men pillage Constantinople for the three days prescribed by Muslim tradition for a city that had resisted capture. They ransacked most of the churches, houses, and shops, destroying as much as they stole. They killed many of the citizens, particularly the remaining Italians, before starting to enslave the rest. Only two districts in the northwest and southwest of the city, the quarters of the Phanar ("Lighthouse") and Studius, were evidently allowed to surrender and remain intact, along with Genoese Galata. Their inhabitants ransomed some of the captives. The sultan freed a few others, but executed the highest Byzantine officials.

Mehmed, henceforth known as the Conqueror, began rebuilding and resettling the city as his capital. He restored the walls of Constantinople itself but leveled those of Galata, where the Genoese were allowed to stay. Preserving Saint Sophia for use as a mosque, he chose a new patriarch, Gennadius Scholarius, a former delegate to the Council of Florence who had become the leading antiunionist. After briefly taking over the Church of the Holy Apostles, Gennadius chose to leave the dilapidated building, which the sultan demolished to build a mosque of his own.

Once Mehmed had definitely decided to capture Constantinople, Constantine XI could hardly have held it for long with the men and money he had. Even several thousand more reinforcements from the West could have done no more than delay the city's fall by a few months.

195. Miniature of the siege of Constantinople from Bertrandon de la Broquière's *Voyage Oversea* of 1455 (Bibliothèque Nationale, ms. français 9087). (Photo: Bibliothèque Nationale, Paris)

The recent development of the large-bore cannon doomed any isolated post so dependent on the strength of its fortifications. Although a full-dress crusade might have made a difference, such expeditions took time and trouble to organize, and had failed so often as to discredit the whole idea. Extreme subservience to the sultan might have gained Constantine a few wretched years, but no more.

After the fall of the capital, and the surrender of Selymbria just afterward, the despots Thomas and Demetrius remained in the Peloponnesus, still trying to subdue the rebels against them. Both the rebels and the despots appealed to Mehmed, who decided for the despots. Requiring them to pay an annual tribute of ten thousand hyperpyra, he sent them an army that suppressed the rebellion in 1454.[13] The Ottomans gradually took over the northern Aegean islands and the Duchy of Athens, but spared the Peloponnesus for the moment.

Although the despots' fiefdoms caused no inconvenience to the sultan, their hereditary claim to the fallen empire was a potential nuisance. Mehmed began to let Peloponnesian landholders submit directly to his rule, thus curtailing the despots' revenues without reducing their tribute. By 1458 their payments were three years overdue, and the sultan led an expedition against them. He was harder on Thomas, who as a unionist had been trying to interest the pope in a crusade. Despite Thomas's hasty remittance of forty-five hundred hyperpyra, Mehmed annexed most of his despotate, including Corinth and Patras.[14] Two years later, when the brothers were quarreling again, the sultan returned to conquer what remained. Demetrius surrendered Mistra. Thomas fled with his family to the Venetian Corcyra, and from there to Rome. While the sultan sent Demetrius into retirement at Adrianople, the pope received Thomas with honor at Rome.

By 1461 the Ottomans had taken all the despots' domains but Monemvasia, which Thomas made over to the papacy. That summer the sultan marched against the pitiful Empire of Trebizond, the last Byzantine splinter state. Confronted with an immense Ottoman army and no prospect of outside help, the emperor David Comnenus surrendered his capital in early September.[15] The little empire's last few towns fell during the autumn. Although David's capitulation saved Trebizond from being sacked, Mehmed deported many of its people to Constantinople. Two years later the sultan executed David and six of his seven sons on a dubious charge of conspiracy.

By the end of 1461, the Turks had eliminated every state that could claim lineal descent from Byzantium. In what had once been Byzantine territory, Venice still held Crete, Corcyra, Dyrrhachium, and several other Greek ports and islands; Genoa held Chios and some ports in the Crimea; the Hospitalers remained on Rhodes; the Tocco family kept Cephalonia and a bit of Epirus; and the crusader family of Lusignan ruled Cyprus.[16] While Scanderbeg gallantly kept up his revolt in Albania, the Serbian principalities had again become Ottoman clients. The Ottomans soon took most of these lands outright. The majority of Greeks remained subject to the sultan until the nineteenth century.

CHAPTER TWENTY-SIX

The Separation of Society
from State, 1204–1461

After the crippling blow of the Fourth Crusade, Byzantium recovered better and survived longer than might have been expected. Yet after 1204 the fate of the Byzantine state became clearly distinguishable from that of Byzantine society. Even at its strongest, and
even along with Epirus and Trebizond, the restored Byzantine Empire
never came close to including all those who could properly be called
Byzantines. In much of Asia Minor, the Balkans, and the islands, Latins,
Turks, or Slavs ruled many people who belonged to the Byzantine church,
shared Byzantine traditions, and often spoke Greek. Meanwhile the Byzantine church kept most of its influence over eastern Christians as far
away as Russia and Egypt, and Byzantine culture came to command more
respect in the West than at any time since the eighth century. Even after
the empire disappeared altogether, Byzantine traditions, the Eastern Orthodox Church, and the Greek language all survived in the East, and to
some extent in the West.

BYZANTINES AND GREEKS

Being a Roman (*Rhōmaios*), as the Byzantines still called a Byzantine,
was mostly a matter of culture and religion. It was not primarily a matter of speaking Greek or of living within Byzantine territory, and it had
nothing to do with race. Byzantium had always had Slavic, Vlach, Albanian, or other subjects who spoke little or no Greek, but were Byzantines nonetheless. If an Armenian, Italian, or Turk settled in the empire,
joined the Byzantine church, and adapted to native ways, he passed for a

Byzantine. Although a speaker of Greek who became a Muslim ceased to be a Byzantine, a Greek-speaking Christian could count as one even if none of his relatives had lived under imperial rule for generations.

After 1204 the Byzantine successor states were overwhelmingly Greek-speaking, but none was a nation-state in the sense that France or England was already beginning to be. While westerners often tried to make sense of the Empire of Nicaea or the restored Byzantine Empire by calling its ruler king of the Greeks, no Byzantine would have countenanced such a title. The emperor was both less and more than that. He was less, because many Greeks lived outside his rule; he was more, because he was still supposed to head a supranational state. He had a right to precedence above other rulers not as the sovereign of the Greeks, but as the successor of the Christian Roman emperors going back to Constantine I.

Nevertheless, during this period some Byzantines began to use the name "Greek" (*Hellēn*), with its ancient definition as an inhabitant of Greece, rather than its usually Christian meaning of "pagan." This revived meaning for the word "Greek" was a feature of the continuing revival of classical culture. The most erudite writers, who took Thucydides or Demosthenes as their stylistic model, gave contemporary cities and peoples the names of the cities and peoples located in the same places in the fifth or fourth centuries B.C. Thus they called Constantinople Byzantium, Adrianople Orestias, Turks Persians, Slavs Scythians, and their fellow Byzantines Greeks. By extension, realizing that the restored empire held approximately the lands of the ancient Greeks and had a population largely descended from them, such scholars came to take pride in the pagan Greek as well as the Christian Roman past, especially in a time of Byzantine political decline. Yet these were the views of a small learned minority, and would have seemed nonsensical or dangerous to most good Byzantine Christians.

The threat or reality of foreign rule, not some sort of Greek national consciousness, was the main new element that worked to draw Byzantines together. The local Byzantine powers that had proliferated around 1204 resolved themselves before long into the three main successor states. Once the Empire of Nicaea emerged as the strongest of these, many Byzantines rallied to its support. Consequently, after 1261 the restored empire suffered less from regional separatism than twelfth-century Byzantium had done. From the middle of the fourteenth century, most divisions in the empire resulted from administrative decisions by the central government rather than local initiative. Even when Byzantium was reduced to isolated enclaves ruled as appanages, their inhabitants usually professed loyalty to Constantinople and to the Palaeologan dynasty.

This relative cohesion permitted the peculiar geographical development of the state that we call the Empire of Nicaea before 1261 and the restored Byzantine Empire afterwards. Starting with Theodore I Lascaris's modest domain in northwestern Anatolia, the Empire of Nicaea expanded into the Balkans, taking Thrace, northern Greece, Albania, and then Constantinople and the eastern Peloponnesus. When the Turks captured its original heartland in Asia Minor, including Nicaea itself, the empire based itself on its new Balkan lands, expanding into Epirus and Thessaly. Buffeted by the civil war of 1341 to 1347, then by the Black Death of 1347 to 1349, the empire lost Albania, Epirus, Thessaly, and the hinterland of Thessalonica to the Serbs. Next the Turks took Thrace and Thessalonica itself, leaving the empire without any of the possessions it had held before 1261. Such a state cannot be understood in regional terms. Nor can regional loyalties explain its prestige among the eastern Christians outside its borders.

Throughout this period, Constantinople kept a seemingly disproportionate significance not only for Byzantines but for westerners, Slavs, and Turks as well. Reasons for this included its past, its trade, and its value as an almost impregnable fortification in a time of military instability. Yet despite some recovery after 1204, and especially after 1261, the city never regained anything like its former size, and was no longer the greatest market in the Mediterranean world. The Black Death damaged it further. Although possession of Constantinople might seem to be a strategic necessity for any state with lands in both Anatolia and the Balkans, first the Empire of Nicaea and then the Ottoman Empire managed to rule possessions all around it without much trouble. Its greatest value was as a symbol. While it provoked the envy of enemies, it also awed them, and owning it surely prolonged the life of both the Latin Empire and restored Byzantium. During the empire's last miserable hundred years, only its capital made it a power that neither westerners, easterners, nor Turks could wholly dismiss.

As soon as the Byzantines retook Constantinople, western Anatolia was no longer absolutely essential to them. Yet it had formed almost the whole Empire of Nicaea for forty years, until John Vatatzes conquered much of the Balkans in 1246. Even after the emperor, the bureaucracy, and much of the aristocracy had left for the recovered capital, western Asia Minor must still have accounted for nearly half the empire's population, agricultural output, and revenue, making it worth defending even at great cost. The emperors knew its value. Michael VIII sent or led repeated campaigns to defend Byzantine Anatolia, and by and large he succeeded; Andronicus II promised the Catalans ruinous sums to defend it before his money ran out in 1305; and Andronicus III made a valiant effort to retrieve some of it as late as 1329.

Although western Anatolia gave rise to several rebellions under Michael VIII and Andronicus II, none of these lasted for long. All but the initial revolt over Michael's blinding of John IV Lascaris seem to have been caused not by disloyalty to the emperor, but by a feeling that he was not doing enough to defend his Anatolian possessions from the Turks. With no natural frontiers to keep out its numerous and warlike Turkish neighbors, western Asia Minor suffered from more foreign attacks than any other part of the restored empire. It was therefore more disaffected and more vulnerable, and became the first part of the empire to fall when Andronicus II lowered Byzantine defenses.

Thrace, in earlier times usually one of Byzantium's more exposed regions, was as secure as any during this troubled period. The Bulgarians were fairly quiescent after John III Vatatzes expelled them from Thrace in 1246. During the next century, the straits and the sea usually kept out the Turks, except when the Byzantines deliberately brought them in as allies. Thrace became the reduced empire's granary, where its great aristocrats had most of their estates. While a few of the earlier landholders seem to have kept their property in Thrace during the upheavals of the early thirteenth century by collaborating with the Latins and Bulgarians, most of the Thracian magnates must have come from western Anatolia, and acquired their lands only after the emperors of Nicaea expanded into Europe. Some were doubtless wealthy refugees from the Turkish advances in Asia Minor, resettled with the help of the government in the years after 1305.

In the great civil war of the fourteenth century most of the aristocracy of Thrace backed John VI Cantacuzenus, himself a Thracian magnate from a family that had served the emperors of Nicaea. Even after his ultimate defeat, most Cantacuzenists kept or recovered their estates. Before the Black Death arrived, Thrace was prosperous and populous. Along with important ports like Rhaedestus and Mesembria, it had several good-sized inland cities like Adrianople and Didymotichus. After the Turks gained a firm foothold at Callipolis in 1354, they still took some thirty years to conquer the interior. Even then, a few coastal cities held out until more were added by the Turkish treaty of 1403. To the end, Selymbria in the south and Mesembria in the north were considered appanages suitable for senior Byzantine princes.

The region of Thessalonica, the ancient Macedonia, was slightly less fertile than Thrace, and farther from Constantinople. Although it formed the center of Theodore Ducas's Empire of Thessalonica, that state had a brief career, like the Latin Kingdom of Thessalonica that preceded it. From the time of John III's conquest in 1246, the region was in Byzantine hands for a century, until the great civil war allowed the Serbs to take the interior. During the eight years beginning with 1342, the Zealot movement at Thessalonica relied on a large and boisterous urban population, which only submitted to John VI when the Serbs were at the gates. Afterward the Byzantines held only the immediate vicinity of the city, while first the Serbs and then the Turks held its hinterland. Since Thessalonica served primarily as a trading outlet for the interior, neither Manuel II in 1387 nor the Venetians in 1430 could hold it for more than a few years against a Turkish blockade from the land side.

The part of Byzantium that fared best during the Palaeologan period was the Peloponnesus, then commonly called the Morea. After Michael VIII acquired it in 1261 as a ransom for the captured Latin barons of Achaea, the Byzantine Peloponnesus soon became a self-sustaining but surprisingly loyal province. It included the fertile valley of Laconia and the growing cities of Mistra and Monemvasia. Except for Monemvasia, the main ports of the peninsula belonged to Venice, but they too provided markets for Byzantine goods. What remained of the Latin Principality of Achaea was too weak to threaten the Byzantine province seriously, but screened it from most other invaders until the Turks began raiding late in the fourteenth century. Though the Black Death struck the Byzantine Peloponnesus along with the rest of the empire, the despots made up for some of the loss in population by importing Albanian settlers. Then the despots used Albanian mercenaries to conquer more Latin territory.

These Albanian immigrants notwithstanding, the Byzantine Peloponnesus remained mostly Greek-speaking. It had a sometimes recalcitrant local aristocracy, which had been reinforced by refugees from other parts of Greece. Under the despot Theodore I Palaeologus, who ruled from 1382 to 1407, Mistra became the empire's second capital, with its own bureaucracy, literati, and artists. Yet the division of the despotate among two or three Palaeologi led to repeated squabbling, and except

196. Aerial view of Mistra, with the Palace of the Despots (center). (Photo: Deutsches Archäologisches Institut, Athens)

for the future emperor Constantine XI the despots were not particularly distinguished men. The little Peloponnesus became the principal Byzantine province only by doing moderately well while the rest of the empire met with disaster.

The only other places under Nicene or Byzantine rule for any length of time were Aegean islands. John Vatatzes of Nicaea recovered Lesbos, Chios, Samos, and Rhodes, and gamely sustained the Greek resistance on Crete, which the Venetians spent more than a century in extinguishing. Michael VIII made use of the mercenary Licario to regain many of the small islands and most of Euboea, then generally known as Negroponte. Although Andronicus II lost most of these conquests later, the empire kept a few islands in the north almost to the end. The Turks used their limited naval power for piracy rather than conquest, while Venice, Genoa, and the other Latin sea powers fought each other more often than they fought Byzantium.

During most of the first half of this period, Byzantium exercised a loose suzerainty over Epirus and Thessaly. The two provinces were usually ruled by separate members of the Ducas family, until the dynasty died out in 1318. Yet their rulers owed their titles of despot of Epirus and sebastocrator of Thessaly to nomination by the emperor, first at Nicaea and then at Constantinople. Although Epirus possessed some good farm-land around its capital at Arta, the region mostly consisted of mountains and hills, which were defensible but poor. Thessaly, the last scrap of the Thessalonian Empire, was more fertile than Epirus but smaller and more exposed to attack. The Ducas family succeeded better at maintaining its autonomy than at projecting its power. Andronicus III finally annexed both Thessaly and Epirus by 1337, and with their natural defenses they should have been easy to hold. But after just eleven years, the civil war and the Black Death so weakened Byzantium that the Serbs overran both provinces with little resistance.

The Empire of Trebizond, though never recovered by the restored Byzantine Empire, ceased to be a major factor in Byzantine politics when it lost Paphlagonia and with it the hope of retaking Constantinople. After giving up Sinope in 1265, the tiny empire held only the Pontus, keeping a weaker grip on part of the Crimea until sometime in the middle of the fourteenth century. The Pontus sheltered behind the Pontic Alps, which gave Trebizond the best natural defenses of any state in the East. Its neighbors were not Byzantines but Turks, Georgians, Mongols, and the Genoese who built trading colonies in Trapezuntine territory. With little false pride, Trebizond's emperors, the Grand Comneni, accepted the suzerainty of the Seljuks, Mongols, and Ottomans in turn. From 1282, when John II of Trebizond married a daughter of Michael VIII, the Comneni also recognized the claims to superiority of the Byzantine emperors. Friendship with the acknowledged emperor of the Romans, who was too remote to pose a military threat, bolstered the Grand Comnenus's authority over his Greek subjects.

In 1332 Basil Comnenus used Byzantine support to usurp the Trapezuntine throne. Basil married and then divorced Andronicus III's bastard daughter Irene, who succeeded him, perhaps after poisoning him, in 1340. A nine-year power struggle ensued, involving Irene, Basil's sister Anna, Basil's uncle Michael, and Michael's son John III, none of whom gained firm control. Meanwhile Trebizond was devastated by the Black Death in 1347, and lost a war with its Genoese colonists in 1349. During these many trials, the Turks established petty emirates within the western Pontic lands, and the Mongols and Genoese seem to have taken over the Crimean province.[1] Basil's son Alexius III of Trebizond, who married a niece of John Cantacuzenus, restored some stability in the latter

197. Alexius III Comnenus of Trebizond (r. 1349–90) and his wife Theodora Cantacuzena. Miniature from an original chrysobull of 1374 at the Monastery of Dionysiou, Mount Athos (MS. Dionysiou no. 4). (Photo: Courtesy of Jacques Lefort)

half of the century by making the Turkish emirs his vassals. On the whole Trebizond held off the Turks better than Byzantium did, retaining more of its original land and lasting eight years longer.[2]

Such were the parts of the Byzantine world that remained under Greek rule, or returned to it. Most of the time the restored empire exercised diplomatic and ecclesiastical influence over other eastern Christian states as well. As before, these included the Slavs of Bulgaria, Serbia, and Russia. They were joined in the fourteenth century by the new Vlach principalities of Wallachia and Moldavia, which by this time may be called Romanian.[3] While Georgia and Cilician Armenia maintained good relations with Byzantium, both were now distant from Byzantine territory. The kings of Georgia were closer to the emperors of Trebizond, with whom they intermarried, while the Armenian kings of Cilicia allied themselves with Latin Cyprus.

Byzantium also had a measure of authority over the Greeks under Latin rule. Even where Latin dominance was continuous, as in Cyprus or Cephalonia, the westerners were too few to change the Greek character of the country. Their subjects came to various accommodations with the Latin government, grudgingly endured nominal union with the western church, and sometimes learned some French or Italian. But their main language remained Greek, adulterated with a few French and Italian loanwords that also became current in the emperor's domains. Most regarded themselves as under foreign occupation, thought of themselves as Byzantines, and were glad to receive any of the emperor's forces that might arrive. The Greeks of Crete repeatedly rebelled with the emperors' help. The only place Greeks were in much danger of Latinization was southern Italy, where they had always been restricted to the coasts and mingled with the Italian-speaking population. Yet even most Italian Greeks continued to speak their own language, and Greek monks like Barlaam of Calabria kept close connections with Constantinople.

As the number of Greeks ruled by Latins gradually diminished, the number ruled by Turks steadily rose. The Turks had greater powers of assimilation than the Latins. There were many more Turks, and they promoted conversion to Islam, which virtually insured that a Greek's descendants would consider themselves Turkish. As the Turks raided and conquered, they enslaved many Christians, selling some in other Muslim regions and hindering the rest from practicing their faith. Besides levying the Muslims' usual head tax on Christians, the Turks adopted the practice of taking Christian boys from their families and raising them as

Muslims, usually for military service in special corps known as the Jan-
issaries. Conversions, Turkish migration, and Greek outmigration increasingly endangered the Greek minority in central Asia Minor. When
the Turks overran western Anatolia, they occupied the countryside first,
driving the Greeks into the cities, or away to Europe or the islands. By
the time the Anatolian cities fell, the land around them was already
largely Turkish.

During the first half of the thirteenth century the boundary between
Muslims and Christians seemed to be stabilizing at the straits, giving
Anatolian Greeks little hope of a Byzantine reconquest and some reason
to emigrate to Europe. After the Turks captured Callipolis, their occupation of the Balkans proceeded in a rapid but haphazard fashion, and
by the time most Greeks realized that the Turks had come to stay no secure refuge remained. Besides, after three centuries of Turkifying Asia
Minor, not many Turks were left to repeat the process in the Balkans,
and few followed their previous course of settling the countryside and
then taking cities. Most Turks who did settle in the Balkans went to the
cities first, where they were eventually outnumbered by migrants from
the overwhelmingly Christian countryside.[4] Thus the pattern was set of
a Christian Greek and Slav majority in Europe and a Muslim Turkish
majority in Asia.[5]

For a century and a half the Ottomans lived in a surprising degree of
harmony with the Byzantine emperors, first as allies and then as suzerains.
As long as an emperor remained at Constantinople, the Greeks under
Turkish rule regarded him as their protector, who could at least negotiate on their behalf with the sultan.[6] When Constantinople fell and the
empire vanished, all eastern Christians found themselves bereft of their
accustomed leader. The Greeks, who still called themselves Romans, had
become merely an ethnic group with a glorious past, no higher in legal
or ecclesiastical status than other eastern Christians of the Ottoman Empire. As Latins and Turks also realized, the final Turkish conquest had a
significance for people who lived far beyond the last pathetic remnants
of Byzantine territory.

THE FRAGMENTED EMPIRE

The Fourth Crusade shattered a tradition of unified government in
the Aegean basin that dated back to the Roman Republic, and wrecked
institutions that were as old as Diocletian and Constantine I. Since the

Crusaders failed to conquer the whole Byzantine Empire, they never replaced its institutions with a single system of their own. Because the Byzantines failed to reconquer everything they had lost, or even to suppress
all the Latin states and the Empire of Trebizond, they were unable to restore the old system. Both Crusaders and Byzantines had to make compromises even within the lands they conquered or reconquered. Western
feudalism worked poorly under eastern conditions, and the fortunes of
the Byzantine successor states were mixed. The Latin Empire, Trebizond,
and Epirus never came to be of much consequence. Nicaea did make itself into a passable imitation of Byzantium, but after holding its own for
about a generation it began a gradual descent into insignificance.

Curiously, however, each successor state enjoyed a dynastic stability
that by earlier Byzantine standards was rocklike. The Grand Comneni
ruled Trebizond as long as its empire lasted, though they sometimes
fought among themselves with encouragement from Constantinople.
The Ducas dynasty ruled Epirus and Thessaly until its male line died
out, and even then its female line was connected with the later rulers
from the Orsini and Tocco families. The Ducas family too had its internal quarrels, partly fomented by the Nicene and restored Byzantine empires. But while the family survived, local loyalty to it was too strong to
allow Byzantium to annex Epirus and Thessaly for good.

The Lascarids remained emperors of Nicaea until the reconquest of
Constantinople. In spite of John IV's minority and Michael VIII's triumph in regaining the capital, the change of dynasty in 1261 caused lingering bitterness. After that, the Palaeologi ruled the restored empire to
the end, for more years than any other Byzantine dynasty. They enjoyed
a loyalty from their subjects that outweighed popular resentments over the
unions of Lyons and Florence, and the glaring failures of Andronicus II
and John V. Dynastic loyalty was the main reason the young and mediocre John V Palaeologus was able to push aside the mature and brilliant
John VI Cantacuzenus, even as a colleague. Although the practice of ruling through relatives presumably strengthened the dynasties, similar practices had been tried before 1204 with much less success. The main difference after the Fourth Crusade was probably the Byzantines' readiness
to rally around the ruling family against the powerful Latins and Turks.

Such a feeling also helps explain the easing of the emperors' troubles
with local separatism and unruly merchants and magnates. While princes
ruling appanages occasionally revolted, they did so rather less than might
have been expected, given their power and the weakness of the central

government. No ruler of an appanage secured lasting independence in this period, and none seized the imperial throne more than momentarily. Byzantium still had many wealthy landholders, some of whom acted as virtual rulers of the towns where they lived and the surrounding regions where they owned their lands. Such men, however, seldom led local revolts. Although John VI Cantacuzenus was a magnate, he claimed the crown as the grand domestic of the army and a friend of the late emperor; he never aspired to rule as a separatist, and his support extended well beyond Thrace, the region of his estates. Magnates and merchants certainly played their parts in the civil wars between 1341 and 1354. Yet each side always struggled to take over the monarchy, not to limit it, and the legitimate dynasty emerged victorious in the end.

At first glance, the great civil war, with its loyalist urban mobs sacking the palaces of Cantacuzenist aristocrats, may look like an uprising of the oppressed against their oppressors. But if the Cantacuzenist magnates oppressed anyone, it was the peasantry on their rural estates, none of whom lived in the cities where the mobs ran riot. And if anyone oppressed the urban poor, it was the merchants, tradesmen, and bureaucrats, scarcely any of whom were magnates. What seems rather to have happened was that the bureaucrats, merchants, and tradesmen led the riots against the aristocrats. To the limited extent that the lower classes took part in the civil war at all, the urban poor seem to have sided with the businessmen and officials, making the cities loyal to the regency, while the peasants seem to have sided with their aristocratic landlords, leaving the countryside generally Cantacuzenist. While envy of rich aristocrats was doubtless a factor, the civil war was nothing so simple as a struggle between rich and poor.

It was, however, partly a struggle between landholders and merchants, of a type already perceptible in Byzantine history during the eleventh and twelfth centuries. In the fourteenth century the fight was for control not only over the central government but also over the cities, where the landholders usually resided. Because cooperation with Italian merchants was necessary to do business, the regency with its mercantile supporters tended to be more sympathetic to Italians.[7] Since most monks and Palamites were suspicious of the western church, they tended to oppose the regency and favor the Cantacuzenists, who moreover included many aristocratic donors to monasteries. Despite all these tendencies, other public and private concerns were also involved, so that some aristocrats, monks, and Palamites backed the regency, and some merchants, bureau-

198. Ruins of the Palace of the Grand Comneni at Trebizond. (Photo: Dumbarton Oaks, Washington, D.C., copyright 1996)

crats, and anti-Palamites backed John Cantacuzenus.

Similar tendencies, subject to similar qualifications, appear to have aggravated the civil troubles at Trebizond between 1340 and 1349. Those conflicts pitted local aristocrats against an urban faction that favored Byzantine nominees to the Trapezuntine throne and was allied to the Byzantine regency.[8] At both Byzantium and Trebizond, the aristocratic side was the weaker, perhaps mainly because aristocrats were perceived as threatening the power that the emperor needed to defend the state. Such a perception was, however, largely mistaken, because aristocrats too, and John Cantacuzenus most of all, saw the dangers that threatened Byzantium.

Given their handicaps, the emperors and other Greek rulers after 1204 were successful in gaining and keeping control over their domains. Starting with some high-ranking refugees from Constantinople but no working central government, Theodore I of Nicaea managed to build up a reasonably efficient administrative structure. Without trying to reconstruct much of the old central bureaucracy, he ruled through courtiers and family members, following a pattern set under the Comneni. Alexius I of Trebizond, who brought along fugitive officials of his own from Constantinople, created a similar government of courtiers in his new capital. Michael Ducas of Epirus did much the same thing at Arta, without the title of emperor or much help from Byzantine refugees. These rulers claimed imperial prerogatives that had briefly lapsed but had long been familiar to their subjects. Even if the successors' rights to such authority were questionable, without possession of Constantinople no other Byzantine had a clearly superior claim.

As under the Comneni, the most important officials of the Lascarids and Palaeologi were relatives of the ruling house, with such titles as despot, sebastocrator, Caesar, or panhypersebastus. Usually a grand domestic commanded the army; a grand duke, the navy. The bureaucracy was normally headed by a mesazon, holding the title that had been given to a general controller in the preceding period and now denoted the nearest thing to a prime minister. There was also a grand logothete, formerly known as the logothete of the secreta, though his departments had changed. The treasury was now an extension of the emperor's private treasury, while the old public treasuries had lapsed. The new chancery was an expanded bureau of the emperor's private secretaries. Other palatine officials had duties that had formerly been performed by civil or military officials. Some titles once denoting high officials, like general logothete, confusingly became mere honorifics. Although imperial relatives and honorary officials were more numerous than before, the real central government was somewhat simplified, and even more dependent on the emperor. Later the despots with appanages had courts, administrations, and revenues of their own, on the pattern of the emperor.[9]

At the local level, Theodore I Lascaris, who at first professed loyalty to his father-in-law Alexius III Angelus, took over the provincial governments of western Anatolia soon after Alexius lost control of them. Alexius I Comnenus of Trebizond and Michael Ducas also set up their original states in lands that had recently been under Byzantine rule. The provincial administration that the successors inherited included the system of tax collection, various pronoia grants, and the themes, which had now become chiefly administrative divisions but were headed by dukes with some military responsibilities. The local magnates and towns, which had already shown tendencies toward independence before 1204, often profited by the ensuing confusion to assert their autonomy further.

The successors did what they could to restore order. The emperors of Trebizond, ruling little more than the old Theme of Chaldia, kept the old thematic subdivisions called turmae and banda. The rulers of Epirus and emperors of Thessalonica, holding middle-sized territories with shifting boundaries, seem to have paid little attention to the themes and created smaller divisions as they went. The emperors of Nicaea retained the Asian themes with their dukes, but in their European conquests seldom tried to revive the themes as anything more than geographical expressions. By the time of the recovery of Constantinople, Michael VIII adopted a more uniform system of smaller provinces, each usually consisting of a town and its region, under a governor with both civil and military powers.[10] The emperors often appointed a leading magnate as governor of his town and region, though gubernatorial terms were kept short.

There was certainly a danger that the towns and magnates might go their own way. They had the chance to choose sides in times of civil war or foreign invasion; but they chose the legitimate emperor surprisingly often. Since they were too weak to look after themselves, they needed the emperor's protection. The emperor also kept control over taxation and pronoia grants through a domestic of the themes, or through separate domestics of the eastern and western themes when the empire had both Asian and European provinces. In the fourteenth century, as Byzantium came to consist of discontinuous segments of territory, the small provinces in outlying areas were grouped into appanages under the despots, which met the need for an intermediate tier of administration.

The resemblance that the Byzantine appanages bore to feudal counties and duchies was mostly superficial. The term "appanage" is a modern borrowing from medieval France, and not an entirely appropriate one. Except for the despotates of Epirus and Thessaly, which were independent states compelled to accept Byzantine suzerainty, the appanages never became hereditary, and functioned within a system of centralized imperial government and taxation. Although western practice probably did contribute to the idea that junior members of Byzantine dynasties should receive lands of their own to govern, the practice owed at least as much to Byzantine family loyalties and a tradition of dynastic government going back to the Comneni in the late eleventh century. The system of appanages worked tolerably well, not only in easing family rivalries but in keeping what was left of the empire together.

At a time when all armies were small by earlier Byzantine standards, the army of the Nicene emperors and Michael VIII was relatively large and strong. In 1211 Theodore I could put two thousand men in the field to defeat the Seljuks. By 1259 well over six thousand men are said to have won the battle of Pelagonia for Michael VIII. Michael recruited still more soldiers after he retook Constantinople. At times when he managed to repel his enemies on as many as six different fronts, he can scarcely have had fewer than ten thousand field troops, not counting the irregulars used to garrison towns. Yet Michael always had trouble paying his men. After the early part of his reign, his only major conquests were made by the self-financing admiral Licario.

Andronicus II let both his army and his navy shrink. By 1304, with most of Asia Minor lost, the seventy-eight hundred Catalans were apparently more than all the emperor's field forces combined. By 1321, Andronicus was trying to raise his standing army to the modest figure of three thousand mercenaries. Even after mustering pronoiars and other soldiers resident in the provinces, the fourteenth-century empire could probably put no more than five thousand men in the field. Without a strong navy, this was barely enough to defend the Byzantine lands in the Balkans, and too few to restrain unruly Turkish auxiliaries. In the later fourteenth century, the Byzantines could no longer muster a field army worthy of the name, and Byzantium ceased to be a significant military power.[11]

Besides continuing the system of pronoia grants and hiring mercenaries, the emperors before Andronicus II provided support for some of their soldiers by settling them together in groups. Among the best Byzantine troops were the Cumans settled by John III along the frontiers in Asia Minor, who numbered two thousand at Pelagonia. The Nicene emperors also settled native Byzantine irregulars in the Anatolian borderlands, some of whom Michael VIII later enrolled in his regular forces. Michael also gave lands near newly reconquered Constantinople to his soldiers of the Thelematarii, his marines of the Tzacones, and his oarsmen of the Proselontes. The same emperor created two standing units of mercenaries, the marines of the Gasmuli and the thousand soldiers of the Turcopuli. Yet throughout this period most of the empire's field soldiers seem to have been mercenaries hired for a term.

Pronoiars contributed most of the heavy cavalry, though they formed a small proportion even of the emperor's regular soldiers. Military pronoia grants seem to have been better regulated under the Lascarids and Palaeologi than under the Comneni and Angeli. Because the grants eventually came to be worth more or less than their original value, the Palaeologi had them inspected, reassessed, and adjusted from time to time.

Michael VIII made some pronoia grants hereditary, and the sons of other pronoiars must often have followed their fathers into the army and kept the grant in the family. But by and large pronoiars seem to have continued to do their service without greatly overstepping their rights. They formed a small class of petty nobles, humble enough for the government to master if it chose. If Andronicus II often chose to tax them instead of mustering them, the reason seems to have been financial shortsightedness on his part rather than military incapacity on theirs. The government appears to have had less trouble in handling military pronoiars than in managing the pronoia grants and tax exemptions that it gave bureaucrats, imperial relatives, and owners of large estates.

As the state declined, the great landholders, including the Church and particularly the monasteries, remained proportionally at least as powerful as they had been before. Although the unsettled conditions of the time ruined some of them, others bargained for privileges from rival rulers who needed their support, or acquired land that poorer and weaker owners were unable to keep. Magnates continued to increase their holdings, until peasants who farmed their own land and paid taxes directly to the emperor seem to have become not only a minority but a rarity. Some peasants turned into tenants through the practice of pronoia, as the taxes owed to a pronoiar became indistinguishable from the rent owed to a landlord. Tenants were still freemen, since they could leave the lands they rented whenever they wished; but before the Black Death, when good land was scarce, peasants had few advantages in bargaining with their landlords. After the plague, vacant land became more plentiful, but most of it soon passed into the hands of the Serbs and Turks. The magnates suffered, but so did all Byzantines.

Despite the Italians' dominance of long-distance trade, Byzantine merchants and tradesmen benefited from the general growth of commerce. The empire tended to lose its farmland before it lost its cities, giving merchants an additional advantage over landholders. In 1348 John VI, probably hoping not just to gain revenue but to placate the merchants who had opposed him in the civil war, finally lowered the trade duties paid by Byzantines to the level paid by Italians. He appears to have succeeded in stimulating Byzantine trade. Yet even after this measure, and the loss of many landed estates to the Turks, most Byzantine magnates must have been richer than most Byzantine merchants. As trade expanded, the magnates used what remained of their fortunes to go into business, and quickly took a leading role. With magnates and merchants beginning to form a unified upper class, the social tensions of the earlier fourteenth century waned.[12] Even if the empire was already past saving, some of the new commercial class may have survived among the Phanariots, the Greek merchants of the Phanar in Ottoman Constantinople.

THE INTERNATIONAL CHURCH

In the end, the Fourth Crusade did far less harm to the Byzantine church than to the Byzantine Empire. The Latin patriarchate of Constantinople and the Latin hierarchy imposed by the Crusaders never gained genuine acceptance from more than a handful of eastern Christians. Instead the Fourth Crusade increased hostility to the western church and loyalty to the eastern. The patriarchate of Constantinople reestablished by Theodore I Lascaris at Nicaea soon became the leader of the whole eastern church, which included many more souls than the Empire of Nicaea or the restored Byzantine Empire ever did. Except in Asia Minor, the Church's membership scarcely diminished from what it had been in 1204. The emperors tried twice to impose a union with the western church, at Lyons and Florence, and both times the eastern church resisted with ultimate success. The Church not only outlasted the empire, but in some ways took its place.

Nevertheless, the Church had to fight hard to maintain itself throughout these two and a half centuries. Distinguished patriarchs alternated with nonentities, and on average patriarchates were brief. For a short time after the exiled John X died in 1206, the very survival of a Byzantine patriarchate was in doubt, as the Latin patriarch of Constantinople put himself at the head of the bishops and clergy of the Latin Empire. In the absence of a Byzantine patriarch, the Epirotes, Bulgarians, and Serbs officially submitted to the western church. The new patriarch that Theodore I had elected at Nicaea in 1208 was of dubious legitimacy. His coronation of Theodore identified the patriarchate with what was then a small and struggling successor state, with several eastern Christian rivals.

The patriarchate at Nicaea, however, made steady gains, since it had no real competitors but the unpopular Latin patriarchate. Gradually Trapezuntines, Epirotes, Greeks under Latin rule, Russians, Bulgarians, and Serbs accepted the Nicene patriarch's authority. Without being much held back by its association with the Empire of Nicaea, the patriarchate did much to secure the empire's claim to be the heir of Byzantium. By 1232 John III of Nicaea and his patriarch Germanus II could approach

199. John VI Cantacuzenus as
emperor and monk. Miniature
from the theological works of
Cantacuzenus (Parisinus graecus
1242). (Photo: Bibliothèque
Nationale, Paris)

the pope as the leaders of the majority of eastern Christians. Relations between the Lascarid emperors and their patriarchs were good, even when
the emperors negotiated for union with the western church. The patriarchs would surely have found an actual reunion more problematic, but
none occurred under John III.

For all the credit he gained by recovering Constantinople, Michael VIII came into conflict with his church almost from the start. Much
of the reason was that the patriarchate owed its position to the Lascarid
dynasty, the last of whom Michael had deposed and blinded. Although
several earlier Byzantine rulers had been able to blind or even kill their
predecessors and make peace with the Church afterwards, the excommunication imposed on Michael by the patriarch Arsenius had a powerful effect. The emperor's deposition of Arsenius set off the Arsenite
Schism of forty-five years. After one unfortunate patriarchal appointment, the emperor found a worthy candidate in Joseph I, who received
him back into the Church in 1267. But the emperor's crime and the Arsenite Schism weakened his standing to advocate union with the western church.

The patriarch Joseph was a staunch antiunionist who refused to attend
the Council of Lyons and retired when the union was proclaimed in

1275. Michael found another respectable candidate for patriarch, John XI Beccus, only to split the Church yet again. While Josephites and Arsenites vied to represent the antiunionist majority at Byzantium, the emperor's rivals in Epirus, Trebizond, Thessaly, Bulgaria, and Serbia denounced and repudiated the union. When the pope also excommunicated Michael in 1281, the Union of Lyons became a dead letter. For all Michael's tenacity in supporting the union, and his agility in avoiding diplomatic disaster, he had made too many enemies to achieve something as delicate as reuniting the churches.

Andronicus II might have had a better chance, had he not lacked Michael's conviction and nerve. Although the devout Andronicus wanted to avoid trouble with his church, even in that he failed. He had to change patriarchs nine times, more than any previous emperor. He restored Joseph I, but then allowed harsh and divisive reprisals against unionists. The next patriarch, the former unionist Gregory of Cyprus, held a council to condemn the unionist view of the procession of the Holy Spirit; but his attempt to define this evanescent difference aroused so much controversy that he had to abdicate.[13] Gregory's successor Athanasius, a godly but unbending monk, in two stormy patriarchates denounced everyone who fell short of his ideals, including the emperor and the Anatolian bishops who fled the Turks.[14] After Athanasius's second abdication, the emperor managed to heal the Arsenite Schism in 1310 only by means of a bizarre ceremony presided over by Arsenius's skeleton. Finally, the patriarch Isaiah refused Andronicus's demand to excommunicate the rebellious Andronicus III, and helped persuade the old emperor to abdicate.

Under Andronicus III, the Church regained a measure of internal tranquility, even seeming ready to reconsider church union, until the outbreak of the Hesychast dispute and the great civil war split the hierarchy again. The patriarch John XIV Calecas was in the thick of both the dispute and the war as a regent for John V, opposing John Cantacuzenus and consequently Hesychasm and Gregory Palamas. The temporary victory of Cantacuzenus, and the permanent victory of Palamas, brought a succession of Palamite monks to the patriarchate. One of them, Callistus I, actually helped John V regain his throne, and none of them seems to have been strongly hostile to the western church. The patriarchs were quite tolerant of John V's personal conversion at Rome, which did not affect them directly. Vociferous opposition to church union only resumed in 1439 with the Union of Florence. Even that union officially lasted till the empire fell, and would presumably have lasted longer if western Crusaders had managed to rescue Byzantium.

The Fourth Crusade gave the Byzantines some obvious reasons for hating westerners. Even after the Byzantines recovered Constantinople, Charles of Anjou and Charles of Valois threatened crusades against the restored empire, and the Union of Lyons failed even to win over the papacy for long. By the mid-fourteenth century, however, the Turks had plainly become a greater threat than the Latins, and had shown themselves the harsher rulers of Greeks. The grand duke Luke Notaras, who was quoted as preferring the Turkish turban to the Latin miter, presumably changed his mind after Constantinople fell, when the sultan condemned him to death with his sons.[15] No important new differences stood in the way of union, and the Council of Ferrara and Florence seemed to have arrived at reasonable compromises, including western acceptance of Byzantine Hesychasm. However, antiunionists still demanded that westerners abandon usages dating from before the eleventh-century schism, like the *filioque* in the Creed and especially unleavened bread in the Eucharist, which neither union tried to impose on easterners. Such intransigence amounted to separatism for its own sake.

Given that many eastern Christians would resist church union on any terms whatever, concluding such a union threatened the authority not only of the emperor but of the patriarch of Constantinople. With the disappearance of the emperors of Bulgaria and Serbia, the Bulgarian and Serbian patriarchates lapsed, and the patriarch of Constantinople again gained jurisdiction over the whole former Byzantine world—if he could keep it. Most of the Slavs and Greeks outside the empire, many already ruled by the sultan, were ready to break with Constantinople rather than accept any union with the western church. The emperor could do nothing to compel them, whatever influence he had within his shrunken domains. The Turks naturally opposed a church union that was meant to promote a crusade against them. After the fall of Constantinople, church union obviously became unsustainable.

Although Latin rulers usually forced their Greek subjects into union with the western church, these unions were as grudging and superficial as the unions of Lyons and Florence. In most cases, the Latin bishops claimed nominal authority over Greek clergy and laity that paid them as little attention as possible. Sometimes a few Greek bishops were allowed to function alongside the Latin ones, though with restricted privileges and little church property. The allegiance of the bulk of the Greek population to the Byzantine church was always clear. Whenever Latin rule ended in some Greek territory, all but a tiny minority returned to communion with Constantinople. Greek resentment of the Latin hierarchies in Latin Greece and Cyprus was a persistent irritant to relations between Byzantium and the papacy.

The Turks, while they generally allowed their Greek subjects to remain in communion with the patriarch, of course favored conversion to Islam, and limited the number of churches and bishops. Most Seljuk rulers were fairly tolerant of Christians, but the Ottomans became less so as their power grew and they saw a chance of extinguishing Christianity altogether in Asia Minor. In the Balkans, where this seemed impossible, the sultans found bishops useful as a means of controlling the Christian population. Mehmed II continued the patriarchate of Constantinople for the same reason. The Turks let church courts keep their jurisdiction over Christians, to whom Islamic law obviously could not apply in religious matters. Like the emperors before them, but even more arbitrarily, the sultans chose patriarchs and bishops, and removed them from office if they proved disobedient or otherwise unsatisfactory.

While the independence of the episcopate suffered from Turkish and Latin interference, and from the divisive issue of church union, Byzantine monasticism became more independent. The reform movement that had begun in the eleventh century maintained itself afterward, and kept monasteries largely free from lay control. Although the Latins took over some monasteries in Greece and the islands, and the Turks destroyed others in Asia Minor, the great foundations on Mount Athos and Patmos survived. The emperors of Trebizond adopted and lavishly endowed the Monastery of Sumela in the mountains south of their capital (Fig. 161). Michael VIII rebuilt and reendowed several monasteries in Constantinople. There the Monastery of the Chora was similarly restored by Andronicus II's mesazon, Theodore Metochites. In the fourteenth century a new monastic center developed in Thessaly, where refugee monks from Athos built houses atop the rock formations of the Meteora ("Midair").[16]

In this period the monasteries of Mount Athos gained a clear preeminence in eastern monasticism, overcoming Latin confiscations, the persecution of antiunionists by Michael VIII, and Catalan and Turkish raids. Athos attracted monks and donations from all of embattled eastern Christianity. Although subjects of the Byzantine emperor usually predominated on the Holy Mountain, as it came to be called, Greeks also

200. Theodore Metochites' monastery Church of the Chora ("Dwelling"), Constantinople (with minaret deleted). (Photo: Dumbarton Oaks, Washington, D.C., copyright 1996)

arrived from Trebizond, Epirus, and the Latin and Turkish states. Serbs, Bulgarians, Romanians, Georgians, and Russians had their own large or small foundations there, and some orthodox Christians from Armenia, Syria, and Egypt made their way to Athos as well. Nuns, however, like all females, were strictly excluded.

The dozens of Athonite monasteries had thousands of monks, most living in common under the *Rules* of Saint Basil, some keeping to themselves as hermits, and many living as virtual hermits side by side in so-called idiorrhythmic monasteries. Athonite foundations gradually acquired lands spreading over much of northern Greece. A growing number of Athonite monks became patriarchs and bishops, including Gregory Palamas himself, whom John VI named archbishop of Thessalonica. While some Athonite monks were illiterate and many had only a basic grasp of theology, their devotion to prayer gained almost universal respect in the Church. Hesychasm developed on Athos, and soon won the Church's full approval.

The most important theologian of the time was indisputably Gregory Palamas, the defender of Hesychasm. Most other important theologians of the fourteenth century wrote either to support or to oppose him. Although Palamas's earliest adversary Barlaam of Calabria returned to Italy after being condemned, an anti-Palamite party persisted in Byzantium. When Palamas's next opponent Gregory Acindynus was also condemned, the opposition was taken up by others, primarily the scholars Nicephorus Gregoras and Demetrius Cydones, though both were prominent Cantacuzenists.

Personal animosities, the civil war, and feelings about union with the western church lent the whole debate over Hesychasm unnecessary rancor. The dispute as to whether the light around God was created or not was hardly a fundamental one, but both sides made charges of heresy that were not justified by what the other side actually believed. Yet the underlying issue was real: the long-standing and in part natural distrust between intellectuals and mystics. When the Byzantine church followed its traditions and decided for the mystics, some intellectuals like Barlaam and Demetrius Cydones concluded that it had no place for them, and joined the western church.

Their conclusion was premature, since in the next century Byzantine intellectuals like Bessarion and Isidore of Kiev brought about the Union of Florence. Yet events vindicated the antiunionists, led by Mark of Ephesus and then Gennadius Scholarius, the onetime unionist who became the sultan's first patriarch of Constantinople. The future of the Byzantine church lay in the East, in the Ottoman Empire and Russia. To maintain itself under Turkish rule, the Church had to concentrate on its spiritual life and keep its flock together. The West could be of scarcely any help. A unionist church would merely have antagonized the Turks and many of the eastern faithful. The unionist position, and to a great extent the intellectual theology of a Barlaam or a Bessarion, required Byzantine independence from the Turks, which it was supposed to preserve by securing a crusade. After 1461, unionism remained practical only for those who lived in the remaining western colonies in the East, or who emigrated to the West.

THE MAKINGS OF A RENAISSANCE

Until the Turkish conquest of Constantinople, the decadence of the Byzantine state had quite a limited effect on Byzantine culture. This is the more remarkable because the Fourth Crusade had done terrible damage to the schools and libraries of Constantinople. The destruction of manuscripts in the fires and looting of 1204 seems to have caused the greatest loss of Greek texts ever to occur at one time, more even than in the Turkish sack of 1453. After the Fourth Crusade the Byzantines had little more of earlier Greek literature than we possess today. Yet the literary, historical, and other works that were lost, however much we would like to have them now, had seldom been read at Byzantium. Any text that had found a significant readership existed in enough copies that some survived the wreck. In the following period the Byzantines labored to make the most of what remained.

Aspiring to be patrons of education, the emperors of Nicaea attracted learned refugees from Constantinople, including the great historian Nicetas Choniates. John Vatatzes supported a small private school at Nicaea under the leading scholar of his day, Nicephorus Blemmydes, a monk who had traveled all over the shattered Byzantine world to acquire his education. Blemmydes tutored the emperor's son Theodore II, who later demonstrated his learning in many classicizing letters. Blemmydes also wrote the first work of the Byzantine period that can properly be called an autobiography, in which he complains of being insufficiently appreciated. Although both Vatatzes and Theodore tried to persuade Blemmydes to accept a public professorship at Nicaea, the disgruntled monk refused it. Instead he set up a monastic school near Ephesus, leaving Theodore to found a school at Nicaea without him.

After recovering Constantinople, Michael VIII restored the public school of philosophy and the patriarchal school that had existed before 1204. Michael's first professor of philosophy was a former student of Blemmydes', the general George Acropolites. Acropolites seems to have continued teaching until the emperor sent him to the Council of Lyons in 1274 to conclude the reunion of churches. Among Acropolites' students was Gregory of Cyprus, a leading teacher himself before he became patriarch of Constantinople in 1283. Gregory taught or influenced the growing number of scholars and writers who preserved the texts that had survived the Fourth Crusade, reviving Byzantine culture in the process.

Although the chaotic forty years after the Fourth Crusade failed to inspire any Byzantine historians, the fifteen years from Vatatzes' conquests in 1246 to the recovery of Constantinople made a stirring story. They attracted George Acropolites, an unlucky general but a successful courtier. While he had scant enthusiasm for the earlier Nicene period, George nonetheless began where Nicetas Choniates had left off, with the Fourth Crusade. By stopping with Michael VIII's triumphant return to Constantinople in 1261, Acropolites avoided the complexities of Michael's later reign, which was not so clearly triumphant as what had gone before. Though Acropolites criticizes Theodore II and admires Michael, his history is short, direct, competent, and seldom judgmental. Without being an outstanding work, it gave an example that renewed the tradition of Byzantine histories in the classical style.

Acropolites' student and continuer George Pachymeres, who became a professor at the patriarchal school in 1277, attempted a much more ambitious history. He started with Michael VIII's accession, in George's own youth, and reached 1308 before death interrupted him. Considerably earlier than that date, Pachymeres saw that the restored empire had been damaged beyond repair. In an effort to understand what had happened, he wrote his history on a scale not seen at Byzantium since Procopius. While his style is peculiar and difficult, and he sometimes leaves the sequence of events unclear as he pursues a variety of themes, the overall effect is intelligent and impressive. Despite his belief that the empire's decline was inevitable, Pachymeres harshly criticizes Michael VIII.

Although Byzantium's modest advances and losses during the next thirty years attracted no contemporary historian, the civil wars between 1341 and 1354 found two. Both writers were defeated Cantacuzenists, whose works show the influence of Pachymeres and are longer than any previous Byzantine's account of his times.[17] The erudite Nicephorus Gregoras, who began his narrative with the Fourth Crusade, devoted much the largest part of it to his own lifetime, breaking off at 1359, just before his death. As both a Cantacuzenist and an anti-Palamite, Gregoras was one of the few men who managed to be on the losing side in both the civil war and the Hesychast controversy. While his history is full of information and often keenly observed, he left it unrevised and unshaped, and the latter part is largely a denunciation of his Palamite enemies. When he died, the Palamites dragged his corpse through the streets of Constantinople.[18]

John VI Cantacuzenus, the only Byzantine emperor to write his memoirs, composed a much more polished history during his long monastic retirement. His work covers the whole age of the civil wars, from the first rebellion of his friend Andronicus III to the final defeat of his son Matthew Cantacuzenus. John's style is classicizing but not pedantic; his narrative, long-winded but also rich in detail. Referring to himself in the third person, Cantacuzenus exploits his intimate knowledge of public affairs without lapsing into autobiography, and defends himself without egotism. Though his opinion that his adversaries were responsible for ruining the empire is obviously not impartial, neither is it far from the truth. The last major history written before the empire's fall, Cantacuzenus's book is one of the masterpieces of Byzantine literature, perhaps the only one written in the late period.[19]

The histories of Pachymeres, Gregoras, and Cantacuzenus were products of a wider revival of learning. Its first notable classical scholar was Pachymeres' younger contemporary Maximus Planudes, who was engaged in 1283 to copy manuscripts for Andronicus II. Among other accomplishments, Planudes was the first Byzantine scholar in centuries to learn Latin well and to make extensive translations from it into Greek. He translated Cicero, Ovid, Saint Augustine, Boëthius, and other Latin classics, of whom Ovid, the author with the most pagan and erotic content, seems to have attracted the most Byzantine interest. Planudes' student Demetrius Triclinius, who taught at Thessalonica, made his own scholarly breakthrough by reconstructing the meters of ancient Greek poetry. Those meters depended on a rhythm of long and short vowels that had been lost in Byzantine Greek, whose vowels were all short. Triclinius's careful analysis allowed him to correct a millennium of copying errors, above all in the tragedies of Aeschylus, Sophocles, and Euripides and the comedies of Aristophanes.

One of the more reflective scholars of the time was Theodore Metochites, mesazon under Andronicus II. In reendowing the Monastery of the Chora, Metochites gave it a large library, and retired there after the abdication of the emperor he had served. Metochites' wide-ranging works, many collected in his *Philosophical and Historical Miscellanies*, show an independent if respectful attitude toward the Greek classics. He sympathizes with Demosthenes for having to deal with a democracy, accuses Aristotle of masking his uncertainty with a deliberately obscure style, and defends his own obscure style by comparing it to that of Thucydides.[20] Metochites imparted his venturesome spirit to his student Nicephorus Gregoras, who became not only a historian but a theologian, philosopher, and scientist.

Though not even Gregoras had much personal regard for his fellow anti-Palamite Barlaam of Calabria, Barlaam was a scholar of a similar stamp. A native speaker of Italian, the Calabrian knew Greek philosophy, astronomy, and mathematics as well as theology. His historic accomplishment was to bring the West into contact with Greek scholarship. While many western merchants had always known Greek, and Latin rulers and missionaries had to learn it after 1204, few western scholars had mastered it since late antiquity. Up to the early fourteenth century, most of them knew about Greek literature only from classical

201. Theodore Metochites, mesazon of Andronicus II from 1305 to 1328, offering his Church of the Chora to Christ. Contemporary mosaic from the Church of the Chora. (Photo: Dumbarton Oaks, Washington, D.C., copyright 1996)

Latin works and from some translations of Arabic translations of Aristotle. After joining the western church in 1342, Barlaam lectured at the papal court at Avignon, tried to teach Greek to the Italian humanist Petrarch, and received a bishopric in his native Calabria. Barlaam was only the first of a succession of Greek scholars from the empire, Crete, and elsewhere to make their names in Renaissance Italy.

One of the few Byzantines who sympathized with Barlaam was Demetrius Cydones, though he was a Cantacuzenist and John VI's mesazon. Cydones learned Latin in the course of his official duties, and he was translating the theology of Thomas Aquinas when John VI fell in 1354. Then Cydones joined the western church, found favor with John V, and tutored John's son Manuel II. Demetrius accompanied John to Rome in 1369, when the emperor made his own submission to the papacy. Meeting with a warm reception in Italy, Cydones liked the country and returned there three times.[21] Cydones' friend Manuel Chrysoloras, another Byzantine convert to the western church, served Manuel II as an ambassador to Italy, France, and England, and taught Italian humanists Greek literature at Florence and Milan.

Thus Byzantine and western scholars had had increasingly friendly relations for about a century by the time of the Council of Ferrara and Florence. Among the learned Byzantines at the council were Bessarion, Isidore of Kiev, the future patriarch Gennadius Scholarius, and George Gemistus Plethon, Bessarion's teacher. Manuel II had relegated Plethon to Mistra as a suspected heretic, with some reason. Plethon was such a thoroughgoing Platonist that he converted himself to a form of Greek paganism, and exhorted the Palaeologi to organize the Peloponnesians into a militarized aristocracy on the model of Plato's *Republic*. Plethon's knowledge of Plato created something of a sensation at Florence, and won him so much respect among Byzantines that he remained unmolested at Mistra until his death in 1452. Only after the fall of Constantinople did Gennadius order Plethon's final work, the *Laws*, to be burned.[22]

If Plethon was the most original scholar of this period, he was far from being the only one who tried to build upon ancient knowledge. Theodore Metochites updated old astronomical tables, or at least pretended to do so. The young Nicephorus Gregoras proposed reforming the Julian calendar to correct the length of the year, though because Andronicus II shrank from unsettling the Church the change had to wait for Pope Gregory XIII in 1582. In the early fifteenth century, the disgraced scholar Mazaris wrote *A Visit to Hades*, a classicizing prose satire like the earlier *Timarion*. It describes conversations with recently deceased courtiers, and execrates Mazaris's place of retirement in the Peloponnesus.

While some of these scholars also wrote poetry, even they seem not to have valued it very highly, and most of the verse of the time was written in a vernacular Greek that they disdained. This popular poetry was inspired by western vernacular verse, and most of it was presumably written in the Greek lands conquered by the Crusaders. The dozen or so fourteenth-century verse romances show awareness of the Byzantine poetry of the twelfth century, but even more familiarity with contemporary romances in French and Italian, some of which they adapted or translated. Greek or crusader authors even produced two vernacular Greek chronicles in verse, the *Chronicle of the Morea* in the Peloponnesus and the *Chronicle of the Tocco* in Epirus, which celebrate the western conquerors.

Art and architecture, although more expensive than scholarship, flourished to the extent of the Byzantines' diminished resources. Michael VIII's efforts to attract artists and restore churches reestablished Constantinople as the artistic center of the Byzantine world. Unlike Byzantine scholarship, which spread to the West but had little impact on eastern Christians outside Byzantine rule, the Byzantine art of this period was shared by Epirus and Trebizond, and in good measure by the Serbs, Bulgarians, Romanians, and Russians. Byzantine painting, though not architecture, also had influence on the West through Crete and Venice. On the other hand, western architecture, though not painting, had a perceptible influence on Byzantium through the Venetians and Crusaders, who built castles and some churches in their conquests and colonies.

The emperors of Nicaea and Trebizond and the despots of Epirus all built palaces and churches on a scale commensurate with their means. The ruins of the Nicene emperors' palace at Nymphaeum show a pleasant if unpretentious building (Fig. 178). What remains of the palace of the emperors of Trebizond in their capital is more elaborate, and influenced by the Gothic architecture of the West (Fig. 198). Trapezuntine churches show a mixture of Byzantine, Georgian, Armenian, and even Turkish elements (Fig. 202). Perhaps the most extraordinary building in

202. Church of Saint Sophia, Trebizond. (Photo: Irina Andreescu-Treadgold)

the successor states is in the Epirote capital of Arta, where the despot Nicephorus I built the Church of the Virgin Paregoretissa ("Comforter") with a high dome perched on three registers of columns (Fig. 172). Its mosaics, however, are rather mediocre.

At Constantinople Michael VIII devoted himself to rebuilding and redecorating buildings damaged in the Fourth Crusade and under the Latins, who had neglected their overlarge conquest. Michael probably constructed the Palace of the Porphyrogenitus at Constantinople (now known as the Tekfur Saray) for his younger son Constantine. Its handsome stone and tile exterior remains (Fig. 182), though its balconies and western-inspired decorations are known only from old drawings. Also likely to be Michael's is one of the masterpieces of Byzantine art, a superb mosaic panel in Saint Sophia of the Virgin and John the Baptist praying before Christ (Fig. 203). That such a work could have been completed soon after the Latin occupation shows that Byzantine artists of the first rank had never ceased to be trained, whether at Nicaea or elsewhere. The reign of Andronicus II, all its disasters notwithstanding, saw no interruption of artistic endeavor. Andronicus's minister Theodore Metochites rebuilt the Monastery of the Chora ("Dwelling"), covering its church with a profusion of mosaics and frescoes (Figs. 14, 29,

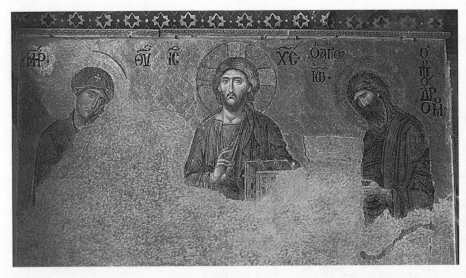

203. Mosaic of the *Deēsis* (Supplication of Christ by the Virgin and John the Baptist) in Saint Sophia, Constantinople. (Photo: Dumbarton Oaks, Washington, D.C., copyright 1996)

204. Apse fresco of the Anastasis (Christ's releasing the dead from hell) from the monastery Church of the Chora, Constantinople. (Photo: Dumbarton Oaks, Washington, D.C., copyright 1996)

201, 204). Though Metochites appears to have spared no expense, the architecture is rather conventional; so are some of the mosaics, like the one over the door depicting Theodore himself offering the church to Christ (Fig. 201). Yet along with artists of average ability Metochites hired some brilliant masters, like the painter of the dramatic fresco of the Anastasis, Christ's releasing the dead from hell (Fig. 204).

From the middle of the fourteenth century, art and particularly architecture dwindled throughout the Byzantine world. The main reason was surely the Ottoman advance. The triumph of Hesychasm, which had a negative but scarcely fatal effect on scholarship, seems to have done art no harm. Among the most accomplished Byzantine illuminations ever executed are those in a manuscript of the Palamite theological works that John VI wrote as the monk Joasaph (Figs. 187, 199). The illuminator was well aware of the text's contents, since he included a scene of the Transfiguration of Christ, radiating the uncreated light that the Hesychasts claimed to see at their prayers. The despots of the Peloponnesus,

205. Vault fresco of the Nativity from the Church of the Virgin Peribleptos ("Much Admired"), Mistra. (Photo: Courtesy of Charalambos Bouras)

which harbored the last scraps of Byzantine prosperity, kept up artistic activity, and continued to add to the imposing Palace of the Despots at Mistra (Fig. 196). Even if mosaics had become too expensive, excellent frescoes still went up in Mistra's churches, such as the strikingly composed Nativity in the Church of the Virgin Peribleptos ("Much Admired"; Fig. 205).

The Turkish conquest did not blight Byzantine culture all at once. Strangely, after a gap of almost a century in Byzantine historiography, four important Byzantine historians appeared just after the fall of Constantinople to record the empire's last years: Laonicus Chalcondyles, Critobulus of Imbros, Ducas, and George Sphrantzes. Also contrary to what one might expect, Chalcondyles and Critobulus, who wrote under the sultan, composed in the most arcane Thucydidean style, whereas Ducas and Sphrantzes, who found refuge on Genoese Lesbos and Venetian Corcyra, use a language much closer to the one they spoke. But all four men had been educated before the city fell, and had similarly educated contemporaries to read their works. A generation later, the break-down of the Byzantine system of higher education brought a virtual end to the tradition of secular literature in the Greek East. Venetian Crete still harbored some Greek scholars, and Greek religious art of high quality survived in parts of the East. Rather later than the scholars, Greek artists made their way to Renaissance Italy and elsewhere in the West and often found favor. The most famous of them was the sixteenth-century Cretan Domenikos Theotokopoulos, better known as El Greco.

Up to the fall of Constantinople, Byzantine scholars and artists showed at least as much knowledge and skill as those of contemporary Italy. Italian scholars were glad to learn from Byzantines like Barlaam and Bessarion, who became leading figures of the Italian Renaissance. Plethon was as innovative a thinker as any to be found in the West at his time. Byzantine art directly inspired Italian artists of the Venetian and Sienese schools. If Byzantium never developed an intellectual and artistic renaissance comparable to that of Italy, the main reason may well have been that the Turkish conquest cut Byzantine progress short. The invention of printing, which did so much to stimulate and spread Renaissance thinking in the West, came a few years too late to help the Byzantines.

THE PASSING OF THE STATE

Even though the restored Byzantine Empire soon fell into impotence and bankruptcy, this period was not one of uniform disaster for everyone in the Balkans and Asia Minor. The Ottoman Turks, who started their state in Byzantine Bithynia and then expanded over all of what had been Byzantium, enjoyed steady military success, broken only by the invasion of Timur. The Venetians and Genoese, despite ruinous wars with each other and the Byzantines, did good business in the region until Constantinople fell. The Serbs attained their greatest power under Milutin and Dushan, largely at the expense of the Byzantines. Many Byzantine magnates remained wealthy until the mid-fourteenth century, and many Byzantine merchants prospered later still. Even the empire started out well enough under the Nicene emperors and Michael VIII, and temporarily reversed its decline under Andronicus III. The Byzantine world had ample resources, even when the Byzantine Empire had few.

The whole region's economy was as before chiefly agricultural, and dependent on the rise or fall of the rural population. Records for the landholdings of Mount Athos, and in the fifteenth century Ottoman tax

records, show demographic trends broadly similar to those better documented for western Europe. The long-term population growth that had
begun by the year 800 appears to have continued until the Black Death
arrived in 1347.[23] The ravages of the Crusaders, the Bulgarians, the Turks,
and the Catalan Grand Company had only temporary effects in limited
areas.[24] By the early fourteenth century, the remaining European provinces of the empire appear to have been densely settled.

This density was disadvantageous for the peasantry, who had to farm
smaller plots, sometimes in poor land ill suited for agriculture, and to pay
higher rents, since they could find a new landlord less easily than their
landlord could find new tenants. Conversely, the great landholders benefited, because they could raise their rents and buy out still more smallholders. As usual, the rich weathered scarcity and unsettled conditions
better than the poor. The state would only have benefited from increased agricultural production if the government was able to collect its
share. Whether it did or not is difficult to say. Its ability to do so was decreased by the tax evasion of ever more powerful magnates, by the corruption of tax collectors, and by pronoia grants that gave up tax revenues. On the other hand, unsettled conditions tended to leave vacant
land to claim for the imperial estates, which contributed more revenue
to the treasury than private holdings.

Before the Black Death, the empire's cities seem to have been relatively prosperous, even if much of their trade was in the hands of the
Venetians and Genoese. Just before John VI lowered the rates in 1348,
Nicephoras Gregoras reports that the customs duties of Constantinople
totaled 30,000 hyperpyra, and those of the neighboring Genoese colony
of Galata 200,000 hyperpyra. Gregoras should have known the first
figure, but is likely to have exaggerated the second.[25] Since at that time
the Byzantine duties still represented a tenth of the value of incoming
merchandise, plus another tenth of the value of outgoing merchandise,
the volume of trade at Constantinople should have been around 150,000
hyperpyra a year. To include Galata, this figure should probably be at
least tripled, to 450,000 hyperpyra. In the twelfth century, itself a time of
lively commercial activity, Byzantine trade in Constantinople had been
equivalent to some 130,000 hyperpyra, and total trade in Constantinople
to no more than 350,000 hyperpyra.[26] If anything, the twelfth-century
estimates are likely to be too high, while because the guess for Galata is
a conservative one the fourteenth-century estimates may well be too low.
So during the intervening two centuries trade seems to have increased.

206. The fourteenth-century Tower of Christ, Galata, Constantinople, built by the Genoese. The conical roof is a modern addition. (Photo: Irina Andreescu-Treadgold)

The main reason for the increase was probably a great expansion of the Black Sea trade, which the Genoese dominated from their colony of Caffa in the Crimea. Their main business was in grain from the Mongol Khanate of the Golden Horde, but fur and slaves were also important, along with the luxuries that came through Trebizond along the silk route from China and Turkestan. The volume of the Black Sea trade stimulated the economy of Constantinople and the whole Aegean region.[27] The Byzantines in Thrace and Greece also had surplus grain to sell, and the Aegean islands had small but valuable exports. The port of Phocaea had mines that produced alum, used for fixing dyes in wool, and Chios had trees that produced mastic, used in perfumes and chewing gum. In 1329, when Andronicus III drove the Genoese from Chios, the island's revenues came to a princely 120,000 hyperpyra.[28] Most exports from the East seem to have been raw materials, while most imports from the West were manufactured goods. For all their grumbling about westerners, the Byzantines had acquired many western tastes.

Constantinople certainly lost many of its people during and after the Fourth Crusade. The great fires of 1203 and 1204 did terrible damage that the Latins failed to repair. Since the Latins held only small parts of neighboring Thrace and Asia Minor, Constantinople lost some of the trade from its hinterland during the Latin occupation. But Michael VIII's efforts to increase the city's population should have brought it back to more than a hundred thousand. An Englishman and an Arab who saw it shortly before the Black Death still marveled at its size, its beauty, and its commerce.[29] During the great civil war of 1341 to 1347, Constantinople, Thessalonica, Adrianople, and some other towns in Thrace were populous enough to produce urban mobs, who seem to have served the interests of merchants and tradesmen. In 1280, under Michael VIII, Andronicus II reportedly resettled thirty-six thousand people in Tralles after recovering its ruins from the Turks.[30] If a refounded town could be so big, many established provincial towns must have been bigger.

Then the Black Death struck, at first with crippling effect. As already noted, the disease might have killed about a third of the empire's people, but many fewer of the empire's Turkish, Serbian, and Bulgarian adversaries.[31] The plague frustrated John VI's attempt to expel the Serbs from northern Greece, and helped the Turks establish themselves in Thrace. During later outbreaks, the Turks and others who had overrun Byzantine territory caught the plague as well, although they may still have suffered less than the Byzantines. Around the end of the fourteenth century, the population should have started to recover, since the disease had lost some of its virulence and had freed more and better land for the people who remained. By then, however, the empire had sunk too low for its government to profit much from such trends.

Constantinople made a poor recovery in the century between the Black Death and its fall to the Ottomans. Largely cut off from Thrace and Asia Minor, the capital of little more than itself, the city was merely a safe and convenient harbor for ships arriving from the Black Sea. Contemporary estimates of its population cluster around fifty thousand, a figure that seems plausible enough.[32] A Castilian ambassador in 1403 found the city filled with ruins, and no longer one of the world's great capitals. Another Castilian in 1437 found both the imperial palace and the city in deplorable condition.[33] Thessalonica seems to have fared better. Though it had formerly been much smaller than Constantinople, a contemporary Venetian estimated it had forty thousand people in 1423.[34] Even a modest city like Argos in the Peloponnesus is said to have had thirty thousand people, whom the Turks enslaved in 1397.[35] Such guesses cannot be considered exact, but they indicate that the difference in size between Constantinople and the provincial cities had diminished. Since by this time Byzantium was no longer functioning as a single economy, Constantinople had become just another regional center. Only the Turkish conquest began to restore its political and economic predominance.

The Black Death, aggravated by the civil war and exploited by the Serbs and Turks, was probably the main cause of the empire's declining from a small power to a negligible one. What the plague cannot explain is the empire's earlier decline to a small power from an important one. In 1282 the newly crowned Andronicus II probably ruled about 5 million souls. By 1312, after the loss of almost all of Byzantine Anatolia, he probably ruled around 2 million.[36] The empire had lost at least half its population in thirty years. This was the real catastrophe. It resulted from Andronicus II's failure to protect his Anatolian and Balkan possessions from the Turks and Catalans, and to keep the Venetians and Genoese from seizing his islands. Andronicus had dismantled most of his fleet, and was unable to keep paying the exorbitant salaries of the Catalan Grand Company, though he resorted to some extraordinary taxes and confiscations and debased the hyperpyron. Even Andronicus's father Michael VIII had debased the hyperpyron, and was clearly short of cash from the early part of his reign. Granted that Michael made better use of his limited funds than his son did, we may still ask why the empire barely had the money to maintain itself.

Andronicus II took some care with his finances, and a report on his financial plans for 1321 by Nicephorus Gregoras supplies us with our one recorded total for the empire's revenue at any date: 1 million hyperpyra in 1320. Andronicus collected this sum, which was larger than the revenue had been for some years past, by raising the rates of the taxes and collecting them more rigorously than before. From his receipts he planned to increase his standing army to three thousand mercenary cavalry, and his navy to twenty ships. He expected to have enough money left over to meet all his usual expenses, such as entertaining foreign ambassadors, paying tribute to neighboring peoples (seemingly the Turkish emirates), and meeting the many expenses of the imperial family. Andronicus seems not to have planned for any significant surplus or deficit.[37] Although his civil war with his grandson frustrated his plans to enlarge the army and navy, the revenue was collected, and presumably would have sufficed to meet the expenses he anticipated.

The first question is how a revenue of 1 million hyperpyra compares with what the empire had raised before the pronoia grants and tax immunities that characterized the later empire. At the death of Basil II in 1025, the empire seems to have had about 12 million subjects, and revenues of some 5.9 million nomismata. This would have been the equivalent of about 11.8 million of the debased hyperpyra of 1320. Because the empire then had only about 2 million subjects, at the same rate of collection the revenue would have been something like 2 million hyperpyra. This is about twice what Andronicus actually collected. The revenue signed away in military pronoia grants seems to have accounted for not much more than 100,000 hyperpyra a year, which after all supported some five hundred heavy cavalry.[38] Most losses of revenue were of other sorts, and profited various individuals while providing few if any benefits to the state. By 1320, then, the grants, exemptions, and inefficiencies of the preceding three centuries had apparently caused a loss of revenue on the order of 50 percent, quite apart from losses of territory. Before Andronicus II's recent efforts to increase revenue, matters must have been worse.

The next question is how the empire's income was spent. We can at least reconstruct a good deal of the budget as it would have been if Andronicus had enacted his plans. The numbers of mercenaries and ships are recorded. Standard pay for mercenaries at the time seems to have been about 3 ducats a month, equivalent to 72 hyperpyra a year, and the extra pay for the officers can be estimated by analogy with earlier Byzantine practice. The pay of a ship's crew of 154 men at this date can be estimated from the terms of the Byzantine treaty with Genoa of 1261, and comes to about 5,000 hyperpyra a vessel.[39] The cost of uniforms, arms, rations, horses, and fodder can all be estimated by adjusting earlier Byzantine figures to take the debasement of the hyperpyron into account. These estimates indicate that paying and maintaining Andronicus's standing army of three thousand men and standing navy of as many men again would have cost some 500,000 hyperpyra, or about half his budget.

Although Andronicus's pronoiars and irregulars provided for their own support, he also had a palace guard to pay. This was perhaps on the scale of that of John VI, who employed some five hundred Catalans, and on the analogy of ninth-century guardsmen might have been paid about 144 hyperpyra a year, double ordinary mercenaries' pay.[40] Then there were the extra costs of campaigns. We happen to know that in 1321 Andronicus gave the young John Cantacuzenus 50,000 hyperpyra to campaign against the Catalans of Athens.[41] Though this expedition never took place because of the outbreak of the civil war, it should be counted

TABLE 18

Estimated State Budgetary Plan for 1321

Budgetary item	Estimate (millions of hyperpyra)
pay of bodyguards (500 × 144 hyp. × ⅓)[a]	0.096M hyp.
pay of soldiers (3,000 × 72 hyp. × ⅓)[a]	0.288
pay of oarsmen (20 ships × 5,000 hyp.)	0.1
army uniforms, arms, and rations (3,500 × 20 hyp.)	0.07
navy rations (3,080 × 10 hyp.)	0.031
fodder and horses (3,500 × 10 hyp.)	0.035
campaign against Catalans	0.05
nonmilitary expenses	0.33
TOTAL	1.0M hyp.

[a]The fractional multiplier allows for the higher pay of officers.

as a planned expenditure. All these projected military appropriations for 1321 amount to some two-thirds of Andronicus's budget of a million hyperpyra (Table 18). Such a proportion is generally in line with what had been spent on the army and navy in earlier Byzantine times, and would be if anything a little lower than average.

This budget was, however, a plan that never went into effect. It represented considerably more total revenue and military spending than had been customary during the preceding few years. Even this budget, though not neglecting the military, was not that of a state on a full wartime footing. In 1322 Andronicus II agreed to pay 36,000 hyperpyra a year simply for the upkeep of his grandson's court, a sum not much less than the 44,000 hyperpyra a year that the same prince apparently received to pay his mercenary troops. The senior emperor's court must have been much more costly. Even after his abdication, Andronicus II maintained a household that cost 20,000 to 24,000 hyperpyra a year.[42] Gregoras's description of Andronicus's plan for 1321 implies that it allotted the same expenses as usual for the court, entertainment, and tribute, while the additional funds were to go, as an exceptional measure, to the army and navy. In the actual budgets of the preceding few years, military outlays cannot have been much more than nonmilitary ones. A reasonable guess would be a third of a million hyperpyra for each, for a total of around two-thirds of a million.

At this time, however, the empire was facing a military crisis that in proportion to its smaller size rivaled that of the early and middle seventh century. More than half of its population and territory was being lost, and its long-term survival was coming into doubt. Andronicus II did take some myopic emergency measures, such as hiring Alans at half the usual pay only to have them desert, and hiring Catalans at three times the usual pay only to have them revolt when they could not be paid.[43] At least his plans in 1320 were a step in the right direction, and show what could be done even without cutting the expenses of the court. Yet the situation called for far more drastic efforts to increase the size and strength of the armed forces. Michael VIII, Andronicus III, and John VI all showed some of the needed sense of urgency, and during their reigns the empire, in spite of everything, more or less held its own. The slackening that occurred under Andronicus II and John V proved fatal. By the fifteenth century, the empire could barely pay the Ottomans tribute of 20,000 hyperpyra a year.[44] By 1451, Byzantium needed another 20,000 hyperpyra so badly that it risked asking the sultan for them, provoking the attack that sealed its doom.

The Balkans and Asia Minor could still support a great power, and the proof is that the Ottomans built one there. It soon covered all the Balkan and Anatolian lands that the Byzantines had held under Basil II. Moreover, unlike eleventh-century Byzantium, fifteenth-century Turkey had many great conquests ahead of it. These would come to include formerly Byzantine territories in Armenia, Syria, Egypt, Mesopotamia, North Africa, and the Crimea. Nonetheless, even with all these conquests in prospect, the Ottoman Empire of 1461 was to survive only a few more years than the Byzantine Empire had after 1025. The whole lifetime of the Byzantine Empire, even excluding its Roman predecessor, was far longer than that of the Ottoman Sultanate, or of any other empire in history. Byzantine staying power was unique. By lasting as long as it did, Byzantium fostered a society that could live on without it, and that in its way survives today.

Conclusion

207. (previous page) Right leaf of a twelfth-century menologium icon from
the Monastery of Saint Catherine, Mount Sinai, showing the Virgin and Child
and six of the twelve great feasts of the Church at the top, with the saints
commemorated each day during the months from March to August. The left
leaf of the same icon above appears on the title page. (Photo: Courtesy of
Michigan-Princeton-Alexandria Expedition to Mount Sinai)

Conclusion

By the standards of a modern nation, the Byzantine Empire was an artificial state, largely created by its rulers. The form it took after 285 was the result of an administrative division of the Roman Empire made by Diocletian. Constantine I chose the empire's religion and built its future capital. Maneuvering by Leo I and Zeno rescued Byzantium from becoming a plaything of barbarians. Without the determination of Justinian I, the empire would never have expanded to the West. Without the inspired strategy of Heraclius or the prudent management of Constans II, Byzantium would probably have fallen during the seventh century. Its revival from the eighth to the eleventh century was the work of a series of unusually capable rulers, and ceased when that series came to an end. Alexius I rescued the empire from collapse, but it fell to pieces after his dynasty ended. The Byzantium of Michael VIII was a deliberate, if incomplete, restoration of its predecessor. The walls of Constantinople, which had helped save Byzantium several times before, were practically all that preserved the restored empire during its last century.

Byzantium never depended on the perceptions of racial or linguistic unity that define a modern nation-state. While most Byzantine emperors strove to impose religious unity, they never quite succeeded in suppressing heresies, schisms, or religious minorities, and their constant striving to eliminate religious divisions drove their subjects apart almost as much as it brought them together. Most Byzantines, though proud of their empire, assumed that God would care for it without aid from them. They considered it the greatest empire in the world, but this opinion had little to do with how big, strong, or prosperous Byzantium actually was. Most of them considered themselves loyal to the emperor, but such loyalty seldom made them resist someone who overthrew him and took his place. The Byzantines, in short, had nothing much like the modern concept of patriotism.

Yet, as its durability shows, Byzantium's artificiality was as often a strength as a weakness. By and large it overcame the ethnic and linguistic divisions among its subjects. Few of the empire's religious disputes divided its people along ethnic or linguistic lines, and none did so explicitly or completely. Under the pressure of religious idealists, many of them monks, the Byzantine church defended its principles well, and often forced them upon the state. The central role of the state in defining Byzantium led to fairly good government by premodern standards. The bureaucracy was distinguished by its education, competence, and professionalism, and the ruling class usually managed to do whatever needed to be done to preserve the state. Regardless of what leading Byzantines might say or write about their powerful emperor on official occasions, they opposed him when necessary, and at some other times as well. The emperor's power never exceeded that of a western monarch like Louis XIV, who was in much less danger of being overthrown.[1]

The differences between Byzantium and the medieval kingdoms that later evolved into nations can easily be exaggerated. In some ways, for example, the history of Byzantium was rather like that of France. Both began as parts of larger empires. Byzantium began as the eastern part of the Roman Empire that was ruled by Diocletian after 285; France began as the western part of the Frankish Empire that was ruled by Charles the Bald after 843. While each of those larger empires was later reunited for a few years, the divisions that created Byzantium and France turned out to be lasting, partly because they corresponded to a previously existing linguistic divide. Diocletian's portion of the Roman Empire was more or less that where Greek, not Latin, was the culturally dominant language, and Charles the Bald's portion of the Frankish Empire was more or less that where the main language was Old French, not Old German. If Byzantium had lasted into modern times with something like the boundaries it possessed between 750 and 1000, it would probably have developed into a predominantly Greek-speaking nation-state, at least as homogeneous as today's Russia and only a little less so than today's France. As of this writing, France is still some years short of Byzantium's record of longevity.

Byzantium's weaknesses had little to do with its subjects' lack of patriotism or nationalism—feelings that were in any case almost nonexistent before modern times—but did have something to do with their religion. The reluctance of the Byzantine church to accept that ends could justify means (even to the point of insisting that killing enemy soldiers in battle was sinful) led to a feeling that no one could engage in politics, war, or commerce without some moral taint. This put the Byzantines at a certain disadvantage against western merchants or Crusaders, or Muslim Holy Warriors. But the Church could forgive even the worst political sins of someone who performed services to Christianity. While scrupulousness and forgiveness are certainly admirable things, in practice the Byzantines' combination of them decreased respect for the state and for commerce, and perversely increased amorality in public life, because emperors, officials, or merchants despaired of avoiding sin.[2] Yet state power was so pervasive that almost everyone needed it at some time for defense or patronage, and all had to defer to it. Therefore most ordinary Byzantines felt dependent upon the government without admiring it or identifying much with it.

Naturally the eastern Christians conquered by the Ottomans felt even less identification with the Ottoman government, though they were forced into dependence on it too. The Ottoman administration, partly staffed by Phanariot Greeks, was often corrupt. The Turks could be harsh in their treatment of Christians, and the sultans in particular had a taste for murdering rivals that went well beyond Byzantine precedents. The sultans chose most of their patriarchs of Constantinople from Phanariot families, but changed patriarchs frequently, and executed several of them on false or dubious charges of treason. Though the patriarchal academy remained, men interested in secular studies in Greek found nothing better at Ottoman Constantinople than some secondary schools and private tutors. More formal higher education was available only in the West, particularly at Venice and its nearby university town of Padua, until the Phanariot governors of Wallachia and Moldavia founded Greek academies in their provinces.

The Ottoman Sultanate was at least as multiethnic and polyglot as the Byzantine Empire it replaced. The sultans, while professing and promoting Islam, made little effort to favor the Turkish language outside Asia Minor, except by settling some Turks in parts of Europe. Many Albanians and Bosnians became Muslims without learning Turkish. Like Byzantine emperors, the sultans paid scant attention to race or language when resettling people or allowing them to migrate. Thus the Balkans and even Asia Minor came to have a very mixed population. Races,

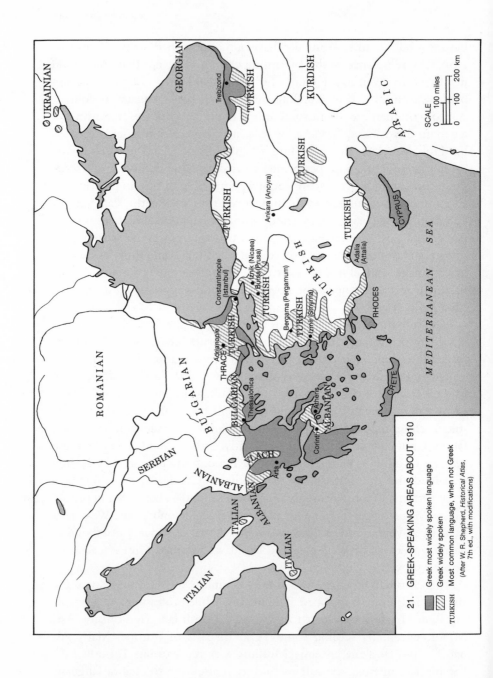

21. GREEK-SPEAKING AREAS ABOUT 1910

Greek most widely spoken language

Greek widely spoken

TURKISH Most common language, when not Greek

(After W. R. Shepherd, *Historical Atlas*, 7th ed., with modifications)

always a mostly imaginary means of classifying people, became hopelessly confused, since many Muslims who spoke Turkish and counted as Turks were the descendants of Christian Greeks or Slavs. Even languages became confused. Although many people who spoke Greek, Serbian, or Bulgarian were still to be found in the lands that had once formed the Byzantine, Serbian, and Bulgarian states, they lived mixed with each other and with people who spoke Vlach, Albanian, or Turkish.

The linguistic map of the Greek-speaking population, who still called themselves *Rhōmaioi* or Byzantines, is difficult to draw and rather controversial, even for the early twentieth century. The only large region with a clear majority of Greek speakers was Greece south of Thessalonica, including the Aegean islands, Crete, and Cyprus. However, most regions that had been predominantly Greek-speaking at the beginning of the Byzantine period still had Greek-speaking minorities of some size. These included northern Greece, Thrace, most of the Anatolian coast, a few pockets and towns in the Anatolian interior, and even two enclaves in southern Italy. A state that consisted of all the areas with substantial numbers of Greek speakers plus some minimal connecting territory would have resembled the Byzantine Empire of the late twelfth century, though less than half of its population would have spoken Greek. Greeks who looked forward to freedom from Ottoman domination were therefore tempted to dream not just of an independent Greece but of a reconstituted Byzantium, including Constantinople and perhaps stretching to Smyrna, Nicaea, Trebizond, and Attalia. The hope of creating such a latter-day Byzantine Empire came to be known as the *Megalē Idea* (Great Idea).

By the nineteenth century, some Bulgarians also conceived the idea of a Greater Bulgaria like the empires of Symeon or Samuel, and some Serbs the idea of a Greater Serbia like the empire of Stephen Dushan. Some Romanians thought of a Greater Romania in Wallachia, Moldavia, and Transylvania. Each of these peoples aspired to take the role that they fancied Greeks had played in the Byzantine Empire, dominating other peoples in a multinational state. The Turks, who already had a Greater Turkey, were of course unwilling to contemplate a country reduced only to regions where a clear majority spoke Turkish. All these claims overlapped, and the linguistic realities were such that no neat boundaries could possibly be drawn between peoples. When national states began to be founded, the situation resembled what would happen if the United States started to break up along ethnic lines, with Swedes, Norwegians, and Germans fighting for parts of Minnesota, and Irish, Italians, and Anglo-Saxons disputing New England.

In 1821 the Greek War of Independence broke out, not in Constantinople, where the Turks were far too strong, but in the Peloponnesus. The revolutionaries had secured the virtual independence of the Peloponnesus and central Greece by 1827. The new state called itself Greece (*Hellas*), since without Constantinople it could hardly claim to be the Byzantine Empire, and it needed the goodwill of western Europeans who idealized classical Greece but knew little of Byzantium. But the Bavarian who became the Greek king in 1832, and the Dane who replaced him in 1863, took the title of emperor (*basileus*) of the Greeks. After gradually gaining territory in northern Greece and the islands, by the end of the Balkan Wars in 1913 the Greek state included most of the regions with clear Greek-speaking majorities, except for Italian-held Rhodes and British-held Cyprus. Since in the First World War the Greeks were hesitantly aligned with the winning side, while Turkey and Bulgaria were losers, in 1920 Greece was able to annex all of Thrace but Constantinople itself, which though nominally Turkish was occupied jointly by the British and French. Woodrow Wilson assigned Trebizond to a newly independent Christian Armenia.

The fairest and simplest boundary that could have been drawn between Greece and Turkey would probably have been at the straits, since that would have left about as many Greek speakers in Turkey as Turkish speakers in Greece.[3] Such a frontier would have put Constantinople, though its Greek speakers were a minority, in Greek hands. The Turkish nationalists, occupied with crushing the Armenians, had already established their capital at Ankara (Byzantine Ancyra). But the allies remained ensconced at Constantinople, and Greece insisted on assuming provisional administration over the region of Smyrna. The Greek army soon began advancing through northwestern Asia Minor. Especially after this Anatolian war inflamed old enmities, hardly any Turks were content to live under Greek rule, nor many Greeks under Turkish rule. The real question was the location of the boundary to which each people would have to adapt.

The Greeks seemed to have the military advantage, but they overreached themselves. The Turks defeated the Greek army near Ankara, drove it from Asia Minor, and burned Smyrna. Having established their military superiority, they recovered Constantinople and eastern Thrace by treaty in 1923. Turkey deported some 1.3 million mostly Greek-speaking Christians to Greece, in exchange for some 300,000 mostly Turkish-speaking Muslims from Greek territory. Only a few Turks were allowed to remain in western Thrace, and a few Greeks in Constantinople, now called Istanbul. The Turks destroyed or defaced many Byzantine churches and monasteries, while the Greeks treated Ottoman mosques in Greece in a similar fashion. Greece became almost entirely Christian and Greek-speaking, while Turkey became almost entirely Muslim and Turkish-speaking. Greece has had to abandon the *Megalē Idea*.[4]

Today the effects of Byzantine civilization vary in the lands that once were Byzantine. Of course later influences have been powerful, and in many cases overpowering. Byzantine traditions remain strongest among members of the Eastern Orthodox Church, which still recognizes the primacy of honor of the patriarch of Constantinople in Istanbul. The Orthodox patriarchates of Alexandria, Antioch, and Jerusalem still have a number of adherents among the substantial Christian minorities in Egypt, Palestine, Lebanon, and Syria. Eastern Orthodoxy is the majority faith in Greece, Cyprus, Bulgaria, Serbia, Romania, Russia, Georgia, Macedonia, Ukraine, and Belarus. Albania has an Orthodox minority of some size, and Armenia is mostly Eastern Christian, though mostly not in communion with the patriarch of Constantinople.

The impress of Byzantine civilization is deep in most of these countries, even as they hasten to become more like Western Europe and North America. In Eastern Europe Communism has reinforced the simultaneous Byzantine tendencies to depend on the government but to distrust politicians and businessmen. Byzantium, the Ottoman Empire, and Communism have left most of these countries with linguistic and religious minorities larger and more diverse than those of most Western European countries. Byzantine, Ottoman, and Communist rule have also suppressed national feelings and discouraged the development of democratic institutions, so that the fall of Communism, like that of the Ottomans, has tended to unleash a sort of nationalism without much regard for minority rights. Eastern Europe is therefore likely to be more turbulent than Western or Central Europe for some time to come. Yet the Orthodox Church remains a traditional, moral, and spiritual force that should not be underestimated, and the history of the Byzantine Empire is a reminder that people of different nationalities can live together as one, over wide areas, for centuries.

Reference Matter

Lists of Rulers

Note that epithets (such as "the Apostate" or "the Blinded") were scarcely ever used until well after a ruler's death, usually to distinguish him from other rulers with the same name. Constantine I, Theodosius I, Leo I, Justin I, and Justinian I eventually acquired the epithet of "the Great" (*ho megas*), meaning "the Elder," to distinguish them from Constantine II, Theodosius II, Leo II, Justin II, and Justinian II. Except where noted otherwise, the lists below are modified from V. Grumel, *La chronologie* (Paris, 1958), 355–59, 372, 376, 380, 388, 403, and 434–37.

Eastern Roman (Byzantine) Emperors (284–1453)

The principal Eastern Roman emperor is listed in capitals, with other rulers (if any) listed under him.

DIOCLETIAN 284–305
    Galerius,   Caesar in Egypt and Syria 293–99
               Caesar in Balkans 299–305

GALERIUS 305–11
    Maximin, Caesar in Egypt and Syria 305–10
             Augustus in Egypt and Syria 310–11
    Licinius, Augustus in Balkans 308–11

LICINIUS 311–24
    Maximin, Augustus in Egypt, Syria, and Anatolia 311–13
    Constantine I, Augustus in Balkans except Thrace 317–24

CONSTANTINE I 324–37
    Constantius II, Caesar in Egypt and Syria 335–37
    Dalmatius, Caesar in Balkans 335–37

CONSTANTIUS II   337–61
Constans I, Augustus in Balkans except Thrace 337–50
Gallus, Caesar in Egypt and Syria 351–54

JULIAN the Apostate   361–63

JOVIAN   363–64

VALENS   364–78
Valentinian I, Augustus in Balkans except Thrace 364–75
Gratian, Augustus in Balkans except Thrace 375–79

THEODOSIUS I   379–95
Valentinian II, Augustus in Balkans except Thrace 382–92

ARCADIUS   395–408

THEODOSIUS II   408–50

MARCIAN   450–57

LEO I   457–74

LEO II   474
Zeno Tarasius, Augustus and regent

ZENO Tarasius   474–91
Basiliscus, rival Augustus in most of East except Isauria 475–76

ANASTASIUS I   491–518

JUSTIN I   518–27

JUSTINIAN I   527–65

JUSTIN II   565–78
Tiberius, Caesar and regent 574–78

TIBERIUS II Constantine   578–82

MAURICE Tiberius   582–602

PHOCAS the Tyrant   602–10

HERACLIUS   610–41

CONSTANTINE III Heraclius   641

HERACLONAS (Heraclius) Constantine   641
Martina, regent

CONSTANS II (Constantine) Heraclius the Bearded   641–68

CONSTANTINE IV   668–85

JUSTINIAN II the Slit-Nosed   685–95

LEONTIUS (Leo)   695–98

TIBERIUS III Apsimar   698–705

JUSTINIAN II the Slit-Nosed (again)   705–11

THEODORA Porphyrogenita 1055–56

MICHAEL VI Bringas 1056–57

ISAAC I Comnenus 1057–59

CONSTANTINE X Ducas 1059–67

MICHAEL VII Ducas 1067–78
    Eudocia Macrembolitissa, regent 1067–68
    Romanus IV Diogenes, coemperor 1068–71

NICEPHORUS III Botaniates 1078–81

ALEXIUS I Comnenus 1081–1118

JOHN II Comnenus 1118–43

MANUEL I Comnenus 1143–80

ALEXIUS II Comnenus 1180–83
    Andronicus Comnenus, regent 1182–83

ANDRONICUS I Comnenus 1183–85

ISAAC II Angelus 1185–95

ALEXIUS III Angelus 1195–1203

ISAAC II Angelus (again) 1203–4
    Alexius IV Angelus, coemperor
    Alexius III Angelus, rival emperor in Thrace

ALEXIUS V Ducas Murtzuphlus 1204
    Alexius III Angelus, rival emperor in Thrace

ALEXIUS III Angelus (in Thrace) 1204
    Hereafter see also Emperors at Trebizond *and* Latin Emperors, *below*

THEODORE I Lascaris (at Nicaea) 1205–21

JOHN III Ducas Vatatzes (at Nicaea) 1221–54
    Theodore Ducas, emperor at Thessalonica 1224–30
    John Ducas, emperor at Thessalonica 1237–42

THEODORE II Lascaris (at Nicaea) 1254–58

JOHN IV Lascaris (at Nicaea) 1258–61
    Michael VIII Palaeologus, coemperor at Nicaea 1259–61

MICHAEL VIII Palaeologus (at Constantinople) 1261–82

ANDRONICUS II Palaeologus 1282–1328
    Andronicus III Palaeologus, coemperor 1321–28

ANDRONICUS III Palaeologus 1328–41

JOHN V Palaeologus 1341–76
    Anna of Savoy, regent 1341–47
    John VI Cantacuzenus, coemperor 1347–54

ANDRONICUS IV Palaeologus 1376–79

JOHN V Palaeologus (again)   1379–91
    John VII Palaeologus, rival emperor at Constantinople 1390

MANUEL II Palaeologus   1391–1425

JOHN VIII Palaeologus   1425–48

CONSTANTINE XI Palaeologus   1449–53

Emperors at Trebizond (1204–1461)

ALEXIUS I Comnenus   1204–22

ANDRONICUS I Gidus Comnenus   1222–35

JOHN I Axuch Comnenus   1235–38

MANUEL I Comnenus   1238–63

ANDRONICUS II Comnenus   1263–66

GEORGE Comnenus   1266–80

JOHN II Comnenus   1280–97
    Theodora Comnena, rival empress ca. 1284

ALEXIUS II Comnenus   1297–1330

ANDRONICUS III Comnenus   1330–32

MANUEL II Comnenus   1332

BASIL Comnenus   1332–40

IRENE Palaeologina   1340–41

ANNA Comnena   1341

MICHAEL Comnenus   1341

ANNA Comnena (again)   1341–42

JOHN III Comnenus   1342–44

MICHAEL Comnenus (again)   1344–49

ALEXIUS III Comnenus   1349–90

MANUEL III Comnenus   1390–1416

ALEXIUS IV Comnenus   1416–29

JOHN IV Comnenus   1429–59

DAVID Comnenus   1459–61

Latin Emperors (1204–1261)

BALDWIN I of Flanders   1204–5

HENRY of Flanders   1206–16

PETER of Courtenay   1217

YOLANDA   1217–19

ROBERT of Courtenay   1221–28

JOHN of Brienne   1228–37

BALDWIN II of Courtenay   1237–61

Archbishops (324–381) and Patriarchs (381–1462) of Constantinople

ALEXANDER   324–37

PAUL I   337–39

EUSEBIUS   339–41

PAUL I (again)   341–42

MACEDONIUS I   342–46

PAUL I (again)   346–51

MACEDONIUS I (again)   351–60

EUDOXIUS of Antioch   360–70

DEMOPHILUS   370–79

GREGORY I of Nazianzus   379–81

NECTARIUS   381–97

JOHN I Chrysostom   398–404

ARSACIUS   404–5

ATTICUS   406–25

SISINNIUS I   426–27

NESTORIUS   428–31

MAXIMIAN   431–34

PROCLUS   434–46

FLAVIAN   446–49

ANATOLIUS   449–58

GENNADIUS I   458–71

ACACIUS   472–89

FRAVITAS   489–90

EUPHEMIUS   490–96

MACEDONIUS II   496–511

TIMOTHY I   511–18

JOHN II   518–20

METHODIUS I 843–47

IGNATIUS 847–58

PHOTIUS 858–67

IGNATIUS (again) 867–77

PHOTIUS (again) 877–86

STEPHEN I 886–93

ANTHONY II Cauleas 893–901

NICHOLAS I Mysticus 901–7

EUTHYMIUS I 907–12

NICHOLAS I Mysticus (again) 912–25

STEPHEN II 925–27

TRYPHON 927–31

THEOPHYLACT 933–56

POLYEUCTUS 956–70

BASIL I Scamandrenus[1] 970–73

ANTHONY III of Studius 973–78

NICHOLAS II Chrysoberges 980–92

SISINNIUS II 996–98

SERGIUS II 1001–19

EUSTATHIUS 1019–25

ALEXIUS of Studius 1025–43

MICHAEL I Cerularius 1043–58

CONSTANTINE III Lichudes 1059–63

JOHN VIII Xiphilinus 1064–75

COSMAS I of Jerusalem 1075–81

EUSTRATIUS Garidas 1081–84

NICHOLAS III the Grammarian 1084–1111

JOHN IX Agapetus 1111–34

LEO Stypiotes 1134–43

MICHAEL II Curcuas 1143–46

COSMAS II Atticus 1146–47

NICHOLAS IV Muzalon 1147–51

1. On Basil I, Anthony III, and Nicholas II, see J. Darrouzès, "Sur la chronologie du patriarche Antoine III Stoudite," *Revue des Études Byzantines* 46 (1988), 55–60.

THEODOTUS II   1151/52–1153/54

CONSTANTINE IV Chiliarenus   1154–57

LUCAS Chrysoberges   1157–70

MICHAEL III   1170–78

CHARITON Eugeniotes   1178–79

THEODOSIUS Boradiotes   1179–83

BASIL II Camaterus   1183–86

NICETAS II Muntanes   1186–89

DOSITHEUS of Jerusalem   1189

LEONTIUS Theotocites   1189

DOSITHEUS of Jerusalem (again)   1189–91

GEORGE II Xiphilinus   1191–98

JOHN X Camaterus[2]   1198–1206

MICHAEL IV Autorianus (at Nicaea)   1208–14

THEODORE II Irenicus (at Nicaea)   1214–16

MAXIMUS II (at Nicaea)   1216

MANUEL I Sarantenus (at Nicaea)   1217–22

GERMANUS II (at Nicaea)   1222–40

METHODIUS II (at Nicaea)   1240

MANUEL II (at Nicaea)   1244–54

ARSENIUS Autorianus[3] (at Nicaea)   1254–59

NICEPHORUS II (at Nicaea)   1259–60

ARSENIUS Autorianus (again, at Constantinople)   1261–65

GERMANUS III   1265–66

JOSEPH I   1266–75

JOHN XI Beccus   1275–82

JOSEPH I (again)   1282–83

GREGORY II of Cyprus   1283–89

ATHANASIUS I   1289–93

JOHN XII Cosmas   1294–1303

ATHANASIUS I (again)   1303–9

NIPHON   1310–14

2. John X was patriarch in exile in Thrace from 1204.
3. See A. Failler, "Chronologie et composition dans l'Histoire de Georges Pachy-mère," *Revue des Études Byzantines* 38 (1980), 45–53.

JOHN XIII Glycys 1315–19

GERASIMUS I 1320–21

ISAIAH 1323–32

JOHN XIV Calecas 1334–47

ISIDORE I Bucharis 1347–50

CALLISTUS I 1350–53

PHILOTHEUS Coccinus 1353–54

CALLISTUS I (again) 1355–63

PHILOTHEUS Coccinus (again) 1364–76

MACARIUS 1376–79

NILUS 1380–88

ANTHONY IV 1389–90

MACARIUS (again) 1390–91

ANTHONY IV (again) 1391–97

CALLISTUS II Xanthopulus 1397

MATTHEW I 1397–1410

EUTHYMIUS II 1410–16

JOSEPH II 1416–39

METROPHANES II 1440–43

GREGORY III Mammes 1443–51

GENNADIUS II Scholarius 1454–56

ISIDORE II 1456–62

Western Roman Emperors (285–480)

The principal Western Roman emperor is listed in capitals, with other rulers (if any) listed under him.

MAXIMIAN 285–305
    Constantius I, Caesar in Britain and Gaul 293–305

CONSTANTIUS I 305–6
    Severus, Caesar in Italy and Africa 305–6

SEVERUS 306–7
    Constantine I, Caesar in Britain, Gaul, and Spain

CONSTANTINE I 307–37
    Maxentius, Augustus in Italy and Africa 307–12
    Crispus, Caesar in Britain, Gaul, and Spain 317–26

Constantine II, Caesar in Britain, Gaul, and Spain 329–37
Constans I, Caesar in Italy and Africa 335–37

CONSTANTINE II   337–40
Constans I, Augustus in Italy and Africa

CONSTANS I   340–50

MAGNENTIUS   350–53

CONSTANTIUS II   353–61
Julian, Caesar in Britain, Gaul, and Spain 355–61

JULIAN the Apostate   361–63

JOVIAN   363–64

VALENTINIAN I   364–75

GRATIAN   375–83

VALENTINIAN II   383–92
Maximus, Augustus in Britain, Gaul, and Spain 383–88

EUGENIUS   392–94

THEODOSIUS I   394–95

HONORIUS   395–423
Constantius III, coemperor 421

JOHN   423–25

VALENTINIAN III   425–55

AVITUS   455–56

MAJORIAN   457–61

SEVERUS   461–65

ANTHEMIUS   467–72

OLYBRIUS   472

GLYCERIUS   473–74

NEPOS   474–75

ROMULUS   475–76
Nepos, Augustus in Dalmatia

NEPOS (in Dalmatia)   476–80

Persian Kings (274–651)

After R. N. Frye, *Cambridge History of Iran* III.1 (Cambridge, 1983) 178. Names in parentheses are Greek forms.

BAHRĀM (Bararanes) II   274–93

BAHRĀM (Bararanes) III   293

NARSEH (Narses) 293–302

HURMAZD (Hormisdas) II 302–9

SHĀPŪR (Sapor) II 309–79

ARDASHĪR (Artaxerxes) II 379–83

SHĀPŪR (Sapor) III 383–88

BAHRĀM (Bararanes) IV 388–99

YAZDGIRD (Isdegerdes) I 399–420

BAHRĀM (Bararanes) V 420–38

YAZDGIRD (Isdegerdes) II 438–57

HURMAZD (Hormisdas) III 457–59(?)

PĒRŌZ (Perozes) 459–84

BALĀSH (Balas) 484–88

KAVĀD (Cabades) I 488–96

ZĀMĀSP (Zamasphes) 496–98

KAVĀD (Cabades) I (again) 498–531

KHUSRAU (Chosroës) I 531–79

HURMAZD (Hormisdas) IV 579–90

KHUSRAU (Chosroës) II 590

BAHRĀM (Bararanes) VI 590–91

KHUSRAU (Chosroës) II (again) 591–628

KAVĀD (Cabades) II Shīrūya (Siroës) 628

ARDASHĪR (Artaxerxes) III 628–30

SHAHRVARĀZ (Shahrbaraz) 630

BŌRĀN (Boran) 630–31

(Ephemeral kings 631–32)

YAZDGIRD (Isdegerdes) III 632–51

Arab Caliphs (632–940)

ABŪ BAKR 632–34

ʿUMAR I 634–44

ʿUTHMĀN 644–56 (Umayyad)

ʿALĪ 656–61

MUʿĀWIYAH I 661–80 (Umayyad dynasty to 750)

YAZĪD I 680–83

MUʿĀWIYAH II   683–84

MARWĀN I   684–85

ʿABD AL-MALIK   685–705

AL-WALĪD I   705–15

SULAYMĀN   715–17

ʿUMAR II   717–20

YAZĪD II   720–24

HISHĀM   724–43

AL-WALĪD II   743–44

YAZĪD III   744

MARWĀN II   744–50

ABŪ'L-ʿABBĀS (al-Saffāḥ)   750–54 (Abbasid dynasty to 1517)

AL-MANṢŪR   754–75

AL-MAHDĪ   775–85

AL-HĀDĪ   785–86

HĀRŪN AL-RASHĪD   786–809

AL-AMĪN   809–13

AL-MAʾMŪN   813–33

AL-MUʿTAṢIM   833–42

AL-WĀTHIQ   842–47

AL-MUTAWAKKIL   847–61

AL-MUNTAṢIR   861–62

AL-MUSTAʿĪN   862–66

AL-MUʿTAZZ   866–69

AL-MUHTADĪ   869–70

AL-MUʿTAMID   870–92

AL-MUʿTAḌID   892–902

AL-MUQTAFI   902–8

AL-MUQTADIR   908–32

AL-QĀHIR   932–34

AL-RĀḌĪ[4]   934–40

4. Al-Rāḍī was the last Abbasid caliph with significant political power, though figure-head Abbasids reigned until 1517.

Fatimid Caliphs of North Africa (909–969) and Egypt (969–1171)

From the *Encyclopedia of Islam*, new ed., vol. II (Leiden, 1965), p. 850.

AL-MAHDĪ   909–34

AL-QĀ'IM   934–46

AL-MU'IZZ   954–75

AL-'AZĪZ   975–96

AL-ḤĀKIM   996–1021

AL-ẒĀHIR   1021–36

AL-MUSTANṢIR   1036–94

AL-MUSTA'LĪ   1094–1101

AL-ĀMIR   1101–30

AL-ḤĀFIZ   1130–49

AL-ẒĀFIR   1149–54

AL-FĀ'IZ   1154–60

AL-'ĀḌID   1160–71

Seljuk Sultans of Nicaea (1081–1097) and Iconium (1097–1261)

SULAYMĀN   1081–85

KILIJ ARSLAN I   1085–1107

SHĀHĀNSHĀH   1107–ca. 1116

MAS'ŪD I   ca. 1116–55

KILIJ ARSLAN II   1155–92

KAYKHUSRAW I   1192–1211

KAYKĀ'ŪS I   1211–20

KAQUBĀD I   1220–37

KAYKHUSRAW II   1237–45/46

KAYKĀ'ŪS II   1245/46–61

Ottoman Emirs (1281–1362) and Sultans (1362–1481)

OSMĀN   1281–1326

ORHAN   1326–62

MURĀD I   1362–89

BĀYEZĪD I   1389–1402

SULAYMĀN   1402–11

MŪSĀ   1411–13

MEHMED I   1413–21

MURĀD II   1421–51

MEHMED II the Conqueror   1451–81

Bulgarian Khans (681–913) and Emperors (913–1018)

For khans to 852, partly revised from V. Beševliev, *Die protobulgarische Periode der bulgarischen Geschichte* (Amsterdam, 1981), 504.

ASPARUKH   681–ca. 701

TERVEL   ca. 701–ca. 718

SEVAR   ca. 718–50

KORMESIOS   750–62

VINEKH   762–63
        Teletz, coruler

UMAR   763

BAIAN   763–65

TOKT   765

TELERIG   765(?)–77

KARDAM   777(?)–ca. 803

KRUM   ca. 803–14

DUKUM   814

DITZEVG   814–15

OMURTAG   815–31

PERSIAN-MALAMIR   831–52

BORIS I Michael I   852–89

VLADIMIR   889–93

SYMEON the Great   893–927

PETER   927–69

BORIS II   969–72 (d. ca. 977)

(Interregnum under Samuel and other Cometopuli)

ROMANUS   ca. 977–97

SAMUEL   997–1014

GABRIEL Radomir 1014–15

JOHN Vladislav 1015–18

Restored Bulgarian Emperors (1186–1393)

ASEN I 1186–96

PETER 1196–97

KALOYAN 1197–1207

BORIL 1207–18

John ASEN II 1218–41

KOLOMAN 1242–46

MICHAEL II Asen 1246–57

CONSTANTINE Tich 1257–77

IVAILO 1278–79

John ASEN III 1279

GEORGE I Terter 1279–92

SMILECH 1292–98

THEODORE Svetoslav 1299–1322

GEORGE II Terter 1322

MICHAEL III Shishman 1323–30

JOHN STEPHEN 1330–31

JOHN ALEXANDER 1331–71

JOHN SHISHMAN 1371–93

Serbian Kings (1217–1346) and Emperors (1346–1371)

STEPHEN the First-Crowned 1217–27

STEPHEN RADOSLAV 1227–34

STEPHEN VLADISLAV 1234–43

STEPHEN UROSH I 1243–76

STEPHEN DRAGUTIN 1276–82

STEPHEN UROSH II Milutin 1282–1321

STEPHEN UROSH III Dechansky 1321–31

STEPHEN UROSH IV Dushan 1331–55

STEPHEN UROSH V the Weak 1355–71

Abbreviations

The following short reference forms are used for works cited more than once in the Notes and the Bibliographical Survey. Works cited only once are not abbreviated and do not appear here.

Ahrweiler, *Byzance et la mer*
> Hélène Ahrweiler, *Byzance et la mer: La marine de guerre, la politique et les institutions maritimes de Byzance aux VIIe–XVe siècles* (Paris, 1966)

Ahrweiler, "Smyrne"
> Hélène Ahrweiler, "L'histoire et la géographie de la région de Smyrne entre les deux occupations turques (1081–1317), particulièrement au XIIe siècle," *TM* 1 (1965), 1–204

Ammianus
> Ammianus Marcellinus, ed. Wolfgang Seyfarth (Leipzig, 1978); trans. with ed. J. C. Rolfe, 3 vols. (Cambridge, Mass., 1935–39)

Angold, *Byzantine Aristocracy*
> Michael Angold, ed., *The Byzantine Aristocracy: IX to XIII Centuries* (Oxford, 1984)

Angold, *Byzantine Empire*
> Michael Angold, *The Byzantine Empire, 1024–1204: A Political History* (London, 1984)

Angold, *Byzantine Government*
> Michael Angold, *A Byzantine Government in Exile: Government and Society Under the Lascarids of Nicaea (1204–1261)* (Oxford, 1975)

Anna Comnena
> Anna Comnena, ed. with French trans. B. Leib, 4 vols. (Paris, 1937–1976); trans. E. R. A. Sewter (Harmondsworth, 1969)

AT
> *Antiquité Tardive*

Attaliates
> Michael Attaliates, *History*, ed. I. Bekker (*CSHB*, 1853)

Avi-Yonah, *Jews of Palestine*
   M. Avi-Yonah, *The Jews of Palestine: A Political History from the Bar Kokhba War to the Arab Conquest* (New York, 1976)
Bagnall, *Consuls*
   Roger Bagnall et al., *Consuls of the Later Roman Empire* (Atlanta, 1987)
Balādhurī
   al-Balādhurī, trans. Philip Hitti, *The Origins of the Islamic State* (New York, 1916)
Balard, *Romanie*
   Michel Balard, *La Romanie génoise (XIIᵉ–début du XVᵉ siècle)*, 2 vols. (Rome, 1978)
Bar Hebraeus
   Bar Hebraeus, ed. and trans. E. A. W. Budge (London, 1932)
Barker, *Manuel II*
   John Barker, *Manuel II Palaeologus (1391–1425): A Study in Late Byzantine Statesmanship* (New Brunswick, 1969)
Barnes, *New Empire*
   Timothy Barnes, *The New Empire of Diocletian and Constantine* (Cambridge, Mass., 1982)
Bartusis, *Late Byzantine Army*
   Mark Bartusis, *The Late Byzantine Army: Arms and Society, 1204–1453* (Philadelphia, 1992)
Belke, *Phrygien*
   K. Belke and N. Mersich, *Phrygien und Pisidien* (*TIB* VII, 1990)
Benjamin of Tudela
   Benjamin of Tudela, *Itinerary*, trans. in M. Komroff, *Contemporaries of Marco Polo* (New York, 1928), pp. 251–322
Bertelè, *Numismatique*
   Tommaso Bertelè, *Numismatique byzantine*, rev. ed. by Cécile Morrisson (Wetteren, 1978)
Bertrandon de la Broquière
   Bertrandon de la Broquière, ed. Ch. Schefer (Paris, 1892); trans. T. Wright, *Early Travels in Palestine* (London, 1848), pp. 283–382
Beševliev, *Protobulgarische Periode*
   V. Beševliev, *Die protobulgarische Periode der bulgarischen Geschichte* (Amsterdam, 1981)
BF
   Byzantinische Forschungen
Biraben, *Hommes et la peste*
   J.-N. Biraben, *Les hommes et la peste en France et dans les pays européens et méditerranéens* I (Paris, 1975)
Blockley, *East Roman Foreign Policy*
   R. C. Blockley, *East Roman Foreign Policy: Formation and Conduct from Diocletian to Anastasius* (Leeds, 1992)
Blockley, *Historians*
   R. C. Blockley, *The Fragmentary Classicizing Historians of the Later Roman Empire*, 2 vols. (Liverpool, 1981–83)

Blockley, *Menander*
  See Menander Protector
BNJ
  Byzantinisch-Neugriechische Jahrbücher
Borkowski, *Alexandrie II*
  Zbigniew Borkowski, *Alexandrie II: Inscriptions des factions à Alexandrie* (Warsaw, 1981)
Bosch, *Andronikos III*
  Ursula Bosch, *Kaiser Andronikos III. Palaiologos: Versuch einer Darstellung der byzantinischen Geschichte in den Jahren 1321–1341* (Amsterdam, 1965)
Brand, *Byzantium*
  Charles Brand, *Byzantium Confronts the West, 1180–1204* (Cambridge, Mass., 1968)
Brooks, "Arabs"
  E. W. Brooks, "The Arabs in Asia Minor (641–750), from Arabic Sources," *JHS* 18 (1898), 182–208
Brooks, "Byzantines"
  Brooks, "Byzantines and Arabs in the Time of the Early Abbasids," *EHR* 15 (1900), 728–47; 16 (1901), 84–92
Brown, *Gentlemen*
  T. S. Brown, *Gentlemen and Officers: Imperial Administration and Aristocratic Power in Byzantine Italy, A.D. 554–800* (Rome, 1984)
Bryennius
  Nicephorus Bryennius, *History*, ed. with introduction and notes P. Gautier (*CFHB*; Brussels, 1975)
Bryer, *Byzantine Monuments*
  Anthony Bryer and David Winfield, *The Byzantine Monuments and Topography of the Pontos*, 2 vols. (Washington, 1985)
Bryer, *Iconoclasm*
  Anthony Bryer and Judith Herrin, eds., *Iconoclasm* (Birmingham, 1977)
Burgmann, *Ecloga*
  See Leo III, *Ecloga*
Bury, *Eastern Roman Empire*
  J. B. Bury, *A History of the Eastern Roman Empire from the Fall of Irene to the Accession of Basil I (A.D. 802–867)* (London, 1912)
Bury, *History*
  J. B. Bury, *A History of the Later Roman Empire from the Death of Theodosius I to the Death of Justinian (A.D. 395 to 565)*, 2 vols. (London, 1923) [1st ed.: J. B. Bury, *A History of the Later Roman Empire from Arcadius to Irene (395 A.D. to 800 A.D.)*, 2 vols. (London, 1889)]
BZ
  Byzantinische Zeitschrift
Cahen, *Turquie pré-ottomane*
  Claude Cahen, *La Turquie pré-ottomane* (Istanbul, 1988)
Cambridge Medieval History
  Joan Hussey, ed., *The Cambridge Medieval History*, 2d ed., vol. IV, 2 parts (Cambridge, 1966–67)

Cameron, *Barbarians*
  Alan Cameron and Jacqueline Long, *Barbarians and Politics at the Court of Arcadius* (Berkeley, 1993)
Cameron, *Circus Factions*
  Alan Cameron, *Circus Factions* (Oxford, 1976)
Canard, *Histoire*
  Marius Canard, *Histoire de la dynastie des H'amdanides de Jazîra et de Syrie* I (Paris, 1951; no more published)
Cantacuzenus
  John VI Cantacuzenus, *History*, ed. L. Schopen, 3 vols. (*CSHB*, 1828–32); German trans. with notes by F. Fatouros and T. Krischer, 2 vols. (Stuttgart, 1982–86; in progress)
Carrié, "Dioclétien"
  Jean-Michel Carrié, "Dioclétien et la fiscalité," *AT* 2 (1994), 33–64
Cecaumenus
  Cecaumenus, *Strategicon*, ed. with Russian trans. and commentary G. Litavrin (Moscow, 1972)
Cedrenus
  George Cedrenus, *Chronicle*, ed. I. Bekker (*CSHB*, 1838–39)
CFHB
  Corpus Fontium Historiae Byzantinae (Washington, etc., 1967–; in progress)
Chalandon, *Les Comnène*
  Ferdinand Chalandon, *Les Comnène: Études sur l'empire byzantin au XIe et au XIIe siècles*, 2 vols. (Paris, 1900–1912)
Chalcondyles
  Laonicus Chalcondyles, ed. E. Darkó, 2 vols. (Budapest, 1922–27)
Chapman, *Michel Paléologue*
  Conrad Chapman, *Michel Paléologue, restaurateur de l'empire byzantin* (Paris, 1926)
Cheira, *Lutte*
  M. A. Cheira, *La lutte entre Arabes et Byzantins: La conquête et l'organisation des frontières aux VIIe et VIIIe siècles* (Alexandria, 1947)
Cheynet, *Pouvoir*
  Jean-Claude Cheynet, *Pouvoir et contestations à Byzance (963–1210)* (Paris, 1990)
Cheynet, "Prix et salaires"
  J.-C. Cheynet et al., "Prix et salaires à Byzance (X^e–XIe siècles)," in *Hommes et richesses* II, 339–74
Choniates, *History*
  Nicetas Choniates, *History*, ed. J.-L. van Dieten, 2 vols. (*CFHB*; Berlin, 1975); trans. Harry Magoulias (Detroit, 1984)
Choniates, *Letters and Orations*
  Nicetas Choniates, *Letters and Orations*, ed. J.-L. van Dieten (*CFHB*; Berlin, 1972)
Christophilopoulou, *History*
  A. Christophilopoulou, *Byzantine History*, 2 vols. (Amsterdam, 1986–93; in

progress); trans. of same, *Byzantinē Historia*, 2 vols. (Athens, 1975–88; in progress)
Chronicle of the Morea
    Chronicle of the Morea, ed. J. Schmitt (London, 1904); trans. H. E. Lurier (New York, 1964)
Cinnamus
    John Cinnamus, ed. A. Meineke (*CSHB*, 1836); trans. C. M. Brand (New York, 1976)
Clavijo
    Ruy González de Clavijo, ed. F. López Estrada (Madrid, 1943); trans. Guy le Strange (London, 1928)
Comnena
    See Anna Comnena
Constantine VII, *De Administrando Imperio*
    Constantine VII, *De Administrando Imperio*, ed. Gy. Moravcsik and trans. R. J. H. Jenkins (*CFHB*; Washington, 1967); with commentary in a second volume by R. J. H. Jenkins et al. (London, 1962)
Constantine VII, *De Ceremoniis*
    Constantine VII, *De Ceremoniis*, ed. J. J. Reiske, 2 vols. (*CSHB*, 1829–30)
Constantine VII, *De Thematibus*
    Constantine VII, *De Thematibus*, ed. with Italian introduction and commentary A. Pertusi (Vatican City, 1953)
Critobulus
    Critobulus of Imbros, ed. D. Reinsch (*CFHB*; Berlin, 1983); trans. Charles Riggs (Princeton, 1954)
CSCO
    Corpus Scriptorum Christianorum Orientalium (Paris, etc., 1903–; in progress)
CSHB
    Corpus Scriptorum Historiae Byzantinae (Bonn, 1828–78)
Dagron, "Minorités"
    G. Dagron, "Minorités ethniques et religieuses dans l'Orient byzantin à la fin du Xe et au XIe siècle: L'immigration syrienne," *TM* 6 (1976), 177–216
Delmaire, *Largesses sacrées*
    Roland Delmaire, *Largesses sacrées et* res privata*: L'*aerarium *impérial et son administration du IVe au VIe siècle* (Rome, 1989)
Demandt, *Spätantike*
    Alexander Demandt, *Die Spätantike: Römische Geschichte von Diocletian bis Justinian* (Munich, 1989)
Dölger, *Regesten*
    Franz Dölger, *Regesten der Kaiserurkunden des östromischen Reiches von 565–1453*, 5 vols. (*Corpus der griechischen Urkunden des Mittelalters und der neueren Zeit*, Reihe A: *Regesten*, Part 1 [Munich and Berlin, 1924–77])
DOP
    Dumbarton Oaks Papers
Ducas
    [Michael?] Ducas, ed. Vasile Grecu (Bucharest, 1958); trans. Harry Magoulias (Detroit, 1975)

Duncan-Jones, *Money and Government*
   Richard Duncan-Jones, *Money and Government in the Roman Empire* (Cambridge, 1994)
Durliat, *De la ville*
   Jean Durliat, *De la ville antique à la ville byzantine: Le problème des subsistances* (Paris, 1990)
Elijah of Nisibis
   Elijah of Nisibis, Latin trans. E. W. Brooks, *Eliae Metropolitae Nisibeni Opus Chronologicum* (*CSCO* 63, 1910)
Encyclopedia of Islam
   Encyclopedia of Islam, new ed., 7 vols. (Leiden, 1960–90; in progress) [1st ed., 4 vols. (Leiden, 1913–34)]
EHR
   English Historical Review
Eusebius, *History*
   Eusebius of Caesarea, *Ecclesiastical History*, ed. E. Schwartz, 2 vols. (*GCS*, 1903–9); trans. G. A. Williamson (Harmondsworth, 1965)
Evagrius
   Evagrius Scholasticus, *Ecclesiastical History*, ed. J. Bidez and L. Parmentier (London, 1898); trans. E. Walford (London, 1854)
Failler, "Chronologie et composition"
   A. Failler, "Chronologie et composition dans l'Histoire de Georges Pachymère," *RÉB* 38 (1980), 5–103; 39 (1981), 145–249; 48 (1990), 5–88
Felix, *Byzanz*
   Wolfgang Felix, *Byzanz und die islamische Welt im früheren 11. Jahrhundert: Geschichte der politischen Beziehungen von 1001 bis 1055* (Vienna, 1981)
Ferluga, *Amministrazione*
   Jadran Ferluga, *L'amministrazione bizantina in Dalmazia* (Venice, 1978)
Fine, *Early Medieval Balkans*
   John Fine, *The Early Medieval Balkans: A Critical Survey from the Sixth to the Late Twelfth Century* (Ann Arbor, 1983)
Fine, *Late Medieval Balkans*
   John Fine, *The Late Medieval Balkans: A Critical Survey from the Late Twelfth Century to the Ottoman Conquest* (Ann Arbor, 1987)
Forsyth, "Byzantine-Arab Chronicle"
   John Forsyth, "The Byzantine-Arab Chronicle (938–1034) of Yaḥyā b. Saʿīd al-Antākī" (diss., University of Michigan, 1977)
Foss, *Byzantine Fortifications*
   Clive Foss and David Winfield, *Byzantine Fortifications: An Introduction* (Pretoria, 1986)
Foss, *Ephesus*
   Clive Foss, *Ephesus After Antiquity: A Late Antique, Byzantine and Turkish City* (Cambridge, 1979)
Frank, *Scholae*
   R. I. Frank, *Scholae Palatinae: The Palace Guards of the Later Roman Empire* (Rome, 1969)

Gascou, "Grands domaines"
Jean Gascou, "Les grands domaines, la cité et l'état en Égypte byzantine," *TM* 9 (1985), 1–89
Gay, *Italie*
Jules Gay, *L'Italie méridionale et l'empire byzantine* (Paris, 1904)
GCS
Die griechischen christlischen Schriftsteller der ersten drei Jahrhunderte (Leipzig and Berlin, 1897–; in progress)
Geanakoplos, *Michael Palaeologus*
Deno Geanakoplos, *Emperor Michael Palaeologus and the West* (Cambridge, Mass., 1959)
Genesius
Joseph Genesius, ed. A. Lesmueller-Werner and J. Thurn (*CFHB*; Berlin, 1978)
Geoffrey of Villehardouin
Geoffrey of Villehardouin, ed. with French trans. E. Faral, 2 vols. (Paris, 1938–39); trans. M. R. B. Shaw, *Chronicles of the Crusades* (Baltimore, 1963)
Gero, *Constantine V*
Stephen Gero, *Byzantine Iconoclasm During the Reign of Constantine V, with Particular Attention to the Oriental Sources* (Louvain, 1977)
Gero, *Leo III*
Stephen Gero, *Byzantine Iconoclasm During the Reign of Leo III, with Particular Attention to the Oriental Sources* (Louvain, 1973)
Gill, *Council of Florence*
Joseph Gill, *The Council of Florence* (Cambridge, 1959)
GRBS
Greek, Roman and Byzantine Studies
Gregoras
Nicephorus Gregoras, *History*, ed. L. Schopen and I. Bekker, 3 vols. (*CSHB*, 1829–55)
Grierson, *Catalogue*
A. R. Bellinger and Philip Grierson, *Catalogue of the Byzantine Coins in the Dumbarton Oaks Collection and in the Whittemore Collection*, 3 vols. (Washington, 1966–73; in progress)
Grousset, *Histoire de l'Arménie*
René Grousset, *Histoire de l'Arménie des origines à 1071* (Paris, 1947)
Grumel, *Chronologie*
V. Grumel, *La chronologie* (Paris, 1958)
Grumel, *Regestes*
V. Grumel et al., *Les regestes des actes du patriarcat de Constantinople*, vol. I, 2d ed., 7 fascicles (Paris, 1972–91)
Harvey, *Economic Expansion*
Alan Harvey, *Economic Expansion in the Byzantine Empire, 900–1200* (Cambridge, 1989)
Hendy, *Coinage*
Michael Hendy, *Coinage and Money in the Byzantine Empire, 1081–1261* (Washington, 1969)

Hendy, *Studies*
    Michael Hendy, *Studies in the Byzantine Monetary Economy* (Cambridge, 1985)
Heyd, *Histoire*
    W. Heyd, *Histoire du commerce du Levant au moyen-âge*, rev. ed., 2 vols. (Leipzig, 1885–86)
Hild, *Kappadokien*
    F. Hild and M. Restle, *Kappadokien (Kappadokia, Charsianon, Sebasteia und Lycandos)* (*TIB* II, 1981)
Hild, *Kilikien*
    F. Hild and H. Hellenkemper, *Kilikien und Isaurien* (*TIB* V, 1990)
Hoffman, *Bewegungsheer*
    Dietrich Hoffman, *Das spätrömische Bewegungsheer*, 2 vols. (Düsseldorf, 1969–70)
Hommes et richesses
    Hommes et richesses dans l'empire byzantin, 2 vols. (Paris, 1989–91)
Honigmann, *Ostgrenze*
    Ernst Honigmann, *Die Ostgrenze des byzantinischen Reiches* (Brussels, 1935) [Vol. III of Vasiliev, *Byzance et les Arabes*]
HUS
    Harvard Ukrainian Studies
Hussey, *Orthodox Church*
    J. M. Hussey, *The Orthodox Church in the Byzantine Empire* (Oxford, 1986)
Ibn Baṭṭūṭa
    Ibn Baṭṭūṭa, trans. H. A. R. Gibb, 3 vols. (Cambridge, 1958–71)
Ibn Bībī
    Ibn Bībī, German trans. Herbert W. Duda (Copenhagen, 1959)
Ibn Ḥawqal
    Ibn Ḥawqal, French trans. J. Kramers and G. Wiet (Beirut, 1964)
Idrīsī
    al-Idrīsī, *Geography*, French trans. P. A. Jaubert, 2 vols. (Paris, 1836–40)
Imber, *Ottoman Empire*
    Colin Imber, *The Ottoman Empire, 1300–1481* (Istanbul, 1990)
Jacoby, "Population"
    D. Jacoby, "La population de Constantinople à l'époque byzantine," *Byzantion* 31 (1961), 81–109
Janin, *Églises*
    R. Janin, *Le siège de Constantinople et le patriarcat oecuménique: Les églises et les monastères*, 2d ed. (Paris, 1969)
Janssens, *Trébizonde*
    Émile Janssens, *Trébizonde en Colchide* (Brussels, 1969)
Jenkins, *Byzantium*
    Romilly Jenkins, *Byzantium: The Imperial Centuries, A.D. 610–1071* (London, 1966)
Jenkins, "Chronological Accuracy"
    Romilly Jenkins, "The Chronological Accuracy of the 'Logothete' for the Years A.D. 867–913," *DOP* 19 (1965), 91–112

JHS
  Journal of Hellenic Studies
JÖB
  Jahrbuch der Österreichischen Byzantinistik
John Catholicus
  John Catholicus, trans. with commentary K. H. Maksoudian, *Yovhannēs Drasxanakertc'i: History of Armenia* (Atlanta, 1987)
John Chrysostom
  John Chrysostom, ed. *PG*, vols. 47–64
John Malalas
  John Malalas, ed. L. Dindorf (*CSHB*, 1831); trans. Elizabeth Jeffreys et al. (Melbourne, 1986)
John of Biclar
  John of Biclar, ed. Th. Mommsen (*MGH, Auctores Antiquissimi* 11, 1894)
John of Ephesus
  John of Ephesus, *Ecclesiastical History*: Latin trans. to 565 A.D. by W. J. Van Douwen and J. P. N. Land, Verhandelingen der Koninklijke Akademie van Wetenschappen, Afdeeling Letterkunde VIII (Amsterdam, 1889); Latin trans. from 565 A.D. by E. W. Brooks (*CSCO* 106, 1936)
John of Nikiu
  John of Nikiu, *Chronicle*, trans. R. H. Charles (London, 1916)
John the Lydian
  John Lydus, *De Magistratibus*, ed. with trans. and notes A. C. Bandy (Philadelphia, 1983)
Jones, *Later Roman Empire*
  A. H. M. Jones, *The Later Roman Empire: A Social, Economic and Administrative Survey*, 3 vols. (Oxford, 1964)
Jones, *Prosopography*
  A. H. M. Jones et al., *The Prosopography of the Later Roman Empire*, 3 vols. (Cambridge, 1971–92)
Joshua the Stylite
  Joshua the Stylite, trans. William Wright (Cambridge, 1882)
JRS
  Journal of Roman Studies
Justinian Code
  Codex Justinianus, ed. P. Krüger (Berlin, 1929)
Justinian, *Novels*
  Justinian, *Novels*, ed. R. Schöll and G. Kroll (Berlin, 1928)
Kaegi, *Military Unrest*
  Walter Kaegi, *Byzantine Military Unrest, 471–843: An Interpretation* (Amsterdam, 1981)
Kaplan, *Hommes et la terre*
  Michel Kaplan, *Les hommes et la terre à Byzance du VIe au XIe siècle* (Paris, 1992)
Karlin-Hayter
  See Vita Euthymii

Karpov, *Impero*
S. P. Karpov, *L'impero di Trebisonda, Venezia, Genova, e Roma, 1204–1461* (Rome, 1986)
Kazhdan, *Change*
A. P. Kazhdan and A. W. Epstein, *Change in Byzantine Culture in the Eleventh and Twelfth Centuries* (Berkeley, 1985)
Kazhdan, *Oxford Dictionary of Byzantium*
Alexander Kazhdan, ed., *The Oxford Dictionary of Byzantium*, 3 vols. (New York, 1991)
Kazhdan, *Studies*
A. Kazhdan and S. Franklin, *Studies on Byzantine Literature of the Eleventh and Twelfth Centuries* (Cambridge, 1984)
King, *Imperial Revenue*
C. E. King, ed., *Imperial Revenue, Expenditure and Monetary Policy in the Fourth Century A.D.*, British Archaeological Reports, International Series 76 (Oxford, 1980)
Kolias, *Léon Choerosphactès*
Georges Kolias, *Léon Choerosphactès, magistre, proconsul et patrice* (Athens, 1939)
Kuehn, *Byzantinische Armee*
Hans-Joachim Kuehn, *Die byzantinische Armee im 10. und 11. Jahrhundert* (Vienna, 1991)
Lactantius
Lactantius, *On the Deaths of the Persecutors*, ed. and trans. J. L. Creed (Oxford, 1984)
Laiou, *Constantinople*
Angeliki Laiou, *Constantinople and the Latins: The Foreign Policy of Andronicus II, 1282–1328* (Cambridge, Mass., 1972)
Lallemand, *Administration*
J. Lallemand, *L'administration civile de l'Égypte de l'avènement de Dioclétien à la création du diocèse (284–382)* (Brussels, 1964)
Lefort, "Population"
Jacques Lefort, "Population et peuplement en Macédoine orientale, IXe– XVe siècle," in *Hommes et richesses* II, 63–82; with additional comments by J.-M. Martin, pp. 83–89
Lemerle, *Agrarian History*
Paul Lemerle, *The Agrarian History of Byzantium* (Galway, 1979)
Lemerle, *Byzantine Humanism*
Paul Lemerle, *Byzantine Humanism* (Canberra, 1986)
Lemerle, *Cinq études*
Paul Lemerle, *Cinq études sur le XIe siècle byzantin* (Paris, 1977)
Lemerle, "Pauliciens"
Paul Lemerle, "L'histoire des Pauliciens d'Asie Mineure d'après les sources grecques," *TM* 5 (1973), 1–144
Lemerle, *Plus anciens recueils*
Paul Lemerle, *Les plus anciens recueils des miracles de saint Démétrius et la pénétration des Slaves dans les Balkans*, 2 vols. (Paris, 1979–81)

Leo III, *Ecloga*
Leo III, *Ecloga*, ed. with German trans. L. Burgmann, *Ecloga: Das Gesetzbuch Leons III. und Konstantinos' V.* (Frankfurt, 1983); trans. E. H. Freshfield (Cambridge, 1927)

"Leo Grammaticus"
See Symeon the Logothete

Leontius
Leontius (Łewond), trans. with commentary Z. Arzoumanian (Wynnewood, 1982)

Leo the Deacon
Leo the Deacon, ed. C. B. Hase (*CSHB*, 1828)

Libanius, *Letters*
Libanius, *Epistulae*, ed. R. Förster (Leipzig, 1903–27)

Liber Pontificalis
Liber Pontificalis, ed. L. Duchesne, 3 vols. (Paris, 1886–1957); trans. Raymond Davis, 2 vols. (Liverpool, 1989–92; in progress)

Liebeschuetz, *Antioch*
J. Liebeschuetz, *Antioch: City and Imperial Administration in the Later Roman Empire* (Oxford, 1972)

Life of St. Nicon
The Life of St. Nicon, ed. and trans. Denis Sullivan (Brookline, 1987)

Lilie, *Byzantinische Reaktion*
R.-J. Lilie, *Die byzantinische Reaktion auf die Ausbreitung der Araber: Studien zur Strukturwandlung des byzantinischen Staates im 7. und 8. Jahrhundert* (Munich, 1976)

Lilie, *Byzantium*
R.-J. Lilie, *Byzantium and the Crusader States, 1096–1204* (Oxford, 1993)

Lilie, *Handel*
R.-J. Lilie, *Handel und Politik zwischen dem byzantinischen Reich und den italienischen Kommunen Venedig, Pisa und Genua in der Epoche der Komnenen und der Angeloi (1081–1204)* (Amsterdam, 1984)

Liudprand, *Antapodosis*
Liudprand of Cremona, *Antapodosis*, ed. Joseph Becker (*MGH, Scriptores Rerum Germanicarum in Usum Scholarum* [Hanover, 1915]); trans. F. A. Wright (London, 1930)

Longnon, *Empire latin*
Jean Longnon, *L'empire latin de Constantinople et la principauté de Morée* (Paris, 1949)

McEvedy, *Atlas*
C. McEvedy and R. Jones, *Atlas of World Population History* (Harmondsworth, 1978)

McNeill, *Plagues*
William McNeill, *Plagues and Peoples* (Garden City, 1976)

Magdalino, *Manuel I*
Paul Magdalino, *The Empire of Manuel I Komnenos, 1143–1180* (Cambridge, 1993)

Majeska, *Russian Travelers*
   George Majeska, *Russian Travelers to Constantinople in the Fourteenth and Fifteenth Centuries* (Washington, 1984)
Makk, *Árpáds*
   F. Makk, *The Árpáds and the Comneni: Political Relations Between Hungary and Byzantium in the Twelfth Century* (Budapest, 1989)
Malalas
   See John Malalas
Malamut, *Îles*
   Elisabeth Malamut, *Les îles de l'empire byzantine, VIIIᵉ–XIIᵉ siècles*, 2 vols. (Paris, 1988)
Mango, *Byzantium*
   Cyril Mango, *Byzantium: The Empire of New Rome* (London, 1980)
Mango, *Constantinople*
   Cyril Mango and Gilbert Dagron, eds., *Constantinople and Its Hinterland* (Aldershot, 1995)
Mango, "Legend"
   Cyril Mango, "The Legend of Leo the Wise," *ZRVI* 6 (1960), 59–93
Mango, *Nikephoros*
   See Nicephorus, *Short History*
Mansi
   G. Mansi, *Sacrorum Conciliorum Nova et Amplissima Collectio*, 2d ed., 53 vols. (Paris and Leipzig, 1901–27)
Marcellinus
   Marcellinus Comes, ed. Th. Mommsen (*MGH, Auctores Antiquissimi* 11, 1894)
Martin, *History*
   Edward J. Martin, *A History of the Iconoclastic Controversy* (London, 1930)
Matthew of Edessa
   Matthew of Edessa and Gregory the Priest, trans. A. E. Dostourian (Ann Arbor, 1972)
Menander Protector
   R. C. Blockley, ed. and trans., *The History of Menander the Guardsman* (Liverpool, 1985)
Meyendorff, *Imperial Unity*
   John Meyendorff, *Imperial Unity and Christian Divisions: The Church 450–680 A.D.* (Crestwood, 1989)
MGH
   Monumenta Germaniae Historica (Berlin and Hanover, 1835–1967)
Michael Italicus
   Michael Italicus, *Letters and Orations*, ed. P. Gautier (Paris, 1972)
Michael the Syrian
   Michael the Syrian, French trans. J.-B. Chabot, *Chronique de Michel le Syrien*, 4 vols. (Paris, 1899–1924)
Miller, *Latins*
   William Miller, *The Latins in the Levant: A History of Frankish Greece (1204–1566)* (London, 1908)

Miller, *Trebizond*
William Miller, *Trebizond: The Last Greek Empire* (New York, 1926)
Miracles of St. Demetrius
See Lemerle, *Plus anciens recueils*
Miskawayh
al-Miskawayh and Abū Shujāʿ, ed. and trans. H. F. Amedroz and D. S. Margoliouth, *The Eclipse of the ʿAbbasid Caliphate*, 7 vols. (Oxford, 1920–21)
Morrisson, "Dévaluation"
C. Morrisson, "La dévaluation de la monnaie byzantine au XIᵉ siècle: Essai d'interprétation," *TM* 6 (1976), 3–47
MS
Mediaeval Studies
Nesbitt, *Catalogue*
John Nesbitt and N. Oikonomidès, *Catalogue of Byzantine Seals at Dumbarton Oaks and in the Fogg Museum of Art*, 2 vols. (Washington, 1991–95; in progress)
Niavis, *Nicephorus I*
Pavlos E. Niavis, *The Reign of the Byzantine Emperor Nicephorus I* (Athens, 1987)
Nicephorus, *Short History*
Nicephorus of Constantinople, *Short History*, ed. with trans. and commentary C. Mango (*CFHB*; Washington, 1990)
Nicholas I, *Letters*
Nicholas I, *Letters*, ed. and trans. R. J. H. Jenkins and L. G. Westerink (*CFHB*; Washington, 1973)
Nicol, *Byzantine Family*
Donald Nicol, *The Byzantine Family of Kantakouzenos (Cantacuzenus), ca. 1100–1460* (Washington, 1968)
Nicol, *Byzantium and Venice*
D. M. Nicol, *Byzantium and Venice* (Cambridge, 1988)
Nicol, *Despotate* I
D. M. Nicol, *The Despotate of Epiros* (Oxford, 1957)
Nicol, *Despotate* II
D. M. Nicol, *The Despotate of Epiros, 1267–1479: A Contribution to the History of Greece in the Middle Ages* (Cambridge, 1984)
Nicol, *Last Centuries*
D. M. Nicol, *The Last Centuries of Byzantium, 1261–1453*, 2d ed. (Cambridge, 1993)
Noble, *Republic of St. Peter*
T. F. X. Noble, *The Republic of St. Peter: The Birth of the Papal State, 680–825* (Philadelphia, 1984)
Obolensky, *Commonwealth*
Dimitri Obolensky, *The Byzantine Commonwealth* (New York, 1971)
OCP
Orientalia Christiana Periodica
Oikonomidès, "Décomposition"
N. Oikonomidès, "La décomposition de l'empire byzantin à la veille de 1204 et les origines de l'empire de Nicée: À propos de la 'Partitio Roma-

niae,'" *XVᵉ Congrès international d'études byzantines: Rapports et co-rapports* I.1
(Athens, 1976)
Oikonomidès, "Évolution"
  N. Oikonomidès, "L'évolution de l'organisation administrative de l'empire
  byzantin au XIᵉ siècle," *TM* 6 (1976), 125–52
Oikonomidès, *Hommes d'affaires*
  N. Oikonomidès, *Hommes d'affaires grecs et latins à Constantinople (XIIIᵉ–XVᵉ
  siècles)* (Montreal, 1979)
Oikonomidès, "Liste arabe"
  N. Oikonomidès, "Une liste arabe des stratèges byzantins du VIIᵉ siècle et
  les origines du thème de Sicile," *RSBN*, n.s., 11 (1964), 121–30
Oikonomidès, *Listes*
  N. Oikonomidès, *Les listes de préséance byzantines des IXᵉ et Xᵉ siècles* (Paris,
  1972)
Ostrogorsky, "Chronologie"
  G. Ostrogorsky, "Die Chronologie des Theophanes im 7. und 8. Jahrhun-
  dert," *BNJ* 8 (1930), 1–56
Ostrogorsky, *History*
  George Ostrogorsky, *History of the Byzantine State*, 2d ed. (New Brunswick,
  1968)
Pachymeres
  George Pachymeres, *History*: Books I–VI, ed. A. Failler, 2 vols. (Paris,
  1984); Books VII–XIII, ed. I. Bekker, vol. II (*CSHB*, 1835)
Paschal Chronicle
  Chronicon Paschale, ed. L. Dindorf (*CSHB*, 1831); partial trans. with notes by
  Michael Whitby and Mary Whitby (Liverpool, 1989)
Paul the Deacon
  Paul the Deacon, *History of the Lombards*, ed. L. Bethmann and G. Waitz
  (*MGH, Scriptorum Rerum Langobardicarum et Italicarum*, 1878); trans. W. D.
  Foulke (Philadelphia, 1907)
Pauly, *Realencyclopädie*
  A. Pauly et al., *Realencyclopädie der classischen Altertumswissenschaft*, 49 vols.
  (Stuttgart and Munich, 1894–1978)
Pero Tafur
  Pero Tafur, ed. F. López Estrada (Barcelona, 1982); trans. Malcolm Letts,
  (London, 1926)
PG
  Patrologia Graeca, ed. J.-P. Migne (Paris, 1857–66)
Philostorgius
  Philostorgius, ed. J. Bidez with corrections by F. Winkelmann (*GCS*, 1981);
  trans. E. Walford in *Sozomen* (London, 1855), 429–528
PO
  Patrologia Orientalis (Paris, 1907–; in progress)
Procopius
  Procopius of Caesarea, ed. J. Haury with corrections by G. Wirth, 3 vols.
  (Leipzig, 1962–64); trans. with ed. H. B. Dewing and G. Downey, 7 vols.
  (Cambridge, Mass., 1914–40)

Psellus
Michael Psellus, *Chronographia*, ed. with French trans. Émile Renauld, 2 vols. (Paris, 1926–28); English trans. E. R. A. Sewter (London, 1953)
Pseudo-Symeon
"Symeon Magister," ed. I. Bekker with Theophanes Continuatus (*CSHB*, 1838)
Raybaud, *Gouvernement*
L.-P. Raybaud, *Le gouvernement et l'administration centrale de l'empire byzantin sous les premiers Paléologues (1258–1354)* (Paris, 1968)
RÉA
Revue des Études Arméniennes
RÉB
Revue des Études Byzantines
RÉSEE
Revue des Études Sud-Est Européennes
RSBN
Rivista di Studi Bizantini e Neoellenici
RSBS
Rivista di Studi Bizantini e Slavi
Runciman, *Bulgarian Empire*
Steven Runciman, *A History of the First Bulgarian Empire* (London, 1930)
Runciman, *Eastern Schism*
Steven Runciman, *The Eastern Schism: A Study of the Papacy and the Eastern Churches During the XIth and XIIth Centuries* (Oxford, 1955)
Runciman, *History of the Crusades*
Steven Runciman, *A History of the Crusades*, 3 vols. (Cambridge, 1951–54)
Runciman, *Romanus Lecapenus*
Steven Runciman, *The Emperor Romanus Lecapenus and His Reign* (Cambridge, 1929)
Russell, *Late Ancient and Medieval Population*
J. C. Russell, *Late Ancient and Medieval Population* (Philadelphia, 1958)
Russell, *Medieval Regions*
J. C. Russell, *Medieval Regions and Their Cities* (Newton Abbot, 1972)
SBN
Studi Bizantini e Neoellenici
Schlumberger, *Épopée byzantine*
Gustave Schlumberger, *L'épopée byzantine à la fin du dixième siècle*, 3 vols. (Paris, 1896–1905)
Schlumberger, *Nicéphore Phocas*
Gustave Schlumberger, *Un empereur byzantin au dixième siècle: Nicéphore Phocas*, new. ed. (Paris, 1923)
Schreiner, *Byzantinischen Kleinchroniken*
Peter Schreiner, ed., *Die byzantinischen Kleinchroniken*, 3 vols. (*CFHB*; Vienna, 1975–79)
Scutariotes
Theodore Scutariotes, ed. [as anonymous] K. N. Sathas, *Mesaiōnikē Bibliothekē* VII (Paris, 1894)

Scylitzes
John Scylitzes, *History*, ed. J. Thurn (*CFHB*; Berlin, 1973)
Sebeus
Sebeus, French trans. F. Macler, *Histoire d'Héraclius par l'évêque Sebêos* (Paris, 1894)
Setton, *History of the Crusades*
Kenneth Setton, ed., *A History of the Crusades*, 2d ed., 6 vols. (Madison, 1968–89)
Setton, *Papacy*
Kenneth Setton, *The Papacy in the Levant (1204–1571)*, 4 vols. (Philadelphia, 1974–84)
Sharf, *Byzantine Jewry*
Andrew Sharf, *Byzantine Jewry from Justinian to the Fourth Crusade* (London, 1971)
Skoulatos, *Personnages*
B. Skoulatos, *Les personnages byzantins de l'Alexiade: Analyse prosopographique et synthèse* (Louvain-la-Neuve, 1980)
SLNPNF
Select Library of the Nicene and Post-Nicene Fathers (New York and Oxford, 1887–1900)
Socrates
Socrates Scholasticus, *Ecclesiastical History*, ed. *PG*, vol. 67; trans. A. C. Zenos, *SLNPNF* (1890)
Soulis, *Serbs and Byzantium*
George Soulis, *The Serbs and Byzantium during the Reign of Tsar Stephen Dušan (1331–1355) and His Successors* (Washington, 1984)
Soustal, *Thrakien*
P. Soustal, *Thrakien (Thrakē, Rodopē, und Haimimontos)* (*TIB* VI, 1991)
Speck, *Artabasdos*
Paul Speck, *Artabasdos, der rechtgläubige Vorkämpfer der göttlichen Lehren* (Bonn, 1981)
Speck, *Geteilte Dossier*
Paul Speck, *Das geteilte Dossier: Beobachtungen über die Regierung des Kaisers Heraclius und die seiner Söhne bei Theophanes und Nikephoros* (Bonn, 1988)
Sphrantzes
George Sphrantzes, ed. Riccardo Maisano (*CFHB*; Rome, 1990); trans. Marios Philippides, *The Fall of the Byzantine Empire* (Amherst, 1980)
Stein, *Histoire du Bas-Empire*
Ernest Stein, *Histoire du Bas-Empire*, 2 vols. (Paris, 1949–59)
Stephen of Taron
Stephen of Taron, French trans. F. Macler, *Histoire universelle par Étienne Asolik de Tarôn* (Paris, 1917)
Stratos, *Byzantium*
Andreas Stratos, *Byzantium in the Seventh Century*, 5 vols. (Amsterdam, 1968–80)
Suda
Suidae Lexicon, ed. A. Adler, 5 vols. (Leipzig, 1928–38)

Symeon the Logothete ("Leo Grammaticus")
"Leo Grammaticus," ed. I. Bekker (*CSHB*, 1842)
Tafel, *Urkunden*
T. L. F. Tafel and G. M. Thomas, *Urkunden zur älteren Handels- und Staatsgeschichte der Republik Venedig*, 3 vols. (Vienna, 1856–57)
Tchalenko, *Villages*
G. Tchalenko, *Villages antiques de la Syrie du nord: Le massif du Bélus à l'époque romaine*, 3 vols. (Paris, 1953–58)
Themistius
Themistius, ed. H. Schenkl et al., 3 vols. (Leipzig, 1965–74)
Theodosian Code
Theodosian Code, ed. Th. Mommsen (Berlin, 1905); trans. with commentary Clyde Pharr (Princeton, 1952)
Theophanes
Theophanes Confessor, ed. C. de Boor, 2 vols. (Leipzig, 1883–85); partial trans. H. N. Turtledove (Philadelphia, 1982)
Theophanes Continuatus
Theophanes Continuatus, ed. I. Bekker (*CSHB*, 1838)
Theophylact of Ochrid
Theophylact of Ochrid, ed. P. Gautier, 2 vols. (*CFHB*; Thessalonica, 1980–86)
Theophylact Simocatta
Theophylact Simocatta, *History*, ed. C. de Boor with corrections by P. Wirth (Leipzig, 1972); trans. with notes Michael Whitby and Mary Whitby (Oxford, 1986)
Thiriet, *Romanie*
Freddy Thiriet, *La Romanie vénitienne au moyen âge: Le développement et l'exploitation du domaine colonial vénitien (XIIᵉ–XVᵉ siècles)* (Paris, 1959)
Thomas, *Private Religious Foundations*
John Thomas, *Private Religious Foundations in the Byzantine Empire* (Washington, 1987)
Thompson, *Goths in Spain*
E. A. Thompson, *The Goths in Spain* (Oxford, 1969)
TIB
Tabula Imperii Byzantini (Vienna, 1976–; in progress)
TM
Centre de Recherche d'Histoire et de Civilisation Byzantines, *Travaux et Mémoires*
Toynbee, *Constantine Porphyrogenitus*
Arnold Toynbee, *Constantine Porphyrogenitus and His World* (Oxford, 1973)
Treadgold, "Army"
W. Treadgold, "The Army in the Works of Constantine Porphyrogenitus," *RSBN*, n.s., 29 (1992), 77–162
Treadgold, *Byzantine Revival*
W. Treadgold, *The Byzantine Revival, 780–842* (Stanford, 1988)
Treadgold, *Byzantium and Its Army*
W. Treadgold, *Byzantium and Its Army, 284–1081* (Stanford, 1995)

Treadgold, *Finances*
    W. Treadgold, *The Byzantine State Finances in the Eighth and Ninth Centuries*
    (New York, 1982)
Treadgold, "Missing Year"
    W. Treadgold, "The Missing Year in the Revolt of Artavasdus," *JÖB* 42
    (1992), 87–93
Treadgold, "Seven Byzantine Revolutions"
    W. Treadgold, "Seven Byzantine Revolutions and the Chronology of Theo-
    phanes," *GRBS* 31 (1990), 203–27
Treadgold, "Three Byzantine Provinces"
    W. Treadgold, "Three Byzantine Provinces and the First Byzantine Contacts
    with the Rus'," *HUS* 12–13 (1988–89), 132–44
Tsougarakis, *Byzantine Crete*
    D. Tsougarakis, *Byzantine Crete from the Fifth Century to the Venetian Conquest*
    (Athens, 1988)
Underwood, *Kariye Djami*
    Paul Underwood, ed., *The Kariye Djami*, 4 vols. (New York and Princeton,
    1966–75)
van Dieten, *Niketas Choniates*
    J.-L. van Dieten, *Niketas Choniates: Erläuterungen zu den Reden und Briefen
    nebst einer Biographie* (Berlin, 1971)
Vasiliev, *Byzance et les Arabes*
    A. A. Vasiliev et al., *Byzance et les Arabes*, vols. I and II (Brussels, 1935–68)
Vasiliev, *Goths*
    A. A. Vasiliev, *The Goths in the Crimea* (Cambridge, Mass., 1936)
Vita Euthymii
    Vita Euthymii, ed. with commentary P. Karlin-Hayter (Brussels, 1970)
von Falkenhausen, *Untersuchungen*
    Vera von Falkenhausen, *Untersuchungen über die byzantinische Herrschaft in Süd-
    italien vom 9. bis zum 11. Jahrhundert* (Wiesbaden, 1967)
Vryonis, *Decline*
    Speros Vryonis, *The Decline of Medieval Hellenism in Asia Minor and the Process
    of Islamization from the Eleventh Through the Fifteenth Century* (Berkeley, 1971)
Whitby, *Chronicon Paschale*
    See Paschal Chronicle
Whitby, *Emperor Maurice*
    Michael Whitby, *The Emperor Maurice and His Historian* (Oxford, 1988)
Wilson, *Scholars*
    Nigel Wilson, *Scholars of Byzantium* (London, 1983)
Wolfram, *History of the Goths*
    Herwig Wolfram, *History of the Goths* (Berkeley, 1988)
Yaḥyā of Antioch
    Yaḥyā of Antioch, incomplete ed. and French trans. I. Kratchkovsky and
    A. Vasiliev, *PO* 18.5, 23.3 (Paris, 1924–32)
Zachariadou, *Trade and Crusade*
    Elizabeth Zachariadou, *Trade and Crusade: Venetian Crete and the Emirates of
    Menteshe and Aydin (1300–1415)* (Venice, 1983)

Zacos, *Byzantine Lead Seals*
    G. Zacos and A. Veglery, *Byzantine Lead Seals*, 2 vols. (Basel, 1972; Bern, 1984)
Zakythinos, *Crise monétaire*
    D. A. Zakythinos, *Crise monétaire et crise économique à Byzance du XIIIe au XVe siècle* (Athens, 1948)
Zepos, *Jus*
    I. Zepos and P. Zepos, eds., *Jus Graecoromanum*, 8 vols. (Athens, 1931)
Zonaras
    John Zonaras, *History*, ed. T. Büttner-Wobst, 3 vols. (*CSHB*, 1897)
Zosimus
    Zosimus, ed. with French trans. F. Paschoud, 3 vols. (Paris, 1971–86); trans. R. T. Ridley (Canberra, 1982)
ZRVI
    Zbornik Radova Vizantinološkog Instituta

Bibliographical Survey

This select bibliography describes the most recent books that I find useful on the history of the Byzantine state and society. Along with many studies of art and culture, I omit most older scholarship that has been incorporated into works cited here; consequently much original and pioneering work is excluded in favor of much that is newer but largely derivative, simply because the later books provide a fuller introduction to the subject. Few articles are here, though additional articles and books appear in my notes. I have usually been unable to include work published later than 1992.

Works cited more than once appear in the forms listed in the Abbreviations, pp. 873–91, even for the first citation; note that primary sources are usually abbreviated to the author's name without a title. I cite the most recently revised editions, omitting unaltered reprints. Secondary works composed in foreign languages are cited in English versions when those exist. For sources, which are in Greek unless otherwise noted, I give only the best available Greek or Latin edition and English translation (or best modern translation for works not in Greek or Latin). I cite Greek and Latin works in the original, without having checked the translations systematically.

After two initial sections, describing general studies and reference works that cover more than half the Byzantine period, the sections of this essay correspond to the parts and chapters of my text. A section for general works in each of the six parts precedes the sections for the chapters. General works on social history appear under Chapters 4, 8, 12, 17, 21, and 26, the summary chapters on society. Since cross-references have been limited to save space, readers who want to find every work listed on a subject may sometimes need to look in as many as five places: the two general sections at the beginning of the whole survey, the general section at the beginning of the relevant part, the section for the relevant chronological chapter, and the section for the relevant chapter on society. In most cases, however, the sections for the part and chapter should suffice.

GENERAL STUDIES

Ostrogorsky's *History*, long the standard survey by a single author, still includes some valuable judgments and references. Its predecessor, A. A. Vasiliev, *History of the Byzantine Empire*, rev. ed., 2 vols. (Madison, 1952), is now mainly of interest for its review of earlier literature. Somewhat more detailed treatment is available in Christophilopoulou's *History*, a teaching manual that reaches 867 in its English translation and 1081 in its Greek original.

Among collaborative efforts, Kazhdan, *Oxford Dictionary of Byzantium*, is of remarkably consistent quality, giving recent and generally reliable views and references on many people, places, and subjects related to Byzantine history. Volume IV of the *Cambridge Medieval History* is usually inferior to Ostrogorsky's *History* for political events but contains some useful chapters on other topics, especially in its second part; it also has convenient classified bibliographies of books and articles published before 1961. Norman Baynes et al., *Byzantium: An Introduction to East Roman Civilization* (Oxford, 1948), is old but sound.

The most recent and best of the topical surveys is Mango, *Byzantium*, though his view of Byzantium is more negative than mine. Louis Bréhier, *Le monde byzantin*, 3 vols. (Paris, 1947–50), shows its age but contains some information that is hard to find elsewhere, particularly in the treatment of institutions in the second volume.

Hendy's *Studies*, an important though difficult book, is the nearest thing to a history of the economy yet written. See also the interesting articles by several authors in *Hommes et richesses*. On trade, Heyd's *Histoire* is old but has not yet been replaced. For agriculture, see Lemerle, *Agrarian History*, a preliminary survey of the problems, and now the more detailed treatment of Kaplan, *Hommes et la terre*; but the view of military landholding in both books is probably mistaken, and Kaplan's postulation of an agricultural decline after the eighth century is implausible.

On daily life, Phaidon Koukoules, *Byzantinōn bios kai politismos*, 5 vols. (Athens, 1948–52), is dry and uncritical but gives extensive references to the sources. On wages and prices, see G. Ostrogorsky, "Löhne und Preise in Byzanz," *BZ* 32 (1932), 293–333, now to be supplemented by J. Irmscher, "Einiges über Preise und Löhne im frühen Byzanz," in H. Köpstein and F. Winkelmann, eds., *Studien zum 8. und 9. Jahrhundert in Byzanz* (Berlin, 1983), 23–33, Cécile Morrisson, "Monnaie et prix à Byzance du Ve au VIIe siècle," in *Hommes et richesses* I, 239–60, and Cheynet, "Prix et salaires."

In the absence of a true history of the army before 1204, see Treadgold, *Byzantium and Its Army*, a preliminary treatment of the main problems. On the navy, see also Ahrweiler, *Byzance et la mer*, a pioneering but hasty work. Jonathan Shepard and Simon Franklin, eds., *Byzantine Diplomacy* (Aldershot, 1992), a collection of conference papers, is the best book to date on that neglected topic.

For ecclesiastical history, see the relevant parts of Augustin Fliche and Victor Martin, eds., *Histoire de l'Église* II–XV (Paris, 1935–64), a successful collaboration. A more recent survey of Byzantine church history, beginning with the seventh century, is Hussey's *Orthodox Church*.

Regional studies covering the whole or most of the Byzantine period are rare, and even the best ones tend to be preliminary and incomplete. For Constantinople, see R. Janin, *Constantinople byzantine*, 2d ed. (Paris, 1964), and now the papers in Mango, *Constantinople*. For the Balkans, see A. Bon, *Le Péloponnèse byzantin jusqu'en 1204* (Paris, 1951), Paul Lemerle, *Philippes et la Macédoine orientale à l'époque chrétienne et byzantine* (Paris, 1945), V. Krivari, *Villes et villages de Macédoine occidentale* (Paris, 1989), and Tsougarakis, *Byzantine Crete*. Also of some use are Robert L. Scranton, *Corinth XVI, Medieval Architecture* (Princeton, 1957), and Ferluga, *Amministrazione*, on Dalmatia. On Italy, see André Guillou and Filippo Burgarella, *L'Italia bizantina: Dall'esarcato di Ravenna al tema di Sicilia* (Turin, 1988). On the Crimea, consult Vasiliev, *Goths*.

For Byzantine Anatolia, a neglected subject, see T. A. Sinclair, *Eastern Turkey: An Architectural and Archaeological Survey*, 4 vols. (London, 1987–90), and for the northern coast Bryer, *Byzantine Monuments*. Among works on specific sites throughout the period, note particularly Clive Foss, *Byzantine and Turkish Sardis* (Cambridge, 1976), and *Ephesus*, Wolfram Hoepfner, *Herakleia Pontike–Ereğli* (Vienna, 1966), and Janssens, *Trébizonde*.

Honigmann's *Ostgrenze* remains useful for the eastern frontier region. Among various surveys of Armenian history, none very satisfactory, Grousset, *Histoire de l'Arménie*, is perhaps the best. For relations with the Arabs and Turks, the *Encyclopedia of Islam* is an unusually valuable reference work. For relations with the Slavs, the safest guide is Obolensky, *Commonwealth*. On Venice, see Nicol, *Byzantium and Venice*.

For demography, Russell, *Late Ancient and Medieval Population*, is convenient but rather careless, while McEvedy, *Atlas*, is a sensible popularization. On Byzantine Jews, see Sharf, *Byzantine Jewry*. On Byzantine Armenians, see E. Bauer, *Die Armenier im byzantinischen Reich* (Erevan, 1978). On Vlachs, see T. J. Winnifrith, *The Vlachs: The History of a Balkan People* (London, 1987).

There is as yet no true history of Byzantine literature as a whole. C. A. Trypanis's *Greek Poetry from Homer to Seferis* (Chicago, 1981) includes Byzantine poetry. On scholarship, see the idiosyncratic but informative Wilson, *Scholars*. Robert Browning, *Medieval and Modern Greek* (London, 1969), supplies a brief but illuminating history of the development of the Byzantine Greek language.

For introductions to the arts, see John Beckwith, *Early Christian and Byzantine Art*, 2d ed. (Harmondsworth, 1979), Richard Krautheimer, *Early Christian and Byzantine Architecture*, 4th ed. (Harmondsworth, 1986), and now Lyn Rodley, *Byzantine Art and Architecture* (Cambridge, 1994). Viktor Lazarev, *Storia della pittura bizantina* (Turin, 1967), is the most comprehensive work on art, while Cyril Mango, *Byzantine Architecture* (New York, 1975), is the best study of the architecture. Anthony Cutler and John Nesbitt, *L'arte bizantina e il suo pubblico*, 2 vols. (Turin, 1986), make a welcome effort to integrate art history with social and other cultural history. Among more specialized studies, Thomas F. Mathews, *The Byzantine Churches of Istanbul: A Photographic Survey* (University Park and London, 1976), and Foss, *Byzantine Fortifications*, are of considerable general interest.

GENERAL REFERENCE WORKS

Encyclopedic surveys of Byzantine literature, with full bibliographies, are provided by Hans-Georg Beck, *Kirche und theologische Literatur im byzantinischen Reich* (Munich, 1959) and *Geschichte der byzantinischen Volksliteratur* (Munich, 1971), and Herbert Hunger, *Die hochsprachliche profane Literatur der Byzantiner*, 2 vols. (Munich, 1978). On the sources for Byzantine history, see J. Karayannopulos and G. Weiss, *Quellenkunde zur Geschichte von Byzanz (324–1453)*, 2 vols. (Wiesbaden, 1982). Although largely superseded by all these, Gyula Moravcsik, *Byzantinoturcica*, 2d ed., vol. I (Berlin, 1958), gives a fuller account of Byzantine historiography.

A guide to editions of the texts is provided by Wolfgang Buchwald et al., *Tusculum-Lexicon: Griechischer und lateinischer Autoren des Altertums und Mittelalters*, 3d ed. (Darmstadt, 1982). For a detailed checklist of the Greek Fathers up to the mid-eighth century, see M. Geerard, *Clavis Patrum Graecorum*, 5 vols. (Brepols, 1974–87). Comprehensive references to hagiography can be found in F. Halkin, *Bibliotheca Hagiographica Graeca*, 3d ed., 4 vols., Subsidia Hagiographica 8A, 47, 65 (Brussels, 1957–84).

For very useful chronological tables and guides to dating, see Grumel, *Chronologie*. For papyrology, see André Bataille, *Les papyrus* (Paris, 1955). On Byzantine legislation, see N. van der Wal and J. H. A. Lokin, *Historiae Iuris Graeco-Romani Delineatio: Les sources du droit byzantin de 300 à 1453* (Groningen, 1985). The laws promulgated in Greek are conveniently available in Zepos, *Jus*, though better editions often exist, some being cited below. The official acts of the government are catalogued in Dölger, *Regesten*.

The official acts of the patriarchate of Constantinople are similarly catalogued in Grumel, *Regestes*. For the acts of ecumenical councils, see Mansi, now mostly replaced for the period up to the seventh century by E. Schwartz et al., *Acta Conciliorum Oecumenicorum*, ser. 1 and 2, 6 vols. (Berlin and Leipzig, 1922–92; in progress); the conciliar acts up to 780 are translated by Henry R. Percival, *SLNPNF* (1899).

For introductions to Byzantine numismatics, see Philip Grierson, *Byzantine Coins* (London, 1982), and Bertelè, *Numismatique*. The best account of the coinage is (or will be) in two complementary works, Philip Grierson and Melinda Mays, *Catalogue of Late Roman Coins in the Dumbarton Oaks Collection and in the Whittemore Collection* (Washington, 1992), which extends from 395 to 491, and Grierson, *Catalogue*, which so far extends from 491 to 1081. See also Cécile Morrisson, *Catalogue des monnaies byzantines de la Bibliothèque Nationale (491–1204)*, 2 vols. (Paris, 1970), and W. R. O. Hahn, *Moneta Imperii Byzantini*, 3 vols. (Vienna, 1973–81; in progress), which should be the most detailed account of all but at present covers only coins from 481 to 720.

For the lead seals that survive from official documents and are of unusual importance for Byzantine history, see V. Laurent, *Le corpus des sceaux de l'empire byzantine*, vols. II and V (Paris, 1963–81; no more published), G. Zacos and A. Veglery, *Byzantine Lead Seals*, 2 vols. (Basel, 1972; Bern, 1984), N. Oikonomidès, *A Collection of Dated Byzantine Lead Seals* (Washington, 1986), and now particularly Nesbitt, *Catalogue*.

For an introduction to the historical geography, see J. Koder, *Der Lebensraum der Byzantiner* (Graz, 1984). For place names and archeological sites, see the volumes of the *TIB* that have been published to date: vol. I, J. Koder and F. Hild, *Hellas und Thessalien* (1976); vol. II, Hild, *Kappadokien*; vol. III, P. Soustal, *Nikopolis und Kephallēnia* (1981); vol. IV, K. Belke, *Galatien und Lykaonien* (1984); vol. V, Hild, *Kilikien*; vol. VI, Soustal, *Thrakien*; vol. VII, Belke, *Phrygien*. These are gradually replacing the obsolete W. M. Ramsay, *The Historical Geography of Asia Minor* (London, 1890). For ecclesiastical geography, see Janin, *Églises* and *Les églises et les monastères des grands centres byzantins* (Paris, 1975).

Classified bibliographies of current scholarship on Byzantium appear in two periodicals, *Byzantinische Zeitschrift* and *Byzantinoslavica*, of which the former gives the more extensive listings. For a select bibliography of recent work with commentary, see Günter Weiss, *Byzanz: Kritischer Forschungs- und Literaturbericht 1968–85* (Munich, 1986).

PART I: 284–457

Among the sources, the only significant secular histories to cover most of the period are the undistinguished compilation of Zosimus, which extends to 410 with a lacuna between 282 and 305, and the unreliable chronicle of John Malalas. Rather better are three ecclesiastical histories: that of Socrates, extending from 305 to 439 and the first to be written, and those of Sozomen (ed. J. Bidez and G. C. Hansen, *GCS* [1960]; trans. C. H. Hartrauft, *SLNPNF* [1890]) and Theodoret of Cyrrhus (ed. L. Parmentier and F. Scheidweiler, *GCS* [1954]; trans. B. Jackson, *SLNPNF* [1893]), extending from 324 to 425 and 428, respectively, but largely dependent on Socrates. The fragmentary ecclesiastical history of the Arian Philostorgius, which originally covered the years from 300 to 425, is also of interest.

The best overall modern history of the period is Stein, *Histoire du Bas-Empire*, which includes the West and covers the years 284–565. More detailed treatment of social, economic, and institutional matters appears in Jones, *Later Roman Empire*, which extends from 284 to 602 and again includes the West. The much shorter complementary volumes of Averil Cameron, *The Later Roman Empire, A.D. 284–430* (Cambridge, Mass., 1993) and *The Mediterranean World in Late Antiquity, A.D. 395–600* (London, 1993), are recent but somewhat careless.

On the barbarian invasions, Emilienne Demougeot, *La formation de l'Europe et les invasions barbares* II (Paris, 1979), is long but a bit superficial. On the Goths, see rather Wolfram, *History of the Goths*, to which Peter Heather, *Goths and Romans, 332–489* (Oxford, 1991), adds some points of value. On relations with the Arabs, see the exhaustive studies by Irfan Shahid, *Byzantium and the Arabs in the*

Fourth Century (Washington, 1984), *Byzantium and the Arabs in the Fifth Century* (Washington, 1989), and *Byzantium and the Arabs in the Sixth Century*, 2 vols. (Washington, 1995). Blockley, *East Roman Foreign Policy*, is a convenient survey.

Important reference works include Jones, *Prosopography*, which covers practically every known historical figure, still Otto Seeck, *Regesten der Kaiser und Päpste für die Jahre 311 bis 476* (Stuttgart, 1919), and now Bagnall, *Consuls*. Pauly's *Realencyclopädie* includes often authoritative articles on almost all people and places relevant to Byzantine history up to 565. Demandt, *Spätantike*, is a detailed and carefully updated handbook. Blockley, *Historians*, discusses the important fragmentary historians in his first volume and in his second gives editions and translations of the texts.

Chapter 1: 284–337

The principal contemporary sources are Lactantius, in Latin, and Eusebius of Caesarea's *Life of Constantine* (ed. J. A. Heikel, *GCS* [1902]) and *History*. Barnes, *New Empire*, provides a good guide to the panegyrics, papyri, inscriptions, laws, coins, and later sources that supplement Lactantius and Eusebius. The fact remains that the evidence for this important period is quite poor.

The standard book on Diocletian, good on political questions but weaker on financial and administrative matters, is now Stephen Williams, *Diocletian and the Roman Recovery* (London, 1985), which mostly replaces the unfinished work of William Seston, *Dioclétien et la tétrarchie* I (Paris, 1946). Franz Kolb, *Diocletian und die erste Tetrarchie: Improvisation order Experiment in der Organisation monarchischer Herrschaft?* (Berlin, 1987), concludes with reason that the tetrarchy was mostly planned rather than improvised.

On Constantine, Timothy Barnes, *Constantine and Eusebius* (Cambridge, Mass., 1981), contains a good summary of current knowledge and the author's discoveries on numerous points. But the most convincing picture of Constantine is still in the modest book of A. H. M. Jones, *Constantine and the Conversion of Europe*, 2d ed. (New York, 1963), which depicts him, in defiance of the scholarly consensus, as far from great. Norman H. Baynes, *Constantine the Great and the Christian Church* (London, 1931), provides a judicious treatment of Constantine's conversion.

Chapter 2: 337–395

Much the best narrative source for the period is the Latin history of the Greek officer Ammianus, of which the surviving portion extends from 353 to 378. For the years before and after Ammianus, the sources are either fragmentary or unreliable. Zosimus improves a bit for this period, probably mirroring an improvement in his source, Eunapius of Sardis, from whom a few independent fragments survive (ed. and trans. in Blockley, *Historians*).

The period as a whole is covered not only by Stein, *Histoire du Bas-Empire*, but by André Piganiol, *L'empire chrétien (325–395)*, 2d ed. (Paris, 1972), an interesting work marred by some bizarre judgments. John Matthews, *The Roman*

Empire of Ammianus (Baltimore, 1989), treats most of the period through a detailed analysis of its main historian. On Constantius II, see for political affairs Chantal Vogler, *Constance II et l'administration impériale* (Strasbourg, 1979), giving a generally positive account of his achievements, and for religious affairs, Richard Klein, *Constantius II und die christliche Kirche* (Darmstadt, 1977), noting that Constantius was not an Arian, a point applicable to Valens as well. Timothy Barnes, *Athanasius and Constantius* (Cambridge, Mass., 1993), may be read with profit even by those who find its view of Athanasius overly hostile.

An immense and repetitious literature exists on the brief and ultimately unimportant reign of Julian. The best book remains J. Bidez, *La vie de l'empereur Julien* (Paris, 1930). Among more recent works, Robert Browning, *The Emperor Julian* (Berkeley, 1976), is sound but lacks full references; Polymnia Athanassiadi-Fowden, *Julian and Hellenism* (Oxford, 1981), is perceptive but distorted by Greek nationalism; Edgar Pack, *Städte und Steuern in der Politik Julians* (Brussels, 1986), is detailed but inconclusive; and G. W. Bowersock, *Julian the Apostate* (Cambridge, Mass., 1978), looks more definitive than it is (see R. Tomlin in *Phoenix* 34 [1980], 266–70).

Ulrich Wanke, *Die Gotenkriege des Valens: Studien zu Topographie und Chronologie im unteren Donauraum von 366 bis 378 n.Chr.* (Frankfurt, 1990), is the only useful book specifically on Valens. Stephen Williams and Gerard Friell, *Theodosius: The Empire at Bay* (London, 1994), is not bad, but less incisive than Adolf Lippold, *Theodosius der Grosse und seine Zeit* (Munich, 1980), taken from his article in Pauly's *Realencyclopädie*. On Theodosius's religious policies, see the rather arid Wilhelm Ensslin, *Die Religionspolitik des Kaisers Theodosius der Grosse* (Munich, 1953), and the livelier N. Q. King, *The Emperor Theodosius and the Establishment of Christianity* (London, 1961).

Chapter 3: 395–457

When Zosimus's narrative ends with 410, and especially when Socrates concludes with 439, the worst-documented period of early Byzantine history begins. The ecclesiastical history of Evagrius begins with 431 but was written much later. Only fragments survive of a succession of contemporary secular historians, Eunapius of Sardis to 404 or so, Olympiodorus of Thebes from 407 to 425, and Priscus of Panium perhaps from 434 onward (all ed. and trans. Blockley, *Historians*). John Malalas is of some use but includes a considerable legendary element. The Latin chronicle of Marcellinus is more reliable but very brief. Nonnarrative sources like the Latin poems of Claudian (ed. Th. Birt in *MGH, Auctores Antiquissimi* 10 [1892]) are often of decisive value.

Bury, *History*, and especially Stein, *Histoire du Bas-Empire*, are the best modern works, but the whole period is in need of a new survey. A good beginning has been made by Alan Cameron, *Claudian: Poetry and Propaganda at the Court of Honorius* (Oxford, 1970), J. Liebeschuetz, *Barbarians and Bishops: Army, Church, and State in the Age of Arcadius and Chrysostom* (Oxford, 1990), and now Cameron, *Barbarians*. K. Holum, *Theodosian Empresses* (Berkeley, 1982), unluckily appeared just when its main conclusions were being refuted by Alan Cameron, "The

Empress and the Poet: Paganism and Politics at the Court of Theodosius II,"
Yale Classical Studies 27 (1982), 217–89. On the Huns, J. O. Maenchen-Helfen,
The World of the Huns (Berkeley, 1973), was unfortunately not quite finished at
its author's death, but for most purposes it replaces E. A. Thompson, *A History
of Attila and the Huns* (Oxford, 1948).

Chapter 4: Society, 284–457

The surviving legislation from the period is preserved in the *Theodosian Code*,
which dates from 438. The *Notitia Dignitatum* (ed. O. Seeck [Berlin, 1876]),
probably drawn up in 408, provides an official record of the structure of the
army and bureaucracy; see most recently R. Goodburn and P. Bartholomew,
eds., *Aspects of the Notitia Dignitatum* (Oxford, 1976). Diocletian's *Edict on Prices*
of 301 (ed. M. Giacchero [Genoa, 1974]) is also of interest. These three sources
are in Latin, though Diocletian's edict includes a Greek translation.

Epistolography and homiletics, particularly the letters of Synesius of Cyrene
(ed. *PG* 66) and Libanius, and the sermons of John Chrysostom, provide valuable evidence for social conditions. So do some orations, notably those of Themistius, though these can give an exaggerated impression of the importance of
the court. Other sources include hagiography, inscriptions, coins, archeology,
and vast numbers of papyri from Egypt.

A. H. M. Jones's *Later Roman Empire* covers almost every aspect of the social and economic history of the time, incorporating evidence from both literary and nonliterary sources. On cities, also see his general work, *The Greek
City from Alexander to Justinian* (Oxford, 1940), and his survey by regions, *Cities
of the Eastern Roman Provinces*, 2d ed. (Oxford, 1971). On linguistic questions,
see Henrik Zilliacus, *Zum Kampf der Weltsprachen im oströmischen Reich* (Hel-
sinki, 1935), Gustave Bardy, *La question des langues dans l'église ancienne* (Paris,
1948), and Paul Peeters, *Orient et Byzance: Le tréfonds oriental de l'hagiographie
byzantine* (Brussels, 1950). On Constantinople, see especially Gilbert Dagron,
Naissance d'une capitale: Constantinople et ses institutions de 330 à 451, 2d ed. (Paris,
1984). On the frontiers, see most recently the papers collected in D. H. French
and C. S. Lightfoot, eds., *The Eastern Frontier of the Roman Empire* (Oxford,
1989).

For the Balkans, systematic treatments can be found in three works that include the earlier period: R. F. Hoddinot, *Bulgaria in Antiquity: An Archaeological
Introduction* (New York, 1975), András Mócsy, *Pannonia and Upper Moesia* (London, 1974), and J. J. Wilkes, *Dalmatia* (Cambridge, Mass., 1969). See also the
tentative study of Velizar Velkov, *Cities in Thrace and Dacia in Late Antiquity*
(Amsterdam, 1977), and the essays in *Villes et peuplement dans l'Illyricum protoby-
zantine* (Rome, 1984). On Greece, see Alison Frantz, *Late Antiquity: A.D. 267–
700*, vol. XXIV of *The Athenian Agora* (Princeton, 1988). On the linguistic situation, see V. Beševliev, *Untersuchungen über die Personennamen bei den Thrakern* (Amsterdam, 1970).

Anatolia in late antiquity is as usual a neglected topic, despite many brief references in archeological reports. But now see Stephen Mitchell, *Anatolia: Land,*

Men, and Gods in Asia Minor, 2 vols. (Oxford, 1993), which extends from about 300 B.C. to about 600 A.D. with an emphasis on Galatia and on religion.

Syria is much better covered. Tchalenko, *Villages,* skillfully exploits the archeological material. Liebeschuetz, *Antioch,* makes good use of the fourth-century literary evidence. Glanville Downey, *A History of Antioch in Syria from Seleucus to the Arab Conquest* (Princeton, 1961), is less perceptive but extends over a wider period. On Palestine, see Avi-Yonah, *Jews of Palestine,* Carol A. M. Glucker, *The City of Gaza in the Roman and Byzantine Periods* (Oxford, 1987), Yizhar Hirschfeld, *The Judean Desert Monasteries in the Byzantine Period* (New Haven, 1992), and Joseph Shereshevski, *Byzantine Urban Settlements in the Negev Desert* (Beersheba, 1991). On Byzantine Arabia, see S. Thomas Parker, *Romans and Saracens: A History of the Arabian Frontier* (Winona Lake, 1985).

On Egypt, now begin with Roger Bagnall, *Egypt in Late Antiquity* (Princeton, 1993). See also Lallemand, *Administration,* and still Jean Maspero, *Organisation militaire de l'Égypte byzantine* (Paris, 1912). The long-influential views of Edward R. Hardy, *The Large Estates of Byzantine Egypt* (New York, 1931), have now been much modified by Jean Gascou, "Grands domaines." On Cyrenaïca, see Denis Roques, *Synésios de Cyrène et la Cyrénaïque du Bas-Empire* (Paris, 1987). All these regional studies have implications for the empire at large.

Less general but still interesting are C. H. Kraeling, *Gerasa: City of the Decapolis* (New Haven, 1938), the same author's *Ptolemais: City of the Libyan Pentapolis* (Chicago, 1962), and J. B. Segal, *Edessa, "The Blessed City"* (Oxford, 1970). J.-M. Speiser, *Thessalonique et ses monuments du IVe au VIe siècle* (Athens, 1984), draws mainly on archeology, while Charlotte Roueché, *Aphrodisias in Late Antiquity* (London, 1989), draws primarily on epigraphy. Some recent local studies, including Greece and Anatolia, appear in Robert Hohlfelder, ed., *City, Town and Countryside in the Early Byzantine Era* (New York, 1982).

On the army, see Ramsay MacMullen, *Soldier and Civilian in the Later Roman Empire* (Cambridge, Mass., 1963), and Hoffman, *Bewegungsheer.* On taxation, now begin with Carrié, "Dioclétien," but A. Déléage, *La capitation du Bas-Empire* (Mâcon, 1945), and A. Cérati, *Caractère annonaire et assiette de l'impôt foncier au Bas-Empire* (Paris, 1975), retain much of their value. H.-J. Horstkotte, *Die 'Steuerhaftung' im spätrömischen 'Zwangsstaat',* 2d ed. (Frankfurt, 1988), provides a corrective to the tendency to exaggerate the oppressiveness of the system of taxation.

On the workings of government, M. T. W. Arnheim, *The Senatorial Aristocracy in the Later Roman Empire* (Oxford, 1972), makes some persuasive observations. J. Karayannopulos, *Das Finanzwesen des frühbyzantinischen Staates* (Munich, 1958), gives a survey of the evidence for financial administration; somewhat narrower in scope but more detailed are two works by Roland Delmaire, *Largesses sacrées* and *Les responsables des finances impériales au Bas-Empire romain (IVe– VIe siècles): Études prosopographiques* (Brussels, 1989). Ramsay MacMullen, *Corruption and the Decline of Rome* (New Haven, 1988), is a good treatment of an important and neglected subject. For a comparison of the eastern and western parts of the empire, see Roland Ganghoffer, *L'évolution des institutions municipales en occident et en orient au bas-empire* (Paris, 1963).

On the triumph of Christianity, the standard work remains Johannes Gef-
fcken, *The Last Days of Greco-Roman Paganism* (Amsterdam, 1978; a translation
of the 1929 edition), to which Ramsay MacMullen, *Christianizing the Roman
Empire, A.D. 100–400* (New Haven, 1984), and Robin Lane Fox, *Pagans and
Christians* (Harmondsworth, 1986), add some new ideas and updated references.
For the most detailed treatment, now see Frank Trombley, *Hellenic Religion and
Christianization, c. 370–529*, 2 vols. (Leiden, 1993–94). On Egyptian religion
and culture, see the studies in B. Pearson and J. Goehring, eds., *The Roots of
Egyptian Christianity* (Philadelphia, 1986). On church property, note Ewa Wip-
szycka, *Les ressources et les activités économiques des églises en Égypte du IVe au VIIIe
siècles* (Brussels, 1972).

On culture, see C. N. Cochrane, *Christianity and Classical Culture* (Oxford,
1940), M. L. W. Laistner, *Christianity and Pagan Culture in the Later Roman Empire* (Ithaca, 1951), G. W. Bowersock, *Hellenism in Late Antiquity* (Ann Arbor,
1990), and especially the essays in A. Momigliano, ed., *The Conflict Between Paganism and Christianity in the Fourth Century* (Oxford, 1963). For theology, Frances
M. Young, *From Nicaea to Chalcedon: A Guide to the Literature and Its Background*
(Philadelphia, 1983), is helpful. The handiest guide to Christian literature of the
time is Johannes Quasten, *Patrology* III (Utrecht, 1960). For oratory, see George
A. Kennedy, *Greek Rhetoric Under Christian Emperors* (Princeton, 1983). For art,
Kurt Weitzmann, ed., *Age of Spirituality: Late Antique and Early Christian Art,
Third to Seventh Century* (New York, 1979), is a convenient introduction.

The economy of the empire in this period is a subject of much debate that
has led to little consensus. Stimulating if somewhat inconclusive studies include
those in King, *Imperial Revenue*, and in *Hommes et richesses* I, E. Patlagean, *Pauvreté économique et pauvreté sociale à Byzance, 4e–7e siècles* (Paris, 1977), and Jean
Durliat, *De la ville*. Roger Rémondon, *La crise de l'empire romain de Marc-Aurèle
à Anastase* (Paris, 1964), puts the problem of decline in a somewhat wider perspective. On society in general, see F. Tinnefeld, *Die frühbyzantinische Gesellschaft*
(Munich, 1977).

PART II: 457–610

The main sources for most or all of this period are the chronicle of John
Malalas, which is at its best from the mid-fifth century to its end in 565, the
chronicle of Theophanes, which was written in the ninth century but includes
some material of value for this time, Evagrius, who ends with 594, and the usually laconic *Paschal Chronicle*.

The comprehensive modern works for the preceding period extend into this
one. Jones's *Later Roman Empire* covers almost the whole, ending with 602.
Stein's *Histoire du Bas-Empire* II runs from 476 to 565, since Stein's plan to continue to 641 was interrupted by his death. The second edition of Bury's *History*
also stops with 565, but the second volume of the first edition, a more cursory
work, continues to 802. Wolfram's *History of the Goths* extends to the mid-sixth
century, and is preferable to Thomas S. Burns, *A History of the Ostrogoths* (Bloom-

ington, 1984). Among reference works, Jones's *Prosopography*, Bagnall's *Consuls*, Pauly's *Realencyclopädie*, and Demandt's *Spätantike* still cover these years.

Chapter 5: 457–518

The sources are mostly the same and almost as bad as for the preceding period, improved only because Marcellinus and John Malalas have more to say as they near their own times. Among historians whose work survives only in fragments, Priscus covered the period to about 474, Malchus of Philadelphia that from 474 to 491, and Candidus of Isauria that from 457 to 491 (all ed. and trans. Blockley, *Historians*). Joshua the Stylite's detailed Syriac chronicle deals with events in Byzantine Mesopotamia between 475 and 506. Procopius of Caesarea occasionally refers to Anastasius's reign as background.

Apart from Bury's *History* and Stein's *Histoire du Bas-Empire*, the period is poorly covered, even considering the poverty of the sources. Nothing detailed appears to have been written on the crucial reign of Leo I. On Zeno nothing specific has appeared since the workmanlike dissertation of W. Barth, *Kaiser Zeno* (Basel, 1894). Walter Kaegi, *Byzantium and the Decline of Rome* (Princeton, 1968), is a rather vague treatment of relations between East and West under Leo and Zeno. Carmelo Capizzi, *L'imperatore Anastasio I* (Rome, 1969), is recent but often superficial. See also Peter Charanis, *Church and State in the Later Roman Empire: The Religious Policy of Anastasius I*, 2d ed. (Thessalonica, 1974).

Chapter 6: 518–565

For this period the sources improve dramatically, and much the best is Procopius of Caesarea. His *History of the Wars* is a detailed narrative of events from 527 to 552 that for the most part he witnessed, while his *Secret History* is an exaggerated but illuminating outburst against Justinian and his associates, composed secretly in 550. Procopius was continued from 552 to 558 by Agathias of Myrina (ed. R. Keydell, *CFHB* [Berlin, 1967]; trans. J. D. Frendo, *CFHB* [Berlin, 1975]). Agathias was in turn continued from 558 by the more talented Menander Protector, whose work survives in extensive fragments. Among sources already mentioned for the previous period, John Malalas, now a contemporary, is particularly detailed and interesting. From the ecclesiastical history in Syriac of the Monophysite bishop John of Ephesus we possess fragments of the part from 521 to 565. With this period the Latin *Liber Pontificalis* becomes a good source for papal history and Rome in general.

Both Bury's *History* and Stein's *Histoire du Bas-Empire* devote almost their whole second volumes to the reigns of Justin and Justinian, and Stein's volume remains the best book on these years. A. A. Vasiliev, *Justin the First* (Cambridge, Mass., 1950), is an exhaustive treatment of Justin's reign. Berthold Rubin, *Das Zeitalter Iustinians* I (Berlin, 1960), treats some aspects of Justinian's reign in numbing detail but is unfinished; the same author's historical commentary on Procopius, *Prokopios von Kaisareia* (Stuttgart, 1954; reprinted from his article on Procopius in Pauly's *Realencyclopädie*), is usually more helpful.

Chapter 7: 565–610

After Justinian's death the sources deteriorate somewhat. Evagrius continues to 594. The fragmentary history of Menander Protector extends to 582. The disorganized but informative Syriac ecclesiastical history of John of Ephesus survives almost complete for the years from 565 to 588. The lengthy but obtuse history of Theophylact Simocatta runs from 582 to 603, with a retrospective account of the Persian war going back to 572. From 603 on these fairly adequate sources fail, leaving little but Theophanes, the *Paschal Chronicle*, and the *Short History* of Nicephorus, which begins with 602.

The contemporary Coptic history of John of Nikiu, which survives in a mutilated Ethiopic translation of an Arabic version, provides valuable but often confusing information on Egypt. The *Miracles of St. Demetrius*, a collection of texts describing how the patron saint of Thessalonica posthumously protected his city, becomes an interesting source for Balkan history with the Slavic siege of 586. Events in the West must mostly be pieced together from scanty information in several Latin sources: John of Biclar's chronicle of Spanish events, Paul the Deacon's *History of the Lombards*, and the *Liber Pontificalis*.

The first edition of Bury's *History* covers the whole period but is inferior to the same author's mature work. The best treatment of the reigns of Justin II and Tiberius II is a monograph by the young Ernest (then Ernst) Stein, *Studien zur Geschichte des byzantinischen Reichs, vornehmlich unter den Kaisern Justinus II und Tiberius Constantinus* (Stuttgart, 1919). For the reign of Maurice, see Paul Goubert, *Byzance avant l'Islam* I–II.2 (Paris, 1951–65), an unfinished and overlong but sometimes helpful study, and especially Whitby, *Emperor Maurice*, which is authoritative for its chosen subjects, Maurice's Balkan and Persian wars. On the reign of Phocas, see the first volume of Stratos, *Byzantium*, which is not very satisfactory but can be supplemented in part by the perceptive comments of Borkowski, *Alexandrie II*.

Chapter 8: Society, 457–610

The outstanding legislative sources are the Latin *Justinian Code*, revised in 534, and especially Justinian's subsequent *Novels*. John the Lydian gives considerable information about the administration despite his lack of intelligence. Procopius's *Secret History* and *Buildings* are enlightening, though unbalanced in both focus and judgment in opposite ways. For the army, the *Strategicon* of Maurice (ed. G. T. Dennis, *CFHB* [Vienna, 1981]; trans. by same [Philadelphia, 1984]) is fundamental. Archeology and papyri continue to be important sources, although inscriptions become rarer. Sermons also fall off, while epistolography and oratory nearly disappear and hagiography has less to say than usual.

Most of the works cited for Chapter 4, above all Jones's *Later Roman Empire*, also cover this period. On the various regions, see the serviceable compilation of Dietrich Claude, *Die byzantinische Stadt im 6. Jahrhundert* (Munich, 1969). On Africa, see Charles Diehl, *L'Afrique byzantine*, 2 vols. (Paris, 1896), and more recently D. Pringle, *The Defence of Byzantine Africa* (Oxford, 1981). On Spain, see

Thompson, *The Goths in Spain*, which has an appendix devoted to the Byzantine province. On Italy, see Brown, *Gentlemen*, a particularly intelligent study. On Mesopotamia, see also J. Lauffray, *Halabiyya-Zenobia: Place forte du limes oriental et la Haute-Mésopotamie au VIe siècle*, 2 vols. (Paris, 1983–91). On sixth-century Egypt, Leslie MacCoull, *Dioscorus of Aphrodito: His Work and His World* (Berkeley, 1988), is of some general interest.

On the *Justinian Code*, see Paul Collinet, *Études historiques sur le droit de Justinien*, 5 vols. (Paris, 1912–52). On civil unrest, see Cameron, *Circus Factions*, a convincing refutation of much earlier literature that interpreted circus violence in political and religious terms. Germaine Rouillard, *L'administration civile de l'Égypte byzantine*, 2d ed. (Paris, 1928), remains of value, treating both civil unrest and administrative corruption in the sixth century.

On the Church in general, see Meyendorff, *Imperial Unity*. On Monophysites, see W. H. C. Frend, *The Rise of the Monophysite Movement: Chapters in the History of the Church in the Fifth and Sixth Centuries* (Cambridge, 1972), which falls prey to some stereotypes, particularly the view that Monophysitism had "nationalist" characteristics. On Chalcedonians, see Patrick T. R. Gray, *The Defense of Chalcedon in the East (451–553)* (Leiden, 1979), which is more careful. On the Church in Syria and Egypt, see R. Devreesse, *Le patriarcat d'Antioche depuis la paix de l'église jusqu'à la conquête arabe* (Paris, 1945), and Jean Maspero, *Histoire des patriarches d'Alexandrie depuis la mort de l'empereur Anastase jusqu'à la réconciliation des églises jacobites (518–616)* (Paris, 1923).

On sixth-century literature, Averil Cameron, *Procopius and the Sixth Century* (Berkeley, 1985), discusses the great historian with little sympathy, mistaking his misanthropy for misogyny; in *Agathias* (Oxford, 1970), she treats a mediocre historian more kindly. The first part of Lemerle, *Byzantine Humanism*, gives a good discussion of the problems connected with education at the time. For an introduction to the art of the period, see André Grabar, *Byzantium from the Death of Theodosius to the Rise of Islam* (London, 1966).

Modern coverage of the problematic but crucial economic history of this period is scanty, and scattered among the general works cited for this and the previous period. Michel Kaplan, *Les propriétés de la couronne et de l'église dans l'empire byzantin (V^e–VIe siècles): Documents* (Paris, 1976), is very limited in scope.

PART III: 610–780

Of all the phases of Byzantine history, this is the worst-documented. Theophanes, covering the whole of it, is the main source, but often shows confusion; his computations of the year of the world generally fall one year behind from 609/10 to 684/85 and again from 725/26 to 772/73 (see Ostrogorsky, "Chronologie," though see below for the years from 684/85 to 714/15). The main supplementary source is Nicephorus's *Short History*, which ends with 769 and has nothing to say about the years from 641 to 668. Later Byzantine chroniclers usually do no more than copy Theophanes.

Many bits and pieces of information can be gathered from Arabic writers. A selection of important excerpts is translated in Brooks, "Arabs," with additions and corrections in E. W. Brooks, "The Campaign of 716–718, from Arabic Sources," *JHS* 19 (1899), 19–33. These are continued from 750 to 813 by Brooks, "Byzantines." For Balādhurī, a major source on Arab-Byzantine border warfare, see rather than Brooks's excerpts Hitti's complete translation. For this period the Syriac chronicles of Michael the Syrian and Elijah of Nisibis also become of some use, though usually for events in the East rather than in Constantinople. The Armenian history of Leontius (Łewond) extends from 632 to 788. The main sources for Italy continue to be Paul the Deacon, who ends with 744, and the *Liber Pontificalis*. Africa is almost a blank.

As a rule these years also have the least satisfactory secondary literature. The first edition of Bury's *History* includes treatment of the whole period, as does Ostrogorsky's *History*, which now becomes fairly detailed. Jenkins' *Byzantium* is informal and uneven. The most comprehensive coverage of the period up to 711 is in Stratos, *Byzantium*, the work of an industrious amateur historian who sometimes goes astray, particularly in exaggerating the empire's control over the Balkans. John Haldon, *Byzantium in the Seventh Century* (Cambridge, 1990), provides the most recent references to other works, but adds little of his own beyond Marxist theorizing.

On the Balkans, see Fine, *Early Medieval Balkans*, and for Bulgaria see Beševliev, *Protobulgarische Periode*, which for this time mostly supersedes Runciman, *Bulgarian Empire*. On Anatolia and the Arabs, see Cheira, *Lutte*, and especially Lilie, *Byzantinische Reaktion*. On Armenia, one may begin with J. Laurent, *L'Arménie entre Byzance et l'Islam depuis la conquête arabe jusqu'en 886*, new ed. by M. Canard (Lisbon, 1980), a hybrid compilation based on a book written in 1919. Kaegi, *Military Unrest*, adds some pertinent material.

Chapter 9: 610–668

Besides Theophanes and Nicephorus's *Short History*, the *Paschal Chronicle* is quite informative until it breaks off in 628, as is the fragment of John of Nikiu from 640 to 646. The poems of George of Pisidia (ed. with Italian trans. and commentary Agostino Pertusi, *Georgio di Pisidia, Poemi* I, *Panegirici epici* [Ettal, 1959]) give a detailed if allusive picture of the reign of Heraclius. On Caucasian affairs and sporadically on Byzantine history, the Armenian history of Sebeus gives some important information until it concludes in 661. The *Miracles of St. Demetrius* does something to fill the gaping hole in our sources for Balkan history.

The most complete history of Byzantium is in the first three volumes of Stratos, *Byzantium*. See also Speck, *Geteilte Dossier*, with dubious conjectures about hypothetical sources but some persuasive conclusions. Pasquale Corsi, *La spedizione italiana di Costante II* (Bologna, 1983), breaks little new ground. Jones, *Prosopography*, continues until 641. On the Arab invasion of Syria, F. M. Donner, *The Early Islamic Conquests* (Princeton, 1981), gives a detailed analysis of the Arabic sources, but by neglecting other sources falls short of being definitive. Walter Kaegi, *Byzantium and the Early Islamic Conquests* (Cambridge, 1992), makes more use of Byzantine material. For the Arab invasion of Egypt, see the old and prudent work of Alfred J. Butler, first published in 1902, *The Arab Conquest of Egypt and the Last Thirty Years of the Roman Dominion*, 2d ed. by P. M. Fraser (Oxford, 1978). For the Balkans, the commentary in Lemerle's *Plus anciens recueils* is actually the best guide.

Chapter 10: 668−717

Here the sources hit their nadir. The main ones remain Theophanes and the *Short History* of Nicephorus, though both are confused and repeat reports that are absurdly biased against Justinian II. Arab chronicles, the *Miracles of St. Demetrius*, and the *Liber Pontificalis* provide more scraps of information.

Volumes IV and V of Stratos, *Byzantium*, cover the years up to 711, not very perceptively. They are better, however, than the popularization by Constance Head, *Justinian II of Byzantium* (Madison, 1972). Lemerle's *Plus anciens recueils* remains valuable for the Balkans, and Lilie's *Byzantinische Reaktion* is important for Anatolia. On the chronology from 685 to 717, see Treadgold, "Seven Byzantine Revolutions," which revises Ostrogorsky's "Chronologie."

Chapter 11: 717−780

From this point our information improves slightly as the common source of Theophanes and Nicephorus's *Short History* becomes better, and both chroniclers approach their own times.

Yet the secondary literature remains deficient, most of all in syntheses. The nearest thing to a general work on Leo III's reign is Karl Schenk, *Kaiser Leon III: Ein Beitrag des Bilderstreits* I (Halle, 1880), a fragment that stops with 720. The only general work on Constantine V's reign is Alfred Lombard, *Études d'histoire byzantine: Constantin V, empereur des Romains* (Paris, 1902), which remains of some use but goes too far in correcting the sources' bias against Constantine. By comparison Iconoclasm under those two emperors has received extensive treatment. See especially the two complementary studies of Gero, *Leo III* and *Constantine V*. On the rebellion of Artavasdus, see Speck, *Artabasdos* (but cf. Treadgold, "Missing Year"). Lilie's *Byzantinische Reaktion* remains valuable for the Arab wars.

Chapter 12: Society, 610−780

The sources for social conditions in this period are so poor that they have led scholars to draw utterly discordant conclusions. The archeological evidence is scanty and equivocal, largely because little Anatolian archeology has been done with Byzantine problems in mind. Any argument from silence is usually worthless because the written sources are so limited.

These include unevenly distributed and problematic hagiographical texts, and three informative but brief law codes: the *Farmer's Law* (ed. Zepos, *Jus* II, 63−71; trans. W. Ashburner, *JHS* 30 [1910], 85−108, and *JHS* 32 [1912], 68−95), the *Rhodian Sea Law* (ed. Zepos, *Jus* II, 91−103; trans. W. Ashburner [Oxford, 1909]), and especially the *Ecloga* of Leo III. The *Ecloga* is the only one of the three that is securely dated (to 726) and definitely an official document. The canons of the Quinisext Council of 692 (ed. Mansi, vol. XI) are also interesting.

On the condition of Asia Minor at this time, now see the careful study of Wolfram Brandes, *Die Städte Kleinasiens im 7. und 8. Jahrhundert* (Berlin, 1989). The first chapter of Treadgold, *Byzantine Revival*, gives a survey of the empire in 780.

For the army and government, the sources and studies relate mainly to the subsequent period. See the preliminary remarks of J. B. Bury, *The Imperial Administrative System in the Ninth Century* (London, 1911), which is otherwise superseded by Oikonomidès, *Listes*. F. Winkelmann, *Byzantinische Rang- und Ämterstruktur im 8. und 9. Jahrhundert* (Berlin, 1985), catalogues the evidence without trying to make sense of it.

On the Church in general, see J.-L. van Dieten, *Geschichte der Patriarchen von Sergios I bis Johannes VI (610–715)* (Amsterdam, 1972), and up to 680 Meyendorff's *Imperial Unity*. On Monotheletism, see V. Grumel, "Recherches sur l'histoire de monothélisme," *Échos d'Orient* 31 (1928), 6–16, 257–77; 32 (1929), 19–34, 272–82; and 33 (1930), 16–28. On Iconoclasm, see the intelligent popularization of Martin, *History*, and the collection of papers in Bryer, *Iconoclasm*.

On cultural decline in this period, see especially the first part of Lemerle's *Byzantine Humanism*. On art and architecture, see Ernst Kitzinger, "Byzantine Art in the Period Between Justinian and Iconoclasm," *Berichte zum XI Internationalen Byzantinisten-Kongress* IV.1 (Munich, 1958), and André Grabar, *L'iconoclasme byzantin: Le dossier archéologique*, 2d ed. (Paris, 1984).

On the economy, see Lemerle's *Agrarian History* and Kaplan's *Hommes et la terre*. Treadgold, *Finances*, remains of some use but should be corrected from Treadgold, *Byzantium and Its Army*. On social conditions, P. A. Yannopoulos, *La société profane dans l'empire byzantin des VIIe, VIIIe et IXe siècles* (Louvain, 1975), and F. Winkelmann, *Quellenstudien zur herrschenden Klasse von Byzanz im 8. und 9. Jahrhundert* (Berlin, 1987), are little more than compilations of the evidence.

PART IV: 780–1025

Although the sources for this period are relatively good, their overlappings and chronological confusion often make them hard to use. Among historical works, the chronicle of Symeon the Logothete is usually the best until it ends in 963, but no text better than its plagiarization by Leo Grammaticus has yet been published. The parallel text now called the Pseudo-Symeon adds some important facts, but also some completely fabricated dates that have misled many scholars. The history known as Theophanes Continuatus jumbles much valuable material together with misunderstandings and fictions until 886, when it begins to copy Symeon the Logothete.

The later chronicle of Scylitzes mostly copies Theophanes Continuatus until 944, while the chronicle of Cedrenus mostly copies Scylitzes. Among eastern sources, Michael the Syrian continues to be of uneven value. The extensive and chronologically helpful Arabic sources for the years from 820 to 959 are conveniently collected and translated as sections of Vasiliev, *Byzance et les Arabes* I and II.2. For the themes in this period, see Constantine VII, *De Thematibus*, and particularly the texts edited in Oikonomidès's *Listes*.

Despite the relative abundance of primary sources, no single scholarly history covers this period in particular aside from Jenkins' *Byzantium*, which is for most purposes inferior to Ostrogorsky's *History*. This lack of a comprehensive work on middle Byzantine history might make little difference if the studies of parts of the period were continuous, careful, and up to date; but on the whole they are not.

Byzantine relations with other peoples are better covered. Besides Vasiliev's *Byzance et les Arabes*, Obolensky's *Commonwealth*, and Fine's *Early Medieval Balkans*, see Robert Browning, *Byzantium and Bulgaria* (Berkeley, 1975), which concentrates on the period from 852 to 1018, and the older but longer account in Runciman's *First Bulgarian Empire*. For Byzantine Italy, still see Gay, *Italie*, which treats the years from 867 to 1071; Gay is updated on various points by von Falkenhausen, *Untersuchungen*.

Chapter 13: 780–842

Apart from the sources already cited, including Theophanes for the period up to 813, see the "Scriptor Incertus" (ed. I. Bekker with "Leo Grammaticus," *CSHB* [1842]), a good but fragmentary source for the years from 812 to 816 whose author was probably Sergius Confessor, and Genesius, which parallels Theophanes Continuatus but is less fanciful. The letters of Theodore of Studius (ed. G. Fatouros, 2 vols., *CFHB* [Berlin, 1992]) are quite informative, as is the abundant hagiography for the second period of Iconoclasm. Brooks, "Byzantines," translates excerpts from the Arabic sources for the years before Vasiliev's *Byzance et les Arabes* begins. This part of Michael the Syrian is better than usual but still not very trustworthy.

The whole period is covered in detail by Treadgold, *Byzantine Revival*. Paul Speck, *Kaiser Konstantin VI*, 2 vols. (Munich, 1978), gives an exhaustive account of the years from 780 to 797, based on a highly subjective analysis of the sources. J. B. Bury continued the first edition of his *History*, which ends with 802, in his *Eastern Roman Empire*, which now is largely outdated but often shows good judgment. Niavis, *Nicephorus I*, which appeared after my *Byzantine Revival* went to press, has some useful points to add.

Chapter 14: 842–912

The main histories are the same as for the previous period. Genesius ends with 886. After that date, Theophanes Continuatus is little better than a copy of Symeon the Logothete, which is the best source but somewhat confused for the period before 867. Other sources are fairly abundant, including laws, military and administrative handbooks, letters, orations, and especially hagiography. The most important single sources are the letters of Leo Choerosphactes (ed. with biography and French trans. in Kolias, *Léon Choerosphactès*), the *Vita Euthymii*, and Constantine VII's *De Administrando Imperio*. The Arabic sources are translated in Vasiliev's *Byzance et les Arabes*. At this point the Armenian history of John Catholicus also becomes relevant.

Since the secondary literature has not adequately sifted the sources, future research is likely to modify the account given in my text. Vasiliev's *Byzance et les Arabes* is helpful throughout; but it has been superseded for the Paulicians by Lemerle, "Pauliciens." Jenkins, "Chronological Accuracy," establishes much of the chronology for most of the period.

Bury's *Eastern Roman Empire* continues up to 867, but does not deal well with the confused sources for those years; on those, see P. Karlin-Hayter, "Études sur les deux histoires du règne de Michel III," *Byzantion* 41 (1971), 452–96. The only book on the reign of Basil I is the largely obsolete A. Vogt, *Basile Ier empereur de Byzance et la civilisation byzantine à la fin du IXe siècle* (Paris, 1908). In the absence of any general study of the long and eventful reign of Leo VI, Kolias's *Léon Choerosphactès* and especially Karlin-Hayter's commentary on the *Vita Euthymii* are the best guides. See also P. Karlin-Hayter, "'When Military Affairs Were in Leo's Hands': A Note on Byzantine Foreign Policy (886–912)," *Traditio* 23 (1967), 15–40.

Chapter 15: 912–963

Symeon the Logothete, by now a contemporary, provides the main narrative up to 948, with a brief continuation, possibly by Symeon himself, to 963. Theophanes Continuatus copies Symeon but makes a few additions up to 948, before becoming the better source for the years up to 961. From 944 Scylitzes begins to add significant material to other sources. Leo the Deacon, the first of the classic middle Byzantine histories by contemporaries, begins with 959. Other Greek sources include Constantine VII's *De Administrando Imperio*, the patriarch Nicholas I's *Letters*, Theodore Daphnopates' *Letters* (ed. and trans. J. Darrouzès and L. G. Westerink [Paris, 1978]), and Nicholas I's other writings (ed. and trans. L. G. Westerink, *CFHB* [Washington, 1981]).

In Latin, Liudprand's *Antapodosis* includes interesting information gathered during the author's embassy to Constantinople in 949. The Arabic excerpts in Vasiliev's *Byzance et les Arabes* II.2 extend to 959. From 937 see the particularly informative history of the Christian Arab Yaḥyā of Antioch. Another valuable Arabic history is that of Miskawayh. The contemporary Armenian history of John Catholicus ends with 923.

Runciman's *Romanus Lecapenus* has aged gracefully and remains the best study for the years up to 945. From 945 to 959, one must use Alfred Rambaud, *L'empire grec au dixième siècle: Constantin Porphyrogénète* (Paris, 1870), and Toynbee, *Constantine Porphyrogenitus*, both of which show some of the diffuseness of Constantine's own works. Because of the frequent Arab wars during this period, the text of Vasiliev's *Byzance et les Arabes* is especially valuable. Canard, *Histoire*, adds many details of Byzantine interest, particularly after 959 when Vasiliev ends. Beginning with 959, see the venerable Schlumberger, *Nicéphore Phocas*.

Chapter 16: 963–1025

The principal sources are Leo the Deacon (to 976, with a brief excursus extending to 989) and Scylitzes, who is sometimes confused but after 976 stands almost alone, since most later histories merely copy him. Beginning with 976 the vivid and brilliant memoirs of Psellus add some information, though he is not yet a contemporary. For the army, the treatise *On Skirmishing* of Nicephorus II Phocas (ed. with commentary and French trans. G. Dagron and H. Mihăescu, Paris, 1986) is of interest. The letters of several important figures of the time, notably Nicephorus Uranus, are edited with commentary by Jean Darrouzès, *Épistoliers byzantins du Xe siècle* (Paris, 1960).

Among Arabic sources, the chief are Miskawayh up to 979, from then to 999 his continuer Abū Shujāʿ (trans. in Miskawayh, vol. VI), and above all Yaḥyā of Antioch (though the Kratchkovsky-Vasiliev edition and translation ends with 1013). Also of some use are the Armenian history of Stephen of Taron, which extends to 1003, and the late Syriac history of Bar Hebraeus.

The secondary literature is generally inadequate. Though the whole period is covered by Schlumberger's *Nicéphore Phocas* to 969 and afterward by the first two volumes of his *Épopée byzantine*, these finely crafted antiques need replacement by a modern study. The dissertation of Forsyth, "Byzantine-Arab Chronicle," unfortunately published only in photocopy, is a good guide to the years from 976 to 1025.

Canard's *Histoire* extends to 1004, but with diminishing detail as the Hamdanids of Aleppo become less important. The story of Byzantine-Arab relations is then taken up by the careful work of Felix, *Byzanz*. While no one has yet given a fully satisfactory account of the obscure history of Bulgaria during this time, Runciman's *Bulgarian Empire* is not bad despite its age, and Fine's *Early Medieval Balkans* gives a recent account of the problems. Matters have been complicated by the nationalism of some Balkan scholars, and by the persistent but baseless idea that Basil II set out to conquer Bulgaria from the start.

Chapter 17: Society, 780–1025

Although the scattered but abundant sources would permit an adequate study of society during this time, no one has written it to date. Earlier secondary works tend to take a pessimistic view of economic and social conditions, but the pessimism seems to derive not so much from the sources as from a desire to explain the failures of the later eleventh century.

The sources include many saints' lives, collections of letters, and military and administrative handbooks, some already cited. See the precedence lists edited in Oikonomidès's *Listes* and Leo VI's *Novels* (ed. with French trans. P. Noailles and A. Dain [Paris, 1944]), the *Book of the Prefect* (ed. with German trans. J. Koder, *CFHB* [Vienna, 1991]; English trans. E. H. Freshfield [Cambridge, 1938]), and Constantine VII's *De Ceremoniis*. The description of Byzantium by the Arab geographer Ibn Ḥawqal is also interesting, despite an obtrusive anti-Byzantine bias.

For the cultural revival, particularly illuminating sources are Photius's *Biblio-theca* (ed. with French trans. René Henry, 9 vols. [Paris 1959–91]; unfinished English trans. J. Freese [London, 1920]) and *Letters* and *Amphilochia* (both ed. B. Laourdas and L. G. Westerink, 6 vols. [Leipzig, 1983–88]). The *Suda* is also of importance. The epic poem *Digenes Acrites* (ed. E. Trapp [Vienna, 1971]; trans. with ed. J. Mavrogordato [Oxford, 1956]) gives some of the flavor of provincial aristocratic life.

The best existing survey of the condition of the empire in this period is the sketch in the first section of Hendy's *Studies*. Toynbee's *Constantine Porphyroge-nitus* gives the fullest general description, but misses some points established by Hendy. Along with the local surveys cited above that extend into these years, see particularly Malamut, *Îles*, which has some wider applicability.

On the army, see Kuehn, *Byzantinische Armee*. On the workings of govern-ment, see especially Oikonomidès's *Listes* and his continuation of it, "Évolu-tion." On the aristocracy, see Lemerle's *Agrarian History*, the studies edited in Angold, *Byzantine Aristocracy*, and particularly Cheynet, *Pouvoir*.

Obolensky's *Commonwealth* includes the best general study of the conversion of the Slavs. On the revival of learning, see Wilson's *Scholars* and especially Le-merle's *Byzantine Humanism*. On the economy, besides Hendy's *Studies*, Toyn-bee's *Constantine Porphyrogenitus*, and Treadgold's *Finances*, see Harvey, *Economic Expansion*, with many useful references and questionable Marxist analysis. See also the first two chapters of Kazhdan, *Change*.

PART V: 1025–1204

While this period is covered by many good Byzantine historians, none treats more than half of it except Zonaras. Zonaras's work extends from the Creation to 1118, but until the very end is mostly an intelligent summary of existing sources—so intelligent that he often seems to have had independent informa-tion when he probably had none. This is the first period with significant docu-mentary sources, principally from monasteries and from Venice. Still occasion-ally useful are the Syriac histories of Michael the Syrian (until 1195) and Bar Hebraeus. The Armenian history of Matthew of Edessa with its continuation by Gregory the Priest (trans. together with Matthew) becomes increasingly in-formative for events in the East up to 1162.

Angold, *Byzantine Empire*, gives a good if concise summary of the state of modern knowledge of the whole period, but his interpretation of internal pol-itics is to be revised somewhat in the light of Cheynet's *Pouvoir*. Chalandon, *Les Comnène*, an excellent work for its time, provides more detail for the years from 1081 to 1180. On members of the Comnenus family throughout this pe-riod, see more recently K. Barzos, *Hē genealogia tōn Komnēnōn*, 2 vols. (Thes-salonica, 1984).

Among studies of the Crusades, the collaboration edited by Setton, *History of the Crusades*, is the most extensive, particularly on peripheral aspects of the sub-ject; but Runciman, *History of the Crusades*, still provides the best continuous narrative. Hans Meyer, *The Crusades*, 2d ed. (Oxford, 1988), is shorter and more recent than these. Of particular interest for Byzantine-Crusader relations is the careful work of Lilie, *Byzantium*.

Nicol's *Byzantium and Venice* becomes more important with the growth of Venetian power in this period. More detailed treatment of Byzantine relations with the Italian city-states is provided by Lilie, *Handel*. For relations with the German Empire, consult P. Lamma, *Comneni e Staufer: Ricerche sui rapporti fra Bisanzio e l'Occidente nel secolo XII*, 2 vols. (Rome, 1955–57).

On the Slavs, Obolensky's *Commonwealth* continues, while Fine's *Early Medieval Balkans* is continued after the 1180's by his *Late Medieval Balkans*. For Hungary, see now Makk, *Árpáds*, which makes progress toward resolving the many ambiguities in the sources. On the Turks, see Cahen, *Turquie pré-ottomane* (the earlier English version, *Pre-Ottoman Turkey* [New York, 1968], is much the same but lacks full references).

Chapter 18: 1025–81

The sources are generally good. Scylitzes remains the basic narrative before he ends with 1057. He is continued to 1079 by "Scylitzes Continuatus" (ed. with Greek introduction and notes by E. Tsolakes [Thessalonica, 1968]), which though inferior to the main history may be a later work of Scylitzes himself. The history of Attaliates extends from 1034 to 1080 and supplies the best narrative after 1057, when Attaliates was personally involved in events and shows sound judgment.

Psellus's memoirs are usually the most insightful source until they end in 1077, but Psellus is far from impartial, especially for the period after 1059 when he eulogizes the reigning Ducas dynasty. The memoirs of Bryennius, which run from 1070 to 1081, are detailed but obviously unfinished. The classic history of Bryennius's widow Anna Comnena includes some coverage of events as early as 1069. Unique among other Greek sources is the *Strategicon* of Cecaumenus, a book of advice with historical anecdotes by a prominent official who may possibly be the same as Catacalon Cecaumenus.

A survey more detailed than Angold's *Byzantine Empire* is lacking for this period. The last volume of Schlumberger's *Épopée byzantine*, though somewhat less critical than the others, remains the most detailed history until it ends with 1057. A good deal of information on the period after 1059 can be found in Demetrios Polemis, *The Doukai: A Contribution to Byzantine Prosopography* (London, 1968), and the same author's "Notes on Eleventh-Century Chronology (1059–1081)," *BZ* 58 (1965), 60–76. Chalandon's *Les Comnène* begins with an account of the years just before 1081.

Felix's *Byzanz* covers relations with Muslim powers until 1055. Thereafter the best guide is usually Claude Cahen, "La première pénétration turque en Asie-Mineure (seconde moitié du XIe siècle)," *Byzantion* 18 (1948), 5–67, though Honigmann's *Ostgrenze* is also helpful up to 1071. A. Friendly, *The Dreadful Day: The Battle of Manzikert, 1071* (London, 1981), while amateurish and unreliable, tries to meet a real need for a detailed explanation of the context of the battle.

The decade after 1071, one of the most momentous intervals in Byzantine history, has been unwarrantably neglected by modern scholars.

Chapter 19: 1081–1143

Until 1118, the two main sources are Anna Comnena and Zonaras, both contemporary and astute, but careless about chronology. Anna Comnena is much the more detailed, and her partisanship for Alexius involves no very serious distortion, though Zonaras's less favorable view provides a corrective. With 1118 the main sources become the histories of Cinnamus and particularly Choniates, though both are much less concerned with this period than with that after 1143. Among supplementary sources, Theophylact of Ochrid's letters and other works supply material for most of the reign of Alexius I. The letters and orations of Michael Italicus, and especially the historical poems of Theodore Prodromus (ed. with German summaries and commentary W. Hörandner [Vienna, 1974]), provide needed information for most of the reign of John II.

Among the Latin historians of the First Crusade and its aftermath, perhaps the most useful for Byzantine history are Raymond of Aguilers (ed. J. H. Hill and L. L. Hill [Paris, 1969]; trans. by the same [Philadelphia, 1968]), Fulcher of Chartres (ed. H. Hagenmeyer [Heidelberg, 1913]; trans. F. R. Ryan [Knoxville, 1969]), and the anonymous *Gesta Francorum* (ed. and trans. Rosalind Hill [London, 1962]). For the Second Crusade, William of Tyre (ed. R. B. C. Huygens, 2 vols., *Corpus Christianorum* [Turnhout, 1986]); trans. E. A. Babcock and A. C. Krey, 2 vols. [New York, 1943]) has more to say about Byzantium.

Chalandon's *Les Comnène* remains the standard treatment of the whole period. Skoulatos, *Personnages*, supplements and updates Chalandon on various points up to 1118. Yet the reign of John II in particular, with its vexed sources, would benefit from a thorough new study.

Chapter 20: 1143–1204

The principal sources for the period remain the histories of Cinnamus (until he breaks off in 1176) and Choniates. At this point the chronicle usually attributed to Scutariotes begins to include information of independent value. Eustathius of Thessalonica's *On the Capture of Thessalonica* (ed. S. Kyriakidis [Palermo, 1961]; trans. with reprinted ed. John R. M. Jones [Canberra, 1988]) supplies an account of events from 1180, leading up to an eyewitness account of the city's sack by the Normans in 1185.

The letters and orations of Michael Italicus continue to be of use for the first part of Manuel's reign, and later those of Choniates become especially informative. Among the crusader historians, William of Tyre remains useful until 1184. The Old French chronicles of Robert of Clari (ed. P. Lauer [Paris, 1924]; trans. E. H. McNeal [New York, 1936]), and particularly Geoffrey of Villehardouin, are essential sources for the Fourth Crusade.

The second volume of Chalandon's *Les Comnène* remains the standard history of Manuel Comnenus's reign, but is now updated in many respects by the interpretive study of Magdalino, *Manuel I.* For the remainder of the period,

Brand, *Byzantium*, offers a clear and detailed narrative. Van Dieten, *Niketas Choniates*, derives many historical details not only from Choniates' speeches and letters but from other sources.

On the Fourth Crusade, apart from general works on the Crusades and Nicol's *Byzantium and Venice*, Donald Queller, *The Fourth Crusade: The Conquest of Constantinople* (Philadelphia, 1977), presents a pro-Venetian interpretation, while John Godfrey, *1204: The Unholy Crusade* (Oxford, 1980), gives a traditional and more likely one. For Genoa, see G. W. Day, *Genoa's Response to Byzantium, 1155–1204* (Urbana, 1978).

Chapter 21: Society, 1025–1204

Among the abundant and varied sources not already mentioned are the *Letters* of John Tzetzes (ed. P. A. M. Leone [Leipzig, 1972]), the *Letters and Orations* of Michael Choniates (ed. S. P. Lampros, 2 vols. [Athens, 1879–80]), and the vernacular poems of Theodore Prodromus (ed. D.-C. Hesseling and H. Pernot [Amsterdam, 1910]). For interesting though brief descriptions of the twelfth-century empire by outsiders, consult the Arabic geography of Idrīsī and the Hebrew account of the traveler Benjamin of Tudela. Among documents, some of particular interest for economic history from the Venetian archives are edited in the first volume of Tafel, *Urkunden*.

A good general treatment of most aspects of society in this period appears in Kazhdan, *Change*. Lemerle, *Cinq études*, treats several topics of general interest for the eleventh century, while Magdalino's *Manuel I* surveys most of the twelfth.

On regionalism, see Cheynet's *Pouvoir*, which largely replaces Jürgen Hoffman, *Rudimente von Territorialstaaten im byzantinischen Reich (1071–1210)* (Munich, 1974). On Anatolia, Vryonis, *Decline*, includes much valuable material but shows an unfortunate lack of scholarly detachment (cf. Vryonis's reply to reviews of his book in *Greek Orthodox Theological Review* 27 [1982], 225–85). Cahen's *Turquie pré-ottomane* covers the same ground more summarily but more judiciously.

On the army and administration, see Kuehn's *Byzantinische Armee* and Oikonomidès's "Évolution" for the eleventh century, and for the twelfth century A. Hohlweg, *Beiträge zur Verwaltungsgeschichte des oströmischen Reiches unter den Komnenen* (Munich, 1965).

On the Church, besides the relevant part of Hussey's *Orthodox Church* see Runciman's *Eastern Schism*, an evenhanded treatment of a controversial matter. On culture, besides Kazhdan's *Change* and Wilson's *Scholars*, see Kazhdan, *Studies*.

On the economy in this period, see especially Hendy's *Studies* and Harvey's *Economic Expansion*. After Grierson's *Catalogue* ends with 1081, Hendy, *Coinage*, becomes the best guide to the coinage.

PART VI: 1204–1461

The events of these years, of a complexity disproportionate to their importance, are relatively well documented. Among several good Greek historians, the only one to cover more than half the period, running from 1203 to 1359, is the long-winded, untidy, but informative Gregoras. The chronicle of Michael Panaretus (ed. O. Lampsides, *Archeion Pontou* 22 [1958], 5–128), though brief and bald, is the only narrative source for the history of the Empire of Trebizond. See also the collection of short chronicles, covering all of Byzantine history but mainly useful for the period after 1204, in Schreiner, *Byzantinischen Kleinchroniken*, which includes a helpful commentary in chronological order in vol. II and an index in vol. III.

Nicol, *Last Centuries*, provides a trustworthy and readable narrative of the history of the restored Byzantine Empire, excluding Epirus and Trebizond. For Epirus, see the same author's *Despotate* I and *Despotate* II. There is no satisfactory history of the Empire of Trebizond as such; the treatment of the empire in Janssens, *Trébizonde*, mostly supersedes the brief work of Miller, *Trebizond*, while Karpov, *Impero*, adds something on Trebizond's foreign relations.

On Latin Greece, Miller, *Latins*, remains valuable; but Longnon, *Empire latin*, is more recent and includes the whole Latin Empire. On the Venetians in the East, in addition to Nicol's *Byzantium and Venice* see Thiriet, *Romanie*; a parallel work on the Genoese is Balard, *Romanie*, though like Thiriet he pays little attention to relations with Byzantium. For papal-Byzantine relations, see especially Setton, *Papacy*. Setton, *History of the Crusades*, retains its usefulness.

Fine's *Late Medieval Balkans* gradually comes to include all of Byzantine history as the empire loses its holdings in Asia Minor. On the Turks, after Cahen's *Turquie pré-ottomane* now see Imber, *Ottoman Empire*. The nearly complete *Prosopographisches Lexicon der Palaiologenzeit*, ed. E. Trapp et al., 11 vols. (Vienna, 1976–91; in progress), is a comprehensive reference work for persons from all but the earliest part of the period, though the entries are sometimes confusingly arranged.

Chapter 22: 1204–1261

The sources for these chaotic times leave important ambiguities and gaps. The histories of Choniates and Geoffrey of Villehardouin cover the repercussions of the Fourth Crusade to 1207. Thereafter the principal source is the contemporary history of George Acropolites (ed. A. Heisenberg with corrections by P. Wirth [Stuttgart, 1978]), drawn upon and added to by the histories of Scutariotes and Gregoras. The very end of the period is included in the knowledgeable if chronologically confusing history of Pachymeres.

The curious *Chronicle of the Morea*, pro-Latin and extant in vernacular Greek verse as well as Old French, Italian, and Aragonese prose versions, supplies some good evidence about Latin rule in the Peloponnesus and nonsense about other regions. The history of the Seljuks of Iconium written in Persian by Ibn Bībī also sheds light on the Nicene and Trapezuntine empires.

The secondary literature becomes fragmented along with the empire. For the Empire of Nicaea, the only connected history is the old study of Alice Gardner, *The Lascarids of Nicaea: The Story of an Empire in Exile* (London, 1912), though it can be partly brought up to date from Angold, *Byzantine Government*. The end of the period is covered by Jean Pappadopoulos, *Théodore II Lascaris, empereur de Nicée* (Paris, 1908), and by the beginning of Geanakoplos, *Michael Palaeologus*, which mostly replaces Chapman, *Michel Paléologue*. All of these are now to be corrected from Failler, "Chronologie et composition."

For the poorly attested history of Epirus and the Empire of Thessalonica, Nicol's *Despotate* I should be updated from the introduction to his *Despotate* II and from Günter Prinzing, "Studien zur Provinz- und Zentralverwaltung im Machtbereich der epirotischen Herrscher Michael I. und Theodoros Dukas," *Ēpeirōtika Chronika* 12 (1982), 73–120, and 13 (1983), 37–109. On the obscure history of the Empire of Trebizond, besides Miller's *Trebizond* and Karpov's *Impero* see A. A. Vasiliev, "The Foundation of the Empire of Trebizond (1204–1222)," *Speculum* 11 (1936), 3–37.

On the Latin Empire, see Miller's *Latins*, Longnon's *Empire latin*, Antonio Carile, *Per una storia dell'impero latino di Costantinopoli (1204–1261)*, 2d ed. (Bologna, 1978), and Benjamin Hendrickx, "Régestes des empereurs latins de Constantinople (1204–1261/1272)," *Byzantina* 14 (1988), 7–221. Fine's *Late Medieval Balkans* is handy for pulling the disparate parts of the story together.

Chapter 23: 1261–1328

The principal sources remain the histories of Pachymeres and Gregoras, with Pachymeres the more important until he ends in 1308. With 1320 begins the uniquely well-informed history of Cantacuzenus, Byzantium's only emperor-historian. The Greek version of the *Chronicle of the Morea* is a major source for the history of the Peloponnesus until 1292. Ibn Bībī continues to be of some help until he concludes in 1280. The Catalan chronicle of Ramon Muntaner (ed. E. B., 2 vols. [Barcelona, 1927–51]; trans. Anna Goodenough, 2 vols. [London, 1920–21]) includes a detailed account of the episode of the Catalan Grand Company, of which Muntaner was a member.

The whole period is covered by Nicol's *Last Centuries*. For the reign of Michael VIII, see Chapman's *Michel Paléologue* and especially Geanakoplos's *Michael Palaeologus*, though its focus on relations with the West leaves it an incomplete picture. The same limitation applies to Laiou's *Constantinople*, which overstates the empire's internal weaknesses so as to minimize the defects of Andronicus II. All three books are corrected on various points by Failler, "Chronologie et composition." The last years of Andronicus II's reign are also covered by Bosch, *Andronikos III*. On the advance of the Turks in Asia Minor, in addition to Imber's *Ottoman Empire* see Paul Lemerle, *L'émirat d'Aydin, Byzance et l'Occident: Recherches sur "La Geste d'Umur Pacha"* (Paris, 1957), and Zachariadou, *Trade and Crusade*.

Chapter 24: 1328–1391

Until the lengthy contemporary histories of Cantacuzenus and Gregoras end with 1356 and 1359, we are amply informed. For the period that follows, skeletal and not very dependable narratives are included in the much later histories of Chalcondyles, Ducas, and the *Chronicon Maius* of Pseudo-Sphrantzes (ed. with Romanian trans. Vasile Grecu [Bucharest, 1966]), which was probably compiled by Archbishop Macarius of Monemvasia in the sixteenth century. The notices in Schreiner's *Byzantinischen Kleinchroniken* become increasingly helpful for these years. Further supplementary evidence appears in documents, orations, and letters, especially those of Demetrius Cydones (ed. R.-J. Loenertz, 2 vols. [Vatican City, 1956–60]), which are dated between 1347 and 1394. Venetian, Genoese, and other western sources are occasionally of assistance.

Nicol's *Last Centuries* is the most detailed study of the whole period, and the best for most aspects of it. Bosch's *Andronikos III* continues through the reign of Andronicus III. On the civil war, Eva de Vries–van der Velden, *L'élite byzantine devant l'avance turque à l'epoque de la guerre civile de 1341 à 1354* (Amsterdam, 1990), is often ill judged but sometimes interesting. On John VI Cantacuzenus before, during, and after his reign, see Nicol, *Byzantine Family*, and especially Günter Weiss, *Joannes Kantakouzenos—Aristokrat, Staatsman, Kaiser und Mönch— in der Gesellschaftsentwicklung von Byzanz im 14. Jahrhundert* (Wiesbaden, 1969).

O. Halecki, *Un empereur de Byzance à Rome: Vingt ans de travail pour l'union des églises et pour la défense de l'empire d'Orient, 1355–1375* (Warsaw, 1930), has largely been superseded by Nicol's *Last Centuries*. A summary account of John V's reign appears in the first chapter of Barker, *Manuel II*. George Dennis, *The Reign of Manuel II Palaeologus in Thessalonica, 1382–1387* (Rome, 1960), also remains of some use.

For the Serbs in this period, see Soulis, *Serbs and Byzantium*. Fine's *Late Medieval Balkans*, Nicol's *Despotate* II, Imber's *Ottoman Empire*, and Setton's *Papacy* continue to be useful.

Chapter 25: 1391–1461

As the fall of Constantinople approaches, the sources improve. Chalcondyles and Ducas become well-informed contemporaries; they are joined by two additional contemporary sources, the melancholy memoirs of Sphrantzes, which begin with 1413, and the pro-Turkish history of the conquest by Critobulus, beginning only with 1451. All four extend past 1461. The short chronicles in Schreiner, *Byzantinischen Kleinchroniken*, remain important. Nearly all the sources for the fall of Constantinople are edited (with Italian translation) by A. Pertusi, *La caduta di Costantinopoli*, 2 vols. (Verona, 1976), and *Testi inediti e poco noti sulla caduta di Costantinopoli* (Bologna, 1983). Also to be consulted are Manuel II's *Letters* (ed. and trans. George Dennis, *CFHB* [Washington, 1977]) and funeral oration on his brother, the despot Theodore (ed. and trans. J. Chrysostomides, *CFHB* [Thessalonica, 1985]).

Nicol's *Last Centuries* and Fine's *Late Medieval Balkans* cover the whole period. The most detailed treatment of the earlier part is Barker's *Manuel II*, which can be supplemented in some respects by Klaus-Peter Matschke, *Die Schlacht bei Ankara und das Schicksal von Byzanz: Studien zur spätbyzantinischen Geschichte zwischen 1402 und 1422* (Weimar, 1981). After the reign of John VIII, which has attracted less interest than Manuel's, the events surrounding the fall of Constantinople are the subject of Steven Runciman, *The Fall of Constantinople, 1453* (Cambridge, 1965), and Donald Nicol, *The Immortal Emperor: The Life and Legend of Constantine Palaiologos, Last Emperor of the Romans* (Cambridge, 1992).

Chapter 26: Society, 1204–1461

For this period several foreign travelers give detailed accounts of the Byzantine world. The most informative are Ibn Baṭṭūṭa for 1325–54 in Arabic, Ruy González de Clavijo for 1403–6 in Spanish, Bertrandon de la Broquière for 1432–33 in French, and Pero Tafur for 1435–39 in Spanish. The Slavonic accounts of Russian pilgrims are chiefly concerned with churches in Constantinople, but give some idea of the dilapidated state of the city (ed. and trans. Majeska, *Russian Travelers*).

This is the only Byzantine period with extensive documentary sources, most of them relating to the Church. Those from Mount Athos, including some of earlier date, are being published in G. Millet et al., eds., *Archives de l'Athos*, 17 vols. (Paris, 1937–91; in progress). The largest collection of other documents is in F. Miklosich and J. Müller, eds., *Acta et Diplomata Graeca Medii Aevi Sacra et Profana*, 6 vols. (Vienna, 1860–90). The fourteenth-century *Treatise on Offices* of Pseudo-Codinus (ed. and French trans. Jean Verpeaux [Paris, 1966]) throws light on the workings of the government.

For a description of the Empire of Nicaea, see Angold's *Byzantine Government*; for Epirus, see Nicol's *Despotate* II; and for Trebizond, see Janssens's *Trébizonde*, supplemented by Bryer's *Byzantine Monuments*. On the Peloponnesus, Denis Zakythinos, *Le despotat grec de Morée*, rev. ed. by Chryssa Maltézou, 2 vols. (London, 1975), adds only a few notes to the edition of 1932–53; it can be supplemented by Steven Runciman, *Mistra, Byzantine Capital of the Peloponnese* (London, 1980). Other regional studies for this period are Catherine Asdracha, *La région des Rhodopes aux XIIIe et XIVe siècles: Étude de géographie historique* (Athens, 1976), Paul Bellier et al., *Paysages de Macédoine* (Paris, 1986), and Ahrweiler, "Smyrne."

On the administration, see Raybaud, *Gouvernement*, though its theoretical discussion is not very helpful, and Lj. Maksimovic, *The Byzantine Provincial Administration Under the Palaiologoi* (Amsterdam, 1988), though it shares some of the disorganization of the administration it describes. On the army, Bartusis, *Late Byzantine Army*, is clear and thorough, with wider implications for society at the time.

On the Church, see D. M. Nicol, *Church and Society in the Last Centuries of Byzantium* (Cambridge, 1979), Joseph Gill, *Byzantium and the Papacy, 1198–1400* (New Brunswick, 1979) and *Council of Florence*, and the first part of Steven Runciman, *The Great Church in Captivity: A Study of the Patriarchate of Constantinople from the Eve of the Turkish Conquest to the Greek War of Independence* (Cambridge, 1968). On Mount Athos, see Emmanuel Amand de Mendieta, *Mount Athos: The Garden of the Panaghia* (Berlin, 1972).

For overviews of the cultural revival, see Steven Runciman, *The Last Byzantine Renaissance* (Cambridge, 1970), and Ihor Ševčenko, "The Palaeologan Renaissance," in W. Treadgold, ed., *Renaissances Before the Renaissance* (Stanford, 1984), 144–71. On education, besides Wilson's *Scholars*, see C. N. Constantinides, *Higher Education in Byzantium in the Thirteenth and Early Fourteenth Centuries (1204–ca. 1310)* (Nicosia, 1982). For scholarly contacts with Italy, see Kenneth Setton, "The Byzantine Background to the Italian Renaissance," *Proceedings of the American Philosophical Society* 100 (1956), 1–76, and Nigel Wilson, *From Byzantium to Italy* (Baltimore, 1992). For an overview of the arts, see André Grabar, "The Artistic Climate in Byzantium During the Palaeologan Period," and Otto Demus, "The Style of the Kariye Djami and Its Place in the Development of Palaeologan Art," both in Underwood, *Kariye Djami* IV, 3–16 and 107–60.

On the economy, besides Heyd's *Histoire*, see especially Oikonomidès, *Hommes d'affaires*, a short but important book. Zakythinos, *Crise monétaire*, also remains of interest.

Endnotes

INTRODUCTION

1. Similarly, in North Africa Punic, another Semitic language, long held out against (Indo-European) Latin, but later, like the native languages of Syria and Egypt, succumbed to another Semitic language, Arabic. (Why Hamitic Coptic should have given way so completely to Semitic Arabic remains mysterious.) All this suggests that the problem was linguistic compatibility rather than the strength of the native cultures, which should have been just as deeply rooted in Thrace or Phrygia as in Syria or North Africa. The apparent survival of (Indo-European) Illyrian as modern Albanian seems to be due partly to the Albanians' isolation in rugged terrain, partly to their living in a borderland between Greek and Latin where the two languages diluted each other's influence.

2. The Greeks and Romans, including the Byzantines, used the word "barbarian" for anyone from outside the Greek or Roman world, though they realized that some barbarians, particularly the Persians, had advanced cultures of their own.

CHAPTER ONE

For basic bibliography, see above, pp. 897–98.

1. The evidence for Diocletian's system of taxation is difficult to interpret, and has been the subject of a long controversy. Here I mainly follow the most recent discussion by Carrié, "Dioclétien," who summarizes previous positions and arrives at the most coherent results to date. I have major reservations only about his skepticism that the *jugum* represented variable amounts of land, as stated in a Syrian law book of admittedly dubious date.

2. For the date, see Hendy, *Studies*, 371–78.

3. These estimates are adapted from those of Jones, *Later Roman Empire*, 1057.

4. See Treadgold, *Byzantium and Its Army*, 44–59.

5. On Diocletian's coinage, see Hendy, *Studies*, 448–62.

6. Since this had long been standard practice for emperors in need of money, there is no reason to doubt the hostile contemporary report of Lactantius 7.11–12.

7. On the events of these years, see now Constantin Zuckerman, "Les campagnes des tétrarques, 296–298: Notes de chronologie," *AT* 2 (1994), 65–70.

8. The Unconquered Sun was said to be reborn at each winter solstice, when the days began to become longer again.

9. That is, a superimposed chi (X) and rho (P); for an example, see Fig. 47, the shield at the far left.

10. Constantine and Licinius began the first numbered fifteen-year cycle with 312, but it seems to have origins in the early empire; see Duncan-Jones, *Money and Government*, 59–63.

11. The account in Zosimus (2.33) of Constantine's creation of regional prefectures, despite modern scholars' criticisms of it, seems to be essentially accurate. All the attested praetorian prefects between 324 and 337, except for four assigned to Africa and one (Evagrius) attached to Constantine personally, appear to have administered the following regions:

Britain, Gaul, Spain: Bassus, Saturninus, Tiberianus
Italy: Aemilianus, Pacatianus
Balkans: Maximus
Anatolia, Syria, Egypt: Constantius, Ablabius.

See the references in Barnes, *New Empire*, 131–39.

12. On the Scholae, see Frank, *Scholae*.

13. Such is the usual but misleading English rendering of the Greek *Hagia Eirēnē* (Holy Peace). The dedication was to the Holy Spirit as the Peace of God, not to a saint named Irene.

14. On the foundation of Constantinople, see especially Cyril Mango, *Le développement urbain de Constantinople* (Paris, 1985), a preliminary study for a projected book on the whole history of the city. On its grain supply, see Durliat, *De la ville*, 185–278.

15. The statement of Libanius, *Oration* 30.6, 30.37, that Constantine used the confiscated temple treasures to build Constantinople should be preferred to the statement in Jerome's notoriously unreliable *Chronicle* that the treasures were confiscated only in 331.

16. On the date of these ministries' creation, see Delmaire, *Largesses sacrées*, 26–38.

17. See Durliat, *De la ville*, 250–53, noting that in 342 Constantius II was able to cut the number of rations to 40,000 without causing problems feeding the city's population.

CHAPTER TWO

For basic bibliography, see above, pp. 897–98, 898–99.

1. For Eusebius's story, which is most unlikely to be true, see Philostorgius, 2.16.

2. For some of the dates that follow, see T. D. Barnes, "Imperial Chronology, A.D. 337–350," *Phoenix* 34 (1980), 160–66.

3. This is the misleading English form of the Greek *Hagia Sophia* (Holy Wisdom). The dedication was to Christ as the Wisdom of God, a description of the Son acceptable to both Arians and orthodox.

4. See most recently Gerhard Wirth, "Julians Perserkrieg: Kriterien einer Katastrophe," in Richard Klein, ed., *Julian Apostata* (Darmstadt, 1978), 455–507.

5. Why Procopius had failed to join Julian earlier and prevent the whole fiasco remains obscure.

6. On the increases in taxation and Valens' measures to halt them, see Themistius, *Oration* 8.113A–C, a source which has both the strength and the weakness of having been delivered before Valens himself in 368.

7. Themistius, *Oration* 8.112A–113C.

8. See W. Liebeschuetz, "The Finances of Antioch in the Fourth Century A.D.," *BZ* 52 (1959), 344–56.

9. Those who do not believe in divination may suspect that this story was made up after Theodosius I succeeded Valens. But see n. 12 below.

10. On the circumstances, see T. S. Burns, "The Battle of Adrianople: A Reconsideration," *Historia* 22 (1973), 336–45.

11. See Hoffman, *Bewegungsheer* I, 444.

12. If the diviners of 371 really had predicted that the next emperor's name would begin with *THEOD-* (see n. 9 above), awareness of this may have influenced Gratian to execute Theodosius's father, who was also named Theodosius, and then to bow to fate and choose the son when a vacancy occurred. For a discussion of the mysteries surrounding the father's execution, see A. Demandt, "Der Tod des älteren Theodosius," *Historia* 18 (1969), 598–625.

13. See Lallemand, *Administration*, 55–57, who dates the creation of the diocese to 380 or 381.

14. For Theodosius's recruiting, see *Theodosian Code* VII, 13.8–11, dating between 380 and 382.

15. Contrary to later opinion, the names "Ostrogoths" and "Visigoths" do not mean "Eastern Goths" and "Western Goths"; in fact, when these names first came into use the Visigoths were settled to the east of the Ostrogoths. "Visigoths" rather means "Noble Goths," while "Ostrogoths" means "Goths of the Rising Sun." See Wolfram, *History of the Goths*, 24–26.

16. The treaty was signed on 5 October, and the transfer of Illyricum had occurred by 9 December, when Flavius Hypatius was evidently prefect of both Italy and Illyricum; cf. *Theodosian Code* XI, 16.15 with Ammianus, XXIX, 2.16. Before this time, military necessity presumably kept Illyricum under Theodosius's jurisdiction.

17. Much about this settlement remains unclear; see most recently Blockley, *East Roman Foreign Policy*, 42–44.

18. On this transfer of troops from West to East and the organization of the two praesental armies, see Hoffman, *Bewegungsheer*, 469–507, who dates both developments to 388. For the numbers, see Treadgold, *Byzantium and Its Army*, 50.

CHAPTER THREE

For basic bibliography, see above, pp. 897–98, 899–900.

1. For a demonstration that Stilicho and the rulers of the East quarreled over Stilicho's claim to be regent for Arcadius—not over a claim that Illyricum belonged to the West, as many have believed—see Alan Cameron, "Theodosius the Great and the Regency of Stilico," *Harvard Studies in Classical Philology* 73 (1969), 247–80.

2. In what follows I accept the essentials of the reconstruction of Cameron, *Barbarians*, revising the previously accepted chronology and reinterpreting the enigmatic account of these events in Synesius of Cyrene's allegorical *De Providentia*. There the good Prince Osiris evidently represents Aurelian, and the evil Prince Typho Aurelian's brother Caesarius, who succeeded him as prefect of the East.

3. I am not persuaded by the redating of Fravitta's death from 401 or (more probably) 402 to "as late as 405" by Cameron, *Barbarians*, 236–52. Such a late date rests on no solid evidence, and depends on two dubious assumptions: that the East and West were on good terms in 402, despite Alaric's invasion, and that John was still powerful enough to force such a controversial measure in 405, after the death of his patroness Eudoxia.

4. Later the surrounding bays and marshes filled in, so that now Ravenna is several miles inland; but at this date it lay within a lagoon like today's Venice, and could not be stormed by land.

5. Eudocia, whose pagan name had been Athenaïs, was the daughter of an Athenian philosopher.

6. See Brian Croke, "Evidence for the Hun Invasion of Thrace in A.D. 422," *GRBS* 18 (1977), 347–67.

7. Theodosius's suspicions linked Eudocia with the former master of offices Paulinus, who was executed, though no proof was forthcoming.

8. On the activities of the Isaurians at this time, which are extremely obscure, see E. A. Thompson, "The Isaurians Under Theodosius II," *Hermathena* 68 (1946), 18–31.

9. This seems the most plausible interpretation of an entry in the *Suda* under "Ardabur" (ed. Adler, A 3803).

CHAPTER FOUR

For basic bibliography, see above, pp. 897–98, 900–902.

1. Grain for Rome was then drawn from North Africa, an instance of the tendency of the eastern and western parts of the empire to become economically independent.

2. See Treadgold, *Byzantium and Its Army*, 58–59. There I also estimate that the eastern army had some 250,000 men in 305, since 50,000 or so soldiers had been transferred to the East from the West by 395. These figures omit the eastern fleets, which had perhaps 23,000 seamen before Diocletian and 32,000 after

him, and the soldiers of western Illyricum, which was part of the East under Diocletian but not in 395.

3. Jones, *Later Roman Empire*, 1057.

4. Each year of the indiction began on 1 September. According to the fifteen-year indictional cycle, years were numbered from 1 to 15, each year 15 being followed by a new year 1.

5. On the wealth of eastern and western senators, see Jones, *Later Roman Empire*, 554–57, and on the taxes they paid at the emperor's accession, see Hendy, *Studies*, 175, 408.

6. On the evidence for landholding in Egypt, see A. H. M. Jones, "Census Records of the Later Roman Empire," *JRS* 43 (1953), 58–64. For more recent findings, see Alan Bowman, "Landholding in the Hermopolite Nome," *JRS* 75 (1985), 137–55, suggesting that townsmen's holdings, some of them quite small, comprised a maximum of 25 percent of that region. For sound criticism of some previous ideas of the size of large estates in Egypt, see Gascou, "Grands domaines."

7. A younger Symeon the Stylite, who emulated the elder one, was to appear in the next century, also in northern Syria.

8. See Louis Swift, *The Early Fathers on War and Military Service* (Wilmington, 1983).

9. On literacy, see William V. Harris, *Ancient Literacy* (Cambridge, Mass., 1989), 285–322, though the moderate decline that he documents in rural Egypt and the Latin West seems much less evident in the well-Hellenized parts of the East.

10. This was Ammonius Saccas, reportedly a lapsed Christian; see Eusebius, *History*, 6.19.

11. See Samuel Rubenson, *The Letters of St. Antony: Origenist Theology, Monastic Tradition and the Making of a Saint* (Lund, 1990).

12. See most recently Jaroslav Pelikan, *Christianity and Classical Culture: The Metamorphosis of Natural Theology in the Christian Encounter with Hellenism* (New Haven, 1993).

13. See Constantine's edict of 334, *Theodosian Code* XIII, 4.1.

14. Synesius, *De Regno* 14D. In typical Byzantine fashion, Synesius borrowed his simile from a classical source, Plato, *Philebus* 21C.

15. On these neglected and poorly attested epidemics, see McNeill, *Plagues*, 103–9.

16. These figures are adapted from the tables in McEvedy, *Atlas*.

17. Tamara Lewit, *Agricultural Production in the Roman Economy, A.D. 200–400* (Oxford, 1991).

18. On Constantinople, see Cyril Mango, "The Water Supply of Constantinople," in Mango, *Constantinople*, 9–18, and Jacoby, "Population." Durliat, *De la ville*, 250–65, first notes that the grain ration in 332–42, which would have fed some 240,000 people, was more than double what the population needed; but then he uses the sixth-century grain ration to estimate Constantinople's population at 500,000 to 600,000, assuming that all of it was consumed in the city. A more likely conclusion is that the ration of the sixth century, like that of

the fourth, included what were in effect large payments in kind, or perhaps rather subsidized sales, to various officials and landlords. This grain they would have sold outside the city at a profit, so that it would have fed many more people than those in the city itself.

19. On Alexandria, see Russell, *Late Ancient and Medieval Population*, 66–67. On Antioch, see Libanius, *Epistula* no. 1137 Wolf = no. 1119 Förster, and cf. Liebeschuetz, *Antioch*, 92–100.

20. John Chrysostom, *In Acta Homilia* 9.3, PG 60, col. 97. When living at Antioch Chrysostom had guessed that about a tenth of the people there were utterly destitute: *In Matthaeum Homilia* 66, PG 58, col. 630. But these are far from being scientific estimates.

21. Note the sensible argument of Donald Engels, *Roman Corinth: An Alternative Model for the Classical City* (Chicago, 1990), 121, that cities over 10,000 could not have supported themselves chiefly by agriculture (though otherwise I find Engels's view of classical cities somewhat overoptimistic).

22. See Tchalenko, *Villages* I, esp. 422–26. But note that he thinks this region may also have benefited from the decline of other olive-growing areas in Greece and the West.

23. Cf. M. I. Finley, *Ancient Slavery and Modern Ideology* (Harmondsworth, 1983), 123–49. Christian influence to the contrary, household slavery declined much less than agricultural slavery and remained significant through most of Byzantine history.

24. John the Lydian, III, 43.

25. For these budgetary estimates, see Treadgold, *Byzantium and Its Army*, 188–95.

26. The calculation for the whole empire around 300, based on Treadgold, *Byzantium and Its Army*, 49–59 and 195, is as follows:

pay of soldiers (581,000 × 12 nom. × ⅓)	9.296M nom.
pay of oarsmen (64,000 × 12 nom. × ¾)	0.96
uniforms and arms (581,000 × 5 nom.)	2.905
fodder and horses (51,000 × 5 nom.)	0.255
campaigns and other military expenses	1.0
pay of bureaucracy	2.0
other nonmilitary expenses and surplus	1.6
TOTAL	18.016M nom.

For the Roman estimates, see Duncan-Jones, *Money and Government*, 45–46, with lower and higher estimates that average 907.5 million sesterces for ca. 150 and 1,537.5 million sesterces for ca. 215. The sesterce was valued at 1/4,500 lb. gold from Nero's reign until 215 and at 1/5,000 lb. gold in 215, so that the sesterce may be calculated at 0.016 nom. before 215 and then at 0.0144 nom.

27. Duncan-Jones, *Money and Government*, 213–47.

28. For numbers and pay around 200, see Duncan-Jones, *Money and Government*, 33–35 (the pay is 1,200 sesterces), with ibid. 45 on the proportion of military spending.

29. This is approximately the conclusion of C. R. Whittaker, "Inflation and the Economy in the Fourth Century A.D.," in King, *Imperial Revenue*, 1–22.

CHAPTER FIVE

For basic bibliography, see above, pp. 902–3.

1. Timothy supposedly received his epithet because he crept about Alexandria at night to plot against Chalcedonians.

2. See R. M. Harrison, "The Emperor Zeno's Real Name," *BZ* 74 (1981), 27–28, for a demonstration that the Isaurian's name was Tarasis (Tarasius) son of Codisas, not, as was once believed, Tarasicodissa.

3. Cf. Frank, *Scholae*, 204–6.

4. For the problems connected with these statistics—the figure for expenditure seems exaggerated by including the regular pay and donatives for the men—see Treadgold, *Byzantium and Its Army*, 189–91.

5. Verina's lover Patricius, not to be confused with Aspar's younger son of the same name, was a Byzantine and a former master of offices.

6. This Zeno was presumably born after Armatus's son Basiliscus-Leo briefly became heir to the throne in 476, but so soon thereafter that the younger Zeno was already an adolescent when he died before 491; see *Suda*, Z 84 Adler. The opinion of some modern authorities that he was Zeno's son by an earlier marriage seems unlikely.

7. The Amals were then the ruling house of the Ostrogoths.

8. This Marcian had married Leo I's younger daughter Leontia, whose first marriage to Aspar's son Patricius had ended either with Patricius's death or by annulment.

9. Many scholars have assumed that these interests camouflaged profound political, religious, and social concerns; but a persuasive case to the contrary has been made by Alan Cameron in his *Porphyrius the Charioteer* (Oxford, 1973) and *Circus Factions*. For additional evidence, now see Charlotte Roueché, *Performers and Partisans at Aphrodisias in the Roman and Late Roman Periods* (London, 1993).

10. See John Malalas, pp. 392–93 Dindorf, dating the incident to the year 543 of the Antiochene Era (494/95).

11. The Isaurians' favorite, Zeno's brother Longinus, died in exile the next year.

12. So John Malalas, p. 394 Dindorf.

13. The facts of the generosity of the allowances and the availability of volunteers are noted by Jones, *Later Roman Empire*, 668–74, though he fails to make the connection of cause and effect. The increase in the field soldiers' pay seems to have been from an average of about 14 nomismata to 17 nomismata, or from 9 to about 12 nomismata excluding the cost of arms and uniforms. See Treadgold, *Byzantium and Its Army*, 149–54 (including a discussion of the later increase in the *annona*, which in effect raised pay to 20 nomismata a year).

14. John the Lydian, III, 49.

15. Joshua the Stylite, 54, p. 44 Wright; cf. Procopius, *Wars* I, 8.1–4.

16. See Treadgold, *Byzantium and Its Army*, 153.

17. Procopius, *Secret History* 19.7, records Anastasius's reserve at 320,000 pounds of gold (23,040,000 nomismata).

CHAPTER SIX

For basic bibliography, see above, pp. 902–3.

1. The source is Procopius, *Wars* VII, 40.5–6, where "Justin," the reading of all the manuscripts, has been emended to "Justinian" by modern editors for no good reason.

2. On the formation of the Army of Armenia see *Justinian Code* I, 29.5; and on its strength see Procopius, *Wars* I, 15.11 (noting that in 530 it was half the size of a Persian force of 30,000); for the strength of the Army of the East in 531, see Procopius, *Wars* I, 18.5 (at I, 13.23, the figure of 25,000 for 530 seems to include temporary reinforcements).

3. See Tony Honoré, *Tribonian* (London, 1978).

4. The opinion of some modern scholars to the contrary, Justinian seems to have contemplated not abdication but a tactical retreat like that of Zeno in 475.

5. Procopius, *Secret History* 24.12–13. Around 395 there had been some 150,000 eastern frontier troops, and even if they had lost 10 percent of their strength there would have been about 135,000 left in 532. Counting pay of 5 nomismata apiece and an additional third for their officers, these would have earned about a million nomismata a year.

6. Yet Julian believed that Christ had taken suffering and death upon himself by a special act of will, so that the consequences of this extreme dogma were almost orthodox.

7. The interpretations of Chalcedon that Justinian promoted to reconcile Monophysites are often referred to as Neo-Chalcedonianism; but this modern term is somewhat misleading, since the movement never had a body of doctrine distinct from Chalcedonianism (which was itself barely distinguishable from Severan Monophysitism).

8. Procopius, *Wars* III, 11.2–20.

9. Procopius, *Secret History* 16.1–5, reports that Theodahad killed Amalasuntha on orders from Theodora. Bury, *History* II, 163–67, corroborated Procopius's story by using the official correspondence of the Ostrogothic court. Apparently Theodora told Theodahad that she was jealous of Amalasuntha; but the empress's real motive may well have been to trick him into giving Byzantium a pretext to declare war.

10. Procopius, *Wars* V, 5.1–4.

11. Since only a part survives of Justinian's *Novel* 51 of 536, which created this command, it remains somewhat mysterious; see Stein, *Histoire du Bas-Empire* II, 474–75.

12. Shāpūr I had captured the city in 256 and 260.

13. On the bubonic plague in history, see Biraben, *Hommes et la peste*, esp. 22–48, and the more general and speculative McNeill, *Plagues*.

14. John of Ephesus, p. 234 Van Douwen–Land. Although John says the

officials gave up counting after reaching this figure, the total can hardly have been significantly higher.

15. See A. van Roey, "Les débuts de l'église jacobite," in *Das Konzil von Chalkedon: Geschichte und Gegenwart*, ed. A. Grillmeier and H. Bacht, vol. II (Würzburg, 1953), pp. 339–60.

16. Belisarius seems to have commemorated this engagement in two surviving mosaics in the Church of San Vitale at Ravenna. See Irina Andreescu-Treadgold and Warren Treadgold, "Procopius and the Imperial Panels of San Vitale" (forthcoming).

17. See Procopius, *Secret History* 24.12–14, noting that the border troops' pay had fallen four or five years behind before finally being suspended in 545.

18. Procopius, *Wars* VII, 36.6, 37.24–26, both evidently refer to the same appointment of Liberius, because the improbable alternative would be that Justinian appointed first Liberius, then Germanus, then Liberius again, and then Germanus again, making the first two changes for no discernible reason.

19. That 550 is precisely the date of Procopius's *Secret History* goes far to explain its wild attacks on Justinian and many others in power. Though even Procopius guessed that the plague killed about half the empire's people (*Secret History* 18.44), he failed to see that six years after the first outbreak had ended its effects were still the main cause of the empire's misery. If written slightly earlier, Procopius's diatribe would have needed to blame the plague more, and if written slightly later it would have found less to blame.

20. These may have been killed by the Byzantines' Lombard allies, whom Narses sent back after they committed various atrocities against the local population.

21. See Thompson, *Goths in Spain*, 320–31, who, however, appears too ready to interpret absence of evidence as evidence of absence of Byzantine occupation. If the second Byzantine expedition arrived before Agila's murder in March 555, it probably came in autumn 554, before sailing became dangerous, not in the winter, as Thompson believes. Since this isolated Byzantine province held out for many years against the much stronger Visigoths, it can scarcely have had such minimal and tortuous frontiers as Thompson assigns it. Nor, Thompson's view to the contrary, could Cordova and Seville have maintained their independence from the Visigoths for so long without joining the neighboring Byzantine forces.

22. Narses may actually have completed the conquest of Italy about 556, and the Ostrogoths at Verona may have rebelled after making an earlier submission; see Stein, *Histoire du Bas-Empire* II, 611 n. 1.

23. Cf. P. Allen, "The 'Justinianic' Plague," *Byzantion* 49 (1979), 11–12, who estimates the mortality at about a third of the population; but she may give too much weight to reports from the cities, where mortality was presumably higher than in the rural areas that contained most of the population.

CHAPTER SEVEN

For basic bibliography, see above, pp. 902–3, 904.

1. This seems indicated by the eastern forces' poor performance in 573.

2. Today's Iranian province of Azerbaijan.

3. On the transfer of troops from the Balkans to the eastern front, see Menander Protector, fragment 25.2 Blockley, noting that the troops were still in the East in 579–80. On the Federates, see Theophanes, A.M. 6074, p. 251 de Boor, who makes their permanence clear by noting that Tiberius named them for himself (presumably *Foederati Tiberiani*), and Evagrius, V, 14, where the impossible number 150,000 seems to be a corruption of the 15,000 reported by Theophanes.

4. See Blockley, *Menander*, 280–81 n. 262 (with p. 218 on the captives), who reads the text of Menander Protector to mean that the Avars were ferried across the Savus near Sirmium into Moesia I, then across the Danube near Singidunum into Slavic ("Scythian") territory. Whitby, *Emperor Maurice*, 87 n. 55, defends the traditional but militarily implausible interpretation that the Avars marched all the way to the Byzantine province of Scythia in the Dobrudja and were ferried across the Danube from there.

5. When Tiberius became Augustus, he took the additional name of Constantine. He counts as Tiberius II in the succession of Roman emperors, Tiberius I being the immediate successor of Augustus.

6. See Averil Cameron, "The Empress Sophia," *Byzantion* 45 (1975), 5–21, esp. 16–20.

7. See John of Ephesus, VI, 28 Brooks.

8. See D. M. Metcalf, "The Slavonic Threat to Greece *ca.* 580: Some Evidence from Athens," *Hesperia* 31 (1962), 134–57.

9. In fact, Ingund died during her voyage from Spain to Constantinople, but this news took some time to reach Childebert, who in any case wanted her son sent to him. Hermenegild was executed the next year, to be venerated as a martyr at the hands of Arians.

10. For this campaign, see Whitby, *Emperor Maurice*, 151–55, who has made a persuasive attempt to sort out some serious chronological confusion in the account of Theophylact Simocatta.

11. The precise figures given by Theophylact Simocatta (VIII, 3) are 4,000 Avars and allies killed in the first battle, 9,000 in the second, 15,000 in the third, and 30,000 in the fourth, with 3,000 Avars, 8,000 Slavs, and 6,200 other barbarians taken prisoner. The figures for the dead are probably estimates, but the prisoners were presumably counted.

12. John of Nikiu, p. 102 Charles, records that the troops on the Danube in 602 had four commanders, who were probably those of these four armies, especially because at that time the armies in the Emperor's Presence were not in or near the capital.

13. Theophanes, A.M. 6098, p. 293 de Boor, and the *Paschal Chronicle*, pp. 695–96 Dindorf, almost certainly refer to the same riot in 603. In the first account, note the unsuccessful attempt of the demarch of the Greens to rally his faction to Germanus in return for a bribe; in the second, note Phocas's burning the demarch of the Greens alive after the riot, presumably as punishment for his key role in the plot. David Olster, *The Politics of Usurpation in the Seventh Century* (Amsterdam, 1993), 76–78, tries to identify the riot of 603 in the *Paschal Chronicle* with a riot of 609 (which he misdates to 610) in Theophanes, pp. 296–

97, disregarding the different names of the city prefects (Leontius in the *Paschal Chronicle* and Cosmas in Theophanes). Olster's book includes several such manipulations in an effort to defend Phocas.

14. See Lemerle, *Plus anciens recueils* II, 69–73, referring to an unsuccessful attack by 5,000 Slavs on Thessalonica, probably in October of 604, that broke a long-standing peace in the area.

15. On this civil war in Egypt, see Borkowski, *Alexandrie II*, 23–43.

CHAPTER EIGHT

For basic bibliography, see above, pp. 902–3, 904–5.

1. On the absence of *limitanei* in Italy, see Brown, *Gentlemen*, 102–5. Since Justinian seems to have found it too difficult to create more such forces by the time he took Italy, he is hardly likely to have created any in Spain.

2. For the practically certain site of Justiniana Prima, see Noël Duval et al., eds., *Caričin Grad*, 2 vols., Collection de l'École Française de Rome 75 (Belgrade and Rome, 1984–90).

3. On the Slavic occupation of Greece in this period, see most recently Maria Nystazopoulou-Pelikidou, "Les Slaves dans l'empire byzantin," *Seventeenth Annual Byzantine Congress: Major Papers* (Washington, 1986), 345–52. On the Avars, see Omeljan Pritsak, "The Slavs and the Avars," *Settimane di studio del Centro italiano di studi sull'alto medioevo* 30.1 (1983), 353–435.

4. Cf. P. Charanis, "Cultural Diversity and the Breakdown of Byzantine Power in Asia Minor," *DOP* 29 (1975), 9–10.

5. See Hugh Kennedy, "The Last Century of Byzantine Syria: A Reinterpretation," *BF* 10 (1985), 141–83.

6. On the sixth-century plague, see Michael the Syrian, II, pp. 235–40 Chabot, where Michael copies a lost portion of the contemporary history of John of Ephesus. On the fourteenth-century plague, see Michael W. Dols, *The Black Death in the Middle East* (Princeton, 1977).

7. For second-century pay (1,200 sesterces), see Duncan-Jones, *Money and Government*, 34; for the value of the sesterce, see above, Chap. 4, n. 26. For Anastasius's pay reform, see Treadgold, *Byzantium and Its Army*, 149–54.

8. On the state of the frontier forces in the later sixth and early seventh century, see Jones, *Later Roman Empire*, 662–63.

9. See especially Thomas, *Private Religious Foundations*, 1–110.

10. Cf. Procopius, *Secret History* 9.10, with ibid. 16.18–25 (and 11.34–36), though he makes no connection between Theodora's own experiences and her abhorrence of pederasty.

11. The paucity of contemporary lives of saints of the late fifth and sixth centuries is apparent from John Nesbitt, "A Geographical and Chronological Guide to Greek Saint Lives," *OCP* 35 (1969), 443–89; the works of Cyril of Scythopolis are almost unique exceptions.

12. For a different view, see Peter Brown, "The Rise and Function of the Holy Man in Late Antiquity," *JRS* 61 (1971), 80–101, who relies on the extravagant claims of a few hagiographers.

13. See Alan Cameron, "The Last Days of the Academy at Athens," *Proceedings of the Cambridge Philological Society*, n.s., 15 (1969), 7–29, slightly modified by H. J. Blumenthal, "529 and Its Sequel: What Happened to the Academy?" *Byzantion* 48 (1978), 369–85.

14. See now Richard Sorabji, ed., *Philoponus and the Rejection of Aristotelian Science* (London, 1987).

15. See now Martin Harrison, *A Temple for Byzantium: The Discovery and Excavation of Anicia Juliana's Palace Church in Istanbul* (Austin, 1989).

16. Procopius, *Secret History* 21.1–2, mentions a punitive tax called the *aërikon* (see Stein, *Histoire du Bas-Empire* II, 442–44), which amounted to 3,000 pounds of gold (216,000 nomismata) a year. If such a hostile author mentions no other new taxes, the presumption must be that there were none of importance.

17. That Africa sent the surplus of its revenues to Constantinople in the sixth century seems clear from the fact that it was still doing so in the seventh, when its position was much more precarious (see Chap. 9, n. 33).

18. See Treadgold, *Byzantium and Its Army*, 188–98.

19. The estimates are again adapted from McEvedy, *Atlas*.

20. Cf. H. Kennedy and J. Liebeschuetz, "Antioch and the Villages of Northern Syria in the Fifth and Sixth Centuries A.D.: Trends and Problems," *Nottingham Medieval Studies* 33 (1988), 65–90.

21. John the Lydian, III, 76, notes that Justinian spent 4,000 pounds of gold (288,000 nomismata) on Saint Sophia during the prefecture of Phocas, which lasted for most of 532.

22. The annual cost of Tiberius's 15,000 Federates may be computed as follows and compared with the estimates in Table 6:

infantry (12,000 men × 20 nom. × ⅓)	0.32M nom.
cavalry (3,000 men × 24 nom. × ⅓)	0.096
remounts (3,000 × 4 nom.)	0.012
TOTAL	0.428M nom.

CHAPTER NINE

For basic bibliography, see above, pp. 905–7.

1. See *Life of Theodore of Syceon*, chap. 152, ed. with translation and commentary in A.-J. Festugière, *Vie de Théodore de Sykéôn*, 2 vols. (Brussels, 1970).

2. Such is the plausible interpretation of the evidence made by Avi-Yonah, *Jews of Palestine*, 261–65.

3. Speck, *Geteilte Dossier*, 33–40, rejects Theophanes' date of 613/14 for the marriage in favor of 622. But Speck's argument cannot be reconciled with Martina's appearance on coins dated as early as the sixth year of Heraclius, which was 615/16 (see Grierson, *Catalogue* II.1, 227).

4. See especially Lemerle, *Plus anciens recueils* II, 85–97, 138–40.

5. So Thompson, *Goths in Spain*, 332–34.

6. For the date, note that the whole entry in the *Paschal Chronicle*, pp. 705–9 Dindorf, is assigned to indiction 4 (615/16) on p. 705. This entry includes the

advance of Shahīn to Chalcedon, which is dated to the same year as the Persian invasion of Egypt (probably 616) by Theophanes, Nicephorus, and eastern sources. The heading that immediately precedes this entry in the *Paschal Chronicle*, for indiction 3 (614/15), probably does not apply to what follows, which appears to have been crowded out of the entry for 616/17 by the chronological calculations that completely fill it as it now stands.

7. The hexagram was probably worth one-twelfth of a nomisma, or 24 folles. Hendy, *Studies*, 494–95, unlike previous scholars, has argued that the hexagram was valued fairly, though in 615/16 (ibid. 498–99) the follis had been reduced in weight as a further economy.

8. See Clive Foss, "The Persians in Asia Minor and the End of Antiquity," *EHR* 90 (1975), 721–47 (also suggesting that Ephesus might have been sacked, though this seems improbable, and he omits the suggestion from his subsequent *Ephesus*, 104–5).

9. Lemerle, *Plus anciens recueils* II, 94–103.

10. See Thompson, *Goths in Spain*, 168–69, who puts the final disappearance of the Byzantine province of Spain between 623 and 625.

11. Ostrogorsky, *History*, 95–100, like the earlier scholars whom he cites, argues that this was the time when the armies were given land grants in specific regions of Anatolia to replace most of their pay, so that they became the "themes" of the subsequent period. Like most recent scholars, I reject this conjecture, which implies that Heraclius had despaired of returning the armies to their original stations, though he soon began fighting to do just that, with ultimate success. As will appear, I date the creation of the themes to the years between 659 and 662.

12. The armies of Illyricum, Thrace, the East, and Armenia, and the two in the Emperor's Presence, had totaled 125,000 men after Tiberius II had added 15,000 Federates to the Army of the East; 80,000 soldiers remained in the armies that developed from these by 780, after they had presumably suffered further losses (see Table 9). Since some troops on the rolls were always unavailable for service and some must have stayed behind to defend Byzantine territory, 50,000 appears a reasonable guess for the mobile force. Note that in 627, when the force was grouped together and combined with some mercenaries, it apparently totaled some 70,000.

13. See N. Oikonomidès, "A Chronological Note on the First Persian Campaign of Heraclius (622)," *Byzantine and Modern Greek Studies* 1 (1975), 1–9.

14. For a persuasive defense of the date of 623 for these events, see Whitby, *Chronicon Paschale*, 203–5.

15. The most detailed (though sometimes speculative) description of Heraclius's route during these campaigns, with clear sketch maps, is I. A. Manandian, "The Routes of the Persian Campaigns of the Emperor Heraclius," *Vizantijskij Vremennik*, n.s., 3 (1950), 133–53 (in Russian).

16. On the last, see C. J. F. Dowsett, "The Name and the Role of Sarablangas or Shahraplakan," *Byzantion* 21 (1951), 311–21.

17. On the loyalties of Shahrvarāz, see Cyril Mango, "Deux études sur Byzance et la Perse sassanide," *TM* 9 (1985), 105–17 (but on the timing, see Whitby, *Chronicon Paschale*, 177 n. 471).

18. The figure of 70,000 without the Khazars, which is plausible but not unimpeachable, comes from Tabarī; see T. Nöldeke, *Geschichte der Perser und Araber zur Zeit der Sassaniden aus der arabischen Chronik des Tabari* (Leiden, 1879), 295. Theophanes, p. 316 de Boor, puts the number of Khazar allies at 40,000 men.

19. See Mango, "Deux études" (above, no. 17), 109–17.

20. On the date of Heraclius's triumphal return, with references for his capture of Edessa and other places in Mesopotamia, see Mango, *Nikephoros*, 185–86.

21. See Philip Mayerson, "The First Muslim Attacks on Southern Palestine (A.D. 633–634)," *Transactions of the American Philological Association* 95 (1964), 155–99.

22. Nicephorus, *Short History*, chap. 23, simply calls John a general, but John of Nikiu (p. 178 Charles) calls him "general of the local levies," the same term he uses for Constantine, a general sent to Egypt in 641 from Constantinople (p. 191 Charles). Since the later "local levies" came from the capital, the earlier ones probably did as well, and both were probably from the praesental armies, whose easily misunderstood title was mistranslated at some point in the tangled tradition of John of Nikiu.

23. Nicephorus, *Short History*, chap. 23, mentions Heraclius's sending two generals to Egypt after John (Theodore was evidently already there): Marinus, general of the Army of Thrace, who was defeated by the Arabs before Cyrus opened negotiations, and Marianus the Cubicularius, who was defeated and killed by the Arabs after Cyrus's negotiations. *The History of the Patriarchs of the Coptic Church of Alexandria*, ed. and trans. B. Evetts, *PO* 1 (Paris, 1907), p. 494, mentions the Arabs' defeating and killing the Byzantine general Marianus (the manuscript reads "Arianus"), and sending the survivors from his army fleeing to Alexandria. (This passage seems to disprove the suggestion of Speck, *Geteilte Dossier*, 400–401, that "Marianus" and "Marinus" are both mistakes for Manuel, a general sent to Egypt in 645.) No other source mentions Marinus. Since Heraclius scarcely had time to send two sets of reinforcements in the fall of 640, "Marinus" was presumably a textual corruption of "Marianus" in one of Nicephorus's sources, not, as Nicephorus thought, a separate person.

24. Mango, *Nikephoros*, 188–89, believes that this agreement, which according to Theophanes staved off the "destruction" of Egypt for three years, was made in 636 or 637 and delayed the attack on Egypt until 639. But the evidence of other sources suggests that the agreement was made in 640 and delayed the final fall of Egypt to late 642, counting the three years inclusively.

25. For the chronology of the events of 641, see Treadgold, "A Note on Byzantium's Year of the Four Emperors," *BZ* 84 (1991), 431–33.

26. Treadgold, *Byzantium and Its Army*, 145–47.

27. Heraclonas ("Little Heraclius") was a nickname; his official name was Constantine Heraclius, and some scholars call him Heraclius II.

28. See John of Nikiu, p. 191 Charles; and n. 22 above.

29. Cedrenus, I, p. 753 Bekker, reports Heraclonas's donative as 3 nomismata per man. Constantine's previous payment seems to have included 5 nomismata of donative besides the usual pay due in the Easter season (see Treadgold, *Byzantium and Its Army*, 145–47).

30. His official name actually became Heraclius Constantine, Constans ("Little Constantine") being a nickname for Constantine, not a real name like that of Constantine I's son Constans I. A few modern scholars more correctly call him not Constans II but Constantine III, referring to his father as Constantine II. Heraclonas seems also to have called himself Constantine on his coins, creating problems of attribution for numismatists that may never be definitively solved.

31. Theophanes, p. 343 de Boor, if his chronology is corrected by the usual one year, dates the attempted coup and death of "Valentinian" (Valentine) after 1 September 644 and before an eclipse that occurred, as he says it did, on 5 October 644. The mention of this eclipse gives Theophanes' date more authority than that of Sebeus (pp. 105–6 Macler), who puts the attempted coup and death of Valentine in the second year of Constans (642/43).

32. This obscure Theodore was apparently not the same as the Armenian prince Theodore Ṛshtuni, or as the general defeated by the Arabs in Syria and Egypt.

33. See al-Nuwayrī, tr. W. M. de Slane in *Ibn Khaldun: Histoire des Berbères et des dynasties musulmanes de l'Afrique septentrionale* I (Paris, 1925), p. 324, who indicates that Janāhā (presumably Gennadius), Gregory's successor, forwarded the usual revenues until the emperor Heraclius (Heraclius Constantine; i.e., Constans) demanded much more, as he did in 664 (*Liber Pontificalis* I, p. 344 Duchesne). Gennadius then expelled the emperor's envoy from Africa, was overthrown by the Africans, and fled to Muʿāwiyah, who launched the invasion of Africa of A.H. 45 (665/66).

34. The rather confused source for the conspiracy is Sebeus, pp. 130–31 Macler.

35. The whole question of the origin of the themes has long been controversial. In what follows I give my own views, which are presented in more detail in Treadgold, *Byzantium and Its Army*, 21–25 (with 72–75 on the Carabisian Theme in particular). The original themes were alternatively called the Opsician, the Armeniacs, the Anatolics, the Thracesians, and the Carabisians.

36. For the Opsician and Anatolic capitals, see Oikonomidès, "Liste arabe." In 668 the strategus of the Armeniacs was at Melitene, but this was an exposed position and seems to have been a temporary residence. By the ninth century the capitals of the Armeniacs and Thracesians were at Euchaïta and Chonae respectively, though they could have changed in the meantime. (Melitene had admittedly been lost.) For Samos as headquarters of the Carabisians, see Peter Charanis, "Observations on the History of Greece During the Early Middle Ages," *Balkan Studies* 11 (1970), 9–10, relying on Constantine VII, *De Thematibus*, p. 81 Pertusi. But strategi were not closely bound to a single headquarters.

37. The reference is in the preface to Constantine VII's *De Thematibus*, p. 60 Pertusi. Though this work was written in the tenth century and much of it is antiquarian nonsense, the author should have had access to state archives, and his antiquarianism has no bearing on this subject.

38. The sources specifically refer to 668, the date of rebellions by the strategus of the Armeniac Theme (Theophanes, pp. 348–49 de Boor, correcting the

chronology by the usual one year) and the count of the Opsician Theme (Jean Gouillard, "Aux origines de l'iconoclasme: Le témoignage de Grégoire II?" *TM* 3 [1968], 295). Because Constans can hardly have organized these eastern themes while he was in the West, they must have been organized before 662.

39. See Hendy, *Studies*, 626, 641. Since only the first of the lead seals in question is of the type used between 654 and 659, it seems to belong to the very end of that period.

40. See Foss, *Byzantine Fortifications*, 131–36.

41. All that is known of Constantine IV's birth date is that he was crowned coemperor in 654. He could scarcely have been born much before 645, when his father turned fifteen, or much later than 653, to make him fifteen at the birth of his own son Justinian II in 668/69. If we split the difference, we obtain a birth date of ca. 649. Constantine must have married by 667, the year before his son's birth, and probably by 662, since Constans is not likely to have left the marriage of his son and heir to occur in his absence.

42. Note that a lead seal dated to 673/74 mentions a "warehouse of Africa" comparable to the warehouses that supplied the soldiers of the themes beginning in 659; see C. Morrisson and W. Seibt, "Sceaux de commerciaires byzantins du VIIᵉ siècle trouvés à Carthage," *Revue Numismatique*, ser. 6, 24 (1982), 234–36.

43. Brooks, "Arabs," 184, believes that the raiders of 665/66 reached Antioch in Pisidia, but al-Yaʿqūbī ("Ibn Wadhih") says only that after wintering in the empire they went to Antioch, which as it is not otherwise specified was presumably Antioch in Syria, their base. On the Hexapolis, see V. Tourneur, "L'Hexapolis arménienne au VIIᵉ siècle et au VIIIᵉ," *Annuaire de l'Institut de Philologie et d'Histoire Orientales* 2 (1934), 947–52.

44. So Pseudo-Codinus, *Origines*, ed. in Th. Preger, *Scriptores Originum Constantinopolitarum* II (Leipzig, 1907), 251–52, probably one of the authentic parts of this often unreliable source. It describes Severus as a strategus commanding the navy, which should mean the strategus of the Carabisian Theme.

CHAPTER TEN

For basic bibliography, see above, pp. 905–6, 907.

1. I see no reason to share the skepticism of E. W. Brooks, "The Sicilian Expedition of Constantine IV," *BZ* 17 (1908), 455–59, who after arguing that the expedition could not have taken place admits in an addendum that it might have.

2. See Lemerle, *Plus anciens recueils* II, 111–36.

3. The Byzantine ducate of Calabria kept a scrap of ancient Calabria around Hydrus (modern Otranto), but the name stuck to the larger part of the duke's command in modern Calabria.

4. Although some scholars have dated these Arab defeats to 678, the fleet appears to have come to grief in a winter storm, and Lemerle, *Plus anciens recueils* II, 128–33, has shown that the Arab attack was over in time for Constantine to campaign against the Slavs in the summer of 678. The erroneous report

that the Arab attacks on Constantinople lasted seven years (Theophanes, p. 354 de Boor; Nicephorus, *Short History*, chap. 34) probably counted from the first Arab attack in 670 to the last in 677, ignoring the interruption from 671 to 674.

5. The Mardaïtes remain somewhat mysterious, but were clearly different from the Lebanese Maronites. See Matti Moosa, "The Relation of the Maronites of Lebanon to the Mardaites and al Jarājima," *Speculum* 44 (1969), 597–608.

6. Both Theophanes, p. 355 de Boor, and Nicephorus, *Short History*, chap. 34, obviously copying the same source, speak simply of "3,000 of gold," but since 3,000 nomismata was a nugatory tribute it was doubtless 3,000 pounds of gold (216,000 nomismata).

7. For the chronology, which is derived from numismatic evidence, see Grierson, *Catalogue* II.2, 512–14.

8. Modern scholars have shown excessive respect for the obviously related accounts of Theophanes, pp. 356–58 de Boor, and Nicephorus, *Short History*, chap. 35, which imply that these Bulgars left the region of the Sea of Azov for the lower Danube only around this time. Bulgars had occupied the northern banks of the lower Danube since the late fifth century, and Kuvrat evidently controlled this area when he expelled the Avars from his land and made a treaty with Heraclius about 632 (Nicephorus, *Short History*, chap. 22).

9. For the date, see Mango, *Nikephoros*, 196.

10. This condemnation of a pope by an ecumenical council has no bearing on the later western doctrine of papal infallibility, as is sometimes said, since Honorius's advice to Heraclius on Monotheletism was not intended as a formal pronouncement.

11. See Lemerle, *Plus anciens recueils* II, 137–62.

12. See R.-J. Lilie, "'Thrakien' und 'Thrakesion': Zur byzantinischen Provinzorganisation am Ende des 7. Jahrhunderts," *JÖB* 26 (1977), 7–47.

13. Elijah of Nisibis, pp. 71–72 Brooks, gives the year as A.H. 65 (18 August 684–7 August 685), but fall 684 is much more likely than spring 685, when Constantine was dying and a peace treaty was being negotiated. This campaign seems to be the same as that described and dated by Cheira, *Lutte*, 147.

14. On the Mardaïtes' military role, see Treadgold, "Army," 115–19.

15. While Theophanes, p. 367 de Boor, mentions these exactions and imprisonments only later, he notes that in 695 some aristocrats had been imprisoned for as many as eight years (p. 369 de Boor), meaning since 687.

16. See Balādhurī, pp. 247–48 Hitti. Though the meager Byzantine sources do not refer to this campaign, the date, circumstances, and terms of the treaty show that it was distinct from others. For the Mardaïtes who went to Hellas, see n. 14 above.

17. Here I disagree with Hendy, *Studies*, 631–34, who revises the chronology, interprets the "Slavic slaves" mentioned on a seal of 694/95 as Slav prisoners of war, and concludes that the official who had this seal sold arms to the Slavs when they joined the army. The natural interpretation, which fits Theophanes' date, is that this official sold the Slavs themselves into slavery after they were dismissed.

18. This event, dated to 690/91 by Theophanes, p. 365 de Boor, must actually have occurred after ʿAbd al-Malik captured Mecca in September 692.

19. According to Constantine VII, *De Administrando Imperio*, chap. 47, this resettlement, which included Cypriots taken prisoner by the Arabs, occurred seven years after Justinian originally removed the Cypriots in 691. Although the unnamed emperor in this passage is usually identified with Apsimar, Apsimar had too little time left in 698 to conclude such an agreement, especially because he promptly attacked the Arabs.

20. Both themes appear for the first time in an Arab list identified by Oikonomidès, "Liste arabe"; but I am not persuaded by Oikonomidès's argument dating the list before 695 because Hellas is omitted (so are the Thracesians, the Carabisians, and the Exarchate of Italy, to fit the erroneous idea that the empire had only six "patricians" in its provinces). In fact, the mention of Sardinia as an independent theme implies a date after the fall of Carthage in 698. Sicily is first attested as a theme ca. 700, and was probably created ca. 699, also as a response to the fall of Carthage; cf. Brown, *Gentlemen*, 48 and n. 20.

21. On the battle at Sisium, see the convincing interpretation of Lilie, *Byzantinische Reaktion*, 115 and n. 36.

22. The unrest at Rome dated to 710, when the exarch John Rhizocopus conducted a purge after the departure of the pope for the East. The unrest at Ravenna should be dated to 709, because it resulted in the exile of its archbishop Felix to Cherson, evidently before Cherson rebelled in 710. The latter fact excludes the transposition of events in the *Liber Pontificalis* suggested by L. Duchesne (*Liber Pontificalis* I, 393 n. 3), who dated the reprisals at Ravenna to 711 and has been followed by most historians.

CHAPTER ELEVEN

For basic bibliography, see above, pp. 905–6, 907.

1. The number of men is given by al-Masʿūdī, *Tanbīh*, trans. B. Carra de Vaux as *Le livre de l'avertissement et de la revision* (Paris, 1896), p. 226, and the number of ships by Theophanes, p. 395 de Boor. These figures are large but plausible, unlike the 200,000 men and 5,000 ships mentioned by Michael the Syrian, II, p. 484 Chabot, which are plainly too many.

2. For Leo's origins, see Gero, *Leo III*, 1–31, who shows that Leo was a Syrian, not an Isaurian as some late sources say.

3. I follow Nicephorus, *Short History*, chaps. 54, 56, who says that the siege lasted 13 months and ended on 15 August. Although Theophanes, pp. 395, 399 de Boor, says that the siege both began and ended on 15 August, he has probably taken too literally a report that the siege lasted a year. The events are treated in detail, if not very perceptively, by Rodolphe Guilland, "L'expédition de Maslama contre Constantinople (717–718)," in his *Études Byzantines* (Paris, 1959), 109–33.

4. They had evidently slipped from imperial control before 733, when Leo was able to confiscate the papal estates of Sicily and Calabria but not those of Sardinia and Corsica.

5. On the whole Arab-Khazar war of 722–737, see D. M. Dunlop, *The History of the Jewish Khazars* (Princeton, 1954), 61–87.

6. See A. A. Vasiliev, "The Iconoclastic Edict of the Caliph Yazid II, A.D. 721," *DOP* 9–10 (1955–56), 23–47.

7. This is the traditional date, and seems to fit the historical context better than the other possible date of 741. Though Burgmann, *Ecloga*, 10–12, prefers the later date, he gives no compelling reason.

8. The *Ecloga* abounds in biblical references (noted in Burgmann's edition). On the death penalty for homosexual acts, cf. *Ecloga* 17.38 with Romans 1.26–32; on mutilation, cf. *Ecloga* 17 *passim* with Matthew 5.29–30 and 18.8–9 and Mark 9.43–48; on divorce, cf. *Ecloga* 2.9.1–4 with Matthew 5.31–32, Mark 10.11–12, and Luke 16.18. (Only in the last case do the scriptural passages supply pertinent justification for the laws.)

9. The case for an edict at this time made by Milton Anastos, "Leo III's Edict Against the Images of the Year 726–27 and Italo-Byzantine Relations Between 726 and 730," *BF* 3 (1968), 5–41, is stronger than the contrary argument of George Ostrogorsky, "Les débuts de la querelle des images," *Mélanges Charles Diehl* I (Paris, 1930), 235–55. But note that the mention of Leo's orders against icons in the *Liber Pontificalis* I, p. 404 Duchesne, cited by Anastos, refers only to icons of saints and includes no clear demand for their destruction.

10. While the evidence is not absolutely conclusive, a good case for this date is made by Milton Anastos, "The Transfer of Illyricum, Calabria, and Sicily to the Jurisdiction of the Patriarchate of Constantinople in 732–33," *SBN* 9 (1957), 14–31.

11. For the date, see Noble, *Republic of St. Peter*, 41–42 and n. 131.

12. The previously accepted date of June 742 for the beginning of the revolt of Artavasdus is almost certainly wrong; on the revolt see Speck, *Artabasdos*, and Treadgold, "Missing Year."

13. Constantine may also have created the Bucellarian Theme at this time to reduce the Opsician Theme further, but it seems more likely that the Bucellarian Theme was created in 767 (when it is first attested), in retaliation for the Opsician's part in the conspiracy of 766.

14. For Sozopetra, see Balādhurī, pp. 298–99 Hitti.

15. Nicephorus, *Antirrheticus* III, 65, *PG* 100, col. 496A–B.

16. Nicephorus, *Short History*, chap. 68, dates the repopulation immediately after the plague, at the time when a Byzantine fleet that happened to be on Cyprus (to gather settlers for Constantinople?) defeated the Arabs. Theophanes, pp. 424, 429 de Boor, also dates the battle on Cyprus to 748 but mentions the resettlement under 756 along with the settlement in Thrace of captives taken in 751; but 756, which seems too late for those two population transfers, is probably only the date of the settlement of captives taken during the campaign of 755, which Theophanes confuses with that of 751 (see n. 19 below).

17. Unlike Lilie, *Byzantinische Reaktion*, 164–65 and n. 11, I am not persuaded by Brooks, "Byzantines," 88 n. 204, who dates the fall of Melitene to 750 rather than 751 on the unwarranted assumption that since the emperor was in Constantinople on 6 June 751 he could not have attacked the Arabs later in that campaigning season.

18. The embassies, dating from 752 to 766, are conveniently catalogued by Dölger, *Regesten* I.1, 38–39, nos. 312, 314–16, 318–20, 322, 325, 326.

19. On this campaign, which Michael the Syrian distinguishes from the one that took Melitene in 751/52 but Theophanes confuses with it, see Lilie, *Byzantinische Reaktion*, 164–65 with n. 12.

20. Theophanes, pp. 432–33 de Boor, mentions a fleet of about 800 ships with 12 horses each, which would have provided mounts for about 9,600 men. This number seems to correspond to the 8,250 men in two cavalry tagmata, plus some Optimates for their baggage.

21. Beševliev, *Protobulgarische Periode*, 212–13, argues plausibly that Vinekh (Sabinus) and Teletz (Teletzes) had previously been corulers, though his case for believing that the Bulgars normally had two rulers during this period is weak.

22. On Stephen, see most recently Marie-France Rouan, "Une lecture 'iconoclaste' de la vie d'Étienne de Jeune," *TM* 8 (1981), 415–36.

23. Here I follow Beševliev (*Protobulgarische Periode*, 224–25) and others in assuming that the reference to October of the eleventh indiction (772) in Theophanes (p. 447.10 de Boor) should be to October of the thirteenth indiction (774).

24. On Leo's reign and death, see W. Treadgold, "An Indirectly Preserved Source for the Reign of Leo IV," *JÖB* 34 (1984), 69–76.

CHAPTER TWELVE

For basic bibliography, see above, pp. 905–6, 907–8.

1. The impact on western Anatolia of the Arab invasions was surely less than that of the Turkish invasion in the late eleventh century, since unlike the Turks the Arabs never migrated into Asia Minor or drove the Byzantines out of whole regions.

2. See particularly André Guillou, "La Sicile byzantine: État de recherches," *BF* 5 (1977), 95–145.

3. On central Italy at this time, see Noble, *Republic of St. Peter*.

4. This fact, not itself controversial, is illustrated by the interesting but speculative study of Richard Bulliet, *Conversion to Islam in the Medieval Period: An Essay in Quantitative History* (Cambridge, Mass., 1979).

5. See Treadgold, *Byzantium and Its Army*, 70–72. Note that after the Excubitors were organized as a tagma they were led by a domestic, not (as before) by a count. Unfortunately, the only book on the tagmata as such, John Haldon's *Byzantine Praetorians* (Bonn, 1984), insists that they were an elite bodyguard far smaller than is recorded in the sources, arbitrarily declaring that evidence that disagrees with his assumptions must be "set aside" (pp. 91–94).

6. The date of the administrative reorganization is not yet fully clear, but most of it seems to have occurred no later than the creation of the themes. Note that one of the new officials, a military logothete, is identified on a lead seal datable to 659–68 also as a commerciarius of a warehouse that apparently supplied the themes (Zacos, *Byzantine Lead Seals* I.1, pp. 227–28, no. 144). Hendy, *Studies*, 409–20, relying on numismatic evidence, suggests a date of about 629 for at least the beginning of the administrative changes.

7. For the military officers, see Treadgold, *Byzantium and Its Army*, 119–35,

141–44, 152–53, and for the civil officials, see Treadgold, *Finances*, 37–46, 98–103, and esp. 111–14.

8. On the location of large private estates, see esp. Hendy, *Studies*, 100–107, who relies on later evidence that appears to reflect long-standing patterns of landholding.

9. See Gerhart Ladner, "Origin and Significance of the Byzantine Iconoclastic Controversy," *MS* 2 (1940), 127–49, and more recently Peter Brown, "A Dark Age Crisis: Aspects of the Iconoclastic Controversy," *EHR* 88 (1973), 1–34. Other interpretations, while legion, are either variations on this theme or unpersuasive.

10. See Ernst Kitzinger, "The Cult of Images in the Age Before Iconoclasm," *DOP* 8 (1954), 83–150.

11. See most recently Paul Alexander, *The Byzantine Apocalyptic Tradition* (Berkeley, 1985).

12. Cf. Lemerle, *Byzantine Humanism*, 82–84.

13. Quinisext, Canon 68 (Mansi, XI, col. 973D).

14. Leo III, *Ecloga*, preface, p. 162 Burgmann.

15. See Averil Cameron and Judith Herrin, eds., *Constantinople in the Early Eighth Century: The Parastaseis Syntomoi Chronikai* (Leiden, 1984), though the editors implausibly assume that their author was making an honest attempt at research and wrote under Leo III rather than some years later.

16. See Foss, *Byzantine Fortifications*, 26–28, 131–42.

17. As usual I refer to McEvedy, *Atlas*.

18. See Treadgold, *Byzantine Revival*, 41 and n. 40.

19. Note that in 768 Constantine V's hoarding in the treasury resulted in a gold shortage that forced farmers to sell food at depressed prices to obtain gold to pay their taxes; see Theophanes, p. 443 de Boor, and Nicephorus, *Short History*, chap. 85.

20. On the treasury in 711, see Theophanes, p. 381 de Boor; on the treasury in 768, see n. 19 above; and on the treasury in 775, see Cedrenus, II, p. 16 Bekker.

21. See M. el Abbadi, "The Finances of Egypt at the Arab Conquest," *Proceedings of the Sixteenth International Congress of Papyrology, American Studies in Papyrology* 23 (1981), 509–16.

22. On these budgetary estimates, see Treadgold, *Byzantium and Its Army*, 188–98.

23. The successful military revolts were those of 610, 641, 695, 698, 711, 715, and 717, since the military revolt of 713 was thwarted by Anastasius II.

CHAPTER THIRTEEN

For basic bibliography, see above, pp. 908–9.

1. The custom of holding shows for imperial brides, which some scholars find hard to believe, is attested by six good and early sources stretching over a century. See most recently L.-M. Hans, "Der Kaiser als Märchenprinz: Brautschau und Hieratspolitik in Konstantinopel 395–882," *JÖB* 38 (1988), 33–52, esp. 46–52.

2. The Theme of Macedonia was located to the east of ancient (and modern)

Macedonia, most of which was still held by Slavs; the theme's confusing name presumably expressed a hope that the Byzantines would soon extend its territory into Macedonia proper.

3. This tribute was meant mostly to be a humiliation, as appears from the extra 6 nomismata, designated as a head tax for the emperor and his son.

4. See Treadgold, "Army," 115–19.

5. For possible identifications of the place, see Niavis, *Nicephorus I*, 243–45.

6. David Turner, "The Origins and Accession of Leo V," *JÖB* 40 (1990), 171–203, among other arguments I find unpersuasive, considers Leo's two wives to be one (cf. Treadgold, *Byzantine Revival*, 196–99, with notes). The reasons for thinking that Leo's first wife Barca was Michael's mistress are the indignation of Michael's wife Procopia at the prospect of Barca's becoming empress in 813, which distressed her more than her husband's abdication; Leo's haste to divorce Barca after Michael's fall; and the absence of controversy over Leo's divorce, which implies notorious adultery by his wife. This hypothesis also helps explain Michael's baptismal sponsorship of Leo's son soon after 803, when Leo was a very junior officer, and Michael's prompt recall of Leo from exile in 811.

7. See Treadgold, "Three Byzantine Provinces."

8. For Michael's criticism of Leo's second marriage, see Pseudo-Symeon, pp. 609–10 Bekker (evidently misunderstood by Genesius, p. 15 Lesmueller-Werner).

9. The account in Treadgold, *Byzantine Revival*, 276–78, should now be supplemented by Jean Gouillard, "La vie d'Euthyme de Sardes," *TM* 10 (1987), 1–101, esp. 39–51.

10. This Alexius was probably the grandson of the Alexius Musele who was drungary of the Watch and then strategus of the Armeniacs in 790 and blinded in 792. The younger Alexius, probably betrothed to Theophilus's daughter Maria in 836 after Theophilus's son Constantine died about 835, is at the center of a chronological confusion in our sources, three of which believe that he actually married Maria, while another assumes that he was already Caesar at Theophilus's triumph of 831. See the references in Treadgold, *Byzantine Revival*, 434, 438, 439.

11. Apparently they fled to Chaldia, which Theophilus then raised in rank from a ducate to a theme.

12. On the beginning of John's patriarchate, which has often been misdated to 832 or 837, see Treadgold, *Byzantine Revival*, 297 and n. 406.

13. The error that the Theme of the Climata was founded in 833 has taken firm root in the secondary literature on the Rus', but is completely unfounded. For an explanation of the mistake and of the correct date of 839, see Treadgold, "Three Byzantine Provinces," 132–36.

14. For Theophilus's reserve, see Theophanes Continuatus, p. 253 Bekker.

CHAPTER FOURTEEN

For basic bibliography, see above, pp. 908–9, 909–10.

1. On the restoration of icons, see particularly the complementary articles of Cyril Mango, "The Liquidation of Iconoclasm and the Patriarch Photios," and

Patricia Karlin-Hayter, "Gregory of Syracuse, Ignatios and Photios," in Bryer, *Iconoclasm*, 133–40 and 141–45.

2. On the foundation and refoundation of this school, which have caused some confusion, see Treadgold, "The Chronological Accuracy of the *Chronicle* of Symeon the Logothete," *DOP* 33 (1979), 185–87.

3. For the date, see Treadgold, ibid., 191–92. Mauropotamus seems to be an alternative name for the Melas River in Bithynia, since both names mean Black River.

4. See Theophanes Continuatus, p. 162 Bekker, and note his reference to renewing the treaty, implying that the treaty of 816, originally meant to last thirty years, was still being renewed at ten-year intervals.

5. See Treadgold, "The Bride-Shows of the Byzantine Emperors," *Byzantion* 49 (1979), 404–7, 411–12.

6. For a more favorable view of Michael than mine, see Henri Grégoire in *Cambridge Medieval History* IV.1, 2d ed., 108–16, and his articles cited there on p. 853.

7. On this Russian attack see especially Cyril Mango, *The Homilies of Photius* (Cambridge, Mass., 1958), 74–82.

8. A strategus of Colonia, replacing a turmarch subordinate to the strategus of the Armeniacs, is first found in 863 (Theophanes Continuatus, p. 181 Bekker).

9. On this campaign, see the reconstruction of George Huxley, "Michael III and the Battle of Bishop's Meadow (A.D. 863)," *GRBS* 16 (1975), 443–50.

10. On Mesembria, see N. Oikonomidès, "Mesembria in the Ninth Century: Epigraphical Evidence," *Byzantine Studies* 8–12 (1981–85), 269–73.

11. The theory of Jenkins, *Byzantium*, 165, 198–99, that Michael's relations with Basil were homosexual is based on a misinterpretation of "chamberlain" as "bedfellow," and seems as groundless as Jenkins' deduction from it that Michael was unable to have children. Four hostile chroniclers describe Michael's debaucheries in detail without hinting at homosexuality, as they would surely have done if they had even suspected it. Cf. the hostile but hardly trustworthy remarks of Theophanes, p. 443 de Boor, on the homosexuality of Constantine V.

12. On this rather bizarre arrangement I follow the carefully documented argument of Cyril Mango, "Eudocia Ingerina, the Normans, and the Macedonian Dynasty," *ZRVI* 14/15 (1973), 17–27.

13. Michael inherited a reserve of 109,000 pounds of gold (7,848,000 nomismata) in 856 (Theophanes Continuatus, p. 172 Bekker) and after melting down 20,000 pounds (1,440,000 nomismata) of gold ornaments he left either 300 or more likely 1,300 pounds (93,600 nomismata) in 867 (Theophanes Continuatus, p. 173 Bekker; Pseudo-Symeon, pp. 659–60 Bekker). The total deficit was therefore some 9.2 million nomismata over 11 years. In 867 Basil I raised 30,000 pounds of gold just by collecting half of Michael's recorded gifts (Theophanes Continuatus, pp. 255–56 Bekker). The total gifts must have exceeded 60,000 pounds (4,320,000 nomismata), because some gifts probably passed unrecorded, because Basil cannot have collected everything he demanded, and because Basil would not have included gifts to himself or to his wife Eudocia Ingerina.

14. Though Photius deduced various propositions from the *filioque* and con-

demned them, none of those propositions logically follows from it. The only point acknowledged by some westerners was that the Creed should not be altered without a church council, and the papacy had not yet officially sanctioned the *filioque* for this reason.

15. On his birth date, often put much later despite unequivocal evidence in the sources, see Treadgold, "The Bulgars' Treaty with the Byzantines in 816," *RSBS* 4 (1984), 213–20.

16. See Ferluga, *Amministrazione*, 165–76.

17. G. S. Radojičić, "La date de la conversion des Serbes," *Byzantion* 22 (1952), 253–56, dates their conversion between 867 and 873. A date soon after the council of 869–70 seems most likely.

18. On the Imperial Fleet, see Ahrweiler, *Byzance et la mer*, 97–99. I would conjecturally date this reform to 870–73 because afterward the empire's fortunes at sea dramatically improved—except when the Imperial Fleet is known to have been absent, as at the fall of Syracuse in 878.

19. The daughter whom Christopher married by 872 must have been born before Basil divorced his first wife Maria in 866. For Basil's four daughters, see the list of tombs in Constantine VII, *De Ceremoniis*, vol. I, pp. 648–49 Reiske. There the two daughters buried in a small coffin presumably died in infancy, while the daughter named Maria was probably Eudocia's because Byzantines seldom named daughters for their mothers. By process of elimination, Christopher's wife should have been Anastasia. The list of tombs also mentions Basil's brother, the domestic of the Scholae Marianus, whose death may have left the vacancy that caused Christopher to be married into the family and appointed.

20. For a satisfactory explanation of the conflicting evidence, see Lemerle, "Pauliciens," 96–103.

21. Cf. Jenkins, "Chronological Accuracy," 100; the conversion should belong to the period between 872 and 877/78.

22. The best treatment of these somewhat obscure events is in Vasiliev, *Byzance et les Arabes* II.1, 52–65.

23. See N. Oikonomidès, "Constantin VII Porphyrogénète et les thèmes de Céphalonie et de Longobardie," *RÉB* 23 (1965), 118–23.

24. See Symeon the Logothete ("Leo Grammaticus," p. 258 Bekker), who dates this campaign, which is for some reason not mentioned in Vasiliev's *Byzance et les Arabes* II.1, after the fall of Syracuse and before Photius's reconciliation with the pope in 879. (Cf. Jenkins, "Chronological Accuracy," 97.)

25. See Lemerle, "Pauliciens," 103–8, who, however, misdates Basil's campaign against Germanicea (and hence the fall of Tephrice) to 878 by preferring the arbitrary dates of the Pseudo-Symeon to the reliable relative chronology of Symeon the Logothete ("Leo Grammaticus," p. 258 Bekker). Vasiliev, *Byzance et les Arabes*, II.1, 86–94, correctly assigns the campaign to 879. Symeon's mention of Christopher's capture of Tephrice ("Leo Grammaticus," p. 255 Bekker) seems to be a somewhat maladroit "cast forward" from Christopher's victory over Chrysocheir in 872.

26. The first apparent attestation of a strategus of Samos comes about 892; cf. Symeon the Logothete ("Georgius Monachus," p. 852 of Bekker's Theophanes Continuatus) with Jenkins, "Chronological Accuracy," 104.

27. See *Vita Euthymii*, pp. 39–41 Karlin-Hayter.

28. By this time the previous domestic, Basil's son-in-law Christopher, had probably died, because all four of Basil's daughters, including Christopher's wife, were in a convent by 886 (Theophanes Continuatus, pp. 264–65 Bekker).

29. For the date of Ashot's coronation, see Maksoudian's commentary on John Catholicus, pp. 272–73; the alliance was probably made in 885.

30. On the title and date, see Andreas Schminck, *Studien zu mittelbyzantinischen Rechtsbüchern* (Frankfurt, 1986), 12–15. The *Eisagōgē* later came to be called the *Epanagōgē* (Restoration).

31. On Basil's forty-book and Leo VI's sixty-book versions, see A. Schminck, "'Frömmigkeit ziere das Werk': Zur Datierung der 60 Bücher Leons VI," *Subseciva Groningana* 3 (1989), 79–114.

32. "Father of the Emperor," meaning the emperor's senior adviser, but twisted by his enemies at court to mean "Father of the Emperor's Mistress," which Zaützes also was.

33. Phocas died about 896, though under his grandson and namesake Nicephorus II Phocas the legend was fabricated that he had lived into the next century and won further victories. See Henri Grégoire, "La carrière du premier Nicéphore Phocas," *Hellenika* Suppl. 4 (1953), 232–54, though Grégoire's reconstruction of Phocas's earlier exploits in Anatolia is questionable.

34. Symeon the Logothete ("Leo Grammaticus," p. 269 Bekker).

35. On Theophano's death, the overall case for the reliability of Symeon the Logothete made by Jenkins, "Chronological Accuracy," 104, which supports the traditional date of 897, seems to outweigh the arguments of P. Karlin-Hayter, "La mort de Théophano (10.11.896 ou 895)," *BZ* 62 (1969), 13–18. The rumors of poison are noted in the *Vita Euthymii*, p. 45 Karlin-Hayter.

36. See Constantine VII, *De Administrando Imperio* 50.111–30 Moravcsik; cf. the commentary, p. 189 Jenkins, for the date.

37. Cf. Vasiliev, *Byzance et les Arabes* II.1, 143–44 and 160–61, and Jenkins, "Chronological Accuracy," 107 (dating the sack of Demetrias to March or early April 901).

38. Vasiliev, *Byzance et les Arabes* II.1, 117, 141–42.

39. See Treadgold, "Army," 93–96, 158–59.

40. For the organizational reform, see Treadgold, *Byzantium and Its Army*, 105–6, 110–11; for the settlements, see N. Oikonomidès, "L'organisation de la frontière orientale de Byzance aux Xᵉ–XIᵉ siècles et le taktikon de l'Escorial," in *Actes du XIVᵉ Congrès international des études byzantines* I (Bucharest, 1974), 295–97.

41. R. Jenkins, "The 'Flight' of Samonas," *Speculum* 23 (1948), 217–35, conjectures not very plausibly that Samonas feigned flight to investigate a supposed conspiracy between the Arabs and disaffected Byzantines.

42. John Cameniates' purported eyewitness account of the sack of Thessalonica (ed. Gertrud Böhlig, *CFHB* [Berlin, 1973]) is of little historical interest and may be a later forgery, as argued by A. Kazhdan, "Some Questions Addressed to the Scholars Who Believe in the Authenticity of Kaminiates' 'Capture of Thessalonica,'" *BZ* 71 (1978), 301–14. Kazhdan's argument rests partly on that of H. Grégoire, "Le communiqué arabe sur la prise de Thessalonique

(904)," *Byzantion* 22 (1953), 373–78, that the sack was the subject of an Arab report—which reached Raqqa three days before Cameniates' date for the fall of Thessalonica—of Leo of Tripoli's taking the large port of "Anṭākiya," killing 5,000 Byzantines and capturing the same number. Grégoire relates this to a later Arab account of Leo's taking an "Anṭākiya" near Constantinople, killing 15,000 and capturing twice as many. More likely, however, the first report refers to a sack of Attalia ("Anṭāliya," a correction once suggested by Vasiliev) earlier in the same expedition, which the later account confused with the sack of Thessalonica.

43. See Schminck, *Studien* (above, n. 30), 98–107.

44. While some scholars have believed this attack to be legendary, indirect evidence in Byzantine and Arab sources corroborates the somewhat embroidered account in the *Russian Primary Chronicle*. See R. J. H. Jenkins, "The Supposed Russian Attack on Constantinople in 907: Evidence of the Pseudo-Symeon," *Speculum* 24 (1949), 403–6, and A. A. Vasiliev, "The Second Russian Attack on Constantinople," *DOP* 6 (1951), 161–225.

45. See Treadgold, "Army," 96–99, 160–61.

46. The *Russian Primary Chronicle* dates this treaty to 2 September 911; see Vasiliev, "Second Russian Attack" (above, n. 44), 170–71, 175.

47. See Treadgold, "Army," 100–121, which includes the numbers.

CHAPTER FIFTEEN

For basic bibliography, see above, pp. 908–9, 910.

1. On Alexander, see especially P. Karlin-Hayter, "The Emperor Alexander's Bad Name," *Speculum* 44 (1969), 585–96, who shows that for Alexander's reign Symeon the Logothete did not use the contemporary annals postulated by Jenkins, "Chronological Accuracy," 111–12. Though Karlin-Hayter doubts that such annals existed at all, the strength of Jenkins' arguments indicates that they did, but that they ended with 912 rather than 913.

2. Bernard Flusin, "Un fragment inédit de la vie d'Euthyme le Patriarche?" *TM* 9 (1985), 119–31, presents a fragment that seems too compressed, too indifferent to Euthymius, and too hostile to Leo VI to be from our *Vita Euthymii*. Its improbable report that the dying Leo had relegated Euthymius to his monastery and restored Nicholas as patriarch contradicts not only the chroniclers but apparently the known text of the *Vita Euthymii*, pp. 113–19 Karlin-Hayter, and agrees only with an assertion of Nicholas I himself (*Letter* 32.496–503 Jenkins-Westerink).

3. The sources' vagueness about the two latter concessions can probably be explained by Byzantine embarrassment that they were made; but P. Karlin-Hayter, "The Homily on the Peace with Bulgaria of 927 and the 'Coronation' of 913," *JÖB* 23 (1974), 29–39, doubts that any coronation occurred.

4. Nicholas I's *Letter* 144 Jenkins-Westerink shows that he and not Zoë sent Nicholas Picingli to be strategus of Longobardia.

5. Cf. Constantine VII, *De Administrando Imperio* 50.159–66 Moravcsik.

6. See Constantine VII, *De Administrando Imperio* 32.81–100 Moravcsik.

7. The grand chamberlain was the paymaster for any soldiers and officials

based in Constantinople who drew pay of less than 72 nomismata (cf. Liud-prand, *Antapodosis* VI, 10). Not realizing this, Runciman, *Romanus Lecapenus*, 58, slightly misinterprets these events.

8. Runciman, *Romanus Lecapenus*, 61–62, 65, misdates the events from Zoë's tonsure to Romanus's coronation in 919 and the coronation of Theodora in 920. On these dates, and on the precedence between Constantine and Christo-pher, see Grierson, *Catalogue* III.2, 526–30.

9. See H. Grégoire, "Le lieu de naissance de Romain Lécapène et de Digénis Acritas," *Byzantion* 8 (1933), 572–74. The form "Lacapenus" is also found. La-cape's exact location is as yet unidentified; see Hild, *Kappadokien*, 85, 168.

10. See R. Jenkins, "The Date of the Slav Revolt in Peloponnese Under Ro-manus I," in *Late Classical and Mediaeval Studies in Honor of Albert Mathias Friend, Jr.* (Princeton, 1955), 204–11.

11. Note that when Jenkins, ibid., 206, dates the arrival of the Bulgars on the Gulf of Corinth to August 921, he is under the misapprehension that Romanus was not senior emperor then; the correct date is presumably August 922, since it followed the suppression of the Slav revolt in November 921 (cf. Constan-tine VII, *De Administrando Imperio* 50.25–70 Moravcsik).

12. This victory over Leo is usually dated to 922, but note the comment of Westerink on Nicholas I, *Letter* 23, p. 537, that it need only be later than Au-gust 922. Symeon the Logothete ("Leo Grammaticus," pp. 309–10 Bekker) dates it between the fall of Adrianople in 923 and the arrival of Symeon of Bul-garia before Constantinople in September 924.

13. The date is corrupt in the chronicles, but Runciman, *Romanus Lecapenus*, 246–48, makes a strong case that the two emperors met on 9 September 924; the year seems confirmed by Nicholas I, *Letters* 30 and 31 Jenkins-Westerink (see Westerink's remarks on p. 540).

14. Although the submission of Melitene is dated to 931 in Vasiliev, *Byzance et les Arabes* II.1, 266–67, the Arab sources say only that the city was under the Byzantines by that time, while Symeon the Logothete ("Leo Grammaticus," pp. 317–18 Bekker) dates its submission around the time of the Bulgar treaty of 927.

15. On the famine, see Symeon the Logothete ("Leo Grammaticus," pp. 315–16 Bekker).

16. On the date of this law, which has often been given as 922, see Lemerle, *Agrarian History*, 86–87.

17. Since Basil was punished for his first revolt by having his hand cut off, he was known as Basil the Copper Hand after the prosthesis he used.

18. See the discussion in Lemerle, *Agrarian History*, 94–97.

19. The other four themes were Charpezicium, Arsamosata, Chozanum, and Derzene. See Treadgold, "Army," 128–30, 162.

20. The source for this campaign, the Arab chronicler Ḍahabī, speaks only of "the domestic," but puts the campaign around the beginning of winter, when Pantherius held that post (Vasiliev, *Byzance et les Arabes* II.2, 240).

21. Theophanes Continuatus, pp. 443–44 Bekker.

22. Here I omit the supposed raid of Sayf al-Dawlah on Siricha and Char-

sianum, dated by three late Arabic sources to fall 956 (A.H. 339, around Jumādā I), which looks suspiciously similar to Sayf's famous raid on Siricha and Charsianum in fall 950 (A.H. 345, around Jumādā II); cf. Vasiliev, *Byzance et les Arabes* II.1, 359, with 342–45.

23. For the date, see J. Featherstone, "Ol'ga's Visit to Constantinople," *HUS* 14 (1990), 293–312, though his views on the children present at the ceremony (p. 306) are not very persuasive.

24. This theme, attested in the *Escorial Tacticon* of 971/75, did not exist in 949, and since it was presumably intended to combat the Arabs of Crete it is unlikely to have been created after 961.

25. On these divisions, cf. Oikonomidès, *Listes*, 329, 330. Not long afterward, in place of the 20 banda and 4,000 men of the united Scholae, its two divisions had 15 banda each, making 30 banda and 6,000 men; cf. *Three Byzantine Military Treatises*, ed. G. T. Dennis, *CFHB* (Washington, 1985), 252.133–38. Probably the Excubitors were similarly expanded when they were divided.

26. On this Cretan campaign, see especially Tsougarakis, *Byzantine Crete*, 58–74.

27. For the location of this battle, the Pass of Cylindrus, see Hild, *Kappadokien*, 218–19.

28. For this campaign, see especially Canard, *Histoire*, 805–17.

CHAPTER SIXTEEN

For basic bibliography, see above, pp. 908–9, 911.

1. Polyeuctus objected that the marriage was the second for both of them, and that Nicephorus had allegedly stood godfather for one of Theophano's sons, making him her spiritual relative. The patriarch not only refused to consider dead soldiers as martyrs, but insisted on the traditional rule that soldiers who killed anyone in battle should do penance.

2. Scylitzes, p. 270 Thurn, dates the expulsion of the Arabs from Cyprus to the second year of Nicephorus (beginning 16 August 964), and it seems to have preceded the embassy of Nicephorus to Sayf in fall 964 (Yaḥyā of Antioch, pp. 794–95 Kratchkovsky-Vasiliev). P. Lemerle, "La vie ancienne de S. Athanase l'Athonite," in *Le millénaire du mont Athos, 963–1963: Études et mélanges* I (Chevetogne, 1963), 93 n. 96, notes that the usual date of 965 seems too late.

3. Leo the Deacon, pp. 56, 57 Hase, twice says that Nicephorus led "forty myriads," or 400,000 men. Since this would have been more than twice as many soldiers as the empire had at the time, it is either a great exaggeration or a mistake for four myriads (40,000), which would be quite plausible.

4. These more easterly themes, which would have been hard to defend before the conquest of Cilicia, were those of Anazarbus, Germanicea, Adata, and Hexacomia. On all these themes, see Oikonomidès, *Listes*, 355–56, 359–60.

5. See Dagron, "Minorités," 177–98.

6. See A. D. Stokes, "The Background and Chronology of the Balkan Campaigns of Svyatoslav Igorevich," *Slavonic and East European Review* 40 (1961–62), 44–57.

7. See K. N. Yuzbashian, "L'administration byzantine en Arménie aux Xᵉ–XIᵉ siècles," *RÉA*, n.s., 10 (1973–74), 143–44.

8. The themes in question are (to the north of Taron) Chantiarte, Chortzine, Cama, Chauzizium, Melte, Artze, and Ocomium(?), (to the east) Chuët, (to the west) Muzarium and Caludia, and (to the south) Erkne, Zermium, Chasanara, and Limnia. On these and the new Ducate of Chaldia, see Oikonomidès, *Listes*, 354, 359–63, and (on Ocomium) 268 n. 26.

9. The best discussion of these laws is in Lemerle, *Agrarian History*, 100–103, 128–31. On the famine, which continued until 969, see Leo the Deacon, pp. 102–3 Hase.

10. This is my suggestion in *Byzantium and Its Army*, 139–41, but the matter remains obscure. Grierson, *Catalogue* III.1, 37–38, has suggested that the tetarteron was modeled on the Arab dinar, for use in Nicephorus's new conquests from the Arabs, but Hendy, *Studies*, 507 n. 293, seems right to reject this suggestion.

11. See von Falkenhausen, *Untersuchungen*, 48–49. Longobardia and Calabria continued to have their own strategi, subordinate to the catepan.

12. Although Oikonomidès, *Listes*, 360–61 and nn. 400, 401, locates the Theme of Edessa listed in the *Escorial Tacticon* in Macedonia, he acknowledges that at this time Macedonian Edessa was usually called Vodena, is not otherwise known to have been Byzantine, and actually became the seat of the Bulgarian patriarchate after the fall of Dristra in 971. These facts argue for Mesopotamian Edessa, which Leo the Deacon, pp. 70–71 Hase, says was taken by Nicephorus.

13. Contrary to the opinion of several scholars, Tzimisces appears not to have abrogated Nicephorus II's law on donations to the Church, though this does seem to have been done by Basil II; see John Thomas, "A Disputed Novel of Basil II," *GRBS* 24 (1983), 273–83.

14. See Treadgold, *Byzantium and Its Army*, 35–36 and n. 46.

15. This number is given by Scylitzes, p. 288 Thurn; Leo the Deacon, p. 109 Hase, seems to round it to 10,000.

16. For the location, just north of Laodicea Combusta, see Belke, *Phrygien*, 205.

17. See Paul Walker, "A Byzantine Victory over the Fatimids at Alexandretta (971)," *Byzantion* 42 (1972), 431–40.

18. Leo the Deacon, pp. 129, 132 Hase, gives the number of ships and notes that the Immortals, for whom he gives no number, were followed by 15,000 infantry and 13,000 cavalry, plus the rear guard and baggage train. Scylitzes, p. 295 Thurn, says that the army's vanguard numbered 5,000 infantry, presumably chosen from the 15,000, and 4,000 cavalry, presumably the Immortals. The numbered troops thus seem to have been 32,000, to which the rear guard should be added.

19. See Treadgold, *Byzantium and Its Army*, 36 and n. 47.

20. For a balanced treatment of the problems surrounding the Cometopuli, see J. Ferluga, "Le soulèvement des Comitopoules," *ZRVI* 9 (1966), 75–84. W. Seibt, "Untersuchungen zur Vor- und Frühgeschichte der 'bulgarischen' Kometopulen," *Handes Amsorya* 89 (1975), 65–98, suggests that the Cometopuli were Armenians settled in Macedonia who rebelled against the Byzantines;

but this suggestion, which is based on a theory of N. Adontz, seems to rely too heavily on a dubious passage in Stephen of Taron.

21. See W. Ohnsorge, "Der Heirat Kaisers Otto II," in his *Ost-Rom und der Westen* (Darmstadt, 1983), 129–72.

22. See M. Canard, "La date des expéditions mésopotamiennes de Jean Tzimiscès," *Annuaire de l'Institut de Philologie et d'Histoire Orientales et Slaves* 10 (1960), 99–108.

23. See Nesbitt, *Catalogue* I, 100–101 (Ras), 195–96 (Morava). The date of these themes' creation must be conjectured; if, as seems likely, it was 973, the *Escorial Tacticon* should be dated before then, though no earlier than 971.

24. See Grousset, *Histoire de l'Arménie*, 494–98.

25. See Canard, "Date" (above, n. 22), 107–8, and cf. Leo the Deacon, pp. 161–63 Hase.

26. See most recently P. E. Walker, "The 'Crusade' of John Tzimisces in the Light of New Arabic Evidence," *Byzantion* 47 (1977), 301–27, although I see no reason to share his doubts that Tzimisces visited Palestine, however briefly. Tzimisces' letter to Ashot III does not really deny that his "conquests" in Palestine had brought him only nominal submissions and token tribute. On the new themes, see Yaḥyā of Antioch, p. 369 Kratchkovsky-Vasiliev, speaking rather vaguely but naming Balaneae and Gabala. Oikonomidès, *Listes*, 261 n. 19, notes that seals confirm Gabala and add Laodicea as a theme. Antaradus should presumably be added as well.

27. Constantine, whose second child Zoë was born about 978, probably took a wife in 976, just after Tzimisces died.

28. On Sclerus and his rebellion, see especially Werner Seibt, *Die Skleroi: Eine prosopographisch-sigillographische Studie* (Vienna, 1976), 29–58.

29. See Scylitzes, pp. 328–29 Thurn, and Yaḥyā of Antioch, p. 418 Kratchkovsky-Vasiliev. Note Scylitzes' report that Romanus went to Vidin, which if it was in Bulgarian hands would have cut off Morava and Ras from Byzantine territory. Runciman, *Bulgarian Empire*, 221, argued that since Scylitzes says Romanus was a eunuch he would according to Byzantine tradition have been ineligible to be proclaimed emperor, as Yaḥyā says he was. But the Cometopuli may have denied that Romanus was a eunuch; or Scylitzes may have confused this Romanus with a eunuch named Romanus captured by Basil about 1003 (Scylitzes, p. 346), since according to Yaḥyā (pp. 431, 446) the Bulgarian emperor Romanus was actually captured in 991 and died in 997.

30. On this famine, see Stephen of Taron, p. 57 Macler.

31. For the geography, see Hild, *Kappadokien*, 93–94.

32. This was the later Monastery of the Iberians, or Iberon (*Ivirōn* in Modern Greek).

33. On the date, see W. G. Brokkaar, "Basil Lecapenus: Byzantium in the Tenth Century," *Byzantina Neerlandica* 3 (1972), 199–234. Cf. Yaḥyā of Antioch, pp. 415–19 Kratchkovsky-Vasiliev.

34. Only one of these, Chuët, was the headquarters of a theme. See M. Canard, "Deux documents arabes sur Bardas Skléros," *SBN* 5 (1939), 55–69.

35. For the sequence of these and the following events, see A. Poppe, "The Political Background to the Baptism of Rus': Byzantine-Russian Relations Be-

tween 986–89," *DOP* 30 (1976), 197–244. On the agreement between Phocas and Sclerus, which some think amounted to a partition of the empire, see Cheynet, *Pouvoir*, 332.

36. On the state of the treasury, see Yaḥyā of Antioch, p. 423 Kratchkovsky-Vasiliev.

37. The origin of the name "Varangian" is disputed, but it seems to mean something like "Faithful"; see S. Blöndal, *The Varangians of Byzantium*, rev. and trans. B. Benedikz (Cambridge, 1978), 4–7. For their number, see Stephen of Taron, pp. 164–65 Macler.

38. Though the earlier view was that the Russians took Cherson from Basil's forces because Anna had not yet been sent to Kiev, see Poppe, "Political Background" (above, n. 35).

39. For the location of his place of detention, the fort of Tyropoeum, see Hild, *Kappadokien*, 297–98.

40. See Yaḥyā of Antioch, p. 431 Kratchkovsky-Vasiliev, whose reference to the capture of Beroea toward the end of the four-year campaign indicates the theater of war.

41. Cf. G. Ostrogorsky, "Une ambassade serbe auprès de l'empereur Basile II," *Byzantion* 19 (1949), 187–94.

42. See Scylitzes, p. 339 Thurn, though here Scylitzes seems to have confused Basil's departure for Syria in 995 with his departure for Iberia in 1000. Scylitzes can hardly be referring to the Iberian campaign of 990, which Basil did not accompany.

43. See Forsyth, "Byzantine-Arab Chronicle," 135–37, showing that the original source was the reliable Aleppine chronicle of al-Shimshāṭī.

44. On this law, see especially Lemerle, *Agrarian History*, 103–5, 112–14.

45. Samuel seems barely to have penetrated the Peloponnesus, to judge from the *Life of St. Nicon*, pp. 140–43 Sullivan.

46. Cf. Scylitzes, pp. 341–42 Thurn, with Yaḥyā of Antioch, p. 446 Kratchkovsky-Vasiliev. Yaḥyā implies the date of 997, which is compatible with Scylitzes' account; the heavy rains suggest the battle took place in the autumn, after Samuel had raided during the summer. Though some scholars have supposed that Samuel conquered much of Greece at this time, the sources indicate the contrary; even Larissa was under Byzantine control, and probably had been since 991.

47. See Yaḥyā of Antioch, pp. 457–58 Kratchkovsky-Vasiliev. Sizara presumably became a theme.

48. These two themes, Teluch and the Euphrates Cities, are first attested about 1030 (Scylitzes, pp. 381, 387 Thurn), but no date after 1000 seems likely for their creation, and the success of the Fatimid raid on Germanicea seems to indicate that they did not exist in 998.

49. Scylitzes, p. 342 Thurn, without mentioning the fall of Dyrrhachium, notes that Samuel controlled it soon after the battle of the Sperchius. Its capture, which can hardly have been by force since Samuel lacked a fleet, probably occurred shortly before the doge Pietro II's expedition to Dalmatia in spring 1000. On the latter, see Ferluga, *Amministrazione*, 191–98.

50. Little Preslav presumably replaced the former Theme of the Mesopo-

tamia of the West. The Byzantines seem never to have lost Dristra, which became the seat of a duke of Paradunavum with authority over the whole Danube frontier. See Nesbitt, *Catalogue* I, 150–52, 173–79, for the seals attesting these commands as well as Mesembria, which may also have become a theme at this time, because no other date seems appropriate. Classicizing Byzantine writers called Paradunavum "Paristrium," Ister being the ancient name for the Danube.

51. Cf. Scylitzes, pp. 342–43 Thurn, who implies that Ashot fled to Constantinople soon after his appointment and found Basil there, evidently before Basil left for Bulgaria. Despite the views of several modern scholars, the Bulgarian occupation of Dyrrhachium seems to have been brief.

52. Scylitzes, pp. 346–47 Thurn, writes of Basil's siege of Vidin, campaign against Scopia, and law on landholding as if they all belonged to the year beginning 1 September 1001; but if Basil took Vidin around the Feast of the Dormition (15 August 1002), as Scylitzes indicates, he could hardly have both campaigned against Scopia and returned to Constantinople in time to promulgate a law before 1 September. A year division must therefore have been omitted before the Scopia campaign, and the law should be dated to 1003. The interpretation of the law in Lemerle, *Agrarian History*, 79–80, differs from mine in assuming that Basil merely prohibited large landholders from turning their estates into tax units distinct from those of their neighbors; this interpretation does not seem to suit Scylitzes' reference to the law as an "unheard-of burden," nor Basil's promise to revoke it later (see Scylitzes, p. 365).

53. For the date, see von Falkenhausen, *Untersuchungen*, 52 and n. 387.

54. See Yaḥyā of Antioch, pp. 461–62 Kratchkovsky-Vasiliev, who says that Basil campaigned against the Bulgarians for four years after 1000. Relying on Scylitzes, p. 348 Thurn, who says that Basil raided Bulgaria annually for some time before 1014, most modern scholars have concluded that Basil continued full-scale warfare from 1004 to 1014. Yet not even Scylitzes says this, and Basil had not even taken the border forts of Pernik and Melnik by 1014.

55. These were the themes of Dryinopolis and Colonia in Epirus and the Theme of Serbia, which probably included Castoria and was named for the city of Serbia in northern Greece, not for the Serbs.

56. It may, however, have led Basil to create a Theme of Chios, which seems not to have existed when the raid occurred about 1024 but did exist before 1028; cf. Scylitzes, pp. 367–68, 373 Thurn.

57. For the reserve (200,000 pounds of gold) see Psellus, I, p. 19 Renauld; for the remissions of taxes, see Scylitzes, p. 373 Thurn. Since most taxpayers were still able to pay the arrears by 1028, the remissions must have been quite recent, and the peaceful interval of 1023–24 seems the most likely time for them.

58. On Basil's hopes for Zoë, cf. Psellus, I, p. 99 Renauld. He can hardly have expected the aged Constantine to reign for long.

CHAPTER SEVENTEEN

For basic bibliography, see above, pp. 908–9, 911–12.

1. See Treadgold, *Byzantium and Its Army*, 75–85.

2. On the Christian majority at Edessa, see Ibn Ḥawqal, p. 221 Kramers-Wiet.

3. See John Teall, "The Grain Supply of the Byzantine Empire, 330–1025," *DOP* 13 (1959), 87–139.

4. So Hendy, *Studies*, 100–107, 135–36, though cf. Cheynet, *Pouvoir*, 235–36.

5. See the remarks of Hārūn ibn Yaḥyā and Ibn Ḥawqal in Vasiliev, *Byzance et les Arabes* II.2, 382–83, 414–16, and Ibn Ḥawqal, pp. 192–93 (the same as the second passage in Vasiliev), 196–97 Kramers-Wiet (not in Vasiliev).

6. See Dagron, "Minorités."

7. See V. Arutjunova-Fidanjan, "Sur le problème des provinces byzantines orientales," *RÉA*, n.s., 14 (1980), 157–69.

8. See Malamut, *Îles*, esp. 465–69.

9. See Gay, *Italie*, 580–92.

10. See Lemerle, *Agrarian History*, 90–114; note that Basil II (Zepos, *Jus* I, 265) singles out a peasant named Philocales who became a palace chamberlain and abused his power to buy up all the land in his village.

11. The themes definitely lost were Ras, Morava, Beroea in Greece, the Mesopotamia of the West, and Edessa. Though parts of the themes of Larissa, Dyrrhachium, and Dalmatia were lost, other parts probably held out. The empire eventually recovered the territory of all but Ras, which became a client state.

12. After 842 these estates were returned to Michael's son the patriarch Ignatius, but by the time of his death he transferred them to Basil I.

13. On the domestic logothete ([*logothetēs*] *tōn oikeiakōn*), see Oikonomidès, "Évolution," 136–40.

14. See Hendy, *Studies*, 85–90, 131–38.

15. Apparently Symeon was called the New Theologian to compare him to Gregory of Nazianzus, often known simply as the Theologian.

16. The standard study of this phenomenon is Obolensky's *Commonwealth*.

17. See Cyril Mango, "L'origine de la minuscule," in *La paléographie grecque et byzantine*, Colloques Internationaux du Centre National de la Recherche Scientifique 559 (Paris, 1977), 175–80.

18. Cyril Mango, "Who Wrote the Chronicle of Theophanes?" *ZRVI* 18 (1978), 9–17, has shown that Theophanes drew heavily on materials left by George, whose work was interrupted by his death; but Mango probably goes too far in maintaining that George wrote practically all of Theophanes' chronicle.

19. On Sergius and the fragments that are probably his, known as the Scriptor Incertus, see Treadgold, *Byzantine Revival*, 376–78.

20. See W. Treadgold, *The Nature of the Bibliotheca of Photius* (Washington, 1980). Though a date of 855 is just possible and other dates have been proposed, Photius's letters and *Amphilochia* refer to so many books not in the *Bibliotheca* that it must be an early work. Illogically, some have argued that Photius's few later references to books in the *Bibliotheca* mean that the work is late; such references show only that, as one would expect, Photius sometimes referred back to books he had read earlier.

21. See Mango, "Legend."

22. On the anthology's complex development through the centuries, now see Alan Cameron, *The Greek Anthology from Meleager to Planudes* (Oxford, 1993).

23. Here I follow the dating of R. Cormack, "The Apse Mosaics of S. Sophia at Thessaloniki," *Deltion tēs Christianikēs Archaiologikēs Hetaireias* 10 (1980–81), 111–26, in preference to the much earlier date proposed by K. Theoharidou, *The Architecture of Hagia Sophia, Thessaloniki* (Oxford, 1988), 148–57.

24. On this building, now vanished, see most recently Paul Magdalino, "Observations on the Nea Ekklesia of Basil I," *JÖB* 37 (1987), 51–64.

25. See Ihor Ševčenko, "The Illuminators of the Menologium of Basil II," *DOP* 16 (1962), 245–76, and "On Pantoleon the Painter," *JÖB* 21 (1972), 241–49.

26. Again I follow McEvedy, *Atlas.*

27. Yaḥyā of Antioch, p. 430 Kratchkovsky-Vasiliev.

28. Scylitzes, pp. 386, 389 Thurn, records that famines in 1032 and 1033 led peasants in the eastern themes to try to migrate to Thrace, an indication that this was already an established pattern.

29. See M.-H. Fourmy and M. Leroy, "La vie de S. Philarète," *Byzantion* 9 (1934), 119, 141.

30. See the *Life of Saint Nicon*, pp. 114–18, 134–36 Sullivan.

31. See P. Charanis, "Observations on the Demography of the Byzantine Empire," in *Thirteenth International Congress of Byzantine Studies, Main Papers* XIV (Oxford, 1966), 8.

32. Treadgold, *Byzantine Revival*, p. 41 and n. 40.

33. See Vasiliev, *Byzance et les Arabes* II.1, 160–61.

34. On the silting of the harbor of Ephesus from the ninth century onward and Smyrna's role as a replacement, see Foss, *Ephesus*, 6, 121–25, 185–87. Ahrweiler, "Smyrne," 34–37, conjectures from the relative silence of the sources that Smyrna was fairly small until 1204, after which she postulates a sudden expansion to account for its newly attested importance; a more plausible explanation would be that the city had already been large but escaped mention in the scanty sources for the earlier period. According to Anna Comnena, XI, 5.4, about 10,000 people were massacred at Smyrna in 1097; the population before the massacre should have been more than twice that, and even larger before the Turkish conquest of 1081. Yet in the absence of useful archeological evidence conditions at Smyrna remain somewhat obscure.

35. See Clive Foss, "Late Antique and Byzantine Ankara," *DOP* 31 (1977), 72–86.

36. According to Leo the Deacon, p. 73 Hase, when Nicephorus II was besieging Antioch he considered it the world's third-largest city in both population and walled area. Russell, *Medieval Regions*, 202, estimates that Antioch had about 40,000 people in 1268, when it was still the largest city in Syria but prolonged warfare had probably left it smaller than in 1025. Cf. Hugh Kennedy, "Antioch: From Byzantium to Islam and Back Again," in John Rich, ed., *The City in Late Antiquity* (London, 1992), 181–98.

37. See Treadgold, *Byzantium and Its Army*, 188–98.

CHAPTER EIGHTEEN

For basic bibliography, see above, pp. 912–14.

1. On his family see J.-F. Vannier, *Familles byzantines: Les Argyroi* (Paris, 1975), with 36–39 on Romanus himself.

2. On Dalassenus, see J.-C. Cheynet and J.-F. Vannier, *Études prosopographiques* (Paris, 1986), 80–82. (Note that in the eleventh century the title "catepan" became practically interchangeable with "duke.")

3. These included the future emperor Constantine X Ducas and probably the future emperor Constantine IX Monomachus, since he had been exiled for seven years by early 1042 (Psellus, I, p. 126 Renauld).

4. See Scylitzes, pp. 386 (famine in northern Anatolia in 1032), 389 (locusts in northern Anatolia in 1033), 393 and 394–95 (hail, probably around Constantinople, and locusts in western Anatolia in 1034), and 399 Thurn (locusts in the Thracesians in 1035). Cf. Matthew of Edessa, pp. 75–76 Dostourian (famine in Armenia in 1032).

5. See Scylitzes, pp. 405 (donatives), 408–9 (sale of offices), 412 (surcharges), and 404 Thurn (conversion of taxes in kind). John and Michael may also have made tentative attempts to debase the coinage, but the evidence for this is ambiguous; see n. 11 below.

6. The Constantinopolitan conspirators included the future patriarch Michael Cerularius, a friend of the exiled Constantine Monomachus, who may also have been involved in this plot. For the sources, see Cheynet, *Pouvoir*, 51–52.

7. For the earlier situation, see Treadgold, *Finances*, 37–39. For Constantine IX's reign and later, see P. Lemerle, "'Roga' et rente d'état aux Xe–XIe siècles," *RÉB* 25 (1967), 85–100 (though unlike Lemerle I believe all the offices in question were purely titular, except for the imperial official of Madytus). That this change was introduced by Constantine seems implied by Psellus, I, p. 132 Renauld; cf. Zonaras, pp. 616–17 Büttner-Wobst.

8. The case for their being summoned by Maniaces is given by A. Poppe, "La dernière expédition russe contre Constantinople," *Byzantinoslavica* 32 (1971), 1–29, 233–68. Poppe failed to convince J. Shepard, "Why Did The Russians Attack Byzantium in 1043?" *BNJ* 22 (1979), 147–212, who stresses the statement of Scylitzes, p. 430 Thurn, that the Russian prince Yaroslav was avenging the death of a Russian trader in Constantinople. Yet this might well have been a reason that induced Yaroslav to support Maniaces against Constantine IX. Especially because Maniaces' army included many Varangians, Yaroslav can hardly have been ignorant of or indifferent to Maniaces' rebellion.

9. For these and the following events, see J. Lefort, "Rhétorique et politique: Trois discours de Jean Mauropous en 1047," *TM* 6 (1976), 272–84; cf. A. Kazhdan, "Once More About the 'Alleged' Russo-Byzantine Treaty (ca. 1047) and the Pecheneg Crossing of the Danube," *JÖB* 26 (1977), 65–77.

10. She died before May 1046; see N. Oikonomidès, "St. George of Mangana, Maria Skleraina, and the 'Malaj Sion' of Novgorod," *DOP* 34–35 (1980–81), 243 and n. 44.

11. Hendy, *Studies*, 233–36, rightly rejects the argument that Constantine meant to increase the money supply to accommodate economic expansion, as argued by Morrisson, "Dévaluation." Though Hendy, *Studies*, 509 and n. 303, notes that Michael IV struck coins that varied between 24 and 19-1/2 carats, Michael's debasement was probably on a small scale and certainly transitory, because at the beginning of Constantine's reign the coinage was not debased.

12. Scylitzes, p. 476 Thurn, mentions this measure after events belonging to 1052 and before events belonging to 1054/55; although he connects it with Constantine's construction of Saint George of the Mangana, finished in 1047, the connection seems simply to be that extravagant building of this sort was what forced such drastic economies.

13. Scylitzes, p. 476 Thurn; Attaliates, pp. 44–45 Bekker; Cecaumenus, pp. 152–54 Litavrin.

14. Leo's real surname was probably Spondylus, Paraspondylus ("Shifty") being a nickname.

15. For the dates, see J. Shepard, "Isaac Comnenus' Coronation Day," *Byzantinoslavica* 38 (1977), 22–30.

16. The fullest (though still not very satisfactory) discussion of Isaac's reforms is Eugen Stănescu, "Les réformes d'Isaac Comnène," *RÉSEE* 4 (1966), 35–69.

17. Cf. Lemerle, *Cinq études*, 280–82.

18. Cheynet, *Pouvoir*, 71, 345 n. 43. Isaac died not long afterward.

19. See Cecaumenus, pp. 252–64 (esp. p. 260) Litavrin.

20. On the circumstances, see N. Oikonomidès, "Le serment de l'impératrice Eudocie (1067)," *RÉB* 21 (1963), 101–28.

21. Attaliates, p. 98 Bekker, speaks of Romanus's youth in 1067, though Romanus must have been at least thirty-four, because his father had died in 1032. Psellus, II, p. 157 Renauld, says that Romanus had been suspected of complicity in his father's allegedly dishonorable plot, but Psellus's chronology is often faulty, and his bias against Romanus is patent.

22. Perhaps the best modern account of Romanus's campaigns in the East is in Hild, *Kappadokien*, 100–105.

23. These generals are said to have included the magister Joseph Tarchaniotes and the domestic of the West Nicephorus Bryennius (Bryennius, p. 107 Gautier), and even Romanus's admirer Michael Attaliates (Attaliates, p. 136 Bekker). Some hindsight may, however, be involved.

24. See C. Cahen, "La campagne de Mantzikert d'après les sources musulmanes," *Byzantion* 9 (1934), 625–27.

25. Morrisson, "Dévaluation," 38–39.

26. See especially J. C. Cheynet, "Mantzikert: Un désastre militaire?" *Byzantion* 50 (1980), 410–38, who supplies estimated numbers (60,000 Byzantines, 15,000 Turks) and the date (26 August 1071).

27. After 1071 no eastern tagmatic troops are found in Anatolia proper (except for the new Immortals recruited about 1075); but when Philaretus nominally ended his rebellion in 1078 he was named domestic of the East, implying that he then commanded the eastern tagmata.

28. The date of 1075 for the recapture of Trebizond, repeated by many scholars as if it were recorded in the sources, can be traced to a plausible conjecture of W. Fischer, "Trapezus im 11. und 12. Jahrhundert," *Mitteilungen des Instituts für Österreichischen Geschichtsforschung* 10 (1889), 185–86.

29. On these new recruits, see Bryennius, pp. 265–67 Gautier.

30. See Morrisson, "Dévaluation," 39–40; cf. Bryennius, pp. 257–59 Gautier.

31. Attaliates, pp. 206–11 Bekker, seems to date Nestor's revolt after Alexius's capture of Russell (1075?) and before a year when a comet appeared, which should be 1076/77; cf. Grumel, *Chronologie*, 473. The latter year was also the time of the famine.

32. See E. Tsolakes, "Ho chronos tēs gennēseōs kai tou thanatou tou Nikēphorou G' Botaneiatē," *Hellenika* 27 (1974), 150–51.

33. Matthew of Edessa, pp. 253–54 Dostourian, describes the famine and chaos in the region at the time.

CHAPTER NINETEEN

For basic bibliography, see above, pp. 912–13, 914.

1. Though Cosmas won his point, he agreed to abdicate a month later in favor of a more pliant patriarch.

2. See W. B. McQueen, "Relations Between the Normans and Byzantium, 1071–1112," *Byzantion* 56 (1986), 427–76.

3. Cf. Zonaras, p. 741 Büttner-Wobst, with Anna Comnena, IV, 4.3.

4. Cf. Anna Comnena, V, 3.2, speaking of the aftermath of the battle.

5. These others presumably included former followers of Nestor, the rebel duke of ten years before, who seems to have died by this time.

6. Cf. Theophylact of Ochrid, *Oration* 5, p. 231 Gautier, with Gautier's commentary, pp. 84–87.

7. The name means "Sons of Officers," though there cannot have been nearly enough officers' sons to man the whole corps.

8. See P. Gautier, "Défection et soumission de la Crète sous Alexis Ier Comnène," *RÉB* 35 (1977), 215–27.

9. On Alexius's monetary reform, see Hendy, *Coinage*, 14–25, 39–49.

10. P. Gautier, "Le synode des Blachernes (fin 1094): Étude prosopographique," *RÉB* 29 (1971), 213–84, has established the date.

11. Which of the two dead sons of Romanus he purported to be is not quite clear. Anna Comnena, X, 2.2, says Leo, but mentions that the pretender claimed to have been at Antioch, as Constantine had been but Leo had not. On the other hand, since this rebel was certainly a fraud, his claims may themselves have been inconsistent. Cf. Cheynet, *Pouvoir*, 99–100.

12. Such is the rough estimate of Runciman, *History of the Crusades* I, 336–41. Though he almost certainly overestimates the size of the Byzantine army as a whole, he is surely right that Alexius could muster no more than 20,000 men in one place. Anna Comnena, XI, 2.2, notes that the Crusaders vastly outnumbered the Byzantine army.

13. Lilie, *Byzantium*, 8–28, argues that Alexius demanded any conquests up

to and including Jerusalem in outright possession, leaving no fiefs to which the Crusaders' oath could apply. But the Crusaders are most unlikely to have agreed to this, and subsequent events imply the agreement outlined here.

14. Anna Comnena's account of Chaka (*Tzachas* in Greek) appears confused. At IX, 3.4, in an account of events around 1092, she mentions Chaka's death when he was stabbed by his son-in-law Kilij Arslan, but at XI, 5.1 she says that Chaka ruled Smyrna in 1097. The two reports can be reconciled by supposing that Chaka's murder actually occurred in 1097, after the Byzantines occupied Smyrna.

15. See Belke, *Phrygien*, 321–22; though Belke's map locates Lampe south of Choma, the course of this campaign indicates that Lampe was in a less exposed position somewhat to the north.

16. Anna Comnena, XIV, 3.5, shows that Acroënus was Byzantine about 1111, and 1098 is much the most likely date for its recovery.

17. The sources for what happened to Laodicea are somewhat contradictory; see most recently Lilie, *Byzantium*, 259–76.

18. As Lilie, *Byzantium*, 275, states, the sources allow a date either late in 1099 or in the first half of 1100; but Bohemund would hardly have spent Christmas 1099 at Jerusalem if a Byzantine army had been near Antioch at that time. A Byzantine presence in Cilicia in 1099 might also have deterred the Rubenids there from calling themselves kings of Armenia.

19. Although the date of this plot is uncertain, Anna Comnena, XII, 7.1, seems to imply that it came shortly before the revolt of the duke of Trebizond Gregory Taronites in 1103/4. If so, the sebastocrator Isaac Comnenus, who was still alive at the time, lived until late 1103, and Anna Dalassena died on 1 November 1102, "a year and a little" before Isaac (Zonaras, p. 746 Büttner-Wobst). Cf. P. Gautier, "L'obituaire du Typikon du Pantocrator," *RÉB* 27 (1969), 244–45.

20. The date of this marriage is uncertain, but it evidently fell between 1104 and early 1106, while Bohemund was collecting his army. It cannot be later, since the couple's first children, a twin boy and girl, were born at the beginning of 1107 (Anna Comnena, XII, 4.4).

21. The technicalities are discussed by Hendy, *Coinage*, 50–64. Though Alexius's basic rules for taxation date from 1106, his final clarification and enforcement of them came in February 1109.

22. Confusingly, Shāhānshāh was sometimes called Malik-Shāh, like the main Seljuk sultan in the East.

23. The precise location of this battle, the fort of Acrocus, has not been securely identified; see Belke, *Phrygien*, 179.

24. Skoulatos, *Personnages*, 39–40 and n. 2, gives a satisfactory explanation of the confused account of Basil in Anna Comnena, XV, 8–10.

25. Constantine was a relative of the region's martyred warlord Theodore Gabras, but the exact relation between the two is uncertain. The duke of Trebizond who rebelled about 1104, Gregory Taronites, may also have been a Gabras and the son of Theodore.

26. The chronology of this whole Hungarian war is uncertain. Here I follow

the reconstruction of Makk, *Árpáds*, 22–27, which if correct explains John's absence from Anatolia between 1127 and 1129.

27. Lopadium is the likely but not certain identification of the city on the coast mentioned by Michael the Syrian, III, p. 230 Chabot.

28. For its act of foundation, see Paul Gautier, "Le Typikon du Christ Sauveur Pantocrator," *RÉB* 32 (1974), 1–145.

29. See L. Petit, "Monodie de Théodore Prodrome sur Étienne Sklitzès métropolitain de Trébizonde," *Izvestija Russkago Arkheologischeskago Instituta v Konstantinopole* 8 (1903), 3–4, 10–11.

30. See Robert Browning, "The Death of John II Comnenus," *Byzantion* 31 (1961), 229–35, who makes a strong case for foul play.

CHAPTER TWENTY

For basic bibliography, see above, pp. 912–13, 914–15.

1. John II had captured Theodore (*Thoros* in Armenian) along with his father Leo in 1137; but after Leo's death, Theodore escaped around 1145 and began to recover his father's Cilician kingdom.

2. "Nureddin" is the usual English form of the Arabic *Nūr al-Dīn* (Light of the Faith).

3. Choniates, *History*, pp. 96–97 van Dieten, gives the figure of almost 30,000 pounds of gold (with 72 hyperpyra to the pound by weight). Most of this probably went to subsidize allies rather than to pay for military operations.

4. For Manuel's changes in military pay, see Choniates, *History*, pp. 208–9 van Dieten, in a section of undated material at the end of his account of Manuel's reign. The date seems to follow from the strength of the army after 1158 despite the loss of so much money in the Italian campaign.

5. Makk, *Árpáds*, 86–88, shows that Béla's succeeding to the throne of Hungary as well as Byzantium, which some scholars believe was Manuel's plan, could have been no more than a remote possibility at this time.

6. *Liber Pontificalis*, II, pp. 414–15 Duchesne; cf. Cinnamus, pp. 219–20 Meineke.

7. Since Choniates, *History*, p. 150 van Dieten, mentions the foundation of Neocastra between the arrest of Alexius Axuch (p. 143) and Manuel's latest Hungarian expedition (p. 151), both datable to 1167, that was probably the year of the theme's foundation.

8. "Saladin" is the usual English form of the Arabic *Ṣalāḥ al-Dīn* (Righteousness of the Faith).

9. Alexius II's coronation took place on 4 March 1171, and the Venetians' arrest occurred on 12 March. On the number of Venetians, see Hendy, *Studies*, 593–94, who suggests that about 6,000 may have been merchants; the rest were presumably employees and dependents of various sorts.

10. Cotyaeum, Byzantine in 1180 (Choniates, *History*, p. 262 van Dieten), would have been difficult to hold before the Byzantines took Dorylaeum, but is unlikely to have been taken later.

11. On this battle, see Hendy, *Studies*, 127–30, with 146–54 for its location.

12. William, who in fact was out for himself, also gave refuge and support to another pretender, Alexius the Cupbearer, a grandnephew of the emperor Manuel.

13. Hendy, *Studies*, 225.

14. See E. Vranoussi, "À propos des opérations des Normands dans la mer Égée et à Chypre après la prise de Thessalonique (1185–86)," *Byzantina* 8 (1976), 203–11.

15. The course of this revolt is somewhat obscure. Here I accept the conclusions of van Dieten, *Niketas Choniates*, 66–78, which follow the principal source, Choniates, and are similar to the reconstruction of Brand, *Byzantium*, 273–74.

16. Van Dieten, *Niketas Choniates*, 62–64, has shown that this expedition occurred in either 1190 or 1191; but Isaac could hardly have felt free to make two lengthy campaigns in 1191, a year of three or four serious rebellions; see Cheynet, *Pouvoir*, 123–25 (esp. no. 170, n. 1).

17. Hendy, *Coinage*, 14 n. 1, notes that the Byzantine hyperpyron was valued at ¼ mark in 1204.

18. The shock of his second deposition seems to have been enough to kill Isaac, though assistance from poison is also possible.

19. According to Geoffrey of Villehardouin, chaps. 254–55 Faral, the Crusaders, after dividing the booty equally with the Venetians and paying them another 50,000 marks, had about 400,000 marks left, not counting booty never turned in for distribution.

CHAPTER TWENTY-ONE

For basic bibliography, see above, pp. 912–13, 915.

1. But most modern maps have exaggerated the area the Byzantines controlled in the twelfth century; see Hendy, *Studies*, 108–31.

2. See C. Toumanoff, "On the Relationship Between the Founder of the Empire of Trebizond and the Georgian Queen Thamar," *Speculum* 15 (1940), 299–312.

3. See Vasiliev, *Goths*, 150–59, though his hypothesis about a revolt in Crimea by the Gabras family is pure speculation.

4. They were Theodore Mangaphas of Philadelphia, who had resumed his rebellion, Sabas Asidenus of Priene, and Manuel Maurozomes in the Meander valley; see below, pp. 710, 712–14.

5. On the beginning of Theodore's activities see Oikonomidès, "Décomposition," esp. 22–28.

6. Hendy, *Studies*, 136–38, emphasizes the tendency for the military aristocracy to have estates in Anatolia and the civil aristocracy to have estates in the Balkans, though Cheynet, *Pouvoir*, 191–98, notes that the two groups overlapped and were not very cohesive.

7. This reestablishment of the Anatolian magnates in the Balkans definitely occurred, but the process is not well documented; see Cheynet, *Pouvoir*, 237–45.

8. Cf. Chap. 19, n. 12 above.

9. The discussion of the pronoia system in Bartusis, *Late Byzantine Army*, 156–90, though based on the more abundant evidence after 1204, applies in broad outline to the later twelfth century.

10. Hendy, *Studies*, 86–89, 132–33, gives a list of such grants, which are sometimes called appanages by an imprecise analogy with late medieval France.

11. On the monasteries during this period, see especially Thomas, *Private Religious Foundations*, 167–243.

12. See J. Grosdidier de Matons, "Psellos et le monde de l'irrationel," *TM 6* (1976), 325–49.

13. See Mango, "Legend."

14. Choniates, *History*, p. 169 van Dieten. The sequence, which spelled the word for blood (*haima*, with *h* not counting as a letter in Greek), was *A*lexius, *I*oannes (John II), *M*anuel, and *A*lexius II.

15. The titles of the men called "professors" here were actually "guardian of the laws" (*nomophylax*) and "consul of the philosophers" (*hypatos tōn philosophōn*), terms implying duties in administration and research rather than teaching.

16. These are Nicetas Eugenianus's *Drosilla and Charicles* and Constantine Manasses' *Aristandrus and Callithea*. Another such romance, Eustathius Macrembolites' *Hysmine and Hysminias*, is in prose.

17. Cf. Cyril Mango, "Les monuments de l'architecture du XIe siècle et leur signification historique et sociale," *TM 6* (1976), 351–65.

18. This much seems certain. But in the mosaic the heads of Zoë and Christ seem also to have been altered, for reasons that are still a subject of controversy; the hypothesis of N. Oikonomidès, "The Mosaic Panel of Constantine IX and Zoe," *RÉB* 36 (1978), 219–32, is technically improbable, but I have nothing better to offer. On the miniature of Michael VII, see I. Spatharakis, *The Portrait in Byzantine Illuminated Manuscripts* (Leiden, 1976), 107–18.

19. See Steven Runciman, "Blachernae Palace and Its Decoration," in *Studies in Memory of David Talbot Rice* (Edinburgh, 1975), 277–83.

20. See especially the complementary articles of Michael Hendy, "Byzantium, 1081–1204: An Economic Reappraisal," originally published in 1970, and "Byzantium, 1081–1204: The Economy Revisited, Twenty Years On," now both available in his *The Economy, Fiscal Administration and Coinage of Byzantium* (Northampton, 1989), studies II and III.

21. See Lefort, "Population."

22. See McEvedy, *Atlas*. On pp. 133–34 the authors write of Anatolia, "The arrival of the Turks meant a drop in the overall population of the country [from 7 million to 5 million by their estimate] because the nomadic and pastoral way of life typical of the Turks at this time cannot support as high a density as agriculture." But the Turks mostly occupied regions on the plateau that were already used for pasture, while most of the farming population stayed where it was, in the western plains. My own guess is that the losses due to the invasion roughly canceled out the natural increase. This would raise the estimate of the population of the whole peninsula to about 7 million, and would put nearly all of the extra 2 million after 1071 in the agricultural regions that soon returned to Byzantine rule.

23. Cf. Jacoby, "Population," figuring an upper limit of 375,000.

24. See Geoffrey of Villehardouin (chap. 251 Faral), who despite his access to good information from former Byzantine officials may have exaggerated somewhat because he was so impressed. On the contemporary population of Venice, see Russell, *Medieval Regions*, 63–65.

25. See Idrīsī, II, pp. 129–30, 133–35, 286–99 (299–302 being copied from earlier works), 302–4, 325–26, 392–93 Jaubert; Benjamin of Tudela, pp. 261–68 Komroff; cf. Sharf, *Byzantine Jewry*, 132–57.

26. Tafel, *Urkunden* II, 208.

27. Idrīsī, II, p. 119 Jaubert; Benjamin of Tudela, p. 267 Komroff.

28. See Kazhdan, *Change*, 31–39, though I suspect that the authors' optimism about Balkan cities and ambivalence about Anatolian ones reflect the fact that the Balkan cities had started from a much lower base. In absolute terms, I doubt their implied conclusion that cities like Ochrid or Castoria were more populous than Sardis or Adramyttium at this time, even though the former had surely grown faster than the latter. Note that after 1204 the strongest Byzantine successor state developed not in Greece but in western Anatolia.

29. Anthony Bryer, "The *Tourkokratia* in the Pontos: Some Problems and Preliminary Conclusions," *Neo-Hellenika* 1 (1970), 36–39, estimates that Trebizond had 6,000 people in the early fourteenth century, but he notes that it continued to have about 6,000 after "as much as two-thirds" of its population was deported in 1461—implying a previous population of some 18,000—and that it had about 34,000 in 1868. Bryer's estimate depends on the statement of Pero Tafur, p. 131 Letts, that Trebizond had about 4,000 people in 1438. But probably Tafur, who in his next sentence calls Trebizond "well walled," was referring only to the small walled town and not to the extensive suburbs, which had no wall. Even in 1461 the population must have been smaller than it was before the plague hit the city in 1347.

30. See Kazhdan, *Change*, 26–31.

31. On this industry see D. Jacoby, "Silk in Western Byzantium Before the Fourth Crusade," *BZ* 84/85 (1991/92), 452–500.

32. Kazhdan, *Change*, 39–46.

33. Oikonomidès, *Hommes d'affaires*, has shown that even in the subsequent period native Byzantines had a considerable role in commerce; in the earlier period it was surely greater.

34. See S. D. Goitein, "Mediterranean Trade in the Eleventh Century: Some Facts and Problems," in M. A. Cook, ed., *Studies in the Economic History of the Middle East from the Rise of Islam to the Present Day* (Oxford, 1970), 51–62.

35. See Hendy, *Studies*, 222, 270.

36. The manuscripts of Benjamin of Tudela vary between making this the daily revenue and the annual revenue. Sharf, *Byzantine Jewry*, 136, 158 n. 4, opts for daily revenue because as annual revenue the figure "would hardly call for comment." But the sum's modest size is a reason for a copyist to change "annual" to "daily," rather than the other way around. Rents were usually collected annually, never daily, and the government is unlikely to have kept track of its trade duties on a daily basis. The decisive point is that a daily revenue of 20,000 hyperpyra would imply an annual revenue of 7.3 million hyperpyra from Constantinople alone, which is utterly fantastic. As an annual revenue the

sum does seem low, but not impossibly so; see Hendy, *Studies*, 598 and n. 201. One might guess that the trade duties, surely the largest item, accounted for about 15,000 hyperpyra.

37. Hendy, *Studies*, 593–99.
38. Tafel, *Urkunden* II, 208–9.
39. See Hendy, *Studies*, 173.

CHAPTER TWENTY-TWO

For basic bibliography, see above, pp. 915–17.

1. For the date of the partition, see Oikonomidès, "Décomposition," 3–28. For the text of the document, see A. Carile, "Partitio Terrarum Imperii Romaniae," *Studi Veneziani* 7 (1965), 125–305, who, however, dates the partition to September 1204.

2. R.-J. Loenertz, "Aux origines du despotat d'Épire et de la principauté d'Achaïe," *Byzantion* 43 (1973), 377–89, doubts that Michael would have left Epirus when he was just organizing his state there; but Michael may well have seen the prevailing chaos as a unique opportunity to seize the Peloponnesus and become a major power.

3. See van Dieten, *Niketas Choniates*, 151–52, for the chronology.

4. Another minor exception was the rocky promontory of Monemvasia in Greece, whose Byzantine population remained under local Byzantine rulers until about 1253. See Haris Kalligas, *Byzantine Monemvasia: The Sources* (Monemvasia, 1990), 71–94.

5. See Loenertz, "Aux origines" (above, n. 2), 370–76.

6. On the date of John's coronation (around 15 December 1221), see Jean Darrouzès, *RÉB* 36 (1978), 276. For official purposes John seems to have used only the name Ducas, and not Vatatzes.

7. On John's campaign, see John Langdon, *Byzantium's Last Imperial Offensive in Asia Minor: The Documentary Evidence for and Hagiographical Lore About John III Ducas Vatatzes' Crusade Against the Turks, 1222 or 1225 to 1231* (New Rochelle, 1992), an article's worth of material published as a book. Vatatzes restored the frontier and fortified Tripolis.

8. On the date of Theodore's coronation, as on some other points of the vexed history of this period, I follow Michael Hendy, who has kindly communicated to me some of the conclusions of his forthcoming fourth volume of Grierson, *Catalogue*.

9. The Byzantine population of Crete rebelled in 1229, and Vatatzes sent help in 1230, but his efforts ended when his fleet was shipwrecked in 1233; see Thiriet, *Romanie*, 97–98. Gregoras, I, 28–29 Schopen, appears to date the conquest of Lesbos, Chios, Samos, and the neighboring islands between Asen's defeat of Theodore Ducas in 1230 and Vatatzes' subjection of Rhodes in 1233–35.

10. Vatatzes' hyperpyra were of 16 karats, or two-thirds gold, rather than the 20½ karats of the previous century; see Hendy, *Studies*, 526–28.

11. Though Baldwin gave the relic to Louis IX of France, it had already been pawned to the Venetians for 13,134 hyperpyra, which Louis repaid. To

house it he built the Sainte Chapelle in Paris, where the crown remained until its destruction in the French Revolution.

12. See Bartusis, *Late Byzantine Army*, 26–27.

13. For the date I follow Michael Hendy (see n. 8 above).

14. Janssens, *Trébizonde*, 82.

CHAPTER TWENTY-THREE

For basic bibliography, see above, pp. 915–16, 917.

1. On this debasement, see Hendy, *Studies*, 526–28.

2. Bartusis, *Late Byzantine Army*, 43–48.

3. Ibid., 54–57.

4. Though formally granted to Genoa by the Mongols of the Golden Horde, Caffa would have been untenable without secure passage through the Byzantine-held straits; cf. Balard, *Romanie*, 114–18.

5. Cf. Pachymeres, I, p. 443 Failler, with I, p. 305 Failler.

6. For Licario's activities, see R.-J. Loenertz, "Les seigneurs tierciers de Négrepont de 1205 à 1280: Regestes et documents," *Byzantion* 35 (1965), 258–65.

7. See R.-J. Loenertz, "Mémoire d'Ogier, protonotaire, pour Marco et Marchetto nonces de Michel VIII Paléologue auprès du pape Nicolas III: 1278, printemps–été," *OCP* 31 (1965), 385–86, 400.

8. Michael remained imprisoned until he died trying to escape in 1307.

9. Although the fall of Scopia is often dated to 1282, see L. Mavromatis, *La fondation de l'empire serbe: Le kralj Milutin* (Thessalonica, 1978), 29–35.

10. Milutin's earlier wives had been princesses from Epirus, Hungary, and Bulgaria.

11. Since from this time Michael received rather wide responsibilities, many modern scholars refer to him as Michael IX, as if he were a senior emperor.

12. Pachymeres, II, pp. 407–8 Bekker (on the rebel officer Cotertzes), and II, p. 390 Bekker (on the proposed confiscations).

13. Cf. Bartusis, *Late Byzantine Army*, 151, and Laiou, *Constantinople*, 186–87. Since Anatolia cannot have been contributing much by this time, the annual revenue can hardly have exceeded the one million hyperpyra recorded around 1320.

14. See Failler, "Chronologie et composition" (1990), 53–82, with 83–87 for a chronological table.

15. The main new silver coin was the basilikon, valued at 12 to the hyperpyron and modeled on the Venetian grosso. See Hendy, *Studies*, 530–35.

16. Pachymeres, II, pp. 599–600 Bekker (misread by Laiou, *Constantinople*, 173 and n. 52).

17. Gregoras, I, 317–18 Schopen.

CHAPTER TWENTY-FOUR

For basic bibliography, see above, pp. 915–16, 917–18.

1. Schreiner, *Byzantinischen Kleinchroniken* II, 243–44.

2. See R. E. Sinkewicz, "The Doctrine of the Knowledge of God in the Early Writings of Barlaam the Calabrian," *MS* 44 (1982), 181–242.

3. The name Hesychasm is derived from *hēsychia* (tranquillity), the state in which the monks sought to receive the vision. For a precise description of their method, see I. Hausherr, "La méthode d'oraison hésychaste," *Orientalia Christiana Analecta* 9 (1927), 100–210, esp. 164–65.

4. Cantacuzenus, I, pp. 393–94 Schopen. The child turned out to be a girl, John V's sister Maria.

5. For the date, in July, see Darrouzès in Grumel, *Regestes* I.5, pp. 165–69.

6. The former view of the Zealots as social revolutionaries depended on a source that has been shown to be irrelevant to either social revolution or the Zealots; see Ihor Ševčenko, "Nicolas Cabasilas' 'Anti-Zealot Discourse': A Reinterpretation," *DOP* 11 (1957), 79–171.

7. See the exhaustive work of Philip Argenti, *The Occupation of Chios by the Genoese and Their Administration of the Island, 1346–1566, Described in Contemporary Documents and Official Dispatches*, 3 vols. (Cambridge, 1958).

8. As with the bastard daughters whom Michael VIII and Andronicus II had married to Muslims, there was no religious ceremony, and the bride remained a practicing Christian.

9. For the date, see Nicol, *Byzantine Family*, 129 n. 3.

10. On the other hand, most of western Europe, its colonies in the East, and the Empire of Trebizond suffered as badly as the Byzantines. See Biraben, *Hommes et la peste* I, 48–55, 71–129, 156–84. Cantacuzenus, III, pp. 52–53 Schopen, mentions losing his own youngest son Andronicus to the disease.

11. On the struggle between these two patriarchs, see A. Failler, "La déposition du patriarche Calliste Ier (1353)," *RÉB* 31 (1973), 5–163. Callistus was restored after the victory of John V.

12. See Franz Tinnefeld, "Kaiser Ioannes V. Palaiologos und der Gouverneur von Phokaia 1356–1358," *RSBS* 1 (1981), 259–71.

13. The tradition that Dushan had been preparing to march on Constantinople at the time of his death seems legendary; his conquests of Byzantine territory had stopped almost five years earlier. See Soulis, *Serbs and Byzantium*, 58–59, and Fine, *Late Medieval Balkans*, 335–37.

14. John, however, failed to expel Manuel Cantacuzenus from the Peloponnesus, and on the advice of the former John VI let Matthew go there as well in 1361.

15. Cf. Schreiner, *Byzantinischen Kleinchroniken* II, 290–91.

16. Since Louis of Hungary had recently conquered Vidin from the Bulgarians, Alexander seems simply to have denied John a safe-conduct to go farther. John apparently considered alternative routes too dangerous, and in view of his later detention by the Venetians he may have been right.

17. For the date, which despite contradictory reports almost certainly fell within the year ending 31 August 1369, see Schreiner, *Byzantinischen Kleinchroniken* II, 297–99.

18. John's negotiations with the Venetians remain rather obscure. Setton, *Papacy* I, 313–20, reckons the nominal value of the Venetians' offer at almost 100,000 ducats (200,000 hyperpyra); Nicol, *Byzantium and Venice*, 304–8, puts

it at 30,000 ducats less, supposing that the Venetians agreed to forgive the interest but not the principal (which seems unlikely, since they were ready to return the security for the loan).

19. Though Manuel went to Thessalonica on his own initiative, John V apparently wanted him to have the city, despite Andronicus's opposition. Cf. Barker, *Manuel II*, 43 n. 119. Theodore took over the Peloponnesus in 1382 after Manuel Cantacuzenus's death in 1380, but had to defeat a son of Matthew Cantacuzenus before gaining full control in 1383.

20. Ignatius of Smolensk, in Majeska, *Russian Travelers*, 100–105 (cf. 408–15), gives the main account of John VII's revolt.

CHAPTER TWENTY-FIVE

For basic bibliography, see above, pp. 915–16, 918–19.

1. Schreiner, *Byzantinischen Kleinchroniken* II, 352–53.

2. On these transactions, see J. Chrysostomides, "Corinth 1394–1397: Some New Facts," *Byzantina* 7 (1975), 83–110.

3. Ducas, pp. 159–61 Grecu, giving the sum as 300,000 aspra. This seems to be the Turkish aspron, then valued at 14 to the hyperpyron, which by this time was only a money of account; see Bertelè, *Numismatique*, 89.

4. Although Murād declared Mustafa was an impostor, and some modern scholars have accepted his claim, it seems to have been mere propaganda.

5. Andronicus, who suffered from a chronic illness, soon became a monk.

6. Ducas, p. 245 Grecu, giving the sum as 300,000 aspra.

7. On the council and related events, see particularly Gill, *Council of Florence*.

8. He is sometimes called Constantine XII because of a misconception that Constantine Lascaris, brother of Theodore I Lascaris of Nicaea, had been crowned emperor in 1204.

9. See Ducas, p. 293 Grecu, giving the sum as 300,000 aspra. Since this was exactly the tribute specified by the treaty of 1424, the Byzantines and Ottomans may actually have been exchanging equal payments for some time. The pretender in detention was Orhan, grandson of the long-dead sultan Sulaymān.

10. Rumeli Hisar is Turkish for "Castle of Rumelia," *Rumelia* (Land of the Romans) being the Turkish name for Turkish-held Europe. The fort lay opposite another on the Asian shore called Anadolu Hisar ("Castle of Anatolia").

11. Chalcondyles, pp. 155–57 Darkó. Since the text on p. 156 gives the number 100,000 without specifying the denomination, 100,000 ducats (320,000 hyperpyra; see Chap. 26 n. 44) is also possible. But Chalcondyles can hardly mean 100,000 aspra (ca. 7,000 hyperpyra), which would have been only a third of the tribute agreed upon in 1424, and less than Mehmed later asked of the despots of the Peloponnesus.

12. Since Constantine had put on the armor of a simple soldier, different stories were told about how or whether his body was identified; but that he died in the battle is not in serious doubt.

13. See Ducas, p. 395 Grecu, for the tribute. At the same time the Serbs were assessed 12,000 hyperpyra a year, the Genoese of Chios 6,000, and the Ge-

noese of Lesbos 3,000. The emperor of Trebizond also paid a tribute, for which no figure is recorded.

14. On the tardiness of the despots' tribute, see Ducas, p. 423 Grecu; on Thomas's payment, see Critobulus, p. 120 Reinsch.

15. See Schreiner, *Byzantinischen Kleinchroniken* II, 499–500, for the date.

16. Cilician Armenia had fallen to the Mamluks of Egypt in 1375.

CHAPTER TWENTY-SIX

For basic bibliography, see above, pp. 915–16, 919–20.

1. Vasiliev, *Goths*, 187–88, notes that as late as 1364 Alexius III of Trebizond claimed to rule the Peratia ("Land Overseas," meaning the Crimea); but Vasiliev reasonably believes that by that date the Crimea had been lost for some time.

2. Cf. Anthony Bryer, "Greeks and Türkmens: The Pontic Exception," *DOP* 29 (1975), 113–49.

3. The Romance-speaking peoples who are called Vlachs south of the Danube came to be called Romanians north of the Danube, though all are closely related to each other.

4. See especially the pioneering article of Ö. L. Barkan, "Essai sur les données statistiques des registres de recensement dans l'empire ottoman aux XVᵉ et XVIᵉ siècles," *Journal of the Economic and Social History of the Orient* 1 (1958), 9–36.

5. After 1453 Constantinople, which was almost as much an Asian city as a European one, became a partial exception to this rule, with a Muslim majority but a large Christian minority.

6. Cahen, *Turquie pré-ottomane*, 168–69, notes inscriptions commemorating Theodore I, John III, and Andronicus II found in churches in Cappadocia, far beyond those emperors' domains.

7. Of course, the Italian origin of the empress Anna of Savoy reinforced this tendency.

8. In the absence of a full study, see Miller, *Trebizond*, 43–57, and Janssens, *Trébizonde*, 100–112.

9. Cf. Angold, *Byzantine Government*, 151–201, Raybaud, *Gouvernement*, 157–206, and J. Verpeaux, "Hiérarchie et préséances sous les Paléologues," *TM* 1 (1965), 421–37.

10. The technical term for such a province was *katepanikion*, though its governor was called not a catepan but simply its head (*kephalē*).

11. On the difficult question of the army's size, see Bartusis, *Late Byzantine Army*, 258–69, though he seems somewhat too ready to minimize the numbers before the reign of Andronicus II.

12. See the perceptive remarks of Oikonomidès, *Hommes d'affaires*, 119–23.

13. See Aristeides Papadakis, *Crisis in Byzantium: The* Filioque *Controversy in the Patriarchate of Gregory II of Cyprus (1283–1289)* (New York, 1983).

14. On Athanasius, see John Boojamra, *Church Reform in the Late Byzantine Empire* (Thessalonica, 1982), and idem, *The Church and Social Reform* (New York, 1993).

968   Notes to Pages 824–40

15. Cf. Ducas, pp. 329, 381–85 Grecu.

16. See D. M. Nicol, *Meteora: The Rock Monasteries of Thessaly*, rev. ed. (London, 1975).

17. Zonaras's history is somewhat longer, but it goes back to the creation of the world.

18. See R. Guilland, *Essai sur Nicéphore Grégoras, l'homme et l'oeuvre* (Paris, 1926), now to be corrected from Hans-Veit Beyer, "Eine Chronologie der Lebensgeschichte des Nikephoros Gregoras," *JÖB* 27 (1978), 127–55.

19. For a good appreciation, see A. Kazhdan, "L'Histoire de Cantacuzène en tant qu'oeuvre littéraire," *Byzantion* 50 (1980), 279–335.

20. See especially Ihor Ševčenko, "Theodore Metochites, the Chora, and the Intellectual Trends of His Time," in Underwood, *Kariye Djami* IV, 17–91.

21. See R.-J. Loenertz, "Démétrius Cydonès," *OCP* 36 (1970), 47–72, and 37 (1971), 5–39.

22. See C. M. Woodhouse, *George Gemistus Plethon: The Last of the Hellenes* (Oxford, 1986).

23. See Lefort, "Population." Although Angeliki Laiou, *Peasant Society in the Late Byzantine Empire* (Princeton, 1977), argues for a significant decrease in population before 1347, Lefort sees none, and most of the conclusions in Laiou's book seem dubious; cf. P. Karlin-Hayter in *Byzantion* 48 (1978), 580–85.

24. For a case study of the impact of Catalan raiding, see P. Karlin-Hayter, "Les Catalans et les villages de la Chalcidique," *Byzantion* 52 (1982), 244–63.

25. Gregoras, II, pp. 841–42 Schopen. Cf. Oikonomidès, *Hommes d'affaires*, 46, and Balard, *Romanie* I, 393–94 and n. 35.

26. These figures are obtained by multiplying the twelfth-century trade duties by 5, and taking 175 percent of the result to convert it into fourteenth-century hyperpyra. In the twelfth century Byzantine trade duties at Constantinople apparently came to about 15,000 hyperpyra, and unpaid Italian trade duties throughout the empire would have come to a maximum of 50,000 (see above, p. 705 and nn. 36, 37). I suppose that about half the Italians' trade was at Constantinople, since about half the Venetian traders were found there in 1171 (see above, p. 648 and n. 9).

27. See A. Laiou, "The Byzantine Economy in the Mediterranean Trade System: Thirteenth–Fourteenth Centuries," *DOP* 34–35 (1980–81), 177–222.

28. Cantacuzenus, I, p. 371 Schopen.

29. Sir John Maundeville in 1322, in Thomas Wright, ed., *Early Travelers in Palestine* (London, 1848), 134: "a very fair and good city, and well walled." Ibn Baṭṭūṭa, II, pp. 506–8 Gibb: "enormous in magnitude. . . . Its bazaars and streets are spacious and paved with flagstones. . . . Within the wall are about thirteen inhabited villages." The last observation suggests a patchwork of vacant and populated areas.

30. Pachymeres, II, p. 595 Failler.

31. See above, pp. 773–74.

32. See A. M. Schneider, "Die Bevölkerung Konstantinopels im XV. Jahrhundert," *Nachrichten der Akademie der Wissenschaften in Göttingen, Philologisch-Historische Klasse*, 1949, 233–44. E. Frances, *RÉSEE* 7 (1969), 405–12, relying

on the reckoning of Sphrantzes, p. 132 Maisano, that 4,773 Constantinopolitans were able to bear arms in 1453, deduces a total of 15,000 to 20,000, which seems much too low. Probably Sphrantzes counted only those with some military training, not all able-bodied males.

33. Clavijo, p. 88 le Strange: "Everywhere throughout the city there are many great palaces, churches, and monasteries, but most of them are now in ruin. It is however plain that in former times when Constantinople was in its pristine state it was one of the noblest capitals of the world." Pero Tafur, p. 145 Letts: "The Emperor's Palace must have been very magnificent, but now it is in such a state that both it and the city show well the evils which the people have suffered and still endure."

34. Zorzi Dolfin, *Cronaca,* cited in O. Tafrali, *Thessalonique au quatorzième siècle* (Paris, 1913), 16 n. 3.

35. Chalcondyles, I, p. 92 Darkó.

36. I adapt these estimates as usual from McEvedy, *Atlas,* figuring that the Byzantine portion of Anatolia in 1282 had about 3 million out of a total of over 7 million people.

37. On this whole budget, see Gregoras, I, pp. 317–18 Schopen.

38. Mark Bartusis, "The Cost of Late Byzantine Warfare and Defense," *BF* 16 (1991), 75–89, esp. 84–85, estimates that there were around 500 pronoia soldiers in the 1320's. In his *Late Byzantine Army,* 166–75, esp. 172, Bartusis reckons the typical income of a military pronoia grant at the same date "in the 150 to 220 hyperpyra range and probably higher."

39. For standard mercenary pay, see Bartusis, *Late Byzantine Army,* 149–53, which supports the alternative pay figure noted by Hendy, *Studies,* 163. For the pay of a standard ship's crew of 154 men, see Hendy, *Studies,* 162, giving the figure of 3,720 hyperpyra in 1261, which I have adjusted to reflect the debasement of the hyperpyron from two-thirds gold in 1261 to half gold in 1321.

40. On John VI's bodyguard, see Gregoras, III, p. 151 Bekker.

41. Cantacuzenus, I, pp. 87–88 Schopen.

42. See Hendy, *Studies,* 205–6; cf. Bartusis, "Cost" (above, n. 38), 81–82.

43. Cf. Bartusis, *Late Byzantine Army,* 151–53.

44. By contrast, Bertrandon de la Broquière (p. 182 Schefer) heard at Adrianople that the sultan's revenues amounted to 2.5 million ducats in 1433. This would have been equivalent to some 8 million hyperpyra, since by that year the ducat was quoted at about 3.2 hyperpyra (cf. Zakythinos, *Crise monétaire,* 29).

CONCLUSION

1. Some modern historians have been too quick to conclude from court rhetoric that the Byzantine emperor wielded absolute authority, or claimed to rule the whole known world. The most that the emperors consistently claimed was that after the fall of the western Roman Empire they were the Roman emperors' only legal successors, and in this they were by their own lights perfectly correct. Of course, like many other rulers ancient and modern, they sometimes gave specious justifications for their actions.

2. The only Byzantine emperor to be generally recognized as a saint was Constantine I, who despite executing his son Crispus and falling into the Arian heresy had given the Church official status. In Byzantine scenes of the Last Judgment an emperor is typically one of several representatives of the damned, and the only royalty among the saved are David and Solomon.

3. On the other hand, the more usual principle that lands should be assigned according to the nationality of most of their inhabitants would have given Greece little more than it had in 1913, because most of the Greeks of Thrace and Asia Minor formed large minorities in areas with bare Turkish majorities.

4. Italy ceded Rhodes to Greece in 1947. Britain refused to cede Cyprus to Greece despite its large Greek majority, and in 1960 made it independent under a constitution guaranteeing special rights for its Turkish minority. This arrangement proved unsatisfactory to both sides, and in 1974 troops from Turkey invaded the island to forestall the union of Cyprus with Greece. A Turkish Republic of Northern Cyprus backed by troops from Turkey still controlled the north when this book went to press.

Index

In this index "f" after a number means a second mention on the next page; "ff" means separate mentions on the next two pages; two numbers with a dash between them mean a continuous discussion over two or more pages; and *passim* means separate mentions on three or more pages with gaps of fewer than five pages.

Library of Congress Cataloging-in-Publication Data

Treadgold, Warren T.
    A history of the Byzantine state and society / Warren Treadgold.
        p.   cm.
    Includes bibliographical references and index.
    ISBN 0-8047-2421-0 (cl.) : ISBN 0-8047-2630-2 (pbk.)
    1. Byzantine Empire—History.   I. Title
DF552.T65   1997
949.5'02—dc21

                                                    97-23492
                                                    CIP

This book is printed on acid-free paper.

Originally published in 1997
The last year below indicates year of this printing:
06   05   04   03   02   01   00   99   98   97